W9-AYL-977

THE OXFORD COMPANION TO BEER

OXFORD
UNIVERSITY PRESS

OXFORD
UNIVERSITY PRESS

Oxford University Press, Inc., publishes works that further
Oxford University's objective of excellence
in research, scholarship, and education.

Oxford New York
Auckland Cape Town Dar es Salaam Hong Kong Karachi
Kuala Lumpur Madrid Melbourne Mexico City Nairobi
New Delhi Shanghai Taipei Toronto

With offices in
Argentina Austria Brazil Chile Czech Republic France Greece
Guatemala Hungary Italy Japan Poland Portugal Singapore
South Korea Switzerland Thailand Turkey Ukraine Vietnam

Published by Oxford University Press, Inc.
198 Madison Avenue, New York, NY 10016
http://www.oup.com

The Library of Congress Cataloging-in-Publication Data

The Oxford companion to beer / edited by Garrett Oliver.
p. cm.
ISBN 978-0-19-536713-3 (hardback)
1. Beer.
TP570.O94 2011
641.2'3—dc23 2011021032

7 9 8 6

Printed in the United States of America
on acid-free paper

CONTENTS

FOREWORD

Is there a more ancient recipe than the one for beer? It is thought that man began brewing beer even before he learned how to bake bread, and that beer was among the provisions that Noah brought on the ark. In ancient times, Egyptians were buried with a supply of beer; by the Middle Ages, beer played such a central role in the culture that it was an acceptable currency with which to pay taxes, settle debts, and donate to the church. Queen Elizabeth I was known to drink ale for breakfast. All by way of saying, it seems that *The Oxford Companion to Beer* is long overdue.

But the timing of its publication is logical. All of that rich history aside, for much of my fermented-beverage-drinking life, we were living in the dark ages of beer. A cultural staple that was for not just centuries but *millennia* made in the home, and later in abbeys and small breweries, had been, by the time Prohibition ended, taken over almost exclusively by multinational companies. These organizations were efficient at turning out bland brews devoid of individual character and deep flavor. Thinking back to my teens and twenties, I saw beer as little more than a means for getting drunk—a beverage often proceeded by the word "light"—and the big producers gave me what I wanted.

Somewhere in my adult life, the tide turned. Part of this was a result of my growing older and beginning to see beer as a drink worthy of appreciation, not just something cold to crack open after a softball game. We're also in the midst of a great renaissance in artisanal brewing. Microbreweries have cropped up all over North America and Europe, with small batch producers turning out wonderfully complex products that showcase beer's wide variety of flavor profiles. Meanwhile, consumers are becoming thoughtful connoisseurs. At the beginning of 2010, when I opened Colicchio & Sons, a contemporary American restaurant in New York's Chelsea neighborhood, I realized from the beginning that I wanted to focus on beer. I started working with my beverage director to select draft beers to feature, focusing on local products as well as the best of the artisanal international brews. There were simply too many good beers to choose from, and I ended up installing 28 taps.

The Oxford Companion to Beer provides an exhaustive account of not only beer's history but its science and its art, at a time when people are more willing than ever to take beer seriously. And if I had to choose one person to be my beer guide and teacher, it would be Garrett Oliver, whose passion for beer is only surpassed by his sheer knowledge on the subject. In this volume Oliver and numerous experts have assembled beer wisdom from around the globe, creating a virtual beer symposium—the scope of which the world has never known. And we, as readers, have a front-row seat.

Tom Colicchio, New York City, February 2011

PREFACE

After water and tea, beer is the third most popular drink in the world. This should not be surprising, as beer is also the most complex and varied of drinks. It can taste like lemons or smoke, coffee or coconuts, bananas or bread, chilies or ginger. Beer can be crisply acidic and earthy, or it can be bracingly bitter and spectacularly aromatic. It can evince a mere prickle of carbonation or flourish on the palate into a fine mousse. It can be enjoyed days after it was brewed or emerge from a bottle more than a century later and produce rapturous delight.

Wine, beer's great rival and table companion, despite its many wonders, cannot begin to approach beer's variety of flavor, aroma, and texture. Because beer can taste like almost anything, it brings superior talents to the dinner table. Beer does not resemble wine so much as it resembles music. Beer predates human civilization and may well have had a hand in creating it. Beer was primary in the minds of ancient peoples, who carved word of it into stone, painted images of it upon temple walls, built cities fueled by its manufacture, and carried it with them into the afterlife. Beer built castles in Bavaria, great ships upon the Baltic Sea, the power of the Hanseatic League, and modern industry in London. Many of the American founding fathers brewed beer, and it has graced the tables of the White House for more than 200 years. Across the sweep of world history, at the cutting edge of technology, on the tables of the rich and the poor, in almost every human situation of any real note, you will find beer.

Why then, we must wonder, is so little written of beer today? Perhaps we must blame its ubiquity, its rapid industrialization and past standardization, and its societal even-handedness. Beer is a thing we think we know, yet right below the surface lies a fascinating world of flavor, aroma, art, and science. It is a world many of us are now rediscovering, as we seek to reconnect with our food and drink. We are brewing beer in our homes, talking about beer with our friends, and bringing beer back to the dinner table where it has always been and always belonged. This renaissance is thrilling, but when the editors at Oxford University Press came to me and asked me to become editor-in-chief of a first edition of *The Oxford Companion to Beer*, my first instinct was to politely refuse. I am a brewmaster by trade, and brewing is itself a profession that takes over one's life, pleasantly but insistently. How could any brewer make time for such a great task and, more important, do justice to it?

Yet as I looked around at the information about beer that was available on bookshelves, I started to realize that a lot was missing. There wasn't a single source to which a brewer, an enthusiast, a homebrewer, a restaurant beverage director, a beer distributor, or a beer novice could go and find answers to many questions he or she might have about beer. What's more, much of the modern world of beer and brewing seemed to be missing from the shelves altogether, whether those shelves were physical or internet based. Many of beer's most fascinating aspects are scattered throughout professional journals or textbooks, or are passed down in families over generations, hidden behind brewery walls, or, especially if it concerns craft brewing, barely written about at all.

Pressed forward by family, friends, and colleagues, I took on this task, and now, a few years later, we have it at hand. Let me be clear that this book is not the work of one person; in fact, it is quite the opposite. As befits a book about a social drink, *The Oxford Companion to Beer* has grown into a grand collaborative project. I truly believe that it is possible to say, without any fear of successful contradiction, that *The Oxford Companion to Beer* is the most comprehensive book ever published on the subject of beer. Our 166 contributors represent a brain trust, a compendium of remarkable brewing talent and experience from more than a dozen countries. They are academics and master cellarmen, agronomists and pub brewers, brewmasters of large international breweries, and homebrewers. I certainly hope that this isn't the last book of its kind, but it is surely the first.

A few words about the organization and purpose of this book: We have sought to present beer in all its aspects—historical, cultural, stylistic, biographical, technical, agronomic, organoleptic, and artistic. This is not a listing or directory of breweries or individual beers—there are many excellent books that cover such territory, many of them written by our contributors. We have included entries on breweries that are widely regarded as culturally significant, but given the many thousands of excellent breweries in the world, we have not made an attempt to cover them all.

The Oxford Companion to Beer comprises over 1,100 articles or entries, presented in alphabetical order. In this, it resembles a classic encyclopedia. It is heavily cross-referenced, in order to allow the reader to best explore subjects that often branch out in many directions. Entries range in length from a few dozen words to several thousand, and inevitably cover some subjects that could themselves fill entire books. Here we seek to give the reader the essential information necessary for a good understanding of the subject at hand. Beyond its most basic levels, brewing often becomes a highly technical pursuit, and we have not shied away from this aspect of the craft, although we have hopefully avoided details that are too dry and esoteric to be of interest to anyone but scientists. We do not, for example, include diagrams of molecules here, although we sometimes make mention of their structures and actions; we trust that any such graphics are these days a few clicks away on the internet and best accessed through those means.

Beer has its own form of terroir, but the ingredients needed for beer-making have traveled the world for hundreds of years. In this aspect, brewing is much like cooking—ingredients and cultural influences may come from many sources. Beer is brewed in all corners of the world, but we have focused individual entries on the great brewing nations, countries clearly developing new brewing cultures, and the history of beer within those societies. Where a particular city or region has made a notable contribution to brewing history, it has also been given an individual entry.

We have provided information about many of the most influential barley varieties, and their particular qualities and lineages. There are more than 100 entries about hops. There are individual entries on 11 hop-producing countries, and where those countries have more than one significant growing region, we have a separate entry for the region itself. All significant modern hop varieties (and a few historical ones) have individual entries giving significant details of their lineages, technical properties, and usage within the brewhouse. Beyond these there are technical entries about other aspects of hops, from aromatic and bittering compounds to specific techniques used for dry hopping.

Beer styles, of course, have individual entries, although they will also be mentioned in other places throughout the book. Beer style is a cultural phenomenon, and thus somewhat subjective or arguable, and we treat it as such. The reader will therefore find these entries to be enlivened by the contributors' individualistic impressions, as we believe they ought to be; we will each find our own well-informed subjectivities on these fascinating and rapidly evolving topics.

Most measurements in the book are mentioned in both American units and metric units. Beer and wort gravities are given in degrees Plato. The reader will find various conversion factors within the back matter. While it would clearly be impossible to list every beer organization, magazine, festival, and online resource, the appendixes will give readers a good start on finding further information they may wish to seek. A synoptic outline arranges subjects by general grouping, such as "Biographies" and "Festivals and Competitions," and it is hoped that this will help the reader navigate the book more easily and in various ways. In a work of this scope, despite our best efforts, there will inevitably be inadvertent omissions and errata. Comments from learned readers will surely inform and improve future editions.

Many of life's great moments happen at the table, whether these be the tables in our homes, in our restaurants, or in our pubs. The world of beer, this great culture, is worthy of far more respect than it has ever enjoyed, and it is capable of producing far more joy than most people realize. We hope that this volume will help you discover more of that joy for yourselves and pass it along to others.

There are many thanks to go around, more than I can possibly list here. Our contributors are uniformly busy people, and they have given generously of their time and expertise. Peruse the short contributor bios at the back of this book; only then will you realize what a diverse and eminent group of people brought this work to fruition. This volume is partially a product of many warm, sunny days spent indoors, surrounded by books and computers instead of trees and fresh air. I am profoundly grateful for everyone's hard work. I want to thank originating editor Benjamin Keene for coming to me with this idea in the first place; this book would not exist if not for his vision. I also want to thank my stalwart Oxford editors, Grace Labatt and Max Sinsheimer, for their sheer doggedness and their steadfast belief that we would get this done. I want to convey all of our thanks to our august Advisory Board—Dr. Charles W. Bamforth, Dr. Patrick Hayes, Dr. George Philliskirk, Dr. Wolfgang Stempfl, and Dr. Keith Villa—each of whom read through hundreds of entries and provided feedback. Graphic artist Charles Finkel, a friend to many in the beer world, curated our photos and illustrations, adding many from his personal collection. When we came knocking, the eminent hop scientist Dr. Val Peacock dropped what he was doing and agreed to become our technical advisor on hops, devoting weeks of work to make sure that our hop-related entries were as clear and airtight as we could make them. Special thanks also to Steve Parkes, Dick Cantwell, and Pete Brown for pitching in so gamely and always being available at the other end of the line. Even if obliquely, I feel I must thank Jancis Robinson, editor in chief of *The Oxford Companion to Wine*. Although we never spoke, her *OCW*, a work of brilliant clarity and erudition, sat beside my desk for years, setting a both a fine example and a sharp spur to the flank.

Above all, I want to thank Horst Dornbusch. Already a remarkably prolific contributor to the *OCB*, late in the project Horst set his normal life aside and joined the editorial team as associate editor. He worked tirelessly every day thereafter, and his combination of brewing and historical knowledge, energy, clear-headedness, and humor has made an enormous contribution to this work. He is a modest man of immodest talents, and I consider him a partner in this enterprise and a fast friend.

I also wish to thank my family and friends, who pushed me forward and then listened to me talk about this project constantly for years, and yet were still willing to share a beer with me. Big thanks go to my partners at The Brooklyn Brewery, particularly Stephen Hindy, Eric Ottaway, and Robin Ottaway, who gamely tolerated my odd and attenuated schedule at the brewery, where I sometimes no doubt seemed like more of an opinionated wraith than a solid presence. I have, even more than usual, stood upon the shoulders of my brewing team, Andrew Ety, Tom Villa, Thomas Price, Christopher Basso, and Daniel Moss. I am moved also to think of my friend the late seminal beer writer Michael Jackson, who by all rights should have been in this chair. I think we have carried the flag well, and I can only hope that he'd have been proud of us.

This book is dedicated to everyone who has ever stood facing the mash tun, hoping to conjure deliciousness, joyous conviviality, and a small measure of magic.

Garrett Oliver, New York City, March 2011

TOPICAL OUTLINE OF ENTRIES

This outline offers an overview of *The Oxford Companion to Beer,* with entries listed in the following subject categories:

Breweries and Brewing Companies
Other Companies
Abbey and Trappist
Beers and Beer Styles
Other Types of Beer
Other Beverages
Regions
Beer Industry
Historical
Culture and Customs
Festivals and Competitions
Organizations
Education and Institutions
Biographies
Food and Ingredients
Beer Containers, Vessels, and Equipment
Characteristics
Mash and Mashing
Fermentation
Brewing
Post-Fermentation
Chemistry
Measurement
Yeast
Wheat
Hops, General
Hops
Hop Regions
Barley, General
Barleys
Malts and Malting
Bacteria
Viruses and Diseases

Breweries and Brewing Companies

Achel Brewery
Adnams Brewery
Affligem Brewery
Alaskan Brewing Company
Amstel Brewery
Anchor Brewing Company
Anheuser-Busch
Anheuser-Busch InBev
Arthur Guinness & Sons
Asahi Breweries
Asia Pacific Breweries Limited
Augustiner Bräu
Ayinger Brewery
Ballantine IPA
Baltika Breweries
Barclay, Perkins & Co.
Bass & Company
Beamish & Crawford
Belhaven Brewery
Blue Moon Brewing Company
Boddington's Brewery
Boon Brewery
Boon Rawd Brewery
Bosteels Brewery
Boston Beer Company
Boulevard Brewing Company
Brooklyn Brewery
Budweiser Budvar
Caledonian Brewery
Cantillon Brewery
Carling O'Keefe Limited
Carlsberg Group
Christoffel Brewery
Coors Brewing Company
Courage Brewery
De Koninck Brewery
Desnoes and Geddes Limited
Dogfish Head Craft Brewery
Dortmunder Actien Brauerei
Dubuisson Brewery
Dupont, Brasserie
Duvel Moortgat
Duyck, Brasserie
Eggenberg Brewery
Einbecker Brauhaus AG
Erdinger Weissbräu
Foster's
Fuller, Smith & Turner
George Gale & Co. Ltd.
Goose Island Beer Company
Greene King

Grolsch Brewery
Hacker–Pschorr Brewery
Harvey & Son Ltd.
Heineken
Hofbräuhaus München
Hook Norton Brewery
Hürlimann Brewery
Huyghe Brewery
InBev
Ind Coope & Sons
J.W. Lees Brewery
Kaltenberg Brewery
Kirin Brewery Company
Köstritzer Schwarzbierbrauerei
Kronenbourg Brewery
Labatt Brewing Company Ltd.
La Chouffe
La Choulette Brewery
Leffe Brewery
Liefmans Brewery
Lion Nathan
Löwenbräu
Magic Hat Brewing Company
Marston's Brewery
Meux Reid & Co.
Miller Brewing Company
Moctezuma Brewing
Molson Coors Brewing Company
Moretti Brewery
Murphy's Brewery
New Albion Brewing Company
New Belgium Brewing Company
New Glarus Brewing Company
Pabst Brewing Company
Palm Breweries
Paulaner Brauerei GmbH & Co. KG
Peroni Brewery
Pilsner Urquell
Pinkus Müller
Porterhouse Brewing Company
Pyramid Breweries, Inc.
Radeberger Group
Redhook Ale Brewery
Ringwood Brewery
Rodenbach
Rogue Ales
Russian River Brewing Company
SABMiller
Samuel Allsopp & Sons
Samuel Smith's Old Brewery
Sapporo Beer
Schneider Weisse Brewery
Scottish & Newcastle Brewery
Shepherd Neame Brewery
Sierra Nevada Brewing Company
Sinebrychoff Brewery
South African Breweries Ltd.
Spaten Brewery
Staropramen Brewery
Stroh Brewery Company
Suntory Group
Theakstons
Thomas Salt and Co.
Timothy Taylor Brewery
Traquair House Brewery
Trommer's Evergreen Brewery
Truman, Hanbury, Buxton & Co.
Tuborg Brewery
Uerige Brewery
U Fleku
Vapeur Brewery
Wadworth Brewery
Whitbread Brewery
Worthington Brewery
Young's Brewery

Other Companies

Briess Malt & Ingredients Company
Cargill
Durst Malz
Hopunion LLC
Krones
Lallemand
Perlick
Schulz Brew Systems
Weyermann® Malting

Abbey and Trappist

abbey beers
Andechs
Chimay
Cistercian order
De Kluis (Brewery)
Koningshoeven Brewery
Orval Brewery
Rochefort Brewery
Trappist breweries
Weltenburger
Westmalle Brewery
Westvleteren Brewery

Beers and Beer Styles

ale
altbier
American amber ale
American brown ale
American pale ale
American wheat beer
Baltic porter
barley wine
beer style
Belgian red ale
Berliner weisse
Bière de Garde
Bière de Mars
bitter
Black and Tan
blonde ale
bock beer
Bohemian pilsner

Other Types of Beer

Other Beverages

Regions

České Budějovice
Chicago
China
Czech Republic
Denmark
Edinburgh
Egypt
Finland
Flanders
France
Germany
Holland
India
Ireland
Italy
Japan
Kent, England
Kulmbacher, Germany
Manhattan, New York
Mexico
Milwaukee, WI
Moravia
Munich
Netherlands, the
New Zealand
Nord-Pas de Calais
Norway
Pajottenland District (Belgium)
Philadelphia
Pilsen (Plzeň)
Poland
Russia
Scotland
Southeast Asia
South Korea
Spain
Sri Lanka
Sweden
Switzerland
Ukraine
United States
Wales
Wallonia

Beer Industry

adulteration
advertising
apprenticeship
bulk transport
cellarmanship, art of
distribution
environmental issues
global warming
health
immigration (effects on brewing)
labeling information
labels
law
marketing
storage of beer
taxes
women in brewing

Historical

ale-conner
ale pole
ale-wives
Austro-Hungarian Empire
Bacchus
beer gods
brewing in colonial America
bride-ale
cakes and ale
coaching inns
East India Company
Free Mash-Tun Act (1880)
Goed sakken
gruit
hekt
history of beer
Hofbräu
Industrial Revolution
London and Country Brewer, the
near beer
Ninkasi
Prohibition
Reinheitsgebot
St. Gallen
stuykmanden
Sumer
temperance
three-threads
zymurgical heraldry

Culture and Customs

ale houses
art, beer in
beer gardens
Beer Orders
Beer Street (by William Hogarth)
beer weeks
beer writing
bottle collecting
breweriana
brotzeit
BYOB
drinking customs
drinking songs
last orders
pub games
public houses (pubs)
scooping
serving beer
social media
taverns
ticking
tied house system

Festivals and Competitions

Beer Judge Certification Program (BJCP)
Great American Beer Festival
Great British Beer Festival
judging beer
Oktoberfest
Oregon Brewers Festival
World Beer Cup

Organizations

American Homebrewers Association (AHA)
American Malting Barley Association, Inc.
American Society of Brewing Chemists (ASBC)
Brewers Association
Brewers' Company
Campaign for Real Ale (CAMRA)
Cask Marque
Durden Park Beer Circle
European Brewery Convention (EBC)
European Union

Education and Institutions

Beer Academy
Brewing and Malting Barley Research Institute
brewing schools
Cicerone
Doemens Academy
Heriot-Watt University
Institute of Brewing & Distilling (IBD)
Katholieke Universiteit van Leuven
Master Brewers Association of the Americas
Siebel Institute of Technology
University of California, Davis
VLB Berlin
Wahl-Henius Institute of Fermentology
Weihenstephan
White Labs
Wyeast Laboratories
Wye College

Biographies

Anheuser, Eberhard
Ballantine, Peter
Bamforth, Charles W.
Bruce, David
Busch, August IV
Carter, James Earl, Jr.
Catherine the Great
Celis, Pierre
De Clerck, Jean
Deleye, Abbot Dom Gerardus
Dorber, Mark
Dreher, Anton
Eckhardt, Fred
Franklin, Benjamin
Gambrinus, Jan
Geary, David
Grant, Bert
Groll, Josef
Grossman, Ken
Guinness, Arthur
Hansen, Emil Christian
Harwood, Ralph
Herrera, Don Alonso de
Hildegard von Bingen
Hodgson, George
Jackson, Michael
Jefferson, Thomas
Judong, Father Andselmus
Koch, Jim
Lewis, Michael J.
Linde, Carl von
Luitpold, Prince of Bavaria
Maytag, Fritz
Narziss, Ludwig
Papazian, Charles
Pasteur, Louis
Ramses II
Ruppert, Jacob
Sedlmayr, Gabriel the Elder
Sedlmayr, Gabriel the Younger
Stewart, Graham
Washington, George
Wheeler, Daniel
Wittelsbacher family
Yuengling, David G.
Zastrow, Klaus

Food and Ingredients

beechwood chips
bog myrtle
borage
Brewer's flakes
brown sugar
buckwheat
candi sugar
carrageenans
cereals
chamomile
cheese (pairing)
chocolate

cooking with beer
coriander
corn
corn sugar
Curaçao oranges
food pairing
gelatin
gum arabic
heather
hemp
herbs
honey
isinglass
juniper
maize
manioc
micronized grains
millet
mint
molasses
nutmeg
oats
organic ingredients
pine, fir, and spruce tips
priming sugar
rice
rice hulls
rye
sage
sorghum
spices
sugar
syrups
vanilla
woodruff

Beer Containers, Vessels, and Equipment

aluminum kegs
ball roaster
barrel
Baudelot cooler
beer analyzer
beer engine
Bier-Drive tanks
bottles
bottle sizes
bright tank
bung
calandria
candle filter
carbonation stone
carboy
cask
cask breather
cereal cooker
cleaning in place (CIP)
coolship
copper
crown cap
drinking vessels
drum roaster
fermentation vessels
flip-top
flotation tank
germination-kilning vessels (GKV)
glassware
Golden Gate kegs
grant
growler
Grundy tank
gyle
hammer mill
heat exchanger
Hoff-Stevens kegs
hogshead
hydrometer
keg
kettle
keystone
lauter tun
manometer
mash tun
oak
roller mill
Saladin box
Sankey kegs
sheet filter
shive
solera
sparkler
spear
spile
Steel's Masher
stein
Strainmaster
swan neck
tap
underback
whirlpool
widget

Characteristics

acidity
aftertaste
aging of beer
anti-foaming
aroma
astringency
beer clean
beer spoilers
bitterness
bloom
bright beer
Burton snatch
caramel color
carbonation
chill haze
clarity
cling
colloidal haze
color
colorants
esters
faults in beer
flavor
flavor wheel
foam
friability
fruity
haze
infection
lightstruck

mouthfeel
off-flavors
phenolic
sensory evaluation
shelf life
solventy
sourness
triangular taste test
umami
viability

Mash and Mashing

adjuncts
congress mash
decoction
dry milling
grain out
grits
infusion mash
invert sugar
mash
mash filter
mash fork
mash hopping
mashing
protein rest
saccharification
stuck mash
temperature-programmed mash

Fermentation

accelerated batch fermentation
attenuation
batch process
bottom fermentation
brandhefe
Burton Union system
concrete (fermenting in)
conditioning
continuous fermentation
fermentability
fermentation
finings
green beer
high kräusen
in-line carbonation
Irish moss
kettle finings
kräusening
maturation
open fermentation
pitching
refrigeration
rousing
secondary fermentation
skimming
top fermentation
Yorkshire square
zymurgy

Brewing

additives
adsorbents
aeration
analysis
automation
Bentonite
bioluminescence
blending houses
boiling
brewhouse
brewing process
brewmaster
brewpub
cask conditioning
centrifugation
chillproofing
clarification
cold break
contract brewing
craft brewing
Dalton's law
Darcy's law
deaerated water
diatomaceous earth
direct firing
drauflassen
drip back
extracts
extreme brewing
filtration
final gravity
first runnings
high gravity brewing
homebrewing
hot break
hot liquor
hot-side aeration
lagering
lautering
microbes
microbrewery
mixed-gas dispense
parti-gyle
perlite
pumping over
quality control and assurance
run-off
silica gel
sparging
spent grain
sterile filtration
Stokes' law
tannins
trub
underletting
vacuum evaporation
vorlauf
water
wort
yield

Post-Fermentation

barrel-aging
bottle conditioning
bottling
canning
counterpressure
effluent
fobbing
gravity dispense
gushing
jetting
mixed-gas dispense
papain
pasteurization
racking
residual sugars
scuffing
staling
ullage

Chemistry

acetaldehyde
acetic acid
acetyl CoA
acid
acidification
adenosine triphosphate (ATP)
alcohol
aldehydes
alkalinity
alpha amylase
amino acids
amylases
amylopectin
amylose
anthocyanogens
antioxidants
butyric acid
calcium carbonate
calcium chloride
calcium oxalate
calcium sulfate
caproic acid
caprylic acid
carbohydrates
carbon dioxide
chromatography
citric acid
dextrins
dextrose
diacetyl
diastase
dimethyl sulfide (DMS)
(E)-2-nonenal
enzymes
ethanol
ethyl acetate
fatty acids
ferulic acid
flocculation
4-vinyl guaiacol
4-vinyl syringol
free amino nitrogen (FAN)
fructose
fusel alcohols
gibberellins
glucans
glucose
glycogen
gypsum
Henry's law
hydrogen sulfide
iodine
iron
iso-alpha acids
isoamyl acetate
isovaleric acid
lactic acid
linalool
lipids
Maillard reaction
maltotriose
melibiose
myrcene
nitrogen
nucleic acids
organic acids
oxalates
oxidation
oxygen
pentanedione
pentose
peracetic acid
pH
polymerase chain reaction (PCR)
polyphenols
potassium metabisulfite
proteins
proteolysis
PVPP
pyruvate
reduction
sodium chloride
starch
sucrose
terpenes
vicinal diketones
woodruff
xanthohumol
xylose
zinc

Measurement

alcoholic strength and measurement
apparent extract
aroma unit (AU)
Balling scale
Belgian brewing degrees
bitterness units
calories
color units EBC
dissolved oxygen (DO)
evaporation rate
firkin
hectoliter
homebrew bittering units
hot water extract
International Bitterness Units (IBUs)
kilderkin

Kolbach index
Lintner
liter degrees per kilogram
Lovibond
original gravity
pin
pint
Plato gravity scale
quarter
real degree of fermentation (RDF)
real extract
shilling system
specific gravity
standard reference method (SRM)
strike temperature
Zentner

Yeast

acid washing
ale yeast
autolysis
Brettanomyces
cauliflower stage
dry yeast
ethanol-tolerant yeast strains
immobilized yeast reactor
killer strains
lager yeast
respiratory-deficient mutants
sterols
wild yeast
wine yeast
yeast
yeast bank
yeast nutrients

Wheat

Einkorn wheat
emmer
spelt
wheat

Hops, General

adhumulone
adlupulone
alpha acids
American Hop Museum
aphids
bittering potential (of hops)
caryophyllene
cohumulone
colupulone
dry hopping
farnesene
first wort hopping
geraniol
hedge hops
hop back
hop breeding and selection
hop extracts
hop isomerization
hop oils
hop pellets
hops
hop seal
hop shortage (aroma varieties)
hop utilization
hulupones
humulene
humulone
late hopping
lupulin
lupulone
Noble hops
oast house
resins
sulfuring (of hops)
wet hopping

Hops

Admiral (hop)
Ahtanum (hop)
Amarillo (hop)
American Tettnanger (hop)
Bačka (hop)
Bramling Cross (hop)
Brewer's Gold (hop)
Bullion (hop)
Cascade (hop)
Challenger (hop)
Chinook (hop)
Citra (hop)
Cluster (hop)
Comet (hop)
Crystal (hop)
CTZ (hop)
East Kent Golding (hop)
Eastwell Golding (hop)
Eroica (hop)
Farnham (hop)
First Gold (hop)
Fuggle (hop)
Galena (hop)
Glacier (hop)
Golding (hop)
Green Bullet (hop)
Hallertauer Magnum (hop)
Hallertauer Mittelfrueh (hop)
Hallertauer Taurus (hop)
Hallertauer Tradition (hop)
Herkules (hop)
Hersbrucker Spät (hop)
Kent Golding (hop)

Liberty (hop)
Lublin (hop)
Mount Hood (hop)
Nelson Sauvin (hop)
Northdown (hop)
Northern Brewer (hop)
Nugget (hop)
Opal (hop)
Pacific Gem (hop)
Palisade (hop)
Perle (hop)
Pilgrim (hop)
Pioneer (hop)
Premiant (hop)
Pride of Ringwood (hop)
Progress (hop)
Saaz (hop)
Santiam (hop)
Saphir (hop)
Serebrianka (hop)
Simcoe (hop)
Sládek (hop)
Smaragd (hop)
Sorachi Ace (hop)
Southern Cross (hop)
Spalter Select (hop)
Spalt (hop)
Sterling (hop)
Strisselspalt (hop)
Styrian Golding (hop)
Target (hop)
Tettnanger (hop)
Ultra (hop)
Vanguard (hop)
Warrior (hop)
Whitbread Golding Variety (hop)
Willamette (hop)

Hop Regions

American hops
American hops, history
Australian hops
Chinese hops
Elbe-Saale hop region
English hops
French hops
German hops
Hallertau hop region
Idaho (northern hop region)
Idaho (southern hop region)
New Zealand hops
Polish hops
Slovenian hops
Spalt hop region
Tettnang hop region
Ukrainian hops
Willamette Valley hop region
Yakima Valley hop region
Žatec hop region

Barley, General

acrospire
aleurone layer
barley
barley diseases
barley harvest
beta glucanase
beta-glucans
dormancy (of barley)
endosperm
endosperm modification
ergot
flaked barley
Hordein
husk
lodging resistance
malting barley
maltose
modification
pericarp
respiration
rhizome

Barleys

Alexis (barley)
B1202 (barley)
Barke (barley)
Bere (barley)
CDC Copeland (barley)
CDC Kendall (barley)
Chariot (barley)
Chevalier (barley)
Flagship (barley)
Golden Promise (barley)
Halcyon (barley)
Haná (barley)
Harrington (barley)
Klages (barley)
Kneifl (barley)
Krona (barley)
Legacy (barley)
Maris Otter (barley)
Morex (barley)
Optic (barley)
Pipkin (barley)
Robust (barley)
Sissi (barley)
Stander (barley)
Steffi (barley)
Tradition (barley)
Triumph (barley)

Malts and Malting

acidulated malt
amber malt
aromatic malts
base malt
biscuit malt
black malt
caramel malts
caramelization
Caramunich (malt)
Carapils (malt)
Caravienne
chitting
cold water extract
couching
Crystal malt
diastatic power
dried malt extract
floor malting
germination
grist
kilning
liquid malt extract (LME)
malt
malting
maltodextrins
malt syrup
melanoidins
milling
Munich malt
pilsner malt
Rahr Malting Company
roasted malts
six-row malt
slack malt
smoked malt
snap malt
steeping
two-row malt
weevils
wet milling
wheat malt

Bacteria

acetic acid bacteria
bacteria
Gram stain
lactobacillus
lag phase
Obesumbacterium proteus
pectinatus
pediococcus
Zymomonas

Viruses and Diseases

Aspergillus niger
barley yellow dwarf virus
downy mildew
Fusarium
hop mosaic virus
smut
Take-All
Verticillium wilt

abbey beers are beers produced in the styles made famous by Belgian Trappist monks, but not actually brewed within the walls of a monastery. Today, the terms "Trappist," "Trappistes," and "Trappisten" or any similar derivation comprise an "appellation *(controlee)*," an indicator of origin. See TRAPPIST BREWERIES. As of 2011 only seven breweries in the world are allowed to use the Trappist designation, but this was not always so. Some people are surprised when they learn that monasteries always produced alcoholic beverages. Self-reliance is a central tenet of many monastic orders and monasteries, and monasteries once had vast land holdings from which to support themselves. Monks grew their own food and made their own drink. In Europe in the Middle Ages, wine was considered safe, but people knew that water, which can harbor many diseases, could be dangerous or even deadly. As monasteries spread from the grape-growing lands of southern Europe to the grain-growing areas of northern Europe, many shifted to the production of beer rather than wine as part of their daily sustenance. The Cistercian Order, founded in the 1100s, gave rise in 17th-century Normandy to "the Cistercian Order of the Strict Observance" at Abbaye de la Trappe. These monks of northern France, known as the Trappists, brewed very good beer and sold and traded it to the outside world.

Monastic life in northern France came to an abrupt halt in 1796. As the French Revolution spread, all monasteries in the country were sacked and looted, and the monks scattered into the countryside. From the 1830s onward, Trappist monasteries were slowly restored in Belgium. Brewing halted during World War II, but resumed in the 1940s. Over time, the beers reacquired a reputation for high quality, and it is here that trouble began. Soon there were Trappist beers produced by brewers who had never set foot in a monastery. Some brewers were more honest, establishing relationships with actual monasteries and remitting some of their profits to the monks. Others simply put a picture of a monk on the label, named a beer after a saint or a local monastery ruin, and reaped the profits for themselves. For a while, the monks largely tried to keep a serene distance from controversy, but when the Veltem brewery of Leuven launched a beer called Veltem Trappist in 1960, Abbaye Notre Dame d'Orval retained lawyers and filed a legal challenge.

On 28 February 1962, the Belgian Trade and Commerce court in Ghent issued its ruling: "the word 'Trappist' is commonly used to indicate a beer brewed and sold by monks pertaining to a Trappist order, or by people who would have obtained an authorization of this kind . . . is thus called 'Trappist,' a beer manufactured by Cistercian monks and not a beer in the Trappist style which will be rather called 'abbey beer.'" Today, the International Trappist Association protects the designation and issues the authority to use the logo reading "Authentic Trappist Product." Only beers produced at the Belgian monasteries Abbaye Notre-Dame de Scourmont (Chimay), Abbaye Notre-Dame d'Orval (Orval), Abbaye Notre-Dame de St. Remy (Rochefort), Abdij der Trappisten Westmalle (Westmalle), St Benedictus-Abdij (Achel), and St Sixtus Abdij (Westvleteren) and the Dutch monastery Abdij Onze Lieve Vrouw van Koningshoeven (La Trappe) may be called Trappist.

Clockwise from top left: American beer label, c. 1890; Brazilian beer label, c. 1900; Scottish beer label, c. 1940; American beer label, c. 1933; Swiss illuminated manuscript, 17th century; German colored lithograph, c. 1900. PIKE MICROBREWERY MUSEUM, SEATTLE, WA

Undeterred, secular breweries have continued to name their beers "St Something" and use images of monks on labels, but provenance is now clear to those paying attention. Abbey beers are produced by everyone from tiny brewpubs to the world's largest brewing company, AB InBev. See LEFFE BREWERY. Although the Trappist beers have exerted a clear influence on brewers worldwide, the term "Trappist" does not describe a single style and neither does the term "abbey." The term is specific enough to be vaguely useful, but broad enough to be frustrating. Some of these beers are pale, and some are dark; some are sweet, but most are dry. Some are at least partly bottle conditioned, but others are filtered. Abbey ales do, however, tend to have a few attributes in common. They are all top-fermented ales and often employ very warm fermentations, with temperatures ranging up to 86°F (30°C). Warm fermentations combine with Belgian yeast strains to produce a range of fruity and spicy flavors. Many of the beers are strong, with most ranging from 6% alcohol by volume (ABV) to 9.5% ABV, although there are outliers at either end of that range. Darker beers tend to attain color through the use of dark candi sugar as opposed to roasted malts, and other sugars are widely used. A few are spiced, but most are not.

Under the abbey ale umbrella there are some clear styles. Tripel (triple) is a strong golden ale style pioneered by Westmalle. See TRIPEL. Tripels have burnished, deep gold color and ABVs from 7% to 10%, with most settling in around 9%. The best examples are low in residual sugar, but may show a sweet-tasting malty fruitiness on the palate. Hop aroma is subdued and well integrated, and most have light snappy bitterness and vigorous carbonation. Despite their strength, good tripels are subtle, and they pair well with a wide range of foods. Dozens of tripels are produced in Belgium, but craft brewers in the United States and the rest of the world now brew many dozens more, some of them excellent.

The dubbel (or double) style, although somewhat less popular in the United States, is still widely produced in Belgium. These beers are dark ales, usually russet brown, with ABVs ranging from 6% to 7.5%. These are also usually technically dry, but most show a gentle caramel sweetness on the palate. The highly caramelized candi sugar syrup that produces the color also gives these beers an almost raisin-like fruitiness. Bitterness tends to be gentle. These can be great food beers, using their caramel character to harmonize with dishes featuring seared, roasted, or fried flavors.

From here, designations become less steady. A style sometimes referred to simply as "Belgian strong dark ale" or "abbey ale" intensifies the character of the classic dubbel, bringing more alcohol and fruit character at ABVs of 8% to 9.5%. When well brewed, these can make fine matches to lamb and game meats. Above this range, all bets are off, and waggish craft brewers, rarely Belgian, produce "quadrupels" at ABVs up to 14%. Although the names "dubbel" and "tripel" are of obscure origin, it is generally understood that a rising number always corresponded to rising strength. Just as some producers of California zinfandel can't resist the allure of 16% blockbusters, so some craft brewers are attracted to similar strengths. And like California trophy wines, some quadrupels can show a wonderful plummy, figgy fruit quality, but many are merely hot. The Belgian brewer will often mutter under his breath that these beers are distinctly un-Belgian, but the American, Brazilian, or Danish beer enthusiast who loves "quads" is entirely unconcerned.

At the lighter end, distinctly Belgian but rarely seen, there is the "abbey single" or table beer. These are interpretations of the beers that Trappist monks make for themselves, which tend to be very light in both body and alcohol, rarely reaching even 5%. Although the actual Trappist versions never see the marketplace, secular brewers, having tasted the beers on monastery visits, are sometimes moved to try their hand at the gentlest of the abbey styles.

See also SINGEL.

Oliver, Garrett. *The brewmaster's table.* New York: Ecco, 2003.

Rajotte, Pierre. *Belgian ale.* Boulder, CO: Brewers Publications, 1992.

Trappist Beers and Monks. www.trappistbeer.net (accessed November 30, 2010).

Garrett Oliver

accelerated batch fermentation is an attempt to gain economic advantage through the production of more beer with the same equipment in less time. If even a few days can be shaved off of the fermentation period needed to produce beer, there can be considerable increases in a brewery's overall capacity. There have always been many strategies for accelerating fermentations. However, care must be taken because flavor changes will occur when fermentations are accelerated by any of these methods.

Fermentation rates can be accelerated in several ways. Both the lag phase and the active fermentation phase can be shortened by increasing the yeast pitching rate. The initial fermentation temperature can be increased, as can the temperature of the active fermentation. Breweries can also speed up fermentations by blending actively fermenting beer with fresh, aerated wort (a form of kräusening; see KRÄUSENING). A higher fermentation temperature will increase the metabolic rate of yeast and the fermentation speed, but the profile of aroma compounds in the finished beer may change unfavorably. Fermentation times can be shortened by using powdery (non-flocculent) strains of yeast or by mechanically stirring the fermenting wort. The yeast can also be roused toward the end of fermentation by the injection of carbon dioxide or by using a re-circulating device.

Flavor changes may occur because of changes in yeast growth patterns with modifications in fusel alcohols, esters, and vicinal diketones (particularly diacetyl) occurring. Therefore, even though the fermented wort may have reached limit attenuation more quickly, proper maturation is still required. Some industrial brewers have sought to shorten the maturation period as well, using technologies such as the immobilized yeast reactor. See IMMOBILIZED YEAST REACTOR.

See also FERMENTATION.

Graham G. Stewart

acetaldehyde is an organic compound found in almost all plant materials and the most common of the aromatic chemical compounds called aldehydes. See ALDEHYDES.

Acetaldehyde is closely associated with ethyl alcohol (ethanol) through reduction (addition of electrons) and oxidation (removal of electrons) reactions. Acetaldehyde is produced in the early stages of fermentation and is reduced to ethanol in the latter stages of fermentation. Acetaldehyde is the immediate product of the metabolism of alcohol in the human body.

The body oxidizes ethanol back to acetaldehyde as the first step in its processing of alcohol. Beer containing excessive levels of acetaldehyde is characterized by the aroma and taste of green apples. People vary in their sensitivity to acetaldehyde, but beyond its presence as a background note, it is generally considered an off-flavor in beer.

If the yeast is not sufficiently active, either because it is not healthy or because the fermentation temperature is too low, too much acetaldehyde may remain in the beer. Bacterial infections can also interfere with yeast fermentation, leaving elevated levels of acetaldehyde in beer.

Acetaldehyde is further metabolized in the body by acetaldehyde dehydrogenases to acetate. In some people, acetaldehyde dehydrogenase enzymes are inefficient in metabolizing acetaldehyde. This can cause the well-known "flush" response observed when some people drink alcoholic beverages. This effect is genetically determined and is most prevalent in persons of Asian descent. It involves a reddening of the skin associated with a dilation of its capillaries.

Bev Robertson

acetic acid, the acid contained in vinegar (at 3%–6%), is also the main volatile fatty acid in alcoholic beverages. As the main acid generated from fatty acid metabolism in yeast, it is a key component (along with ethanol) in the generation of ethyl acetate, which is the most common flavor ester in beer. See ETHYL ACETATE. Acetic acid (CH_3COOH) is a weak, monocarboxylic volatile fatty acid produced by yeast as a natural by-product of metabolism, but it may also be produced by Acetobacteria (spoilage organisms). Acetobacter (acetic acid or vinegar bacteria), a genus of aerobic bacteria, can turn ethanol to acetic acid during fermentation if excessively aerated. This acid can also be generated from the oxidation of acetaldehyde and is thereby involved in complex reactions of flavor-generation during wood maturation of beer.

If present in amounts above the perception threshold, acetic acid conveys a sour vinegar taste and aroma to beer. However, this is not usually an issue in brewing, as most beers are produced under stringent quality controls to minimize both contamination and oxidation. Acetic acid is also not an issue in properly packaged beer, where oxygen is usually absent. In lambic beers and some other sour beer styles, acetic acid can be a desirable component that adds to the complexity of the flavor and aroma profile.

Gary Spedding

acetic acid bacteria typically oxidize ethanol to form acetic acid (vinegar) and are used for commercial vinegar production. This family of Gram-negative bacteria (Acetobacteriaceae) encompasses some 10 genera of which the most common are Acetobacter, Gluconobacter, and Gluconacetobacter. See GRAM STAIN. These bacteria generate energy by the incomplete oxidation of sugars, alcohols, and other carbon compounds to produce organic acids as end products. With ethanol as a carbon source, they accumulate acetic acid. Upon prolonged incubation, most can "overoxidize" the acetate to produce water and carbon dioxide (Gluconobacter strains are unable to further metabolize the acetate). Acetic acid bacteria must have a generous supply of oxygen and cannot grow in its absence. Colonies of acetic acid bacteria can be detected on culture media containing insoluble calcium carbonate and ethanol as carbon source. The acid produced by the bacteria dissolves the chalk, leaving a clear zone around the colony.

Acetic acid bacteria are widely distributed, particularly on plants and fruits and in the air, and will cause severe spoilage of beer if allowed access in the presence of oxygen. Because they are acid- and ethanol-tolerant and not inhibited by hop compounds, they grow rapidly in beer, producing acid off-flavors and turbidity. However, as long as the beer is properly stored and oxygen levels are low, acetic acid bacteria are not a problem. It is for this reason that they most commonly cause problems in cask-conditioned beer during dispense.

See also ACETIC ACID and BACTERIA.

Yamada, Yuzo, and Yukphan, Pattarapom. Genera and species in acetic acid bacteria. *International Journal of Food Microbiology* 125 (2008): 15–24.

Fergus G. Priest

acetyl CoA is an activated form of acetic acid, in which the acetate is coupled with Coenzyme A. It is a critically important molecule that takes part in the metabolism of all living organisms. Acetyl CoA can "donate" acetate in a wide range of reactions, including:

(a) the formation of esters and thioesters. Examples of esters produced by brewing yeast are iso-amyl acetate (banana-like flavor, prominent in Bavarian wheat beers) and ethyl acetate (pear-like flavor, commonly found in warm-fermented beers) while a prominent thioester is methyl thioacetate (cooked cabbage flavor)
(b) the synthesis of fatty acids and sterols, which are important membrane constituents of yeast
(c) the synthesis of organic acids: the reaction of acetyl-CoA with oxaloacetate to form citrate is the first step in the tricarboxylic acid cycle, which performs a key function in many living organisms for the provision of energy and building blocks for new cellular material.

See also ACETIC ACID and ORGANIC ACIDS.

Berg, J.M., Tymoczko, J.L., & Stryer, L. *Biochemistry*, 5th ed. New York: WH Freeman, 2002.

Charles W. Bamforth

Achel Brewery is the newest and smallest of seven approved Trappist monastery breweries. More formally known as the Brouwerij der Sint-Benedictusabdij de Achelse Kluis, it is located at the Abbey of Saint Benedict in the northeast Belgian border town of Achel, although part of the abbey actually lies in Holland.

The brewery opened in 1998, following the sale of some land around the abbey to raise money for the project. The abbey had been home to a brewery before World War I, but its copper kettles were pilfered by the invading German army. After the war, the monastery supported itself by raising cattle and growing and selling fruits and vegetables. In the late 1990s, however, a brother in the community was quoted as saying, "Beer is the most suitable product for an abbey."

The abbey recruited the revered Brother Thomas, who had brewed at Trappist Abbey of Westmalle, to help launch the new brewery. Brother Thomas also brought the Westmalle yeast, which is still used to ferment the Achel beers. Achel (pronounced Arkul) built the brewery on the site of an old dairy barn and for a time only served their beers on premises. A bottling line was later added and the abbey currently produces about 3,000 hl (300,000 liters) per year. Bike paths wind their way through the monastery site and are very popular with visitors.

The brewery's Achel blonde 5° and Achel bruin 5° are only available at the abbey pub. Bottles available in the United States, Belgium, and an expanding international market include the Achel 8° blonde and bruin served in 11-oz bottles and distinguishable by the color of the bottle caps. The blonde has a white cap and the bruin a gold one. There is also a bottled-conditioned Achel Trappist Extra, a complex, strong, dark ale with 9.5% alcohol by volume in 750-ml bottles.

See also TRAPPIST BREWERIES.

John Holl

acid. The general definition of an acid is any compound that yields H+ (hydrogen ions or protons) in solution or a chemical that reacts with alkalis (bases) to form salts. Solutions with pH values below 7.0 are acidic (see PH). In beer the term often pertains to sour, tart, acidic, and pungent aroma and/or taste. In most beer styles, notable acidic character is considered undesirable.

Most acids in beer are organic acids and include, most commonly, acetic (vinegar flavor), pyruvic, lactic (sour milk-like flavor), malic, and citric acid (strong tartness). They derive from raw materials, wort boiling and, mainly, yeast metabolism. Lactic and acetic acids can also derive from unwanted or uncontrolled microbial contamination. See ACETIC ACID and LACTIC ACID. The fall in pH during fermentation (typically by about one unit, for instance, from 5.20 to 4.20) depends in part on organic acid excretion.

These and other acids in beer influence flavor both directly, when present above their threshold levels, and by their influence on beer pH. Lactic acid, which is relatively weak, is sometimes used in the brewery for water composition and pH adjustment purposes (as the anions can aid the brewing process or promote flavor enhancement from raw materials). Stronger mineral acids, such as sulfuric acid and phosphoric acid, are used for passivating stainless steel and for cleaning brewing vessels and tanks. Phosphoric acid may also be used in acid-washing to reduce or eliminate bacterial infections in brewing yeast. Peracetic acid is an effective no-rinse sanitizer for brewery applications. Ascorbic acid (vitamin C) is sometimes used in beer as an antioxidant.

Gary Spedding

acidification is the process of lowering the pH of a solution until it falls below pH 7.00. Brewers will sometimes acidify the mash and/or wort to effect certain changes, via pH, of the efficiency of brewing or to alter the flavor profile of the final beer. In general the process involves the use of acids, acidic salts, or microbial fermentations (generating acids biologically) to shift the pH of the mash, wort, and ultimately the resulting beer to the desired final levels. Brewers require a clear understanding of water chemistry, mash reactions and wort reactions, and chemistries to use acidification to the full effect. The general quality of water for brewing as well as the emulation of world-famous brewing waters can also be attained via adjustment by food-grade acids and acidic salts.

Various enzymes participate during beer production; for example, in the mashing process, starch-to-sugar conversion takes place and proteins are subject to breakdown to peptides and amino acids to provide nutrients for yeast. These enzymes all work at their own best or optimal pH values. The brewer ultimately has substantial leeway in adjusting conditions to best promote the enzymatic reactions taking place. Acidification provides one powerful way to selectively influence the process and final beer stability.

Average malts when mashed will result in a pH of about 5.65–5.75. This pH is usually above the optimum for many of the important enzymes involved in beer production. Acidification techniques can reduce the pH to 5.40 and promote the activity of most enzymes involved in the conversion of the components in malt to desirable wort constituents. Fermentation will then be more efficient and the final beer flavor improved. Better colloidal stability—reduced potential for hazes to appear in the beer—can also be attained and beer is often lighter in color, which some consumers prefer. Flavor will be rounder, fuller, and softer and hop bitterness more pleasant and not "lingering."

Because of the German Reinheitsgebot purity laws of 1516, German brewers must resort to biological acidification of the mash because they cannot add exogenous acids or salts to the brewing water, mash, wort, or beer. See REINHEITSGEBOT. Acidification involves steeping malt, which naturally harbors lactic acid bacteria (beer-acidifying lactobacilli, with the preferred strain being Lactobacillus delbruckii), under defined conditions (sometimes following inoculation of specific strains of lactobacilli) to result in lactic acid production. Through the use of the collected acid "wort" or use of the "acid or sour-malt" (2%–10% added to the mash), a resultant lowering of the pH in mash, wort, and beer can be attained. The propagation is not unlike a sourdough culturing.

Brewers may also inject a lactic acid strain into a portion of wort. Following fermentation, a portion of the acidified wort is pasteurized to kill off the bacteria and then returned to the brewing process. This biological acidification is stated to provide superior results to simply adding commercially available lactic acid. If they do not have to follow the German purity laws, brewers can also add hydrochloric acid or sulfuric acid to mash and/or wort in specified amounts to adjust the pH in a similar manner.

Although water chemistry is highly complex, some simple adjustments to the pH of the water can be attained. Sulfuric and phosphoric acids as well as lactic acid (see also above) and acidic salts such as calcium chloride, calcium sulfate (gypsum), and magnesium sulfate (Epsom salts) can be used to lower the water pH to render its quality more suitable for brewing. Generally, here the brewer is lowering the alkalinity of the water by the acid adjustments, but the ions added such as calcium, magnesium, chloride, and sulfate also aid in promoting enzyme chemistry during mashing and final beer stability and in promoting flavor development in general and the quality of the hop flavor.

See also ACIDULATED MALT and PH.

Gary Spedding

acidity is a term referring to sour, tangy, or tart flavors derived from organic acids. Technically, acidity is the state of being acid—having the properties of an acid or the extent to which a solution is acid. See ACID. Acidity relates to the degree of sharpness of the taste of beer. Many organic acids and carbonic acid (carbon dioxide gas), when dissolved in beer, determine the acidity level. Of relevance to the consumer, acidity is detected via taste and can also be determined by titration against a standard base. When beer is analyzed in a laboratory, the acidity (percentage acid in a sample) is expressed as if all the acidity were present as lactic acid, but this is done for convenience; the acidity figure actually includes any acid present following degassing to eliminate carbon dioxide. See LACTIC ACID.

Almost all drinks that are considered refreshing and "drinkable" contain some notable acidity as part of a balance against sweet elements. The total concentration of "acidity" is typically described in the literature as 220–500 parts per million (ppm), adding to the pleasing tartness of beer. However, this seems rather low, because measurements of 0.1% to 0.3% acidity (expressed as lactic) are typical in beer, which would calculate out to 1000 to 3000 ppm. All-malt worts produce higher amounts of acidity in beer than do malt-adjunct worts. It is a generally assumed rule of thumb that most typical malt-adjunct beers will show about 0.1% acidity and all-malt beers closer to 0.2%. Light beers can be as low as about 0.07% acidity (or 700 ppm).

Beer is thus slightly acidic, with 100% barley malt lager beers having a pH in the range 4.00–5.00. Ales vary a little more, typically pH 3.00–6.00. Sour beer styles such as Belgian lambic, Berliner Weisse, and the new generation of craft-brewed sour ales can get as low as pH 3.30. Although the acidity level is largely driven by organic acids, the carbonation level also lends to the acidity content of these beer styles. See CARBONATION.

Abnormally high acidity can be an indication of bacterial infection of wort and/or beer. Microbial contamination issues (lactobacillus strains, for example) leading to abnormal acidity are usually perceived by the brewer or consumer before any testing would show the defect. See LACTOBACILLUS. Acidity in beer actually helps protect it because many pathogenic and food-spoilage microorganisms are unable to grow in high-acid (low-pH) environments. To some extent the acidic nature of beer, along with the carbon dioxide (carbonic acid acidity), lack of oxygen, and the presence of significant amounts of alcohol, has helped make beer a safe, potable beverage throughout history.

See also BERLINER WEISSE, LAMBIC, and SOUR BEER.

Gary Spedding

acidulated malt is a pale malt (color: roughly 3 to 6 EBC/1.7 to 2.8 SRM) that has been subjected to a lactic acid fermentation after kilning and a second finishing drying cycle. The lactic-acid bacteria reside naturally in the malt. The purpose of acidulated malt is to reduce the pH value of the mash. Proper mash pH (5.4 to 5.6) helps assure the enzymatic performance on which the brewer relies to break down gums, proteins, and starches. It also leads to proper wort pH, which affects yeast performance during fermentation and the final flavor profile of the resulting beer. Every 1% of acidulated malt (by weight) of the total grain bill reduces the mash-pH by 0.1 point. In highly alkaline mashes, acidulated malt can make up as much as 10% of the grain bill.

The optimum wort pH of most barley-based beers is 5.2, and of most wheat-based beers is 5.0. Measurement of the pH values from the mash-in to the finished beer informs the brewer if a pH correction is necessary and how much acidulated malt, if any, should be used in the mash.

Acidulated malt is widely used in Germany, where the Beer Purity Law (Reinheitsgebot) proscribes the direct use of acids in the mash, the wort, or the finished beer. See REINHEITSGEBOT.

See also MALT and PH.

Thomas Kraus-Weyermann

acid washing of yeast is an effective method to remove contaminating bacteria from cropped yeast prior to repitching. It is commonly used in breweries that reused their yeast for many generations. Yeast can be washed every generation or whenever contamination is suspected. Food-grade phosphoric acid is recommended to acidify the yeast slurry down to pH 2.2–2.5; the temperature should be maintained at 2°C–4°C for 2 h with gentle stirring to protect the cells against damage. It has been demonstrated that a combination of an ammonium persulfate wash acidified with phosphoric acid was more effective at removing most bacteria. Some lactic acid bacteria may show resistance even to the treatment; however, hop resins can be added as an extra precaution. The washing process will not remove wild yeasts, which are resistant to low pH. Whether pitching yeast is negatively affected by the washing process has been the subject of many studies, and many brewers view acid washing as a person might regard a life-saving drug with powerful side effects—as a last-ditch resort. However, some breweries employ yeast washing as a regular part of their yeast handling and culture maintenance. Under standard brewing conditions, with the procedure carried out correctly, the yeast should remain healthy. Yeast slurries harvested from high-gravity brews or under poor physiological conditions may result in a loss of cell viability resulting from the acid treatment. Acid-washed yeast must be pitched into wort directly after treatment. It is important to note that acid washing should not be necessary if hygiene standards are kept high, yeast is stored for a minimum period of time between brews, and is not reused for more than 5–10 generations.

Cunningham, S., and G. G. Stewart. Effects of high gravity brewing and acid washing on brewers' yeast. *Journal of the American Society of Brewing Chemists* 56 (1998): 12–18.

Simpson, W. J., and J. R. N. Hammond. The response of brewing yeast to acid washing. *Journal of the Institute of Brewing* 95 (1989): 347–54.

Sylvie Van Zandycke

acrospire is the sprout of a grain seed, the beginning of a new plant. In the field, after the snow has melted and the moist soil is being warmed by the spring sun, the acrospire grows in a spiral from one end of the seed—hence its name of acro"spire"—while rootlets develop at the other end. As the acrospire grows, enzymes in the grain become active, too, which breaks down nutrients so that they can be readily absorbed by the emerging plant. This process is called "modification" and involves the alteration of the molecular structure of the kernel material, which consists mostly of complex proteins, carbohydrates (starches), glucans (cellulose), and lipids (fats). See MODIFICATION. In the malt house, this process is imitated through the steeping of the grain at the beginning of the malting process and its subsequent germination in an air-, moisture-, and temperature-controlled box. The size of the acrospire, therefore, is a good visual indicator of the progress of modification.

If germination continued, all the nutrients the brewer tries to preserve for beer-making would be used up by the plant for its own development. The maltster, therefore, interrupts germination when the acrospire is about 75%–100% of the length of the kernel. At this point, there is just the right balance between the resources converted by the enzymes and the resources consumed by the acrospire. The grain is then kiln-dried, and the dead acrospire and rootlets are knocked off through mechanical agitation.

Thomas Kraus-Weyermann

additives. Brewing is a very traditional and natural process that does not generally call for the use of the sorts of additives found in many other modern foods. Most beers from most breweries are essentially additive-free; the natural raw materials and the biological processes involved in brewing are perfectly capable of producing excellent, tasty, healthy, and stable beer entirely without assistance from the additive industries.

Nonetheless, modern chemistry does sometimes find its way into the brewhouse. Additives used in brewing are categorized according to their purpose of use. Here we do not address the large group of so-called technical aids like salts and acids for water adjustments, enzymes, finings, and chemical stabilizers (insoluble chemicals that are not found in the finished beer) used for ensuring lasting clarity of filtered beers, etc. Nor do we address "alternative raw materials" like adjuncts, unmodified hop extracts, natural fruits, or herbs and spices. These are covered elsewhere.

In all markets the use of additives is regulated by the national and local food safety authorities. Regulations often take the form of a "positive list" detailing all additives allowed for brewing in that market and how they must be declared on the packages. For example, the EU positive list specifies the E-numbers that should be used in the ingredient declarations on the labels or cans. Regulations may also take the form of specific legislation prohibiting certain—or all—additives in beer.

Chemically Modified Hop-Based Additives

This group of additives covers a wide range of different commercial products (e.g., rho-, tetra-, and hexa-iso-alfa-acid-extract), all being produced by various chemical modifications (reduction processes) of CO_2 hop extracts. When used, primarily for industrial lager beer, these are added to finished beer just before packaging and offer the brewer several advantages: avoidance of skunky (lightstruck) flavors that might otherwise form in non-protective clear or emerald glass bottle (see LIGHTSTRUCK), a smooth and easily controlled bitter flavor, high solubility in beer, and enhanced head retention.

Enhancers of Chemical Stability

By far the most commonly used agents for enhancement of chemical stability are the technical aids belonging to the silica group and the PVPP/nylon group, covered elsewhere in this book. See ADSORBENTS and PVPP. These substances affect the ability of a filtered beer to maintain its clarity over long periods of time and at very low temperatures. But some breweries, mainly standard lager breweries in lesser developed markets, still use older technologies for this purpose.

One of these products is PVP (polyvinylpyrrolidone), a beer soluble substance which is a type of "plastic precursor" that is inert to virtually anything but polyphenols, to which it has a high affinity. When added to a beer, the PVP will immediately react with the polyphenols in the beer forming insoluble PVP/polyphenol precipitation that can then subsequently be filtered out of the beer. If not precipitated and removed, the polyphenols will eventually, under stress by time and/or temperature, react with some of the soluble proteins in the beer and form colloidal and eventually insoluble complexes causing a visual haze in the beer.

Another chemical stabilizer, nowadays rarely used in brewing, is the enzyme papain (the name stems from the Papaya fruit where this enzyme is abundant and from which it can be isolated), but sold under the commercial name Collupulin. When added to filtered beer, this proteolytic enzyme will degrade the proteins in the beer, including those that would eventually react with the polyphenols to form haze. Adding enzymes that are still active when the beer is consumed is prohibited in many countries, and regardless of legal implications, Collupulin—although very effective as a chemical stabilizer—also degrades foam-active proteins in the beer, thus reducing the head retention of the beer. As a result of both of these deficiencies it has fallen out of use in developed countries.

Enhancers of Flavor Stability

The chemical agents used for improvements of flavor stability are probably the most widely used additives in brewing. Especially for standard mass-market lager beers, they can be very effective with respect to improving the shelf life of these beers. See SHELF LIFE. The main culprit by far, in terms of spoiling the flavor of beer, is oxygen. Through a series of very complex chemical processes, oxygen reacts with many of the aroma and flavor active compounds in the beer, gradually replacing the fresh and desirable flavors with cardboard-like, papery, and stale flavors. While there are positive forms of oxidation (see AGING OF BEER), when used by brewers the term is almost always associated with these negative flavor effects. Thus, logically, the substances used to reduce or postpone such undesired flavor deterioration are called "antioxidants."

The most commonly used type of antioxidants in beer are sulphites. These very effective compounds all contain free sulphite that not only reacts with free oxygen but also with a large number of those "oxidation precursors" (aldehydes, most importantly) that would eventually be further oxidized into staling compounds. Sulphites are also naturally occurring in beer as they are produced as metabolites by the yeast, but the level varies significantly with both yeast strain and brewing process. This makes control of sulphite levels difficult for brewers who add sulphites to beer, especially in regards to markets where there are legal limits for total sulphite in beverages. Most countries regulate the level of sulphites in beer as they are well known to be allergenic. The majority of wine on the market also contains added sulfites.

Another important antioxidant used for beer is ascorbic acid (Vitamin C). The way ascorbic acid works to prevent or delay staling and oxidation is similar to that of the sulfites, but it is not as effective. Also, ascorbic acid may even under certain (but not well understood) circumstances act in the opposite way, namely as an oxidizer. Ascorbic acid is allowed in beer in most markets.

Color Regulating Agents

As is common in wine and liquor, the color of beer may be adjusted upward (toward higher color) by the use of a number of compounds. The most important is caramel color. See CARAMEL COLOR. A related product is Farbebier (German for "coloring beer"), a product developed in Germany as a coloring agent allowed by the Reinheitsgebot (German purity law). See REINHEITSGEBOT. Although totally undrinkable, Farbebier is technically an extremely dark beer brewed with black malt exclusively, and therefore it may used without label declaration in most countries.

There are two normal reasons a brewer may use coloring agents in beer. The first is as a color corrective, used in small dosages as a final correction of the color of a wide range of beers. But it may also be used as part of the actual construction of a beer. As coloring agents are—at normally used concentrations—virtually without aroma or flavor, they can be used for producing dark beers with much less roasted aroma, flavor, and taste than would result from using dark malts to achieve the same color. An industrial brewer may thereby use a form of food coloring to give a beer the appearance of rich flavors where none may actually exist.

Taste and Flavor Regulators

A wide range of different compounds may be used at all stages of production (including just before packaging, allowing brewers to produce a number of different "products" from the same "base beer") so descriptions here cannot be comprehensive. Acids—the most common is lactic acid—may be added to give desired tartness, sugars added to increase body and mouthfeel, and various natural or artificial extracts or essences of fruits and herbs added to give non-beer related aroma, taste, and flavor. A good example of these is the recent fad of adding lime flavorings to mass-market lagers.

Foam Stabilizers

The use of foam stabilizers in brewing is obviously associated with situations where the head (see FOAM) formation and retention (how well the head of foam forms and how long it takes to collapse and disappear) on a given beer is considered insufficient for consumer acceptance. In most cases the "natural" deficiency of head properties of a given beer is due to either the use of very large proportions of adjuncts (carbohydrate sources that provide no foam potential), very poor malt quality, or processing problems (addition of foam suppressors during fermentation, excessive foaming during fermentation, excessive CO_2 scrubbing of the beer to remove oxygen, incidental addition of surface active cleaning agents, etc.) causing the beer to lose its inherent foaming abilities.

The only widely used foam stabilizer is called PGA (propylene-glycol-alginate), which is sold under a range of commercial names. This compound is an extract from certain types of seaweed that is subsequently chemically modified. PGA, whether purchased in powder or pre-dissolved form, is slurred in deaerated water, yielding a very viscous solution that is then mixed into the beer. The PGA acts by means of its extremely high surface tension that it lends to the beer, thereby creating much more durable foam bubbles when the beer is poured. This ersatz foam tends to have substantially different aesthetic qualities than natural foam, a fact that the consumer may or may not notice.

Kunze, Wolfgang. *Technology brewing and malting*, 3rd international ed. Berlin: VLB Berlin, 2004.

Anders Brinch Kissmeyer

adenosine triphosphate (ATP) is a molecule that is a universal energy store. It comprises one xylose sugar, the adenine base, and three phosphates. One of the phosphates is linked through a high-energy bond which, when split, fuels reactions such as biosynthesis, transportation, etc.

ATP is generated in catabolic processes such as glycolysis ("sugar breakdown"). In turn, ATP is consumed in reactions that demand an input of energy, e.g., the biosynthesis of cellular materials in anabolic reactions.

The detection of ATP can be used as a rapid test for the hygiene status of equipment and products. Wherever there is or has been growth of microorganisms in locales that have not been efficiently cleaned (e.g., in the Cleaning in Place [CIP] systems that are widely used in modern breweries to clean vessels and pipes), the soil will contain ATP. This can be detected through ATP bioluminescence. A swab swept across a surface is broken into a reaction mixture that includes a substrate luciferin and an enzyme called luciferase. (This is the enzyme whose action leads to the light generation in firefly tails.) If ATP is present, then the reaction can proceed, with the production of light. The intensity of light production is proportional to the amount of ATP present and, in turn, to the amount of contamination present. ATP testing is considered a powerful tool for quality assurance in modern breweries.

Berg, J.M., Tymoczko, J.L., & Stryer, L. *Biochemistry*, 5th ed. New York: WH Freeman, 2002.

Charles W. Bamforth

adhumulone, one of five identified alpha acid analogues in hop resin, the others being cohumulone, humulone, prehumulone, and posthumulone. Collectively, these alpha acid analogues serve as the precursors to iso-alpha acids, the predominant contributors of bitterness in beer. Adhumulone levels in hops are typically constant at 15% of the total alpha acid content across all varieties, whereas cohumulone and humulone levels vary (20%–50%) depending on variety. Pre- and posthumulone are minor constituents. Only slight differences in molecular structures differentiate all analogues of the alpha acids. In the case of adhumulone, the side group of the molecule is 2-methylbutyryl. Oxidation of hops leads to cleavage of this side group and the production of 2-methylbutryic acid, which has a distinctive, pungent odor similar to Roquefort cheese. This is why oxidized hops are often described as "cheesy."

See also ADLUPULONE, COHUMULONE, and HUMULONE.

Thomas Shellhammer and Val Peacock

adjuncts are alternative sources of extract used to replace a proportion of the malt. While they may be used as cheaper sources of extract, it is just as likely that they are used to impact some element of product quality such as color (either to darken or lighten it), flavor, or foam. Alternatively their use makes sense if there are prevailing taxation considerations that make low malt use advantageous, for instance, the legislation in Japan that spawned the development of Happoshu and Third Category drinks. See JAPAN.

Liquid adjuncts (sugars/syrups) are usually added in the wort boiling stage. They may be sugars extracted from plants rich in fermentable sugars, notably sucrose from cane or beet. The sucrose may be hydrolyzed by the enzyme invertase to produce its component monosaccharides, glucose and fructose, in the somewhat sweeter "invert" sugar. Alternatively they may be sugars produced in factories by the acid or (more likely these days) enzyme-hydrolysis of starch, especially from corn (maize). By selection of enzyme and processing conditions a range of products can be realized that differ in their composition, notably their degree of fermentability (see table). Liquid adjuncts are frequently called "wort extenders" because they allow an extension of brew house yield through obviating the need for extra milling, mashing, and wort separation capacity.

Solid adjuncts are added in mashing, because they require the enzymes from malt or exogenous enzymes to digest their component macromolecules. Solid adjuncts are based on diverse cereals, notably unmalted barley, wheat, corn, rice, oats, rye, and sorghum. There is also interest in pseudocereals such as buckwheat and proso-millet, primarily in the context of beers for people suffering from gluten intolerance.

In turn, solid adjuncts can be in different forms: whole cereal, grits, flour, flakes, torrefied, or malted (in the context of malt that is other than the standard malt used for producing the beer style concerned). There has been some consideration of extrusion cooking of cereals but the resultant products have a very low bulk density and therefore tend to have unfavorable transportation economics. The high gelatinization ("melting") temperature for corn, rice, and sorghum demands that these cereals require treatment at higher temperatures than barley, oats, rye, or wheat. If such cereal is in the form of grits (produced by the dry milling of cereal in order to remove outer layers and the oil-rich germ), then it needs to be "cooked" in the brew house.

Alternatively the cereal can be pre-processed by intense heat treatment in a micronization operation. The whole grain is conveyed beneath an intense heat source (500°F/260°C), resulting in a "popping" of the kernels (c.f. puffed breakfast cereals) to produce so-called torrefied cereal. In flaking, grits are gelatinized by steam and then rolled between steam-heated rollers. Flakes (like grits and flour) do not need to be milled in the brew house, but micronized (torrefied) cereal does.

Cereal cookers are made of stainless steel (or occasionally copper) and incorporate an agitator and steam jackets. See CEREAL COOKER. The adjunct is delivered from a hopper and the adjunct mixed with water at a rate of perhaps 15 kg/hectoliter of water. The adjunct will be mixed with 10%–20% of malt as a source of enzymes. Following cooking the adjunct mash is likely to be taken to boiling and then mixed with the main mash (that is at a relatively low mashing-in temperature, say 113°F or 45°C), with the resultant effect being a rise in temperature to allow conversion of the starch from the malt. This is called "double mashing."

Sugars and Syrups

	% Glucose	*% Maltose*	*% Maltotriose*	*% Dextrins*	*Other*
Dextrose	100	—	—	—	—
Corn syrup	45	38	3	14	—
High maltose	10	60	—	30	—
Maltodextrin	~0	1.5	3.5	95	—
Sucrose	0	0	0	0	100% sucrose
Invert sugar	50	0	0	0	50% fructose

From Bamforth, C.W. (2006)

While adjuncts are widely derided by beer enthusiasts for their wide use in major beers (to lighten color and flavor), many uses of adjuncts are quite traditional. Indeed the very long-standing use of certain adjuncts in some of the mainstream beers renders their use as being traditional for those beer styles. American colonialists often supplemented the mash with whatever starch was at hand; pumpkin was a particularly popular adjunct. Many Belgian and Belgian-style beers use a form of sucrose called "candi sugar," which is often caramelized to add color and flavor to beers. See CANDI SUGAR. In particular, dark candi sugar, usually in the form of a heavy syrup, gives many dark Belgian-style beers distinctive raisin-like caramel flavors. These sugars, frequently used as up to 20% of extract, are highly fermentable and can help beers attain very low residual sugar profiles. Craft brewers use various sugars to attain high gravities in beer styles such as barley wine, "double IPA," and other strong ales. Honey is another popular adjunct, and may be added in the kettle. Honey is also often added post-fermentation, where it adds sweetness and honey aromatics.

Bamforth, C.W. *Scientific principles of malting and brewing.* St Paul, MN: American Society of Brewing Chemists, 2006.

Goode, D.L., & Arendt, E.K. "Developments in the supply of adjunct materials for brewing." In *Brewing: New technologies*, ed. C.W. Bamforth, 30–67. Cambridge: Woodhead, 2006.

Stewart, G.G. "Adjuncts." In *Handbook of Brewing*, eds. F.G. Priest & G.G. Stewart, 161–175. Boca Raton, FL: CRC Press, 2006.

Charles W. Bamforth

adlupulone is one of four identified beta acid analogues in hop resin, the others being colupulone, lupulone, and prelupulone. Adlupulone levels are low (10% to 15% of total beta acids) but consistent across different varieties. Colupulone levels vary (20% to 55% of total beta acids) depending on variety, as do lupulone levels (30% to 55%). Structurally, these analogues are very similar to their alpha acid counterparts except that beta acids have a third prenyl group attached to the center ring. As a result of this structural difference, these acids do not isomerize and therefore iso-beta acids are not created. Furthermore, beta acids are virtually insoluble in wort; thus, only trace levels can be found in beer. The oxidation products of beta acids (hulupones), however, are present in aged hops and can be found in beer, and they confer bitterness. As hops oxidize, the bitterness that comes from iso-alpha acids diminishes because of alpha acids oxidation, but this is somewhat offset by the presence of bitterness from the hulupones. The ratio of alpha acids to beta acids ultimately dictates to what degree the bitterness will diminish as hops oxidize. Higher levels of beta acids in the raw hops will result in a slower decline of bittering power as hops degrade oxidatively. Qualitatively, however, the bitterness conferred by hulupones is considered coarse.

See also COLUPULONE, HULUPONES, and LUPULONE.

Thomas Shellhammer

Admiral (hop), an English hop high in bittering potential and showing typical English aroma, bred by Peter Darby at the Wye College from Challenger and Northdown parents. Admiral has high alpha-acids levels (13%–16% w/w) and moderate oil levels (1.0–1.7 ml/100 g) with an aroma that is described as "pleasant," or "English." It has moderate storageability and is only slightly resistant to verticillium wilt. It was developed to replace Wye Target as a high alpha variety but did not actually take hold commercially because it did not have sufficient tolerance of verticillium wilt. It was recorded as moderately resistant in its first test but it soon became obvious during the farm trial stages that it lacked sufficient resistance to withstand infection in most of the hop areas where the disease was endemic. It was released as a variety known to show only slight resistance; however, it had to be classified as "resistant" to distinguish it from the highly susceptible varieties such as Fuggle or Goldings. The variety Pilgrim (released to UK growers in 2001, and registered for PVR (plant variety rights) in 2006) has replaced Wye Target to a much greater extent than Admiral. At the 2009 harvest, there were 114 acres (46 ha) of Admiral grown with an average alpha-acid content of 16.4%. Of this area, 104 acres (42 ha) were grown in the UK and 10 acres (4 ha) in Belgium.

Thomas Shellhammer, Alfred Haunold, and Peter Darby

Adnams Brewery (Adnams Sole Bay Brewery) is based in the seaside town of Southwold in Suffolk, England. A brewery was founded on the site, behind the Swan Inn, in 1396 by Johanna de Corby. In the 19th century the brewery was owned by a local maltster who sold it to George and Ernest Adnams in 1857. Their brewery became a public company in 1891 and the Adnams were joined in partnership in 1901 by members of the Loftus family. Both families have continued to run the brewery to the present day: Jonathan Adnams is the current chairman, following the retirement of Simon Loftus, who turned the company from a small regional brewery into one with a national presence.

Adnams specializes in cask-conditioned beer and uses East Anglian Maris Otter malting barley and such traditional whole hops as Fuggles and Goldings. See FUGGLE (HOP) and GOLDING (HOP). Their beers are widely admired. A substantial investment in the first decade of the 21st century has seen a new brewhouse installed that uses the continental system of mash mixers and lauter tuns. The flagship brands of Bitter and Broadside and a strong winter beer, Tally Ho, have been joined by a golden ale, Explorer, and a rolling program of seasonal beers, including such European styles as kölsch, German wheat beer, and Belgian abbey ale.

A new warehouse, built outside Southwold in the village of Reydon, is environmentally friendly, with a grassed roof that captures rain water for washing casks and delivery trucks. Adnams owns 74 pubs, mainly in Norfolk and Suffolk, but with one in London. Bitter and Broadside are sold throughout England.

Roger Protz

adsorbents are solid materials that are added to beer, usually after primary filtration, to bind (adsorb) the compounds that produce haze. A range of substances in beer can combine as the beer ages to produce particles large enough to reflect light and cause turbidity. Primary among these substances are polyphenols and proteins.

The most common commercial adsorbents are silica gel, which selectively binds the haze-promoting proteins, and polyvinylpolypyrrolidone (PVPP), which binds polyphenols. PVPP can be used either as a powder or in the form of impregnated secondary filtration sheets. In either instance the PVPP, which is quite expensive, can be regenerated and then reused. Silica gel and PVPP are combined in several commercial products for ease of use. Adsorbents are not considered additives because they are completely filtered out of the beer along with the adsorbed proteins and polyphenols after treatment.

See also SILICA GEL.

Priest, Fergus G., and Graham G. Stewart, eds. *Handbook of brewing*, 2nd ed. Boca Raton, FL: CRC Press, 2006.
Siebert, Karl J., and Penelope Y. Lynn. Mechanisms of adsorbent action in beverage stabilization. *Journal of Agricultural Food Chemistry* 45 (1997): 4275–80.

Ritchie S. King

adulteration is any situation where a person sells something of commercial value that is subject to some type of fraud, and beer is no exception. We can expect with fair certainty that adulteration of beer reaches back well into antiquity. For many centuries, however, most Europeans may have had little expectation as to what beer should be. Although the average modern beer drinker may see beer as a grain-based drink flavored only with hops, many flavorings and ingredients beside these were once common. Before hops became standard in Europe and then the UK, a spice and herb blend called gruit was used to bitter beer. See GRUIT. Other grains, particularly rye, oats, einkorn, and spelt, were routinely used in place of barley and wheat malt. Honey or fermented mead might be blended in to create braggot. See BRAGGOT.

The idea of adulteration is, therefore, somewhat related to intentional fraud. In medieval England, an official bestowed with the title "ale-conner" was empowered by towns and great manors to prevent and punish the adulteration of beer. See ALE-CONNER. The ale-conner was essentially a sanctioned beer taster who could haul a brewer or publican into a local court if the beer was found to be unpalatable or somehow suspect. In 1516, the Reinheitsgebot was established in Bavaria, prohibiting brewers from making beer from anything but barley, malt, hops, and water. Although historians argue about the reasons behind the law, the

Reinheitsgebot is widely considered the first real consumer protection law in Europe.

In the early days, many adulterations were relatively harmless, even if they were fraudulent. Any substance containing spicy heat, horseradish, for example, could be used to simulate the warming effects of alcohol. When other spices became available, brewers used them—chilies, black pepper, and ginger were all used to create an illusion of strength. The consumer, convinced that he was getting a strong beer, could be induced to pay more for it. Aged beers were also considered valuable, and a dash of vinegar in a young beer could suffice to give it the slightly acetic character that many beer drinkers once prized in beers that had been "vatted." Both the European age of exploration and the commercialization of the beer industry brought more dangerous frauds to beer.

By the mid 1800s, Cocculus indicus, a berry from India containing the alkaline poison picrotoxin, was widely used in British porter, where it gave a powerful narcotic effect. The minutes of a House of Commons committee meeting indicate some of the substances seized from British breweries' stores: "cocculus extract, coloring, honey, hartshorn shavings, Spanish juice, orange powder, ginger, grains of paradise, quassia, liquorice, caraway seeds, copperas (iron sulfate, used to create foam), capiscum, and 'mixed drugs.'" By 1849, William Black, author of *A practical treatise on brewing*, was forced to conclude that "however much they may surprise, however pernicious or disagreeable they may appear, he has always found them requisite in the brewing of porter, and he thinks they must invariably be used by those who wish to continue the taste, flavor, and appearance of the beer. And though several Acts of Parliament have been passed to prevent porter brewers from using many of them, yet the author can affirm, from experience, he could never produce the present flavored porter without them. The intoxicating qualities of porter are to be ascribed to the various drugs intermixed with it. It is evident that some porter is more heady than other, and it arises from the greater or less quantity of stupefying ingredients. Malt, to produce intoxication, must be used in such large quantities as would very much diminish, if not totally exclude, the brewer's profit."

Things were somewhat better in Germany, but even German beers didn't escape slight of hand. The German journal *Archiv der Pharmazie* divided "the adulteration of beer into two classes: the use of correctives to restore a spoiled beer, and the use of substitutes for malt and hops. Probably most of the evils arise from a too sparing use of the proper materials to furnish a strong and therefore durable beer. The beer, weak in alcohol and extract, grows sour, and the acid is neutralized with alkalies and chalk."

German brewers were also discovered to have used absinthe, aloe, and Heracleum spondyllium (cow parsnip) as hop substitutes and glycerin for flavor and body. And although Germany had long been associated with all-malt beer, German brewers constantly experimented with other grains, publishing results in scientific journals. In 1870, *Chemical News* printed an article about the use of rice in beer, asserting that a beer brewed in Weisenau, containing one-sixth rice and five-sixths barley malt, had been found quite pleasant.

Over the past 100 years, various chemicals have been used as preservatives in beers. These have ranged from largely harmless levels of sulfites, still sometimes used in Europe, to formaldehyde, although the latter was never so widespread as rumored. Today, the European Union tightly regulates beer ingredients, as does the Food and Drug Administration (FDA) in the United States, and the idea of adulteration becomes harder and harder to fathom. The most popular mass-market beers in the world use corn and rice to replace a fraction of the malt in the mash. Colonial Americans used everything from pumpkins to peapods in beer, and today's American craft beers might be flavored with lemongrass, whole chilies, cacao beans, or reincarnated gruit. The sugars that are anathema to the Bavarian brewer are an important ingredient in the finest Belgian beers. Once eschewed by the craft brewer, hop oils and extracts are becoming more common in India pale ales, where the addition of gypsum has long been expected. Flavored malt beverages are common (see FLAVORED MALT BEVERAGE), but in 2010 the FDA decided that several caffeinated versions were adulterated, briefly leaving many craft brewers to wonder whether their coffee stouts might soon be banned. Today's beer drinker has a hope and expectation of general wholesomeness from the beer set before him, and that expectation is widely justified. Beyond this, however, we may consider that the idea of adulteration has largely moved into the realm of philosophy.

Bickerdyke, John. *The curiosities of ale & beer*. London: Ayer, 1889.

Cornwall, H. B. Adulteration of beer. *Public Health Papers and Reports* 10 (1884): 106–15. www.ncbi.nlm.nih.gov (accessed December 1, 2010).

Garrett Oliver

advertising. Sitting quietly in a glass, cask, or bottle, beer is not always its own best spokesperson, and needs some help getting the word out about its quality, availability, and origin. The earliest advertising vehicles were very simple. In the days of ancient Sumeria, a Brewster would announce the availability of fresh ale by hanging a bush above her door. In medieval times, this symbol of a bush or a broom was known as an ale stake, with the simple message, "We have beer." Early tavern or brewpub signs were visual advertising, appropriate for an illiterate clientele. Very little evidence for graphically branded beers exists prior to the mid-19th century, although it is clear that certain breweries enjoyed wide fame. In 1876 the Bass red triangle was the first trademark for any product to be registered in Britain, although the mark had been in use for decades prior to that date.

Modern advertising for beer began in the 1880s with the development of polychrome lithography, which allowed complex and colorful imagery to be applied to a paper or metal surface. Posters became an important advertising vehicle, especially in Europe, where notable artists such as Alfonse Mucha, A. M. Cassandre, and Ludwig Hohlwein produced memorably creative examples. One of the most notable was a series of posters by John Gilroy for Guinness in the 1930s and 1940s, featuring slogans like "Guinness is good for you," with striking imagery such as the famous toucan balancing a pint on his beak.

In the United States, images of alluring women or smoke-belching breweries were preferred, but the most famous American brewery lithograph is the 1896 Budweiser piece, *Custer's Last Fight*. Adolphus Busch had a few extra scalpings added to an existing painting, making it more sensational. Busch was also famous for handing out "Stanhope" pocketknives with a peephole showing his portrait.

Enameled metal signs were also popular advertising pieces and because of their durability were most often used for exterior signage, advertising the brands available in saloons. Point-of-purchase advertising also included trays, mirrors, glassware, tap knobs, coasters, and back-bar pieces made of plaster, metal, and eventually plastic. Neon beer

Trade card, c. 1884. Modern advertising for beer began in the 1880s. PIKE MICROBREWERY MUSEUM, SEATTLE, WA

signs started to appear after Prohibition. Many of these pieces were dazzlingly beautiful; all are now highly collectible.

Mass media beer advertising did not begin until after World War II. Full-page ads in general-interest magazines became popular. One famous print campaign, *Beer Belongs,* was commissioned by the United States Brewers Foundation. It featured illustrations of common lifestyle activities along with beer and food images, positioning beer as "America's beverage of moderation." The idea was to undo some of the damage to beer's market share that had been done by Prohibition. Between 1945 and 1956 at least 136 of these ads appeared, although during that period per capita consumption of beer actually dropped.

In the 1950s, radio broadcasts became important along with sponsorship of baseball and other sports. As soon as the medium appeared, beer advertisers made the leap to television. Budgets took a huge jump in the 1970s, after Philip Morris took control of Miller, and for the first time targeted women as well as men. Spending reached a peak in 2007 (Anheuser-Busch spent $1.36 billion in marketing that year) and has declined since.

The most significant television campaign for an American beer is almost certainly McCann–Erikson Worldwide's "Tastes great, less filling" campaign for Miller Lite. The product, which had been languishing as a diet beer for women, was repositioned as a beer that could be consumed in larger quantities (less filling). By linking with eccentric celebrity athletes in a humor-filled campaign, Lite became a roaring success, forever changing the beer industry. With this success, Miller's volume nearly doubled between 1973 and 1977, and in 1992 Miller Lite displaced Budweiser as the number one beer in America.

British beer advertising has tended to be more tongue in cheek and occasionally edgy. Brewery Shepherd Neame first brewed its now-popular beer Spitfire in 1990 to commemorate the 50th anniversary of the Battle of Britain. Ever since, the advertising for Spitfire has often referenced World War II and taken some glee in tweaking the Germans. The early 2000s campaign "No Fokker comes close" certainly caught people's attention. Some other British brewery advertising lines have become classics, such as the one for Cardiff's Brains Brewery: "It's Brains you want."

Over the decades brewery advertising has been much criticized for sexism, irresponsibility, appeal to underage drinkers, and other transgressions. In the United States the Beer Institute adopted an Advertising and Marketing Code to address criticism and offer its large-brewery members some guidance on what to avoid—mainly advertising to those below the drinking age. Since 2005, the European Union has had a similar "audiovisual directive," implemented by industry groups in each country, but some countries, like France, have banned all alcohol advertising on television and billboards. Restrictions tend to follow a society's attitudes about alcohol in general. On the proactive side, larger breweries and brewery associations have campaigns designed to deter underage drinking and drunk driving.

Randy Mosher

aeration. Yeast about to begin a brewery fermentation requires a certain amount of oxygen to fuel some of its biochemical pathways, notably the production of unsaturated fatty acids and esters. It is normal practice to add oxygen to wort prior to fermentation; absence of sufficient oxygen will hamper yeast reproduction and can lead to poor fermentations. Historically aeration may have simply meant allowing the wort to cool in the presence of air or by dropping the wort into a fermentation vessel from above. Modern brewing practice dictates that oxygen be added directly to the wort after it has been cooled. Either filtered compressed air or oxygen from a cylinder is used and introduced into the flowing wort via a sintered metal device, a pumice stone, or Venturi device. The solubility of the oxygen in wort is lower than in water because of the dissolved solids already in the wort. The stronger the wort, the lower the solubility of the oxygen. For wort at 12°Plato and using air as the oxygen source, the maximum amount of oxygen that can dissolve in wort at normal wort collection temperatures is between 7–8 ppm. Using pure oxygen, figures in the 35–40 ppm range can be achieved depending on the temperature. Calculating the amount of oxygen dissolved in the wort is possible but depends on the temperature of the wort and the oxygen as well as their relative flow rates. Brewers will generally place a dissolved oxygen measuring device downstream to achieve consistent dissolved oxygen concentrations. Some brewers have experimented with direct oxygenation of yeast slurries, arguing that this reduces the extent of undesirable oxidation of wort components.

See also OXIDATION and OXYGEN.

Steve Parkes

Affligem Brewery. There has been commercial brewing at or near the site of the Affligem brewery in Opwijk, northwest of Brussels, since 1790, with the De Smedt family holding sole ownership from 1832 until 1984. Their first major brand was Op-Ale in 1935, a hoppier version of the Speciale pale ales that took root in Belgium around 1900. The business survived two world wars and in 1970 took over the brewing of beers for the Benedictine Abbey at Affligem, which had itself brewed at times, well into the 20th century. However, the family was reluctant to make the necessary investments required to compete in a market desirous of blond lagers and increasingly dominated by larger producers. In 1984 they sold half the company to their then brewery manager, Theo Vervloet, and passed him its stewardship. Vervloet applied his considerable abilities to single-mindedly making the plant more productive and the business more efficient, without compromising production standards. Its Affligem brands grew well enough for them to gain the contract to make beers for the Abbey of Postel, and others.

By 1999 Brouwerij De Smedt (or BDS) had revived to the extent that the family withdrew altogether, selling their shares to the Dutch brewer Heineken, who may have become the first truly global brewer but until that point was conspicuous by its absence in Belgium. The deal created Affligem BDS and ensured that the beers went global, with a guarantee that they would continue to be brewed only in Belgium until 2031. Heineken also bought much of Vervloet's shareholding with the right to buy the rest upon his retirement, which they did, in 2010.

Tim Webb

Africa, traditional brewing in, has a long history. The ancient Egyptians brewed beer and tribes throughout the African continent also brewed beer long before any European settlers brought their brewing techniques to Africa. Beer in Africa today has two main influences: tribal traditions passed down for centuries and European settlement. Europeans, especially the Dutch and British, brought different techniques and expertise to brewing starting in the 15th and 16th centuries. Traditional tribal brewing methods are, however, still a strong part of African brewing culture.

Traditional brewing methods have remained an important activity throughout Africa despite commercial breweries producing variations of traditional African beers. It is still a key aspect of the rural economy, where traditional beer is brewed for local markets. It is also brewed for all varieties of ceremonial and cultural occasions and gatherings.

Traditional brews go by many different names depending on the location. Southern Africa has *chibuku, umqombothi, utshwala, joala,* and *doro,* depending on the subregion, and western Africa *shakparo.* Kenya has *chang'aa,* Botswana *khadi,* Central Africa Republic *hydromel,* and Ethiopia *araque, katila,* and *talla.* Botswana, Zambia, and Malawi all have chibuku shake-shake (a commercial variety made from sorghum and maize). In Zimbabwe, shake-shake is called "scud." Uganda has *tonto, mwenge, murumba, marwa, kweete,* and *musooli.* Ghana has *pito, burukutu,* and *akpeteshie.*

By any name, sorghum beer is the traditional beer of Africa. It is also referred to as opaque beer because of its cloudiness. It is made both rurally and commercially throughout the continent. Tribes continue to make their own varieties, using locally available ingredients for additional flavor. Commercial breweries also make different varieties depending on the subregion.

Historically, the Bantu-speaking tribes carried the art of brewing sorghum with them as they migrated south. Women were the traditional brewers of African beers and men the traditional consumers. Even today, women prepare the traditional brews for the market, weddings, ceremonies, and other celebrations.

African tribes have been brewing forms of sorghum beer longer than is recorded in history books. Sorghum malt and grain has been the main ingredient for centuries. As the availability of different grain and starch sources grew, maize (corn), millet, and cassava root were used as adjuncts to the sorghum beer to produce different flavors.

Sorghum

Sorghum, a genus of numerous species of grass, is widely grown throughout Africa, either raised for grain or used as a fodder plant. It is also used in pastures in tropical regions of Africa. Sorghum is native to the African continent, and most species of sorghum can survive high temperatures and drought.

Sorghum beer brewing is the one of the largest consumers of sorghum grain in Africa. Grains have been selected over centuries based on their malting qualities. High-tannin, soft endosperm, red, and brown grains were and are the most favored for brewing in Africa.

Sorghum beer is often cloudy and yeasty, with a sour lingering aftertaste. It is brownish-pink in color. Higher pH levels produce a more pronounced pink coloring. The alcohol content of traditional brews ranges from 1% to 8% alcohol by volume (ABV) depending on fermentation time. Most traditional sorghum beers, however, are lower in alcohol, 3% to 4% ABV. Many traditionally brewed sorghum beers still contain maltotriose, the last sugar fermented by yeasts during fermentation. Some amino acids and peptides are also usually present.

Traditional sorghum beer is consumed in an active state of fermentation, usually within a day or two of production. Today it is sold in various plastic containers or clay pots, still foaming. The more foam around the container, the fresher it is considered and the better for consumption.

The Traditional Method

The first step in traditional sorghum beer production is malt production. Traditional household malting takes place in open yards where the sorghum grain is either added to water or mixed with a slurry of wood ash, soaked overnight, and drained. The grain is then spread on grass mats, kept moist, and allowed to germinate. The resulting malt is then dried, usually between grass mats. The malt is then ground by hand to produce a rough powder. Sorghum malt is often used in porridges and other recipes, in addition to beer production. Today, it is also commercially available in powders.

The sorghum malt is then used alone or in combination with other malts and grains. Maize and millet malts and grains are the most commonly used in addition to sorghum. Cassava root is also used throughout Africa as a grain alternative in addition to sorghum malt.

The malt and grain mixture is soaked overnight in warm water. This overnight fermentation produces lactic acid and the characteristic sourness of traditional African beer. The mixture is then cooked again, cooled, vigorously mixed, and placed in a larger container. It is covered with a blanket and kept in a warm place to encourage further fermentation for several days.

Traditionally, no yeast is added to the final fermentation. Native yeasts present on the grain, malt, and brewing vessels are responsible for the alcohol production. The primary yeasts found in traditional African beer are strains of *Saccharomyces cerevisiae.* Today, yeast from the previous batch of beer, or even purchased yeast, might be added to a new batch.

In western Africa, a sweeter, nonsour version of sorghum beer is more popular than in southern and eastern Africa. It is called by different names depending on the subregion: *dolo, chapalo, pito, burukutu, bilibili,* or *amgba.* The initial souring or lactic acid fermentation is avoided. *Pito,* common in Ghana, Nigeria, and Togo, is made from sorghum and varies from slightly sweet to slightly sour and is light yellow to dark brown in color depending on the malts, grains, and other adjuncts used.

Maize

Although sorghum is the oldest ingredient in African brewing, maize (corn introduced from the New World) is frequently used as an alternative and adjunct to traditional sorghum beer. Maize malt and grain are used to produce a lighter colored beer with a mellower flavor than typical sorghum beer. Most traditional maize beers also use some sorghum malt to achieve a slightly sour and darker finished beer.

Umqombothi is a traditional beer made from maize, maize malt, sorghum malt, and water (and wild native yeasts to produce the alcohol). It has a distinctive sour aroma from the sorghum malt and is usually low in alcohol (3% to 4% ABV). The beer has an opaque tan color and a thick gritty consistency from the maize.

Umqombothi is traditionally prepared with equal parts crushed maize, maize malt, and sorghum malt to which warm water is added. It is made outside and cooled outside, rather than in the home. The mixture is left overnight to begin fermenting and bubbling, producing the characteristic sour odor of sorghum beer. The mixture is then cooked, cooled, and poured into a larger container. It is stirred vigorously, covered, and left in a warm place to encourage further fermentation. A match lit near the fermenting mixture is used to determine whether the brew is ready—if the match blows out quickly, it is ready; if the match does not blow out, the beer will be left to continue fermenting. Once the mixture has fermented, it is filtered through large strainers to collect any excess corn and poured into a large drum, known as a *gogogo*. The local beer is sold at markets, served to visitors, and used in special celebrations and ceremonies.

Other Ingredients

In addition to maize, traditional brewers throughout African also use locally available herbs and fruits to flavor their beers. Some plants that are used make the sorghum beer bitter or give it floral notes. Starchy crops (cassava root and banana), which grow naturally and easily in some areas, are also used in addition to sorghum malt and grain to create a sweeter regional beer.

Tella is a traditional beer brewed in Ethiopia and surrounding areas. It is brewed traditionally with teff, maize, and gesho. Teff is a species of lovegrass native to northeast Africa. It is used as a wheat alternative in many parts of the region and as an alternative to sorghum in this traditional beer. Gesho (*Rhamnus prinoides*) is a bittering agent, with the stems used as hops would be during the brewing process. *Tella* is made using the same method as traditional African sorghum beer.

Oshikundu (in Namibia), or *oyokpo* (in Nigeria), is a traditional beer made from fermented millet, a cereal crop, sometimes with the addition of sorghum for a souring effect. The method of production is the same as for other traditional African beers. Millet is a popular crop in this region of Africa because of its ability to survive poor soil and heat. Millet produces a nuttier, sweeter flavor in the beer.

The cassava root, rich in starch, is also traditionally used in African brewing, particularly in the sub-Saharan and tropical regions of Africa. Cassava is widely grown and used throughout Africa. The tubers are cut up and boiled and then mashed and added to sorghum malt or other malts and grains. The mixture is then prepared and fermented in the traditional method, without the addition of yeast. The cassava root produces a sweeter, lighter colored beer. The flavor, aroma, and color vary depending on the grains and malt used to brew the beer from region to region.

In some parts of southern and central Africa, hibiscus flowers are also added to the traditional brewing process. Like most traditional brews, it has many different names, such as *karkanj* in the Republic of Chad. The brew has a tropical flavor and rose-like aroma. It is a sweeter version of the traditional sorghum beer and is not made with excessive lactic acid production in the initial fermentation.

Bananas and plantains are often used in east Africa to produce the traditional beer of the region. Bananas are mashed and mixed with malt and grains (often sorghum) and brewed in the traditional method, producing a sweet, orange-colored beer. The bananas used in these beers are not the sweet variety sold in supermarkets, but a starchier potato- or plantain-like variety.

Commercial Brewing of Traditional African Beers

Traditional African beers are an important part of the rural economy, sold at local markets and made at home for all occasions. Most commercial breweries in Africa focus on lager or English styles of beer. There are, however, a few breweries that produce sorghum beers to appeal to the traditional markets.

The most popular in southern African countries is chibuku, made by a subsidiary of SABMiller. This thick, brown, commercial version of a traditional ceremonial drink is slightly sour and has 4% ABV. In South Africa, chibuku is made from sorghum. In other parts, maize is also used and is often the primary ingredient. Consumers in Botswana, Zambia, and Malawi know it as chibuku shake-shake because drinkers have to shake it before drinking to mix in the maize sediment at the bottom of the container.

United National Breweries also makes a sorghum beer using maize as an adjunct, sold throughout South Africa. United National Breweries' traditional beer is made in the Zulu traditions of the area and is drunk in a state of active fermentation. It is pinkish in color, sour, and slightly sweet.

In the United States, the Sprecher Brewing Company of Wisconsin produces a commercial *shakparo*, a West African style sorghum beer. It is made exclusively with sorghum malt and millet, keeping with the West African traditions. The company markets Shakparo ale as a gluten-free beer.

In 2009, SABMiller also began producing a light lager version of traditional African sorghum beer using cassava root. Cassava root is widely available throughout Africa and is a cheaper alternative to maize and millet. The company replaced the maize in its beer with cassava root to produce a reduced-price beer to appeal to consumers drinking traditional brews. The beer produced is a clear lager type beer, as opposed to the opaque versions of traditional brews.

See also PORRIDGE BEERS.

Africa Insight. "Kenya: In the African beer brewing pot ferments an occasional crisis." April 2010. http://www.allafrica.com/ (accessed February 1, 2011).

Frederiksen, Richard A., and C. Wayne Smith. Wayne. *Sorghum: Origin, history, technology, and production*. New York: Wiley, 2000.

Hardwick, William A. *Handbook of brewing*. Boca Raton, FL: CRC Press, 1995.

Haw, Greason. "Getting to grips with the gogogo." *Daily Dispatch*, July 1999.

Mosher, Randy. *Radical brewing: Recipes, tales & world-altering meditations in a glass*. Boulder, CO: Brewers Publications, 2004.

Okambawa, Richard. "Shakparo: A Traditional West African Sorghum Beer." http://www.brewery.org/brewery/library/Shakparo.html/ (accessed March 11, 2011).

Sefa-Dedeh, S., A. I. Sanni, G. Tetteh, and E. Sakyi-Dawson. Yeasts in the traditional brewing of pito in Ghana. *World Journal of Microbiology and Biotechnology* 15 (1999): 593–97.

Anda Lincoln

aftertaste refers to the flavors and aroma sensations that linger after food or drink is no longer in the mouth. The general associations of the word tend toward the negative—we even refer to the memory of an unpleasant experience as leaving a "bitter aftertaste." Mass-market lagers are often advertised as being "clean" or "crisp," with some ads having gone so far as to claim "no aftertaste."

In the world of wine and food, however, a fine aftertaste is widely considered a desirable attribute. A person who enjoys oysters will be as impressed by lingering sensations of fresh sea air as by the oyster itself. A wine with little aftertaste is referred to as "short" and the term is pejorative. What we refer to as a sense of taste is mostly a sense of smell. The tongue only perceives sweet, sour, salt, and bitter, and umami, a savory sensation produced by glutamic amino acids. Located at the peak of the nasal cavity, our olfactory receptors react to molecules carried by air and can detect up to 10,000 different compounds, many of which may linger in our perception long after a beer has been swallowed.

Aftertaste, therefore, is complex and will include both tongue/palate impressions and olfactory impressions. A hoppy India pale ale, properly brewed, will not disappear instantly from the tongue, but leave a clean, sharp bitterness. It will also leave a pleasant echo of resiny hop aromatics that invite the next sip. A well-made Imperial stout may leave a combination of roast acidity and hop bitterness, but hopefully without an excess of drying astringency. Olfactory sensations may include caramel, chocolate, coffee, and fruit. If the beer is barrel-aged in American oak, there may be an overlay of vanilla and coconut.

A pleasant aftertaste in beer is a matter of recipe design, brewing technique, and raw materials. A good aftertaste is a critical part of a beer's overall drinkability. Water chemistry is particularly important; trace metals in brewing water can lead to metallic aftertastes, and carbonate waters can give hop bitterness a lingering harshness. Improper sparging of the mash will release excess tannins, giving beer an astringent aftertaste. A nicely brewed pilsner, however, while very "clean," will leave a fine-boned, appetizing sharpness and a sense-memory of freshly baked bread. Even the lightest of beers should possess an aftertaste, and it is up to the brewer to create impressions that beckon rather than repel.

See also BITTERNESS, SPARGING, UMAMI, and WATER.

Garrett Oliver

aging of beer, an aspect of beer connoisseurship that is rapidly being rediscovered by modern breweries, beer enthusiasts, serious beer bars, and restaurants. Here we must distinguish *aging* from two other terms: *maturation* and *staling*. The term maturation refers to the relatively short controlled aging period employed by the brewery to transform freshly brewed "green beer" into a drink suitable for sale. Traditionally this maturation takes place over a period as short as 1 week or, in the case of certain beers, a few months. Staling refers to the onset of unwanted and unpleasant flavor, aroma, or appearance caused by inappropriate aging and/or exposure to heat, light, oxygen, and other harmful factors.

Beer *aging*, on the other hand, is deliberate, or at least felicitous. Many wine enthusiasts are of the opinion that wine is the only beverage that can benefit from aging, but this is not nearly true. In fact, the vast majority of wine is incapable of aging well and is designed to be consumed as soon as it leaves the winery. If aging is attempted, these wines will become stale. Precisely the same is true of beer—most beer is at its best the day it leaves the brewery and, depending on conditions, it has a limited shelf life, often measured in months and rarely exceeding a year. However, certain beers, kept properly, will improve and deepen with age, becoming increasingly complex and even profound.

Whereas most beer throughout history has been meant for consumption within days, weeks, or a few months, certain beer types have always been meant to age further. One of these is Belgium's range of lambic beers, complex and acidic wheat beers entirely fermented by wild yeast and bacteria living in the brewery and its environs. See LAMBIC and WILD YEAST. Lambics and similar beers have probably been made for more than 1,000 years and are traditionally aged in oak barrels. One or two years of aging in barrels is normal for lambic, and bottled styles such as Gueuze can age for many years further. Because of the interactions between its complex microflora, the aging of lambic is unique among beers. In some ways it resembles the aging and affinage of cheese, where continued action by bacteria and molds will help develop the cheese to the height of its flavors. In lambic, the microflora represent the biggest influence over the period of aging, but other factors are at work as well.

Oxidation, although usually considered a form of damage at virtually all stages of the brewing process, is an important part of the deliberate aging of both beer and wine. The difference between unwanted damage and desirable evolution is both qualitative and subjective. Beers that cannot age well, such as pilsners, are admired for their fresh, bright qualities, all of which will eventually be lost over a relatively short period of time. In such beers, oxidation tends to be rapid and somewhat violent, replacing malt flavors with unpleasant notes of black currant or tomato, followed by an impression of wet cardboard. These negative changes tend to be accelerated and compounded by dissolved oxygen in the original beer, oxygen in the headspace of bottles, and elevated aging temperatures (above 20°C, or 68°F). Certain esters will decrease in aged beer (such as banana-like isoamyl acetate), but other esters tend to increase, leading to wine-like flavors. Hop bitterness decreases over time, as does hop aroma. Hop aroma tends to degrade first to tropical fruit-like flavors, which can be pleasant, but then to less desirable tea-like flavors.

In beers that are age worthy, such as barley wine, slow oxidation and breakdown of various compounds will create a different set of new flavors as the old ones recede. Barley wine is a beer style that was originally designed to age and was traditionally never consumed young. See BARLEY WINE. In such beers negative flavor developments, if they arise at all, may be masked by more powerful positive aromatics within the beer. Rich bread-like malt flavors can become nutty and then toffee-like, eventually oxidizing to almond-like flavors reminiscent of sherry. Further aging can bring on leathery flavors that can be harmonious with the whole. Roasted malt character can change from "fresh coffee" to "dark chocolate" and eventually to "rich old Madeira," picking up complex licorice notes along the way.

Many factors of beer aging are non-oxidative and not fully understood. As compounds break down, the components become available for new reactions, and new flavors, mostly esters and aldehydes, are formed in a fashion that can be difficult to predict. In bottle-conditioned beers, the complexity is compounded by presence of yeast. While the yeast remains alive, it can slowly synthesize new flavors, and the flavors of the beer may become more profound. The eventual death of the yeast can result in more typical "meaty" or "soy sauce" autolysis flavors, but it can also result in the toasty hazelnut-like aromatics that are highly prized in vintage Champagnes. Over time, however, bottle-conditioned beers tend to lose their foam stability because enzymes released by yeast autolysis break down the proteins responsible for foam formation. Old bottles of strong beers such as barley wines and imperial stouts can also throw a crust of sediment, even if the beer was originally filtered. Therefore, old bottles should be kept upright for at least 24 hr before pouring and then poured carefully to avoid sediment in the glass.

Although beer aging is highly complex, we do know that some beer types tend to age better than others. Strong beers tend to be more age worthy than beers that are lower in alcohol. Beers that age well tend to have relatively high hop bitterness, but are more malt forward than hop forward in their aromatics. Relatively high residual sugar confers an advantage (barley wines, imperial stouts, old ales), but some dry styles can fare well. Strong dark Belgian Trappist and abbey ales, for example, tend to age well, despite their relative lack of residual sugar. Although it is not always true that darker beers age better than paler beers, it does tend to be the case, with lambic styles and some Belgian tripels as notable exceptions. Pale beers tend to darken over time, but dark beers may become slightly paler as their color compounds combine with other elements and sediment out. As with age-worthy wines, beers that are destined to be beautiful after 10 years or more of bottle age will tend to first experience a tough, inexpressive, and disjointed youth.

Although slow oxidation can be positive, rapid oxidation is almost always negative for beer flavor, and brewers wishing to see longevity in their beers will avoid oxygen pickup throughout brewing and packaging.

The best storage conditions for aging bottled beer are similar to those for aging wine. Most beers age best at "cellar temperatures" of approximately 11°C to 13°C (about 52°F to 55°F). Colder temperatures will retard the aging process; much warmer temperatures can accelerate aging, but the results will tend to be less pleasant. Bottles of beer should be stored upright and in the dark. Aging wine bottles on their sides prevents drying and shrinkage of corks, but this is generally not a problem for beer because most beers are sealed with either a crown cap or a compressed Champagne-style cork. Very old bottles will sometimes be closed with straight corks, but these are often covered in wax to prevent shrinkage and ingress of air. Most beer enthusiasts are not blessed with perfect conditions for beer aging at home. At home, often the best that can be done is to keep the beer in a dark place where summer temperatures are moderate. Intentional aging of beer in kegs is far less prevalent than aging of bottles. However, well-brewed kegged beers can store well, usually at relatively cold temperatures (around 4°C [40°F], the average temperature for normal storage of non-pasteurized kegged beer), for 10 years or more.

As interest in "vintage beer" grows, many brewers have started printing the production year on the labels of their age-worthy bottles, a practice that was previously limited to a small number of breweries. Some high-end restaurants and enthusiast bars feature vintage beer collections, but supplies are naturally limited. Today, breweries sometimes struggle to provide the market with enough aged beer, so many are establishing their own in-house aging regimes, not too dissimilar to those of good wineries.

Although barley wines and imperial stouts aged for 10 or 20 years are not unusual, some beers possess considerably greater longevity. In 2006 the Worthington White Shield Brewery at Burton-on-Trent found some 200 bottles of Bass Ratcliff Ale 1869, a barley wine brewed to commemorate the birth of a member of the Ratcliff family, who were partners in Bass. The 137-year-old beer was found to be in astonishingly wonderful condition and reminded tasters of a fine old Amontillado.

See also BASS & COMPANY and IMPERIAL STOUT.

Vanderhaegen, Bart. The chemistry of beer aging—a critical review. *Food Chemistry* 95 (2006): 357–81. http://www.sciencedirect.com/ (accessed January 19, 2011).

Garrett Oliver

Ahtanum (hop) is a hop cultivar grown originally by the Yakima Chief Ranches. Ahtanum is reported to be an open-pollination cross among Brewer's Gold, Fuggle, East Kent Golding, and Bavarian aroma hops. The variety's name is derived from early Yakima Valley hop history when Charles Carpenter brought hop rhizomes to the area and grew them on his homestead at Ahtanum, now a small community west of Yakima. The cultivar has never been popular with large breweries. Thus, acreage is low. It has been favored, however, by many craft brewers. The cultivar is tolerant to downy mildew (Pseudoperonospora humuli). See DOWNY MILDEW. It matures in mid- to late season and typically yields 800 to 1,000 kg (1,760 to 2,200 lb) per acre. Ahtanum has an alpha acid range of 5.7% to 6.3%, a beta acid range of 5% to 6.5%, and a cohumulone range of 30% to 35%. Its aroma profile is floral, citrus, and piney, with grassy notes. The essential oil content is 50% to 55% myrcene, 16% to 20% humulene, 9% to 12% caryophyllene, and <1% farnesene, which makes it similar in aroma characteristics to Cascade, Centennial, and, to a lesser extent, Amarillo. It is typically used as a late or dry aroma hop, especially in American craft-brewed pale ales, India pale ales (IPAs), and "double IPAs."

Matthew Brynildson

Alaskan Brewing Company is a regional brewery located in Juneau, Alaska, and was the first brewery in the state capital since Prohibition. As of 2009, Alaskan Brewing Co was the 11th largest craft brewery in the United States, selling 126,000 barrels of beer.

The brewery was founded in December 1986 by Geoff and Marcy Larson. Geoff Larson was trained as a chemical engineer and became a homebrewer prior to opening the commercial brewery. His wife, Marcy, was an accountant and aspiring bush pilot. Doing research on brewing in Alaska, Marcy Larson discovered a newspaper account of a beer brewed by the nearby Douglas City Brewing Co that was in business from 1899 to 1906. Geoff Larson recreated that beer as Alaskan amber ale, the brewery's first commercial beer, the first 250 cases of which were bottled, labeled, and boxed by hand.

Today, the Alaskan Brewery is at the forefront of innovative sustainable practices. In 1998, they were the first American craft brewery to install a carbon dioxide reclamation system and have since added a grain dryer and a mash filter press. The brewery produces five styles year-round and two seasonal beers, along with a recently launched limited-release series using a newly built 10-bbl pilot brewery.

In the winter, they also release their famous (and much imitated) Alaskan smoked porter, first introduced in 1988 using malts smoked with local alder wood. Geoff Larson is the co-author of *Smoked Beers*, published by Brewers Publications in 2001.

Larson, Geoff, and Ray Daniels. *Smoked beers: History, brewing techniques, recipes*. Denver, CO: Brewers Publications, 2001.

Jay R. Brooks

alcohol is an organic compound in which the hydroxyl group (-OH) is attached to an alkyl or substituted alkyl group. The most notable alcohol in a brewing context is ethanol (ethyl alcohol) and of course the words "ethanol" and "alcohol" are frequently used synonymously in this context. See ETHANOL. However, beer contains a diversity of alcohols, including traces of methanol, propanol, iso-butanol, 2-methylpropan-1-ol, iso-amylalcohol, tyrosol, and phenylethanol.

Higher alcohols (containing more carbon atoms than ethanol) are sometimes known as fusel alcohols. See FUSEL ALCOHOLS. These higher alcohols are important flavor contributors and their levels are influenced by the strain of yeast and fermentation conditions, notably temperature. Beers containing notable levels of higher alcohols are often described as tasting "hot." Ales tend to contain greater levels of these alcohols than do lagers. For example, propanol levels are typically about four times higher in ales than lagers and iso-butanol levels are three times higher. It has been suggested that higher concentrations of fusel alcohols in beer can be associated with hangovers. If this is true, it is most likely that the aldehydes produced from the alcohols in the body are the culprit.

The alcohols serve as the precursors of even more flavor-potent esters, produced by enzyme-catalyzed reactions in yeast through the coupling of the alcohols with acids. Oxidation of the alcohols leads to aldehydes and ketones and then to acids.

Quantitatively the most important alcohol in beer is ethanol. In addition to its key role in alcoholic beverages where it provides the warming alcoholic note but also impacts the distribution of other flavor-active molecules into the headspace of the beverage, it is used as a solvent, as a gasoline replacement in cars, and as a reactant in diverse industrial chemical reactions. Apart from via fermentation, alcohols can be made by hydrating ethylene derived from the cracking of distilled crude oil, but such "industrial" alcohol is not potable.

See also ALCOHOL STRENGTH AND MEASUREMENT.

Briggs, D.E., C.A. Boulton, P.A. Brookes, and R. Stevens. *Brewing: Science and practice.* Cambridge: Woodhead, 2004.

Charles W. Bamforth

alcoholic strength and measurement in beer is generated as a function of both the quantity of fermentable sugars originally present in beer wort and the extent to which those sugars are actually fermented by yeast. The initial original gravity of wort is a measure of the specific gravity (SG) of the wort at 20°C (where, simplified, water at a standard reference temperature has an SG of 1.0000) and is also known as the original extract. In the brewery this is often measured using a hydrometer. Brewers and winemakers take this as an expression of the sugar content in units of grams of sugar per 100 g of wort. This number is equivalent to a percentage weight/weight. In the brewing industry this measurement is denoted in degrees Plato (°P) and winemakers refer to it as degrees Brix. See BALLING SCALE, HYDROMETER, PLATO GRAVITY SCALE, and SPECIFIC GRAVITY.

As fermentation continues, the sugars in the extract are consumed and the SG of the liquid drops. The brewer monitors the progress of fermentation by following the changing SG (or Plato) value until it reaches a terminal value (the maximum degree of fermentation). However, as sugars are consumed the alcohol content rises and the "extract" in the beer is not read correctly and is regarded as the apparent value (apparent extract). There is a drop in gravity caused by the conversion of the sugars to alcohol, but the gravity also drops because the newly generated alcohol is lighter than water. The real extract (the gravity value not compromised or "obscured" by alcohol) is an important value and can be computed or determined following the careful removal of alcohol from a known amount of the wort/beer. The real extract then represents the true final extract (containing residual sugars and dextrins—more complex carbohydrates, some protein, and the mineral content of the sample) in the beer expressed as grams/100 grams (or percentage terms).

The real degree of fermentation is a measurement of the percentage of the original gravity that was actually fermented, adjusted once again for alcohol content. Not all sugars in the wort will be fermented because wort contains non-fermentable elements, particularly complex sugars. These will be left behind and provide the beer with body and sometimes sweetness. See REAL DEGREE OF FERMENTATION (RDF) and REAL EXTRACT.

The original gravity minus the final gravity (real extract or true final gravity) will produce a value that indicates the amount of fermentable sugars consumed; this, in turn, indicates the amount of alcohol produced (see below). These above values can be used together with equations known to the brewer and brewing chemist to determine the actual exact alcohol strength.

The average strength of beer is between 4.8% and 5.2% alcohol by volume (ABV). However, the range of strength in beer is far wider than that of wine. There are many beers on the market with only 3.5% ABV or below, whereas some beer styles, such as barley wine, commonly reach 12% ABV. Although it is possible to coax beer fermentations to produce beers with more than 20% ABV, these generally require special yeast strains and techniques. In this, they can come to resemble laboratory experiments rather than beers, although some very interesting beers have been produced in this manner. For normal worts and fermentations, alcoholic strength in beer tops out at about 15% ABV, with these beers normally requiring long aging before they become palatable. See AGING OF BEER and ETHANOL-TOLERANT YEAST STRAINS.

Once alcohol is produced in beer, brewers need to measure it. The analysis of beer for alcohol content is an important part of brewing laboratory work both for quality assurance programs and for legal reporting purposes. Results, however, are subject to appreciable variation and, under official methods, the analyses are time consuming and expensive. The history and theory behind alcohol measurement are lengthy and complex and could not be presented in any appreciable detail here, but it is possible to explore the methods by which today's brewing chemists best determine alcohol content in beer.

The production of 1 g of alcohol requires 2.0665 g of fermentable extract. (As originally determined, 2.0665 g sugar yields 1 g ethanol, 0.9565 g CO_2, and 0.11 g yeast. Note: 0.9565 g and 0.11 g add up to a sum of 1.0665 extract *not* converted to alcohol.)

Predictions of alcoholic strength in beer can be made based on these numbers, but they will be approximate. For official and accurate determinations, the alcoholic strength of a beer was historically measured or originally reported in percentage alcohol by weight in the United States, with most of the rest of the world preferring its volumetric content (percentage by volume). As of 2011, the United States allowed reporting by volume for labeling and certification purposes. Alcohol by volume is a measure of alcohol content of a solution in terms of the percentage volume of alcohol per 100 mL total volume of beer (volume/volume). Alcohol by weight is a measure of alcohol content of a solution in terms of the percentage weight of alcohol per weight of beer (weight/weight, also expressed by mass as mass/mass in Europe).

Traditionally most brewers would use a carefully calibrated hydrometer to determine the alcohol content in their beer. Established tables of SG versus alcohol data were then used to compute the alcohol content. Distillations performed on precisely known volumes (or weights) of alcohol added to water led to the generation of an extensive set of tables of data by various agencies and academic laboratories, showing the interrelationships among specific gravity, density, and alcohol by weight and volume. These tables and formulas are now used by brewers and brewing chemists to accurately determine the alcohol content of beer.

Finally, it is to be noted that alcohol may be measured via the hydrometer, distillation, reference to alcohol and solute concentration tables, and sophisticated oscillating U-tube density meters; even refractometers are sometimes used with appropriate algorithms. Near-infrared instruments can measure the specific alcohol peak in a mixture, as can gas chromatography, which is now an approved method for the determination of the concentration of ethanol.

See also CHROMATOGRAPHY.

Eßlinger, H. M., ed. "Analysis and quality control." In *Handbook of brewing: processes, technology, markets.* Weinheim, Germany: Wiley-VCH Verlag, 2009.

Weissler, Harald E. "Brewing calculations." In *Handbook of brewing*, ed. W. A. Hardwick. New York: Marcel Dekker, 1994.

Gary Spedding

aldehydes are organic compounds produced by the removal of hydrogen from (i.e., oxidation of) alcohols. Conversely, the reduction of aldehydes leads to the production of alcohols. In a brewing context, the best known of these reducing reactions is the reduction of acetaldehyde to ethanol.

Aldehydes tend to be highly flavor active, are detectable in lower concentrations than their equivalent alcohols, and can contribute a range of characters to beer, especially to aged beer. Many aldehydes are used in the production of perfumes, giving them their distinctive fragrances. In beer, particular attention has been paid to E-(2)-nonenal, which possesses a pronounced cardboard character. However, quantitatively, the more important aldehyde in beer is often acetaldehyde, with its distinctive aroma of green apples. See ACETALDEHYDE.

Aldehydes will react with sulfur dioxide (metabisulfite) to form adducts that display far less flavor potency than the aldehydes per se. This is believed to be one of the mechanisms by which sulfur dioxide protects beer from staling.

It is also believed that aldehydes produced by the oxidation of alcohol in the body are the prime mediators of hangovers and headaches through their reactivity with diverse components of cells.

See also ACETALDEHYDE, FERMENTATION, and MATURATION.

Briggs, D. E., C. A. Boulton, P. A. Brookes, and R. Stevens. *Brewing: Science and practice.* Cambridge: Woodhead, 2004.

Charles W. Bamforth

ale comprises a broad class of beers brewed using the top-fermenting yeast Saccharomyces cerevisiae. See YEAST.

The recent craft brewing revolution in the United States has taken the English word "ale" and started to give it a whole new meaning. At one time, ale referred to only a few different beers from England. Today, ale has come to include a continuously growing number of beers, some new and some older than England itself.

One common conception of the world of beer is that it is divided into two categories, namely ales and lagers. All beers fermented by "top-fermenting" yeasts, that is, yeasts that tend to do their work at the top of a fermenting vat of beer, are called ales.

All beers fermented by "bottom-fermenting" yeasts are called lagers. Top-fermenting yeast (S. cerevisiae) likes to ferment quickly (2–7 days) and at higher temperatures 15°C–24°C (60°F–78°F), whereas bottom-fermenting yeast (S. pastorianus) ferments more slowly (5–10 days) and at lower temperatures, 7°C–13°C (45°F–55°F). The higher temperature fermentation of ales with S. cerevisiae yields beers with a more fruity, complex flavor profile, whereas the lower temperature fermentation of lagers with S. pastorianus yields beers with cleaner, more directly ingredient-driven flavor profiles. See LAGER and LAGERING.

The idea that beer can be split cleanly into the two groups, ale and lager, is perhaps emotionally satisfying. In real life, however, the menagerie of yeast strains that brewers use does not actually fit so neatly into these two categories. In fact, the behavior of many yeast strains is somewhere between that of true top- and bottom-fermenting yeasts, and their genetics are much more complicated than a simple split between two species. The wide use of unitanks to ferment ales shows this quite clearly, and any experienced ale brewer knows that many yeasts can be "trained," by selection during cropping, to gravitate toward the top or bottom of their vessels. Another problem is that even the term "beer," when used in its general sense, refers to any fermented beverage made from grain. This includes such outliers as the corn-based *chicha* of South America and the rice-based *sake* of Japan, neither of which is generally considered an ale, despite the fact that they are both fermented using top-fermenting yeasts. This confusion over the precise definition of ale is nothing new.

The first instances in Old English of the word "ale" (*ealu*) do not do a very good job of pinpointing an exact recipe for the beverage. It is sometimes referred to as being bitter, sometimes as sweet, sometimes as made with honey, and sometimes as brewed with spices. Whatever the case, the word "ale" was introduced to the English-speaking world by the Danes, who knew the beverage as *öl*.

It was not until the 16th century that hops began to gain popularity as a bittering agent for English brewers to add to their ales. The hop vine was well known in England prior to this point, and the English were familiar with brews made by foreigners using hops. These brews were known to the English as "beers" and differed from England's ale, which was brewed at the time using only water, malt, and yeast. Prior to the 16th century the English took their ale so seriously that brewers who "adulterated" their ale with hops or other spices were subjected to fines. The use of hops and spices in the brewing of beer as opposed to ale, however, was accepted.

Eventually, not even fines were sufficient to keep English ale brewers from experimenting with the use of hops in their ales. They found that adding hops increased both the quality and the longevity of their ale, and gradually the use of hops in ale came to be accepted by English ale drinkers and government officials alike.

Even with this acceptance of the use of hops in ale brewing toward the end of the 16th century, the term "ale" only referred to a select few English brews (most notably pale ale and brown ale) well into the 20th century. Porter, for instance, was considered its own separate brew from both ale and beer until recently. It is for this reason that so many laws in the English-speaking world, many of them still in force, refer to malt beverages collectively as "ale, beer, and porter" specifically; ales differed from beers in that ales used less hops and differed from porters in that they were light in color. Any casual walk around London will reveal pub signs that proudly announce the availability of all three of these beverages.

In fact, the term "ale" only began to become synonymous with top-fermented beers generally as late as the 1980s. References to "German ale" prior to this date are few and far between, with references to "Belgian ale" being all but nonexistent. It was not until the 1980s resurgence of interest in international beer styles, marked by the advent of microbrewing in the United States, that the term "ale" began to be used, somewhat confusingly, to refer to most top-fermented beers.

It is noteworthy that there are also some legal definitions of ale that are both confusing and incorrect. For example, in the state of Texas, ale is legally defined as any malt beverage with an alcohol content of more than 4% alcohol by weight (ABW) and is mutually exclusive of beer, which is defined as any malt beverage with an ABW of less than 4%. This definition disregards any other aspects of the malt beverage, such as it being a high-alcohol lager or a low-alcohol ale. Many brewers have been amused (or annoyed) to find that their strong lagers suddenly need to call themselves ales upon reaching the Texas border.

Thus, the modern conception of ale is extremely young and in a state of flux. Today, the term "ale" refers to beers ranging from the strong, fruity, spicy ales of Belgium to the crisp, clean, hoppy pale ales of the United States. Although there are a few exceptions, ales can usually be recognized by their distinctive, fruity character achieved through warm fermentation using the top-fermenting yeast S. cerevisiae.

Bennett, Judith. *Ale, beer, and brewsters in England: Women's work in a changing world, 1300–1600.* New York: Oxford University Press, 1996.
Bickerdyke, John. *The curiosities of ale & beer,* 2nd ed. London: Spring Books, 1965.
Hornsey, Ian. *A history of beer and brewing.* Cornwall, England: The Royal Society of Chemistry, 2003.

Nick R. Jones

ale-conner, an official appointed by a manor, borough, or town to assay the quality of ale served within a particular jurisdiction. In England, from at least the 1300s on, ale-conners were appointed annually in courts leet, special manorial courts that some lords were entitled to convene. These were courts for small claims and petty offenses. The ale conner, also known as the "ale founder" or more grandly as the "Gustator Cervisiae," was to go from one ale house to the next, tasting the beers and certifying them to be of good enough quality to drink. If the quality of the ale was found wanting, the ale-conner was empowered to drag the offending brewer to the manor court to make restitution. Depending upon the rules of the particular manor, the ale-conner was sometimes also allowed to set the price at which a batch of ale could be sold, or to enforce a manor-wide fixed price for ales.

Given the place of ale in the lives of medieval Englishmen, the role of the ale-conner was taken quite seriously. Here is part of the oath sworn by an ale-conner during the reign of Henry V:

> *And that you, so soon as you shall be required to taste ale of any brewer or brewster, shall be ready to do the same; and in case that it be less good than it used to be before this cry, you, by assent of your Alderman, shall set a reasonable price thereon . . . nor when you are required to taste ale, shall [you] absent yourself without reasonable cause and true . . . So God help you and the saints.*

There is a commonly believed legend that ale-conners once roved the land wearing specially made leather britches. The ale-conner was said to have tested ale not by drinking it but by pouring some of the beer on a wooden bench and sitting down in the puddle. A half-hour later he would rise from his seat, and if the beer stuck his britches to the bench, this was a sign that the beer was improperly brewed. However, some versions of this story hold that stuck britches were a sign of high quality. In any event, it appears that there is no solid evidence that beer puddle-sitting was ever actually part of the assaying process. That said, ale-conners are still appointed to this day all over England. The role is now entirely ceremonial, and sometimes involves solemn robes and sturdy leather breeches, always worn with considerable humor. London still appoints four ale-conners every year, and the appointment remains highly prized.

See also ALE HOUSE.

Bickerdyke, John. *The curiosities of ale & beer.* London, 1889.
Snell, Melissa. "Encyclopedia article (1911)." history medren.about.com/od/encyclopedias/a/1911_encyc.htm (accessed November 30, 2010).

Garrett Oliver

ale houses. The term "ale" comes from the Danish and Saxon *öl* and *ealu,* words implanted on the English by invaders from mainland Europe and Scandinavia. In Anglo-Saxon times, from the 5th century CE, brewing was a domestic pursuit. But the demand for ale was enormous—it was drunk at every meal, celebration, and funeral—and often outstripped supply. Some households built a reputation for the quality of their ale and began to specialize in brewing. When a new brew was ready, a member of the family would tie a branch or part of a bush to a pole placed through the door or a window. See ALE POLE. Neighbors were invited to come in and drink: the ale house, along with a rudimentary sign, had arrived.

The spread of ale houses was slow at first as a result of the domination of the Church. Christianity dampened some of the wilder excesses of Anglo-Saxon times, but ironically the Church not only attempted to regulate drinking but also to corner the production of ale. Monasteries offered accommodation to

Early 19th-century etching illustrating "The Jolly Beggars," a cantata by Scottish poet Robert Burns. Burns wrote it after spending an evening in an ale house with a jovial group of beggars who, he observed, appeared miserable by day. PIKE MICROBREWERY MUSEUM, SEATTLE, WA

travelers and created their own brew houses to supply them with drink. The clerical establishment looked down on common ale houses, as can be seen by the instruction issued by Ecbright, Archbishop of York, to his bishops and priests in the 8th century to provide their own hospices for pilgrims and travelers, and to provide them with home-produced ale and food. As impoverished pilgrims were given extremely weak ale in monasteries, they made use of ale houses en route to partake of stronger brews. (Until it was converted into apartments in the 21st century, there was an ale house in St. Albans in Hertfordshire called the Mile House that stood exactly one mile from the great abbey founded to commemorate the first Christian martyr in England. Pilgrims enjoyed some strong ale there before walking the final mile to the abbey and the more meager offerings of the monks.)

Brewing and retailing of beer have for centuries attracted the attention of tax gatherers. In the 13th century in England a tax known as a "scot" was levied on beer sold in ale houses, using the familiar argument that the tax was needed to combat drunkenness. The tax applied only to ale houses in urban areas or those that stood on open, cultivated land. As most of England was covered by thick forests at the time, it was not difficult to set up rudimentary alehouses that were beyond the reach of the tax man. With wry humor, the beer sold in these illicit ale houses was known as "scot ale," while customers were said to drink "scot free." (The word "scot" is of Germanic origin and has no connection with Scotland.)

In 1267 Henry III introduced the Assize of Bread and Ale to protect the quality of the people's basic food. Ingredients used in bread-making and brewing were strictly controlled and prices for strong and "small" (weak) ale sold in ale houses were laid down. To prevent drinkers from being served short measure, ale could only be sold from pots that carried an official seal. The assize was backed by the rigorously enforced Tumbril and Pillory Statute that fined brewers in ale houses who infringed the law. Repeated infringements received more serious punishment: "If the offence be grievous and often and will not be corrected, then he or she shall suffer corporal punishment, to wit the baker to the Pillory, the brewster to the Tumbril or Flogging." The use of the term "brewster" indicates that brewing was still mainly carried out by women. See ALE-WIVES.

To further enforce the law, the post of ale-conner was created. He was an early version of the excise office, whose task was to visit every ale house with a brewery attached to it in order to judge the quality of the product. According to legend, the ale-conner would ask the brewer to pour some of his or her fresh brew onto a bench outside the alehouse. The conner would then sit in the puddle and after a certain time would rise. If his breeches stuck to the bench, then the ale was considered of sufficient quality to drink. It is more likely that the conner preferred to taste the ale rather than sit in it, as a rhyme of 1608, the Cobbler of Canterbury, implies: A nose he had that gan show,/What liquor he loved I trow;/For he had before long seven yeare/Been of the towne the ale conner. See ALE-CONNER.

The first licensing of ale houses dates from the reign of Edward VI, who brought in two Acts in 1552 and 1553. The legislation strictly delineated the role of three public drinking places: an ale house could sell beer only; a tavern was required to offer food, wine, and other liquors as well as ale; while an inn had to supply food, drink, and accommodation. The Act of 1552 gave justices of the peace the power to license or close ale houses. The licensees had to provide surety for good behavior and the prevention of drunkenness on their premises. A census of drinking premises in 1577 showed there were some 14,000 ale houses, 1,631 inns, and 329 taverns in England. The population of the country was estimated at 3.7 million, which meant there was one license for every 187 people, compared to a license for every 657 people today. The counties of England with the greatest number of ale houses in the 16th century were Yorkshire (3,679) and Nottinghamshire (1,023). Throughout the country, there were 9 ale houses to every inn and 40 to every tavern, an indication that the English preferred the simple pleasures of drinking beer without the trimmings.

The English Reformation of the 16th century broke the power of the Church over brewing and led to the rapid growth of commercial or "common" brewers. Commercial brewers were based mainly in urban areas and for many centuries brewing continued to take place in ale houses. It seemed that both beer drinking and its manufacture would be inhibited as a result of the rise of Puritanism in the late 16th century, with frequent loud attacks on ale houses as dens of iniquity. Philip Stubbes in the *Anatomie of Abuses* (1583) recorded that

> Every county, city, town, and village and other place hath abundance of ale houses, taverns, inns which are so fraught with malt worms [drunkards] night and day, that you would wonder to see them. You shall have them sitting at the wine and good ale all day long, yea, all night too, peradventure a whole week together, so long as any money is left; swilling, gulling, and carousing from one to another, till never a one can speak a ready word. And a man once drunk with wine or strong drink rather resembleth a brute than a Christian man, for do not his eyes begin to stare and be red, fiery, and bleared, blubbering forth seas of tears? Doth he not froth and foam at the mouth like a bear? Doth not his tongue falter and stammer in his mouth? Are not his wits and spirits as if were drowned?

In spite of this fearful diatribe, the period of the interregnum in the 17th century, when Oliver Cromwell ruled a republic between the reigns of Charles I and Charles II, did not lead to any great repression of ale houses, though tax on brewing was increased. The fact that Cromwell had been a farmer in eastern England, the major barley-growing area of the country, made him aware of the importance of brewing to the economy and the well-being of the people. He often stayed in ale houses and inns during his military campaigns. Not surprisingly, ale houses that bore the names of monarchs were encouraged to change their signs, while any suggestions of immodest behavior or "Popery" were frowned upon. The ale house name "Bacchanales," commemorating a riotous drinking festival, thus became the "Bag o' Nails," while "God Encompasses Us" was refashioned as the "Goat and Compasses." "Catherina Fidelis" (a reference to Catherine of Aragon) was turned into the "Cat and Fiddle." Signs that bore a reference to the Virgin Mary, whose emblem was a bowl of lilies, became the prosaic "Flower Pot" while the "Salutation," an early religious sign that referred to the Annunciation of the Virgin Mary, changed to the "Soldier and Citizen," a powerful Cromwellian symbol of the New Model Army.

Ale houses went into decline in the 18th and 19th centuries for political and economic reasons. An epidemic of gin drinking in England in the late 17th century killed thousands of people and led to misery and poverty for many more. Beer was seen as a healthier alternative, as depicted in William Hogarth's savage illustrations of Gin Lane and Beer Street, one a shocking portrait of dissolute behavior, the other of cheery bonhomie. See BEER STREET (BY WILLIAM HOGARTH). Beer drinking was encouraged and more elaborate premises were designed for consumers. The Victorian public house, or "pub" for short, was born.

English society was changing at a fast pace. The Industrial Revolution created factories and an urban class of workers with insatiable thirsts. Early in the 18th century, the development of a new style of beer called "porter" created such demand that commercial brewers, such as Samuel Whitbread in London, built substantial breweries that produced only porter and its stronger version, stout. See PORTER, STOUTS, and WHITBREAD BREWERY. Ale house owners who also brewed on the premises were swamped by the demand and were forced to buy supplies of porter from Whitbread and other commercial producers.

The pressure on ale houses was intensified in the 19th century with the arrival of pale ale. The first light-colored beer, made possible by new technologies that allowed paler malt to be produced, was more expensive than darker beers such as porter. Pale ale appealed to the emerging and more affluent middle class who shunned the coarser ale houses and instead frequented the fancy "saloon bars" of more opulent and respectable public houses.

The modern pub became deeply rooted in British society at the turn of the 20th century, when powerful brewers developed large estates of pubs. These "tied houses" sold only the beers made by the landlords. See TIED HOUSE SYSTEM. Pubs acted as both advertisements and sales outlets for the brewers. They offered such creature comforts as food and wine as well as beer and drove a further nail into the coffin of the simple ale house.

See also PUBLIC HOUSES (PUBS).

Roger Protz

ale pole or "ale stake" was a rudimentary sign used in England in the medieval period to indicate that a household had brewed a fresh batch of ale. In drawings from the period, it is usually depicted sticking out of a window or hanging from a house like a flagpole. In those days all beer-making was domestic, but houses that built a reputation for the quality of their brews might invite the people of the village to come in and drink, becoming an "alehouse." See ALE HOUSES. If the house also supplied wine, a bush of evergreens was tied to the pole.

The practice began in early medieval times and lasted until the Renaissance. It is believed that the ale pole followed the Roman legacy of shop signs that denoted the trades practiced within. A popular inn sign still in use in Britain is the Chequers, which stems from the Roman sign of a chequer board indicating that wine was on sale and money could be exchanged.

Legislation in the 14th and 15th centuries to control the quality of food and drink sold to consumers had an impact on alehouses. An official known as the "ale-conner" had to verify the quality of the beer made on the premises. See ALE-CONNER. The conner visited alehouses when the owners displayed ale poles with branches or bushes attached.

The use of the ale pole went into decline as inns and taverns began to display more elaborate signs. Some signs had religious connections, such as the Cross Keys and the Lamb, while others reflected medieval trade guilds or associations as can be seen in the Elephant and Castle, the sign of the Cutlers' Company. But the ale pole and bush has not entirely disappeared. There are many pubs today called "The Bush." The Bull & Bush in north London achieved fame during the time of the Victorian music hall with the popular song "Down at the old Bull & Bush."

Corran, H.S. *A history of brewing*. Newton Abbot, England: David & Charles, 1975.

Protz, Roger. *Great British beer book*. London: Impact Books, 1997.

Roger Protz

The **aleurone layer** is a layer of living endosperm cells that encloses the outer surface of the starchy endosperms of cereal grains. It is the major enzyme source of malted barley. In barley, this layer is about three cells thick and can be colorless or blue in color. In wheat, rice, maize, rye, millet, and sorghum the aleurone layer is one cell thick. Aleurone cells of barley contain storage lipids, phytin, proteins, and sucrose. The aleurone layer is covered by the testa, pericarp, and husk. Together, the aleurone layer, pericarp, and testa are the major tissues of cereal bran. The primary function of the viable aleurone layer during malting is to produce a wide range of hydrolytic enzymes that contribute to the degradation (modification) of the starchy endosperm. During malting, the germinated embryo produces and secretes gibberellic acid into the adjoining aleurone layer. Gibberellic acid travels along the aleurone layer, inducing it to produce endosperm-degrading enzymes that not only modify the endosperm during malting but also act during mashing to optimize the development of sugars. Enzyme production includes the synthesis of enzymes such as alpha-amylase, endo-beta-glucanses, limit dextrinase and endoproteases, and the activation of enzymes such as beta-amylase and carboxypeptidase, which are located in the starchy endosperm. The phytin of the aleurone layer helps to control wort pH. Foam-stabilizing proteins such as lipid transport protein are derived from the aleurone.

See also GERMINATION and MALTING.

Palmer, G. H. "Cereals in malting and brewing." In *Cereal science and technology*, ed. G. H. Palmer, 61–242. Aberdeen, UK: Aberdeen University Press, 1989.

Palmer, G. H. "Achieving homogeneity in malting." In *Proceedings of the European Brewery Convention Congress*, 232–63. Cannes, France: Oxford, 1999.

Geoff H. Palmer

ale-wives An "ale-wife" or "brewster" is a designation from the Anglo-Saxon period in England, between the 5th century CE and the Norman Conquest, when it was the responsibility of the woman of the house to make sure the men were well supplied with beer. Domestic brewing grew apace following the Norman invasion of England. In the homes of the nobility, ale-wives were employed to supply families with beer. In 1512 the *Northumberland Household Book* showed that the aristocratic Percy family consumed for breakfast a quart of ale [two pints] each "for my lord and lady," a similar amount for "my lady's gentlewomen," and two and a half gallons for the gentlemen of the chapel and children.

As commercial brewing spread, the term "ale-wife" was applied to women who brewed in ale houses. They were often held in poor regard. In one of the Chester Miracle Plays of the 14th century, Christ redeems all the characters from the fires of Hell save for the ale-wife, who admits:

> Some time I was a taverner/A gentle gossip and a tapster/Of wine and ale a trusty brewer/Which woe hath me bewrought./Of cans [brewing vessels] I kept no true measure,/My cups I sold at my pleasure,/Deceiving many a creature/Tho' my ale were nought.

In John Skelton's bawdy poem "The Tunning of Eleanor Rumming," Elinour Rumming is a fictional character who runs a 16th-century pub in Hogsdon, England. PIKE MICROBREWERY MUSEUM, SEATTLE, WA

The hapless woman is carried off by demons and flung back into the mouth of Hell, still holding her short-measure pot. A 15th-century carving of an alewife being thrown into Hell can be seen in the St. Laurence church in Ludlow, England.

Some ale-wives, however, enjoyed good reputations. In the 16th century in England, a brewster named Elynoure Rummynge was said to have a "hideous visage" but her "noppy ale" was declared to be superb.

The growing craft brewing movement allows a number of women to have some fun with the tradition of the ale-wife or brewster. In Lincoln in England, Sara Barton calls her brewery Brewster's and her beer range includes Wicked Women and Belly Dancer.

See also WOMEN IN BREWING.

Corran, H. S. *A history of brewing*. London: David & Charles PLC, 1975.
Protz, Roger. *Great British beer book*. London: Impact Books, 1997.

Roger Protz

Alexis (barley) is a German two-row spring brewing barley bred by Saatzucht Josef Breun GmbH & Co KG of Herzogenaurach near Nuremberg, Bavaria. It was first registered with the Bundessortenamt (the German government crop-licensing agency) in 1986 and subsequently planted in virtually every major brewing barley-growing area of the world. It remained in commercial use for almost twice as long as an average barley variety and was withdrawn from the German recommended list only at the end of 2008. Although perhaps a mixed bag agronomically, Alexis' longevity was well deserved because its brewing qualities were outstanding. On the field, Alexis' maturation, homogeneity, and mildew resistance were average or better than average and its yield, stalk sturdiness, and resistance to rust were moderately to severely below average. In the brewhouse, however, its very low protein and viscosity values, its excellent diastatic power and friability, and its high extract values more than made up for its agronomic shortcomings. See DIASTATIC POWER, EXTRACTS, FRIABILITY, and PROTEINS. Alexis has an impressive genealogy, which goes back all the way to the Czech variety Old Haná agroecotype of the mid-1800s, perhaps the most important historical brewing barley variety ever. See HANÁ (BARLEY). Alexis is a cross between the once popular variety BR1622 and the iconic variety Trumpf, which was bred in 1973 in what was then East Germany. Trumpf, in turn, carried the genes of the venerable Czech variety Diamant, which was a descendant from the Haná lineage. True to tradition, Alexis, although no longer planted ubiquitously, has passed on its favorable genes to several successor varieties, including the highly regarded brewing barley variety Barke, which was bred in 1996 from Libelle and Alexis.

Horst Dornbusch

ale yeast is any one of a number of yeast strains belonging to the species Saccharomyces cerevisiae, used to brew pale, brown, and dark ales, wheat beers, Belgian ales, and many other types of beers. Aside from lager beers and beers brewed by spontaneous fermentations, essentially all beers are brewed with ale yeast as the fermenting organism. Ale yeasts are genetically distinct from lager yeasts in that the latter are hybrid organisms formed by mating between two closely related Saccharomyces species, whereas ale yeasts appear to be purely S. cerevisiae. In contrast to lager yeasts, which tend to gather toward the bottom of the fermentation vessel, ale yeasts are characterized as "top fermenters" because many (but not all) form a thick layer of foam at the top of the wort during fermentation. See LAGER YEAST. However, a better distinguishing characteristic between these two types of yeast is the temperature at which they best ferment: ale yeasts carry out fermentation at moderate temperatures of 18°C to 24°C (65°F to 75°F), whereas lager yeasts are able to ferment at much colder temperatures, 5°C to 14°C (40°F to 58°F). Compared with lager yeasts, ale yeasts also tend to produce more of the esters that lead to fruity and/or complex flavors and aromas; the higher ale fermentation temperatures can also accentuate this tendency. Ale yeasts comprise a diverse group of strains with many different attributes, as can be seen by even a casual perusal of the catalog lists of many of the commercial beer yeast producers. At least 180–200 different ale yeast strains are commercially available, each with different advertised fermentation characteristics and/or flavor/aroma profiles; however, it is not known whether many of the strains are similar or even identical to each other.

See also ALE and YEAST.

Barbara Dunn

alkalinity is a property of liquids. Technically it is the ability of a solution to resist (or buffer) a change in its pH value when acids are added. See PH. The three key ions that contribute to alkalinity are the hydroxide ion (OH^-), the carbonate ion (CO_3^{2-}), and the bicarbonate ion (HCO^{3-}). In water, they react with acidic substances to form salts. Alkalinity ions are thus acid reducers; they increase water's pH value. Depending on the suitability of a given brewing water for a particular beer style, a brewer may use water additives to change the water's pH in the direction of more acidity or more alkalinity.

Alkalinity is often reported as either milligrams of bicarbonate (HCO_3^-) ions per liter or as the equivalent amount of calcium carbonate ($CaCO_3$) in milligrams per liter; the concentration relationship is $CaCO_3 = 0.82 \times HCO_3^-$. For brewing waters it is recommended that the alkalinity should not exceed 100 mg bicarbonate/l, with a value of 50 mg/l being much better.

The use, in specified amounts, of food-grade phosphoric acid, sulfuric acid, or lactic acid or acidic salts such as calcium and magnesium chlorides or sulfates (Wallerstein Lab's Burtonization process, for example) helps to adjust the pH of alkaline brewing waters (by first breaking the buffer capacity). The recommended range for the pH of brewing water is between 6.0 and 7.5. The salts added aid in reduction of alkalinity while providing important ions to further benefit the processes of brewing. For the German Reinheitgebot purity law, neutralization by means of lactic acid fermentation or acidulated malt may also be employed. See ACIDIFICATION.

During brewing, pH is reduced further upon addition of malts and adjuncts, and ultimately a low wort pH results in a number of benefits to the brewer (increased extract yield, increased fermentability, and a decrease in the extraction of harsh tannins and hop bittering compounds). For optimal enzyme activity in mashing, a pH of 5.2–5.4 is desirable.

See also MASHING.

European Brewery Convention. *Water in brewing, European brewery convention manual of good practice.* Nurnberg, Germany: EBC and Fachverlag Hans Carl, 2001.

Hardwick, W. A., ed. *Handbook of brewing*. New York: Marcel Dekker, 1995.

Gary Spedding

Allsopp

See SAMUEL ALLSOPP & SONS.

alpha acids are the principal components in lupulin, the resin of the hop cone. They are of great interest to brewers because they are the main bittering agent in hops. Chemically, alpha acids reside in the soft-resin fraction of the lupulin, which is soluble in hexane. They are expressed as a percentage of the total weight of the hop and exist as complex hexagonal molecules. Alpha acid analogues include humulone, cohumulone, and adhumulone, which, when isomerized to isohumulones (iso-alpha acids) through the boiling process, bring bitterness to beer. Alpha acids in their non-isomerized form are stubbornly insoluble in aqueous solutions such as beer. They are considered only the precursor to the isomerized compounds that are measurable in finished beer. See BITTERNESS. There is some debate among experts as to which of the humulones gives the cleanest bitterness. There seems to be agreement, however, that high levels of cohumulone are an indicator for potentially harsh bitterness. Cohumulone levels are listed on a hop analysis, usually right next to the alpha acid percentage. Many of the classic brewing varieties such as Saaz and Hallertauer Mittelfrueh have very low cohumulone levels.

The alpha acid level of hops is measured in a laboratory. When dissolved in beer as iso-alpha acids, the unit of measurement for bitterness is International Bitterness Units. See INTERNATIONAL BITTERNESS UNITS (IBUS). The hops' alpha acid value is then used by the brewer to formulate a recipe for the beer's final bitterness. Brewers adjust hopping rates based primarily on the selected hop's alpha acid content expressed as a percentage of the hop's weight (commonly in a range of 2%–18%) and on the expected "utilization rate" of that hop in a given brewing system during a particular brewing process. See HOP UTILIZATION. Because the kettle process is inherently less efficient at extracting isomerized alpha acids from hops than a laboratory process can be, the brewhouse utilization rate rarely exceeds 30%. This means that for hops with 9% alpha acids by weight, only a maximum of 3% of the hops' weight will ultimately end up in the beer as bittering. When hops are added to the kettle at different times during the boil, their utilization rates, too, differ. This is because isomerization does not happen all at once, but is a function of the length of time the hop is exposed to high heat in an aqueous solution. Depending on the timing of a hop addition, therefore, utilization rates may vary from as low as 5% for late additions to about 30% for early additions. Hops added after the boil in the whirlpool or hop back do not isomerize efficiently, and those added during dry hopping do not isomerize at all. See DRY HOPPING. When more than one hop variety is used, the contribution of each variety to the beer's final bitterness is calculated separately and then added up.

Hop varieties are often grouped into four categories based on their alpha acid content. There are the low-alpha aroma varieties with alpha acid levels of perhaps 2.5%–6%; there are dual-purpose varieties with alpha acid levels of perhaps 6%–10%; there are high-alpha bittering varieties with alpha acid levels of perhaps 10%–15%; and then there are super alpha bittering varieties with alpha-acid levels of perhaps 14%–18%. Some recent experimental hop plantings have even been assayed at 22%. Many high- and super alpha varieties find their way into hop extract production and are ultimately sold solely for their alpha acid content. Experimental craft brewers, however, have adopted a few super alpha varieties for their unique flavor characteristics.

Hop alpha acid levels are highest at the point of harvest and diminish gradually and continuously during storage because of oxidation. This is especially true of baled whole hops. Refrigerating or even freezing hops after they have been harvested and kiln dried helps to delay oxidation and preserve their alpha acids longer. Hops that have been processed into pellets or into concentrated hop extracts, on the other hand, tend to maintain their alpha acid levels better. World hop production is often measured by the total amount of alpha acids produced in a given harvest year. The annual world alpha acid demand is currently between 7,000 and 7,500 metric tons.

See also BITTERNESS and HOPS.

Matthew Brynildson

alpha amylase is a major mash enzyme of critical concern to brewers in their production of fermentable wort. It digests starch, a large polymer of glucose, into smaller units, exposing it to further digestion by beta amylase. Together these two amylases produce the spectrum of wort sugars essential in the production of a beer. Alpha amylase is an endo enzyme mainly digesting the alpha 1–4 bonds of starch at points within the chain, not at the ends.

To focus on the use of alpha amylase in brewing, it is necessary to look at the needs of a successful mash, in particular the spectrum of sugars required in the final wort. Ideally these should be a suitable balance of simple fermentable sugars—glucose, maltose, and maltotriose—and larger unfermentable dextrins roughly in a 3:1 proportion. Unlike wine, where virtually all of the sugars are fermented, beer is distinct in having residual sugars to provide sweetness, body, and mouthfeel. Dextrins contribute strongly to this and give beer a major part of its character. See DEXTRINS.

A starch molecule is, in essence, a group of glucose molecules linked together. Enzymes break those links. Alpha amylase contributes to the digestion of starch by breaking internal bonds between glucose molecules. As a result it opens up the starch molecule, breaking it into a range of intermediate sizes. Beta amylase further digests these intermediate molecules mostly into maltose—a sugar of two glucose units—but also to glucose itself and to the three-glucose molecule maltotriose. The major limitation to this digestion is the side bonds of starch amylopectin, which are not digested by either alpha or beta amylase. The parts of the starch molecule containing these side bonds form the basis of the important unfermentable dextrins produced by mashing.

The alpha amylase used in the mash comes from the malt, where it is entirely produced in the aleurone layer during malting. See ALEURONE LAYER. In the barley seed, its mobilization is induced in order to digest the starch reserves in the endosperm and provide nutrients for the growing seed. The maltster stops this at the point when enzyme levels are maximal and are preserved in the dry grain ready for use in mashing.

Levels of alpha amylase are typically high in pale malt but are virtually zero in roasted malt due to heat degradation. Levels vary according to malt variety and to malting conditions. Generally six-row barleys have higher levels than two-row barleys due to grains being smaller with less endosperm in proportion to aleurone.

Alpha amylase is not restricted to barley but occurs in most organisms from bacteria to humans. Salivary amylase, ptyalin, is a well-known amylase that initiates starch digestion in the mouth of mammals.

Enzymes tend to have specific temperature and pH ranges at which they will be active—this range is referred to as "optima." Alpha amylase has a significantly different temperature and pH optima than beta amylase. For alpha amylase the temperature optima is higher at around 70°C compared to 60°C–65°C for beta amylase as the enzyme may be stabilized by calcium ions. The pH optima of alpha amylase is also higher at 5.3–5.7 compared to 5.1–5.3 for beta amylase. These differences can result in different wort sugar profiles from mashes conducted at different temperatures and are one means of varying beer character by control of mash conditions.

In traditional breweries, all the enzymes needed for brewing are contained within the natural ingredients out of which the beer is made. However, exogenous alpha amylase is available in purified form from enzyme suppliers and may have different properties according to its origin. These are widely used in the production of "light beers." See LIGHT BEER. The most relevant differences for brewers are thermal and pH tolerances. Heat-labile alpha amylases can be used to supplement malt enzymes or to digest adjunct starch. Because of their heat sensitivity, they will be denatured by pasteurization. Heat-tolerant alpha amylases will, however, survive into the final beer, which may become sweeter over time if residual dextrins are available for digestion into flavor-active sugars.

Commercial alpha amylases may also cause problems if they are impure and contain beta amylase and proteases or if they contain toxins from their bacterial or fungal growth. However, their use is growing in many food industries and will continue to have application in brewing, particularly if novel ingredients are sourced for future beers.

See also AMYLASES.

Briggs, D.E., J.S. Hough, R. Stevens, and T.W. Young. *Malting and brewing sciences*. New York: Springer, 1995.

Lewis, Michael J., and Tom W. Young. *Brewing*. New York: Springer, 2002.

Keith Thomas

altbier is one of the few indigenous German ale styles, along with the blond kölsch from Cologne and the hefeweizens of Bavaria. It is a crisp, clean-tasting, full-bodied beer of usually 4.7% to 4.9% alcohol by volume, with a copper-brown color, firm, lacey white crown of foam, and a malty to nutty bittersweet finish. Altbier evolved over centuries in the Rhenish metropolis of Düsseldorf. Whereas southern Germany is known for its lagers, the Rhineland, like neighboring Belgium, is known primarily for its ales. "Alt" means "old"—an allusion to the old style of brewing, before the emergence of cold-fermented lager beers. The modern altbier acquired its name only in the 1800s, when this Düsseldorf original became threatened by the "new" beer—the lagers of Bavaria and Bohemia, transported there by a growing railroad network.

Altbier is a unique beer style because it requires an unorthodox, "cool" fermentation by a specialty yeast that works best in a temperature range between 13°C and 19°C (55°F and 66°F). Although most other ales are fermented relatively fast and warm at temperatures between 15°C and 25°C (59°F and 77°F) and most lagers are fermented slow and cold at temperatures between 8°C and 13°C (46°F and 56°F), altbier fermentation is somewhere in between. Because of this cool fermentation process, altbier yeast generates fewer fermentation by-products such as esters and fusel-like alcohols. In addition, after fermentation, altbiers—unlike classic British ales, for instance, but like classic Bavarian lagers—are aged in lagering tanks for 4 to 8 weeks at roughly −2°C to 5°C (28°F to 41°F). This slow, lager-like maturation allows the yeast to reabsorb much of the small amounts of esters and aldehydes it introduced into the primary fermentation. Done properly, the result of this complex brewing technique is an unusually mellow and clean-tasting ale of exceptional drinkability. Altbier is traditionally served at about 7°C (45°F) in cylindrical 0.2 to 0.4 l (6.8 to 13.5 oz.) glasses.

The typical altbier is a deep copper to light mahogany color, the result of large additions of carefully kilned, strongly malty-tasting malts, such as Munich or Vienna malts. Some altbiers are also made with a small portion of pale wheat malt, which gives the beers extra creaminess and firmer foam. In most altbiers, these malts are added to a base mash of pale pilsner malt. Some altbiers, however, are made entirely from a single-malt grist of 100% lightly kilned Munich malt. Roasted malts are rarely, if ever, used to color or flavor altbier, because the sharp, acrid notes of these malts are considered an off-flavor for the style. The altbier's mash composition is responsible for the brew's rich and aromatic, malty

Photograph of a Pinkus Müller altbier delivery truck, c. 1930s, in Münster, Germany. PIKE MICROBREWERY MUSEUM, SEATTLE, WA

sweet finish, which is balanced by the bitterness and aroma of so-called noble hop varieties, especially Spalt hops, but also Halltertauer or Tettnanger. See NOBLE HOPS. These hop varieties impart a delicate, often spicy up-front bitterness to the beer, as well as lingering, slightly floral reverberations on the palate.

Historically, the modern altbier evolved from northern German ales that were typical for the region during the Middle Ages. These were strong, well-hopped brews with names like Broyhan and Keutebier, which often contained large portions of wheat malt, perhaps as much as 40%. These medieval beers were of great economic importance in those days, because they served as a crucial trading commodity for the Hanseatic League, the European trading conglomerate of free cities that flourished between the 13th and 17th centuries. A preserved 1540–41 land record of Düsseldorf lists 35 brewers, making mostly Keutebier. Because these tradesmen were familiar with yeast, they often made both bread and beer, and the first brewers' and bakers' guild was formed in Düsseldorf in 1622 to protect the integrity of the local beer.

Four brewpubs in particular have preserved the altbier tradition to this day. They are all located in and around the old town of Düsseldorf. In 1838, Matthias Schumacher opened the world's oldest still-operating altbier pub. He took the local ale as he found it, brewed it slightly stronger, added a bit more hops than was customary at the time, and began aging it in wooden casks. In these modifications lie the roots of the modern altbier as a lagered, bittersweet ale. A decade later, the altbier pub Im Füchschen opened in Düsseldorf's old town. In 1850, Jakob Schwenger started a brewery and bakery, which is now the brewpub Zum Schlüssel, and in 1855, Hubert Wilhelm Cürten, also a baker with brewing credentials, opened his now-hallowed altbier pub, Zum Uerige, which is considered by many the global altbier Mecca. By the 1860s, there were about 100 altbier breweries in Düsseldorf. By the end of World War I, fewer than half remained; by the end of World War II, there were just 18, all of which have since been bought up by large brewing concerns. Only the four brewpubs, Schumacher, Im Füchschen, Zum Schlüssel, and Zum Uerige, remain independent.

See also ALE and GERMANY.

Dornbusch, Horst. *Altbier*. Boulder, CO: Brewers Publications, 1998.
Dornbusch, Horst. *PROST! The story of German beer*. Boulder, CO: Brewers Publications, 1997.
Fonk, Genno. *Altbier im alltag* (Altbier in everyday life). Duisburg, Germany: Merkator-Verlag, 1999.
Langensiepen, Fritz. *Bierkultur an Rhein und Maas* (Beer culture along the Rivers Rhine and Maas). Bonn, Germany: Bouvier Verlag, 1998.

Horst Dornbusch

aluminum kegs are containers once widely used for transporting, storing, and serving beer. The use of aluminum as a material for beer barrels started after the end of Prohibition in the United States in 1933. In older days, most barrels had been handmade of hardwood and hoops and then lined with pitch. The coopers who made the barrels were employed by the breweries, but when Prohibition closed the breweries, it also effectively eliminated the profession of the cooper. When brewing became legal again, there was simply not enough cooperage available to handle the volume of fresh beer that needed to be packaged in a hurry. Industrially made replacements were the only answer. Cast-iron containers were tried, as were those made of stainless steel and aluminum. Compared with wood, metal barrels were easy to sterilize and needed less maintenance, and the beer inside was less likely to spoil. They also could withstand high pressure for carbon dioxide, nitrogen, or a combination of both, which made them suitable for holding virtually any kind of beer. Aluminum also had a few advantages not shared by other metals. It was fairly low cost in relation to its strength, and it was comparatively light weight. Unfortunately, aluminum is also easier to recycle than steel, which made aluminum barrels a favorite target for keg thieves and unscrupulous scrap metal dealers. Aluminum is also susceptible to corrosion by both beer and caustic soda, the principal cleaning agent used in breweries. Aluminum kegs therefore required epoxy linings. As a result of these deficiencies, aluminum kegs are now rarely seen, having been replaced by stainless steel.

Holland, Robert T. The last wooden beer barrels. *Wisconsin Tales and Trails* 7 (1966) 12–16.
Hornsey, Ian S. *Brewing*. Cambridge, UK: Royal Society of Chemistry, 1999.

Tim Hampson and Stephen Hindy

Amarillo (hop) is a proprietary, trademarked aroma hop, also known as VGXP01 c.v. It was introduced and trademarked by Virgil Gamache Farms, Inc, of Washington State in 2000. The variety's genetic origins have not been publicly disclosed and the acreage is very limited. It is grown only in the Toppenish area south of Yakima. It matures mid-season and typically yields 550 to 725 kg (1,200 to 1,600 lb) per acre. It has demonstrated good resistance to both downy and powdery mildew and is moderately tolerant to verticillium wilt. The cultivar is favored, perhaps even loved, by craft brewers, but large breweries have shown little interest. Homebrewers have also taken to Amarillo. Amarillo has an alpha acid range of 8% to 11.0%, a beta acid range of 6% to 7%, and a cohumulone range of 21% to 24%. The aroma profile is floral and citrus-like, with notes of tangerine and apricot. The essential oil content is 68% to 70% myrcene, 9% to 11% humulene, 2% to 4% caryophyllene, and 2% to 4% farnesene, which makes it similar in aroma to Cascade and, to some degree, the recent higher-alpha cultivars Simcoe and Summit. Many craft brewers find Amarillo to be "a hop's hop," with an unusually pleasant aroma that can intensify hop aroma in a wide range of beer styles. Perhaps only its limited acreage has held it back because it shows the potential to eventually become the "next Cascade." Amarillo has found its way into a good number of American craft-brewed pale ales, India pale ales (IPAs), and "double IPAs," where it is often employed as a dry hop. It has also been seen in the Old World, where it is part of the flavor profile of several American-influenced Belgian beers. A few small British breweries have taken notice as well.

Matt Brynildson

amber malt is a traditional British malt made from winter or spring barley. Its principal function is to impart color and flavor to darker ales, especially to porters and stouts, as well as to old ales, mild ales, brown ales, and bitters, and to furnish these with some viscosity and a brownish head. Amber malt was a common type in the 1800s and widely used in porters, where it sometimes made up the bulk of the base malt. For many years amber malt was unavailable, but specialty maltsters have started to produce it again due to demand from craft brewers. Amber malt is made much like typical English pale malt, but after steeping, germinating, and kiln-drying, it acquires its color by undergoing an additional, brief, and severe heating step. In the old days of direct-fired kilns, this final step was carried out over an open fire, which also gave the malt a slight smokiness. Nowadays, the final heat is applied either in an air-heated kiln or, for a more homogeneous product, in a revolving roasting drum at approximately 150°C (300°F). See DRUM ROASTER, ENGLISH PALE ALE, and MALT. When finished, amber malt tends to have a very low moisture content of perhaps 2%–3%, and its color is pale buff to copper in a range of roughly 40 to 65 EBC (roughly 15°L to 25°L). See EUROPEAN BREWERY CONVENTION (EBC) and LOVIBOND. Unlike the old amber malts, modern amber malts have little to no enzymatic power. Because of its intense flavor, which is dry, bready, biscuit-like, slightly toasty, and without any residual sweetness, amber malt usually amounts to no more than 1%–2% of a beer's grist bill. Only in rare cases does it exceed 5%. It is often used in conjunction with such other color malts as brown, crystal, chocolate, or black malt, or roasted barley.

Briggs, Dennis Edward. *Malts and malting*. London: Chapman & Hall, 1997.

Stopes, Henry. *Malt and malting: An historical, scientific, and practical treatise, showing, as clearly as existing knowledge permits, what malt is, and how to make it.* London: Lyon, 1885.

Thomas Kraus-Weyermann

America

See UNITED STATES.

American amber ale is a phrase first used by startup American microbrewers in the 1980s as a simple beer description for consumers, but it soon found acceptance as a formal style name. These beers claim a middle ground between American Pale Ale and American Brown Ale, but often overlap the adjacent categories in significant ways. See AMERICAN BROWN ALE and AMERICAN PALE ALE. Because of their similarity, American-made red ales are usually included in this style. Examples include Bell's Amber Ale, Alaskan Autumn Ale, Anderson Valley Boont Amber, St. Rogue Red Ale, and Mendocino Red Tail Ale.

European beer culture and American consumer sensibilities often clashed in the early years of the United States microbrewery movement. Tradition called for "pale ales" of a deep gold to full amber color, but consumers, taking a literal interpretation, expected "pale" beers to be straw or blonde—similar to familiar pilsners. In response, brewers sought names that more clearly communicated beer identity and the term "amber ale" was adopted by many.

While "pale ale" was a recognized style name that implied a specific set of attributes, "amber ale"—in those early days—was primarily a color description. Many beers labeled "amber ale" were broadly in the pale ale style, but the notation covered other styles with varying attributes including Scottish ales, Irish Red ales, extra special bitters (ESBs), and even German alts. Over time, a formal style description evolved for amber ale that recognized it as an American style, distinct from all its European forebears but closely tied to the American style of pale ale.

A proper American amber ale requires the aroma and flavor of American hops, but the malt bill sets it apart from its pale and brown compatriots. As with American pale ale, two-row malt forms the base. But here, medium- to dark-colored caramel or crystal malts constitute at least 10% of the grist so that the finished beer presents a notable caramel to toffee character. This approach also gives a medium to full mouthfeel or body in the finished beer as well as a perception of malt sweetness in the palate. Brewers avoid the use of black, roast, and even chocolate malts in this style so that the finished beers do not have roasted, burnt, coffee, chocolate, or even heavily toasted flavors.

The "American" part of the style comes largely from American hops, which impart citrus and piney traits to the aroma and flavor of the beer. Expression of hop character may vary from low to high in the aroma—allowing for more assertive maltiness on the nose in some cases. On the palate, hop flavor should be moderate to high, with the citrus or resinous traits leaving no mistake as to the origin of the hops.

When well-brewed, the style supports significant hop bitterness without compromising an overall balance toward malt. Medium to medium-high perceived bitterness (30–40 IBUs) gives balance to the malt character without stealing its leading role.

Like most American ale styles, amber ale offers some fruity esters from fermentation, but these are secondary to the malt and hop traits. The butter or butterscotch traits of diacetyl—distinct and different from the caramel and toffee flavors of the malt—are considered undesirable. See DIACETYL. Many examples are unfiltered and may display a slight haze; bottled examples often include yeast for bottle conditioning, but the residual yeast should not contribute bready or sulfur traits.

American amber ales may be slightly stronger than American pale ale, sometimes up to 6.2% ABV, but may also go as low as 4.5% ABV.

See also MICROBREWERY, PALE ALE, and UNITED STATES.

Ray Daniels

American brown ale, a dark and richly malty ale often well-seasoned with hop flavor and aroma, evolved most recently from the classic English brown ale style. Notable examples include the Pelican Pub & Brewery's Doryman's Dark Ale, Brooklyn Brown Ale, Bell's Best Brown, and North Coast Acme Brown.

American brown ale traces links to English brown ale, mild ale, 18th-century brown porter, and even the stylistically undefined brews of 17th-century England. This style also shows similar influences to other Americanized styles such as American pale ale and American amber ale. See AMERICAN AMBER ALE and AMERICAN PALE ALE. Yet despite the rich heritage and close relations, the modern US brown ales offer a unique formulation and flavor.

Robust expressions of malt, mouthfeel, and alcohol content typify the style. All three of these traits arise from the type and quantity of malts selected and their use in brewing. Built on a base of two-row North American malt like other Americanized beers, this style finds its distinctive traits in the specialty malts employed. Nearly all formulations add medium to dark crystal or caramel malts, which lead to caramel to toffee flavors in the finished beer. To supplement this, darker grains such as chocolate malt, black malt, or roast barley are often added in small proportions to increase color and contribute chocolate or lightly roasted flavors. Various other caramel and toasted malts may be added to enhance these flavors and extend the richness and complexity of the malt palate.

The extensive use of specialty malts, combined with higher mash temperatures, leads to a medium to medium-full mouthfeel in the finished beer. Despite this, sufficient malt is used to reach alcohol contents that range from 4.3% to 6.2% ABV.

The finished beer color results primarily from the grist formulation. Paler examples stick to smaller quantities and lighter types of specialty malts resulting in amber-colored beers (perhaps as low as 15 Standard Reference Method); darker formulations give a dark brown color (up to 35 SRM).

While richly malty, this style—like American pale and amber ales—often exhibits substantial hop character as well. Both formal style guidelines and actual commercial examples indicate that high levels of aroma and flavor hops occur. But unlike some other Americanized styles, these hop expressions may be subdued. Furthermore, the herbal, flowery, or spicy traits of English or noble hops can be substituted for the citrus, piney flavors of American varieties. Thus, American brown ale varies more widely in hop expression than do the related pale and amber ales.

Bitterness levels also vary, but on the whole they tend to provide a solid balance to the malt, keeping sweetness in check without distracting from the rich flavors offered there. Measured levels range from 20 to 40 IBUs.

See also BROWN ALE.

Daniels, Ray, and Jim Parker. *Brown ale*. Boulder, CO: Brewers Publications, 1998.

Daniels, Ray. "Mild and Brown Ales." In *Designing Great Beers*, 215–28. Boulder, CO: Brewers Publications, 2000.

Ray Daniels

American Homebrewers Association (AHA) Founded in 1978 in Boulder, Colorado by Charlie Matzen and Charles Papazian (author of *The Complete Joy of Homebrewing* and current president of the Brewers Association, the AHA's parent organization and the principal trade organization for US craft brewers). See PAPAZIAN, CHARLES. It began with the publication of the first issue of the homebrewing magazine *Zymurgy* and in 1979 held the first National Homebrew Competition and National Homebrewers Conference. In 1983 AHA founded the Great American Beer Festival, which initially was held as a competition for both professional and amateur brewers and is now administered by the Brewers Association. See GREAT AMERICAN BEER FESTIVAL.

The AHA today is an organization of over 19,000 members dedicated to promoting the community of homebrewers. Through its publication of *Zymurgy* and its oversight of a yearly National Homebrew Conference, as well as various events and online information sites fostering competition and education among its membership, it seeks to empower the homebrewing community in improving the quality of its beer. Homebrewing is a popular hobby in the United States, and the AHA estimates that between 500,000 and 750,000 Americans brew at least one batch of beer at home at least once a year.

Despite its amateur origins and leanings, the AHA maintains close ties with professional brewers, both under the auspices of the Brewers Association and directly. With the legalization of homebrewing in the US in 1976, many of today's craft brewers began their brewing lives as members of and participants in AHA programs; its publications were among the earliest instructional documents for a generation of New World professional brewers-to-be. AHA's foundation and growth have proven to be a cornerstone of the revitalization of American brewing, and have influence throughout the world.

See also BREWERS ASSOCIATION and HOMEBREWING.

American Brewers Association. http://www.homebrewersassociation.org/

Dick Cantwell

American Hop Museum is dedicated to preserving, protecting, and displaying the artifacts and history of the American hop growing industry. The museum is located in Toppenish, Washington, in the heart of the Yakima Valley. The Yakima Valley of Washington state grows over 75% of all commercial hops grown in the United States.

The museum first opened in 1993 and is the only museum of its kind in North America. It is located in the former Hop Growers Supply Building in Toppenish, though the 1917 building was originally the Trimble Brothers Creamery. Toppenish is also known as the "City of Murals," and outside the museum there is an excellent one depicting the history of hops in the Yakima Valley that fills an entire side of the building. There is also large antique farm machinery used by hops growers in a fenced-in lot adjacent to the museum building.

Inside, the museum's exhibits include artifacts from all over the country, from the colonial period to the present, including old photographs, publications, hop memorabilia, equipment, hop antiques, and a model of a hop kiln.

Jay R. Brooks

American hops first began in the New England colonies soon after the first English settlers arrived there in 1620. These hops were cultivated varieties of English origin, but they were quickly supplemented with wild New World hops as well as with crosses between cultivated English and wild indigenous varieties. There is some speculation that the quintessentially American hop—Cluster—evolved in this fashion. See CLUSTER (HOP). As settlement moved west, so did hop farming. By the early 1800s, northwestern New York State had become a major hop-growing region, as had Wisconsin and much of the northern Midwest by the mid-1800s. However, because of the high humidity and cold spring weather in these regions, the hop vines were prone to mildew diseases and aphid infestations, and hop cultivation moved to the drier regions further west. See DOWNY MILDEW. By the early 1900s the American hop industry was firmly centered in the Pacific Northwest. Northern California was an important hop-producing area in the early 1900s, but commercial production was largely abandoned by the 1980s. Currently, Washington State, Oregon, and Idaho are responsible for almost all American hop production, and the United States is second only to Germany in acres planted. Because of higher average yields, however, the United States often surpasses Germany in pounds produced. Currently, the United States is responsible for 35% to 40% of world hop production. In the second half of the 20th century, several hop breeding programs were instituted in the United States, which led to the development of

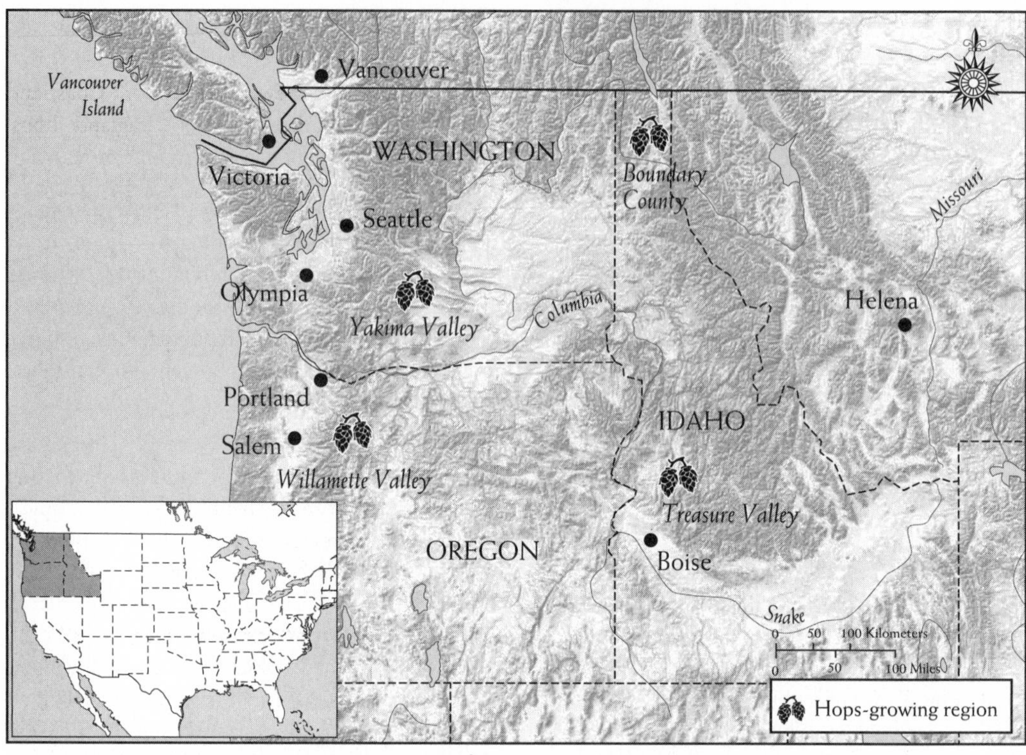

American Hops Growing Regions. GEORGE CHAKVETADZE, ALLIANCE PUBLISHING

many new varieties. See AHTANUM (HOP), AMARILLO (HOP), CASCADE (HOP), CHINOOK (HOP), COLUMBUS (HOP), CRYSTAL (HOP), EROICA (HOP), GALENA (HOP), GLACIER (HOP), LIBERTY (HOP), MOUNT HOOD (HOP), NUGGET (HOP), PALISADE (HOP), SANTIAM (HOP), SIMCOE (HOP), STERLING (HOP), ULTRA (HOP), VANGUARD (HOP), WARRIOR (HOP), and WILLAMETTE (HOP). The Yakima Valley in central Washington is on the dry, eastern side of the Cascade Mountains. It generally accounts for about 75% of all American hop production. See YAKIMA VALLEY HOP REGION. The first recorded hop yard in Yakima Valley was established in 1872, and during the next few decades, the area emerged as a major source of hops. In fact, every hop cultivar grown in the United States today is currently grown in Yakima Valley. But the Yakima Valley's most important hops, from a commercial point of view, are its high-alpha varieties. The Willamette Valley in Oregon is on the wet, west side of the Cascade Mountains. It is America's second-most important hop region. See WILLAMETTE VALLEY HOP REGION. The first hop garden there was established near Eugene in 1869. Today, the center of Oregonian hop production is farther north, between the cities of Portland and Salem. Nowadays, the Willamette Valley usually accounts for about 10% of American hop production, whereas in earlier times, Oregon outproduced Washington. Although the Yakima Valley gives precedence to high-alpha bittering hops, the Willamette Valley concentrates on aroma hops. High-alpha hop varieties tend to be particularly sensitive to mildew diseases and thus do not do well in Willamette's wet spring weather; the exceptions are Nugget and Newport, which are mildew tolerant.

Current hop production in Idaho is centered near the town of Caldwell, slightly west of Boise. Relatively small amounts are also grown in northern Idaho near the Canadian border. Hop farming in the Caldwell area did not start until the mid-1940s. The climate is hot and dry, similar to that of the Yakima Valley, which is why this area, too, specializes in high-alpha hops. Only about 8% of all American hops are grown in Idaho.

See also IDAHO (NORTHERN HOP REGION) and IDAHO (SOUTHERN HOP REGION).

Val Peacock

American hops, history, is essentially the evolution of a collection of native wild-type genotypes, a few transplanted European varieties cultivated from imported rhizomes, and US-developed cultivars. The resulting portfolio of hop varieties is used for both aroma and bittering in brewing. A number of private and publicly developed cultivars have been released by US breeding programs. These include Willamette, Nugget, Cascade, and Galena. American hops are genetically quite variable, which is not surprising considering their diverse derivations from both native American and European genetic sources. As hop cultivation spread out from its origin in central Europe, growers undoubtedly selected those hop plants that seemed best adapted to local growing conditions and that were most desired by the local breweries. These early hop selections were likely chosen from among local wild hop plants that had some favorable characteristics for brewing and perhaps desirable agronomic traits as well. In time, the most suitable plants would prevail and eventually transplanted to other growing areas. Settlers played an important role in transporting desirable hop genotypes into new growing areas. The same goes for the migration of European hops overseas into North America as well as the migration of hops from the East to the West Coast of the New World.

Brewing in North America began with the arrival of European settlers, who considered beer a staple of life, nearly as important as bread and water. Although hops were occasionally imported from Europe, the early pioneers carefully evaluated their potential homestead sites and the surrounding countryside not only in terms of the suitability for growing grain and raising cattle, but also for the availability of wild hops for beer brewing. They likely selected the best native hop plants around them, just as their European ancestors had done. The first cultivated hops were introduced into the United States from Europe by the Massachusetts Company in 1629 to stabilize local hop availability. Hop cultivation spread along the Eastern seaboard as new towns and communities provided support for hop production. The Puritans, for example, were such successful hop producers that they could eventually ship excess hops to the Quakers in Philadelphia. The Puritans also created a system of small land grants for hop gardens.

The soil in much of New England was not as productive as in the Ohio Valley, which is why New England farmers experimented with specialty crops, including hops. This effort coincided with a rise in commercial brewing on the East Coast and thus a ready market for New England hops. Massachusetts became an important hop growing region, in part because of an 1806 law that required inspection and grading of all hops produced for export. Hops that passed this inspection were considered of the highest quality in the United States, and growers were able to obtain premium prices for them. Thus, by the late 1700s and early 1800s, the New England states became the dominant American hop growing region. At its peak, in 1836, New England hop production reached 654,100 kg (1,441,936 lb), a substantial amount considering that hops were primarily hand-picked at that time.

New York State hops quickly gained a reputation for high quality for several reasons. In 1819, New York instituted an inspection law for hops similar to the earlier one in Massachusetts. Then, in 1825, the Erie Canal opened, which provided convenient shipping from Albany to the midwestern United States. Finally, a series of crop failures in England dried up hop imports and forced American breweries to rely on domestic hops. By 1839, New York produced approximately 32% of US-grown hops, but 20 years later, that amount had risen to 88%.

As the US population continued to grow and expand westward, demand for beer, and the raw ingredients for beer, also grew. Because hop production was very profitable, growers in other states soon tried to plant it. By 1850, hops were being cultivated as far south as Virginia, Alabama, Arkansas, Georgia, and Mississippi and as far west as Ohio, Wisconsin, Michigan, Iowa, and Wisconsin, whose major city, Milwaukee, was about to take off as America's beer capital. See MILWAUKEE, WI. A major aphid outbreak in Eastern hop yards turned out to be a boon for Wisconsin growers and gave them a major toehold in the market. In 1867 Sauk County in Wisconsin produced some 1,814,400 kg (4,000,000 lb). To put this in perspective, this is about the same amount that is currently produced in the Tettnang region of Germany in an average year. See TETTNANG HOP REGION. Recurring aphid infestations and downy mildew problems eventually caused the New York hop production to decline, and by 1899, the Pacific Coast states had already surpassed it. When Prohibition was imposed in the United States at the end of World War I, hop growing in New York was abandoned for good. See PROHIBITION.

Hop production began on the Pacific Coast sometime around 1850 when hop yards in Oregon and California were established. The hop industry there grew quickly in the 1870s and 1880s, in part through exports, because of disastrous harvests in Europe during that time. Also, California growers in particular had an agronomic advantage over their eastern American counterparts because the dry summers and mild winters allowed a significant hop crop within a year from planting, whereas it typically took 3 years to produce the first crop in the East. Although there were some outbreaks of hop aphids and red spider mites in California, yields were generally quite good. California growers were also the first in the United States to adopt the high-trellis system for hop production on a large scale. It greatly reduced production costs by eliminating the need to replace hop poles every year. Hop yields in Oregon were not as high as those in California or Washington, but the quality was generally very good. Oregon-grown Fuggle even became popular in England. See FUGGLE (HOP). Much of the Oregon acreage was devoted to the cultivation of Late Cluster, a likely derivative of the English Cluster, with the rest planted with Early Cluster and Fuggle. By the early 1900s, Oregon surpassed both California and New York to become the top hop-producing state, a position that the state held well into the 1940s.

A little more than a decade after hop growing had taken hold in California and Oregon, farmers in the Puyallup Valley of western Washington State experimented with raising hops. Because the soils were fertile and insect infestations low, yields there turned out to be excellent. Records indicate harvests of 1,800 kg/ha (roughly 1,600 lb/acre). Hop production moved into Washington's Yakima Valley in the mid-1870s. The Yakima area was even warmer and drier than the Puyallup Valley, which made hop aphids less of a problem. See YAKIMA VALLEY HOP REGION. By the mid-1890s, the Yakima Valley was already the largest hop-growing area in Washington State; since the 1940s, it has been the principal hop-growing region of the United States.

Whereas the early settlers in the New World had to rely on indigenous hop plants or on plants generated from imported rhizomes, starting in the late 1800s, systematic breeding programs began creating new cultivars either from successful European varieties or from progeny of European cultivars hybridized to indigenous native American hops. Late Cluster, an important early American hop, is thought to have been a hybrid of English Cluster and a native American male hop plant. Early Cluster is believed to have arisen as a mutant found in an Oregon-grown Late Cluster yard around 1908. Although these origins of the old hop cultivars cannot be determined with certainty, many of them have served as genetic foundations for modern hop cultivars.

Cultivated hop (Humulus lupulus L.) is composed of five botanical varieties: Hl var lupuloides, Hl var neomexicanus, and Hl var pubescens, all from North America; Hl var lupulus from Europe; and Hl var cordifolius from eastern Asia and Japan. According to recent genetic analysis, the three North American Humulus botanical varieties contain the greatest genetic diversity, whereas the European group is the most homogenous. Recent molecular genetics–based research into hop cultivars, breeding lines, and male accessions has revealed that all hop cultivars derive from only two genetic sources—purely European ancestry and hybrids of European and native American ancestry.

The US government sought to establish a hop breeding program in 1904 but abandoned the effort almost immediately. It took until 1931 for the US government to launch a successful hop breeding program in Oregon. This program is still in operation today, as part of the U.S. Department of Agriculture Agricultural Research Service (USDA-ARS). It is located on the campus of Oregon State University in Corvallis. Many successful hop cultivars have been released by the program, some in cooperation with other research institutions. Several private hop breeding programs are also active today, and many have produced commercially successful—and generally patented—hop cultivars.

Today, hop cultivars developed for the American market are bred either as replacements of previously successful cultivars or as new cultivars with significantly different trait profiles. For example, the cultivar Willamette was developed and released by the USDA-ARS program in 1976 as a Fuggle replacement. Fuggle is an English cultivar released in 1875 with a pleasing aroma profile. It has been very popular worldwide, but has poor agronomic characteristics and generates low yields. The very popular Cascade is an American original, too. Its unique, grapefruit-like profile has become the signature aroma and flavor of many North American craft beers. Cascade was developed and released by the USDA-ARS program in 1972. Like Willamette, it contains some Fuggle heritage and probably some native American ancestry as well.

From a global perspective, the American hop industry is, of course, relatively young compared with the well-established and tradition-rich European hop industry. Nonetheless, a dynamic and growing craft beer movement, a substantial and genetically diverse pool of native varieties and their hybrids and descendants, and an active hop research community all bode well for the future of American hop farming, the American hop industry, and the American brewing industry.

Brooks, S. N., C. E. Horner, and S. T. Likens. *Hop production*. Washington, D.C.: U.S. Government Printing Office, No. 240, 1960.

Brooks, S. N., C. E. Horner, S. T. Likens, and C. E. Zimmerman. Registration of Cascade hop. *Crop Science* 12 (1972): 394.

Haunold, A., C. Horner, S. Likens, D. Roberts, and C. Zimmerman. Registration of Willamette hop. *Crop Science* 16 (1976): 739.

Neve, R. A. *Hops*. London: Chapman & Hall, 1991.

Schwartz, B. W. "A history of Hops in America." In *Steiner's guide to American hops*. New York: S. S. Steiner, Inc, 1973.

Small, E. S. A numerical and nomenclatural analysis of morpho-geographic taxa of *Humulus. Systematic Botany* 3 (1978): 37–76.

Small, E. S. The relationship of hop cultivars and wild variants of *Humulus lupulus. Canadian Journal of Botany* 58 (1980): 676–86.

Smith, D. C. "Varietal improvement in hops." In *Yearbook for 1937*. Washington, DC: USDA, 1937.

Shaun Townsend

American Malting Barley Association, Inc. The American Malting Barley Association (AMBA) is a nonprofit trade association of brewing and malting companies based in Milwaukee, Wisconsin. Its mission is to encourage and support an adequate supply of high-quality malting barley for the malting and brewing industry and increase our understanding of malting barley. AMBA addresses this mission by aiding the development of new malting barley varieties and through the encouragement of a suitable farm policy safety net for barley producers.

New malting barley varieties require improved agronomic and quality characters to keep malting barley competitive with other crops so that growers continue to plant and produce an adequate supply of suitable quality for the industry. A national barley research infrastructure of personnel, facilities, and operating funds to conduct appropriate research is necessary to develop malting barley varieties that fit the needs of its members, from adjunct to all malt brewing. AMBA provides direct support to the national barley research infrastructure through its University Grant Program (about $400,000 per year) for applied barley breeding and related support programs, including basic malting quality research. In addition, AMBA manages the National Barley Improvement Committee, which prioritizes national needs and lobbies the federal government for funding of barley research.

Agricultural policies are addressed in cooperation with the National Barley Growers Association and individual state barley organizations. Efforts to ensure equity with competing crops and providing the greatest return possible for barley producers drives agricultural policy.

American Malting Barley Association, Inc. *American Malting Barley Association, Inc.* http://www.AMBAinc.org/ (accessed September 1, 2010).

Scott E. Heisel

American pale ale. One of the first Americanized styles brewed by start-up microbreweries in the 1980s, American pale ale came about when American ingredients were used to emulate British pale ale. The resulting beer showcased citrus and piney flavors from US hops, kindling their wide popularity with American beer drinkers and laying the groundwork for a "hops" race to India pale ale and beyond. Commercial examples of the style include Deschutes Mirror Pond Pale Ale, Great Lakes Burning River Pale Ale, and Sierra Nevada Pale Ale, which many consider to be the originator and prototype of the style.

The American amateur homebrewing that fueled microbrewing in the 1980s was learned largely from British literature on the subject. Thus, many early beers mirrored the traditional styles of England,

Ireland, and Scotland. While some brewers hewed to traditional interpretation, others quickly adapted the basic styles with North American ingredients and sensibilities.

One of the earliest innovators was Sierra Nevada Brewing Company, founded by Ken Grossman and Paul Camusi in Chico, California. See SIERRA NEVADA BREWING COMPANY. They produced their first batch of Sierra Nevada Pale Ale on November 15, 1980. It shared many traits with English bitter or pale ale, including pale and caramel malts, finishing hops, and pronounced bitterness. Despite these similarities, the resulting beer was distinctly American as it was flavored with US Cascade hops and, at 5.6% ABV, was stronger than commonly consumed English ales.

Hops define the unique American pale ale flavor. Late kettle additions and dry hopping with US varieties such as Cascade, Centennial, Columbus, Simcoe, and Amarillo impart the signature citrus and piney traits to the aroma and flavor. Grassiness may sometimes result from dry hopping.

Kettle hop additions supply medium to high bitterness (30–45 IBUs). Brewers use water low in calcium carbonate (<75 ppm) and often add calcium sulfate to achieve a crisp, clean bitter flavor.

Malt plays a supporting role, supplying a solid base for the hop expression but remaining in the background on the palate. Grists consist primarily of American two-row malt supplemented with a small portion (<10% by weight) of light to medium crystal or caramel malt for a hint of caramel or toffee flavor. Some brewers include small amounts of kilned specialty malts (e.g., biscuit, Vienna) to impart enhanced toasted notes. Most formulations give beers that are gold to amber colored (5–14 SRM).

Most American pale ales show evident but restrained fruity ester aromas achieved through use of fairly neutral ale yeasts. Many examples are unfiltered and display a slight haze; bottled examples often include yeast for bottle conditioning. Beers in this style should not have diacetyl character and residual yeast should not contribute bready or sulfur traits.

As hundreds of new breweries started production in the 1980s and early 1990s, many made beers broadly in the American pale ale style. Over time, brewers recognized two distinct variations, known as American amber ale and English pale ale. American amber ale follows the same hopping but increased use of dark caramel malts to achieve a deeper amber color and a more assertive and caramel-like malt flavor. English pale ale follows a formulation nearly identical to American pale ale overall but uses English hop varieties which generally results in a more earthy, herbal hop character.

The alcohol content of commercial examples ranges from as low as 4.5% to as high as 6.2%, although the upper end of this range overlaps with that of India Pale Ale—another closely related style. Indeed, a number of Great American Beer Festival medal winners in this category have been labeled or considered India Pale Ales, such as Anchor Liberty Ale, New Holland Mad Hatter, and Bridgeport IPA. Historically, the popularity of highly hopped pale ales supported demand for the more intensely hopped India Pale Ales and ultimately for the extreme hop levels of the newly coined styles "Imperial" or "Double" India pale ale.

See also ENGLISH PALE ALE, INDIA PALE ALE, PALE ALE, and UNITED STATES.

Daniels, Ray. "Bitters and Pale Ale." In *Designing great beers*, 152–74. Boulder, CO: Brewers Publications, 2000.

Foster, Terry. *Pale ale*. Boulder, CO: Brewers Publications, 1999.

Ray Daniels

American Society of Brewing Chemists (ASBC) is the society developed out of the Analysis Committee of the United States Brewers Association (USBA) that was pursuing standardized methods for the US brewing industry prior to prohibition. See PROHIBITION. Following Repeal in the fall of 1934, meetings between the Master Brewers Association of the Americas (MBAA) and USBA led to an agreement that there should be an initial focus on malt analysis. This was followed by consideration of methods beyond malt and on October 11, 1935, the name "American Society of Brewing Chemists" was adopted, with headquarters at the Wahl-Henius Institute in Chicago and 24 member companies. Membership was then opened to individual members with a call to submit research papers to annual meetings. At the meeting in Cleveland on June 17, 1938, the by-laws were adopted establishing the structure of ASBC as it essentially is today. A Technical Committee was formed to continue the work on methods of analysis and annual meetings were set up at which papers were read. The *Proceedings of the American Society of Brewing Chemists* were first published in 1940, becoming the *Journal of the American Society of Brewing Chemists* in 1976.

In 1977 a joint planning committee of the ASBC and MBAA worked toward a scientific meeting encompassing both organizations, leading to the first World Brewing Congress in St. Louis, Missouri, in September 1984.

A network of local groupings within the ASBC developed from initial gatherings in Cincinnati and Philadelphia in 1952. Local sections were formally recognized in 1966, with New York holding the first such assembly. The ASBC is now headquartered as part of Scientific Societies in St. Paul, Minnesota. "ASBC methods" for the laboratory analysis of various parameters of beer quality are considered standard throughout the US brewing industry.

Charles W. Bamforth

American Tettnanger (hop), German hop growers quickly point out, is a very different hop from German Tettnanger from Tettnang. See TETTNANGER (HOP). This is also apparent from the official U.S. Department of Agriculture listing of hop cultivars, in which U.S. Tettnanger has number USDA 21197, whereas Tettnanger-Tettnanger has numbers 21496 and 21497. American Tettnanger is a heat-treated, cultured clone of Swiss Tettnanger (UDSA 61021), a hop grown just on the other side of Lake Constance. Some believe Swiss Tettnanger to be a descendant of Tettnanger-Tettnanger; others feel that it is essentially a British imposter. The exact genealogy of American Tettnanger is in dispute, but the original plant material may have gotten mixed up, probably inadvertently, with another hop material, possibly Fuggle. Another theory suggests that the heat treatment somehow altered the hop. In any case, the characteristics of the resulting hop have more in common with Fuggle than with Tettnanger-Tettnanger. The latter has a red-striped bine, about as much beta as alpha acids, and an oil profile with a much closer resemblance to Saaz than to Fuggle. The American Tettnanger, by contrast, has a green bine without a red stripe, about half as much beta as alpha acid, and an oil profile more in line with Fuggle than Saaz. The aroma and brewing characteristics of American Tettnanger, too, are more Fuggle-like than Tettnanger-Tettnanger-like.

American Tettnanger was widely grown in Washington and Oregon during the 1980s and 1990s, mostly for Anheuser-Busch. But after this brewery curtailed purchases in 1997, acreage dropped drastically and little is currently grown. American Tettnanger has 3.5% to 8.8% alpha acids; 2.1% to 4.4% beta acids, and 24% to 31% cohumulone. Its storage stability is good, with 70% of the alpha acids remaining after 6 months at room temperature. Yields are fair to poor, however, at 1,000 to 1,300 pounds per acre.

USDA. Hop Cultivar Descriptions. http://www.ars.usda.gov/pandp/docs.htm?docid=14772

Val Peacock

American wheat beer is a beer style popularized by American craft breweries, generally using malted wheat for 30% or more of the grist and fermented with either lager or neutral ale yeast. Hop character and bitterness levels vary from low to medium, but all examples display a mild, flourlike malt flavor. Beers brewed in this style do not exhibit the clove, cinnamon, or nutmeg traits or high levels of banana-like esters that are hallmarks of the Bavarian wheat beer styles. Examples of American wheat beer include Widmer Hefeweizen, Pyramid Hefeweizen, and Shiner Hefeweizen.

Wheat, in malted and unmalted forms, has long been used in making beer as evidenced by several classic European styles using the grain: wit, lambic, Berliner weiss, and Bavarian hefeweizen. Historically, these styles have often accounted for a significant portion of beer sales in their respective regions.

Before the 1980s, beers were rarely made with wheat in the United States. American wheat beer developed during that decade as start-up microbreweries emulated European styles, especially Bavarian hefeweizen. The resulting beers looked like the original, but offered a novel flavor experience.

The key to the American wheat beer's flavor stems from yeast selection and fermentation practices. Early brewers used their regular ale or lager strains rather than a Bavarian weizen yeast, a practice that continues today. This approach gives American wheat beer a subdued fruitiness while eliminating the phenolic, clovelike traits associated with German weizen strains.

While American brewers use malted wheat like the Germans, they generally use less—as little as 30% of the grist and rarely more than 50%. The balance of the grist comes from pale two-row malt. A huskless grain, wheat malt does not deliver the same lightly toasted flavors found in barley malt. Recipes are generally formulated to result in a beer with 4%–5.5% ABV and the soft, flourlike flavors from wheat malt give the style a relatively mild flavor and good drinkability. A slightly tangy light acidity is common.

The resulting beers are pale yellow to gold in color and the high protein content of wheat malt contributes to a hazy or cloudy appearance common to the style. Like their German counterparts, American brewers often sell wheat beers unfiltered so yeast may be present—occasionally to such an extent that it contributes to the cloudy appearance of the beer. Despite this, bready yeast flavors are not seen as an accepted style trait.

While hop usage varies, the relatively light malt base means that hopping must be kept in check to prevent overwhelming the beer. Bitterness may range from 10 to 35 IBUs but is usually at the lower end of this range and generally perceived as low to moderate. Many examples use flavor and aroma hopping with American varieties for a low to medium citrus or piney trait. European aroma hops are occasionally used for a similar level of floral or spicy effect.

Despite significant flavor differences between American and German wheat beers, many US brewers use the German words "weizen," "weiss," or "hefeweizen" in naming wheat beers made in the American style. As a result of this twisting of the nomenclature, consumers rarely know whether to expect the traditional German flavor profile or the American flavor profile when buying US-made wheat beers.

American wheat beer has been a popular base for making fruit beers. See FRUIT BEERS. Raspberries were often used in the 1990s, but less assertive fruits are more often used now. The pale color and mild flavor of American wheat beer can allow easy expression of fruit traits.

See also WHEAT and WHEAT MALT.

Hieronymus, Stan. *Brewing with wheat: The "wit" and "weizen" of world wheat beer styles*, 1st ed. Boulder, CO: Brewers Publications, 2010.

Ray Daniels

amino acids. Proteins, especially enzymes, occupy a unique and important position in cell metabolism, and their biosynthesis from amino acids is one of the less secretive aspects of biology. Proteins are mostly constructed of linear, covalently bonded chains of amino acids.

From a brewing point of view, free amino acids are of most significance during fermentation, where they are the most readily available nitrogen source for yeast. See FREE AMINO NITROGEN (FAN). They are derived from malt and wort, and are critical to fermentation performance and beer quality. The uptake of wort amino acids involves a number of permeases: a broad-spectrum general amino acid permease (GAP) and several specific for an individual acid. Sixteen different amino acid transport systems have been identified in yeast (12 being constitutive and 4 (including the high-affinity GAP) being regulated by nitrogen sources already present in wort—called nitrogen catabolite repression).

A typical all-malt wort contains some 19 amino acids and these are taken up by yeast at differing rates. In order to achieve a good, rapid, fermentation the α-amino acid content of wort should be not less than 100 mg l^{-1}, preferably in the region of 150–200 mg l^{-1}. There should also be a balance of amino acids for the yeast to utilize. Commercial yeast nutrients often provide trace zinc and a range of amino acids.

Boulton, C. A., and D. E. Quain. *Brewing yeast and fermentation*. Oxford, England: Blackwell, 2001.
Hornsey, I. S. *Brewing*. Cambridge: Royal Society of Chemistry, 1999.

Ian Hornsey

Amstel Brewery was the now-defunct competitor to Heineken, located near the center of Amsterdam in the Netherlands. It opened its doors on the Mauritskade in Amsterdam on June 11, 1870 as De Pesters, Kooy & Co. Two years later its annual Pilsner production had risen to 10,000 hectoliters and in 1890 it was renamed "Beijersch Bierbrouwerij De Amstel" (The Bavarian Amstel Brewery) after the river close by. Cooling for the lagering of their pilsner was made possible by taking ice from the nearby canals in the winter and storing it in specially made double-walled cellars to provide sufficient cooling during the warmer months. Amstel was taken over by rival Heineken in 1968 and its Mauritskade brewery was demolished in 1982. Only the head office (now used as a college) on the Mauritskade dating from 1930 and a product line of beers using the Amstel name still remain. Its fruity Pilsner is now brewed using its own proprietary yeast strain at the Heineken Zoeterwoude facility, while its special beers (e.g., Bock) are brewed in Den Bosch. Amstel beers, while being targeted at the average no-nonsense beer drinker, are typically more pronounced in character than their Heineken counterparts. Experimental brews are often launched under the Amstel name to prevent tarnishing the Heineken image should they fail to succeed. Amstel Bock was the first Bock beer brewed in the Netherlands when it was released as "Winter" beer in 1872 and is widely regarded to be the "reference" for the Dutch variation of this style. The American market is only familiar with Amstel Light (3.5% ABV), a low-calorie lager introduced by Heineken in 1980. It remains a leading foreign light beer brand in the United States.

See also HEINEKEN.

Derek Walsh

amylases are widespread in nature, and, as well as plants, they are found in animals and are produced by many microbes. Once the endosperm cell walls have been breached and starch granules have been ruptured (both of these events are the result of enzyme activity), starch is available for degradation. In cereals, the mixture of enzymes responsible for partially or totally degrading starch is called diastase. See DIASTASE. This complex mixture does not have a precise composition, and diastase from a raw grain will be different from that after it has been malted. Most of the activity of diastase can be attributed to the activities of two enzymes, alpha and beta amylase, and, to a lesser extent, gamma amylase (together, the amylases), although many other enzymes are also present.

In the brewery mash tun, most starch degradation is the result of amylase activity, but *in vivo*, for example, in a barley plant, other enzymes will be involved as well. The concerted action of the amylases produces mainly maltose, but it leaves detectable amounts of undegraded dextrins. A pH-promoting general amylase activity is around 5.3. See DEXTRINS.

Diastase was the first enzyme to be isolated, albeit in an impure state, by Persoz and Payen in 1832. It was obtained by precipitating the enzyme out from an extract of malt with ethanol. It came out as a yellowish, amorphous, tasteless powder, and it was found to be able to break down starch, first into dextrins and then into the disaccharide maltose. In the brewhouse, diastase activity in malt is measured as diastatic power and the units of measurement are in °Lintner (°L). See DIASTATIC POWER.

Barley contains appreciable levels of latent beta amylase (glucan 1,4-alpha maltohydrolase), which is located in the endosperm. During malting the enzyme becomes active and starts to degrade starch slowly, a process that continues in the mash tun. In the absence of other enzymes, beta amylase is unable to degrade starch granules. It is, however, able to carry out (effect) a stepwise attack on amylose, dextrins, and soluble starch chains in solution.

In barley, beta amylase occurs in "free" (soluble) and "bound" (latent, or insoluble) forms. The latter is attached to insoluble proteins through disulfide linkages. When malting, during the steeping of grain, the level of free beta amylase can fall, but during subsequent germination, nearly all of the beta amylase becomes free and the bound form disappears.

Barley does not contain alpha amylase (glucan 1,4-glucanohydrolase), but this enzyme develops in the grain during malting and then gets to do most of its work in the mash tun. Copious quantities of alpha amylase are synthesized in the aleurone layer that surrounds the endosperm.

Synthesis is a response to gibberellic acids secreted by the embryo, and much of the alpha amylase is then secreted into the endosperm. Alpha amylase is an endo-acting enzyme (endoglucanase) in malt and catalyzes the hydrolysis of internal alpha 1,4-glycosidic bonds at random within the starch molecule. Such an attack is slower on short-chain dextrins, is slower near the chain ends, and does not occur in the vicinity of alpha(1→6) branch points. Isoenzymes of alpha amylase are known and have been much studied. Parallel with the formation of alpha amylase during malting is the formation of limit dextrinase, which can hydrolyse the alpha 1,6 linkages in dextrins.

Thus, unlike beta amylase, alpha amylase acting alone can attack starch granules and will steadily degrade them to a complex of sugars (including dextrose), maltose, oligosaccharides, and dextrins during mashing. Alpha amylase requires calcium ions (Ca^{2+}) for activity, and, if necessary, the brewer can add gypsum (calcium sulfate, $CaSO_4$) to the mash tun to ensure a sufficient presence of this cation. Both alpha and beta amylases from malt are active during mashing, although the latter is more heat labile and will not survive very long at elevated temperatures.

Alpha amylase (known to zoologists as ptyalin) is, of course, found in human saliva, where it will break down ingested starches to dextrins and, eventually, maltose. Ptyalin is inactivated by the low pH of gastric juices in the stomach. The enzyme has played an important role in the evolution of beer because, to initiate fermentation, many ancient indigenous peoples would chew their starch-containing raw material and then expectorate the bolus into a vessel intended for fermentation. Via this simple method, fermentable material could be obtained for brewing purposes.

The practice of prechewing grain for subsequent feeding to infants, the sick, or the elderly developed many moons ago, and the use of saliva to hydrolyze starch was likely the original way of initiating fermentation. Perhaps the classic example of this is *chicha*, a beverage of many South American native tribes. See CHICHA. Indeed, it is thought that the very name of this drink emanates from "chichal," a word that translates as "with saliva" or "to spit." Most chicha was made from the indigenous crops manioc and/or maize (the latter mainly in regions conquered by the Incas). Chewing was the only means of imparting amylolytic enzymes into manioc root.

See also ALPHA AMYLASE, MALTING, MASHING, and WORT.

Briggs, D. E. *Malts and malting.* London: Blackie, 1998.
Briggs, D. E., J. S. Hough, R. Stevens, and T. W. Young. *Malting and brewing science, volume 1: Malt and sweet wort,* 2nd ed. London: Chapman & Hall, 1981.
Hornsey, I. S. *Brewing.* Cambridge: Royal Society of Chemistry, 1999.
Pollock, J. R. A., Ed. *Brewing science,* volume 1. London: Academic Press, 1979.

Ian Hornsey

amylopectin. This polysaccharide comprises between 65% and 85% of the starch molecule and is a branched glucan polymer produced by the formation of *α*-(1→6)-branch linkages between adjoining linear (i.e., *α*-(1→4)-linked) glucan chains. The other component of starch is amylose. It is the breakdown of these two starch components that creates the various sugars found in wort.

The distribution of glucan chain lengths and branch point clustering within amylopectin allows short- to intermediate-sized glucan chains to form double helices that can pack together in organized arrays, and this forms the basis of the semi-crystalline nature of much of the starch granule matrix. Starch granule formation is governed by both the semi-crystalline properties of amylopectin, as determined by the length of the linear chains of amylopectin, and the clustering and frequency of *α*-(1→6)-branch linkages.

Chemically, amylopectin has similarities to the animal storage compound glycogen, and both structures are produced by the same overall class of enzyme (glucan synthases). The majority of the *α*-(1→6) linkages in amylopectin will survive a "normal" brewing process.

Amylopectin, which is preferentially broken down during the malting of barley (or, at least, the chain length of the molecule is reduced), has one reducing chain end and numerous non-reducing glucose residues at the branch ends (amylose molecules have single reducing and non-reducing glucose residues at their chain ends). Therefore, when iodine solution is used for a starch conversion test, amylopectin imparts a reddish tint, whereas amylose gives the blue color.

Barsby, T. L., A. M. Donald, and P. J. Frazier. *Starch: Advances in structure and function.* Special Publication 271. Cambridge: Royal Society of Chemistry. 2001.
Briggs, D. E. *Malts and malting.* London: Blackie, 1998.
Briggs, D. E., J. S. Hough, R. Stevens, and T. W. Young. *Malting and brewing science, Vol. 1: Malt and*

sweet wort, 2nd ed. London: Chapman and Hall, 1981.
Hornsey, I. S. *Brewing*. Cambridge: Royal Society of Chemistry, 1999.

Ian Hornsey

amylose. The sugars in wort are derived from the breakdown of starches contained in malt and any adjuncts that may be used in the mash. Starch can be separated into two parts, amylose and amylopectin, and these two different types of glucose polymer are synthesized simultaneously and then incorporated into the starch granule in very different ways. Amylose, a hydrocolloid, comprises largely unbranched α-(1→4)-linked glucan chains and does not appear to participate in the formation of the ordered part of starch matrix. Around 30% of barley starch is comprised of this polymer, and, within the starch granule, amylose molecules appear to be interspersed in a single-helical or random-coil form between amylopectin molecules. Evidence suggests that amylose synthesis is dependent on, and even controlled by, amylopectin synthesis.

The suitability of cereal starches for their intended uses is dependent on their amylose/amylopectin ratios. Historically, amylose has been determined by the measurement of its iodine-binding capacity (e.g., colorimetrically). Unfortunately, the test can be deceptive—amylopectin-iodine complexes also form and these may lead to overestimation of amylose. There are now methods by which amylopectin can be sequestered (for example, by binding it with the lectin concanavalin A), which renders it unavailable for reacting with iodine. Molecules of amylose consist of anywhere from 200 to 20,000 glucose units, depending upon starch source.

Barsby, T. L., A. M. Donald, and P. J. Frazier. *Starch: Advances in structure and function*. Special Publication 271. Cambridge: Royal Society of Chemistry. 2001.
Briggs, D. E. *Malts and malting*. London: Blackie, 1998.
Briggs, D. E., J. S. Hough, R. Stevens, and T. W. Young. *Malting and brewing science, Vol. 1: Maltand sweet wort*, 2nd ed. London: Chapman and Hall, 1981.
Hornsey, I.S. *Brewing*. Cambridge: Royal Society of Chemistry, 1999.

Ian Hornsey

analysis refers to the measurements made on raw materials, process streams, and products. Analysis is critical if a beer is to be produced consistently and within specification. Indeed, those specifications are developed on the basis of suitable and reliable analytical methods.

Within the brewing industry there are two major sets of standardized analytical methods. These are the methods of the European Brewery Convention and the American Society of Brewing Chemists (ASBC). The methods within these compendia address the chemical, microbiological, physical, and sensory attributes of raw materials, process streams, and beer. They are rigorously evaluated for their reliability such that, if the same method is used in different laboratories on the same sample source, those laboratories would be expected to arrive at the same value. If a given laboratory does not generate a value in keeping with those from other laboratories, then they have a problem that must be resolved. These types of "ring analyses" are widely used within bigger companies to ensure that all laboratories are generating reliable numbers. Ring analysis can also be performed between groups of different companies, and indeed the ASBC operates such a service.

Analysis may be performed by trained quality control staff, although simpler procedures may be performed "at line" by the operators who are running the brewery processes. Beyond this, analysis may also be performed "in-line" by specific sensors that relay analytical values either to a computer screen for interpretation or preferably to a feedback control system that will correct any drift from desired values and return the process to "in specification" running in real time.

American Society of Brewing Chemists. *Methods of analysis*. CD-Rom, 2009.
Bamforth, C. W. *Standards of Brewing*. Boulder, CO: Brewers Publications, 2002.

Charles W. Bamforth

Anchor Brewing Company is a craft brewery in San Francisco, California that produces steam beer, one of the few American beer styles (see STEAM BEER). Anchor has also been both inspirational and influential upon the craft beer industry as a whole, especially in its early days.

The Anchor Brewery is San Francisco's only remaining historical brewery from the gold rush era, having originally been founded by George Breckle around 1874 as the Golden City Brewery on Pacific Street. In 1896, it was bought by German brewer Ernst F. Baruth, along with his son-in-law Otto Schinkel Jr, and renamed Anchor Brewery. After it was destroyed in the 1906 San Francisco earthquake, the brewery was rebuilt at 18th and Hampshire streets.

Shortly after reopening once Prohibition was repealed in 1933, fire consumed the brewery and it was again rebuilt at 17th and Kansas streets, and then moved again in 1961 to 8th Street. The brewery struggled on under a variety of owners until 1965, when it was again on the brink of being closed. At that same time, recent Stanford graduate Fritz Maytag was a fan of their Steam Beer, which he enjoyed at his favorite North Beach restaurant, the Old Spaghetti Factory. See MAYTAG, FRITZ. When Fred Kuh, the restaurant's owner, told the young heir to the Maytag washing machine empire of the brewery's plight, Maytag paid a visit to the brewery and ended up buying a majority interest in it.

When he bought Anchor Brewery in 1965, it was one of dozens of similar regional breweries struggling to compete against the big national brands. Maytag spent the next several years learning everything he could about brewing. He visited breweries in England, studied old texts, and investigated steam beer, one of America's few unique beer styles. Anchor began bottling its current version of steam beer in 1971, striving to emulate the pre-Prohibition brew, the recipe and procedure for which had been lost by 1933. It marked the beginning of a prolific and innovative decade.

Anchor then bottled its first Porter in 1974, and even though porter is originally an English beer style, no brewers in England were making the style any longer. They then released the unprecedentedly hoppy Liberty Ale on April 18, 1975, to commemorate the 200th anniversary of Paul Revere's ride. It was one of the first beers to use Cascade hops, today the most popular hop variety used by craft brewers.

The first Anchor Christmas Ale, a brown ale, came the same year. Shortly thereafter, they began creating a new recipe, often spiced, and a new hand-drawn tree label, each year. Old Foghorn, the first barley wine-style ale to be brewed in America in modern times, debuted the following year.

In 1979, having outgrown the brewery on 8th Street, the brewery was moved to its present location on Mariposa Street, in an old coffee roastery that was built in 1937 on nearby Potrero Hill. In 1984, to celebrate their fifth anniversary in the new location, they brewed a wheat beer, which was possibly the first American wheat beer since prohibition. They also embarked on a series of special brewing projects, including the Sumerian Beer Project to make Ninkasi Beer, based on a 4,000-year-old Sumerian recipe, and a spruce beer based on colonial recipes. In 1993, Anchor added an in-house distillery where they make rye whiskey and pot-distilled gin.

In late April of 2010, Maytag announced he was selling the brewery, along with the distillery, to the Griffin Group of Novato, California. The Griffin Group is an investment company owned by Keith Greggor and Tony Foglio, who have extensive experience in the alcohol business, primarily with spirits such as Skyy Vodka.

Jay R. Brooks

Andechs is a Benedictine monastery ("Kloster" in German) located atop the appropriately named Holy Mountain, overlooking Lake Ammersee, just outside Munich, Germany. Kloster Andechs boasts a stately baroque basilica, but its fame is perhaps rivaled by that of the monastery's brewery. The Klosterbrauerei makes several types of Bavarian beer, all highly regarded, including a 5.5% alcohol by volume (ABV) weissbier and a 4.8% ABV helles. However, Andechs' best-known beer is perhaps its 7.1 ABV doppelbock, the modern interpretation of the medieval monks' "liquid bread." In Bavaria, doppelbock is universally made only in late winter, for the Lenten season, but at Andechs it is a year-round beer. Andechs is a packaging brewery, but it also has a beer hall on the monastery premises as well as a beer garden with an absolutely spectacular view, which on a clear summer day extends all the way to the glacier-capped Alps in the distance. There is evidence of brewing by monks at Andechs going back to the 12th century, when the place became a monastery. It became a Benedictine abbey in 1455, when it also acquired its official brew rights. Around that time, the church, which was started in 1430, also became a destination of pilgrimage, and the location acquired its current name of Holy Mountain. Swedish troops damaged the church during the Thirty Years War (1618–1848) and a lightning strike in 1669 did further damage. The church was rebuilt to its present state by 1675.

Today, Andechs beers are brewed in a modern high-tech brewery that was completed in 1984 just below the old monastery buildings and the beer garden.

See also MUNICH.

Andechs. http://www.andechs.de/ (accessed January 29, 2011).

Kloster-Andechs. http://www.destination-munich.com/kloster-andechs.html/ (accessed January 29, 2011).

Horst Dornbusch

Anheuser, Eberhard (1805–1880) was the co-founder of what would become Anheuser-Busch Brewing Company (see ANHEUSER-BUSCH and INBEV) in St. Louis, Missouri, brewers of the American beer Budweiser.

Anheuser was born in Bad Kreuznach, a town in western Germany along the Nahe River, a tributary of the Rhine River. With his two brothers, he immigrated to the United States and settled in St. Louis, Missouri in 1842. A soap and candle maker by trade, he founded a successful soap factory and became wealthy.

Around 1859, Anheuser became a major creditor in the failing Bavarian Brewing Company founded by George Schneider less than 10 years before. Schneider was ultimately unable to pay Anheuser, who acquired the brewery to satisfy the debt, and began running the brewery business, renaming it E. Anheuser & Co. Though not a brewmaster, Anheuser was a shrewd businessman and had the wherewithal, and cash, to keep the brewery going.

In March of 1861, Anheuser's 17-year-old daughter Lilly married Adolphus Busch, who owned a successful brewing supply company. On the very same day, his older brother Ulrich married another of Eberhard Anheuser's daughters, Anna, as well.

A few years later, Adolphus Busch joined his father-in-law at the brewery, buying a stake in the company in 1865. When Eberhard Anheuser passed away in 1880, Busch became president, and the brewery became known as the Anheuser-Busch Brewing Association.

Jay R. Brooks

Anheuser-Busch, the legendary American brewing company whose roots go back to 1852, ceased to exist as an independent entity when it was acquired in a hostile takeover in 2008 by the Belgian brewing giant, InBev. See INBEV. The new company is named Anheuser-Busch InBev and is headquartered in Leuven, Belgium. It is currently the largest

Etching of Anheuser-Busch malt houses in St. Louis, c. 1850. PIKE MICROBREWERY MUSEUM, SEATTLE, WA

brewery group in the world, with annual sales at the time of the merger of US $36.4 billion, approximately 25% of the global beer market. The former A-B now operates as Anheuser-Busch Companies, Inc, based in St Louis, Missouri.

History

Adolphus Busch was a charismatic, multilingual, and very ambitious German immigrant who arrived in St Louis in 1857 at the age of 18. After 2 years as a salesman for a brewery supplies company, he started his own company in 1859. This put him in close contact with St Louis' brewing industry.

About that time, Eberhard Anheuser, a successful local soap manufacturer, had taken control of the failing Bavarian Brewery. In the course of his sales calls, Busch became friendly with Anheuser and also with his attractive young daughter, Lilly. When he married her in 1861, he joined the family and later bought into the business as well, which in 1879 was renamed the Anheuser-Busch Brewing Association. When Anheuser died in 1880, Adolphus Busch became president. At the time, the brewery was producing about 4,680 hl per year (4,000 barrels). In the next 41 years, Busch managed to turn it into one of the world's largest breweries and became the grandest beer baron of the era.

Busch was one of the first entrepreneurs to envision and create a national brand in the United States, a task made doubly difficult by the extremely perishable nature of the product. Like all business visionaries, Busch was swift to adopt the emerging technologies of the day and supported the developments of those he thought could be useful to his plan.

Busch was one of many Germans with brewing connections to arrive in the United States in the mid-19th century. Prior to this time, very little beer had been consumed in the country (approximately 4 l [1 US gal] per capita in 1800), and vast swaths of the nation—especially the South—were nearly devoid of beer. Because of climate, soil, and difficult transportation, spirits were a cheaper and more practical drink in the early United States than beer. That all changed with the push into the nation's fertile heartland and the arrival of beer-loving German immigrants like Adolphus Busch beginning in the 1830s.

Armed with a formidable personality and a ferocious work ethic, Busch was able to build a highly sophisticated brewing operation along with a sales and distribution network that covered much of the country.

Adolphus Busch was instrumental in the development of refrigerated railcars around 1874, even before they were adopted by the emerging meatpacking industry in Chicago. He created an extensive network of ice depots in the South and West from which to refill the rail cars. With mechanized bottling and the pasteurization process developed by Louis Pasteur in the 1860s, Busch's beer could arrive in good condition to any major market. See PASTEUR, LOUIS. Adolphus Busch made a great show of shipping a Budweiser beer to Europe and back and challenging anyone to tell the difference from a fresh beer that had never traveled at all. By 1901 A-B had reached 1.17 million hl in sales (1 million barrels) and was shipping beer around the globe.

The oncoming storm of Prohibition was swirling ferociously by the end of the 19th century and accelerated into the 20th as anti-German sentiment built in the run-up to World War I. See PROHIBITION. Like many breweries, Anheuser-Busch showed a lax attitude about the crime and low moral standards that plagued many of the saloons it owned, and this fueled the antisaloon movement. In 1919, the Volstead Act became law, despite Busch's strident lobbying at the highest levels of government, and Prohibition began.

Prohibition closed many breweries and was enormously disruptive to all the rest, but A-B had enormous resources and many non-beer business interests to help it survive: diesel engines, corn syrup, ice cream, and even a railroad. As with most brewers, A-B marketed a near beer (Bevo) and sold huge quantities of malt syrup and yeast, more than a little of which ended up in the glasses of American homebrewers. See NEAR BEER. Assuming control of the brewery upon Adolphus' death in 1913, August Busch Sr guided the company through the difficult times of Prohibition and kept the brewery relatively strong compared with its competitors. In 1934, worn out and gravely ill, August Sr took his own life. Adolphus Busch III took control.

The decade that followed was a time of rebuilding. The drinking public had been profoundly changed by Prohibition. Spirits-based cocktails gained a modern stylishness; beer was increasingly seen as old-fashioned and, worse, fattening. The old saloon system had been disrupted, but nothing legitimate had taken its place. World War II was a further interruption and brought more changes to the drinking public. Beer consumption would not reach pre-Prohibition levels until the 1970s. In 1946, Adolphus Busch III died, and the hard-charging August II, known as "Gussie," took over the business.

The 1950s and 1960s were a period of slow growth and enormous price competition. Budweiser outsold its rival Schlitz in 1957 and became the number one beer brand in the United States. Most of America's regional breweries went out of business by the early 1970s, leaving fewer than 100 operating breweries in the United States. The spectacular implosion of the huge Schlitz brand in the late 1970s resulting from bad technology and poor public relations allowed A-B to snap up a good portion of the Schlitz market share, but despite this, A-B itself was not in the best of health.

Profits were slipping and under August II Anheuser-Busch was in the grip of an increasingly inflexible and unfocused leader. Although Busch had installed Richard Meyer as president in 1971, Busch retained the CEO title and kept a tight grip on the reins. The company was badly in need of more modern management and marketing techniques. In 1974, August III was named president and began plotting a palace coup, ousting his father and taking over the company the following year. His father never forgave the betrayal. August III assembled a team of MBAs and modern marketing specialists, and, spurred on by the aggressive marketing tactics of competitors, especially Miller, the young Busch invested in media advertising and sports sponsorships at levels that had never been seen in the beer business. At its peak in 2007, A-B spent $1.36 billion in marketing, about one-third of which was media advertising.

Miller Brewing Company emerged as A-B's archrival, and the competition got very personal. See SABMILLER. Miller president John Murphy allegedly kept a voodoo doll named "August" in his office. Battles were fought in court, in the media, and at the Federal Trade Commission over ingredients, beechwood chips, too-heavy light beer, and alleged deceptive advertising of the German brand Löwenbrau contract-brewed by Miller for the US market.

Most troubling to A-B, Miller's wildly successful 1975 launch of Miller Lite had taken the beer world by storm. A-B was unprepared and reluctant to take their flagship Budweiser brand in that direction, feeling that the light fad would quickly burn itself out. It was not until 1982 that they launched Budweiser Light, later shortened to Bud Light. With the company's full attention and huge amounts of money, Bud Light finally surpassed Miller Lite in 1997. The downside was that much of the growth of Bud Light came at the expense of the company's flagship, Budweiser, and in 2004 Bud Light overtook its namesake.

In 2006, August Busch IV was named President and CEO, succeeding Patrick Stokes who had run the company since 2002, the first non-family CEO. Busch IV continued until 2008, just prior to the InBev acquisition, and still maintains a seat on the board of directors. Dave Peacock is the current Anheuser-Busch Companies, Inc, President and CEO, reporting to Luiz Fernando Edmond, Zone President for Anheuser-Busch InBev's North American zone.

Controversies

Adolphus Busch appeared as an honest enough man by the standards of 19th-century industrial barons, but there are documented records of his attempts to fix prices in a gentlemen's agreement with Pabst and perhaps others, and his relish in crushing competitors was legendary.

As early as the 1930s, the company was charged with unfair trade practices, mostly related to free merchandise given to retailers, a practice regulated or prohibited in most states. Accusations, indictments, and settlements occurred over the decades. In 1977, the company admitted to $2.6 million in "questionable payments," paying the government a $750,000 settlement and promising to end the practice.

In the late 1980s A-B was criticized for advertising that seemed to promote beer to underage drinkers, most notoriously using the character of "Party Animal" Spuds McKenzie, a small but pugnacious dog. The pup was retired, but concerns over youth drinking still surface from time to time, especially over flavored malt beverages, whose soda pop flavors seem custom-tailored for the young drinker. The company launched a responsible consumption campaign, "Know When to Say When," in 1985.

In 1996, troubled by the success of Boston Beer Company's Sam Adams brand, A-B launched a series of attack ads, questioning its Boston heritage, and unsuccessfully tried to stir up labeling regulators along similar lines. Boston Beer fought back and eventually prevailed, but the fracas damaged Sam Adams' sales for several years.

In 1998, A-B issued a mandate to its distributors called "100% Share of Mind," which pressed for the ejection—often at fire sale prices—of non-A-B brands in a wholesaler's portfolio, the idea being that without such distractions distributors could give the A-B brands their full attention. Brewers have applied similar pressures to distributors for decades, but this proved to be a very contentious and unpopular program. With thin profit margins and mainstream brands declining, A-B's leverage with wholesalers is not what it used to be, and the policy is no longer in effect.

As with any family dynasty, the Buschs have had their fair share of scandals and deep, dark secrets over the years. In 1991, Avon Books published *Under the Influence*, an unauthorized book by Peter Hernon and Terry Ganey about the family and its role in the company, with 5 decades of intimate family matters laid out for the world to see. It quickly became a best-seller.

Brands

Prior to Prohibition, A-B made a wide range of beers of different colors, strengths, and price points, including Anheuser-Busch Standard, Original Budweiser, Pale Lager, Exquisite, Old Burgundy, and Faust. Most are long forgotten now, despite the occasional attempt to revive brands like Faust.

The flagship product is Budweiser, named for a Bohemian brewing town called České Budějovice. Budweiser was one of the first of the type of pale, dry beers brewed with a proportion of adjuncts—in this case, rice—which thins out the body and tames the high protein inherent in many North American barleys.

Bud Light is an important brand extension, having overtaken Budweiser in sales in 2004. It has been extended into a constellation of flanking brands such as Chelada (made with Clamato, a clam-flavored tomato juice drink), Bud Light Lime, and Bud Light Golden Wheat. Budweiser American Ale was released in 2008, attempting to capture some craft beer credentials for the core brand.

Michelob (also named for a Czech brewing center) is a so-called "ultrapremium" brand that was first brewed in 1901 as a draught-only beer aimed at better restaurants and clubs. In 1961 it was first bottled in a distinctive tapered bottle. Although Michelob has generated worthwhile sales for A-B, it has never been a huge seller, failing to compete well against imported brands like Heineken in the US market.

Michelob also serves as a platform for the company's more "experimental" beers—Michelob Light preceded Bud Light by 4 years. Today, Michelob is the name on a line of "craft-like" beers that includes Amber Bock, Pumpkin Spice, and other seasonals and also headlines the upscale light beer, Michelob Ultra. A Belgian-style Witbier called Shock Top is part of the group, but without the Michelob name attached to it. Although successful in some markets, these products do not appear to have caught on with consumers interested in more characterful genuine craft beers from independent producers.

Bud Select was introduced on Superbowl Sunday in 2005. The original marketing position was a bit unclear, although later efforts did hint that the product was lower in carbohydrates and calories than regular Bud. Now it is the standard-bearer of lightness, with Budweiser Select 55.

A-B also produces lower-price beers, most important the "popular price" Busch and Busch Light products. Launched in 1955 as Busch Bavarian, the name was shortened to Busch in 1979. Another low-priced product, Natural Light, was introduced in 1977.

Over the years, A-B has introduced dry, ice, low-carbohydrate, and other more specialized products, some of them brewed and packaged to resemble Miller products, reportedly in the hopes of stealing share from their rival. In the past decade A-B has flirted with flavored malt beverage products also known as "alco-pops," with sales results that were perhaps not worth the controversy. A-B produces a malt liquor, King Cobra, but has never had a big share of the category. See FLAVORED MALT BEVERAGE.

A Very Big Business

In the United States, A-B owns 12 breweries: St Louis; Newark, New Jersey; Los Angeles; Houston; Columbus, Ohio; Jacksonville, Florida; Merrimack, New Hampshire; Williamsburg, Virginia; Fairfield, California; Baldwinsville, New York; Fort Collins, Colorado; and Cartersville, Georgia. A-B's brands make up 48.5% of the US market (2008), just under 120 million hl (100 million barrels).

A-B has significant interests outside the United States. Budweiser/Bud is a strong and growing brand in the British Isles, China, Brazil, and elsewhere. Additionally, A-B functions as a distribution partner for a number of brands imported into the US market.

A-B also holds some equity in the craft beer market. In April 2010, A-B acquired 100% ownership of Chicago's Goose Island Brewing. A-B also owns 25% of Red Hook Ale Brewery, as well as 40% of Craft Brewers Alliance (formerly Widmer Brothers Brewing), which owns 100% of Kona Brewing Co and 49% of Coastal Brewing (Old Dominion and Fordham brands). Most of the high-profile craft breweries have been approached with talk of an equity proposition by A-B, and A-B InBev's involvement in the craft sector will likely grow over time.

A-B also has domestic and international partnerships with other brewers. It owns 50% of Mexico's Grupo Modelo (famous for the Corona brand) and, until recently, 7% of the Chinese brewer, Tsingdao, which has since been sold.

In addition to the breweries, A-B invested in significant vertical integration and at the time of the merger owned eight barley elevators, five aluminum can plants, three malt plants, three seed facilities, two hop farms, two rice mills, two bottle plants, a railcar company, and a railroad, along with assorted other related business like recycling ventures.

In 1959, A-B formed Busch Entertainment Corporation to manage several Busch Gardens attractions, which had grown out of the family's fondness for showy gardens and fantasy farms. In 1989, A-B purchased the Sea World parks, eventually becoming the fifth largest amusement park operator in the world. After the InBev merger, the division was sold to The Blackstone Group.

Postmerger

At the time of the 2008 merger, the company was anticipating US $1.5 billion in postmerger "synergies." To come up with those efficiencies, the new management cut some 1,600 positions in St Louis as of the beginning of 2010. As is typical for acquisitions of this type, costs are being cut. Office sizes, employee pensions and insurance, corporate jets, smart phones, accounts payable, advertising expenditures, and many other areas have been targeted to take advantage of postmerger efficiencies and pay off the enormous debt incurred by the takeover.

See also ANHEUSER, EBERHARD, BUDWEISER, and BUSCH, AUGUST IV.

Hernon, Peter, and Ganey, Terry. *Under the influence: The unauthorized story of the Anheuser-Busch dynasty.* New York: Simon & Schuster, 1991.

Ogle, Maureen. *Ambitious brew.* Orlando, FL: Harcourt, 2006.

Plavchan, Ron. *A history of Anheuser-Busch, 1852–1933.* New York: Ayer, 1975.

Randy Mosher

Anheuser-Busch InBev is the largest beer company in the world and is the result of a 2008 hostile takeover of the American brewing giant Anheuser-Busch by the Belgian beer company InBev. See ANHEUSER-BUSCH and INBEV.

In late June of 2008, InBev made an offer of $65 per share to acquire Anheuser-Busch. That offer was quickly rejected by A-B. After contentious negotiations and maneuvering over the subsequent 2 weeks, InBev increased their offer to $70 per share, which was accepted by the shareholders of Anheuser-Busch in mid-July of 2008. The total price InBev paid for A-B was approximately $52 billion.

Anheuser-Busch InBev (ABI) had combined revenues of $36.8 billion in 2009 and employs 120,000 people worldwide. The company maintains its headquarters in Leuven, Belgium. ABI stock is traded on the Euronext Stock Exchange (Ticker: ABI) in Brussels and they have a secondary listing on the New York Stock Exchange (Ticker: BUD).

As of early 2011, the CEO is Carlos Brito, originally from Brazil. He joined AmBev in 1989 and became the head of that company in 2004. After the AmBev/Interbrew merger in August 2004, he headed the North America division before becoming CEO of InBev in December of 2005, a position he retained in the restructured ABI.

The company divides their international business into six "operational zones," which consist of North America, Latin America north, Latin America south, western Europe, central and eastern Europe, and Asia. The company owns and operates 152 beverage plants worldwide, including 138 breweries in 15 counties. Of those, 19 are in North America, 55 in South America, 39 in Europe, and 35 in Asia.

ABI owns over 200 brands of beer, which they market in 30 nations. They have the number one market share in at least 10 countries, are second in 10 more, and are number three in 5.

They consider three of their most popular brands to be global: Beck's, Budweiser, and Stella Artois. They characterize Belgian brands Hoegaarden and Leffe as multicountry brands and refer to Brahma (popular Brazilian beer available in 20 countries), Bud Light (accounting for half of US light beer sales), Chernigivske (the most popular beer in the Ukraine), Harbin (a Chinese brand), Jupiler (Belgium's most popular beer), Klinskoye (the second best-selling Russian beer), Michelob (the fourth best-selling American premium beer), Quilmes (Argentina's best-selling beer), Sedrin (another Chinese brand), Siberian Crown (a popular Russian brand), and Skol (the best-selling Brazilian beer and fourth in the world) as "local jewels."

Other familiar brands ABI owns include Alexander Keith, Antarctica, Bass, Belle Vue, Boddingtons, Bohemia, Diebels, Franziskaner, Labatt, Kokanee, Löwenbräu, Oranjeboom, Spaten, Staropramen, and St Pauli Girl.

In the UK, ABI also has licensing or exclusive bottling agreements for Castlemaine XXXX, Estrella-Damm, and Tennent's.

In addition to their own breweries, ABI also has a 50% equity interest in the operating subsidiary of Mexico's largest beer company, Grupo Modelo, makers of the popular Corona beer.

MacIntosh, Julie. *Dethroning the king: The hostile takeover of Anheuser-Busch, an American icon.* New York: John Wiley & Sons, Inc., 2011.

Jay R. Brooks

Anselmus of Achel

See JUDONG, FATHER ANSELMUS.

anthocyanogens (flavan-3,4-diols), also known as proanthocyanidins or leucoanthocyanidins, are a group of polyphenolic compounds that provide most of the tannins that are important in terms of beer stability. Both malt and hops are sources of these compounds (also named "pro-tannins"), in roughly equal amount, with "aroma" hop varieties containing higher levels than "bitter" ones. When it comes to barley-based tannins, six-row varieties tend to contain higher levels than two-row varieties, and crops grown under maritime conditions usually have lower levels than those grown far inland.

Anthocyanogens are readily able to polymerize (both with themselves and with other polyphenols, notably catechins—which are not anthocyanogens *per se*), although free forms are invariably present as well. This polymerization is a first step on the path to haze formation. It has been known for more than 50 years that the colloidal stability of beer is inversely related to the concentration of anthocyanogens in wort. Anthocyanogens can pass through the brewing process and end up in finished beer, where they may be converted into tannins and then interact with proteins to give unwanted hazes. The importance of wort polyphenols to the colloidal stability of beer has led to there being many analytical methods available for their detection. In the past, some brewers would add formaldehyde to the mash-tun; this would reduce anthocyanogen in the resultant wort (and enhance beer shelf life), but it would also reduce wort fermentability. This is no longer practiced. Oxygenating the mash also achieves a similar result.

A number of post-fermentation treatments are available for improving the colloidal stability of beer, including activated carbon, bentonite, silica gels, and polyamide resins. Thanks primarily to extensive work by plant breeders at Carlsberg, there are now a number of proanthocyanidin-free (PA-free) malting barleys that can produce haze-free beers.

Briggs, D. E., J. S. Hough, R. Stevens, and T. W. Young, *Malting and brewing science, vol. 1: Malt and sweet wort,* 2nd ed. London: Chapman and Hall, 1981.

Pollock, J. R. A., ed. *Brewing science, vol. 1.* London: Academic Press, 1979.

Ian Hornsey

anti-foaming agents are sometimes added by brewers to either boiling wort or fermenting beer to reduce the size of the foam cap on top of the wort. This antifoaming agent takes the form of a liquid silicone material that works by reducing the surface tension of the wort. The reduction of surface tension also prevents the release of foam-positive wort components, enhancing foam formation in finished beer. In the kettle, anti-foaming agents help prevent dangerous boilovers. Used in the fermenter, reduction of the foam cap provides the advantage of increasing the working capacity of the vessel.

Typical fermentation vessels require up to 30% headspace above the liquid level, especially when vigorous ale fermentations are employed. Other benefits may include better hop utilization because of reduced bitterness loss associated with normal foaming and easier cleaning of vessels. Silicone-based antifoaming agents are removed during filtration and/or centrifugation and should not survive into the finished beer.

See also FOAM.

Steve Parkes

antioxidants are naturally found in beer and may have a positive effect on health. An antioxidant is a substance that protects against the oxidation of other molecules. Oxidation is defined as the loss of electrons. Antioxidants function by interfering with the siphoning of electrons from molecules. They may do this by themselves being preferentially oxidized, thereby preventing other materials being oxidized; by blocking the action of oxidizing systems; or by donating electrons. Antioxidants may be endogenous (i.e., native to the raw materials of brewing), exogenous (i.e., added), or both.

Examples of endogenous antioxidants are polyphenols (such as catechin), phenolic acids (e.g., ferulic acid), and Maillard reaction products and enzymes (notably superoxide dismutase, catalase, and peroxidases). See MAILLARD REACTION, PHENOLIC, and POLYPHENOLS. Exogenous antioxidants would include ascorbic acid, which, although present (as vitamin C) in many living systems, is not substantially present in those organisms significant in brewing. Sulfur dioxide (metabisulfite) is both endogenous (it is a product of yeast metabolism) and exogenous.

Antioxidants in a brewing context have two significant roles. First, they protect against the oxidation of wort, yeast, and beer, thereby extending beer shelf life and yeast viability. Second, their presence in beer is relevant to the impact of beer on the health of the drinker. The antioxidants in beer are derived from both the malt and the hops, but the levels found will depend on the style of beer and the raw materials and brewing processes used. Beer contains more than twice as many antioxidants as white wine (of equivalent alcohol content) but only half the amount in red wine, although the antioxidants in beer tend to be smaller molecules than in wine and may be more readily absorbed by the body. Researchers working on animals have suggested a direct effect of antioxidants in beer to reduce the risk of cardiovascular disease.

Halliwell, B., and J. M. C. Gutteridge. *Free radicals in biology and medicine*. New York: Oxford University Press, 2007.

Charles W. Bamforth

aphids are small insects, Phorodon humuli (Schrank), also known as the Damson-hop aphid, which can have a devastating effect on the hop plant resulting in substantial yield decline and a reduction in cone quality. This is one of the dominant hop pests in the Northern Hemisphere and its impact on a hop yard can result in significant yield loss up to complete devastation of a crop. The aphid overwinters as eggs attached to various Prunus species (i.e., sloe, plum, cherry plum, damson), and in early April, wingless female insects hatch and give birth to an average of four more generations of wingless female aphids. After several generations, winged female arise and migrate to the hop plant when the weather warms above a flight temperature threshold (when minimum daytime temperature is greater than 13°C). They reproduce on the hop leaves and feed on the sap in the phloem strands in the hop leaves, thereby weakening the hop plant and in some cases causing defoliation. Toward the end of August, they migrate back to the Prunus winter host, mate, and lay eggs on or near the buds of the host plant, and these will hatch the following spring. The aphid causes yield declines when high numbers of aphids feed on plant sap during the growing season. Much of the economic damage, however, occurs late in the summer when the aphids enter the hop cone to feed since they are protected from insecticides and can cause heavy damage to the cone. Heavily infected cones appear brown and are prone to shatter during picking and drying. The excreted honeydew from aphid infestation can serve as a medium for sooty mold fungi on hop leaves and cones, and in instances with high levels of mold the hop cones are unmarketable. Furthermore, several viruses can be transmitted by these aphids, including Hop mosaic virus and American hop latent virus, and these may also negatively impact plant health. Control of aphids is often carried out using organophosphates, carbamates, endosulfan, and/or pyrethroid sprays. However, because some of these have been used exclusively for long periods, the Damson-hop aphid has developed resistance to many of these compounds. Use of natural enemies such as ladybird beetles (Coccinellidae), anthocorids, and lacewing and hoverfly larvae has been used successfully by hop growers, provided environmental conditions are more favorable for the predators than for the aphids.

Thomas Shellhammer and Shaun Townsend

apparent extract is a direct measurement of the dissolved solids in brewers wort, gauged according to specific gravity. See SPECIFIC GRAVITY. A substantial portion of the dissolved solids will be removed from the wort during fermentation by the action of yeast, so the progress of the fermentation may be monitored by measuring the disappearance of these solids. However, the measuring method compares the weight of the dissolved solids with that of water. As the fermentation progresses the solute is no longer pure water but is a mixture of water and alcohol.

Alcohol has a specific gravity substantially lower than water. This means the "true" or "real" extract is greater than that measured directly, hence the term "apparent extract."

See also EXTRACTS.

Steve Parkes

apprenticeship is a professional training concept that originated with the rise of tradesmen guilds in Europe in the Middle Ages. It is based on what we would now call a polytechnic approach to education. Its principle is learning by doing, which was the only way most people in the Middle Ages could learn anything of substance; the vast majority of people were illiterate, except for a few learned monks. Apprentices started work in the employ of a master, usually at age 10 to 15, who for about 3 to 7 years taught them a trade. The master also provided food and lodging and was sometimes paid for the training he dispensed. In exchange for the privilege of being trained, apprentices had to agree to continue to work for their masters for a fixed period after they had become skilled. Brewery apprentices would learn the nuts and bolts of the profession, but they also did the backbreaking grunt work, such as shoveling the germinating grain on the malt floor, stoking the fires under the malt kiln and the brew kettle, milling the dried grain, carrying brew water from the well to the kettle to be heated for the mash, ladling hot mash in and out of the kettle for decoctions, cropping yeast off the fermenting beer, filling and sealing casks of finished beer, and loading heavy casks into horse-drawn drays for delivery. Finally they would learn how to distinguish between good and bad raw materials, how to manage fermentations at different ambient temperatures, and even how to formulate recipes. Once a master had certified an apprentice's skills, the new brewer would eventually take his leave to become an itinerant journeyman, working for different brewmasters to further hone his craft. Finally, a journeyman might settle down, become a master himself, run his own brewery, and train his own apprentices . . . and the training cycle would repeat itself.

The entire system was strictly regulated by guilds, which, for brewers in medieval times, were often combination guilds for both brewers and bakers. Because the European countryside in those days was populated mainly by serfs that were essentially owned by their feudal lords, guilds first sprang up only in the chartered cities with their free burghers. There, the guilds formed oligarchies of competence in otherwise static societies. As a guild member, a person's station in life might be based on what he could actually do, rather than his family affiliations. Guilds had their origins in primitive Germanic, often religious, brotherhoods. The first documentary mention of guilds dates back to decrees by Emperor Charlemagne (742–814). Medieval guilds promoted the economic welfare of their members by regulating entry into as well as advancement within the profession, setting fixed labor rates, discouraging competition, suppressing unaffiliated labor, and setting quality standards. The guild members, in turn, had to submit to the discipline of the guild rules, which included, importantly, the training system of guild-certified apprentices, journeymen, and masters. By being closed shops, the guilds eventually acquired local monopolies over the making of the products of their trades, and the guild houses became centers of social, economic, and often political power. Eventually, the guilds gave rise to modern trade unions.

Echoes of the old guild apprenticeship system remain in place in Germany. In the modern German system, private employers in combination with public vocational schools now provide strictly formalized 3-year apprenticeship programs, which are supervised no longer by guilds, but by local affiliates of the German chamber of commerce. Apprentices receive practical on-the-job training and a modest pay, financed by authorized employers. Brewer apprentices alternately work in a brewery and study at a vocational brewing school. There is some flexibility regarding the duration of the alternating blocks of work and study, from a week or two to several months. During their apprenticeship, apprentices cannot be dismissed by their training breweries. The apprenticeship period ends with a test; those who pass can call themselves journeymen brewers and seek regular full-time employment or they can enroll in further studies at a school to become certified brewmasters. Only companies with brewmasters or maltmasters on staff who are also government-certified holders of educators' licenses may participate in apprentice training programs. This polytechnic training regimen functions in parallel to academic brewing education tracks offered by universities. See BREWING SCHOOLS.

By international standards, the German apprenticeship system is perhaps the most regulated path for entry into the brewing profession, whereas practices in North America rank perhaps among the most lenient. It is not uncommon for a craft brewery in the New World, for instance, to employ brewers who learned their craft strictly by trial and error, often as homebrewers or brewery apprentices without formal training. Considering that the German beer culture has not developed a new beer style for almost 100 years, whereas the North American craft brewing scene has become the undisputed leader in global beer style developments, it might be interesting to speculate whether the German apprenticeship is likely to produce brewers most interested in brewing traditional beer styles to perfection, whereas the much looser North American system is more likely to produce brewers more eager to innovate and experiment with new ingredients and processes. Each system and culture appears to retain certain advantages, a fact reflected by a very recent emphasis on creativity in German brewing education, and a new focus on the importance of practical brewery internships in the United States.

See also BEER STYLE.

Bishop, Morris. *The Middle Ages*. Boston: Houghton Mifflin Company, 1968.

Bloch, Marc. *La société féodale (Feudal Society)*. Paris: Les Éditions Albin Michel, Paris, 1982.

Brauer & Mälzer—Der Körper. http://www.brauer-und-maelzer.de/html/koerper.htm/ (accessed January 21, 2011).

Horst Dornbusch

Argentina is the second largest country in South America and the eighth largest in the world by land mass. It was first explored by Europeans in 1516 and derives its name from the Latin word for silver. Argentina became an independent republic in 1860, with Buenos Aires as its capital. Stylistically it is perhaps the most European of Latin American countries, especially when it comes to cuisine. A wave of investment and immigration from Germany, Spain, and Italy in the middle of the 19th century deepened European connections. Southern Europeans helped turn it into the world's fifth biggest wine producer. Founded in the 1860s by Alsatian colonists, Argentina's first brewery was known as el egido de la Ciudad Autonoma de Buenos Aires. The principal beer types were based on central European styles of lager and wheat beer.

Based in the capital of Quilmes, Partido (Buenos Aires province), the Quilmes Brewery was founded in 1888 by German immigrant Otto Bemberg and by 1920 had become the country's biggest brewery. It remains so today. Quilmes' most popular beer is the light lager "Cristal" and they also brew a bock and stout. By 2010 Quilmes brewed 17 million hl (14,486,854 US bbl) annually, had 75% of the home market, and was a global exporter. In 2002, Brazilian brewers AmBev bought 37.5% of Quilmes and in 2006 InBev (passim, now ABInBev) raised the stakes to 91%. See ANHEUSER-BUSCH INBEV. The brewery sponsors the national football and rugby teams.

In 1912, another German immigrant, Otto Schneider, founded the eponymous brewery in Santa Fe. The brewery was acquired in 1995 by Compana de Cervecerias Unidas Argentina (CCUA), a division of Chilean multinational CCU, who in turn had investment from Anheuser Busch. CCUA is the importer of Heineken, Budweiser, Corona, and Guinness and, in 2009, was the second largest brewer in Argentina with 16% of the market.

The third largest brewery in Argentina is Isenbeck, founded in 1893 and owned by the German brewery Warsteiner until 1990, when it was closed.

It reopened in 1994 under local ownership and was acquired by SAB Miller in November 2010.

The European beer influence on Argentina is still powerful, and this is especially visible at festivals. Fiesta de la Cerveza (Oktoberfest) has been celebrated by the Germanic population in San Carlos and Esperanza since 1863. A town in Cordoba, Villa General Belgrano, was founded in 1930 by Europeans who chose the area for its Alpine qualities and has celebrated Oktoberfest every year since. Celtic lineage is celebrated as Dia den San Patrico (St Patrick's day).

Despite some severe financial shocks to the economy, beer production has grown at an average of 13% per annum since 1980, moving to consumption of 15.7 million hl (13,379,000 US bbl) or 40 l (10.5 gal) per capita in 2007. The financial crisis of the early 2000s placed severe restrictions on all imported goods, including beer, and this hastened the birth and rapid growth of Argentine *cervecerias artesanales* (craft brewers). As of 2010 there were 70 microbreweries and 800 distinctive brands brewed in a wide range of styles. Buenos Aires is home to Buller Brewing, Barba Roja, and Otto Mundo, which exports to North American Free Trade Agreement members, Spain, and Italy. Additionally, El Bolson and Kunster are thriving in Patagonia, whereas Antares has several brewpubs throughout the country. Craft beer accounts for only 0.2% of the Argentine market but has doubled to 36,000 hl (30,678 US bbl) since 2006 and is expected to maintain high growth through the next decade.

Glenn A. Payne

aroma. Some neuroscientists feel that among our five senses, aroma is perhaps the most powerful. The sense of aroma ties directly into the most primitive parts of the brain, evoking pleasure, disgust, recognition, and memory. A strong aroma can transport the human mind directly into the past, over years or even decades, to a particular place or moment. Most of what we think of as our sense of "taste" is actually based on aroma.

The tongue senses sweetness, sourness, saltiness, bitterness, and perhaps umami, but the nose perceives everything else. After the visual appeal, aroma is usually at the forefront of a beer experience but can also be a large part of the lingering finish as residual volatiles feed back into your nose and stimulate your olfactory sense. In beer, especially full-flavored beer, aroma is exceedingly important.

We are all aware of aroma as a major sense, although we aren't always conscious of it moment to moment. In fact, many of aroma's effects are subtle and subliminal. It is, of course, a well-recognized animal sense providing essential information about the environment, food, and other animals. In humans it is particularly important in assessing, and appreciating, the character of food and beverages and, of course, beer.

Aroma detection involves specific sensory receptors in the nose being stimulated by volatile chemicals in the air we breathe. Aroma appreciation involves not just the receptors but interlinking neurons, the brain pathways, and psychology, particularly learned experiences of attraction and aversion. As a result it is much more than a "smell it and like it" effect and involves numerous inputs that will modify our responses.

Taking these parts in turn, however, we should look first at the physiology of the nasal cavity and the sensory organs that detect aroma.

Two of these sensory organs can be identified in the nasal cavity—the sensory receptors themselves and the trigeminal nerves. These occur in different parts of the nose with the trigeminal receptors being located at the entrance and the sensory receptors at the top of the cavity.

These two groups of receptors also respond to different stimuli: the trigeminal to physical stimuli such as cold air and high concentrations of carbon dioxide, the sensory receptors to specific aroma molecules. Beer contains elements from both of these groups and it is important to look for their balance to judge a beer's character. Low temperature and carbonation in beer will stimulate the trigeminal receptors while hop, fruit, and alcohol aromas among others will stimulate the sensory receptors.

Analysis of beer aromatics has identified major and minor groupings. Major beer aromas are those present at levels greater than twice their threshold level, the level at which most humans can detect them. These would include fruit aromas, floral elements, sulfur-based compounds, volatile hop aromatics, and fusel alcohols. Other aromas will be less distinct, but low levels of two or more aromas can act synergistically to create a combination aroma. This is particularly evident with fruit aroma produced from a number of esters or stale aroma produced from a range of oxidized compounds. See FRUITY.

Detecting aroma requires more than just breathing while you drink. To accentuate the aroma, it is important to coat the surface of the glass with beer—this requires a swirl before smelling. Coating the glass surface allows a thin film of beer to evaporate into the air, making the aromatic molecules available to your olfactory receptors. Breathe deeply and bring the air up into the top of your nose; a few sharp sniffs gives a better assessment than one long snort. In addition, note the aroma generated as you swallow. This arises retro-nasally from the back of the nose and can provide a more sensitive detection where less concentrated aromas become more evident in the aerosol generated by swallowing.

It is possible to simply appreciate the aroma from smelling without specific analysis—a great beer would be far less pleasant if we were forced to consider it analytically at every sip. Unconsciously, however, we do respond with pleasure or displeasure and judge the beer appropriately. More consciously we can use recognition skills to identify specific aromas and assess their suitability and balance in the context of a beer.

Knowing beer aromas requires both practice and a mental flavor directory. Specific aromas arise from specific organic chemicals and having exposure to these provides the reference for identification. For the professional brewer or taster, training is required so that an aroma is correctly associated with the corresponding chemical. It also requires standardization of language. This is easy with specific aromas such as diacetyl, which smells of butter or butterscotch, or the ester iso-amyl acetate, which smells rather like bananas. See DIACETYL and ISOAMYL ACETATE. However, less distinct smells may lead to personal impressions that may not correlate. Saying that a beer has the smell of an attic is too imprecise as attics have a wide range of aromas to different people.

Individually we respond differently to aromas, both from our genetic makeup and from experience. Taste training allows us to identify aromas and profile a beer, but our inherent abilities of aroma detection may vary widely. Typically we are more sensitive to some aromas than others, and one person may vary considerably in their specific sensitivities than another. This is one reason why we have different beer preferences. Interestingly, for example, it's recently been discovered that many people are genetically unable to smell a major hop aromatic component called linalool, which has a floral aroma. This has implications for the brewer, since some hop varieties (Saaz, for example) are heavy in linalool, which can make up the majority of that hop's aroma. It is therefore possible to add to a beer an aromatic element that many people cannot smell at all. It is also interesting to note that recent studies show that some aromatics can intensify the perception of a trigeminal flavor. Therefore, an intensified hop aroma can make a beer seem more bitter to the tongue and to the mind, even when actually bittering compounds are not intensified. Our senses are complex and not always easily separated or explained.

Aroma detection is also affected by hormones and emotion. We also respond differently to a beer if we are in company and according to our impression of the environment. We eat food faster in brightly lit conditions and many aromas are now recognized as enhancing the sales potential of shops. Studies are yet to identify the specific effects of beer aroma on consumption, but there is evidence that most people consider a fresh hop aroma to be desirable in a beer, even if they cannot identify the aroma. Undoubtedly a large range of aroma components come together and influence our unconscious individual selections.

Keith Thomas

The **aroma unit (AU)** was proposed by Nickerson and Van Engel to quantify the "hoppiness" of a given hop sample just as bitterness in beer is quantified using the international bitterness unit. They define the AU as the sum of the 22 hop aroma component profile (HAPC) constituents, measured in parts per million (μL/kg of hops or μL/L of wort or beer).

Because hop aromatic character is attributable to hop essential oil, it would not be unreasonable to think that the amount of oil in a hop sample would provide a means of estimating its hop aroma content. Gas chromatography has helped researchers to identify more than 250 essential oil components. Of these, 22 have been reported to affect hop aroma, and they have been divided into groups: humulene and caryophyllene oxidation products, floral-estery compounds, and citrus-piney compounds. It is these 22 that constitute the HACP (see table).

Twenty-Two Hop Aroma Component Profile Constituents

Oxidation products	*Floral-estery compounds*	*Citrus-piney compounds* *Caryolan-1-ol*	*Geraniol* D*-Cadinene*
Caryophyllene oxide	Geranyl acetate	l-Cadinene	
Humulene diepoxides (A, B, and C)	Geranyl isobutyrate	Citral, nerol	
Humulene epoxides (I, II, and III)	Linalool	Limonene limonene-10-ol	
Humuleneol	—		*a*-Muurolene
Humulol	—		*b*-Selenene

A hop's total oil content can indicate the overall quality of a hop sample, especially if there is a good idea of what the normal oil content for that specific hop should be. This method may be valuable to brewers when they are buying hops from afar and sight unseen. But because many factors affect essential oil production and preservation in hops, every growing season holds the potential for significant variation in both the total amount of oil and the composition of the oil, even for a single variety. Hops do essentially have "vintages," and some are notably better, or at least different, than others.

The total oil content figure, therefore, does not provide useful information about the actual composition of the hop oil and is not necessarily a good indicator for evaluating a hop sample for potential hoppiness and/or aroma quality. Additionally, no significant relationships were found between AUs and the key hop oil constituents myrcene, humulene, or alpha acid levels. However, some commercial breweries report that taste panels have found that hop aroma, hop taste, and dry hop aroma have correlated very well with AUs. The aroma unit therefore remains a controversial concept and individual brewers must determine whether it is a measurement that they find useful and are willing to trust.

Nickerson, G., and L. Van Engel. Hop aroma component profile and the aroma unit. *Journal of the American Society of Brewing Chemists* 50 (1992): 77.

Christopher Bird

aromatic malts, a type of specialty malt that contributes a high degree of pronounced malty flavors and aromas to beer and has a color of about 20° SRM/Lovibond. Aromatic malts are produced when germinated barley is kiln dried at higher temperatures, typically 220°F (104°C) or greater, and at higher residual moisture content for a longer period of time than most base malts. The high kiln temperatures and length of kilning at higher temperature and moisture create more pronounced malty flavors and aromas through intensified Maillard reactions. See MAILLARD REACTION. Both two-row and six-row barley can be used to produce aromatic malts, though the use of two-row barley is more common. Aromatic malts are related to the darker range of the Munich malt style, which are also more highly kiln-dried but at slightly lower temperatures and shorter times than those used to produce aromatic malts. See MUNICH MALT.

Aromatic malts are generally used for up to 10% of the grist in beers that benefit from intensely malty flavor and aromatics, such as bocks, brown ales, and Munich Dunkels. Depending upon the maltster, aromatic malts may have some diastatic power (enzymes) for the conversion of starch to sugar in the brewing process.

While the use of highly dried malts dates back centuries, modern aromatic malts owe their clean, malty flavors to the modern kiln that is capable of reaching, maintaining, and uniformly applying high temperatures and controlled drying rates for consistent flavor and color development.

David Kuske

art, beer in, has a rich heritage in the art world, including fine art depicting beer, brewing, and people enjoying it. Although many people associate art more closely with wine, a survey of art history shows that beer has been well represented throughout time in paintings and sculpture from cave paintings to modern museums.

Beautiful Color (oil on wood painting), c. 1900, by the German artist Hugo Kauffmann. PIKE MICROBREWERY MUSEUM, SEATTLE, WA

Ale Cans (watercolor on paper), 1964, by the American artist Jasper Johns (b. 1930). © BOLTIN PICTURE LIBRARY/THE BRIDGEMAN ART LIBRARY NATIONALITY

Beer's prominent position in everyday life on every continent and in every culture is depicted in still-lifes of bottles, glasses, and tankards, in landscapes showing barley, wheat, and hops being grown and harvested, and in myriad paintings of celebrations showing people enjoying their beer.

One famous example is the French artist Edouard Manet's "A Bar at the Folies-Bergère." It was painted in 1882 and depicts a female server behind a bar containing bottles of Bass ale with its iconic red triangle.

Another more modern example is American artist Jasper Johns' watercolor "Ale Cans," which is a pair of Ballantine ale cans that have been bronzed and mounted on a base, although the labels remain intact.

Early civilizations like the Sumerians and Egyptians have left behind sculptures of people brewing, along with paintings on clay that have also survived. As art evolved, it continued to depict the familiar, including 14th-century monks brewing and peasants drinking at harvest celebrations. Later, this became particularly true of Dutch and Flemish artists, who showed a flare for painting everyday scenes that included tankards of beer and tavern scenes.

Although many, if not most, artists at one time or another included beer in their work, a few famous painters who did so include Edgar Degas, Juan Gris, Pablo Picasso, Rembrandt, August Renoir, Rubens, and Vincent Van Gogh. Beer art has even been political at times, especially in the form of political cartoons. In 1751, British artist William Hogarth took things a step further, issuing his famous prints *Beer Street* and *Gin Lane*. Meant to be viewed side by side, *Beer Street* depicts healthy, happy people drinking beers while dancing together in the streets, whereas *Gin Lane* shows a dank street of poverty, neglect, and wanton abandon. Not surprisingly, Hogarth's purpose was to suggest that beer was far better for society than gin; British society agreed and soon the Gin Act closed small gin shops and curbed the drastic overconsumption that had swept the nation.

See also BEER STREET (BY WILLIAM HOGARTH).

Lemoine, Serge, and Marchand, Bernard. *Painters and beer*. Paris: Éditions d'art Somogy, 1999.

Jay R. Brooks

Arthur Guinness & Sons are the brewers of the world-famous Guinness Stout family of beers. Arthur Guinness began brewing in Dublin in 1759. Initially he produced other ales, but seeing the success of imported porter from England, he completely switched to producing this popular beer style by 1799. He even reversed the flow of the beer trade at the time, sending exports from Ireland to England. By 1815, Guinness' beer was so well known that wounded officers at the Battle of Waterloo were calling for it by name.

The second Arthur Guinness (1768–1855) issued an "extra stout porter" in the 1820s, which eventually became known as just Guinness Stout. He made Guinness the largest brewer in Ireland. His son Benjamin (1798–1868) turned Guinness' brewery at St James's Gate into the largest brewery in the world, with its stout sold around the globe. A franchise was granted to McMullen of New York in 1858; Speakman Brothers of Melbourne started distribution in Australia in 1869. The familiar buff label with its harp trademark first appeared in 1862 and in 1878 a new brewhouse was built under Edward Guinness (1847–1927).

By 1910 the ever-expanding plant was producing 2 million hogsheads (54 UK gal, 64.8 US casks) of stout a year. It was a vast enterprise, with enough fermentation capacity to hold 30,000 barrels at any given time. In Dublin, the brewery became a city within a city, employing an army of men complete with its own power station and internal railway system. One quarter of a million wooden barrels were stacked in vast mountains on the 64-acre site.

Sales were so strong that Guinness only felt the need to begin extensive advertising in 1929, with the first official poster carrying the famous slogan "Guinness is good for you." Soon its advertising gained iconic status, notably with artist John Gilroy's striking posters from the 1930s, such as a man carrying a girder under the slogan "Guinness for strength." In 1936 a second brewery was opened at Park Royal in London to keep up with demand in England. E&J Burke of New York City came to dominate Guinness exports into the United States and in 1934 built the Long Island Brewery in the New York City borough of Queens to brew their own beers after the repeal of Prohibition. When Burke ran into financial difficulties during World War II, Guinness bought the company and began brewing Guinness there in 1948, making it the first Guinness brewery outside Ireland and the UK. But the venture was not a success and closed in 1954.

After World War II, the family company began to look beyond the stout at the center of its business. Guinness re-entered the ale trade after taking over Cherry's of Co Wexford in 1952 and then in combination with English brewing giant Ind Coope through Irish Ale Breweries, notably with a beer called Phoenix. The firm's bicentenary was celebrated in 1959 with the planning of its own Harp lager, brewed in Dundalk. Smithwick's of Kilkenny was next, in 1965.

But the black stuff remained the flagship beer, and not just at home. Since 1962 Guinness has built breweries around the world in Nigeria, Malaysia, Cameroon, and Ghana. In addition, the stout is brewed under license from Canada to Africa and Australia, whereas exports continue to flow out of Dublin. When £180 million was invested in a new brewery in Dublin in the 1980s, 40% of production was for export. Today, Guinness is brewed in 48 countries and is sold in a further 100, with Nigeria the largest market after the UK, having overtaken Ireland in 2007. Around the world, people enjoy 10 million pints of Guinness every day. Guinness is coy about revealing specific market figures, but sales have been declining in traditional markets like Ireland and the UK while rising in Africa. The company is now targeting Asia.

As familiar as the beer may seem, there is not one Guinness Stout, but several. The stout varies in strength and character depending on the market. Most use unmalted roasted barley and are heavily hopped to give the beer a ruby–black color and dry, roasted, bitter flavor, notably still to be found in bottled Guinness Extra Stout or Original (4.2%). The kegged draught version (4.1%), first introduced in 1954, is much smoother and creamier owing to the nitrogen dispense system. The last wooden casks of cask-conditioned Guinness were filled in 1963 and the last pint of "plain porter" was poured in 1973. The bottled and draught stouts are so different that in 1988 a canned "draught" Guinness was launched using a "widget" to burst nitrogen out of the beer and recreate the smooth brew served over the bar, followed in 1999 by a bottled version. See WIDGET.

Stronger stouts are brewed for export, notably Foreign Extra Stout (widely called FES; 7.5%), which is today the oldest version of Guinness, having first been brewed in 1801. It accounts for 40% of all Guinness sold around the world. There is also a mellow Special Export (8%) for the Belgian market. These beers are partly blended using specially matured stout. St James's Gate also exports concentrated versions of mature stout to blend into beer brewed abroad to provide the characteristic flavor and color. Because FES is matured for long periods with a high hop rate, it develops an aged vinous flavor from high levels of lactic acid, giving a thirst-quenching characteristic popular in tropical climates. Stronger Guinness is especially popular in Africa and the Caribbean. Guinness does its best to use local materials, brewing their beer with sorghum in Benin and Nigeria.

Guinness took over United Distillers in 1986. A further merger with Grand Metropolitan in 1997 to form Diageo saw the combined company become the world's largest alcoholic drinks company and biggest whiskey producer with 30 distilleries.

In recent years the company has tried to broaden the Guinness brand but with limited success. Beers have included Guinness Light, Brite, Bitter, Red, Gold, and Breo, a wheat beer. Most were soon withdrawn. The latest, released in 2010, is Guinness Black Lager. Declining sales saw the Park Royal Brewery in London close in 2005. Sales have declined in Ireland and most European markets in recent years, but risen in Africa. The company now also looks to Asia for future growth.

Byrne, Al. *Guinness times, my days in the world's most famous brewery.* Dublin: Town House, 1999.
Hughes, David. *A bottle of Guinness please.* Wokingham, Berkshire: Phimboy, 2006.
Sibley, Brian. *The book of Guinness advertising.* London: Guinness Books, 1985.

Brian Glover

Asahi Breweries traces its beginnings to the establishment of the Osaka Beer Brewing Company in 1889. The Asahi Beer brand was launched in 1892 and the following year garnered a Grand Prix award at the Chicago World's Fair. The company opened its first beer hall in 1897 and in 1900 released Japan's first bottled beer. The company merged in 1906 with Japan Beer Brewery Ltd and Sapporo Beer Co to form Dai Nippon Breweries.

In 1949 Dai Nippon Brewers was divided into Asahi Breweries Ltd and Nippon Breweries Ltd as part of the government's Economic Decentralization Act. In 1958, Asahi released Japan's first canned beer under the Asahi label.

In 1982, Asahi signed an agreement with Lowenbrau of Germany and began licensed production and sale of the beer in 1983. In 1988, Asahi signed an agreement with Bass Exports of the UK and began the import and sale of Bass pale ale.

In 1987, the brewery released Asahi Super Dry, causing a sensation in the Japanese beer industry. Super Dry experienced explosive sales that eventually pushed Asahi ahead in the market. It is now positioned neck and neck with Kirin beer for sales in Japan.

Asahi further solidified its position in the Japanese market in 2009 with the import of the popular Hoegaarden Belgian white ale on draught and in bottles.

Asahi currently produces a wide range of beer products, mostly in mass-market lager styles. Many are of the popular low-malt variety called happoshu, which are taxed at a lower rate than regular beer. Asahi stout, released in 1935, is still brewed today as an 8% alcohol by volume (ABV) beer, broadly in the foreign extra stout style. Asahi Kuronama Black, a 5% ABV dark lager, appeared in 1995 and is sometimes found outside of Japan. The Asahi Beer Hall, designed by the French architect Philippe Starck in 1990, is one of Tokyo's most eye-catching modern buildings.

Bryan Harrell

Asahi tanks

See FERMENTATION VESSELS.

Asia

See CENTRAL ASIA and SOUTHEAST ASIA.

Asia Pacific Breweries Limited (APB) is a joint venture between Fraser & Neave Holdings Bhd, a drinks company headquartered in Kuala Lumpur, Malaysia, and the Dutch beer-maker Heineken. Heineken has maintained a strong presence throughout Asia Pacific following on the Netherlands' historical colonial links in the region. Listed on the Singapore stock exchange, APB was established in 1931 under the name Malaysian Breweries Limited (MLB). The company opened its first brewery in Singapore a year later and launched its iconic Tiger beer. Its catchy advertizing slogan was "Time for a Tiger," which become the title of author Anthony Burgess' first novel in his trilogy *The Long Day Wanes*. To reflect its growth in the region, MBL was renamed Asia Pacific Breweries Limited in 1990. Now APB operates a network of 36 breweries in 13 countries—Singapore, Cambodia, China, Indonesia, Laos, Malaysia, Mongolia, New Caledonia, New Zealand, Papua New Guinea, Sri Lanka, Thailand, and Vietnam—with sales in some 60 countries. In addition to Tiger, APB brews more than 40 beers for its regional markets, including Heineken, Anchor, Baron's strong brew, and ABC extra stout. It also produces Gold Crown in Cambodia, SP lager in Papua New Guinea, Tui in New Zealand, and Larue in Vietnam. In 2006, APB opened the Archipelago Brewing Company, a microbrewery with a pub outlet, producing classical European-style beers alongside innovative specialties.

Asia Pacific Brewers Limited. http://www.apb.com.sg/ (accessed February 16, 2011).

Tim Hampson

Aspergillus niger, also called "black mold," is a fungus common in breweries and malteries. The name Aspergillus niger is derived from the dark, nearly black spores of the fungus. A. niger grows in soil around the world and is a frequent food spoiler, while the metabolites of A. niger can also damage many materials—even glass and optical lenses can be corrupted by them. A. niger is useful in the food industry for the production of citric acid. The fungi metabolize acid under low pH conditions and when there is an absence of iron in the substrate. The optimum growing conditions are at a temperature between 95°F and 98.6°F (35°C–37°C), although A. niger is able to grow at temperatures between 42.8°F and 116.6°F (6°C–47°C) and a pH value between 1.5 and 9.8. This robust nature makes the mold difficult to eradicate in the brewery environment, and frequent cleaning may be necessary to keep it at bay.

In breweries A. niger is most commonly found in the fermentation and lagering areas, especially where condensation occurs on refrigerated equipment. It can also be found in bottling areas, where it can cause severe problems because of the high motility of the spores. Although the mold spores normally do not damage beer, spores detectable in packaged beer can be an indicator of poor brewery hygiene. Therefore, in some countries an elevated count of A. niger spores in beer leads to prohibition of sale.

See also BEER SPOILERS.

Gerrit Blüemelhuber

astringency is often listed as a "taste" but is as much a physical sensation of beer as it is a flavor. Although not particularly hard to define, it is often confused with bitterness and is easily misdiagnosed in tasting profiles. While some balanced astringency can be pleasant in certain beer styles, notable astringency is generally considered to be a flavor fault in beer.

A simple analogy of astringency without the bitterness is the dryness produced by a strongly brewed cup of tea. Tea releases similar phenolic compounds to beer and causes similar physical responses of a dry mouth, a slightly grainy feel and, after time, a thirstiness—in part to clean the palate.

Astringency results from phenolics, particularly polyphenols in beer. Phenols arise from the husks of malt and the stems of hops and polymerise to polyphenols during brewing and in beer maturation. These polyphenols include drying, mouth-puckering tannins. Polyphenols are attracted to protein molecules causing them to co-precipitate both in the boil and later as beer matures. However, some remains to provide astringency when beer is tasted.

In the mouth polyphenols are also attracted to proteins—particularly those of the mouth epithelium. A consequence of this is that they contract the mouth surface, providing an impression of dryness.

As with most flavors an optimal amount is acceptable, excess is not. Well-crafted beers will contain only enough astringency to balance bitterness and sweetness. Poorly crafted beers cause uncomfortable dryness and a desire to move to a different drink. Excess levels may arise from specific ingredients but most often from poorly managed sparging, after the mash, particularly with high pH liquor. See SPARGING. In these conditions oversparging drains phenols from the grain husks leading to an aggressively dry beer with a harsh aftertaste. Injudicious use of spices and herbs can also lead to astringency and medicinal sensations on the palate.

Keith Thomas

attenuation involves the removal of sugars and production of alcohol by yeast during fermentation such that the wort becomes less dense and viscous and is thus thinned-out or attenuated. The use of the hydrometer or saccharometer for measurement of attenuation during a fall in specific gravity of fermenting wort was introduced to brewing in late 18th-century England. See HYDROMETER. Determination of temperature, brought in a few years earlier, and gravity measurement were the first quantitative process control measures made available to the brewer.

The extent of attenuation achieved in fermentation of wort to beer is often given as the difference between the starting gravity of the unfermented wort and the gravity of the finished beer, expressed as a percentage of the starting gravity. Thus, if the wort has a starting gravity of 15°Plato and the finished beer a gravity of 3°Plato, then the percent attenuation would be $(15 - 3)/15 \times 100 = 80\%$.

Because alcohol produced during fermentation has a lower density then that of water, measurement of the beer gravity overestimates the extent of sugar removal from the wort and the calculation above yields what is termed the "apparent attenuation." To determine the "real attenuation," it is necessary to remove the alcohol by distillation before measuring the beer gravity and use this figure in the determination of percent attenuation of the wort. Real attenuation is about 80% of the measured apparent attenuation in normal circumstances.

Briggs, Dennis E., Boulton, Chris, A., Brookes, Peter, A., and Stevens, Roger. *Brewing science and practice.* Cambridge: Woodhead Publishing Limited, 2004.

Sumner, James. John Richardson, "Saccharometry and the pounds-per-barrel extract: the construction of a quantity." *The British Journal for the History of Science* 34 (2001): 255–73.

Ray Anderson

Augustiner Bräu is Munich's oldest brewery. Founded as an Augustinian monastery in 1294, the site has been a brewery at least since 1328. The original brewing license allowed the monks to make beer for their own consumption as well as to sell it

Postcard, c. 1920, depicting the Augustiner Bräu brewing complex. On-site brewing operations date back to at least 1328. PIKE MICROBREWERY MUSEUM, SEATTLE, WA

tax exempt for profit. The brewery remained in monastic hands until 1803, when Napoleon Bonaparte forced all church holdings in Bavaria to be passed into the hands of local secular authorities, and the Augustinian monastery became the property of the State of Bavaria. In March 1829, Anton and Therese Wagner purchased the dormant Augustinian brewing license and turned the brewery into a private commercial enterprise. Today, four of the six major Munich beer brands (Spaten, Löwenbräu, Paulaner, and Hacker-Pschorr) are wholly or partially owned by international brewing concerns, and the Hofbräuhaus is owned by the State of Bavaria. Only Augustiner is still independent. It is a closely held corporation, majority owned by the Edith-Haberland-Wagner Foundation, a charitable trust set up in 1996 by the last Wagner heir, a great-granddaughter of the founder. Augustiner is also unique in others ways: the brewery does not advertise at all and, unlike most other German breweries, it does not make light or low-alcohol beers or any sorts of beer mixes. In its brewery vaults, it still has a rare 19th-century floor-malting operation, which contributes pale malt to several of its eight classic Bavarian beers. Finally, much of its draught beer is still dispensed from traditional wooden casks, even at the annual Munich Oktoberfest. These unorthodox business practices have made Augustiner-Bräu a modern paragon of Munich's vibrant, traditional beer culture.

See also BAVARIA and MUNICH.

Personal communications from Werner Mayer, CEO, Augustiner-Bräu Wagner KG, Munich.

Horst Dornbusch

Australia had an association with beer starting through the English, even before they set first foot ashore. On August 26, 1768, Captain James Cook set off from England to sail to the Pacific Ocean on a mission for the Royal Society to observe and track the transit of Venus across the Sun. Cook had developed a strong interest in treating the disease scurvy because in those times its devastating effect on sailors was a major factor in limiting the length of safe sea voyages. Cook had been reasonably successful with his anti-scurvy trials using a number of foodstuffs and he had developed a strong, but incorrect belief in the value of beer as an anti-scorbutic. When Cook set sail in 1768 there were 4 tons of beer on board the *Endeavour*. Captain Cook's account of his discovery of the east coast of Australia during this voyage stirred much interest in England, but it was some years later and after the American colonies achieved independence before a decision was taken to send a fleet to establish a colony in Australia. In 1788, 18 years after Cook had sailed up the east coast of Australia, it was Captain Arthur Phillip who chose and named Sydney Cove, now known as Circular Quay and adjacent to the Sydney Opera House, as the site to establish the new colony.

Governor Phillip and his officers drank four glasses of porter to toast success to the colony. This was followed by a salute of musket fire from the marines and three cheers from all assembled, including the convicts. Beer had arrived in Australia.

Times were tough in the new colony and maintaining a supply of food and beer was just one of many difficulties. Nobody knew how to grow crops successfully in the unfamiliar and rather sandy soil with different seasonal influences and rainfall patterns. Food was often brought in from nearby Norfolk Island. Over the next few years the second and third fleets arrived and the colony hovered on the brink of starvation. The first and only government-owned brewery to be built in Australia started in 1804, in part to undermine an illegal rum trade. The government hoped that regular availability of cheap beer with moderate alcohol content would reduce the preference for rum and the drunkenness that had become so prevalent. Lack of good ingredients, lack of knowledge, staff problems, and an ongoing preference for rum all undermined the viability of this government enterprise and after a year the brewery closed.

The Australian affection for the "larrikin" (hooligan) and derision for the "wowser" (puritan, the larrikin's nemesis) probably have links to the decades of convict transportation that gave birth to the new nation. The imposition of harsh laws and exaggerated punishments, widespread corruption, and class distinction in a colony barely able to survive was likely shaping the psyche of a nation. Many of the convicts showed that they were more likeable, industrious, and respectable than those who had put them there or watched over them as convicts.

One who fits the description is the first fleet convict, James Squire. Squire is credited with the first successful cultivation of hops in the colony, in what is now understood to be quite a marginal location. He is also considered the first brewer of the colony given that he brewed with hops and barley. At one point Squire was caught stealing horehound, a bittering herb, from the government store, and he was given the lash. However, Squire was later awarded a cow from the government herd by the governor in recognition of his hop-growing achievements. Squire ultimately became a respected leader in the community, running a farm, a successful brewery, and Malting Shovel Tavern, a bakery and a butcher shop. He married several times, had more than one mistress, and ultimately had a large number of children. When this larrikin entrepreneur died in 1822, his funeral was the largest seen in the colony to that time.

The colony grew slowly but by 1828 there were 10 breweries in Sydney and regional breweries were being established farther afield. Poor technology, a lack of microbiological understanding, and a warm climate hampered any scale-up by breweries. Beer quality was generally poor and remained so for a number of years. In particular, beer quality was inconsistent and there were many changes in ownership and closures as the industry struggled with the challenges.

The latter part of the 19th century saw major change. The population grew. As convicts were freed and free settlers arrived, the country saw a new enthusiasm. Breweries started in every new location; any town of a reasonable size would have had several. Beers had been influenced by English styles, but local ingredients and environment meant the ales produced were not ideal in quality or style for the hard-working people looking for a big drink to slake a big thirst in a hot country. Experimentation led to the use of sugar as an adjunct to reduce the nitrogen level of the worts made from high-protein barleys. A lighter, drier style of colonial ale emerged and found favor, and the localization of beers better suited to the climate made headway.

In many cases publicans brewed their own beer, and during several gold rushes shanty towns appeared and the demand for beer or other alcoholic drinks quickly followed. Record-keeping was poor, and many operations were just entrepreneurial endeavors, akin to homebrewing, quickly assembled to take advantage of a commercial opportunity. There was little regulation and less interest. Many beers were adulterated with strange substances to overcome bad tastes or odors—brewers did not want to toss out bad beer in the face of high demand. Some beers were actually dangerous and brewing gained a generally poor reputation.

The government, however, supported the industry, which provided a source of revenue to the government, direct employment of the populace, and a substantial indirect employment as well. However, drunkenness remained widespread. The latter half of the 19th century in many ways was chaotic, but there were signs of change coming.

Against the background of growing demand and variable-quality local beer, some imported beers from Europe proved popular with those able to pay. The new lager style of beer from Germany found favor in Australia. The microbiological control benefits of this cold process were especially suited to Australia and a number of enterprising brewers saw an opportunity to move toward this technology. The earliest lager breweries in the 1880s did not survive long. However, two notable breweries both launched lager onto the market in 1889. Foster's Brewery in Melbourne and then Castlemaine Brewery in Brisbane both successfully brewed lager and helped popularize the new style. See FOSTER'S. By the beginning of the 20th century new scientific understandings were being applied by some progressive colonial brewers. Their understandings gave them new opportunities to better control the brewing process and improve quality. This was a pivotal time where the old colonial ways and bad beer were coming under pressure. Those who did not adapt to the newer ways and improved brewing techniques ensuring better quality would gradually disappear. The future of the industry in the 20th century would require breweries with better equipment and economies of scale and brewers with knowledge of new brewing science.

Australia's large brewers today have a heritage dating back to the 19th century. They were the breweries that survived the dramatic changes in technology, commercial challenges, and the upheaval of two world wars. The large size of the country relative to its population presented difficulties for a modern market. Up until the 1960s most major breweries were independent and based in a capital city or major town in each of the states.

Drinkers were very parochial about their local beer brands and they seldom crossed state borders. Economies of scale in brewing marketing and distribution saw the consolidation of breweries continue. Most of the large individual breweries are now part of a larger corporation. The Carlton and United Breweries are part of the Foster's Group. The United Breweries refers to a number of significant 19th-century breweries such as Foster's, Victoria, Abbots, and other Melbourne or Victorian breweries that were part of a consolidation. In 2009 Kirin of Japan acquired the Lion Nathan Breweries that came out of the consolidation of Lion Nathan of New Zealand, Bond Brewing, the South Australian Brewing Company, and J Boag & Son in Australia. See LION NATHAN and NEW ZEALAND. The Coopers Brewery in Adelaide is still privately owned. Individual brands such as VB reflect the Victoria Brewery heritage, although the brewery no longer exists. Another Foster's-owned brewery, Cascade in Hobart, is the oldest operating brewery in Australia dating back to 1832. Coopers dates back to 1862 but operates on a new site. Castlemaine Perkins has brewed on the same site since 1878, whereas Boag's of Tasmania has been brewing on the same site since 1882. Australians still have a reminder of the colonial brewing past in terms of both historic breweries still operating and the historic brand names available in the market.

The craft-brewing industry in Australia is well established and growing. Most people regard the Sail and Anchor Pub Brewery to be the first successful craft brewery in Australia. It started in 1984 in Western Australia and its success inspired many others to follow. Shortly after, Matilda Bay Brewery was also established in Fremantle by brewer Phil Sexton as a specialized craft brewery selling to the pub trade rather than a pub-located brewery. On the east coast in Picton near Sydney, Geoffrey Scharer started brewing at his pub in 1987 and in 1988 Chuck Hahn established the Hahn Brewery in Sydney, which now operates as the Malt Shovel Brewery. Australia's *Beer and Brewer* magazine totals the breweries in Australia at 130. More than half of Australia's craft brewers are found in two states. The state of Victoria has the most at 38, followed by Western Australia with 32. The major national brewers are involved in craft-style brewing, with Lion Nathan owning the Malt Shovel Brewery that produces James Squire and other brands of craft-style beers as well as the Knappstein Brewery. Carlton and United breweries produce the Matilda Bay brands. Major retailer Woolworths has developed a strategic partnership with Western Australia's Gage Roads craft brewery to supply private-label beer exclusively to the retail chains outlets. Contract brewing of craft beer brands is also established. In Sydney, Australian Independent Brewers built a greenfield brewery on the outskirts of Sydney specifically to brew beers under contract and a small number of other craft brewers also contract brew.

Australia today has a population of 20 million people. Per capita beer consumption peaked around 1979 at 135 l per year but has since declined to just less than 90 l. During this period a separate mid-strength category of around 3.5% alcohol by volume was born and is still growing, with the leading mid-strength brand XXXX Gold now the second largest selling beer nationally.

There are a number of beer competitions in Australia, some run in association with festivals and some run by pubs or local regional brewers associations. The oldest and most established is the Australian International Beer Awards. Run jointly by the University of Ballarat and the Royal Agricultural Society of Victoria, this competition is the second largest in the world in terms of number of entries.

Australia has a hop-growing industry in the southern states of Tasmania and Victoria. The most widely used bittering hop for traditional Australian lagers is the Pride of Ringwood or newer Super Pride. See PRIDE OF RINGWOOD (HOP). A range of other varieties is also grown for local and export markets including aroma varieties.

Barley is also grown in plentiful supply in several states. The total Australian barley crop is of the order of 7 to 8 million tons, with approximately 2 to 3 million being classified as malting barley. Approximately 1 million tons is malted to supply both domestic brewers and the export market. Malting barley is also exported.

Although the per capita consumption of beer has decreased from its high point, the decline has almost stabilized. There has never been a greater choice of beers on the Australian market, and beer is gaining proper recognition as a legitimate partner to food at the restaurant table. New craft brewers continue to start up and the traditional larger brewers are innovating and bringing new tastes to the market.

See also FOSTER'S and LION NATHAN.

Beer and Brewer Australia. http://www.beerandbrewer.com/ (accessed March 10, 2011).
Deutscher, Keith M. *The breweries of Australia—A history*. Melbourne, Australia: Thomas C. Lothian Pty Ltd, 1999.

Bill Taylor

Australian hops account for slightly less than 1% of world hop acreage and world hop production; and Australia accounts for about 1% of world beer production. At face value, this suggests that Australian domestic hop supply and demand are in balance. However, most beers made and consumed in Australia are international-style lagers of fairly low bitterness and only moderate aroma profiles, and they are often lightened with the addition of cane sugar and flavored with hop extracts and oils. See INTERNATIONAL PILSNER. Add to this the fact that roughly three-quarters of Australia's hop production is in high-alpha varieties and less than 1% in aroma varieties and it becomes clear that Australian hop growers regularly produce surplus bittering hops for export. Not surprisingly, the key market for Australian hop exports is the burgeoning beer market in Asia, especially in China—markets dominated by some of the world's lowest-hopped beers, with bitterness often barely above the taste threshold. To put this in perspective, China now produces almost one-quarter of the world's beer volume of about 1.8 billion hl (approx. 1.5 billion US bbl) annually, but only about 10% of the world's hops. In addition to serving their domestic market, it is toward this export market that Australian hop growers orient their production. The main Australian hop regions are the states of Tasmania and Victoria; the main varieties grown there are the high-alpha varieties Millennium and Super Pride. Together these two varieties amount to almost one-third of Australian hop production, followed by Pride of Ringwood and Topaz, which together account for roughly one-quarter. The other varieties of note are Cluster and Victoria. See CLUSTER (HOP) and PRIDE OF RINGWOOD (HOP). Pride of Ringwood is an Australian-bred high-alpha hop from the Carlton and United Breweries Ringwood Research Station in Melbourne, Victoria. It was released in 1953 and has been Australia's dominant hop variety since the 1960s. It has a pleasant aroma and an average alpha acid rating of about 9% to 10.5%. It is considered the archetype source of "Australian" beer flavor. This hop is also one of the progenitors of the Australian-bred Super Pride, bred by Hop Products Australia's Rostrevor Breeding Garden in Victoria and released in 1987. It is a seedless high-alpha variety with a mild aroma, but an alpha acid rating of approximately 13.5% to 15%, several percentage points higher than that of its mother, Pride of Ringwood. Victoria, also bred by Rostrevor, is a seedless high-alpha variety with about 11.5% to 14.8% alpha acids. Released in 1976, Victoria is widely used as a source of varietal CO_2 extract. Topaz, another Rostrevor product, was released in 1985. It is an agronomically robust variety that was selected almost exclusively for its high average alpha acid content of 15.5% to 18%. Millennium is a high-alpha triploid cultivar that was bred in the United States by the Barth-Haas group and released for commercial production in 2000. It has a profile similar to that of Nugget and CTZ. See CTZ (HOP) and NUGGET (HOP). In Australia it achieves alpha acid values of 13.5% to 15%. Finally, Australian-grown Cluster, which is an old American variety, tends to have a slightly lower alpha acid rating there than in its homeland, achieving 3.8% to 5% versus 4.5% to 5.5% in the American-grown Cluster.

Barth-Haas Group. *The Barth Report*. http://www.barthhaasgroup.com/images/pdfs/barthreport20092010_english.pdf/ (accessed January 7, 2011).
Hop products Australia. *Australian varieties*. http://www.hops.com.au/products/australian_varieties.html/ (accessed January 7, 2011).
Michael Jackson's Beer Hunter. *But what about Australian beer?* http://www.beerhunter.com/documents/19133-001371.html/ (accessed January 7, 2011).

Horst Dornbusch

Austria was once a world superpower. That was in the late Middle Ages, when, from its capital of Vienna, the Austrian dynasty, the House of Habsburg, ruled not only what we know as Austria but also virtually all of Europe—with the exception of France, Britain, Russia, and Scandinavia. As a result, German beer history and Austrian beer history are inextricably intertwined.

Politically, the stories of Austria and Germany began to diverge only in 1806, when, following a debacle against Napoleon at the Battle of Austerlitz, the last Holy Roman Emperor of the German Nation, the Habsburg Francis II (1768–1835) renounced the crown. This ended 844 years of the First German Reich. Importantly, it also meant the beginning of an Austrian empire, with the former Francis II of Germany metamorphosing into Emperor Francis I of Austria. The new empire immediately went on an expansion spree, mostly in an easterly direction, soon adding most of the Balkans, as well as Bohemia, Moravia, Slovakia, Hungary, and even parts of present-day Ukraine, Romania, Poland, and northern Italy to its realm. In 1867, the new entity became the Austro-Hungarian Empire, which lasted until the end of World War I, in 1918. Although Austria was quick to establish its own identity after its split from the old German empire, it took Germany another 65 years before it formed its own new empire, the Second Reich, in 1871—this time under the guidance of Chancellor Otto von Bismarck, with the Prussian House of Hohenzollern on the throne and Berlin as the new capital.

As much as Austria went its separate ways politically after the Napoleonic Wars, it was not able to break loose from German beer culture. In fact, one can argue that Austria continued to contribute as much to the German beer culture as it borrowed from it. In 1841, for instance, the Schwechat Brewery outside Vienna brought out the Vienna lager, which was—next to the Märzen brought out simultaneously by the Spaten Brewery of Munich—the first systematic attempt at brewing an amber lager. The Schwechat Brewery was owned by Anton Dreher, who also had major facilities in the Hungarian capital of Budapest and the Italian seaport city of Trieste at the Adriatic Sea. See DREHER, ANTON, MÄRZENBIER, SPATEN BREWERY, and VIENNA LAGER. The first pilsner beer style, too, brewed by Bavarian brewmaster Josef Groll at the Burgher Brewery of Pilsen, in Bohemia, in 1842, has a decidedly Austrian component, namely its German branding. Bohemia was then part of the Austrian Empire; thus, whatever happened in the land of the Czechs also had to have a name in the official Austrian language, which is German. This is why the beer that was destined to become the model for perhaps 9 of 10 beers brewed in the world today was—and still is—known worldwide as Pilsner Urquell and not by its native designation of Plzeňský Prazdroj. The Dreher operation was also one of the world's first breweries to install Carl von Linde's revolutionary invention of refrigeration for lagering tanks. See LINDE, CARL VON. Although the Spaten Brewery of Munich was the first to take delivery, in 1874, of von Linde's original "cold machine," Dreher's brewery in Trieste was the first to take delivery of von Linde's second-generation "improved ice and chilling machine," in 1877. That machine ran in Trieste for the next 31 years.

Today, there are some 70 packaging breweries in Austria as well as more than 100 small breweries and brewpubs. Most of them are concentrated in upper Austria. Austrians drink as much beer per capita as do their German neighbors—roughly 1,00 l per year. The Austrians and Germans are surpassed only by the leading Czechs. The most popular beer style in Austria is "Austrian Märzen," a filtered lager that holds about 60% market share. Austrian Märzen ought not to be confused with Bavarian Märzen, however. Whereas the latter tends to be malt accented, amber to copper in color, with an alcohol by volume (ABV) between 5.5% and 5.9%, the former is more like a Munich Helles with a golden–yellow color, with a balance of malt and hops, a gentle to moderate bitterness, and an ABV that tends to stay below 5%. Märzen is the most important beer style for just about every brewery in Austria, just as pils is the most important beer style for virtually every brewery in Germany. Austria's largest privately owned brewery, Stiegl of Salzburg, makes a Märzen called Stiegl Goldbräu, which is Austria's most popular bottled beer. Stiegl was founded in 1492 and now makes more than 1 million hl (852,168 US bbl) of beer per year. Next to the Märzen, Stiegl makes a large portfolio of beer styles including a popular pils, as well as such specialty brews as brown beer, Altbier, red ale, Christmas honey beer, and stout. Brauunion (BU), which is owned by the Heineken Group and holds more than 50% of the Austrian beer market, produces a popular Märzen too, under its Gösser brand. Another BU brand, Zipfer, considers its Urtyp, a pilsner style, its most important beer. Another BU brewery, Hofbräu Kaltenhausen near Salzburg, makes Edelweiss, which is Austria's leading weissbier.

The structure of the Austrian brew industry is very decentralized and half of it consists of small, regional brewers. In this respect, Austria resembles Germany. This structure sets both Austria and Germany apart from North America, where only a few brewing giants tend to dominate the overwhelming share of the market. In Canada, perhaps 9 of 10 beers consumed are made by either Molson or Labatt; in Mexico, they are made by Modelo or FEMSA; and in the United States, perhaps 8 of 10 beers are made by Anheuser-Busch, Miller, or Coors. The presence of many mid-size and small breweries makes for a great diversity of beers in Austria, probably more so than in Germany, because Austrian brewers are not restricted in their ingredients the way German brewers are by virtue of that country's Beer Purity Law. See REINHEITSGEBOT. Among Austria's smaller breweries, perhaps the best known internationally is Schloss Eggenberg, the producer of the legendary high-alcohol Samichlaus lager. See EGGENBERG BREWERY. Also well known is Trumer, a pils brewery in Salzburg, which has a subsidiary in Berkeley, California, which makes an identical pils. Among the specialty beers produced by Austria's small breweries, one notable oddity is a kübelbier (literally, "bucket beer") made by the Hofstettner Brewery in the Mühlviertel region of upper Austria. This beer is fermented in open troughs made of granite that was quarried nearby. A new creative wave of Austrian brewing is typified by the Viennese brewpub 1516, named after the year the German Beer Purity Law was promulgated. The name seems more a taunt than an oath of Austrian fealty to German brewing culture, especially because the brewpub produces everything from American-style India pale ales to beers made from quinoa.

Sepp Wejwar

Austro-Hungarian Empire. With the Compromise of 1867 the Austrian-based empire of the Hapsburgs struck a deal with the Hungarian Magyars, establishing a joint monarchy that encompassed the several peoples of a sprawling land between the unifying German and Italian states, Russia to the north and the Balkan kingdoms to the south. The new alliance would last until the conclusion of World War I and constituted a lumpy cohesion of numerous ethnicities embracing several religious ideologies and speaking over a dozen different languages. Even before the time of its dissolution in 1918 approximately 10% of its population of roughly fifty million would have emigrated to other lands, principally to North America. Along with simultaneous waves of emigration from Germany and Italy in the late 19th century, the population balance not just of Europe but also of the newly swelling lands across the seas was changed forever.

Where the history of brewing is concerned, it is this mass population shift, combined with the advances in yeast technology and industrialization taking place in Europe in the mid- to late 19th century, that brought about the worldwide lager revolution and redistributed Western and Central Europeans who would become the world's dominant brewers for the next 100 years. One cannot necessarily attribute the efforts of every German-speaking brewer in St. Louis, Milwaukee, Cincinnati, Buenos Aires, or Qingdao to the historical alterations of Franz-Josef's Austria-Hungary, but just as certain events set the stage for the upheavals of war, so did they prefigure the activity that enwrapped the industry of world brewing during this period.

Migrations can be triggered by many things, and the 19th century brought about myriad considerations for movement. Industrialization created incentive for a general migration to the cities from the country; social unrest such as the failed revolutions of 1848 fostered discontent and a popularly felt need for escape; realignments of political and ethnic consideration bred both possibility and aversion; and with word trickling back from participants in earlier waves of migration to the Americas and elsewhere, a great deal of movement was inevitable.

Many German-style breweries that remain a part of our landscape were established immediately before and during this time. The large breweries of St. Louis and Milwaukee—Anheuser-Busch, Miller, Pabst, Schlitz, Lemp, and others—were able to take advantage of arriving waves of German-speaking workers to people their expansions. Slightly later arrivals were able perhaps to work first for those earlier established, and then, when the time came, to strike out for themselves. Adolph Coors was one of these later arrivals. Less specifically and less easily traced, much of the brewing culture that today lives on in South America, Africa, Australia, and Asia was largely sparked by immigrants looking to create opportunities in their new homes, using brewing expertise or at least awareness brought from the Germanic cultures of their origin.

It may seem convenient to link the societal unrest of the mid-19th century with the unrest of discovery then rocking the brewing world. But simultaneity cannot help but establish at least the possibility of relation. The isolation of pure lager yeasts and the founding of new beer styles dependent on greater technical achievement by Anton Dreher in Vienna, Gabriel Sedlmeyer in Munich, Emil Hansen in Copenhagen, and brewers in the Czech city of Pilsen (as well as through the immunological experiments of Louis Pasteur, who did much of his work with brewing yeasts) captured the world's fascination with brewing innovation. When the Czechs, Bohemians, Moravians, Germans, and Austrians spread outward into the wider world, they were liable to carry with them their enthusiasms. They did not sweep all brewing culture before them, but they did establish a way of doing things wherever they went. At the same time emigrants from the winemaking regions of Italy and Hungary were busy themselves spreading world wine culture.

Not all migration by the various Central European peoples was so dramatic. Much was within Europe, as national and ethnic groups sought their enclaves or repatriated to traditional lands. Much was within established borders, and as such is even more difficult to trace. But movement of any kind spreads and strengthens culture, whatever other chaos it may create.

One irresistible footnote to the strangely entwined histories of the Habsburgs and beer is the fact that the Emperor Franz-Josef's younger brother Maximilian was emperor of Mexico for the 3 years until his execution by firing squad in 1867 (the same year as the Austro-Hungarian compromise). Some years later, in 1890, a consortium of German- and Spanish-speaking brewers would establish the Cuahtémoc Moctezuma Brewery in Monterrey. Arguably their most distinctive product, Dos Equis (amber), would prove to be one of the world's most enduring examples of a Vienna-style lager. See MEXICO.

See also AUSTRIA, MORAVIA, and VIENNA LAGER.

Encyclopedia Britannica, 1911 ed., s.v. Austro-Hungarian Empire.

Eurodocs. http://eudocs.lib.byu.edu/ (accessed April 15, 2011).

Habsburg Source Text Archive. http://www.h-net.org/~habsweb/sourcetexts/.

Twain, Mark. "Stirring Times in Austria." *Harper's New Monthly Magazine,* March, 1898, pp. 530–540.

Wien Viena. http://wien-vienna.com/ (accessed April 15, 2011).

Dick Cantwell

autolysis. Brewing yeasts are remarkably robust organisms armed with strong cell walls and protective abilities to survive in acid conditions and alcoholic solutions. However, they are not immortal and will eventually succumb to a variety of stresses during fermentation, conditioning, and prolonged storage. Autolysis is the final result of these stresses, where the vacuolar membranes inside the yeast disintegrate; releasing hydrolytic enzymes that cause the cells to burst open, releasing the contents of the cell into the beer. The word "autolysis" essentially means "self-destruction."

This autolysis has a number of consequences, the two most important of which are flavor changes and enzymatic digestion.

Flavor changes are readily noted as the general characteristic sometimes termed "yeast bite." This is generally a sharp, bitter taste with a meaty and sulphury edge caused by some of the amino acids and nucleotides present in yeast. If yeast is in high concentrations, these compounds can increase the pH of the beer and alter its acidity, also changing flavor. Finally, lipid release may increase the chance of rancidity. The meaty aroma of autolyzed yeast is so powerful that it is an important flavor additive in the food industry, adding "meat" flavor to everything from soups to "barbecue flavor" potato chips.

Enzymatic digestion is particularly related to proteases which leak from the cell and then digest the proteins in beer. A major consequence of this is a reduction in head retention, resulting in turn in a rapid collapse of foam and the impression of a flat beer. Hazes may be accelerated. In bottle-conditioned beers, enzymatic digestion of complex sugars into simpler sugars can actually re-start fermentation by still-living yeast cells in the bottle, causing over-carbonation and other problems.

Many causes may be cited for autolysis, not least simple old age. However, poor handling of yeast and beer will accelerate autolysis. Common examples are high temperatures, particularly above 25°C, or sudden changes in temperature at pitching or at chilling, and osmotic shock where yeast is pitched into high gravity worts. Some yeast strains may be inherently sensitive to conditions such as high alcohol, high carbonation, and high acidity and autolyse faster than others. In other conditions extensive re-pitching of yeast from batch to batch may create stress, as can the presence of contaminants including lactic acid bacteria and other yeast species.

While autolysis flavors are generally considered negative in beer, they are often considered positive in wine, especially vintage Champagne, where they comprise a large part the famed "sur lie" (on sediment) flavor and aroma. This aroma is often described as "toasty" or "hazelnuts" in the wine context, and the flavors are considered to be consistent with umami characteristics. Similarly, when bottle-conditioned beers are aged on yeast, similar flavors can eventually arise from autolysis, and in balance with other flavors and aromas, they can be very pleasant.

See also AGING OF BEER, FLAVOR, and UMAMI.

George Philliskirk

automation is the use of software and hardware to perform processes otherwise performed by humans. Brewing is, in most instances, a batch process, and for thousands of years every batch was made by hand. Since the early days of the Industrial Revolution, brewers have sought to reduce manual labor and focus brewers' attentions on beer quality. Today, even relatively small breweries and brewpubs (and the occasional zealous homebrewer) may employ automated processes. The primary benefit of automation is that it makes the most brewery operations "hands free" and thus renders the operator able to tend to other items. It may also, of course, allow for reduced manning. Other benefits include consistency, because automation excludes errors unique to humans, such as forgetfulness, lack of oversight, or variation between different operators. Simple automation can be as basic as a computer chip with one input (e.g., from a temperature probe and one output) to a cooling valve. The essence of more complex automation is a programmable logic controller (PLC) with many inputs and outputs, a personal computer (PC) with a human machine interface (HMI), communication cables that connect the PLC to the PC, and various hardware components installed throughout the brewing process. The operator selects and executes a program stored on the PC, which loads the program onto the PLC. Once loaded onto the PLC, the program runs independently of the PC. The program has within it a series of steps, written by a computer programmer at the behest of the brewing authority, and each step may also include a series of parameters, which must all be met before one step can advance to the next. In an automated brewhouse, many programs run simultaneously and often in synchronization with one another. The program is written to simulate what the brewer had previously performed manually. For example, for a valve to open, a signal is sent from the PLC as an output to a pneumatically actuated butterfly valve. If a proximity switch does not register that the valve has successfully opened in the prescribed amount of time, then a monitoring fault alarm is typically displayed on the HMI. The process will be suspended indefinitely awaiting investigation by an operator.

For automation to be possible, many types of sensors are required to successfully replicate what can be performed manually by a person. Such sensors include empty pipe detection for knowing when a pump has emptied a vessel, pressure sensors for monitoring lauter cake differential pressures and head pressure, pressure transducers for converting a pressure into a level of a vessel, and temperature sensors (there are many different types of sensors for each process). Very critical to automation is a proportional, integral, derivative controller (PID controller). A PID controller will typically be installed anywhere where precise control is required of the process and thus not in instances of simply on or off or open and closed. As the PLC sends a command to a hardware component, the PID controller looks at the result and then promptly makes small adjustments if it over- or undershoots the target. It does this constantly as long as the controller is engaged. Typical processes in a brewhouse that utilize PID controllers are the steam valves for making hot water and boiling wort, the lauter speed control and differential pressure control of lautering speed and efficiency, and the wort cooling valve, which controls the flow of ice water through a heat exchanger to cool hot wort into a fermenter. Depending on the budget for and applications within a brewhouse, there may be many other uses for PID controllers such as yeast pitching and turbidity meters or other instrumentation.

For many experienced brewers, a transition to automated systems is jarring, but necessary. Small breweries grow larger, outstripping their ability to perform every operation manually. When the imperative arrives to brew perhaps 8 to 10 batches of beer wort per day, automation becomes virtually the only way that a brewery can continue to grow. Once the automated programs are optimized and all functions are satisfactory, the desired operations will be executed the same way every time; programs do not rewrite themselves and brewers new to automation learn to trust and value its advantages. Well-designed systems are highly flexible and allow brewers to make changes when necessary and to program new recipes easily.

Jeremy Marshall

Ayinger Brewery (Privatbrauerei Franz Inselkammer) has been brewing classic Bavarian beers in the tiny village of Aying, south of Munich, Germany, since 1878. Although Ayinger's brewing techniques and selection of ingredients are strictly traditional, its brewing equipment is completely modern and fully automated. Ayinger is dedicated to operating its brewery with a minimum amount of environmental impact by engaging in ecologically sound and sustainable practices. See ENVIRONMENTAL ISSUES. It sources most of its brewing barley and wheat from surrounding farms, whose fields are fertilized in part with wholesome organic waste from the brewery itself. Hops for Ayinger beers come exclusively from the Hallertau region, only a short distance away, northeast of Munich. Ayinger's brewing water is pumped directly from a 176-m-deep (approximately 560-foot-deep) aquifer next to the brewery. This water source is rich in carbonates, which makes it particularly suited for brewing dark, malt-accented beers. The brewery produces about 150,000 hl of beer annually. Among its dozen authentic Bavarian beer styles, perhaps the best known is the Alt-Bayerisch dunkel, a mildly hopped, deep mahogany, full-bodied beer with a rich finish. Perhaps its most famous beer worldwide is the Celebrator doppelbock, a strong winter lager of 6.7% alcohol with dominant malty notes but surprisingly little residual sweetness in the finish. The golden jahrhundert-bier (centenary beer), first brewed on the occasion of the brewery's 100th anniversary, has about 5.5% alcohol, a spicy upfront bitterness, and a honey-like aroma. Other popular Ayinger beers include the Ur-weisse, a traditional Bavarian dark wheat ale; the Bräu-weisse, with the typical clove and banana fragrance of a Bavarian hefeweizen; and Liebhard's kellerbier, an unfiltered lager, left hazy with yeast. Ayinger is a family-owned brewery, and the local populace treats owner–proprietor Franz Inselkammer as if he were mayor or perhaps even a benevolent prince.

See also BAVARIA.

Ayinger Brewery. http://en.ayinger-bier.de/?pid=263/ (accessed December 24, 2009).

Personal communications from Franz Inselkammer (owner) and Gertrud Hein-Eickhoff (export manager).

Horst Dornbusch

B1202 (barley) is a springtime, two-row malting barley developed by the Barley Breeding Program of Anheuser-Busch in 1998 from a cross of RPB70-268/2B75-1223//Klages for the specific purpose of beer production. Adapted in Canada but mostly produced in Montana, Idaho, and Wyoming, it is compared to other popular varieties such as Klages because of its higher seed plump percentage and stronger stem. Since its creation, it has consistently been one of the top varieties of barley. It is protected under the Plant Variety Protection Act of 1970, which grants US breeders 25 years of control over new plant varieties.

Jai Kharbanda

Bacchus, the Roman god of wine, is otherwise known as Dionysius to the Greeks. He is more traditionally associated with wine, the vine and grapes as well as being the inducer of madness and ecstasy; this frenzy is known to the Romans as *bakkheia*. Though Bacchus is one of the 12 Olympians, it is generally understood that he was an outsider and not of classical Greek origin. He is one of Zeus's sons and considered by Silenus, the Greek God of Beer and Drinking, to be his mentor. Indeed, since Silenus is not part of the Roman pantheon of gods, Bacchus assumes some of the attributes of his drinking companion. Bacchus, along with King Gambrinus and other historical or mythological figures associated with drinking, has often been depicted in classical beer art and advertising.

See also BEER GODS.

Jai Kharbanda

Bačka (hop) was developed from a landrace in the Bačka region (pronounced Batchka) of Serbia. It was added to the U.S. Department of Agriculture hop cultivar collection at Oregon State University in 1956. Little is known about the genetic makeup of this hop. In its native environment, it is moderately high-yielding (about 2,017 kg/ha; 1,800 lb/acre), but performed poorly in field tests in Oregon, where it matured medium late and was susceptible to downy mildew. Its alpha acids generally range from 3% to 5%, but of late they have been disappointingly low, sometimes not even reaching 3%. The essential oil content is about 50% myrcene, 24% humulene, 12% caryophyllene, and traces of farnesene. Bačka is being marketed worldwide as a European-type aroma hop with "noble" characteristics.

Kisgeci, Jan, A. Mijavec, M. Acimovic, P. Spevak, and N. Vucic. *Hmeljarstvo*. Novi Sad, Yugoslavia: Poljoprivredni Facultet, University of Novi Sad, 1984. With English summary.

Wagner, T. *Gene pools of hop countries*, 68. Zalec, Yugoslavia: International Hop Production Bureau, Institute for Hop Research, 1978.

Alfred Haunold

bacteria are microscopic organisms, typically a few micrometers (thousandths of a millimeter) in size, with a simple, single-celled structure. They have diverse physiologies and are widely distributed in the environment from the upper atmosphere to the deep sea and from deserts to ice fields. Many are intimately associated with animals and plants. Genetic evolutionary analyses have revealed three major divisions (or domains) of all life on this planet, of which two are bacterial in nature: Archaea (thought to represent the first life forms) and Bacteria (the "true bacteria"). The third domain, Eukarya, comprises plants (including fungi and yeast) and animals. Beer is an inhospitable environment for bacteria because of its low pH (high acidity), lack of nutrients (the yeast has consumed the easily-assimilated sugars and amino acids), relatively high ethanol concentration, lack of oxygen, and presence of inhibitory hop compounds such as the iso-alpha acids. Consequently, of the many thousands of genera and species of bacteria, few can grow or even survive in beer. Notably, no human pathogenic bacterium has ever been associated with beers. Some bacteria generate their energy by respiration, using oxygen as we do, or perhaps nitrate, which is reduced to nitrite in the process. Alternatively, they can ferment sugars in the absence of oxygen to produce, for example, lactic acid or ethanol. Some bacteria are restricted to respiration or fermentation, whereas others are more versatile and can switch between physiologies. In breweries, bacteria are largely seen as spoilage organisms. Bacteria associated with beer and breweries include acetic acid bacteria, lactic acid bacteria, Obesumbacterium, Pediococcus, Pectinatus, and Zymomonas species. Some beer styles, however, involve bacteria in their normal production, including lambic beers, Berliner weisse, and modern sour beer styles produced by adventurous craft brewers.

See also ACETIC ACID BACTERIA, FAULTS IN BEER, LACTIC ACID, LAMBIC, PECTINATUS, PEDIOCOCCUS, OBESUMBACTERIUM PROTEUS, SOUR BEERS, and ZYMOMONAS.

Priest, Fergus G., and Iain Campbell. *Brewing microbiology*, 3rd ed. New York: Kluwer Academic/Plenum Publishers, 2003.

Fergus G. Priest

Ballantine IPA was an India pale ale legendary among aficionados, brewed from 1890 into the 1990s by the Ballantine Brewing Co. of Newark, New Jersey (later owned in turn by Falstaff Brewing and Pabst Brewing). Ballantine IPA spanned two eras of IPA glory, that of the late 19th century in Britain and the revivification of the style several decades later by American craft brewers. Maintaining traditional brewing methods such as dry-hopping and aging in oak for up to a year, as well as distilling extract from whole Bullion hops for use in conditioning, this IPA introduced many drinkers to ales of substantial character and inspired many brewers to emulation. See BULLION (HOP).

Cited by Michael Jackson as "wonderfully distinctive . . . an outstanding American ale unique in its fidelity to the East Coast tradition of Colonial ales," Ballantine IPA in its heyday boasted a bitterness of 60 IBU, a strong hop aroma and 7.5% ABV; it also held a lofty price point among domestic beers (around 5 US dollars for a six-pack in the late 1970s). Over the years, and as the sites of its brewing moved from Newark to Cranston, Rhode Island (1971) and then to Fort Wayne, Indiana (1979), aging times were reduced and hop bitterness diminished. The oak tanks in which it was aged gave way to lined Cyprus wood and then stainless steel, and eventually alcohol strength was cut to 6.7%.

Though long out of production, Ballantine IPA remains a touchstone for the brewers and beer drinkers who remember it. It introduced many Americans to the IPA style and inspired many brewers to attempt to recreate it.

See also INDIA PALE ALE.

Falstaff Brewing Company fansite. *History of Falstaff beer and the Falstaff Brewing Corp.* http://www.falstaffbrewing.com/ (accessed March 10, 2011).
Glaser, Greg. *The late great Ballantine.* Modern Brewery Age. March 27, 2000.
Jackson, Michael. *The new world guide to beer.* Philadelphia, PA: Running Press, 1988.
Tomlinson, Thom. *India pale ale.* Brewing Techniques, March/April and May/June 1994.

Dick Cantwell

Ballantine, Peter (1791–1883) was a Scottish immigrant to the United States who founded the Ballantine Brewing Company.

Ballantine was born in Dundee, Scotland. He immigrated to the United States in 1820, settling in Albany, New York. There he learned to brew and by 1830 had opened his own brewery. A decade later, he moved to Newark, New Jersey, in order to be closer to the lucrative New York City market and partnered with Erastus Patterson to lease General John R. Cumming's old High Street Brewery that had been built in 1805, which the pair operated as the Patterson & Ballantine Brewing Co.

Five years later, in 1845, Ballantine quit the partnership and built a new brewery along the Passaic River, which became a successful ale brewery. In 1857, Ballantine brought his three sons—Peter H., John, and Robert—into the business with him. Twenty years later, P. Ballantine & Sons was the fourth largest brewery in the nation and the only ale brewery among the top 20.

Around this same time, the brewery began using the iconic three-ring logo, with each ring symbolizing purity, body, and flavor. The rings are technically known as Borromean rings and were also an early symbol for the Christian trinity. Legend has it that Peter Ballantine came up with the design after seeing the rings that were left on a table by the condensation on beer glasses.

When Peter Ballantine passed away in 1883, his sons continued running the brewery until the last one, Robert, passed away in 1905. The brewery then passed to George Frelinghuysen, who was married to Sara Ballantine, his granddaughter.

Jay R. Brooks

Balling scale is a measurement (expressed as °Balling) of the concentration of dissolved solids (mainly sugars) in a brewery wort. The concentration of dissolved sugars in the wort is an indicator of the potential alcoholic strength of the beer, as it is those sugars that the yeast will ferment into alcohol. The solids concentration can be measured most simply by using a hydrometer, an instrument used for measuring the specific gravity of a liquid (see HYDROMETER). Alternatively, the solids concentration of wort can be measured using a refractometer, an instrument for measuring the refractive index of a liquid.

The measurement scale was devised by the German chemist Karl Balling, who in 1843 established a set of tables relating the weight percentage of sucrose solutions to the specific gravity of the solution at a temperature of 17.5°C (63.5°F). The Balling scale has been largely superseded by the Brix and Plato scales, although all three scales are essentially the same. See PLATO GRAVITY SCALE. The Balling and Brix scales are more commonly used in the wine industry to measure the sugar concentration in grape must and are rarely used in commercial brewing, whereas the Plato scale or specific gravity measurement is used to measure wort solids concentration. British brewers use the specific gravity figure multiplied by 1,000 to express wort "gravity"; a specific gravity of 1.048 becomes 1048 or 48 "degrees of gravity." As an approximation, by dividing the degrees of gravity by four a figure for °Plato, °Balling, or °Brix can be derived, that is, 48 degrees of gravity approximates to 12 °Plato, Brix, or Balling. This, in turn, represents a sugar solution of approximately 12% by weight.

George Philliskirk

ball roaster is one of the earliest industrial devices for roasting such foodstuffs as coffee, cacao, cereal, chicory, malt, and nuts. Roasted malts and grains, when used in the mash, can impart color and roasted flavors to beer. Roasted malt flavor and color are integral to a number of beer styles, especially porters and stouts. Depending on the technique employed, ball roasters can also be used to produce caramelized malts.

Developed in the mid-19th century, the ball roaster's roasting chamber was an enclosed, rotating, ball-shaped iron container. It replaced the traditional flat, open pan, which was the common roasting equipment in the more distant past. Roasting pans tended to yield uneven results, because some seeds or beans invariably ended up being only partially roasted, while others were lightly to severely scorched. Such over-roasted foods were too acrid to taste pleasant. The ball roaster, on the other hand, needed to be hand-cranked on an axle above its heat source of charcoal, coke, or coal. This caused the contents inside to tumble constantly. The roasting process, therefore, was slow, even, and controllable. Used with skill, the ball roaster could deliver roasted and caramelized malts of consistent quality with exactly the flavor and aroma characteristics desired. The basic technology of the ball roaster has changed little since those early days, except for the cranking power, the heat source, and the capacity. The hand crank is a thing of the past, and the preferred heat source nowadays is gas.

The first patented rapid gas roaster was produced in Germany in 1899. While early roasters had a capacity of perhaps 5 kilograms (approximately 12 pounds), they eventually grew to sizes that could roast hundreds of pounds of malt per batch. In the United States, these roasters were known as "K-balls," the "K" standing for "kugel," the German word for "ball" or "sphere." Some were used in the US malting industry well into the 1990s, but these days the ball roaster is largely used for roasting small-batch coffees. The roasting machines in modern malting plants today are computer-controlled, cylindrical drums that can produce up to 3.5 tons of roasted malt, caramel malt, or roasted barley per batch.

See also DRUM ROASTER and ROASTED MALTS.

Thomas Kraus-Weyermann

Baltic porter, an offshoot of the 18th-century porter style, channeled through the history of imperial stout. In the late 1700s, Henry Thrale's Anchor Brewery in London, famous for its dark porter beers, shipped a strong version into the Baltic countries. Much of the beer was bound for Russia, whose empress, Catherine the Great, had developed a liking for it. As a result of imperial connections, sometimes real and often imagined, the beer style became known as imperial stout or Russian imperial stout. In 1795, Matthew Concanen, the author of *The History and Antiquities of the Parish of St. Saviour, Southwark*, said of Thrale's beer at that time:

> The reputation and enjoyment of Porter is by no means confined to England. As proof of the truth of this assertion, this house exports annually very large quantities; so far extended are its commercial connections that Thrale's Entire is well known, as a delicious beverage, from the frozen regions of Russia to the burning sands of Bengal and Sumatra. The Empress of All Russia is indeed so partial to Porter that she has ordered repeatedly very large quantities for her own drinking and that of her court.

The name "entire" refers to the original name for porter. More than a dozen London breweries produced strong export porters at the time, and through agents they shipped beer through the Baltic ports into Sweden, Finland, Russia, Latvia, Lithuania, Livonia (now split between Latvia and Estonia), and Poland. In 1819 the Russian émigré Nikolai Sinebrychoff began producing his own version outside of Helsinki, Finland. Sweden started brewing strong porter in the late 1700s when William Knox came from England to Gothenburg and built a brewery there. By 1836, the Scottish émigré David Carnegie had set up nearby and began brewing Carnegie Porter. As lager brewing reached the Baltic countries in the mid-1800s, many of the breweries there saw no need to maintain their warm-fermenting ale yeasts. These beers quietly became cold-fermented lagers, losing some of the fruity character that the ale yeasts had imparted. Malts changed too, with early brown malts giving way to blends of pale and "black patent" malts.

Today, a number of breweries in the Baltic region and beyond produce strong porters. Few have retained their original strengths of over 10% alcohol by volume (ABV), but they typically show a strong, licorice-like roast character and the high bitterness that would have been common in a beer designed to travel. Most land between 6% and 8% ABV. Both the Sinebrychoff and the Carnegie breweries were eventually acquired by Carlsberg, and both still produce full-bodied, bottom-fermented porters at their respective breweries in Falkenberg, Sweden, and Kevala, Finland. These are dark brown rather than black, quite dry, and almost vinous, with notes of chocolate and raisins. In recent years, American craft brewers have picked up the style as well, seeking to make smooth, strong, roasty lagers with notable aging potential.

Concanen, M., and A. Morgan. *The history and antiquities of the Parish of St. Saviour, Southwark*. Kent, England: J Delahoy, 1795.

Jackson, Michael. *Michael Jackson's beer companion*, 2nd ed. Philadelphia: Running Press, 1997.

Thrale, David. "Russian Imperial Stout." http://www.thrale.com (accessed March 15, 2011).

Garrett Oliver

Baltika Breweries is the largest brewery in Russia, producing one of Europe's best-selling beers. The success of Baltika Breweries was no fluke; it was a well-planned and executed venture within the Leningrad Association of the Beer Brewing and Nonalcoholic Beverages Industry in Soviet-Era Russia. In 1978, construction began on what would become the Baltika brewing facility in St Petersburg, following a design prepared by the Gipropishcheprom-2 Institute. When the construction was completed in 1990, the new company was named Baltika Brewery, but this was not yet a brand name. It was not until 1992, when the brewery underwent reorganization, that the Baltika brand was created with the exclusive intention of producing the highest quality European beer using classical technology.

The Baltika brand was quickly hailed as the most popular beer on the market, beating out what had become a domestic Soviet market full of low-quality light beers. In 1997, Baltika purchased a controlling interest in the Donskoye Pivo factory in Rostov-on-Don and in October 2000 they added the Tula Brewery. In 2006, Baltika Brewery merged with three other Russian breweries, Vena, Pikra, and Yarpivo, and the new group took on the name Baltika Breweries, better reflecting what the entity had become. In 2008, The Carlsberg Group purchased about 89% of Baltika and, as of 2010, Baltika Breweries maintained a domestic market share of 40% and were responsible for 70% of all exported Russian beer. As of 2009, 270 million l (2,300,853 US bbl) of Baltika brand beer was sold abroad, and the company's Russian facilities are capable of producing 5.1 million hl (approx. 4.3 US bbl) per month. Baltika produces about 30 different beers, including Tuborg, Carlsberg, and Kronenbourg. Most beer sold on the export market is broadly in the international pilsner style, although there are several permutations available.

Baltika Brewery. *History of Baltika Brewery*. http://eng.baltika.ru/m/41/the_history_of_baltika_breweries.html (accessed March 15, 2011).

Baltika US. *History*. http://www.baltikabeer.com/ (accessed March 15, 2011).

Carlsberg Group. *Baltika Breweries*. http://www.carlsberggroup.com/Company/Markets/Pages/Russia.aspx (accessed March 15, 2011).

Jonathan Horowitz

Bamberg, Germany, a modest-size town in the Franconia region (northern Bavaria), appears on cultural maps for its well-preserved medieval architecture and on beer maps for brewing smoke-flavored beers with techniques preserved from the same period. With a population of 70,000, Bamberg supports eight breweries (a ninth, Maisel, closed in 2008); two are notable producers of "rauch" or smoked beer. See RAUCHBIER.

The Schlenkerla brand made by Heller Bräu Trum (annual production approximately 15,000 hl or 12,800 US barrels) illustrates the range of styles that may be offered in smoked form from a heavily smoked märzen (the style most often offered with smoked flavor) and Ur-Bock to more lightly tinged weissbier and helles. The smaller Spezial Brewery offers a more traditional range that keeps to the dark lagers with dunkel, märzen, and seasonal bock offerings. Although Schlenkerla has been widely exported, Spezial has rarely been seen outside its home region.

The smoke flavor in these beers comes from malt kilned directly over a wood fire. Green malt enters the kiln at the end of germination and is heated by the wood smoke for a full 24-h cycle. Beechwood fires the kilns, but only after being dried under cover for 1 to 2 years to reach optimal seasoning.

The one exception to this technique is Schlenkerla's slightly smoky helles, which contains no smoked malt but picks up the flavor from yeast previously used in the more heavily smoked beers. Both Schlenkerla and Spezial make their own smoked malt on micromalting equipment of approximately 4,000 kg (10,000 lb) per batch within their facilities. Across town, Weyermann Malting produces smoked malt in larger lots for other brewers both in Germany and abroad.

See also WEYERMANN® MALTING.

Larson, Geoff, and Ray Daniels. *Smoked beers*. Boulder, CO: Brewers Publications, 2001.

Ray Daniels

Bamforth, Charles W. "Charlie" (1952–) is the Anheuser-Busch Endowed Professor of Brewing Science and the Department Chair, Food Science & Technology, at the University of California at Davis, a position he has held since 1999. See BREWING SCHOOLS.

Bamforth was born in Great Britain and grew up in the Lancashire area of northwest England. He received a BS in Biochemistry 1973 from the University of Hull in Yorkshire. He also was awarded a PhD in 1977 and a doctoral degree in 1993, both from the University of Hull.

Before joining the faculty of UC Davis, Bamforth was the director of research at Brewing Research International (now known as Campden BRI Brewing Division) from 1991 and held a variety of positions with Bass Plc, including Quality Assurance

Manager, Research Manager, and Senior Projects Manager from 1983 to 1991. Prior to that, Bamforth conducted research into brewing science at the Brewing Research Foundation and the University of Sheffield.

His academic affiliations also include fellowships with the Institute of Brewing, the Institute of Biology, and the International Academy of Food Science and Technology. Bamforth is a member of the editorial board for the *Journal of the Institute of Brewing* and the editor-in-chief of the *Journal of the American Society of Brewing Chemists* and is on the editorial board of the *Technical Quarterly of the Master Brewers Association of the Americas.*

Bamforth is a prolific author on the subject of beer and brewing. He has published over 260 academic papers on the specifics of beer foam, beta-glucans, dimethyl sulfide, and flavor stability and more generally for trade publications, magazines, and newspapers. He has also written several books, including the textbooks *Scientific Principles of Malting and Brewing* and *Standards of Brewing,* along with general interest books such as *Beer: Tap into the Art and Science, Grape vs. Grain,* and his most recent, *Beer Is Proof God Loves Us.*

Jay R. Brooks

Barclay, Perkins & Co. was one of London's largest breweries for more than 150 years. It was formed in 1781 when chief clerk John Perkins and Robert Barclay, a member of the Barclay banking family, purchased Henry Thrale's Anchor brewery from Henry's widow, Hester. Famed lexicographer Dr Samuel Johnson, a friend of the Thrales, commented, "Sir, we are not here to sell a parcel of boilers and vats, but the potentiality of growing rich beyond the dreams of avarice."

The brewery fared well under its new owners. By 1809, with an annual output of more than 325,000 hl (260,000 barrels) it was not only the largest brewery in London, but the largest in the world.

As with other London brewers, its fortunes were based on porter, the first beer to be brewed on an industrial scale. In the early decades of the 19th century Barclay Perkins produced exclusively porter and stout. As porter's popularity began to wane after 1840, the brewery expanded its range to include mild and pale ales.

The company's legacy to brewing is their legendary Russian stout, first produced for the Russian royal court in the 18th century and brewed continuously for more than 200 years. The final brew was in 1993.

Barclay Perkins was one of the first breweries in London to brew lager. The initial experimental brews were conducted during World War I. In the 1920s a specialist lager brewhouse was constructed and a Danish brewer hired to run it.

Barclay Perkins merged with close neighbor Courage in 1955 but continued to brew until the early 1970s.

See also COURAGE BREWERY.

The London Metropolitan Archives. http://www.cityoflondon.gov.uk/Corporation/LGNL_Services/Leisure_and_culture/Records_and_archives/. This archive houses the Barclay Perkins brewing records (accessed March 10, 2011).

Pudney, John. *A draught of contentment: The story of the Courage group*. London: New English Library, 1971.

Ron Pattinson

Barke (barley) is a German-bred two-row spring brewing barley variety developed by Josef Breun GmbH & Co. KG of Herzogenaurach, Bavaria, and introduced in 1996. It quickly gained a reputation for exceptional agronomic, malting, and brewing performance, and rapidly became one of the most popular brewing barley varieties worldwide. Its genetic progenitors are two successful older barley varieties: Libelle, a highly leaf-rust-resistant variety introduced in 1974, and Alexis, introduced in 1986. See ALEXIS (BARLEY). Alexis, in turn, is a hybrid of Trumpf, introduced in 1973, and a wild barley variety selected for its disease resistance. This genetic heritage gives Barke comparatively short, strong stalks as well as a superior resistance to many common barley diseases, including leaf rust, leaf scald, net blotch, and mildew. Hectare yields for Barke, therefore, are fairly high in most growing environments. Outside of Germany, Barke has been planted throughout Scandinavia and in the UK, France, and South America.

In the malting plant and in the brewery, Barke is favored because of its relatively large overall kernel diameter, good kernel homogeneity, good germination potential, superior diastatic power, excellent extract yield, high apparent attenuation, moderate levels of soluble nitrogen, and low beta-glucan values. Its friability rating is average. See FRIABILITY. Also, worts from Barke-derived base malts tend to maintain their color well during the kettle boil, which is why Barke malts are particularly popular for making blond ales and lagers, especially Pilsners. In the finished beer, Barke can impart a rich malt aroma and contribute a creamy head with good foam stability.

Thomas Kraus-Weyermann

barley is the primary cereal used as the source of carbohydrates for brewing beer. It is designated Hordeum vulgare, a species of monocotyledonous grass, of the family Gramineae, which originated in the Fertile Crescent of the Middle East (formerly Mesopotamia and its surroundings, now Syria, Iraq, and neighboring lands). See SUMER. The wild barley H. vulgare spontaneum is still to be found there. Used as a cereal for bread-making several thousand years ago, it is speculative how ancient civilizations discovered how to convert the plant's starch into fermentable sugars that could then be fermented to a palatable beverage. It is likely that the first brewing was done with barley bread, and that the beer was distinctly different from today's beverage.

German chromolithograph of "Getreide Arten" (grain varieties), from the book *Bilder zum Anschauungs-Unterricht für die Jugend* ("Pictures for the visual instruction of the young"), first printed in 1835. The illustration shows unripe ears of barley. PIKE MICROBREWERY MUSEUM, SEATTLE, WA

The cereal spread north into and across Europe, becoming domesticated and improved for local agronomic conditions and weather as it went. It is a versatile crop, and is now grown in regions from the equator to the subarctic, from sea level to great altitudes, in areas of substantial rainfall and in deserts.

Modern breeding techniques have produced excellent varieties that deliver benefits to growers in all parts of the world, but the selection of a small number of strains in the middle of the 20th century to be the parents for modern elite lines has resulted in a relatively narrow gene pool for current maltsters and brewers. There are now many landraces of barley in different regions of Europe, fortunately held in academic collections, which retain different characteristics from the original genetic properties of ancient barleys. These landraces are not purebred varieties, but are instead a mixture of strains that results in a consequent breadth of the gene pool. It is certain that these older types of barley will provide wonderful resources for breeding improvements, and that they are needed in barley, as in other major crops, to meet the challenge of feeding the world during the 21st century.

Varieties were first selected from the best of the plants observed in the field by growers, an early example being Chevalier, which was selected in 1824 in England. See CHEVALIER (BARLEY). Old barley varieties could grow to a height of 1.8 m (in the works of English artist John Constable, who worked in the 1820s, the crop may be seen at the agricultural workers' shoulder height) but breeding for shorter, stiffer straw has reduced the height of modern varieties to 0.7 to 0.9 m. Taller varieties may still be grown for a dual purpose: as grain for animal feed, and as straw for thatching roofs.

Individual grains of barley vary tremendously in size. Units of measurement include thousand corn weight (TCW) which may vary from 5 to 80 g, although malting varieties fall into the middle of this range at 30 to 45 g. Thickness varies from 1.8 to

4.5 mm; as this is a critical measurement for brewers to be able to set their malt mill correctly, it is best to have a narrow range of thickness. Although the length of a barleycorn may vary from 6 to 12 mm, for several centuries the barleycorn was the base standard of length for England and Wales. The inch (25.4mm) was defined as three barleycorns, so an average corn was deemed to be 8.5 mm in length—but there was plenty of room for argument over such a natural standard!

Barley, although supplanted by wheat as a cereal of choice for bread-making in most of the world, still ranks as the fourth cereal by tonnage grown annually. It is important for animal feed, barley breads, and in other cookery as flour, flakes, or whole corn (often dehulled or pearled), and for malting to produce the primary ingredient for beer-brewing and whiskey production. Although other cereal grains may be made into malt, barley really is the pre-eminent cereal for this process. Its husk offers protection against the damage caused by handling the grain, particularly the regular turning to separate the grains during germination. The high moisture content of the grains at this stage renders all cereals more fragile. The husk then acts as the filtration medium in the brewhouse, allowing the brewer to achieve bright worts and have better control of fermentation conditions and subsequent flavors.

Cultivated barley is classified in various ways. Common distinctions are between winter and spring sown grain, and between two-row and six-row. In shorthand, these lead to general classifications of, for example, 2RW (two-row winter), or 6RS (six-row spring). There is a further distinction made between feed and malting varieties.

Two-Row or Six-Row?

Barley has six spikelets arranged in triplets that alternate along the main spike that forms the spine of the ear of barley (the rachis). In wild barley only the central spikelet of each three is fertile, while the other two are sterile. This condition is retained in those cultivars known as two-row barleys, which then appear to have two rows of corn, one along each side of the ear from top to bottom. A single mutation in the barley gene can result in fertile lateral spikelets, producing six-row barleys, with six rows of corns along the length of the ear. Six-row barleys have four of the corns from any set of six slightly thinner than the other two; the smaller corns are also twisted as they grow from their position on the rachis. This diversity of corn size makes six-row barley less attractive to brewers for two main reasons: the small corns have a lower starch content and higher protein content (and hence lower alcohol potential), and the mills in the brewhouse are most easily set to produce an optimum grist when the malt corns are even in size. However, it is the totality of the economics in the supply chain from the farm to the beer glass that influences exactly which type of barley is grown for the maltster and brewer to use—so the agronomic yield to the farmer may be greater from a six-row variety, and this can outweigh the loss of carbohydrate in the small corns. In Europe, the result is mostly two-row varieties with an occasional six-row variety emerging from the breeding program for a few years, which can compete successfully before becoming outclassed. However, six-row varieties are extensively and successfully grown and used in the United States and elsewhere in the world for malting and brewing.

Winter or Spring?

Certain varieties need to be sown in the autumn; these are known as "winter" varieties because they are in the ground over winter. However, severe continental winters will kill most barley varieties—barley is not hardy enough to survive extreme cold—so countries in a continental land mass will generally grow and malt spring varieties. Winter varieties have agronomic advantages—in particular, they lead to higher yields and earlier harvesting. This latter benefit brings with it earlier sale of the crop and payment for it, extended use of combining equipment, early availability of land for tillage for the following crop, and good utilization of equipment and manpower, plus the opportunity to sow the following crop—perhaps high-yielding winter wheats—at the optimum time. Having arable land covered over winter helps to prevent run-off of nitrogen into watercourses. On the downside, winter crops are exposed for longer to diseases and will need additional fungicide sprays (unless they are bred to be resistant). Spring barley gives the opportunity for excellent weed control. For example, the pernicious weed blackgrass is related to barley and cannot be selectively killed, so allowing it to germinate on fallow soil over winter gives the opportunity to use a general weed killer in the spring before sowing barley as the commercial crop. Spring varieties yield best when sown as early as possible, allowing for the end of severely cold weather and then dependent on the land being dry enough for the farmer to be able to take his machinery across it.

Malting or Feed?

The best malting varieties will take up water rapidly during steeping, commence germination rapidly and evenly, and deliver high enzyme activity and high extract potential in a friable grain of malt. See FRIABILITY. The endosperm of such a variety is likely to be mealy—that is, floury—and apparently rough to the eye when the grain is dissected. In contrast, "steely" grains are smooth and apparently hard—the endosperm structure is more tightly packed, and water less readily taken up. Steeliness tends to increase with nitrogen content: feed barley is grown for agronomic yield, whereas malting barley is grown to a protein specification. Nitrogen fertilizer applications are therefore carefully controlled on malting barley to avoid procuring a high-protein grain at harvest that is not acceptable to the maltster. Typically acceptable nitrogen levels are 1.6%–1.9% (10%–12% protein) on a dry matter basis in two-row varieties, although higher levels may be specified in North American varieties, particularly when the anticipated brewing use is with high levels of adjuncts that will both dilute wort nitrogen and require higher enzyme levels to convert the additional starch from these adjuncts in the mash vessel. Feed varieties receive fertilizer applications to maximize their yield; consequently grain nitrogen contents are high—of the order of 1.8%–2.4% (11%–15% protein). The balance between carbohydrate and protein in feed barley is then taken into account by feed compounders when designing or producing animal feed rations.

When a farmer is choosing whether to grow barley for the feed market or the malting market, he will expect to be able to charge a premium for the latter sector. This is because malting varieties tend to yield less than feed and less nitrogen can be applied during the growing season in order to meet maltsters' specification—reducing yield further still—so there is a direct effect of fewer tons/hectares that needs to be recognized by a higher price per ton. There is also a risk factor with growing malting barley: that of possible failure to meet specification. With feed barley, the specification is not onerous. Potential malting barley that lacks germinative capacity, has pre-germinated, or is not acceptable for other quality reasons will be downgraded to the feed market. The grower, consequently, needs a risk premium to account for the occasions when this happens to his crop.

Grain Structure

The key physical feature for the maltster is the distinction between the embryo and the endosperm. The embryo is the baby potential plant. The endosperm, which accounts for around 75% of the weight of the grain, is the food reserve that will see the growing embryo through its first few days until it can produce leaves. These will harness the sun's energy to fuel continued growth to maturity as a new barley plant. See ENDOSPERM.

The main component of the food source is carbohydrate, stored as starch in granules, but there are also storage and functional proteins, which will be needed for the growing corn to develop material for new cells to grow.

The other primary features are the husk (comprised of palea and lemma wrapped around opposite sides of the corn); the pericarp, also surrounding and protecting the whole corn; the testa, which is a barrier to inward diffusion of salts and outward diffusion of sugars, amino acids, and other solubles from inside the grain; and the aleurone layer, which receives a signal from the embryo to start growing and which releases enzymes into the endosperm to start to mobilize the food reserves to feed the embryonic plant. See ALEURONE LAYER.

The embryo has several important features: the scutellum, which releases the messenger molecule gibberellic acid to stimulate the aleurone layer; the coleorhiza and coleoptile, which will develop into root and shoot, respectively; and the micropyle, a small hole in the proximal (embryo) end of the grain. Water enters readily through the micropyle during steeping, and it is also the exit route for the chit and subsequent growing rootlets that develop in the first days of malting. Hydration of the embryo is the signal for the baby plant to start growing.

The malting process aims to harness the natural growth tendency of the barley grain, allow it to proceed to a certain point, and stop it there, producing a package of natural compounds that can be further processed by the brewer to produce a nutritious wort for fermentation by yeast. The key concept is that of the nutrient package: the barley plant needs energy from carbohydrate and the building blocks for proteins, plus the vitamins necessary for its biochemical processes, to proceed, and so does the yeast. It is the maltster's and brewer's role to adapt the life process and materials of the barley to feed the yeast.

Accordingly, as the embryo is hydrated and sends out the gibberellins to call for nutrition from the endosperm, the maltster is looking for enzyme development to start to break down the cell walls of the starch granules in the endosperm and to deliver raised levels of amylase activity into the grain, but not to allow these amylases to break down too much starch before delivery of the malted grain to the brewery. See MALTING. The main enzyme groups are the glucanases and proteases, which break down the cell walls, and the amylases, which break down the starch cell contents. See AMYLASES. β-amylase is naturally present in barley; α-amylase is developed almost entirely during malting. Other hydrolytic enzymes that break down complex carbohydrates also develop during malting. The breakdown of the cell walls is vital and must be nearly complete at the end of malting, as the material in the cell walls is viscous in solution and can slow run-off in the brewhouse and cause beer filtration difficulties and possibly hazy beer. This breakdown must be achieved with little digestion of the starch, as it is the starch that is the valuable component of the grain—it is the material from which alcohol will be derived after further breakdown to sugars during mashing and fermentation of these sugars by yeast. The starch in the endosperm is packed into granules which themselves are embedded in a protein matrix inside the cells. The starch granules are in two distinct size ranges, from 1.7 to 2.5 μm and from 22 to 48 μm. The smaller granules are digested during the normal malting process, while the large granules remain whole, except in cases where germination proceeds too far and the malt becomes overmodified. See MODIFICATION.

The physical characteristics of the two sources of starch are different with respect to their gelatinization temperature. Gelatinization is a phase change (similar to that in water when changing from ice into liquid) in which starch moves from a semi-crystalline phase to an amorphous phase. The large starch granules gelatinise at 140°F–149°F (60°C–65°C) and are readily hydrolyzed in their amorphous phase by amylases during mashing in the brewhouse. Starch in the small granules has gelatinization temperatures in the range 167°F–176°F (75°C–80°C), and so is not broken down by mash amylolytic activity and will form a paste that will slow run-off from the mash and cause haze in the beer that may be problematic at the later filtration stage.

Barley for Malting

Sound storage after harvest of any cereal crop is essential to protect the quality and against commercial losses. Threats to malting barley include mold, insects, mites, rodents, and birds. The vertebrates can be excluded from grain stores physically, and minor infestations can be cleared up quickly by suitable bait. Protection from the remaining hazards is best achieved through control of moisture and temperature. In warmer, drier climates, grain will come off the combine harvester at a suitable moisture content (around 12%), in more temperate climates it will be 14%–15%, and in wet climates it may rise to over 20% in rainy harvest seasons. The usual level of moisture regarded as safe for storage is 12%, although some maltsters are experimenting with 14%. At or below 12%, insects and mites will not proliferate. At 14%, the temperature becomes important, and ideally should be less than 50°F (10°C) within a few weeks of drying. In warmer countries, such a temperature is not possible without refrigeration, which is usually too expensive, so some losses to insect infestation may be expected. There are chemical insecticide protections, but fewer with tightening legislation, and again, these can be expensive. As a curative, fumigation with phosphine is feasible in closed silos, but much more difficult in flat stores. In either case, expert supervision is required.

Failure to protect against these threats to the corn can lead to loss of dry matter through the grain being eaten by the infesting species, to food safety issues with direct contamination, and to more serious food safety concerns with storage mycotoxins from mould growth. Local moist conditions in grain can undo otherwise good work looking after the bulk—the warmth of mold growth and insect infestation in a moist area can lead to condensation elsewhere in the bulk, with further infection and infestation possible as a result.

Sound storage will give the shelf life of over 12 months that is needed for one season's barley to be processed in the maltings until the following crop becomes available.

Dormancy

In the natural cycle, cereal seeds have a disadvantage if they germinate immediately upon becoming ripe, as they will be attempting to grow into plants at the wrong time of year, with adverse weather conditions likely. Perhaps the clearest example is with spring varieties, which should not germinate until sown in the spring. The natural protection against early germination is dormancy, and this can be bred into or out of varieties. Too much dormancy gives maltsters problems with starting to malt the new season's barley at a reasonable time after harvest, say, 6 to 10 weeks. Too little dormancy and the barley may start to shoot while still on the ear of a plant in the field during a wet harvest period. In a bulk of grain that is likely to exhibit unacceptable dormancy, storage may take place at 104°F (40°C) for a period of weeks to break this dormancy. This temperature should not be extended into several months, as there would then be an increased risk of insect infestation. See DORMANCY (OF BARLEY).

Specification of Barley for Malting

A maltster will want to put together a bulk of barley that is consistent throughout and meets certain quality standards. When barley is presented for delivery against a contract, the intake laboratory will check for variety, germinative capacity (GC), nitrogen content, moisture, and corn size profile, and will ensure that it is free from other cereal and weed seeds and free from mold and insects. Several of these parameters are commercial. For instance, failure to meet exactly the moisture specification may lead to an adjustment in the price to be paid for the consignment. The ability to germinate, however, is key to being able to process the grain, and it is an absolute hurdle for quality for acceptance to a maltings or intermediate store. The threshold is set by reference to the standard achievable by the supply chain from the farm through storage and is commonly a minimum of 98%. Any corns that do not germinate will pass through to the brewing process with unmodified gums, proteins, and carbohydrates that will lead to problems in the brewery. Small amounts can be accommodated by the surplus natural enzymes from the malt, but larger amounts will cause additional processing time and cost.

GC testing at intake can prevent dead corns from being delivered to the maltings. The test also shows those corns that may have started to germinate in the ear, termed "pre-germination," and may continue germination on subsequent steeping, or may not, which can cause subsequent process problems and cost.

Once in store, to determine readiness for transferring barley into process, a test for germinative energy (GE) is carried out, which involves incubating 100 corns on a filter paper in a Petri dish, moistened with 4 ml of water, for 3 or, less commonly, 4 days, removing chitted grains each day. (Barley kernels that have been properly steeped and now show evidence of root growth are referred to as "chatted.") GE scores of at least 98% are desirable, showing that grain has been stored with no loss of viability and that dormancy has been broken. An indication of the vigor of the grain sample is given by the daily count of chitted corns: the earlier that corns chit, in general, the better. In a parallel test, by wetting the filter paper with 8 ml of water, a measure of the water sensitivity (WS) of the grain can be made. The additional water maintains a film of water over the surface of the grains (limiting the amount of oxygen available to the embryo to start germinating) and gives an indication to the maltster of the appropriate steeping regime—lengths of wet periods and dry periods—for that barley.

Barley for Flavor

Brewers have long been interested in whether the variety of barley can influence the flavor of the resulting malt and the flavor of the beer made from the malt. In the early 20th century Hugh Lancaster, in his book *Practical Floor Malting*, praised the "finest qualities of sound clear-grown Chevaliers" for the delicate flavor they could bring to pale ales. Most brewers have been content to brew with malts that presented no processing difficulties, and to achieve malt flavor variations in their beers by different malt specifications. The variety Pipkin, popular in the UK in the late 1980s and 1990s, was known to produce a high level of the precursor for formation of dimethyl sulphide (DMS) during the brewing process. See DIMETHYL SULFIDE (DMS). DMS is a characteristic aroma and flavor in many lager beers. Those brewers of lager who did not want DMS character, and some brewers of ales, either decided completely against the use of malted Pipkin, or ensured that their maltsters utilized process conditions (higher temperatures during kilning) to ensure that the DMS precursor was reduced.

Most recently, in the first years of this century, there has been investigation into the flavor of Maris Otter and its effect on beer. See MARIS OTTER (BARLEY). To avoid the effects of the brewing process and hopping, it has been demonstrated, by tasting of biscuits baked with flour from malted Maris Otter, that the variety does have a distinct taste. Such variation in flavor is small compared to that induced during the malting and brewing processes, but nevertheless, this flavor difference has added to its appeal for brewers who look for differentiation and heritage in their malt. Consistent beers can be produced by brewers with malt from different barley varieties, but this is an area of brewing that will witness more work to try to understand and develop the different flavors of barley varieties as a further point of differentiation between beers.

Craft brewers, in their search for deeper malt flavors in their beers, are showing a particular interest in "heirloom" barley varieties. As the topic of barley varietal flavor comes to the forefront, there is hope that barley breeders may yet develop efficient but flavorful crosses from older varieties.

Environment

The carbon footprint of barley is similar to other cereals, the principal components being the manufacture of nitrogen fertilizers and the emission of nitrous oxide from the soil during the growing season. These two factors alone account for 80% of the greenhouse gas emissions of intensively farmed barley. The remaining emissions are associated with the use of diesel fuel to power tractors and combine harvesters, those associated with manufacture of other inputs, any post-harvest drying, and those coming from storage and haulage of the crop. The most promising area for reductions would seem to lie in a switch to organic materials—compost, anaerobic digestate, and sewage sludge—to replace the industrially produced fertilizer, and in establishing a better understanding and subsequent control of the mechanisms of production of nitrous oxide in the soil.

Being a relatively low-nitrogen crop, the input of fertilizers is a little lower than for other cereals on an acreage basis, but not by weight of cereals produced. Similarly, nitrate run-off again is slightly lower for malting barley than from other cereals as a result of less nitrogen input per area.

The crop is fairly drought tolerant, which will prove an advantage, as water is now forecast to be in deficit in many parts of the world in the coming decades.

There can be no question that barley is a crop with a strong past and a bright future.

Bamforth, Charles W. *Beer: Tap into the art and science of brewing*. New York: Oxford University Press, 2003.
Briggs, D. E. *Malts and malting*. New York: Blackie Academic & Professional, 1998.
Briggs, D. E , J. S. Hough, R. Stevens, and T. W. Young. *Malting and brewing science*. Norwell, MA: Kluwer, 1999.
Hornsey, Ian. *Brewing*. Cambridge, England: Royal Society of Chemistry, 1999.
Lancaster, Hugh. *Practical floor malting*. The Brewing Trade Review, 1908.
Palmer, G. H., ed. *Cereal science and technology*. Aberdeen, Scotland: Aberdeen University Press, 1989.

Colin J. West

barley diseases. Barley is the fourth largest food crop in the world and disease has a major impact on its contribution to human food supplies. The major diseases affecting barley are fungal, particularly mildew, head blight, smut, Rhyncosporium, and Ramularia. Barley Yellow Dwarf Virus and Barley Stipe Rust are the most prevalent virus infections. In addition, a number of insect pests attack barley, particularly aphids, but also worms and beetles.

Many barley diseases are common to wheat, and this makes combating them critical to the security of food resources. Barley is more adaptable than wheat and other cereals, being able to grow at higher altitudes and in drier and more saline environments. However, this wider ecological range means that a broader range of diseases may develop.

Barley cultivation has always been a constant battle between managing growth and fighting disease. The development of high barley yields and of specific malting varieties has continued for decades and has been a perpetual leapfrogging of increased resistance to disease being overcome by the evolution of new virulence factors increasing disease prevalence.

The incidence of most plant diseases varies according to climate, geography, and agricultural practice and differs considerably according to the resistance of varieties to specific diseases. Barley is no exception, and high levels of disease are typically associated with moist conditions and often with cool temperatures which typically favor fungal growth. Viruses are often spread by aphids, whose populations can rise rapidly when conditions are favorable, resulting in a subsequent surge in crop disease. See APHIDS.

Barley disease also varies with the age of the plant with some diseases affecting young shoots, others prevalent on leaf and shoot, and others only evident on maturing seed grains.

The different tissue locations of barley diseases are listed below:

Leaf and stem	Net blotch	Pyrenophora teres
	Spot blotch	Bipolaris sorokiniana
	Speckled leaf blotch	Septoria passerinii
	Scald	Rhynchosporium secalis
	Stem rust	Puccinia graminis
	Leaf rust	Puccinia hordei
	Powdery mildew	Blumeria graminis f. sp. Hordei
	Barley Yellow Dwarf Virus	
Head and seed	Head blight	Fusarium species
	Loose smut	Ustilago nuda
	Covered smut	Ustilago hordei
	Ergot	Claviceps purpurea
Root and crown	Common root rot	Cochliobolus sativus
	Take all	Gaeumannomyces tritici graminis var
	Pythium root rot	Pythium species

Barley disease symptoms on leaves include a yellowing often with the development of darker necrotic spots or patches, although mildew grows externally as white powdery masses of fungus. Infection of stems causes blackening and weakening leading to collapse, while infection of roots results in local rotting, poor plant support, and stunted growth. On seed heads infection can discolor and shrivel grains as the fungi digest the internal structure. Ergot is distinctive as the barley ears show the fungus protruding between the corns.

Some diseases are systemic but require environmental triggers to cause plant damage, while others reside in the seed and develop in the next generation of plants. Ramularia, for example, develops progressively as the plant grows, but symptoms may not appear until the level of light is sufficient to trigger synthesis of phytotoxins.

While most diseases reduce plant growth and the yield of corns, some also provide longer lasting impact and affect grain quality. Fusarium infection is particularly relevant for this as many species produce poisonous mycotoxins during growth. These toxins are part of the fungus attack on the plant but are also harmful to animal health, producing neurological effects at high concentrations and carcinogenic effects at low levels. Mycotoxins may survive malting and pass into beer, and brewers require malt to be checked for purity before use.

Other effects of barley infected with fungi are the production of hydrophobins. These act to reduce the surface tension to assist in spore release by the fungus but can induce early flocculation of yeast during fermentation. Similar factors may be involved in inducing gushing in beer by enhancing gas release on dispense.

Management of barley diseases depends on pesticides, particularly fungicides, but also on good agricultural practices. Many diseases may survive over winter on crop residues left in fields and their removal is therefore important. Pesticides are often used in preventing and limiting barley disease but require timely application and are often overcome by resistant mutations developing in the disease organism.

Breeding barley varieties for resistance to specific diseases may only provide short-term relief and more integrated approaches are now being adapted, including a mixture of partial resistance, crop rotation, and hygienic management. In addition, early warning of disease outbreaks is required to allow local action and to anticipate variety choice and practices for future years. In many cases the gross appearance of barley disease may be too late to treat. The use of molecular testing to identify the disease in the barley tissues before disease appears is desirable alongside modeling to predict the course of disease and direct treatment. Future approaches to barley disease management in the light of global climate change and increased sensitivity to the environment will require more understanding of specific diseases and inventive action.

Keith Thomas

barley harvest is the cutting, threshing, separating, and cleaning of individual barley grains from the mature barley plant. Depending upon variety and climate conditions, barley grows from 12 to 48 inches tall. The tightly packed spikes or ears of seed kernels can take from 40 to 55 days to fully ripen after flowering and droop down when ready to harvest. Growers closely monitor and test mature plants for grain size, protein content, and moisture. For malting barley, the moisture content at harvest tends to be between 12% and 17%, whereby 12.5% is considered ideal. In the silo, the moisture level must be kept below 14%. The optimum protein level for brewing barley is between 9.5% and 11.5%.

Harvesting by "direct head cutting" involves cutting the ripened ears off close to the stem, high on the plant, to minimize debris. The crop is then threshed to separate the individual grains from other plant material and cleaned of foreign matter. Swathing, by contrast, involves cutting the plant low, leaving a short bed of stubble that supports the long interlaced stems and ears off the ground, where the crop is allowed to dry in the field before being gathered and threshed. Excessive handling, however, can break, crack, or abrade the barley kernel, rendering it useless to the malt house and brewer. Dry grain, properly stored, will last for months or even years.

Barley is still harvested by hand in very small fields and plots. Mechanized harvesting equipment—called combines—is often used that combines cutting, threshing, and cleaning into one process. This produces barley grains ready for immediate use or storage. In the United States, barley yields are often listed in bushels. This is a volume, not a weight measure, whereby 1 US bushel equals 35.24 l. This way of measuring yields make the result independent of the grain's moisture content. In the metric world, on the other hand, yields are often given in kilograms or metric tons (1,000 kg) per hectare, whereby 1 hectare equals 2.47 acre. Because this is a weight measurement, two identical "yields" can be quite different depending on the barley's moisture content. Consequently, there is no simple mathematical conversion formula between bushel yields per acre and metric-ton yields per hectare. For obvious reasons of climate, soil conditions, prevalence of pests and diseases, barley varietal differences, and agricultural methods, yields can range very widely across the world. In terms of bushels, yields of 100 to 150 bushels per acre of brewing barley are considered desirable. In much of Europe, farmers might consider yields of roughly 6 to 9 metric tons per hectare (6.6 to 9.9 US tons per 2.47 acres) satisfactory for winter barley or roughly 5 to 8 metric tons per hectare (5.5 to 8.8 US tons per 2.47 acres) for spring brewing barley.

"Barley Production in Western Australia." Government of Western Australia Dept of Agriculture and Food, 2007. http://www.agric.wa.gov.au/PC_92005.html?=1001 (accessed April 11, 2011).

"Crop Profile for Barley in Colorado." Ft Collins, CO: Colorado State University, 2002. http://www.ipmcenters.org/cropprofiles/docs/cobarley.pdf (accessed April 11, 2011).

Mike Laur

barley malt extract

See LIQUID MALT EXTRACT (LME).

barley malt syrup

See LIQUID MALT EXTRACT (LME).

barley wine is the strongest of beers and while not always literally approaching the alcohol content

American barley wines. CHARLES FINKEL

of wine, usually surmounts the strength of ales referred to as "strong" and "old," to which they are related. See OLD ALES. The first beers we now think of as barley wine sprang from the British farmhouse tradition, often as beers brewed from the first runnings (strong worts) of multiple-brew single mashes, which were infused a number of times to yield worts of diminishing strength. This system is known as partigyle and is still employed in some British breweries. See PARTI-GYLE. Barley wines are often brewed to alcoholic strengths of 10% ABV, and sometimes more.

The early development of the barley wine beer style began in the mid to late 18th century in breweries attached to aristocratic great houses in England. At first, such beers were too expensive to produce on a commercial basis. Using new techniques to produce pale malts, they began to brew very strong ales exclusively for the use of these wealthy households. In 1736 the seminal book *The London and Country Brewer* makes mention of very strong ales brewed "as to be of a Vinous Nature." These beers would often be aged in wood for a year or more before serving, and were brewed "to answer the like purpose of wine" at the table. This was considered important in the days when difficulties between England and the wine-producing countries to the south could interrupt wine supplies for extended periods of time.

In 1854 the brewers Bass, Ratcliff, & Gretton of Burton upon Trent began production of a single-brew barley wine they called simply No. 1, its label adorned with a single red diamond. This diamond was registered as Britain's second trademark, following the still-familiar Bass Ale red triangle. The dark beers of Bass bore a brown diamond. No. 1 was a ponderously strong beer, beginning its fermentation at a specific gravity of 1.100 (about 25° Plato). No. 2, another barley wine, was somewhat smaller at 1.097. Bass No. 1, as it is still known, was brewed almost continuously (with a 10-year break from 1944 to 1954) until its discontinuation in 1995. It remains the standard (though today only in memory) against which other British barley wines are measured.

Bass No. 1 was distinctive not only for its single brew method of production but also for its paleness, owing in part to increased understanding of the economic feasibility of pale malt. Prior to this development, barley wines had been mainly dark amber to brown in color, employing more cheaply available darker malts. Other brewers followed suit with pale versions such as Tennent's Gold Label and Fuller's Golden Pride. A dark and noteworthy barley wine, Thomas Hardy's Ale, has been produced by a succession of brewers, beginning with Eldridge Pope in 1968 and concluding in 2009 at O'Hanlon's Brewing Co. See THOMAS HARDY'S ALE. The Hardy ale was purported to age for 25 years and more. The effects of age and the greatness of the beer are subjects hotly debated among beer aficionados. Today, several UK breweries carry on the classic barley wine tradition, perhaps most notably J.W. Lees of Manchester, who produce J.W. Lees Harvest Ale.

With its roots in British traditions, barley wine as a style enjoyed a substantial second flowering among American craft brewers, beginning with the production by Anchor Brewing Co. of its Old Foghorn in 1975, and followed shortly afterward by Sierra Nevada Brewing's Bigfoot. Within several years barley wine had become something of a seasonal showoff among small American brewers, who released small batches of it for the Christmas season as thanks for loyal patronage throughout the year. It can be argued that as barley wine production in the UK has waned since the discontinuation of Bass No. 1 and others, the American craft brewing scene has been instrumental to maintaining the vitality of the style. See CRAFT BREWING.

For the brewer, barley wine is a difficult and expensive beer to produce, requiring great amounts of materials, procedural vigilance, and time, which it may be said constitutes the fifth vital element of its production (along with malt, hops, water, and yeast). Like its early cousins old and strong ale, barley wine is intended to be laid down, the fortitude of its flavors sometimes requiring a year or more to mellow to an enjoyable integration. Its alcoholic strength also commonly prescribes its sale in small glasses and six-ounce "nip" bottles.

A range of interpretation exists across barley wine's geography, not only between British and American versions but from one side of the North American continent to the other. Generally and historically, and no doubt owing in part to the relative proximity of supply, the barley wines of the West Coast are substantially hoppier than their eastern counterparts. Where British examples are noteworthy for pronounced alcoholic and sherry-like flavors, a pure-bred northwest US version is fierce in hop bitterness and aroma, even after the time ordinarily counted upon to diminish hop character. The American Northeast, with perhaps stronger ties to UK brewing traditions and tastes, generally produces barley wines in a kind of mid-Atlantic meld, tending more to the sweet and strong, with tempered flavors of age.

In a sort of historical resonance with the emergence in the mid-19th century of barley wines paler than their antecedents, American barley wines in the 1990s took a turn for the paler as well. This, combined with the fierce hop qualities evident in the bolder examples, took the first steps toward the development of a new style whose other parent was India pale ale. Double, or "Imperial" IPAs displayed the alcoholic strength of barley wine along with the layers of hop bitterness, flavor, and aroma long associated with IPA, another staple of American craft brewers arguably rescued from the scrap heap of British brewing tradition. See DOUBLE IPA. "Double IPA" is, these days, a more popular strong ale than barley wine, but barley wine remains atop the scale as the biggest of beers.

Allen, Fal, and Dick Cantwell. *Barley wine*. Boulder, CO: Brewers Publications, 1997.

Jackson, Michael. *The beer companion*. Philadelphia, PA: Running Press, 1993.

Jackson, Michael. *The New World guide to beer*. Philadelphia, PA: Running Press, 1988.

The London and country brewer, 2nd ed. 1736. http://www.pbm.com/~lindahl/london/. This is a scanned copy and is also available as a single pdf file at http://www.pbm.com/~lindahl/london/all.pdf/.

Dick Cantwell

barley yellow dwarf virus (BYDV) is a member of the luteovirus genus and is closely related to cereal yellow dwarf virus. It is the most common viral disease of cereal plants and has a serious economic impact, reducing yields from infected crops by 2%–79%. The virus affects barley, wheat, oats, maize, and rice, and also infects wild grasses, which serve as year-round reservoirs of the virus and can trigger new outbreaks. It is transmitted through the saliva of aphids, which feed by piercing the phloem (vascular tissue) of the plant. Symptoms of the disease include yellowing of leaves, reduced height, reduced root growth, delayed heading, and yield reduction. Younger plants are most susceptible, and the only current mechanism of control is through application of insecticides to remove aphids from the crop.

Studies show that BYDV infection results in a reduction of kernel plumpness and higher proportion of thin seeds. In brewing practice, this can lead to higher total protein, higher wort protein, and lower extract. The virus is found worldwide, with different species prevalent in different areas. Transgenic plants expressing resistance genes have been produced under research conditions and show sustained resistance to viral infection.

Department of Primary Industries, Victoria, Australia: Note AG1113, August 2003, Updated July 2009. "Barley Yellow Dwarf Virus (BYDV) and Cereal Yellow Dwarf Virus (CYDV)." http://new.dpi.vic.gov.au/notes/crops-and-pasture/cereals/ag1113-barley-yellow-dwarf-virus-bydv-and-cereal-yellow-dwarf-virus-cydv/ (accessed March 17, 2011).

Edwards, M. C., Fetch, T. G., Jr., Schwarz, P. B., and Steffenson, B. J. Effect of barley yellow dwarf virus infection on yield and malting quality of barley. University of Nebraska, Plant Disease Central website resources, 2001.

University of Nebraska at Lincoln. "Barley yellow dwarf." http://pdc.unl.edu/agriculturecrops/wheat/barleyyellowdwarf/ (accessed March 17, 2011).

Zhang Z, Z Lin, and Z Xin. Research progress in BYDV resistance genes derived from wheat and its wild relatives. *Journal of Genetics and Genomics* 36(9) (2009): 567–73.

Martha Holley-Paquette

barrel, a container made from wooden staves. The construction may be "slack" or "tight." Slack barrels have been made since Roman times for dry goods—hence, for instance, cracker barrels—whereas tight

Photograph, c. 1935, of a Pinkus Müller brewhouse-style restaurant in Münster, Germany. The decorative barrel portrays Jan Gambrinus, the mythical Flemish king of beer. COURTESY OF PINKUS MÜLLER

barrels for wet goods such as beer and wine, as well as for oil, olives, fat, vinegar, sauerkraut, and pickles, came into use only in the early Middle Ages. Barrels often come by different names depending on their size and function. There are firkins and hogsheads for beer and pipes for Port and Madeira wines. Most barrels are made from staves of hardwood, often oak, bound together by metal hoops into a bulging cylinder. The bulge, which makes it easy to roll and spin the barrel, is called a bilge. The barrel's head and bottom are flat and each is secured into the staves by a grove called a croze. This allows the staves to protrude above the head and bottom in a ring called a chime, which makes it easy to grip and roll the barrel.

The quality of the barrel depends largely on the expert selection of the wood. Straight-growing trees are preferred. The staves are split from the felled trees and planed. Then they are piled up in tiers in the open, where they age and season for several years, while air and water reduce the wood's green, unpleasant, tannic flavors. During the barrel's construction, the cooper moistens the staves and then lights a small wood fire inside the emerging barrel to heat the wood and make it more pliable for bending into the typical barrel shape. The fire chars or "toasts" the inside of the barrel. Toasting levels range from light to medium to heavy, which, in turn have an impact on the flavors of their contents, be it wine or whiskey. Used toasted or charred barrels are highly sought after by specialty brewers for barrel aging. See BARREL-AGING.

However, barrels that are intended as simple containers rather than aging vessels do not take a prior detour through a winery or distillery. Instead, they are often coated on the inside to keep the beer from making contact with the wood. In years past, the material of choice for lining barrels was pitch, a type of tar. Nowadays, the protective blanket between the beer and the barrel tends to be made from various modern, inert, elastic, sturdy, rubber-like materials.

Wooden beer barrels are still used—commonly for gravity dispensing—by several traditional breweries, such as the Altbier Brewpub Zum Uerige in Düsseldorf and the Rauchbier Brewery Schlenkerla in Bamberg, both in Germany. See ALTBIER, GRAVITY DISPENSE, RAUCHBIER, and UERIGE BREWERY. A few British breweries still use wooden casks. As of 2011, the Wadworth Brewery of Wiltshire employed England's last fully trained master cooper for the upkeep of the brewery's wooden casks. Theakstons and Samuel Smith's still do limited trade in wooden casks, and Marston's Pedigree has the distinction of actually being fermented in barrels through the Burton Union sets. See BURTON UNION SYSTEM, MARSTON'S BREWERY, SAMUEL SMITH'S OLD BREWERY, and THEAKSTONS. In 1963, British barrel enthusiasts founded the Society for the Preservation of Beers from the Wood, their aims being exactly as described.

Barrels are typically fitted with several openings for filling, cleaning, and emptying, as well as for air to enter the barrel as the liquid is drained. The opening for cleaning, sanitizing, and filling is called a belly bung. The opening for emptying the barrel via a tap or a beer engine is called a keystone, kept shut with a stopper. See BEER ENGINE and CASK. During tapping, the keystone stopper gets pushed into the beer. For venting, a classic British cask has a shive with a center hole for a stopper called a tut and a hard wooden peg called a spile, the latter being hammered into the tut. The spile can be removed and reinserted during poring to vent the cask.

Society for Preservation of Beers from the Wood. http://www.spbw.com/wood.html/ (accessed January 30, 2011).

Horst Dornbusch

barrel-aging. For most of us, the sight of wooden barrels brings wine most readily to mind, but this would not always have been so. For centuries, in the days before the manufacture of metal containers became commonplace, the wooden barrel was among the standard containers for storing and shipping just about any liquid. Water, beer, wine, olive oil, rum, chili sauces, vats of fermented fish paste—all have been stored and traveled the world in wood. Originally there was no particular intention to have the wood impart its own flavor to the liquid it held; the barrel was simply the container at hand. "Sweetness," or at least a lack of sour character, was the most that people expected from a barrel in terms of flavor.

Decades into the 20th century, most beer was delivered to the bars of the world in wooden barrels. These were heavy oak barrels built to withstand the pressure of the carbonation within. They were usually tapped very much as British casks are tapped today, by driving a heavy wooden or metal tap through a reinforced aperture with a thin spot in the center. See CASK. Some British breweries use such wooden casks to this day, though none for the majority of their production.

Many beer enthusiasts, having heard tales of India pale ale (IPA) traveling the seas for months in large wooden barrels, have supposed that wood flavors were common in these beers. In fact, at least from the early 1800s on, brewers worked hard to avoid wood flavors in beer, and contemporary writings give the impression that they were successful in this. New barrels, usually made of oak, were often filled with successive soakings of boiling water and hydrochloric acid to remove wood flavor. See OAK. Only once the barrel had been rendered neutral was it thought fit to hold beer. German and later American brewers lined their barrels with pitch, minimizing both wood flavor and leakage.

In time, stainless steel tanks, fermenting vessels, and kegs have taken over a beer industry obsessed with sterility and concerned about costs and ease of use. Today, craft brewers, particularly in the United States, have once again brought wood into the brewery, but this time the purposes are entirely different. The barrel is no longer a mere container. The modern brewer ages beer in wood so that the wood will influence the flavor and aroma of the beer. Here we speak mostly of varieties of oak, though other woods are in use as well. Chestnut, ash, poplar, cedar, acacia, cypress, redwood, pine, and even eucalyptus have been used for barrels with varying success. Oak, however, remains the wood of choice for most barrels. When heated and steamed, oak is easily bent into barrel staves, and the structure of the wood renders it watertight. The same qualities once prized for ships are still prized for barrels. Though there are surely variations upon these themes, the modern brewer has essentially four different but often interlocking qualities that he wants from barrel-aging.

Wood Flavors

Oak, even though watertight, is porous, and contains a complex array of flavors that can be extracted

A brewer at the Avery Brewing Company in Colorado prepares a blending session for barrel-aged beers. JONATHAN CASTNER PHOTOGRAPHY

into beer. In the United States, where barrel-aging has recently become commonplace among craft brewers, the most common barrel in use is the bourbon barrel. By US law, whiskey designated as "straight bourbon" must be aged for a minimum of 2 years in *new* American white oak barrels. This means that a barrel can only be used once to age true bourbon whiskey, a fact that turns a used barrel into a surplus item for a bourbon distillery. American oak has powerful flavors, and these are accentuated by charring of the barrel interior before the barrel heads are affixed. Each distillery will use its own blend of oak and its own level of charring, leading to distinct differences in the sorts of flavors that brewers can derive from the used wood. Used bourbon barrels were once cheap and easily available, but those days are over. As of 2011, prices easily reached as high as $200 per 200-liter barrel, and increased competition from other brewers and from whiskey producers in Scotland, India, and China seems likely to drive prices ever skyward.

Wine barrels are usually made from either French oak or American oak, though oak from parts of Eastern Europe is also in use. French oak is denser, more mildly flavored, and far more expensive than American oak, as its flavor contributions are felt to be more sophisticated and balanced. American oak is more powerfully flavored and therefore tends to be used more sparingly in wine production, where it can easily overwhelm the flavors of the wine itself. Below, the major wood flavors at work are addressed.

Lactones, lipids contained within the oak itself, make up a large part of the aroma we associate with oak. In lower concentrations, it strikes the nose as simply "oaky" and pleasantly herbaceous, but higher concentrations can become rose-like, with the highest concentrations giving powerful impressions of coconut. Open air seasoning of oak staves tends to decrease lactone content, but charring of oak can bring this character foreword. As a result, both the seasoning of the wood and the char of the wood will affect its flavor. Balanced with other flavors, lactone character can be highly pleasant, but in excess, many people will find it cloying.

Phenolic aldehydes are derived from lignins, complex polymers that make up part of the oak structure. Phenolic aldehydes, the most important of which is vanillin, are degradation products of lignin, and are formed under the influence of gentle heat or mild acid. Vanillin, of course, gives a vanilla-like flavor, and it is the main ingredient in artificial vanilla food flavorings. The mild heat applied in barrel toasting for wine barrels tends to promote the conversion of lignin compounds to vanillin. Charring, however, while leaving some vanillin intact, can break down lignin compounds to simpler steam volatile phenols, and these are responsible for smoky and medicinal flavors in the wood and any beers later aged in it. Other phenolic compounds include guiacaols (sweet spice, cinnamon) and eugenol (clove).

Hemicelluloses are part of the wood structure, polymers made up of several simple sugars. Upon heating, these compounds degrade into their constituent sugars, which then caramelize into furfurals, maltol, cyclotene, and other compounds that give flavors ranging from bitter almond to toasty, to sweet caramel and burnt sugar. Maltol, which has caramelized flavors reminiscent of freshly baked bread, is also a flavor enhancer and can increase the perception of maltiness in beer. Furfurals, when in contact with active yeasts, can transform from a bitter almond character to smoky, meaty, and leathery flavors that can be desirable in certain aged beers.

Oak tannins are hydrolysable substances that break down into other flavor-active compounds in the presence of beer. While tannins can lend astringency, they are broken down to a large extent by toasting of wine barrels and to a greater extent by bourbon barrel charring. Any previous resident of the barrels is likely to have extracted a large proportion of the tannins, and there is rarely enough left behind to trouble the brewer. Tannins are also powerful antioxidants and therefore provide something of a buffer to the inevitable oxygenation that occurs through porous woods.

Previous Residents

Concurrent with the flavor of the wood itself may be the flavor of whatever beverage the barrel held previously. While some brewers do buy new barrels, this is relatively rare; not only are they very expensive, but their flavors can be overwhelming. The spirits or wine a barrel previously held will have extracted a lot of this flavor but also left much intact and possibly imparted its own flavors. Before whiskey is aged in barrels it is clear in color and referred to variously as "high wine," "white dog," "new make spirit," or the somewhat pejorative "moonshine." It is very strong, up to 160 proof, and can be packed with agricultural character, some of the flavors of the corn, wheat, rye, or barley that went into the original whiskey mash. Some brewers feel that they can detect the influence of the sour mash technique used for bourbons and some Tennessee whiskeys, though distillers insist that sour mashing is a mere pH adjustment technique used to aid fermentation. Alcohols, soaked up to an inch into the wood, may also be extracted into beer, bringing higher alcohol flavors and grappa-like notes.

Beers have also been aged in barrels that previously held Calvados or applejack, lending fresh apple and cider flavors to beer. Though most Scotch whisky barrels originated as bourbon barrels, the second use for the Scotch can bring powerful flavors of its own, especially if the whisky was made from heavily peated malts. British brewers, with these Scotch barrels readily at hand, are experimenting with these barrels and deriving a wonderful array of malt and peat flavors from them.

Especially in wine-rich California, previously used wine barrels bring a whole other range of flavors, both from the wine itself and from the microflora that fermented it. Red wine barrels can lend a pink tinge and notable berry flavors, while white wine barrels can show grape varietal characteristics, especially from riesling, gewürztraminer, and other powerfully flavored grapes. Chardonnay barrels are more common in the US, and tend to be more variable, probably because the grape expresses itself so differently depending upon terroir and winemaking technique. At its best, chardonnay can impart flavors of tropical fruit, peaches, roses, and other pleasant flavors into its barrels, and these flavors can transfer well to paler beer styles. In Italy, a great wine-producing country suddenly boasting more than 300 craft breweries, barrel-aging is quickly becoming a natural part of the craft beer culture. Within a short period of time, we can expect to see more Italian beers aged in wine barrels, perhaps lending flavors from the famed Barolos of Piemonte and the esteemed traminers of the Alto Adige.

Oxygen

Oxygenation, whether desired or not, is an integral fact when aging a beverage in barrels. Oak is porous and oxygen slowly makes its way into beer through the wood. In wine, slow and steady oxygenation is an important part of barrel maturation and produces, particularly in red wines, more agreeable flavors. Over the past 20 years, wine-makers have actually instituted a technique, dubbed micro-oxygenation, that mimics the effects of slow oxygen transfer through barrels. This has allowed tank-aging of cheaper wines, where the heavy cost of barrel-aging may not be justified.

Brewers are taught from their first days in the industry that oxygen is an enemy to be avoided at all costs. See OXIDATION and OXYGEN. Oxygen is largely unwelcome in the mash vessel and the kettle, and after oxygen is introduced during cast-out to help initiate yeast reproduction, it is afterwards anathema. But slow oxidation is a part of all aging of beer, whether in barrels, bottles, or kegs, and when properly controlled, it can impart pleasant flavors. Hop bitterness softens considerably over months, malt flavors can step further forward, and flavors can marry into complex sherry-like notes that seem more than the sum of their parts. Carefully managed, many beers will develop positive flavor characteristics rather than the musty, papery flavors we associate with more violent uncontrolled oxidation. Over-oxygenation, however, can allow the development of acetic flavors, as acetobacter bacteria thrive in aerobic environments. As with any form of aging, oxidation will occur more slowly at lower temperatures.

Biological Diversity

Microflora other than normal brewing yeasts are increasingly a friend to the craft brewer interested in the creation of a wider range of flavors than Saccharomyces yeasts can create. Barrel-aging is traditional for lambic beers and is almost always practiced in the creation of the new generation of sour beer styles. See LAMBIC and SOUR BEER. It has long been known that although many yeasts and bacteria find their way into lambic beer during the cooling process, many others will await the fermenting wort inside the receiving barrels. Lambic brewers sometimes scour their barrels between uses, but this does not eliminate wild residents under the surface of the barrel walls and between the staves. Wood not only harbors wild yeasts and bacterial strains, allowing their easy transfer from one batch of beer to the next, but they provide the slow oxygenation that is crucial for the development of such complexing agents as Brettanomyces yeasts. See BRETTANOMYCES. These microflora are often unwelcome in the brewery's main facility or in tanks where they could wreak havoc on more "normal" beers, and barrels provide a place for them to live, work, and grow without tying up tank space or acting as contaminants in other fermentations. Interestingly, research indicates that seasoning and toasting of oak can break down wood cellulose into cellobiose, which then provides additional nutrients for Brettanomyces yeasts.

Racking and Storage

Most brewers rinse barrels when readying them for use. In the case of bourbon barrels, rinsing removes loose wood char, which the brewer does not want ending up in finished beer. Some soak barrels in very hot water, which may reduce any biological contamination, but also removes notable barrel flavor. Others trust to the bacteriostatic quality of the cask-strength bourbon that the barrel previously contained, and prefer to leave the barrel untouched. In all cases brewers will prefer to get barrels as soon as possible after they've been emptied. This not only lowers the risk of bacterial infection but also the risk of leaks due to drying and shrinkage of the wood. Barrels are sometimes flushed with CO_2 before being filled, and then set on barrel racks if they are needed.

Temperature is a major determinant of the extent and quality of barrel flavors, especially in barrels that are seeing their first use after spirits or wine. At warmer temperatures, above 60°F (15.5°C), wood flavors and those of the previous barrel tenant will develop quickly in the beer, but those flavors can often be rough, coarse, or hot. If allowed to age out over time, they will diminish and can gain finesse. Warmer temperatures also speed evaporation of liquid through the wood, so there may be need to top up barrels more frequently. Finally, warmer temperatures encourage oxidation and the development of any yeasts or bacteria that may reside in the barrel, desired or unwelcome as they may be. Some brewers of sour beers will allow barrels to rise to ambient warehouse temperatures, even though these may reach well over 90°F.

Conversely, colder temperatures will slow developments and tends to allow greater mellowness.

Brewers will each decide their own golden mean, depending on whether they are merely aging for wood character or trying to cultivate microflora. For the former purpose, most settle in the 50°F to 60°F (10°C–15.5°C) range when it is attainable.

Barrels are also often staging areas for various steepings and for aging on fruit. Everything from the traditional cherries used to make kriek, to other fruits, cacao nibs, and various other spices may be introduced into the barrel for aging along with the beer. Barrel-aging, a technique seemingly emerging out of the past, is in fact appearing in new forms every day, bringing new flavors to craft beers around the world.

Ackland, Tony. "The composition of oak and an overview of its influence on maturation." http://www.homedistiller.org/oak.pdf/ (accessed December 7, 2010).

Robinson, Jancis. *The Oxford companion to wine*, 3rd ed. Oxford, England: Oxford University Press, 2006.

Garrett Oliver

bars

See PUBLIC HOUSES (PUBS).

base malt is malt that has enough enzymatic activity, notably diastatic power, to ensure that starch conversion occurs during mashing. It usually accounts for the largest percentage of malt in a beer recipe (anywhere from 60% to 100%). The remaining percentage may be made up of specialty malts, unmalted grains, or adjuncts that may not have enough enzymes to convert their own starches to sugars during mashing. In essence, the base malt provides for the production of fermentable sugars and free amino nitrogen for the yeast to consume during fermentation. The entire grist bill represents the substrate but the base malt provides both substrate and enzymes.

When selecting a base malt for a given recipe, brewers are interested in several factors, some of which are included in a standard malt analysis sheet: moisture content, potential extract, color, protein content, and diastatic power. Brewers also want to know the barley (or other grain) variety, place of origin, and type.

Most often, but not always, base malt is a two-row or six-row pilsner or pale ale malt. For example, a pale ale recipe may comprise 85% base malt (pilsner or pale ale) and 15% specialty malt. However, in German weissbier, wheat is the base malt, sometimes up to 60%, with pilsner malt making up the remaining balance. Some other specialty beer may use other base malts. Traditional German märzenbier can be made from 100% Munich malt, which concentrates that malt's toffee-like flavors.

Noonan, Gregory J. "Malted barley." In *New brewing lager beer*. Boulder, CO: Brewers Publications, 1996.

Palmer, John J. "Understanding malted barley and adjuncts." In *How to brew*. Boulder, CO: Brewers Publications, 2006.

Damien Malfara

Bass & Company was a British brewery, based in Burton-on-Trent, that became one of the most recognized brewery brands in the world. Bass' red triangle logo and its flagship beer, Bass pale ale, once traveled the world, spread by the ships of an advancing empire.

Founded by William Bass in 1777, the brewery saw remarkable growth in its early years, with ale sent to Russia in 1784 and to North America by 1799. For much of the history of the flagship brand it was known as an India pale ale because of its shipment to British forces overseas. More than a century later, the brewery would quietly drop the word "India" from its official packaging.

By 1850 it was producing more than 100,000 UK barrels (137,250 US barrels) per year. By 1888, the Bass brewery complex covered 145 acres of land and employed more than 2,500 workers, with output approaching the million-barrel mark.

In 1926 Bass and Co acquired the nearby Worthington brewery and continued to produce that brewery's popular White Shield, a bottle-conditioned pale ale. That would continue until 1977 when the brewery discontinued the brand and licensed the recipe to a smaller brewery. In the 1960s Bass continued to grow, merging with Mitchells & Butler, and later that decade became the UK's largest brewery following the acquisition of Charrington United Breweries, brewers of Carling. The new company was named Bass Charrington Ltd and would later become known as Bass PLC.

Celebrated for more than just the flagship Bass pale ale, the brewery produces a number of beers that would introduce new styles to the world and several that would continue to entice new generations of beer drinkers. Bass was the first brewery to use the term "barley wine" for a bottled beer named No. 1 in 1903. Although it was widely distributed for decades, it currently is brewed sporadically.

In 1902 Bass' King's ale was released to commemorate a visit by Edward VII to the brewery. Corked-finished bottles that occasionally surface are sought after by collectors. Equally as desirable are bottles of Ratcliffe ale, brewed to celebrate the birth of a brewery director's son in 1869. The ale was also cork finished and cellared, intending to be drunk on the boy's 21st birthday.

These beers, the Bass flagship ale, along with general distribution to a global audience, would add to the legend and allure of the brewery, making it a household name not only in the UK but also around the world.

The company would diversify, purchasing and managing pubs throughout the UK, acquiring the Holiday Inn hotel chain and expanding that brand to include several other properties, including Holiday Inn Express and Staybridge Suites. It also purchased several soft drink companies. By this point in the 1990s the company had grown so large that it had a separate division dedicated to its beer efforts named Bass Brewers.

In 2000, however, the company decided to focus its efforts on the lodging and hospitality industry, shed its namesake product, and sold brewing operations to Belgium-based Interbrew S.A. for $3.5 billion. Monopolies legislation demanded that Interbrew dispose of a large slice of their breweries and brands, notably Carling Black Label. The buyers were Coors.

Interbrew would later merge with Brazilian beer company AmBev, creating InBev to create the behemoth Anheuser-Busch InBev, the largest brewing company in the world. Bass pale ale was added to the global portfolio of the company. Bass pale ale is made at Anheuser-Busch InBev's Samlesbury Brewery in England and is available around the world. For most of its existence the flagship beer was known as Bass India pale ale, although in the 1990s it was rebranded as just Bass pale ale.

Bass has a number of historical distinctions in both brewing and general history arenas. Because of its popularity and impressive exporting in the 1800s, its red triangle logo became the first registered trademark in the UK in 1876. That triangle is clearly visible on beer bottles depicted in Edouard Manet's 1882 painting "A bar at the Folies-Bergère" and in dozens of paintings by Picasso.

Over the years, the various owners of the Bass brand have played up its historical importance with a number of vague claims and advertisements, including that Napoleon Bonaparte enjoyed the brew so much that he sought to build a Bass brewery in France or that pints of Bass inspired Edgar Allan Poe and relaxed Buffalo Bill Cody. There is even a claim that famed explorer Sir Earnest Shackleton drank Bass ale while on his expedition to reach the South Pole in 1921–22. These claims are murky at best.

One historical truth that cannot be refuted is that the RMS Titanic was carrying 500 cases (12,000 bottles) of Bass ale when it sank in the Atlantic Ocean in 1912. During expedition and recovery efforts of the ship in the late 1990s, nine bottles were found and lifted to the surface from the debris field.

Today, the ale is enjoyed at pubs around the world, where the corporate owners say it is still made following the original recipe. The result is an amber-colored brew with a light, burned, roast aroma. It is made with English malts and hops and is brewed with two strains of yeast that give it a malty, slightly nutty flavor. In the United States it is served at 5.1% alcohol by volume.

Bass ale is frequently used as the bottom ingredient in a Black and Tan, where a pub glass is half filled with the pale ale and, using a specialty spoon, a stout is poured on top, creating a two-layer beverage where the stout floats atop the pale ale. See BLACK AND TAN. This can be created with most pale ales and stouts, but marketers behind Bass have pushed the brand as the key ingredient in recent years, even releasing a specialty, triangle shaped spoon, an homage to its famous trademark.

Bass pale ale is served on draught and in a variety of bottles sizes and cans in more than 50 countries across the world.

See also BARLEY WINE, BURTON-ON-TRENT, and INDIA PALE ALE.

Bass: The story of the world's most famous ale. Burton-on-Trent, England: Bass, 1927.

Pederson, J. P. *International directory of company histories*, Vol. 38. Farmington Hills, MI: St. James Press, 2001.

John Holl

batch process is the name given to the process of producing a beer in individual processes, vessels, and time frames, as opposed to a continuous process that involves a steady flow of ingredients through the plant and equipment. See CONTINUOUS FERMENTATION. A batch process takes place in individual vessels such as a lauter tun or a fermenting vessel. Each process is normally started and finished in the same vessel. Each discrete, individual batch is usually given a specific "brew" or "gyle" number but may be subject to blending with other batches later in the process.

Several breweries experimented with continuous brewhouses and fermentations in the 1970s and 1980s, but most returned to batch processes after experiencing production control and quality issues. Beer is brewed using batch processes in tanks and vessels, for example, in the brewhouse, fermentation, and maturation areas, whereas filtration and packaging can be regarded as continuous processes carried out on each particular "batch" of beer.

Paul KA Buttrick

Baudelot cooler. Jean Louis Baudelot (1797–1881), was born in France, and studied engineering in Belgium. Though he claimed several inventions, fame came in 1856, when he patented a liquid cooler, specifically intended for the brewing industry. A cousin who was a brewer presented him with the fact that until then beer worts had to be cooled in a shallow vessel (cool ship) and stirred during a whole night—a process that easily took 8 hours. See COOLSHIP. Worse, the continuous exposure of the worts to the air resulted often in unwanted inoculation and infected beer. Yet exposure was mandatory because beer yeasts need oxygen at the outset of fermentation. Therefore, the wort needs to be well aerated. Baudelot envisaged a fine double copper sheet overlaying copper tubes (first cylindrical, later elliptical in cross-section) wherein cold water (spring water or icewater) ran countercurrent to the worts. The worts were collected on top of the cooler in shallow tray, and then finely dispersed, flowing over outside of the copper sheets, which were being being cooled internally. In this way, cooling took place in less than a quarter of the original time needed, limiting exposure to contaminating microbes, while aeration was assured. Hot wort flowed like an undulating waterfall down the exterior of the cooler, emerging cool and aerated at the bottom. It was a massive improvement that led to beer of much better quality and stability.

Baudelot opened a brewery (later taken over by his son) after patenting his invention, which was nonetheless shamelessly copied. The brewery served for experimenting and bettering his designs. Others also worked on his patent, not least in the US, where a new type was patented as late as 1939.

Though plate heat exchangers and shell-and-tube coolers have taken over, Baudelot coolers are still with us. In industrial/chemical plants, ultrafast cooling is still done by contemporary Baudelots, and in Germany, at least one commercial brewery still uses a stainless steel Baudelot today.

Joris Pattyn and Jonathan Downing

Bavaria, the southernmost of the 16 states of the Federal Republic of Germany, is the undisputed cradle of the world's lager beer culture. There, in the northern foothills of the Alps, where summers are hot and winters are cold, many of the world's major beer styles have emerged, some by happenstance, some by design. These include helles, dunkel, märzen, Oktoberfest, kellerbier, rauchbier, schwarzbier, and bockbier in all its variations (doppelbock, maibock, weizenbock, and eisbock among them). In addition, Bavaria has spawned an ale, hefeweizen (also known as weissbier or weizenbier), the world's most popular wheat beer, as well as its dark relation, the dunkelweizen, and its filtered version, the kristallweizen. Other, less common Bavarian styles include zoiglbier, zwickelbier, landbier, dampfbier, erntebier, dinkelbier, and roggenbier. Even the flagship brew of the Czech Republic, the pilsner, has Bavarian roots: It was a Bavarian brewmaster, Josef Groll, who was hired by the Měšťanský Pivovar (Burgher Brewery)

Three Bavarians engage in a drinking contest in a Munich beer cellar, 1952. The beer hauler (center) emptied the three-liter stein the fastest, while the waitress (left) and plumber (right) were runners-up. PIKE MICROBREWERY MUSEUM, SEATTLE, WA

in 1842 to reform beer making in the Bohemian city of Plzeň (Pilsen). See GROLL, JOSEF. In the process, Groll created Plzeňský Prazdroj (Pilsner Urquell), the world's first blond lager, largely by applying his Bavarian brewing techniques to the local barley, hops, and water.

Bavaria is also the world's most important source of hops, supplying about one-third of the global hop demand, especially in so-called noble aroma varieties. In addition, its fields produce some of the world's best brewing barley and wheat, and specialty malts made by Bavarian maltsters are sought after by breweries on all continents. Bavarian beers, invariably made from home-grown raw materials, tend to be rich and malty, with a delicate up-front bitterness and an aromatic, malt-accented finish.

There are few places in the world where beer is as firmly interwoven with the daily culture of its inhabitants as in Bavaria. Bavarians call their way of life *Gemütlichkeit*—an inimitably Bavarian form of conviviality—and beer is an integral part of that *Gemütlichkeit*, a basic food, the people's daily "liquid bread." In the summer, Bavarians favor their pale beer, the straw-blond, easy-drinking helles and the refreshing, effervescent hefeweizen with its slight clove, banana, and bubblegum aromas. In the fall, they switch to the amber and stronger Oktoberfest beer. Around Christmas, the bock beers come into their own. In the depth of winter, around Lent, it is time for the strong and nourishing doppelbock, while, in the spring, when the days get longer again, the beer of choice becomes the amber-to-blond, medium-strong maibock (May bock). See DOPPELBOCK, HELLES, and MAIBOCK. In recognition of the uniqueness of the Bavarian beer culture, the European Union, in 2001, granted the designation "Bavarian Beer" the status of a "Protected Geographical Indication," which is akin to a controlled appellation.

No matter which season, when Bavarians sit down for a beer, they like to take their time. In the summer, beer gardens under the shady canopy of chestnut and linden trees offer oases of respite from the struggles and stresses of the daily grind, even in the big bustling cities. There are some 80 beer gardens in Munich alone. In the winter, cozy beer halls, some centuries old, offer warmth and comfort. The beer in these places is usually served in liter or half-liter mugs (roughly pint- or quart-size glasses with sturdy handles). And Bavarians know how to celebrate with beer: Springtime is official *Starkbierzeit* (strong beer season), fêted with doppelbocks indoors, while fall is always Oktoberfest time, the last big outdoor bash of the year. The 2-week-long Munich Oktoberfest has become the biggest party in the world, attracting some six to seven million visitors each year. See OKTOBERFEST.

Bavaria's beer-making goes back to the late Bronze Age, if not further. An earthenware amphora, discovered in 1935 in a Celtic chieftain's burial mound in Kasendorf near the northern Bavarian city of Kulmbach, has been dated to about 800 BCE. It is considered the oldest evidence of beer-making in continental Europe. Its dried-up content has been identified as the residues of a black wheat ale flavored with oak leaves. The brewers who made this beer belonged to the so-called Hallstatt culture, a Celtic people, who then occupied an area roughly between the present-day border of France and Germany, and the Danube basin near Vienna, Austria. Yet, by the beginning of the modern era, at the time of the Roman conquest of Central Europe, invading Germanic tribes from the east had driven the Celts to the western edge of the Continent and across the present-day English Channel to the British Isles. The first Celtic settlements began to appear in Britain around the second half of the 5th century BCE. Of course, the Celts took their beer-making skills with them, which may make them the ancestors not only of the German but also of the British and Irish beer cultures.

Meanwhile, in Central Europe, the Germanic tribes continued to make beer, too, because, like all good conquerors, they usurped the achievements of the vanquished. A key piece of evidence of the continuity of beer-making in Bavaria is an archeological dig at the outskirts of Regensburg on the banks of the Danube. This site contains a complete brewery, replete with malting facilities, a deep well, and a fire pit for heating a mash-brew kettle. It dates from 179 CE, when Castra Regina (Regensburg) was a walled-in encampment for the Emperor Marcus Aurelius' Third Italian Legion of some 6,000 elite troupes and their Germanic servants, prostitutes, and artisans, including brewers. The fortification was built as a bulwark against the Marcomans, a confederation of marauding tribes that were threatening the northeastern flank of the Roman Empire. The Romans usually scoffed at the primitive brews of the Germans, but for the outpost at Regensburg, the local beer just had to do, because it was next to impossible to supply that many thirsty souls with wine from across the Alps. Oddly, therefore, the oldest evidence of a complete brewery in Bavaria is a Roman structure.

Brewing in Central Europe, until the late Roman period, was mostly women's work. While the man of the household tilled the fields of barley, wheat, and oats, the lady of the house attended to both the stew and the brew around the domestic hearth. Her beers were usually flavored with herbs, known as "gruit," such as bog myrtle, gale, juniper, mugwort, woodruff, and yarrow. See GRUIT. But that division of labor between the sexes began to change when Christianity arrived in Bavaria in the 6th century CE, by way of Irish missionaries, who had set out from the Emerald Isle to eradicate paganism in Central Europe. These monks established missionary outposts and small monasteries along the old Roman roads, which gradually became centers not only of preaching and contemplation but also of brewing. And as the monasteries grew, so did their breweries. Over time, brewing knowledge accumulated among the learned and literate cloistered friars, and brewing techniques and beer quality improved. Nuns, too, who might have been domestic beer-makers had they not chosen the habit, became accomplished convent brewsters. As some of the monks and nuns specialized in beer-making, brewing gradually evolved from a common household activity to a recognized profession. In the process, monks discovered the bitter flower of the hop plant as a perfect beer flavoring and preservative. The oldest written reference to hops is a document from 768 CE found in the Benedictine Abbey of Weihenstephan outside Munich. Within just a few centuries, hops would replace gruit as a beer flavoring in virtually all of Europe, except for the British Isles. In 1040 Weihenstephan obtained its commercial brewing license. In 1803, as part of the Napoleonic Secularization of French-occupied Europe, including Bavaria, Weihenstephan become the property of the State of Bavaria. Today, it offers one of the world's leading university programs in brewing studies and is still a commercial brewery, which makes it the world's oldest continuously operating brewery. See WEIHENSTEPHAN.

As brewing in the monasteries and convents of the High Middle Ages improved, beer became a source of wealth for the religious orders, which, not surprisingly, attracted the attention of the secular feudal lords in the countryside and the patrician merchants in the cities. Soon rival court and burgher breweries sprang up, yet beer quality in the hands of lesser-trained brewers declined. Especially in the summer, beer in Bavaria would often taste sour or worse—from microbial infections, as we now understand. But the first microbes were only observed in 1673, by Antonie van Leeuwenhoek, the Dutch inventor of the microscope; and the definite proof that microbes are responsible for both fermentation and putrefaction had to wait until Louis Pasteur's groundbreaking 1876 work *Études sur la biere, ses maladies, causes qui les provoquent, procédé pour la rendre inaltérable, avec une théorie nouvelle de la fermentation* (Studies on Beer: The diseases of beer, their causes, and the means of preventing them, with a new theory of fermentation).

See PASTEUR, LOUIS. To microbiologically ignorant medieval Bavarians, however, the causes of their defective summer beers were a complete mystery. Their fermentation took place in open, usually wooden, and invariably unsanitary fermentation vessels. There is no doubt that, aside from benign brewer's yeast, airborne bacteria were also regular residents in these vats. To cover up the off-flavors of their summer beers, brewers would resort to all sorts of beer additives, including soot, oxen bile, chicken blood, salt, pith, chalk, legumes, rushes, tree bark, even poisonous mushrooms. In the cold Bavarian winters, on the other hand, bacteria were rarely able to survive and thus winter beers tended to be much more palatable.

Given the feudal order of things at the time, therefore, there was only one remedy for bad beer in Bavaria: regulation. Thus was passed a decree, in the city of Augsburg, in 1156, insisting that a brewer's bad beer "shall be destroyed or distributed among the poor at no charge." In 1363 the 12 members of the Munich city council assumed the role of beer inspectors. In 1420 they decreed that all beer must be aged at least 8 days before it could be served, and in 1447 they ordered that brewers may use only barley, hops, and water for their beers. In 1487 Duke Albrecht IV of the House of Wittelsbach, the ruling dynasty in Bavaria since 1180, forced Munich brewers to take a public oath to adhere to the 1447 decree. Finally, on April 23, 1516, the Bavarian Duke Wilhelm IV issued the now-famous *Reinheitsgebot* (Beer Purity Law) for his entire realm. See REINHEITSGEBOT. It, too, stipulated that only barley, hops, and water be used in Bavarian beers. That decree has remained in force ever since and, by 1906, it had metamorphosed into a law for all of Germany, which makes it the world's oldest food safety regulation. In the 16th century, however, it did not achieve the desired end, because summer beer continued to be bad in Bavaria. In 1553, therefore, Wilhelm's successor, Duke Albrecht V, went one step further: He simply forbade brewing altogether between the Feast of Saint George (April 23) and Michaelmas (September 29).

This 1553 decree had enormous, mostly unintended, consequences for the entire world of beer. It not only cleaned up Bavarian beer, but it inadvertently also caused all Bavarian beers henceforth to be lagers, because all ale-making yeasts go dormant below roughly 7°C (45°F). Only lager-making yeasts are still capable of fermenting beer at cold winter temperatures. Also, because of Albrecht's decree, brewers had to work overtime in late spring to make enough beer for the hot summer months, for which they made relatively strong beers, of perhaps 6% ABV, that would keep well. These brews of spring became soon known as March beers (*Märzenbier* in German)—forerunners of the modern Märzen beer style. See MÄRZENBIER. These March beers were stored in casks in cool cellars, tunnels, or caves. From this practice stems the term "lager," because *lagern* is the German word for "to store." Duke Albrecht's summer brewing prohibition was rescinded only in 1850, at which time brewers had learned to fill their lager cellars with ice cut from frozen lakes in the winter. Where there was no lake, brewers would erect wooden scaffolding called "ice gallows." On frosty days, they would spray these with water until icicles formed, which they would then knock off and throw into the cellars. By 1872 a Bavarian engineer, Carl von Linde, had invented a refrigeration system for lagering tanks, which, for the first time, allowed lagers to be brewed all year, anywhere. As we now know from hindsight, the two 16th-century decrees, the Reinheitsgebot and the summer brewing prohibition—issued within a span of four decades—changed not only Bavarian brewing but world brewing techniques forever. In Bavaria they led to a gradual evolution of the everyday brew from a murky, often rough concoction to the modern, clean, all-barley-based lagers in all their splendor and variety. Worldwide, too, perhaps 9 out of 10 brews are now lagers.

The original Bavarian winter lager was a beer we now know as dunkel, meaning "dark." See DUNKEL. In the days before the invention of the indirect-heated malt kiln by Daniel Wheeler in England in 1817, virtually all beers were some shade of dark, because malt was dried in direct-fired kilns, which always left some kernels slightly to severely scorched. Depending on the heat source, the malt also tasted more or less smoky. The darker versions of the dunkel became known as schwarzbier ("black beer"), while the smokier versions became rauchbier ("smoke beer"). See RAUCHBIER and SCHWARZBIER. Today, the city of Bamberg in central Bavaria is still the center of rauchbier-making. See BAMBERG, GERMANY. Old-fashioned Bamberger rauchbier is made from smoked malt that is kilned over open fires of aged beech wood. The dunkel remained Bavaria's most popular beer style well into the 1890s, when it was replaced in popularity by a straw-blond lager style, the helles (meaning light in color), which was first brewed by the Spaten Brewery of Munich in 1894.

But not all traditional Bavarian beers are lagers. A curious exception is the weissbier ("white beer") or hefeweizen ("yeast wheat"). This brew is a refreshing, effervescent pale ale—usually unfiltered and thus yeast-turbid—made from at least 50% wheat malt. The rest is barley malt. Weissbier became a popular brew in southeastern Bavaria in the 15th century, when the noble House of Degenberg of the village of Schwarzach obtained a feudal monopoly for brewing it. In the 16th century, weissbier found itself in technical violation of both the barley-only provisions of the Reinheitsgebot and the seasonal limitations of summer brewing prohibitions, which stirred up a decades-long conflict between the Degenbergs and the ruling House of Wittelsbach. In 1556 Duke Albrecht V declared wheat beer "a useless drink that neither nourishes nor provides strength and power, but only encourages drunkenness," and explicitly outlawed wheat beer-making by ordinary brewers—except for the Degenbergs, who got slapped with a special beer sales tax. But in 1602 Baron Hans Sigmund of Degenberg, the last of the Degenberg clan, died without leaving an heir, and, by the feudal rules of the day, the wheat beer privilege reverted to the Wittelsbachs. This led to a sudden reversal of official Bavarian beer policy: Duke Maximilian I, Albrecht's grandson, brought the Schwarzach brewmaster to Munich, built a new "white" brew house (near the present-day Hofbräuhaus in downtown Munich at Am Platzl Square), and eventually forced every innkeeper in his realm to purchase wheat beer from the many Wittelsbach-owned breweries. In 1872, during a dip in weissbier popularity, the Wittelsbachs sold the weissbier privilege to a private company, the Georg Schneider Brewery, which is still today a leading weissbier maker. In the late 20th century weissbier made a surprising comeback in public taste, and, at the beginning of the second millennium it overtook helles as the most popular beer style in Bavaria, garnering more than one-third of the market share there. See WEISSBIER.

The glory of Bavarian beer's past, however, is no guarantee of its future. In modern times, Bavarian beer finds itself strangely in trouble—perhaps the victim of its own success, because, when a thing becomes ubiquitously good, its exceptional quality is often no longer recognized, except by people looking in from the outside. As the globalized economy now offers Germans, including Bavarians, such "cool" new experiences as Shiraz from Australia and bourbon from Kentucky, and as these beverages are embraced mostly by the young, beer—the drink of generations past—begins to look more like an "old hat." German beer statistics tell the story: Overall German beer consumption decreased from roughly 114 million hl in 1991—the first year of all-German statistics after the fall of the Berlin Wall—to less than 100 million hl per year in 2010. In Bavaria, the number of breweries dropped from 726 to fewer than 630 during the same period. Wine, by comparison, was able to increase its per-capita consumption by about 10% just during the first decade of the new millennium.

These negative trends left the German brew industry with excess capacity and, because roughly half of Germany's approximately 1,300 breweries (as of 2010) are located in Bavaria, the state naturally suffered the brunt of the fallout. In addition, because the structure of the Bavarian brew industry, much like that of the North American craft brew industry, is fragmented into many small players, few of them have had the resources to ride out a long-term slump. Many breweries that did not close were taken over by larger players. In order to maintain capacity utilization, albeit at a razor-thin margin per unit, many of the very large breweries still operating, such as Oettinger, have been offering a 10-liter case of beer for a consumer price of about four Euros since the start of the millennium. This amounts to between US$4 and US$6 depending on the exchange rate, or about US$1.25 per US six-pack! There is one emerging sign, however, that offers hope for the future of Bavarian beer: Small brewpubs are making a comeback. These are modern, American-style establishments, but with traditional and indigenous beer style portfolios.

In the near term, therefore, Bavaria is likely to experience the same structural adjustments seen in many other mature beer cultures around the globe. While mid-size packaging breweries are struggling, the emerging bifurcation of the industry between big industrial beer-makers, who are getting bigger through mergers, acquisitions, and economies of scale, on the one hand, and small, artisanal beer-makers, who combine tradition and innovation to keep beer interesting, will probably continue. But it remains to be seen if Bavarian beer—artisanal and/or industrial—will be able to retain its hitherto unchallenged status as the people's daily "liquid bread." It is not likely that the answer will be known for a few more decades to come.

See also GERMANY, LAGER, and MUNICH.

Bayerischer Brauerbund (Bavarian Brewers Federation). http://www.bayerisches-bier.de/ (accessed August 10, 2010).

Deutscher Brauer-Bund e.V. (German Brewers Federation). http://www.brauer-bund.de/ (accessed August 10, 2010).

Dornbusch, Horst. *Bavarian helles.* Boulder, CO: Brewers Publications, 2000.

Dornbusch, Horst. *PROST! The story of German beer.* Boulder, CO: Brewers Publications, 1997.

Pohl, Werner. *Bier aus Bayern* (Beer from Bavaria). Grafenau: Morsak-Verlag, 1988.

Horst Dornbusch

Beamish & Crawford is a brewery operating in Cork City, Ireland, from 1792 to 2009, best known for its Beamish stout. In 1792 Protestant butter merchants William Beamish and William Crawford purchased a brewery at Cramer's Lane in Cork City; it had been in production since 1641. The new venture, dubbed the Cork Porter Brewery, focused on the production of porter. Porter, predominantly imported from London breweries, accounted for 25% of the Irish beer market at the time. Beamish & Crawford brewed 12,000 UK barrels of beer in its first year. In 1795 Dublin MP Henry Grattan had the excise tax on beer in Ireland rescinded, ushering in a new period of growth for Irish brewers. By 1807 production at the Cork Porter Brewery had topped 100,000 barrels. Beamish & Crawford remained the largest brewery in Ireland until it was surpassed by Guinness in 1833.

Beamish & Crawford's signature half-timber Counting House was built in the 1920s and is a Cork landmark. The company was sold to Canada's Carling O'Keefe in 1961. In 1987 Australia's Fosters purchased the Carling O'Keefe group, and in 1995 Beamish was sold to Scottish & Newcastle. Scottish & Newcastle was acquired by Heineken in 2008, and the company closed the Beamish Brewery in May 2009. Beamish stout is now produced at Heineken Ireland, formerly Murphy's Brewery in Cork City, on the north side of the city. Annual production of Beamish stout currently totals around 150,000 hl. Beamish stout is a classic example of the Cork-style stout, with chocolate malt flavor more dominant than the roast barley favored by Dublin brewers. It is also notable for its floral hop aroma.

Abram Goldman-Armstrong

beechwood chips, mentioned prominently on Budweiser packaging. About 1400 tons per annum of beechwood chips are used by Anheuser-Busch InBev as a lagering aid in their beers. The "chips" are actually strips or shavings, 3 mm thick and 450 mm long, and have a spiral shape. The three-dimensional form of the chip prevents packing in the bottom of the maturation vessel and allows beer to circulate through the chips. Though the consumer might imagine otherwise, the chips are not meant to flavor the beer. The chips are subjected to an extended period of boiling in sodium bicarbonate prior to use, apparently to remove any vestiges of flavor that they might otherwise impart to the product. Their sole role would therefore appear to be to add a substrate for the carriage of yeast, allowing a greater surface area of yeast to be exposed to the circulating beer than would be the case if the yeast were lying as a packed sediment on the bottom of the vessel. This can aid the lagering process, as beer contact with yeast is critical for the reduction of diacetyl and other off-flavors that remain at the end of active fermentation. The chips are added to the horizontal maturation tank before filling; the beer is then kräusened in the tank and aged for approximately 3 weeks. See KRÄUSENING. The chips are re-used several times in "chip tanks" until they are too degraded for further service.

These chips were, for a long period, produced by Millington's in Tennessee, from US-grown beech. The advent of a more aggressive tendering procedure has since resulted in the company losing the contract and going out of business, although the chips are still produced in the United States.

Prior to 2002 the majority of the chips were sent to landfill but about one third (approximately 400 tons) was composted in that year. According to the Anheuser-Busch InBev website, the chips are composted after use.

Owens, Mike. ksdk.com. "Former supplier of beechwood to A-B says he was kicked to the curb." http://www.ksdk.com/news/local/story.aspx?storyid=173201/ (accessed March 11, 2011).

Chris Holliland

The **Beer Academy** is a UK-based not-for-profit educational body dedicated to helping people understand, appreciate, and enjoy beer sensibly. It was founded in 2003 by a small group of beer enthusiasts at the famous White Horse pub in Parson's Green, London, and it quickly attracted support and start-up funding from brewers large and small, beer retailers, trade associations, and consumer groups. The funding allowed the Beer Academy to establish courses taught by experienced ex-brewers and to publish training and course materials, with the first course starting in early 2004. The courses range from 90-min introductory sessions to half-day, 1-, 2-, and 3-day accredited courses, often tailored to specific client needs, as well as open public sessions held at venues throughout the UK. The students are mostly employees in the beer and brewing industries, as well as consumers and journalists. The Beer Academy also functions as an informed arbiter and authority on such issues as the definition of beer styles, matching beer and food, and beer and health issues. In 2007 the Beer Academy became part of the Institute of Brewing and Distilling.

See also INSTITUTE OF BREWING & DISTILLING (IBD).

The Beer Academy. http://www.beeracademy.co.uk/ (accessed February 16, 2011).

George Philliskirk

beer analyzer is the name given to a range of commercial instruments marketed for their utility in measuring various components of beer (and wort). The best known of these instruments is the SCABA, a system first launched in 1979 that measures specific gravity, alcohol, pH, and color. Thus, the instrument will provide calculated data for Original Extract, Apparent Extract, Spirit Indication, Apparent Fermentation, and Real Fermentation.

Charles W. Bamforth

beer clean is a term that refers to the cleanliness of a vessel used for drinking beer, generally made of glass. Beer clean glassware is critical for the proper presentation and consumption of beer. While all beverages should be served in clean glassware, beer is more sensitive to contaminants than other beverages such as wine or spirits. Any residue of dirt, oil, or soap will affect the taste, aroma, and foaming properties of the beer. Even if a residue cannot be seen, smelled or tasted, it can ruin a beer almost instantly by collapsing the foam. See FOAM. It can also prevent "lacing," the term for foam that clings to the glass in rings as the beer is consumed. See CLING.

A quick sensory evaluation of the glass may reveal if it is beer clean or not. First, the aroma should be evaluated to ensure that no abnormal scents are present. Then the glass can be held up to a bright light to determine if any residue is present in the form of oily smudges, fingerprints, lipstick, and so forth. It is sometimes difficult to determine if glassware is beer clean, as many types of residue are almost invisible. Therefore, several simple observations can be made to decide if a glass is clean enough to showcase a beer.

The easiest observation is to pour beer into a glass and inspect the foam and bubbles. If the bubbles rise to the surface of the liquid and die off quickly, there could be a cleanliness problem. (It should be noted that some beers do not exhibit rich, dense heads of foam, such as light beers and high-alcohol beers.) Additionally, if bubbles are observed forming on the inside surfaces of the glass and rising to the top, then it is likely that dust or a dirty residue is present.

Another important observation can be made while rinsing the inside of the glass. The water should be repelled from the surface of the glass in sheets and not in beads. If beads form, then the glass can be considered unclean. If the water flows off the surface in sheets, the glass is most likely beer clean.

A quick test for beer clean glassware is to rinse the glass and then sprinkle crystalline sugar or salt on the inside of the glass. If the crystals stick to the surface of the glass, then it is clean. If the crystals do not stick, then a residue is present on the surface of the glass. If the glassware is found to be unclean, then it should be rewashed with detergent and hot water and allowed to air-dry on a rack. Spots should not appear when the glass is dry.

Several companies manufacture special detergents that are formulated specifically for cleaning beer glassware. These detergents generally have a high pH and contain a sequestering or chelating agent and are very effective at removing most residues from the surface of glassware. At home, glasses vigorously cleaned with a sponge and dishwashing detergent, then thoroughly rinsed with clean water, should emerge beer clean with little difficulty. See GLASSWARE.

Keith Villa

A **beer engine,** also known as a hand pump, is a uniquely British dispensing device that is specifically appropriate for traditional cask-conditioned ales. The beer engine is a piston pump that allows the casks to be kept in a cooler cellar below the bar and the beer to be pulled or drawn up to the bar. Cask-conditioned beers have lower carbonation than standard beers because they are usually served at about 11°C to 14°C (approximately 52°F to 57°F). If a cask-conditioned ale were served through a standard dispensing system, the gas pressure and colder temperature would increase the carbonation of the beer, which would then lose its ideal balance of flavors. See CASK CONDITIONING. Conversely, dispensing fully carbonated beers with a beer engine would yield relentless foam. A simple gravity tap is suitable for a cask-conditioned ale if the proper cask temperature can be maintained, but a beer engine is imperative if the cask is in a remote location. See GRAVITY DISPENSE.

A version of the beer engine was patented by the prolific British inventor, locksmith, and hydraulic engineer Joseph Bramah in 1797. The modern beer engine has changed little since the early 1800s; it consists of a simple piston attached to a long, sturdy handle. Check valves assure that beer flows only in one direction, up from cask to glass. Traditionally, all beer engine parts were made of brass, but a British law passed around 1990 mandated that all parts in contact with beer henceforth had to be made of plastic or stainless steel. Beer engines are designed to dispense a half or a quarter (Imperial) pint per pull. Proper beer engine installations have some measure of cooling all the way up the beer line and the piston chamber should be insulated. Operating a beer engine in a busy pub is hard physical work, requiring patience, skill, and muscle. Experienced bartenders will switch back and forth between using their right and left arms to pull pints—otherwise they may suffer the so-called barman's bicep, where one arm grows noticeably larger than the other.

See also SWAN NECK.

CAMRA. *Campaign for Real Ale.* http://www.camra.org.uk/ (accessed November 20, 2010).

Brian Hunt

beer gardens are open-air spaces where beer is served at rather simple tables, often under trees. Beer gardens are considered a core element of southern German beer culture, but the concept has been copied and modified to fit into any beer oriented gastronomical environment. While large beer gardens like the ones in Munich only evolved in the 19th century, the roots of the beer garden culture are much older. The oldest legal document regulating taverns in Bavaria was the "Lex Bavariae" dated 1244—it made the innkeeper (owner of a "legitima taberna") a regular profession. It says that no one should drink wine or beer unless in a legalized tavern. The text does not mention if these taverns were allowed to have beer gardens, but old pictures show people dancing and drinking outside, so most probably it was a custom to drink in the garden. Before these regulations were established in medieval cities noble guests and officers would be invited into a burgher's home (which preceded the more professional taverns of later times) to have food and drink but lower ranking people would be served jugs of beer outside—and be encouraged to bring their own food. Up until today it is a custom in

Ayinger Brewery's Liebhard beer garden in Bavaria, Germany. BRAUEREI AYING FRANZ INSELKAMMER

many Bavarian beer gardens to bring food and even a personalized beer stein to a beer garden.

Many medieval towns were granted the right to brew beer, which actually meant that they could sell the beer that was brewed by the town patricians (burghers who owned a house made of stone and had some right to vote on a city level). This gave a boost to the development of a—albeit small-scale—brewing industry that developed the beer styles that became typical for the town. These brewers (some, but not all of them licensed inn-keepers) soon began to build cellars on the outskirts of their cities to store and mature their brews. These cellars were a core element in the development of lager beer—if they were cold enough, bottom-fermenting yeasts would grow there. By the 17th and 18th centuries some of these cellars had gained some popularity especially among students because there was always fresh and cool beer at hand. To keep theses cellars cool, brewers would plant tree varieties featuring large masses of leaves (preferably water chestnut) that could substantially lower the surrounding temperature by evaporating water through their leaves. These trees would also provide shadow for those sitting "auf dem Keller" ("atop of the cellar") where the brewer was allowed to sell his beer (but again no full meals). Later brewers were also allowed to accommodate guests indoors; therefore, some beer gardens have adjacent beer halls featuring similarly simple furniture and the same limited offer of drinks (beer and not much else) and food that can be found outside year long. Notable examples are the Löwenkeller and the Augustiner Keller in Munich.

Munich's beer gardens became extremely popular in the 19th century. Breweries grew in size—and so did their gardens. Today the largest beer garden in the world is the Hirschgarten in Munich seating 8,000 guests (1,200 in a serviced area with full food service; the rest is self-service) with a choice of beers brewed by Augustiner, Herzogliches Brauhaus Tegernsee, and Schloßbrauerei Kaltenberg. However, its fame is challenged by the slightly smaller beer garden around the Chinese tower in Englischer Garten serving Hofbräuhaus-beers. Both gardens were formerly owned by the royal family of Bavaria and opened to the public in the last years of the 18th century.

During the 19th century the concept of the beer garden was exported to other regions of Europe and in fact the whole world—often along with beer from Bavaria. Bavarian style dark lager was the typical product to be found there at the time. In large capital cities like Berlin and Vienna these gardens were often the venue for concerts of military bands and some masterpieces of classical music (including many waltzes by Johann Strauss) were first performed in front of a beer drinking audience in these popular gardens.

By the middle of the century the beer garden hit America. Stanley Baron writes in his book *Brewed in America* that German style beer gardens were popular in San Antonio, Texas, where one-third of the population was German (which includes some immigration from Austria and Bohemia) in 1856. For New York City Baron records: "The Bowery in New York City became particularly famous for a number of beer gardens that were established on that street in the 1860s . . . These beer-gardens are generally spoken of approvingly, because they provided entertainment for simple hard-working families, and offered a wholesome antidote to the corrupt and licentious gin-dives or dancing parlors that were also current in New York and other cities. At the beer-gardens entrance was free." Baron quotes Edvard Winslow Martin (pseudonym of James Dabney McCable) who wrote in his book *The Secrets of the Great City* (1868): "Beer and other liquids are served out at a small cost . . . The music is a great attraction to the Germans. It is exquisite in some places, especially in the Atlantic Garden, which is situated in the Bowery, near Canal Street." The Atlantic Garden was on the eastern side of the Bowery in the block south of Canal Street, closer to Bayard St, in the same block where the Thalia and the Windsor Theatres were. Today this is where the Manhattan Bridge ends. The area east of the Bowery and north of Division was known as "Kleindeutschland" ("Little Germany") until the 1870s. In 1871 *Harper's Monthly* wrote a piece on the Atlantic Garden: "On every side there are family groups, father, mother, and children, all merry, all sociable, all well-behaved and quiet. There is not the remotest danger of insult or disturbance, or need of the presence of any policeman."

After the end of prohibition the beer garden became an all-American institution, made popular again by the famous song "Roll Out The Barrel" (a composition by Czech composer Jaromir Vejvoda originally titled "Modřanská polka" and later "Škoda lásky" which means "Wasted Love") performed by the Andrews Sisters. The same tune is played in beer gardens back in Germany with a different text and title called "Rosamunde." Today, the beer garden is making a comeback in many areas of the United States. In New York City, the Bohemian Hall in Astoria Queens, the city's only surviving old beer garden, is once again bustling. It was built in 1910 and on warm days still seats thousands of people under soaring old trees.

Baron, Stanley. *Brewed in America*. Boston: Little, Brown, and Company, 1962.
Homberger, Eric. *The historical atlas of New York City*. New York: Holt, 1998.
Rauers, Friedrich. *Kulturgeschichte der Gaststätte*. Berlin: Alfred Metzler Verlag, 1941.

Conrad Seidl

beer gods. Benjamin Franklin supposedly once said, "Beer is our best proof that God loves us and wants us to be happy." The quote is likely apocryphal, but the sentiment is surely nothing new. Throughout the millennia, as mankind gave thanks for the miracle they felt beer to be, they gave thanks to various gods they credited with the gift. These ancient deities were often associated with drinking, agriculture, and harvest as well as, on occasion, with merriment and festivities. Look closely into most ancient cultures, and you will find gods and goddesses of beer.

Perhaps primary among them was Ninkasi, the ancient Sumerian goddess of brewing who not only gave beer to the world but also was brewer to the gods themselves. She is of particular importance not only because she is female but also because she appears around 4000 BC, making her the oldest of the beer deities. Also female and credited with the invention of beer is the Zulu goddess Mbaba Mwana Waresa who, like many other deities related to beer, is also the goddess of agriculture and harvest. Her legend also includes a search for romance and true love on earth and in combination with beer, this made her beloved among the Zulu. Yasigi is another important African female deity who looks after beer, dancing, and masks, a combination that makes her sound very festive.

The Egyptian god Osiris is said to have led his people away from cannibalism and toward farming, and although this made him the god of agriculture, he is also seen demonstrating how to brew beer. After Osiris' death at the hands of his brother—who intoxicates him with beer before their duel—he is resurrected and assumes the dual role of god of the underworld. He is usually described as wearing green, which represents the life cycle, along with a crown; however, he is dressed as a mummy and is nourished through offerings of beer. Before his reanimation, the brewing grains emmer and barley are supposed to have sprung from his body as a gift to humankind.

In later centuries, Europeans credited the gods with the gift of beer as well. Raugaptais and Raugutiene, part of Baltic and Slavic mythological pantheon, were a god and goddess partnership specifically devoted to fermentation and beer, respectively. Not surprisingly, they are both described as being very attractive. From Czech tradition comes Radegast, who in addition to being the god of hospitality, is also said to have created beer, which presumably helped him in his duties. Apparently hospitality is hard work, because the famous statue of Radegast in the Czech Beskydy Mountains depicts him as a strong, tall, and powerful figure. Aegir, a Norse god who is probably best known for his role as king of the sea, is also credited with beer and brewing. He was known for throwing frequent parties for the other gods, where his guests were plied with copious amounts of strong beer.

Jai Kharbanda

The **Beer Judge Certification Program (BJCP)** is a US-based organization that certifies beer judges and sanctions beer competitions. It was founded in 1985 by the American Homebrewers Association in collaboration with the Home Wine and Beer Trade Association. Although the BJCP has been an independent organization since April 1995, its officers still collaborate with the American Homebrewers Association on various projects.

The BJCP is perhaps best known for its Style Guidelines, which break down beer into approximately 80 distinct styles and substyles. These guidelines were originally written by a BJCP committee, which has updated them several times. The BJCP Style Guidelines provide a detailed description for each listed beer substyle, as well as for various kinds of mead. They contain an explanation of the appropriate aroma, appearance, flavor, mouthfeel, and overall impression for each substyle and provide a number of measurable parameters, including bitterness color and alcoholic strength. The guidelines also name commercial examples of beers that exemplify each style. The BJCP Style Guidelines are used as reference tools by both brewers and beer judges. They are available on the BJCP website along with a large number of other judging and competition resources.

The website also contains information for those interested in completing the exam to become a BJCP Judge. The BJCP exam is written and combines short-answer questions, essay questions, and a tasting component. A BJCP Study Guide is available online to assist candidates in preparing for this exam. The website also provides a list of upcoming exams, which can be held anywhere that qualified BJCP members are available to administer and proctor the exam.

There are different certification levels that can be achieved within the BJCP. The basic levels are Recognized, Certified, National, Master, and Grand Master. Advancing from one level to the next requires a minimum grade on the BJCP exam, as well as a certain number of experience points, which are earned by judging competitions and by volunteering to assist with BJCP administration. There are currently more than 3,400 beer judges registered with the BJCP. Fewer than 40 people have accumulated the many years of experience and service required to reach the rank of Grand Master.

Hundreds of beer competitions are sanctioned by the BJCP every year and the number is steadily increasing. These competitions are run according to strict guidelines outlined in the BJCP Sanctioned Competition Handbook. The beers submitted must be judged against the Style Guidelines, and they must be judged blind. Although the BJCP was originally conceived to provide judges for homebrew competitions, since 2001 the organization has also sanctioned and supplied judges for an increasing number of commercial competitions. These include the Great American Beer Festival and the World Beer Cup, in which thousands of professionally brewed beers are entered and judged.

Beer Judge Certification Program. http://www.bjcp.org/

Mirella G. Amato

Beer Orders were introduced in the UK following a report in 1989 by the Monopolies and Mergers Commission (a UK government agency) on the supply of beer. They sought to widen consumer choice in pubs by restricting the number of pubs owned by the six largest brewery companies (Allied, Bass, Grand Metropolitan, Imperial, Scottish and Newcastle, and Whitbread) that accounted for 75% of British beer production, and to allow their tenants to sell one brand of cask-conditioned beer not produced by them. This was known as the guest beer provision. They also removed the tie on non-beer drinks. The orders were intended to increase competition in brewing, wholesaling, and retailing.

Various amalgamations took place in an attempt to bypass the effect of the orders and several large pub-owning but non-brewing companies, known as pubcos, such as Punch Group, Normura, and Enterprise Inns were created as well as many smaller ones. Alongside this came a significant increase in the number of small independent breweries created to take advantage of the freeing up of the retail market.

After 10 years the Office of Fair Trading made an examination to determine whether the orders were still relevant and declared against their usefulness. None of the so-called big six brewing companies existed in their original form and consequently most of the orders were repealed. The government view was that the brewing industry had markedly changed and the orders had served their purpose. As they stood they were pointless regulations. The beer orders were finally revoked in 2003.

See also TIED HOUSE SYSTEM.

Barrie Pepper

beer spoilers are microorganisms that can change the flavor, aroma, or appearance of beer in a manner deemed undesirable by the brewer. Although there is some overlap, brewers seek to divide spoilage organisms into the categories of "beer spoilers" and "wort spoilers," with the latter largely inhibited by alcohol, pH, and/or the anaerobic environment created by yeast fermentation. Spoilage organisms are mostly limited to about 40 species of yeast and about 50 of bacteria.

A purist might argue that any organism beside a pure yeast culture would be a spoilage organism. Another perspective, possibly more lambic-tinged, could easily find over a dozen other bacteria and yeasts that would give desirable qualities when grown in some beers. Many brewers, especially craft brewers in the United States, are now welcoming a larger range of microflora. Therefore, the concept of "spoilage" is very much based on the wishes and expectations of the brewer and consumer. See LAMBIC BEERS and SOUR BEERS. By making sweet wort, the brewer is purposefully creating the ideal food source for the brewery's yeast. It is an excellent meal for many other creatures as well. Although perhaps 80% of all yeast and bacteria would eat the sugars in wort, brewers limit the potential spoilers in many ways, starting with the pH, temperature, and nutrition of the wort. Boiling the wort sterilizes it and allows the brewer to introduce the desired inoculation; the brewer starts with a blank slate from a microbiological standpoint. This is a contrast to traditional winemaking, where any organism on the skin of the grape would remain alive and eventually ferment the wine, with the winemaker seeking to encourage some organisms and discourage others. In both beverages, fermentation lowers the pH and creates alcohol, two developments that some spoilage organisms will not survive.

The organisms that do survive can wreak considerable havoc in finished beer. The simplest symptoms of spoilage contamination are haze in the beer or muddled, "unclean" flavors. Furthermore, off-flavors such as buttery (diacetyl), vegetable (dimethyl sulfide), sulfurous, medicinal (phenols), and even putrid (butyric acid) can be formed. Beers may become soured by lactic acid bacteria consuming starches or sugars and creating lactic acid or by acetic acid bacteria combining oxygen with alcohol to produce acetic acid.

See also BACTERIA, DIACETYL, OFF-FLAVORS, QUALITY CONTROL AND ASSURANCE, and WILD YEAST.

Priest, F. G. *Brewing microbiology*, 3rd ed. New York: Kluwer Academic/Plenum Press, 2003.

Brian Hunt

beer stone

See CALCIUM OXALATE.

Trade card, c. 1870, for the Feigenspan Brewery Company in Newark, New Jersey, highlighting its numerous beer styles and local appeal: the logo "P.O.N." stands for "Pride of Newark." PIKE MICROBREWERY MUSEUM, SEATTLE, WA

***Beer Street* (by William Hogarth)** is an etching published as a print in February 1751. It idealistically contrasts the wholesomeness of beer drinking with the degradation that results from unbridled gin drinking as depicted in the artist's companion piece, *Gin Lane*. Deregulation of the production and sale of spirits led to excessive consumption of gin in London between the 1720s and the 1750s. *Beer Street* and *Gin Lane* together represent a morality tale aimed at the lower classes who were considered to be the main offenders. Starvation, infanticide, squalor, despair, and madness stalk Gin Lane with a shocking central image of a bare-breasted woman, sodden with gin, unknowingly spilling a child from her arms so that he tumbles to the ground. These images are contrasted with the thriving commerce, healthy industrious populace, and general bonhomie of *Beer Street*. Both prints show drinking, but in *Gin Lane* it is instead of working, whilst in *Beer Street* it is the well-earned relaxation of workers with the tools of their trade around them enjoying foaming tankards of ale. Only the pawnbroker suffers in *Beer Street*. As the prints sold for one shilling (5p) each, they would have been beyond the pocket of the poorest, but they were widely displayed and were snapped up by the voting classes. A few months after the prints appeared the Gin Act was passed, increasing the price of gin and restricting its availability. The "gin craze," which was already on the wane, subsided—a rare case of art influencing public opinion and legislation.

See also BEER IN ART.

Lander, Dorothy A. "Art as temperance activism." In *Alcohol and temperance in modern history: An international encyclopaedia*, ed. Jack S. Blocker, Jr., David M. Fahey, and Ian R. Tyrrell, 64–72. Santa Barbara, CA: ABC Clio, 2003.

Ray Anderson

beer style, a much-debated concept of critical importance to both the brewer and the consumer, but often misunderstood by those who have benefited most from its influence. Beer style is, at its base, the codification of all parameters that group particular beers together, such that they can be recognized, replicated, discussed, and understood.

Humans instinctively crave patterns and differentiations. We want to know whether a particular animal is a deer or an antelope, whether Pluto is a planet or just a big rock, whether Japanese sake is to be called a "beer" or a "wine" or perhaps sits apart from each of these.

For thousands of years, cultures all over the world have always differentiated types of beer, just as they have differentiated other types of food. The modern concept of beer style is sometimes compared with taxonomy, where all the world's living things are grouped by kingdom, phylum, class, order, family, genus, and, finally, species. This describes the natural world, and the things that it describes can be considered objectively true, even if one disagrees with the groupings.

Beer, of course, is man-made and therefore subjective. To speak of beer style, then, is more akin to speaking of a type of food—such as hollandaise sauce. As any chef or culinary student knows, hollandaise sauce is an emulsion of egg yolks and butter, usually flavored with lemon juice and some type of pepper. It is mildly tangy, has a pale yellow color, and is completely opaque, with no lumps or traces of oil. If one adds tarragon, or curry powder, or mint, or orange zest, or tomato puree to hollandaise sauce, it may be transformed into sauce béarnaise, sauce café de Paris, sauce Paloise, sauce Choron, or sauce Maltaise. One can argue, successfully, that hollandaise sauce was not always what it is today, but as a result of this "food taxonomy," chefs, cooks, and consumers are able to use a common language to describe food.

This, then, is the true basis of beer style. A beer's style will encompass its color, its level of carbonation, aroma, aspects of its flavor, the brewing technique used to make it, and the often-rich history from which it derives. When someone mentions "German pilsner," then, we know that the color is clear and golden, the carbonation is moderately high, the aroma is fresh and floral with bready notes of malt and perhaps a whiff of sulfur, the bitterness is snappy, the palate is dry, and the beer had a cold fermentation by a lager yeast strain and emerged at about 5% alcohol by volume. We also know that it was essentially invented in the city of Pilsen in Czech Bohemia by a Bavarian brewmaster in 1842 and has formed the foundation for most of the beer consumed in the world today.

From one word, then—pilsner—the brewer and consumer can derive a huge amount of information. The world of wine, variously broken as it is into classifications, regions, grapes, wine types, etc, remains a mystery to many people. When a wine label says "Barolo," what does this mean? Barolo is a type of wine, but to understand it, you need to know that it is named after the town of Barolo and that it is grown in five towns in Piemonte, Italy, from the nebbiolo grape; there is no Barolo grape. When the label says "Barbera," on the other hand, we need to know that barbera is a grape, not a place, and Barbera can be grown anywhere. "Champagne" is a place and a technique of wine-making; all Champagnes have some things in common, and this approaches the idea of style. Sauternes are even more so, because it is grown in one place, is always sweet, is always golden, can be made from three grape varieties, is affected by botrytis, etc.

Although we tend to imagine that the modern concept of beer style is itself ancient, it is not. In fact, it is not even old, having been essentially invented out of whole cloth by the late beer writer Michael Jackson in his seminal 1977 book *The World Guide to Beer*. See JACKSON, MICHAEL. Although Jackson mined the work of earlier writers such as Jean De Clerck to form his concepts, the term "beer style" appears to be solely his invention, and other beer writers have searched in vain for earlier uses of it. See DE CLERCK, JEAN. Whereas some beer styles, such as pilsner, porter, tripel, dubbel, and Weissbier clearly already existed and were well understood when Jackson arrived on the scene, others were disparate threads of a cloth that Jackson wove together. When he saw a number of similar russet-colored sour beers in West Flanders, Belgium, sharing a common set of flavors, aromas, brewing techniques, and yeast strains, he grouped them together into a style he called "Flemish Red"—something the Flemish themselves had never heard of.

Germany, especially through its intricate tax laws, had already codified many beer styles, at least in some fashion. But many other countries had no such tradition, and Jackson applied his new taxonomy widely, particularly in unruly Belgium, and created a system by which beer flavor, beer culture, and beer history could be understood by ordinary people. Building on Jackson's work and earlier work of his own, beer writer Fred Eckhardt self-published the influential book *The Essentials of Beer Style* in 1989. See ECKHARDT, FRED. Along with Jackson's works, Eckhardt's book had a large effect on his fellow homebrewers and on the budding American craft brewing movement that was growing out of the homebrewing culture. In 1985 the American Homebrewers Association spawned the Beer Judge Certification Program (BJCP), which was designed to provide trained judges to preside over homebrewing competitions. The BJCP latched onto Jackson's and then later Eckhardt's style designations and built from them a codified beer taxonomy that now informs the judging of commercial beers at the Great American Beer Festival (GABF), the World Beer Cup, and many other competitions around the world. As of 2010, the competition guidelines of the GABF recognized 78 individual beers styles in addition to dozens of subcategories. See BEER JUDGE CERTIFICATION PROGRAM (BJCP), GREAT AMERICAN BEER FESTIVAL, and WORLD BEER CUP.

Scarcely more than 3 decades later, the idea of "beer style" is well rooted in popular culture. All beer publications written in English use the term, as do most written in other languages. When non-specialized media refer to beer, and particularly to traditional European or craft beers, beer style is almost always invoked. Brewing schools, cooking schools, and sommelier programs all base many of their teachings upon the idea of beer style.

Inevitably, however, there is a backlash against the very idea of beer style. Some beer historians point out, entirely correctly, that many beer styles have changed over time, some of them so much that they would probably now be unrecognizable to their own progenitors. Modern beer styles, they say, are merely a snapshot of time within the evolution of a culture and are therefore unreliable and unworthy of codification. Some rather grumpy older traditionalists grumble that when they were young, there were not "all these styles—there was just beer." Many younger beer enthusiasts and brewers see the concept of beer style as a straitjacket, a construct that seeks to blunt the sharp edges of creativity by taming something that ought to live freely in the world. Like many artists, they bristle at attempts to define them and their work, preferring to let the work stand on its own and speak for itself, preferably quite loudly. The blogosphere is alight with talk of "style Nazis," scheming ultraconservatives who seek to prevent valiant brewers from making the beers they want to make.

As the debate rages on, however, perhaps it best to consider the consumer. Now faced with a vast and glorious range of beer, the modern beer consumer faces a dizzying jumble of bottles, taps, and labels, all vying for attention. Someone who is looking for a bright, bitter, hoppy pale beer might decide to look for an India pale ale (IPA). Someone looking for a softer, effervescent, fruity beer well suited to brunch dishes might reach for a Belgian Witbier. Another consumer searching for an after-dinner beer to enjoy in front of his fireplace might decide upon an imperial stout. Without beer style, there is no nomenclature, and without nomenclature the brewer has a hard time conveying to the consumer much idea of what is actually in the bottle. And when brewers misuse the names of existing beer styles, the consumer can be confused, or worse, think that beer is a drink without any history or background. As brewers create new styles, therefore, it is to be hoped that they will coin new names to accompany them. How to explain beer to the novice, when some brewers speak of Black IPA? People know what Champagne is because the word Champagne *actually means something*. Winemakers can make whatever wines they wish, but Champagne is *never* going to be a red wine. This is not a restriction upon creative winemaking—it is a simple but important matter of nomenclature. Like makers of non-Champagne sparkling wines who claim that their misuse of the word "Champagne" is a form of "shorthand," some brewers will claim the same for their "hefeweizen" with no Bavarian weizen yeast character.

Ironically, those who rail against beer styles seem not to have noticed that creativity is based upon memory. Bloom's Taxonomy, the influential construct used for everything from business training to education, shows a pyramid with "Knowledge and Remembering" at the bottom, with "Understanding," Describing," and "Explaining" above, and the ultimate goal of "Creativity" at the peak. Understanding this, it can be no wonder that the country that took up Michael Jackson's style guidelines with such fervor is also the country that has developed what is arguably the most dynamic, creative, and increasingly influential beer culture in the world—the United States. The great musician does not resent the sheet music, the great baker does not resent the baguette, and the best wine garagistes do not resent classical Bordeaux. Beer styles are simply forms, structures, and collective memory, in other words, a place to start. Art does not spring solely from itself, devoid of a past. For the brewer, far from being a straitjacket, the concept of beer style defines the places in which modern brewers will set up their own springboards of creativity. For the consumer, beer style is an illuminating lamp upon the flavors, histories, and cultures behind all these bottles that beckon so alluringly from the shelf.

Garrett Oliver

beer weeks are a recent phenomenon, primarily in the US, where restaurants, bars, and other institutions in a city or region host a large variety of different beer-themed events over multiple days. As seems appropriate for a "beer week," the festivities often last longer than 7 days, with 10 days the apparent norm. The stated goal of most beer weeks is to showcase the local beer scene, increase tourism, and introduce beer in new and different ways to both the neophyte and seasoned beer lover alike. These usually include not just traditional beer festivals but also beer dinners, specific food and beer pairing events (such as cheese, chocolate, charcuterie, etc.), and many other innovative events that display beer in new ways. The 2010 New York City Beer Week featured dozens of dinners at many of the city's best restaurants and even an India pale ale tasting aboard a full-rigged 165-ft clipper ship.

The first typical modern version of a beer week is Philly Beer Week, which debuted in March of 2008. Originally inspired by beer writer Michael Jackson's events for an earlier "food week" called The Book and the Cook, the original Philly Beer Week spanned around 375 events over 10 days. Now permanently moved to early June, the granddaddy of beer weeks comprised over 900 events in 2010.

In addition to Philadelphia, established beer weeks are held in the San Francisco Bay Area (February), Seattle (May), Ohio (July), New York (September), Baltimore (October), and San Diego (November). There are now nearly 40 beer weeks, taking place in communities such as Alaska, Boston, Charlotte, Denver, Los Angeles, Milwaukee, Sacramento, and Washington, D.C.

Jay R. Brooks

beer writing is an occupation where a journalist or author's primary area of expertise involves writing about beer, brewing, and related topics. Although the number of full-time beer writers is growing as interest in beer increases, the number remains relatively small compared with many other similar fields, such as wine writing or food writing. Many beer writers also cover related topics or other alcoholic beverages such as wine, spirits, or cocktails. Others write part-time while working at an entirely different job, although sometimes within the beer industry.

British writer Michael Jackson is generally credited with creating the profession of beer writer when he began writing exclusively about beer and whiskey in the mid-1970s. See JACKSON, MICHAEL.

In the UK, the British Guild of Beer Writers was founded in 1988 as a trade association "to improve standards of beer writing and extend the public knowledge of beer" and includes, in addition to writers, photographers, illustrators, broadcasters, and people working in public relations. Currently, the British Guild of Beer Writers has over 150 members.

In the United States, the North American Guild of Beer Writers was active through the 1990s but ceased operations before 2000 because of a decline in the number of beer publications paralleling a drop in the craft beer industry during the same period of time. As of the close of 2010, several North American beer writers were making plans to launch a new Beer Writers Guild. In the meantime, as within other areas of writing, beer writing online has proliferated.

As the craft beer industry rebounded beginning in the late 1990s, so too did the number of magazines devoted to covering beer. Today there are more beer magazines, both trade and consumer publications, than at any time prior, offering increased opportunities for writers whose expertise includes beer. Some of the most popular beer magazines in the US include *All About Beer, BeerAdvocate, Beer Connoisseur, Beer Magazine, Beer West* (covering the American west coast), the *Celebrator Beer News*, and *DRAFT*. The Brewing News produces seven regional beer newsprint publications and the Ale Street News publishes one nationwide, with additional inserts in select regions. In addition, there are magazines devoted to all beverages, including beer, such as *Imbibe* and *Mutineer*. Homebrewing periodicals include *Brew Your Own* and *Zymurgy*, which is published by the Brewers Association.

Likewise, a renewed interest in beer has also created an increased demand for books on the subject, and in the past decade the number of beer books has grown exponentially, with perhaps more in print today than at any time in history.

Beer books examine the topic from a variety of angles, including the tried and true traditional subjects like brewing textbooks and related technical literature, guidebooks, histories, and breweriana. But many new subgenres have risen in popularity, such as books on beer appreciation, brewer memoirs, homebrewing, cookbooks, and books on food and beer pairings.

Michael Jackson's *World Guide to Beer* (1977; updated 1991) and his later *Beer Companion* (1993; updated 1997) were two of the most influential early books on beer and set the standard for later offerings.

Homebrewing is the most popular type of beer book, with Charlie's Papazian's *The Joy of Homebrewing* having seen three additions, 25 reprintings, and nearly a million copies sold.

Despite the up-to-the-minute information on the Internet, guidebooks to microbreweries and beer travel continue to be popular, with several publishers even expanding their series of guides to breweries within a particular state.

In the past few years, books educating readers on beer appreciation are feeding the public's appetite for knowledge about the intricacies of enjoying beer. A few notable examples include Randy Mosher's *Tasting Beer* (2009), *The Naked Pint* (2009), by Christina Perozzi and Hallie Beaune, and two by University of California Davis professor of fermentation studies Charlie Bamforth, *Beer Is Proof That God Loves Us* (2010) and *Grape vs. Grain* (2008).

Garrett Oliver's 2003 book, *The Brewmaster's Table*, although not the first book on food and beer, sparked a resurgence on the subject, leading to renewed interest in beer and food, both for pairing the two and for cooking with it.

More recently, writing about beer has expanded online, and the number of beer blogs has exploded, written by both professional writers creating an online presence for themselves and amateur beer bloggers launching writing careers through their work online. There are estimated to be more than 700 blogs devoted to beer, many with large followings. In the fall of 2010, the first Beer Bloggers Conference was held in Boulder, Colorado, with just over 100 beer bloggers in attendance, with both a US and a UK conference scheduled for subsequent years.

Jay R. Brooks

Belgian brewing degrees are an obsolete calculation of the gravity of beer stipulated by Belgian law for the payment of taxes. It was developed as a practical way to analyze both regular and acidic (lambic and other sour style) beers, as the presence of acid led to errors in other methods.

Belgian brewing degrees were calculated after performing three analyses on the beer. First, the residual extract (n) of the beer was measured by distilling off the alcohol and analyzing the weight of the residual material left in the liquid. Using the standardized Doemens–Plato conversion table, this was converted to degrees Plato. See PLATO GRAVITY SCALE. Second, percent alcohol by weight (A) was measured by analyzing the specific gravity of the distilled alcohol from the beer sample. Using a standardized alcohol conversion table, the amount of alcohol in a 100-gram sample was determined. Third, the acidity or volatile acid content (c) of the beer was measured using standard titration techniques with alkali. Knowing n, A, and c, the original gravity (p) of the beer being analyzed was calculated as:

$$p = n + 2A + 1.5c$$

The original gravity obtained was converted to specific gravity by means of a Doemens–Plato conversion table. The factor 0.0013 was then subtracted. Finally, Belgian brewing degrees were obtained from the second decimal place of the resulting number. For example, if the final number calculated was 1.0641, the official Belgian brewing degrees would be 6.41. Tax and beer classifications were then based on this number.

Until the early 1990s, many Belgian breweries still used the Belgian gravity scale, but it has largely fallen out of favor with the Plato scale's increasing prevalence. There are a number of Belgian beers, however, that are still named after their original gravities expressed in Belgian degrees, for example, Rochefort 6, 8, and 10.

See also TAXES.

Keith Villa

Belgian red ale is a specialty of the northwestern province of Belgium, West Flanders. The beer is characterized by a red to brown hue and a balanced but assertive acidity. The fermentation process is typically done through a mixed fermentation of yeast and lactobacilli, followed by a long aging on oak barrels. This brewing and fermentation process is closely related to that of the Belgian sour brown ales, and although English speakers now differentiate the two styles, the Belgians do not; they use the term "sour brown beer" for both.

Belgian red ales are regional session beers with alcohol contents hovering around 5% alcohol by volume and show a mild refreshing tartness. The Rodenbach Brewery of Roeselare has long been the anchor of this category of beer. See RODENBACH. In the early 1870s Eugene Rodenbach did an apprenticeship in a brewery in England and came back with a process that was very close to what Obadiah Poundage described as the origin of porter beer. Fresh beer was blended in the pub—and later in the brewery—with beer that had been aged for 2 years on oak barrels and acquired a distinctive sour complexity. See PORTER.

The Rodenbach Brewery makes two different brews. Both brews are made from a base Munich malt of around 9 European Brewery Convention (4.5 standard reference method), some caramel malts, corn grits, and spices. They are lightly hopped for a bitterness of around 12–20 international bittering units in the beginning of the boil. The heavier beer, with an original gravity of around 13° Plato, goes through a week-long mixed lactobacilli–yeast fermentation. The settled yeast is removed and the beer goes through a primary aging of 6 to 8 weeks in horizontal tanks at around 15°C (59°F) to settle the remaining yeast and develop the lactic acid anaerobically. The secondary aging follows with 18 to 24 months in vertical oak vats, each holding between 100 and 660 hl (85 to 560 bbls). The beer microbiology develops mainly lactic acid, acetic acid, and the ethanol esters of those acids, ethyl lactate and ethyl acetate. The wood is porous and cannot be sterilized, so the microbiology is different from barrel to barrel, containing Saccharomyces and Brettanomyces yeast and lactic and acetic acid bacteria. A sturdy pellicle (skin) forms on top of the beer, bound by filamentous yeasts. After the secondary aging in oak, the beer used to be bottled straight as Rodenbach Grand Cru. Today, the assertive sourness of the Grand Cru has been cut down by dilution with a lighter blending beer. The lighter blend beer is brewed at 11.5° Plato with the same weeklong mixed fermentation, followed by an aging for 4 to 6 weeks in stainless steel metal tanks to further develop some lactic sourness. The lighter brew blended at higher proportions to the wood-aged beer leads to a very drinkable, thirst-quenching red-brown ale, simply called Rodenbach.

At one time, the Rodenbach Brewery used to sell its yeast to breweries within a 50-km (30-mile) radius of Roeselare, and these breweries made their own Belgian red, sour brown, or other beers with it. Sharing yeast has been very common in breweries in Europe. The mixed yeast slurry was used for mixed fermentation in Ichtegems from the Strubbe Brewery, Liefmans and Goudenband from the Liefmans Brewery, Oerbier from the Dolle Brouwers, Vichtenaar and Duchesse the Bourgogne from Verhaeghe Brewery, Felix from Brouwerij Clarysse, and Damy Brewery in Olsene. Some breweries used this yeast also for bottle conditioning or even to ferment a Tripel with it, as in the Guldenbergs Brewery. Regional and family politics led to some breweries maintaining their own processes, such as the Bockor, Bavik, and Van Honsenbrouck breweries focusing on a regular main fermentation with a long aging on wood afterward leading to beers like Bellegems Bruin, Petrus, and Bacchus.

Rodenbach stopped distributing their yeast in 1999, leading to no small resentment and resulting in new fermentation strategies at the surrounding breweries. Brewers had relied on long-established processes within their own breweries that were based upon symbiosis with Rodenbach, but now they faced a challenge as their yeast supply vanished. Breweries like Liefmans started to maintain their own mixed fermentations. Strubbe Brewery changed to wood aging to make the Ichtegemse Grand Cru. The Dolle Brouwers puts part of the beer through a souring fermentation in a separate tank.

When traditionally brewed, the sour red beer style is complex, balancing a backbone of lactic acidity with sherry-like fruit notes. The best of them can be very elegant and wonderful with food. Rodenbach and other sour beer brewers have struggled to transition from being strong local brands to players on a larger stage. The segment has always been a minor but relevant part of the Belgian beer scene. See BELGIUM. Red ales are exported worldwide as unique specialties but have gained a foothold in the United States with the growth of the craft brewing industry.

It now seems that Belgian red ales will develop niche markets where creative brewers are active. Sour beers are late to arrive in a developing craft beer market as we see in the United States, Italy, and, to a lesser degree, France, Canada, Japan, and a few other countries. In the United States in particular, they have helped, along with lambics, to spark an entire new category of sour beers. The endeavor to work with microorganisms other than yeast is always a risky step for a brewery; it involves intentionally culturing microbes that most breweries do their best to eradicate. However, the production of such beers is a creative outlet for brewers who have explored the classic sour styles and wish to attempt new and interesting iterations within the genre.

De Bruyne, Michiel. *De Rodenbachs van Roeselare*, 218–25. Roeselare: Belgium: Edicon BVBA, 1986.

Poundage, Obadiah. Letter. *London Chronicle*, November 4, 1760.

Peter Bouckaert

Belgium is to beer what Cuba is to cigars and France is to wine. The Belgians, a tough prickly people with a sense of history that comes from Belgium's position wedged between former rivals France, Germany, and the Netherlands for centuries, have held onto a greater range of their ancient brewing traditions than any other country in the world. As keepers of a certain cultural flame, Belgian beers have in recent decades provided inspiration to thousands of brewers the world over. The Belgian brewers, proud of their beers but vaguely bemused by foreign attentions, remain idiosyncratic and independent, not least of each other.

In 1579 Hainaut, Artois, and Douai, three Catholic provinces of the southern Netherlands, sought independence from the Protestant north and went in search of a protector. The Spanish king Phillip II stepped forward, offering them administrative freedom and a stringent defense of the faith. Now known as the Spanish Netherlands, the province plotted a difficult course between its neighbors, with constant warfare along its southern border with France. A battleground during the War of the Spanish Succession, the Spanish Netherlands was handed to the Austrian Habsburg dynasty in 1714. Such peace as this brought was not to last for long because the War of the Austrian Succession saw France invade the province in 1745, finally coughing it up in 1748. Instigated by the French revolution, an uprising drove the Austrians out in 1789, setting up 5 years of war in which the possession of the province shifted constantly. In 1795, fledgling Belgium became part of France and in 1815 was folded into the Kingdom of the Netherlands. This arrangement was not to last either. Tension was constant between the Dutch-speaking north and the French-speaking south, with southern Catholics in particular bristling under the rule of the Dutch Protestant King William I. In 1830 Belgium revolted and gained independence under the Saxe-Coburg king Leopold in 1831.

In the following years, the monasteries that had been sacked and burned during the French revolution reopened and built their breweries, although they were not to become famous for many years. Many breweries produced styles of beer based upon oats and wheat as well as barley malt. Some were very sweet, some dry, some intentionally sour, and others unintentionally so. Almost all remained top-fermented. English pale ales, and then Czech and German pilsners influenced the creation of new beers in the early 1900s, when cheap foreign imports flooded the Belgian market.

World War I brought the German army, who stripped out all the brewing equipment they could find for its valuable copper, and many breweries never reopened. But after the war, Belgian beer began to bounce back. In 1919, a new law banned the sale of distilled spirits in bars and cafes, a rule that was not rescinded until 1984. Brewers strengthened their beers to meet the demand for more robust drinks. While retaining relatively lighter beers for themselves, the Trappist monks began to produce stronger, more complex beers for public sale. As they met with success, they were widely copied, and Belgian beer as we know it started to emerge. World War II saw many breweries interrupted with the brewers burying their kettles out in nearby fields to save them from the German army. As soon as the war ended, the brewers started digging.

It is not surprising that the Belgian outlook on the world has a unique character. Belgium remains

Tin photo of the De Koninck brewery team, based in Antwerp, Belgium, c. 1900. PIKE MICROBREWERY MUSEUM, SEATTLE, WA

split along religious, linguistic, and political lines. Belgian beer combines French flair, German precision, and Dutch sturdiness into a unique range of beers that often defy the idea of beer style. It is important to point out that the majority of beer sold in Belgium, as almost everywhere in the world, is a variant of pilsner. When we speak, therefore, of "Belgian beer," we refer to top-fermented beers showing uniquely Belgian character.

If you ask three Belgian brewers what defines Belgian beers, it is likely that you will get three different answers. Surely, however, one answer is yeast. Throughout Europe, over centuries, brewers passed yeast from one brewery to another until certain areas began to express a *terroir* of fermentation, a regional character that links them. We see this in the weissbiers of Bavaria and it is equally evident in Belgium, where top-fermenting yeasts tend to produce spicy, fruity, complex flavors, often driven by strong worts and very warm fermentation temperatures. Most Belgian beers, even when they seem to express some sweetness, are well attenuated and have very little residual sugar. As a result, hop bitterness is usually kept low because there is little sugar to balance it.

Whereas most Belgian beers are based on pilsner malts, others use pale ale or Vienna malts. Wheat is used in witbiers and in Payottenland's spontaneously fermented lambics, but finds its way into other beers as well, along with oats, spelt, and other grains. The hop sometimes has partners in the kettle. Orange peel, coriander, star anise, grains of paradise, black pepper, and other spices, sometimes announced by the brewery but often not, may give background flavors. Although Belgian brewers are often exasperated to hear that foreigners tend to think of Belgian beers as "spiced," the fact remains that they are widely if subtly used. Also unique to Belgian beer is the use of very dark caramelized sugars. Invert sugar is used in England as well, but in darker Belgian beers it often replaces dark malts, providing most or all of the color. In doing so, dark candi sugar replaces coffee and chocolate malt flavors with flavors of crème brûlée and raisins.

In other beers, pale candi sugar is used, often to lighten the character of strong beers and allow them to become dry, very drinkable, and sometimes almost spirituous. In general, these beers can be excellent peers for pairing with food.

The méthode Champenoise brings sparkle to wines, but it first brought bubbles to beer, and bottle conditioning of some sort is more common in Belgium than anywhere else in the world. Some beers are partially carbonated in tanks before being primed with yeast and sugar to achieve a minor refermentation, but the best beers are bottled flat and gain all their carbonation during conditioning. These often emerge with wonderfully complex aromatics, very high carbonation, attendant voluminous rocky foam, and a scintillating pinpoint mousse on the tongue. In Belgium, such beers are poured carefully to avoid disturbing the sediment of yeast at the bottom of the bottle.

Perhaps what defines Belgian beer more than anything else is a sense of stubborn individuality. Belgian brewing is a realm of non-conformists and *garagistes*, many of whom seem content to tirelessly tilt at the windmills of change, sometimes for decades. If this means keeping a day job and brewing at the weekends, so be it—the Belgian brewer defines himself and will not be fenced in. Many brewers seem to be radical and conservative at once, unwilling to try anything new, yet still creating beers that taste like no one else's.

In many ways despite themselves, Belgium's brewers have exerted a large influence on modern craft brewing, particularly in the United States. In the 1980s and 1990s most American craft brewed beers grew directly out of British brewing traditions, but once these seemed fully mined, attention turned to Belgium, aided greatly by the writings of the late beer writer Michael Jackson. Where once Belgian brewers may have seen imitation as a threat, they now see the intended flattery, and in turn the United States has become a key market for Belgium's finest beers. Indeed, it is easier to find many of them in the shops, bars, and restaurants of Brooklyn, New York, than it is to find them in Brussels. American craft brewers now make dozens of tripels, dubbels, abbey ales, saisons, and witbiers. Some, fascinated by the bracing acidity of Belgium's lambics and sour brown and red ales, have invented an entire new breed of sour and "wild" beers. Bottle conditioning is on the rise. Belgian-influenced beers are also now easily found in Canada, Italy, Scandinavia, Switzerland, Brazil, and beyond. Germany has been held back by its clinging to the Reinheitsgebot, but that is slowly changing.

Slowly, the influence has crept back in the other direction as well. Belgian brewers are experimenting with bold hop character, long the signature of the American craft brewing movement. Many of these beers are not yet wonderful, but they do show potential, and it will no doubt be interesting to see what develops as the Belgians delve deeper into the worldwide craft brewing community.

See also ABBEY BEERS, ACHEL BREWERY, BELGIAN RED ALE, CHIMAY, DUBBEL, FLANDERS, GUEUZE, JACKSON, MICHAEL, KONINGSHOEVEN BREWERY, KRIEK, LAMBIC, ORVAL BREWERY, ROCHEFORT BREWERY, TRAPPIST BREWERIES, TRIPEL, WALLONIA, WESTMALLE BREWERY, and WESTVLETEREN BREWERY.

Garrett Oliver

Belhaven Brewery is claimed to be Scotland's oldest brewery, established in 1719 by John Johnstone in Dunbar, Lothian, Scotland. Its original two wells and some vaults in the brewery date from the 16th century.

In 1815 it changed its name to Dudgeon & Co. At this time, the "shilling" terminology was widely used to categorize beers in Scotland. The shilling term was originally an invoice price but was later useful as an indicator of ascending beer strengths. In 1846, with the arrival of railways, Dudgeons focused on producing malt for sale, while still producing small quantities of beer, particularly for the local and military trade. The malting portion of the company closed in 1970 and in 1972 the company changed its name to the Belhaven Brewery, with a brewery and seven tied public houses. See TIED HOUSE SYSTEM. This company was then sold to Clydesdale Commonwealth Hotels Ltd. There have been further owners; in 2005, with 275 tied public houses, it was sold to Greene King, based in Bury St Edmunds, England. See GREENE KING.

As of 2010, the company still produced traditional cask ales and bottled beers at Dunbar within the Greene King Group including 80/- (Eighty Shilling Ale), which is one of its oldest and most traditional brands. The bottle beers are now packaged at the groups' Bury St Edmunds site.

See also SCOTLAND.

Belhaven Brewery. http://www.belhaven.co.uk/.
Donnachie, Ian. *A history of the brewing industry in Scotland*. Edinburgh, Scotland: Jon Donald Publishers Ltd., 1979.
Richmond, Lesley, and Alison Turton, eds. *The brewing industry: A guide to historical records*. Manchester, England: Manchester University Press, 1990.

Chris J. Marchbanks

Bentonite is a natural, clay-like material of volcanic origin, which is geologically a form of montmorillonite, a smectite clay. It is a complex sodium, calcium, and aluminum silicate, and when hydrated it becomes a powerful adsorbent that can be used to clarify beer.

Montmorillonite, a term first used in 1847, was named after the French town Montmorillon, near Poitiers, where it was first mined. Its origin can be traced to ancient volcanic eruptions whereby fine volcanic ash particles were carried by winds and deposited in discrete layers that metamorphosed over time from the "glassy" state to claystone. The term "Bentonite" was first applied in 1898 to a particularly highly colloidal clay found in the Cretaceous beds near Fort Benton, Montana, and the product is still mined in this state. Some of the largest and highest quality deposits of Bentonite occur in neighboring Wyoming, from which the product takes on the alternative name "Wyoming clay."

Bentonites are usually composed of about 90% montmorillonite, with the residue consisting of feldspar, gypsum, calcium carbonate, quartz, and traces of heavy metals, and it is these metallic impurities that impart any color to the mineral. In the pure state montmorillonite is almost white.

In the brewery, Bentonite is used as a stabilizing (chillproofing) agent and is used to bind and remove haze-forming proteins. Negative charges on Bentonite bind with positively charged proteins, forming a precipitated complex. The reaction yields copious quantities of sediment, which is an inconvenience for brewers, as the sediment has to be removed by filtration. For this reason, the role of Bentonite has been largely superseded by other products, such as silica hydrogels. Bentonite is still widely used in the wine industry, where it will bind with phenols and tannins, clarifying the wine.

See also ADSORBENT.

Hornsey, I. S. *The chemistry and biology of winemaking*. Cambridge: Royal Society of Chemistry, 2007.
Hough, J. S., D. E. Briggs, R. Stevens, and T. W. Young. *Malting and brewing science, vol. 2, Hopped wort and beer*, 2nd ed. London: Chapman & Hall, 1982.

Ian Hornsey

Bere (barley) (pronounced "bear") is an ancient barley landrace, likely Britain's oldest cultivated cereal. It was widely grown across Britain until more modern, high-yielding barleys were developed. A six-row spring barley adapted to the short growing seasons of northern areas, bere is currently grown on limited acreage in the Scottish Islands. Modern development of the grain was by Dr Geoff Sellars of the Orkney Institute of Agronomy, and its commercialization has been similar to the expansion of the use of spelt grain as a premium product.

"Bere" has its origins in the Old English word for barley, "Bœr." It is synonymous with "Bygg" or "Bigg" barley, terms likely derived from the old Norse word for barley, "Bygg," which itself originates in the Arabic for barley. All of the Scandinavian languages used bygg for barley. Once in the UK, bygg came to be spelled "bigg."

Numerous sources state that not only the name but also the grain itself came with Viking colonists to Orkney. However, analysis of the genetic makeup of bere barley races from various Scottish islands and from Scandinavia are all distinctly different and must, therefore, have evolved each on its own island. No doubt the Vikings found barley there on Orkney and called it by their usual name for it.

Agronomical problems with the ancient grain include susceptibility to lodging and powdery mildew, variable grain size, and high levels of protein. Bere can produce quite spectacular protein deposits in the kettle after boiling of the wort. Additionally, bere grain is relatively high in nitrogen, which reduces alcohol yield. Earlier planting dates and the addition of growth regulators have ameliorated some of the problems, and the grain is used today primarily for specialty whiskey, beer, and local bread products.

Beer brewed from bere barley has a distinctive, pleasant, smoky flavor with a slightly bitter aftertaste.

Loudon, John Claudius. *An encyclopedia of agriculture: comprising theory and practice.* London: Longman, Hurst, Rees, Orme, Brown, and Green, 1831.
Rickards, Sir George Kettilby. *The statutes of the United Kingdom of Great Britain and Ireland.* London: His Majesty's Statute and Law Printers, 1822.

Chris Holliland and Shaun Townsend

Berliner weisse is a beer style originating from the region around Berlin, Germany, which developed gradually from the 17th to the 20th century. Its main characteristic is a mild sourness and tartness with a light and fruity character, which led to the nickname "Champagne of the North."

The origins of Berliner weisse are murky at best. There are several competing theories surrounding the development of the style. One theory holds that the Huguenots, French immigrants to Berlin in the early 18th century, developed the beer after migrating through Flanders and picking up techniques from brewers of Flanders brown and red ales. See FLANDERS. Another theory points to a popular beer called *Halberstädter Broihan*, supposedly popular in Berlin in the 1640s; even this is said to have been a copy of an unknown beer brewed in Hamburg. Some claim that there have been historical mentions of Berliner weisse as far back as the 1570s.

What we do know is that wheat beers brewed around Berlin were not originally sour but rather light and easy to drink compared to the heavier brown beers. Most of the beers were about 3% ABV and used a mash of approximately 50% barley and 50% wheat. Interestingly, the wort was not boiled and the amount of hops used was quite low. Given that the wort was not boiled, the hops were not typically added in the kettle. Instead, hops were boiled with water (concurrent with the mashing process) and then this boiled hop infusion was blended into the mash to increase the mash temperature. This was a version of an infusion mash, one which may have allowed early brewers to achieve different mash temperatures without decoction. See DECOCTION and INFUSION MASH. Hops were also added to the mash, allowing a freer run-off of wort from a lauter tun, in which a layer of straw was used as a false bottom.

With no wort boiled to effect sterilization, one can easily imagine the huge diversity of microorganisms that survived into the cooled wort. It was necessary to start the fermentation quickly enough to suppress most of the spoiling organisms. Even so, heat-tolerant lactic acid bacteria survived and synergistically fermented the worts into beers with a dry and lightly acidic character. This was not true spontaneous fermentation as is carried out in lambic beers—yeast was pitched, but carried both yeast and bacteria from previous fermentations. Other organisms survived wort production; malt has plenty of its own lactic bacteria. Fermentation took place in wood (and wood, being porous, is difficult to sanitize).

We can therefore differentiate between three production steps where acidification could have taken place:

1. During the mashing process (if the mash stood too long, especially at low temperatures)
2. During fermentation (mainly caused by yeast cross-contaminations)
3. During storage (mainly micro flora in the storage containers)

The result was a range of beers with vastly differing levels of acidity, and although acidity was not uncommon in beers of the 17th and 18th centuries, the variability of the beer meant that it often failed to meet a consumer's expectations.

The modern Berliner weisse developed relatively late, during the 19th century, and numerous Berlin breweries specialized in its production until the style started to wane in the 1950s. The technology applied in these breweries was very similar to the brewing process in earlier times, with the main difference being that fermentation was better controlled, especially with respect to the ratio of yeast and lactic acid bacteria during fermentation and lagering (the average bacteria concentration was approximately 20% of the yeast concentration).

Berliner weisse has not always been a low-gravity beer. Some were brewed at normal gravities, then either consumed straight or watered down at the beer hall, either by the house or by the consumer. To cut the varying acidity levels, the addition of various syrups became popular over the years, with the most common being bright green woodruff syrup or bright red raspberry syrup.

At the height of its popularity in the 19th century, Berliner weisse was the most popular alcoholic drink in Berlin, with almost 700 breweries producing it. But the intervening years have not been kind to Berliner weisse. Within Europe, it enjoys protection as a sort of *appellation controlee*; Berliner weisse can only be produced within the city limits of Berlin. That honor, however, has not saved it, and it has become a rare specialty, produced by only two full-scale commercial breweries, Berliner Kindl and Schultheiss. These breweries no longer use a yeast/bacterial blend to ferment the beer; the bacterial fermentation is conducted separately and the beer is blended for a defined acidity. The beers are very pale, slightly hazy, and effervescent, with a light tang. They are refreshing oddities but show little complexity.

In the last few years, however, Berliner weisse has enjoyed a revival among artisanal brewers. Small experimental brews have been conducted in Germany, and the resulting beer found to be very fine and complex, with no need for any syrups. American craft brewers have also taken to producing Berliner weisse, which is taking its place within the nascent culture surrounding sour beer styles. Even though the United States is far from Berlin and its appellation controlee, it is the place where production and enjoyment of this compelling old beer style is likely to flourish in the future.

See also GERMANY and SOUR BEER.

Fritz Briem

beta glucanase is an enzyme that hydrolyzes β-glucans. The most important β-glucanases for brewing are those that break down the β-glucans located in the cell walls of the barley endosperm. See BETA-GLUCANS. High levels of β-glucans in brewing raw materials are to be avoided as they can cause problems, particularly in wort production and beer filtration. β-Glucanases are important in that they are needed to break down the complex β-glucan molecules to smaller units. There is a wide range of such enzymes, differing in the specific bonds that are broken.

The most important such enzyme in barley is endo-β→3, 1→4-glucanase (sometimes called endo-barley-β-glucanase) which potentiates the hydrolysis of a β1→4 linkage adjacent to a β1→3 linkage, thereby leading to a rapid diminution in the viscosity of β-glucan solutions. The enzyme is essentially absent in raw barley, but is synthesized during germination and functions during malt modification to remove the problematic β-glucans. The enzyme is extremely sensitive to heat and if the enzyme is required in the brewhouse grist, for example to deal with residual β-glucan in poorly modified grain or adjuncts rich in β-glucan such as raw, roasted, torrefied, or flaked barley or oats, then the green malt must be kilned at a lower onset temperature with progressive ramping to a non-excessive final curing temperature. Furthermore, mashing needs to commence at a reduced temperature (e.g., 40°C–50°C or 104°F–122°F) if the β-glucanase is to function at that stage. Alternatively, more heat-tolerant microbial β-glucanases can be added to the mash. These include the enzyme from Bacillus subtilis, whose specificity is very similar to that from malt, or glucanases derived from fungi such as Aspergillus, Trichoderma, or Penicillium, which comprise mixtures of enzymes with different specificity, including endo- and exo- β1-3- and β1-4-glucanases. As a consequence they are much more comprehensive in their removal of glucan.

Yeast cells can be "opened" by the action of lytic enzyme, which is β1-3 glucanase derived from snails that degrades that particular glucan, a key structural feature of the yeast cell wall.

Hrmova, M., and Fincher, G. B. Structure-function relationships of β-D-glucan endo- and exohydrolases from higher plants. *Plant Molecular Biology* 47 (2001): 73–91.

Charles W. Bamforth

beta-glucans are polymers in which residues of the monomer glucose are linked through glycosidic linkages in the β-configuration. These linkages can be between different carbon atoms on the glucose molecule. In a brewing context there are two significant β-glucans, found in barley and yeast respectively.

In the cell walls of the starchy endosperm of barley is a highly polymerized β-glucan in which β linkages are either between the number one and four carbons of successive glucoses or between the one and three carbons. In most of the molecule there is a β1→3 linkage occurring after every third or fourth β1→4 linkage. The occurrence of the β1→3 linkages tends to break up regularity that makes solely β1→4 linked glucoses (viz. cellulose) highly crystalline and resilient to attack.

Barley β-glucans are highly viscous and can cause a number of problems in brewing, notably reduced rates of wort separation and beer filtration and also the formation of hazes, gels, and precipitates. On the other hand, they do represent soluble fiber and barley β-glucan on that basis is touted for its healthful properties.

A different β-glucan is found in the cell walls of yeast, where it accounts for 30%–60% of the total material and affords rigidity. Here, the linkages are β1→3 and β1→6. Whereas the barley β-glucan is linear, that from yeast comprises a backbone of β1→3 linked glucosyls, with branches linked to the backbone by β1→6 bonds.

See also BETA GLUCANASE and GLUCOSE.

Jin, Y-L., Speers, R.A., Paulson, A.T., & Stewart, R.J. Barley beta-glucans and their degradation during malting and brewing. *Technical Quarterly, Master Brewers Association of the Americas* 41 (2004): 231–240.

Charles W. Bamforth

Bier-Drive tanks are horizontal, stainless steel beer-serving tanks that are designed to be filled via transfer hoses from mobile, usually truck-mounted, beer delivery tanks. The Bier-Drive system was developed and patented by the German company EDS Schwiekowski of Schöningen in Lower Saxony in the 1970s. It is designed for the convenient delivery of bulk quantities of ready-to-serve beer from the brewery to large on-premise accounts, much the way tank trucks deliver heating oil to private households and businesses. The system is very economical and practical because it eliminates the need for kegs, which are always expensive, labor intensive to clean and to fill, heavy to handle, and often stolen for their scrap-metal value. Bier-Drive tanks come in sizes of 500 and 1,000 l (132 and 264 US gal) and, just like beer tanks in brewery cellars, they are manufactured for various pressure ratings (up to 3 bar), as well as with and without cooling jackets for either ambient or individual tank cooling. Unlike brewery tanks, however, Bier-Drive tanks have a disposable plastic inner liner, which keeps the beer from making contact with the inside tank wall. The liner is replaced every time the tank is filled. Thus, a Bier-Drive tank does not need to be cleaned and sanitized. Also, the beer is less likely to get infected by microbes and protected against undesirable uptake of the gas—be it air, carbon dioxide, or nitrogen—used to pressurize it. The beer is pushed out of the tank to the dispensing tap by means of air or gas applied between the tank and the plastic liner. Because Bier-Drive tanks can also be used as serving or bright tanks without the liner, they are much sought after as used equipment by brewpubs.

Bier-Drive. http://www.bierdrive.de/ (accessed February 16, 2011).

Anders Brinch Kissmeyer

Bière de Garde Considered the only widely acknowledged French contribution to specialty brewing, *Bière de Garde* claims heritage to farmhouse breweries that were once ubiquitous within French Flanders, an area now encompassing the French departments du Nord and Pas-de-Calais and the Belgian province Hainaut.

The name "Bière de Garde" roughly translates to "beer for keeping," a reference to the old practice of brewing a stronger beer to store as provision for the warmer months of the year, when conditions were not as hospitable for brewing. Before mechanical refrigeration, brewers made beer during the cooler months to be served within a few weeks of brewing. These brews made early in the season were intended for immediate consumption and tended to be lower in alcohol content, typically 3%–4% by volume. Toward the end of the brewing season it was not uncommon for the last brews of the season to be made stronger to allow them to be stored during the rest of the year. The higher alcohol content would have helped retard spoilage during months of storage. A similar practice applied to Saison, a Belgian specialty ale which also originated on farmhouse breweries in the French Flanders region. French Bière de Garde and Belgian Saison form the style family known as Farmhouse Ales. See SAISON.

The farmhouse heritage of Bière de Garde is well-established but written historical documentation is scarce. In an 1880 work entitled *L'industrie de la Brasserie* by L. Figuier, the author describes "Bière de Garde de Lille" as "a highly special brew that was aged in large, wooden barrels for six to eight months before serving." It is described as having a "very vinous flavor, which was highly regarded by the customers." A 1905 paper titled *The Beers and Brewing Systems of*

Northern France by British brewing scientist R.E. Evans describes Bière de Garde as popular in Lille and other large towns, as a beer "purposely allowed to become sour and at the same time acquiring a vinous flavor."

Whatever flavor characteristics Bière de Garde may have exhibited in the past have certainly evolved to a different profile in modern interpretations. Improvements in process control and ingredient quality and a much deeper understanding of brewing science have combined to make Bière de Garde adapt to modern times. A no less powerful influence is the nearly universal consumer preference for the crisp, clean taste of lager beer. All of these factors have influenced the evolution of not only Bière de Garde but also that of virtually all recognized beer styles (with perhaps the notable exception of lambics). Today, the rapid rise of interest in craft-brewed beer and the slow decline in the popularity of industrial lagers have provided an environment for further growth of the style.

Credited with pioneering the style as we know it today is Brasserie Duyck's Jenlain Bière de Garde, an obscure brand, first bottled in the 1940s, that grew to prominence as a cult beer in the late 1970s among French college students. See DUYCK, BRASSERIE and JENLAIN ORIGINAL FRENCH ALE. Most contemporary producers of Bière de Garde acknowledge Jenlain as the archetypal example. Prior to Brasserie Duyck's redefining of the style, Bière de Garde was served as a draught beer and, true to its farmhouse origins, was made lower in alcohol (in the 3%–4% range as compared to 6%–8% in modern versions) in order to sustain but not inebriate farm workers. Brasserie Duyck reinvented the style by essentially doubling the alcohol content and set a new standard by offering Bière de Garde in a cork-finished "Champagne" bottle, allowing for year-round consumption. This became the benchmark for French specialty brewing; other producers followed suit.

Spurred on by the success of Jenlain Bière de Garde and by growing interest in French specialty beers at home and abroad, other small brewers began producing their own interpretations of Bière de Garde. Of those that survive today (undoubtedly more regional breweries have closed than have survived) Brasserie La Choulette, Brasserie Thellier, Brasserie Castelain, and Brasserie St. Sylvestre were regional brewers who participated in the revival of French specialty brewing in the 1970s and 1980s. Each of these breweries had a long history of producing low-alcohol "table" beers or mainstream lager beers before reinventing themselves as specialty beer producers in the 1980s. Exploiting the niche of being a specialty producer gave these breweries a chance at survival—a better alternative to the futile effort of trying to compete directly with large national brands.

Modern Bière de Garde can vary considerably among the various interpretations on the market today. This is a result in part of the French tendency to distinguish products by location, rather than by adhering to predetermined style parameters. However, the widespread use of a proven style name, such as Bière de Garde, has been embraced by many in an effort to ensure success. This has led to confusion and even consternation among beer aficionados and casual consumers alike.

Generally speaking, "classic" Bière de Garde is amber in color and exhibits a dominant malty flavor without being cloying on the palate. Hop character is generally in the background but certain varieties lend a subtle, spicy note. Fermentation character is generally minimal as some producers have continued to employ the lager yeasts and lager brewing techniques used in their previous incarnations as regional producers of mainstream beers. Other brewers do use genetic "ale" yeasts but at generally cooler temperatures in an effort to minimize esters and other fermentation by-products. Some examples exhibit a "cork" note (not to be confused with the less pleasant character of "corked" wine) that adds a decidedly rustic nuance. A well-made Bière de Garde is subtle in its complexity and requires "revisiting" time and again to fully reveal its charms.

See also FRANCE.

Brasserie La Choulette. http://www.lachoulette.com/ (accessed March 14, 2011).

Evans, R. E. *The beers and brewing systems of northern France* (223–38). Birmingham, England: Institute of Technical Brewing, 1905.

Jackson, Michael. *Beer companion*. Philadelphia: Running Press, 1993.

Jenlain—La Brasserie. http://www.jenlain.fr/ (accessed March 14, 2011).

Markowski, Phil. *Farmhouse ales*. Denver, CO: Brewers Publications, 2004.

Woods, John, and Rigley, Keith. *The beers of France*. Wiscombe, Bristol: The Artisan Press, 1998.

Phil Markowski

Bière de Mars is a French term that literally translates into "March Beer" in English. It refers to a type of low-alcohol lambic beer that was made in Belgium and was quite popular until the start of the 20th century, when production declined and eventually ceased. It is closely related to the faro style of beer but was much weaker in gravity and alcohol, and kept unsweetened. See FARO.

Bière de Mars was traditionally made from the second and/or third runnings from the lauter tun during the production of lambic beer. The net result and goal of the brewer was to make a refreshing drink during the warmer months of the year. The flavor of Bière de Mars most likely was not as good as lambic, geueze, or other ales because the wort from second and third runnings would have been very high in tannins that would have given an almost mouth-puckering astringency to the beer. Interestingly, while many European brewers made stronger beers to be released in the month of March, such as bock, the brewers of Belgium tried to make faro and Bière de Mars as refreshing, low-alcohol alternatives. This somewhat contrary or rebellious way of brewing has been a trademark of Belgian brewers for the last couple of centuries. During the 1990s the Frank Boon Brewery in Belgium reintroduced a type of Bière de Mars that was labeled as Lembeek's 2%. See BOON BREWERY. It was a lightly spiced lambic style of beer with 2% ABV. Although refreshing, this brand failed to find a market and production ceased.

The traditional method of brewing Bière de Mars includes a lambic grist of 30%–40% raw wheat and 60%–70% malted barley. The hops used were typically Belgian and included varieties from the southern Belgian hop-growing region around the town of Poperinge, such as Northern Brewer and Brewer's Gold. All hops used in lambic production were stored to reduce the oil and alpha-acid content and therefore to reduce the potential flavoring and bittering components. The intentionally aged hops were used mainly for their antimicrobial effect. Mashing was carried out to optimize the growth of microorganisms associated with spontaneous fermentation and favored high levels of free amino nitrogen and unfermentable sugars. To obtain this type of wort, the brewer would mash in the grist at a low temperature around 30°C (86°F), and use a stepped decoction to increase the mash temperature up to a high near 80°C (176°F). See DECOCTION. Multiple holds at various temperatures were carried out, resulting in a very long day for the brewer.

The first runnings from the lauter tun were used for lambic production, while the second and third runnings from the lauter tun were isolated for faro and Bière de Mars production. In the brewkettle, whereas typical beers are boiled from 60 to 90 minutes, lambic styles could be boiled up to 5 hours, always using aged hops. After boiling, the wort was transferred to a coolship, a shallow, large open tank where the wort was cooled and allowed to be infected by airborne microorganisms that began the spontaneous fermentation. See COOLSHIP. Brewing traditionally took place only in the colder months of the year so that the wort would cool quickly—1 to 2 days—using only the ambient air temperature. Usually, the coolship was located on the roof of the lambic brewery and was well-protected from the elements, except for strategically positioned air holes and vents to allow the air to circulate from inside the brewery to the exterior and vice versa. After the wort had started fermenting, it was transferred to oak barrels where the Bière de Mars finished fermenting and could be aged for several months before being served in the warmer months.

In the United States and France several craft breweries have introduced Bière de Mars varieties that differ from the historic Bière de Mars found in Belgium. The French versions are usually called "Bière de Printemps" ("spring beer") and are stronger versions of Bière de Garde, usually containing around 6% or 7% ABV. See BIÈRE DE GARDE. They are also usually brewed with only the best malts and hops available so that the flavor has a fuller malt taste with pronounced hop character. The US versions of Bière de Mars are also brewed in the newer French tradition and have high alcohol contents (6%–7% ABV) with full malt and hop flavors. Craft brewers such as New Belgium, Jolly Pumpkin, and Southhampton Publick House all have offered modern versions of Bière de Mars.

See also BELGIUM and LAMBIC.

Keith Villa

bioluminescence is an analytical technique used to detect microbial contamination in the brewing process by measuring the presence of adenosine triphosphate (ATP) in samples taken in the brewery. See ADENOSINE TRIPHOSPHATE (ATP). The detection and measurement of ATP indicates the presence of living cells because ATP is broken down when cells die. The analytical method involves the use of the luciferin–luciferase enzyme system, which fireflies use to emit light. In the presence of oxygen and ATP, the enzyme luciferase produces light that can be measured. The quantity of light emitted is related to the amount of ATP present and therefore to the quantity of living cells present at the time of sampling. Up to 1,000 microbes per sample can be detected in a few minutes, although the method is unable to discriminate between specific types of microorganism. The technique is used in breweries to monitor the cleanliness of the brewing plant and equipment and is preferred to traditional microbiological analysis because of its speed and its relative simplicity. It can be used routinely by plant operators to assess the effectiveness of cleaning regimes. More traditional microbiological sampling routines can take several days to obtain a result. The technique is used predominantly in larger breweries because of the high cost of the system. However, because the method does not require the skills of a trained microbiologist to monitor microbiological contamination, it is likely to eventually find application in smaller breweries.

George Philliskirk

biscuit malt, a style of highly flavored specialty malt, is produced using a drum roaster. Biscuit malt is produced when germinated, kiln-dried barley is then roasted at high temperature but for a relatively short roasting time, resulting in a color of about 30° Lovibond/SRM. The high temperature applied to the malt at low moisture content, also known as dry roasting, develops the unique toasted, warm bread, biscuit, and especially nutty flavors and aromas characteristic of this malt type and the beers in which it is used. Biscuits malts have no diastatic power (enzymatic action) due to the high temperatures applied during roasting.

Biscuit malt is a relatively recent type of malt made possible by the invention of the first drum roaster in the early 1800s during Britain's Industrial Revolution. The nutty flavors of biscuit malts make them popular when brewing brown ales, where they can make up as much as 10%–15% of the total grist bill.

The toasted, nutty flavors of biscuit malt also make it popular for usage at low percentages, adding subtle flavors and aromas to beer styles such as pale ales, amber and red ales and lagers, and bock and Oktoberfest/märzen beers.

In darker beer styles such as stouts and porters, low percentages of biscuit malt can help develop greater complexity and increase malt aroma.

David Kuske

bitter, despite the recent ubiquity of thin golden lagers in the country's pubs, is the national drink of England. The word "bitter" describes a particular type of cask-conditioned draught ale, and in many pubs "a pint of bitter" remains a standard order for beer.

The British have been using the word bitter to describe pale ales since the early 19th century, although the term did not entirely take hold until almost a century later. The style, such as it is, is broad, covering a range of colors, tastes, and strengths. Despite popular myth, bitters are not traditionally only tawny brown in color. In 1899, one of the great early beer writers, Alfred Barnard, penned the following description for a popular West Country bitter: "A bright, sparkling beverage of a rich golden colour and possesses a nice, delicate hop flavour." Another contemporary described a bitter as being "straw coloured."

The term "bitter" came into common use before the use of pump clips to identify different beers or brands. Brewers themselves called the beers "pale ale," but ordinary customers began to identify them as bitters. There was nothing on the bar to tell customers they should be asking for pale ale, and so they requested a bitter to show they didn't want the sweeter, less-hopped mild. Until recently, most beer consumed in the UK was cask-conditioned beer on draught, served in pubs. Because the customers were calling the beer bitter, the term stuck and even the brewers began to use it.

Most British brewers produce at least one bitter. Cask conditioning and service by beer engine or gravity dispense is traditional (although these days bitter is sometimes filtered, pasteurized, and even bottled, processes that tend to shear away the beer's best qualities). The beers are universally fermented at warm temperatures by ale yeasts. The color ranges from an almost pilsner-like golden hue to a full mahogany, and the strength may be anything from a low 3.0% alcohol by volume (ABV) to a more steadfast 5.5%. Often a brewer will produce at least two bitters—one at a lower strength and the other stronger; in this case the weaker beer will be known as just bitter or "ordinary" and the other "best" or "best bitter." Best bitters tend to be in the mid 4% range, with anything stronger designated by another name, sometimes "special bitter." The hop content of bitter can range from a light, gentle bitterness to something more substantial and tongue tingling, although typically they will have a bitterness of around 30 (international bitterness units). It is not unusual for a brewer to "dry-hop" the beer by adding a handful of whole hops to each cask, allowing extra, fresher hop aromas to suffuse into the beer. See DRY HOPPING and INTERNATIONAL BITTERNESS UNITS.

The mash is normally made from a lightly toasted pale malt, with the Maris Otter barley variety still particularly favored by the most traditional of brewers. See MARIS OTTER (BARLEY). A small amount of a caramelized crystal malt may be added for color and additional flavor. Some brewers add invert sugar, which has a soft toffee flavor. The sugar is actually expensive when compared with the price of malt and is primarily used for taste rather than to provide cheaper fermentable material.

Bitters are traditionally hopped with the great British varieties of Fuggles and Goldings, grown in the hop fields of Kent, Herefordshire, Worcestershire, and Oxfordshire. These hops are renowned for their moderate bitterness and their piney, fruity aromatics, which remain prominent in the flavor profile of many bitters. Today, however, Britain's oft conservative brewers also look to other parts of the world for flavorsome hops to add to their recipes.

Britain's bitters are almost more of a family of related beer styles than one distinct beer style. Bitters are hard to codify, and the style is very broad. The breweries' individual ale yeasts are major determinants of flavor, with yeast lending orangey notes to one bitter and banana notes to another. Traditionally they have also varied greatly from region to region. Hoppy bitters, like Shepherd Neame's Canterbury Jack, a pale beer with a pronounced citrus aroma, are found throughout Kent, London, and the Thames Valley.

The Midlands was renowned for its sweeter bitters; Marston's Burton bitter is an example. West Country bitters are typically fruity, whereas South Wales was the home of particularly malty bitters. Smoother, creamier bitters can be found in Yorkshire, and Manchester was renowned for its fruity, dry beers. Other bitters are called by the name "IPA" even when neither the bitterness nor the strength properly merits the title (although truer forms of India pale ale are re-emerging in Britain). Scotland was known for its fuller bodied "lights" and "heavies." Other styles are still being developed, such as brightly hoppy, golden-hued "summer bitters" well suited to summers that seem warmer than they once were.

Bitter is the signature ale of Britain's brewers, with their skill exemplified by the ability to produce beers with only about 3.5% ABV, yet with so much flavor and character.

Bitter and British pubs are almost inseparable companions. Bitters are "running beers," an old term for beers that are best drunk fresh and are not meant to age for a long period of time. They are not for sipping but for drinking, preferably by the pint and over a good conversation. Although foreigners sometimes describe bitters as "warm and flat," they are actually best served at cellar temperature, 11°C–14°C (50°F–55°F). No one wants "warm, flat beer," least of all a veteran bitter enthusiast.

Today many North American brewers brew a bitter. Hale's Ale and Redhook (formerly the Independent Ale Brewery) launched their versions in 1984, as did others in Canada. Served on draught, they are often stronger than British bitters and tend toward a higher carbonation, which changes their nature. Many craft brewers, particularly in the United States, but elsewhere around the world as well, have been trying their hands at cask-conditioned bitters. Although good cellarmanship remains rare outside of the UK, many of these breweries are making delicious versions of bitter.

See also BRITAIN, CASK CONDITIONING, CELLARMANSHIP, ART OF, FUGGLE (HOP), GOLDING (HOP), MARSTON'S BREWERY, and SHEPHERD NEAME BREWERY.

Barnard, Alfred. *The noted breweries of Britain and Northern Ireland*. London: Sir Joseph Causton & Sons, 1889.

Hornsey, Ian S. *Brewing*. Cambridge, UK: RSC Paperbacks, 1999.

Jackson, Michael. *Beer companion*. London: Mitchell Beazley, 1993.

Tim Hampson

bittering potential (of hops) is an estimate of how much bitterness a sample of hops can deliver to finished beer. The potential is primarily a function of the alpha-acids content of the hops. Brewers and growers will loosely classify hops based in part on ranges of hops alpha acid content; for instance "aroma" hops have 3%–9% alpha acids by weight, "bittering" hops have 5%–13%, and "super alpha" hops have 11%–18%. Bittering potential is also affected by factors that affect both hop acids dissolution during wort boiling as well as boiling time and temperature. The form of the hops affects how well the hop acids are dispersed into wort, and liquid hop extracts are the most efficient in this regard followed by pelletized hops and then by whole cone hops. Hops added at the beginning of a long boil will have greater potential to impart bitterness while hops added at the end of the boil or to finished beer will have much less potential to increase bitterness. The bitterness in beer and wort is measured instrumentally using two different approaches. A liquid extraction using 2,2,4–trimethylpentane (also known as iso-octane) and subsequent analysis in a spectrophotometer leads to the International Bitterness Unit (IBU); however, there are compounds other than iso-alpha-acids, such as some polyphenols and residual hop acids, that will be extracted by iso-octane thereby yielding an IBU value that is typically higher than the actual iso-alpha-acids content. Individual hop acids can also be measured via high performance liquid chromatography. Brewers use a measure called "hop utilization" to gauge effectiveness of converting insoluble hop alpha-acids into soluble iso-alpha-acids, and this is calculated as the amount of hop iso-alpha-acids in the finished beer relative to the amount of alpha-acids added during the brewing process.

See also HOP UTILIZATION, INTERNATIONAL BITTERNESS UNITS (IBUS), and ISO-ALPHA ACIDS.

Thomas Shellhammer

bitterness is one of four individual tastes that are sensed by different areas of the human tongue. The others are sweet, sour, and salty, which require no explanation, but bitterness is often confused with the physical sensations of burning and astringency or dryness. Just as vintners must balance the acid:sugar ratio to produce a wine with drinkability, brewers must balance the sweetness derived from the malt with bitterness derived from hops and sometimes other sources. If the sweetness is not counterbalanced with bitterness, the beer will seem sweet and flabby tasting on the palate and the drinker will tire of the beer quickly. Whether very strong or barely perceptible, bitterness is critically important to beer flavor.

Alpha Acids

The alpha acids are the main source of bitterness from hops. Iso-alpha acids, produced from the alpha acids during the wort boil, are the main source of bitterness in beer. See HOP ISOMERIZATION and ISO-ALPHA ACIDS. The alpha acids themselves are not very water soluble and only traces are found in beer. Hops are dosed into the brew kettle largely based on alpha acid content, and the brewer seeks to hit a target bitterness level. The bitterness in beer is measured by the International Bitterness Unit (IBU). See INTERNATIONAL BITTERNESS UNITS (IBUS). The IBU measurement detects not only iso-alpha acids in beer but also other compounds, which may or may not be derived from hops and may or may not contribute to bitterness. Compounds from dark malt and oxidation products of hop resins also contribute to measured IBUs. Some of these compounds contribute to perceived bitterness; others do not.

Simple methods to determine iso-alpha acid content in beer are not used to measure bitterness because of the contribution of these other compounds. Industry dogma is that the standard IBU test is the best analytical method to measure perceived bitterness in beer. See ALPHA ACIDS.

Alpha Acid Homologs

Note that the term "alpha acids" is plural. This is because there are three main alpha acids and several minor ones. The major alpha acids are humulone, cohumulone, and adhumulone. See ADHUMULONE and COHUMULONE. These alpha acid homologs have different utilization rates in the brew kettle, and the corresponding iso-alpha acids have different bittering profiles and foam properties in beer. See HOP UTILIZATION. But to a first approximation, they are all considered the same and are called collectively "the alpha acids." These differences are important. The relative amount of these homolog alpha acids is a function of hop variety. Tradition has it that the so-called aroma hops are lower in cohumulone than less desirable hops and that iso-cohumulone in beer has a harsher, more lingering bitterness than the other iso-homologs. This is not universally accepted, but is a majority view. Pleasantness of bitterness is an individual judgment and about two-thirds of tasters seem to prefer low iso-cohumulone beer, whereas the rest prefer higher iso-cohumulone beer. Iso-cohumulone is also lost more quickly as beer ages than the other iso-homologs—this will result in quicker staling. See STALING. Knowing that cohumulone is not valued by brewers, hop breeders tend to select lower cohumulone in new cultivars, so this distinction is being blurred with time.

Beta Acids

The beta acids are of secondary importance only when compared with the alpha acids. The beta acids are completely insoluble in cold water and beer and, unlike the alpha acids, do not isomerize to more water-soluble compounds when boiled. The beta acids themselves do essentially nothing in the brewing process, but their oxidation products formed as baled whole hops age are arguably more bitter than the iso-alpha acids, are quite water soluble, and end up in finished beer at high utilization rates. See HULUPONES. The alpha acids also oxidize as baled hops age, but their oxidation products, although quite water soluble, are generally not very bitter. As a result, as hops age, they lose bittering potential caused by the loss of alpha acids, but gain bittering potential caused by increased beta-oxidation products. If the amount of alpha and beta acids is roughly equal, the overall bittering potential of the hops remains fairly constant with aging. Traditional aroma hops, excluding the English ones, tend to have as much or more beta than alpha, but the higher alpha bittering hops generally have much less beta than alpha.

This does not mean that the bittering profile from aroma hops does not change as the baled hops oxidize. The measured IBUs and the intensity of the bitterness of beer made with aged aroma hops will be roughly the same as that of beer made with the same amount of fresh hops, but the bitterness of the former will be harsher and more lingering. Just as there are qualitative differences in sweetness from different sources (aspartame, sugar, saccharine) and different kinds of spicy heat from various chilies, there are qualitative differences in bitterness from hops. The bitterness from the iso-alpha acids from fresh hops is very different from the bitterness of deteriorated hops or from so-called reduced iso-alpha products. These differences are not trivial.

Reduced Iso-alpha Products

As beer is exposed to light, it will develop a sunstruck or "skunky" aroma if the beer contains iso-alpha acids. See LIGHTSTRUCK. This can be inhibited by "reducing" either the carbon–carbon double bonds on the side chains of the iso-alpha acids with hydrogen (the same process as hydrogenating corn oil to margarine) or the ketone on the bottom side chain with sodium borohydride. The former process produces what are known as "tetra" products (under different trade names) and the latter process produces products known as "rho." Use of these products can inhibit the formation of sunstruck aroma, but the bittering profiles of beers made with these products are vastly different than those made with natural hops. Beer packaged in green or clear glass tends to develop this skunky off-aroma more quickly than beer in brown glass. This encourages brewers to use these "reduced" hop products when using clear glass. This is one reason why beer in clear bottles often tastes quite different than beer in other packages.

The relation between measured IBUs and perceived bitterness no longer holds in beers made with these products. Beers made with rho products tend to have lower perceived bitterness than their measured IBUs would indicate; beers made with tetra products have higher bitterness than expected.

Beer Aging

Alterations in bitterness occur not only because of the aging of hops but also during staling of beer. The iso-alpha acids in beer are sensitive to oxygen and are removed as beer ages. The rate of deterioration is a function of time, temperature, initial oxygen content in the package, and how quickly oxygen enters the sealed package. Generally, beer will lose about 20% of the iso-alpha acids (and about 15% of the measured IBUs) after 8 months at room temperature. The resulting oxidation products are not detected by the IBU analysis and are not considered bitter. Hence, as beer ages, the bitterness decreases.

Polyphenols

Both hops and malt are sources of polyphenols in beer. This is a wide class of compounds with a number of important characteristics. Some polyphenols can complex with proteins in beer and form haze. Others have antioxidative properties that may retard the staling of beer. Polyphenols also add astringency, or a quality of dryness, to beer. This latter property is often confused with true bitterness. Some polyphenols are believed to modify the bitter impression of the hop acids, mellowing the beer while adding complexity and body. See POLYPHENOLS.

Hop Oil

When hops are added to the brew kettle, most of the hop oil is distilled out quickly with the evolving steam. Enough may remain to contribute to the aroma of the beer, but not enough to contribute to bitterness. But, when hops are added during or after fermentation, hop oil is dissolved directly into the beer, resulting in a strong aroma of hops and often an oil "burn." See DRY HOPPING. Whether this oil burn is true bitterness or confused with bitterness is in dispute, but its presence definitely increases perceived bitterness. The oil itself is not detected by the IBU analysis; however, small amounts of unisomerized alpha acids or xanthohumol dissolved directly into the beer during dry hopping will increase measured IBUs. See XANTHOHUMOL. As a practical matter, it is unlikely this would be more than a 1 IBU increase. See HOP OILS.

pH and Bitterness

The iso-alpha acids are weak acids. This means they exist in two forms in solution—the dissociated ionic form and the non-dissociated form. The ionic form, which is more abundant at higher pH, is more bitter than the non-ionic form. As a result, the bitter perception of beer is reduced at lower pH. See PH.

Alcohol and Bitterness

Many consider the taste of alcohol bitter. Higher concentrations of alcohol in wine are reported to increase perceived bitterness, but only at concentrations above 10%. Studies of this in beer are lacking, perhaps because the effect is small, below 10%. Alcohol would tend to suppress the dissociation of the weak iso-alpha acids mentioned in the previous paragraph, which would, in theory, reduce bitterness. This may counteract any increase from the alcohol itself.

Malt Roasting

The color compounds formed as malt is roasted will contribute to the bitter taste of beer, just as the roasting of coffee beans gives bitter flavor to espresso coffee. In beers made with very dark malts, this can be a significant portion of overall perceived bitterness. The color compounds from dark malts are more water soluble in general than the iso-alpha acids, so they do not contribute as much to the measured IBUs. It is rare that they would increase measured IBUs by more than 2–3 units. Their contribution to perceived bitterness can be much greater than this. Some stouts may derive as much of their bitter character from roasted malts as from hops. See ROASTED MALTS.

Mineral Content

Non-distilled water contains varying amounts of dissolved minerals. Many of these can have profound effects on the flavor of the water and also on the flavor of beer brewed with it. Brewers have long known that beers brewed from water containing high levels of calcium sulfate will tend to exhibit pleasantly crisp, snappy hop bitterness. Conversely, those brewed from alkaline water containing high levels of calcium carbonate will tend to show broader, coarser hop bitterness. This is among the reasons that many brewers of pale ales and India pale ales often add calcium sulfate to their brewing water or directly to the kettle; this is called "Burtonization," after the famously sulfate-rich waters of Burton-on-Trent in the British midlands. Very soft water is said to give a delicate quality to bitterness, making such water suitable for brewing classic pilsner. See CALCIUM CARBONATE and CALCIUM SULFATE.

Temperature

Lower temperature suppresses the perceived bitterness of all beverages—beer is no exception. For this reason, different styles of beer should be served at different temperatures for maximum enjoyment. The bitterness of a beer once served may increase, if it is allowed to warm substantially before it is finished.

Carbonation

Carbonation affects the flavor of beer in a number of ways. When carbon dioxide is dissolved in water, it forms carbonic acid. This increases the titratable acidity of the beer, increasing sourness. Also, as carbon dioxide bubbles are formed on the tongue, a characteristic "bite" is sensed, even in carbonated water. The higher the carbonation level, the more bite. The bite and sourness generated by high carbonation may increase perceived bitterness.

See also CARBONATION.

De Keukeleire, Dennis, et al. "Beer lightstruck flavor—the full story." In *Hop flavor and aroma, Proceedings of the First International Brewers Symposium*, ed. Thomas Shellhammer, 1–16. St Paul, MN: Master Brewers Association of the Americas, 2009.

Peacock, Val. "The international bitterness unit, its creation and what it measures." *Hop flavor and aroma, Proceedings of the First International Brewers Symposium*, ed. Thomas Shellhammer, 157–66. St Paul, MN: Master Brewers Association of the Americas, 2009.

Shellhammer, Thomas. "Hop components and their impact on the bitterness quality of beer." *Hop flavor and aroma, Proceedings of the First International Brewers Symposium*, ed. Thomas Shellhammer, 167–82. St Paul, MN: Master Brewers Association of the Americas, 2009.

Val Peacock

bitterness units, known widely as the international bitterness unit (IBU) or sometimes the shortened form bitterness unit (BU is the internationally accepted unit for describing bitterness in beer). For brewers, the IBU is an important metric for defining beer styles, beer flavor, and a particular beer's "trueness to brand." The IBU measurement is an important quality control measurement because it gives information regarding bitterness intensity. More specifically, it is a measure of iso-alpha acids and other bitterness compounds present in wort or beer where 1 IBU is equal to 1 mg/l or 1 ppm iso-alpha acid in solution. Brewers calculate the expected IBUs of their beers when formulating a recipe or incorporating a new hop into a beer. Beers can range from 1 to about 100 IBUs. The saturation point of iso-alpha acid in beer is approximately 110 IBUs. Brewer's initial calculations are only an estimation of bitterness and the true IBUs of a beer must be measured. IBUs measured in the original wort will drop dramatically during fermentation, and therefore wort IBUs and beer IBUs are two very different things. IBUs are measured in a brewing laboratory by either ultraviolet (UV) light spectrophotometric assay or high-pressure liquid chromatography (HPLC) methods. The UV method is common and is often done even in small brewery laboratories. It tends to be less accurate in measuring specifically iso-alpha acids, whereas the HPLC methods performed in larger, more sophisticated brewery labs are very accurate. HPLC can detect, separate, and measure specific analogues and non-iso-alpha acid bittering compounds that can originate in the hard resins, beta fraction, or other hop fractions. Trained flavor panelists are able to taste and approximate IBU values quite accurately. However, the sweetness and malty component of a beer can counterbalance and cover the bitterness in a beer, making it harder to determine the IBUs by taste, especially in higher-gravity, more assertive beer styles. IBUs do not give any information about the quality of bitterness. To use wine as an example, it is possible to measure a wine's tannin content, but this measurement does not convey whether tannins are smooth and well integrated or rough and astringent. It is the same with the IBU, which should be of far more interest to the commercial brewer and brewing scientist than to the consumer, who will learn relatively little about beer flavor from a number. Measured IBUs in beer, like tannins in wine, decrease as a beer ages. A barley wine that may be very tough and bitter in its youth may therefore become supple over a number of years if aged properly. Examples of typical IBU ranges in various beer styles include the following: American light lagers (5–10 IBUs), Bavarian hefeweizens (8–12 IBUs), amber lager (20–25 IBUs), American pale ale (35–40 IBUs), American India pale ale (IPA; 55–70 IBUs), and "double IPAs" and American barley wines (65–100 IBUs).

Matthew Brynildson

Black and Tan is a beer cocktail composed of one part bitter, amber ale, pale ale, or pale lager and one part stout or porter. It is traditionally poured at the bar so that the two beers layer, often with the darker beer in the top half of the glass. "Black and tan" is also a term used by more than a dozen US breweries for bottled products that consist of similar blends. Examples include Yuengling Original Black and Tan, Saranac Black & Tan, Mississippi Mud Black & Tan, Hoppin' Frog Bodacious Black and Tan, and Michelob Black and Tan.

The fact that beers have different densities creates the opportunity to layer two beers in a glass as showcased by the traditional Black and Tan pour. Draught Guinness Stout is often used as the dark beer because its low specific gravity or density allows it to float on top of many other beers. A spoon (often specially fashioned for the job) facilitates the layering when placed with the round side of the bowl facing up to deflect and spread the top beer. This prevents churning and mixing of the two beers during pouring.

The term "Black and Tan" undoubtedly originated from England; the *Oxford English Dictionary* cites its first use to signify the drink in a slang dictionary in 1889. The drink is rarely seen in Ireland, where some may take the term "Black and Tan" as a reference to the uniforms of British paramilitary forces who opposed Irish independence in the 1920s and were widely known as black and tans. Because consumers in England have ordered blends of ales in pubs and alehouses since at least the early 1700s, similar mixtures under various names have no doubt been common for hundreds of years. The Black and Tan is one of the few to survive to the present day, if largely as a vaguely amusing bartender's stunt.

See also COCKTAILS.

Ray Daniels

black beer

See SCHWARZBIER.

black malt, or "black patent malt" as it used to be known, is a grist component used purely for color, flavor, and aroma. It contains almost no extract in terms of fermentability, and it is devoid of any enzymic activity. Colored malts generally are heated to high temperatures while the grain is still moist, but in highly colored grains, such as black and chocolate malts, the temperature in the roasting drums is up to 230°C (446°F), a temperature high enough to denature all enzymes. With a moisture content of 3.5%, and a color of over 1300° EBC (500–600° ASBC), black malt would typically be used at rates of around 3% to 5% in a grist.

Historically, black malt was a key ingredient of early 19th-century porter beers, into which it probably imparted a somewhat astringent taste, and, perhaps a smoky aroma. The invention of the process for making black malt is credited to Daniel Wheeler, who produced it using his new drum roaster in 1817. At the beginning of the 19th century, London porter brewers were restricted to using brownish malts for coloring their beers, and they would (often illegally) use various colorants for increasing beer color. Using a modified coffee roaster, Wheeler invented a method (which he patented, hence "patent" malt) for roasting malt at an elevated temperature without charring. The result gave "extractive matter of a deep brown color, readily soluble in hot or cold water . . . A small quantity of which will suffice for the purpose of colouring beer or porter." The huge Whitbread brewery in London was the first to take this new product on board in 1817, and other large brewers soon followed. This development was a large and lasting change in the flavor of modern dark beers.

See also DRUM ROASTER, PORTER, and WHEELER, DANIEL.

Briggs, D. E. *Malts and malting*. London: Blackie, 1998.
Cornell, Martyn. *Beer: The story of the pint*. London: Headline, 2003.

Ian Hornsey

blending houses are establishments specializing in the finishing, aging, blending, packaging, and sale of beers brewed outside their own premises. The practice of blending wine is commonplace; many Champagne houses blend and finish wines they have bought from others, Scotch blending houses are well respected, and "new make spirit" flows like water between distilleries, but few are familiar with similar traditions in beer. Breweries have always blended beer within their own houses, and it was once common for even large breweries to produce beer that was transported long distances in barrels, later to be bottle conditioned and sold by others. Britain's porter beer style is said to have grown out of blends put together in pubs out of various beers, the most famous of these being a blend called "three-threads." Often such blends would contain some fresh beer, some "stale" beer (stale meaning old, and it was not a pejorative term), and perhaps a dash of something else.

In the Payottenland region of Belgium, lambic was once routinely blended by houses that did not actually produce the wort. The vagaries of spontaneous fermentation have always meant that one cask of lambic beer was often quite different from another, even if they had been filled with the same wort. Each oak barrel of lambic represents its own individual ecosystem of microflora. Some barrels may become fruity, others sour, and yet others touched with an acetic tang. A lambic blending house would buy lambic barrels, often from a number of different producers, and blend the lambics in large wooden vats called foeders (or foudres in French), producing a new beer to match the house style and the desires of their customers. Some of these houses specialized in gueuze, which is always a blend of old beer and young fresh beer, gaining complexity from the former and vitality and eventual sparkle from the latter. Others would take things a step further, buying barrels of wort that had barely started their fermentations and then shepherding them through fermentation, years of aging, and finally blending and possible bottling.

In this respect, a lambic blending house was similar to an affineur of cheese, who may buy the cheese mere days after it is made, but then age it out to ripeness and put the house stamp on it. The lambic blender, therefore, was rarely simply a merchant or *négociant*. The past tense used here is intentional—whereas free-standing lambic blenders once dotted the countryside outside of Brussels, few are left. Hanssens of Dworp was until recently the only pure blending house left in Belgium, turning out fine, sharply bracing beers in traditional and experimental styles. As of 2011, however, things are stirring, and it seems certain that as interest in sour beer styles rises worldwide, more artisans will hear "the call of the blending foeder."

See also GUEUZE, LAMBIC, and PORTER.

De Wolf, Aschwin. http://www.Lambicandwildale.com/ (accessed December 12, 2010).

Oliver, Garrett. *The brewmaster's table*. New York: Ecco Books, 2003.

Garrett Oliver

Blenheim (barley)

See CHARIOT (BARLEY).

blonde ale, also referred to as "golden ale," is a bit of a catch-all term, though it usually refers to a beer in the same general family as cream ale and kölsch. These blonde ales feature a low to moderate original gravity that is fermented out very low for a crisp and dry finish with a detectable malty sweetness that is like bread or toast rather than caramel. The color is usually a bright full gold, and the grist is often just pilsner malt. Blonde ales are generally very smooth, and perfumy ester qualities are kept to a minimum. Low to moderate hop bitterness (15–25 IBU) is best achieved without using high alpha American hop varieties due to the delicate flavor structure. Most good examples show some hop aroma, but this tends to be the gentler German aroma varieties rather than the flashier American ones. Strengths of 4.5% to 5.5% are typical. Blonde ales are supposed to be easy-drinking and very approachable and though this sounds simple, it isn't. Brewing them requires skill, because any flaws will be noticeable. Though the hop bitterness is more generous than that of the old cream ale style, brewers seek to use soft water, as harder, alkaline waters can turn the bitterness harsh. Blonde ales can pair very well with delicate white fish and poultry dishes that are not burdened with heavy sauces. Blonde ales are best enjoyed fresh without cellaring, though it should be mentioned that there is an emerging new style that ages blonde ale in neutral wine barrels along with Brettanomyces and/or lactic acid bacteria and these products do age gracefully. Of course, this moves these beers away from the traditional meaning of "blonde ale," but some brewers enjoy using the name anyhow, perhaps as a fun opportunity to throw a curve ball to the beer-drinking public.

See also BRETTANOMYCES, CREAM ALE, and KÖLSCH.

Jeremy Marshall

bloom is a cloudy condition on the surface of glass bottles that can appear after a period of time, especially on re-usable bottles that have been run several times through a washer and filler. Bloom is a chemical reaction and part of the aging of glass. Technically, residual mobile ions, such as sodium ions, leach out of the silica sol and react with ambient moisture ($SiONa + H_2O \rightarrow SiOH + NaOH$). The newly formed sodium hydroxide, or lye, (NaOH) gradually dissolves the glossy outer layer of the glass and turns it hazy. This may take months, but will not occur in dry and relatively cool environments. There are various methods of removing bloom. Just washing a bottle with water can remove minor bloom, but severe bloom requires a soaking for about five minutes in HCL (at around pH 4) and a subsequent rinse. To retard bloom, many glass manufacturers apply a protective coating of sulfur, fluoride, or Freon compounds to their bottles.

See also SCUFFING.

Glass on Web. www.glassonweb.com/ (accessed on May 14, 2010).

Csilla Kato

Blue Moon Brewing Company was started in 1995 by Keith Villa, PhD, brewmaster, and Jim Sabia, marketer, as a craft-beer operating unit of the Coors Brewing Company (now called MillerCoors), headquartered at the Sandlot Brewery at Coors Field in Denver, Colorado (later renamed the Blue Moon Brewing Company at the Sandlot). See COORS BREWING COMPANY. The name stems from the vision that unique, great-tasting beers come into existence only once in a blue moon. All products were developed and tested at the Sandlot Brewery.

Originally, four products were offered including Belgian White, Nut Brown, Honey Blonde, and a seasonal autumn ale called Pumpkin Ale. Over the years, the multiple offerings were discontinued in order to concentrate on the company's biggest seller, Blue Moon Belgian White, also simply referred to as "Blue Moon." This is a version of the Belgian witbier style, packaged, unfiltered, and flavored with orange peel and coriander. See WHITE BEER. Through national distribution, a low-key marketing effort and consumer self-discovery, by 2009 Blue Moon Belgian White grew to become the single largest craft or pseudo-craft brand in the United States. Blue Moon also helped to popularize the Belgian White style of ale and to introduce American consumers to Belgian styles of beer.

Blue Moon was brewed in Utica, New York, from 1995 to 1997. Production moved to Cincinnati, Ohio, from 1997 to 1999, then to Memphis, Tennessee, from 1999-2001 and, from 2003-2008, to both Montreal, Canada, and Golden, Colorado. In 2008 production was moved to Eden, North Carolina, and Golden, Colorado.

In addition to Blue Moon Belgian White, the company also sells seasonal beers and limited release offerings, such as Grand Cru. Blue Moon remains a wholly owned subsidiary of MillerCoors.

See also CRAFT BREWING.

Keith Villa

bock beer, a strong beer with an original gravity above 16 degrees Plato and a typical alcohol content beyond 6.5% ABV. The style originated in the lower-Saxonian town of Einbeck, Germany and has many regional and commercial variations. Some of these claim to have historical roots, and others are simply experimenting with the effects of certain ingredients and/or certain yeast strains on a wort of high gravity. While most bock beers are bottom fermented lagers, there is a broad range of top fermenting beers that also fall into the category, with weizenbock being the most prominent among them. Many strong ales of British, Belgian, or American origin are "bock beers" by the legal standards that have been established in many European countries for proper taxation, even if they are considered nothing of the sort in their home countries.

It is generally assumed that the first commercial bock was brewed in the German town of Einbeck, halfway between Hannover and Kassel. Einbeck had won fame for brewing and exporting a very

Poster stamp, c. 1875, advertising Thomasbräu Bock, produced by Paulaner, one of the big six Munich breweries. PIKE MICROBREWERY MUSEUM, SEATTLE, WA

tasty strong beer in the middle ages. In 1368 Einbeck joined the Hanseatic League, which helped find customers for the beer from Einbeck in Scandinavia, Russia, Britain, and Flanders. These were markets that were already acquainted with strong beers from other Hansa member cities like Rostock that had joined the league about a century earlier. The oldest written record mentioning beer from Einbeck is a receipt for two casks of "Einbecker" sold to the town of Celle on April 28, 1378. A key factor for the success of Einbeck's product was a unique system of quality control that had been established by the city council. Dozens of burghers were entitled to malt their own grains (barley and wheat, which accounted for one third of the grain bill) and make beer in their own cellar, but none of them was allowed to possess his own brewhouse. The brewing equipment was owned by the city and the city council employed professional brewers who would take the brew kettle to the homes of those burghers who wanted to brew. The brewmaster, being a civil servant to the city, had to check the malt, oversee the actual brewing process, and later certify the finished product before it could be sold or exported.

The streets of Einbeck's historical town center are still lined with colorful timber-framed buildings from the 15th and 16th century that have extraordinarily large gateways. These had to be wide enough to bring in the brew kettle when it was moved from one town house to the next in the row. The procedure made sure that all beer brewed in Einbeck followed the same recipe and met the same quality standards regardless of which household had brewed it.

This early form of standardizing a product came along with a set of marketing ideas that seem to come right out of a textbook for modern branding although they have been applied half a millennium ago. The beer from Einbeck was tested at one of the leading laboratories of its time at the medical faculty of the university of Salerno where it was described as "vinum bonum" ("good wine"). In 1521 when the church-reformer Martin Luther, one of the most prominent men of his time, had to defend his program at the Diet (General Assembly) in Worms he brought along a jug filled with beer from Einbeck that he drank in public praising it as the "best drink one can know." And most of all, Einbeck did a good job in branding its product as "Ainpöckisch Pier," a term that was soon shortened to "Oanpock" by Bavarian consumers and later "a bock bier," hence the name.

Shipments of the strong bock beer were growing. In 1578 the town of Munich spent 562 guilder on bock beer imported from Einbeck. It was time to copy its success. In 1617 Elias Pichler, a master brewer from Einbeck, was hired for the Hofbräuhaus in Munich to brew a Bavarian version of "Oanpock," which became extremely popular especially in lent periods when strong drinks ("liquid bread") had to replace at least some part of the food in the diet of a pious Catholic. This is why to this day many bock beers are labeled "Weihnachtsbock" or "Osterbock" for Christmas and Easter, respectively. Contrary to common belief these beers are not meant to celebrate the holidays but to be consumed in the weeks preceding them. For lent in spring an even stronger version of bock beer, "doppelbock," is brewed every year in many Bavarian breweries, some breweries also brew a "Maibock" to be consumed in May.

Most of the bock beers are golden to amber in color, but some can also be reddish or even black. A relevant commercial example for this style is the "Zipfer Stefanibock," the best-selling bock beer in Austria, and of course the "Ur-Bock" from Einbecker

Brauhaus, the only surviving brewery in Einbeck city. The small Plank brewery in Franconia brews an award-winning weizenbock and the "Masuren-Dunkel" from Browar Kormoran in Poland is an example of a typical dark bock. Many—but not all—bock beers tend to be full-bodied to slightly sweet and malty with a floral or fruity note. They are generally not hop-driven beers, and bitterness is kept to a moderate level. It should be noted that bock beers tend to age very well, with some able to cellar for many decades.

Conrad Seidl

Boddington's Brewery. In 1832 Henry Boddington joined the Strangeways Brewery in Manchester, UK, which had been founded by Thomas Caister and Thomas Fray in 1778. Henry quickly rose to a partnership in 1847 in the brewery, now called John Harrison & Co. He became sole proprietor of the business in 1853. Under his management and that of his successors from the Boddington family, the company became a major regional brewer, producing close to 560,000 barrels (650,000 hl) by 1985. The company largely grew organically, having purchased only three smaller brewers (Bridge Brewery in Burton, 1869; Hull's Brewery, Preston, 1900; Isle of Man Brewery, ca 1907), until acquiring Richard Clarke & Co. of Stockport in 1962.

The Boddington family's share holdings had fallen to about 40% in the 1930s, making the company a target for other brewers, and Allied Breweries made a bid in 1969. This was unsuccessful, fended off with help from the Whitbread Investment Company, who brought Boddington's under their protective umbrella. See WHITBREAD BREWERY. Boddington's remained independent, buying up Oldham Brewery in 1982 and Higson's of Liverpool in 1985. Their 280 pubs were a valuable prize and Whitbread took over the company in 1989. Whitbread took Boddington's distinctive pale gold bitter cask-conditioned ale, famous for its high hop bitterness, nitrogenated it, made it somewhat bland, and turned it into a mass-market brand. In 2001 Whitbread sold its brewing business to the Belgian company Interbrew (later to become InBev, now Anheuser-Busch Inbev). See INBEV. Boddington's brewery was closed in 2005; only the brand lives on, as a part of the portfolio of the world's largest brewer.

Jacobsen, Michael. *200 years of beer*. Manchester, England: Boddington's Breweries Ltd, 1978.

Terry Foster

bog myrtle. Also known as "sweet gale," and scientifically as Myrica Gale, bog myrtle grows, as its name might suggest, in marshlands in the northern latitudes. It was traditionally one of the primary elements of gruit, the flavoring and preservative blend of herbs used in brewing beer before the common use of hops, and it continues to be employed as an antiseptic, a sedative, an expectorant and an anti-itch medicine in herbal treatments. See GRUIT.

Bog myrtle has played a substantial part in the history of brewing in Britain, Ireland and Europe, and into nearly modern times in Scandinavia, where it is known as "Pors." It is nearly ubiquitous in mentions of gruit mixtures, and continues to be used by homebrewers and small traditional craft brewers in the areas in which it is found. It grows in swampy lowlands at the edges of lakes, ponds, and rivers in the boreal reaches of England, Scotland, and Ireland, northern Europe, nearly throughout Canada, and in the United States in areas approaching the forty-eighth parallel, as well as in Alaska. Henry David Thoreau mentioned it in his unfinished manuscript *Wild Fruits* in the 1850s.

In beer, bog myrtle imparts a somewhat astringent and resinous flavor and mouthfeel. It can be used as a partial hop substitute or as an herbal additive, either in the boil or in the fermenter, where interaction with alcohol can better integrate its overall effect.

Buhner, Stephen Harrod. *Sacred and herbal healing beers: The secrets of ancient fermentations*. Boulder, CO: Siris Books/Brewers Publications, 1998.

Graeve, Maud. *A modern herbal*. New York: Harcourt, Brace, 1931.

Thoreau, Henry David. *Wild fruits: Thoreau's rediscovered lost manuscript*. New York: W.W. Norton & Co., 1999.

Dick Cantwell

Bohemia is the northwestern part of the Czech Republic comprising about two thirds of the country.

Historically Bohemia was a kingdom (from 1158 until 1918) within the Habsburg and later the Austro-Hungarian Empire. Many of the famous Czech brewing towns are situated in Bohemia including Budweis (Ceské Budejovice), Krusovice, Pilsen, Prague, Saaz (Žatec), and Velké Popovice. Bohemian brewing became famous in the 13th and 14th centuries when some of the aforementioned towns were granted brewing privileges and banlieu rights (which meant that within a certain distance of the town only beer brewed by the town's burghers could be legally sold). Part of this fame might be credited to the hops from (and of the variety of) Saaz (Žatec). Hops of that origin were considered so valuable that the hop bales were branded with the town's official seal and that it was legally prohibited to export hop sprouts out of Bohemia. The brewing industry suffered greatly during the 30 Years War (1618–1648), which wiped out two thirds of the population and saw local nobility and town councils on the losing protestant side. Brewing privileges were revoked and many breweries were taken over by Catholic nobility loyal to the Habsburg emperor. It was not until the invention of the pilsner-style beer by Josef Groll in 1842 that Bohemia was put back onto the map as a leading brewing country. In the three decades following the invention of pilsner beer the whole industry changed dramatically, as brewers abandoned their traditional warm-fermenting techniques for the new cold lager fermentations. Pilsen's technology was widely copied across the region and was more or less unchanged for more than a century, especially since the western obsession with producing "cleaner tasting" beers was not shared by Bohemia's communist rulers in the second half of the 20th century. The traditional Pilsner beers, with their somewhat darker color and their sometimes noticeably buttery diacetyl content, would come to define something that was understood as "Bohemian-style pilsner."

See also CZECH REPUBLIC, DIACETYL, PILSNER, and SAAZ (HOP).

Conrad Seidl

Bohemian pilsner, a beer style that retains closer links to the origins of the "pilsner family" of lager beer styles than any other type. The town of Pilsen (Plzeň in Czech) is the capital of Czech Bohemia, and it is here that Bavarian brewer Josef Groll brewed the original pilsner beer in 1842. That brewery is now called Plzeňský Prazdroj, better known as Pilsner Urquell, which means original source. However, within the Czech Republic, only beer from Pilsen is called pilsner, even when it is brewed in the same style. For the Czechs, pilsner is essentially an appellation contrôlée, and German brewers respect this by calling their similar beers by the truncated name "pils." To the rest of the world, Czech beers such as Staropramen, Gambrinus, Krusovice, and Budweiser Budvar represent a style called Bohemian or Czech pilsner.

Eventually, the German pilsner brewers refined their pils beers into a style that became distinct from the Bohemian originals. They are very much lager beers, cold-fermented and aged for up to 90 days. Whereas German pilsners eventually became paler, reaching for a bright yellow color, the Czech beers are deep gold, sometimes even showing hints of red, although the brewing grists are invariably 100% pilsner malt. Part of this is caused by differing malts and water, and some of it may be caused by darkening of the wort by oxidation in open grants as the wort runs from the lauter tuns. See GRANT and HOT-SIDE AERATION. Decoction mashing remains common in the Czech breweries, and this may have a darkening effect as well, also perhaps bringing a deepening of malt flavors. Hops tend to be the local floral Saaz variety and they are used more assertively. Whereas the average German pilsner today has a bitterness of 28 International Bitterness Units (IBUs), the Czech pilsners are usually closer to 35 IBU, making them notably snappier. Balanced against this is a bit more malt sweetness, a slightly toastier malt flavor, and sometimes even a small whiff of diacetyl, a buttery-tasting compound created by yeast and aggressively opposed by most lager brewers. Altogether these qualities make the Bohemian pilsner a more full-bodied version of the style than the German one, and some beer festival competitions separate the two into their own categories.

Garrett Oliver

Bohemian Red (hop)

See SAAZ (HOP).

boiling wort is one of the most crucial and complex aspects of the brewing process. In the days before people developed the ability to fashion metal vessels, wort was often run into wooden or stoneware vessels and heated to the boiling point by the addition of glowing-hot stones. Today there are very few types of beer where the wort is not boiled. Among the better-known types is the Finnish traditional beer called Sahti, for which the wort is merely heated; see SAHTI. Though they knew nothing of microbes, ancient brewers soon learned that beer made from boiled wort lasted longer and was healthier to drink.

The boiling of wort serves various functions:

- inactivation of residual enzymes from the mash
- isomerization of bittering hop α-acids
- sterilization of the wort
- removal of unwanted volatiles
- precipitation of unwanted proteins as "hot break" (trub) (See HOT BREAK)
- concentration of the wort

During an effective boil, all of these goals can be accomplished, usually in under 90 minutes. But achieving an effective boil is not as simple as it sounds. With the exception of the conversion of dimethyl sulphide (DMS) precursor (S-methyl methionine) to free DMS (a compound with an often undesirable aroma reminiscent of cooked corn; See DIMETHYL SULFIDE (DMS)) a reaction fundamentally impacted by time and the duration of the boil, the other chemical and physical events in boiling are generally quantified empirically by measuring evaporation rate. Water is usually boiled off at a rate of about 4% per hour.

Vigorous mixing is mandatory for the effective coagulation of proteins to form flocks, although shear forces need to be minimized if such flocks are not to be subsequently disrupted, making the unwanted protein difficult to remove. Polypeptides need to be denatured during boiling so as to manifest their optimum foam-stabilizing properties, although this simultaneously increases the extent to which they are lost owing to their elevated hydrophobicity.

When hops are boiled in wort, the bittering alpha acids are isomerized; it is only then that they become soluble and can be extracted into the wort. See ALPHA ACIDS. At 212°F (100°C) in wort of pH 5.2, approximately 1% of the total alpha acid is isomerized every minute. Wort boiling, therefore, takes time.

The end result of boiling is impacted greatly by the vessel configuration and the heating regime, as well as by the composition of the sweet wort and of any other materials introduced to the vessel (sugars and syrups; clarification aids; and, of course, hops and hop products).

The rate of transfer of heat from condensing steam to wort is greatly impacted by the area of the heating surface and the temperature difference between the steam and the wort (ΔT). If unwanted cooking reactions are to be avoided, it is best to maintain a low ΔT. Establishing the appropriate surface area is important and influenced by any fouling and by refreshment of the boundary layer through wort flow. Pumping the wort will facilitate heat transfer but then hot break integrity is jeopardized.

Boiling is carried out in kettles, sometimes referred to as "coppers" because of the metal from which they were originally fabricated. These days they are usually made from stainless steel, but sometimes contain some "sacrificial copper" to bind sulfur compounds such as hydrogen sulfide. But the modern brewer must be careful; over-heating will "burn-on" and caramelize sugars, and lead to the formation of undesirable "cooked" flavors, darkening of the wort, and possibly to carbonyl substances that contribute to aged or stale character in beer. For centuries most wort boiling was done in large direct-fired pots with wood, coal, or gas flames roaring beneath them. Today, direct firing is largely avoided for the reasons above.

There are many shapes for kettles. The essential criterion is the extent to which a "rolling boil" can be achieved. It is only when the boil is vigorous that there will be efficient steam volatilization of off flavors, effective precipitation of proteins and polyphenols, etc.

The kettles used by most small breweries today employ low-pressure steam jackets within the walls of the vessel. Most larger modern kettles feature an internal (or external) bundle of heater tubes (calandria) through which the wort passes upwards before striking a spreader plate that returns the wort to the surface. In the spraying, volatiles escape. An example of such a system is the Stromboli, produced by Krones of Germany.

In dynamic low-pressure boiling systems that allow for a rapid evaporation of volatiles while reducing overall water evaporation, the pressure is raised and lowered between pressures of 1.0 bar and 1.2 bar (corresponding to temperatures of 100°C–102°C [12°F–215°F] and 104–105°C [220–221°F]); this occurs six times per hour. Every pressure release stage leads to an instant boiling of the kettle contents, with attendant sweeping away of volatiles.

The Merlin system, also produced by Krones, is claimed to allow quality beers from worts despite evaporation rates as low as 4%. It comprises a vessel containing a conical heating bottom for boiling and evaporating wort. The whirlpool, below the Merlin device, serves as a collection vessel for wort. A pump circulates wort between the vessels. Wort is lautered into the whirlpool, at the end of which the wort is pumped as a thin film over the conical heating surface of the Merlin. The thin film, high flow rate, and turbulent flow ensure that heat transfer is very good with a very low temperature differential between steam and wort, as well as very good volatile stripping. Over a 40- to 60-minute period the wort passes four to six times over the heating surface, with just 1.5%–2.5% evaporation and low thermal damage of the wort. The whirlpool is insulated, so breakdown of DMS precursor occurs therein. The contents of the whirlpool are in rotation throughout boiling, with good separation of hot break, so the "rest" can be as short as 10 minutes. Wort is pumped once more over the heating surface en route to the cooler, in which "stripping" phase the free DMS formed in the whirlpool is driven off virtually completely.

There is a physical limitation to the surface area that can be achieved with internal devices, which shifts the focus to heating systems outside of the kettle. One such example is Symphony™ from the Briggs company, with its very large heater surface area that is some four- to five-fold greater than the norm. This large area allows a much lower ΔT with the attendant benefits in terms of lessened "cooking" and also the facilitation of more brews between cleans. The substantial surface area and low ΔT make for huge quantities of small vapor bubbles, maximizing the liquid/vapor interface area and promoting trub formation and volatile stripping. See TRUB. Lower evaporation rates are possible with savings in energy costs.

External systems can be used over a wide range of brew lengths; they overcome the disadvantage of internal heaters in that the latter cannot be used until submerged below wort level.

The PDX Wort Heater uses direct steam at speeds of 3,000 feet per second to break wort into mist droplets with a huge surface area, thereby allowing for the efficient stripping of volatiles.

The Ecostripper comprises a sequence of wort kettle, whirlpool, wort stripping column, and cooler. In the stripping step, the unwanted volatile compounds are purged by clean steam injection. The stripping column is filled with packing to ensure a large surface area and the wort flows downwards counter to steam. The claims are that this saves energy through reduced boiling; heat recovery; less color development; and less heat abuse.

See also WORT.

Leiper, K.A., & Miedl, M. "Brewhouse technology." In *Handbook of brewing*, eds. F.G. Priest & G.G. Stewart, 383–445. Boca Raton, FL: CRC Press, 2006.

Charles W. Bamforth

Boon Brewery in the Belgian village of Lembeek on the banks of the River Senne can trace its origins back to 1680, when a certain J. B. Claes purchased a farm and converted it into a brewery and distillery. Lembeek is considered by many the architypical home of the Belgian sour beer style called lambic and its derivatives. In fact, according to one theory, the name "lambic" is simply a mispronunciation of Lembeek. According to another theory, however, lambic is a mangled form of "alembic," the French word for a pot still. At one point in the 1800s, there were more than 40 breweries in operation in Lembeek, and many of them were distilleries as well. The Claes Brewery changed hands in 1860 and was renamed Brasserie de Saint Roch, which, 15 years later, bottled its first Gueuze, a blended lambic style. A malt house was added to the brewery in 1890. In subsequent decades the premises were subdivided and sold several times until, in 1977, Frank Boon, a commercial blender and marketer of Gueuze, purchased the site and renamed it Brouwerij Boon. In 1986, Boon moved his operation to a new site in the center of Lembeek, where he installed a modern brewhouse and cellar. In 1990, he entered into a 50/50 joint venture with the Belgian Palm Brewery, and in October of that year, he finally produced his first batch of his own lambic. Within the 2 decades since, annual production at Boon has increased from a mere 450 hl (383 US bbl) the first year to well over 11,000 hl (9,374 US bbl). Because lambics and their derivative styles are well-aged beers, the amount of lambic held in oak barrels at Boon at any one time exceeds 1 million l (approx. 8,522 US bbl), which is reputed to be the largest stock of lambic anywhere. Today, the Boon portfolio includes just about all varieties of lambic beer. Among these are the Champagne-like, 2-year-old Oude Geuze Boon (Boon has his own unique spelling of the word "Gueuze"), the select Geuze Mariage Parfait, the Faro Perte Totale made from half young and half old lambic with the addition of candi sugar and spice, the Kriek Boon and Oude (traditional) Kriek Boon cherry lambics matured in large oak foudres, the Framboise Boon raspberry lambic, and the dark, hop-aromatic, and slightly coffeeish Duivels Bier (devil's beer), which is brewed with dark malt and candi sugar. The Boon beers are largely traditional, if not as bone dry as most lambic enthusiasts would have them; the beers featuring the prefix "Oude" are more concentrated and avoid the modern sweetness.

See also FRAMBOISE, KRIEK, LAMBIC, and PALM BREWERIES.

Brouwerij Boon. http://www.boon.be/ (accessed January 24, 2011).
Palm Breweries. http://www.palm.be/ (accessed January 24, 2011).
http://tiac.net/~tjd/bier/boon.html/(inactive).

Lorenzo Dabove

Boon Rawd Brewery is best known for its German-style lager Singha and the distinctive mythical lion emblazoned on its packaging. The renowned beer writer Michael Jackson once described it as "an outstanding pale lager that would attract attention anywhere in the world." Singha is brewed from 100% barley malt, giving the golden beer a full-bodied character and flavor. Printed on the neck label of each bottle of Singha are the words "by royal permission," which refer to the fact that the company received a seal of approval from HM King Rama VII, a distinction it earned on October 25, 1939. Founded by Phraya Bhirom Bhakdi, Boon Rawd had become the first Thai brewery 6 years earlier. Born Boonrawd Sreshthabutra, Bhakdi traveled to Germany and Denmark in 1930 to observe European brewing practices before launching his enterprise. His son, Prachuab Bhirom Bhakdi, was the first brewmaster in Thailand.

In the 1970s Boon Rawd began to sell Singha internationally. Boon Rawd claims to have introduced the concept of the beer garden to Thailand during the 1980s. The company is still family owned and operates three breweries in Thailand. In addition to Singha and Singha Light, their beverage business now includes bottled water, soda water, green tea, and an energy drink called B-ing, along with two other beer brands, Leo and Thai Beer. With a production capacity that exceeds 12.7 million barrels annually, it remains the largest brewer in Thailand and distributes Singha to over 40 countries.

Boon Rawd Trading International Co., Ltd. *Boonrawd.co.th.* http://www.boonrawd.co.th/ (accessed June 14, 2010).
Hamson, Tim. *The beer book.* New York: Dorling Kindersley, 2008.
Jackson, Michael. *The new world guide to beer.* Philadelphia: Running Press, 1988.
Singha Corporation Co., Ltd. *Leobeer.com.* http://www.leobeer.com/ (accessed June 14, 2010).

Ben Keene

borage (Borago officinalis L.), a hardy annual, also called "starwort," was once known as one of the four "cordial flowers most esteemed for cheering the spirits," and it is most probably a native of Syria and other parts of the Mediterranean basin, but now naturalized in most parts of Europe.

The fresh herb has blue flowers with a cucumber-like fragrance and has been regularly used in herbal medicine since the time of the ancient Greeks. It has been said, notably by the Greek physician and botanist Dioscorides (ca. 40–90 AD; author of *De Materia Medica*), that the plant was the "Nepenthe" described by Homer in the fourth book of his *Odyssey.* Nepenthe literally means "medicine of sorrow," or "the one that chases sorrow away," on account of the fact that when it is taken with alcohol the imbiber is said to enter a state of absolute forgetfulness. In a similar vein, Pliny the Elder named the plant *Euphrosinum* because it was believed that it brought happiness and joy to the user.

Borage is widely used in traditional soups and salads throughout Europe, and it is particularly popular in the Liguria region of Italy, where it is used to fill ravioli and pansotti pastas. There are various suggestions for the naming of the plant, one being that it is derived from "barrach," a Celtic word meaning "man of courage." Another maintains that "borago" is a corruption of "corago" (which literally means "I bring heart"). As a medicinal herb, it has diuretic and emollient properties.

In northern Europe, borage has been used as a beer flavoring since medieval times, and was almost certainly sometimes a component of gruit, although the secrecy surrounding that beer component precludes absolute identification. An ancient drink known as "cool tankard" was made with wine (or strong beer), water, lemon, sugar, and the leaves and flowers of borage. The traditional version of the classic cocktail "Pimm's Cup" includes a garnish of borage leaves, but these days most bartenders replace this with the more readily available slice of cucumber.

See also GRUIT.

Buhner, S.H. *Sacred and herbal healing beers.* Boulder, CO: Siris Books, 1998.
Grieve, M. *A modern herbal.* New York: Dover, 1971.
Gunther, R.T. (ed.) *The Greek herbal of Dioscorides.* Oxford, England: Oxford University Press, 1933.
Hornsey, I.S. *A History of beer and brewing*. Cambridge: Royal Society of Chemistry, 2003.
Unger, R.W. *A History of brewing in Holland 900–1900.* Leiden, England: Brill, 2001.

Ian Hornsey

Bosteels Brewery is a classic, mid-size family brewery in the small village of Buggenhout, in East Flanders, central Belgium. Founded in 1971, the brewery has been run by the Bosteels family for seven generations. Although family breweries everywhere are under pressure to keep up with the multinationals on the one hand and with and the versatile micros on the other, Bosteels seems to have found its market niche. Between 2002 and 2010, Bosteels' sales have gone from 25,000 to 65,000 hl (21,300 to 55,400 bbl).

After extensive investment in modern brew equipment in 1953, the Bosteels added an emporium of music halls, where the brewery's bottom-fermented Salamander sold in massive quantities. This attraction fell out of favor in the 1970s, but a renewed interest by beer drinkers in specialty ales more than made up for the decline in entertainment revenues. One of the unique Bosteels beers is the Pauwel Kwak, an ale that is world famous for the stemless coachman's glass in which it is served. The beer's name means "babbling Paul," a reference to a legendary local coachman who just couldn't keep his mouth shut. The glass is shaped so that it can be hung on the coach, keeping the driver's hands free for reining the horses. Then there is the Tripel Karmeliet, a multigrain brew of wheat, oats, and barley, served in an attractively etched tulip glass. One of the Bosteels' ales is called "The Same Again," which make you wonder what they were thinking when they gave that brew such a tongue-in-cheek name. A most unusual brew is the DeuS Brut des Flandres. This brew, whose name is reminiscent of the Latin "dues" for "God," is made at Bosteels, but then shipped across the border to the Champagne region of France, where it is finished by the *méthode champenoise* like an actual champagne. The result is a fine-pearly, truly *pétillant* beer of supreme elegance and delicacy that is best served in a champagne flute. Just as eager as the brewery is to introducing innovative beers, it also has no hesitation to discontinue brews that do not sell. Thus, abandonment was the fate that befell such traditional Bosteels brews as Cupido (an ale), Buggs (a low-alcohol beer), and Prosit Pils (a lager and the brewery's oldest product). Next to the sophisticated glassware and attention-getting idiosyncratic names that ensure notoriety for Bosteels beers, it certainly has not hurt that the brewery has also been a reliable award winner at many international beer competitions.

Joris Pattyn

The **Boston Beer Company** is one of the largest American-owned brewing companies, best known for its line of all-malt beers under the brand name Samuel Adams. The Boston Beer Company was founded by Jim Koch, Harry Rubin, and Lorenzo Lamadrid in 1984, along with Rhonda Kallman, a colleague of Koch's from Boston Consulting Group, who was made a founding partner and vice president of sales in 1985. See KOCH, JIM. As of 2011 the company was publicly traded on the New York Stock Exchange (Ticker: "SAM"), employed over 750 people, and produced nearly

2 million barrels annually. Net revenue for fiscal year 2009 exceeded $415 million.

The first beer produced by the company, Samuel Adams Boston Lager, was based on a recipe created by Koch's great-great grandfather Louis Koch and was first sold on Patriots' Day in 1985.

The brand name Samuel Adams was chosen to honor the American Revolution leader, who is also believed to have been at least a maltster, although some accounts do suggest he was a brewer, too. For example, in Ira Stoll's "Samuel Adams: A Life," the author reports that Jim Koch was "once offered for sale a receipt for hops signed by the patriot Samuel Adams."

The beer was hand-sold in the beginning, and by the end of their first year production was about 500 barrels. Later the same year, it was selected as "The Best Beer in America" in The Great American Beer Festival's Consumer Preference Poll (and the subsequent 3 years), which figured heavily in early advertising of the brand. The second Samuel Adams beer the company released was their Double Bock, which went on sale in 1988.

By 1992, the brand was distributed nationally in every state and by 1994 was the best-selling specialty beer in the country. In the early 1990s, sales were around $50 million annually, but by the mid-1990s had risen to over $200 million, with 1.2 million barrels produced.

All of Boston Beer's early production was on a contract basis, brewed initially at the Pittsburgh Brewing Co in Pennsylvania, and later at still others, such as Stroh's, Blitz-Weinhard, and Miller breweries. In 1988, the company renovated the former Haffenreffer Brewery in the Jamaica Plain neighborhood of Boston, which today is a tourist destination. A pilot brewery there also conducts research and development and brews specialty beers for limited release. Separate corporate offices are also maintained in downtown Boston.

In the mid-1990s, Boston Beer purchased the Hudepohl-Schoenling Brewery in Cincinnati and in 2005 completed a major renovation and expansion. In 2008, a third brewery was acquired in Breinigsville, Pennsylvania. Today, all Samuel Adams' beers are produced at company-owned breweries.

The Boston Beer Company went public in 1995, selling Class A Common Stock (which have very limited voting rights) on the New York Stock Exchange, whereas founder Jim Koch owns 100% of Class B Common Stock, which is the only class with full voting rights.

Over 30 different beers are produced under the Samuel Adams label, with Boston Lager still accounting for the majority of the company's sales. In 2002, Sam Adams Light was introduced, making it one of the first low-calorie light beers produced by a craft brewery. In addition to Boston Lager and Sam Adams Light, nearly a dozen seasonal beers are released each year along with several series of beers. These include, to date, the Brewmaster's Collection (consisting of 12 different beers), the Imperial Series (with 4 beers), and the Barrel Room Collection (with 3 beers).

In addition to the flagship beers and the other series, Boston Beer has also produced a number of specialty beers. Triple Bock, released in 1994, was one of the company's first specialty releases and one the first extreme beers produced in America. Triple Bock was an 18% alcohol by volume (ABV) non-carbonated beer sold in a distinctive, small 0.25 l (8.45-oz) dark-blue bottle. That was followed by Millennium Ale in 2000 (at 20% ABV) and Utopias, made every 2 years since 2002 (with the current version at 27% ABV). Utopias is currently the strongest beer made in the United States. Each of these beers has been made in limited quantities.

In 2006, the company began working with TIAX Laboratories of Cambridge, Massachusetts, to develop a proprietary glass. Comparing designs of dozens of glasses and testing different configurations for nearly a year, they designed the new glass to maximize such properties as nucleation, volume-to-surface ratio, and foam retention. The glass was released in 2007 and is claimed to enhance the flavors of Samuel Adams Boston Lager.

In addition to the Samuel Adams brand, the company owns the trade names Hardcore Cider Company and the Twisted Tea Brewing Company, under which they produce the alcoholic products hard cider and hard iced tea. Both lines are purposefully kept separate from the Samuel Adams brand.

The company also works closely with the homebrewing community and sponsors a contest called the Longshot American Homebrew Contest in which homebrewers are invited to enter their beers in regional competitions. Regional winners are then judged in a final, where three are selected as winners. The Longshot winners have their beers produced by Samuel Adams under the Longshot label, with their pictures on the label and sold in a mixed six-pack.

Baron, Stanley. *Brewed in America, the history of beer and ale in the United States.* Boston: Little, Brown and Company, 1962.
Kahn, Joseph P. "With new design, foam follows function." http://www.boston.com/ae/food/articles/2007/06/20/with_new_design_foam_follows_function/ (accessed February 8, 2011).
Stoll, Ira. *Samuel Adams: A life.* New York: Free Press, 2008.

Jay R. Brooks

bottle aging

See AGING OF BEER.

bottle collecting, the hobby of collecting older-style beer bottles, began growing in popularity in the United States during the 1970s with the publication of the Kovels' price list book on antique bottles. The Kovel book together with the *National Association Breweriana Advertising* in 1972 served as a starting point for many interested in learning more about beer bottle collecting. Today, collectors often focus on a particular type of bottle or bottles from a particular geographical area. Popular brewing styles include porter and ale, brown stout, and various lagers, whereas Philadelphia, New York City, and Brooklyn have provided the greatest variety of producers in the United States.

Bottles entering collections are usually obtained in one of three ways. The first and most sought after bottles are those in "attic" or near-mint condition. Such examples come from old houses or the breweries themselves and show little evidence of actual circulation. Still others are found by scuba divers or along waterways by search or happenstance. Finally, older town dumps have been productive as well. In recent years many 19th-century beer bottles have been discovered by bottle diggers who unearth them in old garbage dumps and long-abandoned urban privy pits.

The Industrial Revolution by the 1830s brought more durable glass beer bottles to the United States in significant numbers. Bottles until the 1860s were typically hand blown into a blank or embossed mold using a hollow tube called a blowpipe or pontil rod. The glassblower would skillfully work the far end of the molten glass before breaking the bottle free of the rod, leaving either a circular "open" or "iron" pontil mark on the base. These are highly prized by many collectors. Mechanization of the process later simplified beer bottles to smooth bases with "blob tops" until the 1904 Owens Automatic Bottling Machine standardized most bottles into "crown tops," the genesis of the modern beer bottle.

See also CROWN CAP.

Guest, Gary. *Antique beer bottles of old New York,* 4th ed. New York: Guest, 2004.
Kovel, Ralph, and Terry Kovel. *Kovels' complete bottle price list,* 5th ed. New York: Crown, 1979.
Odell, John. *Digger Odell's sodas, mineral waters, porters & ales.* Mason, OH: Digger Odell, 2009.

Erik Fortmeyer

bottle conditioning, also known as "bottle refermentation," is the original method by which beer in the bottle is made sparkling. Today, most beer gets its carbonation from the injection of exogenous carbon dioxide under pressure. The bottle-conditioning technique involves bottling beer that contains little or no carbon dioxide and then adding priming sugars that yeast will ferment in the bottle. This refermentation (so called because it is performed after the original fermentation of the beer is already finished) gives off carbon dioxide, which dissolves into the beer, giving it natural carbonation. In this context the word "condition" refers directly to the carbon dioxide (CO_2) content of the beer; brewers refer to "bringing a beer into condition." Bottle conditioning, when done properly, can result in a beer with a finer, silkier texture of carbonation, superior foam retention, more complex flavors, longer shelf life, and better aging ability than beers that are "force carbonated." As a rule, the technique of bottle conditioning is capable of producing some of the world's most sophisticated beers. In commercial practice, however, bottle conditioning has never been a simple affair.

History

Until the Middle Ages, almost all beer was consumed flat, that is, without appreciable carbonation. With the advent of modern barrel making, the

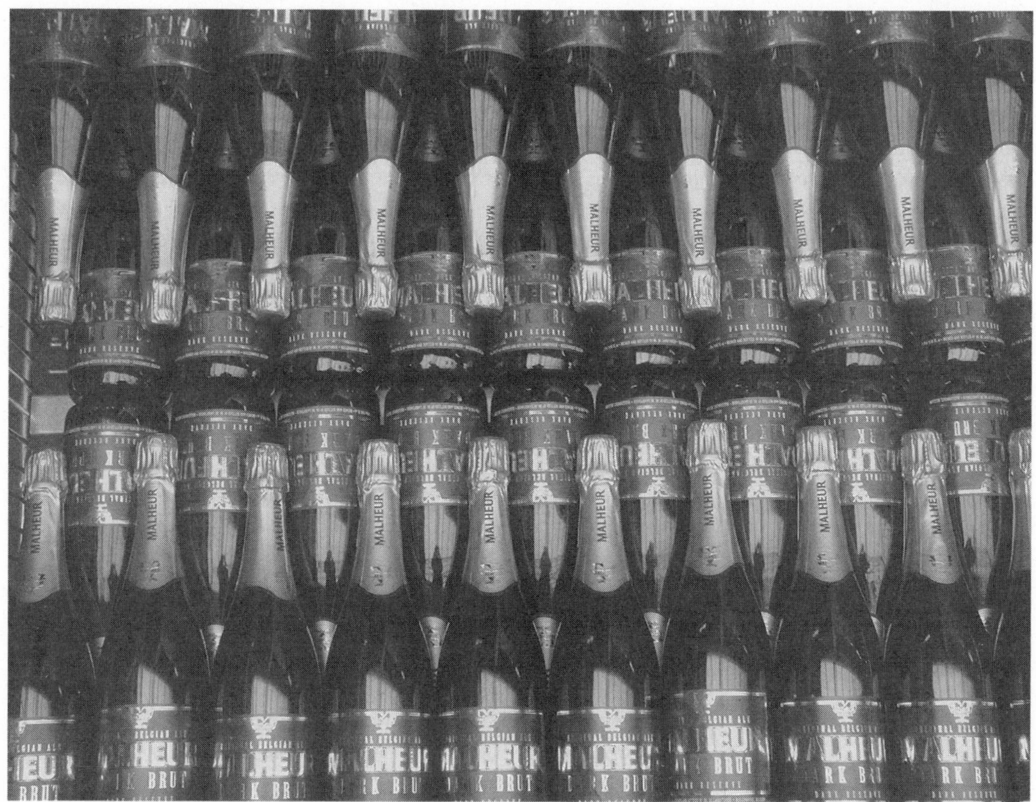

Malheur Dark Brut Ale undergoing a bottle conditioning that will naturally carbonate the beer. Bottle conditioning involves adding sugar and yeast before bottling, triggering a refermentation that produces natural carbonation with a delicate texture. COURTESY OF MANU DE LANDTSHEER (MALHEUR BREWERY)

world saw the first vessel that was physically able to hold a carbonated liquid under pressure. In those days, however, brewers had only a dim understanding of fermentation and very little knowledge of yeast. Barrels were made strong to withstand continuing fermentation over time, which often occurred whether the brewer intended it or not. Eventually, however, they learned that carbonation in the sealed barrel could be induced by the addition of extra wort or other sugars after the main fermentation had finished. See BARREL.

As small-scale commercial bottle manufacturing emerged in the 1600s, brewers and vintners alike showed interest in bottling their wares. Although carbonation was then considered a fine quality for beer, it was generally considered a detriment to wine. Brother Pierre Pérignon, later better known as Dom Pérignon, became treasurer of the Abbey of Hautvilliers, in the Champagne region of France, in 1668. Among his duties was the management of the abbey's cellars. Here, fermentations often started off in the autumn after harvest, but weather quickly turned cold and fermentations would cease, only to start again spontaneously in the spring. Any resulting carbonation was considered a problem for bottled wine because the weak bottles of the day would often burst under the pressure. Ironically, far from being the "father of Champagne," Dom Pérignon did everything he could to prevent wine from refermenting. Even once sparkling wine became fashionable, throughout the 1700s only a few thousand bottles of Champagne were produced annually, and half of them were lost to bursting.

Brewers, however, fared better. By the 1700s they were well accustomed to the production of sparkling beverages, and they used that knowledge earlier, better, and faster than did the winemakers. This is not surprising since the average brewer might have dozens of opportunities a year to produce beer, but the winemaker had but one chance per season. Belgium, England, and Germany took the lead.

In Belgium, the development of bottled gueuze, where young, partially fermented lambic beer is blended with older, fully fermented beer, gave Belgian brewers an increasing understanding of bottle refermentation. In traditional gueuze making, which was often carried out by an independent blender, the young beer, still containing residual sugars, provides the sugar for the secondary fermentation in the bottle. See BLENDING HOUSES and GUEUZE. Trappist monastic brewers, who were far more learned than most other brewers of the day, further developed the techniques for other types of beer as well. The British led the way in the manufacture of strong bottles specifically designed to hold high pressure. By the late 1700s, newspapers in Calcutta carried advertisements for bottled India pale ale.

Technique

No matter how it is carried out, bottle conditioning requires absolute cleanliness in both brewing and bottling. The beer will have sugar added to it and then spend a period at warm temperatures; this is a perfect environment in which to grow any unwanted spoilage organisms. The simplest and oldest form of bottle conditioning involves adding a measured amount of sugar to freshly fermented beer and bottling it immediately. This is the technique used by most homebrewers who bottle their beers. This technique uses the original fermentation yeast, still suspended in the beer, to consume the added sugars and produce the carbonation, usually within a few weeks.

This method, although it is common among amateur brewers and usually works perfectly well in that setting, is not suited to commercial brewing. Yeast that has just performed a primary fermentation is not the best candidate to perform refermentation. At this point the yeast is in a depleted state and is in a low pH environment, stressed by its own ethanol in solution, and will be further stressed by the pressure building in the bottle. Such yeast may or may not perform the task at hand suitably or within a predictable period of time, which is why most commercial brewers introduce new yeast for bottle conditioning. Sometimes this yeast is of the same strain that fermented the original beer, sometimes it is another brewing yeast strain, and sometimes it is a wine yeast; the aggressive strain Pris de Mousse, often referred to as "Champagne yeast," is a popular choice.

The most effective methods involve the removal of the original fermentation yeast before redosing. This allows the brewer to be certain that the bottle contains only fresh, healthy yeast of the strain desired. At this point, the amount of priming sugar, which will fuel the refermentation, must be calculated. The amount is dependent on three factors: the carbonation level desired in the finished beer, the CO_2 content of the beer at bottling, and the amount of fermentable sugar still remaining in the base beer. Most brewers will seek a carbonation level between 2.5 and 4 volumes (5–8 g/l). The former value is typical of most bottled beers on the market, whereas the latter value typifies the higher carbonation with which Belgian specialty beers are particularly associated.

To determine how much fermentable sugar the base beer still contains, the brewer performs a test called a "rapid fermentation," colloquially called a "rapid." By adding a large amount of yeast to warm beer in a flask and preferably stirring it for 24–48 hours, the brewer can see how much further the beer ferments; this final gravity becomes part of the refermentation calculation because the beer is likely to reach this value during the refermentation process in the bottle. Failure to take this residual fermentable sugar into account can result in overcarbonation and attendant gushing or, at worst, bursting bottles.

Even beer that seems to be flat will contain carbon dioxide. This can be measured with sophisticated equipment, but lacking this, brewers can assume that most beers fermented at temperatures around 20°C (68°F) will contain approximately 0.75 volumes (1.5 g/l) of CO_2 after fermentation. This small amount of CO_2 figures into the equation. The amount of carbonation in the bottle after bottle conditioning is a function of three simple parameters: how much CO_2 is already in the beer, how much total fermentable sugar is present after priming sugar is added, and how much of that fermentable sugar will actually be consumed by the refermentation yeast. For most applications, priming sugar will be between 8 and 12 g/l. See PRIMING SUGAR.

Priming sugar is usually glucose, dextrose, or sucrose, all of which produce clean flavors and are highly fermentable. These are available either in granulated form or in syrups, the latter typically containing an average of 66% sugar solids. In either case, the sugar will be added as a hot syrup, with the heat having guaranteed the syrup's sterility. Once the syrup is evenly blended into the beer, the yeast is added.

Yeast concentrations will vary depending on a wide range of parameters, including shelf-life expectations, the desired appearance of the beer, and the time within which the brewery requires the refermentation to be finished. Typical additions range from a low of 200,000 cells/ml to a maximum of 2 million cells/ml, with about 1 millions cells/ml found suitable for most types of beer. Although it is possible to grow yeast specifically for this purpose, today many breweries use reconstituted dried yeast for refermentation. Modern dried yeast production techniques provide a range of excellent strains that can be used for refermentation, and the use of dried yeast allows the brewer to make the yeast addition highly accurate and repeatable. See DRY YEAST.

After the yeast is blended in, the beer is bottled warm, usually at 15.5–21°C (60–70°F), and the bottles are placed into warm storage at 21–25°C (70–77°F). Although it is possible to bottle the beer cold and allow the bottles to warm up in storage, this technique often results in stuck refermentations because the yeast may not emerge from dormancy. The onset of refermentation should be rapid and is generally complete with 2 to 3 weeks; many brewers find that a short period of cold storage thereafter is beneficial for flavor and appearance. Except for those few wishing to make some nod toward Champagne, bottle-conditioned beers do not undergo the processes of *remuage* and *dégorgement* associated with the *méthode Champenoise,* where the yeast is settled into the neck of the bottle and then removed after refermentation. For beer, the yeast is allowed to settle to the bottom of the bottle, where it can continue to help the beer evolve over time.

Because they are restricted by the "German Beer Purity Law," German brewers use a different technique for bottle conditioning. See REINHEITSGEBOT. Rather than adding priming sugar, they add a precisely dosed blend of wort and yeast called "speise," a word meaning "food." The speise provides both the fermentable sugar (along with unfermentable wort sugars) and the yeast necessary to perform the refermentation. This is most often seen in the production of traditionally bottle-conditioned hefeweizen (weissbier). However, most hefeweizen on the market is bottled with yeast, but is pasteurized beer that has not undergone bottle conditioning. Fortunately, some artisanal brewers continue to produce bottle-conditioned hefeweizen.

Modern Variants

The rise of filtered beer styles and the pressures of modern commercial production saw a decline in bottle conditioning over the 20th century. Some breweries, rather than abandoning bottle conditioning altogether, developed variants on the traditional techniques. Most beers bearing labels that claim that they are "bottle conditioned" are in fact only partially so. Partial bottle conditioning initially involves force carbonation of the beer, usually to about 2.2–2.5 volumes (4.4–5 g/l) of CO_2. This carbonated beer is then dosed with a smaller amount of yeast and priming sugar, and the beer undergoes a somewhat truncated refermentation in the bottle. Even some of the famous Trappist beers are now made by this method, which is obviously capable of producing very pleasant results. The modern technique has many advantages, including shorter refermentation times, the ability to add less yeast in the bottle, lower oxygen pickup on the bottling line, and something of a safety net should the refermentation not finish properly. However, both tasting and analyses clearly show that full bottle conditioning provides for more complex flavors in the finished beers.

With the rise of craft brewing worldwide, bottle conditioning is once again on the rise, if only on a relatively small scale. Some larger breweries have taken up partial bottle conditioning of a belief that the active yeast will remove oxygen from the beer and extend shelf-life, but this is only partially true. Yeast can remove small amounts of dissolved oxygen from beer, but very little from the bottle headspace air, which means these benefits will only attain to breweries using sophisticated brewing methods and very good packaging equipment. An increasing number of small artisanal breweries are using bottle conditioning to rediscover the complexity of flavor, aroma, and texture the process can bring to their beers. Producers of modern sour beer styles are using bottle conditioning to advance the effects of bacterial strains added in the bottle. The addition at bottling of alternative yeasts such as Brettanomyces can produce a wide range of potentially desirable aromatics as well. Like the affinage of traditional cheese, bottle conditioning is a traditional but difficult high-wire act that can bring about wonderful results when applied by skilled and judicious craftspeople.

See also BRETTANOMYCES and SOUR BEER.

Derdelinckx, Guy, B. Vanderhasselt, M. Maudoux, and J. P. Doufour. Refermentation in bottles and kegs: A rigorous approach. *Brauwelt International* 2 (1992): 156–64.

Robinson, Jancis. *The Oxford companion to wine*, 3rd ed. New York: Oxford University Press, 2006.

Garrett Oliver

bottles are today the most common package for beer worldwide. Although the bottle now strikes us as the natural package for beer, this was not always so. Historically, beer has not always been served as an effervescent beverage. In antiquity, beer was a flat beverage that was simply served in amphorae, crocks, buckets, leather sacks, or pitchers, sometimes imbibed communally through straws or by passing the drinking vessel around. The Romans invented the art of glass blowing and made simple bottles in which they may have sometimes stored wine. We know, however, that in this era bottles were rare and were not the main storage vessels for wine or, in fact, anything else. The 17th century saw glass making become a major commercial concern, and by the late 1600s glass bottles were common in European upper-class households. In the meantime, beer had moved into oak barrels. As soon as mankind had learned the art of tight, liquid-holding, metal-hooped cooperage in the early Middle Ages, beer could be kept in casks under modest pressure and poured by gravity. See GRAVITY DISPENSE. It took the Industrial Revolution, however, with its enormous advances in material science and fabricating technologies before cheap, pressurized, portable beer containers became possible. Specifically, beer needed the emergence of a glass industry in the late 19th century to become the widely distributed commodity that it is today, with beers made centrally at ever-larger breweries for shipment to entire regions, countries, and even the world. The first automated glass bottle manufacturing machine was invented only around 1900 by an American, Michael Joseph Owens (1859–1923), who first put used it in production in his Owens Bottle Machine Company, formed in 1903 and the forerunner of the current glass-making giant Owens-Illinois Inc.

The difficulty with beer is that it is at its best when it is effervescent, that is, when the container is under pressure. This represents a technological and economic challenge. The technical challenge is that the material must be impermeable to both liquids and gasses, it must be strong, and preferably it should also be lightweight and easy to produce. The challenge is economical because beer, unlike Champagne, for instance, is the common person's everyday drink. This means that the investment in the packaging must be amortized by the sale of the relatively low-priced—compared with many other alcoholic beverages—content. Most beers, therefore, cannot be put in bottles that are very expensive to produce.

Glass had many practical advantages over the old casks. People could now purchase beer in small amounts and easily travel with it or bring it home to the dinner table. The bottle did have one crucial drawback: it does not block sunlight. Sunlight is the great enemy of any hopped beer's flavor and shelf life, because it provides the ultraviolet energy for a highly undesirable photochemical reaction, during which the bittering agents iso-alpha acids react with sulfurous fermentation trace elements and dissolved oxygen to produce 3-methyl-2-butene-1-thiol, a compound that gives an unpleasant "skunky" flavor in concentrations as low as 0.4 parts per trillion. See LIGHTSTRUCK. Trained tasters can detect the results of this reaction after as little as 30 seconds of exposure to bright sunlight. The reaction is fastest in clear bottles, which do not impede light at all. It is slightly slower in green bottles, which cannot block the frequency of light that is most responsible for the skunking process. Green bottles, despite their ubiquity, remain poor packages for beer. Brown bottles have optimum (although not perfect) blockage ability, but they, too, can only delay, not prevent, the inevitable effects of light. The beer can, which in the minds of many beer aficionados is often associated with uninspiring mass-produced beers, is ironically often the best packaging, because metal is entirely impermeable to light. See CANNING.

Because beer is under pressure, the natural optimum shape for a beer container would be a sphere. It is a simple law of physics that, in a round container, every part of the container receives the same amount of radial, outward pressure, which means there is no weak spot for the container to burst. Beyond this requirement, however, there is an almost infinite opportunity for designers to shape the bottle, mostly for marketing reasons. Hand-blown bottles from the 1600s are almost uniformly onion shaped, but today almost all beer bottles are taller than they are wide. They have straight-side bodies and then taper at the top to form a pouring neck. Bottles from the 1800s often have attractive shapes with low, squat shoulders and long, elegant necks, but these broke more easily than modern bottles. Modern beer bottles tend to be straight sided, mostly because automatic labeling machines work most reliably with flat rather than bulgy surfaces. Unless they are cork-stoppered and wire-cage "Champagne-style" bottles for bottle-conditioned beers, they also feature a lip around which a crown cap can be crimped. See CROWN CAP. Alternatively, they may be closed with a wire-bale top, also referred to as a flip-top. Although fairly expensive compared with crown caps, wire bales are now making a comeback, especially in Germany, where recently enacted deposit laws encourage the use of very sturdy, returnable bottles that are cleaned and refilled perhaps 50 times.

Although Europe and most of the world uses and accepts recycled glass beer bottles, the American consumer does not. Recycled bottles, despite the best attempts by brewers and glass manufacturers, will show telltale scuff marks at the shoulder, and the American consumer tends to reject these bottles as unsanitary. Oddly, there seems to be an exception for bottles of mass-market beers when they are sold at bars rather than at retail in shops.

Although the most common shape and size is a long-necked bottle containing 33 cl (12 US oz), many shapes and sizes are used. Belgian brewers in particular have favored their own bottle shapes, with some types of 750-ml bottles having become commonplace both in Belgium and then in the United States, especially for beers that are Belgian inspired. Many American craft brewers put beer in 650.5 ml (22 US oz) bottles that are colloquially known as bombers. For reasons that are unclear, this bottle is very popular in some US markets and virtually anathema in others. In the United Kingdom, the imperial pint (568 ml) remains a popular size, and many shapes are used, some of them handsomely recalling shapes from the late 1800s and early 1900s. And as Italy enters the craft beer scene with typical Italian flair, we are now seeing further stylistic evolutions of the glass bottle.

See also BOTTLE CONDITIONING.

Horst Dornbusch and Garrett Oliver

bottle sizes for beer are standardized in most countries around the world, but this was not always the case. Early beer bottles in the UK frequently came in sizes known as the "reputed pint," equivalent to one-twelfth of an Imperial gallon, 13 Imperial fluid ounces, 378 ml, or the "reputed quart," 26 fl oz. The reputed pint is close in size to the regular modern US beer bottle size, the standard "longneck" 355 ml (12 US fl oz).

The reputed pint and reputed quart had been largely replaced in the UK at the beginning of the 20th century by bottles in Imperial pints and quarts, 568 ml and 1136 ml, respectively. However, stronger ales and barley wines were frequently sold in bottles holding one-third of a pint, 6.66 fl oz, known as a "nip."

In the United States, standard bottle sizes varied between 325 and 385 ml (11 and 13 US fl oz), before settling at 355 ml. Other beer bottle sizes included the "split," 6 US fl oz, for stronger beers. Larger bottles are usually 650 ml (22 US fl oz). This has become a popular size for American craft-brewed beers, as is the Champagne-style 750-ml bottle, often with a cork and wirecage. At the other end of the quality spectrum is the infamous 40-oz bottle, which has itself nearly become a synonym for cheap, nasty "malt liquors," strong adjunct-driven beers peddled by mass-market brewers. In Canada the standard bottle size is 341 ml (12 Imperial fl oz).

After the mandatory use of metric units in the UK came into force in 1995, many British brewers used 550-ml bottles, although most have now changed to a standard 500-ml bottle. Smaller-size bottles in the UK are generally 275 ml or, more commonly, 330 ml. In Europe the EU standardized 330-ml bottle is common, although in the Netherlands a 300-ml bottle is frequently found.

Larger bottles are generally 750 ml, and these are particularly popular in Belgium.

In the Northern Territory of Australia the "Darwin stubby" is a 2-l beer bottle, originally four Imperial pints (2.27 l), sold to capitalize on the region's reputation for beer consumption. Two-liter bottles, with ceramic swing tops, are also found in Germany.

Magnums (1.5 l) and larger sizes are occasionally seen, although these tend to be collector's items or display bottles, usually filled by hand at the brewery.

See also BOTTLES.

Martyn Cornell

bottling. Breweries have been bottling their beer since the pre-industrial era, although bottling only first really took-off with the development of modern industrialization in the latter half of the 19th century. This was because glass bottles became much cheaper and much more accessible with the introduction of mass production. Partially as a result, many breweries started selling their beers into ever more distant markets.

It is difficult to generalize about the current importance of the different types of bottling, as this varies significantly from market to market, depending on the level of technology, tradition, culture, legislation, and geography. The different types of bottling technology used by breweries large and small today can be divided into the following categories:

Bottling of Returnable Bottles

Modern bottling lines for returnable bottles can handle anything from a few hundred up to about 100,000 bottles per hour. Such a bottling line will normally look like this: Empty bottles from the market are received in crates that are placed on a conveyor leading to the unpacker where the bottles are lifted unto a separate conveyor. The empty crates are normally washed in a tunnel before being transported to the packing end of the line. The bottles are then fed upside down into the baskets in the bottle washer, a large machine where the dirty bottles are transported through a number of different compartments where they are sprayed with and submerged in both caustic and clean water, thoroughly rinsing both their interior and exterior (including

Postcard depicting bottling machinery, c. 1910. PIKE MICROBREWERY MUSEUM, SEATTLE, WA

removal of old labels). The conveyor then transports the clean bottles to the either visual (very rare these days) or automatic inspection by an empty bottle inspector (EBI) for any remaining traces of liquid or dirt. It is worth noting here that in recent years, beer consumers in the United States have roundly rejected returnable bottles, apparently thinking them unsanitary. They are now exceedingly rare, and the tell-tale scuffed shoulder of the returnable bottle has almost vanished from store shelves.

Whether brand new or recycled, the bottles are then fed into the filler, a large rotary device connecting the bottles to the bowl containing the beer ready for filling. But before beer is filled into the bottles, the air is sucked out of them to remove the harmful oxygen. This may happen either once or twice—single or double pre-evacuation—which is always followed by a pre-pressurisation with pure CO_2 that serves to both provide a "beer friendly" atmosphere in the bottles and aligns the pressure in the bottle with the one in the tank, making sure that the subsequent filling can take place without the beer foaming. When the bottles are full, they enter the rotary capper where caps/crown corks are applied to the bottle mouths and squeezed tightly onto them.

In a large brewery the next step will usually be the tunnel pasteurizer, another very bulky machine that is essentially a huge shower with water increasing in temperature in the first half of its length and decreasing in the last half, controlled in such a way that each bottle gets a heat treatment that is sufficient to destroy any live microorganisms during its passage through the pasteurizer, leaving the bottled beer microbiologically stable. The pasteurized bottles are then fed to the labeller, and finally a full bottle inspector (FBI) that automatically checks filling height, capping, and labelling. From here the bottles will be conveyed to the *packer* where they are automatically packed into six-packs, cases, and/or crates.

Aseptic Bottling

On an aseptic bottling line there is no tunnel pasteurizer. Frequently, the task of ensuring microbiological stability of the beer is instead achieved by flash pasteurization or sterile filtration (see STERILE FILTRATION) of the beer before filling. This enables physically smaller lines which may cost less, but at the same time, since the beer is not pasteurized after filling, this technology sets very high demands on the technology of the filler, the general level of hygiene and cleaning, and the brewery's microbiological quality control.

Bottling in Plastic Bottles

This technology was introduced in the 1990s and made possible by progress in the quality of PET and PEN bottles with respect to their barrier properties, the protection against CO_2 escaping from the bottles and oxygen entering them. Both these phenomena are detrimental to the quality and shelf life of the bottled beer. Bottling lines for plastic bottles are very similar to aseptic glass bottling lines, as the bottle material does not allow tunnel pasteurization. On the most advanced of such bottling lines, the bottles are "blown"—produced from small plastic cartridges by hot air in moulds—just before entering the filling line.

The introduction of plastic bottles for beverages, including beer, on a large industrial scale took place in the 1970s following advances in the plastic industry allowing production of containers from either materials that in themselves provide sufficient barrier properties or producing these from composites—several layers of different plastics—giving combined, satisfactory wall qualities. Besides being much lighter than their glass counterparts, plastic bottles offer advantages with respect to safety, as they don't break easily. Further, a new plastic bottle is significantly cheaper than a similar glass bottle. The most commonly used material is PET (polyethyleneterephtalate), a compound in the polyester family, that can be used as a single layer bottle for beer with a shelf life almost as long as glass bottles. A newer and still more expensive type of plastic for bottles is PEN (polyethylenenaphtalate) having the advantage over PET that its barrier properties is superior to PET and that it can be washed with caustic just like glass bottles, allowing PEN bottles to be used as returnable bottles for beer or other carbonated beverages. While consumers in many parts of the world are used to seeing beer in plastic bottles, the American consumer has yet to warm to this packaging, and it remains a rare sight. Recently, however, some mass-market brewers have introduced plastic bottles that have the same general appearance as glass bottles, and these are now increasingly seen at public venues such as stadiums.

Manual or Semi-manual Bottling

Many different types of very simple machinery are available to brewers, allowing them to bottle very cheaply. In comparison to the technologies described above, these simple types obviously suffer from the disadvantages of having very low capacities—sometimes only up to a few hundred bottles per hour—and being very labor intensive. Consequently, this technology is found mostly in small craft breweries, and often in connection with bottle conditioned and barrel aged beers.

Anders Brinch Kissmeyer

bottom fermentation is a process using yeast strains that work effectively at lower temperatures 5°C–10°C (41°F–50°F), causing the yeast to work less vigorously and create carbon dioxide more slowly. This results in less turbulence in the beer and yeast precipitating early in its life cycle. Bottom fermentation is usually associated with lager yeasts. See LAGER.

The term "bottom fermentation" was first used in Bavaria in 1420. Traditional beers of the time were ales. The ale's warm 17°C–25°C (63°F–77°F) and turbulent top fermentation carried the yeast to the foam on top of the beer where it often formed a thick mat and was harvested and used to start the next batch. Brewers in Bavaria, however, found it advantageous to attempt fermentation and storage in cool caves at the foothills of the Alps, where it was possible to ferment beer even in summertime. Until this development, warm weather meant that brewing had to cease, as bacteria overwhelmed the yeast in warm fermentations. In the caves, a different yeast started to emerge—a yeast that could ferment at cold temperatures, that is, temperatures at which spoilage bacteria struggled. This new type of yeast fermented more slowly and less vigorously than ale yeast, never formed much foam on the surface, and when finished, sunk quickly to the bottom of the vessel. From there it was collected and used in the next batch of beer. Over time, selection of yeast from the bottom of the vessel naturally favored yeast types that precipitated well, and these became known as "bottom-fermenting" yeasts. This type of yeast was finally isolated in a pure culture by Dr Emil Christian Hansen in 1883 and named Saccharomyces carlsbergensis. See HANSEN, EMIL CHRISTIAN.

While warm fermentations by ale yeast strains can be very rapid—as short as a few days—the cold temperatures of bottom fermentations required longer fermentation times, often 10 to 14 days. Lower temperatures of bottom fermentation slow down the rate at which the yeast consumes sugars in the beer. Further, only the top layer of the settled yeast comes into contact with the beer and is able to continue fermenting it. After active fermentation is completed, the beers tend to have immature flavors and need a period of cold storage referred to as lagering. Breweries specializing in bottom fermentation often use fermenting vessels that are short and wide, and will sometimes install platforms in the vessel to catch precipitating yeast, thus increasing contact between beer and yeast. This is the true purpose of the "beechwood strips" made famous in advertisements for AB-InBev's Budweiser beer.

Over the past few decades many breweries and laboratories have developed ale yeast strains that ferment quickly at warm temperatures, create typical ale flavor and aroma profiles, then drop to the bottom of the fermentation vessel, easing their collection from cylindro-conical tanks. This has blurred the distinction between "top-fermentation" and "bottom-fermentation." Furthermore, yeasts that conduct cold bottom fermentation were previously considered to be a different species from those that work by top fermentation. The species name for bottom-fermenting yeast, *carlsbergensis,* gave way to the name *uvarum*. Taxonomists have now decreed all lager yeast to be Saccharomyces pastorianus, an organism that seemingly arose from a coming together of S. cerevisiae and S. bayanus.

See also TOP FERMENTATION.

De Clerk, Jean. *A textbook of brewing,* Vol. 1. London: Chapman & Hall Ltd, 1957.

White, Christopher. 7 fascinating facts about yeast. *Brew Your Own*, February, 1998.

Young, Thomas W. "History of Brewing." http://www.britannica.com/ (accessed May 1, 2010).

Curtis Dale

Boulevard Brewing Company began in 1988, when founder John McDonald started construction of the brewery in a turn-of-the-century brick building on historic Southwest Boulevard of Kansas City, Missouri. The brewery's name comes from its location on the boulevard. A vintage Bavarian brewhouse was installed, and the first batches of beer were produced in the fall of 1989. The first keg of Boulevard pale ale was delivered that November, in the back of McDonald's pickup truck, to a restaurant located a few blocks away. Since opening, the brewery has undergone three expansions: in 1999, 2003, and 2005. The most recent expansion increased brewing capacity to 600,000 barrels per year. In 2009 the brewery produced 140,000 barrels, making Boulevard one of the 10 largest craft breweries in the United States.

As of 2010, Boulevard sold beer in 19 states, largely in the Midwest. Boulevard, like many other modern craft breweries, considers itself a participant in the revival of the regional brewery tradition in the United States. Boulevard brews five seasonal varieties and eight beers that are available year-round. The majority of the volume is contributed by two brands—pale ale and unfiltered wheat. Boulevard also brews the Smokestack Series, which is an award-winning line of artisanal beers introduced in 2007 and packaged in 750-ml bottles. This series includes both permanent selections and limited edition brews.

Keith Villa

braggot. Brewing does not always produce beer but in some applications creates a mixed product. Braggot is one of these: it is a beverage produced from both malt and honey and is in essence a mixed drink, part beer part mead. Historic references suggest braggot is a Celtic drink from at least the 12th century; it is mentioned in *The Canterbury Tales*. In such times honey was the major source of sugar and braggot would have been a common and distinctive drink in medieval Europe.

Various options are possible depending on the balance of malt and honey used, but in strict terms there should be more honey than malt to distinguish braggot from a honey beer. See HONEY. Braggots may be made by combining separately fermented beer and mead, or the combination may be made at the outset of brewing, with the honey added to the kettle. In addition hops and spices may be included to give the drink various flavor characteristics. Ideally hop character and bitterness should balance any residual sweetness of the honey. The source of honey also contributes to the specific character, which varies with different types of flowers frequented by the bees, and also during the year according to the seasonal nectar they gather.

Historically specific versions of braggot were also distinguished by the range of hops, herbs, and spices added, with some of these being selected by the customer in the bar. Today this is only possible if the braggot is brewed at home. Commercial braggot is now rarely seen in bars, although versions are available from adventurous craft brewers, most of them in the United States.

In production a careful balance and selection of malts and honey is required as each can provide conflicting flavors that may not always blend well. Lighter malts are generally used and the brew may be strong in alcohol, normally at least 6% and occasionally up to 12% by volume.

Keith Thomas

Bramling Cross (hop) is a traditional English variety that was bred in 1927 by Professor Ernest S. Salmon at Wye College in Kent, England, and released commercially in 1951. It was a cross between the Bramling (a Golding clone that had become popular in the 1860s) and a male seedling of the Canadian Manitoban wild hop; hence the name. The breeding goal at the time was the preservation of the hardy qualities of the Manitoban in a classic British hop, especially with respect to mildew and wilt resistance. Salmon also looked for improved yields and earlier ripening. The result was a hop with a fruity aroma, black currant and lemon notes, and good alpha characteristics. Until the 1980s, it was a rare hop in British brewers' repertoire. Among the few breweries reported to use it were Harvey & Son of Lewes, Sussex, and Ruddles Brewery of the East Midlands. See HARVEY & SON LTD. Bramling Cross has an alpha acid range of 6% to 8%, which makes it a general-purpose kettle hop, although British craft brewers also appreciate its black currant and lemon notes. It has been used in imperial stouts as both an aroma and a bittering hop. It is grown mainly in Britain in Kent and Sussex. Many growers and brewers still know it by its trial number OT48. It sends up its shoots quite early in the season and matures by the end of August—although in years with a warm, dry spring, it may show some spring dormancy with a resultant yield reduction. The bine is strong and the cones are of medium size and nicely shaped for comfortable hand picking.

Darby, Peter. The history of hop breeding and development. *Brewery History* 121 (Winter 2005): 94–112.

Adrian Tierney-Jones

brandhefe literally "burnt yeast," is the German name for the brownish residues found on the sides of an emptied fermenting vessel. Usually seen as a ring near the top of the vessel, brandhefe is composed of dried-up yeast, albumen, and hop resins and must be carefully removed after each use of a fermenting vessel. It is a tough, tacky material, and is not always easy to remove. Contrary to its name, it does not consist primarily of yeast, but actually contains proteins and hop resins that make it dark and sticky. The brandhefe is mainly the dried remains of the froth built during the early stages of bottom fermentation, the so-called Kräusen. This froth, which is built up by evolving carbon dioxide, "washes out" undesirable flavors, including some rougher-tasting hop components, from the fermenting young beer. The Kräusen turns dark and eventually brown or even black as the contained hop resins dry out. In the latest phase of primary fermentation, the froth collapses and if not skimmed off sticks to the sides of the vessel, where it can be removed after the vessel is emptied. Traditional lager brewing recipes call for the removal of all dark parts of the Kräusen before racking the beer to a maturation tank, an operation that can only be performed when open fermenters are used in traditional lager beer breweries. In modern cylindroconical fermenters most of the brandhefe will stick to the inner walls or ceiling of the fermenting vessel, but several brewers argue that some of the harsh bitterness in certain modern pilsners may be the result of incomplete removal of brandhefe.

Wahl, Robert, Henius, Max. *American handy-book of the brewing, malting, and auxiliary trades*. Chicago: Wahl & Henius, 1901.

Conrad Seidl

Brasserie à Vapeur

See VAPEUR BREWERY.

Brasserie d'Achouffe

See LA CHOUFFE.

Brasserie Dubuisson

See DUBUISSON BREWERY.

Brasserie Dupont

See DUPONT, BRASSERIE.

Brasserie Duyck

See DUYCK, BRASSERIE.

Brazil. While Brazil was a colony of Portugal from 1500 until independence in 1822, the history of beer in Brazil begins in 1634, when Dutch colonizers arrived for the first time, carrying provisions of beer. That era lasted only until 1654, leaving Brazil without beer (or at least European types of beer) for 150 years. In 1807, England sent her armies to defend Portugal against Napoleon, forging close ties between England and Portugal. Partially as a result, English merchants established businesses in Brazil and made porters and pale ales available in major cities around the country. It took more than 50 years for the first local artisanal beers, now produced by large waves of German immigrants, to appear. The Germans colonized the southern part of the country and the first breweries were located in the states of Rio de Janeiro, São Paulo, Santa Catarina, and Rio Grande do Sul. However, most of them struggled to survive. As a tropical country, Brazil didn't have an ideal climate in which to cultivate good barley and hops. Both ingredients had to be imported from producing countries, which was particularly difficult and expensive at the time. Beyond that, refrigeration wasn't yet available, making the lives of brewers very tough in a country where the temperature easily reaches 40°C (104°F). At these ambient temperatures, contamination by wild yeast and bacteria was hard to stave off, and batches of beer often spoiled before they could reach the market.

It was only in 1888 that the two major Brazilian breweries, Cia. Cervejaria Brahma from Rio de Janeiro and Cia. Cervejaria Antartica from São Paulo, were founded. After many years duelling for market share, Brahma acquired Antartica in 1999, becoming a major player in the world beer market. The new company was named Ambev, which later merged with the Belgian giant Interbrew to become the second biggest brewery in the world, called InBev. In 2009, the Belgian–Brazilian brewery managed to acquire the largest brewing company in the world, Anheuser-Busch, to create a new company, named Anheuser-Busch Inbev. As of 2010 InBev accounted for more than 68% of the Brazilian beer market, mainly brewing mainstream light lagers such as Skol, Brahma, Antartica, and others. Other major brewers in Brazil are Grupo Schincariol, which accounted for 12.3% of the beer market, Cervejaria Petropolis, with its Itaipava brand, with 9.7% of market share and Femsa, mainly with its Kaiser brand, which recently sold its beer operation to Heineken, with 7.5%.

Since the beginning of the 1990s, with the resurgence of several craft breweries inspired by classic styles created in Europe, a small beer revolution has taken place in Brazil, attracting enthusiastic beer consumers to the world of specialty beers.

The Brewpubs Dado Bier, Cervejaria Bork, Cervejaria Colorado, Krug Bier, and Alles Bier started their operations during this time, and the renaissance was underway. They first tried brewing light versions of pilsner like the bigger breweries, but soon found that this wasn't to be their niche. In 1999 Cervejaria Baden Baden was founded and introduced new styles into the market such as a Barley Wine named Baden Baden Red Ale, an award-winning stout, a German-style pilsner, and a bock. Three years later, Cervejaria Eisenbahn was founded in Blumenau, Santa Catarina, with a line up of well made German-inspired beers, including a schwarzbier, weizenbier, kölsch, a highly credible dunkel, and even a Belgian-inspired beer re-fermented like Champagne. Blumenau, a place that looks rather like a small German city, even holds a large well-attended Munich-style Oktoberfest every year, startling visitors who expected to find caipirinhas in Brazil rather than weissbier. Cervejaria Colorado has been particularly creative, adding regional Brazilian ingredients such as manioc roots, natural brown sugar, and local honey to their beers. German brewers have even given an award to Cervejaria Bamberg for their well made smoked beer, as they did before with some Eisenbahn, Baden Baden, and Colorado beers.

Of course, bigger brewers have not failed to notice the burgeoning Brazilian craft beer scene, and Grupo Schincariol, mainly known for its popular mass market brand Nova Schin, has acquired the three largest craft breweries in Brazil: Devassa, Baden Baden, and Eisenbahn.

Yet in 2010 virtually every month saw the opening of a new brewery in Brazil and consumers, journalists, and restaurateurs are starting to understand that Brazil now produces another great drink besides the native cachaça. Approximately 100 craft breweries are now running in the country and it will not be surprising if Brazil eventually gains a reputation as a diverse and creative brewing nation.

Juliano Borges Mendes

Brettanomyces is a genus of yeast traditionally associated with old stock ale from 19th-century Britain and well-recognized as being responsible for tertiary fermentation in Lambic and Flanders red ales. Considered an integral part of terroir in a few select, barrel-aged red wines, Brettanomyces has historically been considered a "wild yeast" because of its spoilage capabilities and the characteristically funky flavors and aromas it can produce. Descriptions range from "floral" even "earthy" to "horse-blanket," and where the winemaker blanches, the craft brewer rushes in. Today, Brettanomyces in the brewery is increasingly anything but wild; many craft brewers are culturing this fickle organism and purposefully using it to gain complex characteristics in their beers, like a new paint on an ever-broader canvas. Craft brewers casually refer to the yeast as "Brett," a name that sounds appropriately like a new friend.

Since the first literature was published on this yeast in the early 20th century, nomenclature of the genus has changed multiple times, leading to confusion between the terms "Brettanomyces" and "Dekkera." Brettanomyces is the asexual budding form known as an anamorph and Dekkera the sexual reproducing form known as a teleomorph. These are the same organism in different forms, which have not been observed simultaneously. The genus of Brettanomyces has five species, of which two are currently used in brewing, Brettanomyces bruxellensis and Brettanomyces anomalus. A third strain, Brettanomyces custersianus, has possible application in brewing but is yet to be used in a commercial beer. Brewers show little regard for scientific nomenclature and instead brewers will often refer to a species by its strain name, which confusingly is usually the old nomenclature that yeast scientists no longer use. Strains such Brettanomyces lambicus and Brettanomyces claussenii are actually Brettanomyces bruxellensis and Brettanomyces anomalus, respectively.

While modest amounts of research concentrated on Brettanomyces during the 20th century, its natural use went on unaffected. The Trappist beer Orval shows the iconic use of Brettanomyces as a secondary fermentation yeast, and even the spontaneous Lambic brewers producing one of the oldest styles of beer, tip their hat to this complex yeast. See LAMBIC and ORVAL BREWERY. Although frequently considered a Belgian yeast due to its previous lack of use in beers of other origins, one would be incorrect to make this assumption, as Brettanomyces can be found all over the world. Indeed, the name "Brettanomyces" literally means "the British yeast." Increasingly, however, it is becoming the American yeast.

Craft brewers, particularly in the United States, have embraced the use of Brettanomyces, especially in conjunction with oak barrels. Brewers hoping to add complexity to their beers have turned to old traditions and started putting beer into oak barrels for aging. Modern-day brewers have been inoculating barrels with different strains and observing the changes in ester profiles, leading to the addition of unique flavors and aromas. Not much research has concentrated on the beneficial effects of Brettanomyces in brewing, and thus brewers who are inoculating barrels are just learning how versatile this yeast can be. One such use of Brettanomyces is in conjunction with bottle conditioning. See BOTTLE CONDITIONING. Beer styles that traditionally would have naturally contained Brettanomyces are now being recreated in the new world, and the addition of Brettanomyces at bottling has been carried out with notable success. Unlike more traditional brewers' yeasts, Brettanomyces is hard to control, and harder yet to predict. Adventurous brewers take this as a challenge, one that can sacrifice strict control for the reward of exciting results.

One feature of Brettanomyces is its ability to produce certain acids. In the presence of large amounts of oxygen, acetic acid production can be high, as Brettanomyces oxidizes ethanol and residual sugars into acetic acid. See ACETIC ACID. During barrel aging, small amounts of oxygen diffuse through the oak quickly being scavenged by Brettanomyces cells, and producing a crisp acidity. When using Brettanomyces for bottle conditioning oxygen is minimal so less acidity is produced leaving clean Brettanomyces flavors.

A common misconception is that beers produced with Brettanomyces are sour. Brettanomyces is not a souring organism; lactic acid bacteria are needed to create truly "sour" beers. Brettanomyces will not give more then a small tartness when used as the sole secondary or primary fermenting yeast. More important effects include the production of new esters and the reduction of other esters. Isoamyl acetate, a compound responsible for a banana-like aroma, is greatly reduced during Brettanomyces secondary fermentations while ethyl acetate and ethyl lactate appear in greater quantities. Recently it has been shown that when Brettanomyces is used as the primary fermentation yeast, two flavor-active esters are produced at detectable levels. Ethyl caproate and ethyl caprylate produce fruity, pineapple aromas and floral, apricot, tropical fruit aromas, respectively. Depending on the strain and technique used, these two esters can be produced at levels three to five times what trained tasters can smell, and so they appear to be important characteristics of an all-Brettanomyces fermentation. Volatile phenols are another group of compounds characteristic to Brettanomyces fermentations. The amounts produced vary depending on the strain and can leave crisp clove aromatics or horsey, medicinal aromas. Balanced with other aromatics, these phenols can become part of a unique and even beguiling beer aroma.

Modern Saccharomyces yeasts give today's brewers much to work with, but inevitably some brewers want more, and many see Brettanomyces as one way to remove the leash of obvious commercial acceptability. Primary fermentations using 100% Brettanomyces yeast are true examples of the art and creativity seen in craft brewing around the world. Only a handful of brewers have produced Brettanomyces primary-fermented beers, and as no traditional style exists, each of the beers so produced is unique, leaving interpretation open to the consumer.

Bouckaert, P. "Brewery Rodenbach: Brewing Sour Ales." *Lambic Digest* 846 (April 1996). http://hbd.org/brewery/library/Rodnbch.html/ (accessed September 2008).
Scheffers, W.A. On the inhibition of alcoholic fermentation in Brettanomyces yeasts under anaerobic conditions. *Cellular and Molecular Life Sciences,* 17 (1961): 40–42.
Van Oevelen, D., F. De l'Escaille, and H. Verachtert. Synthesis of aroma compounds during the spontaneous fermentation of lambic and gueuze. *Journal of the Institute of Brewing* 82 (1976): 322–326.
Yakobson, Chad. *Primary fermentation characteristics of brettanomyces yeast species and their use in the brewing industry*. MSc. Thesis. Heriot-Watt University, 2010.

Chad Michael Yakobson

breweriana refers to any beer or brewery-related item that is considered collectible. Breweriana includes everything from branded paper napkins to bottles, to pottery jugs and mirrors. If it's about beer, someone, somewhere, will collect it with devotion.

The dominant collecting bent of any particular country depends on the local beer-drinking culture. In Britain or Germany coasters (also called beermats) are common and few enthusiasts can resist collecting at least a few. In the United States the pub culture isn't as strong as it is in Germany or the UK, and people tend to drink more beer at home. Not surprisingly, can collecting is the dominant desire, with enthusiasts' garages often transformed into temples of tin.

Mid-18th-century English Spode porcelain depicting cherubs and hops. PIKE MICROBREWERY MUSEUM, SEATTLE, WA

While almost anything can be considered collectible, breweriana does tend to break down into several categories upon which we can elaborate:

Coasters or beermats: Simple woodpulp mats were patented in Dresden, Germany, in 1892 by Robert Sputh, before spreading around the globe after World War I. Older examples tend to be thick and pitted, genuinely made to absorb spilled beer. Modern versions are much thinner but more colourful, primarily acting as promotional cards. A collectors' group appeared in Austria as early as the 1930s. Tegestologists (the UK name for enthusiasts) formed the British Beermat Collectors Society in 1960. The mats can soon stack up. Leo Pisker of Vienna had a collection of 63,000 from 100 countries by 1982.

Bottle labels: Like mats, they provide a merry walk down memory lane, recalling many lost breweries. But one difference with labels is their length of history; labels have been fixed to bottles since the first half of the 19th century. Then, once machines sped up laborious hand-bottling after 1880, attractive oval designs replaced the earlier simple circular pieces of paper. Oblong labels dominate from the 1950s. The first collectors' organization, the Labologists Society, rolled into life in 1958 with the help of Guinness, which promoted the pastime from its export office in Liverpool. Soon similar organizations sprang up around the globe.

Bottle tops: As well as the main label, collectors also sought the thin strips of paper stretched across the stopper, often with the words, "Observe that this label is unbroken." But these disappeared thanks to an American inventor, William Painter, who in 1892 patented the crown cork. This simple metal cap, which could be easily applied by machine, gradually took over from wire-caged corks, screw-stoppers, and swing-top porcelain plugs. Carrying the brewery logo, they provided drinkers with something new to keep. Many breweries also provided complementary openers branded with their name.

Bottles: Some like to save the full bottle, though this is mainly reserved for special editions.

In Britain, the many bottles issued for royal jubilees and weddings were often kept for display. Some also like to collect earlier thick embossed glass or stoneware bottles and those with fired-on labels.

Cans: Beer was not canned until the 1930s, with Krueger Brewing of New Jersey leading the way in the US in 1935. See BEER CANS. Felinfoel of Llanelli in Wales canned beer in the same year with its cone-top tins, which are now highly prized. Light and handy for the new home refrigerators, the can proved a big hit, notably in America, where beer can collecting has become the dominant area of breweriana, backed by the Beer Can Collectors of America club since 1969.

Showcards and posters: Most breweriana collectors like to own a few of these, as their attractive designs are ideal for hanging on the wall. They date from as early as the 1830s and some famous artists, such as Alphonse Mucha in France, created stunning examples.

Mirrors: These are the ultimate collectors' wall-hangings. Early ones can be elaborately engraved while later ones are transfer-printed.

Ashtrays: Until the recent smoking bans, many breweries produced branded ashtrays, ranging from quality china and brass to cheap tin and plastic. Older, heavy match-strikers are harder to find.

Trays: Another common but attractive item of breweriana, often depicting breweries that have long since disappeared.

Water jugs: Stylish pottery jugs were provided by many breweries for whiskey drinkers.

Glasses: Branded and specially shaped glasses are popular in countries like Belgium, where drinkers expect to receive their beer in the matching glass. In Germany more robust pottery steins are eagerly collected, and better examples can sell at auction for many thousands of euro.

Other forms of breweriana include beer engine pump-clips and beer taps, brewery figurines and model drays, ties and T-shirts, playing cards and bar games, clocks and books. See BEER ENGINE. Simpler ephemera range from leaflets, share certificates, and price lists to bills, postcards, and matchboxes. There is surely something for everyone.

Cornell, Martyn. *Beer memorabilia.* London: Apple, 2000.

Wilson, Keith. *An introduction to breweriana.* Northampton, England: Brewtique, 1981.

Brian Glover

Brewers Association The (BA) is the trade association of craft brewers in the United States. It was formed in 2005 by the merger of the Association of Brewers (AOB), which originated in 1983 in Boulder, Colorado (where the BA is still headquartered), and the Brewers Association of America, a grouping of regional brewers that started during World War II to ensure that small brewers got their fair share of war-rationed raw materials like grain and tin. The BA brought together the brewers of America's craft brewing revolution and the heritage brewers who had weathered the consolidation of America's brewing industry after Prohibition. See PROHIBITION. From its inception and as of 2011, the president of the BA is Charlie Papazian, founder of the AOB and author of *The Complete Joy of Homebrewing*. See PAPAZIAN, CHARLES. The BA, a not-for-profit organization, is governed by a 15-member board that in 2010 included 9 packaging brewers, 4 pub brewers, and 2 homebrewers. The board members are elected by their respective memberships. As of 2010, the BA membership includes 452 packaging breweries, 655 brewpubs, 261 allied trade members, 161 wholesaler members, and 17,113 homebrewer members; membership is international. The homebrewers are all members of the American Homebrewers Association, a division of the BA. In addition to its professional division and homebrewing division, the BA represents craft brewers in the national political arena and runs the Great American Beer Festival in Denver, the annual Craft Brewers Convention, and the World Beer Cup competition. See GREAT AMERICAN BEER FESTIVAL. It also runs other special events and publishes statistics, magazines, and books, while acting as a central source on beer-related topics for the national press. The mission statement of the BA is "to promote and protect small and independent American brewers, their craft beers and the community of brewing enthusiasts."

Brewers Association. http://www.brewersassociation.org/ (accessed March 8, 2011).

Stephen Hindy

Brewers' Company. Also known as the Worshipful Company of Brewers, this is one of the oldest of the London City guilds. Guilds were made up of businessmen who had joined together, ostensibly to protect themselves and their trade. The oldest written evidence we have of a guild of brewers is to be found in a 1292 entry from the London Letter Book. Headed "Edward, etc. to the Warden and Alderman of the city of London, etc.," it commences: "Whereas it has been shown to us by certain brewers, citizens of London, that they had been prejudiced as to their franchise in relation to their trade by our Sheriffs of London, and by those appointed by us to hear plaints in London, and we have already you to enquire into the matter. . . ."

Over the ensuing centuries, this organization was to evolve to become the Wardens and Commonalty of the Mistery of Brewers of the City of London, and would assume the position of fourteenth in order of precedence among London's 84 Livery Companies. There is no record of exactly when the Brewers formalized their association, but it is likely that, given the importance of ale in the medieval diet, they were one of the earliest guilds.

When the Brewers Guild received its first charter it was known as the Guild of St. Mary and St. Thomas the Martyr (Thomas à Becket). Why Becket was chosen is unclear, but legend has it that after his martyrdom in 1170, the numerous pilgrims that made their way to Canterbury quaffed enormous quantities of ale along the way, thus making brewers very happy.

The importance of ale/beer in the Middle Ages can be gleaned from the fact that a London poll tax in 1380 records over 1,000 brewhouses in the city, which worked out at one for every dozen inhabitants. The original Brewers' Hall was first recorded from 1403, but the grand old building in Addle Street was destroyed by the Great Fire of 1666. Its replacement stood until the Second World War, whence it was destroyed by bombing. The Brewers' Company still exists to support the industry in London and southern England, with the new Brewers' Hall now located in Aldermanbury Square, London.

Ball, Mia. *The worshipful company of brewers: A short history*. London: Hutchinson Benham, 1977.

Hornsey, I. S. *A history of beer and brewing*. Cambridge: Royal Society of Chemistry, 2003.

Ian Hornsey

Brewer's flakes are cereal grains that have been precooked or pregelatinized and then rolled into dried flakes. The use of flaked grain helps brewers overcome certain obstacles in the brewing process. Brewer's corn flakes and rice flakes are the most common and are used at up to 40% of the grist bill for making American-style standard lagers and light lagers. The flakes are added directly to the mash and do not require a separate liquefying or cooking step. This makes them simpler to use than whole rice or corn grits, which must first be gelatinized in a separate vessel called the cereal cooker. Corn and rice flakes are adjuncts that lighten the body and flavor of the beer, resulting in a clean, crisp flavor. As with any adjunct, corn and rice flakes will decrease the amount of foam in the beer and may necessitate the use of yeast nutrients to ensure the fermentation progresses to completion. Brewer's flakes are also made from pregelatinized oats and are sometimes used by brewers who wish to increase the mouthfeel of a beer. Oat flakes are usually added to the mash at 2% to 20% of the grist bill when making oatmeal stout and occasionally Belgian-style white ales. The glucans in oat flakes do add body and texture, but they can make lautering and filtration difficult. Brewer's flakes from precooked rye are used when making rye beers. Like oat flakes, rye flakes are used at a relatively low percentage. Rye has a strong, almost peppery flavor and also contains high levels of beta-glucans and protein. Rye flakes are rarely used for more than 25% of the grist. Although not as commonly used, brewer's flakes can also be made from precooked unmalted barley and wheat. Grists for Irish stouts sometimes contain barley flakes, which are felt to add body to a beer style that can otherwise be somewhat thin on the palate.

Keith Villa

Brewer's Gold (hop) is the earliest of the English high-alpha hops and a sister to Bullion. See BULLION (HOP). It was selected by Professor Ernest S. Salmon of Wye College in 1919 from among wild American hop genotype BB1 seeds that were pollinated by an English male hop. The genotype BB1 was discovered near Morden, Manitoba, Canada, and cuttings were collected in 1916 by Professor W. T. Macoun, Dominion Horticulturist for Canada, and sent to England. There, the wild hop was established in the Wye Hop Nursery in 1917, but it died during the winter of 1918–19. After extensive testing, Brewer's Gold was released in 1934. A large number of modern hop cultivars and breeding germplasm, particularly in bittering hops, are descendants of Brewer's Gold. Although still grown commercially, Brewer's Gold has largely been replaced by modern high-alpha cultivars with better disease resistance and more desirable agronomic properties. Brewer's Gold yields are about 2,000 to 2,700 kg/ha (roughly 2,200 to 2,600 lb per acre) and cones typically contain 9% to 10% alpha acids and 5% beta acids. Essential oil content is fairly high at approximately 2.0 ml/100 g of dried cone, with myrcene (67%) being the dominant component. It is largely considered a bittering hop, and few brewers seem to feature itas an aroma hop in their beers. One of the problems associated with Brewer's Gold is its poor storage potential, and bales must be refrigerated quickly.

Salmon, E. S. Two new hops: Brewer's Favourite and Brewer's Gold. *Journal of the South East Agricultural College* 34 (1934): 93–105.

Shaun Townsend

The Rochefort Brewery, or Brasserie de Rochefort (Abbaye de Notre-Dame de Saint-Rémy), is a Trappist brewery in Belgium. Its copper brewhouse is among the most beautiful in Belgium. MERCHANT DU VIN

Brewers of Europe, the

See EUROPEAN BREWERY CONVENTION (EBC).

brewhouse is the name used for the room where brewing takes place, but the word is also used for the vessels used in the creation of hopped wort for fermentation. A typical brewery is constructed in a logical sequence so that the heating steps, or "hot side," take place in one area, and the cooling steps, or "cold side," take place in another area. The area containing the hot side is called the brewhouse. A brewhouse contains the major tanks, or tuns, for preparation of hopped malt extract, called wort, which when cooled and fermented will be transformed into beer. Most brewhouses also have a large tank for storage of hot water, also called "hot liquor." In sequence, the first tank to be utilized in a brewhouse is the mash mixer or mash tun, into which ground malt, or grist, is added along with warm water, resulting in a porridge called the mash. The primary purpose of the mash tun is to convert the starches in malt into simple sugars for yeast to ferment. After the mash tun the mash is transferred to the lauter tun, which is actually a large filtration vessel. Lauter tuns have an interior floor that is much like a filter screen and is referred to as a false bottom. The mash enters the lauter vessel and forms a bed, called a filter bed, on top of the false bottom mainly caused by the husks. The liquid, or extract, is then filtered through the bed and transferred to the kettle. In the kettle, boiling takes place along with the addition of hops and/or spices. After boiling, the wort is cooled and then sent to the fermenters or to the cold side of the brewery, where yeast is added and fermentation takes place.

When referring to "the brewhouse," commercial brewers are often referring to the actual set of vessels that comprise the hot side of the operation. It is therefore common for a brewer to say "we have a 50-hl brewhouse" or "our brewhouse was made in Germany," in which case the reference is to the vessels and not to the room itself.

See also BREWING PROCESS, KETTLE, LAUTER TUN, and MASH TUN.

Keith Villa

Brewing and Malting Barley Research Institute The (BMBRI), based in Winnipeg, Manitoba, Canada, provides research grants for projects related to the improvement of malting barley varieties, production, processing, and performance.

Specifically, the BMBRI works with Canadian grain growers to produce varieties that will meet the needs of brewers in North America and around the world. They also provide information and resources to brewing industry members who support production and marketing of Canadian malting barley, malt, and beer.

As of 2010, BMBRI members included nine leading North American malting and brewing companies, including Anheuser-Busch InBev, Sierra Nevada Brewing Co, and MolsonCoors Canada. Members have access to research work and facilities, and BMBRI represents their interests to barley growers, government bodies, and agricultural policymakers.

Founded in 1948, the BMBRI recognizes the importance of continued support to the scientific community for further work in both basic and applied research that will lead to new developments in malting barley breeding.

Brewing and Malting Barley Research Institute. http://www.bmbri.ca/ (accessed February 28, 2011).

John Holl

brewing in colonial America. One of the earliest orders of business by colonists to any new land has generally been, once food and shelter have been reasonably secured, the generation of some kind of fermented beverage. Native fruits, grapes, or berries might engender the production of wine, but as malt is both portable and stable, the materials for making beer can be brought along for rapid utilization, especially when the colonists themselves are from lands where beer is brewed. Given a scarcity of evidence by the earliest presumed beer-drinking explorers of the New World, the Norse in the 11th century, and the assumption that Spanish settlements in Florida would likely have centered on the pressing of the local muscadine grapes for such refreshment, we must move first to the English colonies in Virginia and Massachusetts for the dissemination of Old World brewing culture.

Just the same, it seems to have taken some time for the settlers in the Virginia colony of Jamestown to produce their own beer. Following the exhaustion of supplies of the English beer brought along on the voyage of 1606–7, the Jamestown settlers were reduced to drinking only water and even to trading essential tools with incoming sailors for the beer they held onboard. In 1609 the Governor and Council of Virginia advertised for brewers to come to the colony, and even into the 1620s a lack of decent beer was decried. Finally, in 1629, John Smith reported in England that the colony boasted two brewhouses and produced beer made both of barley malt and malt made from the native corn.

In landing at Plymouth on Cape Cod in December of 1620 instead of along the Hudson River as planned, and purportedly because of dwindling beer supplies, William Bradford's words have become legendary: "For we could not now take time for further search or consideration, our victuals being much spent, especially our beer . . ."

In Massachusetts as in Virginia the self-generated production of beer took time to become established (at least on a scale larger than home or farmhouse brewing), with orders for equipment to be sent from England appearing in the early 1630s, and the licensing of commercial brewers following a few years later. Malt was generally imported, but in 1640 an address of "Maulsters (maltster's) Lane" was recorded in Charlestown (now part of Boston). It is interesting to note that laws remain active today in the Commonwealth of Massachusetts linking brewing with the cultivation of barley. Hops were discovered growing wild, but were neither gathered nor cultivated in either of the English colonies in quantities sufficient to entirely supplant either importation or alternative.

The incentive to produce beer from scratch in the colonies was great. Beer imported from England took up valuable space aboard ships, and often was not fit to drink after voyages lasting months under less than optimal storage conditions. Actual deaths were ascribed to the consumption of spoiled beer, but given the anti-pathogenic property of any alcoholic beverage—a blessing in areas where water supplies are dubious—it is most likely that the evidence linking bad beer with fatality was circumstantial. Imported ingredients for making beer were also expensive and in short supply. The result was a certain amount of homespun improvisation of ingredients for both fermenting and flavoring. A substantial attempt was made to establish maize malt as an alternative to that of barley; in 1622 John Winthrop Jr presented a paper to the Royal Society on the malting of maize. Molasses figured prominently in the fortification of brewing worts; also employed were peaches, persimmons, Jerusalem artichokes, peas, pumpkins, and even corn stalks. Spruce is often mentioned as a flavoring and preservative.

Modern craft brewers might find familiar—at least in spirit—the list of alternative fermentables ascribed to colonial brewers, particularly pumpkin. As popular and widespread as its use has become in the fall offerings of many brewers, from the smallest to the largest, it is resonant to mark its use in some of the earliest American-produced beers. Contrary to emerging fully formed from the brow of modern ingenuity, today's "Imperial Chocolate Pumpkin Porter" and "Ginger Pumpkin Pilsner" have their roots in colonial resourcefulness. Pumpkins grew wild in the colonies and when blended with malt, pumpkin starches could easily be broken down into sugars in a mash.

At about the same time as the English settlers were finding their feet in Massachusetts and Virginia, the Dutch were establishing outposts in Port Orange (now Albany, New York), Port Nassau (now Camden, New Jersey), and most notably in New Amsterdam, later to be known as Manhattan. Within several years both breweries and maltings were established in the Dutch towns, employing barley and hops grown in the New World. By the 1640s Dutch brewers and maltsters were exporting their wares to the other colonies, among them Virginia, where tobacco had supplanted other crops as more profitable, and indeed served as a currency alternative to cash. The mid-Atlantic and southern colonies, including Maryland, Georgia, and the Carolinas, also relied on imports of beer and its materials from the north for similar reasons. Such hops as were not imported from abroad were likely to come from New England or what would now be designated upstate New York. More perhaps than the beer produced in the other, more provincial colonies, the Dutch-produced beer of New Netherland was widely praised for its quality.

New Amsterdam, in addition to growing into the first American cosmopolitan city, was the first real New World center of brewing and its culture. Several breweries were established in the 1640s and 1650s, and by the time the English took over the colony in 1664 there were at least ten serving a population of some 1600. A number of these brewers became wealthy and influential men, active in government. Of the so-called nine men that petitioned against the autocratic Peter Stuyvesant for municipal government of the city, four were brewers. As the Dutch expanded their territories farther outside of the city, plans for new settlements invariably included a brewery. Brewing families arose, the families Bayard and Rutgers notable among them, the latter producing four generations of brewers.

It is important to note that it was in the cities that brewers made the greatest progress toward commercial viability. A robust tavern culture existed to serve the population in New Amsterdam and in Boston, and since these cities were both seaports, there were ships to outfit with beer. Military garrisons also needed beer.

Philadelphia became the next great American brewing city, presaged by William Penn's land grant of 1680 from Charles II and his plans for the city, which included facilities for brewing. Not long after his arrival in 1682 Penn chronicled progress in the colony, describing a beer made with molasses, sassafras, and pine; recognizing the growing prominence of malt beer; and making mention of a local brewer, William Frampton. By the century's end there were several malt houses and breweries, as the population of the city overtook that of New York. Beer from Pennsylvania was exported to the southern colonies, and even onward to Barbados.

It may seem incongruous to the modern sensibility that religious leaders central to the establishment of the earliest colonies of the New World would so heartily encourage the development of brewing. Whether by the New England Puritans or Pennsylvania Quakers—even the Baptists of Roger Williams's Rhode Island—beer was embraced as a near-necessity of life and culture. Initially it was no doubt viewed as a safer bet than any questionable water supply. But it was largely in contrast with spirits—which of course led more quickly to drunkenness and its problems—that beer's relative virtue lay. Spirits took up less physical space than beer on incoming vessels and didn't spoil, and hence were more easily imported. Spirits could also be more readily manufactured from many agricultural bases. Without beer as a moderate option it was feared that drunkenness would become rampant. In fact various leniencies of taxation were employed toward beer in order to favor its production and sale over stronger liquors, as well as to encourage greater independence from foreign sources of supply. This distinction would take on greater importance as the gradually coalescing colonies approached their bid for autonomy from the Crown.

As one of the merely domestic arts, brewing was practiced in the homes and farmsteads of the New World by many who settled there, without distinction of national origin. The commercial breweries that arose were often first established and run by either Englishmen or Dutch, with an occasional Scottish, Irish, or German name appearing. The Germans of course would have their day as the dominant New World brewing immigrants in the 19th century as territories farther west were settled, but prior to the American Revolution their numbers were relatively small. Early on brewers were immigrants themselves, but, as in other apprenticeship trades, arrangements were struck for the peopling of the brewers' ranks. By the mid-17th century much of the first-hand brewing culture was home grown.

While Philadelphia and New York boasted brewing dynasties and imposing production facilities, the practitioner of the brewing-related arts probably best known to posterity from pre-Revolutionary times is Samuel Adams of Boston. This is for various reasons, not least among them the modern beer from Boston Brewing Co. bearing his name. Variously credited with having been a brewer, evidence suggests that he malted grains rather than brewed beer on his way to a celebrated political career. Adams published remarks in the form of advertisement that served both his callings, urging the embrace and consumption of American-produced beers to the exclusion of foreign offerings. This early version of the now familiar "buy American" refrain carried increasing weight with the sundry indignities of English taxation that began to be heaped upon the colonists.

For in fact the English needed money. The conclusion of the Seven Years' War in 1763 left resources diminished and the American colonists with a feeling of relative safety from the French to the North. They were hence extremely reluctant to submit to the new taxation imposed by the British, some of it having directly to bear on the brewing and tavern trades. The back and forth of the Stamp Act of 1765, the various embargoes on British shipping enacted by the colonists (1765, 1770, and 1774), and other impositions of taxation and dictatorial reaction by the British both encouraged home generation of goods (malt and hops among them) and hastened the onset of war.

With the interruption of supplies of beer and the materials for brewing from abroad, it became even more necessary to brew beer with American-produced agricultural goods. Several recipes have come down to us chronicling the use both of traditional ingredients and alternatives perhaps more readily available. The most famous is a recipe for small (weak) beer transcribed in the diary of George Washington while serving in the Virginia militia (1737), which today rests at the New York Public Library. See SMALL BEER. The correspondence of Thomas Jefferson and James Madison indicate a first-hand knowledge of brewing as well. Both Benjamin Franklin and General Jeffrey Amherst saw fit to commit recipes for spruce beer to posterity, though both were somewhat on the rudimentary side. In contrast, a set of "Directions for Brewing Malt Liquors" discovered in the body of a letter of Joseph Clarke, general treasurer of the Rhode Island colony, shows a more sophisticated awareness of the processes of brewing—in this case both a first and a small beer from the same mash—as well as the importance of sanitation. Nonetheless, there is a highly empirical spirit to the recipes left from this time, relying as they do on appearance and intuition rather than such later implements as thermometers and hydrometers, to say nothing of refrigeration and its modulation. Somewhat bizarre, in fact, is a recipe that appeared in the Virginia Gazette in 1775 describing the process of brewing a beer made from chopped and pressed corn stalks. The use of herbs and flavorings other than hops persisted well into the 19th century.

Efforts have been made in recent years to recreate the beers of the colonial period. In September of 2005 a judging panel at the Great American Beer Festival selected a recipe by brewer Tony Simmons for Poor Richard's Ale, a beer to be brewed nationwide by several dozen commercial breweries in celebration of the tercentenary of Benjamin

Franklin's birth. See GREAT AMERICAN BEER FESTIVAL. Poor Richard's recipe employed a range of malts in emulation of those likely used during the period, as well as corn, molasses, and Goldings hops. Others have taken it upon themselves to stage brewing reenactments at public events and historical locales such as Pennsbury Manor, the restoration of William Penn's estate, where they employ methods appropriate to the limitations of the colonial period such as mashing and fermenting in wooden vessels and boiling over a wood fire. It may as well be noted that despite his much-quoted aphorism that "Beer is proof God loves us and wants us to be happy," Franklin himself was more a wine drinker than a beer lover; his household accounts testify to only occasional consumption of beer.

It is to be assumed that the beers produced commercially up to and into the Revolutionary years would have been executed with greater consistency and mastery than these essentially home recipes, which at times call for things such as the use of a blanket to shelter a fermenting brew and keep it warm. It was as true then as it is today that a brewer of bad or inconsistent beer does not long stay in business, and there is ample evidence of continuity where the brewers of the pre-Revolutionary cities are concerned. The beers produced were certainly ales, of varying color from pale to dark, with hopping rates addressing balance and preservative effect rather than strength of flavor. With the use of wooden fermentation vessels it is a certainty that a flavor component derived from resident microflora would have been present alongside that imparted by the pitching of yeast, or "barm," all the more reason for quick sale and consumption, especially in the case of beers of lesser strength. Spent yeast and grains were also sold by brewers as secondary products, presumably primarily for cattle feed.

Nor were the colonies untouched by brewing fashion imported from the mother countries. Porter as a distinct style began to be brewed around 1720 in London, and while it never enjoyed the degree of popularity in the colonies as it did at home, it was brewed and consumed then as now by its loyal adherents. Perhaps the most historically notable porter brewer of the age was Robert Hare of Philadelphia, an immigrant himself from London, owing to his frequent supply of beer to George Washington, who pronounced it the best porter in that city. Washington procured his beer from Hare by way of Clement Biddle, a merchant whose role as a middleman prefigured the modern use of agents and distributors. So devoted was Washington to Hare's porter that on hearing of the brewery's destruction by fire in around 1790 he extended instructions to procure what stores might remain.

Once independence was an accomplished fact, brewers in the various colonies participated heartily in ratification celebrations, held for the most part on July 4, 1788. As professional revelers of a sort their contributions were a natural outgrowth of their wares, but in many cases their political activities prescribed enthusiasm in the triumphs of the fledgling nation. The parade in Philadelphia, for example, included brewers whose hats were decorated with barley sheaves and hop vines, and who bore a standard with the simple motto "Home brew'd is best."

See also HISTORY OF BEER and UNITED STATES.

Baron, Stanley Wade. *Brewed in America: The history of beer and ale in the United States.* Boston: Little, Brown & Co., 1962.

Smagalski, Carolyn and Rich Wagner. *Beer historian brews colonial ale.* http://www.bellaonline.com/articles/art64142.asp (accessed April 1, 2011).

Smith, Gregg. *Brewing in colonial America.* http://www.beerhistory.com/library/holdings/greggsmith1.shtm (accessed April 1, 2011).

Smith, Gregg. *Beer in America: The early years 1587–1840.* Boulder, CO: Brewers Publications, 1998.

Dick Cantwell

brewing process, a term that, taken literally, should describe the entire process of making beer. However, among professional brewers this term has come to refer to the process used to produce sweet wort in the brewhouse.

The technical objective of brewhouse operation is to render soluble the insoluble components of malted barley and any other grains, to separate them from the spent grain husk, to boil the extracted sugary liquid with hops to add flavor and aroma, to remove off-flavors and troublesome material, and then to cool the wort to an appropriate temperature for enabling the action of yeast.

The malted barley and most other cereal grains must be crushed to expose the starch inside, enabling the solubilization in hot water of the endosperm of the grain. Milling is generally carried

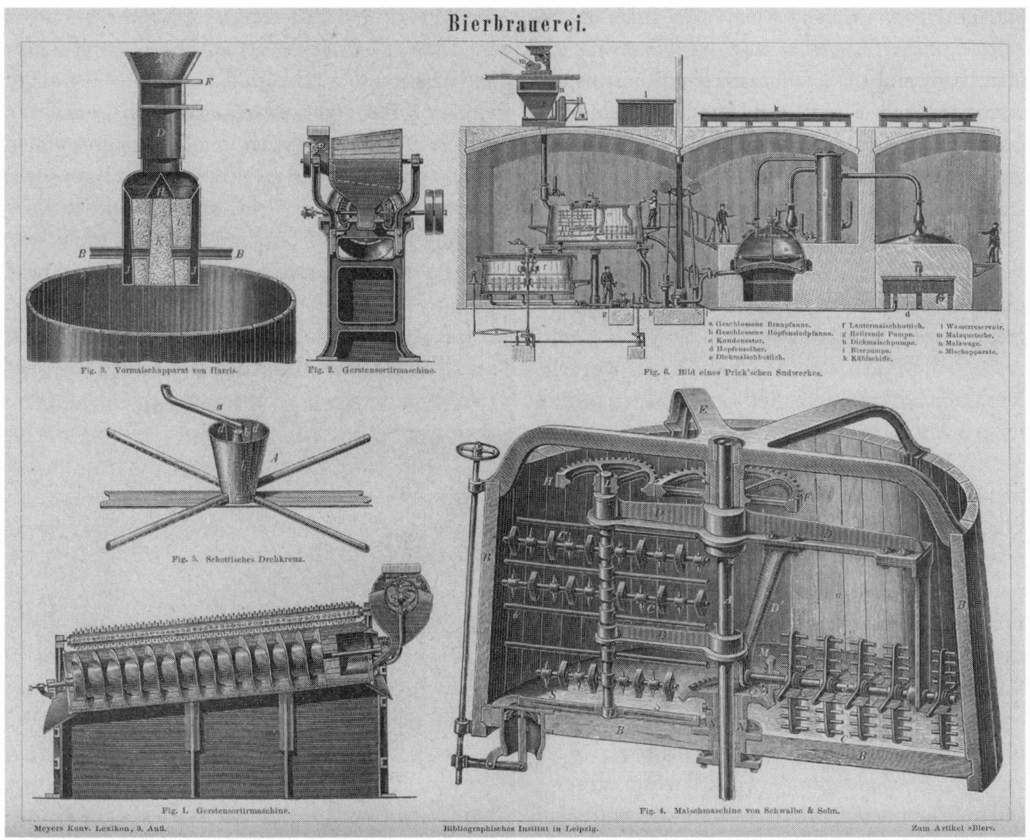

Mid-19th-century German etching depicting a brewery cross-section. PIKE MICROBREWERY MUSEUM, SEATTLE, WA

out in such a way as to avoid damaging the husk of the barley malt. This is because the husk contains several components detrimental to beer quality, but mainly because the husk acts as a filtration medium during the wort separation process. The resulting crushed malt is known as *grist*.

The grist is blended together with hot water (sometimes known as "brewing liquor") in a mash vessel, creating a porridge called the *mash*. In a modern brewery the mash vessel will be jacketed, steam heated, and fitted with a stirring apparatus. In a more traditional British brewery, or in a small microbrewery or brewpub, it may simply be an insulated vessel with a false bottom fitted with screens. In this "infusion mash tun" the enzymatic starch conversion and the separation of the resulting wort occur in the same vessel. Regardless of which type of vessel is used, it is important at this stage to control the temperature of the mash because the heat-sensitive enzymes working to break down the barley starch into a range of fermentable and nonfermentable sugars have overlapping temperature ranges in which they are most effective. If the mash temperature is too low, then conversion will be very slow; if the temperature is too high, then the enzymes will be denatured and no conversion will occur. Although mash programs vary widely, the standard "optima" for enzymatic conversion of malt starches is approximately 65°C (149°F). Most of the enzyme action responsible for breaking barley starch down into fermentable and nonfermentable sugars ceases early during wort collection. Either the mash will be heated to a temperature that denatures the enzymes (this is called "mash-off" at approximately 76.5°C/170°F) or sparging (rinsing) at similar temperatures will accomplish the same goal. Any enzymes that remain active will later be denatured by heat in the kettle.

Once the endosperm of the barley is solubilized into sugars, then the wort must be recovered from the spent grains. This is achieved by draining the wort through the vessel false bottom using the intact barley husk as a filter medium. When a separate mash mixer is used for the mashing process (as opposed to the aforementioned infusion mash tun), the entire mash is transferred to a lauter tun, which is a specialized vessel designed to optimize the conditions for wort separation. It is essentially a large sieve that holds grain husk in place while the wort is rinsed away into the kettle. The separated spent grain is usually sold as cattle feed.

Once the wort is collected from the spent grains, it must be boiled. Boiling the wort is a vital part of the process, and how it is carried out affects the final beer quality and flavor in many ways. Although there are a great many reactions occurring during the kettle boil, the principal one of interest is the isomerization and subsequent solubilization of the bitter substance alpha acid from the added hops. Boiling the wort also essentially pasteurizes it, rendering it free from any bacterial contamination. Boiling completely ceases the enzyme activity and fixes the carbohydrate composition of the wort and hence the dextrin content of the final beer. Under the favorable conditions of wort boiling, proteins and other polypeptides present in the wort will combine with polyphenols or tannins. Boiling also can destroy a protein's secondary and tertiary structure, causing it to become hydrophobic and insoluble. This is desirable because most of these proteins are unwanted in the finished beer. These compounds form a solid precipitate called "trub," which is removed from the wort prior to fermentation.

The wort must be clarified and chilled prior to adding yeast for fermentation. Solid spent hop cones will be strained from the wort using a vessel with a false bottom known as a hop back, whereas smaller particles such as spent hop pellets and precipitated protein are separated using a vessel known as a whirlpool. The whirlpool works by pumping the wort into the vessel using a tangential inlet pipe about one-third of the way up the side of the vessel. This causes the wort to spin, and the forces acting in the rotating liquid cause solid particles to collect in a mound in the middle of the vessel bottom. Clear wort can then be drawn from an outlet close to the edge of the vessel bottom. Historically wort was then chilled by allowing it to cool naturally in large, shallow pans called cool ships. This method is still used for very specialized and rare beer styles. However, in modern breweries the wort is chilled by passing it through a counterflowing plate heat exchanger, which uses cold water to chill the hot wort down to temperatures suitable for the addition of yeast. In the case of ales, that temperature would be between 56°F and 68°F, whereas for lager styles it will be as cold as 46°F to 58°F. The water used for chilling the wort is heated by the heat exchanger, and so both the water and some of the heat are reclaimed. The cooled wort enters a fermentation vessel, where yeast is added. At this point it can be said that the "brewing process" has ended and the fermentation process has begun.

See also BOILING, COOLSHIP, GRIST, HOP BACK, LAUTERING, MASHING, TRUB, and WHIRLPOOL.

Steve Parkes

brewing schools, institutions of higher learning that offer programs designed specifically for aspiring brewing professionals. They provide formal practical and theoretical training in those branches of science and engineering that are relevant for beer making on a commercial scale in a modern brewery. People have brewed for at least 8,000 years, but brewing schools, perhaps surprisingly, are a phenomenon of only the past 150 years. Before that time, brewers essentially learned their craft by doing it and were often taught by family members. In the early Middle Ages, brewing knowledge resided mostly among the learned friars in the monasteries, who, being literate, were able to write down recipes, perfect their techniques, and pass on their knowledge over time. As secular brewing arose in the high Middle Ages, brewers' training became regularized in the form of a three-tier tradesman's training process, in which an aspiring brewer started at the bottom as an apprentice, then took to the road as an itinerant journeyman, finally to settle down as a master brewer. The entire system was regulated by closed-shop tradesmen guilds that issued certificates and controlled both entry into and advancement within the profession.

The beginning of the industrial and scientific revolutions of the 1800s, however, turned brewing irrevocably from an intuitive craft into a process based on sophisticated scientific and engineering knowledge. It became clear that the old practical training provided by the traditional vocational system needed to be supplemented with an academic education, at least for the brewmasters themselves, and possibly for other brewery workers as well. In addition to being able to perform the labor required for malting, mashing, lautering, fermenting, and packaging beer, brewers now need to be able to operate complex machinery, maximize the use of costly raw materials, and maintain the consistent microbiological quality of the final product. As brewing became a marriage of craft, science, and engineering, modern brewing schools stepped in as repositories and promulgators of knowledge that the medieval training system could no longer supply.

In addition to teaching students basic brewing skills, modern professional brewing education also allows students to move on to various specialized fields—from mechanical process engineering to brewing chemistry, microbiology, ecology, raw materials agronomy, and automation technology. Different countries around the world offer varied programs and study opportunities, as well as different certificates and degrees. These are largely based on their different social and cultural traditions, but all brewing schools seem to fall into two categories: institutions that offer primarily academic study programs with a focus on scientific and engineering theory and practice and institutions that offer primarily brewing vocational instruction, more in line with the apprentice and journeyman traditions of the past.

Particularly in Germany these two tracks have a long history. A German university-level brewing education consists of graduate studies either exclusively in brewing science and beverage technology or in a related field, such as biotechnology and food science, which permits a specialization in the field of brewing. A graduate of an academic degree program can generally expect to take a management position in industry in beer production, quality operations, packaging, industrial engineering, or other technological, biological, and biochemical functions in the brewery. The occupational profile of academic graduates also includes careers in laboratories and research institutes.

Perhaps the two most prominent German academic brewing schools, which are also global pioneers in brew science education, are the Versuchs- und Lehranstalt für Brauerei in Berlin (VLB) at the Technical University Berlin (TUB) and the Weihenstephan Center for Life and Food Sciences, Land Use, and Environment at the Technical University Munich (TUM). See VLB BERLIN and WEIHENSTEPHAN. The VLB, whose long name translates to the Test and Teaching Institution for Breweries in Berlin, was founded by German brewers and maltsters in 1883 to conduct research and train brew professionals on all levels. Weihenstephan was founded in 725 as a small Benedictine monastery, which acquired its official brew license in 1040. By 1803, when Napoleon Bonaparte decreed the secularization of all church holdings in French-occupied Europe, Weihenstephan became the property of the state of Bavaria and a small agricultural and brewing school. That school closed in 1807, but reopened in 1822. In 1868, King Ludwig II of Bavaria elevated the school to the rank of a university. Today, the graduate study programs in brewing technology at the TUB and the TUM in Germany lead to a bachelor's degree after 3 years and a master's degree after 5, followed by an optional postgraduate program leading to a PhD. Within Europe, academic education models are now being harmonized as part of the so-called Bologna Process, by which all European universities are to follow the same guidelines for awarding bachelor's and master's degrees. In the wake of these reforms, the traditional German "Diploma Brew Engineer" degree will be phased out at both VLB and TUM, but the "Diploma Brewmaster" will still be offered.

On the practical side is the uniquely German system of "dual vocational training." It offers parallel training in real-world brewing and malting companies combined with professional–vocational training in classroom settings. Students essentially alternate between going to work and going to school. Such programs are structured as 3-year apprenticeships for brewers and maltsters. The only entry and eligibility requirement for such dual vocational training is the completion of a German elementary school or a high school diploma. Doemens Academy of Gräfelfing, near Munich, was founded in 1895 as a German private brewing school specializing in secondary polytechnic training and seminars for certified journeymen. These programs last between a few weeks and 2 years. Some of these tracks allow students to graduate as credentialed brewmasters and maltmasters. See DOEMENS ACADEMY. The VLB, in addition to its strictly academic degree programs, also offers short, full-time educational programs and extension courses, now taught entirely in English, in Berlin, such as a 5-month training course in brewing technology for prospective brewing professionals.

In the UK, the center for academic brewing studies is the International Centre for Brewing and Distilling at Heriot-Watt University in Edinburgh, Scotland. It offers a full-fledged honors and master's degree program in brewing and distilling. See HERIOT-WATT UNIVERSITY. The London-based Institute of Brewing and Distilling in London, which is technically not a school but a charity, offers a range of professional extension courses, training materials, and examinations for people with careers in brewing and distilling. Also in the UK is the School of Biosciences of the University of Nottingham. It offers an Internet-based master's degree in brewing sciences using modern e-learning technology. In Valby, a suburb of Copenhagen, Denmark, the Scandinavian School of Brewing and the Faculty of Life Sciences at University of Copenhagen joined forces in 2010 to launch a common Diploma Master Brewer course, which offers students a bachelor's in food science and technology or a similar degree. In Belgium, the Catholic University of Leuven (Katholieke Universiteit Leuven), which was founded in 1425, has a Center for Malting and Brewing Science as part of its Department of Food and Microbial Technology. Although not offering a systematic brewing study program as, for instance, the VLB or Weihenstephan does, this center is an important brewing science research institution, which organizes international certificate courses in brewing for students with a science background or industry experience.

In the United States, the Department of Food Science and Technology at the University of California at Davis has long been a leader in brewing education. Although better known for its world-class winemaking courses, it offers a specialization in brewing sciences as part of its undergraduate degree program. Available brewing programs there range from short brewing courses to an 18-week program. A similar Department of Food Science and Technology also operates at Oregon State University in Corvallis, Oregon. Finally, the American Brewers Guild offers long-distance courses for working and would-be brewers who cannot attend face-to-face classes. This popular program includes a brewery internship. Other industry-related programs include the World Brewing Academy curriculum, which is a joint venture of Doemens Academy and the Siebel Institute of Technology in Chicago, Illinois. See SIEBEL INSTITUTE OF TECHNOLOGY. This alliance offers courses and programs at educational facilities in Chicago, Montreal, Munich, and Durango, Colorado, which cover the spectrum of brewing technology and are concluded after 3 to 12 weeks with a diploma certificate.

Today, more and more universities all over the world are offering courses and curricula focused on brewing science and technology. These include Dalhousie University in Halifax, Nova Scotia, Canada; Edith Cowan University in Perth, Western Australia, and the University of Ballarat, Ballarat, Victoria, Australia; Massy University in Palmerston North, New Zealand; the International Centre for Brewing and Brewing Engineering at the University of Johannesburg in South Africa; and the Institute Français de Boisson de la Brasserie et de la Maltérie in Vandoeuvie, France.

Brewing schools, of course, are no substitute for a brewer's creativity in formulating beer recipes. Just as art academies cannot instill or replace an artist's innate talent, brewing schools cannot "teach" imagination. However, they can supply training in basic brewing techniques and beer styles as well as the scientific basis for the biochemical and mechanical processes that take place in a brewery. They can also institute a system of standardized evaluations and tests, both practical and theoretical, by which a student's progress and achievement can be measured. Finally, they can certify a student's competence and thus create a cadre of brewing professionals for a burgeoning worldwide brewing industry.

Roland Folz

brewmaster is surely a title that appeals to the imagination; many people seem to place it on a scale somewhere between "quarterback" and "astronaut" when thinking about the perfect dream job. But just as no one thinks about getting sacked by 300-lb behemoths or spending quality time in a g-force simulator, few people consider what the brewmaster's job truly entails.

The brewmaster is, in essence, the chef of the brewery. A chef is responsible for the kitchen

French brewmaster medal, c. 1900. PIKE MICROBREWERY MUSEUM, SEATTLE, WA

equipment, running the kitchen staff, putting the menu together, food safety, inventing new dishes, cooking, and plating and bears ultimate responsibility for every morsel of food that is served at a restaurant table. Similarly, the brewmaster often designs the brewery, trains a staff, keeps the equipment clean and running properly, orders ingredients and brewery supplies, keeps the costs of production in line, designs every beer down to the last detail, supervises the packaging of the beer, oversees quality control, and then follows the beer out into the marketplace to make sure that it always meets or exceeds the expectations of customers. At the end of all this, he or she may represent the brewery in public, train sales staff, and maintain draught lines at a brewpub. Sometimes the brewmaster has a staff, but at pub breweries they may work alone.

It is a balancing act that requires parts of the skill set of a plumber, architect, engineer, electrician, cook, artist, welder, salesman, chemist, accountant, and microbiologist. Many amateur brewers make excellent beer at home, just as many home cooks have serious skills and can prepare excellent food. This leads many to believe that homebrewing resembles professional brewing, but in fact it does not, just as home cooking bears little resemblance to running a professional kitchen.

Just as for the chef, there are many paths to the position of brewmaster. In the United States, the brewmaster's job description has largely shifted from the heavy engineering focus required by large industrial breweries to the far more variegated work of the brewmaster working in a craft brewery. Some spend months or years attending brewing schools, whereas others work their way up through formal or informal apprenticeships and then later through ascending positions at breweries. Sometimes the brewmaster owns the brewery; often he or she does not. Most brewmasters in the United States started as amateur brewers, a fact that has surely led to the wonderful passion and creativity at work in the American craft brewing scene. Also instrumental is the fact that for most American brewmasters today, brewing is their second or third career. This allows them to bring to bear skills and experiences gained in their "previous lives."

In the United States, "brewmaster" is actually a job description, not a formal title. In Germany, the title "braumeister" implies the successful completion of some formal brewing education and the attendant degree. Although there is no US equivalent, the title "Diplom Braumeister" is considered akin to a bachelor's degree in brewing, whereas the "Diplom Ingenieur" might be considered a master's degree. In Britain, the job title is "head brewer," whereas the title "Master Brewer" is reserved for those who have passed the tough exam issued by the Institute of Brewing and Distilling. Regardless of the title used and despite the rigors of the job, an increasing number of people worldwide seem interested in mastering what an early British brewing book called "the whole art and mystery of brewing."

See also BREWING SCHOOLS.

Garrett Oliver

The **brewpub** is a modern business model for an ancient practical concept: serving and selling beer on the premises where it is brewed. One wonders what the reaction of a visitor from brewing's past might be on visiting a modern brewpub, whether one of mistrustful wonderment or essential familiarity. From the bench outside the farmer's brewshed to the Bavarian brewery "gasthaus" to the high-concept brewpub chain, the same processes run common.

Brewing was once, alongside baking and cheese making, the ultimate cottage industry. It was only with industrialization that brewing became disconnected

The Standing Stone Brewing Company of Ashland, Oregon, is a brewpub that serves ales and lagers produced on site in 10-gallon batches. GEORGE RUBALOFF

from the individual beer drinker. Customers who had once perhaps known the brewer personally and taken pride in the success of the owners of their local brewery may have maintained loyalty to the expanded brewing factory on the outskirts of town, even as they regretted the loss of any intimacy with the process. As large and often multinational brewing concerns gobbled up—and often shuttered—these local and regional breweries, the connection of the customer to his or her beer became abstracted by brand and the machinations of commerce. In some countries large breweries bought smaller breweries primarily to acquire the pubs they owned. Then the bigger brewery would narrow the choices for the beer consumer.

In Britain, one vestige of the old days was cask-conditioned beer, or "real ale." As large breweries assumed, and vied for, greater market share, ease of manufacture and maintenance trumped tradition and flavor. They replaced hand pumps and the ethereal softness of cask conditioning with overchilled, highly carbonated draught beer ill-designed for that form of dispense. The Campaign for Real Ale (CAMRA), founded in 1971, may have taken this perceived last straw as a rallying cry to preserve British beer culture, but their message reached a worldwide audience. CAMRA fostered pub culture as well, and it was this sensibility, along with an already active homebrewing scene, that sowed the seeds for the emergence of the modern brewpub. See CAMPAIGN FOR REAL ALE and CASK CONDITIONING.

David Bruce was a beer enthusiast who saw business opportunity in bringing new life to some of the London pubs that were being cast off by larger brewers as unprofitable. Bruce took these pubs and turned them into the first modern brewpub chain. Known as the Firkin chain of pubs (each typically bore the name of an animal along with the word "Firkin," referring to a type of cask, e.g., "Frog & Firkin"), they combined small, fairly primitive brewing systems with erstwhile amateur brewers making particularly flavorful beer. The patrons could see, smell, and hear the beer being made, and the brewery vessels were visible to all. Suddenly, beer was a cottage industry again. Bruce added decent pub food, comfortable interiors, and old-time entertainments such as piano sing-alongs, and people flocked to his pubs. The first of the Firkins, the Goose & Firkin, opened in 1979, and Bruce, every bit the entrepreneur, opened dozens more before selling the chain in 1988. See BRUCE, DAVID.

Homebrewing was legalized in the United States in 1976; two years later the American Homebrewers Association was founded, and later its members would people the approaching American craft brewing movement. In 1982 Bert Grant, a Scottish-Canadian brewer of long professional standing and something of an iconoclast, established the Yakima Brewing and Malting Company, in Washington state, which had a pub as part of its operation. The next year Mendocino Brewing Co opened California's first brewpub in Hopland and was soon followed by Buffalo Bill's Brewpub in Hayward. The American East Coast answered in 1984 with the Manhattan Brewing Company in New York City, which, in addition to operating a large pub replete with peanut shells on the floor and hand-pulled British-style ales at the bar, delivered packaged beer to local accounts in lower Manhattan by horse-drawn cart.

Other parts of the English-speaking world were also affected by the growing early enthusiasm for brewpubs. Following soon after their fellows in Britain and the United States were Spinnakers in Victoria, British Columbia; The Sail and Anchor in Fremantle, Western Australia; and Shakespeare's Tavern in Auckland, New Zealand. Other countries in Europe were perhaps not so in need of a phoenix-like rebirth from an oppressive brewing climate. Brewery gasthäuser and farm brewery taprooms in Germany and Belgium, for example, had operated unabated for centuries. They didn't need the supposedly "new" idea of putting breweries in pubs, but before long, those countries too would see the re-invention of the brewpub in more modern forms.

The typical early brewpub combined a bar serving relatively uninvolved food and a small, 10 to 12 hl (7 to 10 US bbl) brewing system. The two were usually separated by a large window. The brewing equipment was often improvised, sometimes from used dairy equipment now employed as fermenters. Many used old UK-fabricated bulk serving tanks known as Grundies. See GRUNDY TANK. Manufactured in the decades following World War II by a few companies, these tanks usually held 7 barrels of beer, and this dictated the batch sizing of many brewpubs; many brewed either 7 or 14 barrels at a time. New fabricators of brewing equipment arose, sensing opportunity in the growing trend. One American manufacturer, JV Northwest of Wilsonville, Oregon, shifted its allocations of stainless steel to the production of brewery tanks when the demand for saw blades from the diminishing Northwest timber industry lessened. The typical brewhouse consisted of two vessels: a combination mash–lauter tun in which single-temperature infusion mashes were conducted, and a kettle, generally direct fired by a gas burner. A single full-time brewer was most often employed for all brewing and cellar operations. See DIRECT FIRING and INFUSION MASH.

Those who had started the first new brewpubs soon opened others. The Firkin chain may have been the most quickly prolific, but it was not alone in bringing further outlets to a receptive public. Buffalo Bill's within a few years opened a second location in Berkeley (Bison Brewing, 1988). Richard Wrigley, Manhattan Brewing's founder, soon took his franchise to Boston (Commonwealth Brewing Company, 1986) and later to Seattle and Japan. The founders of the Sail and Anchor in Fremantle went on to foster the Little Creatures and White Rabbit chains of breweries there and in other parts of Australia.

In Portland, Oregon, brothers Mike and Brian McMenamin moved from the tavern trade to brewpubs with the opening in 1985 of Oregon's first, the Hillsdale Brewery and Public House in southwest Portland. The McMenamins had worked to change state laws to effect the legality of their enterprises, which by late 2010 numbered in the 60's, including pubs, restaurants, cinemas, hotels, and variously otherwise resuscitated historic buildings in the Pacific Northwest. The McMenamin consortium today constitutes not only one of the most numerous brewpub chains in the United States, but also one of its largest restaurant groups altogether. In large part McMenamin's uses a common aesthetic to decorate their pubs, a sort of hippie-ish, cross-eyed Victorianism employing details such as psychedelic flocked wallpaper, overstuffed furniture, and ornately trippy paintjobs, the latter even extending to the brewery tanks. The Rock Bottom and Gordon Biersch chains are outwardly more conservative, but they each now have dozens of brewpubs.

Brewpubs begin to franchise not only themselves as the 1980s wore on but also the information connected with starting them. Academic programs such as the one at the University of California at Davis, already known for its course in viticulture, were expanded to accommodate the legions intent on gaining the rudiments of knowledge necessary to start new breweries and especially brewpubs. Davis's donnish chief instructor, Dr Michael Lewis, tutored many dozens of future American pub and production brewers. In 1978 Peter Austin, a multi-decade veteran of large breweries in the UK, founded one of Britain's earliest modern small breweries, the Ringwood Brewery in Hampshire. Within only a few years he was hosting a sort of camp for aspirant new brewers, many of whom later started brewpubs. In 1982 he was joined by brewing scientist Alan Pugsley, who would go on to become a Johnny Appleseed of brewpubs, extending the Peter Austin educational franchise to Kennebunkport, Maine, and carrying Peter Austin consulting services to new breweries and pubs in such outposts as China, Nigeria, and Russia and throughout the northeastern United States. Both the Davis and the Austin systems of instruction offered the option of professional consultation, extending to recipe design, equipment procurement and installation, lessons in legal compliance and site selection, and ongoing lab and analytical services.

No doubt the most amusing franchising of the brewpub cabala was started by "Buffalo" Bill Owens, founder of Buffalo Bill's Brewpub in Hayward, California, and Bison Brewing in Berkeley, California. Although he became well known to beer enthusiasts, he is perhaps best known in the wider world as a leading photographer of suburban verité. For a fee in the neighborhood of US$1,500, subscribers would be provided a printed manual of everything needed to know about starting a brewpub. Owens also boldly attempted to trademark the word "brewpub," but he was unsuccessful—the cat was already well out of the bag.

The legal climate for brewpubs was, in the early days, variously accepting and discouraging, depending on what country, province, or state promulgated the relevant laws. In many cases laws were on the books protecting large brewers from either foreign or interstate incursion; this hampered the development of smaller competition. Japan, for example, prohibited small breweries (below a fairly high threshold of production) from even existing. In the United States many state laws dating from the years immediately following Prohibition strictly separated sites of production from places where beer could be served. It was not uncommon for husbands and wives to own one or the other separately and then sell beer to each other. In countries such as Germany, Belgium, and the Philippines, where the ownership or contractual partnership between breweries and serving outlets tended to favor larger breweries, it was the large breweries themselves, such as Paulaner and San Miguel, who began opening brewpubs. But as the McMenamins had done in Oregon, people agitated for changes in the applicable laws. As soon as the law changed, some places exploded with activity, as Japan did in the mid 1990s. In Denmark it was a large brewer, Carlsberg, that played a prominent role in the fostering of brewpubs and a general raising of beer consciousness.

Novelty was the watchword for the earliest brewpubs wherever they arose. Beer was produced in plain sight by actual individual human beings, drawn from kegs, casks, and serving tanks filled right there on the premises, and offered in styles long neglected (or perhaps never before attempted). In many places, people had not seen such a thing for generations. The beers themselves varied in color—usually a scattershot chromatic array including "something pale," "something amber," and "something dark." They also varied in quality. For all the self-proclaimed brewmasters arising by the hundreds, actual mastery of brewing was not nearly universal. In the brewpub's early days, opportunity certainly outpaced expertise, but enthusiasm and loyalty ran high, and patience was rewarded. As further educational materials and opportunities became available (and brewers gained more experience) and as the raw materials accessible to the small producer increased in quality and variety, the brewpub proved to be the cutting edge for the development of new beer styles. Traditional styles as well, sometimes neglected in their countries of origin, found new life in the brewpub. Porter, barley wine, and India pale ale, to name a few English styles then in decline, took on new vitality in the hands of eager, idea-hungry brewers. Later would come witbier and other Belgian varieties, barrel-aged, sour ales, and others of the world's niche beer types. This would become especially true as the craft brewing movement seasoned and consumers demanded not only their old favorites to be available at all times but also new choices to be arising at every turn. Brewpubs in particular could no longer beguile with only 3 everyday choices and a rotating seasonal beer; the pressure was on to offer a dozen. Today it is not at all unheard of for a brewpub to offer 15 to 20 different house-made beers. Unlike the packaging brewery, the brewpub need not expend time, energy, and money on designs, bottles, and tap handles for each beer. This gives the brewpub distinct advantages, including the fact that a good brewer can have full rein over the line of beers available, and commercial concerns are minimal if one or two do not find favor with customers.

There may have been an everyman's sameness to the earliest brewpubs in Britain and America, but the decades since have seen variations on the brewpub theme commensurate with the innovation of the brewers working them. The brick-clad rusticity of a Peter Austin kettle has given way to gleaming copper showpieces such as the Sandlot Brewery at Coors Field in Denver, but left room for the dozens of beers once offered by the Tugboat in Portland, Oregon, fermented in 30-gal plastic pickle barrels and mashed in a plastic Rubbermaid horse trough. And not all have been small. The now-defunct Bardo Rodeo, in Arlington, Virginia, fit around 800 patrons indoors among the various bars, brewing tanks, and auto parts. The Tawandang Microbrewery, serving German-style beers in a giant barrel-shape room to an overwhelmingly local population filling 2,000 seats before a bizarrely eclectic variety show, is Bangkok's largest and most successful restaurant. Brazil as well, long one of the world's largest producers and consumers of beer, has turned its attentions to the variety and possibility of craft- and pub-brewed beer. The brewpub may still be a novelty act, but it is surely one that plays in every town. Perhaps the kettle in the window is the modern equivalent of the old British ale pole, a symbol that says "come on in—we've made you some delicious beer."

Kissmeyer, Anders. The Danish craft beer revolution. *The New Brewer,* March/April 2008.

Dick Cantwell

bride-ale was one of a series of beers brewed to celebrate special occasions, often religious holidays or celebrations; in the case of bride-ale the occasion was a wedding. It is not irrelevant that the marriage feast in Anglo-Saxon times was known as "bredale," and that, in early medieval times, the word "ale" sometimes related to a feast as well as to beer. The first reference we have to a bride-ale celebration comes from an entry in the Worcester MS in the *Old English Chronicle.* Dated 1075, it refers to a raucous feast in Norwich; "there was that bride-ale, the source of man's bale." Then, from Protestant reformer Heinrich Bullinger's 16th-century text *The Christen State of Matrimony* we learn:

> When they came home from the church then beginneth excesse of eatyng and drinking—and as much is waisted in one daye as were sufficient for the two new married folks halfe a yeare to lyve upon.

From the same era "bryde-ale" is mentioned in a commentary on one of Elizabeth I's excessive celebrations at Kenilworth Castle.

In some parts of England, regulations were invoked in an attempt to restrain the outrageous behavior associated with bride-ale consumption. These often bade brewers to refrain from making the wedding beer too strong. In the old Worcestershire town of Halesowen, for example, the medieval Manorial Court Rolls have an entry:

> A payne ye made that no person or persons that shall brewe any weddyn ale to sell above twelve stryke of mault at the most, and that said persons so marryed shall not keep nor have above eyght messe of persons at hys dinner within the burrowe, and before hys brydall daye he shall keep no unlawful games in hys house, nor out of hys house on payne of *20s.*

Ben Jonson, the English Renaissance dramatist, poet, and actor, uses "bride-ale" frequently to mean "wedding feast," and etymologists seem to agree that the modern word "bridal" emanated from this usage.

Bickerdyke, John (pseudonym of Charles Henry Cook). *The curiosities of ale and beer.* London: Leadenhall Press, 1886. Reprint, Cleveland, OH: Beer Books, 2008.

Hackwood, F. W. *Inns, ales and drinking customs of old England.* London: T. Fisher Unwin, 1910. Reprint, London: Bracken Books, 1987.

Hornsey, I. S. *A history of beer and brewing.* Cambridge: Royal Society of Chemistry, 2003.

Ian Hornsey

Briess Malt & Ingredients Company

The is the largest producer of specialty malts for

the brewing, distilling, and food industries in the United States. The family-owned company, a division of Briess Industries, Inc., also hosts a full line of adjuncts, malt extracts, and organics that can be used in the brewing process.

In 1876 a grain trader named Ignatius Briess opened his first malt house in the Moravia region of Czechoslovakia. Within 20 years the company was exporting their malts to Germany, the United States, and Belgium. Unrest in Czechoslovakia brought the family to the United States, where their malt company grew and began a partnership with the Winconsin-based Chilton Malting Company, which would later become part and headquarters of the Briess company.

For decades, Briess used specialized drying machines called K-Ball Roasters to roast malts. These German-made machines were phased out over the years by more modern drum roasters and were last used in the 1990s. See DRUM ROASTER.

The affable Roger Briess ran the company from 1971 until his death in 2001. He was a notable figure in the development of the craft beer industry. A major supplier to the larger and regional breweries, Briess saw potential in the American microbrewery movement of the early 1980s. As more craft breweries opened their doors, Briess was the first company to begin offering both base and specialty malts in smaller 50-lb bags. The company also added milling facilities around this time to provide cracked grain to smaller breweries that lacked the necessary equipment. Briess also developed several recipes it shared with smaller breweries, a tradition that continues today.

John Holl

bright beer is the term used by brewers to describe any beer through which an observer can see clearly. In general terms a beer can be said to be bright if one can read large print through a glass of beer when the paper is held behind the glass. Another way of seeing if a beer is bright is by holding a glass of beer in front of a fine filament light bulb; if the filament is distinct and clear and if the beer has a sparkle it can be said to be bright. There are various degrees of brightness that are quite subjective but easily understood with experience. Beers can be "brilliant," when no particles are visible at all and the beer sparkles with the clarity of glass; simply "bright" if the beer is very clear; "hazy" when the beer has a slight cloudiness to it but is still quite clear (this can also be called a "cast"); "cloudy" when a beer is difficult to see through due to small particles in the beer, often yeast or protein. Bright beer is often the name given to a beer when it has been filtered and all the yeast and protein removed to leave a brilliantly clear beer. A bright beer tank is the vessel a beer occupies before it is packaged into bottle, can, or a larger container such as a keg. Bright beer is not always a term used for filtered beer; some bottle conditioned beer and traditional cask beer in the UK can also be called "bright" when all the yeast and protein has settled to the bottom of the package to leave a bright beer. In the UK, cask beer that has become particularly clear is sometimes referred as having "dropped star bright," the highest level of clarity.

See also CLARITY and HAZE.

Paul KA Buttrick

A **bright tank** is a dish-bottomed pressure-rated temperature-controlled tank used to hold beer in preparation for packaging. The term "bright" refers to "bright beer," beer that has been rendered bright (clear) by filtration, centrifugation, fining, and/or maturation. In most breweries, beer will be filtered after leaving a uni-tank or lagering vessel and be directed into a bright tank. If the beer is to be force-carbonated, then the beer may be carbonated in-line, under pressure, between the fermenter or lagering tank and the bright tank. In this case, the beer should arrive at the bright tank with full carbonation. For in-tank carbonation (or adjustments), the bright tank will be fitted with a carbonation stone, a device through which carbon dioxide is forced, dispersing fine bubbles into the liquid for fast dissolution. Carbonation stones are usually made from either porous stone or sintered stainless steel. After carbonation, the beer is ready to be bottled or kegged (or both) directly from the bright tank. As the bright tank is the last stop before the package, careful attention is paid to quality assurance at this stage. Carbonation is closely checked and the brewery's laboratory will run a series of tests.

In larger breweries, color may be added at the bright tank stage, and adjustments may be made to bitterness and aroma using pre-isomerized hop extracts or hop oils. In craft breweries, bright tanks may play any number of roles besides those enumerated above. As many craft beers are not filtered or clarified, the beer sent into the bright tank may not be bright at all. The beer may have flavors added at the bright tank. The volatile flavors of honey, for example, do not always survive fermentation, and therefore many honey ales have honey added at the bright tank, where it will add some sweetness as well as flavor and aroma. Coffee or coffee extracts are also often added here for similar reasons. Bright tanks are also often used for blending one or more beers to create something new.

Bright tanks are also sometimes used as mixing tanks for beers that are to be bottle-conditioned. Here, the beer will be mixed with priming sugar and possibly with new yeast intended to carry out re-fermentation. The beer is then bottled (or, in rare instances, kegged) from the bright tank. In brewpubs, the bright tank is often also the serving tank; beer may run directly from this tank to the taps at the bar.

See also BRIGHT BEER, CARBONATION, and FERMENTATION VESSELS.

Garrett Oliver

Britain, or Great Britain, is generally considered to be one of the world's great brewing and beer drinking nations. Like its counterparts Germany and Belgium, it has retained its unique tradition and specialness in the face of the globalization and corporatization of the brewing industry. While the United States craft brew movement has assimilated great British styles and in several cases improved upon them, when British brewers do what they do best, they remain peerless in their art.

Britain is best known in the world of beer for two things: cask ale and the great British pub. The British are, famously, a reserved nation, and the pub is a home away from home, a "third place" where people can relax and open up in an informal, benignly anarchic environment in which the rules are randomly devised and collectively imposed. It's also an environment that revolves entirely around beer.

Cask ale is, in most cases, between 3.6% and 4.5% ABV, and served in an iconic English pint (20 oz, or 568 ml, compared to the American 16 oz pint). Whereas, say, an American-style IPA is famous for its assertive hop flavor, or wood-aged Imperial stouts for strong oak or spirituous notes, cask ale is all about balance: the perfect harmony of citrus or floral aromas, caramel and biscuit on the palate, and a dryness at the finish. It's a convivial drink and helps create a convivial atmosphere.

This atmosphere is something that refuses to be bottled, standardized, or easily replicated. While branded chains of pubs have emerged in the UK, they are unloved compared to the hundreds of Red Lions, White Harts, and Kings Heads, which may share a common name and purpose, but are mostly unrelated in terms of ownership.

For its eccentricity, its randomness, its welcome that is at the same time quintessentially British and yet so unlike other aspects of the country, the British pub (and the British beer that fuels it) has become famous worldwide. According to some studies, it is second only to the Royal Family in attractions that lure foreign tourists to British shores.

Britain was notable in that for almost a hundred years, it resisted the tide of commercial lager brewing that swept around the world from Pilsen and Bavaria during the late 19th century. But in the 1970s Britain did succumb to lager, and cask ale was declared to be in terminal decline. Today, Britain resembles the rest of the beer-drinking world much more closely than it once did.

But the global revolution in craft beer brewing has reached British shores too. There has been an explosion of artisanal cask ale brewers, who are now combining a reverence for British brewing tradition that, while important, was threatening to become a little stifling, with a more forward-looking, inclusive appetite for experimentation.

This is the latest stage in a long and uneven history of brewing that has given the world at least two of its most important beer styles.

Early History

When the Roman Empire reached northern Europe, beer was waiting for them, and recent findings suggest brewing was well established in Bronze Age Ireland. But Britain was mostly forested, and therefore unsuitable for growing grain. Mead and spontaneously fermented cider would have been the predominant alcoholic drinks. The Anglo-Saxons colonized Britain in the 4th century AD, and

A team of horses delivers beer from Samuel Smith's Old Brewery, founded in 1758, to citizens of Tadcaster, England. Horse-drawn drays are still used to this day for many deliveries. MERCHANT DU VIN

brought brewing with them. Britain has been a nation of beer lovers ever since.

Brewing, like baking, was an activity every household performed. But some people were better brewers, and others better bakers, and gradually brewing became a commercial activity. A respected brewster (female brewer) would erect an "ale stake" over the door when beer was ready, and people would arrive to buy or barter for it. Clearly, there was something about this particular transaction that encouraged people to linger, and some brewers' homes became alehouses. See ALE HOUSES. These grew to become the focal points of communities, places where business was transacted as well as free time spent. With the average house being little more than a hovel for sleeping in, the ale house was an important center of light and heat as well as communion, literally a "public house."

The first moves to brewing on a larger scale came with the spread of monasteries throughout the country. As well as brewing for large populations of monks, they refreshed pilgrims en route to holy places. The provision of accommodation and food as well as beer saw inns emerge as a more sophisticated alternative to the ale house, and beer production became a little more scientific and standardized.

Medieval brewers used a variety of herbs and other seasonings to flavor their ales, but from the late 14th century hops became increasingly prevalent, after being introduced on a wide scale by Flemish immigrants. Traditionally, "ale" was brewed without hops and "beer" specifically referred to beverages containing hops. The two were quite separate for several centuries. The foreigners became famous brewers throughout London and southeast England, but many drinkers preferred traditional un-hopped ale. By the 17th century, however, hopped beer was increasingly popular. On pub signs today, it is still common to see offerings of "Ales, Beers, and Lagers," as though "beers" remained separate from the other two.

After the religious reformation under Henry VIII, Britain's monasteries were destroyed. Their place was taken by "common brewers." Most pubs brewed their own beer, and perhaps supplied a few smaller local establishments. For some, brewing became a bigger concern than innkeeping, but it remained a very localized activity.

Beer was a vital part of everyday life. It was a source of nutrients, and of clean water when polluted wells and rivers in towns would have carried disease. Beer was used to bathe newborn babies, and weak beer was served in schools and in workhouses to the poor. While Britain has always enjoyed a dubious reputation for drunkenness, for the vast majority beer was seen as something that made the population strong and hearty. When the Prince Regent (the future George IV) proclaimed, "Beer and beef have made us what we are," he was boasting, not complaining.

Porter and the Birth of Commercial Brewing

When the twin drivers of land enclosures and the Industrial Revolution transformed Britain into the world's first modern urban population (of course, Rome might claim that prize), the demand for beer changed shape. Instead of diverse populations working as families, living in small communities on the land they tilled, we now had large, concentrated populations in towns and cities with men working together in factories, mills, and mines. The brewers who could capture the loyalty of the industrial workforce could take advantage of economies of scale, growing rapidly, improving their processes, and undercutting the price of smaller competitors, thereby growing further still. A cycle of consolidation began: when it became cheaper for an inn, ale house, or tavern to buy beer than to brew it themselves, large-scale industrial brewers supplying tens or even hundreds of outlets emerged.

The Industrial Revolution and the brewing industry developed hand in hand, driving each other on. Brewers were among the first to make use of steam power and coke smelting, invested heavily in transport networks, and pioneered microbiology.

The beer style of the Industrial Revolution was porter. Developed as an alternative to mixing together old ale and younger beer, porter is rumored to have been perfected by Harwood's brewery in the London district of Shoreditch in the 18th century. It drew its name from the ranks of porters who carried goods and worked in and around London's markets. A dark brown, full-bodied beer, it benefited from economies of scale and gained consistency and quality from being brewed in larger vats. As it grew more popular, its brewers grew larger, the quality of the beer improved, and it grew more popular still, until it was regarded, in the words of one foreign visitor to London in the 18th century, as "the universal cordial of the populace."

Arthur Guinness was a Dublin brewer who adopted porter brewing after seeing its popularity in London. Stronger versions of the brew became known as "extra stout" porters, eventually abbreviated to simply "stout." Arthur's son, also called Arthur, perfected Guinness stout, which went on to become arguably the world's most famous and iconic beer brand. See ARTHUR GUINNESS & SONS. Back in London, other famous names such as Whitbread, Truman, and Barclay Perkins made their fortunes as porter brewers. See WHITBREAD BREWERY.

Burton, Empire, and IPA

Porter's supremacy in Britain lasted until the unlikely and much mythologized rise of India pale ale. Strong, hoppy beers for the thirsty westerners in British India formed a tiny fraction of British brewing for many years. George Hodgson's brewery in east London was the first to become famous for brewing "East India Pale Ale," but following an altercation with the East India Company, the company sought out brewers in Burton-on-Trent to compete with Hodgson's Brewery.

They went to Burton because this small town had a reputation for brewing beers that stood up well to the rigors of sea travel, after decades of successfully exporting strong, sweet Burton ale to the Russian Imperial Court and other important cities around the Baltic States. This market had dried up, and Burton was left with a highly developed brewing infrastructure and no demand. Then, in 1822, the chairman of the East India Company approached Samuel Allsopp—the largest of the Baltic-focused Burton brewers—and suggested he replicate Hodgson's India Ale. What neither company nor brewer could have known was that when the pale, sparkling ale was brewed with Burton rather than London water, it would reach a condition and quality that far surpassed the original. Burton brewers, led by Allsopp and his bitter rival Bass, grew rapidly to dominate the Indian market. Every other export market within the emerging British Empire soon followed. See INDIA PALE ALE.

By the middle of the 19th century, the small landlocked town of Burton-on-Trent was one of the most significant brewing centers on the planet. As the brewing industry's scientific knowledge developed, it identified the fact that Burton's special brewing water—the combination of minerals and salts it possessed after filtering through layers of gravel—was key to the appeal and longevity of its beers. Brewers from London were forced to open branches in Burton if they wanted to compete in the manufacture of this new, bright sparkling ale.

It's rumored that Britain itself first developed a taste for IPA following a shipwreck off the coast of Liverpool in 1827, after which the locals enjoyed the salvaged India-bound cargo. Such a shipwreck may well have happened—they often did—but this one did not introduce India pale ale to Britain in such a dramatic fashion. Burton pale ales were already on sale, but only in minimal quantities.

India pale ale exploded in domestic popularity in the 1850s. The end of the tax on glass meant glassware became widespread. Compared to a pewter or earthenware mug, glassware showed impurities in beer and made adulteration of beer much more noticeable. Such adulteration was much easier to detect in pale ale than porter. It became a fashionable drink, a "Champagne of malt," according to contemporary admirers. Attempts by a French chemist to suggest that the characteristic bitterness of Burton ales was achieved by adding strychnine was comprehensively refuted by Burton's brewers, with the help of leading doctors of the day. The surrounding publicity—and subsequent endorsements of Burton pale ale from the medical profession—helped propel it to become the most fashionable and sought after beer of the age.

Cask Ale

Huge domestic demand created a headache for IPA brewers. If the beer were not to be sent on the 6-month sea voyage that miraculously conditioned it, it had to be aged in cellars for a year or more, creating a lag between demand and the ability to supply it, and requiring acres of extensive storage space. But the influx of brewing talent to Burton, coupled with the huge scientific advances the brewing industry was making in the late 19th century, held the answer.

Both IPA and porter needed to be stored for long periods to condition, and brewing was confined to cooler months, when wild yeasts were less active. But advances such as microbiology and refrigeration allowed brewing to become a year-round activity. Beer no longer had to be stored, so it could be brewed all year round, and therefore need not be brewed as strong in alcohol. New, lower strength "running beers" emerged, and quickly caught on with the rising middle classes who had to keep a clear head for work. Reforms in taxation in 1880 saw beer taxed on its original gravity, which could now be accurately measured. This incentivized brewers to brew lower strength beers, and the average alcoholic strength of beer plummeted.

Low strength running beers became the norm. With India pale ale so successful, many were soon brewed as weaker pale ales, and their characteristic hoppiness saw them increasingly become referred to as "bitter." Throughout the 20th century, IPA, pale ale, best bitter, ale, and simply bitter became increasingly interchangeable as names for beers in Britain.

What they had in common was live yeast in the cask for a secondary fermentation. This gave beer a natural carbonation and a satisfying complexity and depth of flavor. While some fans erroneously refer to it as "beer the way it has always been brewed," cask ale is undeniably Britain's national drink, unequalled as a style anywhere else. British drinkers continued to enjoy it in great quantities until the final quarter of the 20th century.

The Lager Revolution

While it is incorrect to say that Britain ignored the rise of lager completely (there were British lager breweries dating back to the late 19th century, and lager caught on as a style in Scotland quite quickly) Britain for the most part doggedly stuck with its ale styles as lager swept the rest of the world.

Why? Partly because it had its own pale, sparkling, refreshing beer in the form of pale ale. Partly because refrigeration was much slower in becoming established in the UK than in the rest of the world. Partly because of the British tied house system, which meant that the large global lager brewers struggled to gain a foothold in a country that drank a lot of beer, but did so mainly in pubs owned by ale brewers. And partly due to national pride, a now-disappeared notion that anything British must by definition be better than anything foreign.

This notion of "British Is Best" outlived the Empire that had spawned it, but finally decayed in the 1970s, a decade characterized by economic near-collapse and industrial strife.

Coincidentally, it was also the decade when air travel became affordable to the majority of the population. Britons began taking foreign holidays in larger numbers, mainly to continental Europe. They began acquiring a taste for Italian food, French wine, and European lager beer.

Lager marketers had tried unsuccessfully to persuade the Brits to drink their beers throughout the 1960s and early 1970s. But an advertising campaign by Heineken that made lager seem like a cooler, more fashionable product coincided with a record-breaking hot summer in 1976. This was lager's moment. Over the next 30 years, Britons switched from ale to lager, gaining an international reputation for swilling cheap imitation pilsners, and seemingly abandoning its ale tradition to a niche of geeky enthusiasts.

The Ale Revival

The rapid consolidation of British brewing in the 1950s and 1960s, and the attitude of modernism that drove it, changed the landscape of British brewing. The "big six" brewers emerged, between them owning over 70% of all brewing capacity. In search of efficiencies (in what had until then been a very economically inefficient and naïve industry) they strove to build standardized, national brands, beers that could be brewed in any part of the country, were robust enough to travel long distances, and were able to stand up to bad handling from poorly trained pub landlords and staff.

When cask ale is good, it can be fantastic, as good as any beer, anywhere on the planet. When it is bad, it resembles vinegar, or pond water, or worse. By the dawn of the 1970s, much of it was bad, and brewers phased out cask in favor of keg ale. Filtered, carbonated, and pasteurized in the brewery, keg ale was almost foolproof, never as bad as the worst kept cask ale, but never approaching the heights of a truly great pint of cask. Keg ale and lager, which was also filtered and pasteurized, threatened cask ale with extinction.

The problem with standardization is that it wipes out the exceptionally good as well as the exceptionally bad. Those drinkers who had been lucky enough to have access to great cask ale suddenly found they were drinking vastly inferior keg ale instead. The breweries creating their treasured beers were being bought up by the giants who wanted to get their hands on their pubs, while the breweries themselves were quickly closed.

One group of drinkers decided to do something about this, and formed the Campaign for the

Revitalization of Ale, or CAMRA for short. They coined the phrase "real ale" to refer to traditional cask conditioned beer, and duly renamed CAMRA the "Campaign for Real Ale."

CAMRA was astonishingly successful in raising awareness of real ale and protesting brewer closures. It swiftly became regarded as one of the most successful consumer movements of its day but also benefited from catching a cultural wave that saw people begin to reject modernism for its own sake, and approach traditional, crafted produce with renewed interest.

After its initial success CAMRA stagnated. Its attraction to hobbyists, reverence for tradition over innovation, and militancy that cask ale was the only beer that could be considered worth drinking, gave cask ale a negative image. To be a real ale drinker was to be a bearded, pot-bellied, sandal-wearing geek when lager drinkers were considered cool. Image had become crucially important in beer marketing, with the leading lager brands spending millions on TV advertising campaigns. Not only did ale brands not have the same budgets, ale drinkers rejected the notion that image mattered and did nothing to combat the negative image they were giving their beloved drink.

The stagnation ended in the new millennium, when Progressive Beer Duty gave tax breaks to small brewers, leading to a craft beer revolution in the UK. By now the big brewers that dominated the British market had become or were becoming part of huge multinational corporations that were keen to build global lager brands, and were withdrawing support from once iconic ale brands like John Smith's, Tetley's, and Boddington's. But influenced by tax breaks, a growing market for imported "specialty" beers, and the buzz coming from the craft beer movement in the United States, many British beer fans began setting up as brewers. Unlike the previous generation, these new brewers combined their healthy respect for tradition with an appetite for innovation, with American hops becoming commonplace and techniques such as wood ageing seeing the first genuine innovation in beer for decades. Once seen as a beer category in terminal decline, ale revived and began increasing its share of a declining beer market. By 2010, there were almost 800 brewers in Britain, more than at any time since the 1940s.

While mainstream beer in Britain will continue to be dominated by mass-produced lagers owned by global giants, the future of craft beer in Britain is secure. The beer market remains in steady decline, and economic hardship, crippling government legislation, and changing leisure patterns have led to a sharp reduction in the number of pubs in Britain. But British beer has been served in British pubs for a thousand years now. It would seem arrogant to suggest that it is about to disappear in the near future.

Classic British Beer Styles

- Pale ale—does what it says, covering a broad range from light summer ales that are almost the same color as standard golden lager but with a bit more personality, through to heady, aromatic India pale ales.
- Bitter—the workhorse of the ale world; usually mid-brown, moderate strength, all about the perfect balance of citrus or floral aromas, caramel and biscuit on the palate, with a dry finish.
- Porter and stout—a richer, darker roasting of the malt gives a fuller chocolatey, coffee, sometimes even vinous, flavor.
- Mild—dark, like porter and stout, but usually low in alcohol, full of mocha flavors while managing to remain light and refreshing.
- Old ale and barley wine—strong beers (above 7%) that have been aged to give a vast range of flavor complexity. These are not intended to be consumed by the pint, but they can rival sherry or port as an after-dinner digestive.

Regionality, Local Flavor, and Great Beer Towns

In a world of increasing standardization and homogenization, British beer and pubs provide a welcome point of regional and local difference. The large ale brewers remain regional in terms of their areas of dominance, while many smaller ones focus on providing an area no more than 30 miles' radius from the brewery. Every part of the country now has its own unique specialties.

Having said that, there are some towns and cities worthy of note. London is of course unrivalled for its historic pubs and has seen a belated explosion in the number of craft brewers supplying them.

Derby and Sheffield rival each other for the claim to have the most beers on tap of any city, with the latter felt to be the winner by a narrow margin. Edinburgh is an historic brewing town now enjoying an incredible rise in craft beer appreciation. But all key cities—Manchester, Newcastle, Cardiff, Bristol, Leeds—now have their own brewers and great beer pubs.

Brown, Pete. *Man walks into a pub: A sociable history of beer*. London: Macmillan, 2010.

The Cask Report: Celebrating Britain's National Drink. http://www.caskreport.co.uk./Cornell, Martyn, *Beer: The story of the pint*. London: Headline, 2003.

Pete Brown

Brix scale

See BALLING SCALE.

Brooklyn Brewery is both a leading craft brewer and a symbol of the revitalization of New York's most populous borough. Founded in 1987 by journalist Steve Hindy and banker Tom Potter, by 2010 it had grown to over 107,000 barrels, and become one of the top 20 craft brewers in the United States (out of 1600). Brooklyn Brewery also "played an integral part in revitalizing the Williamsburg [section of the borough] and fostering Brooklyn's renaissance," according to New York City Mayor Michael Bloomberg. That tip of the hat appeared in the mayor's introduction to Steve Hindy and Tom Potter's 2005 book on their origins called *Beer School*. Prior to founding Brooklyn, Steve had honed his writing chops as an Associated Press correspondent in the Mideast (where he witnessed Anwar Sadat's assassination, among other seminal events). While in the Mideast, Steve also developed a keen interest in home brewing, which he capitalized on when he returned to the US.

Brooklyn's original logo was created by designer Milton Glaser, best-known for the iconic "I Love New York" campaign. Early on, Brooklyn Brewery developed a close connection with its local community through sponsorships, events, and media coverage, which Steve proved especially adept at cultivating. Brewmaster Garrett Oliver joined in 1994 and enhanced those ties as a pioneer in beer–food pairings, a frequent media presence, and an author in his own right. The brewery releases upwards of 15 different beers per year, many of them available on draught for only a short time. The beers have won many national and international awards. Brooklyn Brewery has also become a leader in the production of fully bottle-conditioned ales, most of them Belgian-influenced.

Brooklyn retains strong local connections, but it has also paved the way in exporting Brooklyn Brewery's products as well as the craft beer movement around the globe. About 12% of Brooklyn's 2010 volume was in exports. Brooklyn is likely the largest craft exporter, accounting for about 20% of all craft beer volume exported outside the US. It was also the first brewery in the United States to pursue international brewing collaborations, and in 2010 the brewery commenced regular production of collaborative beers with the Italian brewery Amarcord.

Brooklyn also owned its own distribution arm for over a decade, called the Craft Brewers Guild. The pioneering Guild helped spread the "gospel" of craft beer in New York City. It sold Brooklyn's own beers and many other craft and import brands. The Guild was sold in 2003, and that capital infusion enabled Tom Potter to sell his stake to the Ottaway family. David Ottaway and Steve Hindy's friendship dated back to the early 1980s when David was a Mideast Washington Post correspondent. David's two sons, Eric and Robin, are the principal managers of the brewery. Brooklyn Brewery brews in Brooklyn and also under license in upstate New York. In 2010, Brooklyn undertook a major expansion of its brewery that will eventually enable it to brew up to 120,000 barrels in its home borough.

Brooklyn Brewery. http://www.brooklynbrewery.com/ (accessed March 16, 2011).

Benjamin Steinman

Brooklyn, New York, now better known as a hotbed of modern urban culture, was once one of the great brewing capitals of the country. In 1898, when Brooklyn was annexed by the City of New York, there were 48 working breweries in the city. As late as 1960, Brooklyn brewed 10% of the beer consumed in the United States. However, until recently none of the beers produced in Brooklyn ever touted their hometown. Instead, the breweries

The F. & M. Schaefer Co. was one of 48 breweries in Brooklyn at the turn of the 20th century.
Top row: Etching of the Schaefer brewery and malt house, 1880. PIKE MICROBREWERY MUSEUM, SEATTLE, WA
Middle row: Photograph of the Schaefer brewery taken at street level from Kent Avenue, 1948. LIBRARY OF CONGRESS
Bottom row: Beer coaster, 1942. PIKE MICROBREWERY MUSEUM, SEATTLE, WA

of the city for the most part were named after the German families that founded them.

The last two Brooklyn breweries of that era were F. & M. Schaefer Co., known for Schaefer Beer, and S. Liebmann & Sons, which was famous for Rheingold Beer (and eventually adopted the name of its most popular brew). Both closed their Brooklyn facilities in 1976, ending a tradition of brewing in New York City that began with the founding of a Dutch brewery in lower Manhattan in 1413. Schaefer was located on the East River, facing Manhattan, not far from the Brooklyn Navy Yard, a beehive of activity in the 19th and early 20th centuries. Rheingold was brewed on an 18-acre expanse of land in Bushwick, Brooklyn. Both companies sold as much as two million barrels of beer annually in their heyday.

The first commercial low-calorie "light" beer was concocted in 1967 at the Rheingold brewery by the famous brewing chemist and brewmaster Joseph Owades. The beer, unfortunately named "Gablinger's," was a flop. Both companies sponsored the Brooklyn Dodgers, Brooklyn's famous baseball team, and in later years, the New York Mets.

The demise of brewing in Brooklyn was heralded by Schaefer opening a state-of-the-art plant in 1972—in Allentown, Pennsylvania. The rising cost of land, labor, and virtually every other expense in New York City made it impossible for Schaefer and Rheingold to continue to brew beer in the city. Schaefer is still produced by the Pabst Brewing Co. See PABST BREWING COMPANY. There have been several attempts to revive the Rheingold brand, which was best known for the "Miss Rheingold" beauty contest that was said to be the second biggest election in the United States, after the US presidential election.

Most of the Brooklyn breweries were clustered in the Eastern District of Long Island, which had been annexed by the City of Brooklyn in 1855. The Eastern District covered the areas now known as Williamsburg and Bushwick. German immigrants fleeing hard times in Europe poured into the United States in the early 19th century; many settled in the Eastern District. The German lager brewers were attracted by the crystal waters of natural springs fed by the Brooklyn-Queens aquifer. By late in the century, the underground springs had been polluted by the heavy industrialization of Brooklyn. Part of the reason voters approved the annexation by New York City was a desire to connect to the city's remarkable water system, a network of underground tunnels that brought fresh water from the Delaware River and Catskill Mountains.

There were many lesser-known breweries based in Brooklyn. J.F. Trommer's Evergreen Brewery was famous for its all-malt lager beer, Trommer's White Label. See TROMMER'S EVERGREEN BREWERY. It was also known for Maple Garden, a fabulous outdoor beer garden that was crowded with families on weekends. Like many breweries, Trommer's was badly hurt by the 81-day brewery workers strike in 1949. During the strike, many New Yorkers were introduced to beers like Budweiser and Blatz that were shipped into New York City from the Midwest.

There was an area in Bushwick known as "Brewers' Row" where 11 breweries occupied a 12-block area. Many had large underground caverns that were ideal for lager fermentation because they maintained a cool temperature year round. Before Prohibition, many New York breweries owned retail outlets in the city.

Some of the better known Brooklyn breweries were the Consumers Brewing Co., the Excelsior Brewing Co., the Federal Brewing Co., India Wharf Brewing Co., Old Dutch Brewing Co., Piel Brothers Brewing Co., Schlitz Brewing Co., and Welz & Zerwick Brewing Co. The Peter Doelger Brewery owned a bar and restaurant in Williamsburg that still operates under the name "Teddy's." It still has a stained glass window that promotes "Peter Doelger's Extra Beer." Many of the old Brooklyn brewery buildings are still standing and a company called "Urban Oyster" offers tours that begin at the Brooklyn Brewery. Many of the old Brooklyn brewers are buried in Evergreen Cemetery in East New York, across the street from the site of the Trommer's Brewery.

Today, there are three breweries in Brooklyn. The Brooklyn Brewery was founded in 1987 and sold its first beer, Brooklyn Lager, in 1988. See BROOKLYN BREWERY. The Brooklyn Brewery brews beers in Williamsburg, Brooklyn, and under contract in Utica, New York. A second brewery, the Six Point Brewery, is located in the Red Hook neighborhood of Brooklyn. Brooklyn is also home to Greenpoint Beer Works, Inc., brewers for the Heartland Brewery restaurant chain and the Kelso of Brooklyn brands.

See also MANHATTAN, NEW YORK.

Anderson, William. *The breweries of Brooklyn.* Croton Falls, NY: Anderson, 1976.

Stephen Hindy

brotzeit is a German word that technically translates as "bread-time," but has come to mean a hearty snack consumed between the main meals of the day. Bavaria is the center of "brotzeit" culture, and there it most often refers to a snack consumed in the mid-morning, a sort of second breakfast. At 10 a.m., many Bavarian beer halls are full—brotzeit usually includes a beer, most often weissbier. See WEISSBIER.

At one time, brotzeit referred to a between-meal snack eaten by Bavarian farmers and herdsmen, but these days the idea appeals not only to farmers but also to suited businessmen and even many nearby Austrians. Brotzeit almost always includes bread or a soft pretzel and may also feature sausages, cheeses, hams, and sometimes sauerkraut and some vegetables. *Weisswurst,* a bland white veal sausage served with sweet mustard, is considered a particularly classical brotzeit dish.

Brotzeit is naturally a popular time in Bavarian beer gardens, and people sometimes bring their own food from home. The Bavarian Biergarten Decree of April 20, 1999, codifies this old beer garden tradition, specifically stating that one of the defining characteristics of the beer garden is the customer's right to bring his own food.

See also BAVARIA.

Gerrit Blüemelhuber and Garrett Oliver

brown ale is a term covering a broad range of styles united by color and the practice of warm fermentation by ale yeasts. Although the German altbier style fits this description, as do the Belgian dubbel and oud bruin styles, these are rarely referred to as "brown ales," and the term is usually reserved for beer styles with roots in Britain. See ALTBIER, DUBBEL, and OUD BRUIN.

The term "brown ale" can easily be confusing, or at least not much more useful than the term "red wine." At one time, before the advent of pale malt production in the 1700s, most commercial beers could have been describes as brown ales. We see the first mentions of the term in British books of the mid 1700s. At first these beers were made exclusively from brown malt but, with advances in kilning technology, pale malts—which also had the advantage of higher yields—became a cheaper and more reliable alternative. The color and flavor profile was subsequently determined more by modern-style dark malts, crystal malts, and caramelized sugars. See CRYSTAL MALT.

Within England, there are several variants of brown ale. The classic Northern English example is

Newcastle Brown Ale (4.7% alcohol by volume [ABV]) which was first brewed in 1927 not only in response to competition from the growing popularity of pale ales from Burton-on-Trent but also to maximize new developments in bottling technology. See NEWCASTLE BROWN ALE. "Brownness," of course, is relative, and great care was taken to ensure that the Newcastle Brown Ale's color had an appetizing red luminosity—indeed, the development process took 3 years. The result is a beer with a restrained caramel and dried fruit individuality and signature brown ale toffee and nut flavors. More robust northern English examples include Samuel Smith's Old Brewery Brown Ale (known in the United States as Nut Brown Ale) and the richly flavored Double Maxim from the Maxim Brewing Company of Sunderland. See SAMUEL SMITH'S OLD BREWERY. The latter beer was originally brewed by Vaux in 1901 to celebrate the safe homecoming of Lieutenant-Colonel Ernest Vaux from the Boer War, where he commanded the maxim machine-gun detachment of the Northumberland Hussars.

These Northern English brown ales all hover around the 5% ABV mark, which is considered relatively strong in the UK. They are also relatively dry. Southern variants tend to be sweeter and rarely exceed 4.2%. In parts of the south, the Midlands, and the west, a variant called mild was once prevalent. Until the 1950s, cask-conditioned mild outsold bitter, the drink now more closely associated with traditional British beer. Milds are also usually brown, but they tend to be softly hopped, slightly sweet, and low in alcohol, showing light chocolate, caramel, and fruit notes in the center. They are beers meant for long evenings in the pub and are rarely seen in bottles. Conversely, British beers called brown ale tend to be found in bottles. See MILD.

Once every English brewery included a brown ale in its portfolio, but the popularity of brown ales in Britain has declined with the loss of heavy industry and the redeployment of the hardy individuals who rewarded their skilled efforts with glasses of foam-topped dark beer. By the latter half of the 20th century, brown ale had acquired a "cloth cap" working-class image, and people who aspired to office work set brown ales aside in favor of paler beers.

Craft brewers in the United States, unencumbered by any class images surrounding brown ale, have taken the style up enthusiastically and transformed it in the process. Although mild has gained a toehold in American brewpubs and brewers from Utah seem to have embraced the style with a vengeance, there is now a uniquely American variant of brown ale. American-style brown ales are stronger, browner, and hoppier than their English forebears. Most are full bodied and dry on the palate, with strengths ranging from 5% to 6% ABV, and bitterness tends to be moderate, but can be robust. Roasted and caramelized malts are used heavily enough to skirt the edges of the porter style, but the best keep the roast restrained, pushing caramel notes to the fore. Most versions have notable hop aromatics, sometimes brought on by dry hopping. See DRY HOPPING. Craft brewers outside of North America have paid little attention to the brown ale family of styles, but a few versions have recently popped up from Scandinavia to Brazil, and it can be supposed that the evolution of the brown ale will continue apace in future years.

Jackson, Michael. *Beer companion.* London: Mitchell Beazley, 1993.

Webb, Tim. *Good beer guide Belgium.* St Albans, UK: CAMRA Books, 2009.

Alastair Gilmour

brown sugar is any sugar that has a brown color because of the presence of molasses, whether added or naturally present. Most brown sugar available in the United States is made by adding molasses to processed white sugar. In many other countries, brown sugar is usually minimally processed and has a naturally brown color.

Brewing with natural brown sugar made from sugar cane dates back to early colonial times when the highly prized sugar cane plant was successfully transplanted from India into the Americas and the Caribbean Islands by Spanish and Portuguese traders.

As early as 1558 the German beer writer and scholar Jacob Theodor Von Bergzarbern (also known as Tabernaemontanus), in his *Botanical Encyclopedia,* describes how the English often suspended a mixture of sugar, cinnamon, cloves, and other spices in a sack into beer. Tabernaemontanus also mentions that in Flanders when making or serving beer the use of brown sugar was commonplace.

In his 1889 book *The Curiosities of Ale and Beer,* Charles Henry Cook (writing under the pseudonym John Bickerdyke) points at a popular prejudice against sugar derived from the love of English people for the historic drink made of malt, but he also states that there is no fault in beer made with the addition of sugar, although it does give different flavors than malt. It is worth noting that brown sugar, like other forms of sucrose, rarely adds much in the way of sweetness because it is highly fermentable. It does, of course, add to the gravity of the wort and therefore can fortify the strength of the resulting beer.

Naturally brown sugars include dark muscovado and rapadura, which are made from sugar cane juice that is boiled and simply crystallized. Muscovado is usually found in the form of large damp crystals, whereas rapadura, popular in South America, is usually dried into a formed brick. These sugars are very flavorful and can add notable earthiness to dark beers. Demerara and turbinado sugars are tan-colored and usually made from cane juice that is evaporated, crystallized, and rinsed in a centrifuge to remove some of the molasses "impurities." Turbinado sugars tend to have relatively mild sugar cane flavors, but demerara sugars vary widely depending on the origins. They can be quite mild or very complex, adding earthy flavors reminiscent of rum, fruit, and tobacco.

Processed brown sugar generally adds a much simpler, more predictable flavor to beer, allowing it to be used regularly without much fear of variability, although when used in beer it tends to lack the depth and charm of naturally brown sugars. Cane sugars are generally preferred, but brown sugar is also made from sugar beets.

Many craft brewers use natural brown sugars to add interesting flavor notes to beers ranging from Belgian-inspired golden beers to very dark stouts. South American craft brewers have taken a particular interest in their indigenous forms of brown sugar. Presented in oddly shaped cones, slabs, crystals, or blobs, specialty sugars can give a touch of tropical *terroir* to a beverage otherwise made with ingredients grown only in temperate climates.

See also MOLASSES and SUGAR.

Bickerdyke, John. *Curiosities about ale and beer.* London: Swan Sonnenschein & Co, 1889.

Herz. Tabernaemontanus on sixteenth century beer. *Wallerstein Laboratories Communication* 27 (1964): 111–13.

Mosher, Randy. *Radical brewing,* 196–200. Denver, CO: Brewers Publications, 2004.

Unger, Richard W. *Beer in the Middle Ages and the Renaissance,* 93–144. Philadelphia: University of Pennsylvania Press, 2004.

Marcelo Carneiro

Bruce, David (1948-) has played a catalytic role in the craft brewing revival in Britain and beyond. He ran a group of brewpubs in the London area under the generic moniker of Firkin—the name for a nine-gallon beer cask—and proved that beer drinking could be fun as well as pleasurable. The attached breweries were collectively known as "Bruce's Brewery." See BREWPUB.

Bruce learned his brewing skills with two British companies, Courage and Theakston, but was keen to run his own business. In 1979 he raised the finances to purchase a closed pub in a rundown area of south London and reopened it as his first brewpub, the Goose & Firkin. The Goose set the tone for his later pubs: cask-conditioned beer brewed on the premises, bare-boarded floors, simple but good food, and no juke boxes or "fruit machines" (gambling machines that were then ubiquitous in British pubs). Such beer names as Earthstopper and Dogbolter stressed the fun element, underscored by outrageous puns on T-shirts such as "If he nicks [steals] my beer I'll Firkin punch him." In the first two weeks of business, the Goose & Firkin sold as much beer as the previous owners had in 3 months.

The theme proved a great success. Bruce eventually ran 11 pubs, 9 of them with breweries attached. Pub names included Flounder & Firkin, Phantom & Firkin, and Pheasant & Firkin. Beer sales grew five-fold in the pubs he bought and operated. The popularity of the Firkin pubs did not go unnoticed in the United States, where craft brewing was just getting its start in the early 1980s. Many American brewpub operators later credited Bruce as their original inspiration, and he later invested in several American craft breweries.

By 1990 Bruce decided to move on. He became a multimillionaire overnight when he sold the Firkins to the Stakis Hotels group. Within a year, Stakis sold the pubs on to Allied Breweries, which in turn sold them a decade later to a national pub group, Punch Taverns. Punch closed the entire Firkin operation in 2001. In the 1990s Bruce divided his time between charity work for disadvantaged children and a directorship of the pub group Slug & Lettuce. He now runs the Capital Pub Company, a group of un-themed pubs that are quite different in style from the Firkin formula.

Glover, Brian. *New Beer Guide.* Newton Abbot, England: David & Charles, 1989.

Roger Protz

buckwheat is not a grain, in spite of its name. Grains belong to the grass family, whereas buckwheat varieties belong to a family of herbs of Asian origin called Fagopyrum. However, because buckwheat has grain-like properties, it is often referred to as a pseudo-cereal. The buckwheat plant has small, off-white, triangular, edible, fruits called "achenes." These are high in protein, and, like barley kernels, are mostly made of starch. Also like barley, they have endosperms and aleurone layers, and contain the diastatic enzymes alpha-amylase and beta-amylase. See ALPHA AMYLASE and AMYLASES. When ground, buckwheat seeds can be used as a flour substitute. In a beer mash they can be used malted or unmalted as an adjunct. See ADJUNCT. In the finished beer, they add a slightly nutty flavor.

The proportion of buckwheat in a mash may be as high as one-half, though experimental mashes with 100% buckwheat have been reported in brewing literature. However, because of the buckwheat's relatively high protein content, a mash with buckwheat generally necessitates a grist-to-water ratio of 1:4 or thinner to avoid excessive mash viscosity, clumping, and low extract volumes. Buckwheat, unlike most cereal grains, is also gluten-free. See GLUTEN-FREE BEER. Individuals with celiac disease, who cannot drink most beers because of the presence of gluten, can usually tolerate beer made from buckwheat in conjunction with such gluten-free grains as sorghum and/or millet.

Phiarais, Blaise Patricia Nic, Hilde Henny Wijngaard, and Elke Karin Arendt. The impact of kilning on enzymatic activity of buckwheat malt. *Journal of the Institute of Brewing* 111 (2005): 290–298. http://www.scientificsocieties.org/jib/papers/2005/G-2005-1108-310.pdf/ (accessed March 17, 2011).

Wijngaard, H. H., and E. K. Arendt. Optimisation of a mashing program for 100% malted buckwheat. *Journal of the Institute of Brewing* 112 (2006): 57–65. http://www.scientificsocieties.org/jib/papers/2006/G-2006-0406-428.pdf/ (accessed March 17, 2011).

Wijngaard, H. H., H. M. Ulmer, M. Neuman, and E. K. Arendt. The effect of steeping time on the final malt quality of buckwheat. *Journal of the Institute of Brewing* 111 (2005): 275–281. http://www.scientificsocieties.org/jib/papers/2005/G-2005-1012-303.pdf/ (accessed March 17, 2011).

Horst Dornbusch

Budweiser, larger and more famous by far than its European namesake. The American beers called "Budweiser" are made by Anheuser-Busch Companies (A-B), a division of the world's largest brewing company, Anheuser-Busch InBev. Although now widely thought of as being as American as McDonald's, the name is taken from a famous Czech Bohemian brewing center, České Budějovice, which is called Budweis in the German language that was once commonly spoken there. Anything from Budweis, whether it be a beer or a person, might be called a Budweiser. Unauthorized borrowing of place names was commonplace in the 19th century, when Europeans were not worried that American products would cut into their markets or reputations. Later, just as winemakers in France became upset by ersatz American wines labeled "Champagne," the Czechs were to become more than slightly perturbed by American Budweiser.

Most early lagers in the United States were made in imitation of the brown Munich type: all malt, rich, and heavy. With its hotter climate and richer diet, brewers sensed that Americans might be interested in a lighter, more refreshing style of beer. Inspiration came in the form of Bohemian lager, which spread rapidly in Europe after its introduction in 1842.

Brewing this style of beer from American ingredients was not a simple matter. The North American six-row barleys prevalent at the time had very high protein levels and produced beers that were prone to an unsightly haze, especially when chilled, making the product unstable on the shelf. Based on work that had been ongoing in Europe for some time, in 1869 brewing chemist Anton Schwarz published an article called "Brewing with Raw Cereals, Especially Rice" in *American Brewer* magazine.

In the mid-1870s, Adolphus Busch and his brewmaster Irwin Sprule formulated their first Bohemian pilsner recipe, labeling it "St. Louis Lager."

Shortly thereafter, a second recipe was created for Busch's friend Carl Conrad, a liquor merchant and restaurateur in St Louis. Based on the slightly paler and more effervescent "Budweis" beer from České Budějovice, it was sold under the "Conrad Budweiser" name. The recipe contained 23.5% rice in addition to the malt and was hopped with a combination of American and European hops. Rice, rather than corn, was felt to give a crisper, more refreshing edge to the product.

Budweiser was exclusively a bottled product, allowing the label to serve as a guarantee of origin. However, by the late 1870s, the name and label were so widely copied that Busch was forced to sue, and this was to be repeated many times in the decades to follow. Budweiser was the first beer to be bottled and pasteurized on a large scale. This allowed Busch to market the beer far from home. Thanks to an extensive network of refrigerated rail cars and ice depots, Budweiser was very successful in the expanding markets south and west of St Louis and eventually throughout the United States.

By 1882, Conrad was bankrupt. In lieu of payment of a $94,000 debt, the brand was transferred to Anheuser-Busch, but Busch and Conrad wrangled for control of Budweiser until 1891, when Conrad gave Busch perpetual rights to the name. That year, 14 million bottles (5 million l) were sold. In 1901, Budweiser was 65% of total A-B volume, and 761,000 hl (650,000 US bbls) were sold across the United States and in foreign markets, including Asia and South America. Sales for all alcoholic beverages declined in the United States after that date in the run-up to World War I and national Prohibition.

When the company resumed brewing after Prohibition, Budweiser was its main brand and sole focus of its advertising efforts. Diligent marketing and steadfast technical quality helped grow Budweiser, and after trading the top position several times with Schlitz in the decades after Prohibition, it became the number one beer brand in the United States in 1957. Budweiser was itself upstaged in 2004 by its sister brand, Bud Light, launched in 1982, which remains the single largest beer brand in the world.

Battles with Europeans over ownership of the Budweiser name began as early as 1907, when challenges by German and Bohemian breweries were settled by large payments. The matter remained mostly dormant until the mid-1980s as A-B attempted to widen its reach into Europe. Courts in the UK granted both American and Czech Budweisers the use of the name there in 1984. After the fall of communism, A-B attempted to purchase its namesake brewery in Budweis, and at one point the workers went on strike to encourage the purchase. Czech President Vaclav Havel reportedly got involved to stop the sale. Today, detente has been reached. In Continental Europe, A-B InBev's Budweiser is generally known as "Bud," whereas the Czech-brewed Budweiser Budvar brand is called "Czechvar" in the United States. In July 2010, A-B InBev lost another significant battle as Europe's highest court denied their request to register the Budweiser brand in the European Union.

A number of line extensions to the Budweiser (Select, American Ale) and Bud Light (Chelada, Bud Light Lime) brands have been launched with varying degrees of success.

The flagship beer, simply called Budweiser, is an extremely pale lager with a mild, bready aroma, a bit of apple fruitiness, a clean, dry palate, and a crisp finish. The recipe consists of a mix of about 30% four-row barley malt from A-B's own maltings and 40% six-row malt; the remaining 30% is rice grits. The recipe varies by a few percent to hit specific flavor targets depending on the characteristics of the grains available. Budweiser has a standard 5% alcohol by volume from an original gravity of 11.0°.

The brewing process is a modification of the traditional American adjunct mash procedure. The malt mash is given a short protein rest at 120°F (48°C) while the rice grits are brought up to temperature for a short boil, and then the two mashes are combined for a saccharification rest. For many decades, A-B employed a unique wort separation vessel called a Strainmaster, which consisted of a trough-like vessel with a conical bottom and a perforated manifold through which the clear wort is withdrawn. This system offers speed but is a bit less efficient that traditional lauter tuns, and for this reason they have been largely replaced.

Bitterness is low, but noticeable on the palate at 10 to 12 international bitterness units. Hops are mainly US-grown German varieties such as Hallertau, Saaz, and Tettnanger, with some European hops plus high-alpha and non-Germanic types such as Willamette in the mix. This complex hop bill allows brewers to maintain a consistent flavor and aroma despite changing characteristics of hops available on the market.

Prior to chilling, the wort undergoes a special stripping process to remove sulfur compounds, especially dimethyl sulfide. The hot wort is streamed in a filmy layer on the inner surface of thin vertical tubes through which is blown hot, sterile air. This method provides additional evaporation that allows for a shortened wort boil, more or less replicating the effects of the Baudelot wort chillers that the company used until the 1960s.

Fermentation and lagering normally takes 21 days. By traditional standards, lagering is a bit warm, at 7.2°C–8.9°C (45°F–48°F). At these temperatures the yeast does a good job of reducing diacetyl and acetaldehyde (which, contrary to a commonly held notion, is at very low levels in Budweiser) but also allows for a bit of ester development, giving the beer its hint of applelike fruitiness. Bottled Budweiser is pasteurized; draught is not.

The company employs extensive quality control procedures, both mechanized and sensory, a necessity with any packaging brewery, especially one dedicated to producing an identical beer at locations across the globe. In one extreme measure, cans of Budweiser are frozen in liquid nitrogen and tasted years later, a check against slow drift of the famous flavor profile.

In 2008 Budweiser volume was 43.4 million hl (approx. 37 million US bbls), whereas production of Bud Light was higher still at 55.6 million hl (approx. 47 US bbls).

See also ANHEUSER-BUSCH and BUDWEISER BUDVAR.

Baron, Stanley. *Brewed in America: The history of beer in the United States.* Boston: Little, Brown & Co., 1962.
Hernon, Peter, and Ganey, Terry. *Under the influence: The unauthorized story of the Anheuser-Busch dynasty.* New York: Simon & Schuster, 1991.
Ogle, Maureen. *Ambitious brew.* Orlando, FL: Harcourt, 2006.

Randy Mosher

Anheuser Busch and the Budvar Brewery in the Czech town of České Budějovice, also known as Budweis, have fought a protracted legal battle over the rights to the Budweiser trademark. PIKE MICROBREWERY MUSEUM, SEATTLE, WA

Budweiser Budvar is a Czech beer brewed in the southern Bohemian town of České Budějovice, a town better known outside the Czech Republic under its old German name of Budweis. It's the town's name that gives a clue to the reason why, for more than a century, there has been a long and bitter legal battle between two producers of beers labelled "Budweiser."

Anheuser-Busch InBev, the American brewer of Budweiser, claims that its beer is the original. See ANHEUSER-BUSCH. It is true that the St Louis, Missouri, brewery was producing its version of Budweiser some 30 years before Budvar, but this outlook ignores the long history of brewing in Budweis. The south Bohemian town has been a major brewing center for centuries and its beers were given the generic name of Budweiser beer, just as pilsner beer has its origins in Pilsen. The beers from Budweis were so popular at the Bohemian royal court that they were known as the "Beer of Kings." In the 19th century, a brewery owned by German-speaking Bohemians, the Budweiser Burgerbrau or Citizen's Budweis Brewery, was formed from a merger of two smaller companies. It exported its beers widely under the Budweiser trademark.

The Anheuser-Busch brewery in St Louis opened in 1875, owned by two German emigrants, Eberhard Anheuser and Adolphus Busch. Among their portfolio of beers was one labeled "Budweiser," and in subsequent court cases, the company admitted its beer was based on the Bohemian beers.

When sales of American Budweiser grew, it was marketed, with classically American bravado, as the "King of Beers"—not too dissimilar from the "Beer of Kings." In 1895, Czech speakers in Budweis banded together to build a rival to the town's German brewery, Burgerbrau. The new company was called the "Budějovicky Pivovar" meaning the "Budweis Brewery," but this was contracted to "Budvar" for convenience.

When the Czech company attempted to export its beer to the United States, a series of court cases ensued. At first, Budvar was banned from exporting to the United States using the Budweiser trademark, but there were no restrictions on their use of the mark in Europe. However, since the end of World War II, the two companies have fought protracted battles to establish their respective brands throughout the world. The company that manages to register its trademark first can use the full Budweiser label. In some countries the American beer can only be sold as "Bud," whereas the Czech version is known in some markets as Budějovicky Budvar as a result of losing a court case to Anheuser-Busch. The Czech brewery is still state-owned more than 2 decades after the fall of communism. Successive Czech governments have said they will only privatize the brewery if they can find a "suitable partner," a phrase widely understood not to include their nemesis, Anheuser-Busch. But steps are being taken to turn the brewery into a joint stock company, the first steps to privatization.

Budvar bears little resemblance to the American beer of the same name. It has 5% alcohol by volume and 20 units of bitterness and is one of the few remaining large brands still made by the traditional lagering method involving a very slow secondary fermentation. The beer adheres to the German Reinheitsgebot or Purity Law that stipulates that only malted barley, hops, yeast, and water can be used in the brewing process. Budvar is brewed in a particularly beautiful traditional brew house with copper mashing and boiling vessels set on tiled floors. A double decoction mash is used. See DECOCTION. Primary fermentation is in small cylindroconical vessels, with maturing or lagering in classic horizontal tanks in cellars below the brewery where the temperature is held at just above freezing. Lagering lasts for a full 90 days, one of the longest periods of cold conditioning in the world.

Only pale Moravian malt and Žatec (Saaz) whole hops are used. Soft brewing water comes from a deep natural lake beneath the brewery, using a well that dates back several thousand years. The finished beer is refreshing, showing a rich malt and vanilla aroma, and fine, floral hop character. The finish has a fine balance of juicy malt, tangy hop resins, and a delicate hint of apple fruit. The beer retains the deep burnished gold color that is among the hallmarks of the Bohemian pilsner style.

Budvar also brews a 4% version of the beer for the domestic market. In recent years it has added an amber lager called Pardal (Panther) aimed at blue-collar drinkers and sports enthusiasts. Following a major debate within the brewery, Budvar has also added Dark, a black lager of the type produced in central Europe before the advent of modern malting techniques. It has been a success in the Czech Republic and is exported to Britain where some pubs have a special dispense system that mixes golden Budvar and Dark, a mixture known as "Half and Half."

There has been some slight softening in the dispute between Anheuser-Busch and Budvar, with A-B Inbev distributing the Czech beer in the United States under the name Czechvar. In the Czech Republic both Budvar and the older Burgerbrau brewery—known for some years as Samson but now called the Town Brewery—have been granted a guarantee of origin by the European Union that entitles both companies to use the Budweiser trademark.

Protz, Roger. *Complete guide to world beer/world beer guide*. London: Carlton Books, 1995/2009.

Roger Protz

bulk transport (or bulk shipping) relates to the movement of large quantities of beer—other than that contained in bottles, cans, kegs, casks, or demountable tanks that can be used to dispense beer directly to the consumer. Bulk transport is often used where the beer packaging location is separate from the brewery. Although beer can be transferred over short distances by pipelines, most bulk transport is carried out in tanks designed for transport by road, rail, or sea. The filling of these tanks with beer presents challenges not experienced with most other liquids. First, the tanks must be thoroughly cleaned to a high standard to prevent possible flavor taints and contamination with beer spoilage microorganisms. Second, the pickup of oxygen during the beer transfer and filling operations must be minimized to prevent the subsequent development of staling characteristics in the beer. Third, because the beer is often already carbonated, turbulence must be avoided during tank-filling operations because this can generate foam and prevent effective filling. Oxygen pickup can be minimized by careful monitoring of pipe and hose joints and of the seals of beer-pumping equipment, together with the creation of an oxygen-free atmosphere (usually carbon dioxide, nitrogen, or both) in the receiving tank. Pressuring the gases inside the tank can also help to minimize turbulence during filling. Finally, maintaining the beer at low temperatures during transit can also reduce any adverse flavor development and slow the growth of spoilage organisms. Heaters are also used to prevent the beer from freezing during winter. Bulk-shipped beer is normally flash-pasteurized before the tanker is filled. Large breweries that practice high-gravity brewing often bulk ship concentrated versions of their beers. The high-gravity beer is then blended down with sterile deoxygenated water at the receiving location before being bottled or kegged there. See HIGH GRAVITY BREWING.

See also DISTRIBUTION.

George Philliskirk

Bullion (hop) is an early English bittering hop selected by Ernest S. Salmon in 1919 from open-pollinated seeds collected from the wild American accession BB1. Bullion is a sister to Brewer's Gold and was released by Professor Salmon in 1938 after extensive testing. See BREWER'S GOLD (HOP). The female parent BB1 was discovered near Morden, Manitoba, Canada, and cuttings were sent to England in 1916 by Professor W. T. Macoun, Dominion Horticulturist for Canada. In 1917, BB1 was established in a field at Wye College and pollinated by an English male hop. Bullion was selected from the resulting progeny. Bullion is similar to Brewer's Gold in alpha acids (10%) and beta acids (5.4%), and, like Brewer's Gold, it does not store well. It was considered a good "workhorse hop" and, starting in the 1940s, Bullion became a major bittering hop in the United States. It was replaced in the mid-1980s by higher-alpha cultivars with better storage and agronomic performance.

Salmon, E. S. Bullion hop, a new variety. *Journal of the South East Agricultural College* 42 (1938): 47–52.

Shaun Townsend

bung, the hole in the head of a cask, keg, or barrel. It can also refer to the hole in the belly or bilge of a cask and to the devices that seal those holes. The average size of a cask or barrel bung is 1 15/16 inch, although some breweries have used smaller sizes in North America for Hoff-Stevens and Golden Gate kegs.

When referencing the bung as a closure, it is a hard nylon, rubber, or wood stopper used to plug the hole in the head or belly of a cask or keg. The shape is generally a slightly truncated cylinder, and it is usually hammered in to be flush with the container. In traditional English cellaring the bung refers solely to the hole in which the keystone is inserted in the cask head and the shive boss is in the belly of a cask.

See also BARREL, CASK, GOLDEN GATE KEGS, HOFF-STEVENS KEGS, and KEG.

Jonathan Downing

Burton ale was a rich, strong, dark amber ale, probably up to as much as 11% ABV, which predated (and later co-existed with) the pale ales and India pale ales for which Burton–on-Trent, UK (also known as simply Burton), became famous. See BURTON-ON-TRENT. It fit squarely into the category of "brown beers," which were the most common brews in Britain certainly up until the 18th century. Like most British beers up to that time it was not brewed to a definite style, and never really achieved a clear identity even as porter, stout, pale ale, and others emerged as separate entities.

There is evidence that the abbots of the monastery in Burton were brewing in the 13th century. This had ceased by Henry VIII's Dissolution of the monasteries in the 16th century, but by this time small commercial brewers were making ale in the town. In those days ale was produced in its original sense, in that it was not brewed with hops; these came to Burton later, probably in the 16th century.

Burton Ale was brewed by collecting the first and richest wort and fermenting it separately to make strong ale. The grain would then be re-mashed with hot water two or more times and the dilute worts collected and used to make table and small beers. See SMALL BEER.

Burton Ale would have been brewed from malt paler than the brown high-dried malt used for porter, but one that was still much darker than modern pale ale malts. By the 18th century it was still only brewed on a relatively small scale, compared to London porter. But Burton must have obtained a sound reputation by then, for there was a small export trade to London and Hull, after the river was opened to shipping with the 1699 Trent Navigation Act. In the last quarter of the 18th century, with the opening of several canals, Burton Ale was also able to reach Manchester and Liverpool by barge. One result of this improved accessibility to deep-sea ports was that Burton Ale was regularly exported to the Baltic countries, notably Russia. Here it apparently held its own against the strong Imperial Stouts which were being exported from London to the Russian Court.

Such trade came to an end with the Napoleonic Wars, as a result of blockades and embargoes. The Burton brewers saw India as an alternative export destination, developed a method for producing paler malt, and began to brew India Pale Ale. From then on breweries in Burton saw phenomenal growth, outpacing even the great London brewers. In particular Bass became the world's largest brewing company by 1876. See BASS & COMPANY.

Brewing methods too had changed. The practice of collecting separate liquors from the grain mash and making separate beers from had largely ceased. This approach had been superseded by the technique of continuous collection of liquor (wort), coupled with sparging, or sprinkling of hot water on the grain bed. The collected wort would then go to make a single beer, instead of two or three beers of differing qualities.

The popularity of Burton Ale began to fade by the 1830s, however, it was not yet extinct; in 1839 just under half of Bass' output consisted of porter and Burton Ale. By 1865 this proportion had dwindled to some 7% of the total, some of which was described as "export ale," and was presumably Burton Ale, as in 1876 a label for this was trademarked by Bass. It was available in the United States in the late 19th century, and this is where we have the best information on the strength of this beer. Brewers could not measure gravity until almost the end of the 18th century when the hydrometer became a brewing tool; even after this, there is little to be found on analysis of Burton Ale.

In 1908 results of analysis on various beers were published in Chicago, and included two samples of Burton Ale tested, respectively, in 1879 and 1890, and containing 8% and 10% ABV. The authors also quote an 1890 result on a "ninety years old" sample of Worthington Burton at 11% ABV. Interestingly, "Burton Ale" was brewed in North America in the mid-20th century by the Ballantine Company, then brewing out of Newark, New Jersey. This beer was red-amber in color, highly hopped, and aged in lined wooden tanks. This perhaps suggests its brewing was influenced by Burton's pale ale expertise, rather than by its history of strong ale brewing.

A dark brown version of Burton Ale was still in production in the early 1960s, when Ind Coope & Allsopp offered it as a special winter brew. It then disappeared from view, although in the 1970s Ind Coope brought out a pale bitter beer (about 4.7% ABV) and called it Burton Ale, another instance of a British brewer twisting brewing history for marketing purposes.

See also BRITAIN.

Hornsey, Ian. *A history of beer and brewing.* Cambridge: The Royal Society of Chemistry, 2003.

Terry Foster

Burtonization

See BURTON-ON-TRENT and CALCIUM SULFATE.

Burton-on-Trent. By the end of the 19th century, Burton-on-Trent (28 miles north-east of Birmingham) was to become "the brewing capital of Britain," and its beers were highly prized and much-copied. The brewing origins of this Staffordshire town can be traced to the Benedictine Abbey, founded by a Thane of Mercia, one Wulfric Spot, in 1004. In those days, the affairs of Burton were largely controlled by the abbots and their officials. There is some dispute as to the actual date of the foundation of the monastery, as the relevant extant document was not signed or dated. As a result, the town of Burton-on-Trent celebrated one thousand years of brewing history in 2002. According to Sir Walter Scott's *Ivanhoe*, the Abbey at Burton, in the time of Richard Coeur-de-Lion (Lionheart, who reigned 1189-1199), had acquired a lofty reputation for its ale. The earliest historical reference to such eminence for Burton ale comes from a ditty of 1295:

> The Abbot of Burton brewed good ale,
> On Fridays when they fasted,
> But the Abbot of Burton never tasted his own
> As long as his neighbor's lasted.

Also in 1295 there occur some of the first references to the Abbey brewhouse, although there is no documentation of volumes brewed or people employed. It seems as though brewing must have been pretty well confined to households and the ecclesiastic establishments, for in a document of 1319, which itemized the rental of properties in Burton, the population was given as 1,800 souls, not one of whom was engaged in the trade of brewing! Even in those days, the numerous wells in and around Burton, were recognized as being "special" for brewing purposes. The suitability of Burton water for brewing lies in its extreme hardness, particularly in terms of calcium and magnesium sulfates. These so-called gypseous waters promote protein coagulation during boiling, allow high hop-rate usage, and promote yeast growth; the result being the clear, sparkling ale for which Burton became famous.

On the dissolution of the Abbey in 1540, an inventory was made of the brewhouse equipment, and mention was made of large malting house in the Market Place. As was the pattern at the time, brewing migrated to become the province of the pub–brewer, and, in 1604, there were 46 of these serving a population of around 1,500. By the end of the 16th century, beer from Burton's breweries was attaining many plaudits, and it seems as though considerable quantities were being carried out of the town, even reaching London, where, certainly by the 1620s, it was sold as "Darbie [Derby] Ale" and held in very high esteem. Even so, throughout most of the 17th century, brewing remained subordinate to cloth-making and allied trades.

By the mid-18th century, Burton's brewing industry had expanded, but was restricted by limited markets and generally poor transport connections; at this time, each of London's major breweries produced more beer than all of Burton's added together!

Daniel Defoe, in his *Tour Through the Whole of Great Britain* of 1724–1726, remarked: "At Lichfield, the ale is incomparable, as it is all over this county of Stafford. Burton is the most famous town for it . . . the best character you can give to ale in London is calling it Burton Ale, and that they brew, in London, some that goes by that denomination."

A crucial turning point in Burton's brewing industry was a Lord Paget-inspired Act of Parliament of 1699, "The Trent Navigation Act," which permitted opening up of the river. This put the town at the head of one of Britain's largest navigation systems and in direct contact with major ports, such as Hull and Gainsborough (in those days), from where the Baltic ports could be reached. Communications were even better after the Burton section of the Trent and Mersey Canal was opened in 1770, and this brought increased prosperity to the town, which, by the end of the century was a bustling town of some 6,000 people.

The rate of growth slowed during the first 40 years of the 19th century (mainly due to a downturn in Baltic trade). Population in 1831 was still under 7,000, but, during the following half-century there was massive industrial and urban growth (population 46,000 by 1891). This was almost entirely due to expansion of the brewing industry, and, during the last half of the 19th century, there were generally 20–30 breweries in the town, with Bass & Co., and Allsopp's accounting for over 50% of total output.

As with much of the British brewing industry, there has been a major contraction in Burton, with the disappearance of many notable names.

In the past, the town has engendered literary interest, as is shown by these lines from A.E. Housman's *A Shropshire Lad*:

> Say, for what were hop-yards meant,
> Or why was Burton built on Trent?

And it is also mentioned in important historical documents, such as those relating to the imprisonment of Mary, Queen of Scots in Tutbury Castle in 1584, where we are told that she was supplied with "beer from Burton, some three myles off."

Molyneux, W. *Burton-on-Trent: Its history, its waters and its breweries.* London: Trubner & Co., 1869.

Owen, C.C. *Burton-on-Trent: The industrial history.* Derby, England: Breedon, 1994.
Owen, C.C. *The development of industry in Burton-upon-Trent.* Chichester, England: Phillimore, 1978.

Ian Hornsey

Burton snatch is a term, now somewhat antiquated, for the whiff of sulfur on a freshly poured beer. The aroma is particularly associated with beers originally brewed in Burton-on-Trent, England. See BURTON-ON-TRENT. The sulfur smell comes from the presence of sulfate ions in Burton's natural water supply. The water in Burton rises up through a sandstone aquifer, which has a high content of calcium sulfate, more commonly known as gypsum. See CALCIUM SULFATE. The high levels of sulfate in Burton waters (up to 800 ppm) bring a hard dry mineral edge to the bitterness of beers brewed from it, and this makes the water ideal for the production of pale ales.

The characteristic of Burton's water is a happy accident, but a well-suited water supply was once one of the main considerations for situating a brewery, a clear example of "terroir" in beer. In the 19th century, Burton's brewing heyday, sulfate hardness made the water perfect for brewing crisp, clear pale beers. Burton eventually specialized in pale beers, whereas London, where water was naturally hardened by calcium carbonate, specialized in dark porter beer. See PORTER. With the beginnings of scientific investigation toward the end of 18th century, the presence of the Burton salts was recognized, but it wasn't until late in the 19th century that London brewers learned how to treat water, or "Burtonize" it, to increase its sulfate hardness and make it better-suited to the production of pale ales.

The practice of Burtonizing water became widespread in the British Isles and has now spread worldwide. That said, brewers rarely add enough salts to emulate the sulfurous "Burton snatch" aromatic, which remains part of the aroma profile of Burton-brewed Marston's Pedigree, though some aficionados say it is not nearly so pungent as it once was.

Matthias, Peter. *The Brewing Industry in England 1700-1830.* Cambridge: Cambridge University Press, 1959.

Tim Hampson

The **Burton Union system** is a wood barrel fermentation system that was used predominately by the brewers in and around Burton-on-Trent, England, in the mid- to late 19th century. It is also referred as a "Union set." Among the notable brewers who employed this system are Bass Brewery and Marston's Brewery. Marston's is the last brewery in England who still utilizes this system. A Union set is an amazing and strange brewing anomaly, consisting of large wood barrel casks, each 150 imperial gallons in size (about 7 hl), ranging from 24 to 60 in number, which are positioned on their sides in rows, typically suspended off the floor in a wood or metal frame by large metal axles. The barrels are spaced evenly and each is fitted with a bottom valve that leads to a bottom trough. An attemperator cooling coil is installed in each barrel to control fermentation temperature with chilled water. The barrels are linked together by a series of side rod pipes so that liquid can be evenly dispersed throughout the Union from a feeder vessel. A swan neck pipe leads from the top of each the barrel to a top trough, which is suspended over the barrels and is slightly pitched to one end. Connected to this trough, at the lower end, is the feeder trough.

The Union is fed by gravity from the primary fermentation vessels, or squares, with fresh, actively fermenting ale wort, typically 12–24 hours after yeast has been added. At this time in the fermentation process the yeast is very active. The fermenting wort is introduced to the system at the feeder vessel and flows into the barrels through the side rods, flooding the Union. As the yeast ferments, it is forced out of the barrels in foamy bursts, along with some beer, through the swan necks, and into the top trough. Here some of the yeast stays behind while the beer runs down the trough, into the feeder vessel, and back into the casks through the side rods. As the fermentation proceeds, a large amount of healthy, viable yeast is retained in the top trough and the beer in the barrels, now cleansed of its yeast, gradually becomes bright. The yeast is collected from the top trough for subsequent fermentations and is considered of very high quality. After about 6 days in the union, the fully fermented beer can be dropped out of the barrels through the bottom valve and collected in the bottom trough. This beer is then moved to a finishing vessel, blended with other beer, or packaged in casks.

Although the Burton Union system is spectacularly ungainly, it is also oddly beautiful. At the height of the system's use in the 1800s, a large brewery

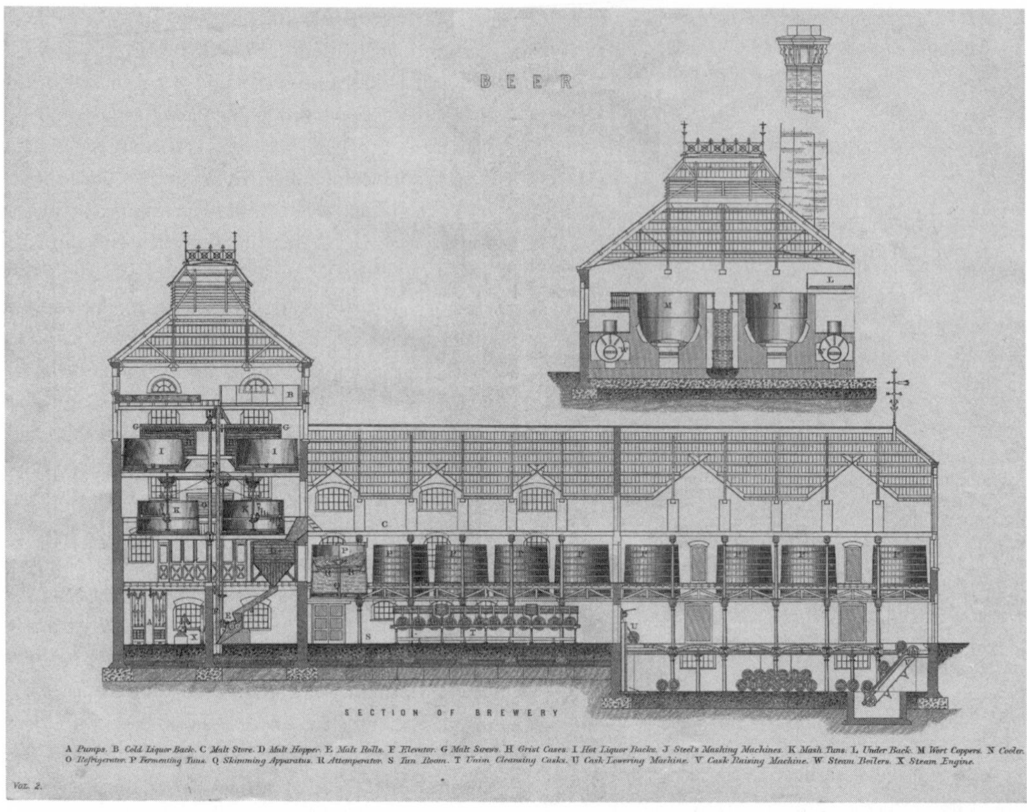

Burton Union systems use a series of 150-gallon wood barrel casks in the fermentation process. Etching, c. 1900. PIKE MICROBREWERY MUSEUM, SEATTLE, WA

such as Bass would have employed dozens of Union sets, each of them capable of fermenting over 300 hl (256 US bbl) of beer at a time. The oak was never used for flavoring the beer, and today the brewers at Marston's also prefer maintaining older neutral barrels and do not select wood based on the flavor that it will impart. Like brewers 150 years ago, they are interested instead in the quality of the yeast and the character of the fermentation that the system produces because of its unique design and materials. The Union system is very labor and capitol intensive to employ and requires constant maintenance by an experienced cooper. Cleaning is difficult and is conducted with large amounts of hot water and manual labor; modern cleaning chemicals and automated cleaning systems cannot be used with wood. This has resulted in the Union process being largely abandoned by British brewers, Bass having discontinued the use of Burton Unions in the 1980s. Today, Marston's uses the Union largely for the production of their flagship Pedigree Bitter.

Firestone Walker Brewing Company in Paso Robles, California, utilizes a modified Burton Union fermentation system (Firestone Union, US Patent 1996) and is the only brewery in the world beside Marston's who is recognized as operating a union set today. The union set is used to produce the brewery's flagship Double Barrel Ale, Walker's Reserve Porter, and Pale 31 beers. Their system does not utilize an elaborate system of swan necks and troughs but rather uses flexible hose and smaller receiving buckets. It consists of new American oak barrels, 227 l (60 US gal) in size, which are toasted inside similar to winemaker's barrels and impart wood flavor to the beer. Firestone Walker's system is not utilized to collect yeast; however, the unique geometry of the system along with the new American oak barrels has a profound effect on the flavor of the beer. In the Firestone process, 24-hour-old fermenting wort is delivered to the individual barrels utilizing a racking cane. The wort is then allowed to ferment without any temperature control in a series

The Firestone Walker Brewing Company in Paso Robles, California, uses a modified Burton Union system that consists of 40 American oak barrels, each with a capacity of 65 gallons. MATTHEW BRYNILDSON

of barrels ranging from 32 to 48 in number. As the beer ferments, brown yeast and foam are pushed from the barrels to a bram back or receiving bucket, and the cast-off foam is discarded. The finished beer has a notable soft and fruity character with a pronounced oaky, vanilla note compared with beer simply fermented in stainless-steel vessels.

Boulton, Chris, and David Quain. *Brewing yeast and fermentation*. Boston: Blackwell Science Ltd, 2001.

Matthew Brynildson

Busch, August IV (1964–) is the former president and CEO of the Anheuser-Busch Brewing Company headquartered in St Louis, Missouri. See ANHEUSER-BUSCH. He is also the great-great-grandson of Adolphus Busch, founder of Anheuser-Busch, and the son of August Busch III, the former chairman, president, and CEO of the company.

Busch was born in St Louis, Missouri, in 1964, the eldest son of August Busch III. His parents divorced when he was 5 years old, and Busch lived with his mother during the remainder of his childhood. Growing up, Busch IV saw his father primarily at the family brewery and under business settings. Busch IV once said of his relationship with his father, Busch III, "I never, ever had a father–son relationship." It was "purely business."

Busch holds a bachelor's degree in finance along with a master's degree in business administration from Saint Louis University. Busch also attended the 6-month Certified Brewmaster course at Germany's VLB Berlin. See VLB BERLIN.

Busch began working at Anheuser-Busch as an apprentice brewer in 1985. Since that time, he has held a variety of positions in management, brewing, operations, and marketing. In 1994, he was named vice president of brand management and 2 years later, in 1996, he became vice president of marketing. In 2000, Busch was promoted to group vice president of marketing and wholesale operations.

Busch IV spent most of his career in marketing, where he launched Bud Dry, a product that ultimately proved disappointing for Anheuser Busch. More recently, he introduced Budweiser Select, Bud Extra (a.k.a. B-to-the-E), and new packaging innovations such as aluminum bottles. He had greater success in steering the company's advertising toward more humorous advertising campaigns, such as the "Budweiser frogs" and the popular "Whassup?" commercials.

Nicknamed "The Fourth," Busch eventually became president and CEO of Anheuser-Busch in December of 2006, succeeding the only non-Busch family member to lead the company, Patrick Stokes. When Busch became CEO, he was fifth-generation family and the sixth member of his family to hold that position.

In 2008, Busch IV presided over the company as the global beer company InBev acquired Anheuser-Busch for approximately $52 billion, or roughly $70 a share. See INBEV. Initially opposed to the takeover, Busch IV attempted to thwart the deal by trying to buy the remainder of Mexico's beer giant Grupo Modelo and employing other strategies to raise his company's value. Eventually, however, InBev increased the offer and a majority of shareholders voted in favor of it. The story of the merger was detailed by Julie Macintosh in her best-selling book, *Dethroning the King*.

After the merger, August Busch IV continued to hold a position on the board of directors of the newly formed combined company, Anheuser-Busch InBev. His new brief was to advise AB InBev on new products, review marketing programs, meet with retailers, wholesalers, advertisers, and the media; scrutinize the quality of Anheuser-Busch's beers; and give advice about A-B's relationship with charitable organizations and local communities.

August Busch IV remains an active member of the Democratic political party and holds black belt degrees in three martial arts.

Arndorfer, James B. "Is he Busch league?" *Advertising Age*. June 25, 2005. http://adage.com/article?article_id=103802/ (accessed January 2, 2011).

Kesmodel, David. "Anheuser CEO fights for his legacy." *Wall Street Journal*. May 27, 2008.

Jay R. Brooks

butanediol

See DIACETYL.

butyric acid, also known under the systemic name "butanoic acid," is a carboxylic acid with the structural formal $CH_3CH_2CH_2COOH$. It is an important flavor compound in a number of foods in addition to beer. However, at concentrations above its beer flavor threshold (2 mg/L), it causes cheesy, rancid, baby vomit, or putrid off-flavors. Abnormal concentrations in beer can arise from infections by anaerobic spore-forming bacteria of the genus Clostridium.

Investigations into the sources of butyric acid and the bacteria involved have shown that glucose and cane sugar syrups being used as kettle adjuncts can be involved. The vulnerable areas during syrup manufacture have been found to be the handling of the starch slurry during glucose syrup manufacture and the sweet water system in cane sugar syrup manufacture. Wort production has also been identified as a potential source of butyric acid both before and after kettle boiling.

Food plant hygiene is essential in preventing outbreaks of bacteria in syrup and brewing plants, particularly during periods of high ambient temperatures and following plant shutdowns. Quality control based on the analysis of butyric acid in adjuncts, wort, and beer and the microbiological detection of anaerobic spore-forming bacteria can prevent butyric acid off-flavors in beer.

See also OFF-FLAVORS.

Graham G. Stewart

BYOB is an acronym that has several possible sources, and even several possible alternative symbolized words. But all have the same ultimate meaning: You are invited to an event, but if you want anything to drink you'll have to bring your own (BYO).

Bring Your Own Bottle, Bring Your Own Booze, Bring Your Own Beverage, Bring Your Own Beer . . . the detail is irrelevant. The initials mean the same thing on party invitations and in unlicensed restaurants across the English-speaking world.

The term can be traced back to the 1950s, though it is uncertain on which side of the Atlantic it was first coined. The fact that it has so many different variations strongly suggests that it emerged spontaneously in different locations.

"BYOB" became popular in England in the 1970s, in the aftermath of the rise of supermarkets that sold drinks more cheaply than pubs, prompting a long-term shift to home-based drinking away from the traditional pub. At the same time Britons also began to eat out in restaurants much more. Indian restaurants in particular would commonly cater to a post-pub crowd, but being unlicensed they would invite people to bring a few cans or bottles from the off-license or supermarket, sometimes in return for a small corkage fee.

Some etymologists believe the term has deeper roots. It has been suggested that in the early 19th century BYOB was society slang for "Bring Your Own Basket" at picnics. Even here, "basket" could well have been a polite euphemism for "booze," but there is no evidence to suggest that this was the main implication.

In the United States, "BYOB" are four letters that warm the hearts of beer lovers everywhere. While it would be considered churlish to suggest that you "BYOB" to a party, BYOB is considered by many to mean "have yourself a royal banquet" when it's allowed at a restaurant. The American restaurant-goer tends to blanche at lack of choice rather than undue expense. Until recently very few restaurants had decent beer lists, and other than bringing the doggie bag home, bringing your own bottle might be the only way to experience a restaurant's food with an interesting beer. While the advent of well-rounded restaurant beer lists is wonderful for beer enthusiasts and neophytes alike, bringing your own remains a special thrill. In many cities, the invitation is usually temporary (and often technically illegal, depending on local laws). Once the establishment has its own license, the cheery notes telling you to indulge yourself tend to disappear pretty fast. In New York City, a place that has long been home to a large south Asian population, "Indian restaurant rows" were among the first incubators for shops carrying a then-bewildering variety of beer. Even in the early 1980s, well before American craft beer became prevalent, shops at either end of one block of New York City's East Village displayed signs declaring "More than 100 varieties of beer!" What most patrons didn't know was that most of the restaurants on the block in question were run by Pakistani Muslims, and this is why the restaurants offered no alcoholic beverages. The then-rare availability of India pale ale right alongside tasty "Indian" food turns out to have been a happy coincidence.

Pete Brown

cakes and ale. Today, the expression "cakes and ale" is synonymous with "the good life" and is a commonly used metaphor for earthly pleasures. The word "cake" also has connotations of something good. The origin is commonly attributable to Sir Toby Belch in Shakespeare's *Twelfth Night*, who asks Malvolio:

> Out o' tune, sir: ye lie. Art any more than a steward?
> Dost though think, because *thou* art virtuous, there shall be no more cakes and ale?

Evidence, however, suggests that the idea of "cakes and ale" is much older, as it appears several times in a version of the ancient *Book of the Dead*, a funerary text containing instructions and advice to help the deceased pass into the afterlife. The following extract comes from the version known as *The Papyrus of Ani*, written c. 1240 BCE and translated by E.A. Wallis Budge in 1913:

> . . . says the deceased to the god Thoth: 'But let the state of the spirits be given unto me instead of water, and air, and the satisfying of the longings of love, and let quietness of heart be given unto me instead of cakes and ale.'

Cakes and Ale has been the title of three books of note, written, chronologically, by Douglas W. Jerrold (1842), Edward Spencer (1897), and W. Somerset Maugham (1930).

Bickerdyke, John (pseudonym of Charles Henry Cook). *The curiosities of ale and beer*. London: Leadenhall Press, 1886. Reprint, Cleveland, OH: Beer Books, 2008.

Budge, E. A. Wallis. *The papyrus of Ani–The Egyptian Book of the Dead*. New York: Dover Publications Inc, 1985.

Ian Hornsey

Calagione, Sam

See DOGFISH HEAD CRAFT BREWERY.

calandria, a tubular heat exchanger that heats wort quickly and efficiently, enabling it to be boiled vigorously in the kettle.

Wort requires a long vigorous boil, normally of 60–120 minutes. Wort boiling releases bitterness from hops, reduces precursors for off-flavors such as dimethyl sulfide, coagulates proteins, and renders the wort sterile. It is an expensive process because the energy costs increase with each minute of boiling.

The calandria can be placed vertically inside a kettle or it can be external to the kettle and linked by piping and a pump. In an internal calandria, convection forces the wort up through the vertical bundle of tubes, where it is superheated by steam. When the calandria is external, the wort is pumped out of the kettle, through the calandria, and then back into the kettle again. Most kettle designs include a dish-shape wort spreader device that suppresses overfoaming, mixes the wort, and drives off unwanted volatiles. A calandria provides a larger area for heating the wort than does a direct fired kettle or those fitted with steam jackets.

The higher temperatures achieved using a calandria, typically up to 104.4°C (220°F) can reduce boil times up to 30% while also increasing hop utilization in brewing systems using hop pellets.

Hornsey, Ian S. *Brewing*. London: Royal Society of Chemistry, 1999.

Kunze, Wolfgang. *Technology, brewing & malting.* Berlin: VLB Berlin, 1996.

Tim Hampson

calcium carbonate ($CaCO_3$) is a precipitate of bicarbonate. Bicarbonate is the critical component in the measurement of temporary water hardness (carbonate hardness). This part of water hardness is defined via the titration of all carbonates, bicarbonates, and hydroxides and is expressed in equivalent amounts of calcium carbonate. This measurement can sometimes be referred to as the alkalinity of water. A high carbonate level in brewing water is generally considered to be negative as it can impart a harsh bitterness in beer, especially when combined with assertive hopping rates. Therefore, removal or reduction is typically desired and can be accomplished through heating or by the addition of acid to water. Via these treatments bicarbonate can be converted to calcium carbonate, a substance that is non-soluble and will precipitate out, reducing overall carbonate levels. However, though calcium carbonate is often considered undesirable, when making dark beers the presence of carbonates can offset the acidity of dark malts. In these situations a higher carbonate level is considered to be a positive attribute of brewing water. Calcium carbonate is formed by the solvent action of carbon dioxide present in rain or surface water, which then reacts with minerals present in the earth such as calcite or dolomite. Munich, Dublin, and London are examples of classic water sources that exhibit high calcium carbonate levels. Porters and stout are both beer styles that tend to benefit from higher calcium carbonate levels in brewing water.

Bernstein, Leo, and Willox, I. C. "Water." In Harold M. Broderick, ed. *The practical brewer,* 13. Madison, WI: Master Brewers Association of the Americas, 1977.

Fix, George. "Compounds Relevant to Brewing." In Marjorie Raizman, ed. *Principles of brewing science,* 13–21. Denver, CO: Brewers Publications, Association of Brewers, 1989.

John Haggerty

calcium chloride is one of the primary components in the measurement of permanent water hardness (also known as non-carbonate hardness). Permanent water hardness is defined by the sum of all calcium and magnesium ions associated with anions such as chloride or sulfate. This part of water hardness is referred to as "permanent" due to the fact that it will not precipitate under the influence of heat. Therefore, calcium chloride is also one of the primary salts used for the boosting of calcium levels in beer.

Proper calcium levels in beer can lower pH, preserve mash enzymes, increase extract yield, improve yeast growth and flocculation, accelerate oxalate removal, and reduce color. The chloride ion is believed to promote a palate fullness, sweetness, or mellowness within the flavor profile of beer. Most water sources contain some calcium chloride; however, rarely do you find it without other components such as carbonate or sulfate present in significant amounts. Dortmund, Germany, is an example of a water source that has a high calcium chloride content and demonstrates those properties attributable to calcium chloride.

Bernstein, Leo, and Willox, I. C. "Water." In *The practical brewer,* ed. Harold M. Broderick, 13–20. Madison, WI: Master Brewers Association of the Americas, 1977.

Kerwin, Larry. "Water." In *MBAA practical handbook for the specialty brewer, volume 1: Raw materials and brewhouse operations,* ed. Karl Ockert, 7–12. Madison, WI: Master Brewers Association of the Americas, 2006.

Kunze, Wolfgang. "Raw materials." In *Technology brewing and malting,* 2nd ed., 69–73. Berlin: VLB Berlin, 1999.

John Haggerty

calcium oxalate (CaC_2O_4) is a crystalline deposit formed by calcium reacting with oxalic acid. Oxalic acid is released from malt during mashing. Calcium oxalate is commonly referred to as "beer stone" and is typically seen as a yellowish-brown deposit in tanks, kegs, and bottles. Calcium oxalate is known to harbor microorganisms if not properly removed; removal is achieved via the use of an acid during the cleaning cycle. The proper rate of reaction, or formation, of calcium oxalate is important in regard to its precipitation from beer. By insuring there is enough calcium in upstream processing then one can insure calcium oxalate forms and precipitates in tanks and not in kegs and bottles where it can create nucleation sites. In this case, nucleation sites are irregularities on a container surface formed by calcium oxalate precipitation that cause carbon dioxide molecules to congregate creating a density of gas that is more than the liquid solution can hold. The formation of such nucleation sites leads to issues such as the uncontrollable release of carbon dioxide from beer (gushing). Additionally, high levels of calcium oxalate (greater than 20 ppm) in the final beer can lead to haze issues. Precipitation of calcium oxalate is imperative in the production of shelf stable beer and can be insured by proper calcium levels in the brewing process. Calcium levels can be improved through the addition of salts such as calcium chloride and/or calcium sulfate to brewing water.

Bamforth, Charles W. "Gushing." In *Scientific principles of brewing and malting,* 167–168. St. Paul, MN: American Society of Brewing Chemists, 2006.

Bernstein, Leo, and I. C. Willox. "Water." In *The practical brewer,* ed. Harold M. Broderick, 18–20. St. Paul, MN: Master Brewers Association of the Americas, 1977.

Compton, John. "Beer quality and taste methodology." In *The practical brewer,* ed. Harold M. Broderick, 293. St. Paul, MN: Master Brewers Association of the Americas, 1977.

John Haggerty

calcium sulfate is a critical component in the measurement of permanent water hardness (also known as non-carbonate hardness). This part of water hardness is defined by the sum of all calcium and magnesium ions that are associated with anions such as chloride or sulfate. It is referred to as permanent hardness because of the fact that it will not precipitate under the influence of heat. Therefore, calcium sulfate is also one of the primary salts used for the improvement of calcium levels in beer. Proper calcium levels in beer can provide the following influences that are generally considered to be positive: they lower the pH, preserve mash enzymes, increase extract yield, improve yeast growth and flocculation, accelerate oxalate removal, and reduce color.

The sulfate ion in this compound is generally thought to promote a drier, more bitter beer. Burton-on-Trent, England is the classic source of water with a high calcium sulfate content, caused by the region's large gypsum deposits. The emulation of this classic water has led to the term "Burtonization," meaning to improve one's brewing water via the addition of calcium sulfate. This water treatment is common for the production of pale ales and India pale ales.

Bernstein, Leo, and Willox, I. C. "Water." In *The practical brewer,* ed. Harold M. Broderick, 13–20. Madison, WI: Master Brewers Association of the Americas, 1977.

Kerwin, Larry. "Water." In *MBAA practical handbook for the specialty brewer, volume 1: Raw materials and brewhouse operations,* ed. Karl Ockert, 7–12. Madison, WI: Master Brewers Association of the Americas, 2006.

Kunze, Wolfgang. "Raw materials." In *Technology brewing and malting,* 2nd ed., 69–73. Berlin: VLB Berlin, 1999.

John Haggerty

Caledonian Brewery was one of more than 40 breweries in Edinburgh, Scotland, when it opened in 1869. Known then as Lorimer and Clark's Caledonian Brewer, like other breweries in the city it was able to draw its famed brewing water from a series of underground wells known as the Charmed Circle. Today, "The Caley" is the only one of these breweries to have survived.

A Victorian tower brewery, Caledonian is the last brewery in Britain to have direct-fired open coppers (kettles), which have a hand-beaten inner dome that concentrates the heat and develops a constant churn and roll of the boiling wort. Connoisseurs say that the direct heat and vigorous boil impart distinctive toffee-like malt flavors to the beers. The flames are now from gas jets, but coal was used until the late 1980s.

The brewery survived two disastrous fires in 1994 and 1998 and was rebuilt. In 1919 it was sold to the English brewer Vaux of Sunderland. In 1987 Head Brewer Russell Sharp led a management buy-out with former Lorimer & Clark Managing Director Dan Kane. When Vaux ceased brewing operations altogether in 1999, Caledonian bought back the rights to the Lorimer & Clark name.

The brewery site and part of the equity was bought by Scottish & Newcastle in 2004, after S&N said it was going to close its nearby Fountain Brewery and was looking for somewhere to brew its McEwan brands.

In 2002 the company's Deuchars IPA won the Campaign for Real Ale's Champion Beer of Britain award. In 2006 Caledonian bought the Harviestoun brewery on the retirement of its founder Ken Brooker.

In 2008 the company fell into the ownership of Heineken as part of the joint takeover of S&N's worldwide operation by the Dutch brewer and Carlsberg; Harviestoun sprung loose and became independent once again. Deuchar's IPA, a pleasant beer, is not actually an IPA at all, but Caledonian 80/- (80 – Shilling) is considered a fine example of Scottish ale.

See also EDINBURGH and SCOTTISH & NEWCASTLE BREWERY.

Tim Hampson

California. The state of California's influence on American beer culture cannot be underestimated. It may have begun brewing a lot later than other states but, given its influence on the contemporary craft brewing scene, it has more than made up for lost time and currently boasts some of the nation's most innovative breweries and beers.

California began brewing nearly 250 years after America's first brewery was formed in Manhattan in 1612. It wasn't until 1849, a year before California was officially an American state, that Californians embarked on their first ale-making endeavors with the Adam Schuppert Brewery opening its doors on the corner of Stockton and Jackson streets in San Francisco.

1849 was a very good time to open a brewery. It was the height of the Gold Rush and more than 300,000 entrepreneurial "49ers" had arrived in California in search of shiny flecks of fortune. San Francisco was rapidly growing from a small settlement into a busy boom town and panning for gold was seriously thirsty work.

Beer was the panner's pick-me-up and by 1852, San Francisco boasted more than 350 bars and pubs serving a population of little over 36,000. By 1860 that number had increased to more than 800 saloons supplied by more than two dozen breweries while San Diego, Sacramento, and Los Angeles, bolstered by the completion of a railroad in the 1870s, also became home to blossoming beer scenes.

The first Sacramento brewery was set up in 1859 by Hilbert & Borchers while San Jose's first brewery was the Eagle Brewery. Californian breweries that opened in the 1850s included the Bavarian Brewery, the Albany Brewery, the American Railroad Brewery, the Union Brewing Company, John Weiland Brewery and, of course, the Pacific Brewing Company which is now known as the Anchor Brewery Company. Between 1890 and Prohibition, the Buffalo Brewing Company in Sacramento was the largest brewery west of the Mississippi.

Californian breweries could call upon a wealth of local brewing ingredients. Hops were first introduced into California in 1854 and, until Prohibition, Sonoma County was a major hops supplier to both California and beyond. By the late 1880s, the recipes for beers brewed as far away as Britain make mention of "California hops." In and around Sacramento, Emil Clemens Horst owned the largest hop acreage in the world and in 1909 was responsible for inventing the hop separator, a mechanical instrument that eased the process of hop-picking.

The vast majority of Californian breweries were set up by German speaking immigrants and, in the late 19th century, they wholeheartedly embraced the new lager beer type which, having been first brewed in the European town of Pilsen in 1842, was fast capturing the imagination of American beer drinkers. In 1875, the Boca Brewery near Truckee produced California's first lager.

However, lager was a beer type brewed with bottom fermenting yeast which performed best at low temperatures. Mechanical refrigeration, first unveiled in the Spaten brewery in Munich during the 1870s, had yet to reach America's Golden State and California brewers, unlike their Bavarian and Bohemian brethren, couldn't store their beer in chilly cellars cut deep into Bavarian mountains.

Even though the temperate Californian climate was hardly conducive to brewing lager, the Germanic brewing community remained loyal to lager yeast and brewed a beer known as "steam beer," also referred to as "California Common." See STEAM BEER.

Synonymous with central California and San Francisco in particular, "California Common" straddled the dividing line between lager and ale. It was brewed using bottom fermenting yeast in wide shallow vessels yet, due to the California climate and the dearth of refrigeration, it fermented at a temperature more closely associated with ale making. It was a hybrid brew borne out of necessity and the "terroir" of its surroundings.

Brewed using local hops and barley, "steam beer" didn't revel in the kind of reverence it receives today and, instead, was a rather rudimentary blue collar

Brochure for the Albion Ale and Porter Brewery in San Francisco, California, which operated from 1875 to 1919. The New Albion Brewery, which in 1976 became the first brewery to open in California following Prohibition and the first American microbrewery, was named in tribute to the Albion Ale and Porter Brewery. PIKE MICROBREWERY MUSEUM, SEATTLE, WA

beer, cheaper than other brews on the bar and associated with the hard-drinking everyday worker.

Following the boom years and the emergence of "steam beer," California's beer scene was to change considerably. First there was consolidation; the emergence of mechanical refrigeration and pasteurization, advances in bottling, and the considerable improvement of the railroads allowed a handful of well-established, mostly German-inflected brewing companies to procure smaller concerns and embark on national distribution.

Between 1873 and 1910, the number of American breweries shrunk from more than 4,000 to approximately 1,500. Yet, in the same period, production grew by 600% to exceed 50 million barrels and, by the beginning of the 20th century, the number of saloons had doubled from 150,000 to 300,000 and drinking emporiums were mushrooming all over California.

However, the dreamy quixotic visions of these saloons were far removed from reality. Principally frequented, and often run, by the kind of folk you'd rather not introduce to your parents, saloons became synonymous with ne'er-do-wells and raucous behavior. They soon bred contempt among a growing temperance movement and beer began being blamed for a burgeoning society's ills. Prohibition, spearheaded by the Volstead Act, was on the horizon.

Some Californian breweries tried to survive the 13-year "noble" experiment by peddling "near beer," chancing their arm with root beer and malt extracts, non-alcoholic drinks, and tonics while some continued to brew beer under the protection of mobsters. However, Prohibition drove the vast majority of breweries out of business and very few survived the double blow of war and the Volstead Act.

Post-Prohibition, it was with a whimper rather than bang that beer returned. Initial attempts to resurrect small breweries were hampered by the Depression, legislative red tape that prevented breweries from owning saloons, and the shift toward drinking at home. It was only the big breweries that were thriving. They enjoyed post-war double-digit growth and the battle for brewing dominance switched to the west coast or, more precisely, the booming state of California.

By 1967 the top four breweries commanded a third of all beer sales yet while the big breweries were busy merging, acquiring, and shrinking into a ball of price-driven homogeny, the seeds of a brewing backlash were being quietly sown in California.

One of the most significant developments, one that was to later oil the wheels of American craft brewing, was the creation in 1958 of a brewing program and pilot brewery at the University of California in Davis. See UNIVERSITY of CALIFORNIA, DAVIS.

Then in 1965, a 27-year-old with no knowledge nor experience of brewing and a lackadaisical interest in beer purchased a ruined, filthy fiasco of a brewery in downtown San Francisco renowned for brewing sour, downright awful beer. The likes of Pabst, Schlitz, and Anheuser-Busch hardly batted an eye, but Frederick "Fritz" Maytag III, new owner of the Anchor Steam Brewery and heir to the eminent Maytag washing-machine empire, fired the first shot across the bows of the big breweries.

Maytag began brewing steam beer again. It was small-batch, brewed with the finest, freshest ingredients. It snubbed hype in favor of history (dating back to 1896) and valued authenticity ahead of advertising. Unwilling and unable to compete on price or the national distribution of the goliaths, it played on its reputation as a loyal, local, west coast hero.

Maytag's timing, and indeed location, was immaculate. In the early 1970s, a revolution was starting against the shrink-wrapped, frozen monotony of modern American food and drink and California was leading the charge. It, more than any other state, proudly flew the flag of epicurean enlightenment and stormed the gates of mass-produced mediocrity.

Boutique wineries were cropping up on the Pacific Coast and in the Napa Valley region yet beer wasn't that far behind. In 1976, in the hippy Northern California backwater of Sonoma, the first microbrewery since Prohibition was set up by Jack McAuliffe, a Navy engineer who'd fallen in love with British ales while stationed in Scotland in the 1960s. The New Albion Brewery may not have lasted long (closing in 1983) but, throughout the craft beer community, McAuliffe is rightly revered for his visionary derring-do. See NEW ALBION BREWING COMPANY.

McAuliffe and Maytag succeeded in igniting the fire under the rocking chair of mainstream American beer but it was the legalisation of homebrewing in 1978 that really fanned the flames and California quickly emerged as the epicentre of a small yet passionate craft brewing scene.

In 1983, Don Barkley, formerly of New Albion, opened California's first brewpub in Hopland and 2 years earlier, Ken Grossman had cobbled together a brewery using dairy equipment, called it the Sierra Nevada Brewing Company and brewed Sierra Nevada Pale Ale. Distinctively hoppy in character, it was a marked departure from the big branded beers and became the golden giant on whose shoulders other West Coast beers now stand.

By 1994, California laid claim to 84 microbreweries and brewpubs (one more than there'd been in all of the United States a decade before) and that number has continued to grow. Nearly two decades on and, from San Diego in the south to Eureka in the north, California remains the jewel in the American craft brewing crown.

When it comes to cutting-edge beer, few cities can rival San Diego. Yet, 20 years ago, things were very different. While San Francisco, Seattle, and Portland were brewing up a craft beer storm in the eighties and early nineties, San Diego remained a wilderness for flavorful beer. Locals were forced to rely on brews produced "up state" rather than their own. After years of living in the brewing shadow of its west coast peers, San Diego's beer scene came into its own in the mid-1990s.

Not content with a dozen maverick craft breweries, a mesmerizing array of switched-on tap-houses and a smattering of brewpubs, San Diego has even got its very own beer style. A strong, hoppy pale ale dubbed "Double IPA" is perhaps the signature beer of San Diego. At strengths often above 10% and with bitterness to burn, it is not a beer style for the meek. Heady "hop monster" beers run amok in San Diego, outselling other styles in leading beer bars such as O'Brien's, Liar's Club, and Hamilton's Tavern.

For all the adulation received elsewhere, boutique beer has never met with a particularly warm welcome in Los Angeles. As to why, no one really knows. Some blame the climate; perhaps L.A.'s hot and sweaty weather stifles pub culture and big beers wilt whenever mercury rises. Yet, were this really the case, neighboring San Diego wouldn't be such a hotbed of craft brewing creativity.

Others contend that Los Angeles is simply too tourist-driven and transitory. No brewery has managed to unite what is essentially a scatter of individual neighborhoods with no discernible center.

Having somehow remained oblivious to the west coast's love affair with craft beer for quite some time, Angelinos are finally getting the taste for craft beer; you just have to look a little harder in Los Angeles than you do in other cities.

And then, of course, there's San Francisco. San Francisco is the center of the California brewing scene. The city played an integral role in the birth of the American craft beer movement and it remains instrumental in today's larger artisan food and beverage renaissance. As for the big brewers, California offers the largest population of any state, and Anheuser-Busch InBev operates breweries in Los Angeles and Fairfield, and MillerCoors' beers flow from Irwindale. Regardless of the type of beer, California is well supplied. As of 2010, there were more than 250 breweries in California, more than any other state in the United States.

Ben McFarland

California common, a somewhat fusty and generic designation for the style more properly known as steam beer. California common has been settled upon by various beer judging and classification entities in compliance with the wishes of Anchor Brewing Company of San Francisco, which retains legal right to any use of the word steam in connection with beer made in America. The steam beer style harkens back to the limitations of lager brewing on America's western frontier, where refrigeration was usually unavailable and colder-favoring yeasts were allowed to ferment at warmer temperatures. The result was a beer of some crispness and sulfur, yet displaying the fruitier esters of a less restrained fermentation. The beer is generally dark amber to brown in color, of medium alcoholic strength. German hop varieties are typically used.

California common is the recognized designation for the sometimes disputed style by the Beer Judge Certification Program, which oversees the judging of homebrewing competitions in the United States. It is also used by the Brewers Association in its judging supervision of both the Great American Beer Festival and the World Beer Cup competitions for professional brewers.

Although some American brewers acknowledge Anchor's right to the term "steam," there are those whose California Commons offer tongue-in-cheek reference to the assertion of trademark, such as Victory Brewing of Downingtown, Pennsylvania's, "dampf" beer (dampf is German for steam). Perhaps more artful is Sly Fox Brewing, of Phoenixville and Royersford, Pennsylvania, whose Gold Rush lager gives the idea without risking offense or action.

See also ANCHOR BREWING COMPANY, JUDGING BEER, and STEAM BEER.

Jackson, Michael. *The New World guide to beer.* Philadelphia: Running Press, 1988.
Mosher, Randy. *Radical brewing: Recipes, tales & and world-altering meditations in a glass.* Boulder, CO: Brewers Publications, 2004.

Dick Cantwell

calories are a measurement pertaining to the energy value of food. Beer is a food item and contains components providing energy value or calories to the consumer. The methods used to calculate energy value vary depending upon sources of caloric information but these are generally close enough for us to adopt the values specified by the American Society of Brewing Chemists. Specifically, beer contains protein (which provides 4 calories of energy/g), sugars and more complex carbohydrates (with 4.0 calories energy/g), and ethanol (7 calories energy/g). Organic acids can provide energy but are not considered significant in beer for caloric intake, and fats (lipids) are not contained in measurable or detectable amounts in beer so can also be ignored.

To determine the calories in beer, the alcohol by weight and the real extract (the extract remaining in beer after fermentation and containing carbohydrate, protein, and the mineral content of the beer) must be known. The mineral content can be obtained by drying down a known amount of beer and then subjecting it to high heat to burn off the organic constituents. The resulting ash is the mineral content of the beer.

In the United States the calories expressed in 100 g of beer is then determined by cal in 100 g of beer = 6.9 × alcohol % by weight + 4(RE – ash), with RE meaning the real extract (Plato) and ash expressed as percentage by weight. The value 4 represents the 4 calories energy value from protein and carbohydrate, as discussed above. If the value obtained from this calculation is multiplied by the specific gravity of the beer, then the calories per 100 ml of beer is obtained. Finally multiplying this number by 3.55 provides the caloric content of a 12 fl oz (standard US) serving size.

Also, if the value from the above equation is needed in SI units, as kJ/100 ml of beer, as now expressed in Europe, then the conversion 1 calorie = 4.184 kJ can be applied. (One calorie US = 1kcal in Europe.)

Depending upon the composition of the beer, the calorie content may vary quite widely from 15 calories/100 ml for a beer with a low alcohol content to more than 110 calories/100 ml for high-alcohol and high-residual-extract beers (one containing large amounts of nonfermentable carbohydrate) such as barley wines. Aside from the matters of technical information for the brewer and basic nutritional information for the consumer, most brewers outside large mass-market breweries consider the calorie content of their beers irrelevant. Just as calorie information is not listed on wine bottles, most craft brewers do not list it on their labels. As craft brewers move beer away from decades of commoditization, talk of calories may once again be left to brewery laboratories.

Gary Spedding

Campaign for Real Ale (CAMRA) is a UK-based consumer organization which campaigns for the promotion of cask-conditioned "real ale" and the traditional British pub. See REAL ALE. CAMRA was founded in 1971 at the most westerly point in Europe—Kruge's Bar in Dunquin, Co. Kerry, Ireland—by four men from the northwest of England in response to the perceived poor quality and blandness of British beer at that time. Cask-conditioned beer was then on the wane, phased out by British brewers who deemed it archaic, expensive, and difficult to maintain and serve. Filtered, force-carbonated keg beers were offered in its place, but CAMRA rejected these and struck back with organized boycotts. Originally called the Campaign for the Revitalisation of Ale, it adopted the name Campaign for Real Ale in 1973. Its stated aims include the protection and improvement of (beer) consumer rights; the promotion of quality, choice, and value for money; supporting the pub as a focus of community life; and campaigning for the greater appreciation of traditional beers, ciders, and perries. Traditional ciders and perries have been offered a place under the tent in recent years.

Membership of CAMRA is open to all individuals, although commercial entities are not eligible for membership, which is well over 100,000. CAMRA members are an eclectic group, with around 1,000 members residing outside the UK (mainly in the United States) and a strong constituency comprised of medical practitioners and clergymen as well as peers of the realm and Members of the UK Parliament. Members have been seen traditionally as "middle-aged men with beards and sandals" but the organization has been making great strides to broaden its appeal, particularly to a younger profile and, more particularly, to women.

The organization is governed by a voluntary, unpaid national executive, elected by the membership. It has over 200 local branches to which members usually affiliate. The branches organize local beer festivals, publish newsletters and run websites in addition to a range of social events (usually involving visits to pubs and breweries) as well as campaigning on behalf of local pubs and breweries threatened with closure.

Beer festivals are an important part of the CAMRA events calendar and showcase regional beers, ciders, and perries. The festivals are organized by the local branches who supply voluntary, unpaid members to operate them. Beer supplied to these festivals must meet strict criteria laid down by CAMRA. Beer that is dispensed using carbon dioxide or a carbon dioxide/nitrogen mix is disqualified from entry, much to the disquiet of those brewers producing unpasteurized beer which is not dispensed either directly from the container or through the agency of a hand-pull tap. Each festival usually operates an awards system whereby the beers at the festival are assessed by a panel of CAMRA members. Awards are made in a number of classes, usually corresponding to ABV range or style. These awards are much coveted by local brewers and are usually exploited commercially by promotional activities in the local market. Success at the local branch festival level also results in the winning beers progressing to regional judging competitions, with further progression ultimately to the national awards at the Great British Beer Festival held in August each year at a London location. See GREAT BRITISH BEER FESTIVAL. Here, 10 different classes of beer (bitter, best bitter, premium bitter, special bitter, strong bitter/ale, golden ale, mild, speciality beer, new brewery, and bottle-conditioned beer) from the regional award winners are tasted by an expert panel. Awards are made in each class with the accolade "Champion Beer of Britain" given to the outstanding beer. This award is greatly cherished by the brewer of the winning beer, although it can be an embarrassment in that many smaller breweries are unable to meet the demand that the attendant publicity generates.

CAMRA publications range from the monthly newspaper *What's Brewing* and the periodic *Beer* magazine through to the highly regarded annual *Good Beer Guide*. A range of specially commissioned books on beer, pubs, and brewing are also published by CAMRA, including a series of "Guide" books like the *Good Bottled Beer Guide* and the *Good Beer Guide Belgium*. *What's Brewing* reports on current issues affecting beer, cider, and pubs in the UK, with a strong slant on those particular issues which are subject to CAMRA's campaigning zeal. These campaigns vary from support for breweries and pubs threatened with closure through to the prickly subjects of beer supply to pubs, licensing laws, beer duty (tax), and many more. As the largest single consumer group representing beer and pubs, CAMRA opinion carries considerable weight both within the brewing and pub businesses in the UK but also at the government level, where the voice of CAMRA is heard and respected.

The promotion of great beer in good pubs is at the heart of the annual *Good Beer Guide*, a compilation of the top 4,500 pubs in the UK together with a comprehensive listing of all breweries, large and small, and their main beer brands. The list of approved pubs is compiled by CAMRA members whose primary criterion for assessment is cask-conditioned beer quality, using the assumption "that if a landlord keeps his beer well and pours perfect pints then everything else in his pub—welcome, food, accommodation, and family facilities—are likely to be of an equally high standard." Good pubs are listed in the *Guide* according to region and location, with information on pub opening hours, food availability, accommodation, and the range of beers available. Pubs included in the *Guide* will proudly display a "Good Pub Guide" notice at the entrance to the pub, a symbol of quality. The *Guide* is an essential companion to anyone traveling in the UK who wishes to enjoy the delights of traditional British beer.

The overall effect of CAMRA on the quality of British beer is widely lauded, but the organization is not without its detractors. Some argue that CAMRA may have saved "real ale," but has stunted the further development of British beer by casting aspersion upon quality beers and excellent pubs that lie outside its tight designations. A good example of such controversy centers around a device called a "cask breather," which would allow beer drawn from casks to be replaced with a non-pressurized layer of flavor-neutral carbon dioxide as opposed to air. While proponents laud the device and say that it would allow more cask-conditioned beer to be sold in modern pubs at better quality, CAMRA derides the cask breather as an unnecessary and unwanted intrusion into the traditional cellar. Pubs using the device must face de-listing from *The Good Beer Guide*, a fate which usually has deleterious effects on their trade. This ongoing dispute highlights CAMRA's unique place in British beer culture; it is doubtful that any other consumer-based organization can claim such influence over the beer brewed and served in their home country.

Campaign for Real Ale. http://www.camra.org.uk/ (accessed March 17, 2011).
Cornell, Martyn. *Beer: The story of the pint*. Headline Book Publishing, 2003.

George Philliskirk

Unibroue's Maudite ("Damned") ale label is a depiction of a Quebec tall tale from the days of Nouvelle France, when canoe-paddling voyageurs (fur traders) spent their winters in the northern forests. When one team of voyageurs tried to return home to Montreal for the holidays, with the rivers frozen, the devil appeared and offered to fly their canoe home through the air, provided they not invoke the name of God. But one scared voyageur could not hold his tongue and yelled "oh my God," at which point the canoe crashed, and they were never heard from again. COURTESY OF UNIBROUE

Canada is a nation of beer drinkers. While wine sales have been growing for the past few decades, beer continues to account for over half of all alcohol consumed in the country (51.1% of legal-aged alcohol consumption in 2008, versus 20.2% for wine, according to the Brewers Association of Canada). Canadians drink almost 70 liters of beer per capita per year; that figure includes every man, woman, and child in the country. Including only people of legal drinking age, the average Canadian consumes just under 90 liters of beer each year. In some provinces and territories, the annual per capita consumption of beer is as high as 160 liters.

The Canadian beer market is dominated by a pair of companies owned by or merged with larger international conglomerates. Labatt Brewing Company Ltd., owned by Anheuser-Busch-InBev, controls 42.9% of the Canadian beer market, by volume. See LABATT BREWING COMPANY LTD. Molson Coors Brewing Co. controls 41.9%. See MOLSON COORS BREWING COMPANY. Sleeman Breweries Ltd., which began in 1988 as a small craft brewery and now has roughly 5% of the Canadian market, is owned by Japanese brewing giant Sapporo. Molson Coors is the creation of the 2005 merger between Montreal-based Molson Inc. and Colorado giant Coors Brewing Company. The largest brewing company still exclusively Canadian-owned is privately held Saint John, New Brunswick-based Moosehead, which has somewhere between 2% and 3% of the national market.

Just as Canadian viewers flock to American TV, music and movies, so too do Canadian beer drinkers flock to American beer brands, which are heavily advertised in Canadian media, and US networks and publications available in Canada. In 2008 the top two selling beers in Canada were Budweiser and Coors Light, with approximately 13% and 12% of the market, respectively. Both are brewed in Canada (Budweiser by Labatt and Coors Light by Molson-Coors), an arrangement that predates their breweries' current ownership structure. The sales of these

American brands, albeit brewed in Canada, are included in Labatt and Molson's market share figures. So too are beers that they distribute, but don't brew, in Canada, such as Heineken and Corona (Molson-Coors) and Stella Artois (Labatt). Molson Canadian and Labatt Blue, which were for over two decades the top-selling two brands in the country, now rank third and fourth, respectively. Budweiser has been the country's top-selling brand since knocking former No. 1 Molson Canadian off its perch in 2004. The vast majority of the country's best-selling brands are pale lagers designed to appeal to a mass market.

Craft Breweries

Since the mid-1980s, a growing number of craft breweries have taken a small but growing share of the Canadian beer market, buoyed by consumer demand for more flavorful beers than what the major brewers were offering. In 2008 they controlled an estimated 4% of the national market, but had a significantly larger chunk in some provinces. In Quebec, craft breweries have a 5% share of the provincial market, according to estimates from several industry sources.

The first modern Canadian craft brewery was tiny, now defunct Horseshoe Bay Brewing, established in 1982 in Vancouver. It was followed soon after by Vancouver's Granville Island Brewing (1984), Brick Brewing and Wellington Brewery in Guelph, Ontario (1984 and 1985, respectively), and Montreal's McAuslan Brewing Company (1989). Also of note during the 1980s was the opening of several brewpubs, including a number in the British Columbia capital, Victoria (most notably Spinnaker's and Swan's), and one in Halifax, Nova Scotia. Much of the beer produced by the early microbreweries was English-style ale. Since then, microbreweries across the country, most notably in Quebec, have gone on to produce a wide variety of beer styles, ranging from "double IPAs" to Belgian ales and barley wines. See DOUBLE IPA.

In British Columbia, notable microbreweries include Phillips and Granville Island. Alberta-based Big Rock is one of the bigger craft breweries in the country. In Ontario, there are roughly 35 craft breweries, many concentrated close to Toronto, with most specializing in English and German styles. On the east coast of Canada, Propeller Brewing Company and Garrison Brewing Company of Nova Scotia, and Pumphouse Brewery of Moncton, New Brunswick, fly the craft flag. The country's northernmost craft brewery is the Yukon Brewing Company, based in Whitehorse.

The major breweries have dealt with the small but growing movement in a few different ways, for instance, by setting up small subsidiary breweries with a different selection than standard macro-brewed product, distributing more imported beer, and buying existing craft breweries. Molson has broadened its "pub-style" Rickards line. In 2005 Molson bought Creemore Springs Brewery Ltd., a microbrewery established in 1987 in Creemore, Ontario. Beer aficionados worried at the time that the big brewery would tamper with Creemore's highly praised lager, broadly in the pilsner style, but Molson seems to have lived up to its word to leave production of the beer alone. In spring 2010 Molson completed its purchase of Vancouver's Granville Island Brewing.

History

Beer was probably introduced to Canada by French settlers in what is now Quebec in the 17th century. While arguments have been put forth for various candidates to be the first person to have brewed in Quebec (then known as Nouvelle-France), in all likelihood the correct name is lost to history, as in those days brewing was largely a home affair. Still, three of the usual candidates for the first non-home brewer are Frère Ambroise, Louis Prud'homme, and Jean Talon. Frère Ambroise, a monk, was the brewer at the first "institutional" (i.e., non-home) brewery in Nouvelle-France, just outside current-day Quebec City. It was established in 1646 for the refreshment of Jesuit priests. In 1650 Prud'homme was granted a royal decree to run a brewery in Montreal. In 1670 Talon, the Intendant (the region's chief civil administrator), created a brewery in Quebec City. *La Brasserie du Roy* produced 4,000 barrels (880,000 liters) per year before it closed shortly after Talon returned to France in 1672. One person not usually given credit for being the first known brewer in Quebec is Marie Rollet. Rollet was the wife of a Parisian pharmacist named Louis Hébert, who settled in Quebec in 1617. As mentioned in Mario d'Eer's *Le Guide de la Bonne Bière du Quebec*, Rollet acted as a communal brewer for the then-tiny colony, which numbered roughly 60 or so settlers.

After the French were defeated by the English in 1759, brewing in Quebec and the growing colony of Upper Canada (today Ontario) again became a largely home-based affair for another few decades. In 1786, however, a young Englishman named John Molson gained control of a small, faltering brewery in Montreal. The popularity of his brews grew and Molson soon became the largest brewery in Quebec; today, the seventh generation of his family is still involved with the company that bears his name. See MOLSON COORS BREWING COMPANY. In 1847 an Irishman named John Kinder Labatt took over a small brewery in London, Ontario. Just as Molson's brewery became a regional powerhouse in Quebec, so too did Labatt's brewery earn a growing following across southern Ontario.

The beers brewed by Molson, Labatt, and other brewers of their time were largely English-style ales. Lagers came to Canada later, with the settling of the Canadian prairies by immigrants from central Europe.

By the time Prohibition rolled around before World War I, there were 118 breweries across Canada. After Prohibition ended by 1930 in all but one province, there were just 69. See PROHIBITION. Many of those that remained had survived by brewing beer for the American market; consuming alcohol was illegal, but in some provinces, producing it was not. Canadian authorities turned a blind eye to shipments of beer supposedly destined for Cuba or elsewhere, when it was clear it was being shipped across the St. Clair River to Detroit in a rowboat.

After Prohibition ended, surviving breweries were subject to a wave of restrictions on where and how beer could be sold. Succeeding waves of consolidation in the industry—most notoriously driven by horse-racing and industrial magnate E.P. Taylor from the 1930s through the 1960s—meant that by the late 1970s, three companies (Molson, Labatt, and the company Taylor had built into Carling O'Keefe) controlled well over 90% of the Canadian beer market. In 1989 Molson purchased Carling O'Keefe, becoming what was then the largest brewer in Canada, and fifth-largest in the world. See CARLING O'KEEFE LIMITED.

Distribution and Regulation

Canadian breweries must navigate a complex maze of distribution, tax, and production regulations. As the regulation of alcohol consumption and production is largely a provincial responsibility, the challenges vary widely across the country. Several provinces grant favorable tax treatment to brewers who operate locally.

In Ontario, the most heavily populated province, the beer distribution system is essentially a two-tier affair. Roughly 80% of the Ontario beer market is controlled by Brewers Retail, which began in 1927 as a brewers' cooperative warehouse system as the province came out of prohibition. Thanks to industry consolidation, Brewers Retail is now owned by Labatt, Molson (49% each), and Sleeman (2%). While other brewers may distribute their beers through the chain's locations, called The Beer Store, craft breweries complain that the listing fees are unaffordable. The other main distribution channel for beer in Ontario is the Liquor Control Board of Ontario (LCBO), which controls roughly 20% of the market. The LCBO also sets minimum prices for all beer sold in the province. All products stocked at LCBO stores must go through a lengthy, rigorous approval process. As in other provinces, brewers may sell beer out of their own brewery, but there are no corner store or grocery sales.

In Newfoundland and Labrador, beer is sold in the government-run Newfoundland Labrador Liquor Corporation (NLC) stores, and in corner stores. To access the much wider distribution found in corner stores, however, a brewery must operate locally. Labatt and Molson each operate a small brewery in the provincial capital, St. John's.

In Quebec, out-of-province breweries must establish their own warehouse and get a distributor's license if they want access to grocery stores and dépanneurs (corner stores), which are much more widespread than the government-operated *Société des alcools du Quebec's* network of stores.

In all 13 provinces and territories except Alberta, an official government agency acts as the importer of record for beer (and all other alcohol) from outside the province; most breweries use a local agency to help navigate each province's regulations. In some cases, a brewing company can ship straight to retailers if they also have a brewery in the province, even if the beer being shipped is brewed elsewhere. This has led to the establishment or purchase of some small breweries by bigger companies, in order to avoid dealing with the provincial agencies.

In Alberta, the government has privatized the retail, import, and warehousing business; the Alberta Gaming and Liquor Commission (AGLC) regulates the industry and collects revenue from alcohol sales.

See also DISTRIBUTION and TAXES.

Quebec

In addition to being the first part of Canada where brewing occurred, Quebec is significant to the Canadian beer scene for another reason: it is home to some of the most creative and talented brewers in the country.

There are roughly 75 breweries in Quebec, including dozens of brewpubs, serving a population of approximately 7.8 million people. In contrast, neighboring Ontario, with a population of just under 13 million, has between 40 and 50 breweries, including no more than 12 brewpubs.

There are breweries quite literally from one end of the province to the other, producing a far wider array of styles than breweries elsewhere in Canada. Close to the western border with Ontario, *Ferme Brasserie Schoune* produces several ales, including a creditable attempt at a gueuze. In the windswept Magdalen Islands in the Gulf of St. Lawrence in the east, *à l'Abri de la Tempête* makes several fine beers, some with locally grown barley malted at the brewery.

In the Montreal area alone, there are 30 breweries, including roughly 20 brewpubs. McAuslan Brewing Company makes a very good range of mostly English-style beers, including St. Ambroise Pale Ale and the luxurious St. Ambroise Oatmeal Stout. Dieu du Ciel, which began as a brewpub, makes some excellent beers, ranging in style from dry-hopped Belgian strong ales, to a coffee-flavored imperial stout, and a Belgian wheat beer flavored with hibiscus flowers.

Perhaps the most influential craft brewery in Quebec is Unibroue, located in the Montreal suburb of Chambly. Started in 1991 by businessmen André Dion and Serge Racine, Unibroue is arguably one of the finest producers of Belgian-style ales to be found outside of Belgium. In 1992 the brewery got a massive publicity boost when Quebec singer Robert Charlebois bought a small stake.

Belgian brewery Riva did some initial consulting for Unibroue, but the brewery has since gone on to create a wide range of ales on its own. Its flagship beer is the spritzy, citrusy *Blanche de Chambly*, but Unibroue specializes in stronger abbey ales, including the decadently rich, strong (9% ABV) *Trois Pistoles*. Most of Unibroue's beers are bottle-conditioned. The brewery also features compelling artwork on all its labels, many of them based on traditional Quebec legends and stories. Other more recent Quebec craft breweries have followed in Unibroue's footsteps, both with a sizeable Belgian stylistic influence, and in the use of elaborate artwork on their labels. In 2004 Unibroue was purchased by Ontario-based Sleeman, which itself was bought by Japan's Sapporo in 2006.

Quebec is also home to Canada's best beer festival, the annual *Mondial de la Bière* in Montreal. Mondial (in English, the Montreal Beer Festival) attracted 80,000 visitors in 2009. They were lured by 450 beers from 98 breweries, with roughly a quarter of the breweries being from Quebec. There is also a good selection of products from Quebec's cider producers, including the local specialty, ice cider.

There are several explanations for the vibrancy of the Quebec beer scene; the truth is probably found in a combination of factors. One explanation is that Quebecers have a greater openness to exploring good food and beverage than other Canadians, partly thanks to the French cultural influence in the province. Another more prosaic explanation is that thanks to the ability to sell beer in grocery stores and corner stores, Quebec brewers are able more easily to explore a variety of beer styles. Rather than having to supply an entire chain of government-run stores with a new beer, they can make a small pilot batch, and send it to a few independent corner stores. If it sells successfully, they can produce more; if not, there's not much damage done. Another factor that favors Quebec breweries is the set of obstacles faced by brewers based in the other provinces.

Coutts, Ian. *Brew north: How Canadians made beer and beer made Canada*. Vancouver: Greystone Books, 2010.

D'Eer, Mario. *Le guide de la bonne biere du Québec* (Guide to good beer of Quebec). Montreal: Trécarré, 2009. A comprehensive look at Quebec's vibrant craft breweries, their beer, and the history of beer in the province.

Pashley, Nick. *Cheers: A history of beer in Canada*. Toronto: HarperCollins, 2009.

Sneath, Allen Winn. *Brewed in Canada*. Toronto: Dundurn Press, 2001.

Josh Rubin

candi sugar is one of many possible adjuncts, or non-malt fermentables that a brewer can add to a beer in the search for unique flavors. See ADJUNCTS. Candi sugar is most widely used in Belgium for the production of special and Trappist ales. There are several types of candi sugar, ranging from light to dark, and virtually all brewers use it in liquid form. The flavor of candi sugar can be very clean and sweet at the light end and very caramel-like and toffee-like at the dark end. The method of candi sugar production by the sugar producers in Belgium is proprietary, but generally involves heating beet sugar with water in the presence of various salts to create Maillard reaction products, thus caramelizing the sugar to different degrees. See MAILLARD REACTION. When added to wort, candi sugar is fully fermented and results in a beer with lighter body and more alcohol because it is more fermentable than malt sugars. This is one of the reasons that many Belgian beer styles are notably drier than most types from other countries. Typical usage rates are from 10%–30% of the original gravity.

Brewers often use the lighter-colored candi sugar for lighter-colored beers such as tripels and special golden ales. The darker-colored sugars are used in dark beers such as dubbels. Here the dark candi sugar gives flavors of high-temperature caramel, raisins, and even burnt sugar. Even though the color of dark candi sugar is similar to that derived from many roasted malts, the flavors are entirely different; for example candi sugar generally does not give coffee-like notes. Often, beers that include candi sugar are high-alcohol beers with a deceivingly smooth drinkability.

Many homebrewers use candi sugar in crystallized, hard candy form. These crystals are either dark or light and are added to the brewkettle. They are used to recreate many of the famous Belgian styles of beer.

See also BELGIUM.

Keith Villa

The **candle filter** is a type of precoat or pressure filter and is predominantly used for clarification of beer that has been fermented and lagered, although other applications, such as sterile filtration or wort filtration, are possible. The name comes from the shape of the filter element, which is a long, thin cylinder that resembles a candle. The earliest type of candle filter was developed by Wilhelm Berkefeld of Germany in the 1890s for water purification. For the brewing industry, candle filters were developed for beer filtration in the 1950s and 1960s. They remain popular today. The candles are mounted inside a cylindrical pressure vessel that receives unfiltered beer. The candle itself is the septum that holds the filter aid, which could be diatomaceous earth, perlite, cellulose, or other materials, during the solid–liquid separation. The candles themselves do not perform any filtration. It is the filter aid which coats the candle that does the actual filtration. Most commonly, candles are fabricated from metal, almost exclusively stainless steel today or ceramic, although other materials are possible. Early candles were composed of stacked washers with small dimples to create a gap between them, allowing liquid but not filter aid to pass through. Today, candles are made from wedge or v-wire and have much greater precision than older types. Unfiltered beer passes from the outside of the candle, through the filter cake, and into the center of the candle. This now filtered beer passes up through a mounting plate or manifold holding the candles and out of the filter housing. Most candles are mounted to the top of the filter housing, but some models have a bottom-mounted candle. For the purposes of beer filtration, there is no difference in the mounting position.

Kunze, W. "Beer filtration." In *Technology brewing and malting*, 7th ed., 401–416. Trans. by T. Wainwright. Berlin: VLB Berlin, 1996.

Murray, K. "Liquid–solid separation." In *An introduction to brewing science and technology*, Series 2, Vol. 4, *Engineering (including distillation)*, 77–84. London: The Institute of Brewing, 1993.

Andrew Fratianni

canning beer was a tricky and revolutionary development in packaging. The very first beer sold in a can was Krueger's Finest Beer, brewed by the Gottfried Krueger Brewing Company of Newark, New Jersey, which was founded in 1899 by Gottfried Krueger, a German immigrant. It was a shipment of only 2,000 cans that left the brewery in 1933, shortly after the ratification of the 21st Amendment to the U.S. Constitution, which repealed the 18th Amendment and thus ended Prohibition. The beer went on sale not in Newark, but in faraway Richmond, Virginia. That first beer can was a flat-top, welded-seam, heavy-gauge tin can, coated on the inside and made by the American Can Company (CanCo) of Pacific Grove, California, which was founded in 1901. To open the can, the consumer had to punch a hole in the top with a sharp implement like a church-key style opener. The development of this first can, however, was quite a feat. CanCo had started experimenting with beer cans in 1909, but abandoned the effort soon thereafter, because beer in a can is capable of generating in excess of 80 pounds per square inch (psi) of pressure, which can cause the container to leak or even burst. The cans manufactured at the time could not even take 40 lb psi of pressure, let alone 80 psi. Just as troubling, the cans had no lining, and beer is acidic; the reaction between the beer and the tin left the beer with an awful metallic tang. Finally, cans had to be inexpensive enough to be attractive compared with established glass bottles, especially those that could be refilled as returnables. Despite these obstacles, CanCo made another attempt in 1921, although Prohibition was still in force, and the potential market was still limited. CanCo managed to solve both the pressure and the inner coating problems in 2 years. When Prohibition was finally lifted, the Krueger Brewery became CanCo's first customer, on a trial basis.

CanCo may have solved some of the can's technical problems, but there was still the issue of consumer acceptance. The Krueger Brewing Company, therefore, decided to test market this revolutionary beer in a can in a distant location, just in case the new container flopped. Gottfried Krueger did not want to risk his brewery's reputation in his home market along the Northeastern seaboard. Subsequent market surveys, however, revealed that 91% of consumers who had tried the test cans approved of the new packaging, and 85% even claimed that the beer tasted more like draught than did bottled beer. As a result, on January 24, 1935, the brewery packaged its other beer, Krueger's 3.2% ABV Cream Ale, in cans, too, and introduced both beers in its entire sales area. See CREAM ALE.

The first release of beer in a can was so successful that soon thereafter it was imitated by other breweries, first in the United States, then around the globe, and events accelerated. By July 1934, Krueger's production had increased fivefold compared with its pre-can days. In September 1934, CanCo patented its vinyl-type lining under the trademark of "Keglined." In August 1935, Pabst became the first major brewery to offer its beers in cans, followed by Schlitz a month later. By the end of 1935, 37 American breweries canned their beers. On December 3, 1935, the first canned beer outside the United States was released by the small Felinfoel Brewery Company of Llanelli in Wales, UK. Over the years, beer cans not only gained in popularity but also became better. In 1937, the Crown Cork & Seal Company, the inventor of the crown cap, perfected an electrolytic tin-plating process, which allowed it to introduce a two-piece, drawn, necked-in steel can that was sealed with a crown cap. See CROWN CAP. The new can was given the branding of "the Crowntainer" and was made to hold a US quart of beer (slightly less than a liter). In 1958, the Hawaii Brewing Company moved beyond tin, introducing its Primo brand in the first aluminum beer can. In 1965, ring-top cans hit the market; these had a metal tab with a finger loop—a tug removed a tab from the lid, opening the can. By 1969, canned beers outsold bottled beers for the first time in the United States.

Proponents of canned beer point out that the can has several advantages over glass bottles. Importantly, they are cheaper to transport, because they are lighter and stack better than bottles. At one time, canned beer was prone to excessive oxidation, but that is largely a problem of the past. Any metallic flavors would now likely be a figment of the consumer's imagination, although anyone drinking beer directly from a can might be thought to deserve whatever he gets. Cans have the advantage of being impermeable to light and thus can give beer a longer shelf life, especially if the beer is to be stored in a well-lit environment. See LIGHTSTRUCK. Paradoxically, however, as the can improved in quality, it also declined in respectability, because as more and more mass-market beers were canned, cans became increasingly associated with cheap, not premium, beers. As the craft brewing movement got underway in the early 1980s, early microbreweries ignored the can, looking upon it as a plebian package. Even if they'd wanted to use cans, most could probably not have afforded the expensive equipment needed. The can remains popular; today, Anheuser Busch packages about 10% of its volume in kegs, splitting the rest almost evenly between cans and bottles. It seems that the can has finally arrived on the craft beer scene as well. Smaller, less expensive canning lines are now available, and small breweries are jumping onto the can bandwagon, some with both feet. One of the pioneers of this development is the Oskar Blues Brewery of Lyons, Colorado, which canned its first pale ale in 2002, using a recently developed small canning line. Bucking the previous low-rent image, canned craft beer appears to be developing a sort of retro-chic, especially as consumers decide that they want flavorful beer in the fishing boat as well as on the dinner table. As of 2011, there are almost 50 small canning breweries in the United States and Canada, and that number is rising. Cans are highly recyclable. Anheuser-Busch, for instance, claims that it has recycled 460 billion aluminum cans since it started its recycling operation in 1978. There clearly still is a future for the beer can.

Anheuser-Busch Packaging Group. http://www.anheuser-busch.com/ABPackaging.html/ (accessed January 27, 2011).

Anheuser-Busch Packaging Group Fact Sheet. http://qa.anheuser-busch.com/mediakits/CorpMediaKit/A-B%20Packaging%20Fact%20Sheet6-19-08.pdf (accessed January 27, 2011).

http://www.bcca.com/history/beer_can_history.asp (accessed January 27, 2011).

Beer Can History. http://beercanhistory.com/ (accessed January 27, 2011).

Beer Can History. http://www.beercannews.com/BEER_CAN_HISTORY/beer_can_history.html/ (accessed January 27, 2011).

Felinfoel Brewery Company Ltd. http://www.felinfoel-brewery.com/ (accessed January 27, 2011).

January 24, 1935: First Canned Beer Sold. http://www.wired.com/thisdayintech/2011/01/0124first-us-canned-beer/ (accessed January 27, 2011).

Oskar Blues Brewery. http://www.oskarblues.com/ (accessed January 27, 2011).

Horst Dornbusch

Cantillon Brewery is a traditional, authentic lambic brewery located in Brussels, Belgium. It makes a full spectrum of sour, very dry, and highly effervescent lambic-style brews including gueuze, faro, and kriek. See FARO, GUEUZE, KRIEK, and LAMBIC. Brasserie Cantillon Brouwerij was founded in 1900 by Paul Cantillon, himself the son of a brewer, and his wife, Marie Troch. Today the brewery is run by the cantankerous lambic traditionalist Jean-Pierre Van Roy, and his beers are widely revered among lambic enthusiasts. Cantillon is still family owned, and neither the equipment nor the brewing methods have changed much in more than a century. Perhaps the biggest change came in 1999, when the brewery switched entirely to certified-organic brewing, except for its fruit beers, for which there are simply not enough organic cherries and raspberries available. All Cantillon lambics and lambic-derived beers are spontaneously fermented, aged in oak casks, and then blended from different batches and vintages. They are packaged in thick, cork-stoppered, and crown-capped bottles and refermented in the bottle for 1 year before they are released for sale. Because of this artisanal, old-fashioned beer-making process, no two packaged batches are alike, and each has its own character. If kept in a cool and dark environment, Cantillon beers can be laid down for up to 20 years. Half the brewery's production is in gueuze. Perhaps the brewery's second most popular beer is its kriek, which it makes only once a year from a truckload of freshly picked sour cherries. These are placed in oak or chestnut casks and immersed in roughly 18-month-old lambic for a secondary fermentation that is initiated by the microbes both in the lambic and on the skins of the fruit. Once enough fruit colors and flavors have been extracted, the beer—now transformed into kriek—is racked off the fruit, which is then immersed a second time in lambic for a second round of secondary fermentation and a weaker extraction of colors and flavors. The two varieties of kriek are blended half and half before bottling. Other brews from the Cantillon Brewery include Rosé de Gambrinus, a framboise (raspberry) lambic, and Fou' Foune, an apricot lambic. The Grand Cru Bruocsella Cantillon is a select straight lambic that has been aged in oak casks for 3 years, whereas Gueuze Lou Pepe comes from a blend of lambics of the same age (not different ages as in the regular gueuze) from different barrels then refermented with "liqueur d'expédition" as Champagne makers do.

The Lou Pepe Kriek and Framboise are made using twice as much fruit as the regular versions. Vigneronne is a Cantillon fruit lambic made with white grapes, whereas Saint-Lamvinus is made with merlot and cabernet-franc grapes. The brewery's Iris is the only non-lambic beer. It is brewed from an all-pale ale barley malt mash, spontaneously fermented as a regular lambic, then after 2 years in the barrel, it gets a second fresh hopping 2 weeks before the bottling. See DRY HOPPING.

See also BELGIUM and LAMBIC.

Brasserie Cantillon Brouwerij. http://www.cantillon.be/ (accessed January 24, 2011).

Lorenzo Dabove

caproic acid, the common name for hexanoic acid, a short-chain saturated fatty acid that can be created by the metabolic activity of yeasts. It is one of three fatty acids named in relation to Capra, the genus of goats; the others are caprylic and capric acids. The names are derived from the high amounts of these fatty acids found in goat's milk, which give the milk its characteristic odor and flavor.

Caproic acid gives a normal flavor in goat's milk, but it is usually not desirable in beer. In beer it has a pungent, sweaty, cheesy aroma. It is excreted by yeast during extended lagering at warm temperatures and high yeast cell counts. The condition of the yeast also influences fatty acid excretion and beers fermented warm under pressure show increased concentrations of these fatty acids (and corresponding esters) during lagering. Normal amounts of hexanoic acid are in the 1–2 ppm range, whereas increased amounts can have negative effects on both foam and taste. To avoid these effects, brewers often remove yeast as soon as feasible after fermentation. Where time is an issue, a centrifuge is sometimes used between fermentation and lagering tanks, although in this case the process is usually calibrated to leave some yeast behind to assist in maturation.

"Wild" Brettanomyces yeast strains tend to produce caproic acid in large amounts, and although this creates flavors unsuitable for most beer styles, some brewers may desire it as a complexing agent. Caproic acid is a major feature of lambic aromatics and beers intentionally inoculated with Brettanomyces cultures will often show distinctly "funky" characteristics.

See also BRETTANOMYCES, CAPRYLIC ACID, and LAMBIC.

Back, Werner. *Ausgewählte Kapitel der Brauereitechnologie* (Selected chapters in brewery technology), Nürnberg, Germany: Fachverlag Hans Carl GmbH, 2005.

Narzißß, Ludwig. *Abriss der Bierbrauerei* (Summary of the beer brewery), 7th ed. Weinheim, Germany: Wiley-VCH Verlag GmbH & Co KGaA, 2005.

Wolfgang David Lindell

caprylic acid, the common name for octanoic acid, a medium-chain saturated fatty acid. Caprylic acid has an unpleasant, fatty, oily, rancid aroma; like caproic acid, it is excreted by yeast during adverse conditions.

The corresponding ethyl ester, ethyl caprylate (also known as ethyl octanoate), contributes to beer aroma and flavor and can be described as fruity, floral, banana-like, pineapple-like, or even brandy-like in its pure state. It tends to go hand in hand with development of a yeasty flavor that may or may not be desirable, depending on the concentrations and the style of beer.

See also CAPROIC ACID.

Back, Werner. *Ausgewählte Kapitel der Brauereitechnologie* (Selected Chapters in Brewery Technology). Nürnberg, Germany: Fachverlag Hans Carl GmbH, 2005.

Narzißß, Ludwig. *Abriss der Bierbrauerei* (Summary of the Beer Brewery), 7th ed. Weinheim, Germany: Wiley-VCH Verlag GmbH & Co. KGaA, 2005.

Wolfgang David Lindell

caramel color is the most common of food colorings, making up 90% of all substances added to food and drink to effect a color change. While dark color in most beers is the result of roasted malts in the mash, the color of beer may also be adjusted upwards by the use of a number of compounds. Caramel color (also called "couleur" or "colouring sugar," EU positive list E-number 150) is produced by boiling sugar and adding ammonia as a catalyst, causing the formation of compounds giving the product an extremely high color (up to more than 50,000 EBC units).

The reason for using caramel color in beer is twofold; it is used in small amounts as a final correction of the color of a wide range of beers and sometimes as part of the actual recipe construction of a beer. As coloring agents are—at normally used concentrations—virtually free of aroma and flavor, they can be used for producing dark beers with much less roasted aroma and flavor than would result for using dark malts to achieve the same color. It also allows a brewery to create more than one "product" out of a single beer. Especially in mass-market brewing, this allows a very mildly flavored beer to achieve a bolder appearance. Product names include the American "Porterine," so-called for its supposed ability to turn ordinary golden lager into "porter" and the German Sinamar, which is formulated to meet the requirements of the Reinheitsgebot. While Belgian dark candi sugar also gives color, it is not the same as the colorants mentioned here; dark candi sugar is a major flavoring component as well and can also be a major fraction of fermentable sugar.

Where caramel color is used, it is normally added to finished, filtered beer as the part of a final adjustment before packaging.

Kunze, Wolfgang. *Technology brewing and malting*, 3rd international ed. Berlin: VLB, 2004.

Anders Brinch Kissmeyer

caramelization is a complex and poorly understood series of pyrolysis reactions (decomposition caused by high temperatures) that occur in carbohydrates when they are subjected to intense heating under relatively dry conditions. There is a dehydration of the sugars, followed by their condensation. Isomerization, fragmentation, and polymerization reactions occur, variously leading to the development of an assortment of flavors and color.

In a matrix such as malt, there are of course diverse carbohydrates, but in pure sugar systems the caramelization temperatures are 110°C (230°F) for fructose, 160°C (320°F) for glucose, and 180°C (356°F) for maltose.

Caramels are complex mixtures of diverse components, including high-molecular-weight colored substances. In commercial operations, caramels are produced by heating sugar (most frequently glucose), sometimes with agents such as ammonia or sulfite. Processes may involve at least 1 week at ambient temperature, with an ensuing 90°C (194°F) overnight stand and then approximately 3 hours at 120°C (248°F). In the early stages of caramelization, diacetyl is produced—hence the butterscotch flavor of caramels. See DIACETYL. Other flavor substances produced include hydroxymethylfurfural, hydroxyacetylfuran, hydroxydimethylfuranone, dihydroxydimethylfuranone, maltol, and hydroxymaltol.

The high-molecular-weight color components of caramel are positively charged and therefore relatively stable in beer. Where used in brewing, caramel can either be added during the wort boiling stage or to adjust color downstream. In Belgian brewing, caramelized dark candi sugar syrup is used to bring color and flavor to dark styles such as dubbel. See CANDI SUGAR.

Rather than using caramels as colorants and/or flavorings in beer, many brewers choose to use caramelized malts. These are produced by the intense heating of stewed malts. These range from the comparatively light carapils (color specification perhaps 15–30 EBC) through to Crystal (color specification perhaps 75–300 EBC). See CARAPILS and CRYSTAL MALT.

In Carapils production, the surface moisture of green malt is dried off at 50°C (122°F) before stewing over 40 minutes. In this stage there is a promotion of carbohydrate and protein breakdown to provide substantial levels of sugars and amino acids. Sometimes high-protein-content malt is used. Thereafter the temperature is increased to around 100°C (212°F), followed by curing at 100°C–120°C (212°F–248°F) for less than 1 hour. Crystal malt is prepared as for Carapils, but the first curing is at 135°C (275°F) for less than 2 hours. It will be appreciated that apart from caramelization reactions between sugars, there will also be Maillard reaction events in these processes. See MAILLARD REACTION. These malts have pronounced toffee, caramel, sweet characters but lack the burnt harshness of the more heavily kilned malts in which roasting is applied to dry pale malt starters.

Caramelized flavors are very important flavor components in many styles of beer and can form the backbone of a beer's ability to pair successfully with many foods. Harmonization of a beer's caramelized flavors with similar flavors in sautéed, roasted, fried, or grilled foods can provide beer pairings that are substantially different than those achieved by wine. See FOOD PAIRING.

Charles W. Bamforth

caramel malts, as the name implies, impart a strong caramel flavor to beer, which is the result of an extra stewing process that takes place during malting, usually in a roasting drum, between germination and kilning. See MALT. In a modern malting plant, the green malt is kept at a temperature of approximately 64°C and 72°C (147°F and 162°F) during stewing. This ensures that the endosperms, in effect, are "mashed," and the starches are turned into a sugary liquid that is trapped under the husk. Subsequently, the stewed grain needs to be dried, either in a kiln at about 90°C (roughly 195°F) for a pale malt or in the roasting drum at perhaps 200°C (roughly 390°F) for a darker malt. The stewing and drying causes the liquefied sugars to caramelize into solid, semi-crystalline, glassy, long-chain, unfermentable dextrins. Melanoidins form during this process, too. See MELANOIDINS. Because the caramelized sugars cannot be degraded during mashing in the brewhouses, they contribute directly to wort gravity. They are also responsible for malty-sweet flavors, a deep color, a complex aroma, a fuller body and mouthfeel, and improved foam retention of the finished beer.

Historically, caramel malts were produced from green malt in a kiln covered with a tarpaulin. The tarpaulin reduced evaporation as the kiln was heated to perhaps 60°C to 75°C (140°F to 167°F) and kept at that temperature for up to 2 hours. To dry and caramelize the grain, the tarpaulin would then be removed and the temperature raised while the grain was being ventilated.

Many maltsters label their caramel malts in terms of their color values, such as Caramel 10, Caramel 40, or Caramel 120. These are numbers on the Lovibond scale (L). See LOVIBOND. The higher the number, the darker the malt. For an approximate conversion of Lovibond into EBC (European Brewery Convention) values, simply multiply them by 1.97. At the low end of the color scale are caramel malts of as low a 2°L (approximately 4 ECB), which are often marketed as Carapils® or Carafoam®. These are typical additions, up to 5% to the grist, to the mashes of Central European blond lagers. At the other extreme are virtually black, roasted caramel malts of more than 500°L (almost 1,500 EBC). These, too, are used very sparingly, often in porters and stouts, where they rarely exceed 5% of the grist. Caramel malts between these extremes are particularly favored in such beer styles as amber ales and lagers, red ales and lagers, Märzenbiers, and bock beers, where paler versions may account for up to 40% of the grist. However, when used in high proportions, darker caramel malts can bring acrid astringency.

Briggs, D. E. *Malts and malting.* London: Blackie, 1998.
Briggs, D. E., Boulton, C. A., Brookes, P. A., and Stevens, R. *Brewing: Science and practice.* Cambridge: Woodhead Publishing, 2004.
Briggs, D. E., Hough, J. S., Stevens, R., and Young, T. W. *Malting and brewing science, volume 1: Malt and sweet wort,* 2nd. ed. London: Chapman & Hall, 1981.
Hornsey, I. S. *Brewing.* Cambridge: Royal Society of Chemistry, 1999.

Ian Hornsey

Caramunich (malt) is a version of crystal malt that provides a caramel character to a beer, particularly a continental lager or pilsner.

As with all crystal malts, it is germinated but not dried before being roasted at between 230°F and 266°F (110°C–130°C). The grains are thus wet internally when they roast and this allows a wider variety of chemical reactions to develop than if the grains were dry. The most distinctive of these reactions are the caramelization of sugars and the Maillard reaction between sugars and amino acids. See MAILLARD REACTION.

The products of these reactions provide caramel and toffee characteristics as well as a light roasted flavor. Because of the high temperatures and high water content during roasting, caramunich malt contains little, if any, enzyme activity, making it only suitable as a flavoring malt rather than a diastatic malt.

Caramunich malt differs from standard crystal malt in that it is produced from lager malt. This may be incompletely modified in its processing and consequently have high levels of protein, which will enhance the flavor development during the roasting, giving a high level of Maillard products. Because of this caramunich is often used to provide depth of flavor to dark lager beers as well as contributing to color.

In addition many of the compounds in crystal malts are able to absorb oxygen and so protect beer from oxidation reactions. Small proportions of crystal malts are thus often added to improve stability and shelf life.

See also CRYSTAL MALT.

Keith Thomas

Carapils (malt) is a highly modified pale malt that takes its name from the words "caramel," which is melted and crystallized sugar, and "pilsner," which is a blond lager beer style first developed in the Czech city of Pilsen in 1842. See PILSNER. Whereas regular pale malt is gently kiln dried at temperatures ranging from 50°C to 84°C (122°F to 183°F), Carapils is best dried evenly in a heated drum, which allows for the precise control of airflow, moisture, and temperature. For the production of Carapils, the drum is heated to at least 110°C (230°F) and rarely above 160°C (320°F). At this temperature, malt sugars caramelize, which means they change their molecular structure and become glassy and unfermentable. Caramelization also gives the malt a slightly nutty flavor. The higher the temperature in the drum, the darker will be the Carapils color and the stronger will be its flavor. Most Carapils, however, is of roughly the same color as kiln-dried pilsner malt (about 2.5 to 5 European Brewing Convention or 1.5 to 2.4 Lovibond). See PILSNER MALT. In pale ales and lagers, Carapils rarely exceeds 5% to 10% of the grain bill, whereas in heftier beer styles, such as bock beer, it may constitute as much as 40% of the mash. In finished beer, the addition of Carapils can produce more foam and better head retention and leads to a fuller body and mouthfeel. Although many brewers use the term Carapils generically, it is actually a trademarked brand name. Drum-dried and drum-roasted caramel-type malts were first developed by Weyermann Malting of Bamberg, Germany, which has held a trademark registration for the name Carapils under the international Madrid Agreement for intellectual property since 1908 in all countries except the United States, where Carapils is a registered trade mark of the Briess Malt & Ingredients Company of Chilton, Wisconsin. See BRIESS MALT & INGREDIENTS COMPANY and WEYERMANN MALTING. In North America, Weyermann markets its pale caramel malt under the trade name of Carafoam.

Thomas Kraus-Weyermann

Caravienne is a specialty caramel or crystal malt named after the Vienna lager, the beer style in which it is an indispensable part of the grain bill. See VIENNA LAGER. Made from two-row spring barley and kilned to a color value of roughly 40 to 60 European Brewery Convention color units (approximately 15 to 23° Lovibond), Caravienne imparts deep reddish color hues to beer. To produce Caravienne in the malting plant, sprouted green malt is gently drum dried with only moderate venting to contain the moisture. This steeping process denatures all enzymes. In the brewery, Caravienne, like all caramel malts, must be used with enzyme-rich base malts. The moist drying produces glassy, crystalline acrospires consisting of dextrin sugars that are unfermentable by yeast. These sugars provide the beer with extra body, contribute a gentle, slightly aromatic sweetness and maltiness, and make for a fuller flavored finished beer. Despite its Austrian-sounding name, Caravienne is also popular in other brewing cultures, especially in Belgium. It may comprise between 5% and 20% of the total grain bill in such beers as altbier, Belgian abbey-style beers, Belgian red ales, bockbiers, cream stouts, English bitters, Scottish ales, and even some American India pale ales. In these beers, Caravienne can play an analogous role to that of Munich malt or Carapils.

See also CARAPILS (MALT).

Thomas Kraus-Weyermann

carbohydrates are quantitatively the major organic materials in nature. In polymeric form they comprise the main food reserves in living systems, e.g., starch in cereal endosperms and glycogen in yeast. They also have important structural roles, for example, they comprise the β-glucans and pentosans in the starchy endosperm cell walls of grain, the cellulose in the husk, and the glucans and mannans in the cell wall of yeast. Carbohydrates also form a part of the structure of some proteins (*glycoproteins*).

Carbohydrates have the general formula $C_x(H_2O)_n$; i.e., they are essentially "hydrates of carbon." All sugars are carbohydrates, including the various sugars that are fermented by beer yeasts. Glucose, one of the simpler carbohydrates (sugars), has the formula $C_6H_{12}O_6$. See GLUCOSE. Because it has six carbon atoms it is a hexose, from the Latin prefix *hex* for six, c.f., "hexagonal." Sugars with five carbon atoms are called pentoses, from the Latin prefix *pent* for "five"—e.g., "pentagon"—and examples are xylose and arabinose. Polymers of sugar units containing five carbons are known as *pentosans*. Polymers of hexoses are called *hexosans*. Polymers of glucose are known as glucosans, or more commonly, *glucans*. Examples include starch but also the β-glucans from barley that can present major problems for brewers. See BETA-GLUCANS.

Carbohydrates can interact with amino acids to form flavorsome, low-molecular-weight and colored, high-molecular-weight materials (melanoidins) through the Maillard reaction that occurs under the high heat conditions of kilning and (to an extent) wort boiling.

Davis, B.G. & A. J. Fairbanks. *Carbohydrate chemistry*. New York: Oxford University Press, 2002.

See also GLYCOGEN and STARCH.

Charles W. Bamforth

carbonation. While levels differ widely, carbonation is one of the defining features of beer. The effects of carbonation strongly influence a beer's mouthfeel, flavor, aroma, and appearance. Beer without carbonation is said to be "flat," and this is an apt description, as the beer is likely to be dull and lifeless. The two main products of the fermentation of wort sugars are ethanol and carbon dioxide gas. The carbon dioxide is readily soluble in the beer. According to Henry's law, "at a constant temperature, the amount of a given gas dissolved in a given type and volume of liquid is directly proportional to the partial pressure of that gas in equilibrium with that liquid." See HENRY'S LAW. So in a closed vessel such as a bottle, cask, or brewery tank the amount of carbon dioxide dissolved in the beer will vary according to the temperature of the beer and the pressure of the carbon dioxide in the headspace.

Carbonation is measured in two ways. One of these methods compares the volume of dissolved gas with the volume of liquid (vol/vol), while the other measures the weight of gas in solution compared to the volume of liquid (g/l). The device used for measuring the concentration of carbon dioxide in solution uses the principles of Henry's law. A sample of the beer is placed in a specially designed closed container with a measured amount of headspace. The sample is agitated, either by simple shaking, or by passing a small electric current through it, to obtain an equilibrium between the gas in solution and its partial pressure in the headspace. By measuring the temperature of the sample, and the partial pressure in the headspace, the carbon dioxide in solution can be calculated. This is traditionally done using a chart that compares partial pressure and temperature but modern machines have calculators built in.

After primary fermentation an unfinished beer in an open vessel will contain around 1.0–1.2 vol/vol (2–2.4 g/l) of dissolved carbon dioxide, while a beer matured in a closed cylindroconical vessel, with a top pressure, may contain up to 2.5 vol/vol (5.0 g/l) of dissolved carbon dioxide. Traditionally, carbonation to the level required for serving was achieved in the brewery by transferring the beer into a closed vessel with some residual fermentable sugar, and allowing the fermentation to finish. In bottles, the practice of bottle conditioning involves the addition of priming sugar to finished beer, sometimes with fresh yeast. Once the beer is bottled, the yeast consumes the priming sugar, gives off carbon dioxide inside the bottle, and naturally carbonates the beer. Modern production methods allow for carbon dioxide to be added directly to beer using a porous stone or sintered steel rod. See BOTTLE CONDITIONING, CARBONATION STONE, and HENRY'S LAW.

See also CARBON DIOXIDE.

Steve Parkes

carbonation stone, a device used to diffuse carbon dioxide into beer. It may be made of naturally porous stone, porous ceramic, or finely sintered stainless steel. Usually used inside a brewery bright tank or a brewpub serving tank, the carbonation stone is a hollow cylinder, capped at one end, into which carbon dioxide is forced under pressure. The CO_2 diffuses through the stone, emerging on the exterior in very small bubbles. Under pressure, the small bubbles of CO_2 dissolve into the beer before they can reach the surface. Carbonation stones may also be used in-line. A carbonation stone can be used to carbonate flat beer, to add CO_2 to beer with inadequate carbonation for packaging or service, or to scrub dissolved oxygen from beer or water. Whether made of stone, ceramic, or sintered steel, the devices are colloquially known as "stones."

Garrett Oliver

carbon dioxide is a gas produced by yeast during fermentation and creates the "fizz" or "condition" characteristic of beer. In the anaerobic fermentation process, yeast converts the sugars in the wort to, primarily, alcohol and CO_2. Surplus CO_2 is often collected and used later for boosting the level of CO_2 in the finished beer (see CARBONATION). In cask-conditioned beer the CO_2 is generated principally in primary fermentation but a small amount is produced in a secondary fermentation to give the beer a gentle "tingle" ("condition"). The same principle applies in the production of bottle-conditioned beers. Priming sugars—small additions of sucrose or glucose—are often added during filling of the cask or bottle to stimulate the secondary CO_2 generation by the residual yeast. See REAL ALE. Keg, bottled, and canned beers often have additional CO_2 added, usually post-filtration. Beers with this post-fermentation CO_2 are sometimes known as "brewery-conditioned" beers.

CO_2 will dissolve quite readily in beer, with solubility increasing with decreasing temperature. The content of CO_2 in a beer is often expressed in terms of volumes of gas at standard temperature and pressure per volume of beer or in grams of CO_2 per liter of beer. As an approximation, one volume of CO_2 is equivalent to two grams of CO_2 per liter. Cask-conditioned beers have CO_2 levels of around 1.2 vols, whereas keg beers range typically from 2–2.6 vols and bottled and canned beers slightly higher. Knowledge of the precise level of CO_2 in a keg beer is important in that gas pressure in the dispense line from keg to tap needs to be adjusted to the level of the beer in the container to prevent excessive foaming ("fobbing") of the beer as it is delivered into the glass. See FOBBING.

The high solubility of CO_2 at low temperatures is exploited in beers that are served very cold (34–37°F, or 1–3°C). As the beer is taken into the mouth, the rough surface of the warm tongue forms a focus ("nucleus") for the CO_2 to come out of solution. This creates a sharp tingle on the tongue, which can be perceived as refreshing but can sometimes be almost painful; it is known by brewers as the "CO_2 bite." This "bite" is caused by carbonic acid created when CO_2 is dissolved into an aqueous liquid. The lower the beer temperature, the higher the dissolved CO_2 level and the greater the bite. This sensation combines with hop bitterness to form the backbone of a beer's palate sensation and a balance to the sweetness of malt. Without carbon dioxide, most types of beer would be considered unpalatable.

The evolution of streams of gas (CO_2) bubbles from the base of a glass of beer is viewed as being aesthetically pleasing and can aid in foam retention. This rise of gas bubbles can be enhanced by scratching or etching the base of the glass to create nuclei for gas evolution. In the UK branded glasses are often etched with distinctive brand logos to enhance the visual appeal of the beer in the glass.

The foam on a glass of beer is also largely a result of CO_2 evolution out of the liquid, and beer foam is largely comprised of the gas. See FOAM.

George Philliskirk

carboy. Many craft brewers at work today conducted their first amateur fermentations inside a carboy. A carboy is a large container made from different types of glass and plastic depending on the application, and used for storing and serving liquids including beer and yeast slurries. Five-gallon glass carboys were once commonly used to hold purified water and spring water for dispense by water coolers; these are now replaced by plastic vessels of a similar shape.

In brewing they are mainly used by home brewers as fermentation and aging vessels with either an airlock or bung in the top to prevent contamination by airborne microbes. Unlike plastic buckets sometimes used for homebrew fermentations, carboys are easy to make airtight. In a lab setting they are used for storing quantities of media, sterile water, and chemicals cleanly and safely. Some breweries also use them for propagation of special yeast and bacterial strains.

Carboys range in volume between 1 and 15 US gallons (4–60 liters), with the most common size being 5 gallons. Smaller sizes are sometimes simply called jugs while larger sizes are "demijohns" (except in England where a demijohn is 1 UK gallon). Their shape can vary but is generally flat bottomed with straight sides and high shoulders tapering to a narrow (1–3 inch) neck. Some demijohns have round or cone shaped bottoms and are supported by wicker or plastic webbing.

Jonathan Downing

Cargill, a global producer and marketer of food, beverage, and agricultural products, as well and financial and industrial services and products, is a supplier of a wide array of specialty malts, liquid adjuncts, and flavors to the brewing industry. As of 2010, Cargill was the largest privately held company in the United States.

Cargill was founded by W.W. Cargill in 1865 as a grain storage facility in Conover, Iowa. From those humble beginnings, Cargill has grown into one of the largest privately owned companies providing agricultural products and services to the brewing industry around the world, with operations in sixty-seven countries and 138,000 employees worldwide. The company is now headquartered in Wayzata, Minnesota.

Cargill is one of the largest maltsters in the world, with malting facilities in nine countries: the United States, Canada, Belgium, France, Spain, Holland, Germany, Russia, and Argentina. Cargill has worked for years to develop a network which allows it to source bulk and specialty malts both domestically and overseas. In addition Cargill has two technical centers, one in Belgium and one in the United States, which include a pilot brewery and state-of-the-art micro-malting facility.

Cargill Malt's Specialty Products Group supplies not only its own Cargill-branded malts but also imported specialty malts from Dingemans, Gambrinus, Muessdoerffer, Pauls, and Warminster, and brewers flakes from Gilbertson & Page. Cargill also develops and supplies several adjunct ingredients to breweries around the world, making it possible for brewers to produce a wider variety of beer styles and flavors, regardless of location.

Cargill Incorporated. Cargill. http://www.cargill.com/ (accessed May 11, 2010).

Jeff Mendel

Carling O'Keefe Limited is a Canadian holding company that acquired a large number of Canadian breweries through a series of acquisitions and mergers between 1930 and 1967. Previously known as Canadian Breweries Ltd, the holding company was re-named in 1973, shortly after its original owner, E.P. Taylor, sold it to cigarette maker Rothman's of Pall Mall. In its day, Carling O'Keefe was known as one of the "big three" breweries along with Molson and Labatt. See LABATT BREWING COMPANY LTD. and MOLSON COORS BREWING COMPANY. Together, these three breweries accounted for the vast majority of beer sold in Canada from the 1950s to the 1980s.

The name Carling O'Keefe is taken from two historical Canadian breweries that had amalgamated with Canadian Breweries in the 1930s. They were Carling Breweries Ltd, from London, Ontario and O'Keefe Brewery Company from Toronto, Ontario. Of these two brands, the best known is Carling. Carling was founded in 1840 by British-born Thomas Carling. When E.P. Taylor acquired the brewery in 1930, he expanded the brand into the US (through a partnership with Brewing Corp of America later re-named Carling Brewing Company Inc), and into England where Carling remains a very popular brand to this day. When O'Keefe Brewery was acquired by E.P. Taylor in 1934, it was one of Canada's most cutting edge brewing facilities, having been the first company in Canada to install a mechanically refrigerated storage facility.

In 1989, Carling O'Keefe merged with Molson Breweries Canada Ltd to become Molson Companies Ltd, now Molson Coors Brewing Company. Three Carling O'Keefe brands are currently available in Canada as part of the Molson Coors portfolio: Carling Lager, Carling Black Label, and O'Keefe's.

See also CANADA.

Bowering, Ian. *The art and mystery of brewing in Ontario*. Burnstown, Ontario, Canada: General Store Publishing House Inc, 1988.
Heron, Craig. *Booze: A distilled history*. Toronto: Between the Lines, 2003.
Sneath, Allen Winn. *Brewed in Canada: The untold story of Canada's 350-year-old brewing industry*. Toronto: Dundurn Press, 2001.

Mirella G. Amato

Carlsberg Group, as of 2010 one of the top five brewing companies in the world, based in

Copenhagen, Denmark. Carlsberg was founded in 1847 by Jacob Christian (JC) Jacobsen (1811–87) on a hill outside the city of Copenhagen, where Jacobsen had been running a traditional, small town brewery that he had taken over from his father. The new brewery was named after JC's son, Carl, born in 1842, and an adapted version of the Danish word for mountain, "bjerg." JC was very interested in science, having been heavily inspired by his father who, without any academic background whatsoever, had followed lectures at Copenhagen University by the leading scientists of the day. JC believed that the art of brewing could be vastly improved by applying a scientific approach, and he was very open to new developments in brewing.

In 1875 he founded the world's first brewery-owned and -run research facility, the Carlsberg Laboratory, where some of the foremost scientists in the world carried out both basic and applied science supporting the brewing industry. Scientists who worked at the Carlsberg Laboratory included SPL Sørensen, who developed the concept of pH, Johan Kjeldahl, who devised the analytical principle used for centuries to determine proteins, and Emil Christian Hansen, who invented and introduced at Carlsberg the use of pure yeast cultures in brewing. See HANSEN, EMIL CHRISTIAN. In the laboratory's mission statement, JC Jacobsen wrote that no finding or invention made here could be kept secret, but must be shared with the world at large.

JC had already started experimenting in his old town brewery with the fundamentally new method of bottom fermentation, but the lack of cold cellaring possibilities, essential for brewing these beer styles, made this very laborious and only partly successful. See BOTTOM FERMENTATION. He managed, however, to earn enough money to build a new brewery designed specifically for bottom fermentation, using all the newest technology, including mechanical refrigeration.

JC Jacobsen's sphere of interest expanded far beyond his role in brewing. He belonged to a group of prominent members of society who felt that they had an obligation to use their position to create social progress. JC's success as a brewer quickly made him a very wealthy man, and instead of spending his money on a lavish lifestyle he formed the Carlsberg Foundation. The Carlsberg Foundation continues to this day to return the profits of the brewery back into Danish society by supporting mainly the sciences, cultural purposes, and, after the Foundation merged with The New Carlsberg Foundation, the arts.

The Carlsberg Breweries in the hamlet of Valby, now part of greater Copenhagen, were for many years actually two breweries intensely competing with one another—one owned by JC and the other by his own son. When JC's son Carl came of age he was meant to succeed his father, whether he wanted to or not. JC was as tough, single minded, and patriarchal a father as he was a brewer and employer. So Carl was sent abroad to study brewing—his pleas to his father to allow him to return home were ignored. However, JC must have sensed that the tensions between the two were so profound that letting Carl take up a position in the existing brewery would be unwise. The solution to this problem was true to form—JC built an entirely new brewery, the Annexe Brewery, adjacent to his own, and in 1871 put Carl in charge of it. Regardless, the feud between father and son escalated year by year. Fundamental professional issues related to brewing processes, sales, and marketing separated the two, and Carl decided to build his own, new brewery next door, New Carlsberg, which opened in 1882. The two breweries did not merge until JC's death in 1887.

Carl shared his father's interest in and respect for science, but Carl was even more interested in art. The New Carlsberg Foundation, to which Carl willed his brewery and fortune, was created with the mission of donating art to Danish society, the most brilliant example of which was the creation of the beautiful downtown Copenhagen museum, The New Carlsberg Glyptotek. Likewise, the New Carlsberg Brewery was much more lavishly decorated than the older JC Jacobsen breweries, and today the building is one of the major tourist sights in Copenhagen.

Exports of Carlsberg beer began in 1868, with shipping to Scotland, followed soon after by exports to countries in the Far East and South America. Throughout the 20th century exports continued to increase in real numbers, as well as relative to domestic sales, so in the 1960s the first steps were taken to move production abroad. This international expansion was initially completed through agreements with UK brewers to package under licence because the UK market at that time was very big for Carlsberg. This was followed by license brewing agreements in several markets and, in the

1970s, dedicated, green-field Carlsberg breweries were built in far away countries like Malawi, Hong Kong, and the UK, with many other countries to follow.

Carlsberg was born as a lager beer brewery and has remained true to the lager tradition. Still, few major brewers of this magnitude have maintained a portfolio of bottom-fermented beers as varied as those of Carlsberg. These include the "flagship" "Carlsberg Beer," nicknamed HOF at home, Elephant Beer, dark and strong bock style beers like the Easter Brew ("Påskebryg") and the Christmas seasonal "47," as well the darker traditional beers previously baring the "Old Carlsberg" brewery name, including "Gamle Carlsberg," a Munich-style dunkel and the first beer released from Carlsberg by JC in 1847, and "imperial stout," nicknamed "porter" and actually one of the first Baltic porters in the world. See BALTIC PORTER. On the more conventional side, Carlberg's Tuborg Green is sold in 70 countries.

Today, Denmark is home to a vibrant craft beer revolution. See CRAFT BREWING. Carlsberg rowed into these waters fairly early, experimenting with new beer styles and food pairing in the early 2000s. In 2005, Carlsberg followed up this initiative by establishing a small "house brewery" called Jacobsen in connection with its visitors' center in the oldest existing buildings on the original Carlsberg site in Valby.

Brewing at the main production brewery in Valby was stopped at the end of 2008, and production moved to other Carlsberg breweries in Northern Europe, most important the Fredericia Brewery in western Denmark, now supplying the domestic market with both Carlsberg and Tuborg beers. Carlsberg Group employs over 43,000 people worldwide.

See also DENMARK and TUBORG BREWERY.

Anders Brinch Kissmeyer

carrageenans are extracts of marine algae (seaweeds) used in the brewing of some beers to remove materials that could potentially cause hazes in the finished beers. The carrageenans consist of a family of polymers of polysaccharides found at levels of 2%–7% in red seaweeds. The three main carrageenan-producing seaweeds are Chondrus crispus (commonly known as Irish Moss), Euchema spp., and Gigartina spp. Furcellaran (or Danish agar) is a compound related to carrageenan extracted from the red seaweed, Furcellaria jastigiata. The carrageenans are used in brewing to remove hot- and cold-break proteins from wort and other proteins that would eventually cause hazes in chilled beer. The opposing electrical charges on carrageenans (negative) and wort proteins (positive) lead to interactions that form unstable gels, resulting in the formation of sediments that are separated from the main body of the wort. Carrageenans are natural products and subject, therefore, to biological variability. Consequently, carrageenans are often blended together to produce a consistent product. Carrageenans for use in brewing are described as copper or kettle finings and aid the brewer by reducing wort boiling times (energy saving), reducing "trub" collection time, reducing trub losses, and improving beer stability and filtration performance. See KETTLE FININGS and TRUB.

Irish moss and formulated carrageenans are sometimes used to enhance the effectiveness of fining (clarifying) beer with isinglass. In this situation the carrageenans are known as "auxiliary finings." Because the carrageenans have a similar electrical charge to that of the yeast cells they assist in creating the yeast-isinglass matrix and facilitate a more effective sedimentation process. See ISINGLASS.

Ryder, David S., and Joseph Power. "Miscellaneous ingredients in aid of process." In *Handbook of brewing*, eds. F. G. Priest and G. G. Stewart, 354–355. New York: Taylor and Francis, 2006.

George Philliskirk

Carter, James Earl, Jr (b. 1924) was the 39th President of the United States, serving from 1977 to 1981. A graduate of the United States Naval Academy, he is also a recipient of the Nobel Peace Prize. Beer enthusiasts remain grateful to him for making homebrewing legal in the United States, a development that spurred the modern American craft brewing movement. On October 14, 1978, President Carter signed federal transportation bill H.R 1337 into law. It included Amendment Number 3534, proposed by Senator Alan Cranston of California, authorizing the home production of wine and beer. The practice had grown in popularity in the early 1970s, but a homebrew legalization bill failed to pass the House the year before. With regards to beer, the straightforward language reads as follows:

> "(c) BEER FOR PERSONAL OR FAMILY USE.—Subject to regulations prescribed by the Secretary, any adult may, without payment or tax, produce beer for personal or family use and not for sale. The aggregate amount of beer exempt from tax under this subsection with respect to any household shall not exceed—
>
> 1. 200 gallons per calendar year if there are 2 or more adults in such household, or
> 2. 100 gallons per calendar year if there is only one adult in such household.
>
> For purposes of this subsection, the term 'adult' means an individual who has attained 18 years of age."

Reporting on the news in their journal *Zymurgy*, the American Homebrewers Association noted that H.R. 1337 clarified the definition of the term "brewer" to exclude individuals producing small amounts of beer for personal use. The homebrewing portion of the bill signed by President Carter took effect on February 1, 1979.

The American Presidency Project. *Jimmy Carter: Acts Approved by the President.* http://www.presidency.ucsb.edu/ws/index.php?pid=30022&st=H.R.+1337&st1= /(accessed June 14, 2010).

The Carter Center. *Jimmy Carter—39th President of the United States and Founder of the Carter Center.* http://www.cartercenter.org/news/experts/jimmy_carter.html/ (accessed June 14, 2010).

Congress Passes Homebrew. *Zymurgy*, 1(1): December 1978.

Ogle, Maureen. *Ambitious brew: The story of American beer*. New York: Houghton Mifflin Harcourt, 2006.

Ben Keene

caryophyllene is a bicyclic sesquiterpenoid hydrocarbon and is a constituent of many plant essential oils. Essential oils are the principal aroma components of hop, and constitute 0.5% to 3.0% (v/w) of the whole hop cone; terpenoids are abundant in this fraction. The composition of essential oils is characteristic of the hop genotype and, together with that of bitter acids and flavonoids, has been used for distinguishing different hop varieties. The major terpenoid components of hop essential oil are the monoterpene myrcene, and the sesquiterpenes α-humulene (old name, α-caryophyllene) and β-caryophyllene (often with *iso*-caryophyllene). These hydrocarbons are very volatile and do not survive the boiling process, and so their detectable presence in a finished beer would be due to late-hopping in the kettle, dry-hopping, or addition of a "late hop" extract. Essential oils are also lost during the storage of hop cones.

Sesquiterpenes are built up from a molecule called farnesyl diphosphate (FDP), which after elimination of phosphate yields β-farnesene. This compound, via a variety of complex reactions, produces caryophyllene and other related structures. In the hop, sesquiterpene synthase1 (H1STS1) is responsible for the formation of caryophyllene from β-farnesene. While a precursor, β-farnesene itself is not found in all hop varieties. The essential oil fraction in hops can be isolated by steam distillation, where they can be analyzed by a variety of methods, including gas chromatography. The in vitro synthesis of β-caryophyllene was achieved in the 1960s.

β-Caryophyllene is also a main flavor constituent of black pepper, which was used as a beer adulterant in bygone years; it produced "heat" on the palate that the buyer was meant to mistake for alcoholic strength.

Cane, D. E., ed. *Comprehensive natural products chemistry isoprenoid biosynthesis*. Oxford, England: Pergamon Press, 1998.

Connolly, J. D., and Hill, R. A. *Dictionary of the terpenoids*. London: Chapman & Hall, 1991.

Hough, J. S., Briggs, D. E., Stevens, R., and Young, T. W. *Malting and brewing science, vol. 2: Hopped wort and beer*, 2nd ed. London: Chapman & Hall, 1982.

Neve, R. A. *Hops*. London: Chapman & Hall, 1991.

Ian Hornsey

Cascade (hop), a US-bred aroma hop that is particularly popular with the craft brewing industry in the United States. While it remains popular, it was once so prevalent that it virtually defined the flavor of American microbrewed beer. Cascade was developed by the United States Department of Agriculture's (USDA) hop breeding program in Corvallis, Oregon, and released in 1971. It was the first US-bred aroma hop from this program.

Cascade has low to moderate alpha-acids (4.5%–7.0% w/w) and mid-range oil content (0.7–1.4 ml/100 g). It arose from an open pollinated hop seed collection in 1956, and its parentage includes the English Fuggle, the Russian Serebrianka, and an unknown male. It was originally thought to be similar to the imported German aroma hop Hallertauer mittelfrueh. Its alpha/beta ratio is similar to that German hop, but other quality factors (mainly cohumulone and oil composition) are quite different. Cascade is resistant to powdery mildew and downy mildew, especially in the crown (rootstock), but moderately susceptible in the cone and leaf stage. It matures medium early to medium late and is adapted to both Washington and Oregon, but the major acreage is mostly grown in Washington (total US Cascade production in 2009: 2171 acres, 4.55 million lb, representing 4.8% of total US hop production). Cascade has excellent yield potential, but poor storage stability. Therefore, baled hops of Cascade should be allowed to cool after baling before being placed into refrigerated storage. As a common garden plant for many beer enthusiasts, it is a particularly fast-growing, hardy variety. Cascade aromatics can be described as floral and citrusy, with notes of grapefruit and pine needles.

Thomas Shellhammer and Alfred Haunold

A **cask** is a barrel-shape container used for the production, storage, and service of cask-conditioned beer, widely called "real ale" in the UK. The shape of the cask, longer than it is wide and bulging along its length, evolved more than 2,000 years ago for ease of its manufacture out of wood. It is also a relatively easy vessel to handle manually because even large, heavy casks can be rolled on their sides.

Traditionally casks were made of wood, and these remained common until the mid-20th century. Today most casks are made from stainless steel, but they are also made from aluminum and plastic. Wood casks were strong but they were also heavy, hard to clean, and nearly impossible to sterilize. Unlike a modern keg, the cask has no dispense valves or interior tubes. Instead, the cask has a 2-in. round opening along the belly, through which the cask is filled. Along the rim of one of the cask's circular faces is a smaller round opening through which beer is dispensed. After filling, a plastic or wooden stopper called a shive is driven into the large bunghole on the belly, and a smaller one called a keystone is driven into the tap hole.

The center of the keystone is deliberately weakened, allowing the tap to be driven through it at the pub with a mallet. The center of the shive also has a hole, which is thinly sealed—a hard wooden peg is driven through this. During dispense, air or unpressurized carbon dioxide will enter through this hole, which is also used for regulation of the beer's condition (CO_2 level). See CELLARMANSHIP, ART OF. When set up for service, the cask is "stillaged" (set firmly in place), and the beer's yeast, often aided by finings, will sediment out to the bottom belly of the cask, leaving the dispensed beer perfectly clear.

The grade of stainless steel used for casks is important so as to avoid corrosion. Plastic casks are often made of a laminate of materials and must be impervious to air and impart no flavor to the beer. Aluminum, which cannot be cleaned with alkaline cleaning solutions, is no longer used to make casks, although some aluminum casks remain in service in the UK.

Within the brewing trade there is a family of cask sizes, each with a different name and with volumes that are multiples of each other. The most common size is the firkin, which contains a volume of 9 Imperial (UK) gal, which adds up to 72 Imperial pints, a quarter of a UK beer barrel, or 40.9 l. Other sizes, now rarely seen, are the kilderkin at twice the size of the firkin, the barrel at four times the size, and the hogshead at six times the size.

Hankerson, Fred. *The cooperage handbook*. New York: Chemical Publishing Co, 1947.
Lindsay, William. *Cooperage*. Edinburgh, Scotland: W. M. Lindsay & Son, 1938.
Lloyd, John, ed. *Brewing room book*, 83rd ed. Ipswich, England: Pauls Malt Ltd, 1992.

Chris J. Marchbanks

A **cask breather,** sometimes called an "aspirator," is a demand valve used in conjunction with a beer engine and a carbon dioxide tank for the dispense of cask-conditioned beers. It allows beer drawn from the cask to be replaced with the equivalent amount of sterile gas at atmospheric pressure. See BEER ENGINE. This is a nontraditional and thus controversial method of dispensing cask-conditioned ale because some purists, including the British

Campaign for Real Ale (CAMRA), take the position that the only proper way to pour cask ale is to allow ambient air, not gas, to enter the cask as the beer engine empties it. Such air, of course, not only contains oxygen, which can cause the beer to become stale fairly quickly, but also harbors airborne bacteria, such as acetobacter and lactobacillus, which may quickly have deleterious effects, especially in the presence of oxygen. CAMRA argues that oxygen can actually improve a cask ale's flavors over the very limited number of hours that it is servable after the cask has been broached. They also argue that the use of the cask breather allows ingress of CO_2 into the beer, changing flavor and texture, and that the device is the "thin edge of the wedge," a "crutch" that will ease the way for various other changes to cask beer service. Extensive taste testing has failed to demonstrate that the cask breather has any effect other than to extend the service life of a broached cask by an extra day or two, which is sometimes critical to the trade of smaller, quieter pubs, especially in the countryside. The debate rages on, but CAMRA continues its policy of delisting from its influential yearly *Good Beer Guide* any pub where the cask breather is in use.

CAMRA. *Campaign for Real Ale.* http://www.camra.org.uk/ (accessed November 20, 2010).

Brian Hunt

cask conditioning is the process in which a draught beer retains yeast to enable a secondary fermentation to take place in a cask in the pub cellar. Cask conditioned beer is the traditional drink of the British pub, and served properly, it can be among the most subtle and beguiling of beer types. Beer that is cask conditioned is neither filtered nor pasteurized and is often called cask ale, real ale, or in Britain, traditional ale.

Conditioning is a complex business and the term covers the chemical, biological, and physical changes occurring from when the beer leaves the fermenting vessel in the brewery and is racked into a cask, up to the time that it is dispensed by one of several methods from the cask into a glass ready to be served to the drinker. Achieving the correct "condition" for cask conditioned beers is a skilled job usually performed by the publican or the cellarman. They are often the same person. See CELLARMANSHIP, ART OF.

Most of this activity takes place in the pub cellar and while many breweries transfer beer from fermenting vessels into racking tanks and from there into casks, some also use maturation tanks where the gentle process of secondary fermentation commences. Regardless of which method is used, maturation continues in the cellar. Some beers have a small amount of sugar solution, called primings, added to produce natural carbonation and help create the beer's foam. The residual yeast that is left in the beer after it is transferred to the cask will continue changing the sugars into alcohol and produce carbon dioxide. The process usually reduces the final gravity and this causes a slight increase, say 0.1% ABV, in alcoholic strength. The cask must be vented during conditioning by using a soft spile that allows excess gas to escape. Contrary to much foreign opinion, cask conditioned beer should never be flat. A certain amount of carbon dioxide must be retained in the beer to give it liveliness on the palate; this is the "condition" sought by the cellarman, and without it the beer can become flat and lifeless. The flavor of the beer is materially affected by the secondary fermentation.

The period of conditioning will vary according to the style, strength, and brand of the beer and it is usual for breweries to advise publicans as to what conditioning period is recommended and at what temperature. It can vary widely, between 24 hours and 16 days, and the usual temperature should be 13°C–14°C (55°F–57°F). The beer goes through a stage of "dropping bright," the settling of the yeast and proteins to the bottom of the cask, leaving the beer perfectly clear. This task is accomplished by adding finings to the beer that bind the sediment and carry it to the bottom of the cask. Finings are made, improbably, from isinglass, the swim bladders of sturgeon. Isinglass has been processed so as to do its job without adding any flavors to the beer.

Other changes take place during the maturation period in the cask. The beer can attain flavors from dry hops that may be added at the cask-filling stage mainly for aroma. Strong beers require long periods of maturation and the casks are often stored in the brewery for weeks or months before being released into trade.

The method of dispensing beer from the cask into the glass can vary and sometimes reflects regional tastes. The most common way to serve cask conditioned beer is by the use of a beer engine, a hand-operated hydraulic pump, that draws beer from a cask in the cellar up to the bar. It is commonly called a hand-pull or a hand-pump. The requirement for a head on beer is certain, but the size or density of the foam desired depends on geography. In Yorkshire a tight creamy head is required; in Teeside and the northeast it should be large and loose; and in most of the rest of England and Wales a narrow "string of beads" head satisfies. Electric metered and free-flow systems have lost their popularity and never produced the Yorkshire head. In Scotland air pressure dispense was once predominant but is gradually being taken over by the beer engine. This leaves the age old system of "gravity dispense" where the beer runs from the cask through a tap directly into either a glass or a jug. See GRAVITY DISPENSE. The inconvenience of this system is obvious but some publicans prefer its traditional aspect; the cask can literally be set directly on the bar, kept cool by a refrigerant blanket.

Clissold, Ivor. *Cellarmanship*. St Albans, England: CAMRA Books, 1997.

Barrie Pepper

Cask Marque is a quality control and accreditation organization operated in the UK by an independent, nonprofit body called the Cask Marque Trust (CMT). The mission of the CMT is to maintain the standards of cask-conditioned beer poured in pubs and then reward accredited licensees with a plaque and other promotional material. The CMT logo consists of a silhouetted beer engine and the slogan "A sign of a great pint." CMT was founded in the late 1990s, at a time when the quality of cask-conditioned beer was in decline in Britain. At the time, the CMT estimated that one in five pints was served at an improper temperature. A research team from four leading British breweries—Adnams, Marston's, Morland, and Greene King—determined that the diminishing quality of the British pub experience was largely the result of the then-new wave of nitrogenated beers. Subsequently, a CMT team of 45 brewing industry and quality control professionals conducted unannounced inspections of cask-conditioned beers in pubs that subscribed to the CMT program. By the end of 2010, some 6,750 pubs had been accredited nationally. To start the accreditation process, a pub owner must first apply and pay a nominal fee. The applicant premises are inspected, once in each of two consecutive months. Once accredited, the pub is then inspected twice a year, once in the winter and once in the summer, for compliance with the CMT temperature, appearance, taste, and freshness standards during both the warm and the cool season. The CMT requires that cask beers must be between 10°C and 14°C (50°F and 57°F) in the glass and have the clarity, aroma, and flavor characteristics of the brand that is being poured. They may be served at a lower temperature only if the brewery designed the beer to be poured below the CMT temperature specifications. Lists of CMT-accredited pubs can be located on the Web. The organization has evolved from its roots and now sometimes audits the quality of noncask draught beers as well.

Cask Marque Trust. *Cask Marque*. http://www.cask-marque.co.uk/ (accessed October 12, 2010).
Cask Marque Trust. *The Cask Report*. http://www.caskreport.co.uk/ (accessed October 12, 2010).

Alex Hall

cassava

See MANIOC.

Catherine the Great (Catherine II) reigned as Empress of Russia from July 1762 until her death in November 1796, and it is generally recognized that she was responsible for a revitalizing period of modernization in that country. She oversaw an expansion of the Russian Empire (adding around 200,000 square miles), and during her reign Russia became one of the great powers of Europe. She assumed power after a conspiracy deposed her husband, Peter III. Perhaps Catherine's greatest feat was to enact measures that enabled Russia to be governed more efficiently, and these resulted in the country being divided into provinces and districts.

Catherine agreed to a commercial treaty with Britain in 1766, although she was wary about British military power. One rather unusual outcome of her contact with Britain was her reported predilection for London stout. Henry Thrale's Anchor Brewery in Southwark brewed such a drink, which was exported to the Russian Court from the 1780s onward, arriving via Danzig and the Baltic States. This was a very strong "export stout" with an original gravity of approximately 25 degrees Plato and probably reached nearly 12% ABV. By 1781 Thrale had sold his brewery to his brewing supervisor, John Perkins, and a member of the Barclay banking family. The drink acquired the soubriquet "Barclay Perkins Imperial Brown Stout." When Barclays merged with John Courage in 1955, the beer was rebranded "Courage Imperial Russian Stout," and this beer was brewed in London (where it was matured in oak casks for one year prior to bottling) until closure of the site in 1981. See COURAGE BREWERY. The beer continued to be brewed at other sites until 1993. Though this type of strong stout is now generally known simply as "imperial" stout, the imprimatur began with Catherine the Great, and until recent decades the style was widely known as "Russian Imperial Stout." Today many craft brewers will append the word "imperial" to any beer showing unusual strength, regardless of whether the beer ever actually boasted connections to any crown.

Alexander, J. T. *Catherine the Great: Life and legend.* Oxford, England: Oxford University Press, 1988.
Dixon, S. *Catherine the Great.* Harlow, England: Longman, 2001.
Matthias, P. *The brewing industry in England, 1700–1830.* Cambridge: Cambridge University Press, 1959.
Rounding, V. *Catherine the Great: Love, sex, and power.* New York: St. Martin's Press, 2007.

Ian Hornsey

cauliflower stage of yeast growth occurs when the first yeast head arises from the fermenting wort, particularly in top fermenting beers.

"Cauliflower foam" is named after the appearance of the vegetable and is characterized by a thin, loose appearance. The foam rises high up out of the wort and is typically found after the first 12 hours of fermentation. At this point the yeast will be very active and producing large amounts of carbon dioxide. Large bubbles will be formed and as the surface layer of yeast will be relatively thin, these bubbles will be quite buoyant. Dark trub, made mostly of protein, will also be present in the early head and will provide further stability to the bubbles that rise up into the fermenter headspace, producing a craggy foam.

Cauliflower heads are an important indicator that a fermentation is well under way and should be present within 24 hours of the onset of fermentation. In many breweries the cauliflower head is removed because it is likely to contain dead yeast cells carried over from the previous brew. It is undesirable for these cells to return to the wort where they can release unwanted flavors. An early skimming of these yeasts and of the residual trub is advised in order to obtain a cleaner-tasting beer.

Keith Thomas

CDC Copeland (barley) is a two-rowed malting barley developed at the University of Saskatchewan by Dr Bryan Harvey and Dr Brian Rossnagel. It was registered for sale in Canada in 1999. The variety was named after William Copeland, a farmer in the Elrose area of Saskatchewan in recognition of his support of the barley program. The variety is particularly adapted to that area of the province of Saskatchewan. CDC Copeland was derived from the cross WM861-5/TR118. At the time of its registration CDC Copeland outyielded Harrington by 16% overall and as much as 26% in some regions of western Canada. It is taller but has stronger straw than Harrington. It has larger, plumper kernels than Harrington and better net blotch and stem rust resistance. It is slightly less prone to pre-harvest sprouting. CDC Copeland has higher extract and friability than Harrington and much lower malt beta glucan. Its diastatic power is slightly lower than Harrington but still suitable for high adjunct brewing. This variety has a mild flavor profile and a produces a pale beer color favored by the Chinese market. CDC Copeland is a good blending variety and favored by several large breweries. It is a favorite of farmers and is widely grown in western Canada.

Bryan Harvey

CDC Kendall (barley) is a two-rowed malting barley developed at the University of Saskatchewan. It was derived from the cross Manley/SM85221. It was initially registered, in 1995, for sale in Canada under the name "CDC Lager." There was concern, however, with this name in the Japanese market where the word "Lager" is associated with one brewer, leading to a fear that it would not be purchased by the other Japanese brewers. In order to change the name the University of Saskatchewan successfully took the Commissioner of Plant Breeders Rights to Federal Court and won the case. CDC Kendall was intended as a replacement for Harrington. At the time of its release it showed a 6% yield advantage over Harrington, stronger straw, similar maturity, denser kernels, and greater plumpness. It had better root rot, net blotch, and stem rust resistance. Malting quality of CDC Kendall is superior to that of Harrington in a number of parameters. It has consistently heavier, plumper kernels, higher extract and a lower fine/course difference, higher diastatic power and alpha amylase activity, and much lower beta glucan content (typically less than 50%). This was one of the varieties that started the downward trend in beta glucan content in Canadian malting barley. CDC Kendall is widely grown but acreage is limited because it is grown primarily under contract.

Bryan Harvey

Celis, Pierre, born in 1925, is a Belgian brewer best known for single-handedly reviving the white beer, or witbier, style a decade after its production had ceased.

White beer is an unfiltered wheat ale flavored with coriander and orange peel. Monks in Hoegaarden, a small town east of Brussels in Flemish Brabant, are credited with developing the style centuries ago. For many years, white beer was a specialty of Hoegaarden, but its popularity dwindled following the introduction of lager beers. In 1957, Hoegaarden's last white beer brewery, Brouwerij Tomsin, stopped production.

In the 1960s, Celis was working as a milkman in Hoegaarden. He had once lived next to the Tomsin brewery, had worked there part time, and was familiar with the methods used to create this unique beer. In 1966, he pieced together a brewery, Brouwerij Celis (later renamed De Kluis), and began producing his white beer, named after his town, Hoegaarden.

The beer was well received and production increased steadily. In 1985, however, the brewery suffered a devastating fire. Funds to rebuild came from brewing giant Interbrew (now Anheuser-Busch InBev), who purchased the business outright in 1990.

Celis then turned his attention to the United States, where he founded the Celis Brewery in Austin, Texas, in 1992. There, he produced a white beer called Celis White and several other styles. Despite the high quality of the beer, the company struggled financially. In 1995, Miller Brewing Company (now MillerCoors) acquired a majority stake in the company. Miller closed the brewery in 2001 and sold the Celis brands to the Michigan Brewing Company. In 1999, Celis began licensed production of a Pierre Celis Signature Series of beers, featuring beers under the Grottenbier (Cave Beer) umbrella; early editions of these beers were aged in caves at Riemst.

In 2005, Celis published an autobiography with writer Raymond Billen, entitled *Brouwers Verkopen Plezier—Peter Celis, My Life*. In 2010, Celis turned 85 years old. He lives in Hoegaarden and is no longer active in brewing. He still occasionally attends brewing conferences, where he is instantly recognized and treated like a rock star.

See also INBEV.

Jackson, Michael. *Europe's stylish summer whites.* http://www.beerhunter.com/documents/19133-000113.html/ (accessed November 23, 2011).

Protz, Roger. *Think global, close local.* http://www.beer-pages.com/protz/features/hoegaarden.htm/ (accessed November 23, 2011).

White, John. *Pierre Celis, from Hoegaarden The King of White Beer.* http://www.whitebeertravels.co.uk/celis.html/ (accessed November 23, 2011).

Dan Rabin

cellar beer

See KELLERBIER.

cellarmanship, art of, in the broadest sense, covers the gamut of drinks sold by retail outlets and requires a detailed technical manual. The purpose here, however, is to set out the general principles for the successful management of cask-conditioned ales.

An avaricious brewer may define cellarmanship as the art of serving a continuous supply of saleable beer with the least financial loss. Here, compromises will be made on quality to fulfill the primary requirement of profit maximization.

The cellar of the Pinkus Müller Brewery in Münster, Germany, 1935. COURTESY OF PINKUS MÜLLER

The art of cellarmanship is the successful blend of the aesthetic and the practical, the pursuit of the perfectly matured and carbonated beer and its most stylish dispense. The Anchor at Walbersic website mentions that the goal is

> to promote the most beauty in each cask of beer by developing the most interesting range of sound aromas and flavours; by nurturing wherever possible high levels of natural carbonation consistent with each beer style and, moreover, by serving each beer in a manner and at a temperature that enhances its aroma and flavour profile and creates an appropriate mouthfeel.

The above must follow the disciplines of good husbandry, continuity of supply, and speedy turnover to keep the beer in each broached cask as fresh as possible.

The Techniques of Cellarmanship

Setting a Stillage

The cellarman's first order of business is to secure the cask. A "stillage" is the name given to any solid object that enables a cask of beer to be laid down and prevented from moving. This often involves the insertion of wooden wedges (also known as scotches or chocks) under the cask. It is important that casks be set horizontally with the shive pointing straight at the ceiling. If a cask is stillaged with a forward tilt, sediment will fall to the front of the cask and be concentrated at the tap, leading to fouling of the tap and the need to draw off three or four pints of beer before the clarity and quality of the cask's contents can be judged accurately. If the cask is tilted backward, problems of unstable yeast and finings slurry slipping forward may arise when the cask is tilted to decant the final few gallons. To forestall such problems, individual self-tilting metal sprung stillages are becoming the norm in British cellars.

Conditioning

The purpose of conditioning is to reduce the level of carbon dioxide in the cask, to enable a good finings action to occur, and then to build up the level of carbonation appropriate to the style of beer.

Venting excess CO_2 is achieved by inserting/hammering a porous peg ("soft peg" made of soft wood, usually bamboo cane) into the sealed shive tut, causing a sudden escape of gas and the immediate emergence of fobbing beer. This procedure should be carried out in a controlled way (i.e., the contents of each cask should be chilled to 52°F to 55°F so a relatively calm and nonexplosive purging of excess CO_2 can take place. See SHIVE and SPILE.

It is also important that upon soft spiling, the cask should have an even distribution of finings and yeast. It is sensible to roll each cask vigorously before stillaging, securing, and venting. The time taken for the beer to "work" through the soft peg will vary according to each yeast strain, the concentration of yeast cells per milliliter, and the yeast's general friskiness, along with the amount of residual sugar/primings in the cask and the temperature/state of agitation of the cask. In the case of exceptionally lively beers, it may be necessary to replace the soft peg every hour for a day or more. The pegs sometimes become blocked with yeast and occasionally a plug of dry hops may form underneath the soft peg, preventing the release of gas.

The rule on the amount of time to soft peg beer is that there is no rule. It is entirely dependent upon the yeast fining regime adopted. The object of soft pegging is to reduce the amount of CO_2 to the point at which the finings will prove effective.

But it is important that the cellarman does not overvent the cask. He is preparing the yeast for a marathon journey, not a short sprint, hence the need to vent at low temperatures and avoid exhausting the supply of sugars. The tension to be observed is the need to produce clear beer and the imperative to stimulate good to high levels of CO_2 in solution.

Unfortunately, relatively flat, clear beer has become the norm in Britain. Lazy cellarmen drink with their eyes and then "jazz up" flat beer by forcing it through a tight sparkler. This is not how cask beer is properly served.

Hard pegging should occur when a cask has "worked" to the point where it takes 3 to 10 s for the fob to reform on top of the soft spile after being wiped clean, again depending upon the style and strength of the beer, the yeast/finings regime, and when the beer is required for dispense. The soft peg should be replaced with a nonporous hard spile to prevent the escape of any more CO_2 and to slow down yeast activity.

"Dropping bright" (full settling of the yeast) will now occur and is greatly assisted by a rising temperature. Again, it is a matter of trial and error with the yeast strains used, but research has shown that taking the ambient cellar temperature from 52°F to 54°F up to 58°F to 60°F for about 8 to 12 h produces consistently bright, polished results across the range of ale yeasts used in Britain today. The time needed for a cask to drop bright can vary from 4 h to 4 to 5 days.

Carbonating should now take place after a spell of warm conditioning at 58°F to 60°F. It is important to chill back down to 52°F to 55°F depending on the temperature that the yeast is happy with. The lower the temperature tolerated by the yeast, the greater the level of carbonation possible.

Bass' yeast remains one of the liveliest and most tolerant yeast strains in Britain and will work happily at 50°F. After a 4-week maturation period in the cellar at 50°F to 52°F, the beer has the most glorious, mouth-caressing effervescence that one could wish for.

Maturation

This part of the process of cellaring beers, sadly, is seldom given much attention in practice. However, aging beers not only allows the appropriate level of carbonation to be generated but also allows the beer to dry out the effects of krausen or priming additions, thus taking away any insipid qualities from the palate of the beer. The fresh kiss of yeast, the hallmark of cask-conditioned ale or unfiltered lager, develops further impact and complexity during the process of maturation, be it in a lagering tank or in a cask. Aging also enables the effects of dry hopping to achieve maximum impact after 2 weeks or more in cask, developing its own particular grace and delicacy of aroma.

For beers such as low-gravity dark milds, one would expect to put the beer on dispense in the shortest time possible, perhaps only 4 or 5 days after racking, to promote the slightly sweet, fresh malt character of this supremely quaffable style. See MILD. Ordinary British bitters of 1,040 original gravity (og; 10°P) are cellared ideally for a minimum of 2 weeks to extract the succulent malt characteristics and earthy hop flavors, but stop before the yeast imprint becomes dominant. A period of 2 weeks also fosters the buildup of good levels of carbonation to provide the complementary mouthfeel so sought after.

Traditionally, draught bass was kept for 3 to 4 weeks and old ales have been cellared successfully from 2 months in the cases of lower gravity old ales such as Highgate Old (1,055 og, 13.7°P) or Theakstons Old Peculier (1,057 og, 13.8°P) and for a year or more for Traquair house ale and Adnam's

Tally-Ho (1,075 og, 18.75°P). See BASS & COMPANY, THEAKSTONS, and TRAQUAIR HOUSE BREWERY.

Essential Points for Perfect Dispense

The serving temperature is ideally 50°F to 55°F (10°C–12.7°C), depending upon the style of beer and the ambient temperature. A good cellarman will not excessively chill a rich, biscuity, malty Scotch ale or an ester-laden, vinous barley wine. Therefore, he will pay attention to insulated beer lines (and beer engines) that transport beer from the cellar or chill cabinet to the customers' glass. See BEER ENGINE.

Proper dispense of cask beer involves either tap-fed gravity dispense or beer engines. When the cellarman uses beer engines, he will decide which beers benefit from the use of sparkler attachments to produce a tight, creamy head. Stouts and dark milds can be enhanced by the use of sparklers, but the cellarman will think carefully and experiment before connecting a carefully crafted India pale ale to a sparkler that may blast all the resiny hop oils from the pint.

Each cask broached and put on dispense should be consumed as quickly as possible, ideally within 24 to 48 h unless a cask breather is used. It is a question not only of oxidation and possible acetification setting in, but also of the loss of CO_2. In all but the most carefully prepared casks, such loss will result in a notable loss of freshness and vitality, which matter a great deal to the quality of the beer at hand.

For those preparing pale ales for cask-conditioned dispense, the following quote from the head brewer of Marston's in 1899 provides a rare insight into his perception of quality and indicates just how far brewing techniques had advanced from the 16th century as discussed on The Anchor at Walbersic website:

> An ideal glass of ale should evidence stability, "star" brilliancy, absence of deposit or floating particles, a foaming, tenacious, creamy head, with beads of carbonic acid gas adhering to the sides of the glass; the ale when first poured out being as cloudy as milk, subsequently slowly clearing as the gas in solution rises to the surface of the liquid, forming the close head already mentioned, the flavour also being that suited for the district where it is to be consumed.

See also MARSTON'S BREWERY.

Cellarmanship & Real Ale. http://www.anchoratwalberswick.com/ (accessed April 12, 2011).

Mark Dorber

Central Asia. Its borders are softly defined, but its five primary countries are Kazakhstan, Kyrgyzstan, Turkmenistan, Tajikstan, and Uzbekistan. The region's borders are China to the east, Russia to the north, the Caspian Sea to the west, and Afghanistan to the south. All five nations were former states of the Soviet Union and regained their independence during its collapse in 1991. Since then, all five countries have struggled to find prosperity and stability, with varying results.

Although the inhabitants of the five nations of Central Asia primarily practice Islam, which observes the ruling of the Quran against alcohol in all forms, many locals drink alcohol regularly. While vodka, introduced by the Russians, is the drink of choice, beer is currently gaining in popularity. Favored beers are generally imported from Russian and Europe. Popular beers in the region are St. Petersburg's Baltika, and on-tap favorites are Tian-Shansky and Shimkent from Kazakhstan and Siberian Crown from Russia.

Kyrgyzstan is currently undergoing a significant beer revival. The country's National Statistics Committee reported in early 2010 that one sixth of the country's adults drink beer regularly. The first brewery in Kyrgyzstan opened in Kara-Kol in the 1800s. By the beginning of the 20th century, five breweries were producing beer. During Soviet times, Osh, Kara-Balta, Talas, and Kochkor all had breweries. But during an anti-alcohol campaign of the 1980s production was cut and people moved toward alcohol in other forms.

Currently two major breweries are producing beer in Kyrgyzstan—Abdysh-Ata and Arpa, which together produce more than 90% of the country's beer. Most of it is consumed locally, with small percentages exported to Russia and Kazakhstan.

Beer is primarily sold in cafes and beer stands, although in the city of Bishkek, there are six beer pubs and two breweries, Steinbrau and Blonder Pub.

Central Asia Online. *Beer drinking undergoes resurgence in Kyrgyzstan*. http://www.centralasiaonline.com/cocoon/caii/xhtml/en_GB/features/caii/features/entertainment/2010/04/02/feature-02/ (accessed November 28, 2010).

Lonely Planet Central Asia guide. Victoria, Australia: Lonely Planet, 2007.

National Geographic. *National Geographic Online Guide to Asia*. http://travel.nationalgeographic.com/travel/continents/asia/ (accessed November 28, 2010).

Radio Free Europe Radio Liberty. *Central Asia: Culture Shift Sends Beer's Popularity Soaring.* http://www.rferl.org/content/article/1067941.html/ (accessed November 28, 2010).

April Darcy

centrifugation is the application of radial forces upon an object by moving it in a circle. The object can be gaseous, liquid, or solid. The centrifugal forces increase with an object's density. They also increase with the speed with which the object moves in a circle. The radial force pushes objects toward the outer border of the circle being transited, just as we feel ourselves pressed to the door of a car as it rounds a tight curve.

In a brewery centrifuge, which may also be called a separator or a decanter, these same principles are applied to a liquid—wort or beer. The liquid is laden with various types of suspended particulate, including yeast, trub, and hop residue, each with a different density. When a centrifuge spins the liquid within a round chamber, at a given rotation speed, eventually the heavier components of the liquid, notably trub and yeast, because they experience greater centrifugal forces, will move closer to the chamber's outer wall. Meanwhile, the lightest components, including water and alcohol, will stay closer to the center axis of the rotation chamber. This type of separation is aided further by the fact that the circumference of the circle traveled by the liquid closest to the center is much smaller than the one traveled by the particles along the outer wall. This even further reinforces the separation of particles in the liquid according to their density. In terms of physics, the power of the centrifugal forces is governed by an equation called Stokes' law, and centrifuges in a brewery are constructed to generate truly enormous rotational forces that may be several thousand times the size of the earth's gravitational forces. See STOKES' LAW. Such devices also allow for the draining of the clear, separated liquid from the rotation chamber, while leaving behind the layers of particulate along the wall of the chamber. This is the principle of a functioning centrifuge in practice. Centrifuges in the brewery are employed in several ways. A wort centrifuge can separate hot trub from clear wort even more efficiently than a whirlpool, which is actually a type of low-tech centrifuge. See WHIRLPOOL. A beer centrifuge employed before packaging can reduce the beer's turbidity by separating many or most of the yeast cells from the clear beer. This is particularly useful if the beer is to be packaged unfiltered, but the yeast does not flocculate sufficiently to the bottom of the fermenter. It is possible to link the centrifuge to an optical sensor that measures the turbidity of the beer; properly used, this setup can be used to adjust haze or yeast cell counts in the final package. Likewise, a centrifuge can remove some of the yeast between the end of primary fermentation and the beginning of secondary fermentation or before lagering. If the brewery uses fining agents, these, too, can be removed via centrifuge. See FININGS and KETTLE FININGS. Another favorite location for the use of centrifuges is right before an in-line filter. See FILTRATION. Because the centrifuge removes the bulk of the particulate, the filter medium can perform its function for much longer intervals before it needs to be serviced. A completely different purpose of a centrifuge is beer reclamation. When excess or spent yeast slurry is purged out of the bottom of a fermenter, the liquid part of the slurry is of course perfectly drinkable beer. Some breweries consider it worthwhile to centrifuge the slurry and introduce the reclaimed beer back into the beer flow. Finally, beer can be centrifuged to remove any residual cold break right before packaging. This eliminates, among other substances, some of the protein-type of materials that are directly and indirectly involved in haze formation as well as beer oxidation. See COLLOIDAL HAZE and OXIDATION.

The centrifuge is a useful piece of equipment for a brewery, but they are expensive. As a result, it is unusual to see a centrifuge in a brewery producing much less than 118,000 hl (100,000 US barrels) per year.

Paul H. Chlup

A **cereal cooker** is a brewhouse vessel that enables brewers to use unmalted cereals such as corn (maize) or rice as part of their recipe as well as malted barley. The proportion of rice or maize may vary depending on the beer and normally makes up 20%–30% of the grist. The cereal cooker is very much like a mash mixer; it contains mixing paddles and is heated, usually by steam panels. The raw cereal is added to water to create a porridge, which is then boiled. This boiling gelatinizes the raw starches, making them susceptible to breakdown by malt enzymes in the main mash. After gelatinization, the "cooker mash" will be added to the main barley mash, where barley malt enzymes will break down both malt starches and adjunct starches into sugars. Cereal cookers are generally found only in large breweries that regularly produce beers from mashes with high proportions of raw cereal adjuncts.

See also ADJUNCTS, CORN, and RICE.

Paul KA Buttrick

cereals, grains, or cereal grains are the seed products of grasses (members of the monocotyledonous families Poaceae or Gramineae) that are widely cultivated globally. The word "cereal" is derived from Ceres, the name of the Roman goddess of harvest and agriculture. The major cereal crops in order of annual production (average 2005–2007, FAO) are maize (733 MT), rice (642 MT), wheat (611 MT), barley (138 MT), sorghum (61 MT), millet (32 MT), oats (24 MT), rye (14.6 MT), triticale (12.5 MT), and fonio (0.38 MT).

The general morphology of a cereal grain consists of the husk (present in barley, absent from wheat) that covers the pericarp layer, beneath which is the aleurone layer, the embryo and the endosperm. See ALEURONE LAYER, ENDOSPERM MODIFICATION, and PERICARP. It is from the embryo that the roots and cotyledon of the barley plant would emerge if the barley seed were planted in the field. The husk and pericarp (to a lesser extent) protect the growing embryo during malting so as to enable easy handling during the malting process. The husk is utilized during lautering to form a filter bed to enable efficient wort separation. The role of the endosperm is to provide a source of nutrients and energy that are released by hydrolytic enzymes. In the mature barley grain the endosperm cells are essentially large sacs of starch granules and are not living. The hydrolytic enzymes are secreted initially by the scutellum and then more substantially by the aleurone layer, the outermost layer of endosperm cells that are living. The scutellum is a thin layer (from the Latin *scutella* meaning "small shield") that also acts as nutrient-absorbing cells for the embryo.

Whole cereal grains are a rich source of vitamins, minerals, carbohydrates, fats and oils, and protein. A distinguishing characteristic of cereal grains is their energy storage component, starch, which makes up around 60% of grain weight in barley. See STARCH. It is the degradation of this starch during brewing, by the diastase enzymes (α-amylase, β-amylase, limit dextrinase, and α-glucosidase), that produces sugars that are converted by yeast into alcohol to make beer. The aleurone layer and initially the scutellum are the source tissues for many of the hydrolytic enzymes produced during germination. A notable exception is β-amylase, which is synthesized and accumulated in the grain before harvest.

Cereals can be used for brewing beer either after being malted or as unmalted starch adjunct. There are a number of reasons why malted barley is the cereal of choice for brewing beer. First, barley, after malting, has an optimal balance of enzymes to hydrolyze its polymers (i.e., starch and protein, cell-wall polysaccharide) and those from adjuncts into lower molecular weight substances (i.e., maltose, glucose, amino acids, etc.) assimilatable by yeast. Like other members of the tribe Triticeae (which includes wheat and rye), barley has very high levels of β-amylase (up to 2% of total protein) that assist with the production of wort with very high levels of the sugar maltose. Barley malt also produces cell-wall-degrading enzymes such as β-glucanase and xylanases that efficiently hydrolyze non-starch polysaccharides into smaller moieties that do not hinder brewing solid-liquid separation processes (e.g., lautering and beer filtration) and prevent the formation of undesirable hazes in beer that are related to these components. Malt also contains proteases that hydrolyze proteins into amino acids for yeast nutrition, as well as releasing and modifying other proteins so they can fulfil their enzymatic roles or fully enable their participation in the foam formation. Finally, the above combination of enzymatic processes along with the kilning regime produces a number of the desirable malty flavors and aromas typically associated with beer.

Cereals other than barley are widely used for making beer, but they are typically used in combination with barley malt, either in malted form or as a starch providing unmalted adjunct. Wheat, both malted and unmalted, is a frequently used adjunct. Wheat malt comprises approximately 50% of the grist bill in beer styles such as German Weizens; Belgian Wit or white beers use unmalted wheat. As well as impacting the flavor of these beers, the wheat also imparts the characteristic fine white protein haze that is expected in many of these beers. The addition of wheat, either as malt or unmalted adjunct, also has the reputation for improving foam stability, but this conclusion is questionable and may be based on the generally higher protein contents of wheat grain rather than any specific foam-promoting component contained in wheat. Other cereals widely used for beer production are maize (corn) and rice, which are extensively used in Asia and America. The use of rice adjunct in particular imparts a lighter color and more delicate flavor to the beers produced with it. See CORN and RICE.

In the last decade or so, it has been recognized that barley, like wheat, contains the gluten-like protein segments that aggravate the celiac condition in what is estimated to be up to 1% of the world's population. To provide beer to celiac suffers, brewers have investigated the use of grists that do not contain any barley malt. This has focused attention on malting and brewing with the non-Triticeae cereals such as sorghum and millet and pseudo-cereals such as buckwheat. Although the brewing process is not as efficient as when using barley malt, acceptable commercial beers that are celiac-friendly are now increasingly becoming available. See GLUTEN-FREE BEER.

Evan Evans

České Budějovice in the South Bohemi region of the Czech Republic has had a long association with brewing. It was founded in 1265 by Ottakar II of Bohemia and became a Royal City, used by Ottakar to counter the power of the Houses of Witigonen and Rosenberg. As a result of the purity of the local water, České Budějovice started to brew beer from the 13th century and the city at one time had more than 40 breweries. It became the major brewing region of the Holy Roman Empire and its product was known as the Beer of Kings.

The city and its environs became a German-speaking enclave from the 17th century and it was better known by its German name of Budweis. Beer from Budweis was known and labeled as Budweiser beer. In 1795, German-speaking businessmen merged two breweries in the city and formed the Burghers' or Citizens' Brewery, which used the Budweiser trademark for its exports.

But during the industrial revolution, Czech speakers became the majority population in the area and in 1895 a group of Czechs built a rival brewery, Budejovicky Pivovar, or Budvar for short. It also exported beer using the Budweiser trademark, which led to a series of legal battles with the American brewer Anheuser-Busch. See ANHEUSER-BUSCH and BUDWEISER.

During the communist period that followed World War II, the regime changed the name of the Burghers' Brewery (with its German associations) to Samson, after the name of the main square of České Budějovice. Since the return of the free market, Samson has renamed itself the Town Brewery and it exports beer using the Budweiser label. In the United States, beer from this brewery is sold as "B.B. Burgerbrau" to avoid clashing with Anheuser-Busch InBev, though the label notes that it is "Budweis City Beer." Budvar is a much larger company with a major export role. Within the EU, its beer is called Budweiser Budvar, but in the United States it is marketed as "Czechvar."

See also CZECH REPUBLIC.

Roger Protz

Challenger (hop), also known as Wye Challenger, is an English hop that was developed by Dr Ray Neve at Wye College and was commercially released in 1972. See WYE COLLEGE. It was the result of a cross between a female hop showing high resistance to downy mildew and a male seedling of Northern Brewer. See NORTHERN BREWER (HOP). The development of this hop was funded by the (British) Hops Marketing Board and the Brewers Society for the purpose of creating a hop with disease resistance for growers coupled with a relatively high alpha acid content for brewers. The Wye Challenger was deemed to have met both challenges and thus its name. It ripens in the latter part of the growing season and matures to an alpha acid level of 6.5% to 8.5%. This hop became popular with the former Burton-on-Trent brewery Bass, as well as with many English craft brewers. English regional breweries, too, such as Kent's Shepherd Neame in Kent and Suffolk's Greene King, use it in their beers. Wye Challenger is considered an excellent dual-purpose hop, providing both a full-rounded bitterness and an elegant spiciness with a fruity, earthy character. This makes it well suited for a variety of beer styles including English bitter, extra special bitter, and stout. It is mainly grown in the English counties of Herefordshire and Worcestershire, Kent and Sussex. Small patches of Challenger are also grown in Belgium.

Neve, R. A. *Hops*. London: Chapman & Hall, 1991.

Adrian Tierney-Jones

chamomile (Matricaria chamomilla) is a wild-growing annual herb that originated in western Asia and has spread to Europe, North America, and Australia. It is a member of the daisy family. It may appear as a weed in farmer's fields and can be quite invasive. Chamomile has a robust and pleasant aroma, and the flowers have been widely used as a tea and in herbal medicine since the days of ancient Egypt. It has active compounds acting as antiseptic and it is used to treat headache, stomach problems, wounds, malaria, inflammation and a number of other maladies. Historically, beer-based decoctions were often used as folk medicine.

Chamomile (the whole plant) has been used directly in beer together with sea wormwood to achieve a better keeping quality during summertime. Chamomile supposedly increases, if mildly, the intoxicating qualities of fermentation and adds its medicinal qualities to the beer. From a flavor point of view, it gives orange-like floral notes, but can become astringent if over-used. Its citrusy floral character has made it a popular background note for craft brewers.

See also HERBS.

Per Kølster

Chariot (barley). Chariot is a UK barley variety that was prevalent in the 1990s and 2000s. It was a hugely successful spring variety bred by Plant Breeding International (PBI), the successor to the UK state-owned breeding station in Cambridge (now part of seed-breeding and seed-selling company RAGT Seeds Ltd.). Chariot was bred as a cross between the variety Dera and an unnamed crossing strain, itself a cross between Carnival and Atem. Armed with resistance to mildew, yellow rust, brown rust, and scald (Rhynchosporium), it showed much-improved disease performance compared to varieties available to the grower in 1992, when it entered the UK Recommended lists. As such it produced a large increase in yield from plots not treated with fungicides, compared to established varieties such as Blenheim, a daughter variety of Triumph, which had accounted for nearly one quarter of the cultivated barley acreage in Europe.

In treated plots, the yield remained superior. Good brewhouse extracts and excellent malting, brewing, and distilling performance led to its recommendation by the Institute of Brewing (now the Institute of Brewing and Distilling; see INSTITUTE OF BREWING & DISTILLING (IBD)) in 1993. It became the spring variety of choice throughout the UK—the first universal choice since Triumph—and remained so for a decade until superseded by Optic. Chariot possessed classic malting properties of low wort viscosity and β-glucan. See BETA-GLUCANS. Protein modification was moderate, giving low soluble protein in worts.

PBI were so confident about the quality of this new variety in 1992 that they claimed in their product literature that pubs would soon be named for it. While this was perhaps an overstatement, Chariot was certainly a major step along the quality and yield improvement route in malting barleys at the end of the 20th century. In recognition of Chariot becoming outclassed for agronomic yield by newer varieties, growers reduced its area until it was no longer being grown by 2003, when it was removed from the list of IBD Approved varieties.

Colin J. West

cheese (pairing) is one of the finest food partners for full flavored beers and also among the most traditional. Made side by side in farmhouse kitchens for centuries, cheese, beer, and bread once made up a large proportion of the caloric intake of many societies, particularly in Europe. Indeed, at a stretch, one might even say that all three foods come from the same original source given that both barley and wheat are grasses, and grasses make up much of the diet of cows, sheep, and goats. Today, wine is often thought of as the most appropriate partner for great cheeses, but many wine experts feel differently, with some going so far as to suggest beer as a superior substitute.

Traditional and craft beers have a very wide range of flavor, far wider than that of wine. This is partly because brewing is actually a form of cooking, at least before fermentation is involved. Many ingredients may be used; grains can be caramelized or roasted, spices can be added, and fruit may be infused. Common strengths for beer range from 3% to 12% alcohol by volume, and this allows a wide variation of intensity. The level of carbonation, ranging from a mere prickle to a Champagne-like mousse, will influence texture. Yeasts may bring very different aromas, ranging from bright fruit to pungent earth. All of these features may be brought to bear in the service of cheese pairings.

Cheese itself is a very diverse food, but what nearly all cheeses have in common is relatively high amounts of both salt and fat. Beer generally brings some residual sugar from malt, and this makes a pleasant contrast with salt—anyone who has ever eaten potato chips or other salty snacks with a beer knows this. Both carbonation and hop bitterness provide cutting power that breaks through fats, refreshing the palate. Without carbonation to work through it, the fat in such foods as cheese and chocolate can coat the tongue, physically shielding the taste buds from the flavors of a beverage. This is a common problem for wine and cheese pairings.

Because cheese and beer are so diverse, it is impossible to explore all possibilities here. However, it is possible to provide some ideas about where to start. This is probably best done by looking at the three different milks from which cheese is commonly made and the general types of cheeses these milks produce.

Soft Cow's Milk Cheeses

Here we include bloomy-rinded cheeses such as brie, Camembert, and triple crèmes such as St André and Brillat-Savarin. The paste of these cheeses is usually mildly flavored, with sweet buttery and lactic notes posed against the salt. Many beers will pair well with the paste, but with many of these cheeses, the bloomy rind itself can be the determining factor in the success of the pairing. Bloomy rinds, which are formed by white molds, give an earthy, mushroomy character when the cheese is young. This flavor pairs well with softer farmhouse ales, particularly French bières de garde, which often have their own earthiness. Belgian-style tripels work especially well with triple crème cheeses. As these cheeses age, they become more pungent and the rinds may give a bitterness that interacts poorly with hops. Here it can be best to stick with Belgian and German wheat beers that will match the cheese without adding bitterness to the equation.

Washed-rind Cow's Milk Cheeses

These are what we often call the "smelly" cheeses. Good classic examples are Taleggio, Livarot, and Epoisse. Descriptors for the earthy aromatics range from "forest floor" to "barnyard," but the actual flavors of these cheeses are often very mild. The aromas are derived from the rinds, which have been washed with brine, beer, wine, or sometimes a form of brandy. The washing encourages the growth of certain molds and bacteria, which give the rind orange and green colors and ripen the cheese from the outside in. French bières de garde once again work well, but the best pairings are with non-sour barrel-aged beers showing Brettanomyces influence. The earthy "brett" character mingles perfectly with washed rind cheese aromatics, and the vanilla-like flavors derived from oak work nicely against the sweetness of the milk. Many Brettanomyces-influenced sour beers can work here too, but pairings are best found individually because they will partly depend on the degree and type of acidity in the beer.

Semihard Cow's Milk Cheeses

This category covers a wide range, from tommes to Beaufort and various types of cheddar. Most will have notable acidity, some grassy and fruity flavors, and plenty of salt. Pale ales and India pale ales are a good place to start here. Most of these cheeses work well against hops, meld their fruitiness nicely with ale yeast character, and can pick up on caramel notes derived from specialty malts. German-style and Bohemian-style pilsners also pair well with most of these cheeses.

Hard Cow's Milk Cheeses

Parmigiano-Reggiano, Grana Padano, well-aged gouda, gruyeres, and aged farmhouse cheddars fit here. Most have concentrated, almost explosive fruit and salt, some caramelized flavors, and plenty of umami. Here there are two good directions. One direction is the use of contrast—here once again saison and pilsner are good—with the brightness of the beer balancing the concentration of the cheese. The other direction is to use harmony, and here barley wines make a good choice. The rich malt and fruit character melds with these cheeses, and the residual sweetness of the beer makes a good foil for the salt.

Goat's-Milk Cheeses

Goat's milk cheeses have a bright white paste and tangy acidity. When fresh, goat's milk cheeses have no rind. Fresh goat's milks cheeses are usually at their best when they are only a week or two old and not very far from the farm. These cheeses are very brightly flavored, and good examples show a range of citrus notes. They pair especially well with dry saisons and with wheat beers, especially Belgian-style witbiers. They are also excellent with gueuze. Semiaged versions such as crottins or buttons will have rinds; here saisons may or may not work, depending more on the state of the rind than on the beer. Aged goat-milk cheeses can become very cakey and mouth coating; very high carbonation, usually developed by bottle conditioning, tends to help these pairings work well. Once again, think gueuze and saison.

Sheep's Milk Cheeses

Sheep's milk cheeses are often characterized by a soft, earthy nuttiness. They actually retain a smell of lanolin, an aroma recognizable in lamb chops and even in damp wool. Among the best are made in the French Pyrenees, including the excellent Ossau-Iraty, but the American Vermont Shepherd is also very good. This cheese and others of its type are very well paired with brown ales and porters; the nutty character of the sheep's milk mirrors caramel and chocolate malts particularly nicely. Manchego, although much sharper, is also a good pairing for these two beer styles.

Blue Cheeses

Some blue cheeses are quite difficult to pair because of the sharpness developed by the bluing molds. Danish blues and Roquefort can develop an almost tongue-numbing bitterness that tends to clash with hops. Fortunately, many other blues are full bodied but milder, and these can pair very successfully. Stilton is the royalty of this type, and it combines a powerfully earthy aroma with a rich, buttery, salty paste. Barley wines are very good here, particularly the strong British variant, where plenty of residual sugar teams up with caramel and dark fruit notes to wrap around the cheese. When these beers have a few years of bottle age, the pairing can be profound. Although it may seem counterintuitive, imperial stout often works very well with Stilton also. The roasted coffee and chocolate notes can bring out fudge-like flavors in the cheese, and the beer is one of the few styles capable of matching Stilton's intensity. Aside from Stilton, Gorgonzola Dolce, even when it has become quite runny, can often manage a very fine pairing with barley wine or imperial stout.

Of course this only scratches the surface of pairing possibilities, and the serendipity of the unexpected pairing always awaits. Pairings of fruit beers with fresh dessert cheeses, flights of older cheeses with older beers—those with adventurous palates will surely be rewarded by further explorations.

Garrett Oliver

Chevalier (barley). In the United Kingdom, up until the early 1800s, barley consisted of so-called land races, which were mixtures of types grown from saved seed, and known by exotic names such as "Nottinghamshire Long Ear" and "Old Wiltshire Archer." By the end of the 19th century, by gradual selection and re-selection, a number of malting lines had been developed, the major ones being "Chevalier," "Archer," "Spratt," and "Goldthorpe."

Chevalier dominated the English crop for around 60 years, and only really started to fall out of favor when William Gladstone repealed the Malt Tax in 1880. The tax on malt was replaced by a tax on beer itself, which meant that British brewers sought to brew more economically. Increasing volumes of cheaper malt were imported from abroad, and rice, maize, and other malt substitutes were countenanced. Though under declining acreage at the time, Chevalier was still winning prizes at the Brewers' Exhibition in 1914 (which was to be the last). After World War I, Chevalier was to be replaced by the hybrids, "Plumage-Archer" and "Spratt-Archer," which would dominate the British crop during the inter-war years.

There are several versions of how Chevalier came into existence, the following being from a manuscript *History of Debenham* (Suffolk) of 1845:

> *About the year 1820, John Andrews, a labourer, had been threshing barley and on his return home that night complained of his feet being very uneasy, and on taking off his shoes he discovered in one of them part of a very fine ear of barley—it struck him as being particularly*

so—and he was careful to have it preserved. He afterwards planted the few grains from it in his garden, and the following year Rev. John Chevallier, coming to Andrews' dwelling (which he owned) to inspect some repairs, saw 3 or 4 ears of the barley growing. He requested that it might be kept for him when ripe. The Reverend gentleman sowed a small ridge with the produce thus obtained, and kept it by itself until he grew sufficient to plant an acre, and from this acre (the year being 1825, or 1826) the produce was 11½ coombs.

Chevalier was a two-row, narrow-eared variety originally classified as Hordeum distichum, and several seedsmen developed their own sub-varieties, so that the description came to cover a wide range of narrow-eared forms of barley. John Chevallier's heirs (now Chevallier-Guild) are still involved in fermented beverages, living at Aspall Hall, Debenham, where they operate their successful Aspall Cyder Company.

Beaven, E. S. *Barley: Fifty years observation and experiment*. London: Duckworth, 1947.

Ian Hornsey

Chicago, Illinois, was little more than a marsh in 1833, but it was destined for great things. William Haas and Konrad Sulzer arrived that year with equipment and supplies for Chicago's first commercial brewery. A succession of important names became part owners of the Haas & Sulzer Brewery, including William B. Ogden, Chicago's mayor. The brewery was renamed the Lill & Diversey Brewery around 1841, after William Lill and Michael Diversey took ownership. By 1866 this ale brewery was the largest in the Midwest.

John Huck started Chicago's first lager brewery in 1847. Lager beer was a touchstone for Chicago's swelling German community. Anti-immigrant sentiments were strong, and in 1855, efforts to control Irish- and German-owned saloons caused a bloody clash known as the Lager Beer Riot. One person was killed and many were injured, but the conflict tore apart the nativist political coalition, which had wanted to prevent Irish and German taverns from opening on Sundays. Eventually, the immigrants prevailed.

Chicago's growth outstripped demand, so ambitious brewers in Milwaukee began shipping beer to Chicago. In 1871, the city of Chicago burned to the ground. Nineteen breweries were destroyed, with a value of $2 million. Of course, Milwaukee brewers were quick to rush water, then beer, to the parched survivors. Chicago rebounded at an even greater rate of growth, with plenty of customers for local and out-of-town brewers.

Chicago became an important center for brewing research and education. In 1872, Joseph Ewald Siebel founded the Zymotechnic Institute, and his Siebel Institute still exists as a brewing school today. See SIEBEL INSTITUTE OF TECHNOLOGY. The trade journal *The Western Brewer* was launched in 1876 and another brewing school, Wahl-Henius, opened in 1886. See WAHL-HENIUS INSTITUTE OF FERMENTOLOGY.

In the 1890s huge amounts of English capital flowed into US breweries. By 1900, half of Chicago's brewing capacity was in British hands. With this came notions such as tied houses; one British group invested more than $6 million in brewery-owned bars. Today, dozens of distinctive former Schlitz (also with British ownership) taverns ring the center city, many still bearing the iconic old terra cotta Schlitz globes.

Prohibition was enacted in 1920, and the Chicago beer scene, which Prohibition was meant to smother, instead took on its own flavor. At first, 2.75% alcohol beer was still legal in Wisconsin. Pabst, Schlitz, and others flooded the market illegally. Mobsters like Johnny Torrio got involved in brewing and began to consolidate gang holdings. One holdout, northsider Dion O'Banion, sold Torrio his interest in the Sieben brewery, but not before he tipped off the Feds, who raided the place just as Torrio took ownership. Eventually Al Capone, a former Torrio protegé, edged out his old boss. In one transaction, Anheuser-Busch sold Capone more than 250,000 tapping heads, an indication of the size of the illegal enterprise.

From the end of Prohibition to the 1980s, Chicago's brewing story is the same as that of most US cities: price competition, consolidation, and brewery closings. The last old-time brewery in Chicago, Siebens, closed along with its beloved beer garden in 1967.

The city's first modern microbrewery, a reinvented Siebens Brewpub, opened in 1986. Others followed, including Goose Island Beer Company in 1988, now a successful regional brewer of craft beer with ties to Anheuser-Busch. As of mid-June 2010, the Chicagoland area had more than 30 small breweries and a growing number of bars catering to craft beer enthusiasts.

See also PROHIBITION.

Skilnik, Bob. *The history of beer and brewing in Chicago, 1833–1978*. St. Paul, MN: Pogo Press, 1999.

Randy Mosher

chicha, a term used in Latin America for a fermented beverage made from maize (corn). It is commonly known as *chicha de jora* but also goes by the names *aqa* in the native American language Quechua and *kusa* in the Aymaran language. The Spanish name comes from the word "saliva" or "to spit," based on the method by which it is traditionally produced.

Chicha production has traditionally been the task of women in the household, with the techniques often passed down from generation to generation. The chicha maker chewed on maize to form small balls. The ptyalin enzymes in the saliva broke down the maize starches into fermentable sugars. The maize balls were left out to dry and then made into a porridge, which was strained, boiled, and fermented for 3 to 6 days in large earthenware vats.

Malted maize, called *jora*, has largely replaced salivated maize because it is less labor intensive to produce. *Jora* is made by soaking maize kernels, allowing them to germinate overnight, and then drying them. From this point, the process to make chicha with malted maize is essentially the same as with salivated maize. Depending on the region of Latin America, chicha is also often produced from yucca (cassava) root or quinoa or with the addition of various fruits.

The color of chicha varies depending on the type of maize from which it is made, ranging from pale yellow to burgundy red. When made from yellow sweet maize, it has a pale straw color and milky appearance. The beverage is slightly sour and almost cider like. It is often drunk in an active state of fermentation and has a low alcohol percentage, usually from 1%–3% alcohol by volume.

Chicha has pre-Hispanic origins in Andean South America and was an integral and key part of the Incan economy. Following the Spanish conquest in the 16th century, however, the drink was largely outlawed by the Catholic Church, which forced production underground, converting it from a large-scale industry into something smaller and more artisanal, as it remains today.

Today, chicha is still consumed at chicharias (chicha bars) throughout Central and South America. It is produced in a variety of styles, depending on the region. It is often mixed with strawberries or other

Postcard of a Peruvian man selling chicha, c. 1920. PIKE MICROBREWERY MUSEUM, SEATTLE, WA

fruit to make a *frutillada*. The word "chicha" can also refer to a non-alcoholic beverage, *chicha morada*, made by boiling purple corn with cinnamon, pineapple, and cloves (which is available commercially throughout South America).

Chicha also continues to play an important social role in the more rural parts of Andean South America, where it is part of *la minga* (a word denoting a public group effort) and is used as a ritual payment for help given to neighbors for particularly large or complicated projects such as the construction of a new house.

See also CORN.

Jennings, Justin J., and Brenda J. Bowser. *Drink, power and society in the Andes*. Gainesville: University of Florida Press, 2009.

Llano Restrepo, Maria Clara. *La chicha, una bebida a traves de la historia*. Bogota: Instituto Colombiano de Antropologia, 1994. *Chicha, a drink throughout history*. Used because it is a key work, also not translated into English.

Pardo, B. Oriana, and Pizarro, José Luis. *La chicha en el Chile precolombino*. Santiago: Editorial Mare Nostrum, 2005. *Chicha in precolumbian Chile*. Most works on Chicha have not been translated from Spanish.

Jai Kharbanda and Anda Lincoln

chill haze occurs when a beer is chilled below approximately 1.6°C (about 35°F) and constituents can aggregate to form relatively large colloidal (gel-like) particles. These become visible to the naked eye as a cloudiness or haze. This haze is temporary, however, and completely redissolves when the temperature of the beer rises. Measures taken to prevent chill haze are referred to as "chillproofing." Chill haze is caused by low-molecular-weight polyphenols and larger proteins and polypeptides when cross-linked through weak interactions such as hydrogen bonds. Hydrogen bonds are disrupted when the beer warms up, so the particles are only large enough to be visible when beer is cold. Particles range in size from 0.1 to 1 μm. Minor components of chill haze may also include carbohydrates and metals. The particles may eventually become large enough to precipitate and settle to the bottom of the package, forming a dusty sediment or deposit that, when poured into a glass, will result in a cloudy appearance. Chill haze will usually develop into a permanent condition over time.

The major components of these aggregates are certain classes of proteins and polyphenols that are derived from brewing raw materials, namely malt and hops. Excessive levels of protein/nitrogen, namely soluble protein, in malt will present problems with colloidal stability. As little as 2 mg/l of protein is sufficient to induce a haze of 1 European Brewery Convention unit. Haze-active proteins have been identified as deriving from hordeins that are relatively rich in proline. The haze-sensitive proteins make up only a small percentage of the total protein found in beer. Polyphenols also impart certain flavor characteristics and act as natural antioxidants, preserving the original taste of beer so their complete removal is not always desirable.

See also CHILLPROOFING, CLARITY, HAZE, and PVPP.

Christopher Bird

chillproofing is a term used when a beer undergoes a process to protect its clarity or brightness when it is cooled to very low temperatures approaching 0°C (32°F). With most beers, chillproofing is a very important part of the modern brewing process. The earliest use of a form of chillproofing occurred in the mid-19th century with the brewing of lighter lager beers. The original pilsner beers were stored in caves packed with ice, which helped to chillproof the beer through cold aging. Traditionally beers are chillproofed by being stored at 0°C or below for long periods of many weeks or months. During this time protein and polyphenols derived from malt in the beer coagulate to form larger molecules, which can then be removed by filtration. In the days before beer filtration, the beer was aged long enough for the particles to simply settle out. Most filtered beers are clear and bright when bottled or kegged, but without chillproofing the protein–polyphenol coagulation occurs in the package, and the beer becomes hazy within several weeks. In modern beer production, processing aids are used to shorten the chillproofing process from weeks or months to only a few days. Proteolytic enzymes, which break down larger protein molecules, were some of the first chillproofing aids. Nowadays protein and polyphenol adsorbing materials are often used. Beer that is clear (bright) at ambient temperature but that becomes cloudy when cooled is said to have a "chill haze." Beer with a chill haze will become clear again when it returns to room temperature.

See also ADSORBENTS, CHILL HAZE, and PVPP.

Paul KA Buttrick

Chimay is the name of the Trappist brewery located near the town of the same name in the southern Belgian province of Hainaut. The official name of the abbey is Notre-Dame de Scourmont (Our Lady of Scourmont), but many people refer to it as the Chimay abbey or Bières de Chimay. The abbey was founded July 25, 1850 by a group of 17 Cistercian monks from the Westvleteren abbey in the area of Scourmont, which is immediately outside of the town of Chimay. See WESTVLETEREN BREWERY. The first name given to the abbey was Trappist Abbey of Saint Joseph. The first abbot, father Hyacinthe Bouteca, renamed the abbey as Notre-Dame de Scourmont. Father Hyacinthe also began designing and constructing a brewery to provide additional income for the abbey. In 1862 the brewery was completed and opened for business. True to Saint Benedict's motto "ora e labora" (work and prayer), the brewery provided a means for the monks to work with their hands when not in prayer. The abbey began selling beer to the public almost immediately after opening and became successful. The abbey grew quickly from an initial 16 monks in 1850 to 80 by 1858. By 1875 two types of beer were sold to the public in bottles, both strong ales called *Bière Forte* and *Bière Goudronnee*. In 1944, after World War II, the monks had to restart their brewery after losing their copper kettles to the German army. They enlisted the help of the famous Belgian brewing professor Jean De Clerck, of the Katholiek Universiteit Leuven. See DE CLERCK, JEAN and KATHOLIEKE UNIVERSITEIT VAN LEUVEN. De Clerck helped the monks rebuild the brewery and reformulate their beers to a modern standard. The first beer was released to the public by Easter of 1948. De Clerck's assistance to Chimay led the abbey to be quite successful and the monks showed their appreciation by allowing De Clerck and his wife to be buried in their private cemetery behind the abbey. To this day, proceeds from the sales of Chimay beer support the abbey and charitable work in the community.

Currently the monks of Chimay produce four unique types of beer, which are bottle-conditioned and unpasteurized. The commercially available beers are packaged in crown-capped 33 cl bottles and 750 ml bottles finished with cork and wire-cage. The first is Chimay Red (7% ABV), also known as *capsule rouge* or "red crown" in English. In the 750 ml bottling, this beer is known as Chimay Première. This beer has a deep amber/copper color with a thick, long-lasting head of foam. The aroma and taste are fruity and flavorful, with notes that the monks liken to apricots. The second offering is Chimay Triple (8% ABV), with the 750 ml bottling labeled as Chimay Cinq Cents. It is popularly known as "capsule blanc" or white crown in English. This beer has a deep gold color and is the driest-tasting of the Chimay beers. It is also the most generously hopped, displaying hop character from first sip to the aftertaste. It has an assertive ester character that the monks describe as "muscat and raisin." Several years ago, this beer became available in draught form, in which it has enjoyed considerable success. The third offering is Chimay Blue (9% ABV), which is labeled as Chimay Grande Réserve in 750 ml and special 1.5 l magnum bottles. This beer has assertive alcohol notes in aroma and taste and is balanced with sweet, dark malt character, even though the beer is low in residual sugar. Of the three main Chimay beers, the Grande Réserve is considered the most age-worthy, gaining considerable character over several years. The final beer is Chimay Dorée ("Gold," 4.8% ABV). This beer, brewed in the "singel" style, is not available commercially and is made largely for the consumption of the monks in the abbey, who rarely taste the other Chimay beers themselves. See SINGEL. Chimay Dorée can also be found at the pleasant nearby restaurant/inn L'Auberge de Poteaupré, which has close ties with the abbey.

The abbey is separated from the concerns of the world through its establishment of a secular commercial arm called Biéres de Chimay. Chimay has grown to produce 123,000 hectoliters annually, exporting 50% of that volume to more than 40 countries. While brewing and fermentation take place within the walls of the abbey, the beer is bottled at a separate facility 10 kilometers away.

In 1860 the abbey started a small dairy operation. For the first 15 years the main product was butter and it was sold only to individuals and other religious communities. The quality was not good and by the 1880s, the dairy operation was in danger of closing. One of the monks traveled to the Sept-Fons abbey in the region of Auvergne, France to learn how to produce the flavorful varieties of French cheese.

Chimay then produced cheese for a number of years; eventually the production was relocated to dairies outside of the region of Chimay. Quality is said to have suffered, and in 1980 the Chimay abbey formed a venture with local farmers to bring cheese manufacturing back to the region of Chimay. In October of 1982, the new venture officially opened and a state-of-the-art cheese production facility began operations. This venture has been very successful and is now called Chimay Fromages. Five types of cheese are currently made: "Old Chimay," a hard cheese made with whole milk and aged at least half a year; "Chimay with Beer," a hard cheese whose rind is soaked in Chimay beer; "Chimay Grand Classic," a semi-hard cheese aged for a minimum of 4 weeks; "Chimay Grand Cru," a hard cheese aged for a minimum of 6 weeks; and "The Poteaupré," a semi-hard cheese aged for at least 5 weeks.

The abbey ran a small cured meat company called Chimay Salaisons from 1987 to 1995. Producing a range of sausages, cured meats, and hams, Chimay Salaisons was meant to further diversify the abbey's food production. Production was modestly successful, but the abbey decided to abandon this business completely in 1995.

See also BELGIUM, CISTERCIAN ORDER, and TRAPPIST BREWERIES.

Keith Villa

China. Chinese archeologists report that beer was first produced in China 7,000 to 9,000 years ago, at roughly the same time that other cradles of civilization showed evidence of some form of beer production. By definition, the production of beer requires the use of grain. In China, the grain in question was rice, sometimes supplemented with wheat or millet.

Until relatively recently, beverage alcohol, including beer, did not reach the widespread use in China that it did in other parts of the world. For millennia *huangjiu* (a drink often referred to as "rice wine," though it is technically a grain-based beer) and lao li, another type of early Chinese beer, were drinks associated with ceremony and with the upper classes. Modern brewing, using malted barley and hops, began in China in 1900, when a Russian entrepreneur, Ulubulevskij, founded a brewery in Harbin, in Northeastern China. The area is suitable for the production of grains other than rice, including barley. German and Czech breweries opened soon after. The largest and best-known brewery in China is the Tsingtao brewery in Qingdao in Shandong province in east-central China. It was founded by German settlers in 1903.

At roughly 400 million hl (340 million US barrels) of annual production, China now produces more beer than any other country in the world. It is also one of the few in which total annual production is currently increasing, at 3% to 5% per year. The market is dominated by seven large brewery groups.

There has been considerable consolidation in the brewing industry in China in recent years, with 251 brewing companies now operating 550 breweries. Per capita consumption remains low at roughly 22 liters annually, but is also growing. This compares with roughly 80 liters per capita in the United States and 160 liters per capita in the Czech Republic. Most of the major Chinese breweries have entered into joint ventures with large foreign breweries in order to gain access to modern brewing technology and expertise. The foreign breweries have entered into these joint ventures in order to gain access to markets and distribution systems.

Chinese tastes in beer tend toward the lighter side of the international norm of mass-market light pilsners. Some of the larger breweries have offered a dark lager on special occasions, and some medium-sized breweries have sought a market niche with a more full-bodied pilsner with some detectable hop character, but none of these has been successful.

The craft beer movement has been able to establish a presence in China, but largely for unconventional reasons. One of the leaders in bringing craft beer to China is the Paulaner group, with 11 brewpubs (called beer pubs in China) in 10 Chinese cities. Many independent brewpubs elsewhere in China and Southeast Asia have copied the Paulaner model, which involves a highly visible copper-clad brewery, and a focus on just three beer styles: a helles (literally "bright," implying a blond lager), a dunkel (a dark lager), and a wheat beer. See HELLES and DUNKEL. All tend to be brewed with less bitterness and a highly floral character relative to what one would find at the original Paulaner Bräuhaus in Munich.

Brewpubs emerged en masse in China in the mid 1990s, with eight opening in one year in Beijing alone. The motivation behind this flowering was that the state did not yet have the apparatus with which to collect excise taxes on brewpub beer, and brewpubs promised higher profits. The clientele for these brewpubs was a mix of foreigners working in China and local business types who could afford to pay more for beer as a status symbol. Nevertheless, those brewpubs that ventured away from the Paulaner model to bigger, hoppier beers did not last long, and others offered beers that were poorly made. The market had shed many of these brewpubs by the end of the decade and those brewpubs that understood the local market have survived. As China's rapid economic growth progresses, it remains to be seen whether the Chinese public will develop a taste for beers other than mass-market light lagers.

China Daily, August 24, 2009. www.chinadaily.com.cn/china/2009-08/content_8608336/ (accessed July 25, 2010).

Slocum, John W., Jr., et al. Fermentation in the China beer industry. *Organizational Dynamics* 35 (2006): 32–48.

Bev Robertson

Chinese hops have many different names, but most are closely related to Cluster, whereas others are very similar to Columbus. See CLUSTER (HOP). By world standards, China is not a traditional hop-growing region. Substantial cultivation there began only in the early in the 20th century, with cultivars brought in from Europe and North America. Today, the American types seem to predominate. Chinese hop production in recent years has been roughly 15% of the world total. Breweries in China consume the entire domestic hop production and then some. Essentially no Chinese hops are exported. Most Chinese hop production takes place in the isolated northwestern part of the country.

Val Peacock

Chinook (hop), a US-bred high alpha hop with a spicy, piney hop aroma. This variety was developed by Chuck Zimmermann and released by Steve Kenny in 1985 as part of the United States Department of Agriculture's (USDA) hop breeding program in Prosser, Washington. It has high α-acids (12%–14% w/w) and high oil content (1.7–2.7 ml/100 g). Relative to other high alpha varieties, Chinook has a low beta-acid content (3%–4%). Its parentage includes the English hops Petham Golding and Brewer's Gold and a wild American hop from Utah. Chinook matures late, is moderately resistant to downy mildew, and resistant to verticillium wilt, but is somewhat susceptible to virus infection, especially hop mosaic virus. The variety grows best in the Yakima Valley, Washington but not in Oregon, due to downy mildew problems. Its storage stability is fair to good. Chinook is widely used in American pale ales and India pale ales, where they can show clean bitterness and aromatics of pine needles and grapefruit, but are also considered somewhat "catty" when concentrated.

Thomas Shellhammer and Alfred Haunold

chitting is the initial growth phase of the acrospires and rootlets right after the rupture of the grain's seed coat during the malting process. The seed coat consists of the testa and pericarp layers. These layers protect the kernel's enzyme-containing aleuron layer, which, in turn, envelops the endosperm. See ENDOSPERM. As long as the testa and pericarp layers as well as the husks are intact, they restrict the exchange of gasses and moisture between the endosperm and the environment. Chitting, therefore, is an indication of the awakening of the siloed seed from dormancy and is the first step in the transformation of grain into malt. Chitting accelerates especially during the oxygen-rich ventilated air rests that the raw grain undergoes during the steeping cycle, and it continues into the initial phase of the germination cycle. See GERMINATION and MALT. During chitting, the seeds rapidly take up water (hydration) and oxygen (respiration). See RESPIRATION. As the bursting of the testa and pericarp layers progresses, the seeds' respiration accelerates and the temperature in the steeping vat rises. Proper chitting is essential, because it is a precondition for germination. Irregular chitting would decrease the germination rate and thus result in inhomogeneous malt.

While during normal steeping and germination, chitting is only one step in a lengthy steeping and germination process, on rare occasions, the chitted grain will be moved directly into the kiln after just 3 or 4 (instead of perhaps 7) days in the germination chamber. The result of this short cut is called "chit malt." Such malt is produced primarily in Germany as well as in several other countries, where legislations such as the Beer Purity Law forbid the use of raw cereals in beer making. See REINHEITSGEBOT. Because chit malt is modified just enough to be technically called "malt," it can serve, in essence, as a legal functional substitute for unmalted or roasted barley, which are important elements in the grist composition of many Belgian and British beer styles. Chit malts contain mostly high-molecular proteins and sugars and retain many of the green, grassy characteristics of raw grain. One of its main purposes is to improve the finished beer's body and foam stability. Chit malt is usually only lightly kilned and thus pale; only rarely is it roasted like color malts.

Briggs, Dennis Edward. *Malts and malting*. London: Chapman & Hall, 1997.

Thomas Kraus-Weyermann

chocolate encompasses a wide range of confections and flavors derived from the roasted seeds of the evergreen cacao tree, native to Central and South America. Recent research suggests that cacao was first consumed by native Central Americans in the form of a fermented alcoholic beverage. It is safe to say that the flavors of chocolate are today among the favorite food flavors of people worldwide, and it is not surprising to see that brewers seek to incorporate it into specialty beers. Chocolate-like flavors can be derived from roasted malts, including a variety called chocolate malt, so named because of its color and chocolate-like flavor contribution to beer. The flavor of actual chocolate tends to be somewhat different than that of roasted malt, however, so brewers wanting true chocolate flavor will introduce chocolate or cacao at various points through the brewing process.

Although many homebrewers use commercially available cocoa powder, chocolate bars, or syrups, commercial craft brewers tend to focus on the use of the cacao nibs (chopped beans) themselves. Cacao beans contain fat and, when separated from cocoa solids, this is referred to as cocoa butter. Many commercial chocolate preparations contain cocoa butter, which is of interest to brewers because fats and oils have deleterious effects on foam formation and retention. Depending on many factors, including the means of addition and the fermentation profile, fats may or may not survive into the finished beer. Almost all commercial chocolate contains sugar; other common ingredients are vanilla, peanuts, and milk powder. Those wishing to retain purer flavors will stick with straight cacao or with baker's chocolate. Either can be added to the boil. Another popular method is to age beer on cacao nibs postfermentation. This avoids fat extraction and gives a true cacao flavor and aroma, including fruity elements that can be lost in the production of commercial chocolate. Cacao beans, however, also contain considerable amounts of bitter tannin, and long contact times with beer can leach these astringent compounds out along with other flavors. As with other flavorings, alcohol-based extracts are available, but better producers generally avoid them. Used well, various forms of chocolate can add pleasant notes to porters and stouts, but brewers have added chocolate to many other beer styles with varying success. Some of the most interesting pair the chocolate character with sweet spice and/or chili flavors that recall ancient Mesoamerican drink preparations and currently popular forms of Mexican drinking chocolate.

Fountain, Henry. "Love of chocolate may have begun with cacao beer." *The New York Times*, November 13, 2007 (accessed December 11, 2010).

Spadaccini, Jim. "The sweet lure of chocolate." *Exploratium Magazine Online*, http://www.exploratorium.edu/exploring/exploring_chocolate/index.html/ (accessed December 11, 2010).

Garrett Oliver

Christmas ales is a catch-all descriptive phrase given to special beers made for Christmas and New Year celebrations, often with a high alcohol content 5.5%–14% ABV and marked by the inclusion of dark flavored malts, spices, herbs, and fruits in the recipe.

A medieval instance of a Christmas ale was called "lambswool"—made with roasted apples, nutmegs, ginger, and sugar (honey)—so-called because of the froth floating on the surface. Today's versions tend to be based on old ale, strong ale, and barley wine recipes, using cinnamon, cumin, orange, lemon, coriander, honey, etc. to create a warming, dark, and luscious festive beer. See OLD ALES and BARLEY WINE. This tradition is closely related with the "wassail," a mulled wine, beer, or cider usually consumed while caroling or gathering for the Christmas season.

Most country breweries produce a Christmas or seasonal ale, some with long histories—notably in Belgium, England, Scandinavia, and the United States—which are usually matured for many months. There is no fixed recipe for these special ales as it is an opportunity for the brewer to expand

Beer label for Christmas ale produced by the Peoples Brewing Company in Wisconsin, c. 1940. Peoples was the first brewery in the United States to have an African American owner, Theodore Mack, Sr. PIKE MICROBREWERY MUSEUM, SEATTLE, WA

boundaries and explore new tasty ingredients for Christmas, as the brewer's gift to yuletide. The category includes some of the strongest beers brewed in the world including Samiclaus, which is a rich, aged Doppelbock with 14% ABV, originally brewed by Hurlimann in Switzerland but now in Austria at the Eggenberg Brewery. In the United States, Christmas Ale at Anchor Brewing (also known as "Our Special Ale") contains a different blend of spices every year and helped spawn an interest in Christmas ales in the early days of the craft beer movement.

Buhner, Stephen Harrod. *Sacred and herbal healing beers.* Boulder, CO: Siris Books, 1998.

Harrison, Dr John, and Members of the Durden Park Beer Circle. *Old British beers and how to make them,* 3rd ed. Middlesex, UK: Durden Park Beer Circle, 2003. (Includes recipes for old festive ales, taken from old brewing books.)

Unger, Richard W. *Beer in the Middle Ages and the Renaissance.* Philadelphia, PA: University of Pennsylvania Press, 2004.

Chris J. Marchbanks

Christoffel Brewery is a microbrewery located in Roermond in the southeast part of the Netherlands. It was founded by Brand brewery family member Leo Brand in 1986 and named after the patron saint of Roermond, St. Christoffel. Brand graduated as a Weihenstephan University brewing technician 10 years earlier and had worked at various German breweries and maltings before setting up the brewery. See WEIHENSTEPHAN. He brewed his first batch in a former furniture factory using second-hand brewing equipment on August 2 and officially opened the brewery on September 26, 1986. His first beer was a premium, heavily hopped German-style pilsner simply called St. Christoffel, bottled in 33 cl and 2-liter swing-top bottles. National success was quickly followed by exports to Germany, Belgium, America, and Denmark. Production capacity peaked in the early 1990s and the brewery moved to its current location in an industrial estate and replaced its brewhouse with new equipment, thereby almost tripling its output. Its second beer, Robertus, a strong Munich-style dark lager, was launched in 2003 and followed by a Bock in 2005 (replaced by a Doublebock in 2007), a dry-hopped Imperial Pilsner in 2008 and a dark Bavarian-style Weizen in 2009. All of their beers are free of adjuncts and meet the German Reinheitsgebot standards. See REINHEITSGEBOT. The beers remain notable for their bold character.

There have been many personnel changes at Christoffel and a change of owners since the relocation. The most recent development was a buy-out by the husband (brewing engineer) and wife (general manager) team of Steven van den Berg and Joyce van den Elshout in the fall of 2009.

See also NETHERLANDS, THE.

Derek Walsh

chromatography is a method of separating and analyzing mixtures of chemical components. Chromatography is used by large brewery laboratories to identify and quantify volatile and nonvolatile beer components. Separation occurs by allowing a mixture to travel through an adsorbent matrix so that each compound is ultimately resolved into separate zones based on chemical or physical properties such as polarity, boiling point, or size. The simplest forms of chromatography include separation on paper sheets or specially coated plates or through columns packed with an inert media. Various methods are then employed to detect and identify the different resolved species.

Two sophisticated methods of chromatography are gas chromatography (GC) and high performance liquid chromatography (HPLC). Both provide separation techniques for qualitative or quantitative identification of substances.

Gas chromatography relies on selective adsorption and release (desorption) of volatile components on a stationary phase. Components in a mixture are carried through a column by an inert gas to a specific type of detector where species, via calibration with known compounds, are identified based on retention (residency) time in or on the column.

In the brewery laboratories, GC is used to separate higher alcohols (fusel oils) and esters in beer and phenols (wheat beers) and also vicinal diketones such as the buttery flavored diacetyl compound. Results are related back to the chemical composition of the beer and to its sensory properties. GC results can be used to give early warning of an infection (which may produce diacetyl above normal levels) or simply to provide a "map" of a beer's aromatic properties. In some breweries, GC results are used to determine when a beer is ready to leave its fermenter and be put into a lagering cellar for aging; the decision would depend on diacetyl having dropped into an acceptable range of concentration.

High performance liquid chromatography uses a liquid mobile phase to transport and separate components of a mixture. Mixtures are injected under high pressure into a packed column known as the stationary phase. In the column the mixture is resolved, via adsorption and release (desorption), into its constituents. As for GC methods, different types of detectors are available for appropriate identification. Quantification is also possible via integrated calibration with known amounts of specific compounds. HPLC, unlike GC, is more suitable for separating less volatile compounds. As such it is useful in analyzing sugars in beer and wort, organic acids, and hop iso-alpha acids. Chromatography can provide highly useful information, but it is very expensive and time-consuming to perform, and therefore is rarely employed by breweries producing less than 100,000 hectoliters per year.

Gary Spedding

A **Cicerone** is a person who has completed the exams and requirements of the Cicerone Certification Program, a course of beer study founded by Ray Daniels in 2007. Daniels, a beer author, judge, and senior faculty member of the Siebel Institute of Technology, started the program to provide both the brewing and the hospitality industries with clear certifications indicating defined levels of knowledge in the selection and proper service of fine beer. Daniels repurposed the word "cicerone" (pronounced *sis-uh-rohn*), a word meaning "docent" or a person who conducts others through museums or sightseeing tours, to refer to a person who conducts others through the world of fine beer. The primary certification, "Certified Beer Server," requires fairly basic knowledge regarding beer production, popular beer styles, and proper storage and service. The secondary level, "Certified Cicerone," is far more rigorous and delves more deeply into technical and historical aspects, beer styles and their variations, common beer flaws and off-flavors, tasting skills, food pairing, and more. The ultimate certification, called "Master Cicerone," requires detailed knowledge of many aspects of brewing, as well as a superior understanding of all facets of the beverage in its varied forms. All levels require the passing of written exams, with the advanced levels including tasting exams and essays.

Although it is debatable whether the restaurant and hospitality industry should need specified "beer sommeliers," the rapid rise of the craft beer culture has left a vacuum of knowledge among people studying alcoholic beverages. In theory, a "sommelier" is not just a wine steward; a properly trained sommelier should also be thoroughly familiar with all aspects of beer, sake, cocktails, and all other flavorful alcoholic beverages. The reality is somewhat different, however, and many sommeliers know little or nothing about beer, even after having gone through respected cooking schools or sommelier training programs. Daniels' Cicerone certifications, which he has wisely trademarked, have therefore garnered growing popularity among beer distributors, salespeople, and those in the restaurant trade. Exams are administered throughout the United States on a regular basis, and as of early 2011 the exams had also been offered in Canada.

Cicerone. http://www.cicerone.org/ (accessed December 12, 2010).

Noel, Josh. "Beer's buddy." *Chicago Tribune*, July 11, 2010.

Garrett Oliver

CIP

See CLEANING IN PLACE (CIP).

cirrhosis

See HEALTH.

Cistercian order. In the Catholic Church, when laymen or clergy wish to dedicate their lives to the church, they are organized into groups of men (monks) or women (nuns) called "religious orders." These religious orders are each led by a superior and follow a distinct set of religious rules. The Cistercians are one of the religious orders of the Catholic Church and were founded in the year 1098 in Citeaux, France. Their goal was to break away from the order of the Benedictines, who were supposedly becoming lax at interpreting the Rule of Saint Benedict. The Rule of Saint Benedict is no easy path, comprising a book of 73 chapters that spell out the rules for living together in a religious order. The Cistercians wanted a stricter interpretation of the Rule and to live with greater devotion to the motto of St. Benedict, "ora e labora" (prayer and work).

In the 17th century a sub-family of the Cistercians was created called the Trappists, who advocated an even stricter observance of the Rule. Trappists closely follow three of the Rules: silence, prayer, and living by the work of their hands. In this regard, over the years Trappists have come to make foodstuffs, including beer. There are currently seven recognized Trappist breweries in the world, Koningshoeven in the Netherlands and six from Belgium: Achel, Chimay, Orval, Rochefort, Westmalle, and Westvleteren. Trappist beers are world renowned for their taste and quality. A beer labeled as "Trappist" must be brewed by a Trappist brewery. The Trappist designation is protected by law and widely enforced by the International Trappist Association. There exist many beers similar to Trappist beers produced by secular breweries but these beers are called abbey beers.

See also ABBEY BEERS and TRAPPIST BREWERIES.

Keith Villa

Citra (hop), a trademarked and patented aroma hop released by the Hop Breeding Company LLC (HBC) in 2009. Originally called "HBC 394," Citra is the result of a cross performed in 1990 as part of a controlled breeding program in Washington's Yakima Valley. A single plant was selected out in 1992 and the first commercial plot of 6 acres was planted in 2008. Citra has an interestingly mixed pedigree that can be split out as 50% Hallertauer Mittelfrueh, 25% US Tettnanger, 19% Brewer's Gold, and 3% East Kent Golding. Although classed as an "aroma hop," given its alpha acid content of 11%–13%, Citra can also be used as a bittering hop, especially given that cohumulone is relatively low at 22%–24% of alpha acids. Citra matures mid-season and has moderate resistance to downy and powdery mildew. Yields are average at 1569 kg/ha to 1793 kg/ha (1,400 to 1,600 lbs per acre), and the storage stability is fair.

What sets Citra apart and gives it a bright potential is its uniquely exotic citrusy aroma and very high total oil content, which hovers between 2.2% and 2.8%, about twice the oil of Cascade and among the highest of any hop. The oil has 60%–65% myrcene, 11%–13% humulene, 6%–8% caryophyllene, and notably high linalool at 1%–2%. Many breeders and brewers feel that linalool is closely associated with pleasant hop aromatics in beer. Citra, which was named for its citrusy aroma, also shows notes of gooseberry, tropical fruits, and lychee nuts, along with some "catty" black currant notes than can emerge in dry hopping. The hop's intensity gives it a particularly obvious role in pale ales and India pale ales. Few hops have emerged onto the scene in the past several years with quite the fanfare that Citra has, and the hop seems destined for steadily increasing acreage for some time.

Probasco, Gene, et al. Citra: A new special aroma hop variety. *MBAA Technical Quarterly* 47 (2010).

Garrett Oliver

citric acid is an organic acid found in beer normally within the range of 50 to 250 parts per million. It is produced as a result of yeast metabolism and is a key component of the tricarboxylic acid cycle, which is also referred to as the Krebs or citric acid cycle. Although it contributes to the overall acidity of the beer, citric acid has little impact on the overall flavor. It is sometimes added to increase the acidity of some low-alcohol and nonalcoholic beers where incomplete fermentation fails to increase acidity to an appropriate level. Craft brewers and homebrewers have occasionally used additions of citric acid to lend some tartness to Belgian-style witbier; although some tartness is traditional, it has historically been the result of lactic bacterial activity. Citric acid has also been used as a cleaning agent, particularly in the removal of "beer-stone" from fermentation vessels.

George Philliskirk

clarification is the name given to any process where solids are removed from wort or beer to give a clear liquid. Wort clarification is important because beer produced from clear or "bright" wort tends to be of higher quality. Wort clarification takes place in the brewhouse after it has been boiled in the wort kettle or copper. It may involve a "whirlpool" if hop extracts or pellets are used, or a "hop back" when whole leaf hops are used. Worts that have not been clarified may be slow to ferment, and the resulting beer may be difficult to filter, or may be difficult to clarify in cask using finings.

Beer clarification can involve different processes. Filtration is the most commonly used. Centrifugation is another method of clarifying beer. In this process excess quantities of yeast and protein are removed from beer in the brewery before filtration. Beers are easier to filter if excess solids are removed before final filtration. In traditional cask beer, finings agents such as isinglass are used to sediment yeast and protein during a clarification process that takes place in a cask.

See also CENTRIFUGATION, FILTRATION, FININGS, HOP BACK, and WHIRLPOOL.

Paul KA Buttrick

clarity is the state of "brightness" of a wort or beer. Two fundamental forms of "break" (insoluble) material can lead to a lack of clarity in wort, so-called dirty wort. They are hot break, produced during wort boiling, and cold break that forms when wort is cooled. See COLD BREAK and HOT BREAK. Turbidity in beer can take various forms. Some beers develop precipitates that settle to the bottom of the container. Bits ("floaters") are large discrete particles present throughout the body of the beer and are frequently caused by interactions between added stabilizers such as foam stabilizer and certain colloidal stabilizers. "Haze" describes inherent dullness that pervades the whole liquid and can be caused by diverse materials, including yeast and other microorganisms, protein, polyphenols, starch, β-glucan, pentosan, and oxalate. Turbidity caused by living organisms is called "biological haze." That due to non-living entities is called "non-biological haze." If the haze is present under all conditions it is "permanent haze." If the haze is present only when beer is chilled to 32°F (0°C) but not when the beer is warmed to 68°F (20°C), it is so-called chill haze. See CHILL HAZE. Beers that appear bright but which register a high haze reading (determined by instruments that measure light scattered at 90° to the incident) are said to display "invisible haze" (or "pseudo haze").

Clarity is an important aspect of the appearance of many beers. Many consumers correlate haze with a lack of quality in beers where haze is not expected, e.g., pilsner. Interestingly, however, the rise of craft beer in the United States has resulted in a regional difference in that regard. Many craft beer consumers in the Western United States are not disturbed by haze in beer; in fact, they see it as a positive sign of handcraft. This does not tend to be as true in the East, where clarity remains expected in most beer styles.

See also HAZE.

Bamforth, C.W. Beer haze. *Journal of the American Society of Brewing Chemists*, 57 (1999): 81–90.

Charles W. Bamforth

cleaning in place (CIP) refers to methods used to clean the interior surfaces of pipes, vessels, and tanks without disassembly and often without manual labor. Before CIP became commonplace in the 1950s, brewing process equipment was often disassembled and the parts cleaned individually by hand. CIP is not unique to the brewing industry; it is applied in all industries that process liquids in closed systems.

Tanks, piping, brewing vessels, and packaging equipment in modern breweries are all closed systems. Frequent cleaning of such equipment is necessary to uphold the required microbiological and chemical quality of the beer produced through it. Consequently, cleaning and sanitizing of the brewing equipment must take place in a way that allows the equipment to remain closed and personnel to be kept safely isolated from oftentimes very hot chemical cleaning solutions. In large modern breweries the cleaning processes are so comprehensive and elaborate that automation is often necessary for sufficient control of costs, energy and time management, and consistency. Thus, the concept of CIP in the modern brewing world is not just a convenience; it is in many cases a necessity.

CIP cleaning of vessels takes place by means of liquid dispersal devices mounted inside the vessels as part of the construction. These are normally either static sprayballs or different sorts of rotary jets. These devices, using liquid pressure, direct sprays of cleaning solution toward every part of the internal surface of the vessel. The cleaning solution, often an alkaline detergent or acid solution at elevated temperatures, is then repeatedly circulated through the vessel in a manner not dissimilar to that of a dishwasher. The dispersal device may be designed to gently flow cleaning solution over all interior surfaces or it may be a high-impact jet that uses mechanical as well as chemical energy to remove soils. Piping, pumps, valves, filling machines, and other pieces of processing equipment that do not have internal cleaning devices are CIP cleaned by circulating cleaning solution through the parts that contact beer or wort.

The central unit in any CIP cleaning process is the CIP station or CIP unit. This consists of a number of vessels for cleaning solutions plate heat exchangers for ensuring the correct temperature of the solutions and pumps for circulation of cleaning solutions at the required pressure, and flow rates through the route/equipment to be cleaned. Such units can be automated to any extent desired. In smaller breweries and brewpubs, the same task is often accomplished without a dedicated CIP station, so each brewery devises its own effective cleaning method using pumps, hoses, and other equipment on hand. A corollary to CIP is sterilization in place, which uses similar methods, often with a sterilizing chemical solution, to sterilize interior surfaces of vessels and process equipment.

Kunze, Wolfgang ed., *Technology brewing and malting*, 3rd international. Berlin: VLB Berlin, 2004.

Anders Brinch Kissmeyer

cling is the adhesion of beer foam to the side of a glass during beer consumption. It is frequently known as "lacing." While most drinkers perceive cling to be a desirable attribute of beer, indicative of high quality, there are some who are put off by the phenomenon, as they feel it has a characteristic of dirtiness. Its occurrence depends on the cross-reaction of hydrophobic polypeptides with bitter acids, with the involvement of metal ions that act as bridges. It is a time-dependent interaction and the resultant "solidification" that leads to the foam being in an adherent state takes between 30 seconds and 2 minutes to occur. Cling increases in proportion to beer bitterness and is especially strong when the reduced bitter compounds ("light-stable hop extract") that some brewers use to prevent "skunking" are used. The pattern of lacing also depends on the mode of bittering, with conventional iso-alpha acids offering a finer and less coarse appearance. See ISO-ALPHA ACIDS. Cling is inhibited by shorter chain fatty acids.

Cling depends on the glass surface being clean and free from lipid or detergent and can be assessed by optic instruments that scan the surface of the beer glass after beer has been removed and assess the proportion of the surface that is covered by foam. Alternatively, the Lacing Index procedure evaluates the total amount of cling by recovering the foam from the glass in water and measuring the absorbance of ultraviolet light by the resultant solution. While both of these methods correlate with the total amount of clinging foam, they do not quantify the aesthetic appeal of the lacing pattern, which remains in the eye of the beholder.

Evans, D.E., & Bamforth, C.W. "Beer foam: achieving a suitable head." In *Beer: A quality perspective*, ed. C.W. Bamforth, 1–60. Burlington, MA: Academic Press, 2009.

Charles W. Bamforth

Cluster (hop) is one of the oldest US hops grown in North America. It is considered to be a bittering hop with modest levels of alpha-acids (5%–9% w/w) and low oil content (0.4–0.8 ml/100 g). The rootstock's origin is not known for certain; however, it is believed to have originated from a chance (open) pollination of the English Black Cluster with an American wild male, probably on the east coast of the United States sometime in the late 18th century. There are four different USDA accession numbers for this variety: Yakima Cluster (also termed L-1)–USDA 65102, Late Cluster

L-16–USDA 21011, Late Cluster L-8–USDA 65104, and Early Cluster–USDA 65103. They are all very similar with the primary difference being the time of ripening. All Clusters are very susceptible to downy mildew and therefore cannot be grown successfully in the Willamette Valley of Oregon. They do well in the Yakima Valley, Washington, and Treasure Valley, Idaho. All have excellent vigor and high production potential. The storage stability of Cluster's alpha acids is among the best of all hops in the world and it keeps very well even in non-refrigerated storage. Cluster acreage has declined significantly from nearly 90% of total US hop production in the 1970s to about 1.25% (501 acres with 1.19 million lb production) in 2009. Cluster is often described as having a clean bitterness and a blackcurrant-like aroma. At one time, the vast majority of American beer contained Cluster, but Galena has supplanted it as the most widely grown American hop variety.

Thomas Shellhammer and Alfred Haunold

coaching inns were a vital part of the transportation system of Britain and mainland Europe for some 200 years, from the mid-17th century to the arrival of the railway. Coach travel became possible as a result of improvements to road surfaces. Teams of horses pulled stage coaches and mail coaches, stopping every 7 or 10 miles to change tired horses for fresh ones. The inns provided stabling for horses and food, drink, and accommodation for travelers. Some English towns had as many as a dozen coaching inns. There was intense rivalry between them to wring the highest charges from coach companies for the hire of horses and also to earn substantial amounts from wealthier travelers.

At first coaches were cramped and uncomfortable, but by the end of the 18th century sprung axles and lighter bodies made traveling more pleasant. Nevertheless, there was a rigid class system in operation, with four customers inside the coaches and up to a dozen outside or "up top," sitting alongside the drivers. There were further improvements when the Royal Mail introduced faster coach services in the 1780s to speed letters and parcels around Britain. Improvements to the service meant greater business for coaching inns, which became places of bustling activity: ostlers groomed steaming horses, whereas landlords and large retinues of servants supplied food, ale, and beds to exhausted travelers.

According to one legend, it was the consumption of beer in coaching inns that gave rise to the term "cock and bull story." In the town of Stony Stratford in Buckinghamshire, central England, there were two coaching inns, the Cock and the Bull. Emboldened by tankards of ale, travelers at the inns told tales that grew steadily more exaggerated, to such an extent than any examples of absurd tales became known throughout the coaching system as "a load of cock and bull."

Charles Dickens, whose life straddled both the coaching inn and the railway, has handed down to posterity some memorable images of the inns he visited on his extensive travels. Among those he stayed in were the Great White Horse at Ipswich, mentioned in *The Pickwick Papers*, and the Saracens Head in Snow Hill, London, where Nicholas Nickleby set out on his journey to Yorkshire. While in Yorkshire, Dickens also visited the New Angel in Doncaster, the George in Bradford, and the White Horse and Griffin in Whitby.

William and Dorothy Wordsworth were also great users of coaching inns as they traversed the country. Dorothy's journal is full of references to inns and she waxed lyrical about the Black Swan in Helmsley, Yorkshire, which survives today: "My heart danced at the sight of its cleanly outside bright yellow walls, casements overshadowed with jasmine, and its low, double gavel-ended front." The size and scope of coaching inns can be seen from the history of the George at Catterick in Yorkshire, which was run for some 40 years by Daniel Ferguson. His initials are cut in the stone of the lounge windows. His coaching business was substantial and he often had to employ ploughs and dray horses to work the coaches.

A rival inn in Catterick, the Angel, now demolished, had stabling for 100 horses. But these great inns, with their stables, cobbled courtyards, saloons, restaurants, and bedrooms, were swept away by the railway in the 19th century. Once it became possible to travel at great speed from city to city in a fraction of the time of a coach, the inns that stood on turnpikes and town centers succumbed to the power of the steam engine. Pubs and hotels, often called the Railway, were built alongside stations. Coaching inns were too large to be economic in the new age of steam and most were eventually demolished.

The area of south London known as the Borough was once packed with inns because pilgrims would begin their long treks to Canterbury Cathedral there. The Tabard featured as the starting point for the group of pilgrims in Chaucer's Canterbury Tales. Today the only remaining coaching inn in the district is the George at 77 Borough High Street, London. It was once cheek-by-jowl with several other inns, including the Tabard, the Golden Lion, and the White Hart mentioned by Shakespeare in *Henry VI* and the place where the heroes of *The Pickwick Papers* first met Sam Weller. The George, now owned by the National Trust, which protects buildings of historic interest, was first mentioned in a survey of London in 1598, but it could be older. The George is often called an Elizabethan inn but the original buildings were destroyed by a fire in 1676, although they were faithfully recreated. It has a maze of small rooms, with dark oak paneling, benches, and settles. A gallery runs along part of the exterior and it is claimed that Shakespeare and other players performed from the gallery and the courtyard before the Globe Theatre was built nearby. The atmosphere of the George and its rivals was best described by Dickens: "Great, rambling, queer old places they are, with galleries, and passages, and staircases, wide enough and antiquated enough to furnish materials for a hundred ghost stories."

The George, which could accommodate 80 coaches a week, was once much larger but two wings were pulled down in 1889 by the Great Northern Railway Company to make way for engine sheds at London Bridge Station. The railway finished off most coaching inns and severely truncated the George, one of the most famous of the breed.

Coaching Inns and Beer

The popularity of coaching inns created a great demand for ale and beer, a demand that often outstripped the ability of innkeepers to brew sufficient amounts. Roads out of London to the Channel ports and to the north of England contained dozens of large coaching inns for those leaving and arriving in the capital. Commercial or "common brewers" sprang up to supply beer to innkeepers to supplement their own brews. Visitors from continental Europe to London would have encouraged the move from unhopped ale to hopped bier or beer, which had become the norm in mainland Europe. The demand for hops from London brewers became so strong that hop merchants opened up for business in the Southwark area south of London Bridge: the road out of Southwark was the Old Dover Road—made famous by Dickens in *A Tale of Two Cities*—which led to the hop farms in Kent. In 1868 the Hop Exchange was built in Southwark, almost opposite the George Inn, where fresh hops from Kent could be bought and sold. The exchange still stands and is protected as a "listed building" by the government as a result of its historic importance, although hops are no longer stored and sold there.

Two breweries, both called the Anchor Brewery, grew to a considerable size and fortune in the area around London Bridge and Southwark. Thrale's Brewery, in which Dr Samuel Johnson was a shareholder, dates from the early 18th century. It closed following the death of its owner, Henry Thrale, in 1781 and merged with the rival Anchor Brewery founded by John Courage in 1787. Courage was taken over by members of the Barclay family, who also went into banking with some success. The name Courage was maintained and the Anchor Brewery survived until 1981 when its brands were transferred to a modern plant in Reading. Another substantial brewery in the London Bridge area was Jenners: the Jenner family is still active in brewing as the owners of Harvey's Brewery in Sussex, close to Brighton.

In the city of Chester in Northwest England, the Golden Falcon was a leading coaching inn, with beer supplied by the Northgate Brewery, which closed in 1969. The Liverpool Arms in Chester, which still stands, was built next to the brewery. Until the dissolution of the monasteries under Henry VIII, the monks of Chester Abbey supplied local inns with ale.

Corran, H. S. *A history of brewing*. Newton Abbot, England: David & Charles, 1975.

Dickens, Charles. *Nicholas Nickleby*. Various publishers; letters of Charles Dickens; letters of Dorothy Wordsworth.

Hackwood, Frederick W. *Inns, ales and drinking customs of Old England*. London: Bracken Books, 1985.

Pepper, Barrie (ed.). *Bedside book of beer*. St Albans, England: Alma Books, 1990.

Pudney, John. *A draught of contentment*: The story of the Courage Group. London: New English Library, 1971.

Roger Protz

cocktails. Beer has always had a somewhat ambiguous place in the American art of mixology. The classic drinks of the American bar—cocktails, slings, juleps, punches, coolers, and the like—were based on spirits and fortified wines, with little place for beer. Of the 230-odd drink recipes in Jerry Thomas' 1862 *How to Mix Drinks*, the first ever of its kind and a foundational document for the art, only eight contain beer. (By contrast, a contemporary British manual, with many fewer recipes in total, offers 23.) What's more, of those eight, all but two were obsolete as American bar drinks, and even those—the Ale Flip (spiced and sweetened ale with rum and eggs) and the Ale Sangaree (basically a flip without the rum or eggs)—were holdovers from an earlier age. There was one place, however, that beer was making its way into bartenders' drinks at the time: judging by A.V. Bevill's 1871 *Barkeeper's Ready Reference*, sour beer or ale was sometimes used in the "Western Territories" as a substitute for lemon juice.

In a professional mixologist's hands, the use of beer and ale has certainly progressed since then, but perhaps not as far as its proponents might like. Some of the more creative modern bartenders will sometimes use a gueuze as a souring agent, attempt a variation on a Flip, or round out a long drink with a white ale. Some of the leading bars in the American craft cocktail movement have even gone so far as to have sections of their cocktail menus devoted to beer-based concoctions. The drinks tend to feature all the hallmarks of the movement: handmade ingredients (including such things as ale reduced to a syrup), unusual flavor combinations, and a good deal of technical sophistication. Yet few of these creations, whatever their merits, have gained much traction among drinkers, while the periodic brewing-industry sponsored attempts to promote beer cocktails have yet to succeed in creating a truly popular drink.

On the other hand, beer features prominently in what may be called "folk mixology": mixology that takes place in the field, without the mediation of a trained bartender. The resulting drinks almost always eschew specialized equipment or techniques and involve only one or two additional ingredients.

While their very simplicity makes it difficult to detail their history and evolution, it is safe to say that the popular American beer drinks at least have older European analogs, if not direct ancestors. For instance, take the 1980s-vintage "Irish Car Bomb," a pint of stout with a mixed shot of Irish whiskey and Irish cream liqueur dropped in. While it echoes the 17th-century English drink Pop-In (ale with a shot of raw spirits), it also nods to the 19th-century English Dog's Nose (porter and gin) and the American Depth Charge (a shot glass of whiskey dropped in a mug of beer), without necessarily being derived from any of them. Other drinks, such as the Black Velvet (stout and Champagne) and the Shandy Gaff (ale and ginger beer) are direct imports, the former from Germany and the latter from Britain, and both antedating the Civil War. Yet others are at least North American creations: the United States and Canada might dispute who was the first to mix beer and tomato juice, but whether called a Calgary Red Eye or simply Red Beer, it achieved widespread popularity in both countries in the early 1950s. On the other hand, the Michelada, the up-and-coming beer drink of the 2000s, is from Mexico and is somewhat more elaborate than most folk drinks, combining beer with lime juice, hot sauce, Worcestershire sauce, and liquid "oriental seasoning." Less authentically Mexican is the 1970s-vintage Beer Margarita, which mixes equal parts mass-market lager, frozen limeade, and tequila. In fact, with its improvisational use of mass-market ingredients (frozen limeade for fresh limes, beer for Cointreau) and its utter simplicity of execution, this drink is the very model of the popular American beer cocktail.

Bevill, A. V. *Barkeepers' ready reference*. St. Louis: A.V. Bevill, 1871.

Thomas, Jerry P. *How to mix drinks, or the bon-vivant's companion*. New York: Dick & Fitzgerald, 1862.

David Wondrich

cohumulone is one of five alpha acid analogs in hop resin, the others being adhumulone, humulone, prehumulone, and posthumulone. These analogs differ only slightly from each other in their molecular structures, and together they serve as precursors to iso-alpha acids, the predominant contributors of bitterness in beer. Cohumulone and humulone levels vary between roughly 20% and 50% of total alpha acids, depending on variety, whereas adhumulone levels tend to be fairly constant across varieties, at about 10% to 15% of alpha acids.

Pre- and posthumulone, on the other hand, play only minor roles. Most hop analyses will specifically show a cohumulone percentage. This is because brewers believe iso-cohumulone contributes a rougher, harsher quality of bitterness than other iso-alpha acids. Traditional aroma hops tend to be low in cohumulone, whereas some bittering varieties have higher levels. Because brewers tend to associate low cohumulone with a finer quality of bitterness, hop breeders are favoring new cultivars with low cohumulone levels. When hops oxidize, alpha acids, including cohumulone, change their molecular makeup, producing isobutryic acid, which has a distinctive rancid, sour, cheesy odor. See ADHUMULONE and HUMULONE.

Thomas Shellhammer

cold break is an amalgam of proteins, protein-polyphenol complexes, and carbohydrates that precipitate from wort upon cooling and can contribute to chill haze if left in solution. See CHILL HAZE. Cold break consists of roughly 50% protein, 25% polyphenols, and 25% carbohydrates and lipids. Roughly 15%–25% of these proteins bind to polyphenols, forming protein-polyphenol complexes. The total dry weight of cold break generally varies from 17–35 g/bbl and is dependent on numerous factors, including the degree of malt modification, wort temperature, the mashing program employed, hopping rates, and the presence or absence of adjuncts. Under-modified malts contain fewer polyphenols and beta glucans and thus result in less cold break, as do intensive mashing regiments such as a decoction mashing. Finely milled malt and its degraded husks result in a greater extraction of polyphenols and a consequent increase in cold break. Similarly, adding hops, which contain polyphenols, contribute to an increase in cold break. High gravity worts will also result in an increase in cold break, while the use of adjuncts, generally low in polyphenols, will culminate in less cold break.

Various methods will extract or separate the cold break from the wort. Regardless of the method, rapid cooling of the wort is essential to the precipitation of cold break and its subsequent removal from the wort. Some breweries will transfer the wort to a settling tank either prior or subsequent to yeast pitching to allow the cold break to fall to the bottom of the tank, whereupon it is removed from the cone. Conversely, flotation of the cold break via the introduction of sterile air, whose bubbles bind to the cold break and float it to the surface, can also prove effective at removing cold break. After 2 to 3 hours a brown, compact head forms on top of the wort. The wort is then removed from the bottom of the tank, leaving the cold break behind. These methods are time consuming, however, and fraught with potential for bacterial contamination. Centrifugation of the wort prior to pitching is rapidly becoming one of the more popular methods of cold break removal, yielding removal rates of 50%–60%. Diatomaceous earth filtration offers even greater results. See DIATOMACEOUS EARTH. It is largely accepted, however, that total removal of cold break is undesirable.

Cold break can cause unwanted beer haze, but it is also a source of yeast nutrients, namely sterols and unsaturated fatty acids. Studies have shown that total elimination of cold break can result in slower fermentations, lessened yeast viability, higher acetate ester levels, and an increase in dissolved carbon dioxide levels during fermentation resulting in incomplete fermentation.

Barchet, Ron. "Cold trub: Implications for finished beer, and methods of removal." http://www.brewingtechniques.com/library/backissues/issue2.2/barchet.html/ (accessed April 2010).

Carey, Daniel, and Grossman, Ken. "Fermentation and cellar operations." In Karl Ockert ed. *Fermentation, cellaring, and packaging operations*, volume 2, St. Paul, MN: Master Brewers Association of the Americas, 2006.

Kunze, Wolfgang. *Technologie brauer und mälzer.* Translated by Trevor Wainwright. Berlin: VLB Berlin, 1996.

Geoff Deman

cold water extract is the portion of the malt solids that are soluble in cold water expressed as a percentage of the weight of the malt. The test is carried out at 20°C (68°F) using water with ammonia added to inhibit any enzyme action. It serves as a measure of the degree to which the malt has been modified in the malt house. Figures in the 15%–22% range are considered acceptable. The cold water extract consists of simple sugars, amino acids, and other soluble components produced during the breakdown of the endosperm of barley during malting. See ENDOSPERM. Maltsters producing specialty malts in a roasting drum will deliberately allow the enzymic breakdown of the barley endosperm to continue to near completion, creating very high cold water extract prior to roasting. This provides large amounts of simple carbohydrates and amino acids for the desirable Maillard reactions that occur during roasting. See MAILLARD REACTION. Brewers are less likely to worry about the cold water extract as a parameter of their malt directly, but do use the number as an inference of other characteristics of the malt, such as the degree of modification. They will also track the variation in the number as a measurement of malting consistency.

See also MALTING, MODIFICATION, and ROASTED MALTS.

Steve Parkes

College of St. Gregory and St. Martin at Wye

See WYE COLLEGE.

colloidal haze, a type of non-biological haze in beer. Haze in beer can be formed by either of two main factors: biological (bacteria and yeast) or non-biological agents. Non-biological haze can be amorphous (e.g., starch based) or colloidal. Colloidal systems refer to the presence of one substance suspended within another. Beer colloidal haze is generally the result of protein molecules within the beer joining with polyphenols to form molecules large enough to cause turbidity. Colloidal haze can be a chill haze that is present at 0°C (32°F), but solubilizes and disappears at 20°C (68°F), or it can be a permanent haze that is constantly present in the beer. Colloidal haze is considered a quality problem in pilsner beers, which are expected to be brilliantly clear, but a very desirable aspect of Belgian-style white beers. Two strategies can be employed by a brewer to control colloidal haze: decrease the protein level in the beer or decrease the polyphenol content in the beer. There is much more protein than polyphenol in beer. The most common method of physical stabilization is to decrease the protein level by treating the beer with silica gel, which binds with protein and removes it during filtration of the beer. See SILICA GEL. One drawback to silica gel is that it may remove proteins that are responsible for head stabilization; this effect can lead to poor foam formation and retention. Alternatively, removal of polyphenols can also be achieved by the use of polyvinyl polypyrrolidone (PVPP). See PVPP. PVPP is also removed, along with the haze-causing polyphenols, during filtration. However, PVPP is expensive, so recent years have seen an increase in filtration aids that combine silica gel and PVPP at a lower cost. Hazes caused by dry hopping are also colloidal hazes and are caused by polyphenols from the hops combining with protein, oxygen or heavy metals. Dry hop hazes can be difficult to remove, and many craft breweries practicing dry hopping do not bother to make the attempt because colloidal haze has no effect upon beer flavor.

See also CLARITY, DRY HOPPING, HAZE, and POLYPHENOLS.

Keith Villa

Colonial beer

See BREWING IN COLONIAL AMERICA.

color is an integral and important part of our experience of food and drink, and beer is no exception. When beer is poured into a clear glass, the color is the first thing the prospective beer drinker will notice. Color invariably conjures up expectations, usually subliminal, of the flavor experience ahead. A bright golden beer may lead one to expect refreshment and to recall sunny days spent in beer gardens, whereas a reddish–black beer with a thick brown head may evoke expectations of malty roasted flavors and thoughts of sitting in front of a roaring fireplace. Because color works so powerfully upon the mind, chefs, winemakers, and brewers alike will pay very close attention to achieving the right hues for their creations.

It is ironic, therefore, that color can be an unreliable indicator of flavor. This is because color exists more in the mind than in reality; technically, color is the mere reflection or refraction of light as it strikes an object, solid, liquid, or gaseous. Our eyes register the wavelengths of light they receive, and the brain translates these into the colors we see.

In beer, color is determined in various ways. The most significant source of beer color is pigments in the grain. Both the malted and the unmalted grains used in the brewhouse are kilned dried; the longer the drying process and the higher the drying temperature, the darker will be the grist for the mash and the more opaque will be the beer made from it. See BLACK MALT, CARAMEL MALTS, CRYSTAL MALT, MALT, and ROASTED MALTS. Gently kilned malt may make a beer that is brilliantly blonde, transparent, and sparkling, whereas roasted malts can be used to make beer that is virtually impenetrable by light. Through the judicious composition of the grain bill, therefore, a brewer can make beers of any shade and hue from light straw to amber, copper, red, mahogany, dark brown, and finally black. In addition, adjuncts such as rice, corn, or white sugar can be added during the brewing process to replace malt, resulting in a lighter color.

Similar colors in different beers may be derived from different sources. For example, dark Belgian beer styles such as dubbel often derive their brown color not from roasted malts, but from a highly caramelized invert sugar syrup called candi sugar. See CANDI SUGAR. Candi sugar is highly fermentable and rarely leaves much residual sweetness in beer. The flavors given by dark candi sugar syrup (caramel, raisins, burnt sugar) are quite different than those given by roasted malts (coffee, chocolate), even when the color of the beer is similar. This is one reason why a Belgian dubbel does not taste like an English brown ale. See BROWN ALE and DUBBEL.

Dark candi sugar, which is specifically meant to give both color and flavor to beer, is different from products designed to be pure colorants. Various caramel colors, from malt-derived German "farbebier" to the old American "Porterine," have been widely available to brewers for more than 100 years. See COLORANTS. These can be used to overcome natural variations and adjust the color of a beer to meet a particular specification, or they can be used, like a form of makeup, to completely change the viewer's perception of a beer. A golden beer, when rendered russet–brown by caramel coloring, may be perceived by the consumer as having a far richer flavor than it actually does. It is interesting to note that advertising photos that depict the color of mass-market lagers will often show a color notably darker than the beer is in real life.

Chemical reactions that take place during malting, mashing, and wort boiling can also contribute to beer color. These include the so-called Maillard reaction, often referred to as non-enzymatic browning, during which melanoidins are created. These are responsible for the amber hue in many beers. See MAILLARD REACTION and MELANOIDINS. Traditional lager malts, which are not usually as highly modified as ale malts, tend to have lighter color. Higher modification leads to a higher sugar and amino acid content in the malt, and this produces deeper colors in the kiln or roasting drum. Oxidation during the brewing process or later during a beer's natural aging process can affect beer color as well, typically bringing on a yellow–brown tinge.

Brewers use several more technical methods for distinguishing between different colors and their intensities. One of the earliest methods was a color scale developed by Joseph Lovibond, which is divided into "degrees Lovibond," usually abbreviated as L. See LOVIBOND. This scale is still in use today, particularly in the United States. It is based on a standardized set of color samples that are used for a visual comparison with a beer or wort sample. A very pale beer usually has a Lovibond value of about 2°L, whereas a very dark beer may have values about 30°L. In 1958, the American Society of Brewing Chemists adopted a scale based on the absorbance of a single-wavelength light with a wavelength of 430 nm in beer in a half-inch-diameter jar. It was called the Standard Reference Method (SRM). Conveniently, when SRM values were adjusted by a correction factor of 10, the numbers virtually matched those of the Lovibond scale for identical beers. Maltsters now rate their malts in terms of the Lovibond values for a wort derived from that malt in a standard mash. Beer colors, on the other hand, are now more likely to be given as SRM values. The European Brewery Convention (EBC), being rooted in the metric system, has its own EBC color scale, whereby the conversion between SRM and EBC and vice versa is "loosely" as follows:

$$x\text{EBC} = [(x \times 0.375) + 0.46]\ \text{SRM}$$
$$y\text{SRM} = [(y \times 2.65) - 1.2]\ \text{EBC}.$$

For instance, a golden blonde Pilsner with a color value of 4.5 SRM would be have an EBC color value of 4.5 multiplied by 2.65 minus 1.2 = 10.725 EBC.

As a general rule, yellow to straw blonde beers have color values of 4 to 8 EBC (2 to 4 SRM), pale ales of perhaps 20 to 30 EBC (10 to 15 SRM), and stouts of 70 to 140 EBC (35 to 70 SRM). Colorant additives may have color values as high as 9,000 EBC (3,375 SRM). A pale malt may have a color value of 1.5°L to 2.5°L (roughly 2.8 to 5.4 EBC), a caramel malt 60°L (roughly 160 EBC), and a chocolate malt 350°L (roughly 925 SRM). Various blends of differently colored malts allow the brewer to achieve a wide range of color.

Just as many wine drinkers erroneously equate dark colors with both concentration and high quality, so beer drinkers often conflate darker color with alcoholic strength. In fact, beer color is entirely unrelated to beer strength, and most people are surprised to hear that nearly black draught Guinness has only about 4.2% alcohol by volume (ABV), making it notably lighter in alcohol than American Budweiser, which has about 5%. Conversely a golden-hued Belgian tripel will have about 9% ABV, and a German maibock of similar color can have a great depth of malt flavor and 8% ABV or above.

Another range of colors in beer may be derived from fruit, as is the case in Belgian kriek (cherries) and framboise (raspberries). Colors from fruit may be bright, especially if the fruit was added in the form of juice, or dulled, especially if the beer is barrel aged, where slow oxidation will eventually bring on brownish hues.

Bamforth, Charles W., ed. "Beer: a quality perspective." In *The handbook of alcoholic beverage series.* Amsterdam: Elsevier, 2009.

Daniels, Ray. Beer color demystified—Part I: How to measure beer color in the home and microbrewery. *Brewing Techniques* 3 (1995): 56.

Daniels, Ray. Beer color demystified—Part II: The science of beer color. *Brewing Techniques* 3 (1995): 60.

Horst Dornbusch

colorants are designed to mimic colors that a beer might otherwise have from a normal brewing process, but often without the associated flavors. By far the most important group of colorants used in brewing are the caramel colors and the related malt-based food coloring called Farbebier. People often "drink with their eyes," so just as the colorant Mega Purple is used to give a darker, richer color to wine, so some brewers will seek to do the same to beer. Beer colorants can give beers the same colors as dark malts and the resulting colors can be measured and quantified by the same analytical methods as malt-derived color. They can also be used more sparingly to make minor adjustments to color, correcting inconsistencies in the brewing process or ingredients. Caramel coloring, which is widely used in many foods, is usually produced by heat treatment of glucose syrup, sometimes with food-grade chemical catalysts added to ease the caramelization process.

In most countries if a brewer desires to tint beer with colors outside the normal color range for beer, any coloring agent approved by the relevant authorities for the coloring of food products in general can be used. It should be noted that this is a highly uncommon practice in breweries at large, and in general such use of other colorants is only seen in connection with fruit beers, certain seasonal beers, and occasional oddities.

In Europe, the EU lists all additives to foods that can be marketed in the 27 EU member countries, and only caramel-based colors are approved for beer. This means that any coloring of beer with "non-beer" colors such as red, green, or blue will have to be achieved by addition of natural fruit or herb extracts. The U.S. Food and Drug Administration does not publish a "positive list" for colorants allowed in beer sold in the United States, but it requires any producer or importer to apply for the use of such in each case.

See also CARAMEL COLOR.

The Food and Drug Administration. *Food.* http://www.fda.gov/food (accessed February 17, 2011).

Anders Brinch Kissmeyer

color units EBC (European Brewery Convention) refer to the color of a beer measured in a technical manner. Prior to the development of the EBC method, beer color was estimated qualitatively (and perhaps somewhat subjectively) by comparing colored glass plate references, rendered in a scale known as degrees Lovibond, to samples of beer. The sample beer was then designated as a certain color in Lovibond units. See LOVIBOND. The EBC method is quantitative and involves measuring the beer sample color in a cuvette that is placed in a spectrophotometer at a wavelength of 430 nm. This particular wavelength was selected so that the final measured color was in agreement with Lovibond references. The actual formula for measuring color is

$$EBC = 25 \times D \times A_{430},$$

where D = dilution factor of the sample and A_{430} = the light absorbance at 430 nanometers in a 1-cm cuvette. The EBC color system is used primarily in Europe, whereas North and South America use the Standard Reference Method (SRM) to measure beer color. See STANDARD REFERENCE METHOD (SRM). The two systems are closely related and can be converted in the following equations:

$$SRM = EBC \times 0.508$$
$$EBC = SRM \times 1.97.$$

Additionally, both systems require that the beer sample be free of turbidity for an accurate color determination. The sample must be filtered if the turbidity is measured at greater than 1 EBC turbidity unit.

A typical American mass-market lager measures between 4 and 8 EBC units, whereas a dark stout may measure 100 EBC units or above.

See also COLOR.

Keith Villa

Columbus (hop)

See CTZ (HOP).

colupulone is one of four beta acid analogs in hop resin, the others being adlupulone, lupulone, and prelupulone. Colupulone levels vary across hop varieties from roughly 20% to 55% of total beta acids. Lupulone levels also vary, from 30% to 55%. Adlupulone levels vary in a much narrower range, from 10% to 15%. Structurally, beta acid analogues are very similar, but not identical, to their alpha acid counterparts. The slight structural difference, however, prevents beta acids from isomerizing in the kettle. See HOP ISOMERIZATION. There are, therefore, no iso-beta acids in wort or beer. Furthermore, beta acids are virtually insoluble in wort; thus, only trace levels can be found in beer. When beta acids oxidize into hulupones, however, which happens as hops age, they become wort soluble and confer bitterness. As hops oxidize, the bitterness that comes from iso-alpha acids diminishes, but this is somewhat offset by the contribution of bitterness by hulupones. The ratio of alpha to beta acids ultimately determines the extent to which the bitterness will diminish as hops oxidize.

See also ADLUPULONE and LUPULONE.

Thomas Shellhammer

Comet (hop) is a high-alpha-acid hop developed primarily for commercial production in Washington and Idaho. Comet originated in 1961 as a cross between a female seedling from the cultivar Sunshine and the wild American male accession Utah 524-2 (USDA 58006M). Comet was bred and released in 1974 by the U.S. Department of Agriculture hop breeding program in Corvallis, Oregon. The alpha acid content in Comet ranges between 9% and 12.5%, with an average of approximately 11%, whereas the beta acid content averages approximately 5%. Oil content in dried cones may approach 2.0 ml/100 g. Vigor and yield potential are good, with yields typically ranging between roughly 1,900 and 2,250 kg/ha (about 1,700 and 2,000 lb/acre). By the 1980s, Comet production declined in favor of new higher-alpha cultivars, and the hop has disappeared from commercial production, perhaps in part because some brewers found its "wild hop" aroma properties unappealing. A unique agronomic characteristic of Comet is its bright yellow–green foliage early in the growing season, which darkens gradually as the season progresses—probably an inheritance from its maternal grandparent Sunshine, which also produces conspicuous lemon-yellow leaves.

Zimmermann, C. E., S. T. Likens, A. Haunold, C. E. Homer, and D. D. Roberts. Registration of Comet hop. *Crop Science* 15 (1975): 98.

Shaun Townsend

concrete (fermenting in). Fermenters constructed of reinforced concrete were used by breweries in Europe and the United States from the late 19th century to the mid-20th century. These were usually open tanks and, depending on the brewery's size, varied in size up to 2300 hL (2000 US barrels, 1400 UK barrels). Concrete tanks were very economical to build but expensive to maintain. These vessels could be built on-site using any available space in a vibration-free environment. The cement walls were of solid construction. The primary concern with concrete tanks was assuring that the lining material adhered firmly to the tank surface, since when filled with wort, these vessels tend to bulge slightly. Thus, the coatings needed to be somewhat flexible so as not to tear away from the concrete surface.

Typical liner materials included various types of waxes, enamels, and resins. For better coating adherence, the walls were first lined with a porous layer made up of a mixture of Portland cement, ground glass, and magnesia or bauxite. This mixture formed a suitable base for the final coating of pitch and wax, which protected the beer from off-flavors and microbiological spoilage. The lining/coating materials were applied by craftsmen skilled at this type of task. The pitch and wax coating were resistant to most cleaning solutions and could be damaged by alkali cleaners. Damage on the inside could be repaired quickly with the same material as the initial coating. Concrete fermenters were typically cooled by means of copper attemporation coils which were installed on the side-walls of the vessel. Concrete vessels went out of fashion in breweries built after World War II due to the popularity of glass-lined steel tanks and the advent of stainless steel tanks.

De Clerck, Jean. "Fermentation technique." In *A textbook of brewing*, Translated by K. Barton-Wright. London: Chapman Hall, 1957.

Ray Klimovitz

conditioning, the achievement, post-fermentation, of a particular beer's correct character of maturation and carbonation. As such, "conditioning" is a catchall term that may include lagering, relatively warm aging in a tank, refermentation in the bottle, or refermentation in a cask. The word "condition" is often used to describe the level and texture of carbonation, particularly in the UK.

See also BOTTLE CONDITIONING, CASK CONDITIONING, LAGERING, and MATURATION.

Garrett Oliver

Confédération des Brasseurs du Marché Commun

See EUROPEAN BREWERY CONVENTION (EBC).

congress mash is a standardized small-scale mashing procedure employed to assess malt quality. The procedure is named for the standardized process instituted by the European Brewing Congress (EBC) in 1975. Fifty-gram samples of malt are milled, either coarsely or finely, and then extracted with four volumes of water in a regime that involves progressive temperature-raising in order to mimic temperature-programmed or decoction mashing. After filtration (the rate of which loosely approximates to projected lautering performance), the resulting wort (sometimes referred to as "congress wort") can be tested in various ways. Its specific gravity permits calculation of extract. See EXTRACTS. The extract difference between the worts from the coarse and fine grinds is a measure of malt modification, better modified malts offering higher extract at the coarser setting and therefore a lower "fine-coarse difference." Other analyses made on the wort may include its odor, turbidity, "iodine normality" (time taken for the mash to lose its tendency to stain blue with iodine), pH, color (including after boiling), viscosity, soluble nitrogen content, free amino nitrogen, and final degree of attenuation. See ANALYSIS.

Charles W. Bamforth

continuous fermentation is a method of converting wort into beer in a continuous process, whereby wort is fed into one end of the process and beer is discharged at the other without recourse to holding the beer in a static holding vessel (batch fermentation). The advantages claimed for continuous methods include efficient plant utilization, improved carbohydrate utilization, increased throughput, and consistency. However, microbial contamination, flavor differences with batch fermented beers, and the requirement for continuous processes upstream and downstream from fermentation, particularly in wort production, are major disadvantages this method. Additionally, continuous fermentation is somewhat inflexible in that it does not allow the brewer to respond to fluctuations in demand. In situations where a standard base beer is required before secondary adjustments for different strengths, colors, and flavors, the method has been found viable. Various methods of continuous fermentation have been attempted over the past 100 years or so but with limited success. By far the most successful is the so-called Coutts system which has operated in New Zealand for over 30 years. Beer and recycled yeast are mixed with aerated wort and, after yeast growth occurs, the fermenting beer is passed to succeeding vessels in a cascade system. The total residence time in the fermentation system is about 30 hours. An alternative approach using a single vessel only was pioneered by the British brewer Bass in the 1970s. Known as the "tower continuous fermenter," this method generated a fermentation gradient within a single tank within which a body of yeast was retained within the tower, enabling rapid fermentation rates. However, it was prone to microbial infection and "blow-outs"—loss of the yeast that was effectively washed out of the fermenter. The principle of retaining a mass of yeast within a tower was developed by applying the process of immobilization of the yeast within the fermenter. In this method, the brewing yeast is immobilized on woodchips in a one-stage reactor, thus preventing possible blow-out. This method has been used to brew both stouts and lager beers in Finland, with production times of 20–30 hours and consistent flavor development.

See also IMMOBILIZED YEAST REACTOR.

Boulton, Chris, and David Quain. *Brewing yeast and fermentation*. Chichester, England: Blackwell Science Ltd., 2001.

George Philliskirk

contract brewing, an arrangement where a company brews and packages beer on equipment that it does not own. Although such arrangements have long been common among larger brewers, contract brewing came to prominence in the United States through the founding and subsequent success of the Boston Beer Company, makers of Samuel Adams Boston Lager. First brewed at the Pittsburgh Brewing Company in 1984, the Samuel Adams brand quickly grew in both reputation and volume, its rise unencumbered by the enormous expense of owning the bricks, mortar, and stainless steel used in the production of the beer.

Since then, after several different contract arrangements, the Boston Beer Company now brews all of its beer in its own facilities, but many other companies followed the contract model, helping to establish and solidify the American craft brewing movement in the 1980s. Today, some brewing companies start as contract operations, but many more use contract brewing to supplement their production when they run out of capacity at their own brewing facilities. The host brewery, in turn, is able to turn excess capacity into a steady revenue stream.

Contract brewing arrangements vary widely. Some are distant relationships by phone, whereas others are very hands-on partnerships. In the most attenuated form of contract brewing, the host brewery may essentially provide everything from the recipe to the actual packaged beer, with very little input from the contracting brewer. In these circumstances, the contracting brewery is essentially a marketing company—they provide the identity for the beer and then market and sell it. In other instances, the contracting brewer may bring in their own ingredients and yeast strains, supply the recipe, and specify every small detail of production down to packaging. In the latter cases, a brewer or manager from the contracting brewery will frequently visit the premises of the host brewery, shepherding beer through the system.

Contract brewing also takes differing forms from a legal point of view. In a simple contract situation, the host brewery will buy all the materials used to make the beer, physically brew the beer, and then actually hold legal title to the beer until the contracting brewery takes possession of it. Another form of contract, referred to as "alternating proprietorship" or "alternating premises," emerged out of the wine industry in the late 1990s. In this form of contract, the contracting brewery, now referred to as the "tenant brewery," essentially rents time on the equipment at the host brewery. In this arrangement, all of the ingredients and the resulting beer are owned by the tenant brewery from the outset of the process. In the United States, there are tax implications to the various forms of contract relationships, which are closely regulated by the Alcohol and Tobacco Tax and Trade Bureau.

Although craft beer enthusiasts have sometimes looked askance at contract brewing, it is now so common that the stigma of "not owning the stainless steel" appears to be fading. Issues of provenance and "authenticity" still swirl through craft brewing circles, but both brewers and beer drinkers have recently paid closer attention to the beer itself and the people brewing it than to the brewery's location or ownership. Interestingly, a new class of contract brewer has recently emerged and immediately become the darlings of beer bloggers across the globe. These are itinerant brewers, often referred to (if perhaps distastefully) as "gypsy brewers." These brewers follow the model set by the "flying winemakers" who started to emerge from Australia in the 1980s, making wine all over the world. Itinerant brewers wander the world like homeless ronin, brewing beer at various different breweries. These brewers usually release their beers under a single overall brand name, but the beers themselves may have been brewed anywhere; such a brewer (often a single person) will often have several projects going at once, sometimes in different countries. The image of the itinerant brewer, far from being tainted by the idea of "contract brewing," seems to have captured the American imagination in particular. Perhaps this owes to a certain American fondness for the idea of the wandering gunslinger, traveling the land lightly on horseback, unencumbered by a household, crops, fences, or borders. As information technology and social networks speed and facilitate communications and collaborations among brewers, it is to be expected that the "flying brewmaster" will become more common.

Garrett Oliver

cooking with beer, a practice that almost certainly enjoys as long a pedigree as cooking with wine, even if the former has been less celebrated in culinary circles. Almost any beverage can be incorporated into cooking, but beer has a number of unique qualities to offer in the kitchen. Most cultures that drink beer have at least a few recipes cooked with it, from the classic Irish beef and Guinness stew to beer-battered fish and Belgian waterzooi.

It is undoubted in Belgium that cooking with beer achieves its fullest flower, with an entire range of dishes enticingly dubbed *cuisine à la bière*. Although it was based on long-standing local traditions, cuisine à la bière was codified by Belgian master chef Raoul Morleghem in the 1950s, and his work was highly influential. Today, many of Belgium's best restaurants feature beer-based dishes.

As with wine, the alcohol in beer will flash off during cooking. However, beer is not generally analogous to wine in the kitchen. Most beers have notably less acidity than wine does, and beer has hop bitterness as a complicating factor. One might hesitate to cook with very tannic wine, and very hoppy beer can be similarly difficult to work with. Hop bitterness can be broken down by cooking, but this generally requires at least 90 minutes of simmering or braising. Beers with a strong roast character can be used in cooking, but ought not to be concentrated in sauces because they can become very bitter. Used correctly, beer has much to add to cuisine across a wide range of cooking applications. Cooking can concentrate many of a beer's flavors, and therefore it is always best to use beers that have good flavors in the first place. Beers that one does not wish to drink should probably be avoided in the kitchen as well.

Marinating

Many beers can make the basis of fine marinades to add flavor to meat and poultry. British brown ales and Belgian dubbels, when combined with shallots, herbs, salt, pepper, and garlic, can make very good marinades for beer, pork, and lamb. After the meat is removed, the marinade can be strained and used to build sauces.

Deglazing

After something has been sautéed or roasted in a pan or pot, concentrated, caramelized bits of the food remain stuck to the bottom of the cooking vessel. When dissolved by beer poured into the still-hot pan, those caramelized flavors become an excellent basis for sauces. Use sweeter beers such as doppelbocks if maltier, richer flavors are preferred, but acidic beers such as gueuze can work as well.

Beer Batter

Beer's carbonation adds lightness to batters for fish, onion rings, and other foods, and the beer's residual sugar lends caramelized color and flavor.

HE'LL CHEER

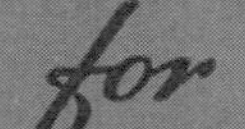

BALLANTINE'S BEER

WHEN your husband comes home hot and tired—try this recipe! Hand him a cool, sparkling glass of beer. But—*be sure it's Ballantine's!* There's nothing like it on these warm, sultry days . . . its mellow refreshing flavor goes right to the right spot.

And for an extra cheer . . . serve him one of the real men's dishes described here . . . just the thing to satisfy his longing for something different!

But remember—to get the full deliciousness of these recipes you need the rich mellow flavor of Ballantine's Export Beer—made by the makers of America's Finest Ale.

THE BEER THAT MAKES A THIRST A PLEASURE

GIVE HIM A PLEASANT SURPRISE WITH THESE

TESTED BEER RECIPES

REAL WELSH RAREBIT

½ bottle of Ballantine's Export Beer
¼ teaspoon pepper
1 teaspoon dry mustard
1 tablespoon Worcestershire sauce
⅛ teaspoon cayenne pepper
½ teaspoon salt
1½ lbs. cut up soft yellow cheese

Heat everything except the cheese in a double boiler or in a chafing dish, or pan over hot water. When very hot, add the cheese stirring constantly until it becomes creamy. Serve at once on toast or crackers.

MACARONI EN CASSEROLE

In salted boiling water, place ½ lb. macaroni. Boil until tender, (about 20 minutes). Drain and add 2 tablespoons of butter and ½ cup milk. Stir well. Place in 3 individual casseroles or one baking dish. On top, place Welsh rarebit made with Ballantine's Beer. Reheat in oven and serve very hot. Chopped bacon or ham may be added to the macaroni if desired.

HAM PATTIES WITH BEER SAUCE

1 lb. smoked ham, ground
1 lb. fresh pork, ground
¼ cup diced green pepper
1 tablespoon diced onion
2 eggs
½ cup rolled corn flakes
Salt—pepper

SAUCE

4 tablespoons brown sugar
½ cup tomato juice
2 cups Ballantine's Export Beer

Combine all ingredients and shape into patties. Saute unevenly browned. Add sauce ingredients and cook slowly in covered pan until tender. The juice may be cooked down until thick and served on the meat as a sauce.

CREAMED DRIED BEEF

¼ lb. dried beef
4 tablespoons butter
4 tablespoons flour
1 pint milk
1 bottle Ballantine's Export Beer

Tear beef into small pieces. Place in cold water and bring to a boil—then drain. Melt butter in frying pan, add the beef and brown. Then add the flour and mix well. Add the milk and beer and stir constantly until mixture thickens. Cook over direct flame for at least 5 minutes. The mixture may then be placed in the top of a double boiler and kept warm until serving time. Serve on toast. Serves 6.

BEER AND ONION SOUP

3 tablespoons butter
1 medium sized onion, sliced thin
1½ cups beef stock
1 cup Ballantine's Export Beer
1 teaspoon salt
1 cup tomato juice
pepper—few grains
2 tablespoons Parmesan cheese

Cook butter and onion together in covered pan until tender, but not brown. Add stock, tomato juice, beer and seasonings; bring to boiling point and keep as hot as possible without boiling.

Dry toast sprinkled lightly with Parmesan or grated cheese may be served on top of steaming soup. The toast should be cut in slender strips, lightly browned and very crisp. Serves 6.

BEER CABBAGE SALAD

1 medium-sized head of cabbage
1 green pepper, shaved
2 tablespoons celery seed
1 teaspoon minced onion
1 cup cooked salad dressing
Season with salt and pepper
½ bottle of Ballantine's Export Beer

Chop or shred the cabbage, add the green pepper and seasoning.

Combine the salad dressing and the beer having both ice cold and beat until smooth. Pour the dressing over the cold cabbage mixture and serve in a salad bowl lined with the crisp green lettuce leaves.

Brochure with dinner recipes using Ballantine's Beer, c. 1933. Ballantine's Brewery, founded in 1840 in Newark, New Jersey, was at one point the fourth largest brewery in the United States. PIKE MICROBREWERY MUSEUM, SEATTLE, WA

Stocks

Meat and vegetable stocks are the principal building blocks of many great cuisines, and beer can replace water or wine when making stock. Use paler beers such as pale wheat beers and golden ales to produce stocks for seafood and chicken dishes and darker beers such as Belgian dubbels and German dunkels to produce stocks for meat dishes.

Stews and Casseroles

Beer can particularly shine in this regard, and carbonnade flamande, a beer-based beef and onion stew, is widely considered the national dish of Belgium. Long, slow simmering breaks down hop bitterness, leaving the beer's malt and fruit flavors intact. Waterzooi, made with either seafood or chicken, is another Belgian dish that can be based on beer.

Desserts

Imperial stouts can be used to make stout-flavored ice cream or combined with ice cream to make delicious floats. Stouts can also be used in a wide assortment of cakes. Barley wines can add excellent flavor to whipped cream. Acidic beers, particularly gueuzes, make bracing and complex sorbets.

Not surprisingly, beer-based dishes are common on the menus of brewpubs around the world. Chefs at high-end restaurants, long used to cooking with wine, are now also looking to beer to bring new flavors and textures to the dinner table.

Garrett Oliver

coolship is the name given to the shallow, open vessels traditionally designed to cool hot wort prior to fermentation. The use of "ship" in the name probably refers to the medieval practice of cooling the boiled wort (or mash) in a hollowed-out tree trunk—not dissimilar to a primitive boat. Before the advent of refrigeration and chilled water, hot wort was cooled by transfer to these shallow, open vessels, where the wort was allowed to cool slowly. These open coolers or coolships with high surface area-to-volume ratios had three functions: cooling, aeration of the wort, and separation of the cold trub. However, these open vessels were fully exposed to the air and consequently subject to microbial contamination. Inevitably, with larger volumes of wort to cool, the coolship dimensions necessary to achieve effective temperature reduction became unwieldy and alternative methods of cooling (usually vertical coolers in which the hot wort flowed continuously as a thin film over a vertical metal surface cooled with chilled water) were introduced.

Coolships still have application in the brewing of traditional Belgian lambic beers for which the large surface area of cooling wort lends itself to spontaneous fermentation (whereby yeasts and bacteria present in the atmosphere, and often in the fabric of the brewery, ferment the wort to create a rich assortment of interesting and challenging flavors). These lambic coolships are often located in the roofs of brewery buildings where louvered shutters are opened to allow entry of the surrounding atmospheric microflora (and sometimes microfauna!) of Belgium into the coolship room. See LAMBIC.

Hornsey, Ian S. *A history of beer and brewing.* London: Royal Society of Chemistry, 2003.

George Philliskirk

Coors Brewing Company began with Adolph Kuhrs, who was born in 1847 in the Rhine Province of Prussia. From 1862 through 1867 Kuhrs worked at several different breweries in Germany and immigrated to the United States in 1868. An enterprising man, he worked various jobs in Illinois before landing in Denver in 1872. By that time, Kuhrs had become Coors. He was looking to start a brewery, but did not have the financial wherewithal and so took on a partner named Jacob Schueler. The name of the brewery from 1873 until 1880 was the Schueler & Coors Golden Brewery. After Coors bought out Schueler's interest in 1880, the brewery was known as Adolph Coors Golden Brewery. Over the years, the company name changed to different iterations of Adolph Coors Company and by 1989 became the Coors Brewing Company. During the Prohibition years in Colorado (1916–1933; Colorado started early), Coors stayed in business by making near beer (nonalcoholic beer) and malted milk. See NEAR BEER and PROHIBITION. The majority of Coors malted milk was sold to Mars Candy Company. Coors also had income from a porcelain plant making pottery and dishwares. These nonbeer ventures provided marginal profit at best and more than once put the company on the brink of financial ruin. But the company held on, and after Prohibition Coors was one of a few breweries that were left largely intact and ready to reopen. Indeed, Coors reopened for business at 12:00 a.m. on April 7, 1933, the precise minute when the Volstead Act was repealed, ending Prohibition. With the playing field essentially cleared, business for Coors quickly ramped up to the point where the brewery was selling every ounce of beer it could brew. Growth did not slow substantially until the 1970s, when intense competition and a boycott by the American Federation of Labor and Congress of Industrial Organizations, a trade union center, joined by other groups, effectively hindered the brewery's growth and profitability. At that point Coors beer was sold mainly in the western United States and so the company began a plan to increase distribution throughout the United States, a goal that was accomplished by 1991, with Indiana being the last state to approve sales of Coors beer. In 1992 all nonbrewing assets were spun off, including Coors Ceramics Company (formerly known as the Coors Porcelain Company), Golden Aluminum Company, and Graphic Packaging Group and held under ACX Technologies. By 2000 most of the nonbrewing enterprises were sold off or merged with other companies, except for Coors Ceramics, which became the sole holding of CoorsTek after ACX Technologies was dissolved. In addition to the Golden Brewery, a second location was added in 1990 when a brewery in Memphis was purchased from the Stroh Brewing Company. The Coors Memphis Brewery operated for 13 years before closing in 2003. In 1987 a beer-packaging facility was built in Elkton, Virginia, in the Shenandoah Valley. This site was converted to a brewery in 2007. Internationally, Coors purchased the malting and brewing assets of Bass Brewers Ltd from InBev in 2002 and renamed it Coors Brewers Limited. In 2005 Coors merged with the Molson Brewing Company in Canada to form the Molson Coors Brewing Company, the fifth largest brewer in the world, with dual headquarters in Montreal, Canada, and Denver, Colorado. In 2008 Molson Coors Brewing Company created a joint venture in the US market with SABMiller called MillerCoors for improved scales of economy. Headquarters for MillerCoors are located in Chicago, Illinois. As of 2010 Molson Coors operated breweries in Canada (all of the former Molson breweries), the United States (all of the MillerCoors joint venture breweries), and the UK (all of the Coors Brewers Limited breweries). See INBEV and SABMILLER.

Throughout its history, Coors has used innovative technologies to improve the quality of its beers. In 1959 Coors developed the first two-piece aluminum can for beverages. Also in 1959, Coors moved away from pasteurization and implemented sterile filtration to stabilize their beer. Coors also started a malting barley research station, which is now located in Burley, Idaho, where new and improved malting varieties are developed. Coors products marketed throughout the years are numerous. However, during the first 100 years of operation, the main product was simply Coors banquet beer, with an Export beer and a Bock beer made in minor quantities until the 1940s. Coors Light was introduced in 1978 and within 25 years became one of the top three beer brands in the United States. In 1994 Coors produced the first flavored malt beverage (widely referred to as "malternatives") under the name Zima. Other beers made by Molson Coors with significant market share include, in the US market, the Blue Moon family of brands, Killian's Red, and the Keystone family of brands; in the Canadian market, the Molson family of brands, the Rickard's family of brands, and Coors Light; and in the UK market Carling, Coors Light, and Grolsch. Other smaller brands around the world include Winterfest, Coors NA, Caffrey's, Cobra, Worthington, and Creemore Springs.

The vast majority of the company's beers are standard American-style lagers made from barley malt and corn adjunct. The brewery at Golden, Colorado, which features a singularly beautiful copper brewhouse, is the largest single site brewery site in the world, with the capacity to produce approximately 20 million barrels of beer per year.

Keith Villa

copper, a metal long valuable in the construction of breweries, but now largely replaced by stainless steel. Copper is malleable and can be formed into sheets, which allowed the engineering of large brewing vessels. The sheets were easily joined to produce leak-proof seals. Copper is also an excellent conductor of heat, which made it the metal of choice in the days when direct firing of kettles was common. See DIRECT FIRING. In Britain, brewing kettles are still sometimes referred to as "coppers." Copper is also, in trace amounts, a nutrient needed by yeast. Wort is mildly acidic and dissolves the small amounts of copper necessary for good yeast health. In beer fermentations, copper acts to reduce concentrations of hydrogen sulfide, a gas with an aroma reminiscent of rotten eggs.

However, copper does have its drawbacks. It is difficult to clean—much more difficult than stainless steel. Although it is malleable, it is also relatively soft and does not have steel's structural strength. Although brewhouses are still made with copper cladding for aesthetic reasons, the interiors of the vessels are almost always stainless steel.

Humans, like yeast, require trace copper (1–2 mg per day in a healthy diet) for normal cellular function. In recent years, much attention has been focused on possible copper toxicity and its implications for brewers. Whether this is a valid concern remains highly debated. The U.S. Environmental Protection Agency limits copper in drinking water to 1.3 mg/l. Copper in high concentrations is surely toxic, both for humans and for many microbes, including yeast. Although the debate continues, it might be noted that many of the world's most beautiful brewhouses, from the Czech Pilsner Urquell to the Belgian Trappist Rochefort, are constructed of copper, and this appears to have had no negative effects on either people or yeast.

Campbell, Kirsteen (Edrington Group). *Brewer and Distiller International* 5 (2009): 35–7.

U.S. Environmental Protection Agency. *Drinking water contaminants.* http://water.epa.gov/drink/contaminants/index.cfm/ (accessed February 28, 2011).

Chris Holliland

coriander (Coriandrum sativum) is the name of an herbal plant that is also known as cilantro or Chinese parsley. Both the leaves and the seeds of this plant are used as an herb in many styles of cuisine, but the leaves are not used in beer because of aromas that some people regard as "sweaty" or "soapy." In regards to beer, coriander refers to the seed of the plant, which is 3–5 mm in diameter and light brown in color. Technically a dried fruit, coriander seed is a spice with a pleasant fruity, citrus aroma when freshly ground. This aroma is very similar to the aroma of hops, a result of the presence of terpene compounds (e.g., linalool) in both coriander and hops. See LINALOOL.

Coriander has been used in European beer since the Middle Ages to provide a spicy balance to malt sweetness. It is an ingredient in several types of beer. The major style of beer that includes coriander as a traditional ingredient is Belgian-style white or wit beer, which originated in Belgium during the Middle Ages. See WHITE BEER. Typically, coriander is added at a dose of 2.11–8.3 ounces per barrel during the last 5 to 20 minutes of boiling in the brewkettle. A short boiling time is required to ensure that the majority of aromatic compounds are not volatilized away. White beer also incorporates orange peel, which together with coriander provides a refreshing fruity, citrus flavor to the beer. The essential oils of coriander are also available as a purified concentrate that can be added to beer after the boiling phase to maximize effect.

Coriander is occasionally used in other types of beers, most often in Belgian beers or those meant to be Belgian-inspired. Much of the coriander sold in the United States is grown in Mexico, but Indian-grown coriander is also available. Many brewers feel that it possesses a brighter, fruitier aroma.

See also HERBS.

Keith Villa

corn. Also known as maize (*Zea mays* L), corn is a member of the grass family domesticated in the Americas in prehistoric times. It is the most extensively grown crop in the Americas; hybrid corn, with its high yield, is especially prevalent. The United States grows approximately half of the world's corn, with the next major growers being China, Brazil, Mexico, and Argentina.

The corn cob comprises individual fruits (kernels) that are approximately the size of peas. An ear contains between 200 and 400 hundred kernels. Compared to wheat, the kernels contain much less protein, and that protein is not of the gluten-type and, as such, is not a problem for those suffering from celiac disease. "Sweet corn" is a variant in which more sugar is accumulated in place of a proportion of the starch.

Corn is a dietary staple in many parts of the world, with uses including polenta (Italy), hominy and cornbread (US), and tortillas (Mexico). Popcorn is made from varieties of corn that explode upon heating. Corn flakes are extensively eaten as breakfast food worldwide (although much of the flavor is actually from malted barley).

In North America, corn cultivation is often on a two-crop rotation, with nitrogen-fixing plants such as soybeans or alfalfa being sown in alternate years. There is increasing use of genetically modified varieties that are more pest-tolerant. Over 80% of the corn crop in the United States is genetically modified, notably "Bt corn," which expresses a toxin from *Bacillus thuringiensis* that targets a grain pest called the European corn borer. Increasingly there is competition for corn between food use and fuel ethanol.

Corn can be used for the brewing of beer in two forms: as a source of starch and as a source of sugar. Corn for brewing can be used in the form of grits, flour, torrified, flaked, or syrups.

Corn is a common adjunct in mass-market beers produced in North America, and is typically used as up to 20% of the grist. Corn produces a lighter color and flavor in beer than barley malt does. Corn grits, more specifically, are the most extensively used form of corn adjunct in the US and Canada. They are produced in a dry milling process that removes the outer layers and the germ, the latter being oil-rich and therefore a source of potential rancidity. The resultant particles are essentially pure endosperm. At very high cost, refined corn starch is a product of the wet-milling of corn. It comprises a very fine powder that is somewhat challenging to handle commercially. Treatment of corn (and other cereals) at around 500°F (260°C) in a process known as torrification leads to a rapid expansion ("popping") of the endosperm, thereby gelatinizing the starch. Subsequent rolling of the grain is used to produce flakes.

Torrified and flaked corn does not need separate cooking and can be used directly in the malt mash, in the case of flaked corn without a need for prior milling. However, corn grits and flour must be cooked before addition to the main mash, for the gelatinization temperature of corn starch substantially exceeds that of barley starch.

The alternative approach is to convert corn starch into sugar solutions by acid or (more likely these days) enzyme-catalyzed hydrolysis. The resultant syrups are added at the wort boiling stage, thereby relieving production pressure on sweet wort production. These syrups are largely devoid of amino acids and therefore there is a limit to their use if nitrogen deficiency in fermentation is to be avoided.

Chicha is a beer-like alcoholic beverage based upon corn. See CHICHA. Corn is also the base for the production of bourbon, which by law must be made from a minimum of 51% of this material. The remainder of the mash bill may be wheat or rye and malted barley.

Watson, S.A. and Ramstad, P.E., eds. *Corn: Chemistry and technology*. St. Paul, MN: American Association of Cereal Chemists, 1997.

Charles W. Bamforth

corn sugar, a common trade name for dextrose (dextrorotary glucose), a monosaccharide, derived from corn. It is also known as glucose. Corn sugar is a highly refined white sugar that shows no corn (maize) character. Glucose is a hexose type sugar with a group of six carbon atoms. Glucose is one of the most common sugars in nature and is the sugar carried in the human bloodstream.

Commercially available corn sugar is made by hydrolysis of corn starch by acids or exogenous enzymes. As a simple sugar, it is easily fermented by yeast and can be used as an adjunct in brewing, usually by addition to the kettle. It generally ferments out completely, leaving no sweetness behind, and is therefore widely used to make beers with dry flavor profiles or to avoid cloying residual sugar in stronger beers. It is also used as a reliable priming sugar for bottle conditioning and cask conditioning.

John Palmer

Corona Extra is the best-selling Mexican beer in the world and the number one imported beer in the United States and Canada. Sold in a distinctive clear glass bottle with a printed-on label, the light "tropical pilsner" style beer, at 4.6% alcohol by volume, is often served in bars in export markets with a slice of lime pushed into the bottle's neck. Although the lime slice has become synonymous with Corona and now makes up part of the brand's image, very few Mexicans drink the beer this way, preferring to leave the lime to tourists and foreigners.

First brewed in 1925 by Grupo Modelo to celebrate the company's 10th anniversary, the beer is light straw in color, light in taste, and has little hop bitterness. Although Corona leads the market in its home country, it is not considered the best of Grupo Modelo's range of beers; others are more expensive in the Mexican market, and Corona was once considered a cheap beer in the United States. Unperturbed by the notion that beers sold in clear glass can become light struck because sunlight reacts with the hops, the brewer says the beer has always been marketed in a see-through bottle "because when you use only the finest ingredients, you've got nothing to hide." Corona's sales have benefitted from a remarkably effective advertising campaign that focuses on relaxation under palm trees on the white sands of Mexico's beaches. Corona is sold in more than 150 countries.

The distinctive crown logo from which Corona takes its name is based on the crown that adorns the Cathedral of Our Lady of Guadalupe in the town of Puerto Vallarta.

Tim Hampson

couching is an old English term for the shoveling of steeped, drained grain onto a malting floor in a heap (a "couch"). See FLOOR MALTING. In traditional British malting, couching is the first of three steps in germination. The others are "flooring" (germination proper) and "withering" (air-drying in a thin layer). A couch retains the temperature of the grain and thus accelerates the uptake of surface water after the wet transfer from the steep. This promotes the completion of chitting and the start of germination. See CHITTING and GERMINATION. The couch is anywhere from 20 to 90 cm high (about 8 inches to 3 feet) and often placed in a rigid, rectangular structure with a flat bottom called a couch frame. In cold weather, couching can last 24 hours or longer, and the couch is often covered with sacks or a tarpaulin to maintain the proper temperature. Once chitting is complete and germination starts, however, the grain begins to give off considerable heat, and it becomes more important to release rather than contain that heat. At this point the couch needs to be broken up and spread out on the floor, in a layer ranging in thickness from perhaps 7 to 40 cm (about 3 to 15 in.). The more advanced the state of germination in the couch and the higher the ambient temperature, the thinner is the layer on the floor to allow excess heat to escape.

Briggs, Dennis Edward. *Malts and malting*. London: Chapman & Hall, 1997.

Thomas Kraus-Weyermann

counterpressure is the pressure used to overcome the tendency of carbonated beer to foam, especially during packaging. Usually, beer is seen without counterpressure; for example, beer that is poured into a glass or that is inside of an open bottle or can. In this case, the carbon dioxide dissolved in the beer tends to form bubbles and rise to the top. This is precisely what counterpressure prevents. When filling a bottle, keg, or other package under counterpressure, the pressure of the CO_2 in the head space of the package is greater than the pressure required to prevent these bubbles from forming. The goal is a "quiet fill" where the package is filled quickly and efficiently with minimal foaming. Typically, a counterpressure of 0.5 to 1 bar (7 to 14 psi) above the equilibrium pressure of the beer is sufficient to prevent excessive foam.

See also CARBON DIOXIDE, CARBONATION, and FOAM.

Nick R. Jones

Courage Brewery. Over the course of more than 2 centuries, Courage was among the best-known names in British brewing. In 1787 John Courage bought a small brewery at Horselydown on the foreshore of the south bank of the Thames, a site now adjacent to Tower Bridge, London (completed in 1892). Brewing may have been carried out at this site as far back as the 16th century. The Borough of Southwark was the center of the English hop trade, and other breweries flourished there, notably that of Barclay, Perkins and Co., which lay to the west of Horselydown, beyond London Bridge. See BARCLAY, PERKINS & CO. Curiously, Courage named his property the "Anchor Brewery," a name already in use for Barclay's concern, one of

London's biggest porter breweries, which had passed through several hands since it was founded in 1616.

Courage died only 6 years later in 1793; his son John did not succeed him until he became a partner in 1811. He became sole owner of the growing company in 1851, having, among other things, purchased wharves on both the east and west sides of the brewery, ensuring good access for shipping in raw materials and shipping out products. Another advantage of the site was that it possessed its own artesian wells, of excellent quality for brewing, for which Thames water was not suited. Some of Courage's land was later sold to the Corporation of London when Tower Bridge was built.

In 1888, although still under the control of the Courage family, the brewery became the limited company Courage & Co. Alfred Barnard recorded his visit to the brewery, and reported that it had produced over 300,000 barrels (490,000 hl, 405,100 US barrels) of beer in 1887. But in 1891 the brewery buildings were set on fire, presumably caused by a malt dust explosion, and the brewhouse burned for several days. Brewing recommenced within a short time, but as the brewery buildings were being reconstructed, Courage & Co. was forced to buy beer from Barclay's in order to meet their commitments to London customers.

In the latter part of the 19th century pale ale, especially that from Burton-on-Trent, became popular. See BURTON-ON-TRENT. But the carbonate water from Horselydown wells was not suitable for brewing such beer. Courage overcame this difficulty by importing pale ale from Flower & Son of Stratford-on-Avon in 1872, and later from Fremlins of Maidstone in Kent. In 1903 the company purchased Hall's brewery at Alton in Hampshire, the first of many such acquisitions. In most cases, Courage desired only to obtain the public houses owned by the companies it bought, and closed the breweries, then supplying the pubs from either Horselydown or Alton as appropriate.

Courage continued to prosper through two World Wars, although there was a hiatus during World War II. Horselydown lay in the area of London Docks, a prime target for German bombers in the blitz on London, and it was duly hit, the brew house destroyed, and even the river wall breached. For a second time reconstruction commenced, although the brewhouse was not to be completed until 1954.

In 1955 Courage and Co. merged with their Southwark neighbor, Barclay, Perkins & Co, to form Courage and Barclay Ltd. Shortly after this there came a period known as "merger mania" started in the brewing industry by Canadian tycoon E.P. Taylor, and which resulted in the formation of several large brewing groups, among them the Scottish and Newcastle Breweries. Courage and Barclay were not immune to this hysteria, and in 1960 the new entity merged with Simonds of Reading, Berkshire, becoming Courage, Barclay & Simonds. This group carried out several further purchases before becoming victims themselves, being bought out by Imperial Tobacco in 1972.

Mayhem, rather than mania, then ensued, for Imperial itself was bought up by the Hanson Trust in 1986. The latter sold Courage on to the Australian company Elders IXL (owners of the Fosters brand), and in 1991 an arrangement was made with the Watney group (owned by Grand Metropolitan) to acquire all of Watney's breweries, with each company's pubs going into a separate group, known as Inntrepreneur. Elders decided to leave the British brewing scene in 1995, selling off Courage to Scottish & Newcastle. This company became known as Scottish Courage, and was the largest British brewer until it too was swallowed up by a greater entity, Heineken Brewing, in 2008.

Barclay's brewery was closed and demolished in 1986. Courage had closed their Horselydown brewery in 1981, transferring production to their more modern Worton Grange plant, near Reading. The Horselydown site had increased in value as the property market in London soared, and it was converted into luxury waterside apartments. The massive building was not destroyed; its river frontage is still magnificent and is visible from Tower Bridge.

Cornell, Martyn. "The Local Brew." In *Beer: the Story of the Pint*. London: Headline Book Publishing, 2003.

Pudney, John. *A Draught of Contentment*. London: New English Library, 1971.

Terry Foster

craft brewing is the descendent of the microbrewing movement that started in the UK in the late 1970s, flourished in the United States in the 1990s, and spread to the corners of the world in the first decade of the 21st century. See MICROBREWERY. Craft brewing is the pursuit of small, independent commercial breweries, making beer by largely traditional means and with largely traditional ingredients, with the goal of making beer that is far more flavorful than the common brands made by large international breweries. As is often the case with cultural movements, there is no single definition of the terminology upon which everyone will agree. However it is defined, craft brewing universally involves boldly flavored beers coupled with a defiantly independent spirit. Although the term "craft brewing" is normally used to refer to breweries that have opened in recent decades, most brewers and beer enthusiasts would agree that many older European breweries also meet the definition.

Craft brewing has taken hold most solidly in the United States, where more than 90% of the approximately 1,700 breweries in the country meet almost any definition of the term. Almost all of these breweries have opened in the past 30 years, and as of 2011 they represented approximately 7.6% of American beer sales dollars. American craft brewers include about 1,000 brewpubs; the other 700 are small packaging breweries (who mostly sell beer outside their own premises), breweries that have become large enough to distribute throughout a region, and a few that have become large enough to sell beer throughout the country. The segment also includes some breweries that produce their own beers partly or entirely under contract at breweries that they do not own. See BREWPUB and CONTRACT BREWING.

Craft brewing usually involves brewing beers that are made entirely or almost entirely from barley and/or wheat malt. Adjuncts, such as sugar, honey, and unmalted grains, are generally used to enhance the flavor of the beer rather than to make it lighter and more acceptable to a mass audience. One of the results is that craft beer flavors tend to be more pronounced than those of mass-produced lagers, which are brewed to be as cleanly innocuous as possible. Hop character, often including bitterness levels several times those of mass-market beers, suffuses

A brewer at the Carolina Brewery in Pittsboro, North Carolina, removes spent grains from the mash tun in a process known as "mashing out." JOSHUA WEINFELD

many craft beer styles. Big hop flavor and aroma are also par for the course, and American craft brewers lead the world in the use of traditional flavor-enhancing techniques such as dry hopping and newer ones such as mash hopping. See DRY HOPPING and MASH HOPPING. Craft brewers have repopularized a range of brewing techniques, including spicing, bottle conditioning, barrel aging, and even intentional souring of beer to help create exciting new flavors. See BARREL-AGING, BOTTLE CONDITIONING, SOUR BEER, and SPICES.

Airline deregulation in 1978 resulted in lower airfares, helping change air travel to Europe from an unreachable luxury to a rite of passage or normal vacation for many middle class Americans. Many of them came back to the United States with fresh memories of the beautiful depth of British cask-conditioned ales, the bright hop quality of German pilsners, and the beguiling complexities of Belgian beers brewed by Trappist monks. Now disappointed by the neutral-tasting lager style that filled virtually every bottle, can, and keg in the nation, many of them started making their own beer at home. When President Jimmy Carter made homebrewing legal in 1978, legions more joined in, looking not for cheaper beer, but for beer with more flavor. Americans taking trips to Europe also brought back a growing connoisseurship in food and drink, a passion that flowered first on the West Coast of the United States.

Becoming a craft brewer strikes many people as a dream job, but the fact is that the road of the craft brewer has never been easy. Surely there are some breweries that have opened smoothly and easily, meeting with instant success. More often, however, the tale is initially one of grit, hard toil, and penury. In the vast majority of cases, the brewer will transition from being an enthusiastic homebrewer working in an unrelated industry to work in a commercial brewery at a fraction of his or her former salary. In the late 1990s, a somewhat predictable shake-out occurred in the American craft brewing industry, leading many journalists to quickly declare that the craft brewing movement was over. Although many breweries did close during this period, the growth rate for the remaining craft brewers recovered within a few years and the segment soon regained its strength. Whereas overall beer sales in the United States have declined over the past several years, craft beer sales have continued to rise sharply, with many breweries enjoying double-digit increases every year. It remains difficult for some brewers to find appropriate distribution channels, but the situation is changing as many distributors come to realize that craft beer may represent their best chances for future growth.

Although craft brewers do compete against each other, craft brewing is generally marked by a cooperative and collaborative nature. Many breweries create, produce, and market special-edition beers with each other, and the outcomes of these collaborations are often widely sought out by enthusiasts. Seasonal and limited-edition beers are also common, and it is not unusual for a brewery to produce 20 or more different beers every year.

Food has become an increasingly important part of the craft brewing movement. Most craft breweries participate in beer dinners on a regular basis, either at their own facilities or at restaurants. This is not surprising; most craft brewmasters have a chef-like outlook on beer and brewing. The wide range of flavors available within both traditional and new beers styles gives these beers remarkable versatility for food pairings. See CHEESE (PAIRING) and FOOD PAIRING.

In the United States, craft-brewed beer is still most firmly entrenched in the coastal cities, with the notable exceptions of Michigan and Colorado, which are each hotspots with dozens of breweries. In terms of market share, craft beer shows particular strength in the Pacific Northwest, with Portland, Oregon, as an epicenter. In Portland, craft-brewed beer has nearly 40% of the draught beer market. Over the past decade, areas of the country that had not previously seemed fertile ground for craft beer, particularly the South, have sprouted vibrant craft brewing scenes.

As of 2011, the craft brewing movement showed remarkable strength in many countries outside the United States. Small breweries have continued their comeback in the UK, which is home to almost 800 breweries. Most UK brewers have remained firmly committed to traditional cask-conditioned British beer styles, and few have ventured into beers influenced by other brewing cultures. There are exceptions, however, and it is to be expected that the UK brewing culture will become increasingly diverse over time. Craft brewing in Scandinavia tends in the opposite direction, with highly creative brewers drawing ideas from many sources, including historical Scandinavian beer styles that had previously become extinct. Italian craft brewers show similar creative flair and a notable focus on Italian food traditions and local ingredients such as chestnuts. Brazilian and Argentinian craft brewers have resurrected the German brewing cultures that flourished in many parts of South America in the 1800s.

The definition of the term "craft brewer" will continue to be controversial. It is worth noting that in some countries the term refers to homebrewing. In 2011 the Brewers Association (BA) in the United States revised its definition to include breweries producing less than 7,040,866 hl (6 million US bbls) per year. According to the BA,

> An American craft brewer is small, independent and traditional. Small: Annual production of 6 million barrels of beer or less. Independent: Less than 25% of the craft brewery is owned or controlled (or equivalent economic interest) by an alcoholic beverage industry member who is not themselves a craft brewer. Traditional: A brewer who has either an all malt flagship (the beer which represents the greatest volume among that brewers brands) or has at least 50% of its volume in either all malt beers or in beers which use adjuncts to enhance rather than lighten flavor.

Craft brewing is an evolving culture, and in many ways the definition is in the eye of the beholder. Within decades it is entirely possible that beers and breweries that are currently seen as "craft" will simply be looked upon as normal or even "classic."

"Big increase in brewery numbers in UK says CAMRA." http://www.bbc.co.uk/news/uk-11323119. (accessed September 16, 2010).

Craft Beer. http://www.craftbeer.com/ (accessed March 22, 2011).

Garrett Oliver

cream ale, once a popular style in North America, can be summed up as a "bigger" incarnation of the standard American mass-market lager. In the days before Prohibition, cream ales were widely brewed in the Northeast and Mid-Atlantic states, where they were often produced to compete with golden lagers. In this, the style bears a resemblance to German kölsch. See KÖLSCH. Compared to modern American mass-market lagers, cream ales have somewhat more bitterness, sometimes more alcohol, and are often lightly fruity. They should be brilliantly clear and have no buttery diacetyl notes, but the "creamed-corn" aroma of dimethyl sulfide (DMS) is common. See DIMETHYL SULFIDE (DMS). Adjuncts such as rice and corn are traditionally employed, though some craft brewers prefer to use all malt. Historical accounts describe brewers using lager yeasts; however, there are also reports of their having used ale and lager yeasts simultaneously for the primary fermentation, or ale yeast for the primary fermentation and lager yeast for conditioning. Others were blends of separately fermented lager and ale. It seems that brewers probably used whatever technique was expedient for each of them, creating beers that could face down popular lagers in the marketplace. Bitterness hops included Cluster and Brewer's Gold or its progeny and aroma hops included US varieties such as Northern Brewer or German varieties. The cream ales that were particularly popular in the Midwest during the pre-Prohibition period are often described as having had notable hop aromatics and bitterness above 30 IBU. After Prohibition, cream ales used many different hop varieties, though by this time hop aroma was very low. In January of 1935 Krueger cream ale became the first American beer to be offered in a can. Current commercial examples include Genesee and Little Kings, and most contain about 10–22 IBU and alcohol of 4.2%–5.6% ABV and very lively carbonation. While the style has at times seemed as if it would fade from history, a slightly ironic sense of nostalgia seems to keep it afloat, and the occasional craft brewer will produce one as a "respectable lawnmower beer." It should be noted that cream ales do not contain any dairy products or lactose and are different from UK term "cream ale," which refers to the creaminess derived from nitrogenation and the resulting tight foam. See NITROGENATED BEER.

Jeremy Marshall

cream stout

See MILK STOUT.

crown cap is the most widely used closure for beer bottles. Although the design of the crown cap looks obvious to us today, beer bottle closures were

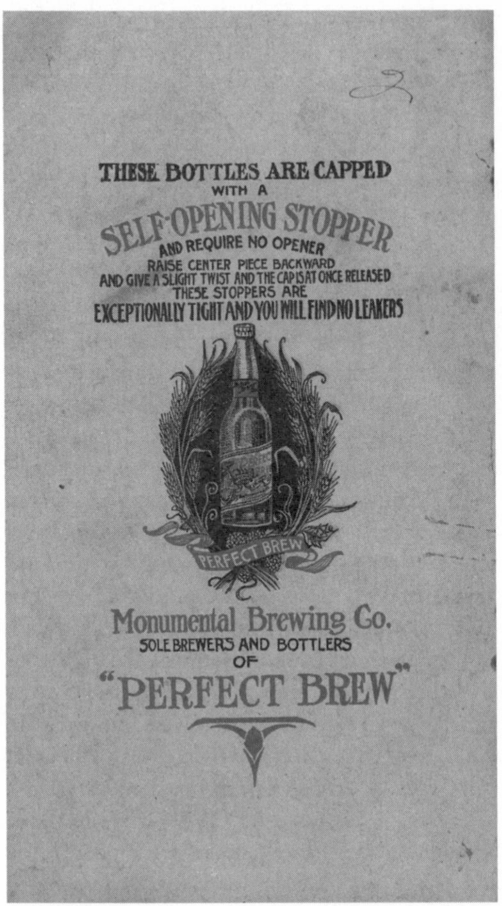

Brochure promising "no leakers" during use of the new crown cap method of bottle closure, c. 1892. PIKE MICROBREWERY MUSEUM, SEATTLE, WA

vexing to 19th-century brewers. For carbonated beverages, the most common bottle closure of the late 1800s was the "swing-top" or "flip-top" design, which had a ceramic plug and gasket held in place by wire spring tension (still occasionally seen today, particularly on bottles from the Dutch brewer Grolsch). These were difficult to make and attach to bottles, and aside from this, they simply did not work very well. Gasket materials were not as advanced as they are today, and swing-top bottles often leaked.

Certainly there was no lack of ideas for solving the problem. Between 1882 and 1890, the U.S. Patent Office received more than 300 patents for bottle stopper designs. In 1892, mechanical engineer William Painter of Baltimore applied for and received three patents for his "Bottle Sealing Device." This metal cap could be crimped onto the bottle by machine, and although it needed some force to remove it, the cap held pressure well without leaking. Dubbed the "crown cap" or "crown cork" because of its flared shape before crimping, he had begun work on the closure in 1889. He was not alone—Alfred Louis Bernardin, Sr, of Evansville, Indiana, was hard at work on similar idea, but eventually Painter won out. He founded the Crown Cork and Seal Company and got to work marketing his invention. His crown cap became the worldwide standard for beer bottle closures. The September 15, 1894, issue of *The Western Brewer* already showed advertisements for the crown cap, with illustrations depicting its easy removal using ordinary household implements such as knives, spoon handles, and even corkscrews.

Not all breweries were quick to take to the new closure, although it worked far better than others and could be easily applied by machines. Eventually, however, there was no denying the superiority of the crown cap, and by the time of Painter's death in 1909, his company had manufacturing plants on four continents. By the 1930s, Crown Cork and Seal made half the bottle caps in the world.

Other than the linings, the crown cap has changed very little since 1892. In 1927 the thin ring of cork under the metal cap gave way to a patented substitute called Nepro cork, and by the mid 1950s this was replaced by polyvinyl chloride. Today there are versions lined with "oxygen-scavenging" materials that will supposedly remove oxygen from the headspace air and extend the freshness of the beer. A twist-off version of the crown cap was invented in the 1960s and is widely used by large breweries, but largely shunned by smaller breweries and craft breweries. Although it requires no bottle opener to remove it, some brewers believe that it is not as good a barrier to oxygen as the traditional crown cap. The twist-off also gained, perhaps unfairly, a reputation as the closure for cheap beer, a tarnished image that has proved durable.

Bull, Don. *Crown Cork and Seal corkscrew*. http://www.bullworks.net/ (accessed January 25, 2011).

Garrett Oliver

Crystal (hop) is an American hop that originated in 1983 as a cross between a tetraploid German hallertauer mittelfrueh and genetic diploid male material with Cascade and German aroma-hop parentage. As such, it can be considered a half-sister to Liberty. See CASCADE (HOP), GERMAN HOPS, HALLERTAUER MITTELFRUEH (HOP), and LIBERTY (HOP). Being a triploid, Crystal produces nearly seedless cones even when grown in the presence of fertile diploid males. Crystal is adapted to the major US hop growing areas in Oregon and Washington. It matures medium-late and averages between 1,300 and 2,300 kg/ha (between 1,160 and 2,050 lb/acre), a yield that is significantly higher than that of its Hallertauer parent. Crystal averages about 3% to 4% alpha acids, 2% to 3% beta acids, and about 21% cohumulone content. The essential oil profile of Crystal is nearly identical to that of Hallertauer Mittelfrueh, indicating excellent aroma potential. Like its Hallertauer parent, Crystal has no measurable farnesene in its essential oil fraction. Crystal is often used in place of German aroma hops in many specialty beers.

Haunold, A., G. B. Nickerson, U. Gampert, D. S. Kling, and S. T. Kenny. Registration of Crystal hop. *Crop Science* 35 (1995): 279–80.

Haunold, Alfred, G. B. Nickerson, Ulrich Gampert, Donna Kling, and Stephen T. Kenny. Liberty and Crystal—Two new U.S.-developed aroma hops. *Journal of the American Society of Brewing Chemists* 53 (1995): 9–13.

Alfred Haunold

Crystal malt is one of the traditional British color malts, next to brown, amber, chocolate, and black malts. During the malting process, it is steeped and germinated like classic, fully modified, pale malt, but then moved wet, with a moisture content of almost 50%, past the kiln directly into a roasting drum. There it is heated without ventilation to roughly 64°C to 72°C (147°F to 162°F), whereupon the contents of the endosperm liquefy and the starch is saccharified by strong alpha- and beta-amylase action. See SACCHARIFICATION. This is also called the "stewing stage." The malt is then dried at a high temperature of approximately 280°F to 390°F (roughly 140°C–200°C.) This is called the "curing stage." It darkens the kernels and causes the malt sugars created through saccharification to crystallize into hard, unfermentable dextrins upon subsequent cooling. In the finished beer, these sugars are responsible for clean, nutty, caramel-like, residual sweetness. The entire drum process may take about three hours, and the finished crystal malt may have a moisture content of only about 5%–7%. Some maltsters nowadays make their crystal malts not in a roaster, but in a kiln. This is considered a more efficient production method, but such crystal malts tend to be less homogeneous and have a much lower moisture content than drum-roasted crystal malts. The exact roasting times and temperatures for crystal malts vary with the desired color, which can range from light, to medium, to dark, in a color band of about 25 to 320 EBC (roughly 10°L–120°L). See EUROPEAN BREWERY CONVENTION (EBC) and LOVIBOND. Some very dark crystal malts may have color values of up to 400 EBS (roughly 150°L). Colors added to beer by crystal malt range from pale honey to dark copper. Crystal malts have no enzymes and are used primarily to enhance a beer's color, flavor, body, aroma, and head retention. However, some brewers will use lighter crystal malts for up to 20% of the grain bill of certain beers.

Briggs, Dennis Edward. *Malts and malting*. London: Chapman & Hall, 1997.

Stopes, Henry. *Malt and malting: An historical, scientific, and practical treatise, showing, as clearly as existing knowledge permits, what malt is, and how to make it.* London: Lyon, 1885.

Thomas Kraus-Weyermann

CTZ (hop) is an acronym for Columbus, Tomahawk, and Zeus, three trade names owned by various private corporations for the same variety of hop, a superalpha cultivar that is capable of delivering about 14% to 18% alpha acids, 4.5% to 5.5% beta acids, and 30% to 35% cohumulone. Some brewers refer to it as "CTZ," whereas others call it by whichever name appends to the company from which they purchase it. In addition to being a powerful bittering hop, CTZ also has some solid, slightly pungent aromas derived from about 1.5 to 2 ml of hop oil per 100 g. The oil palate of this hop is composed of about 25% to 45% myrcene, 12% to 25% humulene, 8% to 12% caryphyllene, and a fractional amount (<1%) of farnesene. CTZ ranks among the most widely grown hops in the United States and is planted in all major American growing regions. In the field, it matures late in the season and shows some susceptibility to powdery mildew, aphids, and mites, but its average yield is still a respectable 2,250 to 2,800 kg/ha (roughly 2,000 to 2,500 lb/acre).

In storage, however, it has little stability and must be processed into pellets or extracts almost immediately and placed into oxygen-free packaging; freezing alone is not enough to preserve it. The development history of the cultivar is not entirely certain, but the plant apparently started its life in the 1980s when Charles Zimmerman—who had worked for the U.S. Department of Agriculture until 1979 and who subsequently held positions with various private hop-processing and trading companies—experimented with diverse genetic hop materials. It is widely assumed that the English high-alpha variety Brewer's Gold as well as several undisclosed American varieties played significant parenting roles in CTZ. Because of its powerful bittering potential, CTZ has become a much sought-after hop by craft brewers experimenting with distinctly American beer tastes, particularly American pale ale, "double IPA," imperial stout, or barley wine. In these brews, this hop is often paired with other typically American hops, including Cascade and Chinook. An American West Coast favorite, CTZ is useful for making "extreme" beers with very high international bittering units because it can deliver a big punch of bitterness without loading up the kettle and/or whirlpool with too much plant material.

See also BREWER'S GOLD (HOP), CASCADE (HOP), and CHINOOK (HOP).

Barth-Haas Group. *Hop production statistics for 2009. The Barth report, hops*. Nuremberg, Germany: Joh. Barth & Sohn. http://www.thebarthreport.com/ (accessed March 8, 2011).

Haunold, Al. IndieHops. *The history of CTZ: The pursuit of hop patent profit*. http://inhoppursuit.blogspot.com/2010/08/indie-hops-exclusive-history-of-ctz.html/ (accessed August 26, 2010).

Hopunion. *Hop variety characteristics*. Yakima, WA: Hopunion USA, Inc., 1995.

Hopsteiner, VDS 65/03. New York: S. S. Steiner, Inc., 2003.

Lewis, Gregory K., and Charles E. Zimmermann. *Hop variety named "Columbus."* U.S. Patent Plant No. 10,956, June 15, 1999.

Townsend, Shaun M. *Genetic marker identification of Columbus, Tomahawk, and Zeus, three super-alpha hop cultivars*. Personal communication, Department of Crop Sciences, Oregon State University, Corvallis, OR.

Brian Yaeger and Alfred Haunold

Curaçao oranges are a citrus fruit grown on Curaçao, a small island nation comprising part of the Kingdom of the Netherlands, and situated in the Lesser Antilles off the northern coast of Venezuela. Spaniards settled the island in 1527 and soon set to planting orange groves. There is argument as to whether the variety planted was Sevilla or Valencia, but what is known is that the oranges didn't grow well in volcanic soil and arid climate of Curaçao. The fruits were small, bitter, and inedible. The colonists kept on trying, and adapting to the local conditions the plant took on new characteristics, the species designation *citrus aurantium currassiviencis*, and a new name, the *laraha*.

While the laraha fruit itself has little value, the peel retains many fine aromatics and is used to produce traditional versions of Curaçao liqueur and triple sec. The Dutch took control of Curaçao in 1815 and, like other spices, the bitter orange peel found its way into Dutch and Belgian beer. It can be used to flavor many types of beers, but it is best known as a traditional ingredient of the wheat-based Belgian witbier. See WHITE BEER. The peel, which is green before drying but turns gray and almost moldy looking upon desiccation, is usually added at the kettle. Brewers have various methods for using it, but most involve steeping the peel in wort for several minutes before the end of boil, taking care not to over-boil it and drive off the desired aromatic oils. After steeping, the peel should be removed from the wort. The aromatics given by bitter orange peel are notably different than those given by the simpler, brighter sweet orange peel. In concentration, bitter orange peel aroma can veer from citrusy to an almost meaty pungency, reminiscent of hot dogs. Therefore, while a valuable flavor in the brewer's arsenal, it is a spice best used sparingly.

Jackson, Michael. *Michael Jackson's beer companion*, 2nd ed. Philadelphia: Courage Books, 2000.

Philbrick, Hope. Spirits of the Caribbean. *Wine report*, February/March 2007.

Garrett Oliver

cylindroconical fermenter

See FERMENTATION VESSELS.

Czech pilsner

See BOHEMIAN PILSNER.

Czech Republic, as home to the pilsner style of beer, is a country that can reasonably claim to be the most important in modern beer history. The Czech lands have had a complicated history, including settlement by the Celts, incursion by the Slavs, invasion by the Magyars, folding into the Holy Roman Empire, attachment to the German-speaking Habsburg monarchy, combination into the state of Czechoslovakia, decades as part of the communist Eastern bloc, and reemergence as part of the West.

Throughout all of this, the Czechs have been steady brewers, making good use of excellent Moravian barley and Bohemian hops. Throughout the Middle Ages, the general populace, from peasants to kings, produced beer within their own households. In 1265, King Přemysl Otakar II founded the town of České Budějovice, known in German as Budweis. The town was granted brewing rights and its burghers quickly grew wealthy selling beer. In 1295, King Wenceslas II of Bohemia founded the town of New Plzeň, shifting the town from a less accessible area several kilometers away. At the confluence of four rivers and a number of important trading routes, this new Plzeň was ready for business. King Wenceslas gave all inhabitants of the town the right to brew and sell beer from their houses, a privilege that throughout Central Europe was generally reserved to noblemen. By the early 1300s, we have records of actual commercial breweries in operation. The Bohemians established guilds and gave beer and brewing a central place in society. In 1588, the Bohemian Tadeas Hajeck printed the world's first brewing textbook.

Czech postcard, c. 1920. The text, from the poem "Pivečko," by the Czech poet Josef Václav Sládek, extols beer's power to mask life's troubles. PIKE MICROBREWERY MUSEUM, SEATTLE, WA

Czech brewing was advancing quickly, but the progress was not to last. The Thirty Years War, which lasted from 1618 to 1648, brought mass death by both violence and plague to much of Central Europe. Beer quality declined and did not fully recover until the early 19th century saw the establishment of several large Měšťanský pivovary "burgher's" or "citizen's" breweries. One of these was eventually renamed Plzensky Prazdroj, meaning "pilsner original source," or "Pilsner Urquell" in German. Here the young Bavarian brewer Josef Groll, using newly developed golden malts together with bottom-fermenting lager yeast brought in from Munich, brewed the original Pilsner beer. See GROLL, JOSEF. The vast majority of beer sold in the world today is a derivation, even if often only an echo, of the beer first made in Plzeň. Years later, fame would come to České Budějovice and its Budweiser Budvar beer, if not always in the fashion the Czechs had hoped for. See BUDWEISER BUDVAR.

Unlike East Germany, where beer quality was quite poor during its communist regime, Czechoslovakia continued to produce fine lager beers in the decades after World War II. Today, of the major Czech breweries, only Budvar is state-owned. The majority of beer sold in the Czech Republic is relatively light lager classified as výcepní; these are brewed from original gravities between 8° Plato and 12° Plato and generally have less than 4.5% alcohol by volume (ABV). What most of the rest of the world refers to as Bohemian or Czech pilsner is called světlý ležák (pale lager) in the Czech Republic. These beers have a full gold color and fine flowery aromatics from the local Saaz hops, with most having between 4.5% and 5% ABV.

Some full-bodied amber Vienna lagers are found (polotmavý ležák), but dark beers referred to as tmavý or Černý ležák or just Černý pivo (black beer) are more common. These were top-fermented beers until the 1890s, when almost all Czech breweries switched to bottom fermentation. They range from dry and brisk to semisweet and malty. Beers having more than 5.5% ABV are referred to as special Speciální, and these range from the famous dark lager at U Fleků in Prague to stronger beers that are cousins to German doppelbocks. Although rare, top-fermented beers are still seen, including weissbiers, which the Czechs claim originated in Bohemia and then migrated to nearby Bavaria. The occasional top-fermenting porter is found as well.

Today, the Czech Republic produces about a half million tons of malt and grows nearly 7,000 metric tons of hops per year, and the country is home to about 125 breweries. The country exports about 3.5 million hl (3 million US bbl) of beer annually, including the famous Pilsner Urquell and Budweiser Budvar, alongside well-known brands such as Staropramen, Krušovice, and Radegast.

Although Czech beers are generally well brewed, choice can be limited. The modern craft brewing movement has been slow to take hold in the Czech Republic, but there are notable signs of a coming flowering of creativity. The number of craft breweries is steadily increasing, influenced by brewing traditions both within and beyond Czech borders. This is helped along by the fact that more bars are willing to try a čtvrtá pípa, or "fourth pipe," referring to a tap at the bar that is independent of any obligations to larger breweries. Specialty beer bars like Prague's Pivovarský klub are popping up around the country, carrying extensive beer lists, and sometimes even vegetarian food—a sure sign of change among the meat-loving Czechs.

Czech Beer and Malt Association. *Report on the Czech brewing and malting industries*. http://www.cspas.cz/ (accessed February 11, 2011).

Ensminger, Peter. The history and brewing methods of Pilsner Urquell. *Brewing Techniques* May/August (1997).

Pattinson, Ron. *Breweries of the Czech Republic*. http://www.xs4all.nl/~patto1ro/czecintr.htm/ (accessed February 10, 2011.)

Rail, Evan. Prague, one pint at a time. *The New York Times*, December 6, 2009.

Garrett Oliver

DAB

See DORTMUNDER ACTIEN BRAUEREI.

Dalton's law. John Dalton (1766–1844) was an English chemist and physicist who studied the behavior of gases. His law of partial pressures, established in 1801, describes how ideal gases behave in a mixture. It states:

$$P_{\text{total}} = p_1 + p_2 + p_3 + \cdots + p_n.$$

In essence, the total pressure in a closed system containing a mixture of gases is equal to the sum of the partial pressures of each of the individual gases.

The implications for brewers are found in the areas of carbonation, dispense, and oxidation of beer where mixed gas systems are found. A mixture of carbon dioxide and air is present in the headspace of a beer bottle. According to Dalton's law, each gas in that mixture contributes to the total pressure in the bottle headspace, while reaching its own partial pressure equilibrium with the gas in solution in the beer below. Thus, oxygen in solution in beer will depend only on the partial pressure of the oxygen in the headspace and not the total pressure inside the bottle, most of which is caused by carbon dioxide. This also explains why most beers, if served through draught systems using a nitrogen-rich gas blend, will eventually lose their carbonation. Though nitrogen pressure can push the beer to the tap, only carbon dioxide pressure can keep carbon dioxide in solution. A failure of the operator of an establishment to understand this principle is often responsible for the service of beer that lacks its original level of carbonation.

See also CARBON DIOXIDE, DRAUGHT BEER, and OXIDATION.

Steve Parkes

Darcy's law describes the flow of liquid through a porous medium. It was formulated by French engineer Henry Darcy in 1856 on the basis of experiments into the passage of water through sand. In a brewing context it is applicable to wort separation and beer filtration, where liquid collection will be fastest through devices of high surface area, small depth, and high hydraulic head (i.e., differential pressure). However, the filter medium is critical—factors influencing permeability include particle size and porosity. Larger particles allow more rapid flow of liquid (less liquid "hold-up"). Less viscous liquids will flow more rapidly.

$$\text{Rate of liquid flow} = \frac{\text{Pressure} \times \text{surface area} \times \text{permeability}}{\text{Depth} \times \text{viscosity}}$$

The designs of the lauter tun and mash filter are very much in accord with Darcy's law. Lauter tuns are very broad with shallow bed depth and depend on husk with minimal damage (c.f., large porosity) and worts that are not excessively viscous. The mash filter does not depend on malt husks, whose function is replaced by the sheets, but the latter cumulatively equate to a very large surface area and the distance between the plates (equivalent to bed depth) is exceedingly small. Furthermore, in a mash filter there is the facility to compress the bed by applying pressure and squeezing out the wort.

See also FILTRATION, LAUTER TUN, and MASH FILTER.

Briggs, D. E., C. A. Boutlon, P. A. Brookes, and R. Stevens. *Brewing: Science and practice.* Cambridge: Woodhead, 2004.

Charles W. Bamforth

dark ale, more of a simple descriptor than a style designation for a particular type of beer. During the early days of the microbrewing movement in the United States in the 1980s, describing a beer as a "dark ale" was a simple way of making plain the fact that the beer at hand was dark in color and therefore different from most beers then available. Although occasionally still seen in the UK, the term is rarely used today because both brewers and beer enthusiasts have become more accustomed to broadly accepted style designations.

There are, however, some exceptions. The designation "Belgian strong dark ale" is often used to describe dark abbey-style beers with strengths above about 8% alcohol by volume, the fuzzy upper limit for the dubbel style. Although the Belgians themselves do not use the term, there are many Belgian beers that fit the name. See ABBEY BEERS.

Although fairly new, the designation "Cascadian dark ale" is gaining some currency as the name of a beer style emerging out of the Pacific Northwest. Sometimes referred to as "black India pale ale," Cascadian dark ale is a top-fermented beer using roasted malts for color but also featuring strong hop bitterness and an effusion of hop flavor and aroma. Perhaps feeling that the name "black India pale ale" was clearly silly, brewers in Oregon and Washington coined a style name that alludes to a mythical republic of Cascadia that would link Seattle to Portland and Vancouver and take a snip out of Alaska. Although the name is tongue-in-cheek, many examples are now produced commercially. Most use dehusked dark malts to avoid a clash between hop bitterness and the acridity that conventional roasted malts can lend to beers. Not surprisingly, just about all Cascadian dark ales are flavored with hops grown in the American Pacific Northwest.

See also INDIA PALE ALE.

Garrett Oliver

dark lager, a broad family of cold-fermented beers with a common heritage that emerged centuries ago out of Bavaria and nearby Czech Bohemia. Before the development of pale malts, all beers were somewhat dark, and that included the lager beers brewed in Bavaria from at least the 1500s on. Over time these became the variants we now know as dunkel and schwarzbier in Germany, černé pivo in the Czech lands, oscura in Mexico, and simply dark lager in the United States. Traditional versions would have been brewed from slightly caramelized Munich malts, but today many are brewed from a pale malt base with additions of caramel and chocolate malts for color and flavor. Although the flavor profiles sometimes become chocolate-like, they tend more toward a clean maltiness with notes of toffee and caramel. Hop bitterness tends to be low to moderate. In the northern Bavarian region of Franconia and in the Czech Republic, many versions are very dark, showing hints of coffee and charming rusticity. These are everyday drinking beers and thus are rarely sweet and usually hover around 5% alcohol by volume.

Many American breweries, harkening back to their shared German heritage, once made dark lagers. These started to fade away in the 1950s as a pale lager monoculture set in. Dark lagers are still produced by some large international breweries; some are entirely credible, whereas others gain their dark appearance largely from caramel coloring. Today, many craft brewers have revived dark lager and it is a favorite on brewpub menus from North Carolina to the Pacific Northwest. Dark lagers are also increasingly popular with beer enthusiasts in Scandinavia, Mexico, Brazil, Argentina, Japan, and beyond. It seems likely that future years will witness a refreshing comeback of dark lagers in many parts of the world.

See also BAVARIA, DUNKEL, LAGER, and SCHWARZBIER.

Garrett Oliver

Davis

See UNIVERSITY OF CALIFORNIA, DAVIS.

deaerated water. Naturally occurring water contains a high concentration of oxygen (up to

10–12 ppm dissolved oxygen), and as oxygen is detrimental to the flavor stability of beer, any water that comes into contact with fermented beer should be "deaerated," or more precisely, deoxygenated.

In the brewing process deaerated water is preferred, if not required, for the following uses:

- Diatomaceous earth (kieselguhr) filtration: to suspend the DE for the filtration process and to precede and follow the beer through the filter. See DIATOMACEOUS EARTH.
- Production of "gravity liquor," the deaerated and carbonated water used for diluting the beer in high gravity brewing. See HIGH GRAVITY BREWING.
- Pushing of beer from tank to tank, to filters, and filling machines
- Suspension of all additives added to finished beer
- All final rinses in cleaning processes for tanks and other equipment used for fermented beer

The methods used for deaerating water vary from very simple to quite complicated and expensive. The simplest is boiling the water, as oxygen has very low solubility in hot water. "Scrubbing" of the water with oxygen-free CO_2 or nitrogen is another method, and finally applying a vacuum to water trickling over a large surface (often in a hollow tube filled with small "fillers") can also be applied. These processes may be repeated or combined to achieve the specified oxygen content required, often 0.01 ppm or lower.

See also WATER.

Kunze, Wolfgang. *Technology brewing and malting*, 3rd international ed. Berlin: VLB Berlin, 2004.

Anders Brinch Kissmeyer

De Clerck, Jean, is known as one of the brewing world's most influential scientists and scholars. Born in Brussels in late 1902, he attended the brewing school at Belgium's famed Catholic University of Louvain, becoming its professor in 1943, a role he would play for the next 30 years.

In 1947 De Clerck founded the European Brewery Convention, and the following year he published his canonical two-volume work, *Textbook for brewing*. His career brought him to a number of breweries, but it was with two that De Clerck made his most enduring marks.

Between World Wars I and II, the Moortgat brewing family commissioned De Clerck to deconstruct the popular McEwan's Scotch ale. He used the yeast he found in the imported beer to make a dark brew that was given the name Duvel, from the Flemish word for "devil." Decades later, when preferences had veered toward lighter-colored beers, De Clerck returned to the Moortgat Brewery to reengineer Duvel, creating the golden strong ale that remains wildly popular today. See DUVEL MOORTGAT.

When De Clerck was summoned to the Notre Dame de Scourmont Abbey in the early 1950s to correct production problems that had made its house beer, Chimay, almost undrinkable, he found that none of the monks was formally trained in brewing. De Clerck arranged for one, Father Théodore, to take his course in Louvain, and eventually the two worked together to create Chimay Blue Label, a dark, strong ale that sent the Trappist brewery on its way to worldwide fame. De Clerck died in 1978 and was buried at the Scourmont Abbey, an honor usually accorded only to its resident monks.

Jackson, Michael. "How Scot's yeast made a Belgian classic ale." http://www.beerhunter.com/documents/19133-000020.html (accessed November 22, 2010).
Jackson, Michael. "In the world of beer the Devil has all the best ales." http://www.beerhunter.com/documents/19133-000816.html (accessed November 22, 2010).
Jackson, Michael. *Michael Jackson's great beers of Belgium*, 6th ed. Boulder, CO: Brewers Publications, 2008.

Nick Kaye

decoction mashing is a traditional and intensive method of mashing. While the method was once used by most breweries, today decoction is a controversial topic among brewers. Many German brewers (among others) claim that it develops malt character, depth, and superior foam. Others feel that it is a waste of energy and time, and is unnecessary now that modern well-modified malts are available to everyone.

The basic principle of decoction is to remove a part of the mash, boil it, and return it to the main mash, which is held at a constant temperature. There are two different aims in boiling one part of the mash:

1. To use physical pulping, which impacts the cell walls of the malt.
2. To raise the temperature of the bulk mash to a defined higher temperature after mixing both parts. (In the days before thermometers, the decoction method made a multi-temperature mash achievable and repeatable.)

The boiling of the grains helps to destroy the cell walls and makes the starches more accessible to the malt enzymes. This is particularly important for under modified malts where boiling helps to break down the cell walls.

There are different types of decoction mashing methods. The archetype is the triple decoction. This very intensive method is, from the current point of view, time-killing and no longer very popular, but it is the basis for understanding the principles behind all decoction methods.

The mash-in temperature is 95°F–98.6°F (35°C–37°C) with one part malt and three parts of water.

The triple decoction mash employs three main temperature rests: the acid rest, the protein rest, and the saccharification rest. At each rest the mash is separated, by interrupting stirring and waiting for a few minutes until there is one part "solid" mash for every three parts "liquid" mash. The thick part of the mash with the main part of the grains is pumped in the mash tun kettle and heated for boiling. The heating must be slow (33.8°F/min [1°C/min]). There can be rests at 143.6°F–149°F (62°C–65°C) or 161.6°F (72°C) during heating. The boiling time is 30 to 45 minutes. In the meantime, the liquid mash rests at a constant temperature of 95°F–100.4°F (35°C–38°C). After mixing up both parts of the mash, the temperature of the full mash will rise to the next (protein)-rest temperature at 122°F–131°F (50°C–55°C). To reach the right temperature a correct calculation of the volume proportions is necessary. The rest temperature and time before pulling the next decoction should be based on the malt that is used.

The next step is similar to the first: separating, heating, and boiling of the thick mash while keeping the liquid mash at the optimal temperature for the enzymes. After the second boiling and recombination of the mash, the rest temperature at 143.6°F–149°F (62°C–65°C) for the amylolysis (conversion of starch to sugars) is reached. Then the stirring stops for 10 minutes and the separation starts again. In contrast to the procedure before, the third decoction step in the traditional triple decoction is the boiling of the liquid mash. This procedure is not logical and is against the basic idea of decoction, because most of the amylase is in the liquid mash and becomes inactivated during boiling. Interestingly, the original idea behind it was to get a sweet and "thick" beer for the Lenten season and keep the degree of fermentation at a low level.

The combined mash temperature after the third mash boiling is at 167°F (75°C) for the saccharification rest. This rest takes about 15 minutes. The duration of the rests and the heating rate can be modified with or without special rests. Therefore, the duration of the triple decoction ranges widely. It lasts approximately 5.5 hours when using dark malts and 3.5 to 4 hours with pale malts. Nevertheless the input of energy is high.

For dark and enzyme-weak malts the triple decoction method could be justified, especially for malt flavor development through Maillard reactions. See MAILLARD REACTION. With the use of well-modified modern pale malts, however, this very intensive mashing with extensive degradation can take a turn for the worse and ruin both flavor and foam stability.

To avoid the waste of energy and possible loss of beer quality, the shortened double decoction is an alternative method. The classic version of the double decoction is a shortened triple decoction. The first acid rest is omitted and it starts with the protein rest at 113°F–122°F (45°C–50°C). The following procedure is similar to the triple decoction described above. Both decoctions use the thick mash for physical pulping and to destroy the starch cell walls to improve enzymatic activity. The liquid part rests at constant temperature for the best exploitation of the enzymatic power. The variations of double decoction are based on different mashing-in temperatures and rests during heating. The duration is between 175 and 215 minutes. Depending on the exact method used, the final attenuation, the color, and the viscosity of the wort varies. Beers produced with double decoction, if the procedure is well-matched to the malts used, can be particularly full-bodied and tend to show very good foam stability.

Finally, the single decoction is always a combination of infusion and decoction to reach all the required temperature rests. There are a number of methods. It is possible to proceed with a standard temperature-programmed mash, achieving the regular rests up to the amylase rest at 149°F (65°C), before separating the mash. The decoction fraction can already be separated at the mash-in temperature and then taken through the steps until boiling. Beers from single decoction wort are considered to be more gentle and fresh, with brighter color.

See also MASHING and TEMPERATURE-PROGRAMMED MASH.

Michael Zepf

degrees EBC

See COLOR UNITS EBC.

degrees Plato

See PLATO GRAVITY SCALE.

De Kluis (Brewery) is a brewery in the Belgian town of Hoegaarden, east of Brussels. It was founded in 1966 by Pierre Celis, a local milkman, in hopes of reviving the white beer, or witbier, style. See CELIS, PIERRE. White beer, an unfiltered wheat ale flavored with coriander and orange peel, was once a specialty of Hoegaarden, but had not been produced since the town's last brewery closed in 1957. Celis would name his new witbier after the town.

Celis set up his original 25-hl (21-US bbl) brewhouse in a barn across from his home. He named it Brewery Celis, but in 1978 renamed it Brewery De Kluis, Flemish for "The Cloister." In the first year of production, the brewery produced 350 hl (298 US bbl) of beer. As the beer's popularity increased, a larger production facility was needed. In 1979, Celis purchased a former distillery and lemonade factory and set up a brewery with a 100-hl (85-US bbl) kettle.

By 1985, annual production of Hoegaarden had increased to 300,000 hl (255,650 US bbl). That year, there was a devastating fire at the brewery. Insurance covered only a fraction of the rebuilding costs. Additional funds were procured from brewing giant Interbrew (now Anheuser-Busch InBev), who acquired partial ownership of the business. Celis had a strained relationship with Interbrew and in 1990 divested his share of the company.

In 2005, the corporate ownership announced its intention to close the brewery the following year and move production to its larger facility in Jupille, 70 miles away. This met with passionate protests in the town of Hoegaarden and the move was never completed. Today, tourists can visit the brewery's Visitors Center and Kouterhof cafe.

See also WHITE BEER.

Anheuser-Busch InBev. "Hoegaarden." http://www.hoegaarden.com/nl-be/home.html/ (accessed January 13, 2011).

Protz, Roger. "Pierre Celis, maestro of white beer." http://www.beer-pages.com/protz/features/hoegaarden.htm/ (accessed January 13, 2011).

White, John. "Pierre Celis, from Hoegaarden. the king of white beer." http://www.whitebeertravels.co.uk/celis.html/ (accessed January 13, 2011).

Dan Rabin

De Koninck Brewery (Brouwerij De Koninck) was founded in 1833 by Johannes Vervliet in Antwerp, Belgium and was originally called *Brouwerij De Hand* ("The Hand Brewery" in Flemish), in reference to a sculpture of a hand nearby. In 1912 the brewery was renamed Brasserie Charles De Koninck (Charles De Koninck Brewery) and has since been run by the Van Bauwel and Van den Bogaert families.

The De Koninck Brewery produces four types of beers. De Koninck (5% ABV) is the largest seller and is made from 100% malt and hopped with only Saaz hops. See SAAZ (HOP). It is the original beer from this brewery. The unique De Koninck ale yeast provides the signature biscuity flavor profile. De Koninck Blond (originally called Anton Blond), introduced in 1999 to celebrate the 400th anniversary of the birth of painter Anthony Van Dyke, is a 6% ABV ale with a pale golden color and higher alcohol. De Koninck Tripel (8% ABV), launched in 1993, is a tripel-style ale that is brewed with organic cane sugar in addition to malt and Saaz hops; this beer is filtered. Winter Koninck (6.5% ABV) is a copper-colored seasonal winter offering.

Throughout the city of Antwerp, De Koninck ale is known simply as "De Koninck" and is generally served in a unique goblet called a "bolleke." The bolleke showcases the creamy head, amber color, and delicate aromatics of De Koninck, and the word "bolleke" has come to be virtually synonymous with the beer itself. Many establishments that serve the bolleke also provide a shot glass filled with fresh yeast from the brewery; this can be added to the beer or drunk on the side.

The De Koninck Brewery enjoyed considerable success in the 1990s, reaching production volumes of 130,000 hectoliters (110,782 US bbls), but it has struggled in recent years. In August of 2010 the brewery was sold to Duvel Moortgat, brewers of Duvel and several other Belgian beer brands, who announced their intent to reinvigorate the brand.

See also BELGIUM.

Keith Villa

Deleye, Abbot Dom Gerardus, was a brother of the Trappist abbey Saint Sixtus of Westvleteren in West Flanders, Belgium. He ascended to the position of Abbot on November 27, 1941, at the age of 36. Four years into his abbacy he changed the focus of the abbey's brewery by limiting its production to serve only the on-premise needs of the monks, sales to the public at the abbey's gates, and a small number of taverns with abbey affiliations. In 1946 the commercial production of the abbey's beers was licensed to a new brewery commissioned for this purpose at the site of a nearby cheese producer in Watou. The Saint Bernardus Brewery, as it known today, has its own monastic history. The site was founded by a group of cheese-making monks from Mont-des-Cats abbey in French Flanders who had fled the French revolution. Just over a hundred years earlier these same monks helped populate the first monastic community at Westvleteren.

Dom Gerardus resigned as Abbot three weeks before his 63rd birthday in 1968 and died in 1997. While full production of beer returned to Saint Sixtus abbey in 1992, the effect of Gerardus' decisions of 1945 can still be observed. Availability of Westvleteren beers is still limited to the needs of the monks, strictly controlled sales to the public at the abbey's gates, and to Café In De Vrede, a tavern with abbey affiliations.

See also WESTVLETEREN BREWERY.

Daniel Paquette

Denmark is a Scandinavian country in northern Europe and home to an increasingly vibrant beer culture. With approximately 5.5 million inhabitants, it is a small country compared to its closest neighbors, Germany and Sweden. That said, Denmark is among the top 10 beer consuming countries per capita in the world. Beer has always been part of the Danish culture as an important beverage, especially as Denmark is too far north to produce wine. As in the rest of Europe, until fairly recently beer was a major provider of calories and was considered far healthier to drink than water, which could rarely be trusted.

The known tradition of brewing in Denmark dates from approximately 1370 BC. At this time many beers were sweetened with honey. The "beer," known as the "Egtved Girl's beer" contained cowberries or cranberries, wheat, bog myrtle, and large quantities of pollen.

The hop is now found as an indigenous plant in most of Denmark. The introduction of hop growing in Denmark is possibly linked to medieval Benedictine, Augustine, and Cistercian monasteries where, as in other countries, beer was regularly brewed. In 1473 the Danish king Christian I ordered hops to be grown in Denmark to reduce German hop imports, and subsequent kings followed his lead, requiring the people to grow increasing amounts over the next 2 centuries. By 1687 there were 140 breweries in Copenhagen, the nation's capitol, and all produced top-fermented ales. In 1845, J.C. Jacobsen got his hands on some bottom fermenting lager yeast while visiting the Spaten Brewery in Munich. He coddled the yeast all the way back to Copenhagen, and that winter started to brew lager beer. By 1847, his new brewery was called Carlsberg, and was to become one of the largest beer brands in the world.

Lager beer swept quickly through Denmark and soon all the old styles were all but gone. From the early 20th century until 2002, almost all the beer consumed in Denmark was pale lager, with Carlsberg and Tuborg very much in the lead and other brands such as Faxe (now Royal pilsner), Hancock, Fuglsang, and Thy pilsner relatively widespread. The interest in speciality beers started in 2002, together with an economic upturn and an increased interest by the public in "the good life." Danes wanted luxury items, they wanted more interesting food, and they particularly wanted more interesting beer. Overall Danish beer consumption dropped, just as it did in other European countries, but small breweries began to proliferate. Between 2002 and 2008, Denmark went from a nation with 19 breweries to one with more than 100. Carlsberg, which still dominates Denmark's beer landscape, got involved through an innovation project called Jacobsen, which brews specialty beers at a small brewery at Carlsberg's visitor's center in the Valby section of Copenhagen.

This recent wave of craft brewing has brought ale brewing back to Denmark, along with a startling level of creativity. The new Danish brewers took inspiration from Germany, Britain, Belgium, and the American craft brewing movement. They also took inspiration from Denmark itself, showing particular interest in local herbs such as bog myrtle, wormwood, and thistle and using regional berries and fruits. Bilberries, cowberries, juniper berries, rose hips, mint, and apples found their way back into Danish beer and the old Baltic Porter style staged a comeback. At Christmas and Easter, most breweries release special beers, many of them based on old Danish winter beer traditions.

In Denmark there is a particular interest in the renewal of indigenous Danish food. In the Nordic countries the weather conditions (hours of sun, rain, and wind) and the type of soil is markedly different compared to other locations in the world. This influences the development of raw materials such as cereal, herbs, and fruits and Danish malting barley is considered to be of very high quality. Experiments are ongoing to bring back old varieties of both malt and hops. To support the overwhelming new number of new beer styles, the Danish Brewers Association launched the Danish Beer Academy and the "Danish Beer Language." The latter was developed to give Danes a few simple and comprehensible tools to get a better grasp of what they now see on their beer shelves. The "language" consists of 110 words describing various aspects of the appearance, aroma, and texture of beer. The Copenhagen Beer Festival, held every May by the Danish Beer Enthusiasts Association, is a large and boisterous affair.

The pairing of beer and food is taken seriously in Denmark, where 13 Michelin stars nestle among only 5.5 million people. In 2010, the Copenhagen restaurant Noma was crowned best restaurant in the world, wresting the crown from Spain's venerable and audacious El Bulli. Noma takes an interest in all things Nordic, and beer is certainly Nordic. Should one go for dinner at the best restaurant in the world, many fine beers will be found on the menu.

Bjørn, Gitte Kjeldsen, Buhl, Bettina. *Scandinavian Brewers' Review* 65 (2008).

Carlsberg visitors center, Copenhagen. http://www.visitcarlsberg.dk (accessed April 19, 2011).

The Danish Brewers' Association. http://www.bryggeriforeningen.dk/ (accessed April 19, 2011).

Ibsen, Morten. Jacobsen original Danish ale. *Scandinavian Brewers' Review* 66 (3), 2009.

Jens Eiken

Derauflassen

See DRAUFLASSEN.

De Smedt Brewery

See AFFLIGEM BREWERY.

Desnoes and Geddes Limited (D&G), a Jamaican brewery best known for its Red Stripe brand of beers. The company was formed in 1918 by Eugene Peter Desnoes and Thomas Hargreaves Geddes and originally made soft drinks, but also sold alcoholic beverages shipped in from abroad. After about 9 years, the pair opened the Surrey Brewery in downtown Kingston. The first Red Stripe beer was produced there in 1928. The now-famous brand was originally applied to an ale, but the beer turned out to be too heavy to suit local tastes. The lager version was developed in 1938 by Paul H. Geddes, son of the company founder, and Bill Martindale. Peter S. Desnoes, son of the company founder, became chairman in 1952. He had started with D&G in 1928 as a salesman. A new plant was built to replace the Surrey Brewery in 1958 on Spanish Town Road. By this time, the sons of the founders were in charge of the business. A new plant was built in Montego Bay in 1966 to satisfy growing demand for soft drinks, which were mainly distributed locally.

Red Stripe beer entered the UK market in the late 1970s and was brewed under license by Charles Wells. Plant capacity was doubled in 1990, one of many expansions over the years. D&G continued to brew other brands including Dragon stout, Guinness, and Heineken.

Drinks giant Diageo acquired a 51% holding in D&G in September 1993, greatly increasing Red Stripe's international distribution capabilities. In 1999, D&G sold its wine and spirits business to Wray & Nephew Ltd., a Jamaican rum producer, and its soda plant to Pepsi Cola (Jamaica), allowing it to concentrate on the brewing business. A new product, Red Stripe Light, was introduced in Jamaica in 2000. In the early part of February 2001, the company held a ceremony to change its name from D&G to Red Stripe Limited. This turned out to be a marketing gimmick employed to pitch D&G as the "world's coolest beer company"—the name Desnoes & Geddes remained on stock certificates and annual reports.

Paul H. Chlup

dextrins are polymers of glucose molecules formed during the degradation of starch in the mashing process. The starch comprises amylose, a straight-chain polymer of glucose linked alpha 1,4, and amylopectin, a branched glucose polymer with alpha 1,4 links in the chain and alpha 1,6 links at the branch points. Starch is derived predominantly from malted barley, although other cereal sources (adjuncts) can also contribute. During the mashing process a series of malt enzymes, notably alpha and beta amylases, break down the starch polymers into smaller units comprising several glucose molecules, which may be arranged either straight chain or in a branch formation. These glucose polymers can be further degraded into much smaller units comprising glucose (a single glucose molecule), maltose (two glucose molecules), and maltotriose (three glucose molecules), which can be utilized by the brewing yeast in fermentation. However, depending on the extent of the enzyme activity, some of the glucose polymers do not degrade completely and are carried forward into the wort. These polymers, which can account for a notable percentage of the total extract, are unable to be fermented by the yeast and remain in the beer at the end of fermentation. In some beers, notably "low-calorie" or "lite" beers, the residual nonfermentable dextrins in the wort are reduced to lower levels through the addition of extraneous enzymes or prolonged mash periods. At high levels residual dextrins can impact the "body" or "mouthfeel" in beers, although they have no flavor of their own. Brewers wishing higher dextrin content in their beers can achieve this through the use of higher mash saccharification temperatures or using dextrin-rich types of caramel or crystal malts as a proportion of the grist.

Lewis, Michael J., and Tom W. Young. *Brewing*, 2nd ed. New York: Kluwer Academic/Plenum Publishers, 2001.

George Philliskirk

dextrose is another name for naturally occurring glucose. Chemical compounds can have two forms or mirror images called stereoisomers. In nature the dominant form of glucose produced is the right-handed isomer called D-glucose, with the left-handed form referred to as L-glucose. D-glucose is commonly referred to as dextrose, the shortened version of "dextrorotatory glucose." Dextrose is a monosaccharide, a simple sugar, and is used as a building block for biological structures or can be broken down to power life-sustaining biochemical reactions. During the production of beer, mashing of grain breaks down many compounds with starch comprising a bulk of the targeted compounds. The starches are broken down by enzymes into the constituent parts, and some of these are dextrose molecules. During the kettle boil some dextrose binds with nitrogen-containing substances in a color- and flavor-forming Maillard reaction. See MAILLARD REACTION. Dextrose, along with other sugars, is consumed by yeast during fermentation and in turn yeast release alcohol, carbon dioxide, and flavor and aroma active compounds. Dextrose is the fermentation sugar first utilized by yeast at the outset of fermentation, so by the end of fermentation it is rarely present in beer above sensory threshold.

In the United States, dextrose is almost exclusively derived from corn starch hydrolyzed with exogenous enzymes. It can, however, be produced from many different starches, including rice, cassava, and wheat. As dextrose is highly fermentable, it facilitates the brewing of very dry high gravity beers. Dextrose is also commonly used as priming sugar for bottle-conditioning.

See also BOTTLE CONDITIONING and GLUCOSE.

Kunze, Wolfgang. *Technology brewing and malting*, 2nd ed. Berlin: VLB Berlin, 1999.

Rick Vega

diacetyl is a flavor compound present in most beers (and many wines), imparting aroma characteristics described as butter, butterscotch, or buttermilk when detected above its flavor threshold of 0.04 mg/l. It is often added to food products to evince a buttery flavor and aroma. Diacetyl (butane 2,3 dione) is generated as a by-product of amino-acid metabolism in yeast during fermentation. A related compound, pentane 2,3 dione, is also produced by the same mechanism but does not have as significant an impact on flavor. The butane and pentane 2,3 diones are collectively known as VICINAL DIKETONES.

Yeast excretes a precursor into the fermenting beer, where it breaks down chemically to produce diacetyl. However, the diacetyl is subsequently reabsorbed by the yeast cell and converted to a compound with no significant flavor characteristics. Failure to reabsorb the diacetyl can result in the beer retaining an unacceptably high level of diacetyl. It is essential that the raw beer is left in contact with the yeast for long enough for the diacetyl to be converted. Yeasts that separate out too early in the fermentation process, often the result of early application of cooling, can fail to complete the reabsorption. Diacetyl is particularly unwelcome in lager-style beers and these beers are often held for a time before cooling is applied, a process known as "warm conditioning" or "diacetyl rest." For this reason, many lager brewers will allow a short-term rise of fermentation temperature to 60°F (15.5°C) or higher at the end of the fermentation.

At low to moderate levels, diacetyl can be perceived as a positive flavor characteristic in some ales and stouts. The amount of diacetyl produced is yeast strain-dependent but wort composition and fermentation conditions are also significant contributors to overall diacetyl levels. Diacetyl can also be formed by certain beer spoilage bacteria (within the group known as lactic acid bacteria), most notably during post-fermentation storage and sometimes in unsanitary beer lines (that is, plastic tubing not cleaned properly) between a keg of beer and the dispense tap.

Lewis, Michael J. and Young, Tom W. *Brewing*, 2nd ed. New York: Kluwer Academic/Plenum Publishers, 2002.

George Philliskirk

diastase. Discovered by French scientist Anselme Payen in 1833, diastase is a complex of malt enzymes that degrade starch in a limited manner during malting but extensively during mashing. Extensive diastase degradation of starch during mashing occurs because starch is gelatinized and solubilized. Mashing and cooking temperatures cause gelatinization and solubilization of starches. The products of diastase degradation of starch are fermentable sugars and dextrins. Malting increases the diastase complex of cereal grains. Enzymes of the diastase complex are alpha amylase, beta amylase, limit dextrinase, alpha glucosidase, and phosphorylase. See ALPHA AMYLASE. During malting, alpha amylase and limit dextrinase are produced in the aleurone layer and beta amylase is activated in the starchy endosperm.

In standard brewing and distilling practices alpha amylase, beta amylase, and limit dextrinase are mainly responsible for the production of the fermentable sugars found in brewers' worts and distillers' washes. Alpha amylase will attack un-gelatinized starch in a limited manner by pitting during malting. During mashing the diastase complex of enzymes will attack gelatinized/solubilized starch quickly to produce the glucose, maltose, maltotriose, maltotetrose, and dextrins found in the wort.

Alpha amylase reduces starch viscosity rapidly, producing a mixture of sugars and dextrins; beta amylase releases mainly maltose and limit dextinase debranches the amylopectin fraction of solubilized starch. The actions of alpha amylase and limit dextrinase facilitate the maltose producing action of beta amylase during mashing. This results in increased fermentability of the wort. Alpha amylase activity is analyzed as dextrinising units (DU) and beta amylase potential is analyzed as diastatic power (DP). DP levels do not reflect alpha amylase levels.

Palmer, G.H. "Cereals in malting and brewing." In: *Cereal science and technology*, ed. G.H. Palmer. 61–242. Aberdeen, Scotland: Aberdeen University Press, 1989.
Palmer, G.H. "Distilled Beverages." In: *Encyclopedia of grain science*, vol.1, eds. C. Wrigley, H. Corke, and C.E. Walker, 96–107. New York: Elsevier, 2004.

Geoff H. Palmer

diastatic power (DP) is the total activity of malt enzymes that hydrolyze starch to fermentable sugars. The starch-degrading enzymes contributing to this process are alpha-amylase, beta-amylase, limit dextrinase, and alpha-glucosidase. The driving force for DP appears to be beta amylase, which usually correlates better with DP than the other starch-degrading enzymes and has the highest activity of all starch-degrading enzymes in malt. Behind malt extract, DP is usually considered the second most important malt quality measurement. For complete conversion of starch to sugars, high levels of barley malt DP are especially important when adding substantial amounts of unmalted adjunct to the mash tun during brewing. See ADJUNCTS. Mashing converts malt starch into fermentable sugars; however, beta amylase and other starch-degrading enzymes are inactivated as the temperature during mashing increases and DP disappears. There is a dilemma in this phenomenon in that as temperatures rise, starch becomes gelatinized and is a better substrate for starch-degrading enzymes. The term "DP" had its origins with the discovery of diastase in barley malt in 1833 by two French chemists, Anselme Payen and Jean-François Persoz. They precipitated diastase from an aqueous mixture of milled barley and found that small amounts could liquefy starch to form sugars, and that it was unstable at high temperatures. This was one of the first reports of the properties of an enzyme. The suffix -ase, commonly used for naming enzymes, was derived from the name diastase. Methodologies for measuring malt DP were developed in the late 19th and early 20th centuries.

Bamforth, Charles W. "Barley and malting." In: *Scientific principles of malting and brewing*, 21–44. St. Paul, MN: American Society of Brewing Chemists, 2006.
Briggs, Dennis, E. "The biochemistry of malting." In: *Malts and malting*, 133–228. London: Blackie Academic & Professional, 1998.
Buchholz, Klaus, Volker Kasche, and Uwe T. Bornscheuer. "Introduction to enzyme technology." In: *Biocatalysts and enzyme technology*, 1–25. Weinheim, Germany: Wiley–VCH, 2005.

Stanley H. Duke and Cynthia A. Henson

diatomaceous earth (DE), a chalk-like sedimentary mineral that is derived from fossilized shell-like remains of marine alga called diatoms. It is also commonly referred to as kieselgur or diatomite. The shells are extremely fine and generally range in length from 40 to 160 μm and in width from 2 to 5 μm, the latter being roughly the diameter of most yeast cells. Because of their microscopic size and porous nature, DE preparations have been used extensively in the brewing industry as a filtering medium.

There are two types of diatomaceous earth, one derived from saltwater and the other from fresh water and the material is mined throughout the world. In the brewing process, the saltwater variety of DE is often used for filtration. DE filters for brewing fall into two categories: pressure leaf filters and sheet filters. These filters are used to clarify beers by trapping yeast and other particulates. DE is available in various grades, with finer grades capable of tighter filtrations. Fresh water DE is often used as a natural pesticide and can help protect grain stores from infestation.

DE has held many functions since it was first used by the ancient Greeks as a building material. Alfred Nobel used DE as a stabilizer for the nitroglycerine he used to make dynamite.

Typically off-white in color, DE resembles talcum powder and is composed of up to 90% silica, with the remained consisting of alumina and hematite.

DE can be dangerous if inhaled and caution is advised when handling the substance. Exposure can cause irritation to the lungs and eyes and prolonged exposure has been linked to severe respiratory problems. Given the health risks associated with DE, the disposal of postfiltration DE is becoming increasingly more regulated.

Antonides, Lloyd E. *Diatomite*. Washington, DC: U.S. Geological Survey, 1997.
Cummins, Arthur B. "Diatomite." In *Industrial minerals and rocks*, 3rd ed. Littleton, CO: Society for Mining, Metallurgy, and Exploration, Inc, 2006.
Kunze, Wolfgang. *Technologie Brauer & Mälzer* (Technology Brewers and Maltsters), 9th ed. Berlin: VLB Berlin, 2007.

John Holl and Wolfgang David Lindell

dimethyl sulfide (DMS) is an organic sulfur-containing molecule with the formula $(CH_3)_2S$. It has a low boiling point (98.6°F or 37°C) and an odor that is generally described as "cooked sweet corn." DMS contributes to the aroma of many foodstuffs, including cooked vegetables (beet, cabbage), tomato ketchup, milk, and seafood, as well as beer, especially lagers. Most people are able to detect it in very low concentrations, typically above 30 parts per billion. It plays a major environmental role in being the principal vehicle by which sulfur is cycled in nature, arising from the breakdown of chemical species within algae, including seaweed, and then evaporating to the atmosphere. There, it is oxidized to dimethyl sulfoxide (DMSO), a moisture-absorbing, high-boiling-point material that returns to earth in precipitation and is subsequently reduced back to DMS by microorganisms.

In beer, DMS can arise from two precursors. The principal one is S-methylmethionine (SMM; also known as DMS precursor, or DMSP), a molecule that develops in the embryo of barley during germination. It is heat-sensitive and is lost to a great extent during malt kilning. Therefore, there tends to be a high survival of SMM in more gently dried lager malts, this SMM being broken down to DMS during wort boiling and in the hot wort stand (the period post-boiling but pre-cooling). It is at this latter stage that the DMS is not purged and survives into the fermenter. Partly for this reason most brewers seek to minimize the hot wort stand and get the wort chilled and into the fermenter as quickly as possible. There is further loss of DMS with the carbon dioxide evolved during fermentation, but the compound is replenished by reduction by yeast of DMSO that is produced during curing of the malt. Wort spoilage bacteria such as Obesumbacterium proteus are especially capable of converting DMSO to DMS. See OBESUMBACTERIUM PROTEUS.

Most brewers regard DMS as an off-flavor, but in moderation it does make a significant contribution to the aroma of many lager beers and indeed has been identified as a key feature of German-style lagers.

Anness, B.J. and Bamforth, C.W. Dimethyl sulfide—a review. *Journal of the Institute of Brewing* 88 (1982): 244–252.

Charles W. Bamforth

direct firing refers to one of the techniques that is used to heat the kettle and boil wort in a brewery. As its name implies, direct firing involves using an open flame under the kettle to heat it up. Historically this was done with coal fires, but today oil or natural gas burners are used. These burners are generally housed in a cast-iron combustion chamber under the kettle that distributes heat across the bottom of the kettle. Sometimes several smaller flames are distributed across the bottom of the kettle to even out the heating. Although direct firing can also be used to heat up mash tuns, this is extremely rare because the mash can easily stick and scorch at hot spots.

Direct fired kettles are found in smaller breweries, with kettles that hold a maximum of 330 hl (281 US bbl), because they are an inefficient way of heating up a very large amount of liquid. There are, however, some advantages associated with the use of direct fire. It is a quick method of heating and can produce a vigorous boil. Brewers can also adjust the flame intensity throughout the boil to achieve rapid temperature changes.

Today, most brewery kettles utilize steam jackets or internal or external steam boilers. These allow for a more even distribution of heat. Direct firing, on the other hand, concentrates the heat at the bottom of the kettle. This results in the caramelization of wort sugars inside the kettle, which can be troublesome to clean. This caramelization will also add caramel flavor notes and color to beer. Although this is desirable in certain styles, it can create a challenge in brewing more delicate styles of beers, such as pilsners. When brewing very pale beers in direct-fired kettles, brewers heat the wort very carefully and keep it in constant motion to avoid a caramelized character. Direct-fired kettles were commonly used in Scotland and traditional Scottish beer styles, like the Scotch ale, are characterized by the flavors and colors that this technique imparts. The only remaining large Scottish brewery to use direct-fired kettles is Caledonian.

See also KETTLE.

Goldammer, Ted. *The brewer's handbook*, 2nd ed. Essex: Apex, 2008. http://www.beer-brewing.com/ (accessed April 18, 2011).

Hough, J. S., et al. *Malting and brewing science*, Vol. 2. London: Chapman & Hall, 1982.

Beer label, c. 1930s, illustrating the direct firing technique, which involves using an open flame to heat a kettle and boil the wort. PIKE MICROBREWERY MUSEUM, SEATTLE, WA

Priest, Fergus G., and Graham G. Stewart, eds. *The handbook of brewing*, 2nd ed. Boca Raton, FL: Taylor & Francis, 2006.

Mirella G. Amato

dissolved oxygen (DO) is a measure of the amount of oxygen gas (O_2) dissolved in solution in wort or beer, as opposed to the total amount of O_2 in a sample, which includes that present in equilibrium with the dissolved O_2, i.e., that present in the headspace. It is typically measured using an oxygen analyzer (oxygen electrode). The solubility of oxygen depends on temperature (gases are less soluble as the temperature is raised) and on the pressure of the gas over the liquid. Henry's Law states that

$$p = k_H c$$

p = partial pressure of gas (in this case oxygen)
k_H = Henry's constant, which depends on the gas, solvent, and temperature
c = concentration of gas in solution

Thus, the more gas that a liquid such as water, wort or beer is exposed to, the more will go into solution. Furthermore, separate gases will respond individually. See HENRY'S LAW.

The concentration of gas dissolved also depends on the concentration of other materials in solution.

The dissolved oxygen content (abbreviated to dO_2) is relevant from the perspective of fermentation control, it being necessary to provide yeast with the correct quantity of oxygen to satisfy its need to synthesize unsaturated fatty acids and sterols. dO_2 is also important in terms of wort and beer stability, oxygen adversely impacting quality and performance by elevating color, cross-linking polymers (leading to reduced rates of wort separation), promoting haze, and causing flavor instability. For this reason, the measurement (and, if warranted, elimination) of dissolved oxygen is a critical element of quality assurance and control for breweries.

See also OXIDATION and OXYGEN.

Bamforth, C.W. & A. Lentini. "The flavor instability of beer." In *Beer: A Quality Perspective*, ed. C.W. Bamforth, 85–109. Burlington, MA: Academic Press, 2009.

Charles W. Bamforth

distribution, the method by which a brewery's beer actually reaches the marketplace. Brewing a great beer is the first step toward success for any brewer anywhere in the world. The second step is getting that beer distributed—getting the beer into the hands of the consumer. Woe shall betide the brewer who underestimates the difficulty of the second step. From the earliest days of brewing, government has had an interest in regulating the production and distribution of beer—to insure the safety of the product, to limit its consumption to people of legal drinking age, and to collect taxes. The structure of beer distribution varies from country to country and even from state to state, or even municipality to municipality, within a country.

In the UK a brewer can be a distributor and own pubs. There are more than 50,000 pubs in the UK. The pub sector is split into three groups—managed, tenanted or leased, and free houses.

There are approximately 9,000 managed pubs in the UK. These are pubs owned by a brewery. The staff of the pubs are employees of the brewery. Decisions on the beers stocked by these pubs will be made by the brewer, and although some beers from other brewers will be sold, the buying decisions will be made by the owning brewer and not the publican. See TIED HOUSE SYSTEM.

The largest group of pubs—about 19,000—are tenanted and leased. A tenanted/leased pub is owned by a brewery or by a pub-owing company and then leased on a short-term or long-term lease to a tenant/lessee. Tenants/lessees are tied for their beer supply at a pre-agreed price, which is likely to be more expensive than the same beer bought by anyone else from a brewer. The owners of the pubs argue that this higher price must be seen in the context of the total rental package the tenant is offered; the tenant, they say, will incur a relatively low capital cost to set up the business. The tenants of pubs owned by national brewers can serve one cask-conditioned beer of their choice from a source of their choice—the so-called guest beer rule championed by the Campaign for Real Ale, a consumer advocacy group. See CAMPAIGN FOR REAL ALE (CAMRA).

In addition, there are about 17,000 "free houses." These are owned and managed by the licensee who makes the decision about which beers are stocked.

In continental Europe it is not unusual for a brewery to own pubs, bars, or even liquor stores. Brewers also will tie retailers to their products through a system of financial loans, whereby the retailer agrees to stock a product in exchange for investment in the business. The investment could include marketing and advertising support, the provision of equipment for draught beer, or even decoration and refurbishment of the premises.

In the UK and Europe, big retail chains sometimes require brewers to pay fees to stock their beers.

In China and many countries throughout the world, brewers pay royalty fees to distributors and retailers, who then agree to sell their beers.

In Sweden the government controls retail beer sales though the Systembolaget, the Swedish Alcohol Retail Monopoly, with the government acting as both wholesaler and retailer. Unless the Systembolaget buys a brewer's beer, it cannot go on sale. The Systembolaget exists "to minimize alcohol-related problems by selling alcohol in a responsible way, without profit motive." Dating back to the mid-1800s, similar monopolies also exist today in Norway, Finland, Iceland, Canada, and some US States. In Sweden, brewers can own and sell directly to bars, restaurants, and hotels.

All of the above-mentioned systems of beer distribution have resulted in a concentration of the beer industry in the hands of small groups of large brewers who could afford to control the distribution of beer and, in some cases, the retail sale of beer.

The United States has a unique and complicated system of beer regulation that was instituted when Prohibition was abolished in 1933. The beer industry in the United States, as in most of the world, became greatly concentrated in the 20th century because of the power of mass marketing and mass distribution. But the US system had some unique features that enabled small brewers to develop their businesses to a greater degree than other countries. See PROHIBITION.

The 21st Amendment of the U.S. Constitution—which abolished Prohibition—provided that the states, not the federal government, would have primary responsibility for regulation of beer and other alcoholic beverages. (Beside tax collection, the only role played by the federal government is to insure that no state makes laws that discriminate against the brewers of other states—the "commerce clause" of the Constitution.)

With some exceptions, most of the states subscribe to the three-tier distribution system. Under this system, a brewer cannot be a wholesaler or a retailer. Wholesalers also may not own retail outlets. Only a retailer—a liquor store, supermarket, restaurant, bar, or hotel—can sell to the consumer. The "tied house"—a bar or store owned by the brewer as in the United Kingdom—was banned in all states. In addition, retail chain stores cannot charge fees to stock beers.

Thus, the wholesaler and the retailer are independent businesses that can make their own choices about what beers they will handle.

States have introduced various exceptions to the three-tier system, the most common being a brewpub, which is both a brewer and a retailer. Some states allow a business to have a part in two of the tiers, allowing breweries to distribute their own and others beers and allowing brewers to sell beer at retail from a store at their brewery.

Most state laws provide that brewers must grant distributors exclusive distribution rights for a geographic area. Many states have "franchise laws," which hold that distributors garner equity in beer brands when they sell brands in their areas. This means that a brewer cannot arbitrarily terminate a distributor's contract without cause. These laws usually provide that the brewer must compensate the distributor if he does terminate the relationship, often for the "fair market value" of the distribution rights.

The various states also have established rules that govern the relationship of the brewer to the retailer. In some states, a brewer may not give promotional items or services to a retailer. In other states, the value of the items is limited. In some states, a brewer can set up and maintain draught lines in a restaurant or bar. In other states, this is prohibited.

The independent wholesalers fostered by the three-tier system have been a key factor in enabling the craft brewing renaissance in the United States. Similar efforts to establish craft breweries in many countries have been stifled by the large brewers' control of the means of distribution.

Tim Hampson and Steve Hindy

Doemens Academy was founded in Munich in 1895 by Dr Albert Doemens as a German private school for brewers. It filled a gap in the traditional, government-regulated German education system, which was then rigidly bifurcated into a trade track with apprentice, journeyman, and master certificates on the one hand, and an academic track with university degrees on the other. Doemens, by contrast, offered a secondary, polytechnic education to certified journeymen, which allowed them to graduate as brew masters and malt masters—a focus that Doemens has retained to this day, as is reflected in its banner motto: "Aus der Praxis für die Praxis" (From practice for practice). In 1965, Doemens reorganized itself into Doemens e.V., a not-for-profit educational institution, which is eligible for public education funding. Later, the Doemens Akademie GmbH was founded as a 100% daughter of Doemens e.V., a for-profit corporation that offers, among other services, consulting to the food and beverage industries, as well as specialized training and seminars, such as a beer sommelier program and a tap system maintenance course. As part of its hands-on orientation, Doemens operates a 5-hectoliter test brewery as well as a small PET-packaging line. In 2000, Doemens and the Siebel Institute of Chicago founded the World Brewing Academy, a joint venture, which offers diploma programs in brewing technology, and for which Doemens serves as the Munich campus. See SIEBEL INSTITUTE OF TECHNOLOGY. All Doemens educational programs take between a few weeks and 2 years to complete. Furthermore, Doemens offers technical seminars which last between 1 and 14 days. Since 1965, Doemens has graduated a total of about 2,000 students.

See also BREWING SCHOOLS and GERMANY.

Doemens. http://www.doemens.org/index.php?id=2&L=1 (accessed March 22, 2011)

Gerrit Blüemelhuber and Horst Dornbusch

Dogfish Head Craft Brewery is an American regional brewery located in Milton, Delaware.

In 2009, Dogfish Head produced 113,362 hl (96,891 US bbl). The brewery is best known for brewing quirky and unique interpretations of international beer styles, often using exotic ingredients and unusual production techniques.

Dogfish Head Craft Brewery grew out of Dogfish Head Brewings & Eats, a brewpub located in Rehoboth Beach, Delaware, started by Sam Calagione in 1995. Dogfish Head was Delaware's first brewpub and was, for a time, the smallest commercial brewery in America, producing all of its beer on a 45-l (12-gal) homebrewing system. In 2002, the company moved virtually all of its beer production to its current facility located in a 100,000-sq-ft converted cannery in Milton, Delaware. At the same time, the company installed a microdistillery at the Rehoboth Beach location to make small-batch gins, vodkas, and rums.

Most of the Dogfish Head beers that have made the brewery famous fall into the "extreme beer" category, including their 120-Minute India pale ale (IPA), an 18% alcohol by volume (ABV) IPA that is continuously dosed with hop pellets during its 2-h boil; Palo Santo Marron, a 12% ABV brown ale aged in a giant tun made of South American palo santo wood; and Sah'tea, a take on the Finnish sahti style of juniper-spice beer, made with black tea, cardamom, and ginger. In the early 2000s, the company's World Wide stout held the unofficial title of world's strongest beer, clocking in at over 20% ABV.

In addition to running the company, founder Sam Calagione is a well-known and unabashedly enthusiastic promoter of both Dogfish Head and craft beer in general. In 2010 Calagione became the subject of his own television show on the Discovery Channel.

Bilger, Burkhard. A better brew: The rise of extreme beer. *The New Yorker*, November 24, 2008.

Brian Thompson

Benedictine monks of the order of Saint Francis of Paola began brewing in Munich in 1634 with permission from the Duke of Bavaria, initially only for their use. But by 1780 they were also selling their brews as extra strong beer under the name of Salvator (Latin for "Savior") to the public. Strong beer called bock ("Billy goat") had been brewed in Munich since 1612, so the monks called theirs dopplebock ("two Billy goats"). PIKE MICROBREWERY MUSEUM, SEATTLE, WA

doppelbock is a strong beer with minimum original gravity of 18 degrees Plato and a typical alcohol content beyond 7% ABV. The style originated in the Bavarian capital city of Munich, Germany and was for a fairly long time synonymous with the Salvator beer brewed by Paulaner. In the late 19th-century breweries that had copied the name "Salvator" were forced by a lawsuit to introduce their own brands of doppelbock beers, but Salvator remained the category defining beer. The beer originated in a convent in the village Au on what used to be the eastern outskirts of Munich in the 17th century when monks following the rule of Saint Franciscus of Paula settled there and began brewing beer. The "Sanct Pater Bier" (later "Salvator"), brewed to celebrate father Franciscus' commemoration day on April 2, was first brewed by Valentin Stephan Sill, called "Frater Barnabas," in 1774. It was a custom to offer a mug of this strong beer to the duke of Bavaria, toasting in Latin: "Salve, pater patriae! Bibes, princeps optimae!" ("Greetings to you, father of our country! Drink, best of all noblemen!"). While the duke was finishing his strong beer (wisely drinking only a small sip at a time) Frater Barnabas was allowed to speak his mind freely. This is re-enacted every year on the Nockherberg when the tapping of the first barrel of Salvator officially marks the middle of the lent period before Easter. Also known as "liquid bread," this beer once helped the monks through the long fasting days of Lent. While Salvator is the most well-known doppelbock, almost 200 other breweries indicate the style by amending "-ator" to the beer's name. Famous doppelbocks are "Animator" (Hacker Pschorr), "Celebrator" (Ayinger), "Impulsator" (Wieninger), "Maximator" (Augustiner), "Palmator" (Prösslbräu), and "Triumphator" (Löwenbräu). Yet there are noteworthy exceptions to that naming convention including "Andechser Doppelbock" and the top fermenting strong weissbier, "Aventinus" from Schneider.

While they can be brewed to any color and made by different methods, doppelbocks are usually reddish-brown bottom-fermented lagers, and generally show a toffee-like, bready aroma and rich malty palate with notable residual sweetness. Hops are usually robust enough to offer some balance, but rarely above 25 IBU.

See also ANDECHS, AUGUSTINER BRÄU, AYINGER BREWERY, and SCHNEIDER WEISSE BREWERY.

Conrad Seidl

Dorber, Mark has been at the forefront of enthusing thousands of people from around the world on the delights and pleasures of beer for more than 20 years. He is widely considered the most accomplished cask cellarman in England. Trained as an economist, Dorber worked in the City of London for a major legal firm in the 1980s but outside the day job his passion was beer, particularly traditional cask beer. His mentor was the great Michael Jackson who both educated and guided Dorber in the beers of the world. Dorber worked in the evenings at the White Horse pub in Parson's Green, south London, acquiring the skills required to keep and serve a great pint of cask beer, with Jackson, a regular at the pub, on hand to sample and savor his work. Eventually the pull of the trade proved too much for Dorber and he gave up his day job to become full-time manager at the White Horse. The White Horse became the Mecca for both beer aficionados and novices from around the world. Staff at the White Horse were also recruited internationally and under Dorber's watchful eye were trained and inspired by the delights of beer. Many returned home to start their own breweries and pubs. In addition to a great range of draught beers, not only cask beers but classic beers from Europe and North America, the White Horse also established a wonderful portfolio of bottled beers, particularly from Belgium, a country to which Mark was a frequent visitor. Dorber is a passionate advocate of matching beer with food and his menus at the pub always included a recommendation on a beer for each dish offered.

Such was the reputation of Mark Dorber and the White Horse that many brewers used the pub as a launch venue for new beers, knowing that a nod of approval from Dorber was the beer equivalent of a royal warrant. In 2006, Dorber and his wife Sophie took over the lease of a charming inn, the Anchor, in the coastal village of Walberswick, Suffolk, close to the home of the Adnam's brewery in Southwold. Mark and Sophie have continued where they left off in London, providing great beers (and wine), excellent food, and a bracing learning environment for the international staff, customers, and beer enthusiasts. Dorber has converted an old barn adjacent to the inn to a state-of-the-art training facility which is used for training courses, most notably through the Beer Academy, an organization that Dorber was not only pivotal in setting up but which continues to enjoy his support and encouragement as a director.

See also BEER ACADEMY.

George Philliskirk

dormancy (of barley) is the inability of mature, viable barley to germinate under favorable conditions. Dormancy is a natural phenomenon in plants that protects seeds from germinating during seed development, which can be advantageous for maltsters after a wet harvest. However, it can be a disadvantage when dormant barley fails to germinate in the malthouse. Barley must germinate vigorously and quickly when steeped during malting if quality, trouble-free malt is to be produced. Malt containing dormant kernels produces less malt extract and more wort beta-glucan, resulting in less beer and problems with poor lautering and beer filtration in the brewhouse. The degree of dormancy in barley varies with variety and storage conditions but weather during harvest and grain silo filling is a significant factor. Barley grown under cool, wet conditions is more dormant than barley grown under hot, dry conditions. The physiological basis of dormancy is poorly understood but has been attributed to the physiological state of the embryo, availability of oxygen to the embryo, and microbial load on the barley. Dormancy will break naturally, given sufficient storage time, but can be hastened by carefully drying barley after harvest to 11%–12% moisture, followed by 2 weeks of warm storage at 25°C–30°C (77°F–86°F) and then cooling to a final storage temperature of less than 17°C (62.5°F). Dormancy is measured by comparing results from a standard germination test (germination energy) to germination results after treatment with hydrogen peroxide (germinative capacity). Dormancy can also be determined by staining longitudinally split kernels with tetrazolium.

See also GERMINATION and MALTING.

Briggs, D. E. *Barley*. London: Chapman & Hall, 1978.

Michael J. Edney

Dortmunder Actien Brauerei, or DAB, is the last remaining large brewery in Dortmund, Northrhine-Westfalia, Germany, owned by the Radeberger Gruppe, which is in turn part of the Dr Oetker group. The brewery was founded in 1868 by three business people (Laurenz Fischer and Heinrich and Friedrich Mauritz) and brewmaster Heinrich Herberz as "Bierbrauerei Herberz & Co" and renamed "Dortmunder Actien-Brauerei" only 4 years later. At the time coal mines in the region thrived and many breweries competed for an ever-growing clientele. Bavarian-style dunkel was the most prestigious beer, but coal miners seemed to prefer the local golden helles (later more specifically defined as Dortmunder Export) that had a character of its own because of the high sulfur content of Dortmund's water. DAB's main rival was Dortmunder Union (DUB)—founded on January 31, 1873—which soon became the fastest growing German brewery of the late 19th century, brewing 75,000 hectoliters (63,913 US bbl) in 1887, 193,650 (165,022 US bbl) in 1900, and one million (852,168 US bbl) in 1929. DAB had reached 100,000 hectoliters (85,216 US bbl) in 1887 but grew at a much smaller pace to reach only 160,000 hectoliters (136,347 US bbl) by the turn of the century, 763,304 (650,463 US bbl) in 1929, and one million (852,168 US bbl) only after World War II in 1959. DUB was run by Fritz Brinkhoff, considered the richest brewmaster (and one of the largest private taxpayers) of his time because he had a contract that guaranteed a huge bonus for the growth of the brewery. He retired after 53 years as a brewmaster and a street in Dortmund and Dortmund's best selling premium beer, "Brinkhoff's No.1," carry his name. DAB and DUB both acquired several other breweries in the town and its surroundings, and both were later bought by Dr Oetker. Production of all remaining Dortmunder brands was moved to DAB's site in 2005.

Conrad Seidl

double IPA is among the most popular new beer styles among craft beer enthusiasts in the United States. Based on the original India pale ale (IPA) style that was revived by the American craft brewing movement in the 1980s, the newly minted "double IPA" (also known as "imperial IPA") seeks to take both alcoholic strength and hop intensity to new levels. See INDIA PALE ALE. Americans tend to feel that "bigger is better" when it comes to many things, whether they be cars or steaks, and beer is no exception. The double IPA is a brashly American expression of hop character, and the best of them are astonishingly bitter, but balance this with dry malt structure and explosive hop aromatics. Most will have bitterness from 65 to 90 international bittering units and the strengths range from about 8% to well over 10% alcohol by volume. Almost all are heavily dry hopped, and some have hops added through the brewing process, starting in the mash. See DRY HOPPING and MASH HOPPING. Most have a honey amber color. For people who love hop bitterness and flavor, these are the ultimate beers, and West Coast beer enthusiasts speak of a "lupulin shift," where drinkers' palates become happily accustomed to very high bitterness.

Vinnie Cilurzo, now owner and brewmaster of the Russian River Brewing Company, is generally acknowledged to have invented the double IPA in 1994 while brewing at Blind Pig in Temecula, California. Others claim earlier versions, but Russian River's Pliny the Elder is still regarded as ranking among the best produced. As of 2011, more than 100 double IPAs were being produced by American craft brewers, and these beers are now beginning to have an influence in Europe and beyond. The style moniker "double IPA" rankles with traditionalists, who feel that it confuses both brewing history and modern consumers. In its heyday, IPA was a well-defined style, and double IPA is a distinctly different beer; perhaps it ought somehow to be named for its native California. The nomenclature has surely already left the barn, however, and triple IPA and quadruple IPA cannot be far behind.

Garrett Oliver

downy mildew is a common plant disease prevalent on many barley varieties and causing yield losses of up to 40%. It is caused by the fungus Erysiphe graminis f.sp. hordei and appears as a distinctive fluffy white mass on leaves, initially as isolated spots but progressing into a complete covering which reduces light penetration resulting eventually to leaf death. Overwintering cleistothecia (closed spore-bearing structures) are eventually produced.

The fungus infects new plants from infected plants nearby or from field residues from previous seasons, often blown or splashed onto leaves by rainfall. Growth of the fungus is predominantly on leaves and less extensive on the flowering head but yield is reduced by its effect on stunting plant growth, reducing the number of tillers produced and the number of corns in each head.

During growth the fungus penetrates the leaf to obtain nutrients and saps energy from the plant. However, the majority of the fungus remains on the upper surface of the leaf. Warm, moist conditions enhance the growth of mildew. Rainfall is not essential but extensive leaf growth due to high nitrogen fertilizer application may encourage growth and enhance its spread.

Resistance to mildew, conferred by various genetic mechanisms, is present in some barley varieties. For example, the *mlo* gene, which controls cell wall development in the barley leaf, can limit the penetration of the fungus. Such resistance genes are important factors in limiting the impact of the disease on current barley production and are under investigation with the hope that their effectiveness can be enhanced.

Keith Thomas

draft beer

See DRAUGHT BEER.

drauflassen (derauflassen) is German for "to put on top of," and, when applied to brewing, refers to putting one batch of wort "on top of" another. The technique behind the term refers to topping up fermenting wort with new oxygenated wort while the fermenting wort is at its peak of fermentation, 24 to 72 hours after its start. The oxygen in the fresh wort will cause the yeast briefly to revert its metabolism back from the anaerobic mode to the aerobic mode, where it multiplies. Once the added oxygen is depleted, the yeast switches back to anaerobic fermentation, converting the fermentable sugars into alcohol and carbon dioxide.

The most common scenarios in breweries calling for the use of the drauflassen technique are the final stages of yeast propagation, when a rather small volume of new yeast is transferred from the laboratory or propagation plant into the main fermentation vessels. Drauflassen then ensures a quick multiplication of the quantity of yeast. The technique may also be used as an emergency procedure in case of a severe lack of sufficient quantities of vital and clean pitching yeast as it enables fermentation of large volumes of wort with small quantities of pitching yeast. The drauflassen stage can be repeated if the starting quantity of yeast is very low. Due to the metabolic stress on the yeast caused by its switching back and forth between the anaerobic and aerobic stages, drauflassen can cause taste and flavor differences to beer fermented in a normal one-stage fermentation.

For some breweries, however, drauflassen is a standard operating procedure, most often used when the size of the brewery's fermenters greatly exceed that of its kettle. In such cases the brewery will usually fill half the fermenter on the first day, followed by the other half on the second day.

Anders Brinch Kissmeyer

draught beer. Beer racked into kegs and served on draught (also spelled "draft" in the United States) is generally considered to be the optimal method to showcase the brewer's art. In the United States, draught beer generally is not pasteurized and is ideally maintained cold through distribution from brewery to glass (although some brewers now choose to flash pasteurize and forego refrigeration). Modern single-valve stainless cooperage—coupled with state-of-the-art cleaning and filling systems—allows beer to be aseptically packaged with very little oxygen pickup or ingress. The stainless keg eliminates degradation from light, as well as potential oxygen ingress through bottle cap seals or flavor influence from can liners that is possible with other beverage packaging methods. When dispensed through a properly maintained and balanced draught system, this allows for optimal brewery-fresh beer to be delivered to the glass. Although draught beer has the potential to deliver the best drinking experience, it can easily be ruined with improper storage and handling through a poorly designed or poorly maintained dispensing system or improperly cleaned glassware. The draught system should be designed and balanced to deliver a perfect pour from the first serving to the last glass. Today's wide range of available beer styles and installation configurations dictate that someone knowledgeable about dispensing system design and the styles of beer to be served is involved in the set-up and balancing of the system to ensure that the brewery's desired gas makeup, carbonation level, and serving temperature are maintained. While it can be excellent, British traditional cask-conditioned ale, sometimes referred to as "draught beer" in the UK, is an entirely different system which we do not address here. See CASK CONDITIONING and REAL ALE.

Cooperage

Modern kegs are almost entirely fabricated from deep-drawn stainless steel and available in a range of common US and European sizes: 7¾ gallons (1/4 bbl) to 15.5 gallons (1/2 bbl) and 20, 30, or 50 liters (5, 8, or 13 gal). Breweries make significant investments in kegs, and they can last for many years. If properly maintained, they can be refilled hundreds of times; but due to theft and unscrupulous metal scrapping, a large percentage of kegs never make it back to the brewery. Marginally successful attempts have been made to fabricate kegs from less expensive coated mild steel, plastic, or "bag-in-a-box" technology, but currently none of these protect the quality of the beer as well as stainless steel. Although several variations exist worldwide, modern keg designs utilize a double-ported top valve that supplies both the dispensing gas and the tapping connection. The valve is connected to a down tube, or spear, that extends to within a 1/4" (7 mm) of the bottom and allows the complete emptying of the keg. During the cleaning and filling cycle at the brewery, the keg is inverted and multiple cycles of detergent, water, and steam are pumped at high pressure through the same fittings before filling.

Keg Delivery and Storage

Kegs of beer should be stored and delivered cold—as close to the dispense temperature as practical. Depending on the temperature, it will take many hours—or even days—to cool a warm keg. Most dispensing and foaming problems are caused by attempts to dispense warm beer. Gas pressure, temperature, and system design are all closely interrelated. Tapping a keg even a few degrees above the desired typical 34°F–38°F (1.1°C–3.3°C) temperature specification for most American beer styles may cause excessive foam and difficulty in pouring. While it is possible to run draught lines at warmer temperatures in order to show certain beers at their best, this requires very careful design and balancing.

Dispensing Gas

Although most beer is carbonated and dispensed utilizing pure carbon dioxide gas, the use of mixed gas blends containing carbon dioxide (CO_2) and nitrogen (N_2) are becoming commonplace—allowing greater dispense system design and flexibility. Remote cold boxes are often utilized to allow easier delivery, loading, and greater keg storage than may be available in a crowded bar or restaurant. The increased pressure required to deliver beer these greater distances would over-carbonate the beer if 100% CO_2 were used, but the low solubility and inert nature of N_2 make a blend of the two gases ideal. Due to oxidation concerns, air should never be used to dispense beer. In the past, some draught-system suppliers marketed air compressors as a way to save money on CO_2 or mixed gas. The oxygen in the air rapidly degrades the beer; unfortunately, such systems are still in use. (Inline beer pumps may also be used to boost the beer-line pressure without changing the carbonation level). Nitrogenated beers (such as some styles of stout) require a higher blend of N_2 and CO_2 to allow proper balance. Several premixed bottled blends are available; or a gas blender can be purchased to mix the two gases on site. Care must be exercised when selecting gas blends so the beer doesn't over-carbonate or lose carbonation during the dispensing period. The dispense gas pressure is reduced using a gas regulator that is set to the equilibrium pressure of the beer in the keg. Beverage regulators must contain a safety relief valve to relieve dangerous system pressure in case of a regulator malfunction.

Dispensing System Design

A properly designed draught system should maintain the brewer's desired carbonation level and gas balance, provide for the appropriate dispensing temperature for the style of beer, allow for a pour rate of approximately 2 ounces (60 ml) per second, and deliver the amount of foam desired. Depending on the installation constraints and physical layout of the system, several different draught-system technologies have evolved; but many components are common to all designs. Best practices call for all-metal system components that come in contact with beer to be made of stainless steel. Chrome-plated brass was commonly used due to its lower cost and ease of manufacture, but the acidic nature of beer and the chemicals utilized in routine draught line cleaning attack the brass and will lead to metallic off-flavors and increased difficulty in cleaning and maintaining good system hygiene. Tubing and other plastic components need to be manufactured of food-grade, approved materials. During installation and design of any dispensing system, the style of beer, CO_2 content, temperature, and elevation are factored in to balance the system for a perfect pour. The simplest—and often best-designed systems—are called "direct draw." Here the keg is located in a cold box either directly behind or below the faucet or "tap." It is important that the lines and fittings are kept chilled to the dispensing temperature to prevent foaming. The keg is tapped using a dual-ported "coupler" that mates up to the top of the keg; this supplies both the dispense gas and beer outlet connection. The coupler also contains a secondary safety relief valve that will relieve potentially explosive pressures in case of a regulator malfunction. The coupler is connected using a short length of vinyl tube with a stainless "tail piece" that connects the coupler and "shank" that goes through the cold box wall or bar "tower" mounting the dispensing faucet. When the distance from the keg to a remotely mounted tap increases—up to a maximum of about 25 feet—chilled forced air is employed in a duct surrounding the beer line to maintain the beer and faucets at or below the cold box temperature to prevent foaming. Long-draw installations are possible—with the kegs being located up to several hundred feet from the faucet utilizing heavily insulated glycol-chilled bundles, or "trunk" lines. These can contain any number of beer lines—surrounding two or more supply-and-return chilled glycol lines—through which refrigerated food-grade glycol is continuously circulated from the cold box to the tap, to maintain the beer at the correct dispensing temperature. Although the use of chilled long-draw systems allows greater design flexibility when situating the cold box and faucets, the added distance complicates system cleaning and increases beer loss. Although not ideal, for temporary 1-day events and picnic use, hand pumps, or "jockey boxes," can be used with either cold plates or coils to chill the beer on the way to the tap; or the keg can be iced down in a large tub. Since hand pumps introduce oxygen, the kegs with them will not keep for more than a day or two after being tapped.

System Cleaning

One of the keys to quality draught beer is a clean and well-maintained dispensing system. Although beer will not harbor pathogens, many common strains of bacteria can grow and taint or sour a poorly maintained draught system. Cleaning should be performed at 2-week intervals, using industry-accepted detergents at proper concentrations and temperatures. The system should first be flushed with cold water to remove any residual beer; then detergent should be circulated for a minimum of 15 minutes—or if no pump is available, soaked for

20 minutes. The faucets and coupler should be hand cleaned, and then the entire system completely flushed with potable cold water before use.

See also DALTON'S LAW.

Draft Beer Quality Manual. http://draughtquality.org/ (accessed April 12, 2011).

Ken Grossman

Dreher, Anton (1810–1863) was an Austrian brewer referred to in some quarters as "The Beer King," thanks to his development of pale lager in the mid-19th century. While not as pale as pilsner, Dreher's creation predated that beer style and can therefore claim to be the world's first commercial pale lager, depending on one's definition of "pale." See PILSNER.

Dreher was born to a father who 14 years earlier had taken over the Klein-Schwechat brewery near Vienna, founded in 1632. As a young man he embarked on a brewing study tour, spending time in Munich, London, and Scotland. He also visited Burton-on-Trent, England, where he later admitted to stealing samples of yeast and wort.

Dreher took over the family brewery in Austria in 1836. Impressed by English pale ale malting techniques, he married English malting with central European bottom fermentation to create a red-hued lager, paler than any commercial beer seen in Europe. It caught on in Vienna and spread rapidly through the Austro-Hungarian Empire. The beer became known as Vienna-style lager, or more commonly as Märzen, as it was brewed in March and stored through the summer until September. See MÄRZENBIER. For more than a century it was the primary beer style at Oktoberfest in Munich, until it was replaced in recent years by a paler, less distinctive lager.

Dreher's brewery became one of the world's biggest, and he became a wealthy and influential man, gaining a parliamentary seat in 1861. His untimely death in 1863, the break-up of the Austro-Hungarian Empire and, later, the withdrawal of the Dreher family from business, mean that he is less famous today than the mighty English brewing houses he almost eclipsed. A company called Dreher Breweries still brews in Hungary under the wing of parent company SAB-Miller. The Schwechat Brewery also still exists, and is now a Heineken brewing plant that creates standard, unremarkable pale lagers.

Dreher's name and influence are not yet exhausted, and his original beer style is still admired and recreated by craft brewers around the world.

See also LAGER.

Pete Brown

dried malt extract (DME) is wort from which nearly all moisture has been removed. See WORT. The production process of DME is very similar to that of instant coffee, whereby the hot wort is sprayed through an atomizer into a heated chamber. Blowers create vigorous air currents within the chamber. As a result of this turbulence, the wort droplets remain suspended, dry out, and eventually settle to the floor of the chamber. DME, unlike liquid malt extract, is never hop flavored, because the hop compounds would not survive the drying process. See LIQUID MALT EXTRACT (LME). To make beer wort from DME, the powdered extract simply needs to be mixed with water to rehydrate it. The ratio of DME to water depends on the desired wort gravity. See ORIGINAL GRAVITY. Once reconstituted, the DME solution can be boiled, hopped, cooled, and fermented like regular wort.

Horst Dornbusch

drinking customs, running from the sacred to the profane, from silly to serious, have long reflected our values, our beliefs, and the trends in our societies. Beer is as old as civilization, and the pleasure and health it provided for early beer drinkers in ancient Egypt and the surrounding lands gave beer a central importance to those societies. The workers who built the pyramids were paid in part with beer and onions, whereas the drink itself was treated with great reverence, as something handed down by the gods. Said a Sumerian poet circa 3000 BCE, "I feel wonderful drinking beer/in a blissful mood/with joy in my heart and a happy liver." Wall paintings from Babylonia show drinkers toasting the goddesses of brewing, whereas in Egypt the brewery owned by the Pharaoh Ramses gave 10,000 (8,522 US bbls) of free beer a year to the temple administrators. The ruling class in Egypt preferred mature beer, which they drank through delicate gold straws to avoid drinking the dregs. The mass of the people, in the manner of the porridge beers still made in parts of Africa, drank beer as soon as fermentation was complete.

It is not surprising that beer, a beverage that essentially convened human civilization, has spawned no end of elaborate custom and ritual. In small African villages the ancient ritual of communal drinking through straws continues, thousands of years after it was first portrayed in art. Surrounding the pot of beer, men with long straws still sit like smokers around a hookah, discussing the issues of the day. In the townships of South Africa, the communal beer cup is passed around the room, with everyone smiling after they've had their sip.

Because most modern beer has European roots, so do many of our beer-drinking customs. The Anglo-Saxons and Vikings who invaded most of northern Europe following the withdrawal of the Romans brought with them a deeply rooted drinking culture along with a custom that endured for many centuries: toasting with drinking horns. The use of drinking horns has also been traced to Ancient Greece, the Gauls, the Thracians, and the Scythians. Xenophon wrote an account of his dealings with the Thracian leader Seuthes in which horns were an integral part of drinking. Diodorus gave an account of a feast prepared by the Getic chief Dromichaites in which drinking horns were made from actual horn but also from wood. Julius Caesar, in *De Bello Gallico*, described Gauls using drinking horns made from the horns of aurochs, a forebear of the ox: "The Gaulish horns in size, shape and kind, are very different from those of our cattle. They are much sought-after, their rims filled with silver and they are used at great feasts as drinking vessels."

Drinking horns are recorded from the Viking period in Scandinavia. The god Thor drank from a horn that was said to contain all the seas of the world, and fittings for drinking horns were discovered at the Anglo-Saxon burial site at Sutton Hoo in Suffolk, eastern England. The elaborate nature of drinking horns shows they were ceremonial vessels used by those of high status. There are references to drinking horns in the Arthurian legend of Caradoc, a tribal chieftain in Cornwall, Devon, and Somerset in England in the 3rd century CE.

A few hundred years later, little beer-selling stands became common throughout the English countryside. The authorities did their best to regulate them, but "ale booths" kept multiplying along the old Roman roads of Britain. Christian kings and their pious legal codes were no match for the vice and pleasure of hearty drinking. The epic Early English poem *Beowulf* from the 8th century CE portrays a society in which serious beer drinking is described as an integral part of any banquet, indeed almost as a religious ritual. By the end of the first millennium, drunkenness had become so rampant in England that King Edgar, who reigned from 959 to 975, decreed, on the advice of Archbishop Dunstan of Canterbury, that any village or town henceforth was limited to only one alehouse. He also ordered that ale may be served only in drinking horns with pins fastened on the inside at prescribed intervals so that, as the law read, "whoever should drink beyond these marks at one draught should be obnoxious to a severe punishment." See ALE HOUSES.

In 1066, the Norman Conquest brought the French and their wine to England, establishing both at the height of English society. Beer was enjoyed in all aristocratic Norman households, but wine became the drink of choice for the nobles, establishing a social hierarchy of beverages that resonates even today. But beer remained the favored quaff of the toiling common people, the now-subjugated Anglo-Saxons. At ceremonies large and small, unhopped ale filled the drinking horns. Corpus Christi College in Cambridge has a large drinking horn that predates the college's founding in the 14th century. It is still used at college feasts. Lavishly decorated horns in the Baroque style, some made from ivory with gold, silver, and enamel decoration, were made in the 19th and early 20th centuries in Austria and Germany. But in general the custom of the drinking horn eventually declined as more puritan attitudes prevailed and indulgent feasting and excessive consumption were increasingly frowned upon.

There is a link between drinking horns and the more modern custom known as a yard of ale. In the United States, there is often a yard glass in college bars, although many patrons may not know what it is used for. The vessel is often used in Britain and its former colonial countries as an initiation ceremony in which a young man, upon reaching the legal drinking age, is required to consume the contents of the glass, usually 3 imperial pints of beer. The glass is 1 yard or 90 cm in length, with a bulb at one end and a trumpet-like flare at the other. If the novice drinker fails to properly rotate the glass as he drinks, a good portion of the beer will end up all over his face, an occasion for uproarious laughter.

The glass is believed to have originated in the 17th century in England when the vessel was also known as a long glass or a Cambridge yard. The diarist John Evelyn (1620–1706) mentions a yard of ale being used to toast King James II but the vessel had more plebeian origins. It was designed to meet the needs of stagecoach drivers who were in a rush to get to their final destinations. At intermediate stops, the drivers would be handed ale in a yard glass through an inn window, the glass being of sufficient length for the driver to take it without leaving his coach. A pub called the Olde Gate Inne in Brassington, Derbyshire, which was once on the coach road from London to Manchester, has a small latched window that was used to hand a long glass to coach drivers. See COACHING INNS.

The system was also used in continental Europe and is recalled in Belgium by the glass produced for Kwak, a strong amber ale. The beer is served in a small version of a yard of ale glass, which is held in place by a wooden stand, with the bulbous end of the glass resting on the base of the stand. According to legend (or at least the Bosteels Brewery, who make the beer), the beer is named after the owner of a coaching inn on the road from Ghent to Mechelen. He was called Pauwel [Paul] Kwak. He brewed his own strong ale and he handed it in special glasses to coach drivers who could place the bulbous ends in their stirrups, flat-bottom metal rings in which they rested their feet. There is a further connection between the yard of ale and the stirrup cup, a vessel filled with beer or other alcohol and used to toast a departing horseman or guest.

The *Guinness Book of Records* says a yard of ale was once consumed in 5 sec. The glass and its ceremonies are used not only in England but also in Australia and New Zealand. The former Australian Prime Minister Bob Hawke once held the world record for drinking a yard. The glass is even bigger in New Zealand and holds more than 2 l (68 oz) of beer. Although no longer much seen outside of tourist shops, the German equivalent is a boot-shaped glass. It supposedly refers to an old military tradition among men stuck in the trenches, communal beer drinking from a leather boot. It is hard to imagine that no other vessels were available, even during battle, and the story may well be apocryphal. What is certain is that, like the British yard, the boot is a trick glass that can quickly deposit beer directly down the drinker's shirt.

Some beer-drinking customs are less uproarious and more plainly social. A widespread drinking custom in Britain and Australia is buying drinks in "rounds." In most other countries, beer is paid for on a tab system—you have some drinks over the course of the evening and then you pay when you leave the bar. But in British pubs there is no table service, so each drink is paid for as it is ordered. This has given rise to the practice of buying rounds: as a group of drinkers enters a pub, one member of the group will say "It's my round" or "My shout" and buy beer for the entire group. There is a powerful social etiquette attached to buying rounds and anyone who fails to "stand his round" is looked down upon as a cheapskate. The rising price of beer in pubs has tended to erode the custom. Groups now tend to break up into smaller ones to reduce the number of beers bought. In Australia, the round system is known as "shouting" and each member of a group is expected to participate.

Chinese drinking etiquette is based on gam bei, which translates as "dry glass" and has a similar meaning to "bottoms up." When the leader of a group or the host at a meal says "gam bei," the rest of the group has to empty their glasses. Drinkers cause offense if they switch beverages: if a toast is made with beer, then beer must continue to be the chosen drink.

Japan is better known for its rice-based sake, but the Japanese actually drink much more beer. When someone walks into a bar, a party, or a backyard barbecue, he will often shout "toriaezu biiru!," which, roughly translated, means "I will start with a beer!" The phrase implies that food may be desired later, but "first things first."

It is fair to say that German speakers have exported more beer-drinking customs around the world than any other culture. Oktoberfests, replete with oompah bands, lederhosen, and giant glass mugs, can be found in autumn almost anywhere in the world. Non-Germans tend to view the German drinking culture as a raucous affair, but it was not always so. Henry Mayhew, in his 1864 book *German Life and Manners as Seen in Saxony at the Present Day*, writes in a chapter entitled "of the beer-drinking customs at Jena," referring to the students of the university there:

> Beer drinking, among the Jena students, can hardly be regarded as wanton indulgence; for there are so many forms and ceremonies connected with it—such rights and duties attached to the "drinking to" and "drinking in response to" another—and it constitutes so intrinsic a part of the academic life of every German university, that the revelries associated with it partake more of the semi-religious orgies of the Bacchantes of old, than they do of mere unmeaning sensual feasts.

Mayhew goes on, at great length (and with little punctuation), to explain the elaborate eccentricities surrounding German beer drinking. Today, some of these customs remain in force and are known to beer drinkers everywhere, including the toast "Prost!" and the attendant vigorous clinking of glasses, something best attempted only with heavy German-style beer mugs. To this day, German college students eschew the "keg stands" and beer pong prevalent in the United States, preferring drinking songs and games of foosball.

American beer-drinking customs, like much of American culture itself, are an amalgam of customs from around the world, with Germany and England the leading progenitors. Many Americans are almost as likely to toast "Prost!," "Kampai!," or "¡Salud!" as they are "Cheers!," and they now have many more interesting beers to toast with. As the American craft brewing movement grows, we will no doubt see new customs built over time. One custom is particularly gratifying to see. There is a growing custom, especially among craft brewers, that the offering of hospitality to visiting fellow brewers is mandatory, even if the visiting brewers are completely unexpected guests. The brewmaster will stop what he or she is doing and offer the visiting brewers a tour and a beer. It seems a custom worthy of brewing's greatest traditions.

See also PUBLIC HOUSES.

Corran, H. S. *A history of brewing*. Newton Abbot, England: David & Charles, 1975.
Eames, Alan D. *The secret life of beer: Legends, lore, and little-known facts*. North Adams, MA: Storey, 2004.
Hackwood, Frederick W. *Inns, ales and drinking customs of Old England*. London: Bracken Books, 1985.
Mayhew, Henry. *German life and manners*. London: Wm H. Allen & Co, 1864.

Roger Protz

drinking games

See DRINKING CUSTOMS.

drinking songs, a type of music that seems more often brought on by beer than by wine or spirits. Drinking songs are sung throughout the world's taverns and pubs and often include some aspect involving alcohol as a main theme or topic of the song.

Most originated as folk songs and virtually every beer culture developed a tradition of drinking songs that paralleled the development of their brewing history, especially in cultures where public drinking places flourished.

It is most likely that drinking songs date back at least as far as the 1st century, but the first record of such songs is the Carmina Burana, an 11th century collection of poems, love sonnets, and songs that includes at least 40 drinking and gaming songs.

Most nations have their own traditional drinking songs, but England, Ireland, Germany, and Russia have by far the most extensive catalogs of examples. Such songs are so popular in Germany that they have their own musical category: the "Trinklieder." Similarly, in Sweden drinking songs are known as "Dryckesvisor." Japanese beer drinkers are also particularly fond of drinking songs, and it's probably

Package of dried hops depicting an all-male glee club, c. 1920. PIKE MICROBREWERY MUSEUM, SEATTLE, WA

no surprise that beer helps fuel the nation's karaoke bars.

The National Anthem of the United States, known as "The Star-Spangled Banner," uses lyrics taken from the poem "Defence of Fort McHenry," by Francis Scott Key, but the melody is from the English drinking song "To Anacreon in Heaven," by John Stafford Smith.

In modern times, English poems such as "John Barleycorn" have been adapted and recorded by rock bands, such as Traffic. Drinking is also a common theme in many American country and western songs, and beer makes frequent appearances in the blues, bluegrass, and rock and roll music as well.

Jay R. Brooks

drinking vessels are more than just functional utensils for holding a beer between its pour and its swallow. In fact, drinking vessels can make the beer, just as clothes are sometimes said to make the person. They are both practical and emotional, and their shape, size, and material are designed to match both the beer and the occasion, because everything has its time and place. Just as most people would never consider drinking a summer ale or crisp lager in a beer garden out of a cognac snifter, one would hope never to be served a *digestif* barley wine in a heavy, sturdy, glass mug with a handle. There are dozens of beer styles—from rich to lean, from hefty to delicate, from velvety to assertive, from honey-sweet to tart—each conveying a different culinary experience; and the aesthetics of the glass, its look and its feel, can accentuate, obfuscate, suppress, or exalt that experience.

Beer-drinking vessels can range from fine, thin, delicate, luxurious stemware to solid, robust, durable, earthenware mugs. Unfortunately, in all too many eating and drinking establishments nowadays,

Left: Salt-glazed stoneware tankard with relief freezes depicting the apostles, Creussen, Germany, 1665. *Middle*: Salt-glazed stoneware jug with applications of coats-of-arms and planets, Creussen, Germany, second half of the 17th century. *Right*: Salt-glazed stoneware tankard with applied coats-of-arms and letters, Creussen, Germany, 1621. COURTESY OF RASTAL GMBH & CO. KG especially in North America, beer—any beer—is uniformly served in a standard, straight-side, wide-mouth shaker pint beaker, made of thick glass and filled without flair, to the brim, often without a head. A properly chosen drinking vessel, in contrast, can bring out a beer's subtle and brilliant hues of color or its impenetrable opaqueness. It can display the enticing promise of a firm, white crown of foam, as well as the lace along the side in the afterglow of a sip well savored. Shape is important, too, because a drinking vessel's grip is part of the prologue to the sensory joys ahead. There is something sensuous about holding a weissbier glass around its slender narrowing just above the base; there is something husky and affirming about the grasp of the handle of a liter mug of helles; there is something elegant about balancing a tulip glass of pilsner or a flute of *biere de saison* to one's lips; and there is something faintly decadent about cradling a chalice of Trappist tripel while enjoying its bouquet. However, there is very little that is inspiring about an overfilled shaker pint glass.

In the central European beer cultures, especially in Belgium and Germany, matching a beer with its proper glass is considered de ri·gueur, and every establishment has several styles of beer glasses conveniently positioned right next to the dispensing taps. There is the flute, which has a slight, stylish bulge just above the stem and a narrowing at the top that traps both the beer's head and the aroma. The flute tends to be favored for beers with a fine-pearly, *péttilant* carbonation, such as Belgian lambic or gueuze. The classic pilsner glass is essentially a straight-side tulip glass. It is great for most pale or amber lagers. In Germany, a stemmed pilsner glass is also known as a pokal. A tulip glass is a short-stem glass, usually about 250 ml (8.5 oz) or so, with a wide bowl that flares at the mouth. It is a perfect vessel for rich, complex, higher-alcohol beers. The large bowl allows for swirling, which helps release aromatics. The flare at the lip directs the beer to the center of the tongue. In Scotland, strong Scotch ales are sometimes served in a pint-size tulip glass know as a "thistle," so-named after the Scottish national flower. A weissbier glass is intended for both pale and dark hazy weissbiers with large, sturdy crowns of foam. These glasses look almost like elegant, oversized, upside-down flutes without a stem. They are usually sized for half a liter (about 16 oz) of beer with plenty of head space to allow for the traditionally high carbonation and the large head it forms. Goblets are stocky, short-stemmed, almost snifter-like, bowl-shaped glasses that can be excellent for strong brews and are often sized accordingly. A chalice is essentially a large-size goblet, often showing off an evocatively ecclesiastical shape. Appropriately, Belgian Trappist and abbey ales are often served in chalices. Mugs are heavy and sturdy glasses with a handle. Most versions are of Bavarian origin and usually come in sizes of one-half to 1 l (16 to 33 oz). Made invariably of very thick glass, they are perfect for straw-blonde German beer-garden quaffs and can be confidently clinked together without fear of breaking them. Some types of glassware move along with the fashions of the day. The British "dimple" mug, a somewhat decorative handled mainstay that first appeared in the 1920s, seems to have faded with 70s bell-bottom trousers and are now rarely seen in pubs. There are cylindrical glasses, ranging in sizes from 0.2 to 0.4 l (6.7 oz to 13.5 oz), which are traditionally used to serve German ales, such as altbier and kölsch, whereby the kölsch glass, known in Cologne as a "stange," meaning rod, tends to be slenderer than its Düsseldorf altbier counterpart. Finally, there is the traditional English ale pint glass. It comes is almost cylindrical and has a bulgy ring below the rim and above the drinker's grip. Should pub conversation grow exciting or one's energy flag, the classic British pint glass will do its best to stay in the hand.

Today, of course, the standard material of which beer vessels are made is glass, but that has not always been the case. Over the centuries beer has been drunk from earthenware, pewter, bronze, china, and even—among the Celtic and Germanic tribes of the Bronze Age—from the hollow horns of aurochsen, the ancestors of all modern cattle. The world's first serious brewers, the Sumerians, drank their beers with straws out of communal crocks. See SUMER. In 10th-century Saxon England, the conventional beer vessel was a wooden tankard made of small staves held together by hoops of wattle or hide, with a solid wood base, and often lined with pitch. In ale houses, these would be passed from drinker to drinker. Some had pegs inside, placed at intervals to indicate how much each person was allowed to drink at any one time. In Germany, people in medieval beer halls used communal drinking pitchers too, only theirs were made of earthenware. Individual stoneware mugs that were high-temperature kilned and glazed with salt for a smooth finish came into wide use there only in the early 19th century. See STEIN. In Finland, the traditional sahti was usually served in a two-handle wooden tankard, called a sahtihaarikka. See SAHTI. Leather, too, had been a common raw material for drinking cups from Neolithic times some 3,000 years ago until the Middle Ages. When wetted and shaped, these were known in medieval England as jacks. During the Tudor period, from the 1400s to the 1600s, fancy, highly decorated jacks would also be called bombards, because they resembled the barrel of the bombard cannon.

Gold, silver, pewter, and glass tankards, often in the shape of a chalice, however, tended to be the beer vessel of choice only for the high and mighty, because of their expensiveness. This only changed in the early 1800s, when new manufacturing techniques made glass much more affordable. Glass is essentially silica-based molten sand. The first evidence of hollow, manmade glass artifacts dates back to Mesopotamia, in the 16th century BC. There is similar evidence of glass manufacturing in Alexandria in Egypt during the 9th century BC. The oldest known description of glass-making is on a tablet from the library of the Assyrian king Ashurbanipal (669–626 BC). It says, "Take 60 parts of sand, 180 parts ash of ocean plants, 5 parts chalk, and you get glass." True enough. By the 1st century BC, the Romans had figured out the technique of glass blowing. By the 1st century AD, glass items, even window panes, were manufactured throughout the entire Roman Empire. But only 4 centuries later, as the Roman Empire crumbled, the art of glass making became all but forgotten. Only in the 11th century did German artisans rediscover the Roman art of glass making and started to produce small bulls-eye-type disks as window glass. This set the stage for the revival of glass as a raw material for utensils, and near the end of the Middle Ages, Venice and Genoa had become the European glass-manufacturing centers. The Englishman George Ravenscroft (1618–81) patented a method of adding lead oxide to glass, and lead crystal was born. By the time the Industrial Revolution rolled around, glass was ready to be transformed for mass production. A German chemist, Otto Schott (1851–1935), laid the foundation for modern industrial glass manufacturing, and the American Michael Owens (1859–1923) invented an automatic bottle glass blowing machine shortly before 1900.

The advances in glass manufacturing in the 1800s were eerily fortuitous for the transformation of beer from a generic daily drink to a social beverage of class, distinction, and variety. The replacement of the stein—in almost universal use until the early 19th century in continental Europe—with the glass mug coincided with the gradual lightening of the color of beer. The latter came about because of technological improvements in malt kilning. The development of truly pale malts meant that beer could now be made deliberately golden, amber, brown, or even black. All over Europe, brewers started to make new, ever paler beer styles, from the märzenbier released in 1841, to the pilsner released in 1842, to the straw-blonde helles released in 1894.

Over the ages, beer-drinking vessels have ranged from humble pots to some of the most highly decorated and beautiful pieces of pottery, glass, and silver in the world. Old German beer steins in particular are highly collected, with the finest examples fetching many thousands of dollars at auction. In modern fine-dining establishments, top restaurateurs are defining new roles for glassware. Restaurants will often eschew clunky or obviously branded glassware in favor of other styles that suit both the beverage and the table. Sometimes these are essentially wine glasses, which are designed for the dinner table and do a fine job of presenting flavor and aroma. Top wine glassmaker Riedel makes fine crystal stemware for beer, both under its own name and through its Spiegelau division. These are sturdily made, but thrillingly thin and perhaps represent the latest evolution of vessels from which to enjoy the world's favorite fermented beverage.

Hackwood, Frederick W. *Inns, ales and drinking customs of Old England*. London: Bracken Books. Reprinted 1985.

Monson-Fitzjohn, C. J. *Drinking vessels of bygone days*. London: Herbert Jenkins, 1927.

Rock, Hugh. *Pub beer mugs and glasses*. Essex, UK: Shire Books, 2006.

Vision2Form Design. *7000 Jahre Glas—Geschichte vom Glas*. http://vision2form.de/glas-geschichte.html/ (accessed January 23, 2011).

Tim Hampson

drip back systems, also known as auto-bac, auto-vac, or Economiser, were once widely used in England and Scotland to recycle cask-conditioned beer that was spilled as it was served by either a beer engine or a Scottish air pressure font. These methods are now rarely used because they are frowned on for hygiene reasons, although some drinkers in Yorkshire, northern England, who demand a thick collar of foam on their beer, defend the system.

To create the head on beer, which has a naturally low level of carbonation, a sparkler is fitted to the spout of the beer engine or font: the sparkler has a tight wire mesh inside it and the beer is agitated as it passes through, forcing carbon dioxide to break out of solution, creating foam. Where a traditional English beer engine and handpump are used, pouring a pint through a sparkler demands some muscular effort by the server because the flow is restricted and the beer is forcefully sprayed into the glass. Some beer inevitably overspills the glass; this is collected in a drip tray and returned to the bulk beer via an injector valve. Today cask beer enthusiasts find the very thought of drip back systems revolting, but they were once quite common. It has often been said that stale beer served through such systems was among the factors that originally led to a decline in the popularity of cask beer in the 1960s and early 1970s.

In recent years these methods have become largely obsolete as a result of the introduction of swan-neck spouts attached to handpumps. See SWAN NECK. These long spouts, with a sparkler attached, reach to the bottom of the glass. Again, the server has to pull hard on the pump to force the beer through the sparkler, but because the spout lies deep in the glass, there is no overflow or wastage of beer.

The British brewer Greene King has developed a two-way beer engine: the server can toggle a switch and produce beer with either a thick collar of foam or a smaller head to meet the demands of customers. See GREENE KING.

See also BEER ENGINE.

O'Neill, Patrick. *Cellarmanship*, 5th ed. St Albans, England: CAMRA Books, 2010.

Roger Protz

Drum roaster in action at the Weyermann® Malting plant in Bamberg, Germany. Drum roasters are used to roast malt, darkening the grains, and providing a nutty or burnt flavor. PHOTOGRAPH BY DENTON TILLMAN

drum roaster is the modern development of an older device, the ball roaster. See BALL ROASTER. Both roasters work on essentially the same principle. They are enclosed chambers that rotate around a horizontal axis and heat up foodstuffs until they darken and acquire a nutty to burned flavor. But, whereas in a ball-shaped roaster grains collect at an uneven depth, in a horizontal drum, fitted with air vents, the material is processed evenly and homogeneously. To produce roasted malt, the maltster places kilned pale malt into the drum for to 2 to 3 h at a temperature of approximately 250°C (482°F). The longer the time and the higher the temperature, the roastier and darker will be the malt. Alternatively, the maltster may place moist green malt from the germination chamber into the drum and heat it there with the vents open or closed. With the vents open, the malt is kilned like regular malt and then turned into roasted malt. With the vents closed, the grain remains moist and undergoes a stewing cycle, at approximately 60°C to 72°C (140°F to 162°F), during which malt enzymes convert starches to sugars, creating caramelized malts. Such homogeneous saccharification is not possible in kilns. After caramelization, the malt may be transferred to the kiln for a final drying to make Carapils®, for instance, or it may stay in the drum with the vents open at about 120°C to 180°C (roughly 250°F to 355°F) to make amber to red caramel malts, such as Caramunich®. In either case, the sugars caramelize into sweet, glassy, crystalline, unfermentable dextrins. Depending upon the degree of caramelization, these malts can lend body, color, flavor, aroma, and foam stability to finished beers. See CARAMEL MALTS, CRYSTAL MALT, AND DEXTRINS.

Thomas Kraus-Weyermann

dry hopping, the addition of hops to beer in the fermenting, conditioning, or serving vessel. For many styles of beer, hops are added throughout the brewing process. Hops added at the beginning of the wort boil are mostly contributing bitterness, those added at a mid-point of the boil add bitterness and some aromatics, and "late hopping," the addition of hops at the end of the boil, is largely intended for hop aroma and flavor (although the reality is that heavy late hopping often adds a large proportion of a beer's bitterness as well). During the boil, highly volatile hop oil components escape quickly with the steam, taking most of the aromatics out of the wort and up the kettle stack. See HOP OILS. Although the use of late hopping, whirlpool hopping, and hop backs can restore essential oils to the wort, some hop aromatics are later stripped away or chemically transformed during fermentation. The purpose of dry hopping is to infuse beer with additional fresh hop flavor and aroma. Dry hopping is a cold infusion technique that not only intensifies hop aromatics in beer but also adds aromatics that are substantially different from those achieved by late hopping. The alpha acids responsible for hop bitterness are not isomerized and therefore remain insoluble during dry hopping, but some tasting trials have shown clearly that the bitterness perception of beer can be increased by dry hopping, although international bitterness unit values may remain unchanged.

Although there can be little doubt that many brewing cultures have used dry hopping over the centuries, the practice is most closely associated with English pale ales and their variants. From the mid 1800s onward, the most common technique was the addition of a large handful of dried whole hops to the cask before filling. As the beer conditioned in the cask over days or weeks, the fresh hop aroma would suffuse the beer. Rather than simply being a tube, the cask tap is perforated with holes at the tapered end, which strains out the hop flowers so they do not end up in the consumer's glass. Although it seems counterintuitive that one could add raw plant material to beer without causing spoilage, hops rarely harbor bacterial strains that can survive well in finished beer's airless, low-pH, ethanol-rich environment.

At the dawn of the American craft brewing movement, many future brewers were inspired by the bright hop flavors of the cask-conditioned ales they had tasted in English pubs. Starved for hop flavor, American brewers took up dry hopping with particular fervor, and today it might be said that intense dry hop character is now widely considered a quintessentially American attribute when it comes to beer flavor.

One reason for this is the aromatic concentration that characterizes modern American hop varieties. Widely derided for decades by British and European brewers, American hops tend to contain considerably more essential oil than their overseas counterparts. A 2006 study showed popular aroma hop varieties such as Czech Saaz, East Kent Golding, and Styrian Golding with aromatic oil contents ranging from 0.4% to 1% of dry weight. When compared with the American hops Cascade (0.8%–1.5%), Chinook (1.5%–2.5%), and Simcoe (2%–2.5%), the difference becomes quite clear. In a very real way, the aromatics imparted by dry hopping have become a natural part of the American beer terroir.

Fresh dry hop aroma, sometimes evocatively described as "hop-sack aroma," is most associated with the monoterpenoid fractions of hop oils. Monoterpenoids are aromatic compounds that are created by most plant species, including common flowering plants, wine grapes, and citrus fruits. In hops, the most important are myrcene (spicy, herbal, also a major aromatic in thyme leaves), gerianol (floral, rose-like, used in many perfumes), linalool (floral, citrusy, minty), limonene (oranges and lemons), and beta pinene (piney and woodsy, part of the aroma of rosemary and basil). Late hop aroma focuses more closely on oxidized forms of the less volatile sesquiterpenoid fractions of hop oils, including humulene (floral, cannabis, hay-like), caryophyllene (peppery, clove, camphor), and farnesene (green apples, lime).

Whereas dry hopping was originally carried out in a cask or barrel, it is now often performed in a fermentating or conditioning tank. The methods are various. The efficacy and quality of any infusion is based upon contact time, surface area, temperature, and agitation (or flow over the surface area). After fermentation, brewers usually cool the beer and allow most of its yeast to sediment out before dry hopping. Far less common is dry hopping during active fermentation, although some brewers do find it effective, feeling that the continuing yeast activity can remove the oxygen inevitably introduced by dry hopping.

Dry hopping with whole flowers is traditional but also relatively difficult. Dried hops float rather vigorously, so keeping them submerged in beer is not always easy. Brewers commonly tie mesh bags full of hops to the bottom of a tank interior, purge the tank of air, and then send beer in, looking to suspend the floating hop bag somewhere in the center of the tank. Alternatively, they will sometimes weigh down a hop bag, hoping to sink it with a heavy piece of sterilized stainless steel equipment. They are often disappointed (and somewhat impressed) to see the bag float back to the surface. Others depend on some form of steel mesh cage inside the tank, usually held in place with a rod. Whatever the method, infusion of flavor from whole hops is relatively slow, because the lupulin glands of the hop flowers are still intact. Oxidation of the hop oils during storage is also a particular concern with baled whole hops. That said, some brewers say they prefer the flavor of beer dry hopped with whole flowers.

In the United States it is more common to dry hop with hop pellets. In hop pellet production, the whole hop flower is milled into a powder, extruded into the pellet form, flushed with inert gas, and then vacuum packed. See HOP PELLETS. In the milling process the hops' lupulin glands are ruptured, exposing the contents to the beer during dry hopping. The pellets quickly break up into small particles upon contact with liquid, and evolution of hop oil character into the beer is relatively rapid. Brewers commonly climb to the tops of tanks and simply pour the pellets in, often through a small pipe fitting that holds a pressure-relief valve. Others have special dry hopping ports built into the tops of tanks. But methods range from the mundane to the ingenious. Many breweries load hop pellets into a small dosing tank and then circulate their beer through it. The most amusing method must be the "hop cannon," a setup that uses a blast of pressurized CO_2 to blow a charge of hop pellets from a chamber through a snaking steel tube into the waiting tank. One brewer reports that dry hopping by this method is highly effective, but takes up to six "shots" of the hop cannon to complete. Apparently the tube of the cannon actually heats up after a few shots, and the brewer must wait for it to cool down before finishing the task.

During the dry hopping phase, it is not uncommon for brewers to either recirculate the beer to resuspend the hop fragments for greater contact or rouse the hops by sending CO_2 bubbles through the bottom of the tank. In cylindroconical tanks, the hops can later be removed in the form of a green sludge. Although this material is usually discarded or composted, it retains its bittering potential and it is technically possible to reuse it for wort bittering.

Regardless of the method, the attainment of dry hop character is also temperature dependent. Hop aroma transfer is faster at warmer temperatures than at colder temperatures. Dry hopping performed at 4.4°C (40°F) may easily take twice as long to achieve similar intensity as the same procedure performed at 15.5°C (60°F). The aroma profile will also be different, perhaps reflecting the differing volatility of the hop oil fractions. Unpleasant grassy, vegetal, chlorophyll flavors can result from extended contact time with dry hops, so most brewers who dry hop heavily try to keep contact time to 1 week or less.

Although lightly applied dry hopping in beer can result in beautifully balanced and aromatic beers, the most expressive use of dry hopping is surely seen in the American India pale ale (IPA) style and the even more intense "double IPA" or "imperial IPA" styles that are becoming increasingly popular. Unfortunately, this bright, hoppy character has a relatively short life. Even when oxygen pickup is minimal, dry hop character tends to oxidize or otherwise degrade notably within a matter of

2 or 3 months, becoming first reminiscent of tropical fruit and finally arriving at a tea-like quality that rarely pleases. Hop polyphenols leached out during dry hopping also can give rise to hazes, although many brewers and beer drinkers do not seem to mind. Beer enthusiasts are enamored with the flavors and aromas that dry hopping brings, but the technique makes beer inherently less stable. Perhaps it is true that the candle that burns twice as bright also burns half as long.

Brynildson, Matthew. Stretching your hop impact. *The New Brewer* 25 (2008).
Brynildson, Matthew. The eternal quest for the ultimate hop impact. *The New Brewer* Nov/Dec (2006).

Garrett Oliver

dry milling is the most common milling process employed in modern brewhouses. Its opposite is wet milling, during which the grist is moistened before it reaches the mill. See MILLING and WET MILLING. Dry milling relies on a roller mill of varying degrees of complexity with two, four, five, or six rollers and complex arrays of vibrating screens to crush the grist kernels—malted and/or unmalted—into smaller particles and to separate grits, husks with attached grits, and flour in preparation for mashing and lautering. See ROLLER MILL. In complex roller mills, the grist is passed sequentially and sometimes repeatedly through consecutive pairs of rollers with different gaps until the desired combination of fine and coarse grinds is achieved. The advantage of dry versus wet milling is its simplicity. Its disadvantage is that it generates dust, with the attendant danger of explosive ignition by sparks.

Kunze, Wolfgang. *Technology brewing and malting*. Berlin: VLB Berlin, 1996.

Horst Dornbusch

dry yeast is a practical alternative to liquid yeast that offers many advantages to the brewer. Many brewers, particularly craft brewers, retain a prejudice against dried yeast because the quality of dried yeast was quite poor during their amateur days. Today, the products available are greatly improved. Dry yeast averages 95% dry matter and 1 g contains between 0.5 and 2×10^9 live cells, depending on the strain. Yeast cultures are grown using a batch (all sugars are added at once while the yeast is fermenting) and then a fed-batch system (the sugars are added slowly so that the yeast produces biomass and not alcohol) and then dried using a fluidized-bed dryer (the yeast remains in suspension in warm air), which is gentle on the yeast. The production process is carefully optimized for each strain so that the yeast will recover and perform adequately in fermentation once rehydrated according to the manufacturer's instructions. Because dry yeast is produced in the presence of large amounts of air, there is no need for aeration/oxygenation prior to inoculation. The quality of dry yeast has advanced because of extensive quality control put in place by the manufacturers; viability and vitality measurements, contamination levels, and genetic integrity are among the tests being performed routinely.

There are numerous advantages to using dry yeast, the most important being a long shelf-life of up to 2 years, non-refrigerated transport, and easy dosage. Dry yeast can be used as a starter for propagation or pitched directly into fermentation and subsequently reused successfully for many generations. The use of dry yeast for bottle conditioning is becoming increasingly popular because of the number of strains available in dry form (brewer's, wine, and distiller's yeast) and the consistency of the product, which in turn can give reliable results. Dry yeast can also be used randomly as emergency stock or to restart a stuck fermentation.

See also YEAST.

Powell, C., and T. Fischborn. Serial repitching of dried lager yeast. *Journal of the American Society of Brewing Chemists* (2011).
Quain, D. The yeast supply chain. *The Brewer & Distiller* 2 (2006): 1–5.
Van Zandycke, S., T. Fischborn, and C. Powell. Bottle conditioning using dry yeast. *New Brewer* Mar/Apr (2009): 65–70.

Sylvie Van Zandycke

dubbel, or double, is one the more popular beer styles to emerge from Belgium's Trappist monastery breweries. Belgians themselves are not often given to defining beers within stylistic borders, but dubbel is one of the few Belgian beer styles that is clearly recognizable. Both Trappist and secular breweries in Belgium have brewed brown beers for centuries, and beers were probably designated "dubbel" or "tripel" based on a fanciful allusion to their relative alcoholic strength. The modern dubbel style was essentially invented by the Trappist brewery Westmalle in 1926. Before then, Westmalle had produced a brown ale alongside the monks' table beer, but the monastery was still recovering from the effects of World War I, and the beer was apparently not reliably good. In 1926 brewer Henrik Verlinden came to Westmalle and worked with the monastery to improve the beer, and the stronger russet-brown "Dubbel Bruin" emerged. It was quickly copied and versions of dubbel are now widely brewed in Belgium and beyond.

Unlike British and German brown beers, dubbel gains much of its color not from roasted malts but from a highly caramelized version of a sugar syrup called "candi sugar." See CANDI SUGAR. Whereas roasted malts tend to give flavors that recall coffee and chocolate, candi sugar gives an aromatic reminiscent of burnt sugar and raisins. The sugar syrup, which appears nearly black, is usually added to a golden wort in the kettle. All dubbels have warm fermentations, and the Belgian yeasts give them distinctive herbal, fruit, and phenol notes. The beers are usually technically very dry, but sometimes taste slightly sweet because hop bitterness tends to be restrained. The best of them are bottle conditioned, but less refined versions are sometimes filtered. Generally speaking, dubbels have at least 6.5% alcohol by volume, but they stray as high as 8%, with beers stronger than this considered to have moved into a different category. Dubbels, unlike their stronger cousins, do not tend to show their alcoholic strength on the palate. Rather than being perfumey, a good dubbel is a balanced and even delicate beer, a surprisingly good pairing for seared scallops or washed-rind cheeses. Although the stronger golden tripel style seems more popular among craft brewers in the United States, the dubbel has recently inspired new beers in Scandinavia, Brazil, Italy, Switzerland, and many other countries.

See also ABBEY BEERS.

Deglas, Christian. *The classic beers of Belgium*. Ypsilanti, MI: G. W. Kent, Inc, 1997.

Westmalle. http://www.trappistbeer.net/westmalle/trappist_mainframeEN.htm (accessed February 7, 2011).

Garrett Oliver

Dubuisson Brewery, also known as Brasserie Dubuisson, is a family-owned brewery located in the town of Pipaix in Southern Belgium. It is one of the oldest breweries in Belgium and certainly the oldest in Wallonia. Founded in 1769 by Joseph Leroy as a farm brewery, it has been passed down through eight generations of family members to the current brewmaster, Hugues Dubuisson. Up until 1931 the brewery remained very small and sold beer only to the farm workers and people in the town of Pipaix. Then, the two Dubuisson brothers, Alfred and Amedee, purchased the brewery from their father, renamed it the Brasserie Dubuisson Freres, Ltd, and began a period of expansion. The brewery now has a modernized brewhouse, cellar, and packaging line in Pipaix. Brasserie Dubuisson is dedicated to the production of all-natural, artisanal beers and has steered clear of private labels and random rebranding. Additionally, the family has built a microbrewery called "Le Brasse Temps" in Louvain-la-Neuve and a brewpub by the same name in Mons, as well as a pub called "Troll & Bush" in Pipaix. The brewery currently brews and distributes 10 different brands of beer. Bush Ambree (12% alcohol by volume [ABV]) is the oldest brand, established in 1933. Bush de Noel (12% ABV) and Bush de Noel Premium (13% ABV) were both introduced in 1991. Bush Blonde (10.5% ABV) was introduced in 1998, Cuvee des Trolls (7% ABV) in 2000, Bush Prestige (13% ABV) in 2003, Bush Blonde Triple (10.5% ABV), Bush Ambree Triple (12% ABV), and Bush de Nuits (13% ABV) in 2008, and the newest offering, Peche Mel Bush (8.5% ABV), in 2009. In 2010, the British brewer Paul Arnott, a veteran of Chimay and Unibroue, became technical director of Dubuisson. Arnott expressed the brewery's wish to remain traditional, but also to become increasingly creative.

See also BELGIUM and WALLONIA.

Keith Villa

dunkel is the dark lager style that for many years was the everyday beer of Bavaria. Although it has

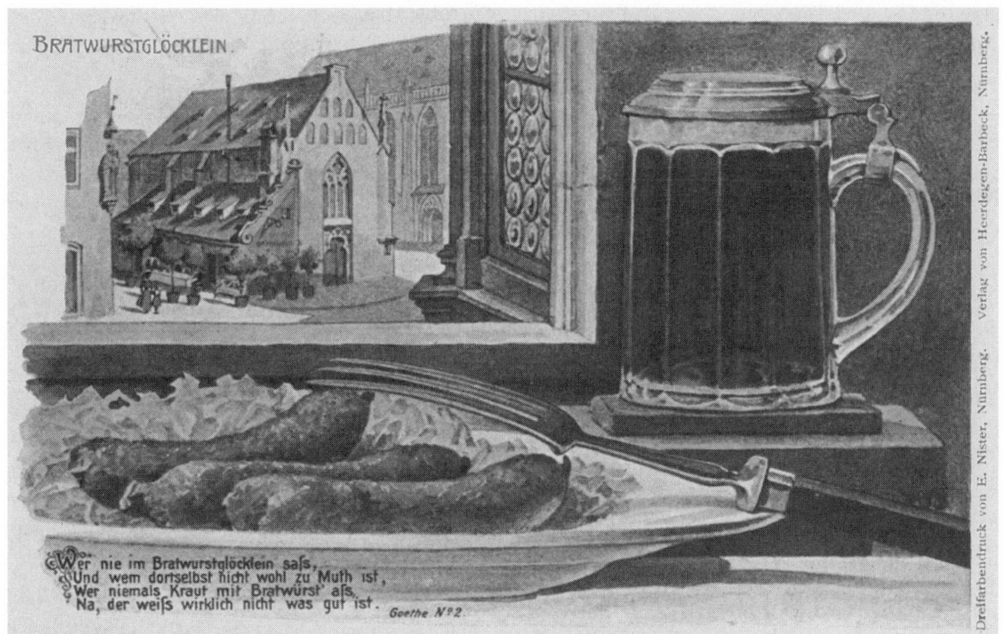

Early 20th-century postcard from Nuremberg, Germany, depicting a traditional pairing of bratwurst, sauerkraut, and dunkel. PIKE MICROBREWERY MUSEUM, SEATTLE, WA

now been dethroned by helles, dunkel can boast a reign that lasted centuries. The German word "dunkel" simply means "dark," and most dunkels have colors that range from a deep reddish mahogany to full, rich brown. The flavor profile is malt-forward, often showing notes of nuts, toffee, freshly baked bread, chocolate, and even licorice, but never veering off into heavily roasted coffee-like accents. Hop bitterness is moderate, with international bitterness units usually in the low 20s, and hop aromatics are subtle. Lager yeasts lend these beers clean flavor profiles; they are round and brisk, with a hint of malty sweetness, but devoid of spice or fruit. They are average in strength and rarely exceed 5.5% alcohol by volume. The best of them are wonderfully direct, deeply satisfying, and a great accompaniment to hearty Bavarian food.

The golden helles may have taken over in Munich, but dunkel remains popular in the city's beer halls. The dark lager still holds sway in Bamberg, Bayreuth, Kulmbach, and Lichtenfels and in the tiny hamlets of Franconia. There, small breweries continue to make dunkel beer exclusively for local markets. They are essentially brewing for their neighbors, and their neighbors seem to have little interest in other beers. The Franconian versions tend to be drier than the Munich versions and the smaller breweries sometimes show charming eccentricities of flavor. Dunkel is traditionally brewed largely from dark Munich malt, which has a toasty, slightly caramelized character. These flavors are often deepened by intensive decoction mashing, which helps develop the toffee-like melanoidin flavors.

To a certain extent, dunkel was the world's first beer style to be fully codified and regulated. When the Reinheitsgebot first came into force in 1516, most of the beer made in Bavaria was an early form of dunkel. The dunkel beer style did not stay home in Bavaria. The Czech černé pivo style is a very close relative, if often slightly sweeter. Dunkel jumped many oceans, and the style was once very popular in the United States and Mexico and also throughout parts of South America, where many Germans settled in the 1800s. Today, many American craft brewers, no doubt inspired by trips into the Bavarian countryside, are starting to brew their own versions of one of the great quaffing beer styles of Europe.

See also MUNICH MALT and DECOCTION.

German Beer Institute. http://www.germanbeerinstitute.com/ (accessed February 2, 2011).

Jackson, Michael. *Michael Jackson's beer companion*, 2nd ed. Philadelphia: Running Press, 1997.

Garrett Oliver

Jackson, Michael. *Beer companion.* Philadelphia: Running Press, 1993.
Markowski, Phil. *Farmhouse ales.* Denver, CO: Brewers Publications, 2004.

Phil Markowski

Dupont, Brasserie is a classic farmhouse brewery located in the agricultural town of Tourpes in the Belgian province of Hainaut in Wallonia, the French-speaking region of Belgium. See WALLONIA. Situated only a few kilometers from the French border, Dupont Brewery is one of a few breweries that survive in an area that was at one time home to hundreds of small farm breweries. It is said that Dupont sits on a site where people have been brewing continuously since 1844. The brewery claims to have been well known for the quality of its beers as long ago as the 1880s. In 1920 Alfred Dupont, seeking to dissuade his son Louis from moving away to start up a farm in Canada, purchased the farm-brewery then known as Rimaux-Deridder. The brewery has been operated by the Rosier family in its current incarnation since 1950.

Well-deserved praise from British beer writer Michael Jackson and many others has helped this distinctive brewery and its outstanding beers thrive in recent decades. The flagship is Saison Vieille Provision, whose name derives from an old farm-brewer practice of making a special beer for provision, or "stock," for use throughout the year. To many beer enthusiasts, Saison Vielle Provision, colloquially known as "Saison Dupont," is the quintessential version of the Saison style. See SAISON.

The brewery produces a couple of unique stronger ales, notably Moinette and Avec Les Bon Voeux de la Brasserie Dupont (a robust holiday beer) as well as a dark Saison, Saison Brune. Dupont also pioneered several organic brews (bières biologique) and the present management has shown marketing savvy by presenting the brewery as a tourist attraction. An on-site bakery was added in 1994 and a cheese-making facility opened in 1995, making several distinctive rind-washed cheeses using a number of the brewery's beers.

Annual production is around 10,000 HL (8,500 US barrels), which is small by any measure. Brasserie Dupont exports to other countries in Europe and to the United States and Japan.

Jackson, Michael. *The great beers of Belgium*, 3rd ed. Philadelphia: Running Press, 1998.

The **Durden Park Beer Circle,** formed in 1972, is a group of homebrewers dedicated to recreating beers from the 18th and 19th centuries. Led by the late Dr John Harrison, they delved into many old brewery records to uncover details of commercial beers from these periods. Often brewers used codes to keep their products' composition secret from would-be competitors. After unraveling these codes to reveal the original recipes, the Circle endeavored to reproduce and critically taste the beers themselves. Some members even developed their own methods of producing old-style malts, such as brown and amber malt, which were no longer available in their original forms.

The group remains active and its research efforts are compiled in a book, which has undergone three revisions and is a mine of information on brewing beers from previous centuries. It contains details on the brewing techniques used to reproduce these beers, together with 131 recipes for such beers as London and Irish porters, stouts (both Imperial and Double), Scotch, amber, mild, March, and October ales. Also included is a section explaining the origin of each of these styles, along with descriptions of their defining characteristics.

Even more interestingly, there is a section showing how to decipher recipes from old brewing texts and brewers' books. Examples are given, including one of a typical brewer's code and its interpretation. Although this small book is aimed at homebrewers, it is a work of some significant scholarship.

Harrison, John, and members of the Durden Park Beer Circle. *Old British beers and how to make them*, 3rd revised ed. Middlesex, UK: Durden Park Beer Circle, 2003. http://www.durdenparkbeer.org.uk

Terry Foster

Durst Malz is a German malting company headquartered in Bruchsal near Karlsruhe in the state of Baden-Württemberg. Founded in 1824 as a small, family-run brewery and malt house, the

Clockwise from top left: Australian beer label, c. 1900; American postcard, 1913; Argentinean beer label, c. 1940; American beer label, c. 1930s; American beer label, c. 1930s; American postcard, 1910; Guatemalan beer label, c. 1900. PIKE MICROBREWERY MUSEUM, SEATTLE, WA

Germinating barley kernels growing new plant shoots, called acrospires. Rootlets emerge from the other end of the seed. The enzymes produced during this phase will later convert malt starches to sugars in the mash.
ADRIAN FODEN, POITOU-CHARENTES, FRANCE

Hop vines cultivated near Alsace, France. The vines climb a series of wires held by tall wooden poles.

The King's Head Pub in London has a variety of "real ales" on tap. The Campaign for Real Ale (CAMRA) coined the term "real ale" to describe unfiltered cask-conditioned and bottle-conditioned beers. CATH HARRIES

Portrait of Jan Gambrinus, legendary king of beer. Pictorial broadsheet (color lithograph) by F. C. Wentzel, Weissenburg, Germany, 1870. PRIVATE COLLECTION/SAMMLUNG HECHT/THE BRIDGEMAN ART LIBRARY INTERNATIONAL

Historical pubs in London. *Clockwise from top left*: The Windsor Castle; Ye Olde Cheshire Cheese; The Marble Arch; The Lamb Tavern; The Punch Tavern; The Blue Anchor; The Mayflower.

PHOTOGRAPHS BY CATH HARRIES, MONTAGE BY CHARLES FINKEL

Home-grown and hand-picked Cascade hops and barley ready for homebrewing in Connecticut. ERIC S. MCKAY

A homebrewer pours malt extract into boiling water to form wort, or unfermented beer. GETTY IMAGES

Bamberg is renowned for its smoke-flavored beers, called rauchbiers. CATH HARRIES

A woman pours cask-conditioned ale using a beer engine, or hand pump, at the Great British Beer Festival in London. © CAMPAIGN FOR REAL ALE LTD. (CAMRA)

Top row, left to right: American beer label, c. 1933; New Zealand beer label, c. 1940; American neck label, c. 1933; American beer label, c. 1933. PIKE MICROBREWERY MUSEUM, SEATTLE, WA

Second row from top, left to right: English beer label, c. 1940; English beer label, c. 1950; English beer label, c. 1920; English beer label, c. 1940. PIKE MICROBREWERY MUSEUM, SEATTLE, WA

Third row from top, left to right: Canadian beer label, c. 1950; Belgian beer label, 1946; English beer label, c. 1946. PIKE MICROBREWERY MUSEUM, SEATTLE, WA

Bottom row, left to right: American keg label, c. 1933; Scottish beer label, c. 1930; American beer label, c. 1933. PIKE MICROBREWERY MUSEUM, SEATTLE, WA

Top left: Salt-glazed stoneware tankard, c. 1665, with relief freezes depicting the apostles. "Apostle tankards" from Creussen, Germany, date almost to the beginning of Creussen stoneware production in the beginning of the 17th century. COURTESY OF RASTAL GMBH & CO. KG

Top right: Carved ivory tankard showing a genealogy of rulers. Probably French, late 19th century. COURTESY OF RASTAL GMBH & CO. KG

Bottom left: Salt-glazed stoneware tankard from the Westerwald region of Germany, c. 1737. COURTESY OF RASTAL GMBH & CO. KG

Bottom right: Salt-glazed earthenware pear-shaped mug from the Saxony town of Annaberg, Germany, late 17th century. COURTESY OF RASTAL GMBH & CO. KG

Top: American barley malt syrup label, c. 1920. Prohibition led many breweries to sell malt extracts as they struggled to cope with the loss of their traditional business. PIKE MICROBREWERY MUSEUM, SEATTLE, WA

Bottom: Early 1930s Japanese postcard. Whereas Prohibition put thousands of American brewers out of business, the Japanese brewing industry flourished in the 1930s, as brewers were able to cheaply procure American brewing equipment. Beer consumption in Japan rose significantly. PIKE MICROBREWERY MUSEUM, SEATTLE, WA

Top row, left to right: Beer label from Guernsey, a British Crown Dependency, c. 1920; Label for Irish beer, bottled in England, c. 1940s; British beer label, c. 1920; Ceylonese beer label (Ceylon is now Sri Lanka), c. 1920. PIKE MICROBREWERY MUSEUM, SEATTLE, WA

Middle row, left to right: Canadian beer label, c.1920; English beer label, c. 1900; Pakistani beer label, c. 1920; Maltese beer label, c. 1920. PIKE MICROBREWERY MUSEUM, SEATTLE, WA

Bottom row, left to right: American beer label, c. 1910; English beer label, c. 1940; Canadian beer label, c. 1950; English beer label, c. 1930. PIKE MICROBREWERY MUSEUM, SEATTLE, WA company focused exclusively on malt making starting in 1885. Today, Durst operates out of three malting facilities with a combined capacity of over 200,000 metric tons per year. Globally, this makes Durst the world's 17th-largest commercial (as opposed to brewery-run) malting company by annual production volume. Its three operations were all former independent maltings that Durst acquired between 1959 and 2000. The Nierstein/Rhine Malting Company moved into Durst ownership in 1959; the Rheinische Malzfabriken Union in Gernsheim/Rhine followed in 1985. In 1992, the three entities, Durst, Nierstein, and Rheinische Malzfabriken, became a single legal entity, which then took over a fourth company, Westdeutsche Mälzerei GmbH in Castrop-Rauxel, in 2000. Substantial investments in focused modernization led to the decision, in 2006, to close down the Nierstein site. Durst now specializes in the bulk production of Pils malt, Munich malt, Vienna malt, and wheat malt, which it exports around the world.

Durstmalz. http://www.durstmalz.com/home_en.html (accessed March 23, 2011).

Gerrit Blüemelhuber

Duvel Moortgat, a family-owned brewery group based in Breendonck, Belgium, best known for its flagship beer, Duvel. Originally Brouwerij Moortgat, the company was founded by Jan-Leonard Moortgat in 1871. After World War I, Albert Moortgat traveled to Scotland and obtained a Scottish yeast that produced an exceptional flavor and introduced it to the brewery. The first beer they brewed with the new yeast was called Victory Ale in celebration of the end of the war. Legend has it that in 1923 a Victory Ale enthusiast in Breendonck referred to the beer as a "real devil" ("duvel" in Flemish), perhaps referring to its well-hidden alcoholic strength. The name stuck, and the beer was soon officially dubbed Duvel. At first this beer was rather dark, but over the years Duvel underwent a transformation so that by the 1970s it achieved the very pale golden color and unique taste that is observed in the modern version. Much imitated, Duvel has become the progenitor of a beer style widely known as Belgian strong golden ale. It shows a voluminous foam and has an herbal aroma that some tasters have compared with pear drops or Poire William. Duvel derives its pale color from a specially kilned pale malt and highly fermentable sugar syrup in the ratio of about 76% malt to 24% adjunct. The unique taste results from the use of the original Scottish yeast during primary fermentation. The rich, dense head is also a unique aspect and is primarily the result of partial bottle conditioning, where the beer is aged in a temperature-controlled environment for up to 2 months. See BOTTLE CONDITIONING. Bottle-conditioned Duvel has 8.8% alcohol by volume (ABV). In the 1960s, the brewery introduced a filtered version of Duvel that did not undergo a secondary fermentation in the bottle, thus retaining some young or "green" flavor with slightly lower alcohol. Bottled versions of this beer are called Duvel Green (6.9% ABV) and have green lettering on the label. In 2008, Moortgat released a draught version of Duvel Green in some markets to mixed reviews. Duvel's unique large tulip-shape glass has become nearly iconic since it was introduced in the 1960s, and the beer is now sold in more than 40 countries.

Duvel Moortgat also brews the Maredsous line of abbey beers, the golden lager Vedett extra blonde, and the Witbier Vedett extra white. The fifth generation of the Moortgat family took the company public in early 1999, while still holding a majority stake. Since then, there have been additional acquisitions; Brasserie d'Achouffe was acquired in 2006, Liefmans in 2008, and Antwerp's Brouwerij De Koninck in 2010. In the Czech Republic, Duvel Moortgat has an ownership stake in Brewery Bernard, and in North America, it owns Brewery Ommegang in Cooperstown in upstate New York.

Keith Villa and Ben Vinken

Duyck, Brasserie is an established regional brewery bearing the Flemish surname of its founder, Leon Duyck. The brewery's principal product, Jenlain Bière de Garde, derives its name from that of the northern French farming town in which the brewery is located—Jenlain, near the Belgian border.

Brasserie Duyck dates back to 1922 and is credited with setting the stage for a French specialty brewing renaissance that began in the late 1970s with the serendipitous success of Jenlain Bière de Garde.

The brewery had historically produced standard lager beers until the unexpected success of Jenlain Bière de Garde ultimately redefined them as a leading French specialty beer producer.

Bière de Gardes were traditionally poured from casks and served for immediate consumption. Brasserie Duyck began to bottle their Bière de Garde in the late 1940s, making it the first to become widely available and therefore setting a standard for the style. Jenlain Bière de Garde existed as a little-known specialty until, by chance, it became a cult favorite with the student population of nearby Lille, the cosmopolitan capital of northern France.

The popularity of Jenlain Bière de Garde transformed the brewery from a small operation to a large regional brewery producing approximately 100,000 HL (85,000 US barrels) in 2009, the majority of which is Jenlain Bière de Garde. The brewery also produces seasonal brews such as Bière de Noel (Christmas), Bière de Printemps (springtime), and many others. Duyck also produces various labels under contract for other brewing entities.

Because of the prominence of its flagship beer, the brewery is more commonly known as "Jenlain."

See also BIÈRE DE GARDE, FRANCE, and JENLAIN ORIGINAL FRENCH ALE.

Jackson, Michael. *Beer companion.* Philadelphia: Running Press, 1993.

Markowski, Phil. *Farmhouse ales.* Denver, CO: Brewers Publications, 2004.

Woods, John and Rigley, Keith. *The beers of France.* Winscombe, Bristol, England: The Artisan Press, 1998.

Phil Markowski

Dwarf hops

See HEDGE HOPS.

(E)-2-nonenal. Formerly known as "trans-2-nonenal," this is a compound claimed to be a principal determinant of beer staling, affording a wet paper/cardboard note to beer. It is also associated with a cucumber aroma and is generally considered an oxidative off-note. E-2-nonenal has the formula $C_9H_{16}O$ and is a degradation product from the oxidation of unsaturated fatty acids. However, it can be produced in other reactions, notably the aldol condensation of acetaldehyde and heptanal.

There is no absolute agreement that this is always a molecule involved in beer staling. It is argued that some beers that display distinct aged character do not display particularly high levels of (E)-2-nonenal, and vice-versa. It is particularly prevalent in beers that have been aged warm, including those that are force-aged in laboratories.

One test sometimes applied is that of "nonenal potential": samples of wort or beer are heated and the level of nonenal produced is taken as an index of propensity to stale.

See also STALING.

Bamforth, C.W., & Lentini, A. "The flavor instability of beer." In *Beer: A quality perspective*, ed. C.W. Bamforth, 85–109. Burlington, MA: Academic Press, 2009.

Charles W. Bamforth

East India Company. Also known as the East India Trading Company, and then the British East India Company, the East India Company was originally formed in Britain for pursuing trade with the East Indies in Southeast Asia. In fact, it ended up trading mainly with the Indian subcontinent and China, where the main items of trade were cotton, silk, tea, opium, and saltpetre (potassium nitrate). From humble origins in 1600, when a group of merchants were given monopoly privileges on all trade with the East Indies, the Company ascended to such a level that it came to be the most powerful economic and political force in India—to the point of ruling the country. The Company's rule in India began in 1757 after the Battle of Plassey and lasted until 1858 when, following the Indian Rebellion the previous year, the British Crown assumed direct responsibility, and the British Raj ensued. The Company's docks were at Blackwall, on the north bank of the River Thames, just east of the City of London. It was dissolved in 1874.

From a brewer's viewpoint, the East India Company is irrevocably associated with one of Britain's great beer styles, India pale ale (IPA). There were approximately 70 ships in regular service in the East India trade, and, apart from general trading, the East India Company was responsible for supplying Britain's numerous garrisons on the subcontinent. The men were desperate for their "home comforts," and regular supplies of cheese, wine, hams, etc. were shipped out. Beer was in great demand and brewers vied to produce a beer robust enough to survive the arduous months-long journey to India. Thus was born the India pale ale beer style, upon which were built the fortunes of many 19th-century British breweries.

See also BRITAIN and INDIA PALE ALE.

Cornell, M. *Beer: The story of the pint*. London: Headline, 2003.

Gardner, B. *The East India Company: A history.* New York: McCall Publishing Co., 1972.
Hornsey, I.S. *A history of beer and brewing.* Cambridge: Royal Society of Chemistry, 2003.
Matthias, P. *The brewing industry in England, 1700–1830.* Cambridge: Cambridge University Press, 1959.

Ian Hornsey

East Kent Golding (hop) is a traditional hop from the County of Kent in southeastern England. Although hops were first planted in the region by immigrant Flemish farmers around the beginning of the 1400s, East Kent Golding was released officially and commercially only a little more than a century ago. It is part of the generic "Golding" family of hops, so named after its breeder. However, whereas hops just labeled Golding or Goldings may be grown almost anywhere, including in the United States, East Kent Golding proper comes only from the eastern portion of Kent. Although any official designation may have come late, the Golding hop was famous by the late 1790s and British brewing books from the mid 1800s make mention of the unique quality of Golding grown in Kent. That said, in 1901 the *Journal of the Royal Agricultural Society of England* made mention of the fact that growers of lesser hops tried to jump on the Golding bandwagon:

> To a beginner desirous of obtaining definite ideas on the nature of hops, nothing is so puzzling or so annoying as the use of the term "Golding". The inquirer soon learns that it is sometimes employed to denote a particular variety, which every grower in the best districts says, and probably imagines, that he grows; and on other occasions, perhaps more especially in districts suited only to the coarser varieties, the term is extended to include a somewhat heterogeneous mixture of kinds possessing few discoverable characters in common except that they are hops.

The writer, however, goes on to explain that there is in fact a true Golding hop, "the history of which is clear enough." "It is thus clear that, although derived from the Canterbury Whitebine, the Golding hop was a specially-selected sort, which had distinct characters of its own."

Errors and confusions of this sort were once common. Styrian Golding, grown mostly in Slovenia, is actually a misnomer, because the progenitors of that hop were varieties of Fuggle. See FUGGLE (HOP) and STYRIAN GOLDING (HOP). East Kent Golding is prized for its aroma, which makes it suitable for dry hopping, but many brewers use it for bittering as well. Like most of the English hop varieties, East Kent Golding is fairly earthy in flavor, and here that quality is combined with apricot and slight notes of spice. East Kent Golding is, next to Fuggle, the classic hop for a traditional English ale flavor. It was a major hop in India pale ale during that style's heyday, and it is still found in many of the best British bitters. The typical analysis of East Kent Golding hops varies greatly with its subvariety, but for the most part, alpha acids range from 4% to 5.5%, beta acids from 2% to 3.5%, and cohumulone levels from 20% to 25%. Humulene averages about 45%. East Kent is particularly susceptible to downy and powdery mildew infections. It is also highly sensitive to verticillium wilt and to the hop mosaic virus. East Kent Golding generally matures early to mid-season up to late season, and the average yield is about 1,500 to 1,800 kg/ha (1,350 to 1,600 lb/acre). East Kent Golding tends to keep well in storage. Although the technical parameters of East Kent Golding no longer make it a sought-after hop for large breweries, its incomparable flavors and aromas have provided that inimitable "je ne se quoi" to the true English pale ale drinking experience, which is now being kept alive and perhaps even expanded by small artisanal breweries all over the world.

The Journal of the Royal Agricultural Society of England, Volume LXII, 1901 (accessed January 14, 2011).

Jon Griffin

Eastwell Golding (hop) is a traditional English hop. It was originally grown at Eastwell Park, close to Ashford, Kent, England. It is very similar to the other types of Golding hops and also bears similarities to Fuggle. See FUGGLE (HOP). It is part of the somewhat generic "Golding" family and shares many of the family's flavor and aroma characteristics, as well as its poor resistance to disease. See EAST KENT GOLDING (HOP). Eastwell Golding alpha acids range from 5% to 5.5%. Beta acids average 3%, cohumulone levels 30%, and humulene levels 25%. The hop generally matures mid- to late season and retains 70% of its harvest-time alpha acids after 6 months of storage at room temperature.

Jon Giffin

EBC (degrees)

See COLOR UNITS EBC.

Eckhardt, Fred, (1926–), homebrewer, influential beer and sake author, and one of American craft brewing's most important and enduring personalities. Author of the 1989 book *The Essentials of Beer Style*, he set out a road map for classical beer styles that was eagerly followed by many brewers during the microbrewing revolution of the 1990s. His first book, *A Treatise on Lager Beers*, was a homebrewing book released in 1969, several years before the hobby was made legal in the United States. A relentlessly upbeat presence in the American Northwest beer scene, Eckhardt's residency in Portland, Oregon, no doubt partly explains why craft beer has a market share of more than 35% in that city.

Eckhardt became enamored with European beer while stationed in Japan during the Korean War as a radio operator in the Marines. The beer on hand in Japan was Denmark's Tuborg. Once back in the United States he came to realize that the United States also had a great beer history that could be revitalized. His own early homebrewing was a blend of published winemaking techniques and his original research of professional brewing texts. He went on to inspire legions of homebrewers and professional brewers alike, writing the first regular beer column in the United States and hosting hundreds of events over more than 2 decades as one of the best known and best loved beer educators in the country. Eckhardt still writes for several publications, including *All About Beer* magazine, and his impish smile and trademark waxed mustache make him instantly recognizable to thousands of beer enthusiasts. Although beer is his primary interest, Eckhardt has also published books on sake, helping spark an interest in craft sake making in the United States.

Garrett Oliver

Ecostripper

See BOILING.

Edinburgh is Scotland's capital city, home to a brewing culture for many centuries. A crag adjacent to volcanic rocks (known as "Arthur's Seat") supports Edinburgh Castle, near which the Augustinian Holyrood Abbey was founded in 1128 CE. Sheltered by the Pentlands Hills, with rich coal seams, fertile soil for grain, and pure water springs, the Abbey was a prime area for the brewing of ale. As the population of Edinburgh increased, many successful breweries arose. By 1598 the Edinburgh Society of Brewers was founded.

The brewery William Younger & Co was founded in the Canongate, in the center of Edinburgh, in the mid-18th century. By acquisitions and mergers it became the Holyrood Brewery, the largest brewer in Scotland, producing 400,000 barrels by 1891 and exporting to the Americas, India, and Australia. The late 19th century saw a demand for low-gravity, pale, bright beers. A higher hop content permitted these beers to travel efficiently, creating a high-quality beer for export. The export beer evolved into India pale ale (IPA)—a high-alcohol, heavily hopped beer that traveled well, particularly to the Indian subcontinent. IPA had its genesis in a London brewery and although brewed in Edinburgh in the early/mid-19th century its production was soon centered in Burton-Upon-Trent.

William McEwan's brewing operation also grew rapidly through mergers and an excellent export trade. Younger's (Abbey and Holyrood) and McEwan's (Fountainbridge) breweries merged in 1931 to form Scottish Brewers, although each retained a measure of autonomy until a full merger in 1959. They were most famous for Younger's Tartan Special, McEwan's 80/-, Younger's pale ale, and McEwan's Export beer. In 1960 Scottish Brewers merged with Newcastle Brewers to form Scottish and Newcastle Breweries Ltd. See NEWCASTLE BROWN ALE and SCOTTISH & NEWCASTLE BREWERY.

By 1937 Edinburgh was the second most important brewing center in Britain, with 23 working breweries.

Scottish & Newcastle Brewery no longer has a production presence in Edinburgh. In 1998 the site of the Abbey Brewery and adjacent land were chosen as the site for the new Scottish Parliament, leading to the demolition of the brewery buildings in 1999. Today Edinburgh only has two full-scale production breweries: the Caledonian Brewery in the Slateford area, founded in 1869, and Stewart's Brewery, founded in 1995.

See also CALEDONIAN BREWERY and SCOTLAND.

Donnachie, Ian. *A history of the brewing industry in Scotland*. Edinburgh: John Donald Publishers Ltd, 1979.

Keir, David. *The younger centuries. The story of William Younger & Co. Ltd 1749 to 1949*. Edinburgh: William Younger & Co Ltd, 1951.

McMaster, Charles. Excerpts from Andrew Smith's "Book of notes on brewing" 1834–1860. *Scottish Brewing Archive Newsletter* No. 12, Autumn 1988.

McMaster, Charles. Further excerpts from Andrew Smith's "Book of notes on brewing" 1834–1869. *Scottish Brewing Archive Newsletter* No. 13 (Winter 1988/1989).

Graham G. Stewart

education

See BREWING SCHOOLS.

effluent is the liquid waste stream from a brewery. Breweries use a significant quantity of water to make beer. Until the 1970s, it was common for breweries to use 30 to 37 l (8 to 10 gal) of water for every gallon of beer sold. This dropped to an average of between 18 to 22 l (5 and 6 gal) by 2010, and some breweries in water-scarce areas have conserved to 11 l (3 gal). The water not leaving the brewery as beer is the effluent.

Much is added to the waste stream. From the brewhouse, bits of grain and hops are most obvious, but the waste stream also includes kettle trub and the dilute wort that is too weak in sugars to use in brewing. From the fermentation and aging cellars come yeast and beer washings from tank cleaning. All stages in brewing use an assortment of cleaners, most commonly caustic soda (sodium hydroxide), acids such as phosphoric and nitric, and detergents and sanitizers, often containing chlorinated chemicals. Effluent is most critically analyzed for biological oxygen demand and total suspended solids.

Thankfully, water quality and sanitation have improved since the days of indiscriminate waste dumping. All breweries in the United States today are regulated as to where this waste effluent goes, and most pay fees both on the volume of wastewater and on the quantity of nonwater material it contains. Left uncontrolled, these costs can be prohibitively high.

As concerns increase about downstream water contamination and as municipal wastewater treatment plants become overwhelmed, breweries are increasingly pretreating this effluent before discharging it to drains.

Kunze, Wolfgang. *Technology brewing and malting*, 7th rev. ed. Berlin: VLB Berlin, 1996.

Brian Hunt

The **Eggenberg Brewery,** a family-run brewery noted for its strong beers, located in the Salzkammergut region of Austria, between Salzburg and Vienna.

The origins of the Schloss Eggenberg brewery date back to the 14th century. The business was acquired by Johan George Forstinger in 1803 and it continues in Fostinger-Stöhr family hands to this day, with the sixth and seventh generations of management in control. The historic brewery in a country manor, or schloss, was almost destroyed by a fire in 1877. It remains the family home but, for production, has been superseded by a modern, airy new brewhouse built alongside it in 2000, which offers spectacular views of Austria's mountain and lakeland scenery through large panoramic windows.

A relatively small player in domestic terms, with approximately 2% of the Austrian market share, Eggenberg has nevertheless forged an international reputation on the back of its strongest beers. Urbock 23° (9.6%) was created specifically for the global market in the 1970s, but it was the acquisition of the Samichlaus brand from Swiss brewer Feldschlössen in 1999 that particularly raised its worldwide standing. This smoothly malty 14% alcohol by volume beer is brewed on December 6 (St Nicholas's Day) every year and lagered for at least 10 months before being released for sale for the following Christmas. At the other end of the scale, Eggenberg is also known within Austria for its pioneering production of low-alcohol beers. Other products in the extensive portfolio include the pilsner-style Hopfenkönig and Nessie, a beer made with whiskey malt.

Schloss Eggenberg. "*History*." http://www.schloss-eggenberg.at/site/en_geschichte.asp?id=71/ (accessed November 24, 2009).

Jeff Evans

Egypt. In ancient Egypt, all segments of society drank beer, from the exalted Pharaoh down to the humblest peasant. Beer was inextricably woven into the fabric of daily existence, as well as being a feature of religious festivals and state occasions, when "special" brews were produced. Most Egyptologists are of the opinion that grain production and distribution, for brewing and baking purposes, underpinned the ancient Egyptian economy and the political organization of that ancient society, and that a study of beer production can provide an insight into the structure of ancient Egypt itself.

Evidence for the production and use of beer in Egypt extending back to the Predynastic era (5500–3100 BC) has long been known. During the first quarter of the 20th century, for example, Flinders Petrie found beer sediments from jars at Abadiyeh, a Predynastic cemetery on the east bank of the Nile, in Upper Egypt, and at Naqada, which is one of the largest Predynastic sites in Egypt (situated some 26 km (16 mi) north of Luxor on the west bank of the Nile). We know from Early Dynastic (3100–2686 BC) written records that beer was a very important commodity and was almost certainly a well-established feature of the culture of that period. It is therefore highly likely that Egyptian brewing had its antecedents in Predynastic times. Indeed, the earliest information available from the Near East and the Middle East indicates that humans knew how to make bread and beer by 6000 BC.

Egyptian woman filtering barley bread to make beer. Painted wood, fifth dynasty (589-618 CE). SCALA/ART RESOURCE, NY

Classical Greek writers credited the Egyptians with having invented beer (an assertion with which modern Assyriologists would contend, and justly so), with Strabo (c. 63 BC–c. AD 21) commenting that "Barley beer is a preparation peculiar to the Egyptians, it is common to many tribes, but the mode of preparing it differs in each." The barley beer of Egypt was called *zythos* by the classical writers, a name that refers to its propensity "to foam."

Even the wine-loving Romans praised Egyptian beer, with Diodorus Siculus (1st century BC), in his *Bibliotheca Historica* (I:3) saying that "They make a drink of barley . . . for smell and sweetness of taste it is not much inferior to wine." He also attributed the invention of beer to Dionysus, a god who was, in crude terms, the Greek equivalent of the Egyptian deity Osiris. The ancient Egyptians believed that beer was invented by Osiris, one of the most important of their deities, whose principal associations were with fertility, death, and resurrection.

For many years, there has been an oft-repeated (and possibly erroneous) notion of how the ancient Egyptians brewed beer. Fairly recent research, and our entry into the genomic age, has enabled archaeologists to reassess the situation. One thing that is indisputable is that, to the ancient Egyptians, beer was sufficiently important to warrant its regular inclusion in the grave goods complex; it was seemingly essential for existence in the afterlife.

It is now evident that in the New Kingdom, at least, two types of barley, two row (Hordeum distichum L.) and six row (Hordeum vulgare L.), and emmer (Triticum dicoccum Schübl.) were used for brewing, while emmer was mostly used for breadmaking. It has been suggested that the use of these cereals and the proportions in which they were mixed may have been one of the characteristics whereby the ancient Egyptians distinguished and named different types of beers. Flavorings (which did not include hops) and other additives, such as dates, could also have contributed to beer style variation.

As Henry Lutz observed, the earliest Egyptian texts, including the Pyramid Texts, enumerate quite a number of different beers, which would necessitate their being brewed with a variety of ingredients or by different methods. Some of these beer types, of which "dark beer," "iron beer," "garnished beer," "friend's beer," and "beer of the protector" may be mentioned, would undoubtedly have been brewed for special occasions. A "beer of truth," for example, was drunk by the 12 gods who guarded the shrine of Osiris. Most beer was consumed when young, i.e., immediately after primary fermentation had terminated, but it is known that the ancient Egyptians knew how to brew beer that possessed an extended shelf life, as well. How this was achieved is unknown, but it was certainly a necessity for funerary beers to be long-lasting, and we find many references to "beer that does not sour" and "beer of eternity."

Information about ancient Egyptian brewing techniques has been heavily dependent on the artistic record, which mainly comprises wall reliefs, wall paintings, statuettes, and models. Such depictions generally show men and/or women grinding/pounding grain, before making it up into small loaves of bread, which are then broken up into small pieces. These were then mixed with water and stirred together in a wide-mouthed jar (forming a sort of mash). The resultant wort was then separated from grain debris through a coarse filter (e.g., a woven rush mesh) and placed in large heated jars, from where it was transferred (being cooled in the process) to another set of jars for fermentation. Beer could then be transferred to smaller, necked containers with clay stoppers for storage/transport.

Fermentation was likely via "contamination" from used equipment, the inoculation by the surrounding air, or an addition of the previous brew. It is possible that specialized brewing environments (such as lambic breweries) were created, where fermentative organisms were harbored. See LAMBIC.

There have, however, been relatively few indisputable findings of Egyptian brewery sites. At many excavated localities, kitchens and bakeries have been identified and brewing has been assumed to have been carried out as well, mainly because of its relationship to bread-making. One huge brewery complex, capable of producing huge quantities of beer, has been discovered at Hierakonpolis, a settlement and necropolis some 80 km (49 mi) south of Luxor, which flourished during the late Predynastic and Early Dynastic periods.

Over the last 20-odd years, Delwen Samuel, now a researcher at King's College in London, has transformed the way Egyptologists interpret New Kingdom brewing technology. She found no evidence of bread being used, but recovered signs of malted barley. Grist for beer from that era, it seems, may have consisted of emmer, barley malt, and gelatinized grain that had been heated while still moist (as crystal malt is today). As Samuel says, "The distinguishing feature of the New Kingdom method of brewing is that it used a two-part process, treating two batches of cereal grain differently, and then mixing them together." We cannot now be 100% certain of brewing techniques used several thousand years ago, but what is certain is that ancient Egypt was home to a relatively sophisticated and fascinating beer culture.

Curtis, R.I. *Ancient food technology*. Leiden, England: Brill, 2001.

Geller, J.R. "From prehistory to history: Beer in Egypt." In: *The followers of Horus*, Eds. R. Friedman and B. Adams, 19–26. Oxford, England: Oxbow Books, 1992.

Hornsey, I.S. *A history of beer and brewing*. Cambridge: Royal Society of Chemistry, 2003.

Kemp, B.J. *Ancient Egypt: Anatomy of a civilization*. London: Routledge, 1989.

Lucas, A. *Ancient Egyptian materials and industries*, 4th ed. Revision by J.R. Harris. London: Edward Arnold, 1962.

Samuel, D. "Brewing and baking." In: *Ancient Egyptian materials and technology*, eds. P.T. Nicholson and I. Shaw, 537–76. Cambridge: Cambridge University Press, 2000.

Ian Hornsey

Einbecker Brauhaus AG, a regional brewery based in the town of Einbeck in Lower Saxony, Germany with an annual output of 800,000 hl (681,734 US bbl). The company claims to date back to 1378—the year when exports of Einbeck's beer were first documented on a receipt issued in the town of Celle, about 130 kilometers (80 mi) north of Einbeck. The Einbeck tourism board claims that the burghers of Einbeck had started brewing long before that and that a professional brewer had been employed here as early as 1351. The popular medieval tales that revolve around the trickster figure

"Till Eulenspiegel" include one in Einbeck where the brewmaster falls victim to one of his not-so-funny pranks. According to that tale, the brewmaster tells Till to add hops to the brew but he throws the brewer's dog (which is also called "Hop") into the kettle instead. This very unlikely story earned Till a statue in Einbeck's town square just across from today's brewery. Einbeck has built its reputation on bock beer and Einbecker Brauhaus still produces three varieties: the golden ur-bock Hell, the dark ur-bock Dunkel, the Mai-ur-bock (a maibock), and as the most recent addition a dark winter bock at doppelbock strength with 18.2° Plato. While these strong beers hold up the old tradition of the style that made the town famous, the brewery's best selling beer, as in most other breweries in northern Germany, is the pilsner, branded "Brauherrn Pils" in Einbeck. In recent years Einbecker Brauhaus has acquired two more regional breweries, Göttinger Brauhaus AG (1988) and Martini Brauerei in Kassel (1997).

Conrad Seidl

einfachbier, a now antiquated German federal beer tax category that was abolished effective January 1, 1993. Literally, the term meant "simple beer" and referred to a beer with an original gravity—measured in degrees Plato—of 2°P to 5.5°P. See PLATO GRAVITY SCALE. For an explanation of the old and the new German beer tax law, see VOLLBIER.

Horst Dornbusch

Einkorn wheat (Triticum monococcum) was one of the mankind's earliest cultivated species of wheat. It is closely related to wild wheat (Triticum boeoticum), and DNA evidence suggests that its likely site and date of domestication was southeast Turkey around 7500 BC. In modern times, cultivation is restricted to areas of southwest Germany and nearby regions of Switzerland. It is only rarely used in brewing. Unlike modern wheat, Einkorn produces hulled seeds, with husks enclosing the grain. Cultivated einkorn wheat ears are very resilient. They stay intact when ripe and do not lose their husks during threshing. However, einkorn seed embryos are easily damaged, making the grain difficult to malt. Einkorn tends to produce highly fermentable worts and can lend beer a mild, vanilla-like flavor and excellent foam stability.

Esslinger, Hans Michael. *Handbook of brewing*. New York: Wiley, 2009.

Heun, M., et al. Site of Einkorn wheat domestication identified by DNA fingerprinting. *Science* 278 (1997): 1312–13.

Italian Brewpub 'Union' Shows Promise. Michael Jackson's beer hunter. http://www.beerhunter.com/documents/19133-000198.html.

Martha Holley-Paquette

eisbock, an extremely strong beer with a typical alcohol content well beyond 7% ABV. This beer undergoes a freezing process called "freeze distilling" that separates water from the other components (alcohol and sugars) to concentrate these. Water has a lower freezing point than ethanol, so the water freezes, leaving the alcohol liquid. When the water ice is removed, the remaining beer is stronger than before. The style seems to have originated in Franconia, reputedly in Kulmbach. The local Reichelbräu brewery (now part of Kulmbacher AG) claims that an apprentice was ordered to move a barrel containing bock beer into warmer parts of the brewery on an especially cold winter evening in 1890. He failed to do so and by the next morning much of the beer was frozen. The ice inside the barrel had extended to a degree where the wooden staves eventually broke. When the head brewer returned to work, he found the barrel busted and a block of ice encapsuling a small amount of dark liquid. This liquid proved to be far tastier than expected: the eisbock had been invented by pure coincidence. This is at least how the story is told in Kulmbach. Interestingly, however, it does not appear in any of the German brewing books of the time. Reichelbräu put their eisbock on the market and "Kulmbacher Eisbock" (also dubbed "Bayerisch G'frorns" meaning Bavarian ice cream) is still one of the few commercially available beers of the style. Another fine example is the "Aventinus Eisbock" by Weisses Bräuhaus G. Schneider & Sohn, aka Schneider Weisse, where the basic beer used is "Aventinus," a weizendoppelbock. Many craft brewers have enjoyed experimenting with the production of eisbocks and other freeze-distilled beers, with some of the beers reaching ABVs of over 40%.

Conrad Seidl

The **Elbe-Saale hop region** is a German hop-growing area that is scattered across the southern part of the former East Germany. See GERMAN HOPS. It has a long tradition of hop growing that dates back to the 12th century. The region's production declined with the rise of the Hallertau area as the juggernaut of German hop production. After World War II, hop farming was collectivized by the communist regime, which created much larger farms than can be found in the rest of Germany today. The average hop farm in Elbe-Saale is almost 125 acres (nearly 50 ha), almost four times as large as the average Hallertau farm. Unlike other hop-growing areas in Germany, Elbe-Saale does not have a cultivar that is uniquely associated with the region. Today not quite 10% of German hops are grown in Elbe-Saale, and almost nine-tenths of that is hops used more for bittering than for aroma. The region's key varieties are Hallertauer Magnum, Herkules, and Perle. See HERKULES (HOP) and PERLE (HOP).

Val Peacock

emmer (Triticum dicoccum) is a low-yielding hulled tetraploid wheat that was the principal wheat type of Old World agriculture in Neolithic and early Bronze Ages. In ancient Mesopotamia, emmer was widely used as the primary ingredient in beer. In ancient Egypt, emmer was the principal wheat (alongside einkorn) that was cultivated from the beginnings of organized farming until the start of the Greco-Roman period after the conquest by Alexander the Great. It was certainly used for both baking and brewing. Its eventual demise in both civilizations began with the introduction of free-threshing tetraploid and hexaploid wheats (first T. durum, then T. aestivum). When and why hulled wheats fell out of favor is one of the big questions in Near Eastern archaeobotany, but it may have been due to increased land salinization (and a consequential shift to barley). In Egypt, during Imperial Roman times, huge quantities of the grain were exported from Egypt to Rome, and emmer gradually lost its popularity and hence primacy as a crop. See WEIHENSTEPHAN.

Emmer evolved from its wild progenitor (T. dicoccoides), which was formed by the hybridization of two diploid wild grasses, T. urartu (closely related to wild einkorn) and an as yet unidentified, species of Aegilops (related to Ae. searsii or Ae. speltoides).

The earliest sign of the pre-agricultural gathering of wild emmer wheat (and wild barley) is from Ohalo II, an early Epi-Palaeolithic (now submerged) site on the southern shore of the Sea of Galilee, dating from circa 17,000 BC. Among the three main Neolithic grain crops (einkorn, emmer, and barley), the wild form of emmer has the most limited distribution; it is confined to the "Fertile Crescent" of the Middle East and Near East.

In Italy, domesticated emmer is known as farro, and it is easily found in supermarkets. Emmer has far more fiber than modern wheat and can be used for baking though it is more commonly used as a whole grain in soups. Today, outside of Italy, it is largely a relic crop occasionally grown in some parts of Europe and southwest Asia (in the Near East it is restricted to the Pontic mountains of Turkey and Iran), although there has been a renewed interest in it of late, especially in health food circles. Malting trials have recently been carried out at Weihenstephan in Germany, and several breweries make emmer-based beers. Emmer has small kernels but relatively large husks, and it therefore tends to produce beers with notable tannic astringency alongside the nutty flavors of the grain.

See also WHEAT.

Harris, D.R., and G.C, Hillman, eds. *Foraging and farming: The evolution of plant exploitation.* London: Unwin & Hyman, 1989.

Hornsey, I.S. *A history of beer and brewing.* Cambridge: Royal Society of Chemistry, 2003.

Nesbitt, M., and D. Samuel, "From staple crop to extinction? The archaeology and history of the hulled wheats." In: *Hulled wheats,* eds. S. Padulosi, K. Hammer, and J. Heller, 41–100. Rome: International Plant Genetic Resources Institute, 1996.

Zohary, D., and M. Hopf. *Domestication of plants in the old world: The origin and spread of cultivated plants in West Asia, Europe, and the Nile Valley,* 3rd ed. Oxford, England: Clarendon Press, 2000.

Ian Hornsey

endosperm. The largest tissue of the barley grain, the endosperm is usually referred to as the "starchy endosperm." Unlike the embryo and the aleurone layer, it is non-living tissue and acts as a food storage organ for the seed embryo. About 60%–65%

of the weight of barley grains is starch and this starch is in the endosperm. In brewing, the mashing process will break down these starches into wort sugars. Starch is composed of large (25 μm) and small (5 μm) starch granules. The large starch granules account for 90% of the total weight of the starch. About 10%–12% of the grain is protein and most of this protein is located in the endosperm as the storage proteins hordein (35%), glutelin (35%), albumin (10%), and globulin (20%). In the starchy endosperm the starch granules are embedded in this storage protein. This association of starch granules and protein in the starchy endosperm helps to give the endosperm its structure. For example, different degrees of compaction of starch granules and proteins can cause the starchy endosperm to be mealy (opaque) or steely (glassy). The starch granules and storage proteins of the endosperm are located in cells of different shapes. The cell walls of the endosperm cells must be broken by enzymes during malting to expose starch and protein to enzymic attack so that wort sugars can be realized. The walls of the cells of the starchy endosperm of barley contain about 70% beta-glucan, 25% pentosan, and 5% protein. Therefore, beta-glucanase enzymes play a significant role in endosperm modification and extract release during malting. The endosperms of other cereals have differing cellular structures, depending on the plant type. The higher the protein content of the starchy endosperm, the lower the corresponding content of starch and eventual brewing sugars.

See also BARLEY and MALTING.

Palmer, G. H. Achieving homogeneity in malting. *European Brewery Congress Proceedings*, 323–63, 1999.

Palmer, G. H. "Cereals in malting and brewing." In *Cereal science and technology*, ed. G.H. Palmer, 61–242. Aberdeen, Scotland: Aberdeen University Press, 1989.

Geoff H. Palmer

endosperm modification is produced by the actions of enzymes that result in the development of brewer's extract in the endosperms of cereal grains during malting. Milling and mashing of malted grains will turn potential extract into "brewer's extract." The potential extract of malted barley develops during the malting process. During malting the germinated embryo secretes natural plant hormones called gibberellins (e.g., gibberellic acid) into the adjoining aleurone layer. See GIBBERELLINS. These hormones induce aleurone cells to produce endosperm-degrading enzymes such as endo-beta-glucanases and pentosanases (cell wall degrading); endoproteases (storage protein degrading), and alpha amylase, beta-amylase, and limit dextrinase (starch degrading). The release of endoprotease enzyme into the starch endosperm during malting activates beta-amylase (maltose producing) and carboxypeptidase (amino acid-producing) enzymes. The main enzymes that cause modification of the starchy endosperm during malting are the beta glucanses and the endoproteases. Factors that influence endosperm modification are the ease and uniformity of enzymic breakdown of the starchy endosperm during malting, the out-of-steep moisture required to promote effective enzymic modification of the endosperm, the uniformity of germination and hormone production, the level of endosperm-degrading enzymes produced, and the procedures used in the malting process.

Some of these factors are determined by varietal characteristics; some are related to malting practice such as applying enough steeping time to ensure that hydration of the grain is optimal and that husk-microbial levels are kept low. During malting, only about 10% of endosperm starch is broken down. However, protein breakdown, which is mainly from hordein, is about 40%, whereas cell wall breakdown, in terms of beta-glucans, is about 90% in well-modified malts. Degrees of endosperm modification can be described as under-modified, well-modified, or over-modified. In under-modified malt, extract development in the brewhouse may be suboptimal and extract may conceal insufficient breakdown of cell wall and protein materials, which could cause problems such as slow wort and/or beer filtration and haze development. In over-modified malts, milling may produce too much flour, slowing wort filtration and lowering extract yield. Protein breakdown may be excessive, which could lead to excessive color development, reduced foam potential, and excessive levels of amino acids. The injudicious blending of malts of different modifications can conceal potential brewing problems, although modification specifications may have been met analytically. All cereals can be malted. However, the principles of modification are unlikely to be identical to that of barley malt. Malted wheat has high foam potential but contains high levels of gluten.

In contrast, malted sorghum is used to make gluten-free beer.

See also EXTRACTS.

Palmer, G. H. "Achieving homogeneity in malting." In *Proceedings of the European Brewery Convention Congress, Cannes, France*, 323–63. Oxford, England: IRL Press, 1999.

Palmer, G. H. *Cereal science and technology*, ed G. H. Palmer, 61–242. Aberdeen, UK: Aberdeen University Press, 1989.

Geoff H. Palmer

English hops were introduced by Flemish farmers who had fled their homeland—a major hop producing area in the High Middle Ages—during the French–English Hundred Years War (1336–1453), but it is not entirely certain when the first hop was cultivated in England. The Flemish settled in Kent in the southeast of England, where, by the mid-16th century, hop cultivation was firmly established. The hop had a hard time getting established in England. By the mid-1400s, ales that were hopped became known as "beer," whereas only unhopped brews continued to be called ales. In fact, while hops were being legislated *into* beer on the European Continent, it seems they were being legislated *out of* beer in the British Isles, notably by King Henry VIII, who in the 1530s—obviously taking time out from his strenuous philandering—forbade the use of hops outright at his court. He considered hops an aphrodisiac that would drive the populace to sinful behavior (such was the pious duplicity of a ruler who managed to go through countless mistresses—not to speak of six wives, two of whom lost their heads in the Tower). Even Samuel Johnson, author of the first *Dictionary of the English Language*, wrote in his seminal work as late as 1775 that "beer" is a "liquor made from malt and hops," whereas "ale" is a "liquor made by infusing malt in hot water and fermenting the liquor." By 1775, however, virtually all British ales were made with hops. Perhaps Johnson should have known better, considering that he wrote much of his *Dictionary* over pints of hopped ale in an alehouse along the Thames called *The Anchor Inn*, in London's Southwark district, just a stone's throw from the Hop Exchange.

During the hop growing season in England, roughly between April and September, the climate in England is wetter and colder than that of continental Europe, which is why, over centuries, very different cultivars survived the natural selection process in England and became commercial varieties. See FRENCH HOPS and GERMAN HOPS. Various "Golding" types can be traced back to the 1790s and Fuggle was propagated by Richard Fuggle in 1875. See FUGGLE (HOP) and GOLDING (HOP). There has been an active hop-breeding program at Wye College in Kent for most of the 20th century, which has led to many recent English varieties. See ADMIRAL (HOP), BRAMLING CROSS (HOP), BREWER'S GOLD (HOP), BULLION (HOP), NORTHERN BREWER (HOP), PILGRIM (HOP), and PROGRESS (HOP). One curiosity that emerged from this program was dwarf hops, which can be grown on low trellises. This greatly reduces both labor costs and losses from wind drift of plant protection sprays. See FIRST GOLD (HOP), HEDGE HOPS, and PIONEER (HOP). Overall, Britain produces not much more than 1% of the world's hops, but its varieties are very distinctive and favored for traditional British-style ales. They tend to be relatively low alpha compared with the world average. Next to the traditional Kent growing region, English hops are also cultivated in Herefordshire near the border of Wales.

Although modern British brewers are making increasing use of hops from far-flung regions (particularly the United States and New Zealand), British hops remain singular. The overall character of English hops trends to a certain stone-fruit earthiness of aroma that is distinctly different from the more citrus-like notes of New World varieties. Indeed, American craft brewers widely use English hops to help bring those flavors to British-inspired pale ales and bitters. Many British beer enthusiasts, although they appreciate New World hops, cannot imagine a classic British bitter without distinctively English hop aromatics.

Val Peacock

English pale ale is a gold-to-bronze-colored beer at 4.5%–5.5% ABV with a noticeable, but not overpowering, hop bitterness (30–45 IBU). Hop character and aroma are muted and somewhat herbal in nature, reflecting the use of English aroma hops, although other hop varieties may be substituted. It is essentially a bottled beer, and these days is usually filtered and pasteurized. However, some examples from newer craft breweries may be bottle-conditioned, and these will be unpasteurized and contain a yeast sediment.

English pale ale is brewed from two-rowed pale malt, with the traditional, floor-malted Maris Otter being preferred by many brewers. See MARIS OTTER (BARLEY). This beer has only a moderate malt flavor, but may have caramel notes, due to the use of a small proportion of crystal malt along with the pale malt, a common practice for British brewers. English pale ale is produced exclusively by top fermentation, and the ale yeast strains suitable for this often produce a variety of esters, which give the beer a fruity character.

Traditionally, English pale ale is hopped with the classic English hop varieties, Goldings and Fuggles. See GOLDING (HOP) and FUGGLE (HOP). Golding hops, from the East Kent area, are often held to give the finest flavor and aroma when added late in the kettle boil. However, the use of other hop varieties, such as Styrian Goldings, is not unusual. Yet other varieties may be added at the beginning of the boil, for these hops provide only bitterness in the beer. American varieties are generally precluded, since these tend to have strong aromas which are too floral, citrusy, and spicy for this style of beer. This has not prevented many British brewers from using American varieties, but the resulting beer might then be considered "American Pale Ale." See AMERICAN PALE ALE.

English Pale Ale derives from Burton-on-Trent India pale ales (IPAs) of the 19th century. When these became popular in Britain, brewers from other areas attempted to reproduce them, sometimes with limited success. But as understanding of water chemistry progressed and brewers learn how to make a creditable IPA, they soon were also making a variety of similar beers at varying strengths. These went by a number of names, such as "sparkling ale," "dinner ale," and "bitter ale," as well as "pale ale."

Early in the 19th century a long-standing British tax on glass was removed, and from then on throughout the century brewers moved to sell more of their beer in bottles, rather than on draught. This trend accelerated with improvements in bottling technology, such as the replacement of corks with screw tops, and with the arrival from America of new techniques for chilling and filtering the beer. It was the larger brewers who led this trend since they already possessed extensive distribution networks. By the early 20th century Bass (who had largely dropped the term "IPA" in favor of "Pale Ale" by 1879) was selling 75% of its home beer trade in bottles. It is not surprising that the British drinking public now associated the term "pale ale" with bottled beer.

But in England bottled beer could never displace the cask-conditioned draught version, and bottled beer reached a maximum of 30% of total consumption by 1939 and held there until the 1960s, when it began a slow decline in popularity. As a result of taxation and changes in popular taste the average strength of English beer also declined, and bitter, in its various forms became the most popular draught pale beer (until lager started to make inroads into the market in the 1970s and later). See BITTER. English pale ale in bottle became a specialty product, although most brewers still produced at least one such beer. Today there are only a few bottled pale ales remaining in the British marketplace. Paradoxically, a number of draught beers called "pale ale" are on the market, but these should more properly be regarded as "bitters."

The famous Bass Ale, once sold in bottles in the US as "IPA," is still to be found on draught, but is now in decline in its home country. Bass itself no longer exists as a brewer; Interbrew UK, a branch of Anheuser-Busch InBev, now owns the brand. In contrast, Samuel Smith of Tadcaster in Yorkshire, a family company that has remained independent since 1847, brews an excellent English pale ale, which has found a good market in the US since around 1980. Another example is Worthington White Shield, with a long pedigree going back to the early Burton IPAs. See WORTHINGTON BREWERY. It remained a bottle-conditioned beer and was brewed in Burton up until the 1980s, when it was moved to other sites in the country by Bass. Its production ceased for a while in 1998. It is now being brewed again at the White Shield Brewery in Burton, part of the National Brewery Centre. But, ironically, the brand is owned by Coors.

See also INDIA PALE ALE and PALE ALE.

Foster, Terry. *Pale ale,* 2nd ed. Boulder, CO: Brewers Publications, 1999.

Jackson, Michael. *Michael Jackson's beer companion.* Philadelphia: Running Press, 1993.

Terry Foster

environmental issues. From grain to glass, all aspects of brewing and delivering beer to the marketplace are burdened with environmental issues, with water and energy consumption being the two primary natural resource considerations. Carbon emissions are primarily proportional to energy consumption. Barley farming and beer production are the largest consumers of water. In the brewery itself, water consumption is expressed as a ratio of water used to actual beer produced. All of these impacts can best be categorized in three broad areas: (a) upstream—the production and transportation of raw materials that will turn into beer and beer packaging; (b) operations—the resource consumption that can be tied directly to the brewery and the process of making beer; and (c) downstream—the transportation and refrigeration of beer after it leaves the brewery.

Glass manufacturing, barley production, and malting make up more than three-quarters of the upstream environmental impact of making beer. See BOTTLING. Glass made with a high percentage of recycled content uses significantly less energy, reducing the glass part of the equation significantly. In countries with national bottle recycling or reusable bottle mandates, the impact of glass as a container for beer is considerably reduced. The embodied energy necessary to make aluminum cans is more than that for glass while its weight for transportation is less, making it comparable overall to glass. Stainless steel kegs make a smaller impact because of their reusable nature. A marketplace strategy using refillable containers and kegs could have terrific benefit for the environment.

Traditional growing methods for barley, which require repeated tilling of the land and application of fertilizers and pesticides, have a heavy environmental footprint. Low and no-till methods could decrease this impact, and organic malts would further reduce the overall equation as fertilizers have a heavy carbon footprint of their own. Because intensive tilling practices disrupt the normal storage of organic carbon in the soil, the assumed carbon offset from this natural process is less likely to be realized. Brewers desire a plump barley kernel, which makes irrigation a general practice although barley can be grown as a dry land crop. Barley is steeped, germinated, dried and sometimes roasted in the production of malt for brewing. Drying and roasting are the most energy-intensive parts of this process, using both electrical and heat energy.

Production of beer at the brewery is the smallest part of the environmental impact calculation. If generally accepted practices are adopted—heat exchange for cooling wort and attention to energy and water consumption and conservation—brewery operations account for less than 20% of the overall environmental impact. Electrical energy production is a significant factor in this calculation, so subscription to high-quality renewable energy programs can make a measurable decrease in overall carbon consumption and emissions. Breweries that are environmentally committed can have carbon emissions that hover around 5% of the beer's total carbon impact.

With a generally accepted industry standard of finished beer-to-water ratio of four and a half barrels of water to one barrel of beer, any effort toward water reduction would be fruitful. Breweries use a lot of water to make beer, especially due to the rigorous and constant cleaning that is necessary during almost every part of the brewing process. A ratio of 3.25 to 1 is considered excellent throughout the world. Many international breweries have set aggressive targets around water usage. See WATER.

Beer is also heavy. Transportation by truck to faraway markets carries a formidable environmental cost. Given that, surprisingly, the largest single impact along the beer supply chain is refrigeration at retail, which weighs in at more than 25% of the total carbon footprint. Beer is best when stored at cool, consistent temperatures. Shelf life stability is an on-going area of concern, especially as beer travels farther away from the brewery. Brewers have two competing imperatives; the first is the need to maintain quality all the way to the beer drinker, and the other is the increasing imperative to cut back on environmental impacts. This will challenge brewers in the coming years, especially with the burgeoning demand for distinctive beers from smaller breweries around the world.

Brown, Rob. *Heineken unveils green targets.* http://www.brewersguardian.com/brewing-features/international/heineken_unveils_green_targets.html/ (accessed June 5, 2010).

The Climate Conservancy. *The carbon footprint of Fat Tire amber ale.* http://www.newbelgium.com/files/shared/the-carbon-footprint-of-fat-tire-amber-ale-2008-public-dist-rfs.pdf/ (accessed May 15, 2010).

Kim Jordan

enzymes are proteins possessing catalytic capability, i.e., the ability to accelerate chemical reactions without being changed themselves at the end of the reaction. The production of beer is critically dependent upon enzymes, whether endogenous enzymes native to raw materials such as malted barley and yeast, or exogenous (added) enzymes of commercial origin. There is a great diversity of enzymes, including amylases that break down starch, β-glucanases that hydrolyze β-glucans, pentosanases that degrade pentosans, and proteinases that catalyze the degradation of proteins. The molecules acted upon by the enzymes are called "substrates;" the materials produced are "products." Traditionally, it is the enzymes naturally present in malted barley that will break down grain starches into sugars during the mashing process, and it is those sugars that will ferment into beer.

Optimizing enzyme activity is crucial to the brewing process and dependent on the style of beer brewed and the materials available. The brewer will carefully manipulate the temperature, time, ionic composition, and material concentrations in wort to ensure that the enzymes work in concert to create the perfect beer.

The more enzyme available, the faster the reaction. The relationship between the rate of an enzyme-catalyzed reaction and substrate concentration is not so simple. At a certain substrate concentration the system becomes "saturated" such that elevating the substrate concentration beyond this point does not lead to the reaction proceeding any faster. This is referred to as "saturation" and occurs because the enzyme binds to the substrate molecule to form an "enzyme-substrate complex" which then breaks down to re-form the enzyme and release the product(s).

The location where the substrate binds to the enzyme and where the reaction occurs is called the "active site." The shape of the protein molecules determines this and the active site might comprise amino acids from quite distinct parts of the enzyme molecule. Stresses such as heat or changes of pH that will tend to change the interactions in the enzyme molecule will disrupt the active site, prevent substrate binding, and destroy enzyme activity. Enzymes differ in their tolerance of heat and pH.

Temperature and pH also impact directly on the rate of the reaction that the enzyme catalyses. All chemical reactions, including those catalyzed by enzymes, are accelerated by heat according to Arrhenius' Law. However, heat also disrupts proteins' three-dimensional organization, thereby deforming the active site. Thus the net rate of reaction observed is a balance dependent on how resistant the enzyme is to heat. Enzymes in mashes such as α-amylase and

Commercial Enzymes Used in Brewing

Enzyme	*Stage added*	*Function*
β-Glucanase	Mashing	Elimination of β-glucans, especially when using barley and oat adjuncts
Xylanase	Mashing	Elimination of pentosans, especially when using wheat adjuncts
Proteinase	Mashing	Production of free amino nitrogen, especially in high adjunct mashes
Amylases	Mashing	Production of fermentable carbohydrate in high adjunct mashes
Glucoamylase (amyloglucosidase)	Mashing or fermenter	Yielding increased fermentable carbohydrate, for production of light and low carbohydrate beers
Acetolactate decarboxylase	Fermenter	Accelerating the maturation of beer by circumventing the production of diacetyl
Papain	Stored beer	To eliminate haze-forming polypeptides
Prolyl endopeptidase	Stored beer	To eliminate haze-forming polypeptides; potential value in producing beer for celiacs
Glucose oxidase/catalase	Packaged beer	Elimination of oxygen

From Lewis and Bamforth (2006)

peroxidases are very resistant to heat, whereas others like β-glucanase, β-amylase, and lipoxygenase are much more heat sensitive. The enzyme α-amylase, essential in starch breakdown during mashing, is also stabilized by the presence of calcium ions.

pH also impacts the catalytic process as well as the stability of the enzyme. See PH. It is likely that the amino acids functioning within the active site will only do so under certain charge conditions and this will be directly determined by the local pH. Most enzymes of relevance in mashing tend to function optimally in the pH range of mashes (between five and six).

Enzymes are susceptible to inactivation by other agents ("inactivators"). One such substance is the copper ion that binds thiol groups. Other molecules ("inhibitors") can block enzyme activity reversibly: i.e., if they are removed then enzyme activity is restored.

See also ALPHA AMYLASE, AMYLASES, and BETA GLUCANASE.

Bamforth, C.W. Current perspectives on the role of enzymes in brewing. *Journal of Cereal Science*, 50 (2009): 353–57.

Lewis, M.J., and Bamforth, C.W. *Essays in brewing science*. New York: Springer, 2006.

Charles W. Bamforth

Erdinger Weissbräu, a family-owned large brewery in the town of Erding, north of Munich, Bavaria, specializing in the production of wheat beer. The annual output was 1.5 million hectoliters (approximately 852,168 US bbl) in 2008, and Erdinger sells more wheat beer than any other German producer. Erdinger Weissbräu dates back to 1886 when the brewery was founded by Johann Kienle. On October 23, 1935 the brewery was acquired by Franz Brombach and renamed Erdinger Weissbräu in 1949. Between 1935 and 1960 the production rose from 3,500 (2,983 US bbl) to 25,000 hectoliters (21, 304 US bbl) per year. When Werner Brombach, then a 25-year-old graduate of economics and brewing sciences, took over in 1965, he realized that Bavarian-style wheat beer was slowly losing ground in a market that favored pilsner-style beer. Wheat beer was popular with older consumers—notably women—and Brombach feared that demand would be down to zero by 1990, when his most loyal customers were unlikely to be around. His answer was marketing-oriented: "Whenever Volkswagen wants to boost their car sales they start an advertising campaign for a new model. And so did I when I introduced "Erdinger Weissbier mit feiner Hefe" (Erdinger Weissbier with fine yeast), a step that was unusual in the brewing industry in the 1960s and 1970s." At that time, beer with yeast was considered "backwards," but Erdinger depicted itself as appealingly rustic. Brombach repositioned it as a typical Bavarian product. The slogan "Des Erdinger Weißbier, des is hoid a Pracht . . ." (Bavarian dialect for "Erdinger Weissbier is a splendor of its own") was introduced in 1971 and made the weissbier a household name. The brand now tries to appeal to a much younger crowd. Weissbier became a lifestyle drink that was closely associated with Bavaria, tourism, and the beer gardens. However, many beer aficionados feel that Erdinger's beers are relatively bland, as they show little of the banana, clove, and fruit aromatics that typify Bavarian wheat beers.

Conrad Seidl

ergot is a disease that affects cereal grains used in brewing—most notably rye, but also wheat and barley. It is caused by the fungus Claviceps purpurea. The fungus produces toxic alkaloids in the affected grain that, when consumed, are poisonous to humans and other animals. Effects of ergot poisoning include convulsions and seizures, vomiting, gastrointestinal distress, gangrene, hallucinations, and often death. Ergot poisoning epidemics have been identified as occurring throughout history, especially in Europe in the Middle Ages, and have been seen in modern times in developing nations suffering from lax oversight of the food supply. However, improved grain cleaning and milling processes have largely eliminated large-scale ergot contamination today. The last recorded epidemic-size outbreak of ergot poisoning occurred in Ethiopia in the late 1970s.

Grain crops are most susceptible to infection in years marked by cold springs and damp, rainy summers; the telltale sign of infection is the presence of dark purplish-black fungal fruiting structures called sclerotia replacing kernels in the grain head just prior to harvest. Reduced yields and significantly reduced grain quality are hallmarks of ergot infection, which, along with the development of poisonous alkaloids, can render the crop a total loss. Rye is the most susceptible cereal grain to ergot infection, although wheat and barley are also affected to an economically significant extent.

Ergot-resistant varieties of rye, wheat, and barley are not available; however, growing other nonsusceptible crops for several years in fields known to have ergot sclerotia in the soil can greatly reduce future infections. Deep plowing can also aid in controlling infection because ergot sclerotia will not germinate when buried under several inches of soil.

McMullen, M., and C. Stoltenow. *Ergot, PP-551 (revised), May 2002.* North Dakota State University Agriculture website. http://www.ag.ndsu.edu/pubs/plantsci/crops/pp551w.htm. Accessed Aug. 7, 2010.

Brian Thompson

Eroica (hop) is a high-alpha American-bred hop released for commercial production in 1982. It derives from an open pollinated seedling that was collected by Dr Bob Romanko in an experimental plot of Brewer's Gold near Parma, Idaho, in 1968. See BREWER'S GOLD (HOP). After more than 80,000 seedlings had been screened for downy mildew resistance, Eroica was judged to be above average. It had very high yield potential and above-average alpha acid content in initial Idaho field tests. It is a half-sister of Galena, a variety that was released for commercial production 3 years earlier. Eroica strongly resembles its maternal parent Brewer's Gold but has a higher alpha acid potential. Alpha acids range from 12% to 14%, beta acids from 4% to 5%, and cohumulone is about 41%. The approximate essential oil values are 56% myrcene, 1% humulene, 12% caryophyllene, and just traces of farnesene. Initially intended as a backup for Galena, Eroica was found to mature too late for commercial hop production and is, therefore, no longer grown in the United States.

Probasco, G. Hop varieties grown in the USA. *Brauwelt International* 1 (1985): 30–4.
Romanko, R. R., J. Jaeger, G. B. Nickerson, C.E. Zimmermann, and A. Haunold. Registration of Eroica hop (Registration Nr. 8). *Crop Science* 22 (1982): 1261.
Romanko, R. R. In *Steiner's guide to American hops*, Book III, 2nd ed, 64–6. New York: Steiner, 1986.

Alfred Haunold

esters represent the largest group of flavor compounds in alcoholic beverages, generating the "fruity" aromas in beer (not including, of course, the direct addition of fruit and fruit flavors in certain beers). The esters are formed by the reactions of organic acids and alcohols created during fermentation. The most significant esters found in beer are isoamyl acetate (banana, peardrop), ethyl acetate (light fruity, solvent-like), ethyl caprylate (apple-like), ethyl caproate (apple-like with a note of aniseed), and phenylethyl acetate (roses, honey).

Esters are produced primarily through the action of yeasts during fermentation and are influenced by three features of the fermentation process: yeast characteristics, wort composition, and fermentation conditions. Brewers look to control all three to produce exactly the flavor and aroma they wish to create in their beers. The selection of yeast strain is very important in determining the type and level of ester found in beer. Some strains are characterized by the production of high levels of isoamyl acetate, most notably in the brewing of traditional Bavarian wheat (weizen; see KRISTTALLWEIZEN) beers, where the distinctive banana (and clove-like) character of these beers is determined by the specific yeast strains used. It has been suggested that the ale strains of yeast ("top fermenters"; see TOP FERMENTATION) are more liable to produce esters than are lager strains ("bottom fermenters"; see BOTTOM FERMENTATION), but it is probable that the higher levels of esters normally found in ales are attributable to the higher fermentation temperatures used in ale brewing. Additionally, the physiological state of the yeast can also influence ester production.

The composition of the wort can also influence ester formation in beer. High dissolved oxygen levels in the wort tend to inhibit ester formation, whereas high sugar concentrations increase ester levels. Higher alcohol beers tend to be marked by high ester levels and the disproportionately high levels need to be accommodated in the application of high gravity brewing to the production of beers of lower alcohol content. See HIGH GRAVITY BREWING. Other wort components such as the levels of free amino nitrogen (FAN), zinc, and lipids also influence ester formation. See FREE AMINO NITROGEN (FAN). High FAN and zinc levels in wort tend to increase ester formation, whereas high lipid content (particularly through a high trub carryover) tends to lower ester levels. See TRUB.

The shape of the fermentation vessels can also impact the production of esters—tall, narrow fermenters tend to produce lower levels of esters than does fermentation in shallow, open fermentation vessels. The effect is attributable to a combination of high hydrostatic pressure and high CO_2 levels in taller vessels. The stirring of fermenters increases ester levels, which is an issue in continuous fermentation systems where excessive amounts of esters are produced. See CONTINUOUS FERMENTATION. Brewers must take these factors into account when brewing specific styles and brands of beer in different brewing locations to achieve consistent ester profiles.

See also FLAVOR.

Dufour, J.-P., Ph. Malcorps, and P. Silcock. "Control of ester synthesis during brewery fermentation." In *Brewing yeast fermentation performance*, ed. Katherine Smart, 213–33. New York: Blackwell Publishing, 2003.

George Philliskirk

ethanol is also known as ethyl alcohol, "spirits," or, even more frequently, simply alcohol. However, there are a great many alcohols, which is a generic term for organic compounds featuring the hydroxyl, –OH, group. Ethanol is a colorless liquid with a boiling point of 173°F (78.4°C). Because of the relative polarity of the –OH group, ethanol is capable of dissolving many inorganic ions as well as organic compounds.

Ethanol is a straight-chain alcohol with a molecular formula of C_2H_5OH and a structural formula. It is a primary end-product of anaerobic fermentation reactions by certain microorganisms, notably yeasts of the Saccharomyces species. See SACCHAROMYCES. In brewing beer, the smaller carbohydrates in wort, in particular glucose and maltose, are converted by yeast during fermentation to ethanol and carbon dioxide. Ethanol targeted for industrial use can be produced as a by-product of petroleum refining.

Ethanol is widely used to dissolve substances marketed for human consumption or contact, including flavorings, colorings, medicines, and perfumes. It is extensively used as a solvent and a reactant in processes in the chemical industries. It is a fuel and is now extensively used as an entire or partial replacement for gasoline in automobiles. It was first used for the latter purpose in 1908, with the Model T Ford.

The structural formula for ethanol was one of the first to be evaluated, in the mid-19th century. As long ago as 1828, Michael Faraday synthesized ethanol by acid-catalyzed hydration of ethylene, a route very similar to that used today to produce industrial ethanol.

Ethanol substantially reduces the surface tension of water. In wine this is responsible for the "tears" or "legs" phenomenon: following the swirling of wine in a glass, ethanol evaporates from the film on the glass surface, leading to an increase in surface tension of the liquid that runs down the glass in channels. The surface tension effect also underpins the observation that alcohol promotes foam formation in beer. However, alcohol destabilizes the foam once formed, as it competes with foam-stabilizing molecules in the bubble wall.

Alcoholic proof is a measure of how much ethanol is present in a mixture. It was formerly determined by adding alcohol in the form of liquor to gunpowder. The level of addition where the gunpowder just exploded was deemed "100 degrees proof."

Ethanol reacts with carboxylic acids to produce esters, important flavor contributors in beer. See ESTERS. This can be catalyzed by acids or by enzymes, notably alcohol acetyl transferase from yeast.

Oxidation of alcohol leads sequentially to acetaldehyde and acetic acid and is most important in living systems, including the human body, where it is catalyzed by the enzymes alcohol dehydrogenase and acetaldehyde dehydrogenase. Acetaldehyde is more toxic than ethanol and its accumulation may be the reason for many of the adverse impacts of ethanol. The reverse reaction whereby acetaldehyde is reduced to ethanol is the key final stage of alcoholic fermentation in yeast, a reaction that ensures the continuation of glycolysis.

Ethanol has a direct impact on the flavor of alcoholic beverages (warming) but also influences the volatility of other aroma compounds. It has psychoactive impacts, with a depressant impact on the central nervous system.

Ethanol is metabolized by the body—it is converted to acetyl CoA and is therefore a source of energy (calories). See ACETYL COA. In excessive quantities ethanol can be seriously harmful to the body, ultimately leading to death. However, in moderate quantities it appears to be the primary causal factor in alcoholic beverages' ability to reduce the risk of atherosclerosis (the build-up of fatty materials in artery walls).

The ethanol content of a beverage is usually measured in terms of the volume fraction of ethanol in the beverage, expressed either as a percentage (alcohol by volume, ABV, or alcohol by weight, ABW) or as alcoholic proof, in the case of distilled beverages.

Fermented beverages containing ethanol are made from diverse raw materials, the chief ones being grain (to produce beer), grapes (wine), honey (mead), and apples (cider). The range is further diversified if the base fermentation product is distilled. Thus, we have whiskies distilled from fermented cereal grains, brandies distilled from fermented fruit juices, rum distilled from fermented molasses or sugar cane, and vodka distilled from diverse start points from potatoes through grain. There may be further infusions with fruits and spices, e.g., gin or fortification of base fermentation products with distilled alcohol, e.g., port and sherry. Applejack is traditionally made by freeze-distillation of cider and the German eisbier in a similar manner from beer.

Oxidation of the alcohol in diverse fermentation products leads to acetic acid (vinegar). Ethanol is toxic to yeast and few yeasts will tolerate concentrations higher than 15% by volume. See ETHANOL-TOLERANT YEAST STRAINS.

See also ALCOHOL.

Jacques, K.A. et al. *The alcohol textbook*. Nottingham, England: Nottingham University Press, 2003.

Charles W. Bamforth

ethanol-tolerant yeast strains are important in brewing beer. When a brewer considers what yeast strain he will use to ferment his beer, there are many qualities he may look for, but the yeast's ability to finish the fermentation is among the most important. All brewing yeasts create ethanol as a by-product of their fermentation of sugars. Once alcohol concentration in the fermenting beer reaches a certain point, however, fermentation will cease. The ability of yeast to continue fermentation in the presence of high alcohol concentrations is referred to as "ethanol tolerance" and is highly dependent on the yeast strain itself. Large breweries often produce high-gravity beers for dilution later in the process. See HIGH GRAVITY BREWING. Many craft brewers produce highly alcoholic specialty beers on a regular basis. In both cases, a common problem when fermenting high gravity wort is that the fermentation often stops short of the brewer's target for alcohol and finished gravity.

For centuries, brewers yeast has been passed down from fermentation to fermentation by harvesting and repitching the yeast sediment. At 3%–5% alcohol by volume (ABV), brewer's yeast is more tolerant of ethanol than most competing microorganisms. In fact, many microbiologists believe that ethanol production evolved as a type of defense mechanism for yeast. But only certain strains will withstand ethanol concentrations above 8%, with some particularly hardy strains able to handle up to 15% in normal fermentations. In recent centuries Belgian brewers in particular have tended to produce a large number of strong beers, and many Belgian yeast strains are quite alcohol tolerant. Some yeasts can ferment past the 8% level, but need coaxing to do so. The addition of nutrients, a high concentration of pitching yeast, rousing, and warmer temperatures will tend to result in greater alcohol tolerance. Some craft brewers have produced beers with ABVs around 20% by slowly dosing additional yeast and additional sugars into fermenting beers; however, many of these beers turn out to be strong but unpalatable. When brewers select yeast strains offered for sale by commercial laboratories, the normal ethanol tolerance of every strain will usually be listed as part of the yeast's profile.

It has been suggested that high ethanol concentrations affect the porosity of the yeast plasma membrane. The yeast cell is then unable to transport nitrogen and sugar into the yeast cell despite their presence in the wort. Without the uptake of these nutrients, the yeast cell "shuts down" fermentation. Ethanol-tolerant yeast strains may have a plasma membrane makeup that gives them a particular ability to survive high ethanol concentrations.

Chris White

ethyl acetate is a compound produced by yeast that is quantitatively the major ester found in both beer and wine. Esters are aromatic compounds formed by the reaction between alcohols and acids. They are widely found in nature and contribute to the aromas of many varieties of fruit. Over 90 esters can occur in beer, and the ethyl esters predominate.

These esters contribute to the overall flavor and aroma of beer, giving a "fruity" quality to a drink that rarely contains any fruit. As ethyl acetate intensifies, however, the aromatic perception can skew from pleasant and "fruity" to "solventy" and "perfumy;" abnormally high levels are therefore regarded as off-flavors. In addition to being produced by brewer's yeast strains (Saccharomyces cerevisiae and Saccharomyces pastorianus), ethyl acetate is also produced in large quantities by the wild yeasts Brettanomyces, Hansenula, and Pichia via aerobic fermentation.

Because ethyl acetate is such an influential part of beer aromatics—for good or ill—brewers seek to control its levels in their beers. Many factors, in addition to the yeast strain employed, have been found to influence the concentration of ethyl acetate formed during fermentation. These include fermentation temperature, where an increase from 50°F to 77°F (10°C–25°C) has been found to increase the concentration of ethyl acetate from 12.5 to 21.5 mg/L. Continuous fermentation results in higher levels of esters as compared to conventional batch fermentation. See CONTINUOUS FERMENTATION. High yeast pitching rates result in lower levels of ethyl acetate. Higher gravity worts can result in elevated levels of esters. Lowering the levels of oxygen supplied to yeast will enhance overall ester formation.

Ethyl acetate arises as a result of the reaction between ethanol and acetyl CoA. Practical measures can be taken to lower ester levels (particularly in high gravity worts), including the production of wort with a suitably low carbon-to-nitrogen ratio and the supply of adequate oxygen at the outset of fermentation, both of which promote yeast growth. The application of pressure during fermentation reduces both yeast growth and ester synthesis.

See also ESTERS and FRUITY.

Graham G. Stewart

etiquette

See DRINKING CUSTOMS.

European Bittering Units

See INTERNATIONAL BITTERNESS UNITS (IBUS).

European Brewery Convention (EBC) is the autonomous scientific and technological arm of the Brewers of Europe, a not-for-profit organization that represents the European brewing sector. Based in Brussels, its mission is to benefit the European brewing sector by facilitating collaboration and the sharing of knowledge between beer producers, maltsters, and academic organizations.

The EBC was founded in 1947 in an effort to bring the brewing industry in post-war Europe closer together by giving them a forum through which to share brewing science and technology. As victors and vanquished re-built their brewing industries after World War II, cooperation between them was crucial and the EBC became a critical conduit for information. The EBC has provided critical scientific research to breweries, governments, and policy makers throughout the course of the establishment of European agricultural standards, environmental policies, and food safety rules over several decades.

While the EBC's main objective is to benefit European brewers, the organization is best known for the EBC congresses, which are held every 2 years. The congresses are among the foremost gatherings in the world focused entirely on brewing science and technology.

In the late 1990s, the EBC started to discuss a merger with the Confédération des Brasseurs du Marché Commun or CBMC. Founded in 1958 and closely allied with the European Community (and later the European Union), the CBMB officially changed its name to the Brewers of Europe in 2001.

After a decade of debate, the EBC and the Brewers of Europe merged in late 2007, giving the European brewing industry a unified voice.

Ordinary membership in EBC is open to national organizations in Europe that represent the majority of the brewing industry in their respective countries. Nineteen European countries are members of EBC.

The board of the Brewers of Europe oversees an executive committee made up of representatives from national member organizations and from major brewing companies. The executive committee plans and executes the organization's activities, while the day-to-day running of the organization is carried out by an executive officer.

European Brewery Convention. www.europeanbreweryconvention.org/ (accessed April 15, 2011).

Karl-Ullrich Heyse and Garrett Oliver

The **European Union** (EU) is a political and economic union of mostly European nations. Its origins date back to a post–World War II political desire to create a lasting peace by integrating the interests of member states.

The initial step was seemingly modest: the creation of the European Coal and Steel Community in 1951, agreed upon by Belgium, France, Germany, Italy, Luxembourg, and the Netherlands. In 1957 these six states signed the Treaty of Rome, broadening economic cooperation by creating a "Common Market" known as the European Economic Community (EEC), later shortened to European Community as interstate initiatives expanded.

In 1973 Denmark, Ireland, and the UK joined the EEC. Membership continued to expand, with Greece joining in 1981, followed by Spain and Portugal in 1986.

In February 1992 the Treaty of Maastricht was signed, creating the EU. The treaty allowed for the creation of a single currency—the euro—as well as closer ties on foreign and security policy and freer movement of people, goods, and services. On January 1, 1993, the EU came into existence.

Post 1993 the EU has continued to integrate nations, welcoming Austria, Finland, and Sweden in 1995. Ten nations, the largest EU enlargement to date, joined in 2004: Estonia, Latvia, Lithuania, Poland, the Czech Republic, Slovakia, Hungary, Slovenia, Malta, and Cyprus. The current membership of 27 nations was reached in 2007 with the addition of Bulgaria and Romania.

The combined beer production of EU member states makes it one of the world's three largest markets, alongside China and the United States, with 363.7 million hl (approximately 310 million US bbl) brewed in 2009. The largest producers were Germany at 98.1 mhl (83.5 m US bbl); the UK, 45.1 mhl (38.3 m US bbl); Poland, 36.0 mhl (30 m US bbl); and Spain, 33.8 mhl (29 m US bbl).

Globally, the EU's best known beer producers may well be Belgium, the Netherlands, and Germany. Belgian production totaled 18.0 mhl (15 m US bbl) in 2008, of which 10.2 mhl (8.5 m US bbl) was exported, a total that includes fellow EU member states as recipients. In the same year Dutch brewers shipped 15.4 mhl (12.8 m US bbl) beyond their borders, much of this as Heineken products destined for the United States; German brewers exported 13.9 mhl (11.9 m US bbl).

Breweries are both plentiful and diverse in EU member nations, as are the styles of beer brewed. All 27 nations can boast brewers, ranging from more than 1,300 in Germany to just 1 in Malta. In 2008 there were more than 3,400 breweries working across the EU—this number is increasing as microbreweries come to life, especially in Denmark and the UK but also in Italy and the Netherlands.

EU taxation policy, as expressed in Directive 92/83/EEC, is intended to harmonize members' excise duties on alcohol and alcoholic beverages, but offers latitude on duty, especially with regard to smaller producers. EU member states may reduce duty as much as 50% below that of their standard national rate, applicable up to a maximum of 200,000 hl (170,434 US bbl) of production.

The effect of such reduced duty rates can be considerable. The UK, which introduced the 50% maximum in 2002 for production to 5,000 hl (4,261 US bbl), has since then had a doubling of the country's brewers, approaching 800 at the close of 2010.

EU taxation policy also mandates a minimum level of excise duty for beer, as shaped by Directive 92/83/EEC. The intention of this legislation was to harmonize excise regimes on alcohol and alcoholic products between EU member states.

The Directive has achieved limited success in meeting this objective. The minimum level of duty, which was not index linked for inflation, is now so

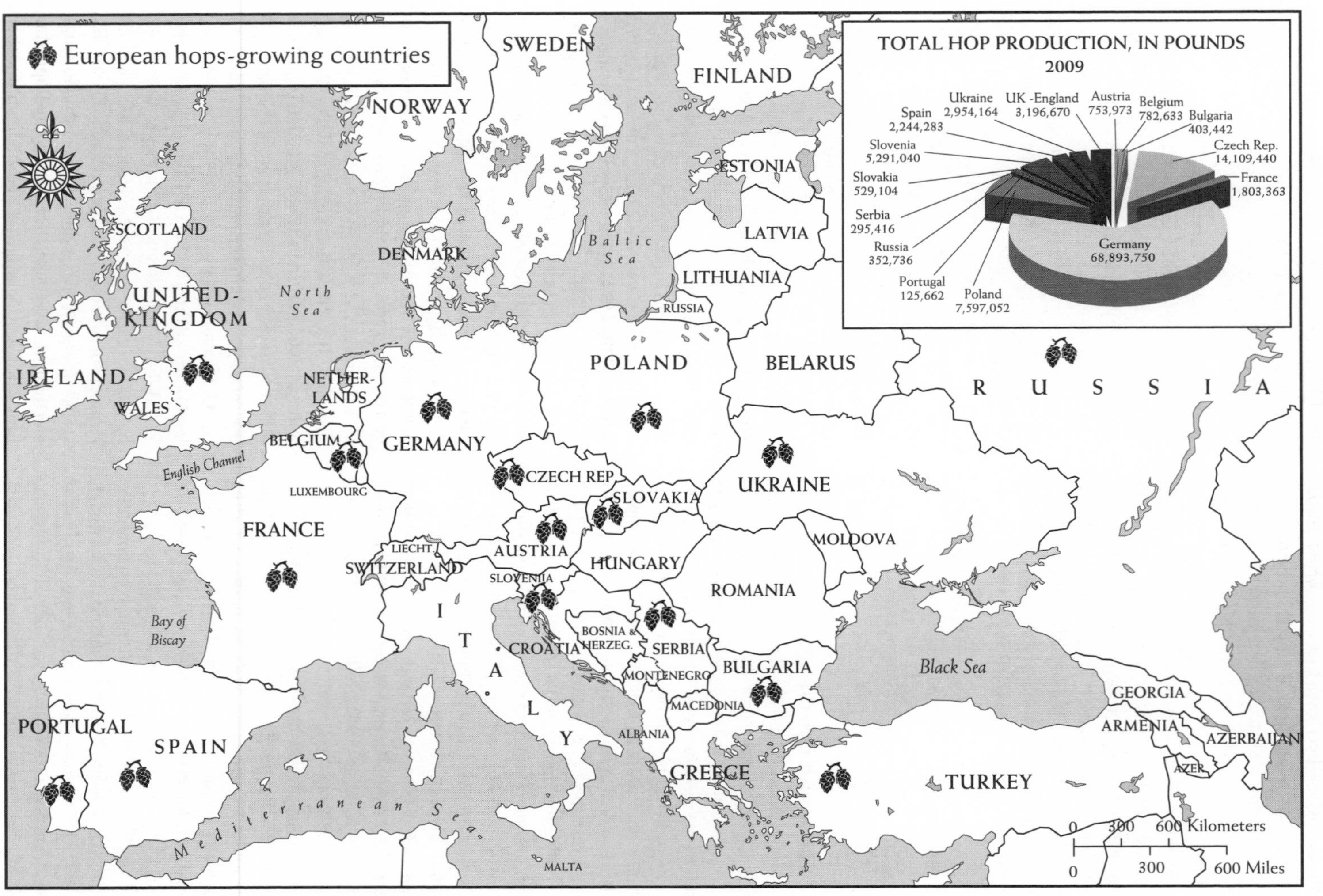

European Hops Growing Countries. GEORGE CHAKVETADZE, ALLIANCE PUBLISHING low at 1.87 euros/hl/per degree alcohol that only one member state, Bulgaria, has excise duty for beer set at this minimum. Finland is currently the state with the highest beer excise duty, at 25.96 euros/hl/degree alcohol.

The result is that neighboring EU states apply widely differing rates of excise duty, encouraging increases in cross-border legal—and illicit—beer imports. This was an issue in the 1990s between France and the UK. French excise duties today remain one-tenth of the UK's, leading to extensive consumer importation well in excess of that intended for personal consumption, rather than for illegal resale. There continues to be extensive importation of cheaper Estonian beer into neighboring Finland.

In 1993 the EU introduced protected food and drink name schemes similar to the Appelations d'Origine Contrôllée system used for wine. Protected Designated of Origin is awarded to products produced, processed, and prepared in a region using recognized methods. Protected Geographic Indication (PGI) recognizes a link between a product and the region in which it is produced in at least one stage of production, processing, or preparation. Finally, Traditional Specialty Guaranteed highlights traditional character in either the product itself or its method of production.

Use of these designations is not widespread, although the Czech Republic is currently the only EU member with PGI status for all beer produced in their country. Such designations can also be surrendered, as was the case for Newcastle Brown Ale when brewing of the beer brand ceased in Newcastle and was moved to Yorkshire. See NEWCASTLE BROWN ALE.

EU legislation also concerns the brewing industry with regard to health policy, for example, reducing alcohol abuse. Legislation for labeling on allergens almost resulted in isinglass, dried swim bladders from fish used to clarify beer and wine, needing to be declared in the mid-2000s. Acting on evidence supplied by the brewing industry and its suppliers, the European Food Safety Authority eventually ruled such allergen labeling unnecessary. See ISINGLASS.

The brewing industry's political agenda is represented by the Brewers of Europe, which is headquartered in Brussels, with its members the national brewers associations of all EU states plus Norway, Switzerland, and Turkey. Beer drinkers' interests are brought to the fore by the European Beer Consumers Union, which believes that beer, one of Europe's natural drinks, deserves the support of the EU.

Karl-Ullrich Heyse and Larry Nelson

evaporation rate, the proportion of the total volume of liquid in the wort kettle that is evaporated as steam expressed as a percentage of the original volume of wort. Brewers strive to achieve a target evaporation rate in boiling their wort. If the evaporation rate is too low, the necessary changes to the wort achieved by boiling may not occur. If it is too high, then energy is being wasted. Historically the target was 10%–15% evaporation over 90 min of boiling, but modern brewers tend to boil for a little over 1 h; as a result, evaporation of 6%–8% of the total liquid volume is now more usual.

Steve Parkes

external calandria

See CALANDRIA.

extra special bitter (ESB) has become the flagship beer of many brewers in the United States and Australia, although most of these beers can trace their roots directly back to the British brewery Fuller, Smith & Turner. The original of the style, Fuller's ESB, is brewed in Chiswick, west London; no British beer has won more prizes from the Campaign for Real Ale in its annual Champion Beer of Britain awards. See CAMPAIGN FOR REAL ALE (CAMRA) and FULLER, SMITH & TURNER. It was named Champion Beer of Britain in 1978, 1981, and 1985 and Best Strong Ale in 1978, 1979, 1981, 1983, 1985, 1987, and 1991, and received a silver award in the Strong Bitter category in 2002.

Fuller's ESB (5.5% draught, 5.9% in bottle) was first brewed as Winter Beer in 1969 and became a regular beer under its current name 2 years later. It is brewed with 90% Optic pale malt, 3% crystal malt, and 7% flaked maize and has a rich coppery amber color. The complex hop recipe includes Challenger, Goldings, Northdown, and Target. The beer is late-hopped in the kettle with Challenger and Northdown, and then dry-hopped with Goldings in the fermentation vessel. Goldings are also used for further dry-hopping in the cask. Fuller's ESB is brisk, with 34 IBUs of bitterness, and many writers have stressed the rich orange fruit character of the beer, with one writer likening it to "liquid Cooper's marmalade."

The finished beer shows a profusion of rich malt, orangey fruit, and peppery hops on the nose, with a full-bodied attack of juicy malt, orange peel, and bitter hop resins on the palate. The complex and lingering finish is beautifully balanced between malt, hops, and tangy fruit, finally becoming dry with a bitter hop resin note.

Though Fuller's zealously guards the name ESB as a trademark in the UK, the beer has become the inspiration for hundreds of beers called "ESB" brewed worldwide, and the style has become particularly prevalent in the United States, where it is a mainstay of many brewpubs. While ESB is now widely considered a distinct style, the parameters have broadened well beyond the original, so that colors between straw and copper, and hop character varying between moderate and strong, are now included. It's generally agreed that the style is malty and fruity, showing sweetness mid-palate, drying to a clean hoppy finish. Most examples have ABVs between 5.5% and 5.8%, which is considered strong in the UK, but not particularly so elsewhere. The annual judging at the Great American Beer Festival now recognizes both English and American variants of ESB, with the latter featuring citrusy American hops over the earthier English varieties.

Roger Protz

extracts are concentrated solutions of sweet wort predominantly mashed from malted barley but can also include adjuncts and in some cases brewed hopped wort. The wort is then evaporated in a vacuum or under reduced atmospheric pressure using the lowest heat possible (below 50°C, 122°F) to minimize any adverse effect on color and flavor. Extracts can be produced to a wide range of standards in regard to sugar profile, protein content, and enzyme activity and can be formulated to produce specific styles of beer.

Starting from a high-gravity mash, the wort is then concentrated to between 75% and 85% solids with a specific gravity of between 1.400 and 1.450 and therefore has the advantage of being stable, protected from microbial growth at room temperature.

Packaging options vary from small cans to 20-l (5-gal) pails through drums and totes up to full tanker loads. Some extracts are dried and can be shipped as flakes or powders in sealed 25-kg (50-lb) bags.

Extracts are used exclusively in some small breweries and brew-on-premise operations, sometimes with the addition of small amounts of grain. They are also widely used by amateur brewers. Larger operations will use them as a supplement or production aid to ensure consistency and quality of wort produced through normal brewing practices. Breweries such as those on U.S. military bases in remote locations use them for their convenience and ease of use to produce consistent and high-quality beers.

Jonathan Downing

extreme brewing, a controversial term describing fun new beers created by craft brewers who want to push the envelope of traditional brewing culture. Although the beers themselves are widely enjoyed, the term "extreme brewing" evokes either an admirable spirit of rebellious creativity or a puerile and cynical attempt to market a manufactured "outsider" image, depending on one's point of view. Given that the rise of the craft brewing movement has been predicated on the transgression of previously confining borders, it is not surprising that the term has been controversial. Although so-called extreme brewing started off as an American craft brewing phenomenon, these beers have had a strong influence on craft brewers worldwide.

Used more often by beer consumers, writers, and bloggers than actual commercial breweries, the term "extreme beer" has been applied to almost any beer that seems out of the ordinary, whether it is a matter of high alcohol, intense concentration of hop bitterness, unusual ingredients, or an innovative technique or inspiration. Some brewers, seemingly out of a juvenile desire to appear "outrageous," espouse a wish to create the "hoppiest beer in the world" or the "strongest beer on Earth" and inevitably set about some scheme to achieve the dubious goal. The crowing brewer, having staked a claim for some silly superlative, is inevitably soon usurped by an upstart claiming the prize for himself.

Many beers that are labeled extreme are genuinely inventive and wonderfully flavorful. Many are strong, but have also undergone complex fermentations, barrel-aging regimes, and meticulous blending to achieve something harmonious and delicious. Whereas most beers have traditionally been made from malted grains, some type of bittering agent, and yeast, modern craft brewers are using everything from maple syrup to chilies, sweet potatoes to lemongrass, edible flowers to lychee fruit. The resulting beers range from disgusting to deeply strange to excellent, but the creativity that can be involved is undeniably refreshing.

Of course, people have been making beer for about 10,000 years, so the idea that one will create something absolutely new is almost surely as hubristic as it is irresistible. Only 250 years ago, colonists in the Americas were brewing beer with native corn, native rice, spruce tips, pumpkins, molasses, green peas, maple sap, wild herbs, potatoes, and just about anything else that might create fermentable sugars and a hopefully pleasant flavor. It might be argued that Italian craft brewers who are brewing beers from their native chestnuts are not practicing extreme brewing, but rather are engaged in very traditional brewing practices that seem unusual only from a very modern point of view. Similarly, strong beers of over 10% alcohol by volume have almost certainly been brewed since the dawn of civilization and have been commercially available for centuries. The growing interest in sour beer styles grows out of lambic brewing, one of the oldest beer traditions in the world. In Central and South America, indigenous people chewed corn so that their saliva would convert starches into sugars for the fermentation of their native chicha beer. Given that beer has such a complex history, what can truly be considered extreme?

Although many beer enthusiasts enjoy the term "extreme brewing," many craft brewers quietly bristle. Having worked and sacrificed for many years to become skilled artisans and craftspeople, they are loathe to see themselves depicted in the public arena as unruly children trying to one-up each other in the playground. After all, they argue, people are not lining up for extreme food, extreme wine, or extreme whiskey—why should brewers allow themselves to be painted with such a pejorative brush? Labels do matter, especially in an environment where wine enjoys a much higher media profile than craft beer does. Craft beer still struggles to be heard by the mainstream media, and many brewers feel that the extreme label is patently unhelpful. Interestingly, many creative artists portrayed as radical or extreme have not enjoyed such titles, from Dizzy Gillespie in jazz in the 1940s and 1950s to the influential modern chef Ferran Adria of El Bulli today. They have argued that they were attempting to make something beautiful rather than being engaged in an attempt to be outrageous at any cost, but such thoughtful sentiments have often fallen on deaf ears.

Other brewers have embraced the term "extreme" wholeheartedly and built the marketing of their breweries around it. When it comes to getting attention from the media, loudness has always been more effective, and that has become particularly true as media evolves away from simple print and television and onto other platforms. If a brewer is willing to do anything for attention, the media will happily follow. What is certain is that brewers will continue to be adventurous souls, creating and recreating flavors that have not been tasted before, at least not in our lifetimes. And there will continue to be those creative brewers who prefer to think of themselves as iconoclasts and others who will continue to wear the words "extreme brewer" as a badge of honor.

Garrett Oliver

farnesene is a component of the hydrocarbon fraction of hop oil. The presence or absence of farnesene (sometimes referred to as beta farnesene) is a distinguishing feature for some hops. In Hallertauer Mittelfrüh and many other (but not all) German varieties; for instance, farnesene is completely absent, while in Czech Saaz, German Tettnanger, all Slovenian varieties, and several American varieties, most notably Sterling, it is present in high levels, at roughly 10% to 20% of total oils. See HALLERTAUER MITTELFRUEH (HOP), TETTNANGER (HOP), SAAZ (HOP), and STYRIAN GOLDING (HOP). Farnesene has a woody, herbal, citrus aroma, sometimes described as floral. Because farnesene is hydrophobic and volatile, the compound itself is usually not found in beer unless the beer has been dry hopped with a variety that contains farnesene—and even then it is present in only very small amounts. However, high levels of farnesene in hops generally correlate well with pleasant, noble-type hop aroma in beer. See NOBLE HOPS.

Thomas Shellhammer

Farnham (hop) was a traditional English hop that is no longer grown today. Originally known as Farnham Whitebine, it is named after the farming town of Farnham in the County of Surrey, some 65 km (40 miles) from London. The town became first known as a notorious coaching stopover on the road to Winchester. Hops were first cultivated there in 1597 and became the area's most important crop, even before wheat, in the mid-1700s, when Farnham hops were regarded as of the highest quality in all of England. The hop is widely mentioned in connection with early India pale ales and was almost certainly a very close relative of the Canterbury Whitebine and Mathon Whitebine, so named because of their very pale green bines and leaves. The boom for Farnhams lasted until roughly the early 1880s, after which East Kent Golding and Fuggle, most of it sold at the Hop Exchange at Southwark in London, began to replace it. But in its heyday, Farnham hops even made it to the New World, where it is known to have been grown in Philadelphia in 1790. This would indicate that Farnham was the likely source of flavor and aroma in the American porters that slaked the thirst of such eminent imbibers as George Washington, John Adams, and Thomas Jefferson, America's first three presidents.

The Journal of the Royal Agricultural Society of England, Volume LXII, 1901 (accessed January 14, 2011).

Glenn A. Payne

faro is a type of sweetened lambic beer traditionally brewed in Belgium. It was widely available throughout the Senne Valley up until the early 20th century. Faro was often made from the weaker runnings from the lauter tun—the second and third runnings—which led to a beer with a lower alcohol content. In the kettle, brewers sometimes added herbs or spices such as orange peel or a little coriander. The fermentation was a natural, spontaneous fermentation by the microbes found in the air around the Senne Valley. The end result was a light-bodied and gently flavored acidic beer that sometimes had hints of spice. Faro was usually sweetened before packaging or on-premise. The brewer would use whatever sweetener was most readily available, including Belgian candi sugar, sucrose, and even saccharin. Sometimes faro was a blend of aged lambic beer with freshly made low-alcohol lambic or even a low-alcohol non-lambic ale. Modern faro is usually stronger in alcohol, 4%–5% alcohol by volume (ABV), compared with historical examples, which would have been around 2%–3% ABV. Kegged versions, which are rare, are flash pasteurized to avoid refermentation of the added sugar. The current production volume of faro is very small, even when compared with other specialty beers in Belgium. Modern examples of faro are made by Belgian lambic breweries such as Brouwerij Lindemans, Brouwerij DeTroch, and Brasserie Cantillon. They are very sweet, showing limited lambic character, and appeal, it seems, to a very small audience.

See also BELGIUM and LAMBIC.

Keith Villa

Farsons Lacto Milk Stout is a sweet, dark beer (3.8% ABV) from the Mediterranean island of Malta.

"Milk stout" is a traditional British ale style brewed with lactose (milk sugar—the beer doesn't contain milk). Lactose cannot be fermented by ale yeast, so it stays behind in the finished beer, resulting in a sweet flavor and smooth body in a beer that's relatively low in alcohol. Historically, in a time of food shortages it was seen as a source of energy among working class families, and it has acquired a reputation as a tonic for the infirm. See MILK STOUT.

So it may seem unusual for one of the most noted examples of the style to be brewed not in the drizzle-gray streets of England, but on a sun-baked Mediterranean island.

Napoleon invaded Malta in 1798, and it was taken by the British 2 years later. It became part of the British Empire, an important staging post on sea journeys to India. British brewer Simonds of Reading began exports to the island in the late 1800s, and in 1927 helped local brewer Farrugia and Sons set up business. The two brewers merged in 1946, abbreviated the name to Farsons, and launched Lacto Milk Stout the same year.

Farsons Lacto Milk Stout is a dark beer with a brown head, a malty aroma, low bitterness, and flavors of chocolate and currants on the palate. The modern beer has lactose and vitamin B added after fermentation, as well as caramel coloring.

As well as its fame as a tonic, the beer is a popular ingredient in Christmas puddings, and enjoys a surge in sales in November.

Simonds Farsons Cisk. www.farsons.com (accessed April 15, 2011).

Pete Brown

Fat Tire Amber Ale

See NEW BELGIUM BREWING COMPANY.

fatty acids, a subcategory of lipids, comprises a range of related organic chemicals that includes fats, oils, and waxes. Their physical properties are largely determined by the length and degree of unsaturation of the hydrocarbon fraction of their molecular structures. The nonpolar hydrocarbon chain accounts for the poor solubility of fatty acids in water while the carboxylic acid group is polar and accounts for the higher solubilities of short-chain fatty acids in water. Butyric acid, for example, with only four carbon atoms is readily soluble in water. The simplest lipids constructed from fatty acids are triglycerides, better known as fats.

Fatty acids are relevant in brewing because they negatively affect the organoleptic stability of beer during aging. The breakdown of unsaturated fatty acids such as linoleic and linolenic acids into staling compounds such as (E)-2-nonenal, known for its typical "cardboard flavor," is well documented. See (E)-2-NONENAL. On the other hand, fatty acids are essential elements in yeast metabolism. Long chain unsaturated fatty acids are used to create other lipids such as sterols in cellular membranes. Instead of supplying fatty acids to the wort itself, brewers will promote synthesis of these fatty acids by generous aeration of the wort, oxygen being required for the desaturation of the molecules. However, interesting work recently done by New Belgium Brewing Company of Colorado suggests that an addition of olive oil to yeast during storage can supply yeast with the fatty acids it needs for cell wall construction and good fermentative capacity. Oleic acid, a fatty acid contained in olive oil, may be capable of supporting yeast health without the destabilizing oxidative effects of wort aeration.

Wolfgang David Lindell

faults in beer, in broadest terms, refer to any attribute found in beer that was not intended by the brewer. It is imperative to understand that faults are not necessarily dictated by sensory preference or even stylistic guidelines, but rather are deviations from a standard developed by the brewer. When discussing faults, context is fundamental; a characteristic considered normal and essential for one beer may be appalling in another. The horsey, barnyard flavors evolved from Brettanomyces may be beguiling as part of a Belgian gueuze, but less so in an American mass-market lager.

Faults can be broken down into two general categories: those derived during the brewing process and those resulting postpackaging. These groups can then be subcategorized into sensory or physical defects.

To assure consistency, product specifications are established for every beer by identifying critical control points throughout the brewing process. Once a control point is identified, a target value is set along with an operating range (normally three standard deviations). Detailed analysis is performed on control points utilizing myriad instrumentation and human methods. Common faults originating in the brewery include bacterial spoilage, ingredient variation, haze, and improper carbonation level.

Bacterial spoilage is perhaps the most feared of beer faults, especially for nonpasteurizing breweries. Ironically, the cooked, oxidized flavor that can be imparted by pasteurization is also often considered a fault. Brewers thoroughly clean and sanitize all equipment that contacts beer to reduce the possibility of contamination. Sanitation is crucial during the entire process, but especially after wort cooling, when wort and beer temperatures are ideal for bacterial growth. Chemical sanitizers, if used improperly, can taint finished beer, so very hot water is often used. Lactobacillus, pediococcus, and acetobacter are common spoilage organisms that can impart sour, tart, buttery, and vinegar-like notes. See ACETIC ACID BACTERIA, LACTOBACILLUS, and PEDIOCOCCUS. They are considered acceptable or desirable in sour beer styles, but not in most others.

Ingredient variance is a major concern for brewers. Beer is comprised of four main ingredients: malted barley (and/or other grains), hops, yeast, and water. Year-to-year barley and hop growing conditions, changes in the water supply, or poor yeast health will result in inconsistent raw materials for brewing. These differences can result in changes in color, hop bitterness and flavor, aroma, mouthfeel, and alcohol content.

Some faults are not olfactory or sensory, but rather, visual. The adage "you taste with your eyes" applies to beer haze. Haze is any cloudiness present in the beer at normal consumption temperature and can be caused by protein–polyphenol complexes, yeast, residual diatomaceous earth DE, or bacterial infection. Filtration, clarifying agents, and centrifugation are employed to reduce these hazes, but beer must be properly aged for optimal quality. The absence of haze can also be considered a fault when discussing certain beer styles that the consumer expects will be served cloudy (e.g., hefeweizen). Improper color is another visual fault. For example, the color of traditional pilsner beer may be pale gold to deep gold, but should not display reddish amber tinges.

Carbonation plays a significant role in beer not only in appearance and head retention but also in flavor presentation. Naturally carbonated beer relies on yeast to produce the proper level of carbonation, whereas forced carbonation uses high-pressure CO_2 mechanically dissolved into solution. Undercarbonated beer will be flat tasting and have difficulty forming and holding a significant head. Overcarbonated beer may result in gushing and will taste harsh, and the "burn" of the CO_2 content will drown out the more subtle flavors in the beer. Again, this is a matter of the expectations of the brewer and consumer. A Belgian saison will usually have a very high, Champagne-like carbonation, whereas British cask-conditioned beers should have a brisk tickle of CO_2 on the palate.

Breweries utilize many practices to assure beer quality, perhaps none as vital as sensory analysis. All sensory analysis revolves around the taste panel. Panelists are selected by their ability to identify flavors and aromas. Because individuals have unique sensitivities and genetic blind spots, sensory scientists must develop and train panelists thoroughly before data become relevant. Panels are conducted in isolated rooms with noise and aroma dampeners. Red lights are often used to hide color differences. Sensory assessments are described as difference or descriptive tests. Difference tests ask whether one sample is different from another and include the triangle test, paired comparison test, and the duo–trio test. Descriptive methodologies require more training and often rank attributes on a scale. Trueness to type tests ask respondents to rank attributes of a sample compared with a known standard. All sensory data are statistically analyzed, often using complex software programs.

Breweries strive to put the best possible beer into package, only to face the inevitable assault of aging. The three biggest causes of faults in packaged beer are sunlight, heat, and oxygen. Light below 550 nm in wavelength causes the breakdown of hop iso-alpha acid molecules, resulting in sunstruck or lightstruck beer. See LIGHTSTRUCK. This skunky flavor and aroma is detectable at concentrations as low as 0.1 part per billion (ppb). Heat and oxygen promote oxidized flavors, perhaps the leading fault in beer in market. Good producers will provide "best by" dates so the consumer can avoid beer that may be past its prime. Packaging methods aim to keep oxygen levels below 80 ppb in the finished product to maximize shelf life, but low levels only slow the aging process; heat speeds the reaction. Oxidized characters are described as papery, cardboard, and vegetal. However, some beer styles are meant to age, and in those, slow oxidation can produce sherry-like flavors that are considered highly desirable, although they would not be accepted in a younger beer.

See also AGING OF BEER, BEER SPOILERS, CARBONATION, HAZE, LAMBIC, OFF-FLAVORS, and SOUR BEER.

Kilcast, David. *Sensory analysis for food and beverage quality control: A practical guide*. Cambridge, UK: Woodhead Publishing Ltd, 2010.

O'Rourke, Tim. Flavour quality. *Brewer's Guardian*, December (2000): 29–31.

Jeff S. Nickel

fermentability of a wort is described as the ratio between the fermentable sugars in wort and the non-fermentable portion of the dissolved wort solids. The fermentable sugars are glucose, fructose, sucrose, maltose, and maltotriose, and generally account for 60%–70% of the total dissolved solids. The degree of fermentability of the wort can be manipulated by the brewer using different mashing techniques and different ingredients. Mashing conditions that favor the action of the enzymes beta amylase and limit dextrinase in the mash create more fermentable worts. Simple sugars can be added to the wort to increase its fermentability. This can also be achieved by the addition of exogenous glucoamylases that generate fermentable sugars from non-fermentable dextrins. This technique is often used to create "low-carb" mass-market beers. Whether all fermentable sugars in any given wort will actually be fermented is dependent on conditions and the yeast strain at hand; fermentability therefore refers only to the sugar profile presented by the wort.

Steve Parkes

fermentation is the process whereby "sugars" are converted by yeast to alcohol, carbon dioxide, and heat. In the brewing of most traditional beer, the sugars are derived mainly from malted barley, although other cereal sources and other plant sugars can also be used. These materials also contribute proteinaceous substances, which in concert with the sugars and added flavoring agents, notably hops, generate the alcohol, flavors, and aromas that we know and love as beer. The fermentation process has been practiced over many thousands of years, with the predilection for consuming alcohol as a common feature of practically all civilizations throughout history. In ancient societies, drinking beer had obvious physiological and psychological benefits (at least with moderate consumption) and also public health advantages; it was safe to drink, unlike many sources of water. Aside from this, the apparently mysterious nature of fermentation lent itself to exaltation in various religious, cult, and ritual ceremonies. Beverages that we can broadly classify as beers have been produced throughout the world for thousands of years. Despite the important place of beer in so many cultures for thousands of years, the nature of the fermentation process remained a mystery until the second half of the 19th century. The role of yeast in the biological transformation of sugars to beer was not fully recognized until microscopists were able to associate their observations with both the production of alcohol by yeast and the spoilage of beer by other microorganisms. However, for centuries before, it had been recognized that what was called "Godisgood" in early English—effectively yeast—was important in the brewing of beer. Nevertheless, despite these empirical observations, the prevailing scientific view was that fermentation was an inanimate, strictly chemical process. Indeed, the word "fermentation" is derived from the Latin *fevere,* meaning to boil, with the implication that the vigorous carbonation arising from fermentation, visually akin to boiling, caused the production of the intoxicating nature and flavors of beer. Louis Pasteur was decisive in persuading the sceptical scientific community of the mid to late1800s that fermentation was the result of the action of yeast on sugars, although by that time many practicing brewers and scientists involved in brewing were already well aware of the role of yeasts, even if they did not entirely understand the process. Furthermore, Pasteur was able to show that other microorganisms were the cause of "diseased" fermentations and that hygienic conditions were essential in the production of beer (and wine) of sound quality. Pasteur's work stimulated a surge in the scientific investigation of fermentation in Europe. At the Carlsberg Laboratories in Copenhagen, the pioneering studies of Emil Hansen on pure culture brewing techniques were quickly adopted by brewers throughout the world. In England, and most notably in Burton-on-Trent, leading scientists of the time including Cornelius O'Sullivan, Johann Peter Griess, and the half-brothers Adrian John and Horace Tabberer Brown were developing the understanding of the scientific basis of brewing and fermentation, much of which underpinned the new science of biochemistry. Throughout the 20th century, research on yeasts at a biochemical and genetic level continued at pace, with the characterization of the type species, Saccharomyces cerevisiae, being of economic importance in brewing, baking, and winemaking. Although it is a single-celled organism, S. cerevisiae is a simple form of a eukaryotic cell in that it has a nucleus enclosing genetic material as chromosomes, which is defined by a membrane. Animal cells, including our own, are also eukaryotic, albeit of greater sophistication. However, the eukaryotic relationship was exploited in that the S. cerevisiae genome was the first eukaryote to be gene sequenced in 1996, paving the way for the sequencing of the human genome 10 years later. It is remarkable that from observations relating to the fermentation of beer, our understanding of our own genetic makeup and biochemical functioning at cellular and molecular level has developed to its current levels, directly impacting our medical well-being. In that context, we should also note that the developments of industrial scale fermentation used in brewing beer were utilized and adapted to the production of antibiotics from the 1940s onward. It is fair to argue that fermentation, and that of beer in particular, has profoundly influenced our physical well-being more than any other development in our social history, perhaps with the exception of the provision of safe water supplies and public health sanitation.

Fermentation is the second of the three principal stages in the brewing of beer and as such cannot be considered in isolation. The first stage involves the preparation of wort, an aqueous medium comprising mainly fermentable sugars derived usually from starch-rich cereals but also assimilable nitrogen, oxygen, sources of sulfur and phosphates, the vitamin biotin, calcium, and magnesium ions, together with trace elements such as copper and zinc. The exact quantities of these substances will vary depending on the source and proportions of the raw materials used. For example, worts derived from grists with a high proportion of nonmalted starch may need supplementing with sources of nitrogen, biotin, and some trace elements to compensate for the dilution of the malt material, which is usually rich in these components. These supplements are called "yeast food" or "yeast nutrients," a reflection of the need to sustain growth of the yeast, at least during the early stages of fermentation. Most worts would be expected to contain about 70%–75% fermentable sugars, glucose, sucrose, and fructose, but mainly maltose and maltotriose. The remaining carbohydrate comprises nonfermentable material, mainly longer chain and branched glucose polymers. Nitrogen requirements for wort are usually measured in terms of free amino nitrogen (FAN); for a wort of specific gravity 1.040 (10° Plato) a typical FAN level would be about 150 mg/l. In addition to variations in raw material sources, the relative level of sugars and nitrogenous materials is profoundly influenced by the conditions of mashing and, to a lesser extent, wort boiling. Low temperatures during mashing (45°C–50°C [113°F–122°F]) favor protein breakdown (proteolysis) and therefore increases in FAN levels. On the other hand, higher mash temperatures (60°C–65°C [140°F–149°F]) reduce proteolysis but increase the activity of amylase enzymes, leading to an increase in fermentable sugars. Thus, by manipulating raw material content and processing conditions, the brewer can adjust wort composition to produce a consistent material ready for the addition of yeast and subsequent fermentation. However, the dissolved oxygen content of the wort is a critical parameter in sustaining yeast growth in the early stages of fermentation. To some extent different yeast strains have differing requirements for oxygen, and worts of varying strengths will also demand different levels. Too much oxygen results in particularly vigorous fermentations, which not only affects beer flavor but also causes excessive yeast growth at the expense of alcohol production. Too little oxygen can cause limited yeast growth, which will result in not only incomplete fermentation but also poor yeast vitality and viability, to the detriment of subsequent repitching of that batch of yeast. Traditionally worts of 1.040 specific gravity would be aerated prior to yeast pitching, giving dissolved oxygen levels of about 6 parts per million (ppm) at 20°C. More modern fermentation systems use oxygen levels at 8–12 ppm, generated by direct injection of oxygen rather than air into the wort stream. The wort prior to pitching should ideally be bright and clear, although it is argued that small amounts of precipitated protein and polyphenol material, called trub or break, can be beneficial in supplying lipids for yeast growth. See TRUB. Brewers vary in their attitudes toward bright worts, with some preferring extremely clear worts, whereas others are content with a slight haze. At the end of the day, it is the success of the fermentation and the stability of the resulting beer that will determine the wort requirements.

Management of the fermentation process is dependent on a number of factors, including the composition and oxygen content of the wort, the quality and quantity of the yeast used for pitching, temperature control in the fermenter, time, and the fermenter design.

Healthy yeast is at the heart of sound fermentation. Unlike traditional winemaking, with the exception of relatively rare "spontaneously fermented" beer styles, brewing depends upon the yeast added by the brewer. The specific strain of yeast is critical to the outcome of the fermentation, not only in the ability of the yeast to metabolize the wort contents to produce alcohol and distinctive flavor characteristics but also in the capacity of the yeast to tolerate its own products of metabolism, most notably alcohol, and the particular attribute of aggregation (flocculation) or otherwise that the yeast strain may normally exhibit. See FLOCCULATION. Brewers jealously guard their yeast strains although catalogs of so-called brewing strains are held in various collections throughout the world and can be obtained commercially. Some brewers, particularly traditional ale brewers in the UK, have used the same brewing strain (or strains) unchanged for decades, relying on serial repitching of the collected yeast at the end of fermentation. However, with repeated repitching some yeast strains exhibit subtle changes in character, particularly in flocculation characteristics, and a decline in viability and vitality. Most commercial brewers will repitch for up to 10 cycles or generations before replacing the yeast with a freshly propagated culture of the yeast grown from a starter culture. Brewing strains can utilize a wide variety of carbohydrate sources, although individual strains will vary in their particular appetites. Ale strains of S. cerevisiae are able to ferment glucose, sucrose, fructose, galactose, raffinose, maltotriose, and occasionally trehalose. Lager strains of S. cerevisiae (sometimes also called Saccharomyces carlsbergensis) are also able to ferment the disaccharide melibiose, whereas S. cerevisiae var diastaticus is also able to utilize some of the higher glucose polymers, called limit dextrins, which are out of reach of the other strains. Ale strains are generically described as "top fermenters" on account of their tendency to form a head or crust on the top of traditional open fermenters at the end of fermentation. Lager strains on the other hand, tend to separate out at the bottom of the fermentation vessel and hence enjoy the description of "bottom fermenters." With modern fermentation systems employing cylindroconical fermenters for both ales and lagers, this traditional differentiation is these days less clear-cut. See ALE YEAST and LAGER YEAST.

Although the primary function of fermentation is to convert sugars into alcohol, for the yeast to fulfill this requirement it must be present in sufficient quantity to effect the transformation. The yeast used to ferment is usually one or several generations old and, as a consequence of storage prior to pitching and the physiological condition at the end of the previous fermentation, it is depleted of nutrients for growth and fermentation. It is said to be in a stationary phase of growth and requires the stimulus of fresh wort nutrients, particularly oxygen, to rebuild its nutrient store and recommence growth and multiplication. Pitched brewing yeast will normally take several hours to adapt to its new environment before growth begins. This period is known as the lag phase and precedes a period of very active growth and metabolism, known as the exponential or logarithmic phase. The yeast will multiply four- or fivefold by a process of budding and build up its nutrient store, while at the same time commencing the conversion of sugars in the wort. The oxygen present at the start of pitching is rapidly used up by the yeast and is not involved in the fermentative process. The sugars present in the wort are taken in to the yeast cell and broken down into smaller units, ultimately producing alcohol, carbon dioxide, heat, and a vast range of other compounds, many of which contribute distinctive flavors and aromas to beer. At the same time, the nitrogenous compounds in the wort are also assimilated by the yeast, and as well as being used in the growth of yeast, they are metabolized and contribute to the rich flavor spectrum. When all available sugars have been utilized, the yeast will begin to use its own carbohydrate reserves (glycogen and trehalose) and effectively shut down its metabolism. This is known as the stationary phase of growth.

The fermentation temperature is critical in controlling the outcome of fermentation and has a significant impact on the development of flavor. Ales are generally fermented in the temperature range of 16°C to 22°C (61°F–72°F) using top-fermenting strains, whereas lagers are fermented much cooler, 9°C–14°C (48°F–57°F), using bottom-fermenting strains. Some beers, particularly Belgian styles, may be fermented very warm, with temperatures reaching almost 32°C (90°F) for some farmhouse ales. See SAISON. The combination of specific yeast strains and temperature generates very distinctive flavor profiles in the beers, with the ales and particularly stouts generally producing fruity/estery characters, whereas the lagers feature much lower ester levels, enabling more of the delicate pale malt characters and hop aromas to manifest on the nose. Fermentation is an exothermic process in that heat is produced and control of the heat generated is essential in fermentation control. Brewing vessels are equipped with cooling equipment of varying levels of sophistication, designed to effect cooling at the appropriate times in fermentation. Cooling is important in moderating yeast flocculation in that it tends to encourage yeast to flocculate. This is necessary at the end of fermentation to facilitate yeast separation, but if applied too early, it can cause incomplete fermentation and leave excessive levels of diacetyl in the finished beer. See DIACETYL.

The progress of the fermentation is usually monitored by following the specific gravity drop and/or increase in alcohol content. Yeast growth and alcohol production deplete the sugar concentration and the pH falls as nitrogenous materials are used up and the yeast secretes organic acids. Flavor compounds are generated during yeast growth, although some volatile components are lost with the exhaust carbon dioxide, whereas other compounds (notably diacetyl) are absorbed and metabolized by the yeast. Traditional ale fermentations at between 16°C and 20°C (61°F and 68°F) will normally take about 4 days to complete, whereas lagers at 12°C will be up to 10 days.

There are many different types of fermentation vessels used in the brewing of beer. This reflects the beer being brewed, the volume required, tradition, the relative age of the equipment, and the type of yeast being used, particularly in relation to the use of top- or bottom-fermenting yeasts. The earliest fermenters were small and probably reflected the availability of local materials, be it clay for earthenware vessels, wooden barrels, or slate (stone) vessels used in Britain. As brewing operations increased in size, metal, particularly copper, was used although the vessels were generally shallow. At the end of fermentation, the yeast was collected from the top of the fermenter and used to pitch subsequent brews.

The introduction of taller, narrower vessels facilitated the selection of bottom-fermenting yeast strains but taller vessels demanded more efficient cooling systems and methods for cleaning. Additionally, tall vessels generate differing hydrostatic pressures, which can impact yeast performance and mitigate against homogeneity throughout the vessel. Nevertheless, this type of vessel has developed into the cylindroconical fermenter that is now used by most of the larger brewers throughout the world and many smaller breweries as well. With facilities for in-place cleaning, carbon dioxide collection, automatic temperature control through cooling jackets, and yeast collection, these vessels can be further adapted to store the beer at lower temperatures after primary fermentation and yeast removal, a process known as conditioning or maturation. These vessels are sometimes known as combined fermentation and conditioning tanks and can have capacities up to several thousand hectoliters.

However, despite the use of these larger fermenting vessels, many brewers still use more traditional methods of fermentation. Rectangular or circular shallow tanks are still used in many small and medium-size breweries, particularly for traditional ales, wheat beers, and classic lagers of central Europe. In Britain, two very distinctive fermentation systems still operate, known as the Burton Union system and Yorkshire squares. In the Burton Union system, now sadly operated in the UK only by Marston's Brewery in Burton-on-Trent, a series of twelve 7-hl oak casks are connected via a "swan neck" to a central trough. Wort is pitched into an open square vessel on the floor above and run into the casks. As fermentation continues, yeast and carbon dioxide are forced through the swan neck and into the top trough. Most of the yeast separates from the part-fermented wort, which is returned to the cask to complete the fermentation. See BURTON UNION SYSTEM. Yorkshire squares are rectangular fermenters, traditionally made of slate but now mostly of stainless steel construction, incorporate a false ceiling. Fermenting yeast rises though a central hole (0.6-m [24 in] diameter with a 5-cm [2 in] rim) and collects on the top of the ceiling, whereas fermenting wort flows back into the fermenter via a series of narrow holes. At the end of fermentation, the collected yeast is removed by suction. See YORKSHIRE SQUARE.

For more than a century, brewers have experimented with the principle of continuous fermentation in which a fermenting vessel is fed continuously with wort, with beer produced in a continuous stream at the same rate as wort addition. Although this type of system has operated in New Zealand for over 40 years, it is not widely used because of difficulties in preventing infections and holding the yeast culture in a steady state. Recently, however, holding yeast on a bed of wood chips has proved to be effective in retaining the yeast. This process is known as an "immobilized yeast" system and is now being used commercially. See CONTINUOUS FERMENTATION and IMMOBILIZED YEAST REACTOR.

Beer at the end of the primary fermentation process is sometimes referred to as "green beer." Before it can be packaged and dispensed, the beer is usually subject to a further processing, which can include secondary fermentation, conditioning, and maturation. In secondary fermentation, the green beer is kept in contact with the yeast after the primary fermentation has ended. This process is most commonly practiced in the brewing of cask ales (also known as "real ale" or "traditional draught"). At the end of the primary fermentation, most of the yeast is removed but a small concentration, usually 0.5 to 2 million cells/ml, is left. A small amount of additional sugar, known as "priming sugar" or "primings," either in the form of sucrose or glucose, is added, which stimulates a secondary fermentation. Very little alcohol is produced (about 0.1%) but the main reason for priming is the generation of additional carbon dioxide, which gives the beer extra carbonation, or "condition," as it is known. Traditionally this primings addition would have taken place in the cask itself but it is now usually added just prior to filling the casks, in a vessel that is known as the "racking tank." See CASK CONDITIONING and CELLARMANSHIP, ART OF.

A similar process occurs in the production of "bottle-conditioned" beers, where secondary fermentation takes place in the bottle. In addition to giving the beer condition, the residual yeast also scavenges any small amounts of dissolved oxygen picked up at the time of filling the bottle. This antioxidant effect can help to extend the shelf life of the beer. See BOTTLE CONDITIONING.

One traditional form of secondary fermentation practiced, particularly in Germany, is known as "kräusening." A proportion of actively fermenting wort is added to beer that is maturing in lager tanks to stimulate secondary fermentation and remove diacetyl and aldehydes, as well as provide additional carbonation. See KRÄUSENING.

See also ALE, LAGER, and LAMBIC.

Boulton, Chris, and David Quain. *Brewing yeast and fermentation*. New York: Blackwell Science, 2001.

Forget, C. *Dictionary of beer and brewing*. Denver, CO: Brewers Publications, 1988.

Lewis, Michael J., and Tom W. Young. *Brewing*, 2nd ed. New York: Kluwer Academic/Plenum Publishers, 2001.

George Philliskirk

fermentation vessels, also known as fermenters or FVs (and occasionally spelled fermentors), are the tanks, barrels, or other vessels where wort is held as it ferments into beer.

Fermentation vessels have always been an essential part of even the humblest home-based brewery. They have been almost infinitely varied over time; almost anything that can hold liquid can be a potential fermenter. That said, the technology used for fermentation vessels has progressed considerably during the past 50 years.

Historical Development of Fermentation Vessels

Historically, the development of fermentation vessels has very closely reflected the development of brewing methods and technology. The first beers were probably fermented in animal-skin pouches and carved wooden bowls. Starting in the early Sumerian and Egyptian civilizations (circa 4000 BC), from whence we have the first written records of brewing, the vessels used were ceramic amphora-like jars, probably up to a few hundred liters in size. These ceramic jars remained the fermentation and storage vessels for most beers (and also wines) for thousands of years.

It is in the period between 500 and 1000 AD that we see the first historical evidence of brewing methods in northern Europe. By this time the preferred fermentation vessel was made of wood, usually oak, and oak remained a preferred material well into the 1800s. See OAK. Raw unlined wood was used at first, but by the 1800s most wooden fermentation vessels were lined with some sort of tar, pitch, or resin. The lining acted as an inert surface that prevented the beer from coming into direct contact with the rather soft, rough, and penetrable surface of the wood. Lined wooden vessels could be cleaned

Cylindroconical tanks at the Paulaner Brewery in Munich. Cylindroconical tanks have a slanted, cone-shape bottoms which, among other advantages, allows brewers to easily remove yeast for disposal or repitching. ROGER PUTMAN

more effectively, thus significantly increasing the stability of the beer against both microbiological infection and off-flavors from the wood itself. Wooden fermentation vessels were constructed in various dimensions—small or large, open or closed, upright or horizontal. Until quite recently, the fermentation vessels at Pilsner Urquell were still a forest of open wooden vats, each on its own pedestal. See PILSNER URQUELL. By the time of the Industrial Revolution, many wooden fermenting vessels were enormous in size. The most famous (or infamous) of them was a fermenting vat at the Meux "Horse Shoe" Brewery in London. See MEUX REID & CO. This wooden fermentation vessel was 22 ft tall and held over a half million liters of fermenting beer. At 6:00 PM on October 17, 1814, one of the 29 giant iron hoops that secured the vessel snapped. The vat burst, causing a chain reaction with surrounding vats, blowing out the wall of the building, and flooding the street. Two houses were washed away and nine people died in the "London Beer Flood."

This incident, among others, spurred breweries to begin looking for other materials than wood for large fermenting vessels. Later in the 19th century most new and expanding large breweries would include square concrete fermentation tanks lined with resin, asphalt, slate, or enamel. Here is a description of a 19th century–style London brewery, as described in 1911:

> The next process is that of fermentation, which is carried on in a splendid room below, the floor of which is constructed entirely of slate. It is known as the "Havelock Room," having been built at the time of the Indian Mutiny, and is shaped like the letter L with dimensions of 210 ft. and 132 ft. Here are contained fermenting vessels of slate and wood, each provided with a copper parachute for skimming yeast, communicating with the yeast tanks below. Each of the vessels holds from 120 to 190 barrels and contains an attemporator to raise or lower the temperature of the gyle at pleasure. This contrivance consists of a series of pipes fixed within the tun and having its inlet and outlet on the outside; by this means it is possible to run hot or cold water through the pipes at any hour.

Active fermentations give off considerable heat, and fermentation temperatures can rapidly rise to a point where flavors and yeast health are adversely affected. The ability to cool fermenting beer was therefore important, especially during the warm summer months. The introduction of mild steel tanks coincided with the spreading use of industrial "artificial" refrigeration. First introduced at Germany's Spaten Brewery in 1871, artificial refrigeration allowed fermentation vessels to be cooled by means other than the "natural" cooling achieved by digging deep fermentation cellars. These cellars had been cooled by vast quantities of ice cut out of rivers and lakes in winter and then placed over the cellar ceilings and below cellar floors. In the early days of refrigeration, cooling of fermentation vessels was achieved either by circulating refrigerated air in the fermentation cellars or by circulating cooled water or brine through metal coils inside the tanks. Normally the coils were made of copper or brass because these materials both conduct temperature efficiently and are not corroded to a major extent by wort or beer. The cooling coils would be placed along the sides or the bottoms of the fermentation vessels. By manually opening and closing the valves on the cooling coils, it was possible to rapidly chill beer, even during active fermentation. However, this method remained primitive and the temperature from vessel to vessel could vary greatly because the tanks were both open and uninsulated.

Around the turn of the 20th century, rapid industrialization brought the widespread use of mild steel for all types of construction. Mild steel became the preferred material for building fermentation vessels. Because mild steel is very susceptible to corrosion by acidic liquids such as beer, direct contact with beer would cause the vessels to rust, giving the beer a notable metallic flavor and aroma. Thus, mild steel tanks had to be lined, and the preferred materials for this were enamel, glass, and later epoxy-type polymer materials. As long as the enamel or glass lining stayed intact, this was a perfectly sanitary and easy-to-clean inner tank surface. However, both enamel and glass are very brittle materials that eventual start to chip and crack, as does epoxy. Many brewery operations remained manual, including tank cleaning, and men had to enter these vessels and hand scrub them after every use. The linings were easily damaged but very difficult to repair.

One thing was improving; although open fermentation was still practiced by some large American breweries into the 1970s, the norm in the United States slowly transitioned to completely closed fermentation. This made fermentation more sanitary and eased the collection and reuse of carbon dioxide created by the yeast.

Around 1920, aluminum became affordable, and many breweries started installing fermentation tanks made of this much lighter metal. Aluminum had the huge advantage of being resistant to corrosion by wort and beer and could therefore be used without having to apply a brittle inner lining. One major disadvantage of aluminum, however, is that it is corroded by caustic soda (sodium hydroxide), which has for many decades been the preferred detergent for cleaning brewery equipment.

Soon after the introduction of aluminum, stainless steel was introduced as a construction material on an industrial scale. This material offered many advantages when used in breweries in general and to this day is the undisputed first choice of material for constructing fermentation vessels. Also, piping, pumps, valves, and almost all other brewery equipment that comes into direct contact with beer are made of stainless steel.

Until the 1960s, whether constructed from mild steel, aluminium, or stainless steel, most fermenters were cylindrical in shape and positioned horizontally. Usually they were stacked in several layers in the fermentation cellars, and it was uncommon to individually insulate the tanks because this was relatively expensive. For this reason, all fermentation vessels were used for primary fermentation only, so when active fermentation had finished, the beer would be moved by means of pumps and hoses to another tank in a separate cellar for the final maturation. Bottom-fermented (lager) beers would be placed for extended periods of time at low temperatures in the lagering cellars, whereas ales would be usually be transferred into a third cellar full of storage or racking tanks before being packaged.

Unitanks (Universal Tanks)

Developments continued during the late 1800s with upright cylindrical vessels, some with sloping or conical bottoms. In 1960s a breakthrough in technology advanced a new principle—primary fermentation and maturation could be carried out in the same vessel. The breakthrough was the modern "cylindroconical" tank, an upright cylindrical tank with a slanted, cone-shaped bottom. These were dubbed "universal tanks," or unitanks for short. Unitanks became widespread in the 1970s, and over the past 40 years the cylindroconical tank has—with a few important exceptions related to the brewing of very traditional beer styles in Belgium and on the British Isles—replaced all other types of fermentation vessels. It has been commonly accepted in the brewing industry that cylindroconical tanks have numerous advantages over all older tank designs:

1. They eliminate the need to move beer while in process, which is a huge advantage with respect to beer quality, process times, space utilization, and production economy.
2. Cleaning, sanitization, and microbiological control are far superior in cylindroconical tanks compared with older tank designs.
3. They can be individually and affordably insulated.
4. The degree of automation required in larger, modern breweries is much easier and less expensive than with older tank designs.
5. Collection of CO_2 during primary fermentation for regeneration (and reuse/sale) is easy in cylindroconical tanks as opposed to the old open fermenters.
6. Cropping yeast is efficient, more selective, and more sanitary in cylindroconical tanks than in the older tank types.

Interestingly, the cylindroconical tank has roots back to patents dating from 1908 and 1927, but the revolution in stainless steel fabrication was necessary to make the manufacture and use of such tanks practical. The proliferation of cylindroconical tanks began in Ireland in the early 1960s, where vertical (i.e., cylindrical tanks standing upright) stainless steel tanks of up to 11,500 hl (9798 US bbl) were in use. In 1965 the Japanese brewery Asahi patented a large vertical tank with a sloped bottom, allowing the yeast to be harvested from the low side. See ASAHI BREWERIES. The first large-scale brewery to install large numbers of cylindroconical tanks was the Rainier brewery in Seattle, Washington, around 1970. These tanks, dubbed Rainier tanks, did have a conical bottom, but with a very shallow cone angle of only 25°. Soon after, it was discovered that a steeper cone angle (70° is the modern standard) gave a more convenient cropping of the yeast that settled in the cone bottom after fermentation. Further evolution and development of the technology of cylindroconical tanks focused on the number and placement of cooling jackets. Cooling jackets are hollow "belts" welded onto the outer surface (but inside the layer of insulation and outer cladding) of the tank and through which coolant (either glycol at subfreezing temperatures or direct expanding ammonia) can be circulated, thus cooling the contents of the tank. The placement and size of cooling jackets are critical to ensure the optimal movement and mixing of the beer during fermentation, thus ensuring the homogeneity that is particularly important in large tanks. During fermentation, the evolution of CO_2 can create powerful currents in the fermenting beer. When jackets toward the top of the tank are cooled, the cooled liquid drops toward the bottom of the tank. At the same time, beer toward the bottom of the tank, warmed by its own fermentation, rises toward the top of the tank, only to be cooled again. This action helps create a circulation and mixing of the liquid, promoting faster, healthier, more complete fermentations.

The overall geometry of tanks was also being explored in the 1970s and 1980s, resulting in taller and slimmer cylindroconical tanks, which saved floor space. However, it was soon found that once these so-called rocket tanks (in reference to their appearance) exceeded a height-to-diameter ratio of 5:1, good mixing could not be achieved and the yeast suffered from excessive hydrostatic pressure. Thus, today cylindroconical tanks are generally built with height-to-diameter ratios between 1:1 and 5:1.

Modern cylindroconical tanks have more than one cooling jacket. This serves two purposes: first, to give the aforementioned optimal thermal movement of the beer during fermentation, and second, to allow the brewer to operate the tank at less than full capacity. A cylindroconical tank will also have a "cleaning device" permanently installed in the top, allowing for easy and automated internal washing of the tank. See CLEANING IN PLACE (CIP). Further, there may be more than one outlet from the tank bottom, allowing the brewer to draw off beer from the tank without inclusion of yeast that has settled in the bottom of the cone.

Cylindroconical tanks were, from their introduction, well suited for being placed outdoors, thus saving space and building costs for larger breweries. Outside tanks are situated in so-called tank farms, where they are placed very closed to each other. This is made possible by the fact that no manual operations or servicing of the tanks take place in the tank farm itself. Rather, all piping to and from the tanks comes from the tank farm and through an adjacent wall to the beer-processing area inside the brewery. All automatic pumps, valves, or swing arms that need to be operated when using the tanks are placed here, largely eliminating the need for long hoses.

State of the Art in Fermentation Vessels

The most modern breweries still use cylindroconical tanks. The next step in process development could be the introduction of continuous fermentation with immobilized yeast. The most recent developments in the technology of these tanks involve what one could call "the accessories" of the tanks in the sense of mechanical mixing (recirculation by pumping from the bottom to the top) of the fermenting beer, as well as advanced control systems that automatically measure and control the progress of the fermentation. See CONTINUOUS FERMENTATION and IMMOBILIZED YEAST REACTOR.

Traditions Maintained

Not all of the traditional tank types have vanished with the introduction of the cylindroconical tank. The requirements of the process involved in brewing traditional English ales have made many large breweries stick to the traditional geometry of square tanks with a "penetrable ceiling," through which the traditional top-fermenting yeasts will accumulate at the end of primary fermentation and from where the yeast can be automatically harvested by a combination of valves and jets. This type of tank is called "Yorkshire Square," referring to its shape and the place where they were invented and became widespread during the 20th century. Modern Yorkshire squares can be as large in volume as cylindroconicals and are also closed and fitted with CIP facilities, thus making them just as easy to automate as cylindroconicals. But because they are more complex, they are also expensive in terms of investment, they take up more space, and they cannot normally be placed outdoors.

Many British breweries maintain the tradition of open fermentation. They feel strongly that the method has positive effects on yeast health and beer flavor. In Bavaria, open fermentation is sometimes used in the production of weissbier and occasionally for lager. Many brewers there believe that open fermentation tends to create a more intense aroma profile in weissbier than does closed fermentation.

Marston's Brewery of Burton-on-Trent, England, is known for having championed the once-common Burton Union system, where fermentation takes place in oak vats and expelled yeast travels between them in open troughs. It remains quite a thing to see, and Marston's brewers claim that the flavor of their flagship beer would not be the same without it.

See also BURTON UNION SYSTEM, FERMENTATION, and YORKSHIRE SQUARE.

Hough, J. S., D. E. Briggs, R. Stevens, and T. W. Young. *Malting and brewing science*, 2nd ed. Cambridge, UK: Cambridge University Press, 1982.

Kunze, Wolfgang. *Technology brewing and malting*, 3rd international ed. Berlin: VLB Berlin, 2004.

University of London, Institute of Historical Research. *A history of the county of Middlesex, Vol 2*. Oxford, UK: Oxford University Press, 1911. Digitized October 12, 2010.

Anders Brinch Kissmeyer and Garrett Oliver

ferulic acid is a phenolic acid found in cellulosic cell walls and in the cell walls of the starchy endosperms of cereals, including wheat and barley.

It is covalently attached to polysaccharides in these walls and is released by the action of an enzyme called feruloyl esterase. Ferulic acid is an antioxidant and has attracted much attention for its potential health benefits, including a possible role in countering cancer. It is a substrate for the enzyme ferulic acid decarboxylase, which converts ferulate into 4-vinyl guaiacol, with its distinctive clove-like aroma. See 4-VINYL GUAIACOL. This enzyme is present in the ale yeasts that are used in the production of weizenbiers, and the clove-like note is an index of authenticity. However, the enzyme is also elaborated by wild yeasts, e.g., Saccharomyces diastaticus, meaning that a clove or spicy note in beers other than weizenbiers tends to be an indicator of wild yeast contamination. Ferulic acid is also used extensively in industry, for example as the precursor of a vanilla substitute.

Ou, S, & Kwok, K.-C. Ferulic acid: Pharmaceutical functions, preparation and applications in foods. *Journal of the Science of Food and Agriculture*, 84 (2004): 1261–1269.

Charles W. Bamforth

filtration is the process of removing solids from liquid by passage across or through a porous medium. The effectiveness of filtration depends on particle size and filter medium porosity. Materials suspended in liquid will remain on or in the filter medium if they are larger than the pore opening. Filtration is widely used throughout brewing, and most beers sold today are filtered to some extent. The range of particle size removal is enormous, from the molecular level (1.0 μm) in water filtration to whole hop removal (1.0 cm) after the kettle boil.

There are two basic types of filtration: depth and surface. Depth filtration, also called powder filtration, uses a convoluted labyrinth of channels in the filter media to trap particles. The media can be diatomaceous earth (DE), Perlite, or other porous media. Depth filtration is often considered rough or primary filtration, though in many small breweries, this is the only filtration performed. Examples are plate and frame, screen, and candle filters. Surface filtration uses a thin film material with pores smaller than the particles to be removed. Particles remain on the surface of the filter while clarified liquid flows through. If the pores are of a defined size (for instance, up to 5 μm), filtration is said to be "absolute" to the pore size. Membrane and cross-flow filtration are examples.

Filter media, sometimes called filter aid, is critical to final liquid clarity. Lautering uses the grain bed, especially husk material, as the filter aid. Sweet wort is drawn through the grain bed and particles are trapped in the matrix. Hop backs use the same principle. The two most popular forms of filter media in use today are DE and Perlite. DE, also known by its German name of Kieselguhr, is a naturally occurring form of silica derived from the calcified skeleton remains of minute planktonic algae. Perlite is similar in nature but derived from volcanic rock and composed of aluminum silicate. The variety and complexity of shapes of these materials form a labyrinth of channels in the filter bed. However, there are pulmonary health risks, such as silicosis, associated with these materials. Handlers, therefore, must wear dust protection. In addition, the disposal costs of filter aids are substantial, which has lead to the development of alternative filtration methods. See DIATOMACEOUS EARTH and PERLITE.

Plate and frame filters consist of vertical plates covered with a filter cloth or pad. Adjacent to the plates are hollow frames that contain the filter aid. These alternate the entire length of the filter and terminate at end plates. Beer is fed into the frames, where media traps solids. Clear beer flows into the adjacent hollow plates and out of the filter through collection tubes. Similar in design is the sheet filter that uses compressed cellulose pads impregnated with DE. There are no open frames, but rather two sets of channeled plates. Turbid beer flows in on one side of the pad, and clear beer exits on the other. Sheet filters have less surface area than other powder filters, and are mainly used as secondary or polishing filters. They are often used after rough filtration, before packaging, and with the proper pads with a porosity of <0.45 μm can be used to produce sterile beer.

Screen filters use hollow mesh screens (leaves) mounted horizontally or vertically along a central shaft, housed inside a cylindrical vessel. In a process called pre-coating, a mixture of beer (or water) and DE is pumped into the vessel and recirculated until all the DE is trapped on the screens, and the liquid is clear. At this point beer is introduced. Because the high solids content of unfiltered beer would quickly blind (clog) the screens or the filter would exceed safe operating pressure, fresh DE is dosed in line with the beer. This keeps the bed labyrinth open by continually creating new channels. The nominal filtration range for screen filters is 3 to 5 μm, which can trap most large particles, including yeast.

Candle filters are similar to vertical screen filters, but instead of leaves, these have hollow, round tubes with narrow slotted openings. Operation is nearly identical, but the increased surface area of the candles allows for faster filtration while using less filter aid. See CANDLE FILTER.

Membrane filters are made of polymer materials and trap particles by virtue of their uniform pore size. They are capable of producing very finely filtered liquids but blind quickly.

Cross-flow filtration improves on traditional membrane filtration by rapidly pumping liquid across the filter surface (usually sintered alumina). Deposited solids are trapped and discharged, leaving the filter surface free from clogging. These filters are often brilliantly designed, but expensive to purchase and operate.

Various processing aids and techniques can reduce the amount of suspended solids before filtration and thus increase filter throughput. These include long, cold maturation times as well as fining agents. These can achieve acceptable clarity though natural sedimentation. Larger breweries sometimes use centrifugation as an alternative to filtration.

Filtration helps stabilize beer and give it a polished, clear appearance. It can also remove elements, such as dead yeast, that otherwise would eventually make the beer unpalatable. That said, especially smaller breweries and brewpubs often prefer to serve their beer unfiltered, because they see no advantage to a clear appearance and feel that something elemental may be lost during filtration. In fact, in several classic beer styles, including hefeweizen and in many Belgian bottle-conditioned beers, yeast turbidity is a defining element of the style.

Broderick, Harold. *The practical brewer*, 2nd ed. Madison, WI: Master Brewers Association of America, 1993.

Kidger, Paul. Solid and liquid separation. *Brewer's Guardian*, July (2001): 26–30.

Lewis, M. J., and Tom Young. *Brewing*. London: Chapman & Hall, 1996.

Jeff S. Nickel

final gravity is a measure of the specific gravity (ratio of the density of the beer to the density of water) or apparent extract of a beer at the end of fermentation. This reading will often be taken with a hydrometer (or saccharometer). While final gravity measures the unfermented substances left in the beer, it does not take into account the fact that the alcohol produced during the fermentation is lighter than water. This skews the reading, rendering it an "apparent extract" as opposed to "real extract." The final gravity is, however, a useful rough measure at the end of fermentation and can be used, in combination with the original gravity, to calculate the approximate ABV of the finished beer.

See also APPARENT EXTRACT, REAL EXTRACT, and SPECIFIC GRAVITY.

Keith Villa

finings are processing aids added to unfiltered beer to remove yeast and protein haze. During fermentation yeast cells and beer proteins largely derived from the malt form a colloidal suspension that appears as a haze. A colloidal suspension forms when very small, charged particles are suspended in a liquid. An electrostatic charge, known as a zeta potential, repels one particle from the next and serves to impede the settlement of the solid particles from the liquid phase.

In beer styles originating in the British Isles this turbidity was traditionally removed by the addition of a solution of a charged polymer solution. Examples include isinglass, gelatin, and gum arabic solutions. In unclarified beer, yeast cell walls carry a negative charge. Isinglass and gelatin solutions are proteins that carry a positive charge. When added to newly fermented beer, the charged finings interact with the yeast and neutralize the zeta potential present on the cell wall. This eliminates the repulsive forces and sticks the yeast cells together to form a larger particle called a floc. These larger particles settle considerably faster than they would otherwise, as dictated by Stokes' law.

The neutralization happens quickly and the use of finings can be remarkably efficient, so much so that it enabled British brewers to present fresh, unfiltered, cask-conditioned beer with a pleasing clarity without the need for filtration or extensive settling time. Some brewers will use finings to reduce the yeast suspended in beer before preparing a beer for filtration.

Preparations intended to precipitate proteins rather than yeast are referred to as auxiliary finings. Often derived from carrageenans or alginates, these preparations carry strong negative charges that attract and form flocs with positively charged proteins. Although yeast finings such as isinglass can be used in conjunction with auxiliary finings, they cannot be added at the same time because each would neutralize the other, rendering both fining agents ineffective.

See also GELATIN, ISINGLASS, and STOKES' LAW.

Ian L. Ward

Finland is a republic in northern Europe with a population of 5.3 million. Yearly beer production is approximately 110 million gallons (416 million liters) and beer consumption, as of 2010, approximately 23 gallons (87 liters) per capita.

In all probability beer has been made in Finland since primitive agriculture reached its then scarcely populated southern shore at about 2000–1500 BCE. Some scholars maintain that agriculture in Finland started because the migrating tribes had accustomed themselves to beer and needed cultivated grain to produce the drink.

Positive evidence of brewing exists from the first centuries CE. The craft was evidently influenced by German tribes; the Finnish word for beer, *olut*, is Germanic in origin, as are many other words related to brewing, even though the Finnish language has no Germanic roots. An often cited example of the status of beer in ancient Finland concerns the national epic poem *Kalevala*, a collection of orally preserved folkloristic poems, the oldest poems predating the arrival of Christianity to Finland. Kalevala describes the birth of the world in 200 lines. The birth of beer, on the other hand, takes 400 lines. In the rustic Finland of Kalevala beer is a communal drink, served at special occasions. The God of Beer was called Pekko. See BEER GODS.

During the Middle Ages the coastal trade centers grew to towns, drawing resident traders from the southern parts of the Baltic. These merchants brought along their own art of making beer, and the brewing soon followed the Central European mode. However, no professional class of brewers as such developed. Generally people brewed for their own household.

The new mode promoted the use of hops instead of bog myrtle, juniper, spruce cones, or natural herbs. Hops had been growing naturally in Finland since the end of the last Ice Age. Some academics have speculated that Finns used hops in their beer before the Middle Ages, but there is no concrete proof of this. In any case, the laws of 1347 and 1442 had austere orders about hop-growing: Every farm had to have a hop garden or pay a heavy fine. Beer and hops were also legal tender for payment of taxes.

At this time (13th to 15th centuries) the art of brewing the Finnish beer style sahti took shape. See SAHTI. The farmhouse-brewers adapted the methods and the equipment of the town brewers to their own ancient brewing tradition. Remarkably, the sahti tradition has survived all twists of history and is still very much alive.

The first attempts to brew beer on an industrial scale took place in the 1750s, but these early ventures failed, as the towns of that time were still too small to support them. The oldest company still brewing, Sinebrychoff, opened in Helsinki in 1819. See SINEBRYCHOFF BREWERY. After the breakthrough of bottom fermentation in the 1850s, industrial-scale brewing took off. In 1907 Finland had 90 active industrial breweries.

The temperance movement in 19th-century Finland was at first directed mainly against distilled spirits, but by the start of the 20th century it opposed beer as well. Political pressure led to the Prohibition Act, which came into effect in June 1919. Some breweries tried to survive Prohibition by making soft drinks and mild malt beverages, but most dissolved or went bankrupt. Illicit distilling and smuggling prospered, and alcohol consumption grew during the late 1920s to a level that was not reached again until 1961. Prohibition was repealed after a referendum was held in 1931.

In spite of the repeal there was no return to free trade in beer. The state took strict control by establishing a monopoly over all alcoholic beverages. The monopoly granted licenses for production of beer to private enterprises. Forty-four breweries got a license to produce beer in 1932.

Nearly all licensed beer was of the continental bottom fermented type, pale lagers. The only still-existing notable exception is Sinebrychoff porter, a world-class imperial stout launched in 1957.

Finland's entry in the European Union in 1995 forced the end of the all-embracing monopoly. However, the state has maintained the monopoly in the consumer retail sales of products over 4.7% ABV. Furthermore, the beer tax in Finland is the highest of all EU countries. In 2010 one liter (2.11 US pints) of 5% ABV beer had a tax of 1.30 euros ($1.75 in Feb 2010). See TAXES.

During the years of strict state control, the brewing industry began to consolidate until three large brewers were left. Only one, Olvi, remains in Finnish hands. The two others are owned by large global brewers: Sinebrychoff by Carlsberg and Hartwall by Heineken. Together this trio has cornered over 90% of the domestic market.

The first Finnish commercial microbreweries were sahti brewers who received their licenses from the government in 1987. During the 1990s microbreweries flourished, totalling over 40 before a recession struck. At the end of 2009 Finland had 30 working breweries.

The existing microbreweries brew ambitiously and produce high-quality beers. The best opportunities to sample their multitude of brews, in addition to the brewpubs themselves, are the Helsinki Beer Festival in spring and the "Suuret oluet–Pienet panimot" (Big beers–Small brewers) festival held in Helsinki during the last weekend of July. A handful of specialist pubs also have microbrews on tap.

As a result of the relaxation of the import regulations in 1995, the variety and quality of the imported beers has expanded. The volume of quality imports is negligible compared to the pale lager business, but the best Finnish pubs have a large variety of beers from all over the world.

Panimoliitto (Federation of the Brewing and Soft Drinks Industry). http://www.panimoliitto.fi/panimoliitto/en (accessed May 27, 2010).

Project Gutenberg. *Kalevala: The Epic Poem of Finland.* http://www.gutenberg.org/etext/5186 (accessed May 27, 2010).

Räsänen, Martti. *Vom Halm zum Fass. Die volkstümlichen alkoholarmen Getreidegetränke in Finnland.* Helsinki: Kansatieteellinen Arkisto, 1975.

Suuronen, Kerttu. *Ohrainen olut.* Helsinki: Otava, 1969.

Tikkanen, Unto. *Suomalaisen olutkirja.* Helsinki: Tammi, 1999.

Turunen, Matti. *Jos täytätte mun lasini. The century of the Finnish brewing and soft drinks industry.* Helsinki: Federation of the Brewing and Soft Drinks Industry, 2002.

Jussi Rokka

fir

See PINE, FIR, AND SPRUCE TIPS.

A **firkin** is a cask used by British brewers for delivery of cask-conditioned beer to the pub. A firkin holds a quarter of a barrel (9 Imperial gal; 10.8 US gal, 41 l). A firkin was originally coopered from wooden staves bound with iron hoops, but is now more commonly made of stainless steel or aluminum. Like all proper casks, it has a hole in one of the curved sides, to which a wooden or plastic bung ("shive") is fitted when the cask is filled. There is a smaller hole in one of the flat ends, or "heads," of the cask, which is also bunged. The bung is knocked out by the tap when the cask is broached. Although other sizes of cask are also used, the firkin is by far the most common.

The name "firkin" marks a milestone in the development of British brewing. The term originates from the Netherlands, as does "kilderkin" (18 Imperial gal; 21.6 US gal). Originally, ale was the common brew in Britain and was made without hops. See ALE. Hopped "beer" was introduced to Britain from the Netherlands, probably sometime before the 15th century; many of the early beer brewers in England were Dutch in origin and used their own terms for the casks in which they sold their products. The beer barrel was established in 1420 at 36 Imperial gal (43 US gal) compared with the ale barrel at 30 Imperial gal (36 US gal). Because hops not only conferred flavor to the beer but also acted as a preservative, beer eventually displaced unhopped ale, and the 36-gal barrel became the standard in Britain.

Kilby, K. *The village cooper*. Haverfordwest, Wales: Shire Publications, 1998.

Terry Foster

First Gold (hop) is an English dwarf variety released in 1995 by the Wye College hop breeding operation. It is a cross between a Whitbread Golding variety and a dwarf male. The First Gold aroma is similar to that of Golding, but it has higher alpha acid levels, which makes it a dual-purpose hop used for both bittering and aroma. Like most English varieties, First Gold exhibits a characteristic earthiness. As an aroma hop, it has a slightly spicy, citrus note that can give beer a faintly orange-like quality. It is perfectly suited for such very English beer styles as extra special bitter. First Gold is widely used for dry hopping. First Gold has an alpha acid range of 6% to 10%, a beta acid range of 3% to 4.1%, a cohumulone range of 32% to 35%, and a humulene average of 19%. It is fairly tolerant to wilts and powdery mildew, but susceptible to downy mildew. It matures in mid-season, with medium-size cones and a good yield of about 1,750 kg/ha (1,540 lb/acre); it stores moderately well. First Gold still has limited acreage, but many brewers like it and it seems likely to grow in popularity. Some yards were fully certified as organic in 2002.

Charles Faram & Co Ltd. *Hop varieties*. http://www.charlesfaram.co.uk/varietydetail.asp?VarietyID=UK-FG/ (accessed November, 17, 2010).

Hopsteiner. *First Gold*. http://www.hopsteiner.com/pdf/uk/First%20Gold.pdf (accessed November, 19, 2010).

Jon Griffin

first runnings, the heavy wort extracted from the mash at the start of the run-off, before any sparging has commenced. See SPARGING. Brewers will typically check the gravity of the first runnings as a rough indicator of the potential extract of the grains in the mash tun or lautering vessel. Gravities for first runnings vary widely depending on the water-to-grain ratio of the original mash and the gravity of the wort the brewer intends to derive from it. It is not unusual for the first runnings of the mash to exceed gravities of 20° Plato (specific gravity 1,080) and above. As the mash is sparged and the sugars are rinsed away, the gravity of the runnings gradually drops and the wort collected in the kettle becomes diluted to its intended gravity.

Very strong beers are sometimes made from concentrated worts that are made up of 90%–100% first runnings and may have original gravities exceeding 25° Plato (specific gravity 1,100). Taking only the first runnings prevents unwanted dilution of the wort but also leaves a high percentage of the potential sugar extract behind in the unrinsed spent grains. The parti-gyle system is sometimes used to extract those sugars into a second wort, thus putting them to use. See PARTI-GYLE. In part-gyling, the first runnings may go to one kettle as a concentrated wort, perhaps to make a barley wine or imperial stout. When sparging commences, the run-off is diverted to a second kettle to make a second, weaker wort, which will be boiled and fermented separately into a lighter beer. See SMALL BEER.

When brewers wish to make very strong beers from the first runnings, but have no use for any weaker wort that would be gained by sparging, the grains may be discharged from the mash or lauter vessel having been thoroughly drained, but never rinsed. Discarding this much malt extract is expensive and somewhat wasteful, but any farm animals fed such sugar-laden spent grain are in for a rare treat.

Garrett Oliver

first wort hopping is a method utilized to deliver additional hop flavor complexity to beer. It is quite probable that this method was initially discovered by accident when a brewer added hops to the kettle very early and then noted a flavor improvement in the finished beer or at least an increase in bitterness. First wort hopping was a common practice around the turn of the 20th century and was a practice used to increase hop utilization. The "rediscovery" research of this method was done in Germany focusing on pilsner style beer. The experiment was carried out in two German production lager breweries. A portion of the late kettle hops (the varieties Tettnanger and Saazer) were added to first runnings in the kettle and allowed to stay with the brew throughout the entire kettle program. The late hop/aroma addition was then omitted. In both test breweries, the beer brewed with the first wort hopping method was preferred organoleptically in blind tasting over the control beers. The panelists reported "a fine, unobstrusive hop aroma, a more harmonic beer, and a more uniform bitterness" when compared to the conventionally hopped reference beer. This would at first glance seem counterintuitive to most brewers since most have been trained to add hops for flavor and aroma toward the end of the kettle program, not before, believing most volatile hop aromatics would otherwise escape the wort. It is important to note that these beers were being critiqued in accordance with accepted and desired European hop qualities and would not likely be consistent with American hop characteristics or American craft brewer's notion of finer hoppy qualities.

In practice, a substantial portion of the hop bill is added to the kettle or wort receiving vessel at the initial stage of the run-off. The hops are then allowed to steep in the wort for the entire run-off and then remain in the wort for the duration of the kettle program. In the case of the rediscovery experimentation, 30%–53% of the entire hop bill was utilized for this addition. The hop charge utilized an aroma variety that was originally slated as the final aroma/flavor addition and normally would have been added 10 minutes before the end of the boil. First wort hopping appears to take advantage of higher pre-boiled wort pHs, thus higher hop component solubility. More important, it acts to drive off lighter oils like myrcene as well as other oils associated with "hoppy" character in finished beer where these characteristics are not desired. De Clerk wrote about a method similar to this where hops are steeped in 122°F (50°C) water prior to being added to the kettle. This was also done to drive off unwanted light hop oils that might otherwise survive the kettle operation and be passed on to finished beer. See DE CLERCK, JEAN.

First Wort Hopping is practiced by a number of craft brewers and is applied to a full range of styles both ales and lagers. It is best suited for beers that call for a "European noble" hop presence or a deep yet subtle and refined hop flavor. This method is not suited for beers that require volatile hop oil presence or fruity hop aroma; in fact, it is a method that works to avoid these characteristics all together.

Modern brewers have limited hop boiling times to a maximum of 90 minutes to avoid harsh flavors that come from thermal breakdown of humulone to humulitic acids. First wort boiling obviously challenges this line of thinking by employing extended extraction times.

See also HOP OILS, HUMULONE, and MYRCENE.

De Clerck, J. *A textbook of brewing*, vol. I, London: Chapman and Hill Ltd., 1958.

Preis, F., and W. Mitter. The rediscovery of first wort hopping, *Brauwelt Int.*,13 (1995): 308–15,

Schönfeld, F. *Handbook of brewing and malting*, vol. I, 1930.

Matthew Brynildson

Flag Porter. Researched and devised by Dr Keith Thomas at the Brewers' Laboratory (Brewlab) in London, Flag Porter is a historical recreation of a porter beer from the 19th century. In 1988 deep-sea divers from the City of London Polytechnic were investigating the wreck of a ship that had sunk in the English Channel in 1825. The divers found bottles of porter onboard the wreck, brought several to the surface, and gave them to Dr Thomas, who found that although the beer had been contaminated by seawater and was undrinkable, some original yeast was still alive inside the bottles. He was able to isolate a few living yeast cells from one bottle and culture them in his laboratory until he had a sufficient amount of yeast to make a batch of beer. The first brew took place in 1988 at the Pitfield Brewery in Hoxton, London, since when the beer has been brewed regularly, mostly for sale in the United States.

Thomas contacted Whitbread, a major brewing group that had been at the heart of the porter and stout revolutions of the 18th and 19th centuries. See WHITBREAD BREWERY. Whitbread supplied him with a recipe for porter from the 1850s, brewed at its former Chiswell Street brewery in the historic Barbican area of London. The recipe for Flag Porter, devised by Thomas, was based on the Whitbread recipe and used pale, brown, crystal, and black malts and was hopped with just one variety, Fuggles. See FUGGLE (HOP). One of the many interesting facts discovered in the Whitbread archive was that the brewery was still using wood-kilned brown malt as late as 1850, at a time when pale ale brewers had switched to malt kilned with coke.

The beer that Thomas created had a second surprise: It was not jet black but dark ruby red in color. He suspects the original may have been even paler.

Despite Thomas' best attempts, such recreations cannot be entirely accurate from a historical perspective. Amber malt, a type no longer produced (and now imperfectly understood), is replaced by crystal malt in the Flag Porter recipe, and the Fuggle hop had not yet been bred in 1825. Bitterness could not be scientifically measured in those days, so Flag Porter's bitterness of 35 IBU is an approximation. That said, the beer is widely felt to provide a window into brewing history. The aromatics are complex, showing tangy, slightly smoky, and nutty notes underpinned by spicy Fuggle hops. The palate is fruity and rich, with notes of bitter chocolate and an intensely dry herbal finish.

Flag Porter was first brewed commercially by a London brewery, then moved to Elgood's in Cambridgeshire before finding its current home at the Darwin Brewery in Sunderland, northeast England. The Darwin Brewery developed initially as a training unit to support the Brewlab brewing school at the local university.

See also PORTER.

Roger Protz

Flagship (barley) is an Australian brewing barley variety developed by the University of Adelaide Barley Program and released in 2005 specifically to suit rice-based adjunct brewing. Varieties from the University of Adelaide are easily recognized by their nautical names such as Clipper, Schooner, Galleon, Flagship, and Commander. Flagship contains a more heat-stable version of the beta amylase enzyme than is present in most varieties and delivers high levels of alpha amylase, which together provide benchmark starch-degrading power during mashing. See DIASTATIC POWER. Flagship also exhibits low levels of the enzyme lipoxygenase, which are largely responsible for the formation of stale flavors in finished beers, especially light beer styles that are very popular in Asian countries today. Although Australian beer consumption per capita is significant, it is almost trivial in comparison with the scale of national barley production. This allows Australians to export about 70% to 80% of their barley crop as malt or malting barley to China, Japan, and a range of southeast Asian countries, where brewers typically use up to 40% rice-based adjuncts. Such adjuncts require malt of high diastatic power and fermentability to degrade the rice starch to fermentable sugars. Flagship, therefore, has become an important variety in Australia, mainly because of its export potential combined with such favorable agronomic characteristics as its good disease resistance, excellent early vigor, good weed competitiveness, and high yields per hectare. In Australia, by contrast, Flagship's specific performance quality profile makes it unsuitable for the production of typical Australian lagers because large breweries that use adjuncts tend to prefer sugar syrup to rice. Sugar syrup, however, requires malt of low, rather than high, diastatic power and low fermentability, which makes such traditional Australian barley varieties as Schooner and Stirling the more typical choice for these beers.

Barley variety sowing guide 2008. http://www.sfs.org.au/resources/BarleyVarietyGuide08SA.pdf (accessed April 19, 2011).

Flagship field guide. http://www.planttech.com.au/pdfs/new_products/flagship_field_guide.pdf (inactive).

Flagship malting barley variety sets sail. http://www.grdc.com.au/director/events/groundcover?item_id=publication-issue57&article_id=482BAD4FC9934E11CB34542B4383E22D (accessed April 19, 2011).

Jason Eglinton

flaked barley is unmalted, cooked, and dried barley that has been rolled into flat flakes. It imparts a rich, grainy flavor to beer and is used in many stouts, particularly Irish stouts, enhancing head formation and foam stability. Flaked barley, which is used directly in the mash mixer along with malt, belongs to a group of pre-cooked gelatinized adjuncts that includes micronized and torrefied whole grains and comprises flaked barley, wheat, flaked maize grits, flaked rice grits, and flaked pearl barley. See ADJUNCTS. These materials are easily handled and yield enhanced extracts compared to untreated raw materials. Because it has been soaked and pre-cooked, flaked barley is relatively soft and is easily broken up in malt mills. To produce flaked barley, whole barley (graded to remove thin grains) is cooked in hot air at 428°F–500°F (220°C–260°C). During cooking the softened material becomes firm with a moisture content of approximately 4%. Flaked barley has an extract value of 72% on a dry weight basis.

Flaked barley and, to an even greater extent, flaked pearl barley (grains from which the husk and surface layers have been removed) can present brewing problems because they contain comparatively large amounts of β-glucan. See BETA-GLUCANS. In order to overcome this problem, flaked barley is often sprayed during preparation with a solution of bacterial enzymes containing α-amylase, β-glucanase, and possibly proteinase. The resulting product has an appreciable cold water extract and does not give rise to highly viscous worts or any other problems associated with β-glucans.

Graham G. Stewart

Flanders is the northern half of Belgium, defined nowadays by the five counties or provinces of East and West Flanders, Flemish Brabant, Limburg, and Antwerp. The official language is Dutch, spoken in a variety of local Flemish dialects.

As with much in modern Belgium its brewing traditions differ from those of the French-speaking south, Wallonia, though they retain some continuity with other parts of old Flanders.

The original 9th-century fiefdom was based around the city of Bruges (now Brugge) but grew in influence such that by the 16th century the Dukes of Flanders ruled an area spanning from Antwerp in the east, via Courtrai (Kortrijk) and Tournai in the south, to the North Sea coast west of Dunkirk, encompassing a swath of what is now northeastern France.

Indeed an ale-brewing culture is far more discernable in the part of France known as French Flanders, which is home to over 50 craft breweries, than in the one-third of present-day Flanders that lies east of the Dijle river, which has barely a dozen.

Before the acceptance of hops as an essential ingredient of beer, brewers would lengthen the shelf-life of their beers by adding herbal mixtures called *gruut* (also grut or gruit) to stall oxidation, bitter the beer, and mask unpleasant spoilage notes. See GRUIT.

The owners of the best gruit recipes held considerable power, particularly in medieval Bruges, and to this day, Flemish beers frequently contain a mix of herbs and spices, at least in part to continue a long tradition of the region.

Another, entirely separate practice that has survived particularly in the southern part of West Flanders province is that of aging (usually brown) ales in oak tuns for long periods, sometimes up to 2 years. Oak-aging allows lactic fermentation to occur and some additional conditioning by slowly working yeasts, turning the beer slightly sour like neatly aged wine, though many varieties are later softened by the addition of younger beer.

This tradition shares a history with English stock ales. The most magnificent examples are at Rodenbach in Roeselare and the smaller Verhaeghe family brewery at Vichte, east of Kortrijk. Others are beginning to revive the practice, though a similar tradition around the East Flanders market town of Oudenaarde has largely died out in recent years.

The region is also at the westernmost point of what some beer historians refer to as "the wheat beer belt," which can trace its origins back as far as the Holy Roman Empire and likely encompassed the wheat beer traditions of Bavaria, Berlin, Belgium, and elsewhere.

Defunct local styles such as Leuven's *peeterman* and various sour and sweeter styles, such as the witbier style revived by Pierre Celis in his De Kluis brewery at Hoegaarden in 1965 were part of that heritage, though none has crept closer to the edge of sane brewing practice than the lambic traditions of the Payottenland region of Flemish Brabant. See CELIS, PIERRE, LAMBIC, and WHITE BEER.

The late 19th and early 20th centuries saw more links between Flemish and English brewing through the influence of George Maw Johnson, the Kentish brewer who became the first editor of the Belgian brewers' house magazine, *Le Petit Journal du Brasseur*.

Johnson is credited with helping to create the soft form of pale ale called Spéciale, suited to the new breweries of the industrial age that were growing in the north of Brabant, and with popularizing light sweet stouts and strong Scotch ales, styles of beer now rarely found in their native Britain but still made by breweries in East and West Flanders.

At the heart of Flemish brewing, however, is a desire to stand out from the crowd by doing things differently. Where lesser brewers will imitate successful beer styles thereby creating a trend, the Flemish brewer craves non-conformity, be it through pushing the limits of accepted brewing practice or simply by creating outrageous glassware.

How else can one explain the presence on a single café beer list of local *streekbieren* (regional beers) as singular and diverse as Anker's lush, deep Gouden Carolus Classic, Dolle Brouwers' near-sharp, burnt Oerbier, Bosteels' honey-sweet Karmeliet Tripel, Boon's razor-edged Oude Geuze, Struise Brouwers' authoritative Black Albert imperial stout, Slaghmuylder's peppery pale Witkap Special, Van Eecke's flowery Hommelbier, and Kerkom's delicate-but-firm Bink Blond.

One explanation for this diversity and originality is that the Flemish are overly used to having their lands invaded and occupied by foreign powers. This happened twice in the last century and dozens of times before that, courtesy of the Spanish, Dutch, Austrians, French, Germans, and others. The Flemish, it seems, prefer anti-authoritarian beers.

At the present time just under 60% of Belgium's active breweries are found in Flanders. The fiscally more conservative north does not offer the same generous start-up packages given to new microbreweries in the south and the gap is narrowing, albeit in part due to younger Flemish brewers setting up businesses there.

On the other hand, Flanders remains home to most of the larger independents, including Duvel Moortgat, Palm, Haacht, and supermarket brewer Martens, plus three Trappist abbey breweries, at Westmalle, Westvleteren, and Achel.

The lack of government support for new brewers also shows itself in a wariness by newcomers to invest in creating a brewery themselves, instead relying on other breweries to make their beers for them, sometimes even hiring out their brewhouse for the day to do so. One such "brewer-for-hire," Proef of Lochristi, has made over a thousand different brands.

Fears that the authorities' disregard of their brewing industry may lead to its demise, however, disregard the nature of the population's spirit.

See also ACHEL BREWERY, BELGIUM, WESTMALLE BREWERY, and WESTVLETEREN BREWERY.

Tim Webb

flavor is the main aspect of any particular beer that distinguishes it from others and one of the major reasons we drink the beers we enjoy. It is also, perhaps, the aspect of beer that has changed the most drastically in the modern age. Technically speaking, most of what we think of as a sense of taste is actually more accurately described as a sense of smell. The overall sensation we think of as "flavor" is a blend between sensory input from the olfactory system and input from the tongue and mouth. The olfactory bulb, located at the peak of the nasal cavity, is studded with thousands of receptor cells, each of these tuned to a particular range of aroma-active molecules that are vaporized into the air. The mouth is linked to the nasal cavity by the retronasal passage, allowing us to fully "taste" food and drink when it is in our mouths rather than only when it is in front of us. More than 1,000 genes, a full 3% of the total number in humans, are devoted to our sense of smell. See AROMA.

Our sense of taste is a far blunter instrument. Humans have about 10,000 taste buds, mostly on the tongue but also scattered within the soft and hard palate, the cheeks, and the lips. Whereas many animals, for example, dogs and cats, have olfactory senses far superior to that of humans, human taste mechanisms are particularly well developed when compared with those of our pets. The palate and the tongue's taste buds only perceive several sensations—sweet, salty, bitter, acid, and the so-called fifth taste, umami, the flavor of glutamates. Recent research suggests that taste buds also perceive fat, but this appears unproven, and because beer contains no fat, we will not address that theory here. See UMAMI.

A group of beer enthusiasts compare beer styles brewed by the Pike Brewing Company in Seattle. Many brewpubs offer numbered "samplers" or flights that emphasize the differences in color, aroma, taste, and aftertaste of their beers. CHARLES FINKEL

Sweetness seems very clear to us, and it is perhaps our earliest memory of flavor. If one thinks of childhood, sweetness pops to mind far faster than saltiness or sourness. The human brain is wired to like sweet things, perhaps because of their high caloric value. Unlike wine, beer almost always contains residual sugars, even if the beer does not taste sweet. Sweet elements derived from malt will be balanced against the hop bitterness, roast bitterness, carbonation, and possible acidity in a beer. Not many beer styles contain notable amounts of residual sugar, and sweetness rarely dominates the palate of beer. However, some stronger styles, such as barley wines, doppelbocks, and Scotch ales, often have semisweet flavor profiles. The sensation of sweetness is more complex than the presence of sugar itself, because other compounds can trigger sensations of sweetness. Alcohol, for example, can seem sweet; stronger beers may seem to be sweet at first, even when residual sugar content is low. Various esters, which the olfactory system will sense as fruity aromatics, will enhance perceptions of sweetness. The brain can combine sensations of actual sugar, alcohol, and esters into a single complex impression of sweetness. Unlike other types of sweetness, actual residual sugar lingers on the palate after beer is swallowed.

Bitterness is the backbone of the flavor of most beer flavor, providing the counterpoint to malt sweetness. Bitterness is derived from various acids in hops, but roasted malts can provide a different type of bitterness as well. Hop bitterness and roast bitterness in beer will intensify each other. Our relationship with bitterness is complicated, cultural, and changeable. In the plant world, bitterness is often a sign of poison, and bitter flavors protect many plants from being eaten by animals. Most humans are able to turn off this "alarm signal," but this differs from culture to culture. For example, Italian food and drink culture seems to be in love with bitterness, as represented by a huge range of popular Italian bitter liqueurs, biting espresso coffee, and the popularity of vegetables such as broccoli rabe and radicchio in Italy. Americans, on the other hand, appear to be less enamored of bitter sensations and are better known for having a national sweet tooth. However, the recently developing popularity of bitter craft brewed beers may signal the start of a change in the American culture of flavor.

There are many qualities of bitterness in beer, just as there are differing qualities of red wine tannins. Bitterness may be quick and snappy, seeming to fade after a few sips, or it may slowly gather and rise as a beer is consumed. Different hops give different types of bitterness, a fact that is empirically observed, but imperfectly understood. Brewers will study analyses of hop varieties, looking for clues to bitterness quality and seeking to create the type and intensity of bitterness they want in their beers. See BITTERNESS.

Although individuals differ, studies show that women tend to have more taste buds than men and that they are more likely than men to be "supertasters," people with acute sensitivity to flavor sensations. This may explain why fewer women than men enjoy bitter beers, especially if this is tied to the evolutionary advantages of having females avoid foods that send bitter warning signals to the brain.

Our perception of saltiness is tied to concentrations of sodium, potassium, calcium, and magnesium ions in our food and drink. In beer, salts will naturally come from brewing water, although brewers may also add them to influence beer flavor. Beers rarely actually taste salty, but a slight sensation of salinity is not uncommon. When added to brewing water in small amounts, sodium chloride can enhance beer flavor, giving a sense of greater palate fullness.

All beer is essentially acidic in nature, with most having a pH between 4.1 and 4.5. However, noticeable acidity is not a major factor in the flavor of most beers. From the dawn of civilization, beer was spontaneously fermented by wild yeasts and bacteria, and acidity was once one of the most prominent flavors in beer. Today, acidity is only assertive in a few beer types, including lambics and fruit beers. Among craft brewers there is a rising interest in acidity, and many look to lambic as an inspiration for the creation of intentionally sour beers. See LAMBIC and SOUR BEER.

Umami, which is Japanese for deliciousness, is the flavor of glutamate compounds, amino acids that form proteins. It is also given by ribonucleotide substances, which are known as powerful flavor enhancers, especially when combined with glutamates. Umami describes flavors underlying those of gamey meat, sea urchin, seaweed, soy sauce, fermented fish sauces, Marmite, mushrooms, ripe tomatoes, and many cheeses, especially Parmigiano–Reggiano, which contains up to 12% glutamate by weight. In beer, meat-like umami flavor is usually considered a fault because it is indicative of unwanted yeast autolysis and breakdown. However, it is a normal part of the flavor profile of beers that are intentionally aged, especially if they are aged on yeast. Here, it often comes across as "toasty" and can come to resemble the "sur lie" (on sediment) character prized in vintage Champagne. In such aged beers, umami can be a powerful factor in the creation of pleasant food pairings, particularly with foods that contain their own umami character. See AGING OF BEER and AUTOLYSIS.

Aside from these five basic flavors, there are other sensations in beer as well. The fizziness of carbonation is both a tactile sensation and a chemical taste sensation (a form of acidity)—the brain combines these to create the "tickle" or "burn" we associate with carbonation. Temperature is critically important to the flavor of beer, and both the palate and the olfactory sense will perceive beer very differently at varying temperatures. Finally, we have the trigeminal reception system, which perceives actual temperature, but also flavor-based sensations such as cooling (mint, anise), burning (chili peppers, alcohol), and numbing (menthol, Roquefort cheese). Astringency is technically not a flavor, but a tactile/trigeminal sensation. That said, we surely perceive astringency as part of flavor. The trigeminal system also senses viscosity—whether a beer "feels" round, soft, or silky or, alternatively, thin and watery.

Flavors not only combine with aroma and trigeminal responses but are also affected by flavors that were previously on the palate. For example, drinking a full-bodied sweet barley wine can give difficulty to other beers served after it, making them taste drier, thinner, and harsher. It is therefore important for trained tasters to pay attention to the order in which beers are tasted, served at the table, or judged. Even our sense of sight affects our sense of flavor, a fact well known to food technologists whose job it is to make commercial foods preparations look appealing to consumers. This effect appears to be linked to the cognitive expectations we associate with color. If a beer looks dark, it tends to "taste" heavier and richer; if it is amber, we look for notes of caramel.

When we drink beer, all of these many aspects combine to create the overall impression we commonly call flavor. Beyond these factors lie our psychological and emotional states, our personal memories, and the environment within which we are drinking. No beer truly tastes the same at the brewery as it does in a pub suffused by the warmth of friends and the smells of perfume and food. Nor will a beer taste the same on a fishing boat as it does in front of a fireplace. Some parts of beer flavor will be measurable and others will not. For those of us who do not analyze beer for a living, perhaps any analysis of beer flavor should largely be a matter of personal enjoyment and the provision of good hospitality.

Garrett Oliver

flavored malt beverage (FMB), an alcoholic beverage made from original base containing malt, but then stripped of malt character and then flavored. These drinks are also referred to as flavored alcohol beverages and colloquially called "alcopops" or "malternatives," among numerous other names. In the United States, FMB production is regulated by the federal government and must be made from a so-called malt base; the malt base itself must be made from at least 25% malt and contain at least 7.5 pounds of hops per 100 barrels of finished product. Most important, of the final alcohol in the product, at least 51% must be derived from malt base. Other countries make FMBs, but only the United States has this strict stipulation about the source the alcohol can come from and the use of hops. In other countries, producers are free to add grain alcohol to their FMBs without penalty, depending on the location.

FMBs originated in the 1990s when producers realized that a malt-based flavored beverage was taxed at the same rate as beer, whereas a spirit-based or wine-based flavored beverage was taxed at significantly higher rates. See TAXES. Additionally, producers exploited a loophole in the tax law—malt-based alcoholic drinks had no upper limit for flavor addition. In this regard, an acid, usually citric acid, was diluted in ethanol to the point where the ethanol was no longer potable, usually 10%. This solution was no longer viewed as ethanol, but rather as "citric acid flavoring," and added to the product to increase the alcohol and minimize the malt or beer flavor. After several years the Alcohol and Tobacco Tax and Trade Bureau closed this loophole by implementing a limit stating that no more than 49% of the final alcohol in the product could come from flavoring.

FMB production starts out much like a beer and then goes through treatment (carbon filtration, reverse osmosis, etc) to remove as much beer and malt flavor and color as possible. The clear, colorless treated malt base is then sweetened, usually with high-fructose corn syrup, and then flavored. Typical alcohol by volume is between 4% and 7%. Top-selling FMB brands in the United States include Smirnoff Ice and Mike's Hard Lemonade. In Europe and Canada, these and other similar products are usually made with spirit bases because other countries offer insufficient tax advantages to FMBs to make them viable products.

Keith Villa

flavor wheel is an internationally accepted tool that describes in a graphical wheel format the flavor terminology of beer. It serves to standardize the terms used in descriptive analysis of beer and enables brewers to communicate effectively about flavor. The original wheel named and described 122 separately identifiable flavor notes (in 14 classes) that can occur in beer. The system was developed from 1974 to 1979 by a joint working group consisting of the Master Brewers Association of the Americas, the American Society of Brewing Chemists, and the European Brewery Convention and stems largely from the input of the late sensory evaluation scientist Dr Morten Meilgaard.

On the wheel each separately identifiable flavor characteristic has its own name; similar flavors are placed together and no terms are duplicated for the same flavor characteristic. The goal is to provide a reference standard compound to be used in spiking (titrated dosing with flavor-active or aroma-active compounds) of beer samples to convey the meaning of each term. This aids in the training of sensory panelists.

From the simplified figure of the wheel it can be seen that the inner portion consists of 14 classes of components. As an example, Class 1 is aromatic, fragrant, fruity, and floral. The first tier then represents the more specific flavors that appear within that class. Class 1 is broken down into alcoholic, solvent-like, estery, fruity, acetaldehyde, floral, and

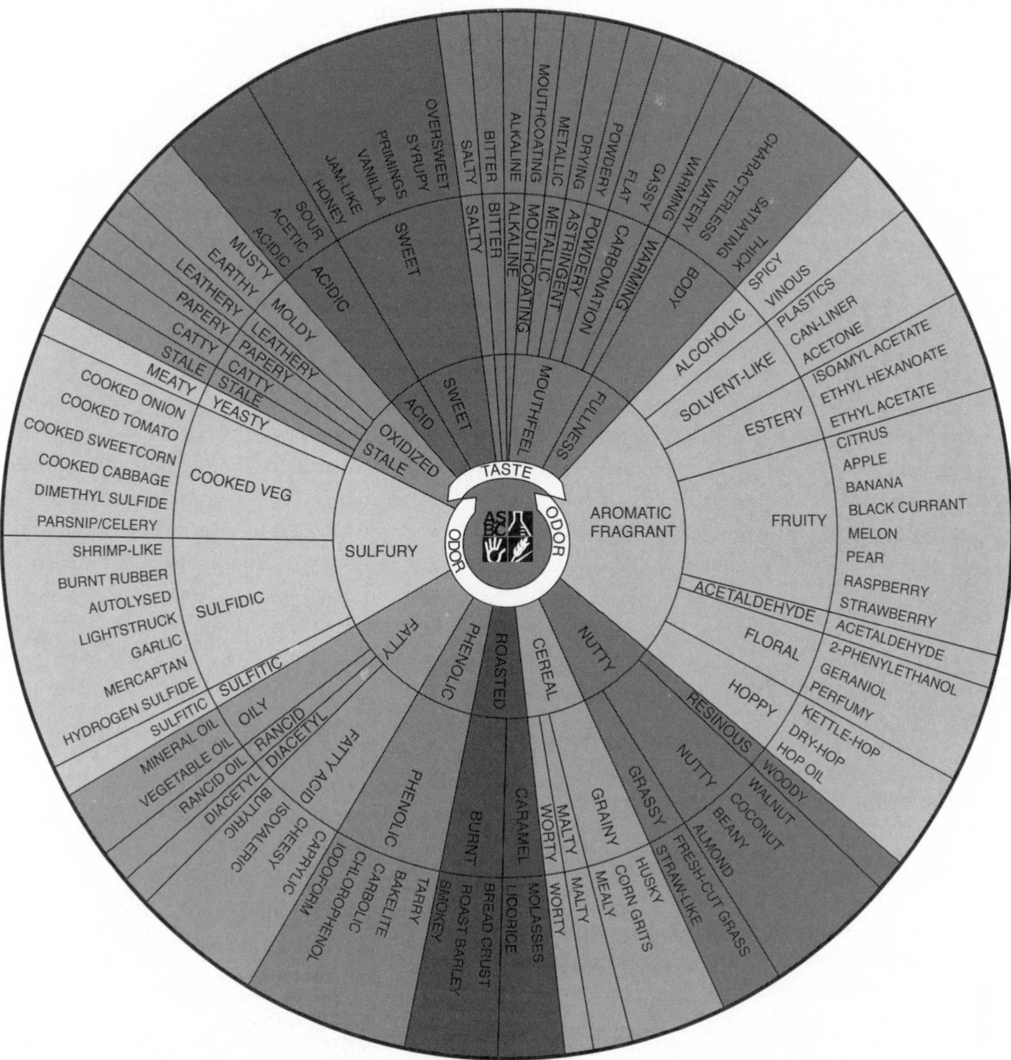

Flavor wheels graphically represent the flavors found in beer and standardize the terminology used to describe beer flavor. REPRODUCED BY PERMISSION FROM THE AMERICAN SOCIETY OF BREWING CHEMISTS, ST. PAUL, MN

hoppy descriptors. A four-digit code is also applied to those descriptor terms. The class and first-tier terms contain common terminology familiar to most people and thus form a vocabulary to fulfill nonspecialist needs. A second tier, not shown in the figure, further refines the flavor notes and becomes more specific and specialized. For example, the term "estery" from the aromatic/fragrant class (Class 1) is subdivided into distinct esters such as iso-amyl acetate, ethyl acetate, and ethyl hexanoate. The other second-tier terms are also subclassified into the distinct flavor notes within the respective groups. Additionally, components are also classified into more diversified physical odor, taste, mouthfeel, warming, and after-taste/flavor sensations.

As terminology and understanding of beer flavor components grow, so, ideally, does the Beer Flavor Wheel. Recently collaborative committees are redefining the wheel to include more aged/oxidized beer flavors, the concept of mouthfeel, and newer, more style-specific flavor components. The time may have come to split up the wheel into several subwheels to better define the new terminology.

See also FLAVOR.

Gary Spedding

flip-top is the colloquial name of a wire-bale bottle closure that was invented by German businessman Nicolai Fritzner in Berlin in 1875. Known in Germany as Bügelverschluss, this closure consists of a pivoting wire spring fastened by a collar that crimps into the bottle's neck. The spring locks a porcelain cap with a rubber gasket tightly to the bottle opening. Before Fritzner, all beer bottles were closed like Champagne bottles, with corks and a wire or string cage. The new closures not only solved the problem of containing high pressure in beer bottles but also made it easy to reclose them. The flip-top remained the standard beer bottle closure worldwide, until it was replaced by the crown cap. See CROWN CAP. In 1877, Nicolai Fritzner received a German patent for his invention, but he was not fast enough to exploit it internationally because he was beaten to the U.S. Patent and Trademark Office by an imitator, Karl Hutter, a German immigrant in Brooklyn, New York, who was granted a New World patent in 1893 for a "Hutter porcelain stopper" invention that was not his, but made him rich.

Bügelverschluss. http://www.worldlingo.com/ma/dewiki/en/B%C3%BCgelverschluss/ (accessed January 27, 2011).

Malted Barley Appreciation Society. vol 15, no 2. http://hbd.org/mbas/pdf/feb08.pdf (accessed January 27, 2011).

Nicolai Fritzner. http://books.google.com/books?id=0hEzAQAAIAAJ&pg=PA2043&lpg=PA2043&dq=Nicolai+Fritzner&source=bl&ots=tg-TI8rpmI&sig=4knasu-VtJmg6Q-17HGP8iAjfaE&hl=en&ei=BpxBTZj5HMT68Ab2v6GzAQ&sa=X&oi=book_result&ct=result&resnum=7&sqi=2&ved=0CDUQ6AEwBg#v=onepage&q=Nicolai%20Fritzner&f=false/ (accessed January 27, 2011).

Horst Dornbusch

flocculation is the tendency of yeast cells to aggregate together, forming a multicellular mass and sedimenting rapidly from the suspended medium or rising to the surface. Yeast flocculation is a complex phenomenon occurring in brewer's yeast under various conditions near the end of the fermentation process. It is a matter of fundamental importance to brewery fermentations.

Flocculation involves the interaction of cell wall proteins of one cell adhering to a receptor site of another cell. Lager yeast strains aggregate into large groups, rapidly sedimenting to the bottom of the fermenter, while ale strains may rise to the surface to form a thick top layer. Flocculation is a reversible process wherein yeast cropped from either the top or bottom of a fermenter and re-pitched into a sugar-rich solution will become disassociated and re-suspended in the wort.

Yeast specialists and brewers often categorize yeast flocculation behavior as being "high," "medium," or "low." High flocculation type strains start to flocculate the earliest, which can leave behind some unfermented sugars or unwanted flavor compounds such as diacetyl. See DIACETYL. Some highly flocculant strains require recirculation of the beer late in the fermentation to re-suspend the yeast, allowing the fermentation to finish to the brewer's satisfaction. Highly flocculant strains do have advantages—namely, they can produce a brighter beer with less suspended yeast, making filtration easier. Producers of cask-conditioned beers will often desire this quality as well, as they want the yeast to drop quickly to the bottom of the cask when fermentation is complete.

Medium flocculation type strains tend to be some of the more commonly used strains and will start to flocculate out as sugars become less abundant. Often they need help in order to flocculate, and this can be accomplished by cooling the fermenter to lower temperatures.

Finally, low flocculation strains are those that stay in suspension well after fermentation has ended. These strains tend to be wheat beer strains in which low flocculation is desirable, as the finished beers are meant to be hazy with yeast.

In working breweries, yeast used over a number of generations can be selected in a manner that may increase or decrease a yeast strain's flocculative tendencies. In a fermenter with a cone bottom, yeast collected from the bottom of the cone will be the yeast that flocculated early, while yeast collected from the top layer of sediment will be yeast that flocculated last. By continuously selecting for these tendencies, many brewing strains can be "trained" to perform in a manner that better fits the brewery's needs.

Boulton, Chris, and Quain, David. *Brewing yeast and fermentation,* 2nd ed. Oxford, England: Blackwell Science Publishing, 2006.

Verstrepen, K. J., Derdelinckx, G., Verachtert, H., and Delvaux, F. R. Yeast flocculation: What brewers should know. *Applied Microbiology and Biotechnology* 61 (2003):197–205.

Chad Michael Yakobson

floor malting was the traditional way of producing malt for brewing before the Industrial Revolution. It was largely a manual process, and today floor malting is considered a niche artisanal practice. A few specialty maltsters in the UK, Germany, and the Czech Republic continue to make floor malts available to brewers, who prize them for the deep, rich flavors. In floor malting, just as in modern mechanized malting, the incoming grain is first steeped in large vats, in an alternating series of "wet" and "dry" cycles. See MALT. Once properly hydrated, the malt is then sent not to a germination chamber, but to a "floor," where it is spread evenly by hand into an approximately 15 cm (6 inch) thick layer. The favored floor material for European floor maltings has always been tiles quarried only in the Bavarian village of Solnhofen. This stone is hard and thin, with excellent thermal dispersion, moisture retention, and wear resistance. British floor maltings have retained their own types of stone floors. While on the floor, the germinating grain must be turned by hand twice a day, 7 days a week, to keep it properly oxygenated, to dissipate heat, and to keep rootlets from tangling the malt into an unmanageable mat. The traditional tools for this hard labor are a wooden malt shovel and a special, iron-wrought rake that often weighs up to 70 lb (30 kg). The rake, dragged arduously through the malt, is simply called a "malt rake" or "puller" in the UK, but in Germany it is known by the very strange name of "wohlgemut," meaning "pleasant disposition." At the proper germination stage, when the acrospires have grown almost as long as the barley kernels, the moist, green malt is sent to a kiln, where it is spread by shovels in a one-half meter (not more than two feet) thick layer. From then on, the drying process proceeds much as it does in a modern kiln, except very slowly, for perhaps 32 to 48 hours rather than the 24 hours that are now common in industrial malting. The temperature in an old-style kiln with floor malt rarely exceeds 85°C (185°F).

Traditional floor malting, unlike modern malting, takes place without any artificial ventilation, which is why green floor malt beds tend to contain more CO_2 than do beds in modern plants. The entire floor malting process, therefore, leaves the malt slightly "under-modified" by modern standards, but it gives the malt a very rich, aromatic flavor that is far more intense than is usually achieved by today's time-efficient, industrial malting procedures. See MODIFICATION. While modern malting plants with mechanized controls can operate year-round, traditional floor malting is not possible during the summer, because barley germinates unevenly once the ambient temperature rises above 14°C (57°F). Uneven germination would cause the malt to lose its pleasant flavor as well as its favorable processing qualities in the mash.

Briggs, Dennis Edward. *Malts and malting*. London: Chapman & Hall, 1997.

Dornbusch, Horst. Brewing with the living past: Floor-malted heirloom barleys for ales and lagers. *The New Brewer* 27 (2010): January/February.

Thomas Kraus-Weyermann

flotation tank is a vessel used to separate cold trub from cold wort in the fermentation cellar. See TRUB. The flotation method relies on sterile, compressed air—between 30 and 70 l (1014 and 2367 oz) of air per hectoliter (26.4 gals)—being percolated into the wort at the beginning of fermentation. The air injection, usually using a ceramic or metal carbonating stone, is best performed within roughly 6 to 8 hours after pitching. Importantly, the yeast must be given enough time before the start of flotation to absorb trace nutrients, especially sterols, from the trub material. However, some brewers perform flotation prior to pitching yeast. As the flotation air is dispersed in the wort, it not only aerates the wort and thus supplies the needed oxygen for the yeast to get ready for its reproductive and metabolic cycles but also forms small bubbles in the wort, to which cold-trub particles cling. As the bubbles float to the surface, they drag the attached trub particles with them. At the top of the wort, the bubbles coalesce into a brown, firm, and compact layer of foam. As time passes, this head of foam may even dry out and become crusty. Once the beer starts fermenting, however, the liquid is racked out from under the trub-laden foam head, leaving the unwanted sediment behind. If the flotation tank is open, the foam layer may also be carefully skimmed off by hand. See SKIMMING.

Although the exact tank shape—horizontal or vertical—for floatation is secondary, tank geometry is important. The depth of the tank's head space must be at least 30% to 50% of the beer's depth. This means that cylindroconical tanks are often too slender for effective flotation. Such tanks would cause an accelerated updraft as the bubbles made their way up the long rise, leading to inhomogeneous flotation at the surface. In cylindroconical tanks, the foam head is also more likely to collapse into the beer during racking, defeating the purpose of the operation. Flotation is most effective if the wort depth does not exceed 4 m (approximately 12 feet). A second, fresh batch of beer may by pumped in underneath an already floatation-clarified wort, in which case the combined worth depth should not exceed 6 or 7 meters (18 to 21 feet). The air bubbles passing through the bottom batch will continue to rise through the top batch and scrub even more trub out of that batch. To keep the surface foaming from becoming too vigorous during flotation—which could prevent the head of foam from firming up properly—the tank can be put under slight pressure, up to about 0.5 to 0.8 bar (roughly 7 to 12 psi). After the beer has been racked, the tank must receive a thorough cleaning, often manually, to remove all crusted-on foam residues.

A key reason for removing cold trub is the trace residues of undesirable compounds it contains. These include varying amounts of fatty acids, polyphenols, undegraded carbohydrates and proteins, and even heavy metals, such as copper and iron, which can take part in oxidation reactions. Reducing these residues can improve the beer's shelf life. However, the practice of cold trub is controversial, with many brewers believing that it can strip wort of nutrients necessary for good fermentations and yeast health. Flotation remains popular in Germany and some parts of Europe, but the technique has become rare in the United States.

Cold trub: Implications for finished beer, and methods of removal. http://www.brewingtechniques.com/library/backissues/issue2.2/barchet.html/ (accessed January 17, 2011).

Narziss, Ludwig. *Die Technologie der Würzebereitung*, 7th ed. Stuttgart: Ferdinand Enke Verlag, 1992 (translation of title: Technology of Wort Preparation).

Oliver Jakob

FMB

See FLAVORED MALT BEVERAGE.

foam, or head, atop a glass of beer is widely considered to be among its most alluring physical traits. It is the main attribute that visually separates beer from other sparkling drinks, and it is also quite important for the mouthfeel of many beers. As one drinks a beer, some of the foam is also consumed, giving the beer a thicker, smoother texture. Brewers, of course, know this, and therefore foam formation and stability are an essential part of overall beer quality. Beer foam has been studied extensively and brewers work hard to make sure their beer has good "head retention."

Beer is, among other things, a supersaturated solution of carbon dioxide (CO_2) and will not foam unless encouraged by agitation or by the presence of nucleation sites such as particles in beer or scratches on glasses. The more CO_2, the more foam will be produced. See CARBON DIOXIDE.

Foam is an inherently unstable phenomenon because of the huge increase in surface area within an aqueous system that is counter to the force of surface tension. That beer foam is stable, unlike that in richly carbonated beverages such as champagne and sodas, is due to the presence of surface-active agents in the beer.

The key physical process leading to the collapse of beer foam is disproportionation. In this phenomenon, gas passes from small bubbles to adjacent larger bubbles, leading to a drastic reduction in the number of bubbles and an increase in the size of remaining bubbles such that they become unattractive. The lower the temperature, the more stable is the foam. More important, it is advantageous to have a uniform distribution of bubble sizes, preferably small bubbles because then liquid beer drains more slowly from the foam, which helps stabilize the head. This focuses attention onto the sites and mechanism of foam formation; devices in dispense taps and deliberate scratching of the bottom of drinking glasses should be such as to enable the production of uniformly small bubbles.

The main foam-stabilizing agents in beer are hydrophobic polypeptides derived from grain. These molecules cross-link with the bitter iso-α-acids derived from hops to render the foam more rigid and not only more stable but also able to adhere to the sides of the glass as the beer is consumed (cling or lacing). See CLING. The reduced hop preparations used to afford light protection to beer are especially good foam stabilizers; however, the foams may appear coarse, lumpy, and less appealing.

Other materials that can support foaming include metals. Zinc is especially efficacious and has an advantage over metals such as iron that were once used in that it does not promote oxidation. Melanoidins have some foam-stabilizing capability, meaning that darker beers frequently have superior foaming properties. Some brewers add foam-stabilizers such as propylene glycol alginate to the beer, and some brewers introduce nitrogen gas into the beer, which gives much more stable foams (though at risk to the aroma of those beers expected to have hoppy notes). This is the reason for the creaminess and retention of the heads on most draft Irish stouts such as Guinness.

The most frequent cause of poor foaming of beer is the presence of foam-negative materials, most notably lipids introduced in the process or as part of food consumed alongside the beer, and detergents that have not been properly washed from the glass or dispense lines.

Alcohol is also foam-negative, so stronger beers tend to have less foam stability pro rata. Also damaging to foam are proteolytic enzymes, either those such as papain added as haze-preventatives, or those secreted from stressed and old yeast. See ENZYMES. Foam is more durable in pasteurized beer because the heat treatment destroys such proteinases.

Deeper heads of foam will naturally tend to last longer. Head retention can be measured by a variety of methods. These include procedures that assess the rate at which liquid beer drains from the foam (e.g., the methods of Ross & Clark and Rudin) and those that assess the extent to which the foam itself subsides (e.g., the NIBEM method).

Though most consumers want and expect to see at least a few centimeters of foam on top of a beer, there are wide cultural differences. In Britain, for example, consumers in the south, when served cask-conditioned ales, widely prefer the liquid level of a pint to nearly reach the rim of the glass. A cap of foam should float above, but no more than that. In northern England, however, the consumer expects a frothier foam, which is often achieved by a device called a "sparkler," attached to the spout of hand-pump assembly. The sparkler causes the beer to spray violently into the glass, which foams the beer even though cask-conditioned beers contain only light carbonation. It is customary to use over-sized glasses, in which the pint measure is marked by a line near the top of the glass, but which leave plenty of room for the foam to feature. The quality of beer foam remains a topic of debate among beer drinkers, though hopefully over pints.

Bamforth, C.W. The relative significance of physics and chemistry for beer foam excellence: Theory and practice. *Journal of the Institute of Brewing*, 110 (2004): 259–266.

Evans, D.E., & Bamforth, C.W. "Beer foam: Achieving a suitable head." In *Beer: A quality perspective*, ed. C.W. Bamforth, 1–60. Burlington, MA: Academic Press, 2009.

Charles W. Bamforth

fobbing is the foaming of beer during processing or dispense. Depending on when it occurs, fobbing can have either negative or positive consequences. Fobbing during wort production can contribute to oxidation that will negatively impact long-term product stability. When used in reference to beer dispense, the term "fobbing" generally refers to excess foaming while pouring draught beer. This results in product loss and subsequent loss for the pub or tavern owner (linking it to the more common layman's definition of fobbing: to cheat or to deceive, i.e., "fob this off on someone"). Multiple factors contribute to excessive draft fobbing. These include incorrect line sizing, incorrect line pressure, uptake of carbon dioxide at the point of origin (i.e., the keg or serving vessel) during or prior to dispense, unclean beer lines, improperly cleaned and rinsed glassware, incorrect beer temperature at the point of dispense (i.e., warm beer), or defects in the beer line. See DRAUGHT BEER.

Fobbing during packaging, particularly bottling, is important in forcing oxygen from the bottle prior to capping. As the bottle exits the filler, foam rises to the top of the bottle, due to the drop in pressure, displacing the oxygen in the bottle's headspace. This is known as "capping on foam." Bottling lines will often employ liquid nitrogen or sterile water "jetters" that disrupt the surface of the beer in the bottle, causing fobbing and ensuring the beer is properly capped on foam. A similar effect can also be achieved by tapping or "knocking" the bottle on its way to the capper or by use of an ultrasonic burst that causes the beer to foam as needed.

Another use of the term "fobbing" refers to cask-conditioned beer which has undergone a secondary fermentation in the cask. Before the beer is ready to serve, the proper level of carbonation must be achieved. When the cask is first vented, it may be quite active, causing fobbing to occur through the hole in the shive. Some cellarmen will wipe away the foam and then use the frequency of its reappearance to decide when it is time to reseal the cask. See CELLARMANSHIP, ART OF.

Evans, D. Evan, and Sheehan, Marian C. Don't be fobbed off: The substance of beer foam—a review. *Journal of the American Society of Brewing Chemists* 60 (2002):47–57.

Kunze, Wolfgang. *Technologie Brauer und Mälzer*. Translated by Trevor Wainwright. VLB Berlin, 1996.

Kunze, Wolfgang. "Beer foam." http://oz.craftbrewer.org/Library/Methods/Other/KunzeFoam.shtml (accessed April 11, 2010).

Lewis, Michael J., and Bamforth, Charles W. *Essays in Brewing*. New York: Springer, 2007.

Geoff Deman

food pairing is one of traditional beer's greatest talents and one of the keys to its growing popularity. Once widely thought of as a great accompaniment to food, beer ceded the dinner table for decades as a pilsner-based monoculture took over in many countries. The renaissance of traditional brewing and the rise of craft brewing have recently brought much attention to beer's versatility with food.

Beer's greatest rival at the table is wine, and many people consider wine exclusively when deciding upon a partner for a dish. Wine is, of course, complex and wonderful, and rare is the craft brewer who does not enjoy it greatly. But any reticence to pair beer with food is unfortunate because beer indisputably has a far wider range of flavor to work with than wine does. The reasons for this are fairly simple—wine is made from a single ingredient, whereas a beer may easily contain a dozen. Beer can be black and taste like coffee or chocolate, it can be brightly acidic and tinged with complex earthiness, it can be bready and gently floral, it can be as smoky as bacon, it can be bracingly bitter and fruity, or it can be rich, sweet, and unctuous. Beer can tread so delicately as not to overwhelm the very lightest fish, or it can bring enough to the palate to match the boldest cheese. Beer can taste like almost anything, including wine. Brewing is much more like cooking than it is like winemaking, and this fact provides the basis for food matching.

An entire book could easily be written about beer and food pairing and many already have been. Here we are only able to provide some principles and guidance in the right direction. All beverage and food matching is—or at least should be—more of an art form than a set of rules. Of course we can drink any beer with any food, and relatively few pairings will turn out be truly unpleasant. However, it is possible to create genuinely transcendent combinations. The flavor experience we are seeking to create is more than the sum of its parts, just as voices in harmony can become exponentially more affecting than they would be alone.

As with any sort of beverage pairing, first we must consider the impact or intensity of the prospective partners. We do not want a powerfully flavored beer to overwhelm a delicate dish, nor do we want a fine-boned beer to vanish from the palate when faced with boldly flavored food. The goal, therefore, is balance. The intensity of the beer will be based on a number of factors that the taster will experience in combination, including sweetness, maltiness (bread-like quality, derived from malted grains), bitterness, roast character, alcoholic strength, carbonation level, and, occasionally, acidity. Although this sounds like a lot of information to process, we process such balances all the time; with a little thought, understanding the intensity of beer comes as naturally as turning the stereo volume to the right level of sound for a dinner party. When it is too loud, you will know it.

In most styles of beer, carbonation gives flavors a refreshing lift. Levels of carbonation vary widely among beer styles, from the light prickle of cask-conditioned ales to the assertive effervescence of saisons. Carbonation provides beer with a physical sensation on the palate but also sharpens bitterness and acidity and cleanses the palate. Carbonation provides beer with cutting power against fats and other mouth-coating food elements. It is restorative on the palate and can make even very heavy dishes such as cassoulet seem far lighter than they might otherwise. Highly carbonated wheat beers, particularly

Venison dish paired with Ayinger's Winterbock. BRAUEREI AYING FRANZ INSELKAMMER

Bavarian weissbier and Belgian witbier, are fruity, lightly bittered, and excellent with egg dishes at brunch. They are also very good with oily fish, such as salmon, sardines, and mackerel.

The range of flavors in traditional and craft-brewed beers gives a large palette of flavors and aromas for pairings based on harmony. Among the most powerful of these is the flavor of caramel, or, more correctly, caramelization. In most beers having colors ranging from amber to copper to deep brown, this color is the result of the use of caramelized malts. Sometimes, as in some Belgian styles, the color will come from caramelized sugar added in the kettle. Caramel flavors are often present in the aroma, often paired with some residual sweetness on the palate. Caramelization is, of course, among the most important flavors in food. When we fry, roast, grill, or sear food, we develop caramel flavors. This can be the basis for harmony and the reason why a brown ale works so nicely with a hamburger, pork roast, or grilled steak. Such pairings may present themselves as obvious, whereas others may require more thought. For example, we may think of a seared diver scallop in a brown butter sauce as a light seafood dish, but in fact much of the flavor of the dish is derived from the caramelization of the surface of the scallop and the butter sauce. A soft brown ale, a Bavarian dunkel, or a Belgian dubbel, each possessing plenty of caramel character, may work better than a paler beer. Other examples include the classic preparation of monkfish with lardons or crispy pancetta and pasta carbonara, prepared with a sauce based on egg yolks and pancetta. Beers with caramelized flavors also provide very good matches for dishes featuring mushrooms and for roasted chicken and game birds.

Many hop varieties, especially American varieties, bring citrus-like aromatics to beers. Dry hopped pale ales and India pale ales (IPAs) often taste of lemons, limes, and oranges. These flavors can provide harmonies with dishes that contain similar elements, whether it is a pork dish simmered with sour orange and achiote or a simple chicken dish in a lemon-based sauce. Many Thai dishes contain citrus juice, and this helps them pair well with beers that show these flavors.

Other beers, such as Belgian tripels and French bières de garde, feature herbal and floral flavors. Dishes strongly flavored with thyme, rosemary, oregano, tarragon, and other herbs tend to work well with them.

Roasted malts, used assertively in porters and stouts and a bit less so in dunkels and brown ales, will bring flavors of coffee and chocolate. These beers can pair very well with grilled meats or vegetables or any dish that develops a slight char in the cooking process. Such beers are sometimes aged in oak barrels, giving them vanilla-like aromatics and a particular affinity with braised beef dishes such as short ribs.

Malt itself, even when pale, has a bready, nutty flavor and will form the basis for any residual sweetness a beer may possess. Although beer is rarely genuinely sweet, many beers have enough malt sweetness to balance the heat of chili peppers or match dishes containing fruit or other sweet elements. Malt sweetness also balances salt in a dish.

Beer almost always starts with two contrasts to food—carbonation and bitterness. These are the backbones of the beer's flavor and provide its cutting power. They also provide intensity, and that is particularly true of bitterness. Hop bitterness cuts through fatty dishes and cleanses the palate. With very spicy food, bitterness can intensify flavors in a pleasant fashion without clashing. Spicy Thai, Szechuan Chinese, Mexican, and Indian dishes often work well with pale ales and IPAs.

Dessert, often thought of as the province of sweet wine, is actually usually better with beer. The maxim in wine—that the wine must be at least as sweet as the dessert—does not hold force with beer. In fact, it is the relief of sweetness from the palate that is the key to success. After a few forkfuls, the palate is overwhelmed by the sugar in most desserts. That is one reason why coffee often seems so pleasant with dessert; it is not nearly as sweet as the dessert. There are many pairings that can work, but bigger beers with some caramel or roasted character tend to do best. With a chocolate tart, for example, we can pair a coffeeish, chocolaty imperial stout. In this pairing, we have both contrast and harmony—the roasted malts match the chocolate, whereas the beer cleanses the palate of sweetness; the dessert can come back tasting fresh. This works in a different fashion with vanilla ice cream, where the pairing is all about pleasant contrasts.

Cheeses are among the greatest partners for beer, so much so that we cover them separately. See CHEESE (PAIRING).

A final word about the order of service: it stands to reason that we serve light dishes before heavy dishes and therefore lighter beers before heavier beers. The previous beer has an effect upon the next one; a prejudice lingers and must be taken into account. A delicate beer that follows a blockbuster is not likely to show its best. It is important to note that sweeter beers will make succeeding beers taste drier, sometimes drier than we might wish.

This principle can be made to work for us when we are serving both beer and wine at dinner. A good example of this is a classic starter dish if a luxurious one—seared foie gras. At most restaurants, this will be served with a sweet wine, and the combination is undoubtedly pleasant. The pleasantries often come to an end, however, when a red wine is served with the next dish; the preceding sweet wine will cause the red wine to taste thin and harsh. By serving a relatively dry beer with the foie gras—say a Belgian dubbel that will harmonize very well—we can avoid such problems. The red wine can follow without incident. Thus, we can observe that the table is not a place for orthodoxy but for pleasure. A little bit of thought regarding the best beer partners for our food can transform ordinary meals into interesting ones on a day-to-day basis. It is a transformation we all can afford and surely deserve.

Garrett Oliver

Foster's is known internationally as the quintessential Australian beer brand. However, it is curiously less popular in its homeland than it is around the world.

Ironically, Foster's was created by two Americans who arrived in Melbourne, Australia, from New York in 1886. The most popular beer style at the time was India pale ale, which, like most beers, was imported. But beer suffered in the extreme Australian heat, and few attempts were made to cool it. This led the *Australian Brewers' Journal* to claim, with remarkable foresight, that lager beer, "supplied in the proper way, in bulk, cold and fully charged with carbonic acid . . . will be *the* drink of Australia."

W. M. and R. R. Foster were not the first to brew lager in Australia, but they went at it with a scale of commitment not seen before. They arrived in Australia with a German-American brewer who had studied in Cologne and a professional refrigeration engineer. They spent £48,000 ($76,690) building a very modern brewery that kept the beer cold and matured it for 6 weeks.

Foster's Lager launched in November 1888 and was widely praised. In the hottest month of the year, it was delivered to hotels (bars) with a free supply of ice. But importers of foreign lager simply dropped their prices to squeeze the Foster brothers out, and after only a year they sold the brewery to a syndicate of businessmen for less than it had cost them to build and returned to New York.

The new Foster Lager Brewing Company continued to struggle, and it soon merged with local rivals Carlton, Victoria, Shamrock, Castlemaine, and McCracken to form what eventually became Carlton and United Breweries (CUB).

Within the CUB portfolio, Foster's—only available in bottles—was seen as a premium brand. It first went international when it was shipped to Australians serving in the Boer War in South Africa and steadily began to build a widespread reputation as a quality Australian beer.

Back in Australia, further acquisitions by CUB saw Foster's competing against other brands in the portfolio. When Foster's Brewery was closed, the brand almost disappeared, but it had already begun to cross state lines in Australia's famously parochial beer market, and orders from Queensland and Western Australia ensured its survival.

But Foster's was dwarfed by draught brands such as Victoria Bitter (VB) and Carlton Draught. With the domestic market stagnant, it launched in the UK in 1971 and the United States the following year. As an Australian export, it was a remarkable success.

With the help of Australian comedian Barry Humphries and his character Bazza McKenzie, Foster's became a cult import brand in the UK. In 1972, the Bazza character appeared in a film that, although critically reviled, made him a household name. By 1975 Foster's accounted for 80% of Australian beer imported into Britain. In 1981 a deal was signed with UK brewer and pub owner Courage to brew the brand under license in the UK. Launched with another Australian comedian, Paul Hogan, Foster's became incredibly popular, and by promoting an ongoing "No worries" Australian attitude, it remains the second largest UK beer brand overall. The lager itself is an unremarkable light international pilsner at 4.1% alcohol by volume (ABV).

Foster's launched in the United States in 1972 and soon acquired a cult reputation thanks to its 750-ml (25.4-oz) cans, which quickly became dubbed "oil cans." Patronage from stars such as Paul Newman and Robert Redford helped it become America's third most popular imported beer for a time, and its continued popularity was again assured by humorous advertising, claiming that "Foster's is Australian for beer." The brand is available today in two variants: a 5% ABV lager and a 5.5% ABV "premium ale."

The European rights to the beer are owned by Heineken International, who brew and sell it in most European countries. In the United States and India, rights are owned by SABMiller, and Foster's is brewed in Canada under license by Molson Coors. In total, it is now available in over 150 countries.

Although the Bazza McKenzie film was banned in Australia, it became a cult hit that helped Foster's gain popularity. A merger between CUB's rivals Castlemaine, Swan, and Toohey's prompted CUB to reposition some of the brands in its portfolio, and Foster's was launched on draught as the quintessential Australian beer, transcending state boundaries. This was supported by a huge marketing spend, including Grand Prix, Olympics, and Aussie Rules Football sponsorships. By the late 1980s Foster's was Australia's best-selling beer.

But with this aggressive promotion, Foster's lost its premium image. Australian drinkers, still fiercely territorial, bridled at the simplistic reflection of themselves it fed back to them, and they migrated back to strong provincial brands such as Castlemaine (Queensland), Tooheys (New South Wales), and Foster's' own stable mate, VB (Victoria). Although state boundaries are now being eroded, particularly by VB, Australians abroad are quick to point out that, far from being "Australian for beer," Foster's is now increasingly anonymous at home.

Pete Brown

4-vinyl guaiacol (4VG) is a member of a group of aromatic, monomeric phenols that includes vanillin and is widely used as a flavoring agent in the food industry. 4VG can be found naturally in most beers (especially ales), but usually well below threshold level. However, 4VG is present in weissbiers (wheat beers), rauchbiers (smoked beers), and some specialty Belgian beers in notable concentrations, generally imparting desirable spicy, pungent, clove-like notes. At higher concentrations and under certain conditions, however, it may present as a medicinal, off-flavor note.

4VG is produced by enzymatic or thermal decomposition of ferulic acid (a hydroxycinnamic acid), found in the husk of barley malt. To a more limited extent, it may be derived from release of the ferulic acid precursor found in wheat malts. With a low flavor threshold of detection at about 200 parts per billion, 4VG can exert a large influence on the flavor of beer. The main production of the compound is yeast strain specific (requiring a specific gene originally called POF for phenolic off-flavor and now renamed PAD1+) but also depends upon other process factors involved in malting and in the brewhouse. Full details of the generation of 4VG have only fairly recently been investigated by Belgian malting and brewing science researchers, who reached the conclusion that the brewer may have more control than once thought over its production. By varying mashing conditions to release more or less of its precursor, ferulic acid, the desired amount of spicy, clove flavor in the beer can be somewhat controlled.

4VG can also be produced by wild yeasts and some bacteria (which harbor the POF or PAD gene with variable degrees of expression). Hence, unless a specific wheat beer yeast strain or a Belgian strain has been used, the analysis of 4VG in beer can often be regarded as an indicator of contamination caused by wild yeast and bacteria in the brewery. Finally, because 4VG breakdown is related to vanilla flavor production, it is now being suggested that the clove-like aroma in fresh specialty beers such as wheat beers and top-fermented Belgian-style ales may shift to sweeter, more vanilla-like flavor impressions as these beers age.

See also 4-VINYL SYRINGOL.

Gary Spedding

4-vinyl syringol (4VS) is a member of a group of aromatic phenols that includes vanillin and 4-vinyl guaiacol but possesses minimal sensory properties compared with the latter compound.

4VS is derived via decarboxylation—the removal of a carbon dioxide molecule—from the precursor sinapic acid (a hydroxycinnamic acid) and is found in beer. It is produced in a similar manner to 4-vinyl guaiacol. See 4-VINYL GUAIACOL. Although no current information exists to show the occurrence of this compound in malt or hops (the usual source of beer phenols), 4VS imparts a smoked or burned note to beer at a threshold of about 0.5 parts per million. It is a compound identified in fresh beers and aged lager beers and may be associated with aged beer flavor. Tasting panelists describe its flavor as "smoky-old beer" or tobacco-like. The smoke used for the production of rauchbier malt has also been suggested as a source of 4VS. Some research has intriguingly suggested that the "wild" yeast brettanomyces might also be capable of producing this flavor, which is usually considered undesirable. If this is so, then the flavor may be apparent in some lambic beers and other beers fermented by brettanomyces yeasts. 4VS is also found in some Bavarian-style weissbiers, where it appears to contribute a smoky background note.

See also BRETTANOMYCES, LAMBIC, and WEISSBIER.

Gary Spedding

framboise (pronounced "frahm bwoz") is a French word meaning raspberry and "frambozen" is a Flemish word meaning raspberries. When speaking of beer, either of these words is used to refer to a very old style of lambic beer that is made with raspberries. Framboise has traditionally been brewed in the small towns west of Brussels, Belgium, in an area known as Pajottenland. See PAJOTTENLAND DISTRICT (BELGIUM). The base lambic beer used in framboise is made by the traditional method using a grist of 30%–40% raw wheat and 60%–70% malted barley. The hops used are typically Belgian and include varieties from the southern Belgian hop-growing region around the town of Poperinge, such as Northern Brewer and Brewer's Gold. All hops used in lambic production are intentionally aged to lessen aromatic oil and alpha-acid content and therefore reduce the potential flavoring and bittering components. The resulting hops are used mainly for their antimicrobial effect.

Mashing is carried out to optimize the growth of microorganisms associated with spontaneous fermentation and favor high levels of free amino nitrogen and unfermentable sugars. After boiling, the wort is transferred to a coolship, a shallow, large open tank generally located near the roof of the brewery. There, the wort is cooled and allowed to be inoculated by airborne microorganisms which begin the spontaneous fermentation. Brewing traditionally takes place only in the colder months of the year so that the wort can cool quickly—that is, in 1 to 2 days—using only the ambient air temperature. Brewing in the warmer months results in the wrong microflora causing "infection" in the beer.

After the wort has started fermenting, it is transferred to oak barrels, where the lambic finishes fermenting. After aging for one season (about 6 months to 1 year) raspberries are added into the oak barrels, where a second fermentation begins. The raspberry addition is traditionally with whole fruit, but today many lambic breweries add a mixture of whole fruit and syrup, or only raspberry syrup. When adding whole fruit, the framboise undergoes another aging period from 1 month up to 1 year, often depending on the needs of the marketplace. Fruit flavor, aroma, and color diffuse into the beer during the barrel aging. The framboise is then bottled and may be aged another several months before being released for sale. When a brewery adds raspberry syrup, the process is much quicker and the framboise can be ready for packaging almost immediately.

Some versions of framboise are very fragrant and can be rich in the natural aroma of raspberry, while other versions have a slight artificial raspberry aroma that has more of a raspberry jam-like character. Either way, the aroma is unmistakably that of raspberry accompanied by the unusual "funky" ester profile found only in lambic beers. In taste, all framboise show raspberry flavors, and like other lambic beers they can be mildly or highly acidic. Perhaps the most distinguishing feature of framboise is the differing level of dryness in various marketplace examples. Some traditional framboise, such as that from the Cantillon Brewery in Brussels, are very dry, quite tart, and full of raspberry character. Other more modern examples, such as those from Belle Vue and Lindemans, have sweetness added to balance the sour taste. Over the years, brewers have used sweeteners ranging from saccharine to corn syrup. Bottled versions of sweetened framboise must be pasteurized. Sugar has long been offered at cafés to allow customers to sweeten their own beers, but most traditionalists look down on lambics that are sweetened at bottling.

The presentation of framboise is often in a small-volume, fluted glass much like a champagne flute. This style of glass highlights the slightly pink to deep red color of the beer and allows the consumer to take in the visual aspects of the beer as well as the rich aroma.

Brewers around the world, and particularly craft brewers in the United States, have recently been inspired to attempt to replicate framboise and other Lambic beer styles. So far, their success has been limited, perhaps because of differences in the mix of microorganisms found in the air in breweries and barrels outside Pajottenland. Lambic purists claim that the correct blend of microflora is part of the unique Senne Valley terroir, and the European Union has shown their agreement by the issuance of an appellation contrôlée for lambic beers.

See also BELGIUM, FRUIT BEERS, and LAMBIC.

Keith Villa

France is so famous for its wine and cuisine that few would pause to consider whether the country had an indigenous beer culture of any significance. In fact, beer is consumed and appreciated throughout France. The northern regions that border the beer-centric nations of Belgium and Germany are, not surprisingly, the most steeped in beer culture. Specifically, these are the departments of Nord-Pas de Calais and Alsace-Lorraine.

Alsace-Lorraine is home to some of France's largest breweries and produces much of the total volume of beer in the nation. Kronenbourg, Fischer

Postcard from Lorraine, France, c. 1910. PIKE MICROBREWERY MUSEUM, SEATTLE, WA

& Adelshoffen, and Meteor are located in Alsace-Lorraine. On the surface, Alsace can appear every bit as German as it does French, a consequence of the area having repeatedly traded hands between the two nations over the past few centuries. Predictably, beers produced here are primarily derivatives of German pilsner and Munich lager styles. There are some examples of original French styles made in the region, notably versions of bière de mars, alternatively known as "biere de printemps" (spring beer), and in fewer cases, bière de noel (Christmas beer). Although these seasonal Alsatian beers are widely available, they are not particularly distinctive in character, generally possessing a somewhat insipid "industrial" flavor profile.

The region most associated with French brewing tradition is Nord-Pas de Calais. It was here that the modern resurgence of French specialty brewing began in the 1970s and 1980s. Although the majority of the producers here are small by any standard, Nord-Pas de Calais is home to the most breweries and produces a more diverse array of specialty brews than any other French department. Perhaps most telling, Nord-Pas de Calais can claim the highest per capita beer consumption in the nation.

Historically, French people have preferred low-alcohol beers with malty accents. Lower alcohol beers were the norm in the days when people could not depend on safe municipal water supplies as they can in modern times. The past popularity of low-alcohol bière de garde and "bock beers" (the French definition is antithetic to the classic, strong German bock beers) in France is historically evident. Their popularity was usurped with the advent of industrialized brewing and the extraordinary appeal of pale lager beers. In the recent resurgence of specialty brewing it stands to reason that bière de garde, considered France's primary contribution to world-class brewing, is a "malt forward" brew, albeit reinvented with a higher alcohol content.

In preindustrial France beer was brewed to serve a local population, which was also the case throughout the "grain belt" of Europe and North America. As the French economy became industrialized, small rural breweries suffered and urban breweries grew with the shift in population. With that change, diversity and regional styles declined as well. In northern France, coal mining was once the primary industry, the large workforce associated with that industry supported many small breweries. Coal mining in northern France has greatly declined from its heyday because much of the coal needs are now imported. The waning rural population meant the end of many small breweries in the beer-loving north. Although this change may not have been unique to France, what is notable is that the French countryside suffered acute devastation in the two world wars, especially World War I. In both conflicts, occupying armies routinely stripped brewing equipment for munitions production. Many small breweries never recovered from such severe insult. This sequence of events resulted in the virtual disappearance of regional styles and a French beer market dominated by German-style industrial lagers.

A renaissance in French specialty brewing began in the late 1970s and continues today. In recent years, small breweries have sprung up throughout France, as they have throughout the United States and the Continent. The *Les 3 Brasseurs* pub brewery chain is particularly widespread, with installations throughout France (plus a few in Canada). A number of small rural breweries have opened expressly to serve a local population. This is a throwback to "the way things once were," a posture the French regard with considerable affection. Although most of these small breweries may not produce overly distinctive brews, they are instrumental in exposing the French people to the many color and flavor possibilities of specialty beer in a market otherwise dominated by typical mainstream lager styles.

The French brewing industry continues to evolve with the specialty segment showing measured growth as a result of increasing market awareness and acceptance. Typical lagers produced by Kronenbourg and Fischer-Adelshoffen, not to mention Heineken and Stella Artois, each of whom have operations in France, continue to dominate the French beer market as they do the rest of Europe. French consumers may require more time to fully embrace their native specialty beers and develop the same level of Gallic pride in their beer as they have with other justly celebrated French consumables. Imported cheese and wine are often dismissed in France, but imported beers from Belgium and Germany are easily found throughout the country. Perhaps one day the terms "bière de garde" and "bière de mars" will occupy a similar space as "Camembert" and "Burgundy" in French hearts and minds.

See also BIÈRE DE GARDE, BIÈRE DE MARS, KRONENBOURG BREWERY, and NORD-PAS DE CALAIS.

Jackson, Michael. *Beer companion.* Philadelphia: Running Press, 1993.
Les Amis de la Bière. http://www.amis-biere.org/ (accessed March 22, 2011).
Markowski, Phil. *Farmhouse ales.* Denver, CO: Brewers Publications, 2004.
Woods, John, and Rigley, Keith. *The beers of France.* Wiscombe, Bristol: The Artisan Press, 1998.

Phil Markowski

Franklin, Benjamin (1706–1790), was one of the founding fathers of the United States, and was perhaps America's first true genius, making numerous inventions such as the lightning rod, bifocals, and the Franklin stove. When he began his printing business in 1725, the very first book he published included descriptions of three types of barley grown in the colonies: two-row, six-row, and winter barley, whose use the author, Francis Rawle, claimed was only good for brewing beer.

Although Franklin preferred wine, he drank beer, too. His correspondence while ambassador to France, for example, makes it clear that he enjoyed beer as well as wine, and he even brought back a brewing recipe for spruce beer. It's likely that he would have enjoyed a pint at Philadelphia's City Tavern in 1774, when newly arrived delegates to the Continental Congress met John and Samuel Adams for a pint. See PHILADELPHIA. Or later, in 1787, at the India Queen Tavern, where a compromise to the U.S. Constitution was hammered out.

But his continuing connection to the beer community is through a famous quotation attributed to Franklin. The phrase "Beer is proof that God loves us and wants us to be happy" can be found in numerous beer books and on countless T-shirts. Unfortunately, it's unlikely that he ever said it. In a 1779 letter to his friend, French economist Andre Morellet, Franklin wrote, "behold the rain which descends from heaven upon our vineyards; there it enters the roots of the vines, to be changed into wine; a constant proof that God loves us, and loves to see us happy."

Jay R. Brooks

free amino nitrogen (FAN) is defined as the sum of the individual amino acids, ammonium ions, and small peptides (di- and tripeptides) in wort. FAN is an important general measure of these nutrients, which constitute the nitrogen that yeast can assimilate during brewery fermentation. FAN is a degradation product of protein in raw materials such as malted barley, wheat, barley, and sorghum. Even if attenuation of wort sugars proceeds normally, production of the same quality of beer is not always guaranteed, suggesting that wort sugar removal alone is not a good indicator of yeast performance. Some brewing scientists regard FAN as a better index for the prediction of healthy yeast growth, viability, vitality, fermentation efficiency, and hence beer quality and stability. Proper FAN levels will be determined by using suitable malts and the correct mashing process. The level of FAN is determined primarily by the extent to which the proteolytic enzymes are able to act. The FAN itself is produced by the enzyme carboxypeptidase, a very heat-resistant enzyme that is present in abundant quantities in most malts and is accordingly seldom in short supply. Its substrates are the peptides that are produced by the proteinases that catalyze the hydrolysis of the storage proteins within the grain. These enzymes primarily act during malting, and so it is the extent of protein modification in malt that primarily determines the amount of FAN that will be developed in mashing. Wort nitrogen is used by yeast to accomplish its metabolic activities, particularly the synthesis of new amino acids and, hence, proteins. The majority of the FAN is consumed within the initial 24–36 h of fermentation, after which yeast growth generally stops. However, differences in FAN uptake between lager and ale yeast strains have been identified. The concentration of wort FAN required by yeast under normal brewing conditions is directly proportional to yeast growth and affects beer maturation. There is also a correlation between initial FAN levels and the amount of ethanol produced. See ETHANOL. FAN is also used by yeast cells to produce a range of metabolic products that affect the flavor and stability of beer, including higher alcohols. Worts produced from certain adjuncts, such as sorghum, tend to be low in FAN, and this deficiency has been shown to cause fermentation problems.

Graham G. Stewart

Free Mash-Tun Act (1880). More accurately known as the "Inland Revenue Act, 1880 [43 & 44 Vict. Ch.20]," this Act changed the emphasis of brewery taxation in Britain from malt to beer. The changes British Prime Minister (and Chancellor of the Exchequer) William Gladstone made were to influence the behavior of British brewers for over 100 years. Instead of a tax on malted barley (instigated in 1660), the brewer was now allowed far more leeway in choosing his raw materials. (A tax on hops had been removed 18 years earlier.) In his budget speech of June 10, 1880, Gladstone stated the aims of the Act to be:

> To give the brewer the right to brew from what he pleases, and he will have a perfect choice both of his materials and his methods. I am of the opinion that it is of enormous advantage to the community to liberate an industry as large as this with regard to the choice of those materials. Our intention is to admit all materials whatever to perfectly free and open competition.

Malt substitutes would henceforth become commonplace, and essential, in years of poor barley harvest. The point of duty now revolved around the volume and strength of wort produced during a brew, and, as a result of experimentation, it was deemed that two bushels of malt should make 36 gallons (one barrel) of wort at an original gravity (OG) of 1057° (approximately 14.9°Plato). See ORIGINAL GRAVITY. This was adopted by Excise as the "standard barrel," and incurred a charge of 6*s* 3*d* (31¼ new pence), which equated to ¼*d* per pint!

The Act also specified that a brewer had to purchase an annual "license to brew" (£1 for common brewers) and must register his premises and each item of brewing equipment (called "the entry"). Notice of 24 hours was required before a brew could commence, and, after carrying out the "normal brewing procedure," as evident from the entry, the worts had to be collected in a gauged vessel within 12 hours of mashing. Possession of a saccharometer (used to measure sugar levels; see HYDROMETER) was now essential for brewers, as were other items of equipment, and many small common brewers and victualler-brewers simply could not afford such things and ceased brewing.

The OG of the "standard barrel" was reduced to 1055° in 1889 because many smaller brewers had difficulty getting a barrel of 1057° wort from two bushels of malt. With minor tinkering, the 1880 acts held sway until June 1993, when duty became levied on the alcoholic strength of the finished beer (ABV).

See also BRITAIN, LAW, and TAXES.

Gourvish, T.R. and Wilson, R.G. *The British brewing industry 1830–1980.* Cambridge: Cambridge University Press, 1994.

Hornsey, I.S. *A history of beer and brewing.* Cambridge: Royal Society of Chemistry, 2003.

Ian Hornsey

French hops come primarily from the key hop-growing region of France, the region of Alsace on the west bank of the Upper Rhine. Politically, for hundreds of years, the region has gone back and forth between Germany and France. Its German name is Elsass. France, and especially Alsace, has been a hop-growing region for many centuries. We know this in part because of a law passed by King Louis IX of France in 1268, which stipulated that, in his realm, only malt and hops were to be used for brewing beer. That was exactly 248 years before the passage of the now much more famous Bavarian Beer Purity Law of 1516, which limited beer ingredients to just barley, hops, and water. See REINHEITSGEBOT. Commercially, however, Alsatian hop cultivation did not take off until the early 1800s. Strisselspalt is the region's main cultivar, but its origins are rather obscure. See STRISSELSPALT (HOP). Some Hallertauer Tradition is also grown there. The region now has its own breeding program and a few new varieties will likely be released there in the near future. Alsace accounts for barely 1% of the world's hop production. In hop-farming towns, however, the hop culture remains strong. As soon as the spring sunshine turns warm, tender young hop shoots show up on dinner menus, dressed traditionally in a Hollandaise-like sauce.

Val Peacock

friability refers to a material's ability to be easily crumbled. In brewing, friability is a measure of the hardness of grains of malted barley. It is, in effect, the grain's resistance to being broken. A friable grain is one that crushes crisply and cleanly into several separate parts. Friability may be easily assessed by chewing a sample, but this requires experience; it is measured objectively with a friability meter.

Friable grains are desirable in brewing because they indicate that the malt is dry and has been well stored. As a result, its enzymes are likely to be active when hydrated in the mash. In addition, proper drying and storage limits growth of mold or other spoilage organisms that could result in problems in brewing. This said, it is important not to over-dry malt; malt with too low a moisture content may shatter during handling and may be powdered by milling, leading to difficulties in the brewhouse and subsequent quality problems in beer.

Friable grains will also crush into suitable sized pieces to provide proper filtration in the mash bed. Softer grains may be termed "slack" and are more likely to be flattened than cracked in milling. See SLACK MALT. Such grains offer less exposure to the mash liquor and take longer for their starch to dissolve and digest. Poorly dried grains or ones that absorb moisture during storage are more likely to be slack. Grains that are improperly modified, and are therefore still hard, are referred to as "glassy" or "steely".

A friability meter tests grains by pressing them at constant pressure against wire meshes and measuring the amount passing through.

Keith Thomas

fructose is a common monosaccharide found in fruits and, to a lesser extent, in malted barley. The word "fructose" is derived from the latin word "fructus" meaning fruit. Fructose is similar to glucose and is considered an isomer of glucose. See GLUCOSE. Both glucose and fructose contain six carbon atoms, twelve hydrogen atoms, and six oxygen atoms, but in different arrangements. Of the saccharides found in malt fructose may contribute less than 3% of the total. Fructose participates in Maillard reactions, bonding with nitrogen-containing molecules to contribute to flavor and color formation in boiled wort. See MAILLARD REACTION. Fructose is fermentable and is converted into alcohol and carbon dioxide by yeast and bacteria. It has earned somewhat of a negative reputation due to synthetically produced high-fructose corn syrups or HFCS content in many of the foods and beverages we consume and the possible deleterious effects on health if consumed too frequently. HFCS is not just fructose but is a blend of glucose and fructose. Fructose tastes sweeter than glucose, especially when fructose is in its five-carbon ring form. Fructose is a major component of honey, making up an average of 38% of sugars.

Rick Vega

fruit beers are beers flavored with fruit rather than alcoholic drinks made from fruit. Thor Heyerdahl in his book *Fatu Hiva* describes people getting drunk on "orange beer" but drinks made from fruit are more properly described as wines. Beers are made from grain and require a conversion step in which fermentable sugar is produced from starch.

Fruits themselves contain only fermentable sugars, usually as fructose, sucrose, or other fermentable sugars and so need only to be squeezed of their juice before yeast is added.

The addition of various non-grain materials, including fruit, to beer preceded the use of hops as both a flavoring and a preservative. Adding fruit to beer has always had a range of benefits. Traditionally, fruit added additional fermentable sugars to the beer, increasing its strength and nutritive value. The taste and aroma of the fruit can hide or ameliorate the flavor of beers that might otherwise be found less than ideal. When added properly by a skilled artisanal brewer, fruit can help create colors, flavors, and aromas unobtainable from grain alone.

The best known fruit beers are from Belgium, with most of them based on lambic beer. Lambic beers are spontaneously fermented by diverse organisms in the brewing environment and most are dry and acidic. See LAMBIC. Traditionally, Kriek, from the Flemish word for cherry, is made by adding large amounts of black Schaerbeek cherries to 6-month old blended lambic beer or sour brown ale. The fruited beer continues its maturation in oak barrels for a year or more until the pulp is consumed by yeasts, and only the stones and skins remain. The beer is then refermented in the bottle. The resulting beer is often acidic and complex, with rosé coloring and attenuated fruit flavors. Hop bitterness and flavor are low due to the use of old hops that have lost their bittering and aromatic compounds; they are mostly there for their preservative value. For both good and ill, fruit beers have increased in popularity, resulting in many ersatz creations. Increased volumes of production, the sweet tooth of a public weaned on soft drinks, and a lack of the traditional cherries have resulted in the wide use of juices, purees, and sweeteners being widely used. Framboise, or frambozen in Flemish, is made in a similar fashion to Kriek, but with raspberries rather than cherries. It has been subjected to similar changes. Many modern fruit beers, even in Belgium, are extremely sweet with a strong taste and aroma of fruit. A whole range of other fruit beers are now being produced based on what are frequently poorer quality beers with added fruit juice or puree. This range includes cherries and raspberries but also peaches (peches), blackcurrants (cassis), and apples (pommes). The majority of these beers seem to have considerable amounts of added sweetener.

In the UK, during the 1970s, young people with a taste for sweet drinks would add blackcurrant cordial to their lager, and the practice would seem to continue today, but now back in the brewery. Some time spent on the Internet or in looking at supermarket shelves demonstrates that many UK brewers are producing fruit beers. The high price of fresh fruit such as raspberries and cherries leads the majority to use extracts, with the more discerning using frozen purees. A rapid survey of the fruit beers available shows that many of the beers produced have overwhelming fruit aromas and taste dominating the nose and palate. Some of these are no longer recognizable as beers.

In the United States, production of fruit beers is becoming popular, and craft brewers have approached fruit from both the modern and traditional angles. The best producers will age beers for months on whole fruit, often in oak barrels. Many of the beers will start off as sour ales and eventually gain much of the character of traditional lambic-based fruit beers. Others will blend in fruit purees or juices, either before fermentation or after. When added post-fermentation, fruit adds sweetness, color, and flavor, but little subtlety or traditional flavors. The least traditional, though the beers are often popular, will add "natural" extracts to their beer, giving them an instant boost of candy-like fruit flavor.

The production of excellent fruit beer undoubtedly requires more effort and time than many brewers wish to expend, but many of the most skilled craft brewers around the world are starting to take a keen interest. We can hopefully expect many fascinating and beguiling creations in years ahead.

Bodensatz Brewing. www.bodensatz.com (accessed January 11, 2011).

Jackson, Michael. *Great beers of Belgium*. Philadelphia: Running Press, 1991.

The Birth of Lambic. www.lindemans.be/start/lambik/en (accessed January 11, 2011).

Chris Holliland

fruity, having the flavor, aroma, or character of fruit. When used in association with beer, fruity is usually a synonym for estery. See ESTERS. During fermentation, especially warm fermentation, yeast will synthesize esters, organic compounds with aromatics that we often associate with fruit.

These include ethyl octanoate (fruity/pineapple), ethyl acetate (pear drops), isoamyl acetate (banana), ethyl hexanoate (apple), and ethyl 9-decenoate (elderberry), among many others. Cold lager fermentations rarely produce prominent fruit-like flavors, and this is one of the major flavor differences between most ales and lager.

Some hop aromatics may also be perceived as fruitlike and are usually reminiscent of citrus fruit. The technique of dry hopping is particularly effective at imparting these compounds to beer. Fruity hop aromatic compounds include limonene (citrus peel), linalool (floral, citrus), and citral (lemon, lime). The aroma of the New Zealand hop variety Nelson Sauvin is reminiscent of passion fruit and gooseberries. Fermentation character and hop character often combine to create complex fruitlike impressions. These will sometimes strike the palate as a form of sweetness, even when little residual sugar is actually present.

Finally, some beers contain actual fruit, usually as a flavoring infusion, although juices may also be used. See FRUIT BEERS. Traditional forms include the better Belgian krieks (cherry) and frambozens (raspberries), most of which are based upon lambics. See LAMBIC. These are tart and complex rather than sweet and very fruity, although the modern latter type has become increasingly popular. Craft brewed fruit beers tend to be either very traditional (long aging in barrels on whole or macerated fruit) or disappointingly ersatz (the addition of so-called natural fruit flavorings).

When fruity flavors are created by fermentations, restraint is usually best. A beer that seems boldly fruity at first often becomes "perfumey" as it warms, unbalancing the palate and decreasing drinkability. For ale brewers, controlling fermentation to produce the correct balance of fruit character in beer is an important part of the brewer's art form.

Garrett Oliver

Fuggle (hop) is a classic old English aroma hop that was found as a seedling in 1861 and introuced by Richard Fuggle some 14 years later. Fuggle saw extensive use worldwide as an aroma hop because of its pleasantness on the drinker's palate and its tolerance to downy mildew (Pseudoperonospora humuli) in the field. Although Fuggle was desirable for brewing, some unfavorable traits caused production problems. In many European growing areas, Verticillium wilt (Verticillium spp.) devastated commercial Fuggle yards, whereas in the United States, relatively low yields were the problem. Although Fuggle is still commercially grown, it has largely been supplanted by agronomically superior cultivars with similar flavor and aroma profiles. Its favorable brewing characteristics, however, have made Fuggle an ideal candidate for parenting in breeding programs. Not surprisingly, it has become the key ancestor for many modern cultivars and breeding lines, including Willamette in the United States. See WILLAMETTE (HOP). Alpha acids in Fuggle average approximately 5%, whereas beta acids average 2.4%. The cohumulone fraction is 27%. Oil content averages approximately 0.6 ml/100 g dried cone and is composed chiefly of myrcene (43.4%), humulene (26.6%), caryophyllene (9.1%), and farnesene (4.3%). Fuggle stores reasonably well. A Fuggle clone was introduced to Slovenia in the early 1900s. It is now marketed as Styrian or Styrian Golding, although it is not a Golding at all, but is identical to the original Fuggle, except for a slightly higher yield potential.

Burgess, A. H. *Hops: Botany, cultivation, and utilization.* New York: Interscience Publishers Inc, 1964.

Shaun Townsend

Fuller, Smith & Turner is one of England's most important real ale breweries and the only brewery to have won the Campaign for Real Ale's Champion Beer of Britain five times with three different beers. See CAMPAIGN FOR REAL ALE (CAMRA) Situated by one of London's busiest junctions, brewing has taken place on the site of the Griffin Brewery in Chiswick, southwest London for more than 350 years. John Fuller became involved in the brewery in 1829 and was joined in 1845 by Henry Smith and John Turner, forming Fuller, Smith & Turner, as it is known today.

The brewery's first CAMRA Champion Beer of Britain winner, Extra Special Bitter (ESB; 5.5% ABV), was launched in 1971, though it was first brewed in 1969 as a seasonal beer known as Winter Beer, replacing a beer named Old Burton Ale. A strong, highly complex beer, it is brewed from pale ale and crystal malts and a heady blend of Target, Challenger, Northdown, and Goldings hops.

ESB followed in the tradition of many British brewers of producing a stronger, richer, mouth-warming beer for consumption during the winter months. However, it quickly became established as a bottled beer available year around. Both pub goers and judges took to ESB, and it won CAMRA's Champion Beer of Britain in 1978, 1981, and 1985. Fuller's has also won that coveted title for two other beers, Chiswick Bitter (an "ordinary bitter" at 3.8% ABV) and London Pride (a "best bitter" at 4.1% ABV).

In the United States, ESB has come to denote a class of beers, which are high in alcohol and full of hop flavoring, but without the assertive hop character of an India Pale Ale. It is said that many of America's craft brewers were inspired to start breweries by their experience of drinking Fuller's ESB in England. See EXTRA SPECIAL BITTER (ESB). As an experiment, Fuller's' head brewer in 2010, John Keeling, has been storing ESB and other of the brewery's beers in oak whiskey casks, which produces luxurious, smoky, peaty flavors.

Since 1997 the company has annually produced a limited edition bottle-conditioned barley wine called Vintage Ale that is brewed with different malt and hops each year. Fuller recommends laying down the Vintage Ale for several years before drinking it. Also of note are the bottle-conditioned strong ale Fuller's 1845 and a creditable London porter.

Beer aficionados credit Fuller's with maintaining a strong interest in cask-conditioned beers, even through years when sales of cask beer have waned. Fuller's has displayed considerable ambition in recent years, and in 2005 bought the brewery George Gale & Co. of Horndean, closing the brewery and acquiring Gale's' brand, along with its tied estate of 111 pubs. See GEORGE GALE & CO. LTD.

See also CASK-CONDITIONING.

London Pride: 150 years of Fuller Smith & Turner. London: Good Books, 1995.

Tim Hampson

Fusarium is a common fungal disease of cereals causing head blight and leading to significant crop losses. Beer brewed with Fusarium-affected grain can contain dangerous mycotoxins and may be prone to gushing. Fusarium primarily infests the seed head of the barley plant, digesting the seed tissues and resulting in shrunken and discolored grains.

The genus is classified in the Ascomyces group of fungi and cultures produce distinctive banana-shaped spores. The mycelia are often pink- or purple-colored and infected barley grains may appear dark.

A range of Fusarium species infect barley, primarily F avenaceum, F culmorum, F graminearum, and F poae, but their prevalence depends on location and climate, with F graminearum most common worldwide. Infection is most likely vectored by plant residues in fields or spread by wind from nearby plants and it affects plants from the flowering head stage onward. In wheat the fungus grows rapidly through the flowering head but in barley it attacks grains separately, causing a patchy appearance.

Mycotoxins, particularly trichothecenes, are often produced by Fusarium infections as part of the fungus's virulence and are highly toxic even at low concentrations—so toxic as to have been considered for possible use as a biological weapon. Fusarium species can also produce hydrophobin proteins that initiate gushing in beer.

Commercial barley is tested for Fusarium infection to prevent contamination of grain stocks, both by visual observation and by antibody or DNA analysis.

See also BARLEY DISEASES and GUSHING.

Keith Thomas

fusel alcohols are by-products of ethanol fermentation. See ETHANOL. More specifically, as many as 45 higher alcohols, those with more than two carbon atoms in the molecule and with higher boiling points than ethanol, represent a major fraction of volatile and nonvolatile compounds in beer. They are considered undesirable in lagers but may positively contribute to ales. The mixture of these alcohols contributes to the general "alcoholic" taste and warming sensation in the mouth and stomach and to the aroma of beer; some of them may also impart a hint of fruitiness. Fusel alcohols are also important in volatile ester formation. Interestingly, the higher alcohols may also be one of the causes of headaches that are associated with the general discomfort of hangovers that follow excessive beer consumption.

The individual alcohols playing the most important role in beer flavor include propanols and butanols conveying alcoholic, wine-like, and ripe fruity notes; active amyl alcohol (a methyl butanol) presenting the characteristic "fusely" or boozy pungent note; phenyl ethanol, producing a pleasant rose or sweetish note; and tryptophol and tyrosol, exhibiting bitter, almond-like, or solvent-like taste characteristics. The yeast strain, fermentation conditions, and wort composition all have significant effects on the combination and levels of higher alcohols formed. Fusel alcohols will be present at higher concentrations in more robust and alcoholic beers such as barley wines and imperial stouts, partly because of stresses inflicted upon the yeast by high ethanol concentrations and more strenuous fermentations. Otherwise, in most beer styles they should not be perceptible or just barely so. As a group, fusel alcohols are a major part of the "alcoholic" perception of beer and overall core beer flavor.

Gary Spedding

Galena (hop) is an American superalpha hop cultivar that has enjoyed considerable commercial success. It was developed by R. R. Romanko in Idaho. Galena originated as open-pollinated seed collected from a Brewer's Gold plant in 1968. It was released for commercial production a decade later. During that time, it was screened under heavy inoculations of downy mildew (Pseudoperonospora humuli), a disease to which it proved moderately resistant. However, Galena is susceptible to powdery mildew (Podosphaera macularis). Plant vigor and yield are quite good, with a production of approximately 1,800 to 2,250 kg/ha (1,600 to 2,000 lb per acre). Its alpha acid content ranges from 8% to 15% and its beta acid content from 6% to 9%. The cohumulone fraction averages about 39%. Essential oils are about 1.05 ml/100 g of dried cones, of which 55.2% is myrcene, 9.2% is humulene, and 4.1% is caryophyllene; with traces of farnesene. Galena is both less floral and less grapefruit-like than the ubiquitous American Cascade hop, but it excels in its crisp and clean flavor profile, which, given the timing of its release, made Galena one of the earliest and most popular bittering hops of many American craft brewed pale ales.

Romanko, R. R., J. Jaeger, G. B. Nickerson, and C. E. Zimmerman. Registration of Galena Hop. *Crop Science* 19 (1979): 563.

Shaun Townsend

Gambrinus, Jan, is the mythical King of Beer and probably the most ubiquitous figure in the crowded pantheon dreamed up by centuries of beer drinkers. Throughout Europe and the Americas, beers, breweries, statues, and even malts bear his name and visage. Also called "The Patron Saint of Brewers" (a distinction also claimed for St. Arnold), in most images King Gambrinus rides a giant cask and is shown replete with an ermine cloak, a crown, and a Falstaffian mug of ale. Like other heroic archetypes, the tales associated with him are many and tall. Perhaps the most grandiose among them has Gambrinus receiving the gift of beer directly from the Egyptian fertility goddess Isis. Another tells of a medieval joint partnership with the devil in which, in exchange for some 30 years' lease on our hero's soul, the deluder teaches him the process and art of brewing. Other tales are military, whether trumpeting his exploits during the Crusades or his aid in breaking the ecclesiastical hold of Cologne and its over-taxed brewers. Still other stories devolve to nothing more than the clever solution to a drinking contest, in which Gambrinus' method of lifting an impossibly large cask involves drinking its contents first.

The stories of Gambrinus, in fact, are a pastiche of historical appearance by a number of actual personages and embellishments of the storyteller's art. Two figures are most commonly mentioned: Jan Primus (John I, 1251–1295) of Brabant, a Burgundian duke who served as "king" of the brewers' guild of Brussels, and Jean sans Peur (John the Fearless, 1371–1419), who in some versions carries the distinction of inventing hopped beer, but whose biography mainly carries a history of courtly and political intrigue. Other possibilities exist as to actual historical antecedent, many dependent on unreliable pronunciation of an actual name, and all

American bronze panel from 1937 showing Jan Gambrinus in high relief. The German phrase roughly translates to "God Save Hops and Malt."
PIKE MICROBREWERY MUSEUM, SEATTLE, WA

eventually giving way to the generally Latinized name Gambrinus.

See also BEER GODS.

Dornbusch, Horst. Born to be (beer) king. *Beer Advocate*. September 21, 2004.

Vogdes, Walt (compiled by); Gambrinus, King of Beer. http://www.steincollectors.org.

Dick Cantwell

Geary, David (1949–) founded, along with his wife Karen Geary, one of the earliest modern microbreweries in the United States and the first in the state of Maine. The D. L. Geary Brewing Co, colloquially known as Geary's, was incorporated in October 1983, making it approximately the 14th microbrewery in America at that time.

In Portland, Maine, in the 1980s, Geary had a chance meeting with the Laird of Traquair House in Scotland, Peter Maxwell Stuart. This led to an internship as a brewer at the Traquair House Brewery. See TRAQUAIR HOUSE BREWERY. Geary was working for a pharmaceutical company selling medical supplies, but when that went bankrupt, he and Karen decided to open a brewery. Geary traveled to Great Britain to work in the 17th-century Traquair Brewery located below the Traquair House manor in Peeblesshire, Scotland, near the English border.

After learning to brew in Scotland, Geary worked for several small breweries in England, including the Ringwood Brewery in Hampshire, England, owned by British brewing legend Peter Austin. There he met Alan Pugsley, a protégé of Austin. Pugsley accompanied Geary back to Maine and spent 2 years at Geary's new brewery, designing and building the brewhouse, which finally opened in 1986.

Born in Massachusetts in 1949, Geary grew up in Portland, Maine, where his family was relocated for his father's job at a trucking company when he was young. He later attended Purdue University in the 1960s, where he met his wife Karen.

In 1989, after 20 years of marriage, D. L. and Karen divorced, but continue to work together at the brewery. Their daughter, Kelly Geary Lucas, also now works for the brewery, possibly ensuring future family ownership of one of the pioneering breweries of the American craft brewing movement.

Jay R. Brooks

gelatin is a protein derived from bovine, porcine, or piscine sources and is used as a culinary gelling agent. It is also used as a fining agent in winemaking and brewing. Gelatin is prepared by making a dilute solution in hot water, cooling, and adding a small quantity of the solution to newly fermented beer. See FININGS.

Gelatin fining was once favored by US craft brewers over isinglass because of availability and cost. With advances in centrifugation and filtration technologies, generally only a few smaller brewpub brewers still use gelatin routinely. Gelatin works by the same mechanism as isinglass, although because of its amorphous structure it binds less tightly to yeast than the highly ordered helical structure of isinglass. See ISINGLASS. As a result, gelatin is generally less effective as a fining agent than isinglass and is usually only suitable for beers served from vessels that are not disturbed (e.g., cellar tanks). In this application brewers are able to serve a pleasing clarity of beer without the need for costly filtration equipment; thus, gelatin served as a useful tool in establishing visual acceptability of early craft beers in the United States.

Ian L. Ward

George Gale & Co. Ltd. was once the most significant ale brewer in the county of Hampshire on the southern coast of England, providing ale for generations of dockyard workers and sailors. Founded in 1847 on the London Road in Horndean, an important coach route from London to Portsmouth, the brewery stood for many years on the site of the Ship & Bell Inn, which was the brewery's tap.

The first brewery was destroyed by fire in 1869 and a new one was built alongside, and extended in 1983. But despite many years of growth, Gale's management concluded that the "rising costs of doing business and red tape, together with the buying clout of its larger rivals, meant a sale was inevitable." The family-owned company, with its 111 pubs, sold out to Fuller's in 2005. See FULLER, SMITH & TURNER.

The most popular of Gale's beers were Butser Bitter (named after a local hill) and Horndean Special Bitter (HSB), but it was the brewery's unfiltered and unpasteurized Prize Old Ale that gave it international renown. First brewed by the brewery's Yorkshire head brewer Barton Mears in the mid-1920s, it was sold in a uniquely shaped corked bottle. A strong brew at 9% ABV, the beer was matured in wooden tanks at the brewery for 2 years before being blended with a younger beer. During the aging it often acquired a torpid character while developing plenty of Christmas pudding fruit, lambic, and gueuze flavors. Its fans say it is best drunk when it is 20 years old, and it is notable as a touchstone of the old ale beer style. See OLD ALES.

Following the takeover, many feared that the iconic beer, with its evolving character, would be lost. But Fuller's head brewer, John Keeling, rose to the challenge of keeping the beer alive, launching Fuller's version in 2007. The first Fuller's vintage was brewed in Horndean in 2005 but matured in West London for 2 years. The cork has gone and is now replaced by a metal crown, enabling the beer to retain its carbonation. ("Finally it has some fizz," said Keeling.) Bottles of pre-Fuller's Prize Old Ale are rare but still obtainable, and many well-kept bottles have displayed extraordinary complexity and character.

Stapleton, Barry. *Gales of Horndean*. George Gale & Co, 1997.

Tim Hampson

geraniol, a compound closely associated with the aromatics of several favorite American hop varieties. It is essential oil found in some hop cultivars. Geraniol is classified as a monoterpenoid alcohol and is a primary component of rose oil, palmarosa oil, and citronella oil. In hops and beer flavor–related chemistry, it is characterized by rose-like, floral, and citrus fruitlike aroma and flavor. Geraniol is also found in coriander, lavender, lemon, lime, nutmeg, orange, rose, blueberry, and blackberry. When oxidized, geraniol becomes geranial or citral. It is found in Cascade, Citra, Centennial, Chinook, Pacific Hallertau, Southern Cross, Motueka, Aurora, and Styrian Golding hops. It is not found in UK Challenger, U.S. Challenger, Alsace Strisselspalt, Spalt Select, Sterling, Czech Saaz, Millennium, or German Magnum. Interestingly, people have differing abilities to perceive geraniol; this difference is thought to be genetically based. One-third of the population has a perception threshold of about 18 μg/l, whereas the remainder of the population has a threshold of around 350 μg/l. Geraniol is also an effective repellent of mosquitoes and is used in many DEET-free repellent preparations. Victories in that regard may be pyrrhic, however, because geraniol is also an attractant of honeybees.

See also HOP OILS.

Matthew Brynildson

German hops comprise more acres under hop poles than in any other country in the world. The second-ranked United States has fewer acres, but its production often surpasses that of Germany. The reason for this is Germany's greater concentration on low-yielding aroma hops. Germany has four main hop-growing regions: Hallertau, some 80 km (49 mi) north of Munich; Elbe-Saale in the southern part of the former East Germany; Tettnang on the north shore of Lake Constance near the Swiss border; and Spalt in Franconia, near Nuremberg, In the Middle Ages, hops were also grown on a large scale in northern Germany, but most of these fields were destroyed during the Thirty Years War (1618–48) and never recovered. There is also some hop growing in the Baden, Bitburg, and Rheinpfalz areas, all near the Rhine River. The tradition of hop growing in these areas goes back centuries, but production is dwarfed by that of the other German areas.

The Hallertau, where almost 90% of all German hops are grown, is also a center of hop research and breeding. The Hüll Hop Research Institute near Wolnzach has been breeding hops since 1926 and has released many varieties. See HALLERTAUER TAURUS (HOP), HALLERTAUER TRADITION (HOP), HERKULES (HOP), OPAL (HOP), PERLE (HOP), SAPHIR (HOP), SMARAGD (HOP), and SPALTER SELECT (HOP). Hops have been grown in the Hallertau region as far back as 736. See BAVARIA. The quintessential German hop is Hallertauer Mittelfrueh, undisputedly one of the world's finest aroma hops. See HALLERTAUER MITTELFRUEH (HOP). It now accounts for barely 10% of German production. Hersbrucker Spät is another aroma variety that was once widely grown in the Hallertau. See HERSBRUCKER SPÄT (HOP). But both classic varieties have been largely replaced by newer, Hüll-bred varieties. See HALLERTAU HOP REGION.

The Elbe-Saale region has a centuries-old hop tradition. Nowadays, it generally produces about 10% of the volume of the Hallertau. Many of its current hop yards were established during the communist East German period. The main varieties are Hallertauer Magnum and other high-alpha hops as well as some plantings of Perle and other aroma hops. See ELBE-SAALE HOP REGION.

The area around the town of Tettnang produces barely 5% of all German hops. It also has a tradition of growing fruit trees and wine grapes. Hop growing started there only in the mid-1800s. The region does have some written records of hop growing as early as 1150, but these early yards were never major producers. The town's namesake Tettnanger hop is most closely associated with the area, but Hallertauer Mittelfrueh and Perle are grown as well. See TETTNANG HOP REGION and TETTNANGER (HOP).

Hop growing near the Franconian town of Spalt has been documented as early as 1341, and during the golden age of hop growing around Nuremberg in the 1500s, Spalter hops were especially prized. In addition to the region's namesake hop Spalter, other varieties include Spalter Select and Hallertauer Mittelfrueh. The region accounts for less than 2% of all German hops. See SPALT (HOP), SPALT HOP REGION, and SPALTER SELECT (HOP).

Val Peacock

German pilsner, more often simply called "pils" in Germany, is a light-bodied and highly attenuated lager beer brewed from 100% barley malt and generally defined as a golden-colored bottom fermented bitter beer showing excellent head retention and a floral hop aroma. Together with its namesake and forerunner, the original pilsner from the town of Plzeň (Pilsen) in Czech Bohemia, German pilsner is the ancestor of the vast majority of beers brewed in the world today. From Heineken to Budweiser, from Peroni to Corona, most commercially brewed beer is golden lager, even if most of them are not made to the same standard as the originals.

That said, the use of the name "pilsner" has been a point of contention since the emergence of the style in the 1840s. For most German brewers (and almost all German beer consumers) there is little doubt that pils, pilsner, or pilsener (the terms are used interchangeably) is a style of German origin. Part of the reason for this may be that the creator of the style was Bavarian born and trained Josef Groll (1813–1887) from Vilshofen near Passau. See GROLL, JOSEF. He was the first head brewer of Pilsen's Měšťanský Pivovar (Citizens' Brewery or, in German, Bürgerliches Brauhaus). And Pilsen was a town with an influential German-speaking minority and the beer style that had made the town a household name came from a German-owned brewery. German breweries started brewing (and marketing) pilsner beers in the early 1870s, about 30 years after Groll had started brewing what we now know as Pilsner Urquell (Plzeňský Prazdroj in Czech). See PILSNER URQUELL. Most of the breweries that copied the style would have insisted that their beer did not differ from the original in appearance, taste, and even analysis.

One of the breweries that is still famous for pilsner in Germany is Simonbräu from Bitburg (now marketed as Bitburger). Theobald Simon introduced his first "bier nach pilsner art" (beer of the pilsner type), in 1883. At the Landgericht Trier (state court at Trier) in 1911 and again at the appellate court in Cologne the next year, Bitburger was sued for unlawfully using the term "pilsner" and they lost both cases. But in 1913 the Reichsgericht in Leipzig (then Germany's supreme court) ruled in favor of Simonbräu as well as Radeberger Exportbierbrauerei that pilsner had become a generic term and Bitburger (and other breweries) could use the term freely for beer brewed in Germany.

They did so in rather modest quantities. Bavarian-style dunkel was far more prestigious, and local beer styles remained more popular. By 1927 there were only 329 breweries producing their own version of a pilsner; by 1939 the number had risen to 458. Even though the world has come to think of pilsner as the quintessential German beer style, only 1 in 10 commercial breweries in Germany brewed the style before World War II.

Change came slowly after the industry had recovered from the devastations of the war. In this era of steady growth many small breweries discovered the virtues of the pilsner style, and they were encouraged to do so by the professors at both Weihenstephan in Munich and the VLB in Berlin. The role of professor Ludwig Narziss cannot be overestimated. Formerly head brewer at Löwenbräu (1958–1964) he was appointed head of the department of brewing technology (at that time Lehrstuhl für Technologie der Brauerei I) in Weihenstephan, a position he held until 1992. See NARZISS, LUDWIG. Narziss taught two generations of German brewmasters how to achieve light-colored and clean-tasting pilsner-style beers by focusing on modern brewing techniques. These included brewing with low levels of oxidation during the mashing, lautering, and boiling phases in the brewhouse as well as implementing state of the art yeast management. Weihenstephan's yeast strain W-34/70 proved to be the most reliable for the production of highly attenuated, crisp, and clean pilsner beers. Therefore, this particular strain became the standard in most German breweries. By the 1970s the German pilsner style differed notably from the Bohemian original. The aroma of diacetyl, a buttery-tasting compound produced by yeast during fermentation, remained somewhat characteristic for a Bohemian style pilsner but had disappeared from most German pilsner beers. The use of the famous Czech Saaz hops, considered style-defining up to World War II, also went by the wayside. German pilsner had diverged into a distinct variant of the style.

Small family-owned breweries from rural parts of North Rhine-Westphalia, among them Krombacher, Veltins, and Warsteiner, modernized their equipment in the 1960s and built breweries large enough to quench the thirst of the beer drinkers in Germany's most densely populated areas in the valleys of the rivers Rhine and Ruhr. Local beers (altbier, kölsch, and Dortmunder export) fell out of fashion along with the large breweries that had dominated the markets in the industrial towns when the country breweries brought their clean tasting (albeit somewhat bland) pilsner beers to the urban beer bars. By the late 1980s about two thirds of the German beer market consisted of pilsner. Pilsner became so popular that beer drinkers built rituals around it, energetically discussing the right dispensing method, which bizarrely came to include such features as a 7-minute draught pour. They claimed that it took this long to build perfect foam, and it took years for many to realize that the beer actually tasted better if served quickly. Beer drinkers also demanded that their local breweries introduce their own pilsner brands. Most breweries did, including those in Bavaria where it had been a common belief that the relatively hard water in southern Germany would not allow brewers to produce authentic pilsner beers; the water from Pilsen is famously soft. Some of the most characteristic examples of the German pilsner style now come from the south—the aromatic Waldhaus pils, the Meckatzer pils, and the Ketterer pils, to mention a few. These beers emphasize the hop aromas of southern German hops, most prominently Tettnanger. See TETTNANGER (HOP). Northern German beers maybe somewhat higher in bitterness, but typically have less hop aroma, with Jever Pils being the most prominent example. In the meantime the right to use the name "pilsner" was challenged over and over again. As late as 1966 Pilsner Urquell (then a state-owned Czechoslovakian National Company) was forced to drop the right to exclusively use the term "Ur-Pils" (a brand name also used by Karlsberg in Homburg/Saar and a couple of smaller breweries).

Today, the straw gold color remains a hallmark of the style, but bitterness has decreased substantially in most examples and now averages about 26 IBUs. See INTERNATIONAL BITTERNESS UNITS (IBUS). A series of analyses carried out by the VLB shows that there has been a steady decrease of bitterness in the hundreds of samples they analyze every year. In 1973 the average German pilsner would have had a bitterness of 34 IBUs, with extreme samples going as high as 50 IBUs, and the low end of the scale having only 16 IBUs. There was little change until 1985, but by 1995 the average bitterness was down to 30, and another decade later it was 27. Statistics from 2008 indicate an average of 26.5 IBUs for German pilsner beers, with the lowest ranking sample having only 13 IBUs and the highest, 37 IBUs.

In the style guidelines for the prestigious World Beer Cup competition, German pilsner is still defined as having 30 to 40 IBUs, but the German brewers themselves have allowed the snappy hop character of pilsner to erode.

As of 2010 it was estimated that beers labeled as pils, pilsner, and pilsener accounted for two-thirds of all beer sold in Germany, with the majority of this beer sold in northwestern Germany where it holds about three-quarters of the market; and a shrinking market in the south, where pilsner accounts for only about one-quarter of total beer sales.

Kisch, Wilhelm. *Besitzstand und verwirkung – Ein beitrag zum recht der bierbezeichnung*. Berlin: Carl Heymanns Verlag, 1941.

Harms, Diedrich. Durchschnittswerte bei bieranalysen. *Brauerei-Forum* 7 (2009): 15.

Voss, Heinrich. Pils bedeutet vielfalt. *Getränkefachgroßhandel* 6 (2010): 8 ff.

Conrad Seidl

Germany has arguably the oldest continuous brewing culture in the world. The origins of German brewing are shrouded in mystery, mostly because the ancient inhabitants of what is now the territory of Germany were illiterate tribesmen who left no written records. We do know from archaeological finds that brewing must have been practiced at least by the late Bronze Age, which lasted in Central Europe roughly from 2000 to 700 BC. Compared with the Stone Age that preceded it, agricultural implements and cooking gear—both essential for raising grain and making beer from it—improved during this period. The most conclusive evidence we have for brewing at this time is an earthenware amphora from around 800 BC. It was found in 1935 in a burial mound of the so-called Celtic Hallstatt culture near the small northern Bavarian village of Kasendorf, some 7 miles west of Kulmbach. See BAVARIA. An analysis of the traces inside the crock identified the content as a black wheat ale flavored with oak leaves. The amphora is now in the Bavarian Beer Museum in Kulmbach.

The first written evidence of Germanic beer making is actually Roman. As the Romans ventured across the Alps, around the beginning of the current epoch, to subdue the barbarians to the north, they sent not only legionnaires to do the fighting but also sophisticated scribes to record the events for posterity. Caesar himself made the first move into Gaul, which is now mostly France, during his Gallic Wars (58 to 51 BC), which he then described in his famous *Commentarii*. But perhaps the most concise descriptions of Germanic customs including brewing come from Publius Cornelius Tacitus (56–117 AD). In his *De origine et situ germanii* (About the Origin and Location of the Germans) he wrote that the Germans were not much interested in hard work—not exactly the image that Germans have today—yet were capable of suffering cold and hunger well. However, he said, they could not in the least endure heat and thirst. And against that nagging thirst, the Germans had a remedy: "*Potui humor ex hordeo aut frumento, in quandam similitudinem vini corruptus.*" (They drank a liquor of barley or other grain that was fermented into a corrupt resemblance to wine.) This, of course, was beer. The Romans generally disdained the German "corrupt" grain-wine, the smell of which the Roman Emperor Julian the Apostate (331–363 AD) once likened to that of a billy goat. However, because it was simply not possible, even for Romans, to freight enough wine from Italy across the Alps to keep the troops in Germany happy, the Romans eventually not only made German beer-brewing their own, but also improved upon it. The evidence for this is a complete Roman brewery that was unearthed near Regensburg, Bavaria, in 1978. It contained all the facilities required for malting,

Photograph of the Pinkus Müller brewpub in Münster, Germany, taken in 1928 at an event celebrating the brewpub's redecoration in a Westphalian style. COURTESY OF PINKUS MÜLLER

mashing, and wort boiling. This site is now considered the oldest evidence of "modern" brewing, in which the old loaves of bread are replaced by mashed grains as the prime raw material for wort sugars. Because the start of mashed brewing in Central Europe has until recently been attributed to early medieval monks, this Roman archaeological find places the discovery of mashing at least half a millennium earlier than had previously been thought. It seems that wine-drinking Romans were the inventors of the modern beer mash, a funny twist in the history of alcoholic beverages.

As the Roman Empire began to crumble and its legionnaires went marching home in the 5th century, the next army to descend upon the Germans was not military but religious in nature, thanks in large part to the influence of a British man named Patricius, later better known as Saint Patrick. He was born around 385 AD not far from present-day Glasgow in Scotland. He was 31 years old when he claimed to have been instructed by a divine voice to go to Ireland and make it Christian. This he did so well that, by the middle of the 6th century, Ireland was thoroughly Christianized and awash in surplus monks. So these friars laced up their sandals and headed for the heathen forests of Central Europe, eager to save Continental souls from eternal damnation. There they set up a string of small Benedictine monasteries as hubs from which they spread the gospel. See ST. GALLEN. It is not clear whether these missionaries had made beer back home, but they clearly started to do so on the Continent. Soon their monasteries were centers not only of preaching and learning but also of brewing. As educated people able to read and write, they kept notes of their brewing. They experimented with new ingredients and discovered the benefits of hops; they tried new techniques and came up with decoction; and they developed new brewing equipment that we now take for granted, including the coolship and the lauter tun. See COOLSHIP, DECOCTION, HOPS, and LAUTERING. Eventually the monks brewed beers not only for their own consumption but also for sale and profit. One such beer-making Benedictine abbey was Weihenstephan, founded in 724. It obtained its brewing license in 1040 and is now considered the

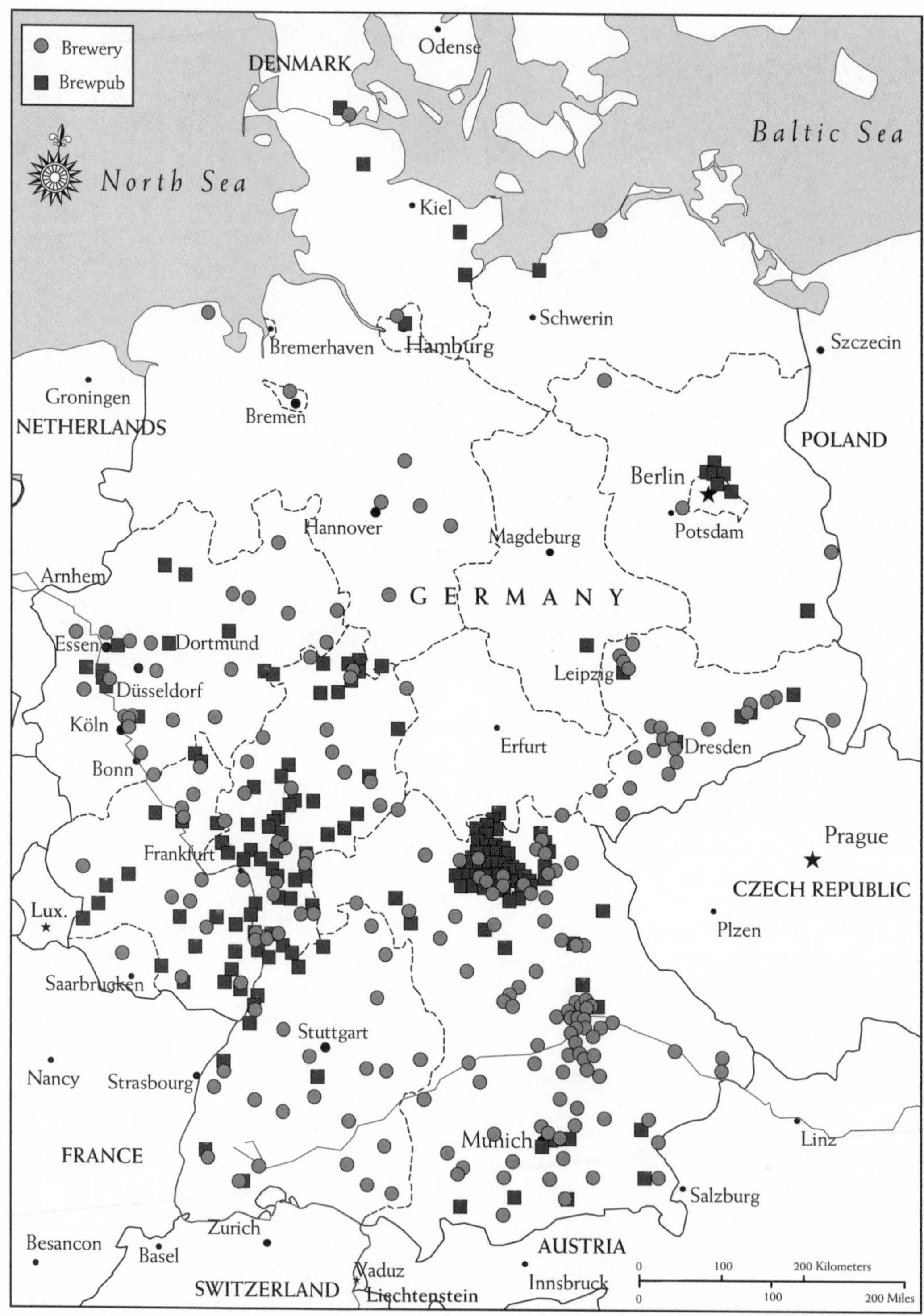

German breweries and brewpubs. GEORGE CHAKVETADZE, ALLIANCE PUBLISHING world's oldest continuously operating brewery. See WEIHENSTEPHAN. Although the period between roughly 500 and 1000 AD is generally referred to as the Dark Ages, brewing was clearly one of its bright lights, because it was in the monasteries that brewing, an erstwhile tribal household chore, became institutionalized. Indeed, for the first time in Europe, brewing actually became a profession.

Monastery breweries were spectacularly successful; as they got richer and more powerful, largely on the profits from beer, the landed feudal lords, the mercantile city burghers, and even the more secular bishops and the mightiest dukes became jealous. Imitation being the sincerest form of flattery, other players of the feudal order soon wanted a piece of the beer action and started their own breweries. This is when breweries started to be identified by their ownership, and if you travel through Germany today, you can still get a sense of the origins of many local breweries. You may encounter a Fürstliches Brauhaus (ducal brewhouse), a Klosterbrauerei (monastery brewery), a Bürgerbräu (burgher brewery), a Bischofsbrauerei (bishop's brewery), a Stadtbrauerei (city brewery), a Gildebrauerei (guild brewery), or a Hofbräuhaus (court brewhouse). Starting with the 2nd millennium, therefore, institutional brewing in Germany, now in several competing hands, took off, and it did so in different directions and with great regional variations.

Many of the new, secular players in the brewing economy lacked the experience of their religious competitors, and in many areas beer quality took a turn for the worse. It seemed that the new brewers were gradually unlearning or ignoring the very knowledge that the monks had so studiously accumulated over many centuries. As beer quality declined, many unscrupulous brewers from the ranks of the old aristocracy and the emerging bourgeoisie started to lower their standards to raise their profits. All sorts of strange, often harmful beer ingredients started to find their ways into the mashes and kettles. See ADULTERATION. Some were cheap starch substitutes, others merely cover-ups for bad flavors. Brewers used legumes and tubers in their mashes and soot, oxen bile, tree bark, poisonous mushrooms, potent herbs, and powerful spices in their kettles and fermenters. Whereas monastery beer was once healthy and nourishing, the new secular brews were just as likely to make people sick as not. There were early, mostly failed, administrative attempts, usually by local city councils, to curb such felonious brewing practices, but it took two very different forces to eventually restore beer quality in the land. One was a powerful commercial incentive, mostly in the north of Germany; the other was a set of strict political edicts, mostly in the south.

During most of the Middle Ages, the center of political power in the German Empire, which then included Austria, was located in the south, where such cities as Nuremberg, Augsburg, Munich, Regensburg, and Vienna functioned as hubs of commerce and influence. The orientation of southern Germany was clearly directed toward Italy, with the all-important Holy See in Rome, the Renaissance culture in Florence, and a great deal of merchant wealth in Venice. Northern Germany, by contrast, was fairly remote from the center of imperial power, and the inhabitants' orientation there was more toward trade, commerce, and the sea. The northern centers were wealthy cities like Cologne, Hamburg, Bremen, Brunswick, Hannover, and Lübeck. By the 13th century, the cosmopolitan merchants in these cities understood that the old feudal order with its licenses, levies, excise duties, and commerce-inhibiting customs tariffs could no longer adequately represent their interests. So they got together to form a protective trading association, soon to be known as the Hanseatic League. The League started out, in 1241, as a compact just between the cities of Hamburg and Lübeck, but soon it had more than 200 member cities. Jointly, these cities opened up the Baltic trade, and they soon had warehouses and permanent agencies in many ports in such places as Russia, Estonia, Sweden, England, Holland, and Flanders. They traded in furs, metals, cloth, salt, dried fish . . . and beer. By cutting out the feudal lords, the League, in effect, had created what might be considered the first European economic union, free of tariffs and national trade barriers. In fact, the League's demand for beer as a trading commodity became so enormous that breweries evolved into the main employers in many port cities. In 1376, for instance, records indicate that Hamburg had 457 burgher-owned breweries; by 1526, it had 531, and half the wage-earning population was engaged in brewing. The principal beer made in Hamburg was called keutebier. It was an ale brewed from a mixture of barley and wheat.

This is not to say that all northern German beers were by any means flawless. Yet some of them became famous well beyond their local areas. The beers from the city of Einbeck in Lower Saxony, for instance, made it all the way to the court of the Bavarian dukes of Wittelsbach in Munich, where the beers were first mispronounced in the local vernacular as "ein bock bier" and then copied in the ducal brewhouse, which is how the bockbier got to Bavaria. See WITTELSBACHER FAMILY. There was the Zerbster Bitterbier from the small town of Zerbst, halfway between Hannover and Berlin, which could boast some 600 breweries in the late Middle Ages. The brew in question was a well-hopped, spicy "bitter beer" made from barley with some wheat. It was first mentioned in a guild document in 1375 and was last brewed in 1949. Duckstein beer from the Lower-Saxony town of Königslutter was another famous brew. It was a top-fermented wheat beer made with very hard local water. Referred to in its heyday in the 16th and 17th centuries in the male grammatical gender as "der duckstein," it was produced by 73 licensed breweries mostly for export. That Duckstein was last brewed in 1898, but the brand has since been revived by the Holsten Brewery of Hamburg, this time as a grammatically transgendered altbier-like brew called "das duckstein." The city of Brunswick, too, became famous for a trading beer called mumme. This was a high-gravity, low-attenuated, syrupy, barley-based brew of legendary keeping qualities and a favorite of the Hanseatic League for shipping to its most distant markets. In Hannover, the most famous trading beer was created by—and named after—Cord Broyhan, a Hamburg-trained brewmaster. His beer reportedly was a well-hopped, perhaps slightly sour ale of wheat and barley, which became one of the most widely distributed beer styles in northern Germany in its day. In fact, it became so profitable that in 1609 the Hannover city council decided to form a producer cartel by limiting the number of burghers who could brew broyhan beer to 317. They then combined the burghers into a guild and turned the guild into a shareholders company. The resulting brewery is still in operation today as the Gilde Brauerei, now owned by Anheuser-Busch InBev.

Whereas the profit motive of the northern merchants provided the impetus for many northern trading beers to be made with good drinkability and keeping quality, no such incentive existed in the south, where the feudal order remained more effective at suppressing the entrepreneurial spirit. There, what was needed to clean up the people's drink was a draconian decree from above, which came in 1516, at least in Bavaria, when, on April 23, on the occasion of a meeting of the Assembly of Estates, at Ingolstadt, north of Munich, Duke Wilhelm IV commanded that henceforth, in his realm, beer was to be made from only three ingredients, water, barley, and hops. Today, this now almost 500-year-old decree is regarded as the origin of the modern German Beer Purity Law. See REINHEITSGEBOT. The decree effectively kept unappetizing and harmful ingredients out of the brewhouse, but it still was not sufficient to ensure the drinkability of Bavarian beer during the hot summer months. In the days before refrigeration, airborne microbial infections would invariably visit the brewers' open fermenters in summertime. Not understanding the true cause of the bad summer beers, Wilhelm's successor, Duke Albrecht V, went one step further and simply forbade all brewing between April 23 and September 21. The effect of this summer brewing prohibition was essentially to turn Bavarian brewing entirely into a lager beer culture, because in the winter only cold-fermenting lager yeasts could still make beer, whereas in the more moderate northern climate the beers were usually warm-fermented ales. See ALE and LAGER.

Although the profit motive in the north and the decrees in the south seemed to have rescued much of German beer in the 16th century, the 17th century was about to deal it a crucial blow. The outbreak of the Thirty Years War in 1618 ushered in more than a century of virtually uninterrupted warfare, which lasted to the end of the Great Northern War in 1721. All major European powers took part in the carnage, usually aligned along religious lines with Austria under the Habsburg monarchy as the head of the Catholic alliance and Sweden as the head of the Protestant alliance. Economic activity came to a virtual halt, and, within a century, Europe had lost about half its population either to war or to starvation. Commercial brewing, which depends on an ample and steady supply of grain, of course had all but stopped too. Even the once mighty Hanseatic League could not survive the conflict and formally dissolved in 1669.

It took almost a full century for Europe, and for brewing, to recover, only to be thrown back briefly into a continent-wide conflict, this time driven by the territorial ambitions of France. After the Napoleonic Wars, however, which lasted from 1799 to 1815, the Vienna Congress reorganized the European map and finally created almost 100 years of relative peace and prosperity. The 19th century turned into a time of incredible progress in science, technology, and industry, interrupted only by two short wars: the 7-week Austro-Prussian War of 1866 and the Franco-Prussian War of 1870/1871. Steam-driven, mechanized production methods combined with metallurgical advances and scientific discoveries such as the microbiological causes of diseases—and of fermentation—led to an unprecedented leap forward in the wealth and health of humanity, in Germany just as elsewhere. In brewing, the development and widespread use of new techniques, tools, and equipment—including the thermometer, the manometer, the hydrometer, indirect-fired kiln for malting, copper brew kettles, refrigeration, pasteurization, beer filtration, and the isolation of pure yeast strains—spawned the development of many of today's classic beers styles. And the new railroad networks made transportation of these new beers possible to markets that had been unreachable before. In Germany, therefore—but also on the British Isles and to some extent in Austria and Bohemia—the 19th century became the *Belle Époque* of new beer styles. Milestones in the development of new German and German-inspired beers include the Paulaner Brewery's Salvator doppelbock of 1835; the altbier, which started to take on its modern specifications in Düsseldorf with the Schumacher Alt of 1838; the Dreher Brewery's Vienna lager of 1841; the Spaten Brewery's märzenbier of 1841; the Pilsner Burgher Brewery's Bohemian pilsner of 1842, which was created there by Bavarian brewmaster Josef Groll; the Spaten Brewery's oktoberfestbier of 1871; the Kronen Brewery's Dortmund Export of 1871; first northern German pilsner of 1872 brewed by the Aktienbrauerei Zum Bierkeller of Radeberg, which has since become the Radeberger Group; the Spaten Brewery's Munich helles of 1894; and the evolution of the pale wiess (white) ale style in Cologne in the 1890s, the forerunner of the modern kölsch, which became codified in the 1920s. See ALTBIER, DOPPELBOCK, GERMAN PILSNER, HELLES, KÖLSCH, MÄRZENBIER, PILSNER, and VIENNA LAGER.

With such a rich recent history to build upon, the 20th century became one of prosperity for German breweries, except, of course during the two world wars and their aftermaths. By the 1970s, German beer drinkers annually consumed about 150 l per capita of almost entirely domestically produced beer. This made Germany the world's second largest beer producer, surpassed only by the huge market of the United States. There were about 2,500 breweries in Germany, many dating back to the late Middle Ages or the beginning of the Industrial Revolution. Most were small producers serving mostly local markets. Traditionally, Germany has always had one of the world's most decentralized brewing industries, and even today, the German market leader, the Radeberger Group with more than a dozen production sites and many more beer brands, holds only about 15% of the national market. See RADEBERGER GROUP.

The fortunes of the German brew industry, however, have turned darker in recent years. During the past 3 decades, German per capita beer consumption has plummeted by roughly one-third, causing Germany, which currently produces slightly below 100 million hl (roughly 85 million US barrels) of beer per year, to drop from second to fifth place among the world's top beer producers. This list is now headed by China with roughly 425 million hl (362 million US bbl), followed by the United States with roughly 230 million hl (195 million US bbl), as well as Russia and Brazil with almost 110 million hl (93 million US bbl) each. During the same period, the number of German breweries has declined by about one-half, either through mergers and acquisitions or because of outright closures. There are barely 1,300 breweries left in the now reunited Germany. There are many theories why Germans, especially younger Germans, appear to be turning away from the universal quaff of their forebears. Some blame the lack of innovation by German breweries who have been focusing increasingly just on pilsners. These tend to be made to a fairly high level of quality, but they are also very similar and difficult to distinguish by the ordinary consumer. The statistics support this argument: pilsner brands now account for more than half of the German beer market. Weissbiers, which are particularly popular in Bavaria, plus helles and pale Export lagers combined, account for almost one-fourth. Beer mix drinks, light beers, and non-alcoholic beers together make up about 10% of the market; and the remaining roughly 10%

is divided among all other styles, including the venerable altbier, bock bier, dunkel, kellerbier, kölsch, märzenbier, rauchbier, and schwarzbier. The large market share of pilsners of similar taste and quality has led to fierce competition among breweries, not through differentiation of the actual beers, but mostly on the basis of price through razor-thin margins. That means that few breweries can afford to build up financial reserves that would allow them to survive even small setbacks. Another factor in the decline of German beer drinking is clearly the country's virtually zero tolerance for drunk driving combined with very stiff penalties for those who get caught.

The only glimmer of hope on the German beer horizon, it seems, is a recent wave of brewpub openings. These new artisanal breweries cater to a small, but growing clientele of German beer connoisseurs who are interested in beer variety and stylistic innovation—a consumer segment that is not averse to experimenting with non-German beers, including traditional British and cutting-edge American styles. To many observers, the German beer culture is now at the crossroads, just as the North American beer culture was some 3 decades ago. It will either spawn its own craft brewing movement, capable of reviving the vast portfolio of German traditional beer styles and of embarking on innovations that make beer interesting again . . . or it will gradually move further and further in the direction of a pilsner monoculture as smaller producers become absorbed or are eliminated by international conglomerates armed with economies of scale and marketing prowess. It would be a rather sad fate for one of the world's greatest brewing nations.

Anonymous. *Der wohlerfahrene Brau-Meister.* Anonymous publisher, 1759 (translation of title: The well-experienced brew-master).

Blankenburg, Christine von. *Die Hanse und ihr Bier—Brauwesen und Bierhandel im hansischen Verkehrsgebiet.* Cologne, Germany: Böhlau Verlag, 2001 (translation of title: The Hanseatic League and its beers—brew industry and beer trade in the Hanseatic commerce area).

Boos, Andreas, Eine Brauerei aus der Römischen Kaiserzeit in Regensburg-Grossprüfening, in *Jahrbuch 2010 der Gesellschaft für Geschichte des Brauwesens e.V.* Berlin: VLB Berlin, 2010 (translation of title: A brewery from the time of imperial Rome in Regensburg-Grossprüfening, an article published in the *2010 Annals of the Society for the History of Brewing* at the VLB in Berlin).

Dornbusch, Horst. *PROST! The story of German beer.* Boulder, CO: Brewers Publications, 1998.

Ehrenfels-Mehringen, Erich v. *Gambrinus.* Duisburg, Germany: Carl Lange, 1953.

Friedrich, Ernst. *Bier.* Künzelsau, Germany: Sigloch, 1993 (translation of title: Bier)

Gerlach, Wolfgang, Hermann Gutmann, Michael Hassenkamp, Udo Moll, and Werner Widmann. *Das deutsche Bier.* Hamburg, Germany: HB Verlags- und Vertriebsgesellschaft, 1984 (translation of title: German beer).

Knaust, Heinrich. *Fünff Bücher, Von der Göttlichen vnd Edlen Gabe/der Philosophischen/hochtheweren vnd wunderbaren Kunst Bier zu brawen. Auch von Namen der vornempsten Biere/in gantz Teudtschlanden/vund von derer Naturen/Temperamenten, Qualiteten, Art vnd Eigenschafft/Gesundheit vnd vungesundheit/Sie sein Weitzen/oder Gersten/Weisse/oder Rotte Biere/ Gewürtzet oder ungewürtzet. Auffs new ybersehen/vnd in viel wege/vber vorige edition/gemehret vnd gebessert.* Erfurt, Germany: Georg Bawman, 1575 (translation of title: Five books about the divine and noble gift, the philosophical, highly valued and wonderful art of beer brewing. Also about the names of the loftiest beers in all of Germany and their names, temperaments, qualities, type and characteristics, health and unhealth, be they wheat or barley, white or red beers, spiced or unspiced. Newly reviewed and in many ways over the previous edition enlarged and improved).

Lohberg, Rolf. *Das große Lexikon vom Bier.* Ostfildern: Scripta, no date (translation of title: The great dictionary of beer).

Schumann, Uwe-Jens. *Deutschland Deine Biere.* Munich, Germany: Zaber Sandmann, 1993 (translation of title: Germany, your beers).

Unger, Richard W. *Beer in the Middle Ages and the Renaissance.* Philadelphia: University of Pennsylvania Press, 2004.

Horst Dornbusch

germination is involved in the production of malt from cereal grains. In cereals such as barley, root (chit) emergence indicates that germination has taken place. However, in the malting process the term "germination" is used to describe the long growth/modification phase between steeping and kilning. The embryo is the germinating organ of the grain. It is composed of the axis and the scutellum. The scutellum is the single (mono) cotyledon of the grain and is a food storage organ. For example, it stores lipids, proteins, and vitamin B like the aleurone layer. The axis contains the shoot and the roots. The shoot is covered by the colepotile. Both tissues constitute the acrospire. The tiny roots are covered by the coleorhizae. Both tissues constitute the chit. Hydration (wetting/steeping) of the embryo at normal temperatures in the presence of air increases its metabolism. Increased metabolism causes the chit and the acrospire to elongate. The acrospire grows slowly along the top of the grain under the pericarp covering layer and exits at the nonembryo end of the grain if the grain is overmalted. The length of the acrospire is used as a modification test. The chit elongates rapidly and ruptures the covering layers before extensive elongation of the acrospires has occurred. This early rupturing of the covering layer by the chit is called germination. During the germination process the axis of the embryo produces gibberellic acid (GA_3). In general, emergence of the chit indicates that gibberellic acid has been transported from the axis to the aleurone layer and that endosperm degrading enzymes are being produced. See GIBBERLLINS.

Dormant grains do not germinate and will not make acceptable malt. Dormancy can be genetic and can be induced by unfavorable climatic (cold) conditions. Dormancy can be broken by warm storage of dried (e.g., 11% moisture) barley. Uneven germination will produce unevenly modified malts. During malting, germinated grains will absorb added gibberellic acid faster than ungerminated (dormant) grains, causing even greater unevenness of modification. Uneven modification is a primary factor in poor brewhouse performance. Absorbed gibberellic acid complements the natural levels of gibberellic acid produced by the embryo. Optimal levels of gibberellic acid will produce optimal levels of endosperm-degrading enzymes. However, some barley varieties do not require additional levels of gibberellic acid to malt well.

Respiration (oxygen uptake and loss of carbon dioxide) promotes germination and enzyme production in malting grains. High respiration and excessive root and shoot growth cause high malting loss. Malting loss reflects potential loss of starches available for mashing. In the past, malting loss was reduced in some quarters by applying potassium bromate. Today, malting loss is controlled by humidity, temperature, and appropriate growth time during the malting process.

Barleys that germinate on the ear in the field or in storage before steeping are described as having pregerminated. Pregerminating potential may be genetic and/or climatic. Pregermination of cereals such as barley and wheat can destroy the processing potential of the grain, encourage microbial growth, and initiate premature enzyme development, which damages the malting potential of barley and the baking potential of wheat.

Germination energy, germination capacity, embryo viability, water sensitivity (vigor in steeping), and the pregermination levels of cereals can be detected using recommended tests.

See also AMERICAN SOCIETY OF BREWING CHEMISTS (ASBC), DORMANCY (OF BARLEY), EUROPEAN BREWERY CONVENTION (EBC), and MALTING.

Palmer, G. H. Cereals in malting and brewing. *Cereal science and technology*, ed G. H. Palmer, 61–242. Aberdeen, UK: Aberdeen University Press, 1989.

Palmer. G. H. *The encyclopedia of seeds, science, technology and uses*, ed M. Black, J. D. Bewley, and P. Halmer, 396–404. Oxford, UK: Cabi, 2006.

Geoff H. Palmer

germination-kilning vessels (GKV) are combination vessels in the malting plant that combine the last two of the three principal stages of the malting process into one. The malting stages are (1) steeping of the grain in cylindro-conical or flat-bottomed tanks to clean and hydrate it; (2) germinating the grain under temperature-controlled humidified air in rectangular or circular vessels to activate enzymes that begin the process of gum, starch, and protein modification; and (3) kilning the grain to dry it and to kill the new plant shoot (the acrospire) and rootlets that started to develop during germination. In a GKV, germination and drying occur within the same vessel without the need to transfer the green malt from a germination box to a kiln. Once germination is complete, the humidified air that was blown through the grain bed is replaced by hot dry air.

GKVs, like single-purpose germination vessels, come in rectangular or circular shapes. They need to be fitted with malt turners to keep the malt rootlets from matting together at the germination phase and to ensure proper aeration during aspiration. During germination, the turners ensure the proper rotation of the batch from top to bottom. This ensures the homogeneity of the finished malt.

GKVs tend to be completely automated. Malt turners in a rectangular GKV move back and forth through the grain bed. In a circular GKV, the floor carrying the grain may revolve instead, while the malt turners are fix-mounted and thus stationary.

See also MALTING.

Thomas Kraus-Weyermann

gibberellins are a group of complex chemical compounds found in plants. Many of these compounds have positive effects on plant growth and development and are regarded as natural plant hormones. They are usually described as GAs. The compound gibberellic acid, which is used in the malting industry to increase enzyme production and accelerate endosperm modification, is a gibberellin. Gibberellic acid is also used to overcome dormancy in some seeds and to produce seedless fruits such as grapes. However, dormancy in barley is not broken by gibberellic acid during malting. At present, 126 gibberellins have been isolated from higher plant tissues such as leaves, fruits, and seeds, and from lower plants such as fungi and mosses. Gibberellins are categorized numerically from GA_1 to GA_{126}. Gibberellic acid is GA_3.

A gibberellin complex was isolated from fungal infected rice plants in Japan in 1926. In 1935 the complex was isolated from the fungus *Gibberella fujikuroi.* This crude complex of natural plant hormones promoted plant growth and development. It also increased alpha amylase production in cereal grains. The first gibberellin to be isolated and identified from the gibberellin complex was GA_1 in 1957. Gibberellic acid was isolated later at Imperial Chemical Industries (ICI) and was applied to malting barley to increase enzyme production and accelerate endosperm modification in 1959. Unlike other gibberellins which are isolated in small quantities, gibberellic acid is isolated in large quantities from the fungus Gibberella fujikuroi (Gibberella moniliforme) and is produced commercially from this fungus. Not all gibberellins have biological activity. Some do not have any obvious actions on plant growth and development. Others like gibberellic acid (GA_3), GA_1, GA_4, and GA_7 are very active and have different actions in different plants. During malting, gibberellic acid will increase alpha amylase development in barley and wheat but not in sorghum.

Palmer, G. H. Cereals in malting and brewing. In *Cereal science and technology*, ed. G. H. Palmer, 61–242. Aberdeen, Scotland: Aberdeen University Press. 1989.

Geoff H. Palmer

ginger beer is not technically a beer at all, but an alcoholic drink invented by the British in the mid-18th century using ginger root and sugar grown in the West Indies. It became popular in various parts of what was then the British Empire as well as in the United States. Today, most genuine ginger beer is made from grated fresh ginger roots, acidified with lemon juice and zest, and sweetened with sugar. Traditionally, this mixture was fermented with a gelatinous substance called "ginger beer plant," a type of starter made from lemon, sugar, and ginger. This blend was left exposed to the ambient air for about a week for spontaneous fermentation with wild yeasts and lactobacilli. The organisms involved were originally identified by the British botanist Harry Marshall Ward in 1887. Some of the ginger beer plant would be added to the main ferment, much like a sourdough mother supplies the leavening for sourdough bread. The volume of alcohol in the brew was, of course, dependent on the amount of sugar and the degree to which it fermented out. Today, ginger is a popular flavoring for craft-brewed beers in the United States and the UK and also among homebrewers. Peeled ginger is usually added to hopped wort in the kettle, and in sufficient amounts it gives not only flavor but also a form of spicy heat. This strong flavor characterizes the ginger beers still widely available in the UK and the Caribbean, but these are now simply soft drinks. Most Americans and Canadians are familiar with a much milder-tasting soft drink variant called dry ginger ale, which became popular in the 1930s and quickly eclipsed the older, more robust versions of the drink.

Chow ginger beer recipe. http://www.chow.com/recipes/10683-chow-ginger-beer (accessed March 29, 2011).

The REAL ginger beer recipe! http://www.instructables.com/id/The-REAL-ginger-beer-recipe/ (accessed March 29, 2011).

Chris Holliland

Glacier (hop) is a modern American variety that was commercially released in 2000 by Dr Stephen

Kenny of Washington State University. Its outstanding characteristics are a fairly low cohumulone content of 11% to 13% and a good yield, averaging 2,135 lb/acre. As far as its breeding goes, Glacier is a genuine mutt, a genetic derivative of nine different varieties of hops, including such international stalwarts as Brewer's Gold, Northern Brewer, Bullion, and East Kent Golding. See BREWER'S GOLD (HOP), NORTHERN BREWER (HOP), BULLION (HOP), and EAST KENT GOLDING (HOP). Not surprisingly, the characteristics of this hop seem to come from everywhere and reveal both German and English leanings. The aroma is a mixture of citrus, fruit, and floral notes, with some earthy English underpinnings, whereas the bitterness is very refined. Beers bittered with Glacier, therefore, tend to have a gently perceived bitterness that can belie high international bitterness units. See BITTERNESS. It also makes a fine dry hop, especially as an accent for pale ales. Glacier has a plump, medium-compact cone and matures in mid-season. It is susceptible to both powdery and downy mildew, but responds well to protective spraying. It stores well, with 71.5% of alpha acids remaining after 6 months of storage at room temperature.

Hopsteiner. Glacier. http://www.hopsteiner.com/pdf/us/Glacier.pdf/ (accessed January 31, 2011).

Jon Griffin

glassware, the proper serving vessel for beer and a vital instrument for shaping our sensory perceptions of drinks. Glassware's role in beer service is complex. Visually, a particular glass will set up a series of expectations. The sight of large chunky glasses on a table will evoke an oncoming period of hearty enjoyment of relatively simple beers with

Photograph, c. 1933, illustrating various classic beer glass shapes as well as a beer comb, used to flatten the head of a beer. Prohibition caused a lack of public knowledge of how to serve alcoholic beverages, an issue addressed in this nationally syndicated photograph. PIKE MICROBREWERY MUSEUM, SEATTLE, WA family or friends. Elegant stemware may send a different signal, perhaps an expectation of more complex beers, of sipping more than drinking, a sign that some genuine attention should be paid. Most of us know this almost instinctually. In a restaurant, when especially large wine glasses are brought to a nearby table, it is hard not to wonder what wine is to be poured into them; one expects that it will be something special.

Beyond the visual/emotional effects of glassware, we have the mechanical and practical aspects. From this perspective, the best beer glasses bear a strong resemblance to wine glasses. The rim, preferably thin and often slightly flared, presents the beer directly to the palate without the sensory interference of a large chunk of glass. The bowl of the glass evolves, holds, and concentrates aromatics emerging from the liquid. Because most of our sense of taste is actually a sense of smell, this aspect is critical. As with wine, any beer that is truly to be tasted rather than simply drunk must be swirled or rotated in the glass. The shape of the bowl makes this easy to do, and as the liquid evaporates from the surface of the glass, the full array of the beer aromatics can become apparent. The bowl also holds the beer's head of foam and a flared rim helps support the foam below.

Below this, the stem supports the bowl and preferably has enough length to accommodate the grip of a few fingers while keeping the bowl clear of the other activities on the table. Beer served in stemmed glassware will maintain its temperature better; the liquid will not be warmed by the heat of the drinker's hand. The stem also makes swirling easier, although this always works best when the foot of the glass remains firmly planted in the table. The foot itself, of course, gives the glass its stability and a sense of presence.

All the aspects above are well served by Belgian-style "tulip" glasses, and similar glassware styles have been adopted by craft brewers worldwide. When appropriate beer glassware is unavailable, there is no reason for any hesitation to use wine glasses, which are well suited to the appreciation of most complex drinks. White wine glasses tend to be the most versatile, but red wine glasses can be appropriate for very strong, complex, or aged beers. See DRINKING VESSELS.

See also SERVING BEER.

Garrett Oliver

global warming refers to the gradual increase in the earth's temperature caused by human activity. The planet gets its core weather temperature from the greenhouse effect, which is a naturally occurring process in which gases trap heat in the lower level of the earth's atmosphere. The rise and fall of greenhouse gases are a naturally occurring phenomenon and the source of the planet's long history of ice ages followed by warming thaws.

In the 1880s, scientists began to notice a gradual warming trend in the earth's atmosphere. Not until the 1950s did they realize that this was likely the result of human activities, such as deforestation and the burning of fossil fuels that became commonplace during the Industrial Age.

According to the Intergovernmental Panel on Climate Change, global warming is "unequivocal" based on the increase in air and sea temperatures worldwide, rates of melting snow and ice, and the rise in average sea levels. If global warming continues unabated, it is predicted that temperatures will rise from 3°F to 7°F by 2100, the greatest rate of increase in the earth's temperature in the past 10,000 years.

The brewing industry is already feeling the effects of global warming in several ways. Energy costs are rising worldwide as the industrial economy's heavy reliance on fossil fuels for energy is affected by escalating oil costs. This increased cost gets passed down the manufacturing chain and affects the production line and packaging costs for breweries.

Prices on key ingredients for brewing are also beginning to rise as the agriculture industry is affected by changing weather patterns. Heat waves in Europe, Australia, and New Zealand in recent years have greatly damaged vital barley crops, reducing quality output. Breweries must pay a premium price for high-quality barley, available now in reduced amounts, or substitute for a lower quality level, which can contribute to lower malt extract, reduced processing performance, and inferior flavors. Hops are similarly affected. In 2009 the Czech Hydrometeorological Institute found that the concentration of bitter alpha acids in the prized Czech Saaz hops has declined 0.06% per year since 1954. The study blamed climate change for the decline of the overall quality of Czech Saaz. Many climate scientists expect global warming to put additional disease pressure on many food crops, including barley and hops.

In light of these events, many breweries are beginning to turn toward better environmental practices, especially through energy conservation and a general reduction of carbon footprints.

Associated Press, Climate change on msnbc.com. "Beer lovers told to beware of global warming." http://www.msnbc.msn.com/id/24011745/ns/us_news-environment (accessed November 10–29, 2010).
Dalton, Rex, Naturenews. "Climate troubles brewing for beer makers." http://www.nature.com/news/2008/080502/full/news.2008.799.html (accessed November 10–29, 2010).
Environmental Protection Agency. http://www.epa.gov/climatechange (accessed November 10–29, 2010).
"Global warming threatens brewery." http://www.czech-netz.com/174/2009-0157/global-warming-threatens-brewery.html (accessed November 10–29, 2010).
National Oceanic and Atmospheric Administration. http://www.ncdc.noaa.gov/oa/climate/globalwarming.html (accessed November 10–29, 2010).
The New York Times "Times Topic" on global warming. http://topics.nytimes.com/top/news/science/topics/globalwarming/index.html?scp=1-spot&sq=global%20warming&st=cse# (accessed November 10–29, 2010).
O'Brien, Chris. "The audacity of hops." http://beeractivist.com/2009/01/14/the-audacity-of-hops-2/ (accessed November 10–29, 2010).
O'Brien, Chris. "Beer and climate change." http://beeractivist.com/2008/07/18/beer-and-climate-change/ (accessed November 10–29, 2010).

April Darcy

glucans are glucose polymers that are present in barley and malt. If not degraded during malting and mashing, they are carried forward into the wort and beer. Strictly speaking, glucans refer to any glucose polymer, although α- linked glucose polymers tend to be called dextrins. In brewing, the shorthand term "glucan" is usually meant to denote beta-linked (1,3, and 1,4) glucose polymers. Glucans are derived predominantly from the cell walls of the barley endosperm. During the malting process the cell walls are partially degraded to release beta-glucans. See MALT. Enzymes that degrade beta-glucans are called beta-glucanases and are formed and activated during the malting process. However, these enzymes are very temperature sensitive and are readily destroyed in malt kilning and mashing. Gentle kilning and mashing regimes are needed to protect these enzymes. Excess amounts of glucans in wort can create problems in mash filtration, causing slow filtration rates and losses of extract efficiency. If carried into the fermenter, glucans can cause slow beer filtration. In the finished beer, they can cause hazes. See CHILL HAZE.

Lewis, Michael J., and Tom W. Young. *Brewing*. New York: Kluwer Academic/Plenum Publishers, 2001.

George Philliskirk

glucose is the building block of starch and as such is the primary source of fermentable material in wort and, subsequently, of alcohol in beer. Chemically, glucose is a polyhydroxy aldehyde, with a chemical formula of $C_6H_{12}O_6$.

In starch, glucose occurs either as long straight chains (amylose) or as branched chains (amylopectin), in which the glucose molecules are joined by either alpha 1,4 or alpha 1,6 linkages. Brewing yeasts are incapable of metabolizing starches. These must first be enzymatically degraded during malting and mashing into mostly maltose, which is made up of two glucose molecules joined with alpha 1,4 linkages, and maltotriose, which consists of three-linked glucose units. Smaller amounts of glucose are also produced during mashing, particularly toward the end of the process. Typically, all-malt wort contains about 7% glucose, 45% maltose, and 20% maltotriose. The remaining roughly 25% of carbohydrates are sucrose and fructose, as well as unfermentable oligosaccharides and dextrins. During wort boiling some of the glucose reacts with amino compounds (mainly from amino acids) to create colored compounds, which both increase beer color and can impart toffee or caramel-like flavors. See MAILLARD REACTION. Glucose can also be added to the boiling process in the form of so-called hydrolyzed starch syrups or glucose syrups. These syrups are derived mainly from corn and wheat, whose starches are converted to a range of carbohydrates, some with high glucose contents. These syrups are used to supplement fermentable sugars derived from malt. In fermentation, maltose and maltotriose are transported into the yeast cell and hydrolyzed (broken down) into glucose. Glucose itself is transported into the yeast cell directly. The intracellular glucose is converted enzymatically into the intermediate compound pyruvate, which, in the absence of oxygen, is then converted to ethanol and carbon dioxide. Glucose is sometimes added to cask-conditioned beers as a priming sugar to initiate a secondary fermentation in the container, generating carbon dioxide to condition the beer and to encourage a small increase in alcohol content. See PRIMING SUGAR. To the human palate, glucose tastes about 70% as sweet as sucrose and is therefore not likely to contribute excessive sweetness to a beer when it remains in solution in small amounts.

Lewis, Michael J., and Tom W. Young. *Brewing*, 2nd ed. New York: Kluwer Academic/Plenum Publishers, 2002.

George Philliskirk

gluten-free beer is devoid of proteinaceous material, derived from certain cereals, that can cause an immune reaction in the small intestine. People with Celiac disease cannot properly digest these proteins, and severe gastric disturbance can result from their consumption. "Gluten" is a word often used generically for storage proteins in plant seeds and more specifically the proteins are called gliadin in wheat, hordein in barley, and secalin in rye. They contain certain sequences of 10 to 20 amino acids that are resistant to attack by proteinases in the digestive tract and which induce damage in the small intestine. Oats are less problematic.

There has been much debate about the magnitude of the problem that regular beer presents, in view of the fact that there is extensive protein degradation and modification during malting and brewing. Nonetheless most brewers err on the side of caution and recommend that celiac patients do not consume "regular" beer, even those produced with sizeable quantities of adjuncts such as corn and rice. See ADJUNCTS. So-called gluten-free beers are made from entirely non-gluten-containing grist materials, such as malted sorghum, buckwheat, and proso (common) millet. The Third Category beers from Japan that are devoid of malt may also be of relevance for this market, as would ersatz products made from bland alcohol bases created by the fermentation of sugar and flavored with hop and other extracts. With regard to more traditional brewing approaches, there is interest in the enzyme prolyl endopeptidase, an enzyme that selectively attacks the proteins that trigger celiac disease.

Arendt, E.K. & Dal Bello, F., eds. *Gluten-free cereal products and beverages*. Burlington, MA: Academic Press, 2008.

Charles W. Bamforth

glycogen is the major carbohydrate in yeast cells. It comprises multiple-branched molecules of glucose linked alpha 1,4 in chains and alpha 1,6 at branch points. It typically makes up approximately 20% to 30% of the dry weight of yeast cells. Glycogen serves as a store for the yeast's biochemical energy, which it uses during the lag phase of fermentation, when growth is limited. See LAG PHASE. Ideally, the glycogen content of pitching yeast should be high, because the glycogen store is rapidly depleted during the first few hours after pitching as the yeast converts glycogen to lipids. Low glycogen levels in pitching yeast are indicative of unsatisfactory yeast handling and are associated with low yeast viability, extended fermentation times, and high levels of diacetyl, acetaldehyde, and sulfur dioxide at the end of fermentation. The glycogen content of yeast can be determined by a number of methods but the simplest is to stain the yeast with a tincture of iodine (Lugol's stain). High glycogen levels stain deep brown, whereas low levels stain a pale yellow.

Russell, Inge. "Yeast." In *Handbook of brewing*, 2nd ed. Fergus G. Priest and Graham G. Stewart, eds., 281–332. Boca Raton, FL: Taylor & Francis, 2006.

George Philliskirk

gods

See BEER GODS.

Goed sakken (literally translated as "good sacks") refers to one of two mashes used to produce wheat beers by parti-gyling in the Low Countries during the late Middle Ages. See PARTI-GYLE. Wheat beers were originally brewed using up to 75% unmalted wheat, which led to filtration problems caused by the high levels of gum substances (glucans) in the grain. In the past, before the wide use of proper mash filtering plates, a *stuykmand*—a tall woven basket that looked like an elongated, stretched, and inverted beehive—was used to separate wort from the spent grains. The following

Leuvens Wit grain bill and brewing method dates from the turn of the 19th century: the brew was split into two different mashes, and assuming that the brewer was using 45.5 kg (100 lb) of grain in total, the technique looked like this: the first sack (60% of the total grain bill) was called the goed sakken and would be composed of 20.9 kg (46 lb) malted barley, 3.6 kg (8 lb) oats, and 2.7 kg (6 lb) unmalted wheat. The second (remaining 40% of the grain bill) was called the "vet sakken" ("fat sacks") and would be composed of 1.8 kg (4 lb) malted barley and 16.4 kg (36 lb) unmalted wheat. Presumably the vet sakken, lacking much malt enzyme to convert the wheat starches into sugars, was rather difficult to deal with. In modern Dutch and Flemish the spelling has changed, and these terms no longer refer to any part of the modern brewing process. Instead, "Goedzak" is currently used to describe an affable but gullible person and "Vetzak" is now a derogatory term used for obese persons.

See also WHEAT BEER.

De Clerck, Jean. *A textbook of brewing*, Vol. 1. London: Chapman & Hall, 1957.

Derek Walsh

Golden ale

See BLONDE ALE.

Golden Gate kegs are a style of beer kegs developed around the early 1950s. Golden Gate kegs were unique in that in addition to the then-standard bung hole, they had two separate ports for dispensing. On the keg top was a built-in valve where the gas inlet fitting connected with a quarter turn. On the sidewall just above floor level was the second built-in valve where the beer line fitting connected, again with a quarter turn of that fitting. Each valve could be removed and serviced by unthreading a lock-ring, ideally with a special tool.

The previous styles that Golden Gate replaced connected solely to the keg top with a quarter turn. Next, the long tap would be driven with a mallet through the keg top fitting, forcing a small wooden plug into the keg, and then the tap was slid down to the bottom of the beer. Beer would invariably squirt out in this process. The Golden Gate design required no mallet for driving in the tap, and the taps being far smaller were much less cumbersome. Each connector fitting had a thick rubber washer to seal onto the keg. When these were old or damaged, they would leak. The beer fitting being low toward the floor could easily be knocked and leak, often out of sight. The kegs were also difficult to empty completely, and it was not uncommon for even a skilled operator to leave a pint of beer in each keg. Golden Gate kegs and Hoff-Stevens kegs competed for market share around the same time. See HOFF-STEVENS KEGS. Anheuser-Busch was the last major brewer to use Golden Gate kegs before the market was taken over by the superior Sankey closed system. See SANKEY KEGS. Many early microbreweries preferred these kegs because they were cheap and the open design made dry hopping in the keg fairly easy. Although they are hard to find today, some have found employment as casks.

See also CASK and KEG.

Broderick, Harold. *Beer packaging*. Madison, WI: MBAA Publications, 1982.

Brian Hunt

Golden Promise (barley) is a classic British spring barley variety, often compared with Maris Otter for its rich flavor. It was also the first variety to be protected under the UK 1964 Plant Varieties and Seeds Act. It was first recommended for growing in Scotland in 1968 and continued to be planted until the 1990s. Golden Promise was bred by Miln Marsters seed company of Cheshire, UK, now part of the French Groupe Limagrain, and was a direct product of gamma ray mutation of the UK variety Maythorpe. It was selected for its short, stiff straw and suitability for contemporary agronomic practice, characteristics largely the result of a mutation that induced the *ari-e*.GP dwarfing gene. This was also associated with even but relatively small grain, characters that made Golden Promise particularly suited to malt production for distilling. Consequently, it was the dominant barley variety grown in Scotland in the 1970s and early 1980s before it was superseded by Triumph, a then East Germany–bred variety, and its derivatives. Golden Promise was, however, susceptible to most common

UK foliar pathogens of barley, but the integration of effective fungicides into management regimes from the 1970s onward enabled growers to control potential problems such as powdery mildew. At its peak, over 30,000 tons of certified seed were produced annually for UK growers. This resulted in a large amount of seed being marketed, especially in Scotland where the distilling industry turned some 400,000 metric tons of Golden Promise into whiskey each year. Although a strong performer in its day, Golden Promise's performance is now so far behind contemporary varieties that such uses are for research purposes only. It is still used by some brewers and is generally available in small quantities as a floor malt. Golden Promise floor malts produce worts showing a soft, sweet character suitable for the production of full-bodied cask-conditioned ales.

The Golden Promise story. Kings Lynn, Norfolk, England: Miln Marsters: The Miln Marsters Group Limited, 1978.

Bill Thomas and Stuart Swanston

Golding (hop) is a traditional English hop that was first released for commercial cultivation more than a century ago, but it has been famous among brewers since the 1790s. It is named after the grower who developed it. Varieties of this hop are legion and have gone by the names Cobbs, Amos' Early Bird, Eastwell, Bramling, Canterbury Whitebine, and Mathon. Golding is grown primarily in the counties of Herefordshire, Worcestershire, and East Kent. It is prized primarily for its aroma, but it can be used for bittering as well. It also makes an excellent hop for dry hopping. Like most of the English hop varieties, Golding exhibits earthy notes as well as a slight spiciness in the aroma. The Golding hop, along with its offshoot East Kent Golding and the princely Fuggle, when married to a full-flavored British barley such as Maris Otter, has set the standard for an unmistakable, classic English ale flavor. Alpha acids in Golding may range from 4% to 7.0% and beta acids from 2% to 2.8%; the average cohumulone content may be about 28%. Humulene averages 45%. In the United States, Golding has been planted from Canterbury Golding stock, with some success, since 1995, but the characteristic English earthiness diminished and the hop's fruitiness increased. Golding is sensitive to various fungal infections, including downy and powdery mildew as well as verticillium wilt. Despite these drawbacks, Golding acreage has increased because of demand. Golding produces moderate average yields of almost 1,675 kg/ha (roughly 1,500 lb/acre). Depending on growing conditions, it can reach maturity anywhere from early to late in the season and stores well.

Charles Faram & Co Ltd. http://www.charlesfaram.co.uk/varietydetail.asp?VarietyID=UK-GO/ (accessed October 29, 2010).

Hopsteiner. http://www.hopsteiner.com/pdf/uk/Goldings.PDF/ (accessed October 29, 2010).

Jon Griffin

Goose Island Beer Company. Founded as a Chicago brewpub in 1988, the Goose Island Beer Company has grown into a major regional brewer that ranks among the largest craft brewers in the United States.

Travel introduced businessman John Hall to regional European beer flavors and inspired him to leave the corporate world to found what is now Chicago's oldest brewing organization. The business began with a 250-seat brewpub tucked into one corner of an industrial building remodeled as an urban mall. Early pub beers like Golden Goose Pilsner were mostly lagers to help introduce the drinking public to the flavorful all-malt formulations of microbreweries, but they soon shifted to the ales that now dominate the brewer's portfolio.

In 1995 Hall—now teamed with son Greg as brewmaster—began packaging and distributing their beer from a second Chicago brewery located on Fulton Street. Built around a fifty-barrel brewhouse and with square footage expanded several times to accommodate growth, this facility now produces in excess of 100,000 barrels of beer per year. In 1999 the Halls leased the short-lived Weeghman Park brewpub facility near Wrigley Field, making it their second Goose Island retail brewing operation and a powerful branding tool.

Leading products include the English-style bitter "Honkers Ale" and American wheat ale "312," named for Chicago's downtown area code. Specialty beers include the pioneering "Bourbon County Stout," which was among the very first American barrel-aged beers, and "Matilda," a Belgian-style beer made using the wild yeast Brettanomyces. See BRETTANOMYCES.

In 2006 Widmer Brothers Brewing Company purchased a significant minority stake in Goose Island; in turn, Anheuser-Busch InBev holds a 40% stake in Widmer Brothers.

See also CRAFT BREWING and CHICAGO.

Ray Daniels

grain out is the physical process of removing spent grain from the mash tun or lauter tun. This is accomplished either by mechanical means (i.e., a stirring mechanism, or mash mixer, in the mash or lauter vessel) or by manual means (i.e., an assistant brewer removing the spent grain by hand).

Larger brewhouses are almost always equipped with a variable-speed, reversible mash mixer in the mash tun or lauter tun that serves the dual purpose of mixing the mash to ensure even consistency and heat distribution and, when run in reverse, pushing the spent grain out of the vessel. Other designs employ a plowing device attached to the lauter knife assembly. The spent grain can then be moved via closed pipes and pumps or via transfer bins to a holding vessel or to trucks or railcars for transport.

In smaller brewhouses, generally under 20 hl (17 US bbl), mash vessels are often not equipped with a mash mixer. In such situations, a brewer will open a manway door and physically move the spent grain into bins using a plastic shovel or similar tool.

See also SPENT GRAIN.

Brian Thompson

Gram stain refers to a procedure for visualizing bacteria under the microscope. It was devised by the Danish scientist Hans Christian Gram in 1884 and is still used widely today. The technique involves soaking bacteria on a microscope slide in a solution of the purple dye crystal violet. This is then complexed with a dilute iodine solution and the cells are then washed with a solvent such as acetone or ethanol. Finally the bacteria are treated with a pink-colored stain such as safranin. Bacteria referred to as Gram-positive retain the original crystal violet/iodine complex and appear purple when viewed microscopically, while Gram-negative types lose the crystal/violet complex when washed with solvent and are stained pink by the safranin.

We now appreciate that Gram-positive and Gram-negative bacteria differ markedly in cell structure. Gram-positive bacteria have a cell envelope composed largely of a unique polymer of sugars and amino acids called peptidoglycan. This large, net-like polymer provides strength to the cell wall in much the same way as cellulose supports the plant cell wall. Gram-negative bacteria have far less peptidoglycan than their Gram-positive counterparts and additionally have a lipid covering termed the "outer membrane." This has important implications for brewing microbiology because the outer membrane impedes entry of hop iso-alpha acids and therefore renders Gram-negative bacteria tolerant to these inhibitory compounds. See ISO-ALPHA ACIDS. Most Gram-positive bacteria are killed by iso-alpha acids but some strains of Pediococcus and Lactobacillus have acquired resistance, either through additional genes (e.g., *horA*) that expel the acid or modifications to their physiology that enable tolerance. See LACTOBACILLUS and PEDIOCOCCUS.

Priest, Fergus G., and Campbell, Iain. *Brewing microbiology*, 3rd ed. New York: Kluwer Academic/Plenum Publishers, 2003.

Fergus G. Priest

grand cru. As craft brewing has expanded over the last few decades, several wine terms have slowly seeped into the beer lexicon. Some of these terms are clear—anyone can understand what a "vintage" beer might be, but some, such as "grand cru," are less so. "Grand cru" is a French term that translates literally to "great growth." The grand cru classification has been used and regulated by the French since the 19th century to refer to vineyards that consistently produce superior tasting wines as a result of their excellent location or "terroir." It is also used by those vineyards to label the wines that they produce, and consumers have responded with high expectations of quality. (The grand cru label is also used by Cognac producers.) As a term that has come to mean "our very finest" (just as the term "vintage" can be applied to a car), beer producers have recently appropriated it. "Grand Cru" has appeared on beer labels since at least the late 1980s; the term is not regulated as it applies to beer.

While grand cru is still too ill-defined to be referred to as an established beer style, we can certainly see a pattern among the beers so labeled. In general, a grand cru beer is a stronger, yet balanced, version of a regular-strength beer from a given brewery and is almost always a limited-production beer, sometimes made for holidays or special occasions. Perhaps following the early example of Hoegaarden Grand Cru, most beers labeled "Grand Cru" are Belgian or Belgian-inspired. Commercial beers with the label range from 6% to over 10% ABV, with better examples showing complexity and balance without harsh alcoholic notes. Some of these are gently spiced. As befits the wine terminology, many of these beers can age quite well, reaching a pleasant maturity within a few years if kept properly.

See also FRANCE.

Keith Villa

A **grant** is a small wort collection vessel, open to the air, placed between the lautering vessel and the wort kettle. The traditional purpose of a grant was threefold: (a) to avoid a potential vacuum in the lauter or mash/lauter tun during wort pumping for recirculation or filling the kettle, which could seal the mash to the false bottom, thus causing turbid worts or stuck mashes; (b) to allow the brewer to asses wort clarity and wort flow; and (c) in larger systems with multiple lauter tun outlets, to determine whether all parts of the grain bed flow sufficiently well or require raking or other measures to improve flow-through. The grant thus serves as a flow buffer. In old tower-style breweries, where brewing vessels are stacked one on top of the other and wort flow is by gravity only, there is, of course, no need for a grant as a vacuum break, but its other uses remain valid.

The simplest grant design is essentially an open-top cylindrical can with wort flowing in from the bottom and being pumped off through a side port. This minimizes wort splashing and thus oxygen

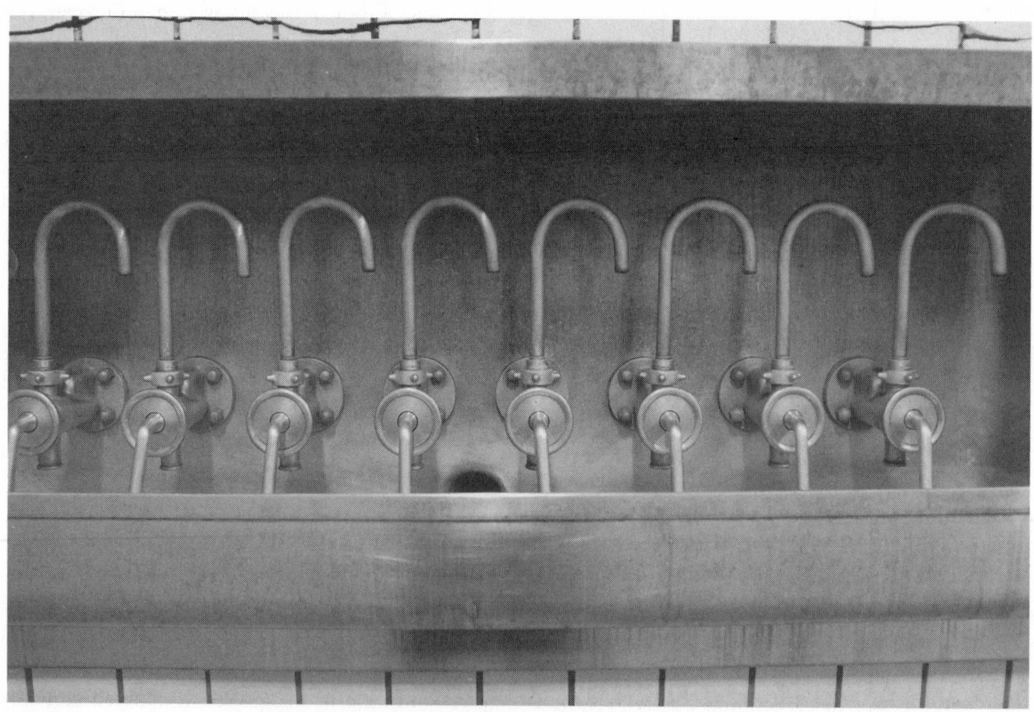

A traditional copper grant at Orval, a Trappist brewery in the Gaume region of Belgium. PHOTOGRAPH BY DENTON TILLMAN

pickup. In traditional breweries, however, especially in Germany and the Czech Republic, the grant is typically a long, shallow copper tub, bordered in regal brass, and fed golden streams of wort by a dozen or more swan-necked lauter run-off tubes. It is a strikingly beautiful design, part of a copper brewhouse that is sure to quicken the heart of any romantic brewer. Unfortunately, it is also a cause for worry, because traditional grants allow plenty of contact between wort and air, and modern brewing tends to eschew hot wort aeration, which can initiate staling reactions. See HOT-SIDE AERATION. In the Czech Republic, wort oxidation from the run-off into traditional grants is partially responsible for the deeper gold coloring than is normally seen in German "pils" beers.

Modern brewing systems usually have no grant at all. Instead they have special valves, often controlled by sensors and complex electronics, to allow wort to flow directly from the lauter tun to the kettle without the risk of a lauter tun vacuum or oxidation. The in-line sight glass used to check for wort clarity is then sometimes called a "grant," although that designation is undeserved by either beauty or function.

Garrett Oliver

Grant, Bert (1928–2001) was an expert on the hop plant and a pioneer of America's craft brewing industry. He was the founder and president of Yakima (WA) Malting and Brewing Co., which brewed Grant's Real Ales. Grant opened one of America's first pub breweries in Yakima in 1982. The brewery later grew into a packaging brewery producing beers that bore the Grant's label. In 1995 he sold the brewery, but continued his association with the brand.

Born Herbert L. Grant in Dundee, Scotland, Grant moved to Toronto at the age of 2 and later got his first brewery job at the age of 16 as a beer taster. He subsequently worked for the Carling-O'Keefe and Stroh breweries and consulted for many breweries around the world, before coming to Yakima in 1967 and helping to build two plants that processed hops with a technique he patented.

Grant carried a vial of hop oil with him to enhance the hop character of the mainstream beers he was forced to drink while travelling. "All beers should have more hops," he declared. Modesty was not one of Grant's traits. With author Robert Spector, in 1988 he wrote *The Ale Master: How I Pioneered America's Craft Beer Industry, Opened the First Brewpub, Bucked Trends, and Enjoyed Every Minute of It.*

In the 1980s Grant tangled with the U.S. Bureau of Alcohol, Tobacco, and Firearms over his claim that beer was a food. He printed labels that listed his beers' vitamins, minerals, and other nutrients. Even though all the information was true, the BATF forced him to stop using the labels.

Grant had a showman's flair and often appeared at beer events in a Scottish kilt and tweed cap. The vanity plates on his white Rolls-Royce declared: "REAL ALE."

See also YAKIMA VALLEY HOP REGION.

Grant, Bert, and Robert Spector. *The ale master.* Seattle, WA: Sasquatch Books, 1998.

Stephen Hindy

gravity dispense is the original method for drawing beer from a cask, before the invention of draught systems. In essence, once the cask was broached with a tap, the beer was simply dispensed directly into a glass without traveling through a beer line. Although this is now rare in Europe, confined to specialty establishments, it is still a relatively common form of dispense for cask-conditioned beer in England. Invented in the early 1800s, the beer engine, or hand-pump, allowed the dispense at the bar of beer stillaged in the cellar below. Before this time, casks sat either on the bar or behind it, and the barman simply opened the tap to dispense a pint. Cask blankets could be employed to keep the beer cool. Today, gravity dispense is mostly seen in country pubs in England, at cask beer festivals, and at the occasional brewpub or craft beer specialist bar in the United States. Some beer enthusiasts particularly enjoy gravity-dispensed ales because they are served with minimum agitation, thus preserving the gentle natural carbonation prized in these beers.

Garrett Oliver

Great American Beer Festival (GABF) is the largest, oldest craft beer festival and beer competition in the United States, conducted annually in Denver, Colorado. The first GABF was hosted by the American Homebrewers Association (which later became the Brewers Association) in 1982. It attracted 22 participating brewers, who served 40 different beers to 800 attendees at the Harvest House Hotel in Boulder and served as the model for every beer festival thereafter.

GABF has become the "Super Bowl of Beer," where commercial beers are judged by expert tasting panels in 79 different style categories. A total of 3,308 US beers were judged against one another at the 2009 GABF. The best in each category are awarded gold, silver, and bronze medals in recognition of their brewing excellence. The competition judging style at the GABF is uniquely stringent and is based on a beer's adherence to set beer style guidelines. All beers are tasted blind, and judges, many of them professional brewers, travel from all over the world to participate in the judging panels. Awards are also presented for Breweries, Brewpubs, and Brewers of the Year.

Popular tasting sessions, open for a fee to the public, allow beer lovers to sample hundreds of different beers from across the United States. Brewers are roughly organized by region within the event venue. The GABF holds the Guinness World Record for "most beers tapped in one location." In 2009, over 49,000 attendees sampled 2,104 beers from 457 brewers during the 3-day event.

A separate GABF "Pro-Am" competition is open to amateur homebrewers, who compete against each other using recipes they have brewed in collaboration with a professional brewer. Additional GABF highlights include demonstrations of cooking, food and beer pairing, beer judging, a beer enthusiast bookstore, and vendors of virtually all things related to beer.

Great American Beer Festival. http://www.greatamericanbeerfestival.com/ (accessed October 4, 2010).

Mike Laur

Great Britain

See BRITAIN.

Great British Beer Festival

Great British Beer Festival (GBBF) is an annual beer festival in the UK organized by the Campaign for Real Ale. See CAMPAIGN FOR REAL ALE (CAMRA). Styled as "the biggest pub in the world," the first GBBF was held in 1977 at Alexandra Palace in London; the festival has been held every year since, with the exception of 1984 (when there was a fire in the hall in which the festival was to be held). Over the years the festival's venue has been in Leeds, Birmingham, and Brighton, but London has been its permanent home since 1991, when it was held in Docklands Arena. It moved to its current home in 2006 at Earls Court after it had outgrown Olympia, where is had been since 1992.

Today the festival hosts more than 600 beers from around the world, though its prime focus is cask-conditioned "real ale," of which more than 450 are from UK brewers. However, it has also become a showcase for craft beers from many countries including Belgium, Czech Republic, Germany, and the United States. Traditional British cider and perry is also available.

The festival is usually held during the first full week in August and runs from Tuesday to Saturday, with more than 60,000 people attending. It is staffed by more than 1,000 CAMRA volunteers. The festival is also home to the prestigious and influential Champion Beer of Britain awards.

The GBBF is complemented by CAMRA's Winter Ales Festival, held in January, which focuses on porter and stouts.

The GBBF was not CAMRA's first large beer festival; that honor goes to the Covent Garden Beer Festival, held in London in September 1975.

Campaign for Real Ale. www.camra.org.uk/ (accessed July 9, 2010).

Tim Hampson

green beer

green beer is beer that has undergone its primary fermentation but has yet to undergo a period of conditioning before packaging. It is perhaps "drinkable" but not ready to drink.

Before it can leave the brewery the beer will require a period of maturation, which, depending on the beer, can be the longest part of the brewing process. This may be as little as a few days for some British cask beers or as long as a few months for very traditional Czech pilsner. See MATURATION. The yeast still has some work to do to remove some of the unwanted by-products of the first fermentation, such as acetaldehyde and diacetyl.

Green beer is often cloudy with unsettled yeast, and in most cases it will eventually need to be filtered or clarified in some fashion unless it is of a type that is meant to be served hazy. Generally speaking, beer is no longer considered "green" when it has reached full maturity of flavor and aroma.

Of course in some parts of the world, cheap industrial beer may be artificially dyed green for St. Patrick's Day; such things, although harmless, are not to be contemplated by beer enthusiasts.

Tim Hampson

Green Bullet (hop) is a popular New Zealand high-alpha variety, released in 1972 by Zealand DSIR (now Hort Research). It is a descendant of a triploid New Zealand "smooth cone" variety. Green Bullet hops have a pleasant slight floral and dark fruit aroma, which is considered unusual, because high-alpha hops tend not to have particularly desirable aromatics. There is also a hint of spiciness in the flavor that is reminiscent of Styrian Golding. See STYRIAN GOLDING (HOP). Green Bullet averages about 11% to 15% alpha acids, about 6.5% to 7% beta acids, about 41% cohumulone, and a tiny amount of farnesene, which contributes floral notes. This hop matures fairly late in the season and produces a moderate to good average yield of roughly 2,350 kg/ha (about 2,070 lb/acre). Considering its antipodal home, Green Bullet is ideal for northern hemisphere brewers needing an off-season hop. Because New Zealand lacks conventional hop pathogens, resistance to them is not a selection criterion for cultivars there. For the same reason, spraying is not required in New Zealand and many hops are available as certified organic. As an added bonus, Green Bullet stores well. Although it is considered a workhorse hop, Green Bullet is respected for providing a good backdrop for the aromatics of classical hops such as Fuggle.

Hopsteiner. http://www.hopsteiner.com/pdf/nz/greenbullet.pdf/ (accessed November 8, 2010).
New Zealand Hops Limited. http://www.nzhops.co.nz/varieties/green_bullet.html/ (accessed November 8, 2010).

Jon Griffin

Greene King is the largest British-owned brewery in the UK. Founded in 1799 by Benjamin Greene, the great grandfather of the author Graham Greene, it's been brewing in the Suffolk town of Bury St. Edmunds for more than 2 centuries. In 1836, the brewery passed into the hands of Benjamin's son Edward under whom production expanded to 40,000 barrels per annum and in 1887, the brewery merged with the St. Edmunds brewery, set up a dozen years previously by Frederick King.

It became one of Britain's largest breweries, boasting 148 public houses and renowned for brewing bitter and Suffolk Old Ale, an ale made by the blending of old and young beers. During the 1920s and 1930s, the brewery then benefited from the boom in bottled beer and built a new art deco brew house in 1938 that helped slake the thirst of Allied servicemen during World War II. By the 1960s, Greene King's pub portfolio had grown to more than 900.

As cask ale floundered during the 1990s, Greene King took a number of smaller regional breweries and pub companies under its wing including The Magic Pub Company, the Marston's southern pub estate, Morrells of Oxford, and the Morland brewery, home to Ruddles and Old Speckled Hen beers.

Greene King further flexed its purchasing muscle in 2005 when it bought Belhaven Brewery in Scotland and Ridley's brewery in Essex before, a year later, buying Hardys & Hansons.

Greene King's flagship beers include Old Speckled Hen, first brewed to celebrate the 50th anniversary of the MG car factory in Abingdon, and Abbot Ale, while Strong Suffolk Ale and Old Crafty Hen are vintage ales revered by connoisseurs. While some British beer enthusiasts have blanched at Greene King's growth and its penchant for brewery takeovers, the company has made an admirably unflagging commitment to the production of cask ale. That said, the brewery's best selling beer is Greene King IPA. Although designated an IPA, at 3.7% ABV and a very modest level of bitterness, it is not an IPA in any sense, but simply an "ordinary" bitter.

Greene King. http://www.greeneking.co.uk/ (accessed October 9, 2010). McFarland, Ben. *World's best beers.* New York: Sterling Publishing, 2009.

Ben McFarland

grist or "ground grist" refers to malt and cereal that is ground (milled) in the brewhouse by a malt mill at the beginning of the brewing process. The mills can be of various designs and contain one, two, and often three pairs of rollers, or in the case of breweries which require a very fine grist, hammer mills. Malt has traditionally been milled in a dry state, but modern breweries often use "wet milling," which can be more efficient. See WET MILLING. The distance between the rollers determines how fine the grist becomes, and this determines the efficiency and speed of the process of extracting wort (malt sugars) from the raw materials.

Grist can be separated into six categories, the three main ones being husk, grits, or flour. The equipment the brewery uses to extract wort from the malt determines the specification of the grist, with British mash/lauter tuns requiring a coarse grind, European lauter tuns a medium grind, and mash filters a fine grind. Breweries monitor and control the milling process by measuring the different proportions of the grist. If a grist has too much flour (too finely ground) the wort separation (run off process) will be too slow. If a grist is too coarse (not finely ground enough) the wort separation will be fast, but the extract yield will be low and the brewing value lost. The term "grist" is also used to refer to the "grain bill" of a beer or the cereal part of the recipe. Therefore, a brewer may refer to a beer "brewed from a grist containing 90% pale malt and 10% crystal malt."

See also MILLING.

Paul KA Buttrick

grits. Brewer's grits are solid cereal adjuncts used by brewers as a malt replacement to make alcohol in beer. The grits are cooked to gelatinize the starches and then added to the mash. A brewer may use grits to make a particular style of beer, to soften the taste of a particular beer, or to decrease the cost of raw materials. Grits are widely used in mass-market beers worldwide, and their use is largely responsible for the lightness of malt flavor in such beers.

Grits have also been used by brewers to dilute nitrogen content when using malt that is very high in protein. As such, German brewers under the Reinheitsgebot law have historically been allowed to use adjuncts, such as grits, to minimize protein haze formation in export beers, but not for beer to be sold in Germany. See REINHEITSGEBOT.

Grits can be made from many different cereals, such as sorghum and rice, but the most common come from corn (maize). See CORN. Corn grits are made by millers who usually employ a tempering (conditioning) and degerming process. In this process corn is cleaned and then tempered with steam to around 20% moisture. The moist kernels are then degerminated, whereby the starchy endosperm is separated from the outer covering and the germ layer. After degermination, the starchy endosperm is dried and cooled then sent through a series of mills and screens to obtain fractions of grits, meals, and flours.

Corn meals and corn flours are used for making snack foods and bakery mixes, while the larger grit fractions are used for breakfast cereals and brewing. The use of corn grits by brewers has decreased over the years and been replaced by corn syrups. This has been a cost-driven change since it is cheaper to purchase highly fermentable corn syrup than to liquefy or cook corn grits in a cereal cooker and convert them to a fermentable form. In recent years, some large European producers of mass-market beers have moved away from the use of corn grits (and syrup) out of concern that genetically modified corn might end up in the brewhouse. This is not presently a concern to the American consumer, but GMO (genetically modified organism) crops are increasingly anathema in Europe. This has led to ironic attempts to use all-malt mashes with enzymes to recreate the light flavor previously attained with the use of corn grits.

Keith Villa

Groll, Josef (1813–1887) was a gifted Bavarian brewer commonly believed to have created the first Pilsner lager. Groll was born in Vilshofen, a small village northeast of Munich in Bavaria. The son of a successful brewer, beer was in his blood but apparently he wasn't easy to get along with. He is described by historians as "a simple man without any manners," and "coarse even by Bavarian standards." His own father declared Groll to be "the rudest man in Bavaria."

Whatever his personal faults, Groll's brewing skill was unmistakable. He was recruited by Martin Stelzer, founder of the Burgher's Brewery of Pilsen in neighboring Bohemia, to brew high-quality beer.

Groll smuggled a Bavarian lager yeast across the border, combined it with the local Saaz hops, soft Bohemian water, and the pale malt that had been perfected by British ale brewers to create a light, golden beer which was christened Pilsner Urquell, or "original Pilsner." See PILSNER URQUELL.

Urquell was not the first golden lager, as is often claimed. But the combination of ingredients gave birth to a new style of beer, one which set the template for 95% of the world's beers today.

Despite that beer's phenomenal success, when Groll's contract expired in 1845 it was not renewed. (Maybe the rudeness and coarseness was just too much, no matter how good his beer was.) Groll returned home to Vilshofen and eventually inherited his father's brewery. He died at the age of 74, at the regular's table in his favorite pub, the Wolferstetter Keller.

See also PILSEN (PLZEŇ) and PILSNER.

Pete Brown

Grolsch Brewery, named after the city of Grol, where it was founded in 1615 by Willem Neerfeldt. Grolsch is the Netherlands' third largest brewer. Bottled in distinctive green swing-top bottles that were introduced in 1897, its pilsner is easily recognized in at least 70 foreign markets. Grolsch was a public company listed on the Dutch stock exchange from 1984 until it was sold to SABMiller in 2008. About 50% of their production is sold within the Netherlands and counts for about 15% of the total Dutch beer market. Grolsch transferred all of its production to a new site in Usselo just outside Enschede in 2003 and closed their Enschede and Groenlo breweries in 2005. A very conservative pilsner brewery, Grolsch only had three beers in its portfolio until they started experimentation with a wide range of spices, fruit essences, and yeast strains in 1995. None of these 40-odd beers has remained on the market, except their mixed-fermentation 11.6% alcohol by volume (ABV) "Het Kanon" (the Canon), and they occasionally release one-off beers for special civic celebrations. The release of two Bavarian-style weizen beers, a 5.5% ABV blond in 2005 and a 6% ABV dark version in 2007, pleasantly surprised many Dutch beer enthusiasts.

See also NETHERLANDS, THE.

Jackson, Michael. *Beer*. New York: DK Publishing, 2007.
European beer guide. http://www.europeanbeerguide.net/ (accessed February 21, 2011).
Grolsch. http://nl.wikipedia.org/wiki/Grolsch/ (accessed February 21, 2011).

Derek Walsh

Grossman, Ken, founder of the Sierra Nevada Brewing Company, was born in Southern California in 1954 and developed very early interests in technical matters. He was only 11 years old when he built a guesthouse annex to his parents' home and not much older when a neighbor interested him in fermentation processes. Upon moving to Chico in 1971, he combined employment in a bicycle shop with studies at Butte College and California State University, Chico, and opened a homebrew and winemaking retail store. During college he constructed, with cofounder Paul Camusi, his first brewery, including drilling all of the holes in the false bottom of his first lauter tun. He never did graduate. The brewery became the Sierra Nevada Brewing Company, named for his favorite hiking and climbing territory. It opened in 1980 in Chico; it is now the seventh-largest brewing company in the United States. Grossman is dedicated to brewing excellence but also to matters environmental and social. He is a principal benefactor for many community groups.

See also SIERRA NEVADA BREWING COMPANY.

Charles W. Bamforth

growler, a container used to take draught beer out of a bar or restaurant for consumption off of the premises. In the United States in the late 1800s and early 1900s most beer was consumed on draught. Families would routinely send someone, usually a woman or a child, to the local saloon to bring home beer for the evening meal. The container used was often literally a galvanized steel pail, sometimes with a lid to prevent the beer from spilling out on the journey. The container, which sometimes apparently rumbled with escaping carbonation, was dubbed a "growler," and the person carrying it was said to be "rushing the growler." Pre-Prohibition saloon-keepers catered to the growler trade, often with a small service window to the saloon referred to euphemistically as the "family entrance." There, it was possible for women and children to rush the growler without walking through the saloon to the bar.

The popularity of the growler was a point of considerable contention in American society. Children lined up outside of factories to pick up pails from working men, rushing them back from the saloon in time for lunch. Antialcohol crusaders, hoping to keep men away from saloons, decried the fact that beer was so easily brought home. It was not unknown for children to sample the beer before it arrived at its intended destination.

The tradition of rushing the growler largely disappeared after Prohibition, but the growler is today reborn as a glass jug used to bring craft-brewed beer home from bars, shops, and brewpubs. The usual size is the US half gallon (1.9 l). These days the jug, filled directly from the taps, does not growl—it has a lid, often a screw cap. Many craft breweries and brewpubs produce some beers that are available only on draught, and beer enthusiasts are understandably very happy to be able to take these special beers home. Growlers have become big business for many small breweries, and some beer shops do a brisk trade in them.

Growlers remain contentious, but for different reasons than those of days past. Brewery owners and beer enthusiasts may be happy about growlers, but the brewers themselves tend to be conflicted. Although some establishments attach a tube to the tap spigot to fill the jug without much foaming, the brewer knows that the beer is losing carbonation and picking up damaging oxygen. The growler is rarely flushed with CO_2 or filled under counterpressure. And although the growler is hopefully clean (customers are often encouraged to recycle them), it is usually not sterile. The establishment filling the growler may tell the customer to drink the beer within a few days, but customers often pay little heed. The growler is also so large that people will often drink part of the bottle and then recap it to be consumed later. Although some wines will stand up to such treatment, beer rarely can. The brewer designs a beer to be served on draught or from a meticulously filled bottle, but the average growler setup can undo the brewer's hard work within seconds. If consumed quickly, the beer may be almost as good as it was at the bar. At worst, it will be the beer equivalent of a fine restaurant meal scraped into a bag, refrigerated for days, and then heated up in a microwave: in short, the brewer's worst nightmare. Some companies are starting to sell "growler filling stations" that are essentially miniature bottling lines; these flush out air, replace it with CO_2, and then fill the growler under pressure. These stations can work quite well, but such systems are expensive. It seems that the growler is back and here to stay, but it remains to be seen whether brewers will insist upon proper quality or look the other way as the cash is counted across the bar.

See also OXIDATION.

Benbow, Mark. "The growler." http://www.rustycans.com (accessed December 18, 2010).

Simonson, Robert. "The new old way to tote your beer." *The New York Times*, January 26, 2010. http://www.nytimes.com/2010/01/27/dining/27growl.html (accessed December 18, 2010).

Garrett Oliver

gruit is a generic term referring to the herb mixtures used to flavor and preserve beer before the general use of hops took hold in the 15th and 16th centuries in Europe. Gruit was most commonly composed of sweet gale (also known as bog myrtle; see BOG MYRTLE), yarrow, and wild (or marsh) rosemary, but could also include other botanicals such as heather, juniper, ginger, caraway, and cinnamon. Hops were also sometimes a part of the mixture. In Britain a distinction was drawn between "ale" flavored with gruit mixtures and "beer" brewed with hops.

Though a taste for hopped beers did arise among brewers and drinkers beginning in about the 11th century, the demise of gruit had less to do with preferential supersession by hops than political, religious, and moral struggles within the individual countries in which it was used. With the Catholic Church having widely held a monopoly on the sale and taxation of gruit, the use of hops in brewing beer was nothing short of a revolutionary act as German princes asserted their independence just as the Reformation dawned. The Bavarian Purity Law (Reinheitsgebot) of 1516 in fact roughly coincided with the earliest public acts of Martin Luther. See REINHEITSGEBOT. Additionally, puritanical interdictions against the use in beer of substances putatively psychotropic and aphrodisiacal as well as the condemnation of the practices of brewsters as tantamount to witchcraft helped hasten the general discontinuation of the production and use of gruit.

Some modern examples of gruit ales do exist, notably Fraoch and Alba by the Scottish brewers Williams Brothers and The Wind Cries Mari by Cambridge Brewing Co. of Cambridge, Massachusetts.

Buhner, Stephen Harrod. *Sacred and herbal healing beers: The secrets of ancient fermentations.* Boulder, CO: Siris Books/Brewers Publications, 1998.

Mosher, Randy. *Radical brewing: Recipes, tales, & world-altering meditations in a glass.* Boulder, CO: Brewers Publications, 2004.

Dick Cantwell

Grundy tank is a term adopted by the North American craft brewing industry for UK-built pub cellar tanks. These inexpensive, mass-produced tanks were fabricated in the 1950s and 1960s and have been utilized at almost every stage of the brewing process. The 8.5 barrel (10 hl) tanks were originally produced for directly dispensing carbonated beer from pub cellars but have also been utilized for fermentation, conditioning, and bright beer storage. Some brewpubs use them as serving tanks. They are now usually sized at 3.5 or 7 US barrels.

While the tanks have found widespread application throughout the UK and North America, they are not without their drawbacks. Among the most notable of these is the large, unwieldy clamp that secures the lid to the standard model; these have occasionally slipped, causing potentially dangerous accidents as the lid blows off under pressure.

"Grundys" have been described as "the Tin Lizzie," "the Model T of tanks," and many other epithets since many have been sold into the North American craft brewing industry since the early 1980s. Many Grundy tanks have been modified, sold, re-sold, modified some more, repaired (often many times) had faces painted on them, and been both feared and cursed by legions of labor-weary brewers.

George Philliskirk

gueuze, an unfruited sparkling form of lambic and the epitome of the art of sour beer production. See LAMBIC. Sometimes called "the champagne of Belgium," gueuze is a blend of two or more lambics of different ages, with the younger beer providing the sugars needed for refermentation in the bottle. Gueuze almost certainly predates champagne and was probably originally served directly from casks. Today, with some rare exceptions, it is considered a bottled beer by definition. Just as some champagne producers buy either grapes or wine to blend their champagnes, so some gueuze producers buy lambic for blending. See BLENDING HOUSES. More often, gueuze is blended from different barrels within a brewery's own production. The traditional gueuze flavor is dry, sharp, and earthy, close to that of unblended lambic, but bottle conditioning and the resulting carbonation give it perhaps even greater complexity and finesse. See BOTTLE CONDITIONING. Like blending wine or Scotch whisky, blending lambics to make gueuze is an art form. The base lambics having been spontaneously fermented, each barrel will have an individual character. Upon tasting, the blender will need to decide whether to use the beer now or hold it further; whether to use the beer for straight lambic or for gueuze; whether to use the beer for the best traditional gueuze or the more commercial variety most houses also produce. Highly aromatic old "stinky" gueuze is considered valuable and will be parsed out carefully in the cellar. These have barnyard aromatics reminiscent of washed rind cheeses; this is not surprising because some of the same wild yeasts and bacterial strains are at work in both the cheese and the beer. Young lambics provide fermentable sugars and bright vibrant flavors to the blend. Aged lambics lend complexity of flavor along with enzymes created by the dozens of microorganisms at work in the cask; these enzymes will break down complex sugars into simple sugars that yeast and bacteria can work upon to create carbonation. Thus, the gueuze blender must not only carefully manage the characteristics of taste and acidity of each different lambic but also make sure that the beer will attain the proper high carbonation desired after bottle conditioning.

The proportions of young and old lambic in gueuze differ from year to year and from one brewer to another. Some brewers use approximately 50% 1-year-old, 25% 2-year-old, and 25% 3-year-old lambic. Others prefer to use two-thirds 1-year-old lambic and one-third 2- or 3-year-old lambic. Special blends may include only 10% young beer.

After blending, the beer is bottled and laid down in cellars for at least 4 to 6 months of refermentation. Some may not be released for many years. When they are eventually served, the bottles may come to the table in a horizontal position; this allows the yeast deposits to remain in place while the beer is poured out sparkling and clear.

Many people do not realize that champagne is essentially a cocktail; almost all champagnes are sweetened to make them palatable to a wider audience. This is not considered traditional for gueuze, but the fact is that it is widely practiced. Except for a few traditional producers, most lambic brewers produce a more profitable sweetened gueuze, and these beers often confuse gueuze consumers. In the late 1990s, some lambic brewers, having tired of what they considered adulterations, founded the association Hoge Raad voor Ambachtelijke Lambikbieren (High Commission of Traditionally-Made Lambic Beers, HORAL), presided over by Armand Debelder of the Drie Fonteinen Brewery in Beersel, Belgium. Every lambic producer and lambic blender is a member, except for Belle-Vue (owned by the multinational company ABInBev) and the ultratraditional Cantillon Brewery, which defers membership because not all members apply traditional methods. See CANTILLON BREWERY.

HORAL's main goal is to protect authentic lambics with a proper denomination, adding the word *oude* (old) to the words gueuze and kriek; today the word *oude* generally guarantees that the beer in the bottle will be unsweetened. HORAL also periodically organizes the Toer de Geuze, an organized bus tour for which almost all gueuze makers open their doors to beer lovers from around the world. For lovers of lambic, it can be something akin to a religious pilgrimmage.

Only 15 or 20 years ago, it seemed that a tidal wave of market forces might sweep true gueuze from the scene, but today the future of authentic gueuze looks promising. At beginning of the 1990s, the total market for traditonal sour gueuze was around 1,500 hl (1,280 US barrels) but by 2006 this number had risen to 6,000 hl (5,130 US barrels). Belgian chefs often pair gueuze with food or cook their dishes following the tradition of "cuisine à la bière." See COOKING WITH BEER. Gueuze, with its cleansing acidity, is a suitable aperitif before a fine meal. Many classical Belgian dishes include gueuze as a main ingredient. In his 2006 book *La Gueuze Gourmande* (*The Delicious Gueuze*), the Belgian food writer Nicole Darchambeau collected some of these dishes; mussels with gueuze, lamb liver with gueuze and mustard, gueuze-preserved goose legs, gueuze-jellied chicken, and guinea-fowl with gueuze and broccoli are all examples of Brussels traditional food. Finally, gueuze can be used as an ingredient in vinaigrette, onion jam, or pleurote mushroom sauce, for special breads, or, as dessert, made into spectacularly sharp, complex, and refreshing sorbets.

Darchambeau, Nicole. *La gueuze gourmande*. Éditions Les Capucines, 2006.

HORAL. *High Council for Artisanal Lambik style beers.* http://www.horal.be/ (accessed March 28, 2011).

Lorenzo Dabove and Garrett Oliver

Guinness, Arthur. The founder of the Guinness brewing empire was born in Celbridge, a town on the River Liffey in County Kildare, Ireland, on September 24, 1725. He has been variously described as an entrepreneur, visionary, and philanthropist. His father was Richard Guinness, who was land steward for Arthur Price, young Arthur's godfather and the vicar of Celbridge. In 1722 Price purchased the small, local Kildrought Brewery and placed Richard in charge of production. Arthur Price became Church of Ireland Archbishop of Cashel in 1744 until his death in 1752, and, in his will, he bequeathed Arthur Guinness (then aged 27) the sum of £100. It was specified that this should be used to expand the brewery.

Accordingly, in 1755, Arthur leased a brewery at Leixlip, a village southwest of Dublin at the confluence of the Liffey and the River Rye. Here, he brewed ale successfully for five years, before leaving his younger brother in charge and setting off for greater things in Dublin. In that city, on December 31, 1759, Arthur managed to secure a 9,000-year lease (at £45 per annum) on a four-acre brewery site at St. James's Gate. In 1761 he married Olivia Whitmore in St. Mary's Church, Dublin, and they had 21 children, 10 of whom reached adulthood. From 1764 they lived at the magnificent Beaumont House in the north of the city, which Arthur had built.

Initially, ale was brewed at St. James's Gate, and the first export consignment consisted of a few barrels shipped to England in May 1769. By 1767 Guinness was the Master of the Dublin Corporation of Brewers and by the time of his death in 1803, the brewery was producing over 30,000 hectoliters of porter per year.

See also ARTHUR GUINNESS & SONS.

Byrne, A. *Guinness times.* Dublin: Town House and Country House, 1999.
Mansfield, S. *The Search for God and Guinness: A biography of the beer that changed the world.* Nashville, TN: Thomas Nelson, Inc., 2009.
Yenne, W. *Guinness: The 250 year quest for a perfect pint.* Chichester, England: Wiley, 2007.

Ian Hornsey

gum arabic is the hardened sap of a handful of species of Acacia tree grown in several countries in northern sub-Saharan Africa, most notably Sudan and Senegal. The sap is harvested by cutting holes in the bark of the tree; after waiting approximately 6 weeks, enough sap will have been exuded for collection. Gum arabic is heavily used in the food and beverage industry as a stabilizer or thickener and falls into the class of substances known as hydrocolloids (others include gelatin and agar agar). The properties that make it useful in food processing have also led to its use in brewing, primarily as a foam stabilizer/head retention agent, but also in fining agents to assist with beer clarification. There has also been at least one claim that a gum arabic solution can also improve beer flavor by stabilizing aromatic compounds in the beer, adding sweetness and coating a drinker's mouth.

Gum arabic's use as a head retention agent comes in two forms: as a solution sprayed onto green malt, which is then used in combination with nontreated malt, and as a powdered or flaked form of gum arabic that can be added later during the brewing process (gum arabic is soluble in cold water, but its solubility increases at warmer temperatures).

Gum arabic's use as a head retention agent/foam stabilizer has been largely overtaken by polypropylene glycol alginate. That shift occurred at least in part because the levels of the active substances in gum arabic can vary widely from harvest to harvest, whereas PGA—being more heavily processed—can be produced to tighter specifications.

See also ADDITIVES.

Imeson, Alan, ed. *Thickening and gelling agents for food.* New York: Chapman & Hall, 1997.

Josh Rubin

gushing, also known as fobbing, is the occurrence of more or less vigorous overflowing of beer upon opening the bottle or can. Generally anything that promotes the rapid release of the gas in beer will cause gushing. Any particulates that form sites for carbon dioxide to gather (called nucleation sites) essentially cause the gas to be released very rapidly.

Gushing has been attributed to several factors. "Primary gushing" is attributed to beers brewed from defective malt (derived from barley harvested under wet conditions) and is apparently the major cause of the issue that shows up periodically in commercial beers. The substances responsible for gushing are hydrophobic polypeptides derived from several mold strains—most commonly those denoted as *Fusarium*. The components have been given the name hydrophobins.

Other causes of gushing fall under the term "secondary gushing" and include but are not limited to the presence of metal ions such as iron, nickel, and tin; calcium oxalate; some isomerized hop extracts; a rough surface (forming the nucleation sites) on the inside of the bottle; and inadequate washing and rinsing of bottles prior to filling. Calcium oxalate can also be an issue. Oxalate anions, derived from the husks of the grains used in brewing, can precipitate out with calcium and form distinct crystals, which form the seeds or nucleation sites for CO_2 breakout. This can be an especially difficult problem for brewers producing bottle-conditioned beers with high levels of carbonation. Brewers encountering gushing caused by oxalate crystals will attempt to ensure that enough calcium is present at the start of the brewing process to allow the precipitation of the oxalate at various stages in the process prior to filtration and bottling. Unfortunately this is a delicate system of chemical equilibrium and calcium addition is not always permanently successful. If enough calcium is used to end up with 80 mg/l of calcium in the finished wort, the oxalate cause of potential gushing will be minimized. In 2001 German researchers argued that 99% of gushing is caused by calcium oxalate in beer.

Prevention of malt-based primary gushing depends on the control of malt quality, whereas prevention of secondary gushing requires the removal of other potential nucleation materials. The treatment of beer with adsorbents and tight filtration can help. Brewers experiencing gushing problems will minimize iron content from brewing water and/or DE filtration medium (leaching caused by reverse flow) and analyze variety-dependent hop alpha acid/polyphenol ratios. In the latter case, polyphenols have been cited as tending to act as gushing promoters, as do very tight naturally derived beer protein clusters.

Of course, at a very basic level, any factor that causes beer to be severely overcarbonated will cause gushing, whether it is improper application of carbon dioxide or overattenuation or overpriming of bottle-conditioned beer. Overattenuation problems are common in bottle-conditioned beers using wild yeast strains such as Brettanomyces, which can continue to ferment out sugars that Saccharomyces strains will not.

Bamforth, Charles W. "Beer: A quality perspective." In *Handbook of alcoholic beverages*, eds. Inge Russell, Charles W. Bamforth, and Graham Stewart. Amsterdam: Elsevier, 2009.

Gary Spedding

gyle is an old term sometimes used (particularly in the UK) to describe a batch of wort or beer as it proceeds through the brewing process. Batches of wort leaving the mashing vessel or mash separator may be distributed into two or more coppers (kettles) for boiling, with the worts often differing in strength. After boiling, the worts can be mixed in various proportions to give rise, after fermentation, to several different beers of varying alcohol content. This arrangement is known as the "parti-gyle" system. See PARTI-GYLE.

George Philliskirk

gypsum is a natural form of calcium sulfate, $CaSO_4$, with varying degrees of water of crystallization (usually 2 H_2O). It is relatively insoluble in water and is the main constituent of permanent hardness in water. When in the crystalline or dry powder form, it is also known as "Alabaster" or "Plaster of Paris."

In brewing it is perhaps best known as the main mineral in the well water of Burton Upon Trent, England, and is widely attributed to be the essential component of the water for pale ale and India pale ale brewing; as such it is the main ingredient in the Burtonizing salts for brewing water treatment. See BURTON-ON-TRENT. It is added by dissolving the gypsum in the mashing and sparging water or directly as a powder into the grist or mash vessels at mashing.

Gypsum's positive effects are to reduce wort pH, improve malt extraction efficiency through enhanced amylolytic activity, give a buffering capacity to the wort, balance the hop flavor for highly hopped beers, improve wort clarity, and remove phosphates and proteins in the wort trub. However, this latter effect of removing phosphate ions (as insoluble calcium phosphate) can be overdone and adversely affect the fermentation if the wort is too depleted of phosphate ions. Similarly a high sulfate content in brewing water and wort can affect the beer flavor, producing the famous Burton stench (sometimes also known as the "Burton snatch" or "sulfur-bite"—a distinctive smell of hydrogen sulfide, which, when concentrated, becomes reminiscent of rotten eggs). See BURTON SNATCH.

The amount of calcium sulfate required or added depends on the base water calcium sulfate content. Brewing water with 150 to 1200 mg/l of calcium sulfate is typical but will be varied according to the wort strength and beer type to be brewed.

See also CALCIUM SULFATE.

Priest, Fergus G., and Graham G. Stewart. *Handbook of brewing*, 2nd ed. Boca Raton, FL: CRC Press, Taylor & Francis Group, 2006.
Scholefield, A. J. B. *The treatment of brewing water*. Liverpool, UK: Privately published, 1953.
Warren, Cyprian A. *Brewing waters*. London: The Brewing Trade Review, 1923.

Chris J. Marchbanks

Hacker–Pschorr Brewery of Munich ranks among Germany's oldest breweries. It was first mentioned in a document dating back to 1417—exactly 75 years before Columbus' first voyage to America. It was then called the "Preustatt an der Hagkagasse" (a brewing place in the Hagka lane), located on the site of the current Altes Hackerhaus beer hall at Sendlingerstrasse 14, halfway between the old city hall at Marienplatz and the Sendlinger Tor city gate. A brewer named Simon Hacker purchased the premises in 1738 and renamed it "Hacker Bräu" (Hacker Brew). In 1797, another brewery owner, Josef Pschorr, acquired control of Hacker Bräu by way of marrying Therese Hacker, but the two breweries remained separate entities until they merged in 1972 to form the Hacker–Pschorr Brewery. The hyphenated brewery name appeared in beer labels for the first time 3 years later. Today, Hacker–Pschorr together with the Paulaner Brauerei GmbH & Co KG is part of the Munich-based Brau Holding International AG, which, in turn, is owned 49.9% by the Dutch Heineken N.V. and 50.1% by the Schörghuber Corporate Group, a diversified enterprise with businesses in hotels, aircraft leasing, beverages, real estate, and construction. Hacker–Pschorr, however, is now a brand without a brewery, because its brewery was closed in 1998, and all its labels are now brewed by Paulaner. There are more than a dozen beer styles with the Hacker–Pschorr label on the market, including a helles, a dunkel, a pils, four weissbiers, an Oktoberfest märzen, and an unfiltered, yeasty doppelbock.

Hackerhaus. http://www.hackerhaus.de/ (accessed January 28, 2011).

Hacker-Pschorr. http://www.hacker-pschorr.de/unternehmen/content/portrait/index.php/ (accessed January 28, 2011).

Hacker-Pschorr. http://www.hacker-pschorr.de/unternehmen/content/fakten/index.php/ (accessed January 28, 2011).

Horst Dornbusch

Halcyon (barley) is a classic English pale ale malting barley. It is a high-yielding, two-row winter barley variety that became rather popular in the 1980s, especially in the UK. It has an impressive genealogy, considering that it was developed from Maris Otter and Sargent. See MARIS OTTER (BARLEY). In its heyday, Halcyon's popularity was based largely on its excellent agronomic qualities of good disease resistance and high yields, as well as its homogeneity, which ensured its excellent performance in the malt house. It was rather low in protein (usually around 9.5%), which made it perfectly suitable for traditional English ale type, single-step infusion mashing. The low protein values also ensured good extract values during lautering. See LAUTERING. Halcyon imbued the beers made from it with a pleasant biscuit component that gave the finished beer a hearty mouthfeel, as well as some depth and complexity of flavor, although not as round and sweet as attributes given by Maris Otter. Many American craft brewers first became familiar with British malts in the late 1980s, and Halcyon was one of the main barley varieties in the imported pale ale malts of the day. However, Halcyon was also considered to have less diastatic power than some of its competitors, a drawback, which is probably the prime reason why it has been superseded by, among other varieties, the even higher-yielding Pearl. Although now rarely grown, Halcyon is still available, mostly as a floor-malted specialty.

See also FLOOR MALTING.

Annual report of the Plant Breeding Institute. Cambridge, England: 1983.

The Country Malt Group: Thomas Fawcett & Sons. *Malt*. http://www.countrymaltgroup.com/fawcettmalting.asp (accessed December 29, 2010).

Keith Thomas

Hallertauer Magnum (hop) was bred by the Hop Research Institute in Hüll, in the center of the Hallertau with Hallertauer Mittlefrueh heritage. See HALLERTAU HOP REGION and HALLERTAUER MITTELFRUEH (HOP). It was released for commercial cultivation in 1993. This hop has an impressive cosmopolitan lineage in that part of its genetic stock is Galena, an American superalpha hop cultivar. Galena, in turn, is partially derived from Brewer's Gold, a hop bred in England that can lay claim to a wild hop from the province of Manitoba in the Canadian Prairies as part of its ancestry. See BREWER'S GOLD (HOP) and GALENA (HOP). With such a global pedigree, this hop seems to have amassed a veritable mosaic of desirable agronomic and brewing qualities, which is probably why Magnum gardens can now be found in all German hop-growing regions as well as in France, Poland, and the United States. In fact, Magnum is the primary high-alpha variety cultivated in Germany. It is a fast and efficient grower that matures medium-late to late in the season, produces a respectable average yield of approximately 2,750 kg/ha (roughly 2,250 lb per acre), and is fairly resistant to verticillium wilt and downy mildew. In the field, its only notable drawback is its susceptibility to powdery mildew (Podosphaera macularis), a shortcoming that led about a decade later to the introduction by the Institute in Hüll of the variety Herkules. See HERKULES (HOP). With an alpha acid content of 11% to 16%, a beta acid content of 5% to 7%, and a cohumulone content of 21% to 29%, its bitterness values are very high, and it stores well after harvest and processing. In beer, Hallertauer Magnum is considered very versatile, contributing a pleasant and harmonic bitterness as well as a hop aroma of delicate, medium intensity with floral and fruity notes.

CMA hop variety portfolio. *The spirit of beer—hops from Germany*. Wolnzach, Germany: Verband Deustcher Hopfenpflanzer, 2005.

Genetic and epigenetic stability of cryopreserved and cold-stored hops. http://etmd.nal.usda.gov/bitstream/10113/21861/1/IND44135548.pdf (accessed March 29, 2011).

Hallertauer Magnum. http://www.hvg-germany.de/images/stories/pdf/hopfensorten/en/Magnum_engl.pdf (accessed March 29, 2011).

USDA named hop variety descriptions. http://www.freshops.com/hops/usda-named-hop-variety-descriptions#usda_id_21670/ (accessed March 29, 2011).

Daniel Paquette and Lydia Winkelmann

Hallertauer Mittelfrueh (hop) is considered the king of German hop varieties and has a solid reputation as one of the world's finest aroma hops. Its name derives from the Hallertau in Germany, the world's largest hop growing region, and from its optimum harvest time in the early middle of the growing season (*mittelfrueh* means "middle-early"). See HALLERTAU HOP REGION. Because of its exemplary delicate and pleasing aroma qualities, this hop is often referred to by hop marketers as the quintessential "noble" hop. See NOBLE HOPS. Mittelfrueh is an old "landrace" hop variety. This designation implies that it simply emerged from the land and that its origins are so old that they cannot be documented with any certainty. It also means that clonal variations in the hop exist because of long periods of separate evolution of different plants. In actuality, as is the case with all landraces, such as Saaz, there has probably been plenty of natural cross-breeding with wild male hops. See SAAZ (HOP). Hallertauer Mittelfrueh has a spicy-herbal, complex aroma and produces a smooth bitterness that fits well into the flavor profiles of most lagers, especially pilsners. See LAGER and PILSNER. The hop may take on some cedar, leather, and tobacco notes as it ages. Its alpha acid content ranges from 3% to 5.5%, its beta acid content from 3% to 5.0%, and its cohumulone content from 18% to 28%. Its total oil content is 0.7% to 1.3%.

Although an indigenous hop of the Hallertau, Mittelfrueh is also grown in the Tettnang and Spalt regions of Germany, where they are referred to as Tettnanger Hallertau and Spalter Hallertau, as opposed to Hallertauer Hallertau. See SPALT HOP

REGION and TETTNANG HOP REGION. Technically, most Mittelfrueh currently grown in all three German areas is "clonal selection 102," a clone selected and propagated by the Hop Research Institute in Hüll in the Hallertau. It owes its selection to its vigor and its conformity to the variety's flavor standards. Through much of the 20th century, Mittelfrueh was the predominant hop grown in the Hallertau.

Hallertauer Mittelfrueh, often referred to as simply "Hallertau," is a low-yielding hop, averaging about 1,250 kg/ha (1,115 lb/ac) that is susceptible to downy mildew and especially to verticillium wilt. Either may be fatal to the plant, especially the wilt. An outbreak of downy mildew in the Hallertau in the 1920s was responsible for the founding of the Hop Research Institute in Hüll in 1926. The new Institute's nearly exclusive mission was to search for hops that were less susceptible to these diseases and then find ways to control the diseases themselves. In the mid-1950s, an especially aggressive strain of verticillium wilt began to spread in the Hallertau and even caused the infected fields to collapse into commercial non-viability. Because all efforts to find effective means of controlling the wilt had failed, the wilt was so widespread by the 1970s that much of the area was replanted with other hop varieties that were known to be more wilt resistant. See BREWER'S GOLD (HOP), HERSBRUCKER SPÄT (HOP), and NORTHERN BREWER (HOP). New aroma cultivars that could stand up to the wilt were also released by the Hüll Institute. See PERLE (HOP). Whereas in 1970, 58% of the Hallertau acreage was planted with Hallertauer Mittelfrueh, by 1990, that number had dropped to only 1.5%. Acreage increased in the 1990s, however, largely because of a continued high demand by brewers around the world and because of—by then—improved agronomic practices. Currently, Hallertauer Mittelfrueh represents slightly more than 10% of all German hop plantings.

Because of the reputation of Hallertauer Mittelfrueh and continued demand for it by specialty brewers, the Hüll Institute continues to be focused on breeding hops with similar brewing characteristics that have made Mittelfrueh famous, but with better disease resistance and higher yields. Of these, Hallertauer Tradition has been the most successful variety. The more recent Saphir and Smaragd show much promise, too. See HALLERTAUER TRADITION (HOP), SAPHIR (HOP), and SMARAGD (HOP).

Many American brewers in the 1970s wanted a secure source of Hallertau, largely because of the wilt-related production problems in Germany. Thus, they explored other options, the most obvious of which was to grow the hop in the United States, where the wilt was less of a problem. Hallertau plant material was, therefore, imported and propagated in the New World. Much of the material was clearly genuine Hallertauer Mittelfrueh, but some material seems to have been mixed up with some other unknown variety, a problem that is not uncommon in the industry. Hallertauer Mittelfrueh plants in Germany produce red-stripe bines, as do genuine plants in the United States, but the questionable Hallertau plants produce green bines without the telltale red stripe, and the hops themselves are more Fuggle-like than Hallertau-like. Because many brewers were subsequently disappointed by the American-grown Hallertau found in the trade, these transplant efforts were largely unsuccessful. One exception is Hallertauer Mittelfrueh grown in northern Idaho. See IDAHO (NORTHERN HOP REGION). The second pathway to a secure source of New World Hallertau was through breeding Hallertauer hybrid hops with better yields, but similar flavor characteristics. See CRYSTAL (HOP), LIBERTY (HOP), MOUNT HOOD (HOP), ULTRA (HOP), and VANGUARD (HOP).

Thomas Shellhammer and Val Peacock

Hallertauer Taurus (hop) is a late maturing hop variety that as released in 1995 by the Hop Research Institute in Hüll, Germany. It has a very high alpha acid content averaging from 12% to 17%. The bitterness character is crisp, which makes it well suited to bittering of German-style lagers. Given its super-alpha character, brewers do not use it as an aroma hop, although its aromatics are delicate and floral. Although brewers probably have not noticed much, there is one thing interesting about this hop—it has the highest amount of xanthohumol of any hop in the world. Although xanthohumol, a powerful antioxidant, is present in most hops in only trace quantities as a share of overall oil content, in Taurus it has been measured to an average of 0.91%. In vitro studies have demonstrated that xanthohumol in fairly high concentrations is an effective cancer chemopreventive agent. This seems likely to open up a new market for the hop besides brewing—in the health preparations and health food sector, where xanthohumol is being aggressively researched. Agronomically, Taurus is fairly resistant to wilt and downy mildew, but it has a low resistance to powdery mildew.

http://www.hopsteiner.com/pdf/germany/HallertauerTaurus.pdf (accessed March 28, 2011).
http://www.hvg-germany.de/images/stories/pdf/hopfensorten/en/Taurus_engl.pdf/ (accessed March 28, 2011).
http://www.sciencedirect.com/science?_ob=ArticleURL&_udi=B6TH7-4CGMX8M-1&_user=10&_coverDate=05%2F31%2F2004&_rdoc=1&_fmt=high&_orig=search&_origin=search&_sort=d&_docanchor=&view=c&_acct=C000050221&_version=1&_urlVersion=0&_userid=10&md5=5d0180322add765935b3592983641459&searchtype=a/ (accessed March 28, 2011).

Daniel Paquette and Lydia Winkelmann

Hallertauer Tradition (hop) is an aroma hop variety developed by the Hop Research Institute in Hüll, Germany, and released for commercial cultivation in 1992, primarily as an alternative to Hallertauer Mittelfrueh, with similar aroma characteristics but better disease and pest resistance and a higher yield. It is widely used by German lager brewers for late hopping in the kettle. Tradition was bred from Hallertauer Gold and an undefined German male. It has a medium alpha acid content of 4% to 8% and good essential oil profile, yielding fine floral aromatics.

http://www.hvg-germany.de/images/stories/pdf/hopfensorten/en/Tradition_engl.pdf/ (accessed March 28, 2011).
http://www.freshops.com/hops/usda-named-hop-variety-descriptions#usda_id_21672/ (accessed March 28, 2011).

Daniel Paquette and Lydia Winkelmann

Hallertau hop region is only a fairly small triangle of land in Germany, some 70 km (43 mi) north of Munich in Bavaria, but it is the largest and perhaps most famous hop-growing district in the world. See GERMAN HOPS. Hops have been grown there at least since 768 AD, the date of the oldest preserved documentary evidence of hop gardens in the vicinity. But hop cultivation remained fairly modest in the Hallertau until the 16th century, when the use of hops as an exclusive beer flavoring became mandated for all of Bavaria by ducal decree. See REINHEITSGEBOT. One of the noteworthy aspects of Hallertau hop farming has always been the small size of individual holdings, most of them family owned for generations. The number of hop farms in Germany has been in decline for several decades. Whereas there were more than 13,000 in the early 1960s, there are now not even 1,500 and fewer than 1,200 of these are in the Hallertau. The total hop acreage, however, has remained fairly constant because the average farm size has grown. Still, the average size of a hop farm in the Hallertau nowadays is about 13 ha (scarcely 32 acres). In the United States, by comparison, a hop farm of even several hundred acres is considered small. Still, the Hallertau region produces almost 90% of all German hops.

The Hallertau has traditionally been divided into 13 so-called sealing districts, each with its own official stamp to certify the authenticity of any hop shipment from the region. See HOP SEAL. In 1992, an additional district, the Jura area across the Danube River, was added to the Hallertau, as was, in 2004, the Hersbrucker area, centered around the small town of Hersbruck, east of Nuremburg. Hersbruck is actually some 150 km (93 mi) distant from the Hallertau, but the objective of this amalgamation was largely to simplify statistics, given the relatively small size of the new districts. For instance, whereas Hallertau proper has about 15,000 ha of hops under cultivation, Hersbruck's hop gardens do not even amount to 1% of that.

Perhaps the Hallertau's most hallowed and traditional hop is Hallertauer Mittelfrueh, one of the four classic, European varieties often referred to as "noble." See HALLERTAUER MITTELFRÜH (HOP) and NOBLE HOPS. Hallertauer Mittelfrueh is an aroma variety whose production has seen many dramatic ups and downs during the 20th century. To cope with the vagaries of this finicky variety, the Hop Research Institute in Hüll was founded in 1926. It has since grown into a world leader in hop research and breeding. Some of the crosses that have come out of Hüll have become successful cultivars not only in the Hallertau but also elsewhere. See HALLERTAUER TAURUS (HOP), HALLERTAUER

TRADITION (HOP), HERKULES (HOP), HERSBRUCKER SPÄT (HOP), OPAL (HOP), PERLE (HOP), SAPHIR (HOP), and SMARAGD (HOP). However, because of terroir-related differences, such as the soil's drainage characteristics, Hallertauer hops cultivated outside the region, including in the United States, may perform very differently from an agronomic perspective. Importantly, their aroma profiles may be very different as well. In the Hallertau, Hersbrucker Spät is considered a more disease-resistant alternative to Hallertauer Mittelfrueh. Hallertauer Tradition was developed as a German aroma hop designed for Anheuser-Busch. Hallertauer Magnum and Hallertauer Taurus are two higher-alpha bitter hop varieties. The English-bred varieties Northern Brewer and Brewer's Gold were brought to the area in the 1950s because of an outbreak of the soil-borne fungus verticillium wilt, against which these British varieties have a well-tested resistance. See BREWER'S GOLD (HOP) and NORTHERN BREWER (HOP).

The Hallertau has long been an aroma hop area, but now high-alpha bittering hops are increasingly grown there as well. See ALPHA ACIDS. Today, almost as much acreage in the Hallertau is devoted to bitter hops cultivation—mostly Hallertauer Magnum, Herkules, Taurus, Northern Brewer, and Nugget—as to aroma hops cultivation—mostly Perle, Hallertauer Tradition, Hallertauer Mittelfrueh, and Hersbrucker Spät.

See also NUGGET (HOP).

Val Peacock

hammer mill is one of several mill types employed in the brewhouse for crushing whole grain kernels—malted and/or unmalted, depending on the beer recipe—in preparation for mashing and lautering. Other designs are wet and dry roller mills. See DRY MILLING, LAUTERING, MASHING, MILLING, and WET MILLING. Whereas most mills do not grind the grist to a flour-like fine power, hammer mills are specifically designed to achieve a perfectly fine grind. In theory, the finer the grind, the easier it is for grain enzymes in the mash to access the grain starches for the purpose of converting them to wort sugars. It also improves proteolysis, which can be important in the case of undermodified malt. See MODIFICATION and PROTEOLYSIS. In practice, however, fine grinds tend to clump in the mash and make the mash too doughy for mash water to flush out the sugars that are produced. Instead, the sugars get trapped. For this reason, hammer mills can be used only in brewhouses that employ a mash filter instead of a conventional lauter tun. See MASH FILTER. The construction of a hammer mill consists of a round, usually horizontal, metal housing. The top of the housing has an opening for the kernels to enter, whereas the bottom half of the housing is perforated and serves as a screening sieve. A spindle is centrally mounted inside the housing. On it are fixed one or more perpendicular disks and from the periphery of each disk protrude many fix-mounted or pivoting flat vanes, bars, pins, or "hammers." Depending on the shape of the hammer, the mill may also be called a pin mill. As the spindle and the disks rotate, the hammers smash the kernels to bits until they are pulverized and fall through the screen, from where they are sent to the mash. There are also vertical hammer mill designs, which operate on the same principle. If used in conjunction with a mash filter, hammer mills yield the most economical wort extraction, but they also add more beta-glucans to the wort, which may cause beer filtration problems later on.

See also BETA-GLUCANS and FILTRATION.

Kunze, Wolfgang. *Technology brewing and malting*. Berlin: VLB Berlin, 1996.

Horst Dornbusch

Haná (barley) is arguably the world's most important foundation landrace for two-row summer brewing barley. Also known as "Old-Haná agroecotype" and sometimes referred to by its German name of "Hanna," this heirloom barley originates from the Haná Valley, a fertile agricultural plain in Moravia, which in the 19th century was part of the Austro-Hungarian Empire and is now part of the Czech Republic. See AUSTRO-HUNGARIAN EMPIRE and CZECH REPUBLIC. Haná malt's early claim to fame was that it made up the mash of the first-ever golden-blond Pilsner lager, which was created in the fall of 1842 by Bavarian brewmaster Josef Groll at the Měšťanský Pivovar (Burgher Brewery) of Plzeň (Pilsen) in Bohemia. See PILSNER. The subsequent global success of the pilsner beer style not only spawned the planting of Haná barley in many countries around the world but also created the impetus for the establishment of a systematic barley breeding program in Austria-Hungary. The program's aim was to propagate Haná's superior agronomic, malting, and brewing properties into other barley varieties for diverse growing environments. One of the most significant results to come out of this pioneering breeding effort was the so-called Proskowetz Hanna Pedigree bred by Emanuel Proskowetz, a Moravian estate owner, economist, and agronomist. Proskowetz Hanna was released in 1884 and planted until 1958. It became the foundation for the next generation of top-performing brewing barleys, perhaps the most significant of which was Opavský Kneifl, bred by Czech botanist F. Kneifl in 1926. Both Proskowetz Hanna and Opavský Kneifl, as carriers of the old Haná genes, passed on their traits to a long succession of highly successful brewing barley varieties, and by the middle of the 20th century, cultivars of Haná origin were considered the best in the world. Of particular genetic importance in the large family of Haná offspring is the Czech cultivar Valtice (or Valtický), developed during the decade before World War II and planted ubiquitously thereafter, as well as the sturdy Czech Diamant, developed between 1956 and 1965, as well as the East German Trumpf (also spelled Triumpf, Triumph, and Trumph), released in 1973. Diamant and Trumpf alone appear in the pedigrees of some 150 barley varieties that have been bred worldwide since the 1970s. In its Czech homeland alone, early 21st-century studies conducted by the Agricultural Research Institute of Kromeriz have found that genes from Haná and its descendants account for the greatest genetic contribution to 137 Czech spring barley varieties developed between 1900 and 1999. The original 19th-century Haná, therefore, although no longer cultivated today, is internationally recognized as the classic genetic progenitor of modern top-quality brewing barleys.

See also KNEIFL (BARLEY) and TRIUMPH (BARLEY).

Jalowetz, Eduard. *Pilsner malz*. Vienna: Verlag Institut für Gärungsindustrie, 1931 (English edition published in Plzeň in 2006).

Kosar, Karel, Vratislav Psota, and Alexandr Mikyska. Barley varieties suitable for the production of the Czech-type beer. *Czech Journal of Genetics and Plant Breeding* 40 (2004): 137–39.

Personal communication with Czech sources (using a translator into German).

Horst Dornbusch

hand pump

See BEER ENGINE.

Hansen, Emil Christian. Dr Emil Christian Hansen (1842–1909) was one of the first directors of the Carlsberg Laboratory, the research facility established in 1875 by the founder of the Carlsberg brewing company, J.C. Jacobsen. See CARLSBERG GROUP. At this time the industrialization of the brewing process in general—and at Carlsberg in particular—had advanced to a stage where breweries had started bottling their beers themselves and exporting the bottled beers to foreign markets. This imposed entirely new demands on the microbiological stability of the beer, and work focused on the need to prevent beer from going sour before being consumed.

Hansen built on the work of Louis Pasteur, who had identified "impurities," such as bacteria, wild yeasts, and molds, in the production yeasts used to ferment beers. Pasteur developed a simple heat treatment process, called "pasteurization," to eliminate these contaminations in finished beer. See PASTEUR, LOUIS and PASTEURIZATION. Hansen's theory was that not only did the production yeasts contain impurities, but they also consisted of numerous populations of different yeast strains, out of which only a few were actually contributing optimally to the fermentations. This led Hansen to his truly revolutionary experimental work: He diluted the suspensions of yeasts he received from the Carlsberg production brewery, and then grew portions of the diluted suspensions in test tubes on sterile wort, continuing the dilution process until growth only occurred in a limited number of the test tubes. Hansen was convinced, correctly, that by this method he could isolate colonies of yeasts grown from a single cell. After a lengthy series of trial fermentations with his different isolates, Hansen was able to identify and grow the ones giving the optimal beer quality and process performance. In 1883 the work was completed and, at the Carlsberg Brewery, for the first time in history, commercial beer was brewed using a pure culture of the best lager yeast available, which was duly named Saccharomyces carlsbergensis (now known as Saccaharomyces uvarum).

Anders Brinch Kissmeyer

Harrington (barley) is a two-row, malting barley developed at the University of Saskatchewan. It was named after Dr J. B. Harrington, a former barley breeder and department head at the University of Saskatchewan. It was derived from the cross Klages///Gazelle/Betzes//Centennial. At the time of its licensing in 1981 Harrington outperformed the commercially grown varieties Betzes and Klages in almost every aspect. It was higher yielding and stronger strawed than either of the other varieties. It had better root rot resistance but otherwise similar disease resistance, except for the spot form of net blotch, to which it is very susceptible. Harrington had greater kernel plumpness and higher extract than both Klages and Betzes; in addition, its diastatic power and alpha amylase activity were higher than that of Klages and much higher than that of Betzes. The Harrington variety modified 2 days faster than its predecessors and thus added 20% to the capacity of malting plants with no additional capital input. It has no postharvest dormancy, so it can be malted straight from the field, eliminating the need for storage to eliminate dormancy and making storage management easier for the malting industry. See DORMANCY (OF BARLEY). After its release Harrington rapidly dominated the acreage in Canada and the United States and remained the primary two-row variety for over 20 years, before it was replaced by its descendants. At its peak Harrington was sown on over 60% of the barley acreage in western Canada and on over 80% in the province of Saskatchewan. It was even grown in countries where it was clearly out of its area of adaptation, such as South Africa, China, and Australia. Harrington enabled Canada to become a major producer and exporter of two-row malting barley. The variety is particularly suited to high-gravity, high-adjunct brewing, which was growing in popularity at the time of its release. This landmark variety set the international standard for malting and brewing quality in a high-enzyme, two-row barley. It proved very forgiving in the malt house and in the brewery. It gave good color, good brewhouse yield, good flavor, and very good beer shelf life. Harrington has been used in the malt blend to make billions of hectoliters of beer in North America, Japan, China, and a number of other countries. It has also been used in numerous crosses for breeding and genetic studies around the world.

See also ADJUNCTS, ALPHA AMYLASE, and KLAGES (BARLEY).

Bryan Harvey

harvest

See BARLEY HARVEST.

Harvey & Son Ltd., also known as Harveys Brewery, is the oldest brewery in the southern English county of Sussex, with a reputation that reaches much farther.

John Harvey built his brewery on the banks of the River Ouse in the medieval town of Lewes in 1790. The original brewery was partially rebuilt in 1880 and stands intact today as a beautiful example of a Victorian Country brewery, one that helps define this popular town and give it its character. (Some of the locals waggishly refer to the brewery as "Lewes Cathedral.") Harveys has remained a family brewer through more than 2 centuries, and the seventh-generation descendants of John Harvey are still active in the running of the business.

Harveys Imperial Stout (9% ABV) is revered worldwide, bottle-conditioned with a distinctive squat, long-necked bottle design. The brewery suggests it can improve for up to a year, but connoisseurs have aged it far longer than that.

Harveys is best known for its Sussex Best Bitter (4% ABV), ubiquitous and beloved in its hometown, with a fanatical cult following throughout southeast England. In December 2006 it was removed from sale at the Lewes Arms by the pub's owners, Greene King. See GREENE KING. This prompted a 133-day boycott of the pub by the population of Lewes that made national headlines across the UK and resulted in an embarrassing climb-down by the larger brewer-cum-pub company.

As well as inspiring such dramatic protests, this pale, hoppy ale was named Campaign for Real Ale's

Champion Best Bitter in Britain 2 years running in 2005 and 2006—just part of the reason why this charming brewery has an international reputation and following that is dramatically larger than its mere size (47,000 UK barrels) would suggest.

Pete Brown

Harwood, Ralph, was an early 18th-century London brewer, who has been lauded as the inventor of a beer called "Entire" or "Entire Butt" (a "butt" being a type of cask). A popular drink at the time was "three threads," a dark beer mixture drawn from three different casks and blended in the customer's glass at the pub. See THREE-THREADS. In 1722 Harwood produced his "Entire" beer which matched the flavor of this mixture in one, labor-saving cask. Entire rapidly became popular with the manual transporters of goods and produce, or porters, and soon the beer itself became known as "porter." See PORTER.

There are several conflicting accounts of the evolution of porter from Entire and of Harwood's role, if any, in it. The first explicit attribution of Harwood as the inventor of porter seems to be in an 1802 article on "The Porter Brewery," written by John Feltham and published in a guidebook called *The Picture of London*. This story—though written many years after Harwood's death and seeming to be of uncertain veracity—appears to be the basis of almost every history of porter in the brewing literature until well into the 20th century.

Harwood brewed at Shoreditch in the East End of London from around 1703, and in partnership with his brother James from 1736. He did not profit from his invention, as did the great porter brewers, such as Whitbread and Thrale. His brewery appears to have remained small, and indeed the Harwoods' company was reported as bankrupt in the *Gentleman's Magazine* in 1747, 2 years before Harwood's death. It is now thought that Ralph Harwood might not in fact have invented porter, and it has been suggested that if a Harwood did so, it was his brother James. The story of Ralph Harwood, therefore, and thus of the "who," "where," and "how" of porter's true origin, remains something of a beer mystery.

Cornell, Martyn. *Beer: The story of the pint.* London: Headline Book Publishing, 2003.

Corran, H.S. *A history of brewing.* Newton Abbot, England: David & Charles, 1975.

Terry Foster

haze is the broad term used for turbidity in beer; however, the term generally covers all forms of instability in beer in which insoluble material appears. As clarity is a desired trait in many types of beer, brewers of these beers work hard to avoid unwanted haze. Haze strictly refers to evenly distributed turbidity throughout the body of the beer, but there may be discrete particles ("bits," "floaters") that appear in otherwise "bright" beer. Precipitates and sediments may also appear, especially in bottle-conditioned or unfiltered beers.

From a technical point of view, there are several different types of haze. One form is so-called invisible haze ("pseudo haze"), which is caused by very small particles that cannot be readily detected by the eye but which scatter light in high intensity. Invisible haze is detected by haze meters that measure turbidity on the basis of the scatter of light at right angles to the incident. These "hazes" constitute a problem only insofar as they force the brewer to make a judgment on acceptability of the beer that contradicts what the instrument is saying. In other words, they present a logistical challenge. This is the reason why many brewers use haze meters that measure light scatter at a narrower "forward" angle, under which circumstances the spurious scatter is not registered.

Visible haze is differentiated into chill haze, which develops when beer is chilled to 32°F (0°C) but disappears when the beer warms to 68°F (20°C), and permanent haze, which is present at all temperatures. It is also differentiated into biological haze, which arises from the growth of living microorganisms in the beer, and non-biological haze, which is caused by a diversity of colloidally unstable non-living materials in beer. These materials include proline-rich polypeptides deriving from the storage proteins of grain, polyphenols (oxidized in the presence of transition metal ions such as iron and copper), starch, β-glucan, pentosans, oxalate, and dead yeast or bacteria.

See also CHILL HAZE and COLLOIDAL HAZE.

Leiper, K.A., and M. Miedl. "Colloidal stability of beer." In *Beer: A quality perspective*, ed. C.W. Bamforth, 111–61. Burlington, MA: Academic Press, 2009.

Charles W. Bamforth

head retention

See FOAM.

health. While wine is currently perceived as being more in keeping with a healthy diet than is beer, there is now growing evidence that it's possible that beer is actually the healthier of the two.

Since the CBS television program *60 Minutes* reported on the role of red wine in countering atherosclerosis (the buildup of fatty materials in the arteries) in 1991, the belief has grown that this is a unique attribute of that beverage. Extensive international studies have now demonstrated that the active beneficial ingredient in this respect is not resveratrol from the grape but rather ethanol and it is just as effective whether it comes from wine of any color, or beer or spirits. See ETHANOL.

Beer is actually more substantial in nutritive terms than is wine. Beer is a significant source of B vitamins (other than thiamine) and contains a range of minerals, notably silicon, which is one of the likely reasons why moderate beer consumption reduces the risk of osteoporosis. Beer contains antioxidants, including polyphenols and ferulic acid, which (unlike many other putative antioxidants) have actually been shown to be effectively taken in by the body. See FERULIC ACID and POLYPHENOLS. It has been suggested that alcohol potentiates the uptake of molecules of this type into the body. Beer contains some soluble fiber and some lower molecular weight carbohydrates that may function as prebiotics (food ingredients that promote the growth of beneficial microorganisms in the lower intestine).

Trade card, c. 1900. Adding water to malt tonic produced a mixture that tasted somewhat like beer, though nonalcoholic. Many breweries made such products in response to the threat of Prohibition, well before Prohibition actually began. PIKE MICROBREWERY MUSEUM, SEATTLE, WA

A 1915 postcard printed in Germany—where the sophistication of the printing industry made such cards cheap and easy to produce—and shipped to the United States. PIKE MICROBREWERY MUSEUM, SEATTLE, WA

Beer stimulates the production of the hormone gastrin, which promotes the flow of gastric juices in the stomach.

There have been several studies that speak to the health benefits of moderate beer consumption, especially in middle age and beyond. This may be both through a direct impact of beer constituents on the body and through boosting the contentment of the drinker.

Performing studies into the specific relationship between consumption of beer and bodily health is not easy, because of the impact of interfering factors. Many studies are based on patients answering doctors' questions about their drinking habits and there is the inevitable likelihood of less than totally honest responses. The other major problem is confounding factors, with aspects of a drinkers' life potentially being the true explanation for a perceived positive (or, indeed, negative) impact that otherwise is ascribed to beer.

As regards atherosclerosis, alcohol lowers levels of LDL cholesterol ("bad cholesterol") in the blood plasma and increases levels of HDL cholesterol ("good cholesterol"). Alcohol also reduces the risk of blood clotting by lessening the aggregation tendencies of blood platelets.

The relationship between risk of death and consumption of alcohol (including beer) is generally described as a U-shaped or J-shaped curve. It appears that the J-shape depicts the relationship between alcohol intake and total mortality, with the U-shape better describing that between alcohol consumption and coronary heart disease. That is, the benefits of alcohol in countering atherosclerosis extend to substantial daily consumption, whereas if all health considerations are considered, then the J-shaped curve suggests an optimum daily consumption of between one and three units if the risk of mortality is to reach its nadir. (One unit is 8g of alcohol.) It has been suggested that the frequency of drinking is also important, with moderate daily consumption being optimal. As regards the claims that wine drinking is superior to that of beer in the interests of countering atherosclerosis, studies have suggested that this is very much to do with other elements of a consumer's lifestyle. Wine drinkers often are wealthier and have a healthier lifestyle and better health care, and they probably have a superior overall diet as compared to many beer drinkers. Wine drinkers are also less likely to smoke. Lifestyle and the rest of one's diet, as opposed to the beer itself, have been shown to be the actual cause of the so-called beer belly.

Some of the hop constituents, e.g., xanthohumol, have been claimed also to function in countering atherosclerosis and other ailments. See XANTHOHUMOL. However, it is questionable whether most beers (even the extreme hopped products in the US craft beer sector) are hopped sufficiently for this effect to be significant. 8-prenylnaringenin from hops is the most potent estrogen yet identified; however, these substances are actually found in extremely low levels in beer. Alcohol, including in the form of beer, destroys the bacterium Helicobacter pylori that is believed to be responsible for ulceration of the stomach and duodenum, and can also cause stomach cancer. Significant purine levels in some beer may exacerbate gout.

It has been suggested that there is a barley polysaccharide in beer that promotes prolactin secretion and therefore milk production in the nursing mother. However, it may be that the relaxing impact of alcohol and hop components is the true promoting factor.

Increased blood pressure (hypertension) is twice as common in heavy drinkers as in light drinkers. Beer drinking in particular has been linked to higher blood pressure. Hypertension is the biggest risk factor for strokes. While moderate drinking (less than 2.1 ounces [60 grams] of alcohol per day) presents a slightly increased risk of stroke as compared to abstinence, it has been claimed that there is actually a reduced risk of stroke for light to moderate drinkers. It seems that it is heavy drinking (more than six drinks per day) and binge drinking that lead to an increased risk. Tyramine and histamine have been found in beers. Tyramine can cause a rise in blood pressure by constricting the vascular system and increasing the heart rate. Such amines can induce migraines and hypertensive crises.

Alcohol speeds up the rate of emptying and filling of the gall bladder—hence people with moderate daily alcohol intake develop fewer gallstones. There is a link between cirrhosis of the liver and excessive consumption of liquor, but less so for beer or wine. However, excessive intake of alcohol can cause fatty infiltrations and a swelling in the liver.

Hop polyphenols inhibit the growth of Streptococci, thereby delaying the onset of dental caries. Furthermore, dark beers contain an unidentified component that inhibits the synthesis of a polysaccharide that anchors harmful bacteria to the teeth.

Moderate drinkers displayed a reduced risk of developing non-insulin dependent diabetes.

There is no consensus agreement about the prime causative agents of hangovers. They are likely in part to be caused by an accumulation of acetaldehyde produced by the oxidation of alcohol, with the aldehyde adversely interacting with brain cells. See ACETALDEHYDE. Headaches may also be induced by biogenic amines found in relatively small quantities in beer. Migraine attacks were more frequently associated with the consumption of sparkling and red wines and spirits than with beer.

A study of multiple sets of twins born between 1917 and 1927 revealed a J-shaped relationship between alcohol consumption and cognitive function, with moderate drinkers performing significantly better than abstainers or heavy drinkers.

Moderate drinkers are said to be more outgoing and enthusiastic about life and less stressed. They perform some tasks better after a drink; enjoy fewer incidences of depression; and fare better when elderly, including as regards cognitive function.

Light to moderate drinking (one to three alcoholic drinks of any type per day) is significantly associated with a lower risk of dementia in those aged 55 years and above. Moderate alcohol consumption may be associated with reduced incidence of macular degeneration. It stimulates appetite and promotes bowel function. Regular consumption of alcohol lowers the risk of incurring Alzheimer's disease; in part this may relate to the silica content of beer.

Hazardous drinking (defined as those occasions when five or more drinks are consumed daily) is associated more with beer than with other types of alcoholic beverages. This correlates with younger, unmarried males.

Alcohol dehydrates the whole body (except the brain, which swells) through a diuretic impact on the kidney, hence the desirability of drinking much water before sleeping following the drinking of alcohol. Beer is more diuretic than is water and is better than water in flushing out kidneys, thereby reducing the incidence of kidney stones.

Alcohol consumption needs to be substantial for it to be a causative factor in cancer. The literature is contradictory on the relationship between alcohol consumption and cancer. Indeed it has been proposed that certain components of beer (such as pseudouridine) might even counter cancer.

As most beers are derived from barley or wheat, it is generally recommended that they be avoided by sufferers of celiac disease who react to prolamin proteins (such as hordein and gluten) and peptides derived from gluten. See GLUTEN-FREE BEER. However, there has been much debate about the extent to which beer actually presents a problem in this context. There is much less protein in beer than in the grist materials from which it is derived, owing to the malting and brewing processes. Indeed, many beers have as part of their grists non-prolamin-containing adjuncts such as rice, corn, and sugar.

The U.S. Department of Agriculture recommends a maximum of one drink per day for women and two for men, a drink being a 12-ounce serving of a regular beer or 5 ounces of wine (12% ABV). And it is stated that at this level there is no association of alcohol consumption with deficiencies of either macronutrients or micronutrients and, furthermore, there is no apparent association between consuming one or two alcoholic beverages daily and obesity.

Bamforth, C. W. *Beer: Health and nutrition*. Oxford, England: Blackwell, 2004.

Bamforth, C. *Grape versus grain*. New York: Cambridge University Press, 2008.

Casey, T. R., & C. W. Bamforth. Silicon in beer and brewing. *Journal of the Science of Food and Agriculture*: In press.

Nutrition and Your Health: Dietary Guidelines for Americans (from the United States Department of Agriculture). http://www.health.gov/DIETARYGUIDELINES/dga2005/report/HTML/D8_Ethanol.htm/ (accessed July 9, 2010).

Charles W. Bamforth

heat exchanger, a piece of brewery equipment designed to quickly raise or lower the temperature of wort or beer. Heat exchangers in breweries are often referred to as "plate heat exchangers" because they are built as a series of plates; a hot liquid flows along one side of the plate and cold liquid flows along the other side. A heat exchange takes place across the plates. The most common heat exchanger is found in the brewhouse. Hot wort at approximately 95°C is run through a heat exchanger, where it is cooled by cold water and/or a refrigerant coming along the reverse side of the plate in the opposite direction. The wort becomes cool (e.g., to 12°C) and ready for fermentation, and the cold water is heated to perhaps 80°C and is returned to a hot water tank, ready to be used in the next brew or elsewhere in the brewery. On average, heat exchangers will be sized so that the entire contents of the kettle can be cooled to fermentation temperature in 45 min or less. A heat exchanger is very energy efficient because the heat originally used to bring wort to the boil is partially reused to heat cold water coming into the brewery. Using refrigerants such as glycol, plate heat exchangers can also be used to cool beer to low temperatures after fermentation, say from 12°C to –1°C, for cold maturation. Heat exchangers may be used in many aspects of the brewing process to heat and cool beer and to heat or cool liquids such as water. Although plate heat exchangers are the most common, other designs of heat exchanger may be used, such as a "shell and tube heat exchanger." Heat exchangers are also used as part of the makeup of flash pasteurization units, which heat beer quickly to pasteurize it, hold it for a short period as it flows through pipework, and then quickly decrease the temperature again.

Paul KA Buttrick

heather (Calluna vulgaris) is a widespread, small bush-like plant that grows on dry, acidic soils. In the northern hemisphere it usually flowers in August and has a strong and pleasant aroma during flowering. Both young shoots of heather and the very aromatic flowering shoots may be used for bittering and flavoring beer. In many areas of Europe, heather was a common component of gruit, a mixture of herbs that was widely used in beer in the centuries before hops became predominant. See GRUIT. Heather shoots are also well known for their coloring characteristics (yellow–brown). Flowering heather is very attractive to bees, and a dark aromatic honey is produced from heather nectar. This honey may be used to produce mead, and it has also been of interest to brewers through the ages. It may be used directly to increase sweetness and alcohol strength and more indirectly as an alternative to traditional brewer's yeast to promote and regulate the spontaneous fermentation of beer. For this use the honey, which contains entrained yeasts, must be nonheated when added to the cooled wort. See HONEY. Furthermore, associated with heather itself is a specific fungal growth (colloquially called "fogg" or simply "white powder"), which possesses a wild yeast capable of fermenting beer. Heather grows wild all over Britain and it is believed that the old tribes of the British Isles, the Picts and the Celts, made beers with heather during the Iron Age. Archeological digs have found heather in the residues of beer-like beverages buried with the dead in their graves, both in the Bronze Age and in the Iron Age. Today, a number of craft brewers are rediscovering heather as an interesting ingredient that can bring pleasant floral aromatics to their beers.

Behre, Karl-Ernst. The history of beer additives in Europe—A review. *Vegetation History and Archaeobotany* 8 (1999): 35–48.

Brøndegaard, V. J. *Folk og Flora. Dansk etnobotanik 4,* p. 121. Publ. Rosenkilde og Bagger, 1987.

Buhner, H.B. *Sacred and herbal healing beers: The secrets of ancient fermentation.* Boulder, CO: Siris Books, 1998.

von Hofsten, Nils. *Pors och andra humleersättninger och Ölkryddor i äldre tider.* Stockholm, Sweden: Akademiska Förlaget, 1960. (Title translated: *Gale and other substitutes and beer-spices in past times.* Includes an English summary.)

Per Kølster

hectoliter is a metric unit of volume equal to 100 liters. It is the major unit of volume used in the brewing industry worldwide. Even in the two countries that have resisted the metric system, the United States and the United Kingdom, the hectoliter is slowly replacing the US beer barrel (117.35 liters) and the UK beer barrel (163.66 liters) as units of beer measurement. Measures equaling "one barrel" differ widely from country to country and between different industries. The metric hectoliter avoids those differences and makes scientific calculation easier. The abbreviation for the hectoliter is "hl."

Gerrit Blüemelhuber

hedge hops is the collective name of a group of English hop varieties originally known as dwarf hops and hedgerow hops. The name was changed to hedge hops after growers thought that hedgerow suggested wild rather than cultivated hops. Hedge hops grow shorter than conventional varieties, often no higher than 2.5 meters (roughly 8 feet), which allows them to be raised on a lower wirework system. They can be harvested by mobile machines that comb the hops from the hedge without needing to cut the bines. This dramatically reduces the labor intensity of hop cultivation and thus the overall cost of production. The compact growth also makes hedge hops more accessible for targeted spraying, which is another cost savings. Hedge hops are cultivated mostly in the West Midlands of England, although there are also breeding programs for hedge varieties in Germany, the Czech Republic, and the United States. The original breeding program for hedge hops was started by Dr Ray Neve in 1977. It was continued by Dr Peter Darby in 1981. The first commercial variety, First Gold, is a Golding-like dual-purpose hop suitable for both bittering and aroma additions that was released for commercial cultivation in 1995, followed by five additional varieties: Herald was released in 1996 and has since been discontinued. Pioneer is primarily a bittering hop that was released in 1996. It may also be used for dry hopping. Pilot, a bittering hop, was released in 2001. Boadicea is a dual-purpose hop that was released in 2005. Finally, Sovereign, a Fuggle-like hop, is used primarily for its aroma. It was released in 2006. See FIRST GOLD (HOP) and PIONEER (HOP). Currently, roughly one-quarter of all hop acreage in the United Kingdom is planted with hedge hops.

Darby, Peter. The history of hop breeding and development. *Brewery History* 121 (Winter 2005): 94–112.

Adrian Tierney-Jones

hefeweizen

See LEICHTES WEISSBEIR and WEISSBIER.

Heineken. Europe's largest multinational brewery was founded by Gerard Adriaan Heineken in Amsterdam, with a major lager production facility in Zoeterwoude, close to Leiden, in the Netherlands. In 1864, Gerard Heineken purchased "Den Hoybergh" ("the haystack") brewery that had been operating in the center of Amsterdam since 1592, and renamed it Heineken's in 1873. In 1874 he opened a second brewery in Rotterdam (which closed in 1968). In 1886 Louis Pasteur student Dr H. Elion succeeded in isolating the A-yeast strain in a Heineken laboratory that is still used in production to this day. A second Amsterdam brewery located on the Stadhouderskade was built to replace Den Hoybergh in 1886. The new brewery switched over to lager production in 1887 and installed refrigeration in 1888. Brewing there ceased in 1988 and after 3 years of renovation the site reopened as the Heineken Reception and Information Center. It was renamed the Heineken Experience in 2001 and after a year of renovation and expansion it reopened to visitors in November of 2008.

In 1929 Heineken starting bottling all of its beer at the brewery, giving the company better control of hygiene and quality. Clever timing ensured that in 1933, only 3 days after the repeal of prohibition in America, the first shipment of Heineken pilsner arrived in New York harbor. (Today it is America's second most popular import beer, after Corona.) Around this time Heineken decided to change its strategy from being a large national brewery to becoming a multinational and when Freddy Heineken started his career in 1942 the stage was set for major changes. In the 1950s the importance of the technical quality of the beer moved to the background and the marketing team began to emphasize the brand instead of the beer. This is not to say that technical advances were ignored—for instance, replacement of all wooden kegs by stainless steel versions began in 1951.

In 1962 Heineken's became "Heineken," replacing "pilsner" as the prominent text on the label. The logo was also revamped by changing the red star to white, accenting the text by changing it to lower case, tilting the second "e" to make it appear to "smile," and placing Heineken on a black banner. To generations of Americans, Heineken's distinctive green bottle became a symbol of "imported quality." Ironically the green bottle also has another effect: It can allow the beer to acquire a "lightstruck" (or, colloquially, "skunked") aroma far more easily than does a brown bottle, which offers better protection from harmful ultraviolet wavelengths of light. See LIGHTSTRUCK.

Heineken opened what is now its special beer production brewery in Den Bosch in 1958 and its major production facility in Zoeterwoude in 1975. It stopped production at its subsidiary Amstel Brewery in 1980 and then demolished it to make way for affordable housing in 1982. See AMSTEL BREWERY. Heineken has used the practice of takeover and closure of competing brewers to increase its national market share since the end of World War I. Examples include 't Haantje in Amsterdam (1918), Griffioen in Silvolde (1919), De Zwarte Ruiter in Maasticht, Schaepman in Zwolle and Rutten's in Amsterdam (1920), De Kroon in Arnhem (1921), Marres in Maastricht (1923), Koninklijke Nederlandsche Beiersch in Amsterdam (1926), Ceres in Maastricht (1931), and Twentsche Stoom Beiersch in Almelo (1934). After the end of World War II many small southern Dutch breweries were offered lucrative Heineken distributorships if they would cease their brewing activities. Faced with the prospect of having to invest heavily to modernize their breweries in an uncertain market, many accepted the offer of a steady income, resulting in a pilsner monoculture in the Netherlands. Van Vollenhoven in Amsterdam (1949), Sint Servatius in Maastricht, and Vullinghs in Sevenum (1952) are typical examples. The Royal Brand's brewery in Wijlre is an exception to the rule. After the takeover in 1989 a great deal of investment, marketing, and distribution via the Heineken network has resulted in Brand growing to become Heineken's third national brand. International takeovers have included the Leopold brewery in Brussels, Belgium (1927), Murphy's brewery in Ireland (1983), Komarom brewery in Hungary (1991), French brewery Francaise de Brasserie (1993), Belgian brewer De Smedt (renamed Affligem Brewery BDS) in 2001, and Austrian brewery group Brau Beteiligungs Aktiengesellschaft, now called Brau Union Ag, in 2003 (in Heineken's largest takeover to date).

Production takes place in more than 125 breweries in seventy countries. Heineken NV is active in more than 170 countries. With a total beer volume of 107 million barrels (125.8 million hectoliters) in 2008, Heineken is one of the world's largest brewers. Only Anheuser-Busch InBev and SABMiller brew more beer. See ANHEUSER-BUSCH INBEV and SABMILLER. Heineken and their subsidiaries produce beer in more than 125 breweries in seventy countries, employ almost 60,000, and sell at least 50% of their beer within the European Union. Some of the more than 200 brand names include 33 Export, Cruz Campo, Zywiec, Birra Moretti, Murphy's, and Star. Heineken produces three products: Heineken Pilsener, Heineken Tarwebok (wheat bock), called Special Dark in America, and Oud Bruin, a dark and sweet low alcohol lager brewed only for the Dutch market.

See also NETHERLANDS, THE.

Sint Servatius Brouwerij. http://www.bierbrouwerijen.org/index.php?title=Sint_Servatius_Brouwerij/ (accessed July 9, 2010).

Derek Walsh

hekt, also spelled "*hqt*" or "*heket,*" as well as a number of other derivations (including *haqu* or *heqa*, according to Arnold), represents "barley beer" in early Egypt. As Murray reported, one of the earliest written records of beer in ancient Egypt is a reference to *hnqt-ndmt*, "sweet beer," which is located on the offering stela in the Dynasty III tomb of Sekherkhabau at Saqqara. Lutz mentions "Nubian beer" as being *hkt* and suggests that this is derived from a root that essentially means "to squeeze" or "to press out." Hrozný maintained that the word was connected with the Babylonian beer *hîqu*, deriving from the word *hâqu*, "to mix," but Lutz disagreed. Lutz's main argument against this suggestion was, "It is hardly possible to suppose that a word like Egyptian *hkt*, which occurs numerous times in texts of every period, should have been borrowed from the Babylonian *hîqu*, a word which is not at all met with frequently in Babylonian texts." Some Egyptologists maintain that the determinative of the word *hqt* was a beer jug.

Zozimus of Panopolis (b. c. AD 250) described the method of brewing *hekt* in ancient Egypt. Details are included in his 28-volume, oft-quoted treatise of the chemical arts, which was written sometime between the end of the 3rd and the beginning of 4th century AD. Unfortunately, some of the lines are not intelligible, but the processes of malting, mashing, and fermenting can be discerned. The account commences, "Take well-selected fine barley, macerate it for a day with water, and then spread it for a day in a spot where it is well exposed to a current of air."

Hekt was likely of low alcoholic strength, because children drank it. As an ancient Egyptian physician recorded, "With hekt the spirit is kept in balance with the liver and blood . . . hekt is the liquid of happy blood and body." Heket (Heqat) was also an Egyptian goddess in the form of a frog, whose strongest association was with childbirth.

See also EGYPT and HISTORY OF BEER.

Arnold, J. P. *Origin and history of beer and brewing.* Chicago: Alumni Association of the Wahl Henius Institute of Fermentology, 1911.

Hornsey, I. S. *A history of beer and brewing.* Cambridge, UK: Royal Society of Chemistry, 2003.

Hrozný, F. *Das Getreide im alten Babylonien: Ein Beitrag zur Kultur- und Wirtschaftgeschichte des alten Orients.* Vienna, Austria: Akademie der Wissenschaften in Wein, 1913.

Lutz, H. L. F. *Viticulture and brewing in the ancient Orient.* Leipzig, Germany: J. C. Hinrichs, 1922 [facsimile produced by Applewood Books, Bedford, MA, 2008].

Murray, M. A. *Saqqara Mastabas, part I. Publications of the Egyptian Research Account 10, British School of Archaeology in Egypt.* London: Bernard Quaritch, 1905.

Ian Hornsey

helles is a pale golden lager that is the everyday session beer of Bavaria, Germany. The German word "hell" or "helles" simply means "pale." In most German-speaking regions ordering a "helles" or "ein bier, bitte" in a pub would simply produce the standard light-colored beer on tap, which is, more often than not, a pils or pilsner. But in Bavaria, style definitions are more differentiated. There, the order of "ein bier, bitte" would most likely be followed by the probing question, "And which beer do you want?" A Bavarian helles is considerably lower in bitterness than a German pils. It is lighter in body and character than a märzen. Helles is a medium bodied, usually straw-blonde beer with an emphasis on clean, bready, malt flavors and floral hop aromas with mild bitterness. In Bavaria, many consider helles the very essence of the summer beer garden. The best have a slightly sulfurous character reminiscent of brewery fermentation rooms. It typically has an original gravity of 11 to 12.5 degrees Plato and 4.7% to 5.3% alcohol by volume.

In the United States, some prefer to call the style "Münchner style helles" after the city where it originated in 1894, although today helles is a style that is brewed in most parts of Bavaria. Until the turn of the 20th century, dark beers had been considered the only "real" Bavarian lager, in part because most Bavarian beer drinkers would hardly have noticed the color of their beers, considering that they were usually served in Keferlohers, the local, grayish version of a beer stein. See STEIN. The beer stein, typically measuring 1 l (33 oz), had remained the drinking vessel of choice in Munich much longer than in the rest of Europe, where cheaper, mass-produced beer glasses had become the norm. It was the new ubiquity of the beer glass that paved the way for pilsner and other light-colored beers; they looked purer and more appetizing in a clear glass than in a mug made of glazed stoneware. See GLASSWARE. "Paler-than-dunkel" lagers were tentatively introduced by Munich's breweries to their home market starting in 1841, with the Spaten Brewery's first märzenbier. See MÄRZENBIER. Then, in 1872, the Franziskaner-Leist-Brauerei came out with its Helles Export Bier, which was not actually a helles, but yielded the foundation recipe of what was to

Helles, meaning "pale" in German, is the session beer of Bavarian beer gardens. The success of the helles style around the turn of the 20th century caused a furor among traditionalists, who considered dark beers the only "real" Bavarian lager. PHOTOGRAPH BY DENTON TILLMAN

become today's Spaten Oktoberfest beer. This was followed in 1893 by an even paler brew, the Münchner Gold, an imitation of the pilsner from Pilsen by Hacker-Bräu (now Hacker–Pschorr). Spaten brewery finally introduced the first "real" helles on March 21, 1894, and promptly sent it for market testing to Hamburg, where it was a hit. The Munich natives, therefore, finally got their first taste of the new brew on June 20, 1895, under the label of Helles Lagerbier, a designation for which the German Imperial Patent Office awarded a registered trademark that same year. Tomasbräu then advertised its version of the helles, also in 1895, as "Thomasbräu-Pilsner—anerkannt vollwertigster Ersatz für böhmisches Pilsener" ("recognized as the most complete substitute for Bohemian Pilsener"). The success of the helles style brought about a stormy meeting of the Verein Münchener Brauereien (the Association of Munich Breweries) on November 7, 1895, where the owners of some of the largest breweries declared that they had no intention of making any pale lagers in the near future. They even drafted a resolution aimed at turning the clock back and forming an anti-pale-lager cartel, which would aim to preserve a local market for dunkel. The result of the meeting was disunity. The brewers who wanted to make helles simply went ahead, and those who did not, did not. The more forward looking of Munich's beer barons, however, recognized that pale beers were the beers of the future, and all brewers soon started to rethink their policies. Still, it took Paulaner until 1928 to introduce its helles. Today, both helles and pilsner are roughly equal in popularity in Bavaria, with each holding about 25% of the market share. In the rest of Germany, however, helles remains virtually non-existent.

A Bavarian Export, incidentally, is the designation for a stronger version of the helles, generally around 5.5% alcohol by volume, and this export ought not to be confused with the Dortmunder Export from Westphalia.

Dornbusch, Horst. *Bavarian Helles*. Boulder, CO: Brewers Publications, 2000.

Conrad Seidl

hemp (Cannabis sativa L.) is botanically closely related to hops. See HOPS. Unlike the hop, it is an annual plant growing from seed every year. Hemp is an extremely vigorous, fast-growing plant with a straight stem that can grow to be several meters tall. Its main use has been as a fiber crop, and hemp ropes were once commonly used on sailing ships. However, because of its resins, which can have a high content of the psychoactive chemical compound Δ9-tetrahydrocannabinol (THC), it is also used as a drug. The concentration of THC is higher in specific selected "marijuana" strains and/or when the hemp is grown in sunny and warm areas. Today hemp is widespread all over the world with partially or completely restricted cropping in most Western countries because of its narcotic potential.

Hemp may have been used in ancient times in beer brewing but very little evidence suggests that it was ever widely used for this purpose. In recent years hemp leaves have been used in Western countries as a substitute for aroma-hopping in a limited number of specialty beers. Other beers have used the seeds, usually lightly toasted before their addition to the kettle. Some have claimed that hemp seeds add a nutty flavor to beer, but many people have found the flavor unattractive. Because of legal restrictions, only materials from cultivars of hemp with a very low content of THC are allowed. The use of hemp in beers, therefore, only adds flavor and aroma and not narcotic effects. If legal, hemp can easily be grown for home use in brewing. That said, it seems fair to say that use of hemp products in commercial beers is more a matter of juvenile titillation than of flavor and aroma. After a brief splash in the 1990s, use of hemp in brewing has largely faded from the scene.

See also HERBS.

Behre, Karl-Ernst. The history of beer additives in Europe—a review. *Vegetation History and Archaeobotany* 8 (1999): 35–48.

Both, Frank, ed. *Gerstensaft und hirsebier: 5000 jahre biergenuss*. Oldenburg, Germany: Verlag Isensee, 1998.

Brøndegaard, V. J. Folk og flora. *Dansk Etnobotanik* 2 (1999): 117.

Buhner, H. B. *Sacred and herbal healing beers: the secrets of ancient fermentation*. Boulder, CO: Siris, 1998.

Hofsten, Nils von. Pors och andra humleersättninger och ölkryddor i äldre tider. *(Gale and other substitutes and beer-spices in past times*. Includes an English summary). Uppsala, Sweden: Akademiska Förlaget, 1960.

Purseglove, J. W. Tropical crops. Dicotyledons. Harlow, UK: Longman Group, 1976.

Per Kølster

Henry's law is a relationship governing the partition of a substance in equilibrium between the atmosphere and the aqueous phase. It states that at constant temperature, the solubility of a substance is directly proportional to the partial pressure p of that substance:

$$p = k_H c$$

Where c is the concentration in aqueous solution (such as beer) and k_H is its Henry's law constant. In beer, Henry's law governs carbonation and the evolution of carbon dioxide (CO_2) out of the liquid during dispense. The law is named after William Henry, an English chemist from Manchester who in 1802 described experiments on the quantity of gases absorbed by water at different temperatures and under different pressures.

Henry's law is most applicable with gases that have not reached their saturation limits, and that do not react with the solvent. Different units of k_H exist in the literature and care must be taken when performing relevant calculations. By comparing k_H for different solutes, one can predict relative solubilities in a given liquid. k_H can also be used to compute the equilibrium concentration of a substance in either the atmosphere or the aqueous phase. Values of k_H are obtained empirically and the approximation is reliable only for substances of low solubility.

One may observe the effects of Henry's law when opening a bottle of beer (or other carbonated beverage). Carbonation levels in typical beers are around 4 to 5 g/l [2 to 2.5 volumes], whereas the equilibrium concentration of CO_2 at serving temperature is around 2.5 g/l. Upon opening a bottle, therefore, the system will strive for equilibrium and bubbles are formed as CO_2 is released into the gaseous phase.

See also CARBONATION.

Wolfgang David Lindell

herbs. While the botanically inclined will often use the word "herb" to describe plants with non-woody stems, the broader use of the word includes flowers and roots as well as leaves. Herbs have always been integral to beer, and they have played many different roles in brewing over the millennia. Today very few beer styles are significantly influenced by the use of any herbs other than the hop flower, but this was not always so.

Historically, herbs were used to stabilize beer, to retard spoilage, to increase palatability and cover brewing failures, to imbue the beer with medicinal qualities, and finally to make beer "stronger" or even hallucinogenic. In the early days of brewing, herbal components of beer might differ from batch to batch, with neither brewer nor consumers expecting much in the way of consistency. Consumers simply demanded that beer satisfy their needs and habits, while brewers did their best to produce reputable beer that people would buy. Those brewing and consuming beer at home used whatever materials were at hand.

In Europe, it has only been little more than 300 years since the hop almost totally displaced other herbs in the brewhouse. Herbs had previously been collected, dried, ground, and often blended and traded as a mixture called "gruit," which was usually added to the kettle during wort boiling. See GRUIT. Before the Protestant Reformation in the mid-16th century, the Catholic Church monopolized gruit production in Europe. During the bubonic plague epidemic of the Middle Ages, specialty "plague beer" was offered as a purported remedy, probably without any significant effect. In this era a comprehensive use of spices coming from "overseas" also became popular, and brewers did not distinguish between local homegrown or collected herbs and imported exotic spices when mixing their gruit.

In the Nordic countries juniper branches and twigs, at least in part because of their antiseptic qualities, were used as a filter during the mashing process. Juniper might also be added when heating the sparge water and during the primary fermentation. See JUNIPER and SPARGING. The resulting beer was strongly influenced by the acting bitter compounds and the aroma of the juniper itself. The Finnish traditional beer called sahti is still brewed using juniper in various ways. See SAHTI.

Examples of other bittering and antiseptic herbs historically used in northwestern Europe are sweet gale, also known as bog myrtle (Myrica gale L.), yarrow (Achillea millefolium), wormwood (Artemisia absinthium L.), heather (Calluna vulgaris), white horehound (Marrubium vulgare), stinging nettle (Urtica dioica), buckbean (Menyanthes trifoliata), the leaves of the ash tree (Fraxinus excelsior L.), and shoots of spruce and fir. Outside Europe the list of herbs and other plants used to bitter beer gets longer still, including species such as hopseed bush (Dodonae viscosa) from Australia, Indian ivy-rue (Zanthoxylum rhetsa) used in rice beers in Vietnam, whiteroot (Gouania lupuloides) used in ginger beer in Jamaica, common hoptree (Ptelea trifoliate) from the United States, shiny-leaf buckthorn (Rhamnus prinoides), used to brew the traditional *tella* in Ethiopia, and quassia (Quassia amara), exported from Brazil and used for centuries as a hop substitute. Almost all of these herbs and plant products add bitterness to balance the sweet flavors of malt, but they also add flavor and sometimes give the beer superior keeping qualities. Herbs have also been used to aromatize beer or for medical or even religious purposes.

The organic chemical composition of an herb depends on the cultivar itself, how it has been grown, and how it is treated after harvest. The valuable compounds are usually best expressed in brewing when the herbs are fresh. Other characters are best expressed if materials are dried and even stored before use (for instance, the hay-like aroma of birch).

The power of the hop flower to significantly extend the keeping qualities of beer eventually spelled the end of widespread use of other herbs. Once brewing became a genuine commercial concern, the hop plant solidified its place in European beers, and from there spread to England and beyond. During the last several years, however, the craft brewing revolution has seen the creation of many new beers inspired by old recipes involving herbs. Examples of herbs used are elder flowers (Sambucus nigra L.) to flavor spring or summer beers (Denmark), mint (Mentha spp.) to flavor stout (Italy), and heather to recreate a traditional ale style (Scotland).

Though herbs can help bring a range of fascinating flavors, they should be used in beer with caution. Some of the traditional medicinal plants have negative effects, and there may be concerns regarding allergic reactions, carcinogenic effects, and other unforeseen problems. Consultation of a pharmacopoeia is therefore recommended before adding herbs to beers brewed at home. Today's commercial brewers are only allowed to include herbs upon approval by governmental authorities.

Behre, Karl-Ernst. The history of beer additives in Europe—a review. *Vegetation History and Archaeobotany* 8 (1999): 35–48.

Both, Frank, ed. Gerstensaft und hirsebier: 5000 jahre biergenuss. Oldenburg, Germany: Verlag Isensee, 1998.

Brøndegaard, V. J. Folk og flora. *Dansk Etnobotanik* 2 (1999): 117.

Buhner, H.B. *Sacred and herbal healing beers: the secrets of ancient fermentation.* Boulder, CO: Siris, 1998.

Hofsten, Nils von. Pors och andra humleersättninger och ölkryddor i äldre tider. *(Gale and other substitutes and beer-spices in past times.* Includes an English summary). Uppsala, Sweden: Akademiska Förlaget, 1960.

Per Kølster

Heriot-Watt University, located in Edinburgh, Scotland, is an important center of brewing education. Heriot-Watt College has functioned as an education facility since the 1920s. In 1903, when there were 36 breweries in the city, the city administration decided to offer courses in brewing. With financial support from the city of Edinburgh, arrangements were made for the Chemistry Department to conduct brewing lectures by practical experts. A 2-year, part-time brewing certificate course was in operation by 1908 and in 1923 a full-time course for undergraduates was available. Prior to 1966, when the college was granted university status, the degree level qualification was known as the Associateship of Heriot-Watt College; this was the forerunner of the present BSc degree in Brewing and Distilling. Similarly, the present Postgraduate Diploma and MSc in Brewing and Distilling, now attracting students from all over the world, can trace their origins to the Associateship in Technical Biochemistry introduced in 1948.

In 1988 the autonomous International Centre for Brewing and Distilling, or ICBD, was established within the Department of Biological Sciences, now the School of Life Sciences. The ICBD has obtained considerable financial support from the brewing and distilling industries in the UK and overseas. At the same time, the Department of Biological Sciences (including the ICBD) moved from the center of Edinburgh to the University's new Riccarton campus, situated on the outskirts of the city.

The undergraduate and graduate programs in brewing and distilling continue to be taught, with the MSc having a distance-learning component. Research activities have flourished and a number of PhDs in Brewing and Distilling Studies have been conferred.

See also BREWING SCHOOLS and EDINBURGH.

Graham G. Stewart

Herkules (hop) was bred by the Hop Research Institute in Hüll, Germany. It was released for commercial cultivation in 2005 and gained quick acceptance, primarily because of its tolerance to powdery mildew, at least compared with the older variety, Magnum, which was released 12 years earlier. Its alpha acid levels range from 11% to 17%, its beta acid levels from 4% to 5.5%, and its cohumulone levels from 32% to 38%. In the field, it has good resistance to the main hop disease verticillium wilt, as well as downy and powdery mildew. Its average yield is a respectable 2,300 kg/ha (2,045 lb/acre). It also stores well. Herkules imparts a harmonic bitterness of moderate intensity. Its aroma is floral and fruity with a slight tang. Given its strong bittering prowess and its solid agronomic performance, the breeders felt justified when they named it after Hercules, the heroic figure of Greek mythology.

CMA Centrale Marketing-Gesellschaft. "The spirit of beer—hops from Germany." In *CMA hop variety portfolio*. Bonn, Germany: CMA Centrale Marketing-Gesellschaft, 2005.

Lydia Winkelmann

Herrera, Don Alonso de, hailing from Seville, Spain, built the first European-style brewery in the New World. He is first heard of in records dated 23 August 1541, when his application for royal authorization to set up a commercial brewery in New Spain (now modern Mexico) was being debated in Madrid by the Council of the Indies. An apparent beer aficionado, Carlos V, King of Spain and Holy Roman Emperor, used the Council of the Indies to administrate his North American territories.

In the city of Nájara, on 6 June 1542, Don Alonso de Herrera signed a contract with the Crown that licensed him to brew beer in the "Indies" for a period of 20 years. He was liable to pay one third of his profits in tax, supervised by the Viceroy, Antonio de Mendoza. The price of beer was estimated at 6 *reales* (20.1 g or 0.7 oz of silver) per *arroba* (approximately 11.5 l).

The Crown, in return, made him *corregidor* (district governor) of an area of the valley of Mexico inside what is now Mexico City where the *hacienda* (estate) "de El Portal," the site of the brewery, was situated. This allowed him, among other privileges, imports free of excise duty.

After early problems, with his Flemish brewers leaving for home or going off to work the mines, production appears to have increased steadily. The last figures we have, from 1552, give a monthly average of 246.5 *arrobas* (about 28 hl). The brewery seems not to have survived its founder.

Luque Azcona, Emilio. Producción y consumo de cerveza en la América colonial: primeras tentativas de Alonso de Herrera en el valle de México. (Production and consumption of beer in Colonial America: First attempts by Alonso de Herrera in the Valley of Mexico.) *Estudios sobre América: siglos XVI–XX*, 921–28. Seville, Spain: AEA, 2005.

Steve Huxley

Hersbrucker Spät (hop) is a traditional Bavarian hop variety. Before there were hop breeding programs for the scientific development of specific hop varieties with select properties, brewers made beer with so-called land races. These were indigenous varieties that had been cultivated from local, often wild, varieties. Hop growers selected and propagated these varieties mostly for such desirable attributes as high yield per hectare and good disease resistance. Hersbrucker Spät is one such variety. It has no pedigree in the classic sense.

It is named after the small town of Hersbruck in central Franconia near Nuremberg, Bavaria, at the northern edge of the Hallertau region where it is still planted on a small scale today. See HALLERTAU. Hersbrucker Spät is a fairly fast-growing, fairly late-maturing hop, and is highly resistant to most diseases, but slightly susceptible to downy mildew. See DOWNY MILDEW. In its heyday in the 19th century, Hersbrucker Spät was one of Germany's most important aroma varieties. While its bittering values are fairly low—between 2% and 4.5% alpha acids—its aroma profile is delicate and complex, with slightly floral-fruity notes that make it still a favorite for traditional unfiltered Franconian beer styles such as kellerbier.

See also KELLERBIER.

CMA Hop Variety Portfolio, "The spirit of beer—Hops from Germany," 2005.

HVG. "Hopfensorten." http://www.hvg-germany.de/de/hopfenanbau/hopfensorten/hopfensorten/ (accessed November 7, 2010).

Lydia Winkelmann

hexanoic acid

See CAPROIC ACID.

high gravity brewing is a term that refers to the process of preparing a type of strong wort with a high original gravity, intended to produce a beer with a high alcohol content. A normal gravity wort is typically in the range of 10°–13° Plato and will result in a beer containing 4%–6% alcohol by volume (ABV). See PLATO GRAVITY SCALE. A high gravity wort is typically considered in the range of 14°–17°Plato and will result in a beer of 6%–8% ABV. A very high gravity wort has a solids content greater than 17°Plato and will usually have an alcohol content greater than 8%.

High gravity brewing is performed by brewers for two reasons. First, it is performed to make a style of beer that has a high alcohol content, such as a German bock, Belgian tripel, or British barley wine. These types of beers are specialty styles and are generally not produced in high volumes.

The second reason a brewer might perform high gravity brewing is to meet high production demand when available brewing capacity is limited. In this regard, a brewer can make a high gravity wort that will become a high-alcohol-base beer to be used as a type of concentrate. At the final finishing steps, the brewer then adds deoxygenated brewing water to dilute the high-alcohol beer to a normal strength. Using this method, it is possible to brew a volume of beer and later increase that volume by up to 100% by dilution. Many major brewing companies and some large craft breweries use high gravity brewing to meet production demand. The technique is technically demanding, because high gravity fermentations typically produce a range of flavors and aromas that are not produced in lower gravity fermentations, and these can skew the desired flavor profile of beers produced by this method.

Keith Villa

high kräusen is a German term, also widely used in English, which refers to the large, billowing, unkempt head of foam that forms on the surface of beer at the peak of fermentation. It refers not only to the foam itself but also to this phase of fermentation; when wort reaches the peak of its fermentation, it is often said to be *at high kräusen*.

The name comes from the German *Hochkräusen* or *hohe Kräusen,* which has the same definition and likely originates from *kräus*, an adjective denoting "wrinkled," "furrowed," or "frizzy." This word is

Top-fermenting yeast throws a heady layer of foam on top of the brew during the vigorous stage of high kräusen at the start of primary fermentation, as shown here in an open fermenter at the Schneider Weissbier Brewery in Kelheim, Germany. HORST DORNBUSCH

often used in reference to a disorderly mane of curly hair (its infinitive *kräuseln* means to wrinkle, ruffle, curl, etc.).

In a traditional fermentation cellar, beer ferments in open vessels that allow the brewer to visually control different stages of fermentation. Low kräusen, the prior stage, has a dense, creamlike, and relatively uniform head of foam. Though white at first, copious amounts of carbon dioxide (CO_2) bubbles congregate particulates from the wort, causing the foam to develop yellowish-brown tips. Metabolizing yeast lowers the pH and causes unisomerized hop bitter compounds and resins to precipitate, along with tannins, denatured proteins, melanoidins, and other coloring agents from both hops and malt. This layer continues to grow, lose density (due to maximum CO_2 production), and darken until it reaches its maximum height during peak fermentation, that is, the high kräusen.

During high kräusen the foam on top of the fermenting beer is intensively bitter and very adhesive. Its appearance depends in part on the composition and concentration of the wort, amount of hops, type, and amount of yeast, fermentation temperature profile, and rate of CO_2 produced. Many of these intensely bitter compounds, some of them carrying coarse flavors, will adhere to the walls of the fermenting vessels during a vigorous fermentation, thus removing them from the beer.

Wolfgang David Lindell

Hildegard von Bingen was a 12th-century abbess of the Benedictine Convent of Rupertsberg near Bingen, on the west bank of the lower Rhine. Born in 1098 at Böckelheim on the Nahe (not far from present-day Frankfurt, Germany), she was probably the first person to describe hops in a scientific manner. During her life, she was a mystic, prophet, composer, brewster, prolific writer on religion and the natural world, and advisor and physician to German Emperor Frederick Barbarossa. In her publications about natural history and healing, she described the influence of various herbs on human health. Her most famous medical work was and still is *Liber Subtilitatum Diversarum Naturarum Creaturarum* (Book about the subtleties of the diverse natural creatures), part I of which is *Causae et Curae* [Causes and cures (of diseases)] and part II, *Physica*. In *Physica*, Hildegard described the preservative qualities of hops when added to a beverage like beer. In the same book, she also mentioned that hop increases melancholy or "back bile," one of Hippocrates' "four humors" of physiology; the others are man's choleric, phlegmatic, and sanguine dispositions. Today we know that hops can relax the nervous system and thus have a calming, sedative effect, which promotes sleep. This insight made Hildegard a progressive in her time, given that her contemporaries recommended hops as a treatment for exactly the opposite affliction, depression. Hildegard also wrote extensively about barley, which she considered beneficial for the stomach and intestines; she recommended a drink made from barley as a restorative after a cold or stomach flu. Many of Hildegard's writings have stood the test of time and are still considered valid by homeopaths and physicians. Hildegard died in her beloved Rupertsberg in 1179 at age 81—an incredible example of longevity at a time when the life expectancy was merely 30 to 40 years. There are those who speculate that her daily ration of well-hopped beer may have given her a life that was as long as it was enjoyable.

See also BEER WRITING.

Breindl, Ellen. *Das Grosse Gesundhgeitsbuch der Hl. Hildegard von Bingen* (The great book of health by St. Hildegard of Bingen), 2nd rev. ed. Augsburg, Germany: Pattloch Verlag, 1992.

http://wolfgang-schuhmacher.com/hildegardvonbingenspiritualitaet/bistumhildegard/bingen/werke.htm/ (accessed October 16, 2010).

Hildegard von Bingen. http://www.hildegard.org/documents/flanagan_biblio.html/ (accessed October 16, 2010).

Catholic Encyclopedia. http://www.newadvent.org/cathen/07351a.htm/ (accessed October 16, 2010).

Horst Dornbusch

The **history of beer,** quite literally, is the history of human civilization. Some anthropologists believe that man moved away from a hunter–gatherer existence to a settled agriculture-based existence largely to grow enough grain to brew large amounts of beer. This appears to be unproven, but the thought that beer would have been a powerful motivation to Neolithic humans would be no surprise. Virtually the entire animal kingdom, from insects to elephants, from fruit bats to monkeys, shows a clear predilection for the consumption

Eighteenth-century etching showing the inner workings of a brewery. PIKE MICROBREWERY MUSEUM, SEATTLE, WA

of ethanol. It is reasonable to believe that we and other animals evolved according to advantages alcoholic beverages can confer. Fruit, when ripe, gives off an alluring scent that tells animals that it is full of sugar and ready to eat. Ripe fruit can become quite alcoholic when naturally present yeasts begin to consume the sugars. Animals get the benefit of the food value of the fruit, but undoubtedly also find a value in the physiological effects of consuming alcohol. The fruiting plants, in turn, derived the benefit of the animal's actions as a disperser of its seeds. One of the great turning points for ancient humanity was the discovery of a method by which sugar could actually be created and fermented into alcohol in the absence of honey or fruit. This technique was the start of what we now call brewing.

As best we are able to determine, brewing emerged more than 5,000 years ago in the grasslands of southern Babylonia, between the Tigris and Euphrates Rivers. Rich alluvial soils supported wild grain plants, and the people there gathered them for food . . . and to make beer. How was the discovery made? It is impossible to be sure. But grain left out in the rain will sprout, essentially starting the malting process and developing enzymes inside the seeds. Someone coming upon a sprouting grain store probably hurriedly went to make bread out of the grain before all of the nutritious starch was lost to the growing plants. Upon heating, the starches, now full of enzymes, liquefied into sugars. And once people had sugars, they knew what to do with them.

Soon the Sumerians settled upon the plains, creating a civilization, the world's first, in Lower Mesopotamia. See SUMER. They began to grow the grains, making them into a form of bread called bappir. In the oldest written recipe known to archeologists, they praised the goddess Ninkasi, whose name means "lady who fills the mouth." Brewer to the gods, Ninkasi taught mankind to make beer too, which they called kas. In a hymn to the goddess, they described her as "the one who waters the malt set on the ground . . . you are the one who bakes the bappir-malt in the great oven. . . . You are the one who soaks the malt in a jar . . . the waves rise, the waves fall." Finally Ninkasi is the one who "pours the fragrant beer in the lahtan-vessel, which is like the Tigris and Euphrates joined." The resulting sugary bread was soaked in water, spontaneously fermented, and then strained. And so beer became part of the day-to-day life of mankind. Beer was healthy, pleasantly mood-altering, and full of nutrients and calories, and to obtain it, people created settled agriculture. At Godin Tepe, in the Zagros Mountains of modern Iran, the evidence remains.

Trade card depicting a 17th-century brewery. The German Liebig Extract of Meat Company, founded in 1840, distributed a series of trading cards illustrating the history of beer. PIKE MICROBREWERY MUSEUM, SEATTLE, WA

Shards of pottery from the Sumerian era are studded with calcium oxalate, a deposit from grain also known as "beer stone." The Sumerian written character for beer is a pictogram of a type of jar, wide at the base and narrowing at the neck. Any homebrewer today would recognize it.

The Babylonians eventually conquered Sumer, and one of the benefits was the adoption of the superior beer-making skills of the people they had vanquished. The Babylonian king, Hammurabi, promulgated laws about just about everything, including beer, which he categorized into 20 different varieties. See LAW.

The beer culture of Sumer also made its way into Egypt. According to Dr Delwen Samuel, who did pioneering work at the Department of Archeology at the University of Cambridge, brewing was well established in the Egyptian predynastic period. By the early Dynastic period, 3100–2686 BCE, it had become an important part of Egyptian culture. Eventually beer, far healthier than water, became the everyday drink of the Egyptian people, from Pharaoh to the lowliest peasant. Great grain stores were built, and the Egyptian economy was underpinned by bread and beer. The god Osiris held in his hands the very stuff of life—fertility, death, resurrection, and the brewing staff. Depictions of people drinking beer from jars through long straws cover the insides of Egyptian tombs. We still have the beer-drinking straws of potentates, handsomely inlaid with gold and lapis lazuli.

When the Greeks arrived in Egypt, they were unimpressed by beer, which they called *zythos*, referring to its foaminess. Preferring wine, they thought of the sprouted malt as a form of rotted grain and disdained the drink the Egyptians derived from it. It was not that the Egyptians did not know wine, but growing grape vines, in many parts of Egypt, was not nearly so easy as growing grain, and Egypt could grow enough grain to feed itself and still have some left for export.

The Egyptians brewed from several grains, including barley and the ancient wheat type, emmer. Texts make mention of many types of beer, some of them clearly designated for ceremonial purposes. They had "dark beer," "sweet beer," "thick beer," "friend's beer," "garnished beer," and "beer of the protector." The gods who guarded the shrine of Osiris partook of the "beer of truth." For funerary purposes, they needed a beer that would last until the afterlife and provided tombs with "beer that does not sour" and "beer of eternity." Massive breweries were built, and both grain and beer were offered in payment for common labor. It is worth noting that brewing was largely the work of women, a tradition that lasted throughout various civilizations until the end of the Middle Ages.

In 332 BCE, the Greeks, led by Alexander the Great, took control of Egypt. Brewing continued apace, but the Greeks, seeing beer as the drink of their rivals and of the conquered, largely disdained it. By the Hellenistic period, Egypt exported beer out of the city of Pelusium, at the mouth of the Nile, to Palestine and beyond. The tax inspectors arrived, carrying titles such as "Inspector of the Breweries" and "Royal Chief Beer Inspector." Alexander's reign as Pharaoh lasted less than a decade, but Egypt was ruled by the Ptolemys until the naval battle at Actium in 31 BCE, after which Cleopatra and her lover Marc Antony took their lives. Egypt became a Roman province.

Ancient Greece and Rome, with plentiful stores of wine, never truly took to beer. But as Rome ranged out from its own lands and sought to build an empire, they made their way over mountains and found on the other side fierce people, often ready for a fight and fortified by beer. Pliny, in his Natural History, noted that "the populace of western Europe have a liquid with which they intoxicate themselves, made from grain and water. The manner of making this is somewhat different in Gaul, Spain and other countries, and it is called by different names, but its nature and properties are everywhere the same. The people in Spain in particular brew this liquid so well that it will keep good a long time. So exquisite is the cunning of mankind in gratifying their vices and appetites that they have invented a method to make water itself produce intoxication."

In the south of present Germany, the Romans encountered the Celts, and in the north they found the Germans, who had followed the Celts into Western Europe out of Asia. These tribes, unlike the Romans, were largely illiterate, but they were fairly proficient at making beer. The nomadic Germans eventually drove the Celts out, across the English Channel into Britain. The Germans and assimilated Celts settled into a network of powerful city-states between the 6th and 7th centuries CE. Slavic tribes settled to the east. As the Roman Empire finally crumbled with the abdication of the last Roman emperor in 476, the Romans, Germans, and Slavs assimilated into each other's cultures, and Western Europe took on Roman Catholicism. Monasteries were set up and became places of learning. To sustain themselves and provide hospitality for weary travelers, the monks established breweries.

During the 500 years of the Dark Ages, from 500 to 1000 CE, brewing continued, but largely without advancement. The light of civilization shone most brightly inside the monasteries, but the monks kept their beer to themselves.

Copper smelting had been used since the Bronze Age, but until now, brewing kettles in Europe had largely been small vessels, suited for households. Now settled into larger communities, Europeans started to build breweries on a scale that had not been seen since the days of ancient Egypt. Breweries moved out of kitchens and into purpose-built facilities, with malting facilities, mashing vessels, fermentation areas, and staffs of trained workers. Coopers made barrels for storage. The flavoring for beer was usually a blend of herbs called gruit, but in some areas the hop was used too. By the early 800s, the monks of the monastery of St. Gallen in Switzerland had built the first full-scale brewing operation in Europe, in many ways hundreds of years ahead of its time. The brewery's floor plan, drawn up in 820, would be essentially recognizable to any modern brewer. See ST. GALLEN.

In the early 1100s, Hildegard von Bingen established the Benedictine nunnery of Rupertsberg, near the town of Bingen on the river Rhine. Later known as St. Hildegard, she wrote a number of books, including the natural history text *Physica Sacra*. In it, she described the hop as a particularly useful plant, one that was excellent for physical health and preserved all sorts of drinks. Over the 1100s, much of Europe's beer was transformed by the use of hops. The Catholic Church, which was making a fair amount of money selling gruit, resisted mightily. But the hop evaded the reach of the Church and began to grow deep roots. Soon central Europe grew into a brewing powerhouse. Ordinances were promulgated to protect grain supplies and beer purity, from Augsburg in 1158, from Paris in 1268, and from Nuremberg in 1293. These were early forerunners of the now famous Reinheitsgebot of 1516, Germany's much vaunted "Beer Purity Law." By the mid-1300s Hamburg became the leading brewing center in the world.

By 1376, 475 of Hamburg's 1,075 manufacturers were making beer. Their techniques were now far advanced over those of any rivals and in 1369 they sent a full 133,000 hl of beer out of the city. On the backs of the brewers, the Hanseatic League, which had been founded by wealthy merchants from Lubeck and Bremen in 1241, grew powerful. The Thirty Years War, from 1618 to 1648, ushered in nearly a century of misery and death in Europe. Warfare raged across the continent, and the population was halved by violence, disease, and starvation. European brewing moved back inside the home. Commercial breweries revived only in the 1700s, with brewers guilds well established throughout central Europe, charged with protecting the interests of a once again increasingly powerful clan of merchants.

In Britain, hops had not yet arrived, but gruit-flavored beer had long been the drink of the people. See GRUIT. When Julius Caesar arrived in Kent in 55 BC, of the people he found there he noted, "They had vines, but use them only for arbors in their gardens. They drink a high and mighty liquor . . . , made of barley and water." Wine certainly arrived in England early, first with the conquering Romans and later with the Normans in 1066. As the Normans assimilated into British society, the upper echelons brewed beer, but kept the Norman taste for wine, and British society separated into a wine-drinking upper class and the beer-drinking masses. Brewing remained a cottage industry though the Middle Ages and was once again dominated by women. By the 1200s, an Assize of Bread and Ale was promulgated, regulating the price and quality of both. Fines for breaking the rules essentially became a form of licensing system, and the records of the fines paid by brewing households allow us to trace the development of brewing families in Britain over generations. See BRITAIN.

Although brewing was a household skill expected of all medieval women, some women, known as alewives, began to set up small commercial operations on a part-time basis. Sometimes they were allowed to open alehouses, and their incomes would provide them with a rare measure of independence. It was virtually the only honest independent work that women were allowed, and they took advantage of it at every opportunity. See WOMEN IN BREWING. After the Black Plague struck England in 1348–1350, demand for ale rose, and female brewers became better established. Soon, however, men and the demands of commerce would conspire to wrest the brew kettle from women's hands.

As hopped beer spread throughout Europe, the preservative effects of the hops meant that beer could be kept longer. Now beer could be made in greater quantities and stored, as opposed to being drunk within a matter of days. Storage and larger facilities required money to build, and women had less to invest with than men did. Slowly, but surely, men began to build larger brewing operations and force women out of their own businesses and into employment in the new breweries. Hops moved into England in the 1400s, and although many people clung to unhopped ale for more than a century, British beer was largely hopped by the mid 1500s.

> So, in the morning, after we had called upon God for direction, we came to this resolution: to go presently ashore again and to take a better view of two places which we thought most fitting for us. For we could not now take time for further search or consideration, our victuals being much spent, especially our beer, and it now being the 20th of December.

And so, in the words of William Bradford, landed the Pilgrims on Cape Cod, Massachusetts, in the small cargo ship Mayflower in 1620. European-style brewing was soon underway on the American continent, but often with whatever could be found or grown. By 1670, the English Quaker John Fenwick arrived to found the town of Salem, New Jersey, and noted that his fellow settlers "straightaway busied themselves in erecting breweries for manufacturing beer for common drink."

As colonial cities grew during the 1700s, so did breweries. City breweries brewed the same sort of beers as were found in England during that time, often supplementing malt with other sugars, such as molasses. Farmhouses brewed with barley malt, wheat, corn, pumpkins, peas, and spices. See PUMPKIN ALE and BREWING IN COLONIAL AMERICA.

In the meantime, the Industrial Revolution in England was giving rise to a recognizably modern brewing industry. As London boomed, dark porter beer fueled the city, and the city fueled the breweries. Brewed from brown malt, heavily hopped, and matured for months, porter beer lasted well enough to be distributed throughout London's thousands of pubs. The erection of enormous porter vats gave brewers the ability to blend large amounts of beer and achieve some level of reliability. The English brewers were voracious in their search for new technologies. In 1784, only 8 years after American independence, Henry Goodwin and Samuel Whitbread installed a coal-fired steam engine in their London brewery. Twenty years later, indirect kilning of malt was combined with the use of thermometers to produce a regular supply of pale malts. Soon, porter brewing eschewed inefficient brown malts, productivity increased, and India pale ale shipped out to Calcutta in huge volumes. See INDUSTRIAL REVOLUTION.

Bavarian brewers, in a skilled display of industrial espionage, stole the secrets of pale malting technology from the British. They then used that secret to take over the world of brewing. Bavarian brewing had been different for centuries. Duke Albrecht V of Bavaria, seeking to protect the populace from spoiled beer, forbade summer brewing in 1553. Brewers made the last beer of the season in the late spring, and it needed to last months until the autumn. Seeking to make beers that could survive the summer heat, brewers had been fermenting their beer in underground caves dug deep into hillsides. Down into the tunnels they dragged ice, hand cut from frozen lakes in winter, to keep the beer cool throughout the year. Over time, their beer, and the yeast that was fermenting it, changed. One species of yeast stepped forward under the cold temperatures whereas another receded. The lager yeast, so named after the German word "lagern," meaning "to store," was able to ferment at low temperatures, outcompete spoilage organisms, settle the bottom of the fermenting vessel, and, after a few months of aging, produce a beer that could last much longer than other beers. By 1840, Bavarian-born John Wagner, using yeast he brought with him from his homeland, was brewing lager beer in a hut next to his Philadelphia home.

Back in Bavaria, in 1841, the first light amber beers emerged from the Spaten Brewery in Munich and from Anton Dreher's brewery in Vienna. Only 2 years later the Bavarian brewer Josef Groll, working at a brewery in the Bohemian city of Plzen, produced the first golden lager beer, the pilsner. See DREHER, ANTON, SPATEN BREWERY, and VIENNA LAGER. Soon, a new railroad network was bringing the sparkling new beer to cities far from Bohemia. Industrialized glass making brought affordable glassware to people previously used to crockery mugs, and the bright golden pilsner beer was made that much more appealing. The introduction of Carl von Linde's ammonia-based mechanical refrigeration technology freed lager brewing from a dependence on natural ice. See LINDE, CARL VON. By 1873 beer could be brewed anywhere there was a decent water supply and at any time of year. Essentially Bavarian styles of beer were soon brewed from Brazil to Tanzania, sweeping ales from most of the world map. England and Ireland held firm against the tide, as did the Rhineland with its kölsch and altbier, and, very quietly, so did tiny Belgium. Keeping fast to its centuries-old traditions of spontaneous fermentation, Belgium kept alive an ancient brewing style, while inside its Trappist monasteries, elegant new permutations of the brewer's art were conjured by silent craftsmen in robes. See ALTBIER, KÖLSCH, and TRAPPIST BREWERIES.

Throughout Europe and the United States, breweries built great empires of commerce in the late 1800s. Britain built its fortunes on ales, whereas central Europe, Scandinavia, and America focused on lagers. By 1900, three of Japan's current top four brewing companies were already well established. Two world wars brought changes to breweries everywhere, but soon one great brewing nation was to leave the trade entirely. Although American lager had already diverged from its European roots, using a proportion of rice and corn to replace malt, it was the 13-year "noble experiment" of Prohibition, from 1920 to 1933, that changed American beer for the next 60 years. See PROHIBITION. When brewing re-emerged from the underground economy in 1933 and America's breweries came back to life, the beer was different. Beer had been gone a long time, and the world had changed. Commerce, technology, and advertising converged to produce the modern American mass-market beer, a technically impressive product with far less flavor than its ancestors. The new beer took its place on shelves next to sliced white bread in plastic bags and slices of "cheese food product," foods apparently impervious to time itself. Americans were happy enough with the new beer, but once they started traveling, they soon realized that they had been missing something.

The 1970s and 1980s saw a time of renewal, first in England's new microbreweries and then in the American West. American craft brewers, inspired by Europe's great traditions, primed by years of experimentation in their own kitchens and believing that brewing can be a jazz-like art form, today spread a gospel of full flavor and creativity in beer.

Dornbusch, Horst. *Prost! The story of German beer.* Denver, CO: Brewers Publications, 1997.
Hardwick, William A. *Handbook of brewing.* New York: Marcel Dekker, Inc., 1995.
Hornsey, Ian S. *A history of beer and brewing.* London: RSC Publishing, 2003.
Meussdoerffer, Franz G. "A comprehensive history of beer brewing." In *Handbook of brewing: Processes, technology, markets,* ed. Hans M. Esslinger. New York: Wiley & Sons, 2009.
Shourds, Thomas. *History and genealogy of Fenwick's colony, New Jersey.* Bridgeton, NJ: G Nixon, 1876.

Garrett Oliver

Hodgson, George, was a London brewer who is often inaccurately credited with "inventing" India pale ale. See INDIA PALE ALE.

Hodgson began brewing on the banks of the river Lea in east London in 1751. His brewery, simply called Hodgson's Brewery, stood close to the East India Dock, from which ships departed for British-ruled India, and Hodgson certainly built up a profitable Indian trade when few other London brewers bothered with it. The quantities were small, the trip perilous, success uncertain. But Hodgson's position by the docks, and his good relations with the captains of the India-bound ships, allowed him to build a profitable trade.

Little evidence survives of Hodgson's brewing exploits, but by 1809 the brewery—now run by George's son Mark—had earned a famous reputation. It dominated the Indian market and was immortalized in verse and prose by writers such as Thackeray. In 1833 Hodgson's became the first brewery to refer to "East India pale ale" in newspaper advertisements.

But Hodgson didn't invent IPA. Imported pale ale was being quaffed in Madras as early as 1717, and other brewers are mentioned by name in Calcutta press ads well before Hodgson. Hodgson exported a version of "October ale," the strong, hoppy ales that were brewed for country houses and aged for years in their cellars. What's most likely is that he adapted his recipe over time, listening to feedback from his customers, and his ale evolved until it suited the market better than any other.

Hodgson's pale ale was eventually supplanted in India by superior Burton-on-Trent pale ales from brewers such as Bass and Allsopp.

See also INDIA.

Pete Brown

Hoegaarden (pronounced "who garden") is a Belgian witbier named after a small town in the Flemish region of Belgium that is famous for the rebirth of the Belgian white ("wit") style of beer. During the 1950s Tomsin, the last white beer brewery in Hoegaarden, closed. The local milkman, Pierre Celis, had worked at the Tomsin brewery as a young man. In 1965, while in his forties, Celis decided to purchase some brewing equipment and start making white beer again. He recreated the recipe based on his experience working at the brewery and from locals who remembered the look and taste of the beer. His new brewery was called De Kluis, meaning "cloister," in honor of the monks who brewed beer in the region during the Middle Ages. The beer was called Hoegaarden, after Celis' hometown.

Sold in dozens of countries worldwide, Hoegaarden is widely considered the standard of the Belgian-white style of beer. It is made from malted barley, unmalted wheat, hops, coriander, and curaçao orange peel. It is very pale in color and hazy with a frothy head of foam. The aroma and taste are citrusy, fruity, spicy, and refreshing, with a light snappy bitterness. The beer is light-bodied, well balanced, and mild in strength and balanced with a deceptively mild amount of alcohol (4.9% ABV).

Hoegaarden quickly became successful in Belgium and elsewhere around the world. By 1985 the brewery was producing 75,000 hectoliters of beer per year, when disaster struck and the brewery burned to the ground. Unable to rebuild on his own, Celis turned to the Belgian brewing group Interbrew (now AB-InBev), who eventually ended up owning the brewery and brand.

See also BELGIUM, CELIS, PIERRE, DE KLUIS (BREWERY), and WHITE BEER.

Keith Villa

Hofbräu literally means "the court's brewery." Hofbräu is the name of several breweries in the

German-speaking countries that were at some point in their history official purveyors of beer to the court or owned by the court. Although Hofbräuhaus in Munich is by far the most well-known (and the only nonprivatized) example, there were dozens of similar breweries in Germany and Austria that operated under that name. See HOFBRÄUHAUS MÜNCHEN. Hofbräu Kaltenhausen, for example, now part of Heineken's BrauUnion branch, was founded in 1475 by the brewer Hans Elsenheimer and taken over by the court of the duke-archbishop of Salzburg in 1486, 103 years before the more famous Hofbräuhaus in Munich went into operation. Other Hofbräu breweries that are still in operation are Würzburger Hofbräu founded by the duke-archbishop Johann Philipp von Schönborn in 1643, Hofbräu Wolters (a family-owned brewery in Braunschweig that was symbolically awarded the title "Herzogliches Hofbrauhaus" in 1882), and Stuttgarter Hofbräu. The brewery in Stuttgart got its name only in 1935, long after the relevant court (to which the brewery, then owned by monks, had been an official supplier since 1591) had vanished. Hofbräu Traunstein was founded in 1612 by the Bavarian duke Maximilian I, owner of the Hofbräuhaus in Munich. The Bavarian sovereign's business model was to build a Hofbräu brewery in every relevant town of the Duchy of Bavaria, starting in Kelheim (this brewery is now G. Schneider & Son) in 1607. For the Wittelsbach family, who laid claim to the monopoly on wheat beer, every so-called Weisses Preyhaus ("white brewhouse" because it brewed weissbier) generated income to balance the budget. Most of these breweries were privatized in the early 19th century and others in another wave of privatization in the 1920s. Only the Staatliches Hofbräuhaus München and Staatsbrauerei Weihenstephan (which was never officially called a Hofbräuhaus although it was nationalized by the court in 1803) are still owned by the state of Bavaria.

Letzing, Heinrich. *Die Geschichte des Bierbrauwesens der Wittelsbacher*. Augsburg, Germany: Wissner, 1995.

Conrad Seidl

Hofbräuhaus München, literally "the court's brewhouse," is the name of a large brewery in Riem on the outskirts of Munich owned by the state of Bavaria. It is also the name of their brewery tap at Platzl in downtown Munich, reputedly the world's most famous tavern. A chain of Hofbräuhaus taverns in Germany and overseas (as well as a chain of brewpubs that brew Hofbräuhaus beers under license in the United States) was launched in 2000.

Several purveyors of beer to the Bavarian court have called themselves "Hofbräu" since the 15th century. The earliest documentation mentions the brewer Berchtold Pörtzl in 1440, who ran a brewery in Sendlinger Strasse in Munich. The Hofkammer, the Bavarian court's ministry of finance, decided to build their own brewery in 1589—primarily to supply the royal court with dunkel (dark) lager beer and weissbier (wheat beer). Later projects, starting with the two wheat beer breweries "Weisses Hofbräuhaus" in Munich and the Weissbierbrauhaus in Kelheim (now "Schneider Weisse") in 1607, were built for the purpose of selling beer to the general public for profit. The Weisses Hofbräuhaus was located at the now well-known address at Platzl in downtown Munich—the wheat beer production was sold off and moved out in 1802. The duke's (and later king's) still thriving lager beer brewery moved into these premises. The brewery tap opened in 1828, making the place so famous and successful that the actual production had to be relocated again in 1896 to make room for an even larger brewery tap. Part of the success story is the well-known tune "In München steht ein Hofbräuhaus, oans, zwoa, gsuffa" ("In Munich there stands a Hofbräuhaus, one, two, chug-a-lug"), composed by Wiga Gabriel in 1936. It is still sung all over the world by every "oompah" band, and the tune is fairly inescapable during Munich's Oktoberfest and all of its many descendants.

Merk, Gerhard, and Hannes Sieber. *Das Münchner Bier*. Munich, Germany: Frisingia Verlag, 1991.

Conrad Seidl

Hoff-Stevens kegs are an American style of keg design. Hoff-Stevens kegs were considered the height of technology in the 1950s and 1960s. These kegs were cleaned and filled on their sides through a hole that was sealed by a wooden bung. The keg is recognized by two different-size holes on the top surrounded by male thread where the short female coupler attached to the keg. Skill was required to thread down the coupler swiftly enough to avoid squirting out beer.

The previous keg styles connected the coupler to the keg top with a quarter turn. Next the long tap would be driven with a mallet through the keg top fitting, forcing a small wooden plug into the keg, and then slid down to the bottom of the beer. Beer would invariably squirt out in this process. Most of these kegs were later converted to Hoff-Stevens.

The similar Peerless keg style also was top-tapped with a two-probe device; however, in these kegs the gas and beer lines were the same diameter and the coupler attached to the keg with a pair of hooks. Olympia Brewing Company was one of the few breweries using Peerless.

Pabst, Schlitz, and Miller breweries used Hoff-Stevens kegs. In 2008, Straub Brewery of Pennsylvania was the last long-standing brewery in the United States to discontinue their use. Production of Hoff-Stevens kegs ended by 1980 because the revolutionary Sankey design became universally accepted as a far superior technology. Fledgling microbreweries that could not afford Sankey kegs and filling equipment survived Hoff-Stevens and Golden Gate kegs, which were now inexpensive. Some small breweries continue to use Hoff-Stevens kegs to this day, but they are becoming rare.

Broderick, Harold. *Beer packaging*. St. Paul, MN: MBAA Publications, 1982.

Brian Hunt

hogshead is an old English term for a large cask used for delivering beer to a pub or for shipping. It contained no less than 54 Imperial gal (65 US gal) and was in common use in Britain, especially in the 18th and 19th centuries. It was a coopered wooden vessel, barrel shaped, and built of tapered staves held together by iron hoops. As with all other casks, it had a large bung or shive hole in the center of one of the staves and a smaller hole in the flat end or head, into which the tap would be hammered when the cask of beer was broached. The hogshead's capacity posed two problems. First, it could be used only in very busy establishments where this amount of beer (432 Imperial pints, each of 20 oz) could be drunk within 2 or 3 days. Otherwise, air, which enters the cask as the beer is being served, could oxidize the beer, bring in souring bacteria, or simply allow the beer to go flat. Second, a full cask weighed close to half a ton. Because it was often necessary to manhandle the hogshead from the dray into the pub cellar, lighter casks such as firkins proved much more convenient. As per capita beer consumption dropped throughout the 20th century, publicans required smaller casks that were both easier to maneuver and faster to deplete. This made the hogshead redundant, and it is rarely seen today.

See also FIRKIN.

Kilby, K. *The village cooper*. Aylesbury, England: Shire Publications, 1998.

Terry Foster

Holland is the name of a maritime region in the western part of the Netherlands that is divided into two provinces, North and South Holland (Noord-Holland and Zuid-Holland, respectively).

Dutch beer label from around 1933. Holland had over 700 breweries at one point in the mid-15th century, before the introduction of coffee and tea caused a steep decline in beer consumption. PIKE MICROBREWERY MUSEUM, SEATTLE, WA

When combined, these provinces include the Netherlands' three largest cities, Amsterdam, The Hague, and Rotterdam, as well as the cities Gouda, Edam, Delft, Haarlem, Leiden, and Alkmaar. It comprises about 13% of the total area of the Netherlands and about a third of the population and contains 25 breweries. The total number of breweries in Holland reached its peak of over 700 in the mid-15th century, with Gouda having the highest concentration followed by Delft, Harlem, Schiedam, Dordrecht, and Rotterdam. Beer was not a luxury but a daily necessity as, having being boiled, it was safer than water. With the introduction of coffee and tea in the mid-17th century beer consumption plummeted and by 1890 only 57 active breweries remained. With the introduction of lager, repressive taxes on low alcohol beers, and two world wars, there were only two breweries left by 1980.

The beer renaissance began in 1984 when the Alkmaarse Brewery opened in the city of Alkmaar in the province of Noord-Holland; although it closed in 1988, it inspired many of the small independent brewers that are now scattered throughout North and South Holland. It remains a very young market with 93% of the brewers and contract-brewers having started after 1985 and 50% of those after 2003.

See also NETHERLANDS, THE.

European Beer Guide. http://www.europeanbeerguide.net (accessed Novermber 4, 2010).

Unger, Richard W. *A history of brewing in Holland 900–1900: Economy, technology, and the state*. Boston, MA: Brill Academic Publishers, 2001.

Derek Walsh

homebrew bittering units (HBUs) are a simple means of assessing the amount of hops required to achieve a specific bitterness in a beer. The number of bitterness units in a beer is simply the number of ounces used times the alpha acid value of the hop, with alpha acids being the active ingredient that will provide the bitterness.

If a beer recipe requires a specific HBU level, then dividing this level by the alpha acid of the hop will provide an estimate of the number of ounces of hops required. For example, a recipe for 5 gal of beer with a HBU of 10 would require 2.5 oz of a hop with an alpha acid of 4%. Hop varieties have different levels of alpha acid and different additions are required to obtain the same bitterness level in the beer.

Standard bitterness units (IBUs) have a chemical definition based on milligrams of the actual bitterness chemical, iso-alpha acid, present per liter. HBUs take into account the bitterness in the hops and allow a simple calculation of hop addition to be made.

However, the actual bitterness in beer depends on additional factors such as the efficiency of the boil in converting alpha acids to iso-alpha acids and the time of hop addition. More exact analysis of the brewing system used will allow for these factors and permit advanced and professional brewing calculations to be made based on IBU values.

See also BITTERNESS.

Keith Thomas

homebrewing is the hobby of brewing beer at home. The process can be as simple as making soup from a can, or for the most advanced homebrewers it can be as technically involved as small-scale commercial craft brewing. The motivation to homebrew for most homebrewers is the fun of making beer at home and the satisfaction of brewing one's own beer. Some homebrewers get into the hobby to save money on purchasing beer, particularly in countries such as Canada, with high beverage alcohol taxes. In the United States, brewing at home offers minimal savings on beer when compared with purchasing beer.

For beer enthusiasts in many parts of the world, homebrewing has become a gateway to starting their own commercial breweries.

Many homebrewers pursue the hobby hoping to understand beer better or to master the complex challenges of brewing to produce beers with a flavor that rivals those they can buy at a store. Homebrewers who achieve such skill find further enjoyment in replicating the world's classic beer styles and then creating beers of their own design.

Homebrewing can be enjoyed in many different ways through a variety of activities. Some homebrewers enjoy the brewing process and its many variations as a technical and logistical exploration, whereas others prefer a simple approach practiced

A homebrewer places an airlock on a large glass water bottle, known as a carboy. It will be used as a fermentation vessel. GETTY IMAGES

as a social occasion with friends. Once homebrewers have attained basic brewing skills, they may challenge themselves to replicate the flavor of a favorite commercial beer or explore beer styles unavailable in their area. Others find no interest in brewing beers like those they might buy and seek to develop innovative beers using fruits, spices, herbs, sugars, and other foodstuffs to create unique flavor profiles.

Once brewed, beers are shared with friends, family, and other homebrewers. In the United States, many clubs and events exist for homebrewers to share and show their beers. Such exchanges offer encouragement and an opportunity to learn improved brewing skills and techniques. Many homebrew organizations conduct competitions where beers are graded and ranked with awards given to the top performers. The National Homebrew Competition run annually by the American Homebrewers Association has drawn more than 6,000 entries in 21 beer style categories.

Skilled judges are needed to judge competitions and a US group called the Beer Judge Certification Program (BJCP) exists specifically to train and test such judges.

Beyond recipe formulation and competitions, homebrewers also enjoy related creative activities such as inventing "brands" for their beers, complete with a brewery name, product name, logos, labels, and other collateral. Although these efforts must legally stop short of offering the beer for sale, the creative activity and sharing with friends offers hobbyists other sources of enjoyment from homebrewing. Many a special occasion has been celebrated with specially brewed and labeled bottles of commemorative homebrewed beer.

Finally, although beer can be brewed in nearly any kitchen, an extensive selection of specialized equipment can be purchased to improve each aspect of the brewing process and expand the capabilities of the home brewery. As a result, some hobbyists devote considerable resources to setting up dedicated brewing space in their home and equipping it with their "dream" system. Some even extend the hobby into the area of equipment fabrication, learning welding and metal working skills to improve their home breweries.

Ingredients

Homebrewers use a variety of ingredients to make beer. The most commonly used ingredients include malt, malt extract, hops, yeast, and water. In addition, homebrewers may use other ingredients, such as herbs, spices, fruits, vegetables, sugars, unmalted grains, and more, giving homebrewers an infinite variety of flavor options when making beer. Ingredients for making just about any style of beer can be found at local homebrew supply shops or online homebrew retailers.

Malt Extract

Malt extract is made from malted barley or wheat to allow homebrewers to skip the mashing process employed by commercial breweries, thus simplifying the beer-making experience. Malt extract is used as the basis for most homebrew recipes, providing the sugars that the yeast consumes to produce alcohol and carbon dioxide. Malt extract comes in a variety of forms. Malt extract can be found as prehopped kits in a can, plain liquid, or in dried powdered form. Malt extract also comes in a variety of colors for making different styles of beer, including extra light, light, amber, and dark.

Malt

Although homebrew can be made exclusively with extracts, most homebrew recipes include some form of malted grain. Specialty malts, such as crystal malt, chocolate malt, and black malt, can be added to extract brews to create different styles of beers such as pale ales, porters, and stouts. It is possible to brew without any extracts by mashing malted grains. All-grain brewing involves mashing base malts such as pilsner or pale ale malts in place of the extract. Unmalted grains such as oats, wheat, or roasted barley are sometimes used in the brewing process as well.

Hops

Like commercial brewers, homebrewers use hops to add bitterness, flavor, and aroma to beer. Bittering hops—hops added early on in the boil process—provide bitterness to the beer to balance the sweetness of the malt. Hops for homebrewers can be purchased as whole flowers, pellets, or more rarely as compressed plugs of whole-flower hops. There are many varieties of hops available to homebrewers, allowing for great diversity of flavors and aromas and allowing homebrewers to make a wide variety of beer styles. Proper hop packaging protects them from air with vacuum packing or nitrogen filling of an air-tight opaque container. Packaged hops should then be stored in a freezer during distribution, at the retailer, and by the brewer until the day of use.

Yeast

Unlike professional brewers, most homebrewers do not brew with enough frequency to regularly reuse their yeast from batch to batch. As a result, homebrewers often buy yeast each time they brew.

Beer yeast is sold in two forms: dried and liquid. Dried yeast is generally found in 5-g packets. Liquid yeast for homebrewers comes in one of two types of packages, foil pouches or plastic vials. Dried yeast is easy to use, can be stored for long periods of time without ill effect, and is generally cheaper than liquid yeast, but dried yeast is limited to just a few strains available to homebrewers. When liquid yeast was introduced in the mid-1980s, the number of different yeast strains available to homebrewers expanded dramatically. There are now scores of yeast strains for brewing a wide range of beer styles.

Water

Homebrewers can use tap water, but chlorinated water can result in harsh flavors in the finished beer. Chlorine can be removed by boiling or filtering. Bottled water is also an option. Factors such as mineral content and pH of brewing water can a have significant effect on beer, although these are of less concern in extract beers than in all grain beers. Certain minerals may be added to beer to achieve flavors found in beers brewed in certain areas of the world; for example, the famous English pale ales of Burton-on-Trent are brewed with the very hard water found in that region. The more common minerals used in brewing include calcium sulfate (gypsum), calcium chloride, sodium chloride (table salt), and magnesium sulfate (Epsom salt). Extract brewers should be aware that the mineral content of the water used by the extract manufacturer will be reflected in the extract itself.

Equipment

Beginner Equipment

The basic equipment used to make extract-based homebrew recipes can be purchased at a local homebrew supply shop or an online retailer for around $80. Much of the equipment includes items likely to be found in a modestly well-stocked kitchen.

- Brew kettle. 8–20 l (2–5 US gal) pot
- Fermenter: 25–27 l (6–8 US gal) food-grade plastic bucket with lid or glass carboy
- Bottling bucket: 25–27 l (6–8 US gal) food-grade plastic bucket
- Airlock and stopper: a device that allows carbon dioxide produced during fermentation to escape from the fermenter without allowing air into the fermenter.
- Thermometer: 0°C–100°C (32°F–212°F).
- Hydrometer: a tool for measuring the density of liquid, used to calculate original gravity, final gravity, and alcohol contents of wort/beer.
- Racking cane: cane-shape rigid tube made from plastic or stainless steel used with vinyl tubing to transfer fermented beer from the fermenter to the bottling bucket.

- Bottle filler: spring-loaded device that allows the user to start and stop the flow of beer while bottling.
- Bottle capper
- Cleaning brushes

Advanced Equipment

Contemporary homebrewers now have available a wide array of advanced homebrew equipment that mimics the equipment used in commercial breweries. A sophisticated and well-equipped homebrewery may look quite like a miniature version of its professional counterpart in a brewpub or microbrewery with stainless steel brewing vessels, pumps, and even microprocessor controls. Those bent on replicating commercial-scale equipment can purchase small cylindroconical fermenters, including some with temperature control capability. In these cases, the homebrewer makes beer using essentially the same ingredients and procedures as a commercial brewer, just on a much smaller scale.

Homebrewing Techniques

Even at the most basic levels, homebrewers must pay close attention to sanitation. The wort produced for fermentation makes perfect food for yeast—and many other organisms. If these other organisms thrive during fermentation, they can impart undesirable flavors in the finished beer. Thus, every brewer must attend to cleanliness and the proper sanitation of their equipment. With care, this can be achieved with any type of equipment, but plastic and rubber items are far harder to clean and sanitize than those made of glass and stainless steel.

Extract Only

The most basic homebrewed beers are made with prehopped extract. There are all-in-one kits like Mr Beer or Coopers Microbrewery that include all of the ingredients and equipment needed for making beer from hopped extract kits, as well as canned extract kits intended for homebrewers who already have the equipment necessary to brew. Many of the extract kits simply require the brewer to stir the extract syrup with water and often additional sugar, add yeast, ferment, and then bottle with priming sugar. Some kits may require an added step of pasteurizing the wort by briefly boiling. Kits that require only a brief boil or no boil at all are capable of making beer, but are really only suitable for a first-time experience. After a brewer comes to understand the process, he or she usually leaves such kits behind. It is, however, possible to make excellent beers using just malt extract and very basic equipment.

Extract with Specialty Grains

Most homebrewers will eventually move on to more involved brewing techniques that allow the brewer greater control over brewing than malt extract affords by itself. Homebrewers can steep specialty grains, including crystal malts and various degrees of roast malts, prior to adding unhopped malt extract. Most extract batches are conducted as concentrated wort boils, meaning that 4–12 l (1–3 gal) of wort is boiled and then topped up with water to 19 l (5 gal) in the fermenter. Hops are added at various points during the boil, depending on the style/recipe being brewed.

The primary advantages of using extracts in brewing are that it requires less equipment (i.e., no mash tun or hot liquor tank) and takes less time and effort to complete. The method of brewing from extract is somewhat limiting, even with specialty grains added, in that grains that require mashing cannot be used with this method of brewing. Thus, styles that derive substantial character from unroasted, uncaramelized, or adjunct grains that need mashing, such as Munich malts, Vienna malts, or flaked barley, cannot be brewed using this method unless extracts containing those malts or adjuncts are available.

All-Grain

All-grain homebrewing, as the name implies, starts with malted grains that must be mashed to convert the starches in the grains into fermentable sugars. All-grain brewing requires the addition of a mash/lauter tun and hot liquor tank to the brewer's equipment. It generally also requires the investment in a larger brew kettle to accommodate a full-wort boil and a wort chiller to facilitate quickly cooling the wort prior to pitching yeast. Homebrewers fashion mash/lauter tuns from plastic coolers, plastic buckets, or large pots with a manifold or false bottom for separating wort from the grains.

All-grain brewing systems can be fairly rudimentary three-tier gravity fed systems to advanced systems using pumps to move wort or hot liquor between vessels. All-grain homebrewers often purchase malt mills that allow them to home-mill their malt prior to brewing. This allows homebrewers to buy bulk uncrushed grain and to have greater control over the crush of the grain they use. As with freshly ground coffee, freshly ground malt also tends to have better flavors than precrushed malt.

The primary advantages of all-grain brewing are that it allows greater control over the brewing process and a wider array of styles/recipes that can be brewed. All-grain brewing also can be substantially cheaper than extract brewing because malted grain is cheaper than extracts for an equivalent amount of fermentable malt sugar. Therefore, the cost for the additional equipment required to brew all-grain batches may be offset by savings on ingredients. All-grain brewing is also a much longer process than extract brewing, typically adding 4 to 6 h more to the brewing day.

Partial Mash

Homebrewers have the option of an intermediary method of brewing between extract with specialty grains and all-grain brewing, and that is partial mash brewing. With the partial mash method, a portion of the fermentable sugars in the wort are derived from a "mini-mash" that is supplemented with malt extract. The mash is conducted in a small pot and sparged through a sieve or colander. This method allows extract brewers to brew beers containing grains or adjuncts that must be mashed, but without needing a full-scale mash tun or hot liquor tank.

Fermentation and Bottling

Most homebrewers produce warm-fermented ales because temperature control, especially at cooler temperatures used in the production of lagers, can be difficult to achieve in the home. After fermentation has taken place in a plastic or glass fermenter, there is usually a short period of aging during which most of the yeast is allowed to drop out. When the beer is ready to bottle, usually within 10–14 days, the beer will be transferred to another vessel and priming sugar will be added. The beer is then bottled. The yeast still in suspension will consume the priming sugar, giving the beer a natural carbonation. This is called bottle conditioning and was the method by which all bottled beer was made sparkling until the late 1800s. See BOTTLE CONDITIONING.

History and Geography of Homebrewing

The brewing of beer for personal use has been a human activity since the dawn of civilization. Some historians argue that the shift from nomadic to agrarian lifestyle occurred primarily from a desire to have a more dependable supply of beer. As a food art, the history of homebrewing runs back thousands of years, and most beer was domestically produced until only a few hundred years ago. Its recent development as a hobby has been not only influenced by technology and societal trends but also uniquely shaped by various facets of alcohol prohibition and taxation in different countries.

United States

In the New World, homebrewing was considered an important family activity among English colonists. In the Old World, water was considered dangerous because water sources were frequently contaminated. Because pathogens cannot survive in it, beer was considered by colonists a safe and nutritious alternative to drinking water. Many of the founders of the United States were homebrewers, including George Washington, Thomas Jefferson, and James Madison.

In the United States, homebrewing had somewhat of a revival when Prohibition went into effect in 1920. With the sale of alcohol illegal, many turned to making beer at home, although the quality of most homebrew produced was notoriously poor. The repeal of prohibition resulted in the legalization of home winemaking, but homebrewing would have to wait until 1979 to become federally legal once again. See CARTER, JAMES EARL, JR.

The biggest impact of prohibition on American homebrewing would not be seen until decades later. Few American breweries survived Prohibition. In the years that followed, the number of breweries in the United States continued to fall, whereas the variety of beer available to American drinkers narrowed to the point where almost all beer sold in the United States was lightly flavored American-style lager. That lack of variety in the beer available became a major incentive for Americans to homebrew, particularly for Americans who had discovered full-flavored beers while traveling in Europe.

The modern rise in popularity of homebrewing in the United States began with the publishing in

1969 of Fred Eckhardt's *A Treatise on Lager Beer*, the first book on homebrewing of the time. See ECKHARDT, FRED. Eckhardt's book was followed by Byron Burch's *Quality Brewing* in 1974 and Charlie Papazian's *Complete Joy of Homebrewing* in 1984, which would quickly become the most popular book on homebrewing in the United States.

Just month's before homebrewing officially became federally legal in the United States, Charlie Papazian and Charlie Matzen formed the American Homebrewers Association (AHA), publishing the first magazine dedicated to homebrewing, *Zymurgy*, on December 7, 1978. The following year the AHA launched the National Homebrew Competition and the National Homebrewers Conference. In 1982, the AHA held the inaugural Great American Beer Festival providing a venue to introduce the American public to a growing commercial craft beer movement in the United States, fueled primarily by homebrewers that had decided to make their hobby a profession. One year later, the AHA added another division, called the Institute for Brewing and Fermentation Studies, to serve the emerging commercial craft brewing community, and formed the Association of Brewers as the parent organization for both associations. See BREWERS ASSOCIATION, GREAT AMERICAN BEER FESTIVAL, and ZYMURGY.

In 1985, the Home Wine and Beer Trade Association and the AHA jointly formed the BJCP to establish a more uniform means of judging homebrew competitions. The BJCP is now an independent organization. The BJCP host exams for certifying beer judges, publishes a set of style guidelines for use in homebrew competitions, and, in conjunction with the AHA, certifies homebrew competitions. By 2009, the BJCP was registering over 300 competitions per year around the world. See BEER JUDGE CERTIFICATION PROGRAM (BJCP).

Homebrew clubs play a distinct role in American homebrewing. The first homebrew club in the United States was the Maltose Falcons, formed in 1974 in Southern California. By 2010, there were nearly 900 clubs spread throughout the country. Clubs play an important role in homebrewing because they provide a venue for sharing knowledge one-on-one with other homebrewers, where homebrews can be sampled and evaluated. Most clubs have monthly meetings, often with guest speakers.

In the early days of the American homebrewing revival, ingredients were often hard to find and/or of poor quality. The quality and variety of ingredients available to the US homebrew market is now vastly improved; homebrewers now have access to essentially the same ingredients that commercial brewers use. The improved quality of ingredients, along with easier access to information via books, magazines, and online resources and a growing variety of equipment options, now allows even novice brewers to make high-quality beer at home. In 2010, the AHA estimated that there were 750,000 Americans brewing at home, a figure that had seen steady growth in the previous 5 years.

United Kingdom

In 1963, the UK legalized homebrewing for personal use without a license. Prior to the change in the law, UK home winemakers had launched an annual national competition in 1959. The competition evolved into the National Association of Amateur Winemakers, which was renamed the National Association of Wine and Beermakers in 1974.

There are now several homebrew clubs throughout the UK, although perhaps the best known among them is the Durden Park Beer Club. The Durden Park Beer Club was formed in 1971 and has since become world renowned for reviving extinct beer recipes from the 18th and 19th centuries. The club originally published *Old British Beers and How to Make Them* in 1976, with the latest revision in 2003.

Once homebrewing was legalized in the UK, many early homebrew kits included cheap materials and very rudimentary instructions and thus resulted in inconsistent and often poor-quality beer. As a result, homebrewing caught on primarily as a method of producing cheap beer; after all, a great pint could be found at the pub. By the 1980s, pharmacy chains (chemists) such as Boots had large homebrewing sections in many of their stores. Before long, homebrewing became associated with penury rather than craftsmanship and its popularity declined for a period of time. Eventually, both technical knowledge and supplies improved and from 1990 onward a second wave of homebrewing began. Quality improved drastically and homebrewing came to have a status image. Today, British homebrewing more closely resembles homebrewing in the United States, although the hobby is not so widespread.

Canada

In Canada, interest in homebrewing has largely been fostered by the high excise taxes imposed on commercially produced alcoholic beverages. Much of the do-it-yourself beer and wine is produced at brew-on-premises businesses, where quality is not necessarily the primary aim. However, Canada is also home to a number of longstanding homebrew clubs that represent more serious homebrew enthusiasts. The Canadian Amateur Brewers Association has been hosting competitions and conferences and publishing information on brewing since it was established in 1984. As with the United States, growth of the homebrewing hobby has contributed to a growing commercial craft beer movement in Canada.

Australia/New Zealand

Australia has a well-developed homebrewing community. Some basic homebrew ingredients are available in grocery stores in Australia, allowing Australians to make cheap homebrew, although higher quality ingredients are available through homebrew supply stores. There are homebrew clubs throughout the country, and there is a national e-mail forum specifically for Australian homebrewers. In 2008, Australian homebrewers led by John Preston established the Australian National Homebrewers Conference as a national non-profit organization. A second conference was held in 2010. The conference is closely based on the AHA National Homebrewers Conference and includes several brewing-related seminars, as well as a national homebrewing competition.

New Zealand has a similarly developed homebrewing culture to Australia, although it is somewhat unique in the realm of home alcoholic beverage production in that it is one of the few countries where home distilling is legal.

Continental Europe

Homebrewing on the European continent is not as well developed as it is in the UK, although there are some pockets of growth. Holland is home to the De Roerstok homebrew club established in 1984. Denmark has a growing homebrewing movement and a robust craft brewing scene. Italy seems to be the country with the fastest growing homebrew culture at the moment, similar to the US homebrewers of the early 1980s. This, in turn, has helped fuel the meteoric rise of Italian craft brewing. See DENMARK and ITALY.

South America

Homebrewing is gaining momentum in Brazil, Argentina, and Chile. As in Italy, the South American homebrewers have established movements similar to those that sprung up in the United States in the 1980s. The Brazilian homebrewers have launched a national annual homebrewers conference and are providing a growing base of enthusiasm for a nascent craft brewing culture.

Asia

In Asia, the country with the most developed homebrewing community is Japan. Homebrewing in Japan is illegal for any beer over 1% alcohol. That said, there are accomplished homebrewers in the country and there are businesses that cater to Japanese homebrewers. In 1999, Ichiri Fujiura of Tokyo won the Homebrewer of the Year Award in the AHA National Homebrew Competition.

Additional Learning

The instructions for making a basic beer can easily be printed on a single sheet of paper but the insights needed to produce quality beer in a range of styles require more in-depth study. Indeed, those who become fascinated with beer find that they can spend a lifetime learning about its many aspects.

The basics of brewing can be found on the Internet and in short guides available from homebrew shops. But anyone interested in brewing more than a couple of batches will want to study further, and many good books are available. In the United States, two print magazines cater to homebrewers: *Zymurgy*, published by the American Homebrewers Association (Boulder, CO), and *Brew Your Own*, published by Battenkill Communications of Vermont.

Beyond this, homebrewers can find a variety of other sources of information from brewers forums that range from local to international in scope, online radio shows, and classes from retailers and internationally known brewing schools.

Daniels, Ray. *Designing great beers: The ultimate guide to brewing classic beer styles*. Denver, CO: Brewers Publications, 1998.

Lewis, Ashton. *The homebrewers answer book.* North Adams, MA: Storey Publishing, LLC, 2007.
Mosher, Randy. *Radical brewing: recipes, tales, and world-altering meditations in a glass.* Denver, CO: Brewers Publications, 2004.
Papazian, Charlie. *The complete joy of homebrewing.* New York: Harper Paperbacks, 2003.
Palmer, John. *How to brew: everything you need to know to brew beer.* Denver, CO: Brewers Publications, 2006.
White, Chris, and Zainasheff, Jamil. *Yeast: the practical guide to beer fermentation.* Denver, CO: Brewers Publications, 2010.

Gary Glass, Ray Daniels, and Keith Thomas

honey can be fermented by itself or with numerous other ingredients to create an assortment of alcoholic beverages. By itself, diluted in water, fermented honey is called mead or honey wine and can be high or low alcohol, sweet or dry, carbonated or still. Used in beer, honey adds a distinctive sweetness and roundness, although in excess it can be perceived as rather cloying on the palate. As one of the sweetest substances found in nature, honey has been gathered by humans since the dawn of man, and all sorts of animals seek it out as a food source. It is created by honey bees from nectar as a food source and stored in hives. Depending on the location of the hives, the honey can take on the flavor of the plants from which it was made. For example, hives located near orange groves produce honey with a subtle orange flavor called orange blossom honey, and hives near clover fields produce clover honey. Nutritionally, honey consists mainly of fructose and glucose with negligible amounts of vitamins and minerals.

The U.S. Department of Agriculture has grading systems for assessing honey color and quality. Color is measured in seven shades on the following scale: water white, extra white, white, extra light amber, light amber, amber, and dark amber. Quality is graded as a composite score based on five factors: moisture content, flavor, aroma, absence of defects, and clarity. Grade A honey must have a score of 90 or higher; Grade B, 80 or higher; and Grade C, 70 or higher. Honey with a score below 70 is classified as substandard.

Honey is usually added to beer in one of two ways. The first method is to add honey during the kettle boil, usually toward the end, where it becomes part of the original gravity of the wort. As a result of its simple sugar profile, honey tends to ferment out completely, and any sense of sweetness derived is usually an aromatic effect rather than residual sugar in the beer. When used in the boil, honey can contribute a wide range of flavor characteristics, from floral (wildflower honey) to seemingly roasted and funky (buckwheat honey).

The other way brewers use honey is postfermentation, where the honey adds actual sweetness to the beer and a more direct honey flavor. Many aromatic volatiles can be lost during fermentation, so adding honey postfermentation allows the brewer to bring a more literal honey flavor to various beers. Brewers occasionally brew other forms of honey beers, including braggott, a drink that was popular in parts of medieval Europe. Braggots are beers containing large amounts of honey in the wort, sometimes more than 50% of the original gravity. As such, they are technically not necessarily considered beers at all, but beverages on the border between beer and mead.

Keith Villa

Hook Norton Brewery, in the village of Hook Norton in Oxfordshire, England, was founded in 1849 by farmer and maltster John Harris. A family-owned brewery, it is run today by his great-great-grandson James Clarke. The brewery produces quintessential English ales and stouts, including Old Hooky, Hooky Gold, and Double Stout, and is fiercely proud that all of its draught beers are cask-conditioned and have never been filtered or pasteurized. See CASK CONDITIONING.

The brewery's six-story tower was built in the late 1890s and was designed by William Bradford, who also drew up the plans for seventy other breweries, including Harvey's of Lewes in Sussex, each bearing his signature of an ornate roofline in a Queen Anne style.

Hook Norton is widely considered to be among the most beautiful breweries in England. Tower breweries were a product of Victorian ingenuity; the movement of liquids through the brewery could easily be achieved if malt and water were winched and pumped to the top of the building, leaving gravity to do the work of transferring liquid down from one vessel to another.

The brewery's motive power is still provided by the Buxton & Thornley 25 hp steam engine installed

The Hook Norton Brewery in Oxfordshire, England, is one of the last working breweries to use a Victorian tower design, in which the brewing vessels used first are placed near the top, and those used last near the bottom. Once liquid is winched and pumped to the top of the six-story tower, gravity assists in moving it along from one vessel to the next. CATH HARRIES

in 1899. It is last steam engine of its age still in regular use for its original purpose in the United Kingdom.

It is not hard to imagine sweating brewery workers in the 20th century using this then-state of the art technology to haul the heavy sacks of malts needed up to the top floor of the brewery, where they would be poured into a grist mill, which is still used today.

But though the brewery has a past, it does not live in it, and over time most of the original vessels have been replaced. For as James Clarke says: "If my great-great-grandfather had known about stainless steel he would have used it."

Eddershaw, David. *A country brewery: Hook Norton 1849–1999*. Oxford, England: Oxford University Press, 1999.

Tim Hampson

hop back is a straining vessel used in traditional brewhouses to separate leaf hops boiled in the kettle before the wort is cooled prior to fermentation. Hop backs can also be used to impart additional "late-hop" character to a beer by flowing the hot wort over fresh hops on its way to the wort chiller. Because these late addition hops have not been boiled in the kettle (boiling drives off some hop volatiles), more of the hop aromatics tend to be retained in the finished beer. A hop back is usually a closed stainless steel (or previously copper) tank designed to take the entire volume of wort from the kettle. The tank is fitted with a slotted false bottom which sits a few centimeters above the floor and has narrow slots comprising 20%–30% of the tank's floor surface area.

Boiled wort is run into the hop back and after a short settling period a filter bed of hops is formed (approximately 30–50 cm deep) on the false bottom. The hot wort is then drained through the filter bed of hops before cooling. The hop bed also traps trub (coagulated protein) which is produced during the boil. The wort run off from the vessel should be clear, as the hops act as a good filter material. High-quality aroma hops are often added the hop back to give beer a special fruity, hoppy aroma. Hops are added at this point because the aroma components are retained in the wort rather that boiled away in the wort kettle. Leaf hops may also be removed from wort by special filters instead of a hop back.

In modern brewhouses, hop backs have been largely replaced by "whirlpool tanks" that separate out hop pellet fragments and protein sediment. See WHIRLPOOL. This is a more efficient separation method because the ability of the hop bed in a hop back to achieve filtration can be variable from batch to batch. In some craft breweries, a smaller hop back may be placed after the whirlpool, imparting extra hop aromatics to pre-clarified wort and to the finished beer.

Paul KA Buttrick

hop breeding and selection is the process by which plant breeders develop new hop cultivars. Many forces play a role in driving the continuous development of new hop cultivars. These include the introduction of new pests and pathogens, the evolution of a pest or pathogen to overcome plant resistance, changing market conditions, entirely new market opportunities, and a desire to minimize the environmental impact of hop production practices. Constant change is normal, so hop breeders engage in an ongoing effort to alter currently available elite cultivars to satisfy the hop industry and to broaden the spectrum of hop flavors available to brewers by breeding entirely new and genetically distinct hop cultivars.

Many believe that hop cultivation began in central Europe in Bohemia (now part of the Czech Republic), Slovenia, and Bavaria, Germany, during the 8th and 9th centuries. Hop cultivation spread to other continents, such as North America and Australia, as Europeans migrated there. Most likely, early hop cultivars were not the product of deliberate breeding efforts but careful selections by hop growers of indigenous wild hops until they had found varieties that were suited for local growing conditions. In time, a select few genotypes became dominant because they possessed the characteristics most sought after by local brewers and growers. Eventually, hops became known as types named after the location where they were found or grown, such as Hallertauer, Tettnanger, or Saaz. Systematic plant breeding programs eventually developed in the late 19th century to replace the simple local selection practices of hop farmers. This was the beginning of formal hop cultivar development and the proliferation of specialized hop varieties.

The earliest known organized hop breeding effort was made in Germany in 1894 and again in 1898. The United States Department of Agriculture (USDA) attempted to establish a hop breeding program in 1904 and 1908 that showed some promise but eventually was abandoned because of federal budget cuts, the onset of World War I, and Prohibition. See PROHIBITION. Eventually, the USDA established a hop research program in 1931 in Oregon. That program is still in operation. In England, hop breeding programs go back to 1904, at Wye College in Kent, where within a few short years, many of the early bittering varieties were developed. See WYE COLLEGE. Other early hop breeding programs sprang up in Denmark, Sweden, the Czech Republic, and Germany. Among the more recent cultivars to come out of Hüll are the high-alpha varieties Herkules, Magnum, and Taurus, while the Slovenian Institute has released Aurora, Celeia, and Styrian Golding. Both private and public hop breeding programs are scattered around the globe in key hop growing regions. Plant breeding is both an art and a science. Science focuses on understanding the underlying genetic mechanism for important traits, the ancestry of individual genotypes, and how their relatedness affects trait expression. It also considers the role played by environmental factors in the expression of the plant's individual character. The art involved in plant breeding comes from the breeder's ability to use scientific information and available tools to identify superior individuals from a vast pool of offspring—a daunting task that much resembles finding the proverbial needle in a haystack.

Humulus genetic material that is available for hop breeders to work with has a long and global history. See AMERICAN HOPS, HISTORY, and HOPS. Hops are thought to have originated in China. According to recent DNA analyses, some 1.05 to 1.27 million years ago a European type diverged from the original Chinese group and inhabits Europe today. More recently, perhaps some 460,000 to 690,000 years ago, a North American group diverged from the

Asian group, and the North American group contains the greatest genetic diversity.

Cultivated hop is dioecious, which means that male and female reproductive organs are borne on separate plants. Hops, just as humans, have one set of chromosomes that determine the sex of the individual. If a plant has an XY chromosome pair, it is male; if it has an XX chromosome pair, it is female. Only female hop plants are used in commercial cultivationbecause only they produce the cones used in brewing. Male genotypes are only used in plant breeding programs because they do not produce cones.

Effective plant breeding in a cross-pollinated species like the hop relies partly on an understanding of relatedness among individuals so that appropriate crosses can be planned to minimize inbreeding. Inbreeding, the mating of related individuals, can uncover negative traits that may result in agronomically unacceptable individuals. Because breweries with successful brands prefer replacement hop cultivars that behave functionally or organoleptically much like the ones they are currently using in their recipes, hop breeders often have to work within narrow genetic confines when developing new cultivars. The danger in this approach is that cultivars can become too closely related, which can hamper future breeding efforts and render the pool of currently grown cultivars susceptible to catastrophic events such as a devastating outbreak of disease or pests. To minimize the chances of such negative outcomes, hop breeders assess the genetic diversity among the genotypes in their breeding collection by evaluating pedigree records and variation in plant traits and using modern molecular biology tools such as genetic markers. This allows breeders to select unrelated parents for crossing in the hope that they will produce genetically diverse progeny.

Although pedigree records are useful for assessing the relatedness among hop genotypes, this information is not always reliable because the origins of many older hop cultivars are not known for certain, especially if they have unidentified indigenous wild plants in their genetic background. Also, some cultivars were developed by open pollination, a technique where the breeder does not pollinate a female flower with a known male pollen source but rather pollination occurs naturally from random males. Although this technique has been used successfully to create genetically diverse progeny, such as Galena, the anonymity of the male parent can complicate future parental selection decisions when using pedigree information.

Molecular biology has provided plant breeders with powerful tools to elucidate genetic structures within available breeding lines and cultivars. Among the tools now available are DNA sequence markers, relatedness computations between individuals, genotype fingerprinting for identification, and gene deactivation to suppress undesirable traits in individuals that might be desirable otherwise. Molecular DNA markers associated with a particular trait allow the hop breeder to select for desirable characteristics much earlier in the plant's life cycle than traditional selection techniques. This can speed up the breeding process and limit expensive field evaluations of individuals known to carry desirable genes. Although hop breeders and researchers currently do not perform genetic manipulations, that is, the insertion of non-hop DNA into hop plants for commercial production, they do use a wide array of genetic analysis tools to make the breeding process more efficient and successful.

In recent years, a number of hop researchers have analyzed DNA extracted from numerous cultivars, breeding lines, and male genotypes in an effort to more fully understand the ancestry of the current breeding stock. This research has shown that, in general, modern hop accessions fall into one of two categories: those with a European-based ancestry and those that are hybrids between European and wild American ancestry. Within these two larger groups, a number of smaller subgroups have been identified based on traits such as sex or regional adaptation. This research has allowed hop breeders to corroborate pedigree records and, in some cases, even clarify disputed ancestry lines. These advancements have improved the planning of appropriate crosses to minimize inbreeding and to maximize potential heterosis (hybrid vigor).

Heterosis is a genetic concept where progeny from a cross outperforms both parents for a given trait. Historically this technique does not appear to have been used much in hop breeding, although it has proven useful in other crops, such as corn, and may benefit hop breeding programs in the future. Heterosis typically occurs when unrelated genotypes are mated and produce diverse progeny with unique gene combinations. The genetic assumption is that the unique alleles (a form of gene) that are brought together biochemically interact in such a way as to enhance the expression of the desired trait. Such traits may be yield, vigor, or disease resistance. Together with pedigree records and molecular marker-based genetic distance estimates, this technique is now considered to have some merit for hop breeding.

A number of hop research programs have begun creating genetic linkage maps that can be used to physically locate—or "map"—important traits on hop chromosomes. Genetic mapping is an important and powerful statistical tool that places numerous molecular markers in linkage groups. Mapping can tie each linkage group to a particular chromosome. Once the order and arrangement of the molecular markers are known, the resulting map can be used by plant breeders and geneticists to associate traits such as disease resistance, which are normally controlled by only one or a few genes, with a marker and then mapped to a physical chromosome location. This allows hop breeders to simply select for the associated marker in the seedling stage, perhaps during the winter in a greenhouse, and be reasonably certain that the selected individuals will be resistant to the respective disease or pest when grown under field conditions.

Some traits, however, are governed by the expression of many genes in combination, and several of these genes may interact in complex ways to influence the trait. Yield is the classic example of a genetically complex trait controlled by many genes. Because markers are physically mapped to a specific chromosomal region, they can be associated with gene clusters that are involved in the expression of genetically complex traits. These types of markers are termed quantitative trait loci (QTL). They allow hop breeders to select individuals in the seedling stage that contain clusters of genes important for expressing the complex trait of interest. Mapping QTLs requires considerable research effort initially to identify and place molecular markers on a linkage map. The greater the number of markers placed on the genetic map, that is, the higher the marker density, the more easily breeders can associate gene clusters with specific markers that are useful in the selection process. Thus, as molecular marker technology improves, so will the quality of the genetic maps constructed with marker technology. Ultimately, molecular markers based upon DNA sequence information will likely predominate, and this will give hop breeders new, powerful techniques for selecting desirable genotypes.

Plant transformation(or genetic modification) may also prove useful in hop breeding, should public opinion ever favor such an approach. Generating a genetically modified organism (GMO) involves inserting a piece of DNA into the host plant, usually via a ballistic device or a bacteria vector. The inserted DNA fragment may be from an entirely different organism or from the host species itself but with some modification to its function. This technique is useful in situations where a desirable individual is deficient in some critical trait such as disease resistance, but is otherwise desirable in its other traits. If a known resistance gene is available, it can be inserted into the desired individual and the transformed individual gains disease resistance to the target pathogen. Transformation can also be used to insert DNA fragments that suppress the expression of undesirable genes. However, current public sentiment would likely not support beer made with GMO hops. Therefore, it remains an open question whether this technology will find use in hop breeding.

Henning, J. A., M. S. Townsend, and P. Matthews. Predicting offspring performance in hop (*Humulus lupulus* L.) using AFLP markers. *Journal of the American Society of Brewing Chemists* 68 (2010): 125–31.

Murakami, A., P. Darby, B. Javornik, M. S. S. Pais, E. Seigner, A. Lutz, and P. Svoboda. Molecular phylogeny of wild hops, *Humulus lupulus* L. *Heredity* 97 (2006): 66–74.

Neve, R. A. *Hops*. London: Chapman & Hall, 1991.

Seefelder, S., H. Ehrmaier, G. Schweizer, and E. Seigner. Genetic diversity and phylogenetic relationships among accessions of hop, Humulus lupulus, as determined by amplified fragment length polymorphism and fingerprinting compared to pedigree data. *Plant Breeding* 119 (2000): 257–63.

Small, E. S. A numerical and nomenclatural analysis of morpho-geographic taxa of *Humulus. Systematic Botany* 3 (1978): 37–76.

Smith, D. C. "Varietal improvement in hops." In *Yearbook for 1937*. Washington, DC: USDA, 1937.

Townsend, M. S., and J. A. Henning. AFLP discrimination of native North American and cultivated hop. *Crop Science* 49 (2009): 600–7.

Townsend, M. S., and J. A. Henning. "Ancestry and genetic variation in hop development." In *Hop flavor and aroma*, ed. T. Shellhammer, 91–8. St Paul, MN: Master Brewers Association of the Americas,

Proceedings of the First International Brewing Symposium, 2009.

Shaun Townsend and Thomas Shellhammer

hop extracts represent one of many processed hop products that are available to modern brewers. More than 50% of all hops used by the brewing industry worldwide are processed into extracts. CO_2 is the primary solvent utilized in the modern process of hop extraction. Prior to this method, hops were extracted using solvents such as ethanol, methanol, and hexane. Ethanol extraction is still practiced on a limited scale. Many brewers feel that the CO_2 method is most effective at selectively extracting the most important components from the raw hop and provides a purer brewing material. Solvent residues are not an issue with this method and the resulting extract is also free of nitrates and residual pesticides. In its unprocessed form, it provides a brewing raw material with fresh hop aroma and flavor characteristics that is very stable after extended periods of storage. This product is typically stored at ambient temperatures prior to use, unlike whole hop products, which must be refrigerated. CO_2 extract contains all of the most important hop components needed for the brewing process, including alpha acids, beta acids, essential oils, and other soft resins. Many brewers believe that beer brewed with these extracts has a typical flavor and aroma, similar to beers brewed with whole hops or pellets. Others feel that ethanol extraction has an edge over CO_2 because of better retention of hop polyphenols and xanthohumol, which they claim can give beer better mouthfeel and shelf stability. Furthermore, researchers at Weihenstephan have found that hop oil components are volatilized out of the kettle more quickly when using any type of extract than they are when hop pellets or whole cones are used.

Regardless of the debate, hop extracts do have their advantages. When extracts are used, the brewhouse can yield more wort because the original plant's cellulose has been removed, making wort separation less difficult relative to whole hop or pellet use. Extracts are also concentrated and thus reduce raw material shipping costs. Utilizing an extract with a measured amount of alpha acid allows for very precise bitterness in the finished beer. It is packaged in cans ranging from 0.5 to 10 kg (1 to 22 lb) as well as drums containing up to 200 kg (440 lb). The smaller package size reduces shipping costs relative to shipping whole-leaf hops or hop pellets. Sophisticated automated hop dosing systems are often utilized to dispense these extracts; however, in many cases the brewer simply pours the extract directly into the kettle. Utilization of these extracts in terms of international bitterness units is typically 35% when added to the kettle. See INTERNATIONAL BITTERNESS UNITS (IBUS). CO_2 extracts are often the starting material for a number of other purified hop extracts, preisomerized extracts, and other modified downstream products such as "Tetra." These modified hop extracts have an even greater utilization and thus higher efficiency when dosed into beer post fermentation and have gained wide favor internationally among brewers of light lagers. Some modified hop extracts provide ultraviolet light stability, preventing the "skunking" reaction, and allowing the beers to be packaged in clear bottles without fear of attendant damage. See LIGHTSTRUCK. Many craft brewers, particularly in the United States, avoid hop extracts entirely, either for philosophical reasons or out of a belief that they are inherently inferior to whole hops or pellets. Proponents, including some craft brewers, argue that hop extracts allow them to dose far more bitterness into their beers than might otherwise be practical. CO_2 hop extracts are now widely used in the production of very hoppy beer styles such as "double India pale ale."

Matthew Brynildson

Hopfensiegel

See HOP SEAL.

hop isomerization is the chemical conversion, during the kettle boil, of insoluble hop alpha acids—or humulones—into bitter-tasting, soluble iso-alpha acids—or isohumulones. Humulones are a part of the sticky resin that resides in the lupulin glands of female hop cones. Isomerization involves the structural rearranging of the humulone molecules, which dramatically increases their solubility in aqueous solutions such as beer and wort. Isomerization, therefore, is the main chemical reaction responsible for the bitter flavor of beers brewed with hops.

The rate of isomerization in the kettle, known as hop utilization, tends to be in the vicinity of 25%–35% for most breweries, sometimes less, rarely more. This is because isomerization depends on several limiting factors. For one, it requires high temperatures, which is why brewers boil bittering hops in the brew kettle, typically for at least 60 minutes. Isomerization is also pH-sensitive and happens faster and more completely the higher the pH value. The pH value of most worts is in the vicinity of 5.4–5.8 at the start of the boil and drops to about 5.2–5.4 during the boil largely as a result of the precipitation of calcium phosphate. Finally, utilization rates decrease as wort gravity increases. Even those humulones that do get isomerized may not all make it into the finished beer to provide bitterness. When proteins precipitate in the whirlpool, for instance, they tend to adsorb isohumulones and pull them down into the trub. Additional isohumulone losses occur during wort cooling, fermentation, and filtration.

Alpha-acid levels in hops are measured as a percent of the hop's weight and that information is provided to brewers by the hop processor. Typical alpha-acid values for hops range between 3% and 20%. This allows brewers to calculate the expected bitterness in their beers—expressed in international bitterness units (IBUs)—based on established hop utilization rates that are specific to their brew systems, recipes, and brewing process. Pre-isomerized hop extracts are available to brewers who wish to add additional bitterness post-fermentation; these extracts are entirely soluble in finished beer.

See also ALPHA ACIDS, BITTERING POTENTIAL (OF HOPS), BITTERNESS, HOP UTILIZATION, HUMULONE, INTERNATIONAL BITTERNESS UNITS (IBUS), and ISO-ALPHA ACIDS.

Matthew Brynildson

hop mosaic virus infects hop plants in Europe, Australia, North America, and China. It infects several other plants in the wild, including tobacco (e.g., Nicotiana clevelandii) and nettles (e.g., Urtica urens). Although many hop cultivars are tolerant, showing no symptoms, Golding-type cultivars are sensitive to the virus. See GOLDING (HOP). In these varietals, hop mosaic virus causes leaf distortion and chlorotic banding (pale patches on leaves) and can significantly reduce yield and plant longevity. In tolerant plants, the prevalence of viral infection is high, and where symptoms are detected they are indistinguishable from the related hop latent virus. Both hop mosaic virus and hop latent virus are members of the Carlavirus genus. Transmission of hop mosaic virus is thought to be largely via insects, with studies showing aphids to be the major vector.

Oregon State University. *An online guide to plant disease control*. http://plant-disease.ippc.orst.edu/disease.cfm?RecordID=605 (accessed April 26, 2011).

Poke, F. S. Hop mosaic virus: Complete nucleotide sequence and relationship to other carlaviruses. *Archives of Virology* 153 (2008): 1615–19.

Martha Holley-Paquette

hop oils, the small, volatile fraction of hops that contribute significantly to the lingering, aromatic character of beer, especially in the finish. They are sometimes referred to as "essential oils." Hop oils are found in the lupulin gland of the hop cone along with hop acids. Oils usually comprise a small 0.5% to 3.0% of the hop's dry weight. Overall oil content is usually expressed in milliliters of oil per 100 g of hops. The oil content of hops varies from one variety to another and can be affected by fertilization. Seeded hops produce less essential oil than do seedless ones. During ripening, hop acids will plateau slightly before or at picking time—typically when hop cones are 21% to 22% dry solids—but they continue to accumulate if the cones are left on the bine. Thus, the timing of the harvest will have an effect on hop oil content as well as hop oil composition. Over 300 components have been identified in hop oils. Because of their chemical complexity and because of the complex chemical reactions in which they are involved during the brewing and fermentation processes, the mechanisms of their contribution to beer flavor are still not fully understood.

Hop oil chemistry is complicated. Basically, these oils can be divided into categories based on their chemical functionality. Some 50% to 80% of oils are hydrocarbons, 20% to 50% oxygen-containing compounds, and less than 1% sulfur-containing compounds. The hydrocarbon fraction has little presence in finished beer. It contains a highly volatile and hydrophobic set of compounds. These compounds have poor solubility and are typically driven out of the wort during the boil and fermentation. If a beer is dry hopped, some compounds will show up in the finished beer, albeit at very low levels. The oxygenated compounds have greater polarity and thus are more water soluble. They are very aromatic, more so than the hydrocarbons, and they impart floral, fruity, herbal, spicy, and woody aromas to beer. These compounds can be found in finished beer, with their amounts dependent on the timing of the hop additions to the kettle, the duration of the boil, and whether the hops were added postfermentation. In general, sulfur compounds have very low detection thresholds (often at levels of parts per trillion), which means that even at extremely low concentrations in the finished beer they can impart notable vegetative, oniony, garlic, rubber-like aromas to beer. Given the susceptibility of hop oils to oxidation in storage, especially in baled as opposed to pelletized hops, the amount of hydrocarbons diminishes and the level of oxygenated compounds increases over time in storage. This is why some brewers believe that mild, but controlled, oxidation of hops can yield more intense aromatic qualities.

The individual hop oil hydrocarbons are made up of isoprene (five carbon or C5) units. Incidentally, the same units can also be found in alpha and beta acids. Overall, more than 40 hydrocarbons have been identified in hop oils, but only few have been found in beer. The four main components of the hydrocarbons are myrcene (C10), a monoterpene, and three sesquiterpenes (C15), caryophyllene, humulene, and (in some hops) farnesene. The presence or absence of farnesene is a distinguishing feature for some hops. For instance, it is completely absent in Hallertauer Mittelfrueh but present—in high levels—in Saaz and Tettnanger. The oxygenated compounds are more diverse and more complex, but they are found in beer and thus are believed to be more important to a beer's hop flavor and aroma. When carbon–carbon double bonds react with oxygen, they can form epoxides. Caryophyllene epoxide as well as humulone mono- and diepoxides can be found in both hop oils and beer. They have spicy and woody aromas. Technically, these are probably the compounds responsible for what hop marketers consider the criterion that separates the "noble" aroma Saaz, Hallertauer Mittelfrueh, Spalter, and Tettnanger from all the other hop varieties. See NOBLE HOPS. Although these varieties tend to be lower in overall hop oil content than others, they can contribute significantly more to hop aroma in beer than many other varieties. Humulene epoxide III is one of the most potent aromatic compounds found in Hallertauer Mittelfrueh. Other oxygen-containing compounds are esters, ketones, and alcohols of isoprene-derived compounds. Oxidation processes on geranyl pyrophosphate (the precursor to myrcene) and subsequent chemical rearrangement can lead to a range of floral, fruity, and citrusy compounds such as linalool (floral–citrusy), nerol (citrus, floral–fresh rose), geraniol (floral–rose, geranium), and limonene (citrus–orange–lemon). Fermentation-derived esters such as 2-methylpropyl isobutyrate and 2-methylbutyl isobutyrate present fruity aromas. Terpenes as a general category serve as a base for over 90% of the total mass of hop oils.

See also FARNESENE, HALLERTAUER MITTELFRUEH (HOP), HUMULENE, and TETTNANGER (HOP).

Thomas Shellhammer

hop pellets are a form of processed whole hops whereby the dried cones are pulverized using a hammer mill and then extruded through a pelleting die to produce a densely packed pellet. The hop cone is a flower-like structure that is both bulky and delicate: beautiful, perhaps, but not very practical in the brewery setting. Developed in the late 1960s, the technology for preparing pellets offers brewers a range of advantages over using whole hops. See HOPS. Whereas whole hops are packed in large bales, pellets are compact and thus easy to store. However, because processing hop pellets is likely to break the hop cone's lupulin glands, pellets are much more sensitive to oxygen than whole hops. For this reason, hop pellets must be flushed with inert gas and vacuum packed in expensive, foil-lined, high gas-barrier bags to minimize their contact with oxygen; and the quality of the packaging's seal is of crucial importance. Shipping hop pellets in oxygen-free packaging greatly enhances their keeping qualities, especially if they are stored at the recommended temperature of below 4°C (about <39°F). If kept very cold, even frozen, pellets can be stored for more than 2 years without significant degradation. In the processing plant, hops are usually milled from several fields and lots and then blended to equalize variations from different sources. Extraneous hop material such as leaves, stems, and non-plant matter are also greatly reduced or eliminated during pelletizing. In addition, brewers can have pellets custom-blended from a combination of different hop varieties. Pelletized hops come in two varieties, Type 90 and Type 45. T-90 pellets are made from the entire hop flower, whereas T-45 pellets are made after much of the vegetative matter has been removed from the flower, which concentrates the lupulin content in the pellets. Because T-90 pellets contain all the vegetative and lupulin material of the hop flower, they function as a full replacement for leaf hops in the kettle. T-45 hop pellets are made the same way as T-90 pellets, except that the hammer milling occurs at a very low temperature of –35°C (–31°F), which prevents the stickiness of the lupulin from impeding further processing. The powder is then sieved to produce a resin-rich fraction containing only about half the original vegetable matter. Then this T-45 powder is sent to the pellet die and the packaging machine. T-45 pellets weigh only about 45% of the weight of the original hop material. One important brewhouse advantage of pellets over baled whole hops in automated brew systems is the suitability for automated hop dosing equipment. This is because pellets flow more reliably and consistently than loose hop flowers. But the physical destruction of the lupulin glands during milling, with the resulting increase in the surface area of the lupulin and the greater exposure to oxygen, is a key disadvantage of hop pellets. Furthermore, processing pellets through a die generates heat, sometimes in excess of 55°C (130°F) if left uncontrolled. This may accelerate oxidation of the hop acids and/or a loss of hop oils. Controlling the processing temperature at the hop processing plant, therefore, is perhaps the most critical variable in initial pellet quality. Because of the overall advantages of pelletized hops, they are used by all sectors of the brewing industry, from the largest brewers to the smallest brewpubs. In the United States, pellets are broadly favored over whole hops and over hop extracts.

Thomas Shellhammer and Val Peacock

hops are the ingredient in beer that provides its backbone of bitterness, increases its microbiological stability, helps stabilize its foam, and greatly influences its taste and aroma.

> For if your ale may endure a fortnight, your Beere through the benefit of the Hoppe, shall continue a moneth, and what grace it yieldeth to the teaste, all men may judge that have sense in their mouths...
>
> Reginald Scot, *The Perfite Platform for a Hoppe Garden*, 1576.

Hops are the flowers or "cones" of Humulus lupulus, a Latin diminutive meaning roughly "a low [slinking] little wolf [plant]," so-named for the plant's tactile qualities, prodigious growth, and wide range. The Humulus genus belongs to the family of Cannabinaceae, which includes Cannabis (hemp, marijuana) and Celtis (Hackberry). Hops are native to the Northern Hemisphere in the temperate zones of Europe, western Asia, and North America and are thought to have originated in China. They are now grown commercially in both hemispheres between roughly 30 and 52 degrees latitude. They are hardy plants that can survive cold winters with temperatures as low as –30°C (roughly –20°F). There are five recognized taxonomic varieties in the genus Humulus: lupulus are European hops; cordifolius are Japanese hops; and lupuloides, neomexicanus, and pubescens are North American natives.

"Noble" hops is a historical and commercial term, which is somewhat arbitrarily assigned to four distinct hop landraces, that is, plants that were domesticated in their respective areas and have become open-pollinated, genetically isolated populations there. These are Hallertauer Mittelfrueh from the Hallertau region of Bavaria; Tettnanger from Tettnang in Germany near Lake Constance; Spalt from Bavaria in Germany, south of Nuremburg; and Saaz from the Žatec region of the Czech Republic. See HALLERTAU HOP REGION, NOBLE HOPS, SPALT HOP REGION, TETTNANG HOP REGION, and ŽATEC HOP REGION. Many hop varieties released in the past century can trace their lineage to at least one of these nobles. Although these four noble hops have been revered for their pleasing aroma profile and gentle bitterness, with alpha acid to beta acid ratios of 1:1, they are notoriously low yielding and highly disease prone.

In the trade, hops come in two basic market classes, bittering and aroma hops, with relatively few hops also being marketed as dual-purpose varieties. Bittering, or kettle, hops are added to the wort near

Harvest day on a farm that grows organic hops, Ashland, Oregon. GEORGE RUBALOFF

the beginning of the boil; and aroma, or finishing, hops, are added any time from 30 minutes before the end of the boil to just at shut-down. They can also be added to the whirlpool, or even later. See BOILING and WHIRLPOOL. The addition of hops to fermented beer is called dry hopping. See DRY HOPPING. This practice adds highly volatile hop essential oils to the beer—oils that in bittering hops evaporate into the brew stack during the kettle boil and may even be scrubbed out of wort during fermentation. The intensity of hoppiness in beer is a matter of beer style specifications and the personality of the brewer. See BEER STYLE and BITTERNESS. Some mass-market American lagers, for instance, refreshing as they may be to many consumers, can leave the drinker feeling as if the brewer had just waved a single hop cone over the kettle. At the same time, some craft-brewed beers clearly push the envelope of hoppiness to the edge of human bitterness tolerance, with the brewers apparently reveling in an almost punishing hop character. Such beers are specialty beers of growing popularity, especially in New World brewpubs, and are slowly catching on in other beer cultures around the world as well, but they are surely not for everyone. See EXTREME BREWING.

Ever since the discovery of hops as a suitable beer flavoring, which occurred probably in the 8th century AD, hops have been added to wort as kiln-dried whole cones. Hops need to lose their moisture as quickly as possible after they are harvested, because otherwise they start to rot within just a few hours. Traditionally, hop kilns were housed in oast houses, which by the 19th century had taken on a distinctive circular architecture, with conical roofs that still dot the countryside of many current and former hop-producing regions to this day. See OAST HOUSE.

Hops are perennial herbaceous plants that live 10 to 20 years, maintaining a perennial root, called a rhizome, a carbohydrate storage structure that is also found in ginger and the iris plant. Each spring the rhizome sprouts a mass of bines that wrap clockwise around anything they contact. Hops grow vigorously up to 15 m (about 50 ft) tall. In most hop gardens, however, they may reach a height of 4 to 9 m (some 15 to 30 ft). During the peak of the growing season in mid-summer, hops bines may add as much as 50 cm (about 20 inches) per week. The bines are herbaceous, although they tend to form woody, secondary growth on the older

Botanical illustration of Humulus lupulus, the scientific name for the common hop. German, c. 1850. PIKE MICROBREWERY MUSEUM, SEATTLE, WA

tissue late in the season. They die to the ground in winter. Unlike vines, which have tendrils, a bine adheres to its support with its large number of rigid, hooked stem hairs called trichomes. These hold the bine to a substrate. Unfortunately for many hop workers, the oils secreted by trichomes can also irritate the skin.

Hops are dioecious (Greek for "two houses"), meaning there are separate male and female plants. Only seedless female hop cones are used in the brewing industry, which is why growers take care to control male plant pollinators in regions where hops are indigenous or cultivated. Male hop plants are less desirable, because they have very small cones that contain only 1/150th of the amount of resin that female cones contain. They also lack some of the essential aroma oils so prized by brewers and beer drinkers. Male plants are tolerated in hop yards only when an open-pollination breeding project is underway. Occasionally a hop plant may turn out to be monoecious, with both male and female flowers on the same plant. But such plants produce only infertile seeds. Modern breeding efforts have produced triploid hop varieties, such as the popular Willamette. See WILLAMETTE (HOP). Such hops are naturally seedless and thus infertile, which, however, is not a problem because most commercial hop varieties nowadays are clonally propagated by cuttings of their rhizomes or some softwood stem tissue; these easily form roots if just kept moist for a few weeks. See HOP BREEDING AND SELECTION.

The hop flower, or cone, is botanically a "catkin." It is an inflorescence that contains a central support called a strig. The strig holds 20 to 60 bracteoles (petals/sepals) along its axis, each with two female floral parts at its base to form a cone-shape flower. The size of the flower varies among hop varieties from an average 2 to 3.5 cm (approximately 0.8 to 1.5 inches) to very large ones of more than 5 cm (2 inches), with shapes varying from round to oblong and somewhat boxy. Lupulin glands, also at the base of the bracteoles, produce the yellow to golden substance called lupulin. It is in the lupulin that the resins—including alpha and beta acids—as well as essential oils are concentrated once the hop cone has ripened.

Alpha acids, also called humulones, which are the sources of most of the bitterness in beer, make up about 3% to 4% of the cone's weight in aroma varieties. In superalpha bittering varieties—which are the most recent products of many breeding programs around the world—they may make up more than 20%. During the wort boil, alpha acids are converted to water-soluble iso-alpha acids or isohumulones, the true bitter compounds in beer. This conversion, or isomerization, is traditionally one of the main objectives of wort boiling and the boiling time must usually be long enough (at least 45 minutes for most hop varieties) to allow isomerization to take place. That said, isomerization can take place in the absence of boiling, so long as the temperature is high enough; mechanical action, surface area of the hop material, and the contact time are critical factors as well. The unit of measurement for hop bittering potential is the International Bitterness Unit (IBU). See INTERNATIONAL BITTERNESS UNITS (IBUS).

Alpha acids are divided into three analogues—compounds of very similar molecular structures: the desirable humulone and adhumulone and the

Postcard, c. 1920, showing workers standing next to a large sack of hops on a farm in Kent, England. A hop press mechanically packed the hops into these sacks, known as "pockets." PIKE MICROBREWERY MUSEUM, SEATTLE, WA

undesirable cohumulone. Cohumulone may make up anywhere between roughly from 15% to 50% of a hop's total alpha acid content, depending on variety. It can also vary greatly from one growing year to the next in the same variety. High cohumulone levels in hops tend to result in lower foam stability and a harsher, often unpleasant bitterness. They are also usually associated with poor aroma profiles. Hops are often marketed, in part, based on their cohumulone content.

As the alpha acids were discovered to actually be three related molecules, the same discovery was made for beta acids, which also come in three analogs: lupulone, colupulone, and adlupulone. The character of a hop, in terms of its bittering and aroma potential, is largely determined by its ratio of alpha to beta acids. The most sought-after aroma varieties tend to have a ratio close to 1:1. Most cultivated hop varieties, however, have a ratio closer to 2:1. Hops with much higher alpha-to-beta ratio are, of course, the modern superalpha varieties. Prior to the 1950s, alpha and beta acids were also called soft resins by virtue of their solubility in hexane, a solvent. Techniques were not developed to separate alpha acids into the three analogues until much later. In early accounts, therefore, all alpha acids were simply referred to as "humulone" and all beta acids as "lupulone." Lupulone provides potent antimicrobial properties and is active against Gram-negative bacteria such as Staphylococcus and Clostridium.

Essential oils in hops are responsible for the distinct hop aroma. Some fresh hops smell very citrusy, such as Cascade, which has a grapefruit–piney bouquet, whereas others, such as Strisselspalt, have a more floral bouquet. The main essential oils in hops are humulene, which has a woody, balsamic aroma; carophyllene, which has a black-pepper, spicy aroma; myrcene, which has a geranium-like, floral aroma; and farnesene, which has a gardenia-like floral aroma. Of these, farnesene is often either completely absent or represented in only miniscule quantities. Other essential oils, such as linalool with its citrus-like bergamot aroma, although present in only tiny amounts, may have a disproportionately high impact on the overall aroma of certain hop varieties.

Hop researchers have identified roughly 300 compounds that are likely contributors to hop aroma profiles. Some of these are pleasant to humans,

Components of Essential Oils in Hop Lupulin

Aroma descriptor		*Essential oil/odorant*
Fruity	Citrus, bergamot	Linalool
	Citrus, balsamic	Limonene
	Citrus	Octanal
	Citrus, soapy	Nonanal
	Pineapple	Ethyl 2-methylpropanoate
	Pineapple	(3E,5Z)-Undeca-1,3,5-triene
	Pineapple	(3E,5Z,9E)-Undeca-1,3,5,9-tetraene
	Apple-like	(+/−)-Ethyl 2-methylbutanoate
	Raspberry	4-(4-Hydroxyphenyl)-2-butanone
	Black currant	4-Methyl-4-sulfanylpentan-2-one
	Fruity	Methyl 2-methylbutanoate
	Fruity	Ethyl 2-methylbutanoate
Floral	Gardenia	Farnesene
	Geranium leaf	Myrcene
	Geranium leaf	(5Z)-Octa-1,5-dien-3-one
	Rose	Geraniol
	Minty	2-Phenylethyl 3-methylbutanoate
Spicy	Black pepper	Carophyllene
	Aniseed, sweet	Anethole
	Soup seasoning	3-Hydroxy-4,5-dimethyl-2(5H)-furanone(sotolone)
Vegetative	Grassy	(3Z)-Hex-3-enal
	Muscat-like, green	(Z)-3-hexen-1-ol
	Bell pepper	2-Isopropyl-3-methoxypyrazine
	Cucumber	(2E,6Z)-Nona-2,6-dienal
	Cooked potato	3-(Methylsulfanyl)-propanal
Nutty	Almond, roasted	3-Methyl-2-butene-1-thiol
Caramelized	Honey	Phenylacetaldehyde
	Honey	Phenylacetic acid
	Sweet, honey	trans-Cinnamaldehyde
	Sweet	3-Hydroxy-2-methyl-4-pyrone
Woody	Balsamic	α-Humulene
	Vanilla	Vanillin
Earthy	Mushroom	Oct-1-en-3-one
	Mushroom, balsamic	Germacrene
Chemical	Cabbage	Dimethyltrisulfane
	Catty, thiol-like	3-Mercaptohexan-1-ol
	Rancid, cheesy	Butanoic acid
	Rancid, sweaty	(Z)-3-Hexenoic acid
Microbiological	Cheesy	3-Methylbutanoic acid
	Cheesy	Pentanoic acid
	Fatty	(2E,4E)-Nona-2,4-dienal

Source: Various studies conducted at Weihenstephan in Germany and the Kyoto University in Japan.
See WEIHENSTEPHAN.

imparting floral, fruity, and spicy notes, whereas others contribute off-aromas that, when present in excess, can negatively impact beer aromatics.

Until well into the high Middle Ages, before hops had become the beer flavoring of choice just about everywhere, brewers used a large variety of herbs, known as gruit in medieval Europe, as well as strange items such as oxen gall, soot, bark, and mushrooms to spice their beers and sometimes to cover up off-flavors. See GRUIT. The presence of hops can be document virtually everywhere where humans had migrated, but it took thousands of years for hops to make the leap from the wild into the brew kettle. The first written description of a hop garden comes from Hallertau. It dates from 768 AD. See HALLERTAU. The first recorded use of hops in brewing dates from 822 AD when Abbot Adalhard of the Benedictine Monastery of Corbie in the Picardy, in northeastern France, made a record stating that his monks added hops to their ales. By the 11th century hopped beer was commonplace in France, and in 1268, King Louis IX issued a decree stipulating that, in his realm, only malt and hops may be used for beer making. Britain, by contrast, seems to have resisted the joys of the hop for a few more centuries, although some early hops must have made it across the Channel, as is evidenced by the remains of a boat holding a cargo of hops and found abandoned in Gravaney, Kent. Carbon-dating of the timbers placed that boat into the 870s AD. For the most part, however, the English considered the hop plant an "unwholesome weed that promoted melancholy." Kings Henry VI and Henry VIII both banned the use of hops in English ales altogether during their reigns. The latter, in the 1530s, justified his antihop stance by declaring the hop an aphrodisiac that would drive his subjects to sinful behavior. Meanwhile, brewers on the Continent moved in exactly the opposite direction, perfecting the use of hops in their kettles. In many places, local authorities even made brewers take an oath that they would flavor their brews with nothing but hops. By the 14th century, a flourishing hop market had developed in Nuremberg, Bavaria, where the hop became known as "green gold," a precious commodity and a source of great wealth for growers and traders alike. By 1516, the Bavarian Duke Wilhelm IV put forth the seminal Bavarian Beer Purity Law, which stipulated that brewers in the Duke's realm may use only three ingredients in beer-making, barley, water, and hops. See REINHEITSGEBOT.

As hops won out over gruit in most parts of the Continent, it became more and more difficult to keep it out of English ales. In fact, a 1604 English statute laments that "of late great fraudes and deceits are generally practised and used by foreiners merchants strangers and others in foreine parts beyond the seas, in the false packing of foreine hoppes and [the hops are] sold with leaves, stalkes, powder, sand, strawe, and with loggets of wood, drosse, and other soyle for the increase of the waight thereof, to the inriching of themselves by deceit." These "great fraudes and deceits" apparently caused England an annual revenue loss amounting to the then-stately sum of 20,000 pounds.

In North America, the early settlers found wild hops, which are native to the New World, but they preferred to brew with cultivated varieties that they had known back home, in the Old World, which they either imported or grew themselves from imported rhizomes. See AMERICAN HOPS, HISTORY. Eventually, as American hop breeding programs were established in the late 1800s, European cultivars hybridized to indigenous native American hop plants started to make their appearance. One such variety is Cluster, a hop believed to be a hybrid between English Cluster and a native American male hop plant. See CLUSTER (HOP).

Hop cultivation takes advantage of the plants' tendency to wind around any support and to produce a large amount of vegetation in a growing season. Early hop yards in upstate New York, in the 1800s, were circular groups of plants growing up on supports that may have been made of hemp twine toward a central pole. Modern hop yards, by contrast, are laid out in a pole-and-cable grid pattern. The poles are placed in the ground at the grid intersections, with the cable connecting the pole tops in all directions. At the beginning of every growing season, V-shape bine supports are strung from the ground to the upper supports, which allow the hop plants to climb skyward. Judicious pruning to just a few bines per plant and careful training of the shoots around the twine help to maximize yields and keep insects and pathogens in check.

Hops are susceptible to many pests, such as downy mildew (Pseudoperonospora humuli) and powdery mildew (Podosphaera macularis formerly called Sphaerotheca humuli). It is now known that resistance to powdery mildew is genetically determined, which allows breeders to select for the chromosomes with that trait. Aphids and spider mites, too, are a perennial problem in hop yards. These are usually controlled with judicious pesticide applications, good agronomic practices, and biocontrol through predatory insects. Finally, there are viruses, such as hop mosaic virus, that can cause severe crop loss and stunting in some varieties. This virus is spread by aphids and is nearly impossible to eradicate. Australia and New Zealand, because of their physical isolation from other landmasses, have entirely avoided many hop pests and diseases and are therefore havens of organic hop production.

The future of hops in beer seems to be assured, but in a bifurcated trajectory. Whereas the consumption of beer—especially of relatively low-hopped beer with IBU values just above the taste threshold—is rising spectacularly in many markets in Asia, Latin America, and Africa, beer consumption in traditional markets has been—and is expected to continue to be—stagnant or declining. In many of these mature markets, however, however, consumer preferences for aggressively bittered brews—some with IBU values at the solubility threshold of alpha acids in wort—and for beers with elaborate and complex aromas are on the rise. For hop breeder, growers, and traders these two seemingly conflicting trends mean that the market push for ever higher superalpha varieties, as well as the market push for ever more interesting aroma varieties, is likely to continue. The superalpha hops will satisfy the brewing industry's demand for generic bittering cultivated under the most economical conditions for a growth market in minimally hopped mass-market beers. The diversification of disease-resistant but much lower-yielding aroma varieties, by contrast, will cater to the high-value market for sophisticated specialty beers. As the flavor and aroma of hops continue to bedazzle craft brewers worldwide, we may now be seeing, after more than 1,200 years of brewing with hops, the "hoppiest" beers the world has ever seen.

Hop Growers Convention. *Proceedings of the Scientific Commission. 2005.* http://www.lfltest.bayern.de/ipz/hopfen/10585/sc05-proceedings-internet.pdf/ (accessed November 1, 2010).

Irwin, A. J., C. R. Murray, and T. D. Thompson. An investigation of the relationships between hopping rate, time of boil, and individual alpha-acid utilization. *American Society of Brewing Chemists* 43 (1985): 145–52.

Kishimoto, T. *Hop-derived odorants contributing to the aroma characteristics of beer.* Ph.D. Dissertation. Kyoto University, Kyoto, Japan, 2008.

Kneen, Rebecca. *Small scale and organic hop production.* http://www.crannogales.com/HopsManual.pdf/ (accessed June 1, 2008).

Nickerson, G. B., P. A. Williams, and A. Haunold. Varietal differences in the proportions of cohumulone, adhumulone, and humulone in hops. *Journal of the Institute of Brewing* 44 (1986): 91–4.

Peacock, V. A., M. L. Deinzer, S. T. Likens, G. B. Nickerson, and L. A. McGill. Floral hop aroma in beer. *Journal of Agricultural and Food Chemistry* 29 (1981): 1265–69.

Steinhaus, M., W. Wilhelm, and P. Schieberle. Comparison of the most odour-active volatiles in different hop varieties by application of a comparative aroma extract dilution analysis. *European Food Research and Technology* 226 (2007): 45–55.

Tomlan, M. A. *Tinged with gold. Hop culture in the United States.* Athens, GA: University of Georgia Press, 1992.

Verzele, M., and D. De Keukeleire. *Chemistry and analysis of hop and beer bitter acids.* Amsterdam: Elsevier Science Publishing Co, 1991.

Victoria Carollo Blake

hop seal (Hopfensiegel) denotes the right of a hop-growing locale in Germany to "seal" its hops, thereby warranting the authenticity of the packaged product. It is a privilege granted by the individual German states and it is strictly regulated. This seal placed on the package assures that the hops within are of the correct type, were produced in the designated area, and were grown and processed in accordance with standardized practices. The custom started first in areas that were able to command a premium price based on the perceived quality advantages of their hop terroir. It was intended to convey a sort of *grand cru* status and prevent fraudulent traders from selling hops under one district name while actually sourcing them from elsewhere. In 1538, the Prince-Bishop of Eichstätt, Bishop Phillip von Pappenheim, granted the world's first hop seal to the Spalt district. In the following years, other districts around Nuremburg were granted the right to seal their hops too, but the Spalt district's seal is the only one in the bishop's original area to have survived to this day. See SPALT HOP REGION. In the mid-1500s many small areas in Bohemia, in the present-day Czech Republic, were also granted the right to a hop seal by local officials. Then, in 1834,

Wolnzach was the first district in the Hallertauer region to be granted the right to use a Hopfensiegel. Many others soon followed. Today, the traditional 13 sealing districts constitute the Hallertau, along with 2 others. In 1992, the Jura region, just on the other side of the Danube River, was added to the Hallertauer region, mostly for administrative reasons. It is now the sealing district of Altmannstein. In 2004, the long-time independent Hersbrucker region near Nuremburg became also part of the Hallertau.

See also HALLERTAU HOP REGION.

Val Peacock

The **hop shortage (aroma varieties)** in 2007 and 2008 hit craft brewers particularly strongly, especially where aroma varieties were concerned. Not only were many small brewers caught without contracts guaranteeing supplies but also growers transferred acreage to more reliably lucrative bittering varieties and in some cases to non-hop crops altogether. The result was drastically higher hop prices for many craft brewers and dramatically reduced availability for the most popular and widely used varieties. For example, within a matter of weeks, prices for Cascade hops on the spot market (non-contracted) increased up to 500%. Supplies long taken for granted were in some cases quickly exhausted, with unprepared brewers literally reduced to begging for the overstock and charitable consideration of their colleagues.

The crisis created both heroes and villains. Some large craft breweries, no doubt more accustomed to the considered acquisition of raw materials than many of their less prepared brethren, offered their oversupply for at-cost sale to those in need. Hop brokers were generally regarded with suspicion as prices skyrocketed and panicked small brewers were pressed into multiyear contracts. Craft brewers traded hops furiously with each other, trying to get their hands on the varieties of hops that had made their beers popular. Many were forced to alter their recipes as supplies dwindled. Craft brewers started to ruefully joke that the next big craft beer style would be mild, referring to the small amount of hops necessary to brew it.

In the years immediately following, growers compensated to some extent by planting fashionable varieties such as Amarillo, Centennial, Simcoe, Chinook, and Citra. A hop glut of sorts soon ensued, fostering further resentments by brewers bound to pay the high prices for which they had contracted during the previous panic; "spot" or non-contracted prices were now often lower. Cultivation of some varieties was increased, only to be pulled back once more in 2010 as high yields and cautiousness by brewers resulted in depressed prices once more. As the market share of craft beer increases and weary growers scramble to react to the realities of their markets, it is anticipated that despite a perception of plenty, a gap is widening once more between supply and demand. Mass-market brewers, who remain the growers' top clients, are looking largely for hop bitterness. The craft brewer, caught in the middle, is looking for lots of hop flavor and aroma as well, but may have increasing difficulty finding them.

Another factor affecting the cultivation, availability, and pricing of both bittering and aroma varieties is the consolidation of the world's largest brewers, particularly in North America. InBev's absorption of Anheuser-Busch and the consolidation of Molson, Miller, and Coors have fostered efficiencies in hop usage and leanness of inventory that have brought about abrupt changes in demand for specific varieties, such as Willamette. Both brewers and growers have suffered from chaotic fluctuations of pricing and cultivation. As stores are exhausted, even varieties considered safe bets by growers may be undercultivated in the future.

For the previous 20 years, a longer period than the careers of most craft brewers, aroma hops seemed as easily available to them as most spices would be to a chef; a quick phone call and the desired hops would be at the brewery within days. Contracts seemed superfluous, and the storm of market forces never rattled the windows of the average craft brewer. As of 2011, those days appear to be over. As craft brewing grows and mass-market brewers seeking to emulate the hoppier flavors of craft beers and aroma varieties suddenly become internationally popular, craft brewers will need to pay very close attention to the realities of a world hop market in which they remain small, if growing, players.

Dick Cantwell and Val Peacock

Hopunion LLC is a specialty hop producer that provides hops primarily to craft brewers. It is owned by six families of hop growers in both Oregon and Washington. It maintains an office in Yakima, Washington, and has six cold storage warehouses and a pelletizing operation. See HOPS.

Hopunion grows its own hops and also processes and stores them. In addition to their own hops—over 30 American hop varieties—they also source hop varieties from the Czech Republic, Germany, New Zealand, the UK, and other regions. The majority of their hops are pelletized, but they also offer whole hops, hop extract, and hop oils. Hopunion also publishes, along with Cargill and White Labs, the *Craft Beer Quarterly*, an industry newsletter.

The company's roots go back to around 1789 when a hop business was founded in Nuremberg, Germany. That international company eventually opened offices around the world, doing business wherever hops were grown. In the United States, their company, Sunnyhops, Inc, purchased the American-owned Western Hop Company in 1986. The two companies were merged together to form Hopunion USA.

The International Hopunion company was acquired by the Baarth Company (today known as the Baarth-Haas Group) in 1999, but 2 years later, in the summer of 2001, general manager Ralph Olson worked with six hop growers from Oregon and Washington to purchase the company outright, renaming it Hopunion CBS, LLC.

Five years later, in August of 2006, Hopunion entered into a strategic partnership with Yakima Chief's craft brewing division and the company's name was altered again, this time to its current name: Hopunion LLC. Changes to the company were initiated after a highly contentious shortage of hops on the spot market in 2007 and 2008.

The two faces of Hopunion, often referred to as Ralph and Ralph, are director of sales Ralph Woodall and GM/Owner Ralph Olson. As of 2011 Woodall's position remains unchanged, but Olson began a 3-year retirement plan in 2008 where over that time his interest in the company will be sold and his responsibilities reduced along a timetable until August 2011, when he will no longer be officially affiliated. During this transition, Don Bryant, a veteran of the alcohol beverage industry, was hired as Olson's replacement in 2008.

See also HOP SHORTAGE (AROMA VARIETIES).

Jay R. Brooks

hop utilization is a calculation used by brewers to gauge the effectiveness of conversion of hop alpha acids into iso-alpha acids during the brewing process. It is focused solely on bitterness yields. Specifically, it refers to the mass of iso-alpha acids measured in finished beer (or in wort if the determination is desired only for wort production) relative to the mass of alpha acids added to the brew kettle. It is important to use total hop acid measurements in beer via high-performance liquid chromatography for this calculation because bitterness unit measurements also include non-iso-alpha acid contributions and are therefore not an accurate quantifier for hop iso-alpha acids. See INTERNATIONAL BITTERNESS UNITS. Hop utilization is typically expressed as a percentage; high values are in the range of 30%–50%, although values as low as 5% are not uncommon, particularly when brewers use late hopping techniques. See LATE HOPPING. Hop utilization is affected by several factors such as the form of the hops used (whole, pellets, pellet type, extracts, isomerized kettle extracts, etc.), the age of the hops, the timing of their addition to the kettle, the nature and length of the wort boil, and the mechanics of downstream processes (nature of fermentation, filtration, and packaging). The key phenomena controlling hop utilization are the dissolution of hop acids into wort, isomerization to iso-alpha acids, and the subsequent removal of some of these compounds from the system. The form of the hops affects dissolution; thus, hop extracts tend to give higher utilization values than do pellets, which, in turn, have higher utilization values than do whole hops. Older hops will yield lower utilization values because, as hops age, the oxidation of alpha acids reduces the amount of bitter precursors in the hops, yet brewers typically work, somewhat incorrectly, with harvest-date hop acid analytical data. The longer hops are boiled, the greater the conversion to iso-alpha acids and hence the greater the utilization. Higher boiling temperatures also increase isomerization rates and thus utilization; conversely, low-temperature boils, common at high altitude, will result in lower utilization. Wort strength is inversely related to hop utilizations; that is, high gravity wort tends to yield lower hop utilization values. This phenomenon is most likely the result of the increased trub formation during high-gravity brewing and its resulting influence on the removal of both alpha acids and iso-alpha acids at the end of the boil. Hop additions that are made late in the boil, in a hop back, or to fermented beer show lower ratios of iso-alpha acid vs. the original alpha acid present since there is insufficient time for isomerization. Consequently, the apparent hop utilization from these additions, or the overall hopping scheme's utilization, will be very low. However, since these late additions are meant largely for aroma contributions, not for bitterness, the low hop utilization values are not necessarily problematic for the brewer, who may consider those hops well used. It should also be noted that many craft brewers typically add the bulk of their hops to the kettle late in the boil, or even at the whirlpool stage, especially for hop-forward beer styles such as pale ale and IPA. Though the utilization may be low, such late additions may still represent a large proportion of the iso-alpha-acid in the finished wort. Even though these hops are not boiled (or not for long), they typically have a long hot contact time with the hops, and some isomerization does occur. Also, iso-alpha-acids are very surface active, and the processes downstream from wort boiling can influence residual iso-alpha-acids levels. For instance, over-foaming fermenters or foam cropping from open fermenters can reduce iso-alpha acids in the finished beer and thereby reduce apparent utilization. The use of preisomerized extracts (known in the hop industry as advanced hop products) can significantly increase utilization because they are already fully isomerized before they arrive at the brewery. They are, therefore, typically added far downstream in the brewing process. In these instances, it is not uncommon to achieve utilization in excess of 90%.

See also BITTERING POTENTIAL (OF HOPS) and ISO-ALPHA ACIDS.

Thomas Shellhammer

Hordein is the storage protein of barley. Cereal proteins have been classified into four major categories based upon their solubility in various solvents. The alcohol-soluble fraction in cereals is composed of storage proteins called prolamines. The prolamines of barley are called hordeins. Hordeins account for approximately 35%–50% of the total seed protein. They are important in brewing for several reasons.

Hordein proteins are rich in the amino acids glutamate and proline, both of which are important to yeast nutrition. Glutamate (glutamic acid) is the amino acid most preferred by yeast and proline is not absorbed at all. As a result, finished beer has higher levels of proline than of any other amino acid.

Another reason is that hordeins such as wheat prolamines (gliadins) are primarily responsible for triggering the autoimmune response that characterizes celiac disease. The amino acid sequences responsible for celiac disease are present in hordeins as well. Wheat beers have been shown to have significantly higher prolamine levels than beers made from only barley or adjunct beers made using corn or rice.

Finally, hordeins are also thought to play a role in beer foaming and haze formation. The proteins have been shown to complex with polyphenolic compounds present in barley and hops, precipitating and resulting in haze. Hordeins, along with other proteins, have been revealed to be important in the favorable formation of beer foam.

Hordein proteins play both positive and negative roles in brewing.

See also PROTEINS.

Scott E. Heisel

hot break comprises proteins and polyphenols that coagulate during the wort boil, eventually clumping together in large enough flocs (chunks) to break out of solution and fall to the bottom of the kettle. The hot break usually occurs anywhere from 5 to 30 min after a vigorous boil has begun. Some brewers add a small amount of hops, as little as 10% of the total hop charge, to the boil at this time. This hop addition helps to precipitate the initial hot break, but it also helps suppress foaming and boilovers in the kettle. A more effective method involves adding some form of carageenan, a seaweed derivative sometimes called Irish moss, to the boil. The addition significantly enhances the clumping action of proteins and polyphenols, facilitating their removal. These "kettle finings" are most often added 10 to 20 min before the end of the boil. Once the boil is complete, brewers can use a whirlpool vessel to separate the hot break material (now, together with any hop fragments, known as trub) from the wort before transfer to the fermentation tank. It is important for whirlpooling to proceed gently because vigorous wort pumping can break up the hot break flocs, making them more difficult to remove. See WHIRLPOOL. In traditional systems using whole hop flowers, the hot break is normally removed by drawing the wort through a bed of hops, either at the bottom of the kettle or in a separate hop back vessel. The hop bed traps the flocs of trub, allowing the brewer to send clear wort to the fermenter. See HOP BACK.

A good hot break is important for the quality of the finished beer. Excess proteins and polyphenols remaining in the wort can cause hazes and other stability problems. Among the polyphenols removed during the hot break are tannins, which, if left in the wort, can lead to both astringency on the palate and unwanted haze formation.

See also KETTLE FININGS and TRUB.

Palmer, John J. *How to brew*. Boulder, CO: Brewers Publications, 2006.

Rehberger, Arthur J., and Gary E. Luther. "Wort boiling." In *The practical brewer*, 3rd ed. St. Paul, MN: Master Brewers Association of the Americas, 1999.

Damien Malfara

hot liquor is heated brewing water, "liquor" being the traditional name given to the water that will later become beer in the brewing process. All other water used in the brewery, such as water used for cleaning, is simply called "water." The term "hot liquor" is widely used in the UK and the United States. Generally hot liquor is used as "foundation liquor" preparing the mash tun for malt, "strike liquor" for mixing with the malt, and "sparge liquor" to sparge over the mash or lauter bed. Breweries using corn or rice would also mix hot liquor with these grains in the cereal cooker. Hot liquor is heated to between 110°F and 170°F for mixing with malt to form the mash and as high as 180°F for sparging. The hot liquor resides in the hot liquor tank until needed in the mash tun, lauter tun, or cereal cooker.

Filtering the incoming liquor to remove contaminants and chlorine is common. Less common are procedures to settle out unwanted contaminants such as silt or iron. Sometimes minerals are added, especially gypsum, to harden the liquor. See BURTONIZATION. The mineral constituents of the hot liquor greatly influence the qualities of the resulting beer. The mineral content will affect the beer flavor and sometimes hard water needs to be softened to become hot liquor that will produce beer with acceptable flavors. Beyond the simple taste desirability lies the need for the water to provide sufficient minerals for brewing chemistry and yeast nutrition.

See also WATER.

Kunze, Wolfgang. *Technology brewing and malting*, 7th ed. Berlin: VLB Berlin, 1996.

Brian Hunt

hot-side aeration (HSA) is the introduction of oxygen in the form of air into hot wort anywhere in the brewing process prior to fermentation. Oxygen is not desired in hot wort because it can combine with lipids, melanoidins, tannins, and other elements to produce undesirable compounds, which can stay in the wort through fermentation, ending up in the finished beer and promoting staling. See LIPIDS, MELANOIDINS, STALING, and TANNINS. Whereas oxidized lipids can make beer taste slightly rancid and give it a pronounced flavor of wet cardboard, oxidized melanoidins can cause finished beer to take on sherry-like flavors (the latter can be desirable in deliberately aged beer, but not in fresh beer). Other oxidation products may slowly break down in the beer, freeing oxygen to transform alcohol into sweetish-tasting aldehydes, giving flavors of toffee and almond. Golden worts will tend to be darkened. Paradoxically, although oxygen in hot wort is detrimental to beer quality, oxygen in cold wort at the beginning of fermentation is essential for the yeast's aerobic growth phase. See AERATION. Fortunately, there is no "cold-side" aeration because of two opposing correlations: The oxidation rate increases with temperature, but the ability of a solution to dissolve oxygen decreases with temperature. This means that very hot wort does not contain enough oxygen for oxidation, whereas oxygen-rich wort at the beginning of fermentation is too cold to permit oxidation. Thus, HSA is a problem only in a temperature band somewhere below the kettle boil and above the heat-exchange temperature. The exact temperature interval in which HSA is a potential problem, however, is a topic of much debate among brewers. But most experts agree that the mash temperature is within the danger zone. Excessive stirring of the mash, therefore, too much splashing during recirculation, and any air pickup during the mash transfer from the mash tun to the lauter tun are among the most likely vectors, along with long hot stands for wort before it is sent to fermentation. All this concern about HSA has led to some fairly extreme measures, such as mash mixing in closed vessels that have been purged of air. However, some traditional breweries, from England to the Czech Republic, do not see hot-side aeration as a quality problem at all. Some aldehydes can be pleasant in certain British ales, and several prominent Czech brewers, using open grants to collect wort from the lauter tun, see the darkened beer color and flavor developments as positive attributes in their beers.

See also GRANT.

Apex Publishers. *The brewer's handbook: Glossary.* http://www.beer-brewing.com/beer-brewing/about_this_title/glossary/beer_brewing_a.htm/ (accessed February 1, 2011).
Bible, C. "When Good Beer Goes Bad." http://www.brewsnews.com.au/2010/02/when-good-beer-goes-bad/ (accessed April 26, 2011).
Miller, D. "The Troubleshooter." http://www.brewingtechniques.com/library/backissues/issue1.4/miller.html/ (accessed April 26, 2011).

Horst Dornbusch

hot water extract, often referred to as HWE, is an analytical measure derived on a laboratory scale of the quantity of dissolved solids derived from malt or other materials used in the brewhouse. Hot water extract analysis is used to measure the brewing value of different malts or adjuncts and can be used to compare cereal varieties and malting processes. See ADJUNCTS. It is used by brewers to compare malts and maltsters and as a measure to ensure malt delivered to a brewery is within a defined specification. Measurement of hot water extract is obtained by measuring the specific gravity of wort derived from a fixed weight of malt (or other material) that is ground in a specified manner at a fixed temperature for a specific time period. This process broadly mimics the mashing process in a brewery. See MASHING. The wort is filtered, the specific gravity measured, and the hot water extract of the sample calculated.

The methods for measuring hot water extract are specifically laid down by the three main brewing institutions, the Institute of Brewing and Distilling in the UK (IOB), the European Brewing Convention (EBC), and the American Society of Brewing Chemists (ASBC). Each method reflects the brewing methods predominantly used in their area, for example, the IOB analysis involves mixing and holding the malt at 65.5°C, reflecting infusion mashing of ale-style beers. The EBC, sometimes called "congress" mash, involves mashing at 45°C and increasing the temperature to 70°C, reflecting the process used in lager brewing. See CONGRESS MASH. The system used by the ASBC is similar to the EBC method. Hot water extract is quoted in a number of ways, for example, liter degrees per kilogram of malt (e.g., 304l deg/kg); in Europe, the practice is to express the extract as a percentage of the dry weight of malt (e.g., 82%).

Paul KA Buttrick

Huangjiu

See CHINA.

hulupones are oxidation products of hop beta acids. Beta acids, lupulones, make up part of the soft resins in hops. They have very low solubility in wort (~1 part per million); thus, only trace amounts survive the brewing process and end up in finished beer. Beta acids are fairly reactive with oxygen and can oxidize to a set of compounds called hulupones, each of which is derived from its beta acid analogue; for instance, cohulupulone comes from colupulone. Because they are not bitter and are only marginally soluble, beta acids do not contribute to beer flavor. However, hulupones are bitter and can contribute substantially to the final flavor of beer. Anecdotal claims suggest that hulupones have an unpleasant bitterness quality. Hulupones are relatively stable once formed and can survive all stages of the brewing process. They can be formed via the oxidative degradation of hops during storage. As hops oxidize, the bitterness that comes from iso-alpha acids diminishes because their precursors, alpha acids, are lost as a result of oxidation, but this is somewhat offset by the presence of bitterness from the hulupones. The ratio of alpha acids to beta acids ultimately dictates the degree to which the bitterness potential will diminish as hops oxidize. Higher levels of beta acids in the raw hops will result in a slower decline of bittering power as hops degrade oxidatively because of the resultant higher levels of hulupones. Hulupones can also be formed during wort boiling because the high temperatures accelerate the reactivity of beta acids. Alternatively, hulupones can form on trub following spent hops separation from boiled wort where the environment is hot and there is plenty of available oxygen. Bitterness contributions can be substantial in the latter case if the trub pile is added to a subsequent batch of beer, as is the case in some breweries.

See also COLUPULONE.

Thomas Shellhammer

humulene is a component of the hydrocarbon fraction of hop oil. It is found with other essential oils in the lupulin gland, where it is formed in the final stages of hop cone maturation. As the hop cone ripens, trace amounts of oxygenated compounds of the essential oil appear first. Caryophyllene and humulene follow next, and finally, myrcene. The ratio of humulene to caryophyllene varies from one hop variety to another, but many brewers consider a good aroma to be one that has a ratio of greater than 3:1. Such hops tend to be floral, herbal, and spicy in character. Some varieties, such as Hallertauer Mittelfrüh and U.K. Kent Golding, may contain 30% or more of their essential oils in humulene, but, because humulene is highly volatile and hydrophobic, only trace quantities of it may actually reach the final beer. Oxidation products of humulene, on the other hand, especially humulene mono- and di-epoxides, can impart significant amounts of aroma to beer. Humulene epoxide III is one of the most potent flavor compounds in Hallertauer Mittelfrüh, for instance, a variety that is high in humulene but relatively low in total oils. Allowing hops that are high in humulene to age in bales for several weeks prior to pelletizing will result in greater amounts of humulene epoxides, as well as other hop oil oxidation products, which some brewers believe can significantly increase the hops's aroma potential.

Thomas Shellhammer

humulone is one of five alpha acid analogues in hop resin, the others being adhumulone, cohumulone, prehumulone, and posthumulone. These analogues differ only slightly from each other in their molecular structures, and together they serve as precursors to iso-alpha acids, which are the predominant contributors of bitterness in beer. Humulone and cohumulone levels vary across varieties, between roughly 20% and 50% of total alpha acids. Adhumulone levels tend to be fairly constant across varieties, at about 10% to 15% of alpha acids. Pre- and posthumulone, on the other hand, play only minor roles. When hops oxidize, alpha acids, including humulone, change their molecular makeup and produce isobutryic acid, which has a distinctly rancid, sour, cheesy odor.

See also ADHUMULONE, COHUMULONE, and LUPULONE.

Thomas Shellhammer

Hürlimann Brewery was a Zurich, Switzerland-based brewery founded in 1836. The brewery was of little note or importance, however, until it was passed down to Albert Hürlimann, a scientist and yeast specialist. Born in 1857, Albert had worked in several other breweries and took a particular interest in the yeasts used for production. By 1914, he expanded the Hürlimann Brewery to include a dozen breweries. The success of the brewery was primarily the result of Albert's discovery of a strain of lager yeast that has a significantly higher resistance to alcohol than other brewing yeasts. Dubbed the Hürlimann strain, this yeast allowed the brewery to develop more potent beers in the years to come, including its signature beer, Samichlaus (Santa Claus), first brewed in 1979. The beer boasted a then-distinctive 14% alcohol by volume—at one time it was the strongest beer in the world. Hürlimann spent over 20 years working to perfect this powerfully malty doppelbock, which was brewed once a year on December 6, St. Nicholas' Day. In addition to its beer, the brewery sold strains of yeast commercially to other breweries.

Although Albert died in 1934, production continued and the Hürlimann Brewery remained in the Hürlimann family for five generations before ultimately merging with the Swiss company Feldschlosschen in 1996. The Hürlimann Brewery closed its doors for good in 1997, the same year in which they produced their last kegs of Samichlaus beer. In 2000, Feldschlosschen was bought by Carlsberg Group, the Danish brewing giant. Also in 2000, the original Hürlimann Samichlaus brewers teamed up with the Schloss Eggenberg brewery to produce a batch of Samichlaus beer, and today they continue to do so annually.

Carlsberg Group—Feldschlösschen Beverages Ltd. http://www.carlsberggroup.com/Company/Markets/Pages/Switzerland_Feldschloesschen.aspx (accessed December 8, 2010).

Nuclear bomb shelters and the world's strongest beers. http://www.beerhunter.com/documents/19133-001423.html (accessed December 8, 2010).

Samiclaus: A beer to be savoured. http://www.ratebeer.com/Story.asp?StoryID=16 (accessed December 8, 2010).

To do: Hurlimann Samichlaus beer dinner at Brasserie Beck. http://www.washingtonian.com/blogarticles/restaurants/bestbites/7929.html (accessed December 8, 2010).

Jonathan Horowitz

husk is the external protective envelope of cereal grains. It makes up about 10% of the seed's mass. It is composed of a number of layers of dead cells with high levels of inert cellulose, lignin, arabinoxylan, and other carbohydrate polymers. It provides a strong barrier to penetration of water and acts as a deterrent to insects that could damage the seed. Silica and antioxidant phenols are also present and provide protection against microbial attacks.

In barley, the husk is composed of three layers and is tightly attached to the underlying waxy pericarp layer, which is also inert and impervious to gas transfer. Below the pericarp is the testa with high levels of lipid material. Together these layers act to keep the barley grain inert for all practical purposes until germination. Abrasion of the husk allows penetration of water and exogenous growth hormones and hastens germination.

The husk is important in brewing because it forms the filter basis for separating solid particles from liquids as the wort is run off at the end of mashing. Cracking of the barley grain during milling should produce large husk particles that can perform the filtration function efficiently. Excessive tearing or crushing of the husk would reduce particle size and produce cloudy worts. The husk imparts flavors to malts, accounting for the tannic "crispness" of many six-row malts. In general, six-row barleys will have a greater husk-to-seed ratio, particularly when there is a notable size difference between the central and lateral kernels. Brewers generally wish to avoid the extraction of astringent tannins and haze-causing polyphenols from grain husk. As a result, they will generally keep sparging temperatures below 77.8°C (172°F) and stop the runoff from the mash when the runoff gravity drops much below 2°P. See SPARGING.

Barley husks are easily colonized by microorganisms, particularly molds such as Fusarium, which can produce mycotoxins and compounds that can induce gushing in beer. Barley grains protect themselves by producing antimicrobial compounds to act against such fungi. One of the modern barley breeding objectives is the development of more resistant varieties that minimize the potential for microbial growth while delivering improved malt quality.

Naked (hull-less) barleys have a free threshing husk, similar to that of wheat, which, if used as the only malt in the mash, will cause a highly compact grain bed that is difficult to lauter. However, advances in mash filtration technology are under development that will make greater use of hull-less malted barleys in brewing possible.

Keith Thomas

Huyghe Brewery was founded by Léon Huyghe in 1906 in Melle, Belgium. It remains the oldest active brewery near the city of Ghent. During World War I, occupying forces seeking local sources for munitions melted down Huyghe's copper brew kettles. Consequently, these large and expensive vessels had to be replaced after the war. In 1938, Brouwerij-Mouterij den Appel became SPRL Brasserie Léon Huyghe and a year later, the company expanded into a larger brewery hall, where it remains to this day. For decades, the brewery's flagship brew was a pilsner, but the brewery eventually phased this beer out, replacing it with a range of beers that might be considered more typically Belgian. Today, Huyghe is best known for its line of strong, bottle-conditioned beers under the Delirium brand with the distinctive pink elephant logo. In addition, Huyghe has acquired and revived other brands. The malty Artevelde Grand Cru was introduced in 1987, with Delirium Tremens following in 1989. A variety of robust, if sweet, fruit beers under the Floris label joined the portfolio in 1993. The success of Delirium Tremens led to the release of its darker cousin, Delirium Nocturnum. Other Huyghe brands include Kira, as well as the interesting Mogonzo, which features five exotic beers inspired by a palm wine made by the Chokwe people of Africa. Mogonzo is made only of fair-trade ingredients, including banana, coconut, quinoa, mango, and palm nut. Huyghe beers are exported to some 45 countries.

Brouwerij Huyghe. *Delirium.be.* http://www.delirium.be/Anglais/Histoire/histoire.htm (accessed June 4, 2010).
Jackson, Michael. *Great beers of Belgium*, 3rd ed. Philadelphia: Running Press, 1998.
Jackson, Michael. *Great beer guide*. London: Dorling Kindersley, 2000.
Kenning, David. *Beers of the world*. Bath, England: Parragon, 2005.

Ben Keene

hydrogen sulfide, H_2S, is a gas that has the distinctive smell of rotten eggs, which easily can overshadow the flavors of fresh malt and hops. Hydrogen sulfide is highly volatile and has a low flavor threshold, measured in parts per billion. Although high levels of hydrogen sulfide are notably offensive to the palate and nose, trace amounts are considered a traditional and accepted characteristic for a few beer styles, particularly English pale ales from Burton-on-Trent. See BURTON SNATCH. These beers have a strong bitterness and dry finish that is heightened by small amounts of hydrogen sulfide. Other beers showing evident rotten egg aromas should be considered poorly fermented and faulty.

Hydrogen sulfide is produced by the normal metabolism of yeast, whereby sulfate ions are taken into the cell and reduced for processing into the amino acids cysteine and methionine. Low nitrogen levels will limit the rate of this reaction, leaving excess hydrogen sulfide to be excreted into the beer. Yeast stress and autolysis will likely occur in parallel, resulting in a complex profile of off-flavors. In addition, hydrogen sulfide may combine with carbonyl compounds to produce even more undesirable off-flavors such as the pungent vegetal and rubbery aromas of mercaptan. Vigorous fermentations, on the other hand, will lead to lower levels of hydrogen sulfide.

Levels of hydrogen sulfide can be controlled by ensuring that nitrogen levels are adequate during fermentation and that some oxygen is available in solution at the outset of fermentation, limiting the reducing condition that promotes hydrogen sulfide formation.

See also OFF-FLAVORS.

Keith Thomas

hydrometer is an apparatus used to measure the density or specific gravity of worts and beers. See SPECIFIC GRAVITY. It relies on buoyancy and has the great value of allowing the brewer to measure how concentrated their worts are, and thus their potential for alcohol production. Hydrometers used in brewing are termed "saccharometers" to reflect their application to sugar solutions.

In construction a saccharometer is a sealed glass tube weighed down with an amount of lead suitable to allow it to float within the density band of the relevant liquid. The tube has a narrow neck that protrudes from the liquid and allows a scale to be read at the meniscus of the liquid. This scale is calibrated to give the density in terms of percentage of sugar, degrees Plato, or specific gravity.

The saccharometer was first applied to brewing in the late 18th century and despite initial resistance soon became indispensible in determining the

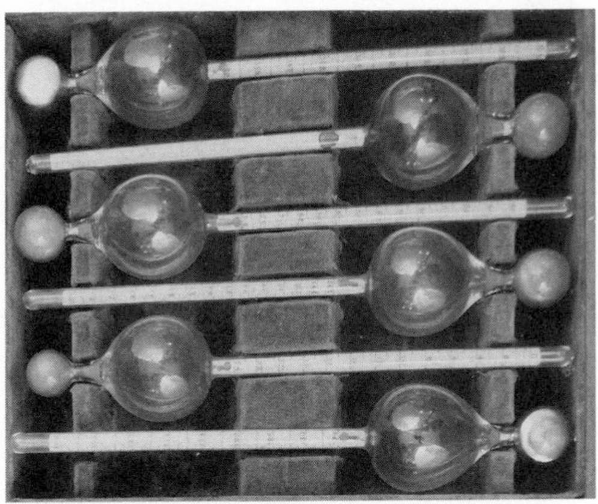

Set of hand-blown mercury hydrometers with ivory measurement rulers. English, mid-19th century. CHARLES FINKEL

strength and consistency of beers. Prior to its application the strength of worts and beers was determined by their taste or stickiness. Part of its promotion was by customs officers seeking a reliable determination of wort strength for taxation purposes.

As wort ferments, the specific gravity falls and the difference between the initial and final levels can be used to calculate the percentage of alcohol using a simple equation. The measurement of specific gravity depends critically on temperature and corrections are required if measurements are taken at a different temperature than that specified. More advanced saccharometers will contain a temperature correction scale inside the glass housing, simplifying calculation for the brewer.

Keith Thomas

ice beer is beer that has been chilled until ice crystals begin to form. These briefly became something of a fashion in the United States, Canada, the UK, and Japan in the 1990s.

The cold temperature was said to force a chill haze and other precipitation, which would then settle or be filtered out, supposedly producing brilliantly clear, clean tasting beers, slightly stronger that that which was fermented. The process is an adaption of freeze concentration, also known as freeze distillation. Water freezes at a higher temperature than ethanol does, so the ice in a lightly frozen beer will contain water, but not alcohol. If the ice is then removed, the remaining beer is concentrated. This technique can be used to make very strong beers, some of which are traditional—the German eisbock is among these. See EISBOCK.

For some years Canadian brewers had been investigating whether freeze concentration could be used to reduce the volume of a bulk beer transported over long distances. The concentrated beer would then be mixed with water and bought back to its sale strength before packaging.

Graham Stewart, who was technical director at Labatt, realized the process was not practical, but thought that the image of "ice" would appeal to Canadian drinkers, especially those who were already concentrating their beers by leaving bottles outside to freeze concentrate them at home. Both Labbatt and Molson (1993) and Labatt (1994) used variations of the technology to bring iced beers to market, beginning the so-called ice wars. These were, in fact, somewhat concentrated, as were the Japanese versions.

American brewers Miller and Budweiser followed on with their own brands—Icehouse and Bud Ice. These generally were simply chilled until they started to become slushy, but little ice was removed and the strength of the beer was raised by less than 1% alcohol by volume. The brewers claimed that this "ice technique" resulted in remarkably smoothness. In reality, the words "ice beer" were simply very appealing and gave marketers free license to send bright shards of ice flying fetchingly across the consumer's television screens. For a few years, the big American breweries brewed many millions of barrels of ice beer, but consumers eventually seem to have realized that the beer was not notably different and the fad went into decline.

Bamforth, Charles W. *Beer is proof God loves us*. Upper Saddle River, NJ: FT Press, 2010.

Hornsey, Ian S. *Brewing*. London: Royal Society of Chemistry, 1999.

Tim Hampson

Idaho (northern hop region) began as a backup site for growing Hallertauer Mittlefrueh. In the 1960s and 1970s, verticillium wilt became a serious problem in the Hallertau region of Germany, threatening the production of the area's famed Hallertauer Mittelfrueh aroma hops. Several large American brewers, who became worried about their Mittelfrueh supplies, decided to take action. See HALLERTAU and HALLERTAUER MITTELFRUEH (HOP). An Idaho hop breeder, Dr Robert Romanko; Ben Studer, the County Agent for Boundry County; and the Hop Merchant S. S. Steiner therefore formed a consortium to search for a backup site in the United States that would be suitable for growing this cultivar. They selected a site near Bonners Ferry, Idaho, which happens to be along the same latitude as the Hallertauer and has a reasonably similar climate. Brad Studer, Ben Studer's son, became the farm manager. The first Hallertauer Mittelfrueh rhizomes (root stock), imported from Germany, were planted there in 1971 and the first harvest was the following year. Coors bought all the hops the farm could produce until 1978, when Anheuser-Busch contracted for 80 acres of production. By 1987, Anheuser-Busch had taken over the farm and began to expand it. Much of the new acreage was planted with virus-free Hallertauer Mittelfrueh obtained from the U.S. Department of Agriculture, whereas the rest of the farm was planted with American Tettnanger as well as various Saaz clones. See AMERICAN TETTNANGER (HOP) and SAAZ (HOP). By 1989, the farm had grown to about 1,700 acres, and by the early 1990s, all of the earlier Hallertauer stock had been replaced. Then, in 1998, the American Tettnanger was replaced with Saaz and Hallertauer. But in the early 2000s, August Busch III, who took a personal interest in the farm, decided to return to the source for the German-derived hop. The virus-free Hallertauer, which was notably different from the original Steiner material as well as from German Hallertauer, had drifted too far. He decided to replace it with Hallertauer Mittelfrueh clone 102, sourced directly from the Hop Research Institute in Hüll, Germany. After a few years, the transition was complete and the farm produced a roughly equal amount of Saaz and Hallertauer only. During 2009 and 2010, however, after the purchase of Anheuser-Busch by InBev, hop acreage at Bonners Ferry was drastically reduced, and as of early 2011 its future remains uncertain.

See also HALLERTAU HOP REGION and VERTICILLIUM WILT.

Val Peacock

Idaho (southern hop region) yields notably different results than hop growing in the northern part of the state. See IDAHO (NORTHERN HOP REGION). In southern Idaho, hop cultivation is concentrated in the Treasure Valley, in the flood plain of the Boise River, some 65 km (40 miles) west of the state capitol of Boise. In contrast to the more moderate climate in northern Idaho, the Treasure Valley is hot and dry, similar to the Yakima Valley in Washington State. See YAKIMA VALLEY HOP REGION. The first hop yard in southern Idaho was established in 1934, a year after the end of Prohibition. Production remained modest until the end of World War II, when a shortage of hops inspired many more farmers to get into the business. Until the late 1970s and early 1980s, Cluster, Talisman, and Cascade were the dominant varieties planted in southern Idaho. Subsequently, these were largely replaced by Galena. See GALENA (HOP). When higher-yielding, high-alpha varieties began to be planted in the Yakima Valley in the 1990s, these were also found to do well in the Treasure Valley. Although some aroma hops such as Willamette and Cascade are being cultivated in the southern Idaho region as well, bittering varieties, as well as the dual-purpose Chinook, are much better suited to the hot climate. However, because summers in the Treasure Valley tend to be even hotter than in the Yakima Valley, identical varieties often yield lower alpha acid values and a bit less aroma in southern Idaho than they do in Washington State.

See also CASCADE (HOP), CHINOOK (HOP), GALENA (HOP), and WILLAMETTE (HOP).

Val Peacock

immigration (effects on brewing), the movement of people from one country and culture to another, has been a major driver of worldwide beer culture for centuries. Food and drink, like music and language, are powerful components of culture, and even when expecting a better life in another land, people take these things with them. The ancient Celts brought brewing to the British Isles when they fled the European continent ahead of advancing Germanic tribes in the second half of the 5th century AD. In 15th-century England, hopped beer was famously introduced by Flemish immigrants. The more people moved, the further their beer cultures spread.

The colonization of North America began in the mid 16th century, and brewing commenced almost immediately. As early as the 1550s, Virginia Colonist Thomas Herriott sent word home of the marvels of the new world, including a native grain—maize—that, he boasted "whereof was brued as good ale as was to be desired." Maize (corn) would feature prominently in American beer history 300 years in the future.

The Pilgrims made an emergency landing in Massachusetts, their beer so depleted the crew was fearful of insufficient supply for the return trip after unloading the colonists. Beer was part of the fabric of life in those days, a matter of survival in the minds of those early settlers. It was safe and wholesome compared with the tainted water supplies they had left behind.

Early settlers did their best to maintain their beer traditions, but it was not easy. Not all of the New World was suited to barley cultivation or fermentation, and transatlantic shipments of malt were expensive and prone to spoilage, as were casks of imported beer. Beer was easy to brew in the central colonies, but tougher in New England and the South.

French and then English colonists managed to brew beer in Canada. By 1670, the governor of New France, Jean Talon, opened a brewery in Québec City, planted hops, and gave himself a brew monopoly. Roughly 2 centuries later, in 1847, an Irish immigrant named John Labatt would found a brewery in London, Ontario, and an English immigrant, John Molson, would found one in Montreal, Québec, in 1876. Today the Molson and Labatt breweries together hold more than 90% of the Canadian beer market.

In the United States, the colonists found the local water supply surprisingly nontoxic, and rum, whiskey, and applejack became cheap and plentiful. Beer was nearly a forgotten pleasure. On an alcohol percentage basis, US per capita consumption of spirits in 1800 was probably more than 100 times that of beer. Despite the efforts of Thomas Jefferson and others to make beer the temperate beverage of choice, spirits ruled America into the mid-19th century.

Change began in the 1830s. Antiaristocracy revolts were roiling Germany, with huge numbers of people being displaced and choosing to emigrate to the New World. For these immigrants, beer was a cherished sacrament and a symbol of their hard-won freedom. The small brewery established in 1838 by Alexander Stausz and John Klein in Alexandria, Virginia, was probably the first commercial producer of lager in the United States Many others followed.

As the German immigrants fanned out to the cities and farms of the America's heartland, they took their love of lager beer with them. However, for decades it was popular mostly among German populations, and every major American city had an area called "Germantown." By 1860, lager represented one-fourth of US beer production (about 1.1 million hl of 4.5 million hl). As the German population swelled, their tippling habits and Sunday beer gardens fueled the fires of Prohibition, which had more than a small amount of anti-immigrant sentiment attached to it. Warfare between "native" (English descent) Americans and the more recently arrived Germans and Irish erupted into pitched battles in the mid 1850s, with bloody riots in Chicago, Louisville, and Cincinnati.

Despite the turmoil, lager beer proved its staying power, and in the decades after the Civil War, it became thoroughly Americanized. German immigrants with names like Pabst, Busch, and Schlitz were quick to seize on the fashion for the new "pilsner" beer and by combining Old World work ethic with the latest technology, were able to create breweries and brands on a scale the world had never seen, several of which continue as major players in the world of beer today. And German immigrants did not go exclusively to the United States. Starting in 1824, waves of German immigrants started to arrive in Brazil, and they quickly set up breweries to provide beer to the burgeoning German-speaking communities. Although German immigration spread throughout parts of South America, it was arguably most influential in Brazil, which retains large pockets of Germanic culture. In the southern town of Blumenau, the Oktoberfest draws over 1 million visitors every year, and much of the currently emerging craft brewing culture harkens back to German roots.

While the British became the dominant colonial power in the 19th century, they too spread their beer and brewing habits with them. One classic example, of course, is the India pale ale, a beer style that might not exist today had it not been for the British Raj in India between 1765 and 1857. See INDIA PALE ALE. In the 1860s, British tea planters set up breweries in then-Ceylon, off the southeastern coast of India. See SRI LANKA. The Germans, by contrast, joined the colonial quest only after the founding the Second German Empire under Bismarck in 1871, when much of the world had already been snapped up by the British and the French. But wherever the Germans were still able to go, they established breweries. In Namibia, for instance, German immigrants established four breweries in the early 1900s, now merged as the Namibia Breweries Limited. In China, Germans established the Tsing Tao brewery in 1903, now one of the largest in China. Austrians, too, left their mark on a faraway brewing culture, that of Mexico. When a complicated set of international intrigues led to the proclamation of the Habsburg Archduke Maximilian as Emperor of Mexico in 1864, Austrian brewers followed in his wake. They brought with them the Vienna lager, a beer style that is probably more popular in Mexico today than it is anywhere else. See VIENNA LAGER.

As the 19th century gave way to the 20th, the American brewing industry had become so Germanized that meetings of the Master Brewers Association of the Americas were often conducted in German. Soon World War I would stir up anti-German emotions in many countries, especially in the United States, where anti-immigrant threads in prohibitionism along with lax oversight of brewery-owned saloons and a rather nonchalant attitude by the brewers led to Prohibition in 1919. Its 14 long years had devastating effects on the brewing industry. See PROHIBITION.

Today the world's beer cultures no longer need to rely on immigrants to fertilize each other. With modern technologies and seamless international trade, brewers now can and do brew just about any beer styles anywhere and then export or license them anywhere, as well. In 2010, for instance, the world's oldest continuously operating monastery brewery, Weltenburg, founded in 1050 on the banks of the Danube in Bavaria, concluded a licensing agreement with Brazil's third largest brewery group, Grupo Petrópolis, for the brewing of Weltenburg beers near São Paulo. Likewise, craft brewers from Italy to the United Sates, from Norway to Mongolia, now brew beers from around the world, often with ingredients from around the world. In this, the modern brewer is very much like a chef, combining cultures as he or she sees fit.

Randy Mosher

immobilized yeast reactor is a device for continuous beer fermentation or processing. See CONTINUOUS FERMENTATION. In conventional batch fermentation, yeast ferments wort while it is in mobile suspension. In immobilized yeast reactors, by contrast, yeast is kept stationary, while wort passes by it. Beer can emerge from this fermentation essentially clear and yeast free. There are two common types of yeast immobilizers. In a fluidized bed reactor, porous glass beads harbor the yeast and float through the beer, whereas in a loop reactor, a fixed, porous silicon carbide (or other ceramic) cartridge contains the immobilized yeast. Because wort flows continuously past the yeast cells, the rate of fermentation is not dependent on the distribution of live yeast cells throughout the fermenter. And attenuation can be rapid, with fermentations requiring half the time they do in conventional batch processing. There are drawbacks, including an elevated level of vicinal diketones and their precursors in the finished beer. See DIACETYL and VICINAL DIKETONES. These can be reduced by raising the beer temperature to convert the precursors to diacetyl and then reprocessing the beer through the reactor again.

In the commercial world, although much research has been done, immobilized yeast reactors have not been made efficient enough to supplant normal batch fermentation. Much research, therefore, concentrates on ethanol production. However, some large breweries do use immobilized yeast reactors for fast diacetyl reduction. During the summer months, when demand is high and tank space is at a premium, some large European breweries process green beer by heating it to force diacetyl from precursors and then using the reactor to absorb the diacetyl. By this method, diacetyl reduction that would normally take weeks is achieved within hours, allowing the breweries to produce acceptable "lager" beer within 14 days from brewing. Immobilized yeast reactors can also be used to conduct partial fermentations used to make certain types of low-alcohol beers.

Horst Dornbusch

imperial is a term until recently reserved for beers specially made for the crowned heads of Europe, but now borrowed by American craft brewers and made unfortunately vague. When used to describe beer, the word "imperial" is now becoming widely used to mean "stronger than usual." The usage is derived from the venerable Russian Imperial Stout brewed in the 1700s by Henry Thrale's London brewery and later by its successors and others. Originally brewed specifically for Czarina Catherine the Great and the imperial court of Russia, this 10% alcohol by volume (ABV) stout eventually became a widely brewed beer style.

In the 1980s, the imperial stout style reemerged at the dawn of the American craft brewing movement, arguably popularized in the United States by Samuel Smith of Tadcaster, England. Although it weighed in at a decidedly "unimperial" 7% ABV, Samuel Smith's Imperial Stout beer had a deep, rich flavor and came dressed in a very stylish bottle and label. Americans were understandably smitten.

American craft brewers, seeking bigger, bolder flavors for their own beers, started to append the word "imperial" to any beer that mimicked an existing style, but boosted the alcohol level and often the hop bitterness as well. First came imperial India pale ale (IPA), followed by imperial brown ale, imperial pilsner, imperial witbier, and even imperial mild. The creativity that went into the beers themselves seemingly abandoned the brewers when it came to naming the new styles. Any beer style that has been given a dose of steroids is now said to have been "imperialized," a term that brings to mind the sudden attainment of superpowers by a comic book hero. The term "double," as in double IPA, is used similarly. Should the brewer feel that imperializing is insufficient, a strong brown ale may become double imperial brown ale, a beer that should certainly vanquish all comers.

Although many of these beers are well made and the prefix "imperial" amuses some craft brewers and beer aficionados, the general public can be forgiven for feeling somewhat confused. A beer that would have been called a hellesbock 20 years ago has suddenly become an "imperial pilsner," even though the beer in question has no imperial connections and is decidedly not a pilsner. One is reminded of Gallo Hearty Burgundy in the half-gallon jug. According to common beer competition rules, imperial IPA starts at 7.5% ABV, scarcely stronger than regular IPA was traditionally. Although some decry the possible ruination of a useful beer style nomenclature, the horse has clearly left the barn. The consumer should therefore not necessarily expect the best qualities of original beer styles in those that have been imperialized. At best, one can hope for some echo of an established beer style, with some of its positive characteristics boosted along with the alcohol.

See also CATHERINE THE GREAT, IMPERIAL STOUT, INDIA PALE ALE, and SAMUEL SMITH'S OLD BREWERY.

Garrett Oliver

imperial stout, among the richest and strongest of beer styles, can also claim to be a history lesson in a bottle. Imperial stout was originally brewed by the major porter brewers in London as an "extra stout" porter for export to the Baltic countries and Russia from the late 18th century onward. It gained its title as a drink supplied to the Russian imperial court of Czarina Catherine the Great. The artist Joseph Farington wrote in his diary in 1796, "I drank some porter Mr. Lindoe had from Thrale's brewhouse. He said it was specially brewed for the Empress of Russia."

Thrale's Anchor Brewery in Southwark had been bought by Robert Barclay and John Perkins in 1781, and it was Barclay Perkins' Russian imperial stout that became the classic example of the style. See BARCLAY, PERKINS & CO. A recipe from 1856 shows it had an original gravity (OG) of 1,107 (almost certainly over 10% alcohol by volume (ABV)) with a resounding smack of bitterness imparted by more than 10 lb of hops to the UK barrel.

But Barclay's was not the only London brewer that became famous for this powerful beer. Reid of the Griffin Brewery in Camden rolled out nothing but stout and porter until 1877, with the strongest regular brew being XX Imperial (1080 OG, or about 20°P), sold on draught at shellfish houses like The Whistling Oyster off Drury Lane. But even this was not Reid's most imposing imperial beer. On a visit in 1889, brewery chronicler Alfred Barnard was shown a store packed with a special export stout for Russia at 1,100 OG (25°P).

Outside London, a few other British brewers also adopted the style. Brain's Brewery in the coal port of Cardiff, Wales, was well known for its mischievous "Little Imp" imperial stout before World War I.

Most breweries did not bottle their own beers in the 19th century, preferring to ship barrels to professional bottlers who then sold the beer under both the brewer name and their own. This left the market open for enterprising middlemen like Belgium-born London beer merchant Albert Le Coq. In 1974 Norwegian divers recovered bottles from the 1869 Baltic shipwreck of the Olivia. They were stamped "A Le Coq" and contained his imperial Extra Double Stout. Le Coq had built up a large trade to Russia. He was so successful that Russian brewers began imitating the style, so to compete effectively Le Coq took over a brewery in Tartu in Estonia in 1910. It proved a troubled venture and was eventually nationalized by the USSR in 1940.

Most other British brewers had abandoned the Russian market before World War I, but Baltic brewers sought to keep the strong stout tradition alive. In Finland, Sinebrychoff, founded by a Russian in 1819, had originally rolled out Koff porter before switching to lager after 1853. But it revived the intensely bitter, roasted beer (7.2% ABV) in 1952. Polish brewers such as Okocim and Zywiec also kept faith with powerful porters, although they were now brewed with lager yeasts and eventually lost much of their powerful roast character. Even Danish lager giant Carlsberg got into the game, brewing a Gammel (old) porter imperial stout (7.5% ABV).

In Britain only Barclay Perkins kept the imperial flag flying, despite the severe disruptions of two world wars, with the focus switching to supplying the home trade with a warming winter stout matured in bottle for at least 1 year at the brewery. And the maturation period grew longer. In 1953, when vintage labels were introduced, the first was for the 1949 batch.

After Barclay Perkins merged with neighbor Courage in 1955, production moved to Courage's brewery by Tower Bridge and then, when that plant closed in 1982, moved out of London to John Smith's of Tadcaster in Yorkshire. The distinctive stout was gradually being lost inside a giant brewing company that was no longer interested in such esoteric beers. During the late 1980s and early 1990s Courage imperial stout emerged every couple of years, with the last in 1993.

But the empire fought back, helped by another drinks merchant, this time in America. Merchant du Vin of Seattle, intrigued by the dark beer's colourful history, encouraged John Smith's family rival in Tadcaster, Samuel Smith, to brew an imperial stout (7% ABV) for export to the United States in the early 1980s. This helped to inspire American interest in the style, with some of the new craft brewers producing bold examples. Today imperial stout is among the most popular strong beer styles among American craft brewers, and the United States now produces more of it than any other country. Modern interpretations sometimes include some time in bourbon barrels, lending rich notes of vanilla and coconut. Albert Le Coq's name and his beer were resurrected in 1999 when American importer Matthias Neidhart commissioned Harvey's brewery in Lewes, England, to brew imperial Extra Double Stout (9% ABV) in his name, using a facsimile of the original label on the corked bottle. And imperial stout has returned to the Baltic countries, with many craft brewers producing one as a winter specialty. Most modern imperial stouts show a rich black color, sharp bitterness balanced against notable residual sugar, and waves of dark fruit melded with chocolatey, coffee-like roast, sometimes trending into licorice notes. They tend to be perfect beers to enjoy in front of a winter fire, and they make fine accompaniments to cheeses and desserts. Good examples, if kept well, can age and improve in the bottle for decades.

Barclay, Perkins. *150th year commemoration.* London: Marshalsea Press, 1931.

Protz, Roger. *Classic stout and porter.* London: Prion Books, 1997.

Brian Glover

InBev was the beer company giant created in 2004 by the merger of the Brazilian company AmBev and the Belgian-based Interbrew. At the time of the merger, Interbrew was the world's third largest brewing company and AmBev was the fifth, by volume. The combined assets of the two made the newly formed InBev the biggest beer company in the world.

Interbrew was the older company, with origins dating back to 1366 with the founding of Brauerei Artois in Leuven. The Belgian brewery would later create the popular international pilsner beer Stella Artois. Beginning in the 1960s, they bought several local Belgian breweries and in 1968 and 1974 acquired two more from the Netherlands. In 1987, the company merged with Piedboeuf, makers of Jupiler beer. At the time, the companies were the two largest breweries in Belgium and the new entity was renamed Interbrew.

In 1995, Interbrew bought the Canadian brewery Labatt and shortly thereafter bought breweries in Hungary and Russia. In 2000, they purchased both Whitbread and Bass in the UK and the German brewer Diebels in 2001. During the same time period, Interbrew also acquired Beck's and Spaten, among other companies in Germany. The following year, 2002, two Chinese breweries were added to their portfolio.

In 2000, the previously family-owned company Interbrew went public and their stock began being traded on the Euronext Stock Exchange in Brussels.

The other half of InBev, AmBev, took its name from a shortened form of "American Beverage Company," a translation of Companhia de Bebidas das Américas. AmBev was itself the product of a 1999 merger between two Brazilian breweries, Brahma and Antarctica. Both breweries were founded in the 19th century, with Antarctica being founded in 1885 as Companhia Antarctica Paulista and Brahma 3 years later, in 1888, as Companhia Cervejaria Brahma.

In 2008, InBev engaged in a hostile takeover of American brewing giant Anheuser-Busch, brewers of the famous Budweiser brand of beer. The result of the merger is the largest beer company in the world, Anheuser-Busch InBev, based in Leuven, Belgium, and run by Carlos Brito, the former head of AmBev.

See also ANHEUSER-BUSCH, ANHEUSER-BUSCH INBEV, and BUSCH, AUGUST IV.

Jay R. Brooks

Ind Coope & Sons began in 1709 when George Cardon opened a small brewery behind the Star Inn in the market town of Romford, Essex, close to the border with London. In 1799 the business was bought by Edward Ind and a bigger brewery was built. Octavius Coope and George Coope joined the company in 1845, which was renamed Ind Coope & Sons in 1886. The brewery produced mainly mild ale, the most popular type of beer in the greater London area, but the development of pale ale in Burton-on-Trent encouraged Ind Coope to open a brewery there in 1856. See BURTON-ON-TRENT. Ind Coope was the first southern brewer to do so and was later joined in Burton by such large London brewers as Charrington and Truman.

Once brewers learned to "Burtonize" their brewing water by adding the sulfates present in the waters of the Trent Valley, most of the breweries from London, Manchester, and Liverpool retreated back to their original plants. Ind Coope, however, remained in Burton as well as in Romford. In 1934 it merged with the major Burton brewery of Samuel Allsopp and became known as Ind Coope & Allsopp. See SAMUEL ALLSOPP & SONS. The company was one of the first UK breweries to produce lager beer in the late 1960s, with a brand called Long Life. In 1961, Ind Coope joined a new national grouping, Allied Breweries, with Ansells of Birmingham and Tetley of Leeds. The group included lager breweries in Alloa in Scotland, which was renamed Ind Coope (Scotland), and the Wrexham Lager Brewery in Wales. Allied invested heavily in a new lager called Skol, which it hoped would become an international brand. Skol was produced by Ind Coope in Burton, Alloa, and Wrexham but never achieved the sales the group had hoped for.

A more successful beer for the group was called Double Diamond. This was first brewed in 1876 by Allsopps in Burton and the name came from its cask mark of two overlapping diamonds: the brewery also produced single and triple Diamond beers. In the 1960s and 1970s, the beer was turned from a cask-conditioned ale into a filtered and pasteurized keg beer and was heavily promoted on television and billboards with the slogan, "A Double Diamond works wonders so have one today."

In the late 1970s, Allied responded to the cask beer revival with a beer called Ind Coope Draught Burton ale, which achieved overnight success. As Allied "rationalized" its brewing operations, the Ind Coope Burton brewery took on such cask beers as ABC bitter, Benskins best bitter, and Friary Meux bitter from closed plants elsewhere in the country. The Burton brewery had greater success with lager when it won the licenses to brew the Australian beer Castlemaine XXXX and the Munich beer Löwenbräu.

The Romford brewery closed in 1997 with Ind Coope best bitter transferred to Burton. Some of the Romford plant was sold to breweries in China. Allied Breweries in 1978 became the brewing division of Allied Lyons: J. Lyons was a major food and catering company in Britain. In 1992, the brewing division was bought by Carlsberg of Denmark, which renamed the division Carlsberg Tetley. Today it is called Carlsberg UK. All of the former Allied breweries have closed with the exception of Tetley in Leeds, but this was planned to close in 2010 or 2011. The only remaining link with Ind Coope is the small amount of Draught Burton ale now brewed in Leeds. That link will be broken when the Tetley brewery closes and the venerable name of Ind Coope disappears into history.

Gourvish, T. R., and R. G. Wilson. *The British brewing industry, 1830–1980*. Cambridge, England: Cambridge University Press, 1994.

Roger Protz

India is the largest country in South Asia, whose brewing traditions come almost entirely from the British who imported beer for their colonial staff in the 18th century. This imported beer became known as "India pale ale," a type of beer with a particularly high quantity of hops to help it survive the 5-month sea voyage from the UK to India. See INDIA PALE ALE.

The first brewery in India was created in the early 19th century in the Himalayan foothills by British general Edward Dyer, who began to produce an India pale ale, called "Lion," using the fresh spring water abundant to the Himalayan foothills around the town of Shimla. This beer was produced until the 1960s, when most other breweries in India at the time were beginning to produce lagers.

Today, the Indian market is dominated by two companies: United Breweries and SABMiller, who also import beers from both Europe and the United States. These two large companies and other smaller breweries have also begun to export beer, such as the Kingfisher and Cobra brands. Through this increasing diversification, the Indian market now has a whole variety of domestic beers, including ales, stouts, and lagers, in addition to the premium imported lagers. In the east and northeast of India there is also a tradition of brewing a beverage made from rice called *Hadia*, which is fermented in large containers and stored underground.

Among Indians, beer consumption has conventionally been low with a current annual per-capital consumption between 1 and 1.4 liters per annum, although recently, as a consequence of improved prosperity and a decreasing average consuming population age, this has increased dramatically. This is particularly true since 2002, owing to reduced beer taxes and improved beer distribution. Nevertheless, the popularity of beer still remains scant, particularly in comparison to distilled beverages like whiskey, rum, and gin.

Datamonitor. "Beer in India Industry Profile." September 2009.

Jai Kharbanda

India pale ale (IPA) is a beer style characterized by high levels of alcohol and hops. It gained its name thanks to its huge popularity in British India and other outposts of the British Empire throughout the 19th century, a result of its keeping abilities on long sea voyages and its refreshing character when it finally reached its destination.

After enjoying phenomenal popularity around the world in the late 19th century, IPA suffered a sudden and steep decline and spent most of the 20th century as a pale shadow of its former self. Toward the end of the century, however, spurred by an explosion of interest in traditional beer styles driven mainly by North American craft brewers, it became the most popular craft beer style on the planet.

Of all beer styles, IPA is the most romanticized, mythologized, and misunderstood. It inspires the fiercest debate, the greatest reverence, and the wildest conjecture in the world of beer.

Why on Earth Did Brewers Send Pale Ale to India?

The problem with trying to pinpoint the birth or invention of IPA is that no one ever referred to it as "India pale ale" until it had been in existence for at least 50 years. IPA is a beer style that evolved over time and continues to evolve today. To understand its development, we need to understand the context that led to it.

In 1600 the British East India Company formed with a single purpose: to become masters of the lucrative spice trade. See EAST INDIA COMPANY. They failed in that, but along the way they discovered a lucrative textile trade in India. They established "factories" in various places along the coast, where traders or "factors" were left when the ships went home, so they could buy fabric when the price was right rather than when English ships were in port.

When they were not buying, there was little else to do, and the factors drank. Madeira, wine, and beer were imported from Europe by the captains of the ships, the "East Indiamen," but were originally available in small quantities at steep prices. Instead, many favored the local alternative. Arak was, by any standards, hardcore liquor. The local nondistilled version was made by fermenting raw palm juice in the hot sun . . . and that was it. Several of the first Englishmen to try it died after a 12-h session, and it went on to claim countless lives. As the factories grew into towns and the numbers of European clerks, lawyers, accountants, and—most of all—soldiers swelled, the death rate soared. The average life expectancy for a European in India was just 3 years. Disease played a significant role, but drink was often blamed. As fleets of ships became more regular and reliable, wealthy merchants were soon enjoying the finest imported drinks in heroic quantities, but the troops could afford little other than arak and died in droves. The need for a lighter, healthier drink soon became apparent.

Pale Ale Arrives in India

Pale ale was common in England from the mid-17th century onward, after the innovation of coke smelting made it possible to consistently control the temperature of malting barley to produce pale malt. It was a premium drink, popular in country houses and upmarket establishments because, being pale, it was harder to adulterate with nasty—even fatal—adjuncts, as was the practice with more common darker beers.

There are records of pale ale being drunk in India as early as 1716, when the President of the colony at Madras, Joseph Collett, was chastised by the East India Company for a phenomenally large monthly drinks tab that included "24 dozen and a half of Burton Ale and pale Beer."

Of course, "pale ale" covers a multitude of different possibilities. In the 17th and 18th centuries, pale ale was effectively anything that was paler than what had gone before. The 18th century saw porter become the first beer brewed in Britain on a truly industrial scale thanks to its incredible popularity, so any beer that was red through to blonde could conceivably have been regarded as pale.

Then there is the issue of strength. Through trial and error and simple accumulated brewing knowledge, any competent brewer knew that high alcohol and large concentrations of hops would help preserve beer over long periods. Country house "stock ales" or "October ales" were brewed to be matured in cellars for up to 10 years, by which time they had attained a condition comparable to wine. A 19th-century Calcutta newspaper ad for October beer suggests that it was these beers that were chosen to survive the long, arduous sea voyage from England to India, the forerunners for what eventually became known as IPA.

In the 1780s, when newspapers were published in Calcutta for the first time, they were instantly full of notices for auctions for the private cargos of ship's captains. These auctions almost always included reference to pale ale, porter, cider, and even small beer, proving that many beer styles were capable of surviving the rigorous sea journey.

The trade in beer was clearly well established by this time, but brand names were nonexistent—they were sold generically. The first pale ale to be mentioned by name was that of Bell's, a Burton brewery, in 1790. Other brewers were soon also mentioned, but in 1793 one name appeared that would change everything—Hodgson.

Hodgson's Pale Ale

Many histories of IPA wrongly credit George Hodgson's brewery in East London with the "invention" of IPA. He did not invent it—his brewery was not even the first to be mentioned by name in the Indian market—but he did evolve an existing beer style until it became phenomenally popular in India, almost to the exclusion of all his competitors.

Hodgson's brewery opened in 1752, close to the East India Docks on the River Thames in London. This was at the height of porter's popularity as a beer style in London, and Hodgson brewed it like everyone else.

But his proximity to the dock meant he came into close contact with East Indiaman captains. He would have heard from them what beer was most popular and offered the captains good trading terms. When George's son Mark took over the brewery, he focused on India more intensively. It was typical for customers to write letters of feedback to brewers, and Mark Hodgson clearly took note of these, adapting his beer to suit the Indian climate and tastes. By 1809, Hodgson's beer was advertised in large block capitals on the front of the *Calcutta Gazette*. Soon, no other pale ale was mentioned by name, and Hodgson's was immortalized in verse and prose.

Hodgson eventually began selling his pale ale in the UK, mainly to families returning from India, and in the 1830s the term "East India Pale Ale" appeared in newspaper ads for the first time. See HODGSON, GEORGE.

Conditioning and Maturation

The beers that eventually became known as IPA are believed to have evolved from October beers, which were brewed to be matured in cellars for at least 18 months before drinking. However, when these beers were shipped without prior maturation, they often arrived in India "ripe," fully conditioned and ready. Somehow, a 6-month sea journey had had an effect that, although not identical to long cellar maturation, was certainly similar.

The passage to India meant sailing out into the Atlantic, through the Canary Islands, and into the open sea. Currents and trade winds meant that ships generally had to sail west when they were trying to go east. After crossing the equator ships would often end up in Brazil and then sail back across the south Atlantic, round the tumultuous, notorious Cape of Good Hope, through the Madagascar channel, across the Indian Ocean, back across the Equator, and arrive in Bombay or Calcutta around 6 months after leaving London or Liverpool.

This was a truly arduous journey, involving temperature fluctuations of up to 20°C and constant movement—often violent movement. Beer therefore had to be assessed before it was auctioned on arrival in India. Rejected beer was sold off cheap, but usually the beer was found to be in perfect condition, and ads describe new shipments as being "fully ripened" and ready to drink.

Allsopp and Burton IPA

Allsopp's was once the largest brewery in Burton on Trent, having built a formidable reputation for its excellent strong, sweet Burton ales across the Baltic, particularly in St. Petersburg. When a combination of Napoleon Bonaparte and crippling Russian tariffs eventually killed off this trade, Samuel Allsopp was desperate to drum up new business.

On a visit to London, Allsopp was entertained by Campbell Marjoribanks, chairman of the East India Company, who informed him that Frederick Hodgson—grandson of George and now head of the company—had given offence to the East India Company and its ships' captains by implementing restrictive trading terms. The Company wanted another brewer to stand against him. Thanks to Allsopp's success in brewing ales that stood up to the rigors of the Baltic journey, they felt he might be the man.

Marjoribanks sent Allsopp samples of Hodgson's ale, which the latter attempted to recreate. The result (allegedly brewed in a teapot) replicated the high alcohol and assertive hop character of the original, but brewed with Burton water—which is rich in gypsum and salts—it was immediately pronounced a far superior beer to Hodgson's. See BURTON-ON-TRENT. According to contemporary accounts it was lighter and more sparkling, ideal for the sultry climate. When it reached India, it quickly broke the London brewer's hold on the market. See SAMUEL ALLSOPP AND SONS.

Bass and Global Domination

Burton-on-Trent is a small town, and brewing is a tight-knit community. Other brewers quickly caught on to what Allsopp was doing and replicated it. Bass had better links within the transport and sales infrastructure to the ports of London and Liverpool and was soon exporting more beer to India than Allsopp.

Bass became a household name, and its distinctive red triangle followed the British Empire wherever it went, becoming the world's first globally recognized brand. Back in Britain, the Great Exhibition of 1851 finally persuaded the British that they had an Empire of which they should be proud. Neither Bass nor any other brewer was present at the Exhibition, but in the years that followed IPA became the drink of fashionable London, a "wine of malt" that was prescribed by doctors for stomach complaints and general well-being.

The Decline of IPA

IPA became the drink of the British Empire not because it was the only beer that could survive rigorous sea journeys, as has often been suggested (in fact, porter was also shipped to India in very large quantities throughout the entire period of IPA's success) but because it was refreshing, light, and tasted better than anything else when served chilled in India's 30°C heat. By the end of the 19th century, thanks to refrigeration, innovation, and a greater understanding of the properties of yeast, lager was commonplace, could be brewed in India, and did the job of refreshment even better than IPA.

But more than that, the pressures exerted by a growing temperance movement meant that excessive drinking became increasingly frowned upon. While lager killed IPA within the beer market, beer itself was displaced in India and other colonies by tea, watery gin, and tonics or various weak blends of whiskey and soda.

For British IPA brewers, the export market disappeared. And although Britain remained one of the few countries not to be seduced by lager, the fortunes of its ales suffered at home too. Changes in the calculation of beer duty began to weigh heavily against the production of strong beers, and there was an increasing demand for weaker products thanks to the growth of white-collar jobs that required a clearer head. Although beers named "India pale ales" were still produced, by the early decades of the 20th century they were pale shadows of their former selves, weighing in at under 4% alcohol by volume (ABV) with none of the heady hoppiness that had once defined them.

Revival

Peter Ballantine, a Scottish brewer, had emigrated to the United States in 1830. A Ballantine IPA, considered pretty true to the style in that it was aggressively hopped, around 7.5% ABV, and, importantly, was aged in barrels for a year, was one of the few characterful beers to survive into the post-Prohibition age. Throughout the 1970s and 1980s Ballantines was acquired and sold by various brewing groups, and the IPA was watered down by successive new owners. It has not been brewed regularly since the mid-1990s. When the American craft brewing revolution began in earnest, brewers looked to historic records for beer styles they could recreate, with beers like Ballantine IPA proving an inspiration. See BALLANTINE IPA.

American hops were discovered to have more intense flavor and aroma than their European counterparts, and traditional IPA proved to be a perfect showcase for them. Bert Grant began brewing in Yakima, Washington, in the early 1980s and believed in using local ingredients. He discovered that hops from the North West, such as Chinook and Cascade, gave a hoppy beer like IPA a striking array of resiny and citrus fruit flavors. Here was an evolution of the style that could in theory still be aged like its ancestors, but delivered bombs of flavor when young and fresh. IPA brewing spread down the west coast of America and then across the country, and IPA became a standard by which craft brewers can be compared.

The appetite for serious hoppy beers grew and led to "double IPAs" or "Imperial IPAs," pushing the boundaries of intensity of bitterness and aroma. See DOUBLE IPA.

Inspired by the American reinvention of IPA, many UK brewers began rediscovering the style. Some of these used American hops, which led to accusations of inauthenticity. But records show that toward the end of the 19th century hops were imported from the United States to be used in IPA because demand was so high that England could not grow enough of its own.

IPA is now the signature of craft brewers worldwide. Fittingly for an export beer, brewers from Australia to Scandinavia are creating new beers, mostly inspired by the American take on the style, but often adding a regional twist of their own.

An Evolving Style

The debate about what constitutes an "authentic" IPA will continue. If one were perfectly strict about it, one could argue that only a beer that has survived the sea journey from Europe around the Cape of Good Hope to India is a true IPA. Because it is no longer possible to do that journey along its original route (all shipping from Europe to India now goes via the Suez Canal), this proviso would be somewhat unrealistic. And in any event, IPA has always evolved. October ales evolved into Hodgson's London version, which was then transformed when brewed in Burton. Brewing records from the mid-20th century would have argued that IPA was a light, refreshing ale of around 3.5%. Once could argue, then, that in its time this was just as authentic as a modern Imperial IPA brewed with malt and hop varieties that didn't exist when Bass was in its prime. Versions of IPA continue to thread the world together and will continue to evolve to suit our tastes.

See also INDIA.

Pete Brown

The **Industrial Revolution** began in Great Britain during the 18th century and gradually spread throughout Europe, North America, and then the rest of the world. Britain was an almost inevitable starting point, because her homeland and Empire provided a vast source of raw materials and an ample market for manufactured goods. Most historians would agree that there were two phases of the phenomenon, the first commencing during the second half of the 18th century and the second starting around 100 years later.

Industrialization proper in Britain commenced around the second half of the 18th century when Richard Arkwright established his first cotton mill and took advantage of the many new inventions available at that time. The foundations, however, were laid a few years earlier, in 1733, when John Kay invented the flying shuttle, a device that allowed a loom to be operated at far greater speeds with half the labor. When James Hargreaves invented the spinning jenny in 1764, the output of an individual worker increased eightfold. At the start of the 18th century, British textile manufacture was a wool-based cottage industry. Flax and cotton were difficult to manipulate with the equipment available in the home and formed only a fraction of raw materials. The influence of the "scientific revolution," which started in the late 17th century, on these early events cannot be overstated. Just as spinning and weaving, previously domestic chores, were taken over by companies operating machinery, so too was brewing transforming from a cottage industry to machine-driven big business. Brewing was gradually divorced from its agrarian roots, and people moved from the fields into the cities to provide labor to the new, large brewing plants.

The harnessing of steam power was probably the singular most important aspect of the Industrial Revolution for brewers. The first (not oversuccessful) stationary industrial steam engine (1 hp) was built by Thomas Savery in 1698 and was designed to lift water, but the first safe and efficient model was credited to Thomas Newcomen. Several of his 5-hp engines were used to drain previously unworkable deep tin and coal mines. Fundamental improvements in the working principles of the steam engine were brought about by James Watt and his collaborator, Matthew Boulton, which resulted in a more constant temperature being maintained in the cylinder. Efficiency no longer depended on atmospheric conditions and was greatly increased, giving a 75% saving on coal usage.

The first brewery to install a steam engine was that of Messrs Cook & Co, at Stratford-le-Bow, just east of London, in 1777. The brewery paid £200 for a small 18-inch cylinder engine from Boulton & Watt. Henry Goodwyn's Red Lion Brewery followed, in May 1784, with a 4-hp Boulton & Watt engine replacing the four actual horses that had worked their grist mill. Whitbread's purchased an engine in June 1784, Calvert's followed a year later, and Barclay Perkins 4 years later. See BARCLAY, PERKINS & CO. and WHITBREAD BREWERY. Most of these engines were originally purchased for milling the vast quantities of grain necessary for large-scale beer production and for various pumping operations but, once installed, they soon found other uses. Indeed, one contemporary (1810) commentator on Whitbread's Chiswell Street Brewery, said:

> One of Mr. Watt's steam engines works the machinery. It pumps the water, wort, and beer, grinds the malt, stirs the mash-tubs, and raises the casks out of the cellars. It is able to do the work of 70 horses, though it is of a small size, being only a 24-inch cylinder, and does not make more noise than a spinning-wheel. Whether the magnitude, or ingenuity of contrivance, is considered, this brewery is one of the greatest curiosities that is any where to be seen, and little less than half a million sterling is employed in the machinery, buildings, and materials.

By 1801, 14 steam engines were operating in London breweries. The breweries that did embrace the new technology were able to expand dramatically. Whitbread, for instance, tripled their annual barrelage (to 202,000) by 1796.

Twenty-five years after converting to steam power, other factors that were to help breweries become larger and more efficient involved iron-making (blast furnace), the rediscovery of concrete, the invention of mechanical refrigeration, and improved transport links (canals, followed by railways) for raw materials and products. In northern continental Europe and the United States, improved refrigeration machines played an exceptionally vital role in the improvement of bottom-fermented beer manufacture and storage, but generally the innovations resulting from the Industrial Revolution in Britain were replicated in brewing industries elsewhere.

Cambridge social anthropologist Alan Macfarlane reckons that one of the largely understudied phenomena occurring immediately prior to the Industrial Revolution in Britain was a surge in population (which had remained static for the previous century). The infant mortality rate halved in the space of 20 years across all classes and in both urban and rural areas. Records show that there was a reduction in the incidence of waterborne disease at this time, and it was argued that a change in drinking habits back to beer (from gin) and the explosion in tea drinking (no other European nation drank more) were behind this. The antibacterial properties of the hop and the health-promoting properties of tea may well have given Great Britain the population capable of fueling the Industrial Revolution.

Dugan, S., and D. Dugan. *The day the world took off—The roots of the Industrial Revolution.* London: Channel Four Books, 2000.

Gourvish, T. R., and R. G. Wilson. *The British brewing industry 1830–1980.* Cambridge, UK: Cambridge University Press, 1994.

Hornsey, I. S. *A history of beer and brewing.* Cambridge, UK: Royal Society of Chemistry, 2003.

Macfarlane, A. *The savage war of peace.* Oxford, UK: Blackwell, 1997.

Matthias, P. *The brewing industry in England, 1700–1830.* Cambridge, UK: Cambridge University Press, 1959.

Ian Hornsey

infection is the introduction or presence of undesirable microorganisms in beer or its raw materials. The severity of infections may range from imperceptible to severe. In the extreme, infections can cause hazes, acidity, or off-flavors and may make the beer appear unsightly or become undrinkable. Although beer infections are not dangerous to human health, allowing infected beer to reach the consumer is quite harmful to any brewery's reputation and business.

Life essentially runs on sweet liquids and many organisms can spoil beer. The term "wort spoilers" is sometimes applied to spoilage organisms that tolerate oxygen well and grow best before fermentation has lowered the wort pH and produced ethanol. Others are referred to as "beer spoilers"—these tend to prefer anaerobic conditions and survive well in lower pH environments and those containing alcohol. The most common organisms considered beer spoilers by most brewers are Lactobacillus, Pediococcus, and wild yeasts including Brettanomyces. Each of these has its own preferred set of nutrients, temperature range, pH range, and growth rate. See BRETTANOMYCES, LACTOBACILLUS, PEDIOCOCCUS, and WILD YEAST. Infection, of course, is in the eye of the brewer and consumer. Certain microbes other than brewer's yeast, although generally considered infections, can be perfectly desirable or encouraged in certain beer styles, including Berliner weisse, lambics, Belgian-style sour beers, and even authentic 19th-century British porters. One brewer's "infection" may be another's "complexity," especially in the domain of sour beer styles. In most beers, however, the brewer desires only the character produced by the yeast added by the brewery and will wish to keep out all other biological actors.

Mankind has been brewing for at least 6,000 years and probably much longer, but consciously managing beer microbes has been practiced only in the past century and a half. Previously, beer had been simply consumed fresh and local before the inevitable spoilage would occur, and although procedures were known that would make less-spoiled beers, the brewers were largely ignorant of the microbiology behind these procedures. The existence of yeast as a microbe was only discovered in 1674 by Antonie van Leeuwenhoek, the inventor of the modern microscope. And it was only in 1859 that Louis Pasteur put an end to the theory of "spontaneous generation," when he demonstrated unassailably and for the first time that living microorganisms are the sole cause of food and beer spoilage, as well as the agents of fermentation. See PASTEUR, LOUIS, and PASTEURIZATION. Pasteur's path-breaking discoveries allowed brewers and other food and beverage producers to develop sanitary procedures that were effective in keeping microbes reliably at bay. Today, of course, pasteurization and other germ-killing techniques are ubiquitous.

After the kettle boil, wort should be perfectly sterile. Thereafter, infection can occur during wort cooling, fermentation, cold transfer, or packaging. The brewer's best weapons against undesirable microbes in the finished beer are proper sanitation in the brewery's cellar and packaging area, as well as the use of sterile bottles and kegs. Many breweries, especially large industrial ones, also sterile filter their beer on the way to the bottling line and/or pasteurize it after packaging. These steps prolong a beer's shelf life by removing or killing potential infectious organisms and thereby make it more probable that a drinkable product reaches the consumer's table. But pasteurization, if improperly performed, can induce stale or "cooked" flavors and aromas. Sterile filtration can remove bacteria but can also strip away flavor, aroma, body, and even color. See STERILE FILTRATION. Bottle-conditioned beers, however, such as many Belgian styles and German hefeweizens, are sometimes flash pasteurized before the reintroduction of live yeast. Classic bottle conditioning, however, does not include this step and therefore requires sufficient sanitation in the brewery to ensure quality and proper shelf stability.

See also ACIDITY, BACTERIA, BEER SPOILERS, HAZE, OFF-FLAVORS, and SOUR BEERS.

Priest, F. G., and I. Campbell, eds. *Brewing microbiology*. Essex, UK: Elsevier, 1987.

Brian Hunt

infusion mash, also called the "single infusion mash" or "British infusion mash," is a mashing technique where hot liquor (hot brewing water) is blended with malts to create a mash that only has one rest, at saccharification temperature. In most modern breweries, a temperature-programmed mash takes place in the mash mixer and the wort is separated in a separate vessel, the lauter tun. The infusion mash, a simpler affair, is carried out in a mash tun, a vessel that might be better described as a "mash/lauter tun." This vessel has a false bottom with screens, and both the mash and the runoff (lautering) take place there. The mash/lauter tun is part of a two-vessel system, alongside the wort kettle. The mash tun is insulated, but unheated; therefore, it is not possible to perform a series of temperature steps. When the mash-in is complete, the correct temperature must have been achieved. This temperature usually ranges between 63.3°C and 68.8°C (146°F and 156°F).

Although the infusion mash seems the most simple of mashing techniques, in professional practice it is virtually an art form. As the crushed grist emerges into the mash tun, it normally goes through some type of hydrator that will mix the grain with the hot liquor before it hits the "foundation liquor" that barely covers the false bottom screens. The texture of the infusion mash is starkly different from that of European-style mashes. Whereas European mashes are somewhat soupy, often with water-to-grist weight ratios at about 3 to 1, the infusion mash is notably thicker. The European mash is thoroughly mixed and contains little or no air, but the traditional infusion mash is fluffy with tiny air pockets, and as the mash-in proceeds, the mash begins to float on a pool of heavy wort that forms below it. Because there are no protein rests or temperature rises, saccharification begins immediately and the starches in the malt begin to liquefy quickly.

If the brewer wishes to achieve a final mash temperature of 65°C (149°F), he or she will need to take account of the temperature of the malt (which may vary depending on the time of year) and the temperature of the mash vessel and then pay close attention to the texture of the mash. If the mash is too wet, it will be too hot; conversely, a mash that is too dry will be too cool. Infusion mashes usually use saccharification rests of at least 1 h, although 90 min is not uncommon. British brewers sometimes claim that the proper conversion of starches takes this long, although European brewers have been heard to joke that the long conversion rest is used just to allow the British brewer a leisurely breakfast.

Sparging of an infusion mash is performed gently, with the surface of the mash kept free of standing water and the mash continuing to float on its wort until the end of the runoff. At very small breweries, the brewer may occasionally cut through the grain bed with a wooden or plastic oar to loosen it and allow the wort to flow more easily. Only at the finish of the runoff is the mash allowed to descend and contact the plates as the last runnings drain off. If the mash is allowed to set down to the plates earlier, a stuck mash can easily result.

Infusion mashes, properly used, can yield excellent results, and they are still widely used at smaller

British breweries and many brewpubs in the United States and around the world. However, because temperature steps are not employed, some types of beers, particularly wheat beers (which normally need a protein rest at a lower temperature), can be more difficult to brew using this technique.

See also PROTEIN REST, SACCHARIFICATION, STUCK MASH, and TEMPERATURE PROGRAMMED MASH.

Garrett Oliver

in-line carbonation, the process of dissolving carbon dioxide (CO_2) into beer as the beer is being pumped from one vessel to another. After fermentation is complete, beer will naturally contain some amount of dissolved CO_2. If this amount alone is not sufficient to give the beer its appropriate level of carbonation, in-line carbonation is often used to increase the CO_2 content of the beer to the desired level. This can be done whenever the beer is being pumped somewhere and is often done between the filter and the bright tank.

Factors affecting the efficiency of this process include time, temperature, pressure, and the size of the CO_2 bubbles being dissolved into the beer. High pressure and low temperature cause CO_2 to dissolve more readily in beer, so in-line carbonation is normally done at around 1 bar (15 psi) of pressure and near-freezing temperatures. Also, small bubbles of CO_2 and long contact time are critical for efficient dissolution. Diffusion stones or venturi jets are often used to produce the small bubbles necessary and are typically followed by a long section of pipe that allows the CO_2 adequate time to fully dissolve into the beer.

See also BRIGHT TANK and CARBONATION.

Nick R. Jones

Institute of Brewing & Distilling (IBD) is an international educational body with a vision statement tasking the organization with "the advancement of the education and professional development in the science and technology of brewing, distilling, and related industries." The IBD has over 4,000 members, approximately half of whom are based in the UK. Members are grouped into regional sections, four of which are in the UK: Great Northern, Southern, Midlands, and Scottish. There are an additional four international sections: Africa, Asia Pacific, Irish, and International (mainly based in North America). Membership classes range from Student through to Standard, Corporate, Master Brewer, and Fellowship levels.

The IBD originated as the "Laboratory Club" in London in 1886, when a group of talented scientific researchers in the fields of biology and chemistry agreed to meet and discuss scientific issues relating to malting and brewing. The *Transactions of the Laboratory Club* was published in that year and was subsequently retitled *The Journal of the Institute of Brewing* in 1890 (the same year the Laboratory Club became the Institute of Brewing) and which continues to publish papers on scientific research related to fermentation, beer quality, distilling, malting, and cereal sciences in four issues annually. In 2001 the Institute of Brewing merged with the International Brewers' Guild, a long-established body representing mainly professional brewers in the UK, to form the Institute and Guild of Brewing (IGB). This body was superseded in 2005 by the IBD to reflect the increasing importance of the distilling industries in the activities of the Institute.

The IBD offers a range of examinations and qualifications in brewing, packaging, and distilling, ranging from the Fundamentals of Brewing and Packaging and of Distilling for nontechnical personnel, through General Certificates in Brewing, Packaging, or Distilling, to Diplomas in Brewing, Distilling, or Beverage Packaging. The ultimate accolade is the Master Brewer qualification, which assesses levels of competence and knowledge in the technical management of the beer production process. The IBD supports its members through a series of lectures, technical visits, seminars, and conferences worldwide as well as publishing the monthly *Brewer and Distiller International* magazine for all of its members.

See also BREWING SCHOOLS.

George Philliskirk

International Bitterness Units (IBUs) are the internationally agreed-upon standard for measuring bitterness in beer. See BITTERNESS. Sometimes referred to by the shortened acronym

BU, for Bitterness Units, IBUs are calculated values composed of the quantity of material in wort or beer derived from hop resin (alpha acids), multiplied by the fraction 5/7. See ALPHA ACIDS. This IBU method was developed in the 1950s and 1960s, when most brewers used unrefrigerated baled hops, which, by the time the hops were actually used in the brew kettle, had often lost between 40% and 80% of their alpha acid–derived bittering potential. Instead they had obtained some 20% to 60% of their bittering power from oxidation products of the hop resins. As a result, the true bitterness in beer did not correlate very well with a simple measurement of its iso-alpha acids, expressed as milligrams of iso-alpha acids per liter of beer. See HULUPONES and ISO-ALPHA ACIDS. The IBU analysis was developed precisely to overcome this discrepancy. The correction factor of 5/7 in the IBU calculation was selected because it was assumed that this was the fraction of hop resin–derived material, which, in the average beer of the day, was actually iso-alpha acids. In beers for which this assumption did not hold, of course, the values for IBUs and milligrams per liter of iso-alpha acids were still not the same.

This has, not surprisingly, led to some confusion. The complexity notwithstanding, for the brewer, IBU values are an important quality control measurement for defining beer flavor and for determining whether a particular batch of beer is true to its style or brand specifications. In practical terms, 1 IBU equals 1 mg/l or 1 ppm of iso-alpha acids in solution. IBU values, therefore, give useful information about a brew's bitterness intensity. There is an elaborate formula that incorporates such variables as hop utilization, which allows brewers to calculate the expected IBUs of their beers during recipe formulation. See HOP UTILIZATION. Beers can range from 1 to about 100 IBUs, whereby the taste threshold for most humans is roughly between 4 and 9 IBUs—different studies suggest slightly different sensitivity intervals, but all within this range. The theoretical saturation point of iso-alpha acids in beer is approximately 110 IBUs, which corresponds to 78.6 IBUs ($5/7 \times 110$). In practice, however, this value is rarely achieved because it assumes that there are no other hop-derived resins in the beer, which is rarely the case. American mass market lagers have typical IBU ranges of 5 to 10 IBUs, Bavarian hefeweizens 8 to 12 IBUs, amber lagers 20 to 25 IBUs, American pale ales 35 to 40 IBUs, American India pale ales (IPAs) 55 to 70 IBUs, and "double IPAs" and American barley wines 65 to 100 IBUs.

IBU values measured in the wort in the brewhouse drop dramatically, and largely unpredictably, during fermentation. This is why wort IBUs and beer IBUs are always two distinctly separate values and a brewer's initial IBU calculations are only estimates of the true bitterness of the finished beer. Measuring the true IBU value of beer requires complicated laboratory techniques such as ultraviolet light (UV) spectrophotometric assay or high-pressure liquid chromatography (HPLC). See CHROMATOGRAPHY. The UV method is more common and can usually be performed even by small brewery laboratories, but it tends to be less accurate than the more sophisticated HPLC method, for which only large laboratories tend to be equipped. Trained flavor panelists, too, are often able to taste and approximate IBU values in beer with reasonable accuracy. However, any strong sweetness and too many malty notes, especially in higher-gravity, more assertive beers, can counterbalance and cover up much of the bitterness and thus make bitterness assessments based purely on tasting more difficult.

Regardless of how IBU values are derived, however, they do not provide information about the quality of the bitterness. In wine, for instance, tannin content can be measured, but this does not tell anything about the smoothness, roughness, or astringency of the wine. Likewise, low-IBU brews, such as many malt liquors, for instance, can taste rough, whereas high-IBU beers, such as well-brewed rich Russian imperial stouts, can taste smooth and velvety. Also, measured IBUs in beer, like tannins in wine, decrease as the beverage ages. Some beers, therefore, may be very tough and bitter in their youth—barley wines tend to be a typical example—but may become supple and balanced after a few years of cellaring.

For all its recent use in the public sphere, where it sometimes even appears in craft beer advertising, the IBU is a laboratory construct that was never meant to leave the laboratory. Its purpose is to help brewers formulate beers and then keep them consistent from batch to batch. The usefulness of the IBU to the beer consumer is highly debatable. Once the beer leaves the laboratory context, many non-iso alpha acid factors, including other hop components, roast character, carbonation, water chemistry, and residual sugar, may exert such influence as to make the IBU an entirely unreliable indicator of actual perceived bitterness.

Bishop, L. R., and Analysis Committee of the EBC. The measurement of bitterness in beers. *Journal of the Institute of Brewing* 70 (1964): 489–97.
Rigby, F. L., and J. L. Bethune. Rapid methods for the determination of total hop bitter substances (iso-compounds) in beer. *Journal of the Institute of Brewing* 61 (1955): 325–32.

Matthew Brynildson and Val Peacock

International Brewers' Guild

See INSTITUTE OF BREWING & DISTILLING (IBD).

international pilsner, according to some, fails to rise to the level of a formal beer category. Nonetheless, any experienced beer drinker knows immediately and intuitively what the concept intends. The German word "pilsner," also spelled "pilsener" or abbreviated "pils," was originally defined as a type of beer that was first brewed, in 1842, in the Bohemian town of Plzen (Pilsen in German) in what is now the Czech Republic. The original pilsner was made only from lightly kilned malted barley, ideally Haná from Moravia, and flavored fairly delicately with Saaz hops. It was conditioned for between 8 and 12 weeks in cold cellars depending on its strength. See HANÁ (BARLEY). It was served clear with white foam and gained success in the middle of the 19th century across central Europe, not least because of the parallel invention of the first affordable forms of clear glassware. It was soon imitated in spades, spreading from central Europe to the rest of the world, shedding quality as it spread.

In 1898, Burghers' Brewery of Pilsen, therefore, tried to set a precedent for the protection of its brand. It went to court in Munich, seeking an injunction against the local Thomass Brewery, which had come out with a blond lager named "Thomass-Pilsner-Bier." The landmark verdict that the German court handed down in April 1899, however, went against the plaintiff. The court argued that pilsner was no longer an appellation, but had become a universal style designation.

In short order, therefore, thousands of new beers were introduced all over the world sporting the words "pilsener," "pilsner," or "pils" in their names. Although virtually all of these were light blond, crystal clear lagers with white foam that managed to attract premium prices, few were truly made in the original pilsner style, which is to say a malt-only mash, Saaz hops, decoction mashing, bottom-fermentation at a controlled lower temperature and prolonged conditioning at near-iced temperature. Pilsner was bowdlerized into a light blond lager that looked the part. It has gone on to be the most copied beer style in the world, appealing particularly to drinkers who want a beer that is relatively light in alcohol and undemanding on the palate. Light lagers are often the only beers available in countries that have little or no ale-brewing traditions. The reasons for the dominance of this style vary from country to country, but commonly feature the growing concentration in the brewing industry and the tendency toward large-scale industrial brewing to serve a mass market deemed to be undemanding in its preferences.

In the United States, for instance, once the brewing industry was relicensed in 1933, after Prohibition (from 1920 until 1933) had wiped out virtually all commercial breweries and the brewing traditions they represented, the surviving companies produced light-bodied golden lager and little else.

Likewise, in Continental Europe, the destruction wreaked by two World Wars between 1914 and 1945 resulted in a considerable reduction in the number of breweries. What the bombs did not destroy, occupying forces dismantled. Brewing kettles especially became prized loot to be turned into munitions.

Because beer drinkers around the world grew accustomed to consuming less flavorful beers and because economic circumstances favored large companies, the drive toward making simpler beers ever more cheaply and in vast quantities became the dominant focus of the post-war brewing industry everywhere. A typical example is Heineken, whose beers are usually made not far from where they are sold. Some versions had an alcohol by volume of no more than 3.2%, as opposed to the original strength of about 5%, yet remain termed "pilsner." After a young Albert "Freddie" Heineken had spent 3 years in the United States studying the American beer market, he concluded that what sells beer is advertising. When he returned home to the Netherlands in 1954 to work in the brewery that his family still partly owned, he set about implementing his ardent belief in branding and marketing. This was the beginning of a pioneering, truly effective global marketing policy for beer. In time many other breweries, too, realized that the foreign-sounding but easily pronounceable name "pilsner" could give even a plain beer a suggestion of exotic excellence.

In the late 1960s, therefore, many larger breweries followed Heineken's suit and embarked on the creation of beer brands that were as easy on the eye and palate as they were easy to make. Rice, corn, corn syrup, glucose, and other cheap sugar sources were often substituted for some of the malted barley in these recipes, the bitterness frequently hovered in the 20 international bittering unit range, and conditioning sometimes took as little as a week, sometimes at room temperature or higher. The result was a wave of cheap, industrial beers that served only to dilute the impact and value of the term "pilsner."

In recent years fewer of the world's most successful brands have been termed "pilsner" by their producers. Perhaps it is just that the term is now meaningless to consumers in the target markets of these beers, although it is more comforting to think that it is a nod to the quality of the past and leaves leeway for an eventual return to making all-malt, well-hopped, and properly lagered brands more deserving of the name in the future. Some brewers of international pilsners, including Heineken and Carlsberg, have recently switched to all-barley brewing. These were not flavor-based decisions, but strategic moves to avoid the public relations stain that would result if genetically modified (GMO) corn ever found its way into their brewhouses. Although Americans have largely accepted GMO agricultural products, they are widely rejected by Europeans. Ironically, brewmasters in these situations are often tasked with making all-malt beers taste as neutral as they had when they previously contained corn. Regardless of the makeup, the international blond lager style, still sometimes labeled pilsner, brewed from India to Russia to Belgium to Mexico, is a golden lager beer with a light body, low bitterness (although notably higher nowadays than mass-market American lagers), very little malt flavor, and a clean profile.

Some 2,000 of the world's estimated 60,000 brews currently include one of the pilsner-derived words in their brand name. Because most of these are mass-market beers, brewers who try to emulate the intentions of the original 19th-century brewmasters of Plzen will have an uphill struggle to differentiate any truly pilsner-style beers in the minds of the consumers, flooded as they are by the images the light lagers of the international pilsner category invoke.

See also PILSNER.

Tim Webb

invert sugar is a brewing adjunct (unmalted source of fermentable extract). See ADJUNCTS. It is manufactured by converting sucrose (derived from cane or beet sugar) with either acids or enzymes to produce a mixture of glucose and fructose. It is called invert sugar because the sugar solution before the conversion (called inversion or hydrolysis) rotates the plane of polarized light in one direction and following inversion rotates the solution in the opposite direction. Fructose and glucose are monosaccharides and are rapidly used by brewer's yeast strains. Liquid invert sugar can be stored at a higher solids content than liquid sucrose or sugar, making it easier for brewers to handle. In the UK, where it is widely used, it is usually delivered either as a syrup or in brick-like loaves. Invert sugar can be supplied at different color levels for use in different beers. For example, "black invert," with a color of 500 European Brewery Convention units, can be used for brewing stouts. Darker invert sugars can lend beers unique caramel flavors that are particular to many British bitters and other ales. Some brewers claim that inverting sucrose prior to addition to the boiling wort results in more rapid fermentation and produces beer with superior head formation.

Graham G. Stewart

iodine is a member of the class of elements called halogens; other members include chlorine, bromine, and fluorine, all of which are more reactive. As a solution of potassium iodide, iodine is used to identify the presence of the amylose component of starch. The helical structure of amylose supplies a matrix within which iodine molecules can assemble, leading to the formation of a blue–black color. After the saccharification steps of the mash, brewers will perform an "iodine test," where potassium iodide is added to a small mash sample. If the starches have converted to sugars, the blue-black color will not form; conversely, the presence of the color indicates that starches remain. In this case, the brewer may decide to extend the mash sequence or take other action.

The second major use of iodine in breweries is as a sanitizing agent. Iodophor, a concentrated liquid containing iodine complexed with surfactants and sometimes acids, is a highly effective sanitizer with limited toxicity and corrosive effects. When diluted to 12 to 15 ppm, it is often used as a "no-rinse" sanitizer, especially for fermentation vessels and other stainless-steel equipment.

http://www.jtbaker.com/msds/englishhtml/i3480.htm (accessed April 26, 2011).
http://www.webelements.com/iodine/ (accessed April 26, 2011).

Chris Holliland

Ireland, despite being a relatively small island nation, has been a brewing powerhouse for centuries. Ireland's contributions to worldwide beer culture have been immense, and in many parts of the world the idea of the Irish pub, whether genuine or faux, remains surprisingly evocative. Ireland's beer history, just as its overall history has always been, is inextricably intertwined with that of England. From the 12th-century colonization of Ireland by the English to the 1801 Act of Union, the famines and independence movements in the 19th century, and the Anglo-Irish treaty of 1921, England has had a large influence over many aspects of Irish life, including its beer.

The earliest form of *beoir* (Gaelic for beer) in Ireland is believed to have been brewed in the Bronze Age. The discovery of a possible brewery site, a *fulacht fiadh* (grass-covered mound), by archaeologists Declan Moore and Billy Quinn in Cardarragh, Co. Galway, led to the test brewing of a gruit (a beer flavored with plants and herbs but not hops) in 2001. Ingredients were barley, bog myrtle, meadowsweet, water, and yeast, resulting in a beer said to be "drinkable and worthy of our ancestor's efforts."

Ireland, like its Celtic cousin, Scotland, has a greater connection to spirits than beer, sharing *uisce beathe* (whiskey) but also having, uniquely, poitin, an Irish form of moonshine that is usually made from barley and sometimes from potatoes. The distilling of poitin was outlawed in 1661 and not legalized again until 1989. The encouragement by the English Parliament to push beer consumption in the 1730s and thus avoid the "immoderate use of spiritous liquors"—best exemplified in Hogarth's 1750 prints entitled Gin Lane—met with limited success in Ireland. Like Scotland, Ireland grows no hops and its beers had to be flavored with imported, mainly Flemish, hops, which were the cheapest available at the time. A 1733 ban on such imports, however, forced Irish brewers to purchase more expensive hops from Hereford and Worcester in England, and sometimes beers were simply brewed without hops altogether or with indigenous herbs as in ancient times.

Records for the 18th century show Irish beer production to be markedly consistent. In 1720–1724, the Irish paid duty on a total of 822,000 hl (+480 hl imported from England); in 1770–1774, 762,000 hl (77,100 hl imported); and in 1790–1794, 818,000 hl (172,000 hl imported). The increase in imports was partly the result of the American War of Independence, which closed these colonial markets off to English breweries. There were also several barley shortages, including two very poor harvests in 1740 and 1741, which triggered the first of the Irish famines. By the 19th century, brewing capacity in Ireland had increased and the Industrial Revolution had taken hold in England. As a result, beer remained within English shores for home consumption. In 1808–1809, for instance, Irish beer production was 1.277 million hl and imports were only 3,680 hl. Duty and English protectionist policies, which both changed wildly during the 19th century, also had a significant effect on Irish beer production in terms of the sourcing of raw materials and how they were used.

In addition to the beer tax, England had also been charging a malt tax since 1697, using the money to finance a number of wars. To ensure that brewers did not avoid paying the malt tax, they were forbidden to use unmalted grist; in 1816 an almost German-sounding law was introduced, which stipulated that only malted barleys and hops could be used in the brewing of beer. The malt tax was repealed in 1880, but as is often the case in brewing, the effects of the tax continued to reverberate through Irish brewing for decades afterward. See REINHEITSGEBOT.

The porter beer style originated in London in the early 18th century but quickly became hugely popular in Ireland as well. It was first brewed in Ireland in 1776, initially just with brown malt. Irish porters were later made from a mixture of pale and brown malts, mostly to reduce production costs. The porter flavor changed again after 1817, with the invention of black patent malt. See BLACK MALT and WHEELER, DANIEL. Now porter could be made cheaper yet, with just 5% of this new, strongly flavored, almost burnt-tasting, dark malt plus 95% pale malt. Eventually, this porter morphed into a "leann dubh" (a dry stout) and, by the start of the 20th century, it had become the principal beer of Ireland, whereas in England pale ales and their variants had already replaced porters in the hearts of the local beer drinkers.

During the potato famine from 1845 to 1849, 1 million Irish died and another 1 million emigrated, mostly to America, but also to England. As a result, the Irish population declined by 20% to 25%. Yet Irish beer production did not decline correspondingly. It was 1.627 million hl 1837, but still 1.482 million hl in 1857. The reason was a growing beer export from Ireland. Guinness had launched its super porter in 1806; it became a single stout in 1840 and in the same year, exports accounted for 53% of the Guinness production. Irish beer production recovered to 3.24 million hl by 1875 and peaked at 5.459 million hl in 1915. With the rise in volume also came a greater concentration of the industry and a precipitous decline in the average beer's original gravity and strength.

Ireland's most famous and most recognizable beer brand, without a doubt, is the iconic Guinness. Arthur Guinness (1725–1807) had started brewing in 1756 and his eponymous brewery has gone on to dominate Irish brewing and become a world force. He set up St. James's Gate brewery, set by the river Liffey, in Dublin in 1759. His first exports to England were 6.5 barrels of bitter, in 1769. Guinness ended his production of bitter in 1799 and concentrated instead on his porter, which he had introduced in 1778. That porter remained in production for almost 2 centuries, until 1974. During those early years, a dispute over a water channel arose that went on from 1775 until 1784. It ended in a peculiar settlement that gave Guinness a 9,000-year lease for the mere sum of £45 a year, after which Guinness embarked on a rapid expansion of his brewery. In 1801, Guinness developed a brew for the Irish workforce in the Caribbean. That brew was then called West Indian porter (a triple). It is now sold as foreign extra stout. Guinness' first exports to continental Europe were to Lisbon in 1811; his first to America were in 1840. By 1870, exports amounted to 10% of total Guinness sales. By the early 20th century, Guinness was the world's largest brewery with an annual volume of 4.8 million hl (1914 figure). After the Irish Free State passed the "Control of Manufacturer's Act" in 1932, the Guinness headquarters moved to London. At that point, the Guinness family still held a 51% ownership in the company. In 1997, Guinness merged with Britain's Grand Metropolitan Holdings plc to form the world's largest drinks company, Diageo. See GUINNESS, ARTHUR.

Only two other breweries have had a national impact on the Irish brew scene and went head to head with Guinness. These were Williams, Beamish & Crawford, and Murphy's, both of county Cork. The former, although reportedly dating back to 1650, was officially founded as the Cork Porter Brewery in 1792. By 1805, it had become Ireland's largest brewery, making some 160,000 hl. The company went public in 1901. It was acquired by Canada's Carling O'Keefe in 1962, then by Australia's Elders IXL in 1987, and then by Scottish & Newcastle in 1995, a company that became part of Heineken in 2008. Murphy's was founded as the Lady's Well brewery in 1854. By 1861 it had reached a volume of 68,600 hl. It peaked at 229,000 hl in 1901. In 1967, Britain's Watney Mann took a controlling stake in the brewery but production fell to 18,000 hl in 1971. The company went onto receivership in 1982 and was taken over by Heineken a year later. In 1984, Heineken launched Murphy's Red. Now that Heineken owned two breweries in County Cork, it decided to close one of them, which spelled the end of the Williams, Beamish & Crawford Brewery in 2009. See BEAMISH & CRAWFORD and MURPHY'S BREWERY. The Irish stout beer style remains one of Ireland's great imports, recognized, admired, and copied worldwide. Even the Belgian–American giant Anheuser-Busch InBev produces an Irish stout, a good indication of the style's cultural reach.

The first lager in Ireland was brewed by the Darty brewery in Dublin, in 1891, but it closed in 1896. The next brewery to try a lager was Regal, based in Kells. It managed to last from 1937 to 1954. Other than

Harp, the only other lagers that have been brewed successfully in Ireland are the long established Heineken-owned or affiliated brands Amstel, Heineken, Fosters, and Carling. Finally, Tennents, a popular Scottish lager in the Irish market, was purchased by the Irish company C&C from Anheuser-Busch InBev in 2009.

Thomas Caffrey founded his eponymous brewery in Belfast in 1897,which was acquired by Charrington in 1967 and ultimately Interbrew in 2000, with brand rights sold to Coors in 2001.

The Letts Brewery Co. Wexford ceased brewing in 1956 but its Enniscorthy ruby red ale was acquired by Coors in 1981 and is brewed under license as Killians.

In the latter part of the 20th century, a wave of microbreweries opened in Ireland, some of them short lived: Balbriggan, Biddy Early, Dublin Brewery, Emerald, Kinsale, McCardle Moore, Dwan–Tipperary, and Waterford. Opening as the second wave were Arrain Mhor, Beoir Chorcha Dhibune, and Galway Hooker, plus Hilden and Whitewater in Ulster. In addition, the successful Porterhouse group has opened brew pubs in several Irish locations and in London's Covent Garden. See PORTERHOUSE BREWING COMPANY.

At the start of the 19th century there were 200 breweries in Ireland, 55 in Dublin alone. By 1960, there were only 8 left, but by 2005, with the advent of microbreweries, that number had increased to 19. Doubtless, this small nation of 3.5 million people will continue to build back one of the world's most influential and enduring beer cultures.

Glenn A. Payne

Irish moss (Chondrus crispus) is a type of edible red seaweed used as kettle (copper) finings. See KETTLE FININGS. It grows abundantly along the rocky Atlantic coasts of Europe and North America. The soft body of the plant consists of 50%–60% carrageenan and was used extensively as a kettle finings agent for the past 200 years or more. Its use peaked around 1970 and then sharply declined as other sources of carageenan were developed. Other sources include Euchema spp. and Gigartina spp., which produce carrageenans with slightly different chemical structures to C. crispus. Carrageenans from these different sources are sometimes blended to optimize performance. However, Irish moss and formulated carrageenan blends are also used as auxiliary finings in cask-conditioned beer, often in conjunction with isinglass. Like other types of fining agents, carageenan works through the ability of its electrostatic charge to gather together oppositely charged materials into large clumps, thus allowing them to settle out more quickly from beer or wort.

John Palmer

Irish red ale. Though the term is rarely heard in Ireland, in other parts of the world it is commonly used to describe a style of reddish-amber or brown ale that has its roots in Ireland. This style of beer is characterized by its color and by its malt profile, which typically includes a caramel or toffee-like sweetness. Irish red ale also traditionally contains roasted malts that provide a dry finish with only a hint of bitterness. Although this style of beer has been brewed and enjoyed in Ireland for many years, it was Coors who popularized the name Irish red ale in the early nineties. At that time, the American public became very interested in specialty beers and a Coors brand called Killian's Irish Red, which had been brewed since 1981 became one of the top selling specialty beer brands in the United States. Coors supported the popularity of this brand with a marketing campaign that highlighted the beer's Irish heritage and distinctive color. First brewed by the Killian family's Lett's Brewery in County Wexford, Ireland, the original beer was called "Enniscorthy Ruby Ale." In the 1950s Lett's Brewery closed and rights to market beer under the George Killian brand were sold to Pelforth Brewery in France and later acquired by Coors, who immediately released George Killian's Irish Red Ale. As it happens, the beer is actually a lager. In Ireland one will find the popular Smithwicks, brewed by Diageo, though there is no reference here to red ale. Many American craft brewers have picked up the Irish red ale mantle, brewing lightly malty easy-drinking beers tinged red by roasted grains. The style is now a mainstay of many American brewpubs.

Cornell, Martyn. *Beer: The history of the pint.* London: Headline Book Publishing, 2003.

Jackson, Michael. *Michael Jackson's beer companion.* London: Duncan Baird Publishers, 1993.

Mirella G. Amato

Irish stout

See ARTHUR GUINNESS & SONS, BEAMISH & CRAWFORD, MURPHY'S BREWERY, and STOUTS.

iron (chemical symbol Fe) occurs naturally in brewing and cleaning water as salts or ions, including Fe^{2+} and Fe^{3+} cations. Iron, however, is usually kept at concentrations of no more than 1 mg/l because at higher concentrations it would have a detrimental effect on the finished beer's taste and color. To keep the iron content in check, brewers often aerate and filter their water before using it. In addition to brewing water, diatomaceous earth preparations used in beer filtration, as well as hot water from fobber jets between the filler and the capper at the bottling line, are also potential sources of iron in beer.

In most finished beers, iron is no more than just a trace element of perhaps 0.1 mg/l. Otherwise, tannins—derived from grain husks and hops—could form chemical linkages with iron ions, which would add slightly metallic or ink-like off-flavors and a brown tinge to the beer. Even these low levels of iron can be damaging to the stability of beer because they potentiate the production of reactive oxygen species that can cause the staling of beer and the oxidation of polyphenols that leads to haze development.

Iron, however, has one positive effect. It promotes beer foam by enhancing the bridge-building capacity, elasticity, and stability of polypeptide chains on the surface of the carbonation bubbles that form the head. In countries where food safety regulations permit, therefore, ferrous salts are sometimes added to beer as foam stabilizers at a dosage of up to 0.6 g/hl, but always in conjunction with reducing compounds that keep the foam from turning a rather unattractive rust brown.

Excessive amounts of ferrous salts in beer are extremely undesirable because ferrous precipitates may serve as nucleation points for large carbon dioxide bubbles inside the bottle, causing gushing problems.

See also GUSHING.

Oliver Jakob

isinglass is a traditional finings, a substance that causes yeast to precipitate out of suspension, leaving beer clear. Isinglass is derived from the swim bladders of certain tropical and subtropical fish. When macerated and dissolved for several weeks in dilute food-grade acids, they form a turbid, colorless, viscous solution largely made up of the protein collagen. This material is known to brewers as isinglass finings. See FININGS. The collagen in isinglass is a highly ordered, positively charged helical polymer. When used as a fining agent it has the ability to settle yeast and beer proteins very quickly and can do so repeatedly. This latter property is essential for cask-conditioned ales, where the casks may be moved several times prior to serving. See CASK CONDITIONING.

There is much speculation as to the first use of this unlikely substance in beer making. The most logical conjecture is that at some point in history a resourceful fisherman used the swim bladder of a large specimen to store his beer, akin to keeping wine in a skin. It is likely that the beer of the day was somewhat acidic, perhaps from lactobacillus or acetobacter contamination. The acidity would have certainly caused some collagen to dissolve and clarify the beer. The observant individual might have noticed a bright, clear beer when pouring it into a drinking vessel.

Traditionally, isinglass for brewing purposes was derived from sturgeon, although modern commercial isinglass is more typically derived from tropical estuarine dwellers, such as the Nile Perch Lates niloticus from Lake Victoria, where it is considered an invasive species. The best quality finings originate in the South China Sea and are identified as Round Saigon or Long Saigon finings. The swim bladder is sun dried at the catch site and then packed for export to markets in China, where it is used to make fish maw soup, or to the UK to make isinglass finings. With the advances in centrifugation and filtration technologies, the use of isinglass has declined and today it is largely confined to cask-conditioned ales, although some American craft brewers also use it to clarify beer without the use of filtration.

Ian L. Ward

iso-alpha acids are the thermally induced isomers of alpha acids and the principal source of bitterness in beer. They are bitter, have surface activity, and are reactive with oxygen and other beer constituents. As a class of compounds, they are composed of individual acid homologs, which are adhumulone, cohumulone, humulone, prehumulone, and posthumulone. The isomerization from an alpha acid into an iso-alpha acid is a chemical process that maintains the alpha acid's original material composition but essentially rearranges the compound's molecular structure, altering its chemical properties and reactions.

Compared with other constituents of beer, such as carbohydrates from malt, ethanol, and carbon dioxide, iso-alpha acids occur at relatively low levels—typically at 8 to 25 ppm and in rare cases as high as 100 ppm. Although only present in minute amounts, even small changes in the concentration of iso-alpha acids can have a disproportionate impact on the beer's flavor, its bitterness, and its overall drinkability. Iso-alpha acids are intensely bitter and have a human detection threshold in beer of approximately 6 to 7 ppm. Because bitterness perception is somewhat subjective, some studies allow for a wider range of 4 to 11 ppm. See BITTERNESS. To put this into perspective, many American lager brands have iso-alpha acid levels at or below 10 ppm, which actually means that a significant portion of beer-drinking consumers may not even detect any bitterness in some American mass market lagers. Different beer styles typically have very different bitterness levels as part of their specifications. European lagers, for instance, may have an average iso-alpha acid content of 20 to 30 ppm, British ales of 25 to 40 ppm, and the wide range of modern craft brewed beers of 10 ppm to 100 ppm.

Iso-alpha acids are formed typically during wort boiling, when hops are added, and alpha acids are extracted from the hops' lupulin glands (or from the hop resin in hop extracts). Isomerization is the result of the effect of heat on the alpha acids. The process is both time and temperature dependent. The longer the alpha acids are exposed to the rolling wort boil, the more alpha acids are converted into iso-alpha acids and the more bitterness is created in the wort and beer. See BOILING. Hops that are added late in the boil, on the other hand, still release their aroma oils—and these will not all evaporate into the kettle stack—but a much smaller proportion of their alpha acids will become iso-alpha acids.

Hop acids can also be isomerized before they are added to the wort kettle. For this there are several approaches. There are preisomerized hop pellets on the market. These are produced by mixing finely milled hops with a small amount of about 1.5% by weight of magnesium oxide. This mixture is then pelletized, vacuum packed, and stored hot at about 45°C (113°F) to 55°C (131°F) for 10 to 14 days. During this time, the small amount of magnesium serves as a catalyst to accelerate the formation of iso-alpha acids. The addition of isomerized kettle extracts is another method. These are prepared similarly to preisomerized hop pellets by mixing magnesium oxide or a potassium carbonate/hydroxide solution with a hop resin extract and then heating the mixture to produce iso-alpha acids. Then there are preisomerized iso-alpha acid extracts, which are produced by separating alpha acids from beta acids after supercritical CO_2 or ethanol extraction and then processing the result further downstream to convert alpha acids to iso-alpha acids. These extracts are used either during fermentation or, more typically, postfermentation to give beer the desired level of bitterness. The unit of measurement of bitterness in beer and wort is the international bitterness unit. See HOP EXTRACTS and INTERNATIONAL BITTERNESS UNITS (IBUS).

Thomas Shellhammer and Val Peacock

isoamyl acetate, a key ester (combination of an acid and an alcohol) present in all beers. See ESTERS. At its flavor threshold (around 0.6 to 1.2 parts per million) it provides pronounced fruity-fresh, banana, or pear drop–like aromas. It is widely used to reproduce banana-like aromatics in artificial flavorings. As with other esters, it is produced by yeast during fermentation and has a major flavor impact in certain beer styles, particularly Bavarian-style wheat beers. In general it contributes to the fruity qualities of beer. See FRUITY. The aroma of isoamyl acetate, which is created by traditional weissbier yeast strains, combines with the phenolic clove-like notes of 4-vinyl guaiacol to form the basis of the typical Bavarian weissbier aroma. As such, the concentration of isoamyl acetate is one of the major separators between the flavors of Bavarian-style weissbier and the so-called American hefeweizen (American-style wheat beer), which generally shows little or no banana-like aromatics. German research has shown that high concentrations of isoamyl acetate in weissbier are partially dependent on a high glucose level in the original wort, which, if desired, can be achieved by a targeted decoction mashing regime.

See also AMERICAN WHEAT BEER and WEISSBIER.

Eder, Michael Josef. Brewing a wheat beer with intensive banana aroma: A European perspective. *The New Brewer*, November/December 2009.

Gary Spedding

isovaleric acid, also known as 3-methylbutanoic acid, 1-pentanoic acid, or delphinic acid, is a natural fatty acid found in many plants, essential oils, old hops, foot sweat, and some cheese. It is characterized by a pungent aroma often described as cheesy (especially referring to aged hard cheeses) or "gym socks." In beer, the flavor threshold of isovaleric acid is in the wide range of 0.1–1.5 mg/l, varying with the taster's sensitivity. Isovaleric acid is a product of the oxidation of hop resins and is often quite pronounced in hops that have been exposed to oxygen over a long period of time. It is also a by-product of contamination by, or fermentation with, Brettanomyces yeasts. See BRETTANOMYCES. The presence of isovaleric acid in beer is usually considered a flaw, but it is considered appropriate as a background note in some English-style ales and can be stronger in beers purposely fermented with Brettanomyces. Excessive isovaleric acid in beer is best prevented by appropriate hop storage and clean brewing practices to prevent wild yeast infections. Because oxygen is the catalyst that forms isovaleric acid in hops, all hops should be stored cold and tightly packed to limit their exposure to the air. See HOPS.

Brewers Publications. *Evaluating beer*. Boulder, CO: Brewers Publications, 1993.
Fix, George. *Principles of brewing science*. Boulder, CO: Brewers Publications, 1989.

Alana R. Jones

Italy is generally considered a center of wine culture and therefore is thought of as a place where beer is an afterthought at best. Perhaps surprisingly, however, Italy has made significant contributions to the world of beer throughout its long history from ancient Rome to the present. Today it has thriving mass market breweries and a creative, exciting craft beer culture. It seems that the ancient Romans probably encountered brewing on a large scale for the first time shortly after Octavian—better known to history as Emperor Augustus (63 BCE–14 CE)—defeated the Egyptian navy under Queen Cleopatra (69 BCE–30 BCE) and her Roman lover Mark Antony (83 BCE–30 BCE) at the Battle of Actium in 31 BCE. See EGYPT. Cleopatra, incidentally, had financed her navy largely from a special tax she had placed on beer. By some reckoning this was the first tax on beer ever. After the loss of their fleet, Mark Antony and Cleopatra jointly committed suicide in 30 BCE, and Egypt became a Roman colony. At that time, Egypt could already look back at thousands of years of beer making. The Romans were less interested in Egyptian beer than they were in the grains from the fertile banks of the Nile, which they usurped for the bread of Rome. Nonetheless, references to beer started to creep into Latin writings after the Egyptian conquest. The first such mention was by the Greek-born Roman historian, geographer, and philosopher Strabo (63 or 64 BCE–approx. 24 CE), who reported that the Ligurians of northwestern Italy and southeastern France lived "mostly off cattle, milk, and a drink from barley." A few years later, the Roman historian Pliny the Elder, who was born in 23 or 24 CE and died in Pompeii during the Vesuvius eruption of 79 CE, wrote about Egyptian beer, which he called zythum; about Spanish beer, which he called caelia and cerea; and about Gallic (French) beer, which he called cerevisia. The Roman writer Publius Cornelius Tacitus (approx. 55–117 CE) visited the newly conquered Germanic regions and made extensive notes about the beer-drinking habits of the local tribes there. In his *De origine et situ Germanorum* (About the Location and Origins of the Germans) he famously wrote, "Potui humor ex hordeo aut frumento, in quandam similitudinem vini corruptus." (The Germans drink a juice from grain, but fermented, which somehow resembles adulterated wine.) But the foreign "grain wine" could not have been very "corrupt," because even Tacitus' own stepfather, the general who was responsible for the Roman conquest of Britain, Gnaeus Julius Agricola (40–93 CE), had, in very un-Roman fashion, three brewers from Glevum (present-day Gloucester in England) in his employ. In 179 CE, during the reign of Emperor Marcus Aurelius (121–180 CE), the Romans even built a full-scale brewery for 6,000 elite legionnaires at Castra Regina (present-day Regensburg) on the banks of the Danube. This brewery was excavated between 1974 and 1980 and is now considered the oldest preserved brewery site where beer was made not from baked bread, as was common for tribal brews at the time, but from mashed grain. See BAVARIA. The spread of beer making in the Roman Empire is further documented in the writings of Saint Benedict of Nursia (480–547 CE), the founder of the order of Benedictine monks, who were to become the most prominent brew monks of the Middle Ages. When Benedict stayed, between 529 and 543, at the Abbey of Monte Cassino in Latium, in central Italy, he composed a set of rules that have served as the model for monastic daily conduct to this day. In it, beer assumed a crucial role, because Benedict considered hard manual labor, at least 5 hours a day, in the fields, the bakery, and the brewery the only road to salvation. To Benedict, food was intended to be simple, and beer was primarily a necessary source of nourishment, not an indulgence. He understood that beer—if made strong enough and from the best grains—was not only thirst quenching but veritable "liquid bread." Thus, Benedict entitled every monk to a substantial amount of daily beer, which, in modern measure, added up to about 1 keg of beer per monk per week! But Benedict also insisted that beer be respected. He forbade drunkenness; any monk who spilled beer was punished by having to stand upright and perfectly still for an entire night.

The importance of beer in the Italian culture, however, declined with the demise of the Roman Empire, in part because of the greater difficulty of growing grains than vines in the Italian soil and climate. Also, beer was considered a drink of the barbarian hordes from up north, who periodically descended across the Alps to sack and plunder Italy and to cause general mayhem. One such marauder was Flavius Odoacer (433–493 CE), a Germanic chieftain who revolted against the Roman Emperor Romulus Augustulus and succeeded in deposing him in 476. It turned out that Romulus Augustulus was to be the last Roman Emperor. In subsequent centuries, the country later known as Italy simply fell apart and split into many different duchies and city states, which became easy prey for invading forces, notably those of France and the German Empire. Much of northern Italy surrounding the Adriatic port city of Trieste, for instance, became Austrian in 1382 and remains so virtually without interruption in 1920, when it was merged with Italy after the post–World War II disintegration of the Austro-Hungarian Empire. The little beer that was consumed in Italy during the Middle Ages, not surprisingly, was consumed mostly in the north of the country, and it was imported. Things changed, however, in the late 18th century, when in 1789 Giovanni Baldassarre Ketter opened the first Italian brewery of modern times, in Nizza Monferrato, Piedmont. Two years later, Ketter sold his brewery to Giovanni Debernardi, who managed to obtain a license for selling beer in all of Piedmont. By 1890, almost 3 decades of the Italian unification in 1861, known as the "Risorgimento," under Giuseppe Garibaldi and Camillo di Cavour, there were some 140 breweries operating in Italy; by the end of the century that number had almost doubled. One of the major forces of large-scale brewing was the Schwechat Brewery near Vienna, owned by Anton Dreher. It was the headquarters of the largest brewing enterprise in all of the Austro-Hungarian Empire, which, in those days, comprised not only Austria and Hungary proper but also Bohemia and Moravia (today parts of the Czech Republic), Slovakia, much of the Balkans, and much of northern Italy. Dreher had breweries not only in Austria, but also in Budapest, Hungary, and in Trieste, where he had founded Birra Dreher in 1896. That brewery was bought by Heineken in 1974. Since 1996, incidentally, Heineken also owns Birra Moretti, founded in Udine, in 1859, by Luigi Moretti; as well as Ichnusa in Sardinia; Messina in Sicily; and Von Wűnster in Bergamo. The other internationally known Italian brewery, Birra Peroni, was founded by Giovanni Peroni in Vigevano in Lombardia in 1846 and moved to Rome in 1864. It is now owned by SABMiller, as are Wűhrer in Brescia and Raffo in Bari. Then there is Carlsberg Italia, which owns Poretti in Varese and Splűgen in Chiavenna. The only major Italian brewery not affiliated with large international concern is Forst in Merano, South Tirol, which also owns Menabrea in Biella.

Today, Italy can boast one of the most exciting and creative craft brewing cultures in the world. Only a decade before, craft breweries were counted in dozens, but by 2011 the number had climbed well past 300 and shows little sign of abating. The story of the Italian beer renaissance will be familiar to anyone who has followed the arc of the American craft brewing movement. Young beer enthusiasts, after enlightening trips to countries with long brewing traditions, opened the first brewpubs in the mid-1990s, mainly in northern Italy, selling fresh new beers to consumers who had become used to drinking almost exclusively bland mass marketed lagers. They took their inspirations from Belgium, England, Germany, and the United States and set about forging a still-evolving idiom of beer that is uniquely Italian. Not surprisingly, the new Italian brewing culture is unusually food driven. Brewers are using varieties of tobacco leaves, smoked teas, beans, nuts, berries, flowers, fruit, herbs, vegetables, spices, sugars, salts, peppers, and more.

The chestnut is a culinary mainstay in many Italian regional cuisines, and more than 30 Italian brewers make chestnut beers. The chestnut, which gives profoundly earthy flavors, is employed in a myriad of forms—dried, smoked, roasted, as chestnut flour, and in powerfully flavored local chestnut honeys. Brewing competitions often include a "birraalle castagne" category ("chestnut beer"), a beer type unique to Italy. There are also interesting fruit beers brewed using local rare fruits and others making use of the traditional spelt grown in areas such as Tuscany, Latium, and Abruzzo. Among the most interesting emerging trends is represented by those beers that are linked to the world of wine. Some brewers, especially those who are former vintners, age beers in oak barrels that previously held local wines, and some add grapes or wine must to the kettle or use wine yeasts to ferment their beers. Italian craft beers sometimes show more flair, style, creativity, and individuality than technical skill, but the latter quality can be learned and the former qualities bode well for the future of Italian craft brewing.

Cooking with beer, as well as the pairing of beer and food, is becoming increasingly popular in Italy. Famed chefs are increasingly adding interesting beer menus to their prestigious wine lists, and they are proud to put Italian craft beers on their tables.

Italy's burgeoning craft brewing scene has started up some relatively large competitions, the biggest of which is "Birra dell'Anno" (Beer of the Year), organized by Unionbirrai. Movimento Birrario Italiano, known as MoBI, promotes beer culture and beer quality, organizing seminars, conferences, competitions, training courses, and tastings, among other activities.

Italian craft breweries produce 200,000 hl (5,282,000 gal) per year, representing 1.5% of the total Italian beer production. Craft beer production has trended consistently upward, whereas production and consumption of multinational mass market lagers have more or less stagnated during the past few years. As of 2010, beer surpassed wine as the favorite fermented beverage of Italians, a development that could scarcely have been imagined only 20 years ago.

Asso Birra. http://www.assobirra.it/tutto_sulla_birra/birra_storia.htm/ (accessed March 30, 2011).

Dabove, Lorenzo. "Italy." In *Beer (eyewitness companions)*, ed. Michael Jackson, 201–6. London: Dorling Kindersley, 2007.

Dabove, Lorenzo. "Italy." In *The beer book*, ed. Tim Hampson, 248–53. London: Dorling Kindersley, 2008.

Konen, Heinrich. "Evidence of the beer trade in the Roman Empire." In *Annual 2010 Annual Compendium of the Society for the History of Brewing*. Berlin: VLB Berlin, 2010.

Microbirrifici. http://www.microbirrifici.org (accessed April 26, 2011). A complete, constantly updated database of Italian microbreweries.

MoBI (movimento birrario italiano). *Beer consumers movement*. http://www.mo-bi.org/ (accessed March 30, 2011).

Wiss-Kotzan, Silke. "References to beer in text books of antiquity." In *Annual 2010 Annual Compendium of the Society for the History of Brewing*. Berlin: VLB Berlin, 2010.

Lorenzo Dabove

Jackson, Michael, (1942–2007) was arguably the single most influential voice in food and drink of the 20th century. Through his writings, lectures, and television appearances he tirelessly promulgated the idea that beer, far from being the simple fizz most people are familiar with, is in fact a fascinatingly diverse and complex drink worthy of great respect and perhaps even love. In spreading this message, he became the spiritual father of the early microbrewing movement and the greatest champion of the craft brewer. He shone a light upon the old brewing traditions of Europe, from the cask-conditioned ales of his native England to the spontaneously fermented beers of Belgium and the obscure, ancient sahtis of Finland. By writing with passion and poetry about the people, the culture, and the flavors of these beers, he surely saved a number of brewing traditions from extinction. Later, as craft brewing took hold in the United States and around the world, his voice launched thousands of breweries and helped remake the modern world of brewing.

Jackson's background did not presage such a future. Born in Wetherby, Yorkshire, he was descended from Lithuanian Jews, a rich heritage of which he seemed to become increasing proud during his life. He spoke often of the hearty Eastern European food he grew up with and once described himself as a "pale-faced kid, whose gloomy Slavic features were not wholly softened by my bubbly dark curls." His grandfather, Chaim Jakowitz, had fled Kaunas, Lithuania, for a new life in Leeds, England. His father, Isaac Jakowitz, married a gentile from Yorkshire and anglicized the family's name to Jackson. The name Michael Jackson was, of course, to become among the most famous in the world, but not for beer. Jackson had good fun with it, occasionally donning a single white sequined glove for comic effect.

Postwar northern England was a hardscrabble place, and Jackson grew up a proud working-class Yorkshireman, an outlook that later informed both his writing and his outlook on life. At 16 he left school and went to work as a trainee reporter on the *Huddersfield Examiner*. From there he moved to London and worked for the *Daily Herald* and later moved to *World Press News*, which he helped transform into the magazine *Campaign*, of which he eventually became editor. In those days, newspaper work revolved around the pub, and it was in London's pubs that Jackson truly fell in love with cask-conditioned beer. In 1976, Jackson wrote *The English Pub*, a heartfelt paean to a culture and way of life he feared was disappearing. The following year *The World Guide to Beer* hit bookshelves, and it was this groundbreaking work that was to make his reputation.

In *The World Guide to Beer*, Jackson postulated the idea that beer could be organized, sometimes clearly, at other times loosely, into styles, and it was through these beer styles that beer's flavor, culture, and history could be understood. In putting forth this concept, Jackson formed the entire basis for our modern understanding of traditional beer. Although anyone who discusses beer now inevitably refers to beer styles, many are unaware that Jackson essentially invented the concept from whole cloth. *The World Guide to Beer* gave Jackson genuine influence within the world of drinks writing, and he quickly brought it to bear, writing dozens of newspaper and magazine articles that described traditional beers, both British and

Michael Jackson, renowned author and "beer hunter," in Munich around 1990. PIKE MICROBREWERY MUSEUM, SEATTLE, WA

foreign in all their nuances. To many, it sounded like wine writing, but to Jackson it was simply good reportage. Beers did have flavors of coffee, chocolate, honeysuckle, bananas, cloves, and smoke, and Jackson wrote about them in a prose style that was direct and deeply studied, yet still sparkled with verve and humor. As the Campaign for Real Ale launched its movement to save Britain's national drink, they found in Jackson a willing ally, although some found Jackson's obsession with the rest of the world's beers a touch too exotic for comfort.

But Jackson did not stay home. A writing assignment in Amsterdam in 1969 had taken him near the Dutch border with Belgium, and there he had discovered an entire new world of fascinating, highly complex Belgian beers. Having opened a door onto the world of Belgian brewing in *The World Guide to Beer*, he brought people there and beyond with his 1990 six-part series "The Beer Hunter." First shown on Channel 4 in the UK and the Discovery Channel in the United States, it was the first television series about beer, taking viewers on a tour through the world's great brewing nations. It has been seen in 15 countries, and the sobriquet "The Beer Hunter" followed him for the rest of his life.

The year 1991 saw the release of two books, *The Great Beers of Belgium* and the ambitious *Michael Jackson's Beer Companion*. Each was a detailed, meticulous, and masterly blend of clear-eyed journalism and romantic polemics. Together, the two books particularly raised the profile of Belgian brewing, and to this day brewers and beer enthusiasts in that country regard him as something of a national hero. Just as the pioneering musicologist Alan Lomax brought the culture of blues and jazz out of the American South and onto the world stage, so Jackson did the same for traditional beer. By the late 1990s it is fair to say that there were few brewers in the world who had not heard of him and many who had been launched into their careers by his writings.

It was perhaps in the United States that Michael Jackson had his greatest impact. His books, lectures, and television appearances fueled both the homebrewing movement and the craft brewing revolution that grew out of it. Hundreds of American brewery owners claim Jackson and his work as their primary inspiration to start a brewery. Followed by streams of fans wherever he roamed across the floor of Denver's huge Great American Beer Festival every year, Jackson was endlessly patient and content to talk, try homebrewed beers, and sign books for hours at a time without complaint. Hundreds of people at a time would show up to his tastings, rambling affairs where his famous "digressions" would include stories of breweries and brewers from all over the world. At American craft breweries in particular, the news that Michael Jackson was coming was often treated with the sort of gravity usually reserved for a state visit. By the time he left the brewery, he was often regarded as a friend. He never learned to drive, but friends and beer fans jockeyed for the honor of picking him up at airports. When he traveled, he sometimes stayed at beer enthusiasts' homes, unable to refuse their insistent hospitality.

Through all of this, Jackson maintained and promoted other passions. He was a great lover of jazz and was deeply conversant with the music, although he rarely wrote on the subject. He did write extensively about whisky and in 1989 produced *The Malt Whisky Companion*, still the best-selling book on the subject. He followed these with *Scotland and Its Whiskies* (2001) and his final book, simply entitled

Whisky (2005), which won him the James Beard Foundation Book Award. Many fans of his beer books barely realized that he was also considered the world's leading authority on Scotch whisky. Overall, Jackson's books have sold over 3 million copies in 18 languages.

Jackson's work won him many accolades, including several Glenfiddich Awards, the André Simon Award, and the Mercurius Award, personally presented to him in 1994 by Crown Prince Phillippe of Belgium.

In his later years, Jackson suffered silently from the effects of Parkinson's disease, a neural disorder, although it was not until 2006 that he disclosed it to the public. Seemingly indefatigable, he continued traveling and writing. Days before he died, he wrote in the magazine *All About Beer* about the indignities of the disease; it was his last piece and one of his best, showing his trademark steely Yorkshire determination and puckish humor. Referring to Parkinsons' effects, he said he planned to write a book entitled *I Am Not Drunk*.

At the opening of the introduction to *The World Guide to Beer* Jackson wrote, "Beer may have been man's staple diet before bread was invented, and these two staffs of life are as comparable as they are closely related. Each can offer an everyday experience or a rare pleasure. In each case, what we seek is a measure of what we deserve." With those words, Michael Jackson began a body of work that seemed to create a new kingdom of beer, populate it with enthusiasts and new brewers, and then expand it to all the corners of the Earth. If any other figure in food and drink during the 20th century had an influence so broad and lasting, it is to be doubted whether any was quite so well loved.

Garrett Oliver

Japan is home to beer's great sibling, sake, and the fourth largest beer market in the world. Although sake is a wonderful and complex drink, in Japan it runs a very distant second to beer. Although there is some indication that beer was introduced to Japan by Dutch traders in the 17th century, it surely did not become established there until the late 1800s. After Commodore Perry signed the Treaty of Kanagawa in 1854, an influx of British and German beer quickly outstripped American beer sales. On August 27, 1869, *The Daily Japan Herald* ran an article declaring that a man named Rosenfeld had opened the Japan Brewery in Yokohama. The Japan Brewery was run by an American, Emil Wiegand, and apparently stayed in business until 1874, having primarily sold its beer to foreigners doing business in Japan. He had had competition from the Norwegian American Johan Martinius Thoresen, who changed his name to William Copeland after emigrating to the United States. Copeland's Spring Valley Brewery opened in 1870 and after some years of success, finally faltered and went bankrupt in 1884. By 1888, this brewery reopened under new ownership, selling a new beer called Kirin. In the meantime, Seibei Nakagawa had returned from Germany to Japan in 1876, having studied brewing there for 2 years. He was appointed chief engineer of the newly built Kaitakushi Brewery in the Aoyama area of Tokyo. This became the first Japanese-owned brewery; when it was sold in 1886 it was renamed the Sapporo Brewery. The Osaka Beer Brewing Company, later renamed after its best-selling Asahi (rising sun) beer, was established in 1889. Japan's three largest brewers were well under way by the 1890s, and the standard beer of Japan, taking after the German and American beers of the day, was a variant of golden export lager. Over most of the next century, Japanese beer changed very little. In 1987 Asahi launched Super Dry, a highly attenuated lager that did not have the heavier maltiness of the beers made by Asahi's rival, Kirin. With a crisp, dry taste similar to beers from northern Germany, Super Dry soon carved out a large share of the market, and in the process many of the other popular lagers became "drier" as well.

However, there were more interesting things slowly happening in the Japanese beer scene. From the late 1980s, Tokyo and other major Japanese cities in Japan were experiencing a small boom in Belgian ales, particularly Trappist beers. A small specialty bar, called Brussels, opened in Tokyo, followed by a few others. Most notable among them is Bois Cereste, a favorite of the late Michael Jackson during his Tokyo visits. Although the popularity of Belgian beer in Japan has been small, the love of these beers by Japanese enthusiasts has been enduring, and interest has steadily grown over the past 20 years. There are now nearly 40 Belgian beer bars in Tokyo and perhaps about half as many spread throughout Japan's other major cities.

Craft beers from the United States have also been imported into Japan since the 1990s, alongside beers from Germany, the Netherlands, and the UK.

Another major shift in the Japanese beer scene occurred in 1994 with the relaxation of brewery license regulations. Previously, yearly production of 2 million l of beer was necessary to license a brewery. This was dropped to 60,000 l annually, enabling the opening of smaller breweries that could produce craft beer, or ji-biru.

Japan's first microbrewery, Echigo Beer of Niigata prefecture, held their opening party in December of 1994 and opened for business the following month. The new brewpub had a design that reminded many of a modern European church, and their beer was based on popular American microbrewed styles of the time. Their pale ale, amber ale, and stout were found to be of surprisingly good quality, and Japanese craft brewing was off and running.

Little by little, the craft brew industry in Japan grew, despite the collapse of the economy around the same time. Although Japanese consumers have a particular appreciation for high-quality food and drink, they were entirely unfamiliar with craft beer, and many Japanese craft brewers seemed not to be entirely familiar with it themselves.

One reason is likely to be the fact that that homebrewing is still illegal in Japan. Without a homebrewing culture—no clubs, no contests, and, in the end, no breeding ground for would-be brewmasters—Japan struggled to build a craft beer culture. Brewers visited from overseas, usually Germany or the United States, but most stayed only months at a time, training local Japanese brewers to brew bolder, more interesting beers.

Some 175 breweries opened in Japan between 1995 and 1999, followed by around 100 more through 2005. Since then, however, new openings have slowed to a trickle, and no great burst of new craft breweries appears to be on the horizon. However, craft beer does have a genuine foothold in Japan. Anyone seeking it there might be advised to visit Beer Club Popeye in Tokyo. Located opposite Ryogoku station, near the famous sumo wrestling stadium, Popeye was founded in 1985 as a western-style pub by Tatsuo Aoki. The pub was an early adopter of Japanese-brewed craft beer. From three taps in 1995, the number grew to 20 in 1998, 40 in 2002, and 70 by 2008. The beer enthusiast contingent that frequented Popeye held Japan's first Real Ale Festival in the early spring of 2003 at the pub. The event spurred them to form a club for beer consumers, first called the Real Ale Club, and then quickly broadened to the Good Beer Club at the founding meeting in January 2004. Some members were soon disappointed that the group did not agitate to lower beer taxes or legalize homebrewing, but the group remains active and hosts regular tasting events. In recent years, a number of pubs specializing in craft beer have sprung up throughout Tokyo and in most other major Japanese cities.

Today, Japan has a very diverse beer culture, and most craft beers are well made and nicely balanced. However, the beer market in Japan is still strongly centered around the mass-produced lagers and low-malt beers produced by the four major brewers. These low-malt beers, called happo-shu, are usually 25% malt or less, with the rest made up by other starches or sugars. Happo-shu can contain up to 65% malt before being reclassified as beer.

This is an important factor because Japanese beer taxes are high—some 222 yen (about US $2.50) per liter. This makes the cost of an ordinary six-pack of standard lager as high as US $15. Taxes on happo-shu are far lower and the drink appeared as a way of offering cheaper beer, with a six-pack costing as little as about US $8. On the other hand, six bottles of the least expensive craft beer will run about US $18 and often nearly twice as much. Japanese craft brewers import most of their ingredients and production equipment, a fact that has allowed foreign craft and traditional beers to enter the market at competitive prices.

As of 2011 there was talk of the Japanese government effecting a significant reworking of beer taxes, and it is possible that any changes will diminish the appeal of low-malt happo-shu while proving advantageous to craft brewers. Still, Japan is a place where dramatic change remains rare, and craft brewers there forge ahead in the knowledge that the path is likely to remain rocky.

Bryan Harrell

Jefferson, Thomas (1743–1826), is most famous as the principal author of the Declaration of Independence and as a politician who later served as the third president of the United States from 1801 to 1809. Like many gentlemen farmers of his day, his estate near Charlottesville, Virginia, included a brewery. Early on, his wife Martha brewed 15-gal batches of beer almost every 2 weeks. But when Jefferson designed his architectural masterpiece, Monticello, early plans included a brewing room and a beer cellar. The execution of these plans, however, had to wait until after Jefferson's retirement from political life. Already in his seventies, Jefferson finally wrote for assistance to English master brewer Joseph Miller, then living in central Virginia. Miller joined Jefferson at Monticello and the pair finally built the brewery. Jefferson also began malting his own grain. Because no barley was grown at Monticello, Jefferson's mashes consisted of a mixture of "wheat or corn," as a plaque at Monticello explains, along with hops grown on his estate. Jefferson preferred bottling his beers and used corks to seal them. Eventually, one of Jefferson's slaves, Peter Hemings, a cook and tailor whom Miller taught to brew, took over brewing operations. By all accounts, Hemings' ales enjoyed a great reputation among Jefferson's neighbors and visitors. Jefferson wrote in an 1817 letter to Miller, "Peter's brewing of the last season I am in hopes will prove excellent. At least the only cask of it we have tried proves so." Hemings had taken to brewing, said Jefferson, "with entire success" using "great intelligence and diligence." In another letter to his successor as President, James Madison, in 1820, Jefferson praised Hemings as "our malter and brewer."

Jay R. Brooks

Jenlain Original French Ale, known in France as Jenlain ambree and traditionally as Jenlain bière de garde, a specialty ale from Brasserie Duyck, is considered by many the standard bearer of the French bière de garde style.

Since its inception in 1922, Brasserie Duyck has brewed a version of bière de garde, an otherwise forgotten traditional ale style with origins in farmhouse breweries once scattered throughout the French departments of Nord and Pas-de-Calais along the border with Belgium.

In the early 1950s Duyck broke with the tradition of bière de garde as a low-alcohol, draft-only product by offering it in large bottles (750 ml) with an elevated alcohol content (7.5%) and a traditional "Champagne" cork finish. These innovations each stand as watermarks in the advent of the French specialty brewing movement. Jenlain is made with three types of malt (pilsner, Munich, and color malts) and three varieties of hops grown in the Alsace region.

Jenlain bière de garde remained an obscure specialty ale until embraced by university students in and around Lille, the cosmopolitan capital of northern France. The French public chose Jenlain bière de garde as the French answer to the increasing presence of imported Belgian specialty beers. This unexpected success transformed Brasserie Duyck from a small regional brewery to a leader in the French specialty brewing industry.

Today Jenlain Original French Ale continues to be the best known example of French bière de garde. Although the product may have a less distinctive character nowadays than it once did, it still maintains an air of rusticity and complexity despite being produced in a state-of-the-art brewery.

See also BIÈRE DE GARDE and DUYCK, BRASSERIE.

Jackson, Michael. *Beer companion*. Philadelphia: Running Press, 1993.

Markowski, Phil. *Farmhouse ales*. Denver, CO: Brewers Publications, 2004.

Woods, John, and Rigley, Keith. *The beers of France*. Wiscombe, Bristol, England: The Artisan Press, 1998.

Phil Markowski

jetting is a method used to expel air from the headspace of a bottle or other container of beer. This method involves using a fine stream of high pressure, and often high-temperature sterilized water, to energize the beer, causing a controlled rise of bubbles and foam from deep within the beer through the headspace just as the closure is placed on the container. Often called "fobbing," this practice has evolved with the development of high-speed packaging lines. Earlier systems included bottle knockers and ultrasonic vibrations and newer systems have experimented with the use of CO_2 or liquid nitrogen rather than water. See CARBON DIOXIDE and NITROGEN.

The most common jetting practice involves a system that treats potable water to deal with any substances that may affect the beer or the system. Chlorine, sediment, and minerals should be removed prior to entering the system to avoid their negative effect on the beer and the machinery.

The water is then pressurized to between 10 and 17 bar (145 to 246 psi) using an adjustable high-pressure air pump that feeds water through an in-line heating source to a nozzle of 0.20 to 0.25 mm (0.008 to 0.010 inch). Pressure, nozzle size, and the distance of the jetter from the capper are all adjusted based on package size and line speed. The settings should be evaluated based on the depth of the jet stream penetration, the control of the foam rise, and finally on the resulting headspace air and total package oxygen results. Nozzles should be replaced or cleaned regularly to ensure a tight, high-energy stream. Out of control jetting can result in air entrapment as well as an unacceptable loss of liquid and improper fill levels.

Donovan, P., R. Currier, R. Blanton, and J. Ross. Liquid nitrogen jetting as a replacement for water jetting: Maintaining O_2 levels while reducing product losses and waste problems. *MBAA Technical Quarterly* 36 (1999): 247–49.

Kronseder, H., and R. Schwarz. New developments in high speed bottle filling technology. *MBAA Technical Quarterly* 23 (1986): 131–35.

Master Brewers Association of the Americas. *Beer packaging*. Madison, WI: Author, 1982.

Weaver, R. L., G. A. Murphy, and T. R. McInnis. A carbon dioxide fobber. *MBAA Technical Quarterly* 10 (1973): 165–68.

Jim Kuhr

J.F. Trommer's Evergreen Brewery

See TROMMER'S EVERGREEN BREWERY.

judging beer, even if informally, is something many professional brewers, homebrewers, and beer enthusiasts do virtually every day. Once competition is involved, however, beer judging moves beyond the act of tasting and acquires a different shape, look, and sound.

In the United States, most beer competitions are judged according to the standards set by the Beer Judge Certification Program (BJCP). Founded in 1985, the BJCP is a nonprofit organization that grew out of the American Homebrewers Association, but has since become independent. See BEER JUDGE CERTIFICATION PROGRAM (BJCP). The BJCP beer judges, once they pass exams issued by the organization, are considered qualified to judge homebrewing competitions sanctioned by the BJCP throughout North America. The BJCP pioneered a style of judging that is based not only on the quality of the beer but also on its adherence to fairly strict style guidelines. Therefore, to win a medal at a BJCP competition, a pilsner must be not only a very good beer but also a great example of the pilsner beer style. See BEER STYLE.

This overall judging style now informs the competitions run by Brewers Association; these are the competitions at the Great American Beer Festival (GABF) and the World Beer Cup (WBC). They are the largest and arguably most rigorous beer competitions in the world, with the GABF judging American commercial beers and the WBC judging commercial beers from more than 40 countries. The 2010 WBC involved 179 judges, mostly professional brewers, from 26 countries, judging 3,300 beers in 90 distinct style categories. All judging is done blind, and judges must be capable of judging dozens of beers per session, while providing comments for the competing brewers and avoiding palate fatigue. The judging is style based and highly technical. Both competitions award gold, silver, and bronze awards in each style category as well as some cumulative awards based on competition scores.

Britain's Campaign for Real Ale runs the Champion Beer of Britain competition at the annual Great British Beer Festival in London. This competition judges a slate of cask-conditioned beers that has been winnowed down by previous competitions and selections. There are six style-based categories judged, and the winner of each category goes on to compete for the title Champion Beer of Britain. The judges, who range from professional brewers to beer writers and well-respected enthusiasts, are asked to judge more hedonically than technically. In a complete departure from the American style of judging, the British competition focuses on how much the judges actually enjoy the beer, even going so far as to ask, "Would you go out of your way to find this beer?" To win Champion Beer of Britain is a huge commercial boost in the UK, and some small brewers have been thrilled to win, only to be swamped by the resulting market demand.

The Brewing Industry International Awards (BIIA), which can trace its roots back to the 1879 Brewers Exhibition in London, takes a middle tack. It is judged by a panel of professional brewers across 9 broad categories that are then broken down into 32 smaller categories. The judging is rigorous but less

Judges evaluate beers at the 2004 Brewing Industry International Awards in Burton-on-Trent, UK. PHOTOGRAPH BY DENTON TILLMAN

style based and puts a distinct value on commercial viability. Unlike other commercial competitions, the BIIA tests alcohol by volume levels for all winning beers, ensuring that stronger beers do not win unfairly by entering categories below their "weight class."

New competitions continue to emerge worldwide from Italy to Australia, each with a unique focus and style. Brewers and enthusiasts argue the merits of each judging style. Despite the number of categories, some find the American style too confining, whereas others appreciate the fact that this judging has well-defined targets. An American judge might find the British judging style too relaxed, whereas the British judge might find the Americans oddly uptight. And both might look at a European-run competition, where lagers and ales sit together in the same categories and wonder what the world has come to.

See also BREWERS ASSOCIATION, GREAT AMERICAN BEER FESTIVAL, and GREAT BRITISH BEER FESTIVAL.

Great American Beer Festival. http://www.gabf.org (accessed April 26, 2011).

Great British Beer Festival. http://www.gbbf.camra.org.uk.

World Beer Cup. http://www.worldbeercup.org (accessed April 26, 2011).

Garrett Oliver

Judong, Father Anselmus, a major figure in the development of Trappist brewing in Belgium. Anselmus was a monk with the Saint Benedictus Abbey of Achel in the province of Limburg in the late 19th century. This was a very short yet prosperous period for this Trappist abbey that began with Achel being granted abbey status in 1871 and ended with the property being temporarily abandoned just prior to World War I in 1914.

While a Superior at Achel's new daughter house in Echt, Father Anselmus is credited with having traveled to assess the ruins of a Trappist abbey in Rochefort, Belgium, on October 11, 1887. Two months later, the former grounds of the Our Lady of Saint Remy abbey (Rochefort) were acquired by Achel and would become one of three daughter houses established during this period (Rochefort, Diepenveen, and Echt).

Rochefort was originally populated by monks in 1464, but the abbey was shuttered and looted in the mid-1790s as the region was transferred from the Austrian Netherlands to postrevolution France. At this time Rochefort's property was sold to a Frenchman named Lucien-Joseph Poncelet, who demolished the church and repurposed the property as a farm shortly after Napoleon was crowned Emperor in 1805.

By the time Anselmus and Achel acquired the farm in 1887, France had a president rather than an emperor and Belgium had survived its own revolution and gained independence. Achel restored the original abbey from its agricultural uses and erected a new church among other buildings. Anselmus was Superior in 1899 when Rochefort first began brewing strictly for in-house consumption. Importantly, he was also present at the "Strictoris Oberservantiae" Chapter meeting that established the Trappist order (officially known as the Order of Cistercians of the Strict Observance) in 1892.

Rochefort officially became an "abbey" in 1912 and released its first two commercial products, "Middel" and "Merveille," in 1952.

See also ACHEL BREWERY, ROCHEFORT BREWERY, and TRAPPIST BREWERIES.

Daniel Paquette

juniper berries and branches have historically been used both as a flavoring for and as a fermentable ingredient in beer. Its use is traditionally common in the Nordic countries, and particularly in Finnish sahti, an ancient beer style that is still produced today. See SAHTI. It has also at times been mentioned as a constituent ingredient of gruit and is of course the primary flavoring botanical in London-style gin.

The use of juniper in brewing is manifold. Sometimes the branches and berries are boiled in the brewing water, rendering an extract with which to conduct the brew. In other cases the branches are used as a rudimentary strainer to separate the wort from the mash in a wooden trough. This is often accomplished with the addition of straw and harks back to primitive brewcraft. And in some instances the mature berries—actually fleshy cone scales rich in dextrose—are used as a source of fermentable sugar.

The medicinal use of juniper is widespread among indigenous, particularly North American, cultures, with citations of effect ranging from contraception to treatment of urinary tract infection to stimulation of insulin production and as a general restorative. Its ubiquity has made juniper a part of lore and utility in many cultures; its species-variety is broad, with native types to be found in Europe, Asia, Africa, and the Americas. It is used for wood, fuel, and food, as well as for ceremonial purposes, and it is no surprise to find it used in the production of beer and other beverages. Its antiseptic properties would also no doubt contribute to a preservative effect.

Buhner, Stephen Harrod. *Sacred and herbal healing beers: The secrets of ancient fermentations.* Boulder, CO: Siris Books/Brewers Publications, 1998.

Mosher, Randy. *Radical brewing: Recipes, tales, and world-altering meditations in a glass.* Boulder, CO: Brewers Publications, 2004.

Dick Cantwell

J.W. Lees Brewery. John Lees, a retired cotton manufacturer, bought land in Middleton Junction in 1828 and built his Greengate Brewery in what was then a rural area of Lancashire. It's now part of Greater Manchester and the brewery prospered as factories with a thirsty army of workers sprang up around it. John's grandson, John William, took over the company, enlarged the brewery in 1876, and renamed it J.W. Lees. Its admirers ever since have called the brewery "John Willie Lees." John William was prominent in both brewing and civil society, twice being elected mayor of Middleton. When William, Simon, Christina, and Michael Lees-Jones joined the company in the 1990s, they became the sixth generation of the family to run the brewery.

The company, which owns 170 pubs in Greater Manchester and north Wales, is fiercely traditional and concentrates on cask-conditioned ales. The range includes Mild, Bitter, a summer beer called Scorcher, and Coronation Street, named after a long-running TV soap opera set in nearby Salford, where much of the action takes place in the fictional Rovers' Return pub.

J.W. Lees is best known for two strong ales. Moonraker (7.5%, bottle and cask) takes its name from a 19th-century tale concerning a group of farm laborers who, after a night on the ale, were returning home and thought the reflection of the moon in a pond was a truckle of Lancashire cheese. They tried to rake the moon from the pond but only succeeded in falling in.

Harvest Ale (11.5% in bottle) is a barley wine brewed every autumn with freshly harvested Maris Otter barley and East Kent Goldings hops. The beer is conditioned in the brewery and released in time for Christmas. It is filtered and pasteurized but ages very well for many years, with bottles from the late 1980s only now starting to peak. It is among the finest examples of the old British barely wine style. In recent years, the brewery has released versions of Harvest Ale that have been matured in casks that have held sherry, port, whiskey, and Calvados.

Gourvish, T.R., and Wilson, R.G. The British brewing industry, 1830–1980. Cambridge: Cambridge University Press, 1994.

Roger Protz

Kaltenberg Brewery in Bavaria is known officially as the König Ludwig GmbH & Co. KG Schlossbrauerei Kaltenberg. Its chief executive officer is Prince Luitpold of Bavaria, a member of the House of Wittelsbach, which ruled Bavaria from 1180 until 1918. Prince Luitpold is the great-grandson of Ludwig III, the last ruling king of Bavaria, who vacated the throne after monarchies were abolished in Germany in 1918. The brewery's headquarters are in the Kaltenberg Castle, some 40 km (approximately 25 miles) west of Munich, which dates back to the 1290s and serves as Prince Luitpold's home. There is a small brewery on the grounds. The brewery also has another production site in Fürstenfeldbrück, where most of its beers are now made. Perhaps the most well known of the Kaltenberg beers is König Ludwig Dunkel, a traditional Bavarian Dunkel lager with a nice balance of mild roasty notes and hop aromatics and a dry finish. The Kaltenberg wheat beer, König Ludwig Weissbier, is a traditional bottle-conditioned hefeweizen, a beer style that first appeared in Bavaria in the 16th century. See HEFEWEIZEN. It is a refreshing, effervescent beer with notes of apple and bananas. In addition, Kaltenberg produces a full spectrum of Bavarian beer styles, including a pils, a helles, and a dunkelweizen.

See also BAVARIA.

Horst Dornbusch

Kaspar Schulz Brew Systems

See SCHULZ BREW SYSTEMS.

Katholieke Universiteit van Leuven, the Catholic University of Leuven, founded in 1425 at the issuance of Pope Martin V, is the oldest operating Catholic university in the world. The original language spoken at the university was Latin, but eventually both Dutch and French became commonly used. The motto of the university is "The Seat of Wisdom" and it is dedicated to the Virgin Mary. It has gone through many changes over the years, including temporary closure by the French and destruction during both world wars. However, the most profound change was the split that occurred in 1968 resulting in two separate universities—one Flemish-speaking located in Leuven called Katholieke Universiteit Leuven, and the other French-speaking located in Louvain-La-Neuve called Universite Catholique de Louvain. This split was the result of the often violent clashes in Belgium between the Flemish- and French-speaking students. The French speakers were perceived to have gotten better treatment by the faculty and the Flemish organized strikes for better treatment.

Both campuses have departments dedicated to research in the field of brewing and are equipped with state-of-the-art laboratories. As such, many publications have appeared from both brewing schools in peer-reviewed journals to advance the knowledge of brewing science. The most famous brewing professor to lead the brewing school of the university was Jean DeClerck. See DE CLERCK, JEAN. DeClerck published many articles and a brewing textbook that was in use for many years. DeClerck was so well regarded that upon his death he was allowed to be buried at the famous Chimay abbey alongside the monks.

See also BREWING SCHOOLS.

Keith Villa

keg, a pressurized container for packaging, transporting, and dispensing carbonated draught beer. Although kegs have been made out of many materials over time, including wood, plastic, and aluminum, the vast majority are now made from stainless steel. The standard beer keg, which once featured curved walls that mimicked barrel staves, is now a straight-side cylindrical container. Above the walls is a rounded rim with hand grips, sometimes coated in rubber, called the chime. In the neck at the top of the container is a spring-loaded valve connected to a drop-tube called a spear. The spear reaches to within a centimeter of the bottom of the keg, allowing almost all the contents of the keg to be served out.

Most types of kegs use a single coupler; this allows gas pressure to enter the keg, forcing beer to leave the keg via the spear. The most common modern keg coupler design is known by the name Sankey, although there is an American variation and a European one; at first glance these appear to be interchangeable, but they are not. Beyond these there are several other coupler designs in use, including the Bass Grundy "G" coupler, still used in the UK, and the German "A" and "M" couplers, all of which slide onto the keg neck rather than twisting on as the Sankey types do.

Two older systems are still occasionally seen—Hoff–Stevens and Golden Gate. Both were unwieldy because of their wooden bungs, which required replacement after each use, and the Golden Gate keg had a gas fitting that was separate from the beer fitting.

Kegs are generally cleaned and filled in an inverted position on a keg cleaning and filling machine. The machine first blows out any remaining beer in the keg and then takes the keg through a rinse, cleaning by hot caustic soda and sometimes acid, another rinse, and steam or chemical sterilization, and then the keg is pressurized and filled.

The standard American keg volume is the American half-barrel, which is 58.6 l or 15.5 US gal. Most European kegs are notably smaller, at 50 l, with many available at 30 and 20 l, sizes that better comply with European labor laws regarding workplace ergonomics. American kegs also come in a range of sizes, with the second most common size being 5 US gal.

Garrett Oliver

Brewmaster at the Full Sail Brewing Company in Oregon, with a keg of Full Sail beer. BLAKE EMMERSON

kellerbier (literally "cellar beer") is an unfiltered, unpasteurized, very yeasty, malty lager from Franconia in central Bavaria, where it is still a summer favorite in local beer gardens. It is usually drunk out of earthenware mugs rather than glasses. An authentic kellerbier should be strongly flavored with aromatic hops and brewed to a märzen strength of about 5% to 5.3% alcohol by volume. More often than not, a kellerbier is deep amber in color, perhaps with a reddish tinge, as the result of a good portion of slightly caramelized malt in the grain bill. If brewed true to style, a kellerbier has very little effervescence, because traditionally it was matured in wooden casks "ungespundet" (literally "unbunged"), with the yeast still active. As the yeast fermented the remaining sugars in the beer and converted these to additional alcohol and carbon dioxide, the gas was allowed to escape through the bung hole. A kellerbier was finished very dry with both noticeable hop and malt notes in balance. The bung ("spund" in German) of the cask was fitted only for shipping. If tapped under atmospheric pressure, therefore, a traditional kellerbier had virtually no foam. In this it bears some textural resemblance to British cask-conditioned ales. Nowadays, kellerbiers are invariably fermented and conditioned in closed stainless steel fermenters, especially when they are bottled or kegged for shipment to distant markets. They also tend to contain less alcohol than in the past and may even be mildly filtered to remove some of the beer's natural cloudiness. Enthusiasts, especially in Franconia, feel that kellerbiers make great aperitifs when served to stimulate the appetite before dinner.

See also BAVARIA, CASK CONDITIONING, and MÄRZENBIER.

German Beer Institute. *Kellerbier*. http://www.germanbeerinstitute.com/Kellerbier.html/ (accessed March 29, 2011).
German Beer Institute. *Zoigl*. http://www.germanbeerinstitute.com/Zoigl.html/ (accessed March 29, 2011).
German Beer Institute. *Zwickelbier*. http://www.germanbeerinstitute.com/Zwickelbier.html/ (accessed March 29, 2011).

Horst Dornbusch

Kent, England, is a county in the southeast of England noted for its hop growing.

Widely known as the "Garden of England," Kent is a fertile area, bordered on two sides by the sea. The gentle climate is conducive to hop production, which was introduced here, it is believed, in the 16th century by beer-loving weavers from Flanders. At its height in the 1870s, hop cultivation claimed more than 31,000 ha (77,000 acres) of the county. That figure has declined dramatically due to imported hops and dwindling UK beer sales.

The industry was historically labor intensive, particularly at harvest time (September), when tens of thousands of Londoners made their annual journey south to pick hops. Their influx fell away from the 1950s with the introduction of mechanical harvesting. Traditional oast houses, used for drying hops, can be seen throughout the county, but many have been converted into private residences. See OAST HOUSE.

It was in Kent that the Fuggle hop was propagated by Richard Fuggle in 1875, but the hop research facility at Wye College, near Ashford, was also responsible for many notable breeding successes until its closure in 2007. See FUGGLE (HOP) and WYE COLLEGE. The unit developed hop strains such as Challenger, Target, Northdown, Progress, Bramling Cross, Admiral, Phoenix, First Gold, and Pioneer.

As well as a number of microbreweries, Kent is home to the UK's oldest active brewery, Shepherd Neame in Faversham, founded in 1698. See SHEPHERD NEAME BREWERY. The company has obtained PGI (Protected Geographical Indication) status from the European Union for Kentish Ale and Kentish Strong Ale, which means only beer brewed in Kent can be so labelled.

BBC. *Legacies*. http://www.bbc.co.uk/legacies/work/england/kent/article_2.shtml (accessed December 9, 2009).
The Hop Farm Family Park. http://www.thehopfarm.co.uk (accessed December 9, 2009).
The Hop Guide. 1st ed. Warwick, England: HRI-HortiTech, 1999.
Dave Hughes. *Hops and Downs* (pdf). http://www.kent.gov.uk/NR/rdonlyres/1913EEC2-B192-4378-9D53-FAB0AFF870D5/0/FoodTrailsHopsandDowns.pdf (accessed December 9, 2009).
The Museum of Kent Life. *Hopping down in Kent*. http://www.hoppingdowninkent.org.uk/index.php (accessed December 9, 2009).

Jeff Evans

Kent Golding (hop) is one of the most traditional and popular of all English hops. Kent Golding is cultivated in Mid-Kent, whereas East Kent Golding comes from East Kent. They are both part of the Golding family of closely related hop varieties. See EAST KENT GOLDING (HOP) and GOLDING (HOP). The Golding is named after a farmer from Canterbury named Golding, who first propagated the hop in the late 18th century for its desirable floral aroma and earthy notes, which have come to symbolize the characteristic flavor of English ale. Golding hop varieties, both Kent and East Kent, are a perfect pairing with Fuggle, a hop named after another Kent farmer, who, roughly a century later, cultivated this other English classic there. Styrian Golding, grown mostly in Slovenia and Austria, incidentally, is a Fuggle variety, not a Golding, despite its name.

With an alpha acid range of 4% to 6%, Kent Golding is widely used as flavoring and finishing hop at the middle and end of the boil, as well as for dry hopping. See DRY HOPPING and LATE HOPPING. As an old hop variety, it does have drawbacks, particularly its susceptibility to downy mildew and hop mosaic virus. Its loose, mid-size cones should be picked delicately or risk shattering during mid- to late-season maturity. After picking, however, it is well regarded for its fairly high storability.

Burgess, A. H. *Hops: Botany, cultivation, and utilization.* London: World Crop Books, Interscience Publishers Inc, 1964.

Haunold, A., S. Likens, C. Horner, S. Brooks, and C. Zimmermann. One-half century of hop research by the U.S. Department of Agriculture. *Journal of the American Society of Brewing Chemists* 43 (1985): 123–26.

Van Valkenburg, Don. A question of pedigree—the role of genealogy in hop substitutions. *Brewing Techniques* October/November (1995): 54–59.

Brian Yaeger

ketones

See VICINAL DIKETONES.

kettle, the vessel in which beer wort is boiled with hops. Proper wort boiling achieves a number of effects, including sterilization of the wort, denaturing of enzymes, extraction of hop components, coagulation of proteins and polyphenols, wort concentration, color development, and the driving off of unwanted volatiles. Modern kettles are designed to carry out these tasks in the most efficient manner possible while still yielding high-quality wort. In the UK, the kettle is often called a *copper,* named after the metal from which many kettles were once fashioned. Hundreds of years ago, the average brewery kettle was essentially a cast iron pot sitting over an open wood fire. Over time these were refined to include furnaces designed to concentrate heat onto the bottom boiling surfaces. See DIRECT FIRING Eventually, the wood was replaced by coal, and the top of the vessel was covered and vented to the outside by way of a stack; this latter innovation reduced the danger of boilovers, which could be deadly in open kettles. The use of coal-fired furnaces had disadvantages as well, not least that the fire in the furnace needed to be shut down once the kettle was empty, lest the undissipated heat deform the vessel. This problem was solved when oil and gas replaced coal for direct firing.

As brewing vessels became more complex, copper replaced iron. Copper is not as strong as iron, but it is more malleable, conducts heat far more efficiently, and resists corrosion better than iron does. Copper's malleability gave rise to the elegant shape of the classical "onion-dome" kettle top, still widely seen in Europe. By the mid-20th century copper was largely replaced by stainless steel, which is stronger and far easier to clean and maintain using modern clean-in-place procedures. See CLEANING IN PLACE (CIP). Direct firing, which could develop some color and pleasant flavors but could also scorch the wort, was set aside in favor of steam heating in most breweries. Steam heating may be internal to the kettle, either through steam jackets within the kettle walls or through a calandria positioned in the center of the kettle. Steam coils and electric elements are also used, but both are rare. External calandrias, through which the wort is circulated in a loop, are also common. See CALANDRIA.

Whatever the design, kettles must evaporate a consistent percentage of the kettle contents and provide sufficient mechanical agitation for protein coagulation and efficient hop extraction to take place. Steam jackets are placed within the kettle walls asymmetrically; thermal currents will set up a rolling boil that thoroughly mixes the kettle contents. Where a calandria is used, the wort will be moved through it, either by a pump or convectively, and dispersed back to the surface of the liquid by an adjustable spreader. Boiling usually takes place at ambient pressures, but some kettles are designed to boil at higher pressure and temperature. This can increase the efficiency of hop extraction, but it may also develop higher color and impede the volatilization of undesirable compounds.

In small breweries and brewpubs, the kettle may include a whirlpool function for the removal of trub and hop pellet fragments. In this case, the vessel will be referred to as a "kettle-whirlpool." See TRUB and WHIRLPOOL. Whereas the combining of these functions saves pace and capital costs, a combined kettle–whirlpool is a compromise that rarely performs either function quite as well as a separate kettle and whirlpool. Kettles that are used to boil whole hops will often have screens fitted to their bottom outlets. At the end of the boil, the wort will be recirculated through the screen until the wort runs clear; it is then diverted through the heat exchanger to the fermenting vessel.

Traditional copper kettle at the Westmalle Brewery in the Trappist Abbey of Westmalle, Belgium. PHOTOGRAPH BY DENTON TILLMAN

Hops, minerals, kettle finings, brewer's syrups, and other additions to the wort may be introduced through the kettle manway or by automated systems that discharge directly into the kettle. Many modern systems, seeking the best possible energy efficiency, will include a heat exchanger system within the kettle stack; the kettle steam is thereby used to heat more water for later use in the brewing process or cleaning.

Hough, J. S., D. E. Briggs, and R. Stevens, eds. *Malting and brewing science*, 2nd ed, vol 2. London: Chapman & Hall, 1982.

Garrett Oliver

kettle finings act to clarify wort by encouraging the agglomeration and sedimentation of haze-active proteins and particles during the boiling and cooling of the wort (i.e., hot break formed at the end of the boil that should consist of large flocs in bright wort and cold break formed on wort cooling that is seen as a heavy, fine sediment in bright wort). All kettle finings are based on carrageenan, a long-chain polysaccharide primarily composed of galactose. The generally accepted mechanism for wort clarification with carrageenan is that negatively charged carrageenan molecules are electrostatically attracted to the more positively charged soluble protein molecules to form soluble complexes, which eventually form larger complexes that interact with microsize particles to become insoluble and flocculate. Carrageenan is denatured by heat and low pH and is therefore added at the end of the boil shortly before whirlpooling. The dosage rate needs to be determined empirically for a particular recipe and brewing conditions to produce the best clarity with the least amount of sediment. The optimization of finings addition is often determined annually when starting the new season's malt or whenever there is a change in the type or supplier of malt. Incorrect addition of copper finings (both over and under) can give poor fining action in the cooled wort and can cause fining difficulties in cask beer. Current commercial preparations of carrageenan can include polyvinylpolypyrrolidone, an insoluble polymer that forms complexes with haze-active polyphenols through hydrogen bonding. The synergism between these two substances produces better beer clarity than either used alone.

John Palmer

A **keystone** is the smaller of the two disposable, circular bungs on a traditional cask, located centrally at the bottom of the face of the vessel. The standard "No. 2" keystone size measures 3.75 cm (1.5 in) in diameter at the front, tapering down to 3.5 cm (1.4 in) at the rear. A broader size, "No. 1," has largely been phased out but remains in limited use by a few British regional breweries.

The outer rim, 0.75 cm (0.3 in) wide on the standard fitting, is deeper than the central plug, with the latter part being shallower to facilitate the tap being manually driven through and being held firm by the wider rim. Traditionally, this fitting would be made of limewood and drilled through in slightly different places at the front and back to ensure a good seal prior to being broached, at the same time allowing for the tapping process to be undertaken without excessive effort. Today plastic keystones are becoming increasingly popular because the material is cheap to manufacture; they also have such sanitary benefits as easier cleaning and the inability to attract fungal growth, which can be a problem with wooden fittings.

Limewood keystones can occasionally split their rims on tapping if not inserted completely flush in the cask's bush or if not pressed in far enough, causing beer to leak out and necessitating a fresh keystone to be inserted promptly. A good cask cellarperson should possess the skill to swiftly replace a split keystone without upending the cask and with minimal beer loss.

For hygiene purposes, it is normal—and courteous—for a sealing bung known as a clip cork to be inserted into the open keystone of a freshly emptied cask as soon as the tap is removed. This prevents insects from entering and breeding and stops potential spillage of yeasty beer dregs on the journey back to the brewery.

Alex Hall

kilderkin is a cask or keg half the size of a UK barrel, holding 18 UK gal (81.83 l) or 22.5 US gallons. Manual handling weight legislation in the UK has made this cask the largest beer container in general commercial use for drayman (i.e., the person who delivers beer on behalf of a brewery) deliveries. Once a common sight in pub cellars, the kilderkin is now relatively rare.

Chris J. Marchbanks

Kildrought Brewery

See GUINNESS, ARTHUR.

killer strains are strains of Saccharomyces cerevisiae that contain a killer factor (sometimes also called a "zymocin"), rendering them resistant to infection by other yeasts. This was first discovered by Makower and Bevan in 1963. Killer strains release a glycoprotein-type toxin that is lethal to sensitive yeast strains. The killer factor has since been found in many other species of yeast as well. Of 964 strains of yeast from the National Collection of Yeast Cultures that were tested in 1975 by Philliskirk and Young, 59 strains were killers. Of those, only 3 were classified as ale strains, although more probably these strains were contaminants of otherwise normal brewing yeast. Yeast can be killer (immune), neutral, or sensitive. Some wine yeast strains are killer yeasts as well. To date, no killer factor has been detected in commercial brewers' yeast strains. However, most brewery strains are sensitive to the killer glycoproteins, which can be carried by wild yeasts. Therefore, should a wild killer strain contaminate a fermentation, it can destroy the culture strain. The only reported case of such an occurrence in the brewing industry was in a continuous fermentation system, where the contaminant killed the brewing yeast culture and then dominated the fermenter. According to Priest and Campbell, if the killer is a Saccharomyces spp. strain, it is particularly difficult to detect the contamination early on. A brewer's strain can be tested for sensitivity to killer strains in the laboratory by checking whether it can grow in the presence of the killer toxin. If it does, it is considered a neutral strain.

Makower, M., & E. A. Bevan. The physiological basis of the killer character in yeast. *Proceedings of the International Congress of Genetics XI* 1 (n.d.): 202.

Philliskirk, G., & T. W. Young. The occurrence of killer character in yeasts of various genera. Antonie van Leeuwenhoek *J. Clin Serol.* 41 (1975): 147.

Priest, F. G., and I. Campbell. *Brewing microbiology,* 2nd ed., 203–4. London: Chapman & Hall, 1996.

Chris White

kilning is the heating of germinated barley to dry it and develop malty, biscuit-like flavors. The largest portion of malt in most beers today is pale malt that is only gently dried at relatively low heat to preserve the integrity of its enzymes. See ENZYMES. Kilning is the final stage in traditional malting, after steeping and germinating, and its techniques and equipment have been developed over many centuries. The kilning process is fairly simple, but its chemistry is complex. See MALT.

Kilning is invariably done in two or three stages. Initially, most of the surface moisture of the germinated grain is driven off. At the final stage, the malt is "cured." The goal is to reduce the grain's moisture content from about 40% to 50% down to at least 4% to 6%. Different maltsters use different temperatures and time intervals for the different kilning phases. A typical sequence is step one at 50°C to 60°C (122°F to 140°F), step two at 65°C to 75°C (149°F to 167°F), and a curing step at 80°C to 105°C (176°F to 221°F). The sequencing of the temperature levels is important. If the grain is heated too moist at too high a temperature, its enzymes would be denatured and thus it would be rendered useless for mashing.

Traditional kiln designs are simple vessels with a heat source at the bottom, one or two floors—perforated for air flow—to hold the grain, and vents at the top for air evacuation. Because kilning is a highly energy-intensive process, most malting plants use various heat exchangers to reclaim heat from the hot air that leaves the kiln.

Keith Thomas

Kirin Brewery Company is Japan's largest brewery and a member of the Mitsubishi group of companies (keiretsu). The forerunner to Kirin Beer was the Spring Valley Brewery founded in Yokohama in 1870 by William Copeland, a Norwegian-born American. The brewery originally produced beers designed to satisfy demand among foreign residents, but it later made efforts to produce beer more favorable to Japanese tastes.

After several shifts in management structure, Copeland ended up selling the brewery to a group of investors, and in 1885 the Japan Brewery was established. Three years later, in 1888, the company released a German-style lager under the Kirin brand, named after a mythical Asian animal that resembles a dragon. The popularity of this product grew so well that in 1907 the Japan Brewery was renamed the Kirin Brewery. The company continued to expand and introduced their Kirin Lemon soft drink in 1928.

The brewery's operations were adversely impacted by World War II, but throughout the 1950s and 1960s the company was expanding into a variety of food- and beverage-related businesses, such as soft drink vending machine operations. In 1972, the Kirin-Seagram Co. was established to produce spirits, with this company later becoming Kirin Distillery.

In 1990, Kirin introduced Kirin Ichiban Shibori, a lager similar in flavor to the original Kirin Lager except that it was not pasteurized but rather microfiltered. This began a shift in flavor in both products, which were gradually made lighter and less bitter. Fans of the original Kirin Lager became increasingly displeased with the product, so Kirin launched Kirin Lager Classic in response. However, Ichiban Shibori has become the brewery's main mass-marketed product. A dark version named Kirin Ichiban Shibori stout (although it is a lager) has been released recently, becoming a replacement for the venerable Kirin stout, an 8% alcohol by volume foreign export-style ale that had been brewed for nearly a century.

Currently, Kirin has a wide array of beer products, including several low-malt "happoshu" brews, and also handles such brands as Budweiser, Heineken, and Guinness in the Japanese market.

See also JAPAN.

Bryan Harrell

Klages (barley) was developed by Dr Karl Klages of the University of Idaho's Department of Agronomy from 1936 to 1962, a pioneering barley researcher with a strong interest in ecology. He is the author of many influential papers, among them Ecological Crop Geography, in which he elaborates on the responses of a wide array of crops to their environments. Klages barley is a cross between Betzes and Domen, whereby the cross has greater diastatic power and delivers more malt extract in the brewhouse than do either of its progenitors. Dr Klages was honored for his contribution to North American barley breeding by having his important innovation named after him. Registered in 1974, Klages became an immediate success, and, starting in 1975, it was the dominant two-row malting barley grown in the Pacific Northwest and in the Northern Plains of the United States and Canada, retaining that prominence for almost a decade. It was succeeded in popularity in 1984 by Harrington, but today Klages still retains a strong following among some established North American craft brewers, who started using it at a time when it was among the first easily obtainable two-row malts for the small-scale brewer.

Harvey, B. L., and B. G. Rossnagel. Harrington barley. *Canadian Journal of Plant Science* 64 (1984):193–94.
Wesenberg, D. M., R. M. Hayes, H. C. McKay, N. N. Standridge, E. D. Goplin, and F. C. Petr. Registration of Klages barley. *Crop Science* 14 (1974): 337–38.

Thomas Blake

Kloster

See ANDECHS.

Kneifl (barley) is one of the most successful spring brewing barley varieties bred between World War I and World War II. Also referred to by its Czech name of Opavský Kneifl (or sometimes misspelled as Kneifel), this variety was developed by the Czech botanist F. Kneifl in 1926 in Opava, in the Czech-Silesian region of Moravia. Kneifl barley is a prominent descendant of an old Czech landrace called "Old-Haná agro-ecotype," which is the barley variety that helped Czech pilsner gain its prominence during the second half of the 19th century. Nowadays, Kneifl is perhaps less well known for the beers that were made from it than for the enormous contribution it has made to the genetic composition of many modern malting and brewing barleys. Once introduced, Kneifl was used extensively in the barley breeding programs of Europe, often in conjunction with Proskowetz Hanna, an older Haná descendant that was bred in 1884. From Europe, the Kneifl genes were spread around the world. Perhaps the most important offspring of Kneifl and Hanna was the Czech Valtice (or Valtický), developed in the decade before World War II. After the war, Valtice, in turn, gave rise to many new cultivars, including the sturdy, short-stem Czech Diamant, whose breeding program started in 1956. Diamant was an x-ray-induced positive mutant. It was released to the fields in 1965, where its stalks grew about 15 cm (6 inch) shorter than those of standard varieties. In addition, it had excellent tillering characteristics and good malting qualities. As a Kneifl descendant, Diamant, too, quickly became a genetic donor to dozens of international spring brewing barley varieties, including Trumpf (also spelled Triumpf, Triumph, or Trumph), which was bred in 1973 in what was then East Germany. Both Diamant and Trumpf have since become exceptionally successful progenitors, with their genes appearing jointly in the pedigrees of some 150 barley varieties bred worldwide since the 1970s.

See also HANÁ (BARLEY) and TRIUMPH (BARLEY).

Jalowetz, Eduard. *Pilsner malz*. Vienna, Austria: Verlag Institut für Gärungsindustrie, 1931.
Kosar, Karel, Vratislav Psota, and Alexandr Mikyska. Barley varieties suitable for the production of the Czech-type beer. *Czech Journal of Genetics and Plant Breeding* 40 (2004): 137–39. http://www.cazv.cz/attachments/5-Kosar.pdf.
Personal communication with Czech sources (using a translator into German).
Petr, J., J. Lipavský, and D. Hradecká. Production process in old and modern spring barley varieties. *Die Bodenkultur*. 53(1) (2002): 19-26. http://www.boku.ac.at/diebodenkultur/volltexte/band-53/heft-1/Petr.pdf.
Vellvé, Renée. World Environment Library. *Saving the Seed—Genetic Diversity and European Agriculture (GRAIN, 1992)*. http://nzdl.sadl.uleth.ca/cgi-bin/library?e=d-00000-00---off-0envl--00-0----0-10-0---0---0direct-10---4-------0-1l--11-en-50---20-about---00-0-1-00-0-0-11-1-0utfZz-8-00&cl=CL3.9&d=HASH0178 37f9ce5227a9aaa108de>=2/.

Horst Dornbusch

Koch, Jim (1949–), is the current chairman and a cofounder of The Boston Beer Co, makers of the Samuel Adams line of beers. See BOSTON BEER COMPANY.

Born into a German-American family that moved to St Louis to brew beer, for five generations the men in Koch's family were brewers. Jim Koch was born in Cincinnati in 1949; Charles Koch, Jim's father, had moved the family to Ohio to take a job at a Cincinnati brewery. But Jim's father discouraged him from pursuing a career in brewing, which he considered a losing proposition in a land of large mass-market brewing behemoths. Jim attended Harvard University in the late 1960s, receiving a BA in 1971.

After college, Koch initially enrolled in a dual degree program at Harvard, but dropped out in 1973 to be an instructor with Outward Board, where he worked outdoors throughout the American West for 4 years. He eventually returned to Harvard and received a dual MBA/JD in 1978. Koch then joined the Boston Consulting Group (BCG), a global management consulting firm, where he worked until 1984.

His time counseling corporate leaders working at BCG inspired Koch to think about starting his own business and he was convinced he could create a niche market within the existing beer market. His father thought he was "crazy," but he was also one of his first investors.

Adapting his great-great grandfather's recipe for Louis Koch Lager, Koch created Samuel Adams Boston Lager, his Boston Beer Company's first beer and still its flagship. Koch launched his beer in April 1985. The first sales of Samuel Adams were conducted one bar at a time, with Koch personally visiting Boston-area bars to persuade skeptical bartenders to stock his beer. Today, The Boston Beer Company is one of the largest American-owned brewing companies and the largest craft brewer in the United States with the Sam Adams brand being one of the nation's most recognizable. And despite long odds, Koch has successfully become the sixth-generation brewer in his family.

Jay R. Brooks

Kolbach index is a measure of the extent of protein modification in beer. It comprises the assessment of total soluble protein in wort as a percentage of the total protein measureable in the malt. This assessment is as performed in the Congress mash. See CONGRESS MASH. When simpler infusion laboratory mashes are used, the equivalent parameter is referred to either as the Soluble Nitrogen Ratio or the S/T value.

The typical value for the Kolbach index in suitably modified malt is between 38% and 42%. Various claims are made concerning the relationship of this parameter to quality aspects of beer such as haze stability and foam. The reality is that the index is nothing more than a gauge of the extent to which proteolysis has occurred during malting. See PROTEOLYSIS. It reveals nothing about the nature of the solubilized proteins and whether they are or are not problematic or beneficial.

Charles W. Bamforth

kölsch is a top-fermented local beer style from Köln (Cologne), Germany. Kölsch beers are characterized by a lightly fruity yeast note in aroma and taste, as well as a pleasant hoppy bitterness. The history of kölsch beer goes back to the year 874 AD. The brewing office of Cologne, which rigorously controlled the production of kölsch, had already been mentioned in 1250. In 1396 representatives of the brewers' guild founded the *Kölner Brauer-Kooperation*, which has been around ever since. In the late 1800s, with imported pale lager from Bohemia making inroads into local markets, the Cologne brewers decided to fight back with a pale beer of their own. They would make the beer golden and hoppy, but continue to use their warm-fermenting ale yeasts. Pilsner beer was thus stopped at the gates, and the modern kölsch was born. In March 1986 the brewers of Cologne renewed the convention that defines a true kölsch ("a light-colored, highly fermented, strongly hopped, bright, top-fermented Vollbier"), how it has to be served (in the famous 0.2-liter (6 oz), tall, straight kölsch-"Stangen" glass), and especially who is allowed to produce it—only the brewers of Cologne. A bright yellow *Vollbier* (beer with original gravity of 11%–12%), kölsch has a prominent hoppiness and is predominantly brewed with barley malt. Fermentation takes place at a temperature between 15°C and 20°C (59°F and 68°F). The original gravity is 11.3% on average, while the alcohol by volume (ABV) is 4.8%.

Many bars in Cologne feature kölsch beer, and the Stangen glassware is carried to the tables in racks containing several glasses. As each glass is only 0.2 liters (6 oz), patrons must order constantly to keep fresh beer on the tables.

Today the Kölner Brauerei-Verband (Cologne Brewers Association) still consists of 20 brewers, only 11 of which are producing kölsch. The annual output in total is approximately 2.6 million hl (2.2 million bbl).

Since 1998 kölsch may be labelled with a European Union logo, thereby joining the ranks of such illustrious regional European specialties as Bordeaux, Chianti, and Champagne. See EUROPEAN UNION.

Still, the style is widely brewed by American craft brewers, who tend to see it as a pleasant bridge from bland industrial lagers to more flavorful traditional beers.

Karl-Ullrich Heyse

Koningshoeven Brewery is the only Trappist brewery in the Netherlands and was founded within the walls of the Onze Lieve Vrouw van Koningshoeven abbey in Berkel-Enschot (near Tilburg and about 12 kilometers [7.5 miles] from the Belgian border) in 1884. It is the most commercial of the seven Trappist breweries and brewing operations were even licensed to Artois (now InBev) from 1969 to 1980 when the majority of the production was pilsner. Development of the current line of beers started in 1982 with the introduction of their Dubbel, the Tripel in 1983, and Quadrupel in 1991, followed by a Blond in 1992. The brewery was fully refurbished in 1989 and again in 1999. They also brewed an Enkel (single) but, being too similar to the Blond, it was dropped in 2000. Finding young able-bodied monks to work at the brewery proved difficult and Koningshoeven set up a company together with national brewer Bavaria in 1999 to assist with operations. The brewery name was changed from Trappistenbierbrouwerij De Schaapskooi to Brouwerij De Koningshoeven. Day-to-day production was soon taken over by Bavaria, and in a widely publicized dispute with the other Trappists they lost their Trappist status until 2005 when the monks agreed to take a more active role in the brewery. Today they brew Bavaria brewery's Moreeke ale, the world's only Trappist witbier, Puur (kölsch) and bock, Tilburg's Dutch Brown Ale for export, and some private labels for contract brewers such as Jopen and Urthel. The latest work-in-progress is a range of barrel-aged beers.

Derek Walsh

kosher beer has been approved as complying with the rules of *kashrut,* Jewish dietary rules. The *kashrut* is interpreted locally by a council of rabbis, each of which has its own purview.

Generally beers made with malted cereal, yeast, water, and hops are accepted as "kosher by default" in most part of the world. In Israel, the United States, and Canada, however, some people consume only kosher-certified products even if they are technically kosher without certification. Kosher certification requires the intercession of a rabbi.

Fining agents such as gelatine or isinglass can potentially be considered non-kosher, although there is a longstanding Rabbinic ruling permitting the consumption of beverages clarified with such flocculants or filtering aids, as some may not accept it.

In addition, there are certain additives, enzymes, and flavorings—such as fruit, fruit syrups, or spices—which would require certification. Furthermore, some higher alcohol beers fermented with a yeast other than typical brewer's yeast would also require certification. The increasing use of hop pellets and hop extracts has raised questions regarding the kosher status of the equipment used to process the hops, but this has yet to become a notable issue.

Kashrut. *The Premier Kosher Information Source on the Internet.* http://www.kashrut.com/ (accessed March 29, 2011).

Tim Hampson and Stephen Hindy

Köstritzer Schwarzbierbrauerei, a brewery located in Bad Köstritz, Thuringia, in central Germany. The brewery is best known for its schwarzbier, a dark lager that made the small town famous. See SCHWARZBIER. They also brew a pilsner for the regional market. The brewery has been producing schwarzbier for centuries, probably from its start in 1543 when it was founded as "Erbschenke" (Hereditary Inn), a tavern with brewing rights that could be passed on within the family of the tenant. This tavern was taken over in 1696 by the counts of the house of Reuss as "Ritterschaftliche Gutbrauerei" ("The Knight's Manor Brewery"). The famous 18th-century geographer Anton Friedrich Büsching (1724–1793) noted that the beer was indeed reddish to black in his day. When he first saw the beer at the duke's table he wondered why such "a dark red wine" would be served in beer glasses. He later learned that the beer was typically brewed in fall and stored in rock cellars below the church to be tapped the next summer. One of the most famous drinkers of Köstritzer Schwarzbier was the poet Johann Wolfgang von Goethe, who sustained himself on beer from Köstritz when he was unable to eat during a period of illness. Early 20th-century print advertisements for Köstritzer show a doctor recommending Köstritzer Schwarzbier as beneficial for health, much like the famous "Guinness is good for you" claim. The professional marketing approach of Köstritzer in the 1920s attracted the attention of the Simon family, owners of the well-known Pils brewery in Bitburg at the time. But Köstritzer remained independent, surviving World War II and 40 years under communist East German rule before Privatbrauerei Theobald Simon, better known as "Bitburger," finally acquired the brewery in 1991. By that time only 7% of the Köstritzer's output was schwarzbier, but Bitburger decided to distribute the beer nationally and it has grown since. At 4.8% ABV, the beer's dark brown color belies an easygoing character showcasing caramel flavors and a hint of smoky, coffee-like roast with very little bite.

Conrad Seidl

kräusening is a German term for the addition of actively fermenting wort as an inoculant to induce fermentation in a different batch of wort or beer. If this method is used to start a new fermentation, a small proportion of a previously brewed, vigorously fermenting wort is removed and added to fresh wort to initiate its fermentation.

This is often a preferred means of inoculation because the kräusen will contain active yeast cells that require limited adaption to the conditions of the new wort. Fermentation begins more quickly and may be better guaranteed than a stored sample of yeast, which may contain many dead cells.

Another application is the use of actively fermenting wort to prime beer when it is being bottled. In this case the kräusen brings sugars and nutrients as well as active yeast to the beer. This is helpful because the beer may have limited sugar left after its fermentation. The addition of this and live yeast cells allows a limited fermentation to occur in the bottle, producing carbon dioxide and secondary conditioning.

Care is necessary when kräusening to minimize the potential for carry-over of contamination by spoilage microorganisms and, in bottle-conditioned beer, to judge the correct level of kräusen needed. Too high a level of kräusening will result in over-carbonation and possible gushing of the beer upon opening.

Kräusening is also traditionally used as a method of conditioning finished beer in a closed tank. In this method, a portion of fermenting beer (kräusen) is added to the finished beer, restarting fermentation. The tank is then "bunged" (closed, so that gas is prevented from escaping), and the carbon dioxide from the continuing fermentation is dissolved into the beer. Many brewers feel that this method can reduce levels of off-flavors such as diacetyl and acetylaldehyde. See DIACETYL and ACETALDEHYDE.

In some cases kräusening may be used to revitalize a dormant fermentation. This may be necessary in producing a very strong beer where high levels of alcohol kill the initial yeast. Kräusening may thus help complete the fermentation.

See also FERMENTATION.

Keith Thomas

kriek is a type of fruited sour beer flavored with cherries. Both the Flemish name, meaning "cherry," and the beer style come from Belgium. Whereas other varieties are made, traditional kriek is based on spontaneously fermented lambic beer. See LAMBIC. It is a specialty beer from the Senne River valley in the Pajottenland, which is part of Flanders, outside Brussels. Traditionally, the cherries for this brew were a uniquely local type, an extremely sour and tart variety called Schaarbeek, which grew only in a very limited area around the small Pajottenland village of Schaarbeek. Schaarbeek cherries are a relatively small fruit, composed of red pulp and a large pit that ends up adding to the flavors. Nowadays Schaarbeek cherries are grown in other parts of Belgium, mostly in Sint Truinden and Gorsem in Belgian Limburg and in Tienen in Flemish Brabant. A similar variety is also cultivated in other parts of Europe, notably in Poland. To make kriek in the traditional fashion, lambic is aged in oak for 12 to 18 months and then transferred into new casks. There, the cherries are introduced to the matured beer whole, macerated, or crushed, and with the pits intact. The dormant yeast and bacteria in the lambic come back to life and ferment the fruit sugars. The amount of fruit varies but is usually about 20 to 30 kg (44 to 66 lb) of fresh cherries per 1 hl (26.42 gal) of finished beer. The longer the kriek remains in the cask on the fruit—from a few months to a year—the drier it gets and the more bitterness it acquires from the pits. Eventually, the brew is racked off the remaining pulp and mixed with some young Lambic for fresh fermentable sugars. It is then bottled or (rarely) kegged for conditioning and the buildup of effervescence as the yeasts consume the residual sugar from the young lambic fraction.

A finished kriek is slightly mouth puckering, refreshing, crisp, and spritzy, with notes of cherry from the fruit, almond from the pits, and complex earthy aromatics from the natural fermentation. It is an ideal beer for sipping out of a Champagne flute on a lazy hot summer afternoon.

Several traditional Belgian krieks are available, with Cantillon Kriek, Cantillon Lou Pepe Kriek, Drie Fonteinen Oude Kriek, De Cam Kriekanlambik, and Boon Oude Kriek enjoying particular respect. There are also many less authentic kriek brands on the market. These tend to be much sweeter than the traditional versions and are often made not with actual sour cherries but with sweetened cherry juice, cherry essence, and syrup added to filtered and pasteurized beers. Although some of these are pleasant diversions with dessert, they are widely derided as ersatz by enthusiasts.

Kriek is usually based upon lambic beer, but some brewers have used other sour beers as platforms for sour cherries. In Belgium there have been versions based upon Flemish red ales and the oud bruin style of brown ale. See BELGIAN RED ALE. In recent years craft brewers, particularly in the United States, have made many enthusiastically sour and interesting versions of kriek. See SOUR BEER.

Cherries are not the only fruit used for refermenting lambics. The other traditional fruit is the raspberry, and a similar technique is employed. Peaches will yield the less traditional pêche, and black currants produce the darkly colored cassis. Any fruit may find its way into a cask, and brewers have experimented with cranberries, blueberries, and even grapes, with varying degrees of success.

See also FRAMBOISE and FRUIT BEERS.

Lorenzo Dabove

Kristallweizen is a filtered weissbier. Although this variant is not as popular as the yeasty Bavarian Hefeweizen, it retains a similar flavor profile. See WEISSBIER and WHEAT.

Horst Dornbusch

Krona (barley) was one of the most popular two-row spring brewing barley varieties in Europe during the last decade of the 20th century. It was bred by SW Seed Hadmersleben of Hadmersleben, a small town in the German state of Saxony-Anhalt, and was first registered with the Bundessortenamt (the crop-licensing agency of the German government) in 1990. Although the use cycle of most brewing barleys tends to be no more than a decade, Krona reigned as a major malting barley for 20 years. The German government only revoked Krona's "recommended" status effective December 31, 2010. The Krona genes, however, will live on in several successor brewing barley varieties, including the immensely popular Pasadena, a cross between Marina and Krona that was first licensed for commercial use in 1998; Annabell, a cross between 90014 DH and Krona that was first licensed in 1999; and Auriga, a cross between a nameless offspring of Viskosa and Krona, on the one hand, and Annabel, on the other, that was first licensed in 2002. Krona was particularly prized for its superior malting and brewing properties, including a low protein content, a favorable modification potential, exceptional diastatic power, a fairly high friability value, a low viscosity value, and a high percentage of plump kernels. These characteristics, which Krona as a progenitor has since passed on to its offsprings Annabell, Auriga, and Pasadena, made Krona an excellent base malt, especially for delicate European lagers.

Braugerstengemeinschaft e.V., *Braugersten-Sortenmappe (German malting barley)*. Accessed through http://www.braugerstengemeinschaft.de/index.php?StoryID=20 (accessed September 25, 2010).

Bundessortenamt. http://www.bundessortenamt.de/internet30/fileadmin/Files/PDF/BlfS_Sonderheft.pdf (accessed September 25, 2010).

Topic Map. http://www.topicmapsforge.org/topicmaps/sorten/topics/gerstensorte (accessed September 25, 2010).

Thomas Kraus-Weyermann

Kronenbourg Brewery (Brasseries Kronenbourg) is the largest brewery in France, part of the Carlsberg group. See CARLSBERG GROUP. Flagship brand Kronenbourg 1664 is the best-selling premium lager in France and the second-largest in the UK.

As the brand name suggests, the brewery was originally founded in 1664 by a Strasbourg, France brewer, Jérôme Hatt. In 1850 frequent flooding inspired the Hatt Brewery to move to higher ground in the Cronenbourg district of Strasbourg. Its beers began to gain popularity across France, and in 1947 the brewery was renamed Kronenbourg. From the 1950s onward it began international expansion and mergers, and was acquired in 1970 by industrial group BSN (now Groupe Danone). Danone sold Kronenbourg to UK brewer Scottish & Newcastle, and in April 2008, when that company was sold to Heineken and Carlsberg, Kronenbourg became part of the latter. In 2010 the brewery dominates its home market with a 33% share and sells in over 70 countries worldwide.

The flagship brand is Kronenbourg 1664, a 5.5% premium lager brewed with Alsace's native Strisselspalt hops. See STRISSELSPALT (HOP). (It is brewed under license in the UK at 5%). While light and unchallenging compared to craft-brewed beers, it does have a whiff of hop character and is superior to many comparable mass-produced lagers.

The brewery claims Kronenbourg 1664 dates back to the foundation of the brewery—hardly likely given that golden lager wasn't created until almost 200 years later. The brand actually launched in 1952 in both France and the UK.

Kronenbourg also produces a small range of other beers under the brand name, including a wheat beer, Kronenbourg Blanc.

See also FRANCE.

Pete Brown

Krones AG is a German-based machinery manufacturer. Founded by the innovator Hermann Kronseder in 1951 near Regensburg in the brewing region of Bavaria, its first machine was a fully automatic labeller for small Bavarian breweries. In 2005 the company absorbed its autonomous subsidiary, Steinecker, under the Krones label and management. Following continuous and healthy growth, the company is today the market leader for all machinery needed in a brewery, from the labeller, bottle filler, and inspector, to all of the brewhouse equipment, as well as the IT systems, logistics, and services.

Krones is a single-source supplier with central engineering and production operations in Germany. Single pieces of machinery, as well as entire brewery projects with numerous interfaces and complex processes, are handled by project management and engineering at company headquarters. While the manufacturing operation is centralized, the service set-up is international.

Besides its brewing know-how, Krones also ranks among the market leaders in aseptic (sterile) filling systems. The qualifications and skill of the brewery staff are significant drivers of product quality. Krones' equipment is considered expensive, but it is also respected as well-built and often innovative.

Krones' success is based on a few crucial strategies: specialized knowledge of mechanical engineering and its customers' sectoral needs; a technical lead in its chosen field thanks to continuously high expenditure on research and development; and a manufacturing operation using state-of-the-art equipment to stringent standards of qualitative excellence. Krones lays claim to more than 1,300 patents, and brewers worldwide are made aware of the company's continuous innovations by focused marketing based around fanciful names for new technologies.

Wolfgang Stempfl

Kulmbacher, Germany, a town in the north of Franconia, Bavaria, where beer has played a major role in the town's economical and social life from the 19th century onward. Since 1996, the local beer scene has been dominated by one major player, "Kulmbacher Brauerei AG," but history has seen a slow amalgamation of erstwhile independent breweries. Reichelbräu (1846) focused on export and gradually took over all the concurrents. Today's Kulmbacher Brauerei is owned by the the Schörghuber group with Brau-Holding International (Heineken) and produces 2.2 million hl annually.

At the start of August, the annual *Bierwoche* (Beerweek) takes place in a big tent in town. Here the erstwhile partition in four major breweries is apparent, even when the former sandlerbräu has been replaced by kapuzinerbräu (wheat beer), whereas once only *festbier* was available. The other three breweries retain their old names: EKU (Erste Kulmbacher Unionsbräu), Reichelbräu, and Mönchshof. Brewing on an industrial scale is still done at EKU and the former Reichelbräu, with Mönchshof having been reshaped into a brewing museum annex microbrewery. This is apt because the brewing site dates from 1349.

Kulmbacher beer is known throughout the world for two strong specialty beers: Kulminator 28, also

German poster stamp, c. 1920. PIKE MICROBREWERY MUSEUM, SEATTLE, WA

known as EKU 28 (referring to the original gravity of 28 degrees Plato), an 11% alcohol by volume *doppelbock,* at one time the strongest lager in the world, and Kulmbacher Bayrisch G'frorns, a genuine *eisbock.*

Historical information. Personal communication with Michaela Knoer of the Gesellschaft fur Geschichte des Brauwesens e.V., Berlin.

Information on EKU Kulminator. Personal communication with Jonathan Downing.

Joris Pattyn and Jonathan Downing

Küppers Kölsch was first introduced into the local market of Cologne, Germany, in 1965, by the Wicküler-Küpper Brauerei GmbH. Kölsch is one of Germany's few traditional ale styles (next to altbier and weissbier) and still holds some 80% to 90% market share in Cologne, its city of origin. See KÖLSCH. The Wicküler-Küpper enterprise started as a small brewpub, founded by Franz Ferdinand Joseph Wicküler, in 1845, in Wuppertal-Elberfeld, some 37 km northeast of Cologne. In 1896 Wicküler merged with another local brewery, the Küpper-Brauerei, and changed its name to Wicküler-Küpper. By 1913 Wicküler-Küpper acquired a 4,000 m2 property in Bayenthal, a suburb south of Cologne. This site was conveniently located close to a rail head and a Rhine River harbor—both great advantages for shipping Wicküler-Küpper beers to distant markets. Küppers kölsch quickly became the market leader in Cologne, much to the chagrin of its approximately two dozen indigenous, more established kölsch competitors, and, within a decade, reached an annual volume of 1 million hl. Over the course of subsequent amalgamations in the German brew industry, Wicküler-Küpper was bought and sold several times, until it became part of the Brau und Brunnen AG, Berlin/Dortmund, in 1994. Brau und Brunnen already owned several other kölsch breweries, including such brands as Gilden, Hansa, Kurfürsten, Meister, Sester, and Sion. In 2002, it combined all of its kölsch holdings into one company, the Kölner Verbund-Brauereien GmbH & Co. KG. With so much production capacity, the Küppers site in Cologne became superfluous and was sold in 2003; but the Kölner Verbund kept the Küppers brand name. Since 2004, Brau und Brunnen, and with it, the Kölner Verbund breweries, are part of the Radeberger Group, Germany's largest brewing conglomerate. Today, all brands of the Kölner Verbund, combined, have been surpassed in output by Reissdorf, which now makes about 0.64 million hl of kölsch a year compared with the Kölner Verbund's 0.55 million hl.

Karl-Ullrich Heyse and Horst Dornbusch

kvass is a mildly alcoholic, lightly sour beer of Slavic origin, commonly made from rye bread or flour and flavored with mint or fruits. It is today available on street corners in Russia, Latvia, Uzbekistan, and many other countries of the former Eastern bloc, where it is often dispensed from mobile tanks, as well as in 2-l bottles, like soda (to which it relates as much as it does to beer). Its production origins are as temporally distant and as vague as many other house-brewed refreshments, but it is said to have been a staple beverage in these parts of the world for thousands of years. Kvass is mentioned in such works of classic Russian literature as Chekhov's *The Cherry Orchard,* Dostoyevsky's *The Brothers Karamazov,* and Tolstoy's *The Death of Ivan Ilyich.*

Like the origins of brewing itself, early versions of kvass were no doubt the result of happy accident, with spontaneously fermented mixtures of water and either stale rye bread or flour yielding a beverage of slight sourness and mild alcoholic content. Commercial versions were more likely to be fermented with added brewing yeast, although home versions would use more commonly available baking yeast. Various fruits have been used to flavor kvass, including lemons, raisins, and strawberries, as well as to mitigate the sourness of the ferment. Today non-alcoholic versions are sold alongside soft drinks such as Coca-Cola. Aggressive efforts by large producers have sought to engender an indigenous pride in kvass, a traditional beverage of the region, against more globalized products.

See also RUSSIA.

Jackson, Michael. *Porter and kvass in St. Petersburg.* Ale Street News, February 1, 1998.

Kvass. http://www.cyberbride.org/kvass.html (accessed 2 May 2011).

Mosher, Randy. *Radical brewing: Recipes, tales, & world-altering meditations in a glass.* Boulder, CO: Brewers Publications, 2004.

Dick Cantwell

Labatt Brewing Company Ltd. is the Canadian subsidiary of AB-InBev and controls roughly 40% of the Canadian market. Created in 1847, when Irishman John Kinder Labatt took over a small brewery in London, Ontario, Labatt now has six brewing facilities across the country, ranging from Creston, British Columbia, in the west to St. John's, Newfoundland, in the east. Labatt produces over 60 brands in Canada, including Labatt Blue, which for many years was the company's flagship product. Originally launched in 1951 as Labatt Pilsner, it was renamed Blue in 1968. Today, the best-selling beer produced by Labatt is Budweiser, also Canada's top-selling brand.

In recent years Labatt has been broadening its Alexander Keith's range of beers. Originally a regional East Coast brand, Keith's has grown into a nationally recognized name. In addition to its flagship India pale ale (which despite the name has precious little hop character), the Keith's brand now includes a dark ale, a wheat beer, a red ale, and a light ale. While a bit more flavorful than Labatt's main products, the Keith's line has nonetheless been met with little acclaim from craft beer drinkers.

In 2007 Labatt took over discount brewer, Lakeport Brewing Company. In 2010 Labatt shifted production of the discount brands from the original Lakeport facility in Hamilton, Ontario, to a Labatt plant in London, Ontario, and closed the Hamilton location.

Labatt started broad distribution of Belgian imports such as Stella Artois, leffe, and hoegaarden after being taken over by Interbrew in 1995. Interbrew (including Labatt) was taken over by Brazil's AmBev in 2004, forming InBev, before the combined company bought Anheuser-Busch in 2008. In addition to AB-InBev products such as Budweiser and Bud Light, Labatt also brews other beers under license, including Guinness Extra Stout.

See also CANADA.

Josh Rubin

labeling information includes precise specifications depending on individual countries' laws, but certain details must be stated on the label of a bottle of beer. In the United States, federal regulations specify that all of the following must be declared: the brand name, the class (type) of beer, the name and address of the bottler/packer or importer, the alcoholic content by weight or volume (if required by the relevant state's law), and the net content. Additionally, the following health advice must be prominently displayed:

> GOVERNMENT WARNING: (1) According to the Surgeon General, women should not drink alcoholic beverages during pregnancy because of the risk of birth defects.
>
> (2) Consumption of alcoholic beverages impairs your ability to drive a car or operate machinery, and may cause health problems.

In the UK, under the Food Labelling Regulations act of 1996, it is essential to declare alcoholic content by volume and a best-before date. Other food laws ensure that the net content is displayed and that the nature of the goods is accurately described. Other countries have similar rulings. In Australia and New Zealand, for example, it is necessary to include a statement of the approximate number of "standard drinks" in the package, a standard drink equating to the amount of a beverage containing 10 g of alcohol at 20°C (68°F).

In addition to the bare minimum of information for legality, brewers all over the world are increasingly choosing to add more detail to their labels as the recognition grows that customers are interested in learning more about the product. These details include ingredients, allergy advice, the history of the brewery, the background of the beer and the beer style, beer and food pairing ideas, units of alcohol, and tasting notes.

See also LAW.

Electronic Code of Federal Regulations. *Title 27–Alcohol, Tobacco Products, and Firearms: Labeling and Advertising of Malt Beverages.* http://ecfr.gpoaccess.gov/cgi/t/text/text-idx?c=ecfr&sid=05b2f6a27b1e95ede836dd6f494b281b&tpl=/ecfrbrowse/Title27/27cfr7_main_02.tpl/ (accessed November 27, 2010).

Labelling of Alcoholic Beverages and Food Containing Alcohol. http://www.foodstandards.gov.au/ (accessed June 10, 2010).

Office of Public Sector Information. *Statutory Instrument 1996 No. 1499: The Food Labelling Regulations 1996.* http://www.opsi.gov.uk/si/si1996/Uksi_19961499_en_1.htm#end/ (accessed December 8, 2009).

Jeff Evans

labels, the paper (or other material) artwork attached to a bottle to provide the name of the beer and other information.

While bottling in some form or another seems to have been around for millennia, the attachment of a label to a glass bottle is a relatively new practice, gaining general usage during the mid-19th century. Up to this point, glassware was manufactured to feature embossed lettering or artwork that depicted the name of the brewery or other details. Guinness was among the earliest companies to switch to paper labels, with examples of its work dating from the 1840s.

Today, labels may also be screen-printed or composed of printed film and are attached to various parts of the bottle, most commonly the front, but also the back (where much of the information is conveyed) and the shoulder or neck. As the trend toward giving beers more colourful names has developed, so has the extravagance of the artwork.

American beer label advertising traditional wood aging. Paper and ink were in short supply during World War II; the simple design of this label, from around 1940, is typical of the period. PIKE MICROBREWERY MUSEUM, SEATTLE, WA

Where once simple, factual designs were employed, now striking illustrations—be they in photographic, sketched, or even cartoon format—are the norm.

The degree of information provided has also increased as consumers seek greater detail about the product. Consequently, alongside often mandatory (dependent on territory) facts and figures such as net content, strength, best-before dates, and medical advice or cautions, many brewers now provide many more details in an effort to inspire and educate the customer. The collecting of labels ("labology") is a widespread hobby.

See also LABELING INFORMATION.

Collections and collectors. *Collections on RIN.ru.* http://collection.rin.ru/cgi-bin/eng/article.pl?id=46/ (accessed December 8, 2009).

The Guinness collectors club. *The Guinness collectors club.* http://www.guinntiques.com/labels/ (accessed December 8, 2009, inactive).

Madgin, Hugh. *Best of British bottled beer.* Weybridge, Surrey, England: Dial House, 1995.

Jeff Evans

lacing

See CLING.

La Chouffe, the colloquial name for Brasserie d'Achouffe, is a regional brewery located in the

Top row, left to right: Belgian beer label, c. 1920; Australian beer label, including offset neck label, c. 1900; English beer label, c. 1920. PIKE MICROBREWERY MUSEUM, SEATTLE, WA

Second row from top, left to right: American beer label, c. 1900; American beer label, c. 1915. PIKE MICROBREWERY MUSEUM, SEATTLE, WA

Third row from top, left to right: American beer label, c. 1910; Belgian beer label, c. 1930; Danish beer label, c. 1900. PIKE MICROBREWERY MUSEUM, SEATTLE, WA

Bottom row, left to right: American beer label, c. 1930s; English beer label, c. 1920. PIKE MICROBREWERY MUSEUM, SEATTLE, WA

Ardennes region of Belgium in the village of Achouffe. It was founded by Chris Bauweraerts and his brother-in-law Pierre Gobron in 1982, when they brewed their first 49 l of La Chouffe in a former pigsty using two antique washing coppers. Their role model was Pierre Celis, and the inspiration for their first beer came from Hoegaarden Grand Cru. See CELIS, PIERRE, and HOEGAARDEN. The unique spicy flavor and the red-hooded, bearded gnome on the label (the "Chouffe," a fanciful local mascot) proved to be a successful combination and sales soared. Demand forced them to replace and expand their brewery six times in the following 25 years. Bottling was moved offsite in 1999 to a facility in Fontenaille, 4 km away. Duvel Moortgat bought the brewery in 2006 and has made several changes, including building a new waste water processing facility, doubling the brewing capacity, and filling in 33-cl as well as the traditional 75-cl bottles. La Chouffe brews the following five beers: La Chouffe (since 1982; 8% alcohol by volume (ABV) and 25 EBUs), Mc Chouffe (since 1987; 8% ABV and 25 EBU), Chouffe Bok 6.666 (since 1991; 6.6% ABV and 35 EBU), N'Ice Chouffe (since 1993; 10% ABV, spiced with thyme and Curaçao peel and 25 EBU), and IPA-Tripel hybrid Houblon Chouffe (launched in 2006; 9% ABV and 50 EBU). Most are fully bottle conditioned. Brasserie d'Achouffe's beers are now exported to more than 20 countries and La Chouffe Blonde is brewed under license by Brasseurs RJ in Montreal, Canada.

Derek Walsh

La Choulette Brewery, originally known as Brasserie Bourgeois-Lecerf, was founded in the late 1970s by Alain Dhaussy, a third-generation brewer and an early player in the French specialty brewing revival. Located in the rural community of Hordain, this classic farmhouse brewery dates back to the 1880s.

La Choulette brews a wide range of specialty ales. The flagship is La Choulette Amber, their take on classic bière de garde which they first introduced in 1981. Prior to introducing a bière de garde in the early 1980s the brewery produced typical lager beers in the German tradition. See BIÈRE DE GARDE. La Choulette produces several variations on biere de garde, including La Choulette Blonde and Les Sans Coulottes. True to La Choulette's status as a specialty producer, it makes a range of seasonal brews, bière de mars ("March beer") for spring and Choulette de Noel, a few fruit ales, and several other brands brewed under contract for other companies.

La Choulette is unusual in that its products are bottled *sur lees* ("with the yeast"), a technique of the past that is no longer practiced by the majority of French specialty brewers. This traditional technique allows the beer to develop additional flavor complexity with age. The products show a charming variability that one would expect from a small farmhouse brewery.

With annual production of around 4,000 hl (3,400 US barrels), La Choulette remains a small boutique brewery. The products are available in France, Italy, Great Britain, and the United States. Mr. Dhaussy, who is passionate about the region's rich brewing history, operates a brewing museum on the site.

Jackson, Michael. *Beer companion.* Philadelphia: Running Press, 1993.
Markowski, Phil. *Farmhouse ales.* Denver, CO: Brewers Publications, 2004.
Woods, John, and Rigley, Keith. *The beers of France.* Wiscombe, Bristol, England: The Artisan Press, 1998.

Phil Markowski

lactic acid (2-hydroxypropanoic acid), also known as milk acid, is a chemical compound that plays a role in several biochemical processes. It was first isolated in 1780 by Swedish chemist Carl Wilhelm Scheele and is a carboxylic acid with a chemical formula of $C_3H_6O_3$. It has a hydroxyl group adjacent to the carboxyl group, making it an alpha hydroxy acid. See ALPHA ACIDS. In solution, it can lose a proton from the acidic group, producing the lactate ion. Industrially, lactic acid fermentation is performed by lactobacillus bacteria, among others. Lactic acid is primarily found in sour milk products, such as koumiss, leban, yogurt, kefir, and some cottage cheeses. The casein in fermented milk is coagulated by lactic acid. In most types of beer, noticeable lactic character (sourness) is considered an off-flavor. In Germany, some breweries will maintain lactic fermentations and use the resulting liquid to make pH adjustments during the brewing process without breaking Reinheitsgebot.

See REINHEITSGEBOT. In other countries, lactic acid may be added directly to brewing water, the mash, or the kettle to make pH adjustments.

Pediococcus is, along with other lactic acid bacteria such as leuconostoc and lactobacillus, responsible for the fermentation of cabbage, turning it into sauerkraut. See LACTOBACILLUS and PEDIOCOCCUS. In this process the sugars in fresh cabbage are transformed to lactic acids, which give it a sour flavor. Pediococcus and lactobacillus bacteria are usually considered contaminants of beer, although their presence is sometimes desired in beer styles such as lambic (gueuze, kriek), Berliner weisse, or Leipziger gose. Certain pediococcus isolates also produce diacetyl, which gives in addition to the sour taste a buttery or butterscotch aroma to beer.

Wolfgang Stempfl

lactobacillus is one of the most common and most feared beer spoilage microorganisms. It belongs to the group of lactic acid bacteria, which also includes pediococcus. There are many species of lactobacillus, including L brevis, L lindneri, and L delbrueckii. Lactobacillus bacteria are Gram positive and rod shaped. See GRAM STAIN. They grow best in environments with a pH value of 4.0 to 5.0 and a temperature of roughly 30°C (85°F). Some species of lactobacillus have a high tolerance for the presence of hop compounds and can survive under anaerobic conditions.

Like brewers yeasts, lactobacillus metabolizes sugars as the main source of energy, but, unlike yeast, it produces lactic acid instead of alcohol. This is a desirable quality for an organism used in making such foods as yogurt, but notable lactic acidity is an off-flavor in most types of beer. Lactobacillus also produces other off-flavors, including diacetyl. Beer with a serious lactobacillus infection will often become hazy.

Although undesirable in most beers, there are a few beer styles for which lactobacillus helps to create part of the beer's characteristic flavor. These include most Belgian sour beers such as lambic, American sour beers, traditional Berliner weisse, and even Belgian witbier, which traditionally showed at least a tinge of lactic acidity.

Malt generally has large populations of lactobacillus on the husks. Some German breweries will use a small amount of malt to inoculate unhopped wort and sour it. This soured wort can then be used for mash or kettle wort acidification without violating the Reinheitsgebot.

There are various methods available for testing for the presence of lactobacillus in beer. These range from simple plating to rapid polymerase chain reaction. See POLYMERASE CHAIN REACTION. Test samples can be taken anywhere from the fermenting vessel to the packaged beer. Testing techniques continue to advance, with the dual goals of quick detection and affordability.

See also BEER SPOILERS, LACTIC ACID, LAMBIC, PEDIOCOCCUS, and SOUR BEERS.

Priest, F., and I. Campbell. *Brewing microbiology,* 2nd ed. London: Chapman & Hall, 1996.

Chris White

lag phase is the period between adding (pitching) yeast into wort and the beginning of fermentation. After its arrival in the wort, yeast requires a certain amount of time to acclimate to its new environment and to shift from dormancy to metabolic activity, that is, to active fermentation. During the lag phase, the yeast turns on genetic pathways that allow it to import sugar and other materials needed for cell replication as well as nutrient absorption (fermentation). The lag phase may last anywhere from 3 to 15 h, depending on such factors as wort type and gravity, temperature, yeast strain, yeast health, pitching rate, and aeration.

During the lag phase, yeast cells rapidly absorb available oxygen. Oxygen is needed for yeast to produce important compounds—most significantly sterols (unsaturated steroid alcohols), which are critical in yeast membrane permeability. Although higher temperatures result in a shorter lag phase, brewers usually keep the lag phase temperature below the temperature at which the yeast will eventually ferment. This is because higher temperatures during the lag phase promote the synthesis of such substances as alpha acetolactate, which is a precursor to diacetyl. See DIACETYL. Overall, however, yeast produces few flavor compounds and ethanol or other alcohols during the lag phase than it does in the fermentation phase.

The pitching rate, too, plays a significant role in the effectiveness and length of the lag phase.

Overpitching can decrease the lag phase, but, because each cell grows the same number of new cells, the result may be too many old, worn-out cells at the end of fermentation. This can lead to off-flavors and low viability if this yeast is subsequently repitched. See PITCHING.

It is also important that the lag phase not last too long, because cool, well-aerated wort is an ideal habitat for bacteria and wild yeast. It is essential, therefore, that vigorous fermentation with the desired yeast begins before any other organisms can gain a foothold. Although most worts will remain stable for at least 24 h, it is best to err on the side of caution and aim for active fermentation within 15 h.

See also FERMENTATION.

Chris White

Other than a temporary closure during Prohibition, the Quandt Brewing Company in Troy, NY, operated from 1859 to 1942. PIKE MICROBREWERY MUSEUM, SEATTLE, WA

lager is one of two overarching families of grain-based beverages that comprise "beer." The other family is ale. See ALE. Although there are countervailing views on terminology, it is generally accepted that all of the world's beer styles belong to one of these two families. Under these families lie further differences that split the world of beer into more than 100 styles, some distinct and some with decidedly fuzzy borders. See BEER STYLE. Lagers are the young upstarts of the beer world, but over the past 150 years lager beer emerged out of central Europe and conquered with amazing speed. Today, approximately 9 of 10 beers consumed around the globe are lagers. Technically, there is only one core difference between all ales and lagers: the type of yeast used to ferment the wort into beer. Simply put, ale yeasts (Saccharomyces cerevisiae) make ales and lager yeasts (Saccharomyces pastorianus) make lagers. See ALE YEAST, LAGER YEAST, and YEAST. Although most ale yeasts ferment wort at relatively warm temperatures, usually between 15°C and 24°C (roughly between 60°F and 75°F), lager yeasts can ferment at relatively cool temperatures, usually between 6°C and 13°C (roughly 42°F and 55°F). Lager yeasts also ferment much more slowly than ale yeasts, produce fewer fermentation by-products, and are considered "cleaner and crisper" tasting than ales by most drinkers. Lager yeasts also tend not to throw a thick, rocky head on top of the fermenting wort during primary fermentation; instead they tend settle to the bottom. This is why lager yeasts are also called "bottom-fermenting" yeasts as opposed to "top-fermenting" ale yeasts. See BOTTOM FERMENTATION and TOP FERMENTATION. If wort has a warm, fast primary fermentation by an ale yeast, it becomes an ale. If it has a cold, slow fermentation by a lager yeast, it becomes a lager. The brewer surely has an intention, but the wort itself is agnostic as to its destiny—it is the yeast that decides its future as a beer.

A pre-Prohibition lager label from The Christian Heurich Brewing Company in Washington, DC. During Prohibition the company managed to stay afloat thanks to its ice plant, which supplied ice to homes, commercial refrigerators, and even, for a time, Congress and the Supreme Court. PIKE MICROBREWERY MUSEUM, SEATTLE, WA

The name lager comes from the German verb *lagern*, which means "to store." This is because lagers are usually matured after fermentation, on the yeast, between several weeks and several months, often near or even below the freezing point. See MATURATION. This maturation period, therefore, is also called "lagering." See LAGERING. During lagering, unwanted flavor and aroma compounds are reabsorbed and transformed by the yeast, which settles to the bottom of the beer, leaving it clear. There is a common perception that lagers are golden, light on the palate, and lower in alcohol, whereas ales are darker, heavier, and stronger. In fact, there is no truth to this whatsoever. The color of a beer has nothing to do with whether it is a lager or an ale nor does its alcoholic content. There are dark and strong lagers just as there are pale and light ales and any combination of these attributes in between. Lagers come in a wide variety of flavors. There are very opaque, almost black, chocolaty lagers; there are smoked lagers; thick, heavy, sweetly malty lagers; amber lagers; deep golden rustic lagers; golden aromatic lagers; straw blond and malty lagers; blond, hoppy, spritzy lagers; and very thin and light quaffing lagers, usually mass-produced with adjuncts. See ADJUNCTS, BOCK BEER, DOPPELBOCK, HELLES, LIGHT BEER, MÄRZENBIER, PILSNER, RAUCHBIER, SCHWARZBIER, and VIENNA LAGER.

For the consumer of beer, the difference between ale and lager is one of flavor and aroma. Lager flavors tend to be ingredient driven rather than yeast driven. The main players on the palate and the nose are grains and hops. Fruity esters and spicy flavors tend to be muted and the flavors direct and focused. Notable fermentation character is usually limited to a fresh whiff of sulfur and often not even that. Ales can be more complex, but well-brewed lagers can be beautiful in their relative simplicity. For virtually all of human history, until roughly the mid-1800s, and unbeknown to the brewer or drinker, beers became either ales or lagers more or less by happenstance, depending on the ambient temperature and overall climate. In temperate environments, ale yeasts tend to become dominant in the fermentation before slower-growing lager yeasts can establish themselves. In cooler climates, especially in the winter, ale yeasts would simply remain dormant, leaving only lager yeasts active in the fermenting wort. Because bacteria would also be dormant during the winter months, beer brewed during the cold season would also be less likely to be infected—cold-fermenting lager yeasts could outcompete bacteria. As a result, winter-brewed beers lasted longer than summer-brewed beers, which often went sour very quickly. This fact did not escape the attention of brewers in central Europe during the Middle Ages. For this reason, Duke Albrecht V of Bavaria decreed in 1553 that henceforth in his realm, all beer brewing had to stop between April 23 and September 29. It was with this decree—perhaps much underappreciated even by beer historians—that Bavaria, with its cold winters in the foothills of the Alps, was moved firmly into the development of lager beer. From then on, by necessity, any beer style developments in Bavaria had to be in lagers. This is why virtually all lager styles brewed the world over today, whether classical or industrial, have Bavarian roots. Eventually ale yeasts largely faded from the scene in Bavaria's cold-brewing culture. The beers made in the run-up to the April shutdown date, now known as märzenbiers (March beers), had to last through the summer until the autumn brewing season and were thus stored, or "lagered," in cellars and caves packed with blocks of ice cut from lakes during the winter. This laborious practice of cold beer storage in central Europe was abandoned only in the last quarter of the 19th century, after Carl von Linde invented mechanical refrigeration for beer storage tanks in 1873. See LINDE, CARL VON.

Since the advent of refrigeration, it has been possible to make lager beer anywhere in the world and in any season. Lager beers, despite being more costly to brew and age, stored and traveled better than ales. By the late 1800s, the new railroads spread lager beer throughout Europe, and from there this once-obscure type of beer was poised to dominate the world of brewing.

Horst Dornbusch, Michael Zepf, and Garrett Oliver

lagering is a form of beer maturation on the yeast that usually lasts for several weeks, if not months, at or near-freezing temperatures, after fermentation and before filtration and/or packaging of the beer. Lagering is employed almost exclusively for bottom-fermented beer styles—hence the name "lager" for these beers—and only rarely for top-fermented beer styles, that is, ales. See ALE, FERMENTATION, and LAGER. Perhaps the best known lagered ale styles are altbier and kölsch. *Lagern* is a German verb meaning "to store." Before the days of mechanical refrigeration, German brewers stored beer in cool, deep caves, especially during the hot summer months. Eventually the lager yeast type, capable of fermentation at cold temperatures, was understood and isolated. Today, the lagering phase of cold-fermented beer production takes place in chilled tanks, and these are often horizontally oriented. During lagering, beer undergoes subtle, but significant, flavor-altering biochemical processes that are responsible for the crisp and clean taste we usually associate with lager beers. Lagering reduces any acetic and lactic acids, for instance, to fruity-tasting esters, whose effects on beer flavor tend to be marginal, because they have a much higher taste threshold to humans than do their precursors. Likewise, any residual acetaldehyde, which can contribute a raw green apple flavor to beer, can decrease by as much as 20% to 70%; 2-3-pentanedione and the volatile, butterscotch-tasting diacetyl, as well as their precursors, are reduced by as much as two-thirds. Diacetyl, which can be detected in tiny amounts, is reduced to fruity-tasting acetoin. Traditionally, when beer reaches the lagering tanks it frequently still contains a small fraction of the sugar that was originally present at the start of fermentation. About four-fifths of this residual sugar is made up of easily fermentable maltose; the rest is mostly maltotriose. During lagering, the total residual sugar content of the beer usually drops by as much as 50%. In the closed lagering tanks, the beer slowly carbonates as the yeast processes the remaining fermentable sugar. If any oxygen was introduced during the transfer to the lagering tanks, it is possible for yeast to scavenge it during the lagering phase, limiting potential damage to beer flavor and appearance.

Traditional lagering can last for up to 3 months, but modern commercial pressures have reduced lagering times substantially at most breweries. In a modern lager brewery, secondary fermentation may or may not occur during the cold storage. If there is to be no secondary fermentation, most brewers will employ a short warm phase (up to 62°F/16.5°C) at the end of primary fermentation; this allows the yeast to ferment residual sugar more completely while absorbing unwanted diacetyl. Today, lagering rarely lasts more than a month and 21 days is fairly standard.

Lagering also has a few mechanical rather than organic chemical effects. It promotes the precipitation of residual colloidal complexes, for instance, that are created in the brew kettle, when large-molecular-chain proteins link up with grain and hop phenols, such as tannins. The precipitation of these complexes has a positive effect on beer stability and reduces protein hazing in the finished product. During lagering, slowly dissipating carbon dioxide scrubs several unpleasant-tasting compounds out of the beer, including sulfur dioxide, which contributes green-beer flavors; dimethyl sulfide, which gives beer vegetal notes; and hop-derived mercaptan, which is partially responsible for skunk-like off-aromas, especially in beer exposed to light.

See also ACETALDEHYDE, DIACETYL, DIMETHYL SULFIDE (DMS), MALTOSE, MALTOTRIOSE, MATURATION, OXIDATION, and VICINAL DIKETONES.

Fix, George. *Principles of brewing science*. Boulder, CO: Brewers Publications, 1989.

Heyse, Karl-Ullrich. *Handbuch der Brauerei-Praxis*. Nuremberg, Germany: Getränke-Fachverlag Hans Carl, 1994 (translation of title: *Handbook of brewery practice*).

Narziss, Ludwig. *Abriß der Bierbrauerei*. Stuttgart, Germany: Enke Verlag, 1986 (translation of title: *Treatise on beer brewing*).

Noonan, Gregory J. *New brewing lager beer*. Boulder, CO: Brewers Publications, 1996.

Horst Dornbusch

lager yeast, Saccharomyces pastorianus, is a bottom fermenting yeast used for brewing lager style beers. It is physiologically distinct from the top fermenting (so called because it forms a thick foam at the top of the wort during fermentation) ale yeast S. cerevisiae in its abilities to ferment at cooler temperatures and to ferment the sugar melibiose. Lager yeast also typically ferments more of the sugars than ale yeast, leading to a crisper taste.

At the genetic level, lager yeast is a hybrid organism between two closely related yeast species, S. cerevisiae and S. bayanus. It is thought to have arisen in response to selective pressures from cold brewing temperatures, and, notably, S. bayanus is much more cold tolerant that S. cerevisiae. Thus, the presence of these two genomes in the hybrid S. pastorianus may have led to its observed ability to carry out fermentation better at cold temperatures than S. cerevisiae alone. This selection for a cooler fermenting yeast may have taken place during successive rounds of cold-temperature fermentations resulting from a 16th-century Bavarian law that prohibited brewing during summer months due to the inferior quality of summer-brewed beers.

Many isolates of S. pastorianus have been collected from breweries since Hansen pioneered pure culturing of yeast in the late 1800s, and recent work has shown that all lager strains in use today likely descended from one of two hybridization events between S. cerevisiae and S. bayanus. In both cases, it is probable that the S. cerevisiae parent of these two original S. pastorianus strains was a strain already being used for brewing ale.

See also BOTTOM FERMENTATION and YEAST.

Gavin Sherlock

Lallemand is a Canadian company that produces yeasts and bacteria for the brewing, baking, wine-making, ethanol fuel, distilling, animal nutrition, and bioingredients industries. For brewers, it offers dried yeasts for the production of both ales and lagers. Founded in Montreal in 1915, Lallemand began yeast production in 1923. In the 1970s, the company added specialty yeasts for distillers and vintners as well as yeasts for homebrewing kits to its portfolio. A decade later, it began opening subsidiaries in Europe, Africa, Australia, Asia, and the United States. In 2000, Lallemand acquired a majority share in the Siebel Institute of Technology in Chicago and, in 2001, purchased the British maker of brewing process aids, AB Vickers Ltd. of Burton-on-Trent. Lallemand now conducts fermentation research in laboratories in Toulouse, France, and Montreal, Canada, and is active in the fields of beer flavor, bottle conditioning, beer clarity, fermentation, microbiology, and yeast handling. Many of its yeasts are marketed under the brand name Danstar.

See also CANADA.

John Holl

lambic is a sour wheat beer style brewed in and around Brussels. By world standards, lambic brewing is rare and the volume brewed is small. At their best, lambic beers are among the most interesting, complex drinks ever created. The fermentation technique reflects medieval and even ancient times,

Empty champagne bottles in the cellars of the Boon Brewery in Lembeek, Brussels, waiting to be washed. The bottles are filled with lambic, corked, and secured with wire cages to hold the pressure that builds up during the beer's final fermentation in the bottle. Such bottle conditioning gives the finished beer a crisp, champagne-like effervescence. PHOTOGRAPH BY DENTON TILLMAN well before the second half of the 19th century, when Louis Pasteur developed new microbiological understandings and Emil Christian Hansen developed a way to breed pure yeast strains. At one time, all beers were made without knowledge of bacteria and pure yeast cultures, and a certain sourness in taste would have been thought of as typical rather than unusual. With the advances of the 20th century, however, brewing equipment improved and brewing techniques became more sophisticated, especially through revolutions in chemistry and microbiology. Brewing became a more controlled process and beer became a more consistent product that did not sour or spoil as easily. It could be brewed, transported, and stored more reliably, which was of significant commercial benefit to the entire beer trade from producer to retailer. Yet, despite this general trend toward controlled brewing practices, brewing lambic beer has remained an enduring and endearing specialty of Brussels and a few villages in the surrounding region of Payottenland.

At the very heart of lambic is a complex fermentation based on locally and naturally occurring wild yeasts and bacteria. In this, they are analogous to the so-called natural wines that are now reascendant among wine enthusiasts. There are two principal fermentation stages in the lambic process, both involving "wild" or native microorganisms. The first stage produces mostly ethanol and lasts about 3 to 6 months. The second stage produced mostly acids and lasts an average of 12 to 24 months. The nature of all lambic fermentations, often described as spontaneous, is largely determined by the local organisms that inhabit the brewery and its environs. The organisms that find a home in brewery barrels and on timbers and walls over time lend a degree of stability to a particular mix of microbes and thus contribute to the unique character of each brewery's lambic. Today the lambic style includes beers that are tart and dry, aged and complex, as well as sugar or syrup sweetened and fruity. In an ironic bow to modernity, some are even sweetened with aspartame or saccharin, a practice viewed as distasteful by enthusiasts.

Lambic brewing reflects a synergy with nature and ancient learnings passed on over generations of brewers. Traditionally, lambics are brewed only between October and April, when the prevailing ambient temperature tends to be below 15°C (roughly 60°F). Importantly, the temperature increase over succeeding spring and summer months stimulates fermentation just as yeast and bacterial activities naturally slow down because of the depletion of fermentable sugars.

Lambics have a number of distinctive features when compared with more common beer styles. Whereas malted barley is part of the mash, so is a high proportion of unmalted wheat, sometimes as much as 30%–40%. This mash composition requires an elaborate temperature regimen to gelatinize and convert most of the grain starches into fermentable sugars. See MASH. Although hops are used in lambics, oddly they are not added fresh, but only after they have been aged for several years. During this intentional aging the hops become stale and oxidized, taking on cheesy, hay-like aromatics. These characteristics are later ameliorated by a long kettle boil and somewhat masked by other aromas in the finished beer. Lambic brewers are less interested in the hops' bitterness and more in their natural preservative qualities. In lambic beers, sweet malt flavors are not balanced by hop bitterness but more by lactic acidity.

In the brew house, lambics can be mashed by decoction or temperature-programmed infusion. See DECOCTION and INFUSION MASH. Typically the mash starts at about 45°C (113°F) with successive rests at roughly 55°C (131°F), 65°C (149°F), and 72°C (162°F). This ensures an adequate breakdown of starches and high-molecular-weight proteins. After lautering, the wort is boiled for up to several hours with the aged hops. Then the wort is pumped into a large, shallow, rectangular copper or stainless steel vessel called a coolship. See COOLSHIP. Because of the large surface area, the wort cools off quickly. The coolship is usually built right under the brewery's roof with louvers or vents in the wall for a good flow of fresh, cool air that is laden with native microflora. Sometimes a large, slow-moving fan enhances air circulation. As the air passes over the surface of the wort overnight, it quickens cooling and, crucially, inoculates the wort with airborne microorganisms. Eventually, the nutritious wort becomes inhabited with an active mix of wild yeasts and bacteria, at which point it is transferred into wooden casks that are generally left open to the atmosphere.

Lambic fermentations have been an object of intense scientific study, which has resulted in the identification of the many organisms involved. A typical lambic fermentation progresses as a relay of competing organisms that, each in their turn, metabolize the wort's nutrients and simultaneously change the wort's chemistry by adding their metabolic byproducts. In this process, as one group of organisms declines, another will start to prosper, grow, and take its turn in changing the ferment. This continues until the last set of microbes has consumed its specific nutrients and made its specific contributions to the beer's flavor. The final result is the typical lambic taste profile (sour, complex) combined with the specific taste profile from the brewery environment in which it was created.

There are essentially two types of fermentation that turn wort into lambic: an alcohol-producing fermentation and an acid-producing fermentation. The fermentation sequence is divided into four chronologically distinct phases. The first phase occurs at temperatures of 18°C to 20°C (64°F to 68°F) and is driven by such enteric bacteria as Enterobacter cloacae, Enterobacter aerogenes, and Klebsiella aerogenes and such wild yeast strains as Kloeckera apiculata and Saccharomyces globosus. Over the course of a month or so, these microbes cause a mixed-acid fermentation that generates both alcohol and carbon dioxide, as well as acetic, lactic, succinic, and formic acids. This mixture of metabolic products eventually alters the chemistry of the ferment to a point at which the activity of these organisms subsides. As the acidity increases, various Saccharomyces species—such as Saccharomyces cerevisiae, Saccharomyces bayanus, Saccharomyces uvarum, and Saccharomyces inusitatus—begin to prosper and ferment most of the wort's sugars into ethanol, as well as some higher fusel alcohols, ethyl acetate, and ethyl lactate. See PH. This second round of fermentation is vigorous and may last up to 6 months, during which overflowing foam may leave a dried crust around the opening of the oak cask.

The next fermentation phase involves Pediococcus damnosus, a bacterium that does well at temperatures above 20°C (68°F) and produces lactic acid and diacetyl. This phase may last for 3 to 4 months.

At the final fermentation phase, two Brettanomyces yeasts, Brettanomyces bruxellensis and Brettanomyces lambicus, begin to work. These reside in the ferment at very low concentrations and give some lambics their characteristic "Brett" taste and aroma, which has been memorably described as "horse blanket." Historically, B bruxellensis was first identified in lambic and appears to be more prevalent in the environs of Brussels, while B lambicus is more prevalent in nearby rural communities. The unique mix of organisms in different locations, therefore, adds to a form of "terroir" and the individual character of different lambic brews. Brettanomyces yeasts ferment any residual extract such as maltotriose and maltotetraose very slowly into small amounts of ethanol and acetic acid. They also synthesize ethyl acetate, ethyl lactate, and tetrahydropyridines—associated with a "mousy" aroma—as well as volatile phenolics—associated with medicinal or barnyard-like aromas—and caprylic and capric acids and esters—associated with "goaty" flavors. Brettanomyces often produce a pellicle, or film, on the surface of the beer in the cask. This reduces the oxidation potential of the cask's content and thus the risk of acetomonas, which are vinegar bacteria, which would make the beer excessively acetic and vinegarlike.

Typical lambic flavors can be challenging on the palate and, if present in excess or out of balance, can cause flavors undesirable even to the most adventurous drinker. Thus, the lambic brewer walks a fine line between creating sensory delight and sensory offense. Although a touch of lactic tartness, for instance, may create an alluring tangy taste just as it does in good Champagne, an intense sourness may make the beer undrinkable. Likewise, a hint of "goatiness" may add an intriguing complexity to the beer, but too much of it may make the beer taste rancid. This is one reason why many finished lambics are often a blend of several batches, sometimes of several years. Nonetheless, sometimes a lambic batch may actually spoil and has to be discarded because the brew may have been exposed to air postfermentation, perhaps from a damaged cask, stimulating acetomonas bacteria and the overproduction of acetic acid.

Lambic beers have evolved over time into several variations on the same basic theme, and modern brewers are still adapting lambics in different geographies and for different export markets. Next to traditional lambics, which are universally very dry, there are now lambic versions on the market that are sweetened to mask some of the brew's "wild" character. This development has been the catalyst for a debate in Belgium and even for the formation of a consumer group, which enthusiastically champions the traditional artisanal style.

Types of Lambic

Lambic

Unblended lambic is uncarbonated, devoid of foam, sour, and available on tap only at a few locations around Brussels and in the producing villages. It often has a cider-like aroma and taste and is generally poured out of an earthenware pitcher and served in short tumblers. It is a highly complex drink and is not exported. If you look at old Flemish paintings such as Pieter Bruegel's "Peasant Dance," the jugs on the tables are typically used for lambic beer.

Bière de Mars

Bière de mars is a partigyle brew made from the second runnings of a regular lambic mash. It is a "small" lambic of indeterminate kettle gravity. See BIÈRE DE MARS and PARTIGYLE.

Faro

This version of lambic is relatively low in alcohol and is sweetened with caramelized brown candi sugar. It is often made from a half-and-half blend of regular lambic and bière de mars. Originally faro was a cheaper "working class" version of lambic, but it is now difficult to find. See FARO.

Gueuze

The most common of the traditional unfruited lambic styles, gueuze (sometimes pronounced "goose," but more often pronounced "gur-zah") is a bottle-conditioned blend of young and old lambic—perhaps at a ratio of one-third to two-thirds—usually sold in a corked and wire-caged bottle. See BOTTLE CONDITIONING. Young lambic still has some residual sugar, which allows for a secondary fermentation in the bottle that builds a high natural carbonation. The blend may contain lambics of several different ages mixed according to the brewer's taste. The older the lambics, the richer they are in Brettanomyces and the more complex and drier will be the gueuze. Conversely, the younger the lambics are, the softer tasting the resulting gueuze. Because the blend depends on each brewer's individual preference, there is no uniform flavor profile for this beer style. This, however, is part of the charm. Most gueuzes have an initial carbonic bite that evolves into a dry, sour, and complex finish. There are also gueuzes on the market that have been sweetened with sugar or an artificial sweetener. The original style is often labeled as "tradition" or "oud," the latter meaning "old" in Flemish. The latter are to be avoided.

Fruit

Several popular styles of lambic incorporate whole fruit, fruit pulp, or juice. These are usually young lambics with the fruit sugars creating a secondary fermentation in the cask. Fruit lambics may have a sour and complex character balanced by the fruitiness. Some fruit lambics are a blend of small amounts of traditional lambic and sweetened and pasteurized fruit syrup. Such fruit lambics taste intensely fruity and clean and may be more akin to fruit-flavored beers than complex lambics.

Kriek is a cherry lambic. It is the original and most popular of the fruit lambics. Its color is reddish with hints of amber, and its foam is pink. Traditionally, the cherries for this brew were an extremely sour variety called schaarbeek that were indigenous to only a very limited area around the village of Schaarbeek outside Brussels. Nowadays the sour cherries are also grown in a few other parts of Europe, especially in Poland, as well as in other parts of Belgium, northern France, and Germany. For traditional kriek, the whole cherry fruit is used, fresh after the harvest, when summer temperatures are still high. After the addition of crushed fruit to the beer in the cask, a secondary fermentation starts within a few days. It can be quite vigorous and the cask often overflows with foam. The cask's bung hole, therefore, may be loosely filled with twigs to prevent cherry pits from floating on the surface and blocking the hole. Interestingly, the twigs are often covered with spider webs, but brewers tend to look kindly upon the spiders because they ensure that no fly or other insect will share in the lambic. Kriek can be matured in the cask for several months as the yeasts consume the cherries. It is traditionally then refermented in the bottle, emerging very dry and fantastically complex.

"Framboise," which is French for "raspberry," as well as black currant and peach, are also frequent lambic fruits. But nontraditional fruit, such as cranberries and strawberries, have been pressed into fruit lambic service by modern experimental brewers.

Such innovation, although considered rather controversial by many traditionalists, has arguably helped the idiosyncratic lambic family of beers to maintain some level of popularity and the lambic beer style to survive. Sweetened fruit lambics tend to be more drinkable to a larger spectrum of palates and may have eased many consumers into tasting the more demanding, traditional versions.

de Keersmaecker, Jacques. The mystery of lambic beer. *The Scientific American*, August 1996.
Esslinger, Hans Michael. *Handbook of brewing*. Weinheim, Germany: Wiley-VCH Verlag GmbH & CoKGaG, 2009.
Guinard, Jean-Xavier. *Lambic*. Denver, CO: Brewers Publications, 1990.
Shanta Kumara, H. M. C., and H. Verachtert. Identification of lambic superattenuating micro-organisms by the use of selective antibiotics. *Journal of the Institute of Brewing* 97 (1991): 181–5.
Sparrow, Jeff. *Wild brews: beer beyond the influence of brewers's yeast*. Denver, CO: Brewers Publications, 2005.

Bill Taylor

lambswool

See CHRISTMAS ALES.

Lao Li

See CHINA.

last orders, such as "Empty your glasses please," or more likely, "Ain't you got no 'ome to go to?" are immortal rantings from "mine host" that will be familiar to everyone who has had a pint in hand at closing time in an English pub. They bring the evening's (or afternoon's) drinking to an end and are prompted by licensing law. In theory, such calls should be less frequent because most British pubs, clubs, and bars are now permitted to serve liquor 24 h a day (there are different laws for England and Wales, Scotland, and Northern Ireland), although relatively few actually do. Many town houses trade from 10 AM until midnight, and clubs, which open early in the evening, might stay open until the small hours. Only a few places are open all night.

Until 2005, British on-license hours were restricted to morning/afternoon (10:30 or 11:00 AM to 2:30 or 3:00 PM) and evening sessions (5:00 PM to 10:30 or 11:00 PM). These hours were different on a Sunday. Such restrictions were introduced "temporarily" during World War I and never rescinded.

The time-honored protocol for closing a session was for the landlord to ring a bell and shout "last orders" 10 min before actual closing time (i.e., 10:50 for 11:00 PM). Precise wording would normally be something like: "Time, gentlemen, please," or "Last drinks at the bar." After this call, the customer has 10 min to purchase drinks. No drink should be served after closing time, and, from then on, the customer should finish his purchase(s) within 20 min.

The relaxation of licensing law was supposedly aimed at bringing Britain into line with the rest of the Western world and to prevent the frenzied activity in and outside of pubs around "last orders," "closing time," and the subsequent ejection of all customers from the premises.

See also LAW, PUBLIC HOUSES (PUBS), and TAVERNS.

Ian Hornsey

late hopping is the addition of hops during the latter part of the kettle boil. During the boil, bittering acids are isomerized from hops into the wort, but the volatile oils responsible for hop flavor and aroma are largely boiled off and therefore lost. Late hopping is employed to keep more aromatic hop components in the wort so that they can later become part of the finished beer. There is no set point during the boil that brewers perform late hopping, but hops added any time within 30 min of end of the boil are generally considered "late hops." Today many beer styles incorporate late hop additions during the kettle boil, and these additions are often blends of different hop varieties. Such blends can become part of the signature aroma of a particular beer. Although late hopping may be a well-accepted technique for adding hop flavor and aroma to beer, the actual mechanism and hop compounds that create these are imperfectly understood. The variety of late hops chosen by a brewer is often based on the aromatic qualities of a particular hop variety. Careful hop breeding has resulted in cultivars with exceptional aromatics, which is why they are often called aroma hops. The substances responsible for hop aromas are essential oils. They make up about 0.5% to 3% of the hop's weight. Essential oils are composed of two fractions: hydrocarbons and an oxygenated fraction. Hydrocarbons, however, which make up 80% to 90% of the essential oil mass, are not necessarily responsible for hop aromas in finished beer, because they are extremely volatile and evaporate during the boil. Oxygenated fractions—made up of terpenes and sesquiterpenes—tend to be more aromatic and are less volatile. Late hop aroma in beer, therefore, may be largely derived from a few intensely aromatic compounds in oxygenated fractions. There is also the possibility of a synergistic effect between several compounds that are each present in amounts too small for the human nose to detect, but which, in combination, may achieve the sensory threshold. Some of these compounds have citrus and floral characteristics. The extent to which they survive the kettle boil, however, depends greatly on the method of late hopping and varies among breweries. In addition, there are additional aromas associated with late hopping that do not appear to be related to the characteristic scent that caused the brewer to select a particular hop variety. American craft brewers have been pioneers in the use of late hopping, not only adding aroma hops in the minutes before the end of the boil but also flavoring the wort with successful dosages of hops right to the very end of the boil. Some brewers wait until the boil is actually over, only adding the final hop pellets before the wort is sent into a whirlpool vessel. To some extent, this practice mirrors the purpose of the hop back, a vessel that strains the wort over a bed of whole hop flowers before it is sent to the heat exchanger and the fermentation vessel. See HOP BACK and WHIRLPOOL. The wort is still hot enough to extract aromatic compounds, but not hot enough to drive them all off. Whirlpool additions can be combined with a hop back for even more intense aroma extraction.

In many craft breweries, the majority of the hops used are part of the late addition. Conventional wisdom has held that hops need to be boiled to provide bitterness to wort, but this is not true. Even when added as late as the whirlpool, late hop additions add bitterness as well as aroma. Isomerization and extraction of hop bittering compounds are a matter of temperature, contact time, and surface area; actual boiling is not strictly required, especially if the wort remains in turbulent motion. The bitterness extraction is inefficient, because the hops are barely boiled, or not boiled at all, but large late hop additions can provide a majority of bitterness in styles such as American pale ale and India pale ale as well as contributing aroma and flavor. The aromatics given to beer by late hop additions are noticeably different than those given by dry hopping, with the latter giving a greener "hop sack" aroma. Late hopping and dry hopping are therefore often used in combination for the production of beers intended to have intense hop aromatics.

See also DOUBLE IPA, DRY HOPPING, and INDIA PALE ALE.

Lewis, Michael J., and Tom W. Young. "Hop chemistry and wort boiling." In *Brewing*, 2nd ed., 269–71. New York: Springer Science + Business Media LLC, 2004.

Chad Michael Yakobson

lautering is a method of separating sweet wort from spent grain. Historically, especially in British ale brewing practice, mashing and lautering often took place in a single vessel, a combination mash–lauter tun. But brewers soon realized that optimizing separate vessels for each part of the process of wort generation and recovery would lead to improved efficiencies and beer quality.

A lauter tun is a circular vessel, often wider than the mash tun, into which the finished mash is transferred. The mash is usually heated to a higher temperature than is needed for enzymatic conversion. This reduces the viscosity of the wort. In the lauter tun, to ease wort runoff, the grain bed is often shallower than it is in the mash tun. Modern lauter tuns are usually constructed of stainless steel and are equipped with slotted false bottoms that are made either from wedge wire or machined solid plates. The wedge wire offers larger openings than a machined bottom, but both allow the unrestricted flow of clear wort through them. There is also an outlet for spraying sparge water over the grain bed to replenish the wort as it drains out.

Most lauter tuns are equipped with a series of rakes and knives that are attached to a rotating assembly, which can be raised and lowered. These knives are angled so that they gently lift the grain and make cuts through the grain bed. This also helps to improve the grain bed's porosity and reduces any pressure differential between the top and bottom of the bed, ensuring an even and easy runoff. A plow is usually also part of the assembly. It can be lowered close to the false bottom to remove the spent grain through a door in the base of the lauter tun. At the very bottom, a lauter tun is fitted with several collection tubes, all of similar flow characteristic, to carry the drained wort away to the kettle or a holding vessel.

Modern automated lauter tuns include sensors that detect pressure and flow rates and feed such data back to a computer that controls the raking system. This optimizes the flow through the grain bed.

In the lautering sequence, first the space under the plates needs to be flooded to a depth of 1 to 2 inches with hot brewing water to warm the vessel and to ease dispersal of the mash when it is pumped into the vessel. The entire stirred mash is transferred from the mash tun to the lauter tun using a specially designed pump. The lauter tun is filled from the bottom up. The mash is allowed to settle for a few minutes before some wort is drawn from the bottom and returned to the top of the mash bed in a process called recirculation or by its German name of vorlauf (literally "prerun"). See VORLAUF. During recirculation, the grain bed serves as a filter material. This continues until the turbidity of the wort decreases to an acceptable level, after which the flow is diverted to the brew kettle.

Once the wort level drops slightly below the top of the grain bed, sparge water sprayed from the lauter tun dome replenishes the liquid in the lauter tun and dissolves more solids from the spent grain. It is possible to match the rate of sparge with the rate of wort recovery so the grains remain immersed at a constant level. Occasionally the rakes and knives can be employed to gently open up the compacted grain bed. Collection of wort continues until the required wort volume is collected in the kettle at the desired strength. See ORIGINAL GRAVITY. The remaining liquid is drained from the lauter tun and the spent grain is removed. It often becomes cattle feed.

Steve Parkes

lauter tun is a vessel for separating the wort from the solids of the mash. See GRANT, LAUTERING, MASHING, and SPARGING. A lauter tun works much like a large sieve. It normally has a slotted, perforated floor, also called a false bottom, which holds the spent milled grains, while allowing the wort to filter through the grain bed and collect in the space beneath; the wort then runs to the brew kettle.

Mashing occurs in a separate mash mixer, in which case the mash must be transferred by a pump to the lauter tun. The mash is usually pumped in from the bottom or side of the vessel to avoid excessive aeration of the mash. See HOT-SIDE AERATION, OXIDATION, and STALING. At the beginning of the run-off, the wort is usually recirculated through the grain bed as a filter mass, until the run-off appears clear through a sight glass in the recirculation plumbing. See VORLAUF. Unless sized for brewpubs or very small microbreweries, most lauter tuns are fit with motorized rakes that cut through the grain bed to give it greater filterability.

Other brewhouses may have a setup in which a single vessel serves as both the mash and the lauter unit, thus eliminating the need to pump the mash. These systems remain common in the UK for performing single temperature infusion mashes. Such mash tuns, like lauter tuns, are fitted with false bottoms. The advantages of a combination mash/lauter tun are less up-front equipment cost and a smaller footprint in the brewhouse. The advantage of two separate vessels for mashing and lautering is that the mash tun can be filled again with a new batch while the previous batch is still running off into the kettle. Thus, a separate lauter tun allows a brewery to produce more brews per day than would otherwise be possible.

Brewing Trade Review July (1961): 781–2.

Gourvish, T. R., and R. G. Wilson. *The brewing industry 1830–1980*. Cambridge: Cambridge University Press, 1994.

Hornsey, Ian S. *Brewing*. London: Royal Society of Chemistry, 1999.

Kunze, Wolgang. *Technology, brewing & malting*. Berlin: VLB Berlin, 1996.

Tim Hampson

law regulating alcohol, its production, distribution, and consumption has existed almost as long as alcohol has been a part of society. As alcohol entered the social life of a community, alcohol control policies developed. Whereas the Sumerians of old Mesopotamia were the first civilization to turn fields of grain into rivers of beer, their conquerors, the Babylonians, turned beer making into a target of governance, especially once Hammurabi (1728–686 BC) took over. Hammurabi ran his realm with an iron fist, and no facet of life, including beer, could escape his "code," which is now considered mankind's first body of laws. The "code of Hammurabi" remains chiseled into a 7-foot-high column of gray–green igneous diorite, which now rests in the Louvre in Paris. In these laws, Hammurabi classified beer into 20 different categories, 8 of which had to be made entirely from barley; others could be made from a mixture of grains. The most highly valued and most expensive Babylonian beer was pure spelt beer. There were also pure wheat beers, thin beers, red beers, and black beers—as well as an aged beer for export, mostly to Egypt, where the thirst for beer was rapidly spreading. He then slapped price controls on both the brewers and the innkeeper, and the first beer laws were enacted.

Since then, communities have experimented with various methods of alcohol control, from heavy taxation to the outright prohibition of all alcoholic beverages. Perhaps the two most famous and most consequential to this day are the Bavarian Beer Purity Law (Reinheitsgebot) of 1516 and Prohibition in the United States (enacted by the 18th and repealed by the 21st Amendments). See PROHIBITION and REINHEITSGEBOT.

The Reinheitsgebot mandated that only barley, water, and hops be used in beer making (the role of yeast in fermentation was still a mystery in those days). But that decree also established firm beer prices for Bavaria, which was a key objective of the decree and is much underappreciated by modern devotees of the brewing techniques that it spawned. In fact, the word "Reinheit" (purity) does not even appear in the original document and only 31 of its 315 words, that is, only 9.85% of the decree, deal with beer ingredients. The rest spell out mandatory summer and winter beer prices as well as penalties for violators of the price control edict. Over the centuries, the edict was amended to include yeast as a legitimate beer ingredient, and the price controls were removed. In their stead, complicated rules were added, permitting the use of malted wheat as well as sugar invert adjuncts, but only for top-fermented beers. It also specified that any brew not following the legislators' ingredients prescriptions could not be called "beer" and detailed the taxes brewers had to pay on their wort. The edict acquired its current name "Purity Law" only in 1918, after an obscure delegate to the Bavarian state parliament called it such during a beer tax debate.

American Prohibition, by contrast, rather than regulating the making, selling, and transporting of alcoholic beverages, simply forbade them entirely. Prohibition, oddly, did not explicitly ban the possession or consumption of alcohol, but only its production and sale. Organized crime and bootlegging quickly became effective at supplying a demand that legal entities no longer could. But the repeal of Prohibition came at a cost: the system of "no" was replaced by a federally licensed three-tier system, which forbade brewers to sell their product directly to an on-premise or off-premise retailer or to the consumer directly. Instead, beer could only be distributed to retailers and the public indirectly, through a middleman called a distributor or wholesaler. The ostensible intent of this complex licensing and distribution system was to eliminate the criminal element from alcohol sales, as well as to blunt the main arguments of the Prohibitionists, namely their opposition to vertically integrated distribution systems that allowed breweries to own distributorships as well as saloons as so-called tied houses and thus create local or regional monopolies and dictate prices. By separating the tiers, it was thought that brewers would have to compete for the portfolios of distributors and distributors would have to compete for the portfolios of retailers and levels of distribution. Although this model makes sense in theory, it has not always had the desired effect in practice. Large national brewers can still grant or withhold such favors as credits to wholesalers and thus place them under duress simply by virtue of the size of the wholesaler's business a particular brand represents. Small breweries may have difficulty getting their beers in front of consumers simply by virtue of the small chunk of business they represent to the distributor in their local market. For the brewer, then, the distributor's attention, or, as it has been termed, "share of mind," becomes almost as important as gaining the consumer's attention and approval. The vertically integrated distribution model, with its dedicated distributors and tied houses, has been replaced by federal and state regulations in the United States, but it is still widely used in Germany, Ireland, and many other countries.

In the United States, individual states were empowered, after Prohibition, to fashion their own particular regulations as to how the three-tier system was to operate in detail within their territorial boundaries. As a result, an incredibly complicated mosaic of different and often conflicting sets of state legislation emerged to regulate commerce in alcohol. Some states reserved alcohol sales exclusively to state agencies; other states created state alcoholic beverage control boards to oversee the licensing of enterprises involved in the manufacture and sale of alcohol. Yet other states have set rules as to which stores might carry alcoholic beverages and which cannot. In some states, therefore, only specialized liquor or "package" stores were allowed to carry spirits, wine, and/or beer; in other states, grocery stores, including supermarkets, were permitted to carry alcoholic beverages. In some states, there were even regulations as to the amount of alcohol beer might contain. Many of these regulations, some of them spectacularly odd, remain in place today.

Although Americans tend to think of Prohibition as uniquely American, it was not—of the Nordic countries, only Denmark escaped any form of severe control during the 1910s and 1920s. Full alcohol prohibition was short in Iceland, lasting only from 1915 to 1922, but beer remained banned until 1989. Sweden's rationing system eventually gave way to today's state monopoly (Systembolaget), and similar systems remain in place in Norway (Vinmonopolet), Iceland (Vínbúðin), and Finland (Alko). Even Belgium, a bastion of brewing culture, suffered a creeping form of liquor prohibition starting in the 1890s.

One of the main goals of alcohol control legislation—often wrapped in the mantle of moral duty, the preservation of public order and decency, the protection of public health, and the curbing of crime—is the generation and control of revenues. In other words, laws regulating alcohol invariably involve taxes on alcoholic beverages as well as licensing fees levied on those enterprises that are engaged in their manufacture and sale. See TAXES. Taxes on beer may come in many forms. There are federal, state, and local sales taxes charged to brewers, wholesalers, retailers, and consumers; excise taxes; and value-added taxes—severally or in combination. In the United States, excise taxes are usually paid by the beer manufacturer, importer, or wholesaler. In many Scandinavian countries all alcoholic beverages carry a heavy sales tax and their off-premise retail sales are often channeled only through government monopoly outlets. Some countries—the United States and Germany included—have lower tax rates on beer than they do on spirits and wine.

Another method of alcohol control—one that is gaining increasing appeal worldwide—is the imposition of a minimum drinking age. In 1984, the United States required all states to raise the minimum drinking age to 21 years. Other countries, which traditionally did not have legal drinking ages, have more recently followed suit with similar legislation. France, for example, enacted a minimum age of 18 for the purchase of alcohol. In most countries, the stated minimum age for purchase of alcoholic beverages is between 16 and 18 years. Many countries do not criminalize consumption of alcohol by minors if they are with their parents.

Most nations also have laws restricting the advertising and marketing of alcoholic beverages. These may range from complete bans of advertising in mass media to strict regulations as to what may or may not be stated in marketing of alcoholic beverages. But beer manufacturers have become creative in working within the marketing restrictions. Beer marketing campaigns subtly target specific groups and involve print, television, and internet media, as well as sponsorships and contests.

Given the myriad of legislative and administrative involvement in the manufacture and distribution of beer and alcoholic beverages in general, the alcohol industry is one of the most highly regulated industries just about everywhere in the world. Each nation has found its own peculiar ways of prescribing what the industry may and may not do . . . and of course, of profiting through fees and taxes from that involvement. Breweries, beer wholesalers, and retailers must adapt to the rules and regulations that govern their businesses in their local environments.

See also MARKETING and TAXES.

Lincoln, Anda, and Brad Lincoln. *21 questions about opening a brewery in the United States*. Beaverton, OR: Dark Train LLC, 2009.

McGowan, Richard. *Government regulation of the alcohol industry: The search for revenue and the common good.* Westport, CT: Quorum Books, 1997.

Anda Lincoln and Horst Dornbusch

Lee's Brewery

See J.W. LEES BREWERY.

Leffe Brewery began when the Leffe monks of the Premonstratensian Order began growing hops, milling grain, and brewing at the Abbaye Notre-Dame de Leffe in Belgium's Namur Province during the 13th century. After surviving a flood of the Muese River in 1460 and then a major fire 6 years later, the brewery began to prosper in the 17th century. Leffe earned a reputation for the quality of its beer and the brewery was enlarged and renovated at this time. In 1796 the abbey was declared the property of the state, although brewing continued in a limited capacity until 1809. At some point during World War I, the original brew kettles were melted down for ammunition. Following World War II, Father Abbot Nys decided to revive beer making on the premises. With the professional assistance of brewer Albert Lootvoet, Leffe brown ale was reintroduced in 1952. Interbrew—now AB-InBev—later purchased the Lootvoet operation in Overijse, Belgium. Today AB-InBev produces five top-fermenting "abbey" beers bearing the Leffe label: blonde, brune (or Leffe dark), Leffe 9°, triple, and radieuse (also known as vieille cuvée). All five are now made at a much larger Stella Artois facility in Leuven with Abbaye Notre-Dame de Leffe receiving royalties from their sale. The Leffe beers are filtered and tend toward sweetness on the palate. Backed by the market reach of the world's largest brewer, Leffe beers are now available in more than 60 countries worldwide. AB-InBev maintains a small museum opposite the abbey that can be toured from April to October. Many of the buildings that are still standing at the abbey, including the church, date to the 17th and 18th centuries.

See also ABBEY BEERS and BELGIUM.

Abbaye Notre-Dame de Leffe. *Abbaye-de-leffe.be.* http://www.abbaye-de-leffe.be/-The-History-/ (accessed June 7, 2010).

Jackson, Michael. *Great beers of Belgium*, 3rd ed. Philadelphia: Running Press, 1998.

Jackson, Michael. *Great beer guide.* London: Dorling Kindersley, 2000.

Leffe. *Leffe.com.* http://www.leffe.com/en-us/het_erfgoed.html#video/ (accessed June 5, 2010).

Ben Keene

Legacy (barley) is a six-row variety of malting barley grown in western Canada and the United States. It was developed by Busch Agricultural Resources Inc as a cross between 6B86-3517 and Excel. It is considered well adapted to the upper midwest and intermountain areas of the United States and Canada. Legacy was recommended in 2001 as a malting barley by the American Malting Barley Association Inc. Legacy matures slightly later than Robust but produces 5%–9% higher yields. It shows moderate susceptibility to leaf and stem rust and moderate resistance to net blotch; it has an intermediate reaction to Fusarium head blight. Legacy is a protected variety under the Plant Variety Protection Act, which provides patent-like rights to developers of unique plant types including barleys and hops varietals.

American Malting Barley Association, Inc. *Barley Variety Dictionary Supplement—Legacy.* http://www.ambainc.org/media/AMBA_PDFs/Pubs/Barley_Dictionary/Legacy.pdf (accessed March 29, 2011).

Canadian Grain Commission. http://www.grainscanada.gc.ca/ (accessed March 29, 2011).

Martha Holley-Paquette

leichtes weissbier is part of a growing German market for light versions of beer styles usually produced as *vollbier*, or beer of moderate alcoholic strength. "Leicht" means "light" in German, and leichtes weissbier is a light version of the classic Bavarian weissbier or hefeweizen. These beers mirror their heavier brethren in most ways, using a grist of more than 50% wheat malt, but are brewed to original gravities as low as 7° Plato and up to 10° Plato. The lower original gravity results in a beer with an alcohol by volume of 2.5% to 3.5%. Leichtes weissbier uses the same yeast strains as regular weissbier and therefore shows the classic phenolic and estery weisse flavors—bananas, cloves, and perhaps a whiff of bubblegum and smoke—although these are naturally subdued. The beers are cloudy with yeast but have a wide range of color, from deep gold to full dark amber. Bitterness is very light, although some brewers compensate by allowing some hop aromatics. The beer is usually served in the typical tall, slender weissbier glass, retaining some dignity on the table. Although some German beer drinkers may be thinking about calories, more of them consider leichtes weissbier to be a fine thirst quencher for hot summer days and an enjoyable restorative after the exertions of sports activity. Today, roughly one of every seven weissbiers produced in Germany is a leichtes.

See also HEFEWEIZEN.

Hans-Peter Drexler

Lewis, Michael J., although born in Wales in 1936, is one of the most influential figures in recent North American brewing education. Lewis graduated from the University of Birmingham in England in 1957, where he also earned his PhD in 1960. By 1962, he was hired at the University of California at Davis as a researcher and in 1964 he set up the brewing program and laboratory at UC Davis, where he stayed for more than 30 years. By the late 1970s, he began university extension classes where he brought previously unobtainable technical brewing knowledge to students needing less than a university degree. During his time as a professor, he brought the science and technology of malting and brewing to nearly 6,000 students from all over the world. In doing so, he allowed for the proliferation of technologically inclined microbreweries, advancements in all echelons of brewing, and widespread beer quality elevation. Through his efforts, UC Davis became one of the preeminent centers of brewing studies in North America. The university honored him with the Distinguished Teaching Award in 1989, and in 1995, Dr Lewis accepted Emeritus status, still continuing his extension and consulting endeavors. He is a prolific writer, researcher, and speaker and the author of *Stout* in 1995, *Brewing* in 2001, *Essays in Brewing Science* in 2006, and more than 100 technical papers. He is a Fellow of the IBD and has been honored with the MBAA Award of Merit and the IBS Recognition Award. Dr Lewis has always been a consummate ambassador and a tireless advocate for well-made beer. His dramatic speaking style, generosity, dry sense of humor, and occasionally nonconformist opinions have educated, challenged, and amused brewing students and professionals for more than a generation.

Brian Hunt

Liberty (hop) originated from a cross between Hallertauer Mittelfrueh and the male genetic material of other German hops, most of them aroma varieties. See HALLERTAUER MITTELFRUEH (HOP). Liberty is a triploid hop, which means it produces nearly seedless cones, even in the presence of fertile male hops. It was released in the United States in 1991. It matures medium early in the season and is well adapted to the growing condition of the hop areas of Oregon and Washington. See WILLAMETTE VALLEY HOP REGION and YAKIMA VALLEY HOP REGION. It averages a modest 1,200 to 1,900 kg/ha (1,070 to 1,700 lb/acre), which, however, is significantly higher than the average Hallertauer Mittelfrueh yield of approximately 1,250 kg/ha (1,115 lb per acre) grown in Germany. Liberty has a soft resin content very similar to that of Hallertauer Mittelfrueh, averaging about 4% alpha acids, 3% beta acids, and about 24% to 28% cohumulone. The essential oil profile of Liberty is also similar to that of Hallertauer Mittelfrueh, and, like Mittelfrueh, it contains next to no farnesene. Because of its flavor characteristics, Liberty is an acceptable substitute for so-called European Noble hop varieties. American craft brewers wishing to create authentic versions of European beer styles tend to like Liberty partly because it shows almost no identifiably American character. It is a particularly good hop for the production of bright, snappy traditional pilsners.

See also NOBLE HOPS.

Haunold, A., G. B. Nickerson, U. Gampert, and P. A. Whitney. Registration of Liberty hop. *Crop Science* 32 (1992): 1071.

Haunold, Alfred, G. B. Nickerson, Ulrich Gampert, Donna Kling, and Stephen T. Kenny. Liberty and Crystal—Two new U.S.-developed aroma hops. *Journal of the American Society of Brewing Chemists* 53 (1995): 9–13.

Alfred Haunold

Liefmans Brewery is a Belgian specialty brewery in Oudenaarde, in the province of East Flanders. The brewery focuses on mixed fermentations using yeast and lactic acid bacterial strains, producing beers that show notable acidity. Since 2008, Liefmans has been part of the Duvel-Moortgat group. See DUVEL MOORTGAT. The brewery's best known beers are a 5% alcohol by volume (ABV) Flanders sour brown ale called Oud Bruin; the 8% ABV Goudenband, which is similar to the Oud Bruin, but heavier; and a 6% ABV cherry ale named Liefmans Cuve-Brut (formerly known as Liefmans kriek). All Liefmans beers are blended, mildly hopped, and made from pale base malts with the addition of dark caramel and roasted malts.

"Oud Bruin" is Flemish for "old brown." After fermentation for a week in open fermenters, the beer matures relatively warm at around 15°C (approximately 60°F) for 4 to 8 months to allow its lactic acidity to develop and mellow. Before packaging, beers from different vats are blended and mixed with fresh beer for priming and refermentation. Until 2007, Liefmans also made an Oud Bruin called Odnar with only 4% ABV.

Oud Bruin is also the base beer for the brewery's kriek (the word is Flemish for "cherry'). Kriek in Belgium can be made from lambic or other base brews. See KRIEK and LAMBIC. After the end of fermentation, the Oud Bruin is put on macerated cherries (about 13 kg per 100 l) and aged in cold, temperature-controlled tanks for a year. See PRIMING SUGAR. Before packaging, this beer is blended with Oud Bruin and Goudenband of different ages. Sour cherries show through against a sherry-like backdrop featuring raisiny flavors and fine acidity.

The oldest written reference to the brewery dates from 1679, when it was owned by a brewer named Vilet. The brewery acquired its current name in 1780 after the marriage of Maria Anth Carola Vilet, heir to the brewery, to Jacobus Joannus Liefmans. The brewery moved out of town, from a location in Krekelput to the current location on the banks of the River Schelde in 1933. The original family owners maintained possession of the brewery until 1974, after which the brewery changed hands several times. The last brew was made at the brewery in 1991, when it was taken over by the Riva Brewery of Dentergem, across the river. There Liefmans wort continued to be brewed, but it was fermented, conditioned, and bottled at the old Liefmans plant. In 2007, Riva went bankrupt, and a year later Duvel Moortgat acquired the Liefmans facility. Now Liefmans worts are brewed at the Duvel Moortgat plant in Breendonk and then trucked to Oudenaarde for fermentation, aging, blending, and finishing.

See also BELGIUM.

Jackson, Michael. *Great beers of Belgium*. Boulder, CO: Brewers Publications, 2008.

Liefmans. http://www.liefmans.be/ (accessed May 2, 2011).

Protz, Roger. *Belgium Part I—Liefmans*. http://www.beer-pages.com/protz/features/belgium-1.htm/ (accessed May 2, 2011).

Peter Bouckaert

light beer, a term that has varied meanings in different parts of the world. In some areas, light beer refers to a beer with fewer residual carbohydrates, whereas in other parts a light beer refers to a beer with lower alcohol than most "regular" beers. In the United States, a light beer is a style of beer that has a significantly lower amount of calories than a comparable full-calorie version. Because the alcohol content contributes the majority of calories in beer, light beers are almost always lower in alcohol than their comparable full-calorie, full-strength variants on a similar style. As a reference, alcohol contains 7 calories per gram, and carbohydrates contain 4 calories per gram. The US governmental regulations for beer, governed by the Alcohol and Tobacco Tax and Trade Bureau (TTB), are not identical to the Food and Drug Administration (FDA) regulations for light products. The FDA defines a light product in regard to calories, as a product that has at least 33% fewer calories than contained in a reference standard calorie product. The TTB defines a light beer as one with a meaningful decrease in calories compared with a reference, full-strength version. Most light beers meet the FDA definition, but many do not. The TTB mandates that beers labeled "light" must have a statement of average analysis on the container that includes the contents per serving for calories, fat, carbohydrates, and protein. Light beer in the United States has become the largest selling segment of the beer market.

Edelweiss was a popular brand for the Schoenhofen Company in Chicago, founded in 1860. This light beer label dates from 1933, the year brewing operations resumed following Prohibition. PIKE MICROBREWERY MUSEUM, SEATTLE, WA

There are four main methods of making light beer. The first method is the easiest and involves dilution of a regular-strength beer with water until the desired alcohol and calorie content are achieved for a light beer. The second method is to decrease the serving size so that the consumer package is small enough to contain significantly fewer calories than a comparable full-strength, full-size serving. As an example, a 12-oz serving may contain 150 calories, but a 6-oz bottle or can will contain 75 calories. The third method is to extend the mashing process so that the natural enzymes in barley break down as much of the carbohydrate material as possible into simple sugars. These sugars are then fermented by the yeast into alcohol and carbon dioxide. After dilution with water, a light beer is the result. The fourth method is to employ exogenous brewing enzymes into the mash or fermenting beer to break down most of the carbohydrates to simple sugars. The sugars are then fermented by the yeast to alcohol and carbon dioxide. After dilution with water, a light beer is the result.

There are many different styles of light beer, but the most famous is light American-style lager. The main commercial examples are Bud Light, Coors Light, and Miller Lite. Light beer had its origins in the 1940s, when the Coors Brewing Company introduced a beer called Coors Light that was lighter in body and calories than the company's premium lager offering. This brand was discontinued at the start of World War II, only to be reintroduced in 1978. In 1967 the Rheingold Brewery brewed a beer aimed at the dieting public called Gablinger's Diet Beer, invented by a chemist named Joseph Owades. The next brewery to launch a light beer was Meister Brau, who debuted Meister Brau Lite. Miller Brewery took over the Meister Brau franchise and reworked Meister Brau Lite into a new brand called Miller Lite in 1973. Through a successful advertising campaign famously offering the supposed attributes "Tastes great, less filling," Miller Lite became the first nationally available light beer in the US marketplace. Coors Light was launched in 1978 in response to Miller Lite and Bud Light followed in 1982. By the late 1990s, Bud Light had become the largest beer brand sold in the United States. These three major brands of light beer appear to be very similar, but they do have unique differences. Although all three are light beers, Miller Lite is the lightest in regard to residual extract (carbohydrates) and Bud Light is the heaviest. Coors Light is in between. All three are lightly flavored and very dry, with each one exhibiting a hint of the unique house flavor of its respective proprietary yeast and brewing technique. All mass market light beers are made with large proportions of adjunct cereals replacing barley malt. Hop bitterness in these beers is barely perceptible, but many consumers regard them as refreshing.

By the late 1990s, an even lighter version of light beer emerged called low-carbohydrate light beer. "Low-carb" light beer is made with exogenous enzymes added to the mash so that virtually all of the carbohydrate is broken down to fermentable sugars. After dilution with water, a very light, low-carbohydrate beer is obtained. Low-carb light beer enjoyed a meteoric rise, but its popularity was short lived and most consumers returned to drinking regular light beer. "Low-carb" beer is now a relatively small part of the US beer market. Contrary to popular belief, the average difference in calories between light beer and similar standard beers is quite small, sometimes less than 20 calories per serving.

Most experts agree that the success of light beer in the US market is caused by a combination of factors, including a very light "non-beer" taste with little bitterness, a low caloric content, and, of course, effective marketing. American-style light lagers are very difficult to manufacture and distribute, but the recent global launch of American brands such as Coors Light will tell us in the near future whether American-style light beer can be successful around the world.

See also CALORIES, CARBOHYDRATES, and NEAR BEER.

Keith Villa

lightstruck. Beer with off–aromas is often colloquially said to be "skunked," but those who have encountered a skunk-like flavor in their beer rarely know how close they are to the truth. Certain compounds in hops are light sensitive and when exposed to strong light a photo-oxidation reaction takes place, creating the intensely flavor-active compound 3-methyl-2-butene-1-thiol (MBT). MBT is one of the most powerful flavor substances known to man. Commonly referred to as "skunky," the pungent odor compound resembles that of the famously malodorous defense spray deployed by skunks.

In 1875 the German chemist Dr Carl Lintner first reported on the formation of an offending taste and obnoxious odor in beer exposed to light. In the 1960s, Yoshiro Kuroiwa suggested that the main constituent of the off-flavor was MBT derived from the photodecomposition of isohumulones, the beer bittering principles, in the presence of a photosensitizer, namely riboflavin (vitamin B_2). Further, the Kuroiwa group established that the blue part of the visible spectrum (350–500 nm) in particular is most efficient in generating lightstruck flavor. In strong sunlight, the reaction can be almost instantaneous, with tasting panels able to detect the aromatic effects of an exposure to less than 10 seconds of full sunshine. Under less deleterious conditions, for example a display cabinet with fluorescent lighting, these reactions still occur, though they may take a number of days or weeks to become noticeable.

This now well-known reaction involves the cleavage in the isopentenyl-side chain of the iso-alpha acids in hops. See ISO-ALPHA ACIDS. This photocleavage is light-catalyzed and results in the formation of a dimethyl allyl radical. Reaction of the radical with sulfur-containing compounds (thiols) forms MBT. Green or clear glass offers little to no protection against this reaction, but brown glass is highly effective, at least against short-term or low-intensity exposure. Aluminum cans or beer stored in kegs offers the best protection against exposure to light. Despite the lack of protection offered by clear and green glass bottles, some breweries persist in using them, the bottle color having become an important part of their branding strategy.

When the bottle offers no protection, modern hop chemistry has brought alternatives for preventing MBT formation from hops. "Tetra" and "hexa" hops are modified by reductions in side-chain double bonds that prevent the photodegradation reaction. These advanced hop products are based on liquid or supercritical carbon dioxide extracts of hops. See HUMULONE. The resins in these are in turn isomerized in alkaline solutions into isohumulones which can be further reduced to produce bittering compounds that do not degrade into MBT. These advanced forms of bittering hops are known as "light stable" products. Their use in brewing yields a beer that is less vulnerable to the deleterious effects of sunlight, although it must be remembered that light can induce other flavor changes in beer that are not related to hops.

Research has recently revealed two unidentified compounds with aromas indistinguishable from the "skunky" aroma used to describe MBT. It is thought that these two new, yet to be elucidated compounds contribute to the overall lightstruck flavor in beer. Perhaps more interesting is the fact that MBT and one of the newly discovered compounds also formed during thermal aging in canned beer in the absence of light.

Lusk, L, et al. Beer photooxidation creates two compounds with aromas indistinguishable from 3-methyl-2-butene-1-thiol. *Journal of American Society of Brewing Chemists* 67 (2009): 183–88.

Christopher Bird

limestone

See CALCIUM CARBONATE.

linalool is a so-called tertiary alcohol of myrcene—a classification based on the molecule's carbon arrangement. It is a potent odorant in hops and beer. As an alcohol, it is considered part of the oxygenated fraction of hop oils and consequently is more soluble in wort and beer than its counterpart myrcene. Linalool has a distinctive floral aroma reminiscent of rose as well as lavender and/or bergamot. It also has citrusy and woody notes. Linalool is found at low levels of perhaps 10 to 100 ppm in hop oils, but it has an extremely low odor threshold for humans—down to 2 ppb in most lagers, for instance. This means it can be a very noticeable component in a beer's aroma. It is commonly present in regularly hopped beers at a range of 1 to 30 ppb, but it may reach as much as 100 ppb or more in dry-hopped beers. Agronomically, linalool concentration in hop oil can vary significantly within the same variety, even in the same hop yard, but from different years—sometimes by as much as a factor of 2. Some researchers believe that linalool serves as a marker for hop aroma in beer, especially when German lagers are flavored with German aroma hops, simply because higher levels of linalool in beer tend to correlate with hoppier aromas in lagers. Nevertheless, linalool is only one of many hop aroma components derived from the many different essential oils in hops.

See also HOP OILS and MYRCENE.

Thomas Shellhammer and Val Peacock

Linde, Carl von was a 19th-century German engineer and one of the world's major inventors of refrigeration technology. See REFRIGERATION. Starting in the middle of the 18th century, many people before Linde had tinkered with artificial refrigeration contraptions, but Linde was the first to develop a practical refrigeration system that was specifically designed for keeping fermenting and maturing beer cool—in Linde's case, Bavarian lagers—during the hot summer months. Linde was born in the village of Berndorf, in Franconia, in 1842, at a time when warm-weather brewing was strictly forbidden in his native Bavaria; no one was allowed to brew beer between Saint George's Day (April 23) and Michael's Day (September 29). This was to avoid warm fermentations, which provided ideal habitats for noxious airborne bacteria to proliferate and caused yeasts to produce undesirable fermentation flavors. Both made summer beers often unpalatable. Summer brewing prohibition had been in force since 1553 and was only lifted in 1850, by which time Bavarian brewers had learned to pack their fermentation cellars with ice they had laboriously harvested in the winter from frozen ponds and lakes. There had to be a better way to keep beer cold . . . and that was just the challenge for a budding mechanical engineering professor like Linde, who had joined Munich's Technical University in 1868. See WEIHENSTEPHAN. The basic principle of refrigeration had been understood for centuries. Because cold is merely the absence of heat, to make things cold, one must withdraw heat. Compressing a medium generates heat; subsequently decompressing or evaporating it quickly absorbs heat from its environment. Devices based on this principle are now generally known as vapor-compression refrigeration systems; apply this to a fermenting or lagering vessel, and it becomes a beer-cooling system. For Linde, the next question was the choice of refrigerant. Initially he experimented with dimethyl ether but eventually settled on ammonia because of its rapid expansion (and thus cooling) properties. He called his invention an "ammonia cold machine." Linde had received much of the funding for this development from the Spaten Brewery in Munich, which was also the first customer to install the new device—then still driven by dimethyl ether—in 1873. By 1879, Linde had quit his professorship and formed his own "Ice Machine Company," which is still in operation today as Linde AG, headquartered in Wiesbaden, Germany. By 1890, Linde had sold 747 refrigeration units machines to various breweries and cold storage facilities. He continued to innovate and invented new devices most of his life, including equipment for liquefying air, and for the production of pure oxygen, nitrogen, and hydrogen. In 1897 he was knighted, and from then on could append the honorific "von" to his surname. He died a prosperous industrialist in Munich in 1934, at the age of 92, and today Linde AG is a leading gases and engineering company with almost 48,000 employees working in more than 100 countries worldwide. For all his many accomplishments, Linde's pioneering work in artificial beer cooling technology is perhaps his most enduring legacy.

Horst Dornbusch

Lintner is an index that measures a malt's diastatic (starch-reducing) power (DP). It is written as "°Lintner" and indicates how much of the grain's starch can be converted by alpha amylase and beta amylase enzymes into fermentable and nonfermentable sugars during the malting and mashing process. See ALPHA AMYLASE. Malts from six-row barley tend to have more enzymes and thus higher Lintner values than do malts from two-row barleys, which, in turn, have higher Lintner values than malted wheat. Roasted malts have no DP. Malts from barleys grown in continental climates tend to have higher Lintner values than do malts from the same barley varieties grown in maritime climates. An extremely well-converted malt, which is well suited for single infusion mashing, may have a DP rating of as low as 35° Lintner. For a top-quality pilsner base malt brewers look for a DP value in the vicinity of 100° Lintner. A typical North American two-row ale base malt may have a °Lintner value of 125 or above. Some six-row malts may have °Lintner values exceeding 160. There is a second measurement of DP in use in the brewing industry, called the Windisch–Kolbach index, expressed as "°WK" and developed by the European Brewery Convention (EBC). See KOLBACH INDEX. The conversion between °Lintner and °WK is

$$\text{DP °Lintner} = (\text{°WK} + 16)/3.5.$$

Dornbusch, Horst. *The ultimate almanac of world beer recipes*. West Newbury, CT: Cerevisia Communications, 2010.

Horst Dornbusch

Lion Nathan is a brewing-centered alcoholic drinks company operating in Australia and New Zealand. Since 2009 it is a wholly owned subsidiary of Kirin of Japan. It is the beer-centered arm of a bigger business, Lion Nathan National Foods, which also produces leading brands of fruit juice and dairy products.

In Auckland, New Zealand, the good quality of the spring water in the Khyber Pass Road area attracted a number of brewers in the 19th century. In 1923 two of these breweries, Lion Brewery and Captain Cook Brewery, joined a merger of the 10 largest breweries in the country to form New Zealand Breweries. In 1977 the name of the company was changed to Lion Breweries; in 1986 it became Lion Corporation, and after a merger with LD Nathan and Company the name changed again to Lion Nathan in 1988.

The Australian part of Lion Nathan also goes back to colonial times. The century-old regional breweries Castlemaine from Brisbane and Tooheys from Sydney merged into Castlemaine Tooheys in 1981. Alan Bond acquired the Swan Brewery in Perth in the 1982 and bought Castlemaine Tooheys in 1987 to form Bond Brewing, only to go into receivership within 2 years.

In 1990 Lion Nathan bought Bond Brewing and merged the Australian and New Zealand brewing businesses to lay the foundations of the modern Lion Nathan. In 1993 the South Australian Brewing

Company of Adelaide was added to the business. Douglas Myers, chairman from the LD Nathan part of the company, sold his substantial shareholding to Kirin in 1998 when he retired. In 2007, the historic James Boag's Brewery of Tasmania was purchased. The latest chapter in the story started in October of 2009 when Kirin lifted its shareholding from just under 50% to full ownership.

Lion Nathan operates major regional breweries in Brisbane, Perth, Sydney, and Adelaide in Australia. Major brands include XXXX, Tooheys, Hahn, Swan, West End, and Boag's. The major breweries in New Zealand are in Auckland, where a new brewery was commissioned in 2009 to replace the old historic Khyber Pass Road site, Christchurch, and Dunedin. The major brands include Lion, Steinlager, Canterbury, and Speight's. Lion Nathan also operates a small number of craft breweries. James Squire and Knappstein are the main craft brands for Lion Nathan in Australia, whereas the Mac's range of beers are their major craft beers in New Zealand.

Bill Taylor

lipids comprise a chemically diverse group of organic compounds, the common and defining feature of which is their solubility in organic solvents and their insolubility in water. There are differing methods of lipid classification taking into account polarity, functional groups, and complexity. Lipids include a broad range of molecules such as "fatty acids": terpenoid lipids (sterols, carotenoids, etc.), tocopherols, glycerides, phospholipids, waxes, oils, and others.

Lipids comprise 2.2%–2.5% of the dry substance of barley, predominantly located in the aleurone layer (60%) and in the germ (30%). Of these, the majority are triglycerides used by the seedling during germination and growth. Therefore, after malting, total lipids are reduced by approximately 25%.

Lipids are present in yeast and comprise 2%–12% of the dry matter of yeast cells. Yeast lipids (mostly phospholipids and sterols) are found along with proteins in the cell membranes, and lipid synthesis is an important part of yeast reproduction. However, lipids ought not to be present in finished beer, where they can cause staling problems and negatively affect foam stability. Brewers will generally avoid the production of cloudy worts, which tend to have high lipid levels.

Lipids negatively affect foam stability as well as aging stability.

Nelson, David L., and Michael M. Cox. *Lehninger principles of biochemistry*, 4th ed. New York: W.H. Freeman and Company, 2005.

Wolfgang David Lindell

liquid malt extract (LME) is concentrated, unfermented brewery wort, a viscous syrup used in brewing—especially homebrewing—as well as in the food industry. LME is a common ingredient in baked goods, confectionery, breakfast cereals, malt beverages, dairy products, and condiments. It is often used as a caramel substitute. Just as wort is produced in many different colors and flavors, so is LME. It may be hop flavored or not. The production of LME through milling, mashing, mash separation, and wort boiling is very similar to that of conventional beer wort. See BOILING, LAUTERING, MASH, and MILLING. Depending on the desired color and flavor, the grist bill for LME is either made up of just one malt type or is a varied mixture of pale and specialty malts. See, for instance, BLACK MALT, CARAMEL MALTS, and CRYSTAL MALT. Mash separation is ideally achieved using a mash filter rather than a traditional lauter tun because wort can be recovered at a notably higher gravity, which reduces the time, energy, and cost during the concentration phase. Once the wort has been boiled, it is usually concentrated further by evaporation until it is made up of roughly 70% to 80% solids. See MALT SYRUP. If it is reduced further, to a powdered from, it is called dried malt extract or spray malt. See DRIED MALT EXTRACT. Finally, the LME is aseptically packaged, usually in a metal can or a plastic Jerry can, for distribution.

Because LME is simply unfermented, concentrated postboil wort, its content is proportionally identical to wort (except, of course, for the water content) and it has all of the normal wort trace elements, including zinc, iron, manganese, potassium, calcium, copper, and magnesium, as well as vitamins and lipids. LME, therefore, can enable yeast growth and sustain its metabolism just as well as any normal wort. Most of the fermentable sugar in LME is in the form of maltose (about 60% to 70%).

For brewing, LME needs to be diluted with hot water to the required gravity, heated to sterilize, and then cooled and fermented like regular wort. LME is available in a large range of formulations, especially for homebrewers, who can choose among many beer style-specific varieties, including wheat, Munich, amber, pils, porter, and stout. Many homebrewers also mix various packaged LMEs for even greater variability. Some LMEs contain additions of diastatic enzymes to allow for the use of unmalted starch adjuncts in the brewing process. See ADJUNCTS, AMYLASES, DIASTATIC POWER, and ENZYMES. Such LMEs, however, must not be heated above 74°C (approximately 165°F) before any desired starch conversion because the heat would denature the necessary enzymes.

Commercial brewers, too, have found many uses for LMEs. Small start-up microbreweries and brewpubs, for instance, may defer the cost purchasing of a mash and lauter tun by brewing with LMEs. Likewise, breweries may find it more efficient to mash and lauter only one wort, usually pale, and blend different LMEs with it in the brew kettle to produce several different beer styles. One special application is the addition of a specially formulated maltodextrin LME, which is rich in unfermentable sugars, to a wort intended for a low-alcohol beers. The unfermentable sugars give the resulting beer a fuller body and enhance its mouthfeel.

See also DEXTRINS.

Evan Evans

literature

See BEER WRITING.

liter degrees per kilogram (l°/kg) is a unit of measurement used by maltsters and brewers to express the amount of soluble extract a malt is capable of delivering. This figure is expressed by determining how many liters of wort at a given strength can be obtained from a kilogram of malt. This figure is important because it enables the brewer to calculate the amount of malt (and adjuncts) needed to brew a given quantity of beer at the required alcoholic strength. The wort strength is expressed in specific gravity degrees where its weight is compared directly with that of pure water. For example, a wort may have a specific gravity of 1.032. Because 1 l of pure water weighs 1 kg, 1 l of this wort weighs 1.032 kg. A typical malt may have a yield of 300 l°/kg. In this case, 1 kg of this malt yields 10 l of wort at a specific gravity of 1.030 or 5 l of wort at 1.060. This relationship can also be used to quickly measure brewery efficiency. If you brewed a batch of wort using 100 kg of malt and obtained 500 l of wort at a specific gravity of 1.056, the malt yield is 500 × 56/100 = 280 l°/kg. This figure can be compared with the hot water extract figure quoted by the maltster to determine the brewery efficiency. The extract potential of nonmalt sources of fermentable extract (adjunct) can also be measured and expressed in liter degrees per kilogram. For example, compared with malt at 300 l°/kg, corn (maize) grits deliver 340 l°/kg and rice flakes 360 l°/kg.

Lewis, Michael J., and Tom W. Young. *Brewing*, 2nd ed. New York: Kluwer Academic/Plenum Publishers, 2002.

Steve Parkes

lodging resistance is a measure of a plant's ability to resist toppling over in the field when confronted with adverse environmental conditions such as high winds or downpours. Toppled grain is extremely undesirable because it increases the danger of noxious microbial contamination, which negatively affects malt quality. Lodging resistance is influenced by many factors, such as root anchorage and the length, diameter, and strength of the stalk. Of particular importance, just prior to harvesting, is the so-called peduncle strength, which denotes the sturdiness of the stem portion between the flag leaf and the ear. Cultivars with shorter peduncles and greater peduncle diameter tend to have greater lodging resistance. The same is true for plants with good resistance to a plant disease called leaf rust. The proper spacing of seeds on the field is essential too, because plants that are too close together compete excessively for light and grow too tall, which decreases lodging resistance. Short, neatly aligned rows of grain, on the other hand, ensure better mechanized harvest efficiency and higher yields per acre and reduce the possibility of fungal disease infestations. High lodging resistance, therefore, results in cleaner grain and better overall grain quality.

Fertilizers, too, influence lodging resistance. For instance, excessive amounts of nitrogen fertilizer, especially if applied at the very early stages of plant development to improve agronomic yields, are correlated not only with higher protein values in barley kernels but also with reduced lodging resistance. Fertilizers containing potassium, on the other hand, tend to enhance stalk strength and thus lodging resistance.

http://www.cals.uidaho.edu/swidaho/Newsletters/Sentinel10.pdf/ (accessed May 2, 2011).
http://www.eau.ee/~agronomy/vol01/p013.pdf/ (accessed May 2, 2011).
(accessed May 2, 2011).
http://www.ndbarley.net/malt_barley.html/(inactive).
http://www.ag.ndsu.edu/ibms/producers/documents/IrrigatedMaltBarleyProduction_001.pdf/ (accessed May 2, 2011).
http://www.ibgs.cz/photos/book_of_abstracts/Session_10.htm/ (accessed May 2, 2011).
http://www.grainscanada.gc.ca/barley-orge/harvest-recolte/2009/qbsm09-qosm09-eng.pdf/ (accessed May 2, 2011).
http://www.sabbi.org/reports/Guidelines%20for%20the%20production%20of%20Malting%20Barley%20Winter%20Dryland%202009.pdf/ (accessed May 2, 2011).

Thomas Kraus-Weyermann

London and Country Brewer, the was a ground-breaking publication in the literature of technical brewing. Eight editions were published, the first in 1734 and the last in 1759. It is one of the most important beer books ever written, as it describes for the first time the use of scientific process for practices that previously had been solely empirical. It explains the many aspects of the brewing process, such as malting and mashing, in technical detail, and in later editions describes how to make clear beer. For the first time the production of pale, amber, and brown malts is described, including the effect of different types of kiln, fuel, and temperature. The book also confirms that most brewers of the time had stopped using wheat for malt and were almost exclusively using barley.

The anonymous author is described as a "person formerly concerned in a public brewhouse in London, but for 20 years has resided in the country." Little is known about the author, but it is likely that he gained his brewing knowledge in London before 1720. The author says the book is written for the many inhabitants of cities and towns, as well as travelers who have for a long time suffered "great prejudices" from unwholesome and unpleasant beers and ales. This the author blames on bad malts, the under-boiling of wort, the use of "injurious ingredients," and the lack of skill of many brewers. He also rails at the heavy taxes put on "malt liquor."

In the book's preface the author says he has "endeavoured to set in sight the many advantages of body and purse that may arise from a due knowledge and management in brewing malt liquors, which are of the greatest Importance, as they are in a considerable degree our nourishment and the common diluters of our food."

See also BEER WRITING.

Anonymous, London & Country Brewer. Project Gutenburg, 2005. http://www.gutenberg.org/etext/8900.

Tim Hampson

The **Lovibond** "52" system for the measurement of color in beer was invented in 1893 by Joseph William Lovibond in Greenwich, England. It involved the visual comparison of standardized colors, in the form of colored glass discs, with samples of beer. This was superseded in 1950 when L.R. Bishop proposed the use of a revised set of slides. Bishop's revised system was adopted as the EBC standard in 1951 and the standard slides were manufactured by Tintometer Co, UK, as they are to this day.

On the Lovibond scale, a pale golden lager might have a color of 2° or 3°, a pale ale 10°–13°, a brown ale or dark lager 17°–20°, all the way through to the near black of imperial stout at 70°.

Inherent errors in visual color comparison due to the age of the standard slides used, the light used to illuminate the samples, the state of the observer, and various other problems meant that consistency across and within laboratories was difficult to achieve using the Lovibond scale. Although the glass color samples are still available and still used, spectrophotometry has largely replaced Lovibond's method. The ASBC spectrophotometric method is called the Standard Reference Method (SRM). Though "degrees Lovibond" and "degrees SRM" are very similar, some feel that SRM gives less information about the actual appearance of the color as opposed to its intensity. In Europe, a different scale (an EBC Method) is used, though this scale is also produced using spectrophotometry. Oddly, in the United States, the SRM method is used to refer to beer color, but malt color is designated in degrees Lovibond. At the lower end of the scale, malt color numbers and beer color numbers are related, but as malt becomes darker, the numbers pull away, reaching more than 500° for black malts. This reflects the non-linear coloring influence of very dark malts, where it may take a very small percentage of the grist to affect wort color.

See also COLOR.

Lovibond. Water analysis and colour measurement. http://www.tintometer.com.

Smedley, S. M. Colour determination of beer using tristimulus values. *Journal of the Institute of Brewing* 98 (1992): 497–504.

Chris Holliland

Löwenbräu is one of the world's oldest and most iconic beer brands. The Löwenbräu brewery is located in Munich and dates back to 1383. Löwenbräu means "lion's brew" in English and its logo is an easily identifiable crest depicting a standing, tongue-flicking lion with a twisted double tail. The name derives from the original brewpub known as Löwengrube (Lion's Den) at house number 17 on a street of that same name. The first documented mention of brewing at the Löwengrube is in the name of Jörg Schnaitter in a Munich tax record of 1524, where Jörg is identified as a "pierprew," which is old German for a beer brewer. Löwenbräu as the name of the brewery at the Lion's Den appears on record for the first time in a Munich brewer registry in 1746. In 1818 a brewer named Georg Brey purchased the Löwenbräu and embarked on an expansion strategy, acquiring additional brew sites and adding bockbier to his portfolio in 1848. By the brew season 1863/1864, Löwenbräu supplied about one-quarter of the entire Munich beer market, which made it Munich's largest brewery.

By 1872, the brewery became a stockholder's company, and a year later, the still famous Löwenbräukeller opened. By 1912, the Löwenbräu annual output reached almost 1 million hl (852,168 US bbl), but it declined by the end of World War I to just about half that volume. A merger with Unionsbrauerei Schülein & Cie., in 1921, however, marked the return of growth. The brewery added a

Löwenbräu means "lion's brew" in English, a name derived from the brewery's original location, the late 14th-century Löwengrube (Lion's Den) brewpub in Munich. The brewery's logo hangs from the shoulder of a cherub in this 1920 postcard. PIKE MICROBREWERY MUSEUM, SEATTLE, WA

weissbier to its portfolio in 1927 and, a year later, even surpassed its prewar volume. Löwenbräu surpassed the 1.5 million hl (1.2 million US bbl) mark in the 1970/1971 brewing season.

Exports, too, become an even more important factor in the Löwenbräu business strategy. In 1974, Löwenbräu arrived in the United States by way of a contract arrangement with the Miller Brewing Company in 1974. The beer marketed under the Löwenbräu name, however, was very different from the all-malt, Reinheitsgebot-guided original. See REINHEITSGEBOT. The recipe adjustment in the direction of an international pilsner, however, hurt the brand and damaged its reputation in the United States. As a result of the fiasco in the United States, Löwenbräu has since shifted to insisting that all its beer brewed abroad under contract be made under its supervision according to the German Beer Purity Law. In 1997, Löwenbräu merged with the Spaten-Franziskaner-Bräu KGaA of Munich and became part of Brau Holding International GmbH & Co. KGaA, which in turn is an entity of the Schörghuber Corporate Group. Effective October 1, 2004, ownership of Spaten-Franziskaner-Löwenbräu-Group was transferred to InBev, now known as Anheuser-Busch InBev, the world's largest brewer. See ANHEUSER-BUSCH INBEV. Within this new worldwide brewing and distribution network, beers marketed under the Löwenbräu brand now maintain strong sales, either as imports or as contract brews, in more than 50 countries.

Anheuser-Busch InBev history. http://www.lowenbrau.com.au/.

Gaab, Jeffrey S. *Munich: Hofbräuhaus & history—Beer, culture, & politics.* New York: Peter Lang Publishing, Inc., 2006.

John Holl

Lublin (hop) is a hop with a fairly obscure background. It is named after the city of Lublin, the center of Poland's major hop growing region. See POLAND. In trade statistics it is also called Lubliner, Lubelska, or Lubelski-Pulawy. Pulawy is the town where the Polish Hop Research Institute is located. Lublin's agronomic and flavor characteristics are very similar to those of the Czech hop Saazer. See SAAZ (HOP). Like Saazer, Lublin matures early, has moderately low yields (average 1,000 to 1,300 kg/ha [890 to 1,160 lb per acre]), and low alpha acids levels, but a very pleasant aroma. Alpha acids range from 3% to 5% and beta acids from 4% to 5%, and cohumulone averages about 23%. The essential oils are composed of 40% to 50% myrcene, 20% to 25% humulene, 6% caryophyllene, and 12% farnesene.

Barth, Heinrich Joh., Christiane Klinke, and Claus Schmidt. *The hop atlas, the history and geography of the cultivated plant,* 251–9. Nuremberg, Germany: Joh. Barth & Son, 1994.

Strausz, David A. *The hop industry of Eastern Europe and the Soviet Union,* 122–51. Pullman, WA: Washington University Press, 1969.

Alfred Haunold

Luitpold, Prince of Bavaria, was born in 1951 as the great-grandson of Ludwig III, the last ruling king of Bavaria. He is a member of the Wittelsbach family, a prominent European dynasty that ruled Bavaria without interruption from 1180 until 1918, when, upon the defeat of the German Empire in World War I, all German monarchies were abolished. Almost from the start, the House of Wittelsbach has been involved in brewing and, over the centuries, has left an indelible mark on beer history: In 1269 Duke Ludwig (Louis) II started the first brewery in Munich, in 1516 the Wittelsbach Duke Wilhelm IV (1493–1550) proclaimed the Bavarian Beer Purity Law (Reinheitsgebot), in 1810 the wedding celebrations of Crown Prince Ludwig I and Princess Therese of Saxe-Hildburghausen became the first Munich Oktoberfest, and in 1868 King Ludwig II of Bavaria established what is still one of the world's foremost brewing universities, Weihenstephan, outside Munich, where young Prince Luitpold went to study brewing science. See WITTELSBACHER FAMILY.

Prince Luitpold at the Kaltenberg castle and brewery in Bavaria. After studying brewing science at the Weihenstephan brewing university, Prince Luitpold became the CEO of the König Ludwig GmbH & Co. KG Schlossbrauerei Kaltenberg, the Bavarian royal family's ancestral brewery. PHOTOGRAPH BY DENTON TILLMAN

In 1976 Luitpold became the CEO of the König Ludwig GmbH & Co. KG Schlossbrauerei Kaltenberg, the Wittelsbach's ancestral brewery, which was opened in 1870 in Kaltenberg Castle. By 2001 Schlossbrauerei Kaltenberg formed a financial, licensing, and distribution partnership with Haus Cramer KG, one of Germany's largest brewing groups, which is best known for its Warsteiner brand. With this increased access to national and international markets, Kaltenberg's annual production grew to about 350,000 hectoliters (298,258 US bbl), and its flagship brand, König Ludwig dunkel, became Germany's top-selling dunkel. In German statistics, dunkel represents about one-third of the broader dark lager category of "dunkel/schwarzbier," which covers roughly 1.7% of the approximately 100 million hl/year (85,216,790 US bbl) German beer market. Kaltenberg's other key brands are König Ludwig weissbier and König Ludwig hell.

See also BAVARIA.

Adalbert, Prince of Bavaria. *Die Wittelsbacher—Geschichte unserer Familie* (The Wittelsbachers—History of Our Family). Munich: Prestel-Verlag, 1979.

Horst Dornbusch

lupulin, small glands that contain hop acids and essential oils. They are observable as a fine yellow powder found deep within the hop cone—a fruiting body, which is technically called a strobile. See HOPS. Pine cones (which have a similar shape) are also strobiles. The cone is made up of bracts and bracteoles that are attached to a central rachis (or strig). The lupulin glands, which are technically called glandular trichomes (specialized epithelial cells in plants that contain essential oils and other secondary metabolites), are found attached to the base of the bracteoles and to a lesser degree to the bracts. They are small, slightly pear-shaped glands roughly 200 μm (0.2 mm) in diameter. Their concentration in hops differs from one variety to another. Given that most of the brewing value of the hop cone is found within the lupulin glands, there have been a number of technical approaches to concentrating or preserving this component. A process for washing hop cones of their lupulin with water followed by sieving, drying, and storage in an inert environment has been developed and patented. Type 45 hops are a pelletized product whereby the hops are milled and then sieved in order to concentrate the lupulin. In this process, 100 kg (220 lb) of whole hops yields roughly 45 kg (99 lb) of concentrated hop pellets, hence the name. Supercritical CO_2, liquid CO_2, and ethanol extraction of hops are techniques for dissolving lupulin, removing it from the hop cones, and recovering it as a solvent-free (in the case of CO_2) or ethanol-based extract.

Thomas Shellhammer

lupulone is one of four beta acid analogues in hop resin, the others being adlupulone, colupulone, and prelupulone. See ADLUPULONE and COLUPULONE. Lupulone levels vary across hop varieties from roughly 30% to 55% of total beta acids. Colupulone varies, from roughly 20% to 55%, but adlupulone stays within a narrower range of 10% to 15%. Structurally, these analogues are very similar, but not identical, to their alpha acid counterparts. The slight structural difference, however, prevents these beta acids from isomerizing in the kettle. See HOP ISOMERIZATION. When beta acids oxidize into hulupones, however, which happens as hops age, they become wort soluble and confer bitterness. See HULUPONES. As hops oxidize, the bitterness that comes from iso-alpha acids diminishes, but this is somewhat offset by the contribution of bitterness from the hulupones. The ratio of alpha to beta acids ultimately determines the extent to which the bitterness will diminish as hops oxidize; higher levels of alpha compared with beta acids in raw hops mean a slower decline of bittering power as hops degrade over time.

Thomas Shellhammer and Val Peacock

Mackeson stout is a dark beer, only 3% ABV, but with a full sweet taste and only a hint of the roasted malt used in brewing it. Mackeson belongs in the sparsely populated sweet stout category. This style was first known as "milk stout," as in the early part of the 20th century brewers were keen to promote the health-giving properties of their products; it is now an illegal label designation in the UK. Milk stouts were so-called because they contained lactose, or milk sugar, a carbohydrate that is not fermented by beer yeasts. Lactose is not as sweet as sucrose or dextrose, so it can add fullness and body to the beer without making it cloyingly sweet. See MILK STOUT.

The beer was originally brewed by Mackeson & Co. Ltd at Hythe, in Kent, England in 1907, a brewery founded in 1669. See KENT, ENGLAND. Mackeson's brewery was bought by a competitor, H. & G. Simonds of Reading, Berkshire, in 1920, who later sold it on to another brewer, Jude, Hanbury & Co. Ltd in Wateringbury, Kent. The latter company along with the Mackeson brewery became part of the Whitbread empire in 1925. Whitbread soon disposed of the draught version of Mackeson, but in bottled form it became a national brand during the 1960s. A stronger version, at 4.9% ABV, known as "Mackeson Triple X," was produced for the American market; it was brewed by the Hudepohl-Schoenling Brewing Company in Cincinnati, Ohio, for a time. A similar version is produced by Carib Brewing in Trinidad. Whitbread itself was taken over by Interbrew, now Anheuser-Busch InBev, and Mackeson Stout is presently a brand of Interbrew UK.

Jackson, Michael. *The new world guide to beer.* Philadelphia: Running Press Book Publishers, 1988.

Terry Foster

magazines

See BEER WRITING.

Magic Hat Brewing Company is an American brewery based in South Burlington, Vermont, founded in 1993 by Alan Newman and Bob Johnson. The brewery made its first sale in early 1994 at the Burlington, Vermont, Winter Blues Festival and soon found its beers on tap throughout the city. Unusually, Magic Hat employs open fermentation and brews more beer by that method than any other American brewery. All beers are fermented by the Ringwood ale yeast strain, which can give signature fruity flavors, but is notoriously difficult to work with. Spurred on by sales from its flagship apricot-flavored ale "#9," Magic Hat quickly expanded distribution and by 1999 was available throughout New England as well as in New York City. Recognizable on shelves by its swirling, colorful, and quirky labels and its whimsical beer descriptions on bottles and packaging, Magic Hat created a loyal following. By 2002, the brewery produced close to 120,000 hl of beer annually (almost 100,000 barrels). By 2008 it was the 12th largest craft brewery in the United States and was able to acquire the West Coast Pyramid Breweries Inc, including its MacTarnahan's brands, for about $35 million.

This gave the brewery distribution on both coasts as well as in the northern states from Maine to Illinois. In 2010, Magic Hat was itself purchased by North American Breweries Rochester, New York, which is one of the companies of KPS Capital Partners, LP, of New York City. Along with Magic Hat's former family of brands, North American Breweries also controls Genesee Brewing Company and its Dundee Brewing brand, and it manages Labatt USA, which sells and markets Labatt beer brewed in Canada.

Interview with chief spokesman Michael Hayes (personal communication 11/2/2010).
Official history from the Magic Hat Brewing Company (Mary Beth Popp, North American Breweries, 11/15/2010).

John Holl

maibock is a traditional strong, malty Bavarian lager. Like the month for which it is named ("Mai" is German for "May"), it is a transitional beer, the perfect drink for the short Bavarian spring. In the Bavarian Alps, May is the brief season between the last thaw and the first bloom, when it is still too cool to linger in the beer gardens, but already too bright outside to hide indoors in the beer halls. Although brewed to bock strength—with about 6% to 7% alcohol by volume and a substantial body—maibock is light amber to deep golden in color. This sets it apart from the darker winter bocks, hence its other name, heller bock (pale bock). Maibock tends to be made from a base of pale pilsner malt with generous additions of Vienna malt, Munich malt, and/or other lightly caramelized malts. See PILSNER MALT. Compared with the winter bocks, maibocks also tend to have slightly more hop bitterness and hop flavor from noble Bavarian hop varieties. Most maibocks are still made by the time-honored and labor-intensive decoction method, during which portions of the main mash are drawn into a separate cooker and boiled there before being returned to the main mash. Decoction ensures optimum conversion of grain starches into fermentable malt sugars, which results in the desired high alcohol content. After fermentation, maibocks are allowed to mature and mellow out near the freezing point for 4 to 8 weeks for a well-rounded finish.

See also DECOCTION.

Dornbusch, Horst. Maibock—A beer for the lusty month of May. *Brew Your Own*, 12 (2006).

Horst Dornbusch

Maillard reaction is a type of non-enzymic browning that adds color and flavor to many types of processed food, including beer. The reaction is named after the French chemist Louis-Camille Maillard (1878–1936), who stumbled on it while trying to replicate biological protein synthesis around 1910. In essence, Maillard provided a chemical explanation for these browning processes that occur in everyday cooking and thus had been empirically known since man began cooking food.

Maillard products are the result of a complex series of chemical reactions between the carbonyls of reactive sugars and the amino groups of amino acids. Maillard reactions are favored or occur more readily at higher temperatures, low moisture levels, and under alkaline (basic) conditions with pentose sugars (i.e., arabinose, xylose) reacting more than hexoses (e.g., glucose), which in turn react more than disaccharides (e.g., maltose). Amino acids also have differing propensities for undertaking Maillard reactions, with lysine and glycine being the most reactive. See AMINO ACIDS. The final products of Maillard reactions are melanoidins (brown nitrogenous polymers).

The most favorable process phase conditions for the formation of Maillard products, proteins or peptides linked to sugars, occur during malt kilning. Kilning, owing to the low moisture content toward the end, is manipulated by maltsters to achieve the various combinations of color and flavor utilized by brewers to produce different styles of beer. See KILNING. Crystal and caramel malts are produced by increasing the kiln temperature of well-modified green malt quickly to 140°F–167°F (60°C–75°C) to liquefy, or rather gelatinize the starchy endosperm. The crystal malt is finished by further drying and heating to produce the caramelized malt. More extreme conditions are used to produce other specialty malts in roasting cylinders by increasing temperatures from 167°F–347°F (75°C–175°C) and then more slowly to 419°F (215°C) to produce chocolate malt and to 437°F (225°C) for black malts. These have substantially higher colors and more intense, potentially harsher flavors.

Maillard browning reactions also take place in the kettle during wort boiling and can develop deeper colors in worts. They also occur during mash boiling phases of decoction mashes, and proponents of decoction mashing often claim that superior depth of malt flavor can result.

Ames, J.M. The Maillard browning reaction—an update. *Chemistry and Industry* 17 (1988): 558–61.

Evan Evans

maize (corn) is used as the primary source of carbohydrates for some traditional beer-like alcoholic beverages in Latin America and Africa and as an adjunct for mass-market beer production throughout most of the world. While most beer consumers might not recognize these beverages as "beer," they are fermented beverages made from grain, and are therefore widely referred to as maize beers. Methods for producing traditional maize beer vary widely, and many of them have changed little for thousands of years. These beverages are generally high in solids and may be thicker and more opaque than commercial beers. They are often consumed at various stages during active fermentation, and consequently do not store well. Traditional maize beer provides calories, protein, and B vitamins in the diet. Maize-based diets are often low in niacin, but deficiency symptoms are uncommon in societies that consume a proportion of the crop as maize beer. Specific types of maize are used, and spices are often added to obtain the color, flavor, and consistency desired to satisfy local preferences. The traditional vats that are used for brewing often serve as a source of naturally occurring yeast and bacteria that carry out the fermentation, but starters from previous batches or other catalysts may also be utilized. For many products, lactic acid fermentation is used to sour the malt or mash prior to alcohol fermentation. Alcohol content varies in traditional maize beers, but it is generally in the 2%–3% ABV range. "Chicha" is a common name for indigenous maize beer produced in the Andes and at lower altitudes in Ecuador, Brazil, Peru, Bolivia, Colombia, and Argentina, but the term also refers to beer made from other plants and some nonalcoholic beverages. Coarse maize flour was traditionally chewed by women prior to fermentation, with the enzyme ptyalin (a type of amylase) in their saliva converted starch to maltose and dextrins. Today, maize is most commonly germinated (malted) to produce amylase for starch conversion in chicha production. Maize malt provides ample alpha-amylase but is low in beta-amylase and has limited quantities of other diastatic enzymes present in barley. Chicha plays an important role in family and social life and in religious and cultural ceremonies. Although primarily a cottage industry today, chicha was once made in large, state-owned breweries and was used as a means of currency during the Inca Empire. Other forms of indigenous maize beer in Latin America include tesguino in Mexico and cauim in Brazil. Maize is used to make traditional fermented beverages in many African countries as well. These beers are sour and opaque and are generally served warm. Maize meal and maize malt may also be mixed in various proportions with sorghum and millet, depending on their relative cost and availability and local traditions. Sorghum and millet are indigenous crops and are preferred for malting, but maize is increasingly used as a starchy adjunct for both traditional beer and commercial lager beer production throughout Africa. Although most traditional maize beer is home-brewed, factory production is well established in some countries in eastern and southern Africa.

Haggblade, S., and W. H. Holzapfel. "Industrialization of Africa's indigenous beer brewing." In *Industrialization of indigenous fermented foods*, 2nd ed., ed. K. H. Steinkraus, 271–361. New York: Marcel Dekker, 1989.

Steinkraus, K. H. Indigenous fermented foods in which ethanol is a major product: Type and nutritional significance of primitive wines and beers and related alcoholic foods. In *Handbook of indigenous fermented foods*, 2nd ed., ed. K. H. Steinkraus, 363–508. New York: Marcel Dekker, 1996.

Jennifer Kling

malt is processed grain seeds—any grain seeds—that have been modified from their natural state by a multistep procedure called malting. Along with water, hops, and yeast, malt is one of the four key ingredients in virtually all beers. The basic malting steps are steeping, germinating, and kilning. For many specialty malts, two other steps—stewing and/or roasting, preferably both in a roasting drum—are used as well. The duration and temperature of these malting steps affect the technical characteristics of the different malts, as well as their flavor and color. Malt varieties range from very pale and sweet to amber and biscuit-like to almost black and coffee-like. The brewer usually selects a combination of malts to formulate a particular beer. Like wine grapes, malting barley is varietal and tastes different depending upon its strain and where it is grown.

Most brewing malt is made from barley and wheat. Taxonomically, these grains belong to the *Gramineae* family, a group of cereal grasses that also includes bamboo, bluegrass, corn, kamut, millet, oats, rice, rye, spelt (also called dinkel), switch grass, and Timothy hay. One of the few nongrains that can be malted is buckwheat, which, despite its name, is actually the edible fruit of a family of herbs called Fagopyrum. See BUCKWHEAT. Grain seeds contain all of the nutrients—mostly carbohydrates, proteins, and fats, as well as many trace elements—that the grasses need for their reproduction. Malting makes these nutrients usable for the brew house.

Seed kernels are hardy, compact enclosures. In barley, they have a shell of two overlapping husk leaves. Unless harvested by humans or eaten by wild life, seeds drop to the ground in the fall and lie dormant during the winter. For compactness, the nutrients inside the kernels have complex molecular structures; and the husks contain tannins—astringent polyphenols that act as preservatives to protect the nutrients against such adversities as mold, rot, and pests. As the rays of the returning sun in springtime melt the snow and warm the soil, the kernels come to life by rapidly absorbing ambient moisture. During this hydration, biochemical changes take place inside the kernels, which initiate the development of roots and shoots, the beginning of new plants. The malting process attempts to harness exactly the same processes that occur in the field—in this case not for growing new plants, but for making beer. Of course there have been many technological changes over the millennia that humans have been malting grains, but the basics of the process remain the same.

After the harvest, the maltster stores the grains in silos and carefully regulates the latter's internal temperature, moisture, and aeration to prevent spoilage. In the case of barley, the kernel's moisture content at harvest time is between 12% and 17% by weight. In the silo, it must be kept to below 14%. Although the kernels are dormant in storage, as they would be in the field, they are alive and will need to absorb small amounts of oxygen, while releasing small of amounts of CO_2; this is the reason for the aeration. Naturally, rodents and other pests must be kept out of the silos as well.

There are strict selection criteria that separate brewing grains from feed grains. In the case of barley, the kernels should be at least 90% homogeneous per sample, preferably with none of the kernels below 2.2 mm in diameter. A batch in which 95% or more of kernels have a diameter of at least 2.5 mm is considered excellent. The average protein content of these kernels should be higher than 10% and lower than 12%. In the case of brewing wheat, the protein content should not exceed 13%.

When the grain is ready to be malted, it is cleaned of any foreign matter such as dust and debris. Next, it is hydrated. This occurs in giant vats that are alternately filled with water and drained. The "wet" phase may last 8 h and the "dry" phase 12 h. Different maltsters use slightly different wet/dry cycles. The steeping temperature is normally between 12°C and 15°C (54°F and 59°F). During the grain's wet immersion phases, air is blown into the vat from the bottom to supply the kernels with plenty of oxygen for respiration and to agitate the content; this action also cleans the grain. The vat is allowed to overflow to float off any dislodged dirt and particulate matter. During the grain's dry phase, air is sucked out of the vat at the bottom to carry away CO_2 exhaled by the respiring kernels and to replace it with air from above. After 20 to 48 h in the steeping vat, the grain has a moisture content of 38% to 46% and tiny rootlets have appeared at each kernel's base. The grain is now considered fully hydrated and is moved into a moisture- and temperature-controlled germination chamber.

There, just as in the field, root development accelerates, and plant shoots appear as well. Both start at the kernel's base. The shoot, called the acrospire, grows upward between the husks and the kernel's body, which is called the endosperm. Germination also involves the activation of enzymes under the kernel's husks. Enzymes reside on a thin skin, called the aleurone layer, which covers the endosperm. They are specialized organic catalysts that initiate—but are not part of—particular biochemical reactions that occur only under narrowly prescribed temperature, moisture, and pH conditions.

Enzymes break down the endosperm's complex nutrients into simpler ones so that these can easily be absorbed as building blocks and energy sources by the embryonic new plant. In the brew house, of course, we don't seek to grow new plants—instead we seek to extract these nutrients for making beer. This enzymatic degradation is called "conversion" or "modification." It softens the hard and starchy endosperm, which makes for easier milling in the brew house. See FRIABILITY and MILLING.

There are three major categories of grain enzymes—cytolytic (cellulose-converting), proteolytic (protein-converting), and diastatic (starch-converting). Cytolytic enzymes such as beta-glucanase break down the kernel's internal gum-like cellulose walls, which hide and protect the kernel's starchy and proteinous nutrients. Once these walls are degraded, proteolytic enzymes such as endopeptidase and carboxypeptidase modify large molecular proteins into smaller ones. The larger the protein molecules, the more likely they are to precipitate out into the trub during wort boiling; the smaller the protein molecules, the more likely they are to make it into the finished beer, where they can contribute to its body, mouthfeel, and foam. After cytolysis, starches become accessible as well. These starches are complex carbohydrate molecules that occur in long chains or as branched structures. They are converted by diastatic enzymes, such as alpha- and beta-amylase, into smaller carbohydrate molecules, that is, into starch fractions called sugars. Alpha-amylase breaks down starches into nonfermentable sugars such as dextrins, whereas beta-amylase breaks down starches as well as dextrins into fermentable sugars such as maltose. This starch-to-sugar conversion is also called "saccharification."

Other significant but minor enzymes in the grain include phytase and lipidase. Phytase breaks down phytic acid and releases phosphorus, whereas lipidase breaks down lipids (fats, oils, and waxes). All grains have germ sacks that contain oil—some more, some less—and barley, fortunately, has unusually low lipid levels. These oils are eliminated in the malting process and do not survive into the brewhouse, where they would cause considerable trouble for brewers.

Mechanically, there are several types of germination chambers. Until roughly the beginning of the 20th century, most germination chambers would have been large, tiled floors with adjustable louvers on all sides for aeration. The moist grain would be spread out on the floor in a layer of perhaps 15 cm (7 inches). There, it would typically stay for 4 to 6 days and begin to sprout. Because germination is an exothermic biological process, the grain needs to be turned constantly—now mechanically, but by malt shovel before the machine age—to release heat given off by the grain. Turning also dissipates CO_2, keeps the grain properly oxygenated, and prevents the rootlets from matting together. For malting to proceed properly on a floor, this grain bed had to be kept at or below an outside temperature of no higher than 13°C to 17°C (55°F to 63°F). In most climates, therefore, malting was possible only in the winter. This labor-intensive malting method is still used by a few boutique malting companies today, and malt produced this way is still referred to as "floor-malted." Many brewers feel that this old method produces malt with superior brewing and flavor characteristics.

In modern malting plants, the germination floor has been replaced by sophisticated, mechanized, and usually automated installations of various designs that allow for malting to happen year round. Modern germinators are equipped with intake and exit grain transfer systems, environmental controls, mechanical malt turners (usually augers and/or rakes), perforated false bottoms for air intake, and fans for air and moisture evacuation. While germinating, the grain is kept in stable condition by humidified cool air blown through the chamber's false bottom. In rectangular germination chambers—such as the Saladin Box, a 19th-century French invention—the malting grain bed may have a depth of roughly 1.20 m (4 ft), and the malt turners move slowly back and forth through the grain bed. See SALADIN BOX. In more recent, circular designs, the malt turner pivots slowly around a vertical axis in the center of the chamber or the malt turner is stationary, and the entire floor that carries the grain revolves instead. Outside Germany, maltsters may spray enzymes grown on biological media onto the germinating grain. This accelerates the process by 2 to 3 days, which reduces production costs. It also allows for the malting of enzyme-poor, lower-quality grains that otherwise may have gone to the feed lot. In Germany, however, such malt treatments are forbidden by the country's Beer Purity Law. See REINHEITSGEBOT.

The temperature of the germination chamber is kept at roughly 13°C to 18°C (55°F to 64°F). The grain remains in the germination facility until the acrospires have grown to roughly two-thirds of the length of the endosperms, which takes anywhere from 4 days to 1 week. At this point, the grain is well on its way to becoming malt, but it is not malt yet. At this stage it is called "green malt." This green malt is then transferred into a drying device, which, depending on the desired malt type, is either a kiln or a roasting drum. In the kiln, hot air is applied to the moist load of grain, primarily to dry it. This kills the developing acrospires but does not destroy the enzymes. Acrospire growth, which generally comes to a halt at temperatures above 40°C (104°F), must be interrupted, because the maltster and brewer want to preserve the modified malt nutrients to make beer, not new plants. Green malt still tastes rather rough and raw, and it requires further biochemical changes to give it the pleasant malty–aromatic quality that we expect to taste in beer. These changes happen only under the influence of heat. Also, because the soggy green malt is a nutritious medium for spoilage organisms, it is highly perishable and must be dehydrated quickly. The malt's water content must be reduced from the 40% to 50% it contains at the end of germination to at least 4% to 6% by weight.

In the kiln, the malt is finished in two phases, drying and curing. The total length of the kilning process varies with the kiln's construction and may take anywhere from 20 h to 2 days. Both stages involve hot air being blown through the malt and the evacuation of the resulting humidity via big fans and exhaust flues. The malt must be completely dry before curing because only dry enzymes can survive the higher subsequent curing temperatures without damage. The malt enzymes need to remain intact so that the brewer can reactivate them later on in the mash. Once the malt's moisture content has dropped to between 10% and 20%, the temperature is raised gradually from a low of perhaps 13°C (63°F) to a finishing temperature of below about 85°C (185°F) for pale malt, such as Pilsner malt, to perhaps 120°C (approximately 250°F) for darker malts. During the temperature ramp-up, which may take about 8 h, the malt traverses through the various active temperature zones of the cytolytic, proteolytic, and diastatic enzymes, much as it does again later in the brewer's mash tun during a step mash. The kilning process, therefore, determines the malt's degree of enzymatic modification. At the final curing phase, at which the malt dries completely, dimethyl sulfide and its precursors are also driven off. See DIMETHYL SULFIDE (DMS). A few maltsters now use installations that allow for germination and kilning to take place in the same unit. See GERMINATION-KILNING VESSELS (GKV). Old-style floor-malting, incidentally, which tends to be less efficient than modern, mechanized malting, generally results in what are now considered slightly "under-modified" malts. After kilning, the finished malt is usually cooled with unheated air to blow off any residual vapors and to prepare it for bulk storage. On its way to the malt silo, the dried-up dead rootlets, called culms, as well as any loose husks and kernel fragments are removed by gently shaking the malt over screens and then passing it through a malt polishing machine.

Another key process that takes place in the kiln is the Maillard reaction, by which sugars and amino acids—the products of diastatic and proteolytic modification—combine to form melanoidins at high temperatures. See MAILLARD REACTION. Melanoidins are brown polymers that give malt its typical malty flavor and aroma. This is why the Maillard reaction is often referred to as nonenzymatic browning. Higher curing temperatures for such darker malts as Vienna and Munich malts promote greater melanoidin formation and are thus responsible for the distinctly toffee-like malty notes in such beer styles as Vienna lager, märzen-oktoberfestbier, and bock.

Malts that have been kilned very quickly are generally considered of lower quality because, during an excessively rapid loss of moisture during the drying phase, the malt's pores may shrink and close. This hardens the kernel and makes it less mealy and more difficult to mill in the brewhouse. Maltsters and brewers distinguish between several different categories of malt, each with different brewing and culinary characteristics: base malts, caramel/dextrin malts, crystal malts, chocolate/roasted malts, and roasted raw grains. Base malts are gently kilned, as explained above, and are usually pale and highly enzymatic. They account for at least half the grist in most mashes. All other nonbase malts are considered "specialty malts." These add varying degrees of color, flavor, aroma, and texture to the finished beer.

Malts that are cured in the kiln, after steeping, germinating, and drying at a high temperature of perhaps 140°C (approximately 185°F), are branded as crystal malts.

Caramel malts require a fourth step, stewing, as part of the malting process. For this, the green malt is sent, after germination, into a rotating, drum-type roaster instead of a kiln. There, it is heated immediately to between roughly 64°C and 72°C (147°F and 162°F), which is the temperature range for strong alpha- and beta-amylase activity. It is kept at that temperature for about an hour. This wet stewing ensures that enzymatic saccharification takes place inside each kernel. The stewed malt is then finished off in the kiln or it stays in the roaster for finishing. If it is finished in the kiln, it is subjected to a drying cycle at about 90°C (roughly 195°F), which causes the sugars to caramelize into hard, glassy, and unfermentable dextrins. If the stewed malt is finished in the roaster, on the other hand, it is subjected to a drying cycle at perhaps 200°C (roughly 390°F), which causes not only the sugars to caramelize into unfermentable dextrins but also the entire kernel to become roasted. The roasting times and temperatures vary with the desired degrees of color and roastiness, but the results are always strongly color- and flavor-intensive malts. Because caramelization completely and irretrievably denatures (destroys) the malt's enzymes, caramel malts rarely make up more than half of a beer's grist bill. Historically, the first pale caramel malt was made by Weyermann and patented in Germany under the brand name of Carapils in 1903. See WEYERMANN® MALTING. Caramel malts impart a sweet maltiness to the brews made with them.

Chocolate malts are slightly stronger in color and aroma than caramel and crystal malts. They are produced by moving regularly steeped, germinated, and kilned—that is, not stewed—malts, after a month-long rest, into a roaster. There, these otherwise finished malts are heated to about 250°C (about 480°F). The resulting finished products are very dark to jet black and when concentrated may taste strongly acrid and bitter. Some maltsters make roast malts directly in the kiln, without moving them to a rotating drum. This method, however, results in less homogeneous products, because of the uneven heat distribution from the bottom to the top of the malt bed.

Certain roasted malts are offered in two forms—regular and dehusked. When malts are dehusked, the barley's tannin-containing husks are removed before the start of the malting process. Husk-free chocolate malts taste very mild, with greatly reduced bitterness and roastiness, but they have the same coloring effects as regular chocolate malts. Roasted chocolate malts, however, must not be confused with roasted barley, roasted wheat, or roasted rye, which are produced like chocolate malts, in a roaster, from raw or malted grains. These slightly harsh-tasting products add not only burnt aromas but also strongly biscuity notes to the finished beer. Neither chocolate malts nor roasted grains—just like caramel and crystal malts—have any enzymes left, and because of their color and flavor intensity, they rarely make up more than 5% of a mash.

Finally, there are several smoke-flavored malts, which are steeped and germinated and then kilned in smoky, direct-fired kilns. These kilns are constructed to allow smoke to filter through the drying grain. Peat smoke is a favorite for whiskey mashes, whereas smoke from aged beechwood logs gives Bamberg-style smoked malt (also known as Rauchmalz) and the Bamberg-style Rauchbier made from it their characteristic flavor. Before the invention of modern kilning and drying techniques, most malts were dried over fires, and many early beers undoubtedly had strong smoky flavors. To this day, malts are major drivers of beer flavor and differences between different beer profiles. The differences in malting are among the reasons why beer has a far wider range of flavor than wine does. Beer can taste of dark chocolate, espresso coffee, caramel, toffee, biscuits, or bread, and malts are the basis for all of these myriad flavors.

Narziss, Ludwig. *Die technologie der Malzbereitung (The technology of malt-making)*, 6th ed. Stuttgart, Germany: Enke Verlag, 1976.

Thomas Kraus-Weyermann

malting is the process in which raw barley or another grain is made ready to become the main ingredient in the brewing process. The grain is steeped in water, then rested under precise conditions to encourage germination, and finally dried in a kiln and/or a roaster. See MALT. Professionally, the person responsible for this process is known as a maltster. Malting is essentially the first step in beer making; the second is mashing, lautering, and

Postcard of a barley kiln, c. 1933. After germination the moist grains are transferred to the kiln, where hot air dries them. This kills the developing acrospires, or new plant shoots, without destroying the enzymes that were released during germination. PIKE MICROBREWERY MUSEUM, SEATTLE, WA

boiling in the brewhouse; the third step is fermentation in the cellar; and the final step is the packaging of the beer in kegs, bottles, or cans.

One of the key functions of malting is to degrade the grain's proteins and to create the enzymes and modify the starches needed for the brewing process. See MODIFICATION. The time and temperatures for each malting step vary from one maltster to the next and from one type of malt to another. The first step of malting is steeping the raw grain in a vat of clean and fresh water. During steeping, which may take up to 2 days, the grain is alternately soaked and then drained in intervals of about 8 h. During this time, the barley corn absorbs water, which, in turn, activates enzymes that reside naturally in the grain and are capable of breaking down complex molecules within the kernel, notably proteins and carbohydrates. It also activates hormones responsible for starting the growth of a new plant. Whereas the moisture content in siloed raw grain rarely exceeds 15% by weight, after the steep it is about 45%.

At this point, tiny roots known as "chits" become visible, and the damp grain is transferred to a germination room, which is usually kept between 16°C and 19°C (61°F and 66°F). There, the germinating barley is well aerated for 4 to 6 days and turned frequently. The turning of the barley keeps the rapidly growing roots from matting together; it also dissipates moisture, heat, and carbon dioxide produced during the grain's respiration. See RESPIRATION. Today, the turning of grain is usually done my mechanical means, but it is a task that has also been done by hand for thousands of years. See FLOOR MALTING and SALADIN BOX.

During germination, the grain enzymes kick their activities into high gear, producing malt sugars, soluble starch, and usable yeast nutrients such as amino acids. See STARCH, SUGAR, and YEAST NUTRIENTS.

Now the grain is ready to be fully dried. For this it is moved into a kiln. See KILNING. The heat of the kiln, which is usually 80°C to 90°C (176°F–194°F) and lasts for approximately 2 to 4 h, kills the embryo of the sprouting grain and preserves its nutrients for beer making rather than for making a new plant. The enzymatic modifications that started in the steeping vessel and continued during germination

Germination chamber at the Weyermann Malting Company®. The long shallow trough, called a Saladin Box, contains the germinating grains. COURTESY OF WEYERMANN® SPECIALTY MALTS

also continue during the initial heating of the grain. As the grain dries out and becomes malt, the enzymes become dormant and modification stops. Later, in the brewhouse, these enzymes will be reactivated by heat and moisture in a mashing vessel. At the end of the process, the finished malt has 3%–6% moisture and can be stored for months.

For specialty malts such as caramel or crystal malts, the process is similar to that for base malts, with some alterations to give specialty malts their variations of color and flavor. Caramel or crystal malts are essentially stewed until their starches liquidize into sugars and then roasted to caramelize those sugars. Roasting done with little moisture does not result in caramelization but develops color and roasted flavors. See MAILLARD REACTION and MELANOIDINS. Higher drying temperatures will result in darker, more flavorful malts, but the malt's enzymes may become permanently denatured. Such malts have no enzymatic power and cannot be used as base malts. See BASE MALT. The flavors of specialty malts may range from toffeelike, to nutty, to coffeelike, to sharp and almost burned tasting. Malt colors may range from golden yellow to pitch black. See CARAMEL MALTS and ROASTED MALTS.

Characteristics of malts will differ partly depending on whether the raw grain used was two-row or six-row barley. Six-row barley malt tends to have more polyphenols and more enzymes than does two-row barley malt. This is principally because the kernels of six-row barley are generally smaller than those of two-row barley, giving six-row kernels a greater husk-to-endosperm ratio. See ENDOSPERM and HUSK. Six-row malt, however, tends to work well with raw adjunct grains, because its higher enzymatic power is capable of converting their starches. See ADJUNCTS and DIASTATIC POWER.

Briess Malt and Ingredients Co. *Malting 101*. http://www.brewingwithbriess.com/Malting101/Default.htm/ (accessed April 4, 2011).

Briggs, D. E., J. S. Hough, R. Stevens, and T. W. Young. *Malting and brewing science. Vol. 1: Malt and sweet wort*, 2nd ed. London: Chapman & Hall, 1981.

John Holl and Wolfgang David Lindell

malting barley is barley developed and grown specifically for brewing beer. Barley was originally domesticated independently in ancient Mesopotamia and Ethiopia; in both areas it was used for beer brewing. Modern malting barley may be either two rowed or six rowed. Two-rowed barley gives a higher extract yield, whereas the six-rowed types have a slightly higher enzyme activity. The flavor and finish of beers produced from either type also differ somewhat, with the six-rowed types being slightly drier in the finish.

Malted barley grain has the potential to provide the perfect balance of carbohydrates and proteins for feeding yeast—and ultimately making beer. "Potential" is the key word. A prerequisite is that the barley has the right genes to produce the necessary compounds in the proper ratios for brewing. For 10,000 years, people have bred barley to achieve this. Simply put, varieties with the right genes for brewing are considered "malting varieties" and those with the wrong genes become "feed varieties." There are stringent testing and approval systems in place to ensure that malting varieties have the traits necessary to meet the needs and expectations of farmers, maltsters, and brewers. Although the needs of each profession differ, there is some general agreement about what the right traits are in a malting variety. Malting barley varieties need to be high yielding, their grain kernels must be of a specified size, the malt extract percentages need to be high, and the wort beta glucan levels need to be low. However, specifications for grain protein and levels of enzymatic activity vary tremendously between brewers. Of particular importance in this regard is the amount—and type—of adjunct used in brewing. Brewers adhering to the Reinheitsgebot find the malting varieties used to brew "low-carb" lagers entirely unacceptable. Brewers of "light" beers despair at the low enzymatic activity of a malt perfect for an all-barley craft beer. Thus, differentiating malting and feed varieties is possible for some traits, but not for others.

These differences in the definition of malting quality lead to elusive targets for plant breeders and geneticists attempting to determine which of the 30,000–40,000 genes of barley are "right" and "wrong" genes for malting. To add yet another variable to this already complex equation, the environment plays a huge role in malting quality. The best available malting variety will produce malt of abysmal quality if grown under conditions of extreme temperature and/or moisture or if it is afflicted by any of the multitude of bacterial, fungal, viral, and/or insect plagues that can attack barley. When things go wrong (as they are increasingly likely to do with climate change), the "malting" barley grown under poor conditions will sorely tax the skills of the maltster and brewer and some of it may have to be sold as lower-value "feed barley." The feed market thus provides a safety net for rejected malt barley, leading to the maxim that "a good malt barley is a good feed barley." The reverse is never true because a variety selected only for grain yield will malt about as effectively and efficiently as gravel. Beta-glucans are good for the human diet, but terrible for beer, turning mashes gummy and the resulting beers hazy.

In actuality, there is no single and simple definition of "malting barley," except to say that it is barley that produces a target profile of characteristics when subjected to malting—a process of controlled germination and subsequent processing for flavor, color, and aroma. Despite many advances in barley breeding, a number of traditional barley cultivars are still used in malting because of their good brewing and flavor characteristics, the British Maris Otter being a prime example of this.

Briggs, D. E., et al. *Brewing: Science and practice.* Cambridge, UK: Woodhead Publishing Limited, 2004.

Per Kølster and Patrick Hayes

maltodextrins are glucose polymers present in wort after mashing. They are not normally utilized by brewing yeasts. See GLUCOSE. Glucose, maltose (two linked glucose molecules), and maltotriose (three linked glucose molecules) are the principal sugars produced during mashing and are readily utilized by brewing strains of yeast. Higher glucose polymers produced as a result of starch degradation during mashing but not utilized by the yeast are left unfermented and are usually carried forward into the beer. These maltodextrins contribute to the "final gravity" of the beer and generate palate fullness, some sweetness, and calorific content to the finished beer. Mashing can be performed in a manner that promotes the production of maltodextrins when greater palate fullness is desired. In light beers these maltodextrins are virtually absent as a result of additional enzyme activity during mashing (sometimes using exogenous industrial enzymes) to effect near-complete starch breakdown to simple sugars. Low-carbohydrate diets (e.g., the Atkins Diet) encourage the use of these light beers because of their low carbohydrate content. However, most types of beer have relatively low carbohydrate content in the first place, and the "low-carb" beers often suffer from a certain thinness on the palate as a result of a deficiency of body-enhancing maltodextrins.

See also LIGHT BEER.

George Philliskirk

maltose is the principal sugar in wort and is derived from the breakdown of starch during the mashing process. Maltose is classed as a disaccharide and consists of two linked molecules of the basic "sugar" glucose. During the mashing process the natural enzymes present in the malt, and notably an enzyme called beta amylase, break down the starch present to create large quantities of maltose, approximately 40% of the total carbohydrate content of the wort. Optimizing maltose production during mashing is dependent primarily on temperature, with a range of 60°C–65°C (140°F–149°F) most suitable for beta amylase activity. Traditional single-infusion mashing is usually carried out within this temperature range. See INFUSION MASH. During fermentation, the maltose present in the wort is transported into the yeast cell and broken down to its constituent glucose molecules before subsequent metabolism into cell components, alcohol and CO_2.

Maltose can also be added to the wort from starch sources other than malted barley. Maize, wheat, and other starch sources can be converted using mainly microbial enzymes to produce syrups containing a range of glucose polymers, with maltose the major component of syrups used in brewing. Special syrups containing high (70%) levels of maltose are known as "high-maltose syrups" and can be used to extend brewing capacity when mashing facilities are limited.

See also SYRUPS.

George Philliskirk

maltotriose is a carbohydrate comprising three linked (alpha 1,4) glucose molecules and is an important fermentable sugar in wort. Maltotriose is generated during mashing as a result of the enzymatic breakdown of starches. In an all-malt wort, maltotriose typically accounts for about 15% to 20% of the total carbohydrate content. So-called hydrolyzed starch syrups (also known as glucose syrups), usually made from corn or wheat, also contain maltotriose produced from starches that are converted by extraneous enzymes into a mix of various fermentable and nonfermentable sugars. Most brewer's yeasts can metabolize maltotriose, but they do so only after all the more easily absorbable sugars, such as glucose and maltose, have been consumed.

Lewis, Michael J., and Tom W. Young. *Brewing*, 2nd ed. New York: Kluwer Academic/Plenum Publishers, 2001.

George Philliskirk

malt syrup or extract is the concentrated (or it can also be dried) form of unfermented brewery wort. Malt syrup is generally produced as a viscous, sticky liquid. Its flavor is, not surprisingly, malty, but distinctly so because of the concentration process during manufacture. Apart from its use in brewing, it is also widely used in baking, confectionery, breakfast cereals, malt beverages, dairy products, and condiments and as a caramel substitute.

The production process through milling, mashing, mash separation, and wort boiling is similar to that of conventional beer production. Depending on the color and flavor attributes desired by the manufacturer, the grist used to produce malt extract will have similar proportions of pale malt and varying proportions of specialty malts (i.e., crystal, chocolate, black, etc.) that are used to produce pale colored lagers and pilsners/pils through darker colored ales to the more intensely colored porters and stouts. The attendant flavor characteristics of these beer styles will also accompany the malt extract produced. These malts are milled and mashed similarly to the normal brewing process. Mash separation is ideally achieved using a mash filter rather than a traditional lauter tun because wort can be recovered at higher gravities (i.e., ~30°P compared with ~20°P, respectively), which saves considerable

Ink blotter, c. 1920. During Prohibition, the Pabst Brewing Company began selling malt extract as an alternative revenue source. PIKE MICROBREWERY MUSEUM, SEATTLE, WA

amounts of energy and attendant cost in the concentration phase. The wort is generally boiled (adding to concentration) and it may be hopped or unhopped depending on the intended use of the product. After this point the wort will be evaporated to approximately 80% solids to produce a thick, viscous liquid or in some cases spray dried to a powdered form. Finally, the malt syrup will be aseptically packaged and then stored and distributed.

Malt syrup is just the concentrated product of the prefermentation; thus, the relative proportions of the various wort components are similar to the wort from which it is derived. Based on a syrup containing 80% solids, the level of protein and free amino nitrogen would be approximately 0.5% and 0.15%, respectively, by weight. The syrup will also contain the appropriate levels of trace elements (i.e., zinc, iron, manganese, potassium, calcium, copper, magnesium), vitamins (i.e., biotin), and lipids ("oils") to enable yeast growth and sustain its metabolism. The syrup is rich in maltose that comprises 60%–70% of the fermentable sugars.

Most homebrewers will be familiar in at least their initial, and often continuing, brewing activities with malt extract that is conveniently provided in a can. Extract brewing avoids the time-consuming and equipment-intensive prefermentation stages of the brewing process. For homebrewing the malt syrup is diluted with hot water to the required gravity, heated (and hopefully boiled, except with some rather lackluster "one-step" kits) to ensure solubilization and sterilization of the wort, and cooled, with yeast being pitched to ferment the wort. For more experienced homebrewers, the addition of various adjuncts, specialty syrups, steeped grains, and different hops provides the opportunity to personalize their beer production.

Malt extracts for brewing are provided to commercial and homebrewers in an increasingly large range of different styles and formulations. In addition to the traditional "standard" (read ale) light and dark malt syrups, more exotic and exciting concoctions such as wheat, Munich, amber, crystal, Carapils, roast malt, etc. are also being produced. Mixing varying proportions of these extracts essentially allows home and professional brewers alike to formulate most of the established range of beer styles. In addition, some malt syrups have various levels of diastatic power enzymes, retained or added, so the unmalted starch adjuncts can also be added and utilized during brewing.

Commercial brewers have also found uses for malt extracts. Some brewers use them as a suitable substrate for yeast propagation when the brewery's own worts are unsuitable or unavailable. Not surprisingly, given the cost of capital startup or because of franchising constraints, some microbrewers and brewpubs also rely on malt syrups and special additions of hops, etc., to produce their beers. Even larger commercial brewing groups have found uses for malt syrups. For instance, in the quest to produce low-alcohol beers that have a palate similar to that of full-strength beer, some brewers include a proportion of maltodextrin syrups that have low fermentability to retain mouthfeel while controlling alcohol content and color. Additionally, the use of specialist malt syrups by small to medium-size breweries can be simply used to diversify the standard wort being produced into a number of different beer styles. This can be relatively easily achieved by blending in the appropriate proportion of specialty malt syrup—such as chocolate malt—for making a stout or porter.

Evan Evans

Manhattan, New York. The first brewery on Manhattan was built in a log house. It was among several structures in a fort erected by Dutch colonists Adrian Block and Hans Christiansen about 1612 on the southern tip of the island. These buildings also were the birthplace of the first white child born in Manhattan, Jean Vigne, who became the first brewer born in America and a prominent citizen. Dutchman Peter Minuit purchased the island from native Americans in 1626 and named it New Amsterdam. In 1629, there were only 350 people in the settlement. "About three years later, however, the West India Company saw fit to build a brewery not far from the fort, on a street which became known afterward as 'Brouwers (Brewers') Straet,'" writes Stanley Baron in his book, *Brewed in America*. Vigne was the brewer. The water for the brewery came from the *Heere Gracht,* a stream flowing from natural springs through Beaver path, now known as Beaver Street. In the 1640s and 1650s, a succession of colonial governors, including Peter Stuyvesant began to collect taxes of the production and sale of beer. The first excise taxes on beer aroused the opposition of the brewers and the citizenry, but the governors did not relent. A 1644 tax amounted to two guilders (80 cents) on each half vat, or barrel, of beer tapped. Half was paid by the brewer and half by the tapster, or retailer. The taxes were used to repair stockades, pay soldiers, and wage war against the Native Americans.

Stuyvesant also waged a crusade against drunkenness and carousing on the Sabbath. Inn keepers were prohibited from serving "any wines, beers, or any strong waters" to anyone but travelers and boarders on Sundays. Violators were liable to fines

Beer label, c. 1934—shortly after the repeal of the Volstead Act and end of Prohibition—from the Fidelio Brewery in Manhattan. PIKE MICROBREWERY MUSEUM, SEATTLE, WA

and suspension of business. Taverns were forced to close at 9 pm in the evening. All retailers of alcoholic beverages were required to obtain licenses. Sale of liquor to Native Americans was forbidden.

When the English took over administration of New Amsterdam from the Dutch in 1664, the Duke of York issued new regulations known as the Duke's Laws which stipulated that ". . . no person whatsoever shall henceforth undertake the calling or work of brewing beer for sale, but only such as are known to have sufficient skill and knowledge in the art and mystery of a brewer."

There were several important breweries in Manhattan. The two most prominent were George Ehret's Hell Gate Brewery, built on the East side of the city where the East River, Harlem River, and Long Island Sound merge in the rough water known as Hell Gate, and the Ruppert brewery, owned by Colonel Jacob Ruppert. He also served in Congress, owned the New York Yankees, built Yankee Stadium, and brought the legendary baseball star Babe Ruth to the team. See RUPPERT, JACOB. The high cost of doing business in Manhattan eventually led to the closing of all the old breweries. Today, the only brewery in Manhattan is the Chelsea Brewing Company, which operates a brewery restaurant in the Chelsea Piers entertainment complex on the Hudson River. Chelsea also sells to some bars and restaurants. The heart of New York City's modern brewing industry was based in Brooklyn, which was annexed by New York City in 1898.

See also BROOKLYN, NEW YORK.

100 years of brewing, a complete history of the progress made in the art, science and industry of brewing in the world, particularly during the nineteenth century; a supplement to The Western brewer. Chicago: H.S. Rich & Co., Publishers, 1903.

Baron, Stanley. *Brewed in America.* Boston: Little, Brown & Co., 1962.

Stephen Hindy

manioc, also known as cassava or yucca, is a root vegetable cultivated in sub-Saharan Africa, Southeast Asia, and throughout South America, primarily for food but also for the production of a type of beer. In its raw form it is mildly poisonous, containing cyanide, but once boiled it becomes edible. Indigenous South Americans such as the Jivaro, the Tupinamba, and the Yudja produce a beer-like drink made from boiled manioc root that is chewed and formed into balls before being allowed to ferment. The chewing introduces the digestive enzyme ptyalin, a form of alpha amylase, which reduces the carbohydrate material to fermentable sugar—the chewing therefore becomes a form of mashing. It is then sometimes reboiled and can be aged for extended periods, resulting in a stronger and more prized beverage. For fermentation, the "mash" is usually blended with water, poured into jars (sometimes buried in the earth and covered with leaves), and left to ferment spontaneously for several days.

Manioc beer is called by various names, among them masato, caouin, and nihamanchi, depending on the tribe and region. The stronger version can be called sangucha shiki. It has been produced for thousands of years for both quotidian and sacramental use. Although these drinks are still produced by indigenous groups in various parts of the world (and the occasional adventurous homebrewer), manioc has not yet found a place in the world of modern brewing.

Buhner, Stephen Harrod. *Sacred and herbal healing beers: The secrets of ancient fermentations.* Boulder, CO: Siris Books/Brewers Publications, 1998.

Capra, Will. *How to brew manioc beer.* http://www.ehow.com/.

Dick Cantwell

A **manometer** is a device for measuring pressure. The international unit of measurement for pressure is the Pascal (Pa). In technical applications, however, the units "bar" or "pounds per square inch" (psi) are in more common use, whereby 100 kPa = 1 bar = 14.504 psi. Manometer readings always indicate an overpressure relative to an ambient pressure, which is usually 1 bar. A reading of 0 bar, therefore, means 0 overpressure, or an absolute pressure of 1 bar.

The quality and reliability of pressure measurements are of outmost importance for the safe and trouble-free operation of a brewery. Manometers are employed, therefore, at several stages of the beer-making process. They measure liquid pressures in piping systems; CO_2 pressures in fermentation and lagering tanks; air pressures in pneumatic valve systems; differential pressures during lautering;

steam, glycol, water, and gas pressures; beer pressures in dispensing systems; and absolute and differential pressures at the bottling line. They can also determine volumes indirectly by means of pressure transducers. High-quality manometers are especially important during filling to avoid potentially hazardous overpressures or inaccurate CO_2 levels in the finished beer.

Modern brewery manometers are usually spring-loaded devices in round, copper alloy, plastic, or stainless-steel housings. The pressure-sensing element may be a Bourdon tube, a diaphragm, or a capsule element. Pressure sensors can also transmit signals to remote devices. They acquire such signals via resistance variations by the piezoelectric effect, strain gauges, or capacitance/inductance measurements, such as by ceramic capacitor. The simplest type, used in many craft brewing setups, is a set of two sight glasses on the lauter tun. One has an inlet above the false bottom, and the other one has an inlet below. Looking at the liquid levels in each tube, the brewer can gain a sense of the differential pressure across the grain bed and adjust the lautering accordingly.

See also LAUTERING.

Oliver Jakob

Maris Otter (barley) is a traditional, two-row, low-protein, winter barley variety with deep roots in English brewing. It is today considered the keystone malt for authentic British ale flavors. It was first bred in 1966 by Dr G. D. H. Bell, the director of the British Plant Breeding Institute (PBI), which was then located on Maris Lane, in Trumpington, England. (In 1990, the PBI moved to a nearby location.) Maris Otter was a cross between two older PBI varieties, Proctor and Pioneer. Whereas Pioneer, bred in 1943, was Britain's first commercial winter-hardy malting barley, Procter is a spring barley that was bred in 1952 as a cross between Kenia, a Danish variety, and Plumage Archer, an indigenous English spring variety that was first bred at Warminster Maltings in 1905.

Maris Otter is considered a very "malty-tasting" pale base malt, which has made it a favorite among traditional cask ale brewers for decades. Using Maris Otter, brewers are able to create beers of relatively low gravity and alcoholic strength, such as "ordinary" bitters, while retaining a genuinely malty flavor profile. After its introduction, Maris Otter quickly became popular with brewers because of its low nitrogen content, excellent malting homogeneity, and good enzymatic strength, which makes it easy to malt and mash. See DIASTATIC POWER, MALT, and MASHING. Although most barley varieties have a commercial life cycle of perhaps a decade from introduction to phase out, Maris Otter kept going strong for almost 3 decades.

Agronomically, Maris Otter thrives particularly well in the maritime climate of the British Isles, but less so in continental climates, which is why it has never become a significant barley crop in such brewing barley-growing powerhouses as Australia, Ukraine, Russia, Germany, France, and the prairies of the United States and Canada. In addition, although a great—albeit high-priced—performer in the malt and brewhouses, farmers consider it an only moderate, even poor, performer in terms of disease resistance and yield. For these reasons, it is no longer listed as recommended by such official bodies as the National Institute of Agricultural Botany of the United Kingdom. For all practical purposes, it has largely been replaced by such varieties as Halcyon. See HALCYON (BARLEY).

In the early 1990s, Maris Otter plantings had virtually ceased. This is when a consortium of Maris Otter loyalists composed of farmers and maltsters were able to acquire the exclusive rights to Maris Otter seeds. By 2002, two companies, H. Banham Ltd. of Norfolk and Robin Appel Ltd. of Wiltshire, purchased Maris Otter as a "brand" and continued to make it commercially available to specialty brewers. Since then, the international demand for Maris Otter has rebounded and remained sufficiently strong to keep small plantings of it viable. Maris Otter has become an "heirloom" variety malt prized by many craft brewers in the UK and the United States. Some of the production is still floor malted, a process that intensifies this barley's natural round, biscuity flavors.

Appel, R. *The malt-stars of Warminster.* Warminster, England: Wiltshire Warminster Maltings, 2010.

Ian Hornsey

marketing, along with its more direct corollary, advertising, is as important to breweries as it is

Postcard, c. 1915, borrowing the title of the popular song "Beer, Beer, Glorious Beer," composed by Harry Anderson, Steve Leggett, Will Godwin, A. E. Durandeau, and E. W. Rogers in 1901. PIKE MICROBREWERY MUSEUM, SEATTLE, WA

to any other sort of company. Beer marketing, however, is highly regulated. Governments use various methods to deal with the perceived marketing impact on increased consumption, from the extreme of banning beer marketing altogether (Norway) to complex regulatory systems. The varying marketing regulations not only are for advertisements but also cover sponsorships, labels, and any promotional materials (coasters, t-shirts, glassware, neon signs, etc). See LABELING INFORMATION and LABELS. In France, for example, brewery sponsorship of sporting events is banned, where in other European countries, it is often prevalent.

In any given country, beer marketing may be subject to more than one regulatory body and set of rules. The European Union has certain marketing regulations, as does each member country. In the United States, the Alcohol and Tobacco Trade and Tax Bureau, the Federal Trade Commission, and the individual states regulate beer marketing.

Generally speaking, beer marketing cannot use misleading statements, advertising that targets minors, and images or statements that associate alcohol with athletic achievement or encourage intoxication. Breweries are also prohibited from making any health claims (Guinness was required to drop its famous "Guinness Is Good for You" campaign decades ago), even if it can be proven that they are entirely true. As of 2011, breweries in the United States were prohibited from printing nutritional information on labels or using it in marketing or advertising.

Given the large list of restrictions, breweries have become creative with their marketing. Many focus on lifestyles and the desires of subcultures (office workers, sports fans, women) and create subtle messages targeting those groups. Beer marketing campaigns for large breweries usually include multiple media avenues (television, print, Internet) and promotional techniques. Product placement in movies and television is a common alternate method of marketing a brand. Point of sale promotions are also part of any beer marketer's tools, including beer-branded merchandise giveaways to consumers.

Many large breweries act as sponsors for various events to target their markets, from sporting events to film festivals and concerts. Stella Artois, for example, sponsors film festivals worldwide. The craft beer segment, which spends very little on conventional advertising, uses various promotional methods to build brand awareness, including point of sale promotions of branded merchandise. Craft breweries focus on the brewery, its story, and its people, connecting to consumers through those stories. Not surprisingly, craft brewers tend to be adept at using social media to spread brand awareness; once established in the public consciousness, Facebook and Twitter quickly became major tools for craft brewers to get the word out about their beers. Small breweries attend festivals, sometimes dozens per year, and often build the brand largely by conversation. They host beer dinners and tastings to promote their brands and to familiarize consumers with craft beer as a whole. As craft beer becomes more prevalent, we can expect the iconography of craft breweries to make an impact. Just as Guinness' rendition of Brian Boru's harp and Bass' red triangle logo are recognized instantly by consumers, so too may craft brewers' marks such as New Belgium Brewing Co's cruiser bicycles become icons for a new generation of beer drinkers.

See also ADVERTISING and LAW.

International Center for Alcohol Policies. http://www.icap.org/ (accessed April 4, 2011).

Pennock, Pamela. *Advertising sin and sickness: The politics of alcohol and tobacco marketing.* DeKalb, IL: Northern Illinois Press, 2007.

Anda Lincoln

Marston's Brewery was founded in 1834 at the Horningblow Brewery in Burton-on-Trent, England as the brainchild of brewer John Marston. In 1898, following a merger with John Thompson and Son Ltd, the brewing moved across town to the Albion Brewery where it became famous for its use of the Burton Union system, a traditional fermenting apparatus based on fermentation in oak barrels. The brewery claims that this system adorns Marstons's ale with a distinctive signature fruity dryness and accentuates the renowned sulphurous "Burton Snatch" aroma.

In 1905, the brewery joined forces with Sydney Evershed to become Marston, Thompson, and Evershed. Between the 1920s and 1960s, the company remained relatively immune to the oscillating fortunes of British ale-making by acquiring a number of pub companies and breweries throughout England.

In 1952, Marston's launched a new pale ale called Pedigree. Brewed on the traditional Burton Union System, it is the brewery's flagship beer and now one of Britain's best-selling ales with more than 40 million pints drunk every year from casks, bottles, and cans.

In 1999, the Marston's Brewery, its beers, and a 918-strong portfolio of pubs was purchased for £292 million by Wolverhampton & Dudley Breweries which, in 2007, changed its name to Marston's PLC. As of 2010, it was Britain's largest independent brewing group.

The company's brewing arm, known as Marston's Brewing Company, now operates five breweries including Wychwood in Oxfordshire, Jennings in Cumbria, the Park Brewery in Wolverhampton, and the Ringwood Brewery in Hampshire. Marston's also now brews Bass Ale and Tetley Cask under licence.

Other Marston's beers include Old Empire, Resolution, and Oyster Stout and the Marston's pub estate now exceeds 2,100 pubs. Marston's is one of only three breweries in Britain that employs its own cooper, and the only brewery in the country to use the Burton Union system.

See also BURTON SNATCH and BURTON UNION SYSTEM.

Ben McFarland

märzenbier is German for "March beer," a golden to deep amber lager style with a full body and a moderate bitterness, which is related to both the oktoberfestbier and the Vienna lager. The historical origins of märzenbier lie in a decree issued in 1553 by the Bavarian ruler Duke Albrecht V, in which he forbade all brewing between April 23 and September 29. The decree was to prevent brewing during the warm season, when, unbeknown to microbially ignorant medievals, ambient bacteria would often infect the Bavarians' beers and quickly spoil them. See BAVARIA and INFECTION. Brewers, therefore, worked overtime in March to make enough beer to last until fall. These March beers were usually brewed slightly stronger than regular beers and they were stored cool, that is, they were lagered, so they would keep better. See LAGER and LAGERING.

As a beer style, however, märzenbier became fixed only in 1841, when the Spaten Brewery of Munich introduced, at that year's Oktoberfest, the first lager officially labeled märzenbier. See OKTOBERFEST. That same year, the Dreher Brewery of Schwechat, near Vienna, also came out with a märzen-like beer, which it called Vienna lager. See VIENNA LAGER. In the ensuing decades, both the märzenbier and the Vienna lager became standard brews in the portfolios of many breweries; and by 1872, the Spaten Brewery first used the name Oktoberfestbier for a märzen-style beer, which it had brewed specifically for that year's Oktoberfest. Today's Spaten oktoberfestbier is still based largely on that 1872 recipe. In the 19th century, of course, these three related beer styles were all made by a double-decoction method, a very labor- and energy-intensive brewhouse procedure that many breweries no longer employ because of the modern availability of highly modified malt. See DECOCTION.

Technically as well as historically, there is a great deal of overlap in the specifications of märzenbier, Vienna lager, and oktoberfestbier; and brewers around the world do not apply these designations consistently on their labels. However, the following general guidelines do apply in most cases. Much of the base malt in a märzenbier and oktoberfestbier, then and now, is so-called Munich malt, a highly aromatic malt with a color rating of roughly 10 to 25 European Brewery Convention (EBC; roughly 3 to 10 degrees Lovibond), whereas much of the base malt in the Austrian brew is Vienna malt with a lighter color rating of roughly 6 to 10 EBC (approximately 3 to 4 degrees Lovibond). See MUNICH MALT. As a result, the märzen and oktoberfest beers tend to be primarily golden amber in color, whereas Vienna lagers tend to have a more reddish tinge. Also, märzen/oktoberfest brews used to be much darker, nearly brown, in the olden days, but there has been a general trend in recent decades toward lightening them, an apparent concession to modern tastes. To North American beer enthusiasts this is often a surprise, because, ironically, North American craft brewers almost always brew märzen/oktoberfest beers to the old style, preferring a fuller color than that of the contemporary German versions. In terms of bitterness, the Vienna brew tends to be just a touch hoppier and drier than the märzen/oktoberfest, with the latter often showing sweet, almost toffee-like maltiness combined with biscuit and bread flavors, as well as plenty of mouthfeel.

In Germany, incidentally, the name Oktoberfestbier is now legally reserved only for the six breweries—Augustiner, Hacker-Pschorr, Hofbräuhaus, Löwenbräu, Paulaner, and Spaten—who may serve their beers at the Munich Oktoberfest. All other breweries may use just the märzen designation for their Oktoberfest-style beers. In other countries, of course, especially in North America, where German law does not reach, märzen/oktoberfest is treated like any other beer style and has seen a great surge of interest, especially in the emerging craft brew sector, although some craft brewers occasionally stray and brew the beer as an ale rather than a lager.

Conrad Seidl and Horst Dornbusch

mash, a porridge-like mixture of ground cereal grains (grist) and temperature-controlled brewing water (often called "liquor"). Mashing, the act of producing a mash, is the first stage in brewing beers of any style in any brewery, its purpose being to convert starch and protein in the grist into sugars and amino acids that are assimilable by yeast. See MASHING. The cereals that make up the mash, the chemical composition, and the volume and temperature of the brewing water are integral determinants of a beer's recipe, final taste, and character. A mash is traditionally made in a mash tun in ale breweries in the UK. It normally contains only malted barley—several types of malt may be used—but sometimes has a small percentage (maximum of 15%) of other cereals such as wheat. The mash in a mash tun is fairly thick compared with mashes used in lager brewing, which are thinner because they take place in a mash mixing or conversion vessel. See INFUSION MASH. A lager mash often goes through a series of temperature rises during which enzymes in the malt differing in their tolerance to heat act successively to produce the liquid sugar extract called wort. See WORT. In traditional ale mashing the wort is run from the grains in the mash tun. Lager mashes are transferred to a mash separation device such as a lauter tun or mash filter in which the wort can be washed out of the mash by spraying with brewing water (sparging).

See also DECOCTION, MASHING, and TEMPERATURE-PROGRAMMED MASH.

Paul KA Buttrick

mash filter, a wort separation device that can be used as an alternative to a lauter tun or a mash/lauter vessel. The mash filter is essentially a plate and frame filter press fitted with series of fine filters for separating spent grist from sweet wort. Whereas older mash filter models were often criticized for providing hazy worts with high levels of unwanted polyphenols, modern mash filters are highly efficient and can produce bright worts with few particles.

In 1901, the Belgian Philippe Meura developed a filter press to improve the mash lautering process. The company that bears Meura's name is still making mash filters. The mash filter, unlike the mash tun, is able to handle very fine grist crushed by a hammer mill, and this ensures exceptional extract recovery. A modern mash filter is a series of polypropylene filters, which can handle grist of up to 100% adjunct because barley malt husks are not required to act as a filter medium, as is the case with a lauter tun.

Once the first wort has been run off into the kettle, sparge liquor can be introduced into the filter and a weaker wort can be extracted. Sparging continues until the required amount of wort has been collected. Some systems allow the mash to be physically squeezed dry after sparging has been completed. At the end of each cycle, the filter is opened and the spent grains, almost dry, are allowed to drop out. A modern mash filter can filter large volumes of wort very quickly, enabling some brewers to process more than 12 brews per day. There are some disadvantages. Compared with a lautering vessel, the mash filter can be difficult to use when a brewery employs a wide variety of mash sizes because the range of optimal loading for the press is relatively small. Some brewers argue that the lauter tun remains a superior mash separation device and produces better quality wort. Mash filters remain rare in the United States, but they are widely used in Europe and other parts of the world.

Kunze, Wolfgang. *Technology, brewing & malting*. Berlin: VLB Berlin, 1996.

Meura. http://www.meura.com/ (accessed April 4, 2011).

Technical feature. *The Brewer International* 3 (2003): 57–59.

Tim Hampson and Stephen Hindy

A **mash fork** was a traditional brewing tool used to manually mix the mash during mashing in to ensure even heat distribution and uniform viscosity and to break up dough balls formed during mashing. Usually made of a hardwood such as beech or maple, a mash fork, with its open lattice design, was able to move easily through a thick mash without risk of breaking. The mash fork played a role similar to that of the lauter rakes in a larger modern brewery. See LAUTERING.

Before the introduction of what we think of as modern brewing equipment and techniques, brewers had to make do with undermodified and inconsistently milled malts and poor temperature control, sometimes leading to gummy mashes that would not run off properly. Skillful use of a well-made mash rake could make the difference between a successful brewing session and a useless mass of wasted grain. Today, the mash fork is largely a thing of the past, although the occasional enthusiastic craft brewer still has one made. They also live on as an evocative symbol of traditional brewing and form part of many heraldic-style symbols used by brewer's guilds and associations, including the Master Brewers Association of the Americas.

Brian Thompson

mash hopping is the addition of hops, typically whole hop flowers, during the mashing phase in the brewhouse process. It is used by a small number of craft brewers to add complexity to their beers. Although the expected hop utilization in the traditional sense is extremely low, it is recognized that mash hopping can impart unique hop flavors to the resulting beer. With this method, there is contact time between the mash and both the soluble and the nonsoluble hop compounds at mash temperatures ranging, depending on beer style and brewhouse process, from 122°F to 170°F, at a preboil wort pH of roughly 5.4 to 5.8. Because the hops remain behind in the spent grain after lautering, they are not exposed to boiling temperatures. Therefore, there is very little expected carryover and isomerization of hop bittering compounds (alpha acids). See ISOMERIZATION. Nonisomerized alpha acids are fairly insoluble in wort, and brewers using this method expect little or no additional bitterness from these hops. See HOP UTILIZATION. If mash hopping is done with pellets rather than whole leaf hops, some bitterness might result, but this would be attributed to hop powder carryover to the kettle during runoff or to a lesser extent, any isomerization that has occurred during the pelletizing process. Bittering acids aside, there will be some carryover of other flavor active compounds; however, similar to other early kettle hop additions, much of the lighter fruity or flowery volatile oils will be lost. Heavier oils, oxidized hop compounds, and other flavor active compounds, on the other hand, can be passed on to the kettle and therefore can make it into the final beer. There are some similarities between this method and first wort hopping in that the flavor active compounds that survive to the kettle are exposed to the wort for a greater period of time prior to the boil. See FIRST WORT HOPPING. The expected hop-related flavor characteristics therefore would be very similar. The hop material being in contact with the mash, wort, and sparge water for the duration of the process no doubt results in some flavor carryover.

There are differing opinions among brewers about what beer styles are best suited for mash hopping. The prominent view is that mash hopping is best suited for lighter styles with subtle hop flavors and textures. But mash hopping has also been used in highly hopped beers, such as "double India pale ales" and other "extreme beer" styles to pack in added hop notes. The subtle notes thus gained, however, are likely drowned out if large hop charges are used downstream. Although it may seem wasteful by some standards, mash hopping with whole flowers has a very positive effect on lauterablity, adding porosity to the grain bed, not unlike rice hulls or other lautering aids. There is some reference to this method of hopping in the traditional production of Berliner weisse, where low hopping rates and very low International Bitterness Units are important to reduce the antimicrobial effect of the hops, which in turn allows for the growth of lactobacillus bacteria in this intentionally sour beer style. See BERLINER WEISSE.

Matthew Brynildson

mashing is the term given to the start of the brewing process, where crushed grains are mixed with water to form a porridge-like mixture called the "mash." It is in the mash that malt and other cereal starches are transformed into sugars and proteins and other materials are made soluble, creating the sweet fermentable liquid called the wort. See WORT. Malt comes from the malting house into the brewery in whole kernels and is then milled to form the grain mixture called "grist." The grist is mixed with carefully controlled amounts of warm or hot water to form the mash. There are three basic types of mashing process: infusion mashing, decoction mashing, and temperature-controlled infusion mashing. Different mashing processes are used in different parts of the world depending on local tradition, the quality of malt available, the equipment used, and the beer styles brewed.

Malt is made from specially grown varieties of malted barley. During malting, enzymes start to break down the main part of the kernel, which is called the "starchy endosperm." The starchy endosperm is made of a framework of cell walls, consisting of mainly hemicelluloses, which is full of starch granules held in a protein matrix. The process of malting and mashing breaks down the proteins, hemicelluloses, and starch into smaller fractions that are soluble and are washed out during sparging to produce wort. See SPARGING. Depending on how the barley is malted, a mashing process is designed to make as much soluble material as possible available in the wort, while avoiding undesirable characteristics.

The different mashing processes are designed to make as much soluble material available as possible from different malts. The mashing process applies different temperatures to the mash that are ideal for breaking down the different parts of the starchy endosperm. Proteases with an optimum working temperature of 35°C–45°C (95°F–113°F) break down the protein matrix holding the starch granules. Glucanases have an optimum temperature of 45°C–55°C (113°F–131°F) and break down the hemicelluloses gums, whereas amylases break down the starch granules and work best at 61°C–67°C (141.8°F–152.6°F).

In the UK most ales are traditionally brewed using an infusion mashing process where good-quality, well-modified malt is mashed into a "mash tun," where it is held at approximately 65°C (149°F) for at least 1 h. During this hour, the malt sugars and other materials are released from the grist by action of enzymes in the malt. The mash is then sprayed with hot water, called sparging (at about 75°C [167°F]), which runs through the mash and out of the mash tun through a slotted false bottom, taking with it all the soluble material that forms the wort, the sweet liquid that the yeast will ferment into beer. This infusion process is sometimes called isothermal infusion mashing, because only one temperature is used. It is made possible because barley-growing conditions in the UK are ideal for the production of very well-modified malt. When well-modified malts are produced, many of the enzymic processes to break down the proteins, hemicelluloses, and gums have already taken place in the malting house. Infusion mashing has always been used in the UK to produce ales, and it remains the simplest mashing process. As the quality of malting barley improves, infusion mashing is used by many craft brewers to brew lagers, wheat beers, and other types of beers. Because the infusion mashing method requires only two brewhouse vessels (a mash/lauter vessel and a kettle) to produce hopped wort, it is still widely used among small breweries and pub breweries.

Most lager brewers and larger ale brewers outside the UK employ a process called temperature-programmed infusion mashing. This process involves heating an infusion mash through a series of temperature rises and then resting the mash at that temperature for a specified period before rising to the next temperature.

These temperature rests are sometimes called "stands." Heating of the mash is carried out by passing steam or hot water through heating panels within the walls of the mashing vessel, which is also fitted with an agitator to ensure good mixing. This process normally starts by mashing the malt at approximately 45°C–50°C (113°F–122°F) into a mashing vessel, sometimes called a conversion vessel. The mash is often held at this temperature for anywhere from 10 to 25 min, during which enzymes work on the protein and gums in the grist to release the starch from which the malt sugars are made. The proteins must be broken down to form amino acids; these are valuable yeast nutrients during fermentation. Higher weight protein materials are also broken down, lest they later contribute to unwanted haze in the finished beer. Other proteinaceous material is also a contribution to beer foam, and too long a stand at 45°C (113°F; called a protein rest or stand) can be deleterious to a beer's foaming quality. After the protein rest, the mash is heated to 62°C–67°C (143.6°F–152.6°F) for the saccharification stand. The enzymes (called amylases) that break down starch and bigger sugar molecules into fermentable sugars work best at this these temperatures. The amount of sugar produced in the mash is largely a function of the amount of grist used. However, different saccharification temperatures will produce different sugars in the wort and therefore different beers. Mashes performed with low saccharification temperatures produce a greater proportion of fermentable sugars in the resulting wort and will produce a drier beer with higher alcohol content. Conversely, saccharification temperatures toward the top of the range will result in less fermentable worts and sweeter, more full-bodied beers, and these will have a lower alcohol content produced from the same amount of grist. The final stage is to heat the mash up to about 75°C (167°F) prior to transfer to a mash separation vessel, usually a lauter tun. See LAUTER TUN. This final heat rise deactivates the enzymes and reduces the viscosity of the wort, thus giving a faster runoff. This is often referred to as "mashing off." Some beer types are best brewed using specially tailored temperature-programmed infusion mashes that will perform different functions. For example, many wheat-based beers are mashed with longer protein rests (wheat having more protein than malting barley) or other rests designed to favor the production of certain flavors in the finished beer. The brewer can therefore fine-tune the wort to create exactly the flavor and aroma desired.

Decoction mashing is the name given to an older temperature-programmed mashing process used by traditional continental brewers, often for lager production. See DECOCTION. Decoction mashing was used before the technology for temperature-programmed infusion mashing was developed and at that time European malts were often undermodified. The process of decoction involves taking a proportion of a mash from a mash vessel into a mash cooker where it is heated to 100°C (212°F) and boiled for a short time. After a specified time the boiled mash is returned to the original mash vessel that is warmed up in the mixing process. For example, a portion of mash at 45°C (113°F) may be taken from a mash vessel and boiled before returning it to the mash vessel. The mash vessel is stirred and the blended mash temperature will rise to a required saccharification temperature of 65°C (149°F). This process may be performed more than once, allowing the mash to achieve a number of temperature stands. Decoction mashing may involve a "single," "double," or even "triple" decoction process, with the latter having become quite rare. Some brewers believe that decoction mashing, although no longer strictly necessary with modern malts and brewing vessels, nonetheless creates greater depth of malt flavor. Many others are sceptical and see the method as needlessly laborious and consumptive of energy.

Variations on decoction processes are also often used when unmalted cereals, usually corn grits or rice, are used as adjuncts in the in the mash. See ADJUNCTS. The unmalted cereal (a small portion of malted barley is also added) is mixed with hot water in a separate vessel (usually referred to as a "rice cooker" or "grits cooker") and this mash is heated to 100°C (212°F). The hard starches in the raw grains gelatinize at this temperature, rendering them soft and susceptible to breakdown by enzymes. When this "cereal mash" is added to the barley malt mash, the enzymes in the malt will convert the now-gelatinized cereal starches into sugars. Almost all American mass-market beers are brewed using a version of this technique, and it is also widely used to produce light-bodied, light-flavored lager beers throughout the world.

See also DECOCTION, INFUSION MASH, and TEMPERATURE-PROGRAMMED MASH.

Paul KA Buttrick

mash tun is a brewhouse vessel used for mixing the ground malt (grist) with temperature-controlled water. This is called "mashing" and the porridge-like result is called the "mash." See MASH and MASHING. The mash is held at a predetermined temperature and time (e.g., at 65°C for 1 h) until the malt starches convert to sugars, and the dissolved malt sugars (wort) are rinsed into the kettle where hops are added. The mash tun is a single vessel where the mashing and wort runoff take place in the same vessel. It is predominantly used for brewing ales and other top-fermented beers, particularly in the UK, using a single-temperature infusion mash.

The traditional mash tun is an enclosed circular vessel of varying diameter with a depth of about 2 m. They were constructed of steel or copper and were insulated on the vertical sides, which were

A brewer at Harveys Brewery in Sussex, England, takes a temperature reading in the mash tun. CATH HARRIES

often clad in wood. The floor of the mash tun has a series of removable plates which sit about 7 cm above the flat vessel floor. The plates have a series of slots approx 50 cm in length and 1 mm wide, which are about 10% of the vessel's floor area. At a predetermined time after mashing, wort is washed from the mash tun by sparging, a rinsing process where hot brewing water, at approximately 75°C, is sprayed over the mash and the dissolved wort is run off from the bottom of the vessel. See SPARGING. The single temperature infusion mash is quite different in texture than the more modern temperature-programmed mash, where the mash attains several temperatures before transfer to a lauter tun. In a mash tun, the mash needs to remain fluffy and somewhat stiff (rather than soupy), retaining some air as it gently floats on top of the wort running off underneath. This is a balancing act requiring some skill on the part of the brewer because if the mash comes to rest directly on the plates, it is likely to become compacted, stopping the flow of wort.

In traditional breweries, the process of mashing, wort runoff, and emptying the mash tun takes about 6 h; in modern breweries two vessels are used to produce wort, a mash mixing vessel and a lauter tun, reducing this time to about 3 h. Because it requires less floor space and one fewer vessel, many small breweries in the UK and brewpubs in the United States continue to use the mash tun and its attendant mashing technique.

Paul KA Buttrick

Master Brewers Association of the Americas (MBAA), founded in 1887 in Chicago, was started as a national association for brewmasters of the United States. This was at a time when the burgeoning city of Chicago in the American Midwest could already boast of a population of well over 1 million. Up to that time there were only local brewers associations in the United States, but forward-looking master brewers felt that these "locals" should be brought under one roof, thereby enabling a more effective exchange of ideas and generally improving the image of the profession of the master brewer.

A call was sent out for a convention of master brewers and, on March 21, 1887, some 90 master brewers, most of whom were members of local associations, assembled in Chicago for the express purpose of forming a national association. Officers were elected, and the newly created association filed for a charter as a not-for-profit corporation in the State of Illinois under the name of the Master Brewers Association of the United States—frequently referred to, in those early days, as the United States Brewmaster's Association. Interestingly, so many of the brewmasters were German immigrants that the convention voted to make German the official language of the Association.

By 1910, the membership had grown to 771, and the Association had 17 affiliated "local" associations. These were called "associations"—not "districts"—at that time. They were Baltimore, Boston, Buffalo, Chicago, Cincinnati, Cleveland, Detroit, Indianapolis, Louisville, Milwaukee, New York, Northern New York, Philadelphia, Pittsburgh, San Francisco, St. Louis, and Northwestern.

After Prohibition became the law in the United States on January 16, 1920, the president of the Association, Robert Weigel, was able to hold the organization together against the odds, until his death in 1926. In 1932, sensing that Prohibition was almost over, the Association held its 29th convention in Detroit and subsequently revitalized old districts and formed new ones. The proposal in Congress of the 21st Amendment on February 20, 1933, signaled the official beginning of the end of Prohibition. That same year, the Association's 1933 Convention and Exposition was held in the city where it was founded, Chicago, which incidentally was also the venue for that year's Century of Progress International Exposition (the "World's Fair"). Prohibition finally ended on December 5, 1933, which was 1 day after Utah, Ohio, and Pennsylvania ratified the 21st Amendment. See PROHIBITION.

The organization's name was changed to "Master Brewers Association of America" at the 1934 Convention in New York. With that name change, the Association became international in scope. It then began giving serious thought to the main purpose for its existence—"technical and scientific inquiry relating to the brewing industry and profession"—and at the 1935 Convention, the Association presented three technical sessions on brewing materials, brewing practice, and ale production. In 1937, at its 50th anniversary convention in Milwaukee, the Association presented its first machinery and equipment exposition. By the time of the 1941 Convention in Baltimore, the work of the Association had increased to such an extent that it was decided that the organization needed a paid executive secretary. From 1942 to 1945 wartime production problems dominated the discussions. At its first postwar business meeting in St. Louis in 1946, the Association presented the first edition of the book *The Practical Brewer*.

The Association continued to flourish and held its first convention outside of the United States in Montreal in 1961. Another great step forward was the 1964 publication of the magazine *Technical Quarterly*. In 1965, the MBAA created the position of technical director.

The MBAA's name was changed to Master Brewers Association of the Americas in 1976 to better reflect the growing international membership of the Association. The second edition of the *Practical Brewer* was published in 1977 and, in 1984, the first edition of the book *Beer Packaging*. The MBAA has cooperative agreements with the American Society of Brewing Chemists (ASBC), with the Institute of Brewing and Distilling (IBD) in the UK, and with the Brewers Association. See AMERICAN SOCIETY OF BREWING CHEMISTS (ASBC) and INSTITUTE OF BREWING & DISTILLING. The MBAA, together with the ASBC, the IBD, the Brewery Convention of Japan, and the European Brewery Convention, sponsors the World Brewing Congress, which is held every 4 years.

Today, the MBAA has more than 2,200 members and is dedicated to providing technical and practical knowledge to all segments of the brewing industry for the continued improvement of products, procedures, and processes, from raw materials through packaging to consumption. It does so by offering professional development education and support, by identifying and communicating technical information and innovation, and by enhancing awareness of emerging issues. Beside holding two courses at the University of Wisconsin each year—the Brewing & Malting course in the spring and the Beer Packaging course in the fall—the Association sponsors pre- and postevent courses at its yearly convention. MBAA members come from all parts of the international brewing industry, from major brewers to pub brewers, to people working in allied professions, and a culture of volunteerism and cooperation exists within its ranks.

Master Brewers Association of the Americas. http://www.mbaa.com/ (accessed May 2, 2011).

Ray Klimovitz

maturation includes all transformations between the end of primary fermentation and the removal of yeast from the beer in preparation for packaging. Although most beer fermentations are technically complete within 3 to 10 days, the vast majority of beers are not yet ready to drink when the yeast finishes its primary work of metabolizing sugars. This is because fermentations tend to produce flavors that are considered undesirable in finished beer. For this reason, beer must undergo some form of maturation to become palatable. Maturation is also referred to variously as conditioning, lagering, and aging.

In traditional brewing practices fermentation and maturation are considered separate steps, but in reality there is significant overlap between the two. Maturation involves many biochemical, chemical, and physical reactions, many of which are not completely understood and elucidated. Vicinal diketones (VDKs, such as buttery-tasting diacetyl and honey-like pentanedione), hydrogen sulfide (rotten eggs), and acetaldehyde (green apples) are primarily responsible for undesirable flavors at the end of primary fermentation. Immature beer is often referred to as "green beer" because it sometimes has the aroma of green apples, the result of elevated levels of acetaldehyde. See GREEN BEER. During maturation, all of these undesirable compounds are reduced, either by the continuing action of the yeast or by other organic chemical pathways.

In a traditional two-vessel process, lager beers are transferred following primary fermentation and cooling (to approximately 0°C–4°C (32°F–29.2°F]), into a separate vessel, where residual sugars (maltotriose and sometimes maltose) are slowly fermented. At the same time, off-flavors are reduced, and the beer becomes carbonated as the yeast continues to give off carbon dioxide. Sometimes kräusening, the addition of a small proportion of fermenting beer, is performed before the beer is transferred to a lagering (cold storage) vessel. See KRÄUSENING. The introduction of active yeast during this process can help the beer mature more quickly and produce vigorous natural carbonation. Cold-fermented beers tend to show more "green" flavors at the end of primary fermentation than do warm-fermented beers—thus the need for the weeks of cold maturation referred to as "lagering."

Ales are traditionally conditioned by relatively warm storage, usually by holding the beer at 10°C–20°C (50°F–68°F). Because most ale yeasts act quickly at warm temperatures, this storage period can be quite short, and many warm-fermented beers are ready to package within 14 days of brewing. In the UK cask-conditioned ales are traditionally matured (conditioned) unfiltered in the cask in the cellar of the retail outlet (bar or public house). Continuing fermentation in the cask gives the beer a light natural carbonation. Isinglass (collagen) is used to adsorb the yeast and other solid material (protein–polyphenol complexes) and settle them to the bottom of the cask, clarifying the beer before service. Bottle-conditioned beers undergo a secondary fermentation in the bottle. This produces carbonation, but these beers normally require further maturation in the bottle before the beer can be released for sale.

The use of secondary maturation vessels can be expensive and cumbersome, and many breweries now ferment and mature beer in the cylindroconical vessels widely known as Unitanks. These tanks employ their own chilling jackets, obviating the need to send beer into another vessel in a cold cellar. The cone-shaped bottoms of the tanks allow easy removal of the sedimented yeast.

There have been a number of attempts by large breweries to develop continuous systems for the brewing process, including continuous maturation. A continuous maturation process has been developed using immobilized yeast cells for accelerated beer maturation. Yeast cells are immobilized on DEAE cellulose particles or glass beads. To achieve rapid reduction of diacetyl in the immature beer, the original fermentation yeast is removed by centrifugation. This clarified immature beer is heat treated (90°C [194°F] for 7 to 8 min) to convert all of the diacetyl precursor (alpha acetolactate) to diacetyl. Care must be taken to prevent oxygen uptake. After the beer is heat treated, it is rechilled and then slowly flowed through a packed bed column containing immobilized yeast cells. See IMMOBILIZED YEAST REACTOR. These yeast cells complete the conversion of buttery diacetyl into flavorless acetoin and butanediol. In addition, other flavor maturation processes occur in a series of undefined reactions. Although brewers have debated whether this practice produces the highest beer quality, it does reduce maturation times from a matter of weeks to a mere 2 h. Some large breweries use their immobilized yeast systems only during the warm summer months when demand is high. By this method commercially acceptable "lager" beer can be produced in as little as 10 days.

See also FERMENTATION.

Munroe, J. H. "Aging and finishing." In *Handbook of brewing*, ed. F. G. Priest and G. G. Stewart, 525–50. New York: Taylor & Francis, 2006.

Quain, David, and Ian Smith. "The long and short of maturation." *Brewer's Guardian* 138 (2009): 56–61.

Graham G. Stewart

Maytag, Fritz (b. 1937), was among the first pioneers of the modern American craft brewing movement. In the summer of 1965, 28-year-old Maytag, an Iowan liberal arts Stanford graduate and great-grandson of the founder of the famed appliance company, often lunched at the Old Spaghetti Factory in North Beach, San Francisco, where he discovered that the brewer of his favorite beer, Anchor Steam, was about to go "belly up." See ANCHOR BREWING COMPANY. On venturing to the brewery and finding a facility that was, in Maytag's own words, "medieval," he nonetheless became enchanted and purchased 51% of the business on September 24, 1965. In 1969 he became the sole owner and proceeded to reinvigorate the company and its flagship brand. He started bottling the beer and launched a series of new beer brands, notably Anchor Porter, Liberty Ale, and Old Foghorn. He also produced the first of his celebrated Christmas ales, which differ every year and have closely guarded recipes. The brewery moved in 1977 to an erstwhile coffee roastery on Potrero Hill.

Maytag founded the Anchor Distilling Company in 1993, whose products include the single-malt rye whiskey Old Potrero and Junipero Gin. He owns the York Creek vineyards, having developed an interest in wine during his time doing humanitarian work in Chile. To all of these he brings the same philosophy of quality and a spirit of helping others.

In May 2010 Fritz Maytag sold the Anchor Brewing Company to The Griffin Group.

Charles W. Bamforth

melanoidins are brown and flavorsome pigments found in malts and malt products. Their structure varies and, in general, melanoidins from darker malts have higher molecular weights than those from pale malts (which are usually more aromatic). The structure of these brown pigments is largely unknown, but they are not the same as the melanins formed in some biological systems by the action of polyphenol oxidase on a substrate such as tyrosine. The formation of melanoidins is not catalyzed by enzymes, and most reactions do not require the presence of oxygen. All are formed by a series of complex processes called Maillard reactions (after the French chemist) and most of these are still imperfectly understood.

What we do know, however, is that reducing sugars interact with amino compounds (e.g., amino acids, simple peptides) to initially yield Schiff bases. These give rise to aldosamines and ketosamines by Amadori rearrangements. The latter may condense with another sugar molecule to form diketosamines, which are unstable and break down to give a range of products including hydroxymethylfurfural and reductones, and some of these products interact and polymerize to melanoidins. Reductones are useful because they consume oxygen and thus stabilize beer.

Melanoidin-producing (browning) reactions first occur during malt kilning and are then carried on during wort boiling. In malt, conditions favoring melanin formation include high temperatures, high moisture levels, and high amino acid and sugar concentrations. Browning reactions are, of course, carried to an extreme in roasted malts, such as chocolate, and in caramels. Because of the above-mentioned Maillard reactions, reducing sugar and amino nitrogen levels will, of course, be reduced during malt kilning and wort boiling. Flavor contributions by malt melanoidins can include bitter or burned flavors but also malty, toffee-like, bready, caramel, coffee, and roasted flavors. This being the case, melanoidins form a basis for the flavor profiles of many beer styles and are also among the major differences between flavors and aromas found in wine and those found in beer.

Briggs, D. E., J. S. Hough, R. Stevens, and T. W. Young. "Malt and sweet wort." In *Malting and brewing science,* 2nd ed. London: Chapman & Hall, 1981.

Hornsey, I. S. *Brewing*. Cambridge, UK: Royal Society of Chemistry, 1999.

Hough, J. S., D. E. Briggs, R. Stevens, and T. W. Young. "Hopped wort and beer." In *Malting and brewing science,* 2nd ed. London: Chapman & Hall, 1982.

Ian Hornsey

melibiose is a sugar that appears in the fermenting beer as the result of an enzymatic degradation of raffinose, which is a minor trisaccharide composed of galactose, glucose, and fructose units. Melibiose is the galactose–glucose disaccharide that is left over following the action of beta fructosidase on raffinose. In lagers, however, melibiose eventually disappears broken down by yeast, whereas in ales it remains intact. This is because lager yeasts develop the enzyme alpha galactosidase that catalyzes the hyrolysis of melibiose, whereas ale strains do not produce that enzyme. This makes melibiose a convenient marker sugar for determining whether a beer was fermented by a top- or a bottom-fermenting yeast strain.

Boulton, Chris, and David Quain. *Brewing yeast and fermentation*. New York: Wiley–Blackwell, 2006.

Fix, George. *Principles of brewing science*. Boulder, CO: Brewers Publications, 1989.

Reed, Gerald, and Tilak W. Nagodawithana. *Yeast technology,* 2nd ed. New York: Van Nostrand Reinhold, 1991.

Horst Dornbusch

Merlin

See BOILING.

Meux Reid & Co. began in 1775 when Richard Meux, in partnership with Mungo Murray, bought Jackson's Brewery in London. Following a major fire in 1763, the partners built new premises in the fortuitously named Liquorpond Street, which is today Clerkenwell Road. Andrew Reid, a distiller and wine and spirit merchant, joined the company in 1793, which was renamed Meux Reid. In 1816 Thomas Meux resigned from the partnership, which became Reid & Co. It took over several smaller breweries in London and the surrounding counties, but in 1898 Reid merged with the large London brewer Watney at the Stag Brewery in Pimlico along with Combe and Co. of Long Acre. The merger created a leading force in London brewing, Watney, Combe, Reid. As a result, Reid's site ceased to brew.

A member of the Meux family, Henry, built a new brewery, the Horseshoe, at the junction of Oxford Street and Tottenham Court Road. It became a major force in porter brewing in London and gained unfortunate notoriety in October 1814 when a wooden brewing vat 6.7 m (22 ft) high burst. The brewery was surrounded by streets of small houses, several of which were swept away by the deluge of beer. Eight people died as a result of drowning or intoxication.

Meux also brewed at Nine Elms in south London. In 1961 the company was sold to Friary, Holroyd and Healy's Brewery of Guildford in Surrey. The company was renamed Friary Meux but only existed as an independent brewery until 1964, when it became part of the new national group, Allied Breweries. The old Meux Horseshoe Brewery is now the site of the Dominion Theatre.

Roger Protz

Mexico, which produces one of the best recognized and top-selling beer brands in the world, has a beer history that is often surprising to foreigners.

Historically, the Mexican beer industry has been greatly influenced by German and Austrian immigrants who started breweries in Mexico during the short-lived (and, in the nearby United States, completely forgotten) reign between 1864 and 1867 of Austrian-born Mexican Emperor Maximiliano I. In the late 19th century this influence continued, and a number of distinctly Germanic breweries were founded. In particular, the Vienna lager beer style took hold in Mexico, remaining popular there long after its memory had largely faded in its native Vienna. By the early 20th century, there were more than 35 independent breweries operating in Mexico, but during the second half of the 20th century the industry went through a period of consolidation. The result of the consolidation was that two large brewing companies now dominate the Mexican brewing industry, Cervecería Cuauhtemoc Moctezuma (FEMSA Cerveza) and Grupo Modelo. The Mexican market is divided almost equally between the two, with Modelo having a slightly larger share. These two Mexican brewing companies are now in turn parts of major international beer companies; Grupo Modelo is partially owned by Anheuser-Busch InBev, and FEMSA Cerveza was bought by Heineken in early 2010 and is now called Heineken Mexico.

Cervecería Cuahtemoc Moctezuma, headquartered in Monterrey, Nuevo Leon, has six production plants. Its brands include Tecate, Carta Blanca, Sol, XX Lager, XX Amber, Bohemia, Superior, Indio, Casta, and Noche Buena. Bohemia is the company's premium brand, covering three styles—Bohemian pilsner, Vienna lager, and a seasonal wheat beer that is similar to a Belgian wit. Noche Buena is a special

A 1947 beer label depicting the Moctezuma Brewery in Orizaba, Mexico. PIKE MICROBREWERY MUSEUM, SEATTLE, WA

seasonal beer in the bock style, produced only around Christmas. Noche Buena has two meanings in Spanish. It means Christmas Eve as well as poinsettia, the typical flower of the Christmas season. Casta started out as a craft beer made by Especialidades Cerveceras, a Mexican microbrewery, which, after a few years in the market, was bought by FEMSA Cerveza, but now is no longer available.

Grupo Modelo, headquartered in Mexico City, has seven production plants. Its brands are the world-famous Corona, as well as Modelo Especial, Modelo light, Victoria, Pacifico, Negra Modelo, Leon, Montejo, Estrella, Barrilito, and Tropical light. Corona is among the top five beer brands in the world in market value. It is also the top imported beer in the United States. Negra Modelo, widely available in the United States, is based on the Vienna lager style. See VIENNA LAGER.

Although Mexico has a great variety of beer brands, it has a very limited diversity of styles. Most Mexican beers are similar to American mass-market pilsners, and most Mexicans think of beer in only two "styles" defined by color—light beers and dark beers.

That said, there is also a growing Mexican craft brewing industry, which as of 2010 was in the very early stages of development. There are fewer than 30 small craft breweries in the country, and most of these have very small brewing systems capable of producing only 1 hl (roughly 0.85 US barrels, or just under 2 kegs) per batch. Among the major craft breweries Cervecería Minerva in Guadalajara, Jalisco, produces four beer styles including the award-winning Minerva pale ale. Cervecería de Baja California in Mexicali, Baja California, makes Cucapa, a brand comprising seven beer styles. Among these are Chupacabras pale ale, an American-style pale ale, and the first Mexican barley wine. Cervecería Primus in Mexico City makes a brand called Tempus, which includes an "imperial altbier" called Tempus Doble Malta and a special-reserve beer called Tempus Reserve Especial. Also in Mexico City is Microcervecería Gourmet La Calavera, which brews eight styles of beer. Following the long-established Mexican–Germanic tradition, Cervecería BayernBrau in Puebla makes a wheat beer called weissbier.

There are also a few brewpubs in Mexico. The best known are Sierra Madre Brewing Co. in Monterrey, Nuevo León; Beer Factory in Mexico City; TJ Beer in Tijuana, Baja California; and Baja Brewing in San Jose del Cabo, Baja California Sur.

Mexico also has its own nascent professional annual beer competition called Copa Cerveza Mexico. It was first organized in 2009 by Maltas e Insumos Cerveceros, a brewing ingredients supplier, with participation by international judges, who ranked more than 50 entries from both Mexico and abroad. The competition is sanctioned by the American Beer Judge Certification Program and seems set to develop further as craft brewing takes hold.

As of today, Mexico's beer culture emphasizes the value of beer as a social drink. Beer is enjoyed at family reunions and soccer games or in restaurants and bars, but is generally not considered an everyday drink to go with meals. Mexican per-capita beer consumption is approximately 52 l per year, which is very low compared with that of many European countries, where a consumption of 100 l per capita or more is not uncommon. But Mexico is also home to several great cuisine traditions, each of which is well suited to pairing with flavorful craft beer. It is possible, therefore, that Mexico's beer future includes not only sunny beaches and clear bottles in iced buckets but also a well-developed beer culture that mirrors the developments to the north.

Jose R. Ruiz

microbes, a shortened name for microorganisms, are living organisms too small to see without a microscope. Single-cell microbes were the first living organisms on this planet. They existed alone for 3 billion years. There is more mass in microbes than in all other life forms combined.

Microbes can be plants such as green algae, animals such as dust mites, fungi such as yeast, protists such as protozoa, and the comparably simpler bacteria and archaea. The only microbes commonly associated with beer are yeasts and bacteria, although fungi do contaminate cereals and hops.

Since Roman times, a few rogue scholars believed there must be living things that were smaller than could be seen. Because this hypothesis could not be proven, the existence of these invisible organisms was rarely taken seriously. In 1675 Anton van Leeuwenhoek built his first microscope and was able to see some of these creatures for the first time. Although he was then able to prove microbes existed, it was centuries later before they were proven to make beer and bread or cause disease. In 1860 Louis Pasteur proved more definitively that not only did microbes spoil or ferment foods but also the food could be made free of these spoilage organisms by heating. This process is known today as pasteurization. See PASTEUR, LOUIS, and PASTEURIZATION. After studying anthrax bacteria, in 1876 Robert Koch was able to prove microbes were the source of certain diseases. Although there were still skeptics, the microbes were by then finally accepted into mainstream science and into the brewing profession.

Priest, F. G. *Brewing microbiology*, 3rd ed. New York: Kluwer Academic/Plenum Press, 2003.

Brian Hunt

The Carolina Brewery team in its Pittsboro, North Carolina, brewhouse, which uses a fifteen-barrel brewing system. JOSHUA WEINFELD

microbrewery, a small brewery making craft brewed beer that is largely consumed outside the brewery premises. Although different people and organizations have various ideas of where to draw the borders regarding the size limit of a microbrewery, almost everyone agrees that breweries producing less than 12,000 hl (about 10,000 US barrels) seem to fit the description. If the brewery sells the vast majority of its beer on the premises, it's usually termed a "brewpub" rather than a microbrewery, although many breweries wear both hats. Because many of these once-tiny breweries have grown over the past 30 years, the term "microbrewery" has slowly faded in favor of the term "craft brewery," particularly in the United States. Microbreweries often seem like a modern concept to non-Europeans, but the fact is that all breweries were once home breweries (the old British alehouses), brewpubs (the well-established German Bräustüberl), or what we would now call microbreweries. It was only in the 1700s that the Industrial Revolution advanced technology sufficiently to make large-scale brewing a practical and profitable enterprise. By the mid 1800s, both large and small breweries had proliferated throughout Europe and the United States.

The term "microbrewery" is of recent coinage, even if the concept is not. As small breweries started popping up in the UK in the 1970s, the word "microbrewery" came to describe the scrappy entrepreneur creating boldly flavorful new beers out of a small building or a shed. In those days, there was no small brewing equipment available, so microbrewers built systems out of old dairy equipment and bought cast-off small tanks from big brewers. The Grundy tank, a small, squat vessel designed by large breweries to be serving tanks for big city pubs, became the mainstay of many small breweries. See GRUNDY TANKS. They held 5 UK barrels of beer (about 7 US barrels) and could be used as fermenters, conditioning tanks, bright tanks, or all three. Better yet, the big brewers were phasing them out, and they were therefore cheap. People built their own mash tuns or contracted welders to make them. In the early days, yeast was usually borrowed from other breweries or bought in dried form, but commercial yeast banks soon provided a range of different yeasts for brewers to work with. See YEAST BANK. The brewer himself was often a homebrewer who had gotten fired up by the idea that he could brew something truly special. It took galvanizing will to prove it, but many rose to the challenge. The British microbrewer was largely producing "real ale," a term coined by the nascent Campaign for Real Ale (CAMRA) to describe cask-conditioned ale, Britain's national drink. As large brewers sought to phase out this delicious but inconvenient form of beer, CAMRA and microbrewers fought to bring it roaring back to life. See CAMPAIGN FOR REAL ALE (CAMRA) and CASK CONDITIONING.

The idea of the microbrewery had a particular appeal in the United States, which in the mid-1970s produced virtually nothing but golden mass market lager. Prohibition, which had brought American brewing to a halt between 1920 and 1933, crushed all the small breweries in the country and few of them ever recovered. The beer monoculture struck many people as stultifying, especially if they had been to the UK or Europe, and some of them decided that America deserved more than one kind of beer. Fritz Maytag, heir to the Maytag washing machine fortune, was first into the fray in 1965. He purchased the old Anchor Brewing Company, a brewery that was founded in the 1800s and had somehow recovered after Prohibition, but had limped into the latter half of the 20th century. The local popularity of his snappy, amber-colored, aromatic Anchor Steam Beer showed others that flavorful beer could be sold in America too. John "Jack" McAuliffe followed with New Albion brewing in Sonoma, California, in 1976, and in 1980 Ken Grossman and Paul Camusi fired the kettle at Sierra Nevada Brewing Company. President Jimmy Carter signed a bill making homebrewing legal as of February 1, 1979, an act that galvanized legions of future microbrewers. See CARTER, JAMES EARL, JR, and HOMEBREWING. The revolution was on. Eventually the West Coast of the United States and Canada became dotted with small companies manufacturing purpose-built equipment for the burgeoning American microbrewing industry.

The beer, too, was revolutionary. Most microbreweries sought to produce the exact opposite of what the big mass market breweries were making. Instead of pale yellow bland lagers, they brewed bold chocolaty stouts, snappy bitter India pale ales, and caramel-accented amber ales. Few of them brewed lagers—because cold fermentation is difficult in the home, most of these former homebrewers came to commercial brewing with little knowledge of lager brewing. In the meantime, there was a whole world of ales to brew, and Michael Jackson's seminal 1977 book *The World Guide to Beer* held the keys to that world, lovingly describing great brewing traditions from his native England and well beyond. See JACKSON, MICHAEL.

The microbrewing revolution has spawned over 1,600 breweries in the United States and about 600 in the UK, but it has also inspired craft brewing movements worldwide. From Japan to Finland to Brazil and even wine-rich Italy, the spirit of entrepreneurship and creativity that typifies the microbrewer has accelerated with a pace that has astonished even the brewers themselves. Most of these once "micro" breweries have grown, and many are not so tiny anymore, even if they are still vanishingly small when compared with the international giants of brewing. The term "microbrewery" eventually became awkward; what do you call a brewery that once brewed for just the local community, but now sends the same beer into markets throughout the country? The term "craft brewery" has therefore come to replace "microbrewery"—it describes a brewery that is still small by international standards, but makes full-flavored beers from largely traditional ingredients using traditional methods. Although the term is fading from use, the Brewers Association in the United States continues to define a microbrewery as a brewery producing less than 17,600 hl (15,000 US barrels) per year.

As the term "microbrewery" fades, however, there is a new player taking the stage—the "nanobrewery." No one has yet set out a clear definition for a nanobrewery, but most are truly tiny commercial operations brewing and selling beer in batches as small as 10–15 US gallons. As of 2011, there were probably only 50 or so nanobreweries in the United States, but many more in the planning stages. As small as nanobreweries may be, they have already caught the attention of American tax authorities, who are quick to remind them that they are not too small to pay federal excise taxes.

Garrett Oliver

micronized grains, principally wheat and barley, are used in brewing as a relatively low-cost ingredient and, in the case of wheat, can contribute to enhanced foam in the beer. Micronized grains are mashed in with the rest of the grist and their starches are converted in the mash by malt enzymes. The term "micronized" is often used synonymously with "torrefied," although the processes of micronization and torrefication differ. In micronization, the cereal grains are subjected to infrared radiation reflected from burner-heated ceramic tiles. The grains are conveyed along a vibrating bed below the ceramic tiles, which results in moisture being driven off the grains, causing the starchy endosperm of the grain to swell and soften. These softened grains can be either rolled ("flaked") immediately to create flakes and cooled or cooled directly. The micronized grains are crisp and friable (rather like "puffed wheat") and can be mixed with malted barley (which is also friable) and milled together, without the requirement for separate milling or grinding equipment, which is necessary with unprocessed, hard grains. In the torrefication process, the grain is passed through a stream of hot air at 260°C and then rolled or cooled directly. Micronized wheat is used by many brewers of traditional British ales at about 10% of the total extract level. The protein in micronized wheat is particularly useful for enhancing foam formation and retention in the beer.

Goode, D. L., and Arendt, E. K. "Developments in the supply of adjuncts for brewing." In *Brewing new technologies*, ed. C. W. Bamforth. Philadelphia: Woodhead Publishing Ltd, 2006.

George Philliskirk

mild is today a relatively low-strength, lightly hopped ale, mainly found on (most is keg or brewery-conditioned) draught in some regions of England and Wales. Despite its low alcoholic strength (around 3.0%–3.5% alcohol by volume [ABV]), it can be quite full bodied, with a sustaining fruity sweetness, sometimes primed with sugar. Most versions tend to be dark ruby brown, but they can be light colored as well. Mild has a blue-collar image, as it is seen as the industrial workers' beer, brewed for drinking in quantity. It is considered a comforting, refreshing pint after a hard day's manual labor, a malty meal in a glass.

But this meek and mild beer once ruled Britain's bars. The *Brewers' Journal* estimated that in the late 1930s mild accounted for more than three-quarters of all beer brewed in Britain. Mass Observation's detailed survey "The Pub and the People," recording working class social life in Bolton, Lancashire, in 1938, stated, "Mild is the most commonly drunk beer. It costs five pence a pint. . . . As well as mild there is best mild, penny a pint more, stronger than the common mild. It is light in color, like bitter, which is seldom drunk here." Most local breweries produced an ordinary mild and a best mild and sometimes three varieties, usually of differing colors—and little else. A landlord questioned at the time estimated that 92% of his trade was mild.

Originally "mild" had been a general term for fresh beer, brewed and sold within a few weeks, unlike the "old" stock ales kept for many months before sale. All beers were once known as mild until they had matured. And because mild did not have to be kept, it was much cheaper. Some drinkers liked to mix mild with old to improve the flavor. The porter beer style developed out of this blending habit. See PORTER.

Although mild was once the basic "running beer" of the bars, it was no weakling. In the past it flexed much more muscle, with double its strength today. James Herbert's *Art of Brewing* of 1866 gives a typical mild ale an original gravity (OG) of 1,070 (15.2°Plato), resulting in well above 6% ABV. In 1880 Chancellor of the Exchequer Gladstone estimated that the average OG of mild was 1,057.

Even in porter-saturated London, mild ale became the dominant drink during the 19th century. Mild also spread to Britain's colonies, notably New Zealand, where English-style ales rather than lager went down well in a climate similar to northern Europe, and a tradition of brewing amber-colored malty "brown" beers developed. Canadian brewer Molson was also brewing mild at its Montreal brewery in 1859, as did brewers in South Africa and Australia.

Mild's robust body was buried by the restrictions of two world wars. The British government wanted beer to become weaker, all the better to have the workforce at full strength in the armaments factories. And although it bounced back from the first conflict to around 1,040 (4%), it never recovered from the ravages of World War II and the long period of rationing that followed. With its strength slashed amid widespread complaints about wishy-washy "war beer," mild never regained its reputation.

Whitbread, which prided itself on the quality of its pale ale, rather dismissed mild in *The Brewer's Art*, published in 1948, as "the X or XX of the public bar" (the "public bar" being the part of the pub separated from the more upmarket "saloon bar"). The London brewer's book described it as "a dark, full-flavored beer brewed from malt that has been heated on the kiln to a higher temperature than the pale ale malts, thereby acquiring a characteristic, slightly burned flavor: "This beer usually has a sugar syrup known as priming added in cask . . . guaranteeing the slightly sweet palate demanded by the drinker of this type of beer. Mild ale is a draught beer brewed for quick consumption." It added that bottled brown ale was usually afiltered and carbonated mild ale.

As Britain recovered, drinkers increasingly turned to the sharper taste of bitter or the consistent promise of heavily promoted bottled and later keg beer. Mild's working-class image did not help. It was increasingly seen as a cheap old man's beer.

As sales slipped so did the quality because mild had less hops and alcoholic strength to protect it once it became a slow seller. Many darker milds were adulterated in unscrupulous pubs, the dark color disguising all manner of ruses. Breweries gradually dropped their milds—or sometimes just dropped the discredited term. McMullen's of Hertford renamed their AK Mild simply AK to boost sales.

But pockets of demand remain, notably in the northwest of England and the West Midlands, where Banks's of Wolverhampton produce Britain's best-selling mild, Banks's Original. Helped by CAMRA's Make May a Mild Month campaign, some craft breweries have had surprising success with their milds, notably Moorhouse's of Burnley with Black Cat. In South Wales, Brain's Dark of Cardiff has gone from being the brewery's best seller to becoming an award-winning niche beer. The historic Sarah Hughes Brewery at the Beacon Hotel in Tipton, near Wolverhampton, has brought back a strong blast from the past, with its famous Dark Ruby Mild at 6% ABV.

In the United States, many craft brewers have developed a respect for mild as a "sessionable" beer style, a beer that has plenty of flavor without the alcoholic wallop of many popular beer styles. Although it is rarely bottled, mild is increasingly part of the roster of the American brewpub.

Brown, Meredith. *The brewer's art*. London: Whitbread, 1948.

Cornell, Martyn. *Amber, gold, and black*. Stroud, England: The History Press, 2010.

Brian Glover

milk stout (also known as "cream stout" or "sweet stout") is a particular type of dark ale (stout) brewed with an addition of lactose, or milk sugar. The milk sugar is unfermentable by brewing yeasts and therefore contributes body and a mild sweetness to the finished beer. The milk sugar also contributes to the mouthfeel of the beer, which is often described as "creamy." Roasted malts contribute chocolate and coffee flavors, and most examples are moderately hopped.

The broad stylistic family of dark ales collectively known as "stout" evolved from the porter style that was popular in the UK in the 18th and 19th centuries. The sweeter milk stouts appeared late in the 19th century. In 1907, the Mackeson Brewery in England, owned by Whitbread (now part of the Anheuser-Busch InBev family of brands), introduced a milk stout that showed a milk churn on the label. See MACKESON. Mackeson's version, which is still brewed, is a low-alcohol beer (3% alcohol by volume [ABV]) with lactose added in powder form to the kettle, next the hops, during the wort boil. Like Mackeson, most milk stouts were relatively low-gravity beers, with most having original gravities around 10°P. After the successful introduction of Mackeson milk stout, other breweries tried their hands at milk stout, but never became major players in that specialty market.

Although it is originally a 19th-century beer style, milk stout did not gain peak popularity until after World War II. Cream stout was once touted as a healthy drink and for a time was used by both lactating mothers and athletes in training. During a period of food rationing following World War II, the British government ordered its brewers to delete the word "milk" from their labels and advertisements and refrain from using any reference to milk in their imagery because the beer did not contain actual milk.

Popularity of the style waned in the UK late in the 20th century, but outside the UK, notably in South Africa, milk stout found aficionados. The South African Breweries, for instance, introduced a 6% ABV Castle milk stout in 2003 and continues to brew it in nine African countries. American craft brewers have also revived the style in recent years, sometimes adopting the "Guinness-style" draught pour (blended nitrogen and carbon dioxide gas) to highlight the sweetness and creamy texture of the beer. Some modern brewers add the milk sugar postfermentation, sweetening the beer before packaging.

See also NITROGENATED DISPENSE.

Brewers Association. *The brewers association guide to American craft beer*. Boulder, CO: Brewers Association, 2009.
Lewis, Michael. *Stout*. Boulder, CO: Brewers Publications, 1995.

Jeff Mendel and Keith Villa

Miller Brewing Company was started by Frederick Miller in 1855. Miller was born Friedrich Eduard Johannes Müller in Riedlingen, Germany, in 1824 and emigrated to the United States in 1854. He purchased the Plank Road Brewery near Milwaukee in 1855; this became the Miller Brewing Company. Miller and his heirs ran the brewery until 1966, when it was purchased by W. R. Grace, who owned it for 3 years. In 1969 the tobacco company Philip Morris took control of Miller and ran it for 32 years, transforming it into the second largest brewer in the United States, largely through successful marketing campaigns. In 2002 the South African Breweries (SAB) purchased Miller to form a new entity, SABMiller, headquartered in London, England. See SABMILLER. By 2007 the US beer market had become highly competitive and to improve synergies, SABMiller merged their US operations with Molson Coors to form MillerCoors. See MOLSON COORS BREWING COMPANY. This company is headquartered in Chicago and its market is only in the United States and Puerto Rico, whereas SABMiller and Molson Coors remain competitors outside of this region. Some of the beer brands that Miller is most famous for include Miller Lite, Miller High Life, Miller Genuine Draft, Milwaukee's Best, and the Hamm's family of brands. The Miller brewery in Milwaukee, Wisconsin, is still considered the flagship brewery of the six former Miller Brewing Company breweries.

See also MILWAUKEE, WI.

Keith Villa

millet is small-seeded species of cereal crops or grains, widely grown around the globe for food, fodder, and beer. Millets do not form a taxonomic group, but rather a functional or agronomic one. Their major similarities are that they are small-seeded grasses grown in difficult agronomic environments—mainly those at risk of drought—in such regions as India, East and West Africa, and China, with India being the main producer of millet (over 10 million tons in 2007) and Nigeria second (over 7 million tons in 2007). The millets include species in several genera, mostly in the subfamily Panicoideae of the grass family Poaceae.

Millets are major food sources in arid and semiarid regions of the world and feature in the traditional cuisine of many others. Because millet contains minimal amounts of glucan, people with celiac disease can replace gluten-containing cereals in the diet with millet. See GLUTEN-FREE BEER. Millets are also used as bird and animal feed.

Millets are traditionally important grains and are used for brewing millet beer in some cultures. Millet beer, also known as *Bantu* beer, is an alcoholic beverage made from malted millet. This type of beer is common throughout Africa and is often served while still fermenting. Millet beer is also produced by the Tao people of Orchid Island, Taiwan along with sorghum. It is the base ingredient for the distilled liquor *rakshi* in Nepal and the indigenous alcoholic drink of the Sherpa, Tamang, and Limbu people. In Balkan countries, especially Romania and Bulgaria, millet is also used to prepare the fermented drink *boza*.

Graham G. Stewart

milling is the physical crushing of malt kernels into smaller particles in preparation for mashing and lautering. The various milling processes need to be manipulated carefully to find a balance between a grind that is too fine and one that is too coarse. See LAUTERING and MASHING. The finer the grind, the greater will be the amount of sugary wort that can be extracted from a given amount of grist. See WORT. In theory at least, finely ground malt flour yields by far the most economical extraction in the brewhouse. In practice, however, the opposite is true; the finer the grind, the more the mash will clump and become sticky, the malt husks having been pulverized along with the starchy endosperm. Pulverized husk cannot not serve to "fluff up" the grain bed for the proper rinsing of sugars out of the

The grist mill at the Hook Norton Brewery in Oxfordshire, England, dates from 1899 and is powered by a steam engine from the same year. CATH HARRIES

mash by the sparge water. See SPARGING. At the other extreme, a very coarse grind, although it would make for a well-draining grain bed in the lauter tun, would reduce the surface area of the grist that is exposed to the grain enzymes. Thus, beta-glucan, protein, and starch conversion could be deficient. See BETA-GLUCANS, PROTEINS, and STARCH. Because both excessively fine and excessively coarse grinds mean a reduction in brewhouse extract yield, the actual grind used by most brewers in the real world is a compromise between theory and practice. For optimum brewhouse efficiency and yield, therefore, the mill must be set to produce a mealy rather than chunky or floury grist, whereby the gap setting depends on many factors: the type, size, hardness, and friability of the kernels; the way the grist has been prepared for milling (wet or dry); and the type of equipment that does the milling. See DRY MILLING, FRIABILITY, HAMMER MILL, and WET MILLING. As a general rule, a combined mash–lauter tun (as is used for single temperature infusion mashes in the UK and in some small breweries elsewhere) requires a fairly coarse grind so as to avoid a poor runoff or stuck mash. A separate lauter tun can usually take a finer grind, which gives better extract efficiency; a mash filter can take an almost floury grind. A mash filter is thus by far the most efficient wort-extraction device, but it is also the most expensive, which is why it is usually employed only in larger breweries. See LAUTER TUN, MASH FILTER, and MASH TUN.

Mill settings, therefore, are always a balance between two incompatible requirements, the maximization of yield and the practical workflow in a brewhouse. At the same time, they have an enormous influence on the biochemical transformations in the mash tun, on brewhouse yields, on the composition and the quality of the wort, and finally on the taste of the beer. A fine, flour-like powder—although the most desirable grind for rapid and optimal enzymatic conversions of all grist components—might also leach too many undesirable substances into the wort and beer, such as silicates, lipids, husk-derived tannins, and large-molecular proteins, which can cause deposits, hazes, and a shorter shelf life. Given the variability of the grist from one harvest year to the next, from one vendor to the next, and between the grain bills for different recipes, milling is as much of a fine art as are the other parts of the brewhouse process.

European Brewery Convention (EBC). *Milling, manual of good practice*. Nuremberg, Germany: Hans Carl Verlag, 1999.

Hough, J. S., et al. *Malting and brewing science, vol 1*. London: Chapman & Hall, Ltd., 1982.

Kunze, Wolfgang. *Technologie Brauer&Mälzer* (Technology for brewers and maltsters), 9th ed. Berlin: VLB Berlin, 2007.

Wackerbauer, K., C. Zufall, and K. Hölsher. The influence of grist from a hammer-mill on wort and beer quality. *Brauwelt International* 2 (1993).

Michael Zepf

Milwaukee, WI, is a city of about 600,000 people on the southwestern shore of Lake Michigan and is the most populous city in the state of Wisconsin. Madison is the capitol of the state, but to beer lovers Milwaukee once had the more esteemed title of "Brewing Capital of the World." In its heyday, during the post–Civil War era in the United States, the name Milwaukee became almost

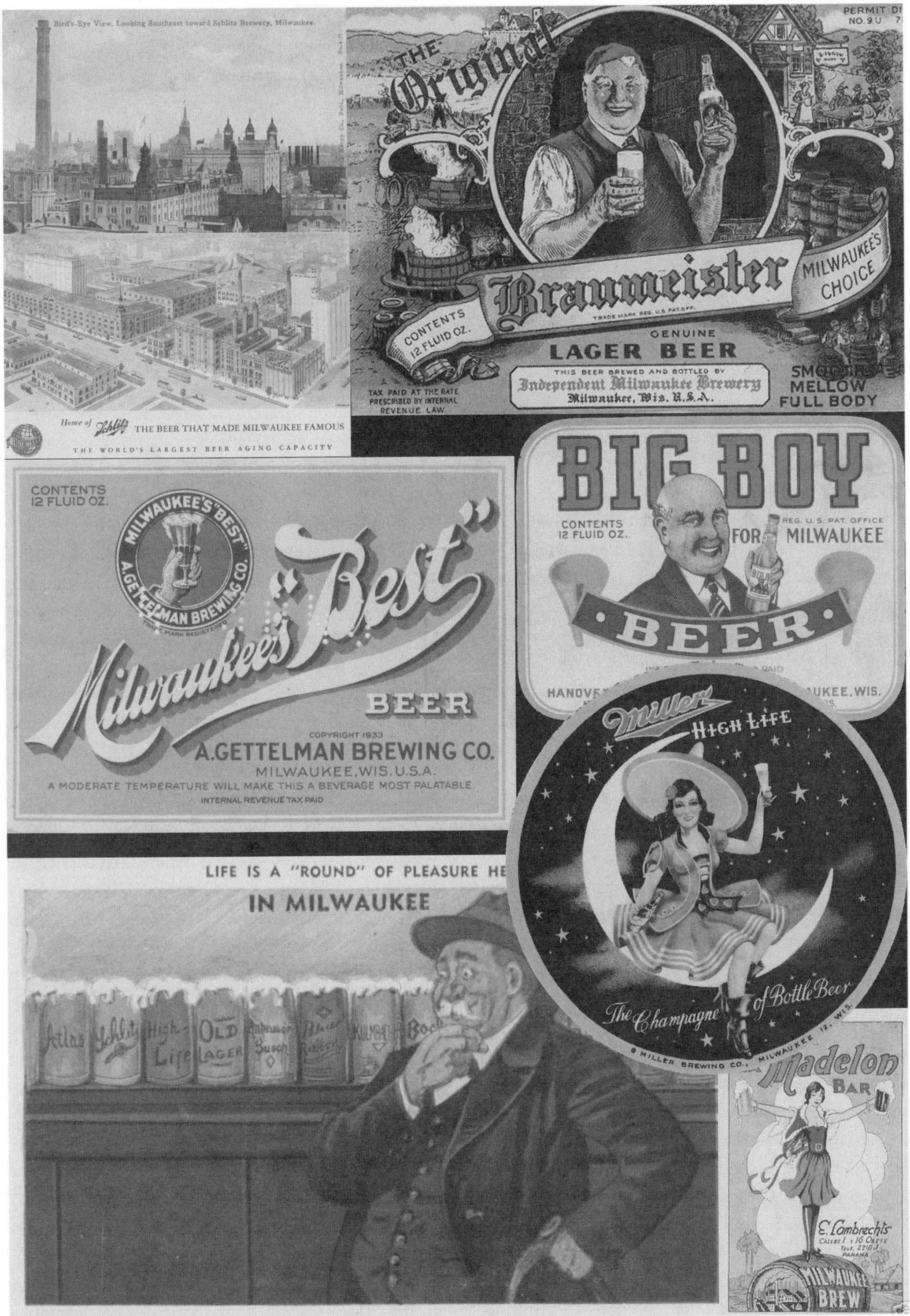

In its heyday Milwaukee was the "Brewing Capital of the World," and "Milwaukee" breweries existed all over the US and even Central America. *Clockwise from top left:* postcard, c. 1933; beer label, c. 1933; beer label, c. 1933; window decal, c. 1933; brochure, c. 1920 (Panama); postcard, 1910; beer label, c. 1933. PIKE MICROBREWERY MUSEUM, SEATTLE, WA synonymous with beer because it was home to four of the United States' largest breweries: Miller, Pabst, Schlitz, and Blatz. In those days, no other city in the world produced more beer than Milwaukee. Today, only Miller—now part of MillerCoors—and Pabst survive as testaments to the city's rich brewing heritage. There were many reasons why Milwaukee gained such importance in American brewing. One was the large number of German immigrants who settled there, starting in the 1850s. With their quest for economic opportunity and religious and political freedom they also brought with them their gusto for beer, particularly lager beer. As soon as German-speaking communities were established, breweries sprung up to meet the demand. Milwaukee's lakefront location combined with cold winters to offer a virtually inexhaustible and cheap source of ice to keep beer cold for traditional German lager brewing. It did not hurt that many of these German immigrants were experienced brewers. Milwaukee was also a major water transportation hub for Lake Michigan, with emerging railroad connections into the agricultural interior of Wisconsin and beyond. Milwaukee's location proved to be perfect for exports of beer as well as such brewing raw materials as barley, wheat, and hops. The trade in timber—essential for cooperage—flourished, too. One freak accident, the great Chicago fire of 1871, almost certainly played a role in the explosion of Milwaukee's breweries, because the Milwaukee breweries quickly filled the need for beer that the burned-out Chicago breweries could no longer meet. Soon after the fire there were regular shipments, especially of Schlitz beer, to devastated Chicago, quickly doubling the brewery's sales. It also earned the Schlitz brand the slogan, "The Beer that Made Milwaukee Famous." Once the genie of long-distance beer shipping was out of the bottle, there was no holding back the beer barons of Milwaukee, and as the Milwaukee breweries got bigger, the talk of mergers, too, became louder. In 1873, Schlitz received a buyout offer from the Tennessee brewer Bratton and Sons. It was rejected. In 1889 three Milwaukee breweries—Franz Falk, Jung, and Borchert—merged to form Falk, Jung & Borchert Brewing Co, which 4 years later was absorbed by Pabst. That same year, a British syndicate hatched a plan to combine Schlitz, Pabst, and Blatz, which Schlitz and Pabst, Milwaukee's two leading breweries at the time, declined. Subsequently, Blatz merged with Milwaukee and Chicago Breweries. In 1902, Schlitz reached the million-barrel-per-year mark (roughly 1.17 million hl), surpassing Pabst as the biggest brewery in the United States. By that time, Milwaukee breweries had become a cornerstone of the Wisconsin economy—as employers, consumers of agricultural raw materials and timber, and sources of spent grain for livestock. Yet, even Wisconsin was not spared the zeal and fervor of the evolving national temperance movement, which became the symbol of an underlying cultural struggle between the state's more ascetic and usually Protestant Anglo-Saxons and the more gregarious and often Catholic Germans. But it took the rise of anti-German sentiment during World War I to eventually put the teetotaling forces over the top nationally. Prohibition, mandated by the Volstead Act of 1919, was devastating for Milwaukee and, not surprisingly, Wisconsin became one of the early and leading states agitating for its repeal. Already in 1926, Wisconsin voters passed a Prohibition-overriding referendum that legalized the manufacture and sale of beer with 2.75% alcohol; 3 years later, they repealed the entire enforcement provisions of Prohibition. Sensing the political winds in Wisconsin, one of its Senators, John J. Blaine, drafted a constitutional amendment for the national repeal of Prohibition, which, after some modifications, was ratified on December 5, 1933, as the Twenty-First Amendment. With the end of Prohibition, many of the Milwaukee breweries sprang back to life, and, after World War II, beers from such brewers as Schlitz, Pabst, Miller, and Stroh became firmly established national brands. But their beers also became very similar, which meant that competition among the big American breweries moved more from actual flavor differentiation to cost cutting. Many breweries also sought salvation in the production of so-called value-priced beers, like Schlitz's Old Milwaukee, introduced in 1955. By the early 1970s, Miller Brewing Company had become a wholly owned subsidiary of tobacco giant Philip Morris, whereas Schlitz became the first victim of the new focus on cheapness. As Schlitz experimented with higher fermentation temperatures and continuous fermentation methods, searching for a faster, more cost-effective throughput of beer through its tanks, it also inadvertently changed its flagship beer. The taste of the beer was different, its stability became suspect, and the brewery went into decline. See CONTINUOUS FERMENTATION. By 1976, Schlitz had dropped to second place in volume behind Anheuser-Busch, and by 1982, it was absorbed as just a shadow of its former self by the Stroh Brewery Company of Detroit, Michigan. As discounting and price promotions by the big national brewers continued, the decline of America's erstwhile unassailable brewing capital could not be stopped. By 2002, even Miller, whose market share had benefited the most from smaller breweries losing ground, was acquired from Philip Morris by South African Breweries. Then, in 2006, the once mighty Pabst Brewing Company closed its Milwaukee production facility and moved its headquarters to Woodridge, Illinois. Two years later, Miller was merged with Coors into MillerCoors. Today, several of the beer brands that once made Milwaukee indeed famous, including Schlitz and Pabst, are now owned by a financial holding company and are brewed under contract, in an ironic twist, by MillerCoors. Milwaukee now enjoys a resurgent craft beer culture led by breweries such as the Sprecher and Lakefront breweries as the buildings of Milwaukee's old brewing giants are quietly converted to condominiums and shopping centers.

Miller, Carl H. *Why Milwaukee*? http://www.beerhistory.com/library/holdings/milwaukee.shtml (accessed October 10, 2010).

Miller, Carl H. *The rise of beer barons*. http://www.beerhistory.com/library/holdings/beerbarons.shtml (accessed October 10, 2010).

Miller Brewing Company. http://www.fundinguniverse.com/company-histories/Miller-Brewing-Company-Company-History.html (accessed October 10, 2010).

Proud history. http://www.millercoors.com/who-we-are/miller-coors-history.aspx (accessed October 10, 2010).

Stephen J. Pittman and Horst Dornbusch

mint, a group of highly aromatic flowering perennial herbs within the genus Mentha and the family Lamiaceae. It spreads via seeds and fleshy rhizomes and grows on humid soils, where it is invasive. Mint originated in the Mediterranean and southwestern Asian regions and is today cultivated internationally, particularly for cooking. There are more than 25 varieties, each with distinctive and distinguishable aromatic qualities. The oil of the herb has a strong aroma and palate presence, and it is used in candies, toothpaste, and other commodities. Mint has a long tradition of use in herbal medicine and has been used in medicinal beers as well. In modern brewing, mint has found little commercial application, although some craft breweries have used it to make some creative and flavorful beers. Mint is more widely used among amateur brewers, who often combine its flavors with those of roasted malts (and sometimes chocolate) to create "mint stouts" and "mint porters." Other interesting applications have combined mint with its partners in cuisine, such as lemongrass. There are various methods of use, and although dried leaves are available, fresh leaves are generally preferred. These can be boiled briefly in water to make an extract to add to the wort, boiled directly in the wort, or added postfermentation as with dry hops. Commercial mint oil preparations are widely available but rarely used in brewing.

See also HERBS.

Per Kølster and Garrett Oliver

mixed-gas dispense is the use of a blend of gases (usually nitrogen [N_2] and carbon dioxide [CO_2]) to serve draught beer. There are two reasons mixed gases are used to dispense beer: either because the beer comes from the brewery with a mixture of N_2 and CO_2 already dissolved in the beer (as is the case with Guinness and other nitrogenated beers) or because extra pressure is required to push beer from the cellar through a very long draught line to the tap.

The physical principle at play in both cases is called Dalton's law, which requires that different gasses in a keg of beer must behave independently of each other. In the case of a nitrogenated beer such as draught Guinness, mixed-gas dispensing is necessary because dispensing a keg of nitrogenated beer with pure CO_2 would cause the N_2 dissolved in the nitrogenated beer to diffuse out of the beer and into the headspace of the keg as if there were no pressure in the headspace at all. The N_2 in the beer would essentially "ignore" the CO_2 in the headspace and diffuse out of the beer until equilibrium was reached between the amount of N_2 dissolved in the beer and the amount of pressure from N_2 in the headspace. As the N_2 left the beer, the CO_2 would likewise diffuse into solution through the same principle. It seems counterintuitive to many people, but the fact is that although the pressure of any gas can be used to physically push a liquid from the keg to the tap, CO_2 pressure is unable to hold nitrogen in solution and vice versa.

The same effect can be noted when dispensing normally carbonated beer with a 75/25 blend of N_2 and CO_2 widely known as "beer gas" or "G-mix" (where the "G" stands for "Guinness"). In this case, normally carbonated beer will lose CO_2 into the headspace and eventually go somewhat flat, except under extreme pressures. If the beer is dispensed to the bar with 20 lb of total pressure, the 75/25 ratio of the gas means that the gas exerts 15 lb of *N_2 pressure*, but only 5 lb of *CO_2 pressure*. The portion of this total pressure for which one gas is responsible is referred to as that gas's partial pressure. See DALTON'S LAW.

Most normally carbonated beer requires 12–15 lb of CO_2 pressure to maintain proper carbonation, but achieving this with a mixed gas containing only 25% CO_2 would require 48–60 lb of total pressure, which is too high for most systems to withstand. At more normal dispensing pressures, normally carbonated beer dispensed with G-mix eventually falls to the same reduced level of carbonation as draught Guinness—the beer the gas was actually meant for in the first place. A failure to understand this basic principle causes many bars and restaurants to end up serving undercarbonated draught beer because they have a mistaken impression that they can serve all of their beers with the same gas blend.

However, a commercial gas blender can be used to achieve customized N_2 to CO_2 ratios, which is useful for pushing beer through long-draw draught systems at a higher total pressure while maintaining appropriate carbonation. To do this, the total pressure in the keg is increased by increasing the partial pressure of N_2 while maintaining a constant partial pressure of CO_2. Thus, an increasing ratio of N_2 to CO_2 will yield higher dispensing pressures without bringing higher CO_2 pressure to bear, thereby avoiding overcarbonation of the keg of beer. Gas blending tends to save establishments money because preblended gas is more expensive than buying the gas separately. Also, the ability to maintain proper carbonation results in happier customers, better beer sales, and less waste.

See also CARBONATION, DRAUGHT BEER, and NITROGENATED BEER.

Dalton, John. On the absorption of gasses by water and other liquids. *Memoirs of the Literary and Philosophical Society of Manchester* 1 (1805): 271–87.

Nick R. Jones

Moctezuma Brewing, the Cuauhtémoc Moctezuma, was founded in 1890 in Monterrey, Nuevo Leon, Mexico. José Calderón and Don Isaac Garza led a group of founders that also included José A. Muguerza, Francisco G. Sada, and Joseph M. Schnaider. They initially invested 150,000 pesos in the creation of the brewery, which began by introducing the brand Carta Blanca to the domestic market.

The brewery found success and over the years obtained more factories, including additional brewing facilities in Tecate (1954), Toluca (1969), Guadalajara (1970), Orizaba (1985), and Navojoa (1991), which installed the most modern equipment on the market. All told, Cuauhtémoc Moctezuma's six plants produce 30,900,000 hl annually and employ over 19,000 people.

The company has enjoyed recent success in large part because of the mainstream consumption of its major US exports, Tecate and Dos Equis, the latter becoming widely known for its "Most Interesting Man in the World" campaign, which began in 2006 and went national in 2009.

In addition to their beer production, Cuauhtémoc Moctezuma has focused on creating projects with social and familial benefits for their workers and country. Some of these include the Sociedad Cuauhtémocy Famosa in 1918, the Instituto Tecnologico de Estudios Superiores de Monterrey in 1943, and the Hall of Fame for Mexican Professional Baseball in 1973.

On January 11, 2010, Heineken International announced that it would be purchasing FEMSA, the organization of which Moctezuma is a subsidiary.

BBC News. http://news.bbc.co.uk/2/hi/business/8451617.stm/ (accessed April 4, 2011).
Book Rags. http://www.bookrags.com/wiki/Cuauht%C3%A9moc_Moctezuma_Brewery/ (accessed April 4, 2011).
Cuauhtemoc Moctezuma Brewery. http://www.cuamoc.com/ (accessed April 4, 2011).
Know Your Meme. http://knowyourmeme.com/memes/the-most-interesting-man-in-the-world/ (accessed April 4, 2011).

Jonathan Horowitz

modification denotes the chemical breakdown of compounds that reside naturally in grain. The process is also known as enzymatic conversion, degradation, or solution. See ENZYMES. For brewers, the key substances in grain are starches and proteins. See PROTEINS and STARCH. In their natural state, starches and protein molecules are much too complex to be suitable for beer making. Starches are carbohydrates that occur in the form of long chains or branched tree-like cluster formations. Carbohydrates can have wide variations in complexity, from highly complex structures such as cellulose (wood), to starches proper, to less complex structures called sugars. Proteins are nitrogen-based compounds. They, too, come in large- and small-molecular form. The degree of modification, then, is the degree to which starches are converted to malt sugars; and long protein chains are split up into smaller ones, including into yeast nutrients called amino acids.

A common method of measuring modification in base malt is the Middle European Analyzing Commission for Brewing Technologies/European Brewery Convention (MEBAK/EBC) Calcofluor-Carlsberg method. This analysis relies on the progressive breakdown of beta glucan-rich endosperm cells as a correlated marker for modification. See ENDOSPERM and GLUCANS. It involves taking kernel samples from a base malt batch after kilning. The sample kernels are then cut longitudinally in half and stained with a fluorochrome solution (calcofluor), which binds with beta glucans and a green dye (called Fast Green FCF) to mask nonspecific fluorescence. When the stained kernels are inspected under ultraviolet light, the unmodified cells appear fluorescent bright blue, whereas the modified cells appear a dull blue. Each kernel in the sample is then assessed as to its percentage content of modified cells. Next, the kernels are counted in six categories of increasing modification percentages (0% to <5%; 5% to <25%; 25% to <50%; 50% to <75%; and 75% to 100%). These data are then used to compute an aggregate modification index, expressed as a percentage value, for the entire batch from which the sample was taken. The brewer will look for a modification level that suits the beer being made and the brewing technique employed. Single-temperature infusion mashes tend to require malts with high modification percentages, but brewers employing temperature-programmed mashes can use less modified malts and those using decoction can use malts that other brewers would find undermodified. See MASHING. Note that the MEBAK/EBC test is not intended for such specialty malts as Munich, caramel, or crystal.

Friability is another, albeit indirect indication of malt modification, which is the capacity of malt to be crumbled or crushed during milling. See FRIABILITY. Like modification, it is expressed as a percentage value and indicates the extent of the grain's mealiness (as opposed to hard "glassiness"). Insufficiently modified malt will be relatively less mealy than properly modified malt. An acceptable base malt should be at least 75% friable; 80% is considered good, whereas 88% is considered excellent. Friability values above 95%, on the other hand, could be an indication of structural defects of the endosperm, often caused by pest infestations.

See also DEXTRINS, DIASTASE, FRUCTOSE, GLUCOSE, MALTODEXTRINS, MALTOSE, MALTOTRIOSE, MELIBIOSE, PROTEOLYSIS, SUCROSE, and SUGAR.

Briggs, Dennis Edward. *Malts and malting*. London: Chapman & Hall, 1997.

Narziss, Ludwig. *Die Technologie der Malzbereitung* (Technology of malt preparation), 6th ed. Stuttgart, Germany: Ferdinand Enke Verlag, 1976.

Thomas Kraus-Weyermann

molasses is a thick, viscous byproduct from the processing of sugar cane or sugar beets into refined sugar. The English term, *molasses,* comes from the Portuguese word, *melaço,* which in turn is derived from the Latin word, *mel,* for honey. In the United Kingdom, molasses is often referred to as "black treacle." Molasses contains notable proportions of fructose and glucose, and usually contains about half as much sucrose as refined sugar.

Until the 1880s, molasses was the most popular sweetener in the United States, partly because it was much cheaper than refined sugar. It has a powerful and distinctive flavor and is often used in baking recipes such as gingerbread, fruitcake, cookies, toffee, baked beans, and more. Although molasses was once cheap, it no longer is, and now often costs twice as much as refined sugar.

Molasses originally arrived in the American Colonies when it was imported from the West Indies to make rum. High taxes were levied on molasses by the British via the Molasses Act of 1733.

However, the duties were widely ignored by the American Colonists, allowing it to become the ubiquitous sweetener of the era.

Due to documented shortages in raw materials for brewing in the mid-1650s, molasses was also extensively used in Colonial beers. As a result, English authorities enacted beer purity laws in an attempt to limit the use of molasses in brewing. But, due to legal loopholes, molasses was still widely used as a brewing ingredient in the American Colonies through the Revolutionary War.

Perhaps the most famous molasses beer recipe is the one that George Washington entered into his notebook in 1754. It is now preserved in the Precious Book Department of the New York Public Library. In a recipe titled "To Make Small Beer," the man who was to become the first President of the United States explained (with spelling and punctuation of the original left intact):

> Take a large siffer full of bran hops to your taste—boil these 3 hours. Then strain our 30 gall[o]n into a cooler put in 3 gall[o]n molasses while the beer is scalding hot or rather draw the molasses into the cooler. Strain the beer on it while boiling hot, let this stand till it is little more than blood warm. Then put in a quart of ye[a]st if the weather is very cold cover it over with a blank[et] let it work in the cask—Leave the bung open till it is almost done working—Bottle it that day week it was brewed.

Molasses is a key ingredient in the modern recipe formulation of Poor Richard's Ale, a beer recipe developed by Tony Simmons, founder of Pagosa Brewing Company, for the (American) Brewers Association. See BREWERS ASSOCIATION. Over 100 commercial breweries in the United States and thousands of home brewers across the globe brewed Poor Richard's Ale in celebration in 2006 on the occasion of the Benjamin Franklin Tercentenary.

Smith, Gregg. *Beer in America, the early years: 1587–1840.* Boulder, CO: Siris Books, 1998.

Trowbridge Filippone, Peggy. Molasses history: Why molasses was edged out by white sugar. http://www.homecooking.about.com/od/foodhistory/a/molasseshistory.htm (accessed December 3, 2010).

Tony Simmons

Molson Coors Brewing Company was created in 2005 with the merger of Coors Brewing Company of Colorado and the Canadian brewing giant Molson. The merger took place to create a company with an operating strength and financial scale to compete effectively as a top-five global brewer. Prior to the merger, Molson had a storied history starting with its founding in 1786 by John Molson. It showed consistent growth over the years and became very profitable. Molson merged with the Carling-O'Keefe brewery in 1989 to become one of the top five breweries in North America. In 2000 Molson expanded further by acquiring the Bavaria beer brand in Brazil. In 2002 Molson purchased the Cervejarias Kaiser brewery in Brazil.

In 1873 German immigrant Adolph Coors founded Coors Brewing Company in Golden, Colorado. The brewery grew gradually to the point where it became the largest single-site brewery in the world, producing approximately 20 million barrels of beer per annum. Coors acquired the Bass brewing facilities in the UK in 2002, but the Bass brand was acquired by InBev. After the merger of Molson and Coors, the majority of the Brazilian brewing unit was sold, leaving the company with a combined 18 breweries: 9 in the United States, 4 in Canada, and 3 in the UK, producing a total of 65 brands. The company is structured as a dual-class ownership entity, with class A and B stock shares. Class A shares hold the majority of voting rights and are majority owned by the Molson and Coors families. Class B shares have minority voting rights and are held by institutions and the general public.

See also BASS & COMPANY and COORS BREWING COMPANY.

Keith Villa

Moortgat

See DUVEL MOORTGAT.

Moravia is the eastern region in what is now the Czech Republic, sandwiched between Bohemia to the northwest and Slovakia to the southeast. It takes its name from the Morava River, a tributary of the Danube. Much of Moravia is a fertile plain that includes the Haná region, an agricultural lowland crisscrossed by seven rivers. The rich soil of Moravia produces many top-quality cereals, including corn and wheat, as well as sugar beet and hops. Its most prized crop, however, is two-row, low-protein, spring barley, about half of which, some 100,000 hectares (247,105 acres), meets the high quality standards of maltsters and brewers. One of the most famous barley strains of the region is the so-called Old-Haná agroecotype, which has become the genetic progenitor of scores of today's most popular brewing barley strains worldwide. Haná malt played a seminal role in the history of brewing when it was used as the foundation malt for the original pilsner, first brewed in 1842 by Bavarian brew master Josef Groll at the Měšťanský Pivovar (Burgher Brewery) of Plzeň (Pilsen) in neighboring Bohemia. Politically, Moravia has a turbulent history. It was first settled by Celtic tribes around 60 BCE. It was occupied by Slavic tribes in the 6th century. From the 10th century onwards, Moravia was part of Hungary, later of Austria-Hungary. At the end of World War I, in 1918, it was made part of Czechoslovakia. During World War II it was briefly part of a German protectorate. With the dissolution of Czechoslovakia in 1993, Slovakia became a separate country, and Moravia became part of the current Czech Republic.

See also CZECH REPUBLIC.

Thomas Kraus-Weyermann

Moretti Brewery, founded in 1859, is one of Italy's oldest operating breweries. The brand takes its name from Luigi Moretti, a wholesale merchant of cereals, wines, spirits, and foodstuffs, including beer. Moretti purchased much of his beer from breweries within the Austro-Hungarian Empire, a regime most Italians reviled because they occupied much of northeastern Italy. So Moretti decided it would be more profitable and patriotic to make his own beer, and he started a "beer and ice factory" in Udine, northeast of Venice. Like other breweries that sprang up in Italy in the second half of the 19th century, Moretti's was influenced by the revolution in brewing that was underway in Southern Germany, Austria, and Bohemia, which relied largely on pale malt and lager fermentation. See LAGER and MALT. He also had one factor in his favor: Udine's soft deep-well water, which was ideal for the pilsner style that had been introduced barely 2 decades earlier in Pilsen. See PILSNER. During his first year in operation, Moretti produced only about 2,500 hl (2,130 US bbl), mostly for his local markets, and his brewery grew slowly, taking about 6 decades to double its output. By the roaring 1920s, however, the Moretti Brewery suddenly took off, producing almost 32,000 hl (27,269 US bbl) in 1921. The Birra Moretti brand had gained enough momentum to carry it through the difficult 1930s, World War II, and the postwar reconstruction period. Evolving from a regional into a national Italian brewery, Moretti surpassed the 1 million hl (852,167 US bbl) mark for the first time in 1991, with the Udine plant running at the limits of its capacity. It was time to move to a larger facility, which was opened in 1992 in San Giorgio di Nogaro, 32 km (20 miles) from Udine. That year, Moretti also changed its corporate name to Castello di Udine. It had now become a sizeable enterprise, which began to attract international attention as a potential take-over target. In 1994, Moretti entered into a partnership with Canadian brewer Labatt, which itself was purchased, a year later, by Belgian brewer Interbrew, which, in turn, is now part of Anheuser-Busch InBev, the world's largest brewer. See LABATT BREWING COMPANY LTD. Moretti's indirect link to Interbrew through Canada, however, did not seem the right fit and the company was acquired in 1996 by Dutch beer giant Heineken. See HEINEKEN. Today, the Moretti brand is exported to more than 40 countries, including the United States, the UK, Canada, and Japan. The company's mainstay product is a generic international pilsner-style lager. See INTERNATIONAL PILSNER. Also in its portfolio are, among other beers, a fairly authentic bock beer called Moretti La Rossa and the malty Moretti Baffo d'Oro.

Lorenzo Dabove

Morex (barley) is a six-row malting variety. It was developed by Dr Donald Rasmusson at the University of Minnesota and released in 1978. The name Morex is derived from the barley's principal attribute—"more extract." It was so named because it produced about 2% more malt extract than did contemporary varieties. This represented a major breakthrough in breeding at the time. Morex has good resistance to the leaf disease spot blotch, and it carries the *Rpg1* gene, which gives it resistance to strains of stem rust that are currently prevalent in the United States. The parents of Morex are Cree and Bonanza. Morex is cultivated primarily in the northern Plains (Minnesota, North Dakota, and South Dakota), where between 1979 and 1991, it occupied more than 10% of the total barley acreage. It replaced the then-dominant varieties Larker and Beacon. Starting in the 1980s, it was replaced by a newer variety, Robust. Throughout the 1980s and 1990s, however, it remained the six-row quality standard for American malting and brewing, which was then established by the American Malting Barley Association, Inc. (www.ambainc.org). In this role, Morex was later replaced by Robust and eventually by Lacey and Tradition. Morex was the key variety used in many genetic studies. Some of these were directed toward an understanding of genes involved in key malting quality traits such as malt extract, diastatic power, and grain protein. Morex has also been the subject of several studies into the regulation of genes during the malting process.

Kleinhofs, A., A. Kilian, M. Saghai Maroof, R. M. Biyashev, P. M. Hayes, F. Chen, N. Lapitan, A. Fenwick, T. K. Blake, V. Kanazin, E. Ananiev, L. Dahleen, D. Kudrna, J. Bollinger, S. J. Knapp, B. Liu, M. Sorrells, M. Heun, J. D. Franckowiak, D. Hoffman, R. Skadsen, and B. J. Steffenson. A molecular, isozyme, and morphological map of the barley (Hordeum vulgare) genome. *Theoretical and Applied Genetics* 86 (1993): 705–12.

Rasmusson, D. C., and R. W. Wilcoxson. Registration of Morex barley. *Crop Science* 19 (1979): 293.

Kevin Smith

Mount Hood (hop) resulted from a 1983 cross between tetraploid (2n = 40) Hallertauer mittelfrüh and a male aroma hop of unknown parentage. See HALLERTAUER MITTELFRUEH (HOP). It was released in 1989. Mount Hood is a triploid, which means it produces nearly seedless cones even when grown in the presence of fertile males. Mount Hood is well adapted to the growing conditions of the US Pacific Northwest region, where it yields about 1,345 to 2,240 kg/ha (1,200 to 2,000 lb/acre). Mount Hood is similar to its German aroma progenitor Hallertauer Mittelfrueh. It has a nearly identical essential oil profile and, like Hallertauer mittelfrueh, contains only traces of farnesene. But it matures later in the season and has a higher yield and about twice the alpha acid content (5% to 8%). Mount Hood is a suitable substitute for so-called European Noble varieties and can be used as an efficient bittering hop as well as for its aromatic properties. Its storage characteristics are poor, however, and Mount Hood requires immediate cold storage or freezing after drying.

See also NOBLE HOPS.

Haunold, A., and G. B. Nickerson. Mt. Hood, a new American Noble-aroma hop. *Journal of the American Society of Brewing Chemists* 48 (1990): 115–18.

Haunold, A., and G. B. Nickerson. Registration of Mt. Hood hop (Reg. Nr. 16). *Crop Science* 30 (1990): 423.

Alfred Haunold

mouthfeel can be defined as the textural attributes of beer, those which produce a tactile sensation in the mouth. The sensations associated with mouthfeel are physical qualities of beer and should be considered a major attribute when evaluating beer, along with aroma and flavor. There are three key attributes recognized in the perception of mouthfeel: carbonation, fullness, and aftertaste. Carbonation is often the first attribute perceived in the mouth. It is felt as a particular sting or tingle that is linked to the amount of carbon dioxide in a beer. Bubble size and foam volume, too, are related to carbon dioxide. Beers pressurized with large volumes of nitrogen have a tight foam and tiny bubbles, which produce a creamy mouthfeel. See CARBONATION. Fullness refers to the perceived weight and flow resistance of a beer while it is being consumed. Terms used to describe fullness are density and viscosity. These are sensations associated with the body of the beer. Whereas wine contains glycerol and other compounds that promote palate fullness, beer often contains unfermentable dextrins in a similar role. These complex sugars, developed during the mashing process, can contribute mouthfeel to a beer without necessarily increasing perceived sweetness. Beers that seem to lack proper fullness might be described as "thin," whereas very full-bodied beers can range from "round" all the way up to "syrupy." "Afterfeel," the final attribute of mouthfeel, is an integral part of a beer's finish. It is associated with the lasting sensations recognized in the mouth. Such attributes as stickiness, astringency, dryness, bitterness, oiliness, or mouth-coating characteristics can leave a well-defined afterfeel that may linger. Although not well understood, mouthfeel is strongly influenced by a beer's raw materials and brewing techniques. Aside from adjustments to ingredients and technique, brewers also can use water chemistry to influence mouthfeel, adding salts such as sodium chloride to enhance a perception of body and complexity.

See also SODIUM CHLORIDE.

Bamforth, Charles. "Eyes, nose, and throat, the quality of beer." In *Beer: Tap into the art and science of brewing,* 2nd ed., 78–9. New York: Oxford University Press, 2003.

Langstaff, Susan, J.-X. Guinard, and Michael Lewis. Sensory evaluation of the mouthfeel of beer. *American Society of Brewing Chemists* 49 (1991): 54–9.

Chad Michael Yakobson

Munich is the capital and most populous city of Bavaria, the southernmost state of Germany. The German name of this city of 1.35 million inhabitants is München, which derived from the Latin and old German designation *apud Munichen,* meaning "near the monks," who are said to have founded the city, most likely in 1158. One of the key events in Munich's early rise to prominence was a bridge that Duke Henry the Lion built across the Isar River, after he had destroyed another bridge near the city of Freising, some 40 km to the north. This rerouted the all-important salt trade and the wealth that came with it through the town "near the monks." In subsequent centuries, Munich never looked back, developing into an important city in politics, culture, and, of course, beer.

Munich's brewing tradition is almost as old as the city itself. Munich's first brewery was started in 1269 by the infamous Bavarian Duke Ludwig (Louis) II "the Severe." There is nothing left of this brewery, but the next one built, founded by Augustine monks in 1294, has since become the secular Augustiner-Bräu Wagner KG, which can claim the title of the oldest continuously operating brewery within the Munich city limits. See AUGUSTINER BRÄU. Hacker-Pschorr Bräu GmbH is another Munich brewery with ancient lineage. It was established in 1417 as *Bräuhaus zum Hacker*. In 1972 Hacker merged with the Pschorr Brewery and as Hacker-Pschorr now belongs to the Paulaner Group, the other member

German postcard, c. 1920, illustrating Munich's wide array of revered breweries. The indecisive gentleman stands beside a phrase that reads, "He who has the choice, has the agony!" PIKE MICROBREWERY MUSEUM, SEATTLE, WA

of which is the Paulaner–Salvator–Thomasbräu AG. Paulaner itself was founded in 1634 by Paulaner monks who had arrived in Munich from Italy in 1627 and soon had a brewery up and running at their Cloister Neudeck ob der Au. The Löwenbräu AG & Co was founded in 1383. It now belongs to the Spaten Group, which, in turn, was acquired by InBev, now AB InBev, in 2004. The Spaten Brewery has a long tradition of innovation. Founded in 1397, it was the first brewery to come out with a märzenbier (in 1841), an oktoberfestbier (in 1871), and a helles (in 1894). In 1922, it merged with the Franziskaner weissbier brewery to take on the legal name Gabriel Sedlmayer Spaten Franziskaner Bräu KgaA.

Despite the many mergers and acquisitions in the brew industry during the past few decades, Munich has remained one of the most important beer cities in Germany and the world. Perhaps its internationally most famous brewery is the Hofbräuhaus. It was founded in 1589 as the private brewery of Bavarian Duke Wilhelm V and is now a commercial brewery and a well-known beer hall in downtown Munich. It is now owned by the State of Bavaria.

Fortuitously for beer making, Munich is located in the midst of one of the best spring barley-growing areas in Europe, as well as next to the largest contiguous hop-growing area in the world, the Hallertau, where roughly one-third of the world's hops are grown. See HALLERTAU HOP REGION. Outside Munich, in Freising, is Weihenstephan, the world's oldest continuously operating brewery, which obtained its brewing license in 1040 AD, when it was a Benedictine abbey. Today, Weihenstephan is not only a commercial brewery but also a brew university, which is part of the Technical University of Munich. See WEIHENSTEPHAN.

Of course, the most spectacular—and most raucous—manifestation of Munich's importance as an international beer center is the annual Oktoberfest. It was first held in 1810 to celebrate the wedding of Bavarian Crown Prince Ludwig of Bavaria and Princess Therese of Saxe-Hildburghausen. Today the Oktoberfest is the biggest beer party in the world, attracting some 6 to 7 million visitors over the span of some 15 days. See OKTOBERFEST.

See also BAVARIA and GERMANY.

Gerrit Blüemelhuber and Horst Dornbusch

Munich malt was first developed as a color and aroma malt by the Spaten Brewery of Munich, Germany in the late 1830s. It was dried using a then-revolutionary, indirectly fired kiln, a change from the direct-fired kilns of the day. See WHEELER, DANIEL. This allowed Spaten to make a homogeneous malt with predictable brewing characteristics. The first beer style made with the new Munich malt, in 1841, is now known as märzen, which is also the forerunner of the oktoberfestbier. Its color is in the mid-20s EBC (approximately 10 SRM, light brown), only half as dark as the standard dunkel of the day with a typical color rating in the mid-40s EBC (approximately 17–20 SRM, dark brown). Outside Vienna, incidentally, a similar malt was developed contemporaneously by the Dreher Brewery. This Vienna malt led to the Vienna lager with a color rating in the mid-30s (approximately 13°L). Munich malts are available in a broad range of colors, from a low of 12 EBC (approximately 5°L) to a high of more than 30 EBC (approximately 12°L). Unlike other aromatic malts—such as caramel, chocolate, and roasted—Munich and Vienna malts are kilned gently at perhaps 50°C to 70°C (roughly 120°F to 160°F) until the moisture content has dropped to 10% to 20% to preserve much of their starch-reducing diastatic enzymes. Any remaining moisture is then quickly driven off during a quick final curing at approximately 110°C (230°F). This initiates the melanoidin-producing Maillard reaction. Melanoidins give beer malty-sweet aromas and deep color. The retention of enzymatic power is important, because this allows Munich malt to be used as a base malt, where it can lend deep malt flavors to beers styles such as märzen.

See also BASE MALT, DUNKEL, EUROPEAN BREWERY CONVENTION (EBC), MÄRZENBIER, STANDARD REFERENCE METHOD (SRM), and VIENNA LAGER.

Thomas Kraus-Weyermann

Murphy's Brewery began in 1854, when James Jeremiah Murphy (1825–97), aided by his four brothers, sold off his distillery and undertook the purchase, for £1,300 (2,472 US dollars), of the buildings of the Cork Foundling Hospital in Cork, Ireland. Named after a local Holy Well, the site became known as the Lady's Well Brewery and began brewing in 1856 under the official name of

James J. Murphy & Co. The brewery was a rapid success and by 1861 produced 64,000 hl (54,538 US bbl) of beer, peaking at 229,000 hl (195,146 US bbl) in 1900. In its heyday, the brewery was a major competitor to Guinness and produced Murphy's porter, XX stout, and a blend of the two, called Single stout. The brewery's robust growth was protected by the tied house system, in which a duopoly in Munster Province was shared with Beamish & Crawford. See TIED HOUSE SYSTEM. A malthouse was built in 1889. This later became the brewery offices and was almost destroyed by a burst vat in 1913. Murphy's was affected by the Irish civil war because four tied pubs in Cork were destroyed by fire in 1920 through UK government action. In 1921 Murphy's was first bottled and in 1924 the first advertising campaign began. In 1953 Lt Col John Fitzjames, the last direct descendent of the founder, became chairman, retiring in 1981. In 1965 Watney Mann took a 30% share (rising to 51% in 1967) but sold to TST, the state rescue agency, in 1971 when production was down to 18,000 hl (15,339 US bbl). Murphy's went into bankruptcy in 1982 and was taken over by Heineken the following year, when the brewery was renamed Heineken Brewery Ireland Ltd. A year later Murphy's Irish red ale was developed for the export market. The first exports were to the United States in 1979.

See also BEAMISH & CRAWFORD and IRELAND.

Glenn A. Payne

myrcene is a type of essential hop oil and the most plentiful hydrocarbon of the hop oils. Like other essential oils, it develops in the hop cone's lupulin gland and is formed throughout the entire hop cone maturation phase. As the hop cone ripens, trace amounts of oxygenated compounds of the essential oil appear first. They are followed by beta caryophyllene and humulene, and finally, by myrcene. The amount of myrcene continues to rise with ripening, while the amounts of beta caryophyllene and humulene do not. The percentage of myrcene, therefore, can serve as an indicator of the hop's ripeness. The ratio of humulene to caryophyllene, on the other hand, can serve as a varietal indicator. Myrcene levels are typically 50% or more of the total oils at harvest time. In some instances, they even exceed 70%, as is often the case with such American varieties as Cascade and Centennial. See CASCADE (HOP). Myrcene has a green and freshly herbaceous aroma that is distinctively "hoppy." It has the lowest odor threshold—13 ppb—of the main hydrocarbons in hop oil, and is, therefore, the most potently aromatic. Beers that have been heavily dry-hopped with American hop varieties can have a pronounced myrcene aroma. Myrcene, however, is very volatile, which means that prolonged boiling causes virtually all of the myrcene to escape through the kettle stack, and very little remaining in the beer. The precursor to myrcene is the chemical geranyl pyrophosphate. Its oxidation, as well as its subsequent chemical rearrangements during the hop growth phase, can lead to a range of floral, fruity, and citrusy compounds. These include linalool (floral–citrusy), nerol (citrus, floral–fresh rose), geraniol (floral–rose, geranium), citral (citrus–lemon–candy like), and limonene (citrus–orange–lemon). See LINALOOL. These latter compounds are considerably more water soluble than myrcene and are, therefore, readily extracted into the finished beer.

See also HOP OILS.

Thomas Shellhammer

Narziss, Ludwig, is one of the world's most renowned brewing scientists and educators of the 20th century. He was born in Munich in 1925 and during most of his working life, for nearly 3 decades, was a leading authority in his field at the Weihenstephan Center of Life and Food Science in Freising, outside Munich. Often called the Harvard of beer, the school, part of the Technical University of Munich, is closely tied to the Bavarian state-owned brewery with which it shares its name. Following an apprenticeship at the Tucher Brewery in Nuremberg, Narziss arrived at Weihenstephan as a student in 1948. There, he received degrees in brewing science and engineering and later completed a doctorate, writing a thesis on the influence of different yeast strains on beer quality. In 1958, he became the brewmaster at Munich's Löwenbräu Brewery. But Weihenstephan didn't let Narziss stray for long. Only 6 years later he joined the faculty at Weihenstephan, taking over the chair of Brewing Technology I. While instructing students in the science of beer making and conducting research on methods in Weihenstephan's test brewery, Professor Narziss at times also served as the school's dean, once from 1968 to 1970 and again in 1990. He also made time available to be a council member of the European Brewery Convention, as well as the organization's president from 1979 to 1983. Narziss has authored and co-authored literally hundreds of papers as well as three seminal text books, *Abriss der Bierbrauerei* (An Outline of Beer Brewing) in 1972, *Die Technologie der Malzbereitung* (Technology of Malt Preparation) in 1976, and *Die Technologie der Würzebereitung* (Technology of Wort Preparation) in 1985. These books have gone through many revisions and editions and are still used as standard student textbooks today. Professor Narziss retired from Weihenstephan in 1992. He still lives in Freising and serves as Professor Emeritus at his venerable alma mater.

The Bavarian State Brewery Weihenstephan. *Weihenstephan Corporate site (video).* http://www.brauerei-weihenstephan.de/index2.html?lang=eng/ (accessed November 16, 2010).

Personal communication (Phone interview November 22, 2010).

Riedl, Veronika. *Prof. Dr. Ludwig Narziss.* http://www.ludwig-narziss.de/ (accessed November 16, 2010).

Nick Kaye

near beer. Colloquially dubbed "near beer" fermented malt beverages containing very low alcohol was the only type of "beer" that could be produced and sold legally during the dark days of Prohibition in the United States (1919–1933). By law, near beer could not contain more than one half of one percent alcohol by volume. Legally, it could not be called beer. It was a pale approximation of real beer, but it enabled many breweries to weather the difficult years when beer was banned in America.

Anheuser-Busch created a near beer brand called Bevo. Miller Brewing Company marketed Vivo, a barley-based beverage, and Milo, a wheat-based near beer. Ads for the Miller products said they lacked "only alcohol to take you back to the good old days." By 1920, the barley product was renamed Miller High Life, but consumers had no difficulty differentiating between near beer and real beer.

William Moeller, a fourth-generation German-American brewmaster who worked for Ortlieb's and Schmidt's in Philadelphia and later Brooklyn Brewery in New York, said: "A near beer is a difficult product to produce without a pronounced mealy or cooked flavor." During Prohibition, most near beers were made by brewing a low-gravity or low alcohol beer, and then boiling away the alcohol until it reached the legal level. Another technique was simply to water down a very low alcohol beer.

The standard for post-Prohibition non-alcoholic beers is the same as it was for near beers. They must not have more than one half of one percent alcohol, and they cannot be called beer. They most often are labeled "non-alcoholic malt beverage." More sophisticated techniques for brewing non-alcoholic beers have developed. The Hurlimann Brewery in Switzerland developed a non-alcoholic beer called Birell that employed a special yeast that limited alcohol yields. The beer then was hopped to mask the pronounced cereal character. Some non-alcoholic beers are made by driving off the alcohol in a vacuum, the latter lowering the boiling point and limiting the cooked character of the beer.

See also PROHIBITION.

Baron, Stanley. *Brewed in America.* Boston: Little, Brown & Co., 1962.

Okrent, Daniel. *Last call: The rise and fall of Prohibition.* New York: Simon & Schuster, 2010.

Stephen Hindy

Nelson Sauvin (hop) is a modern New Zealand variety. It was commercially released in 2000 after an extensive breeding and selection program by the Horticulture and Food Research Institute (HFRI) of New Zealand. The Lion Nathan Brewery, based in Australia and New Zealand, worked with HFRI on pilot brewing and sensory evaluation. See LION NATHAN. The sensory selection was directed toward fruity floral flavor characters. The final hop cultivar showed a unique and intense fruity flavor described as gooseberries, passion fruit, and grapefruit with hints of melon, descriptors often used for the locally grown Sauvignon Blanc wine. Grown in the Motueka Valley near Nelson, this hop with a Sauvingnon Blanc-like aroma was thus named Nelson Sauvin.

The first commercial use of the hop was in the Lion Nathan limited-edition beer Mac's Aromac in mid-2000. Nelson Sauvin is well-suited to craft beers, seasonal beers, and specialties where distinctive flavors are featured. This hop, of 13% alpha-acid content, is principally used as an aroma variety.

The fruit aroma and intensity are impactful, and judicious use or blending with other varieties is often practiced. In 2009 Japanese researchers identified some of the flavor compounds specific to Nelson Sauvin. Isobutyric esters, including 2-methylbutyl isobutyrate, influenced the green apple and/or apricot-like fruity flavor. Novel thiols, 3-sulphanyl-4-methylpentan-1-ol and 3-sulphalyl-4-methylpentyl acetate, had a grapefruit-like and/or rhubarb-like flavor similar to that found in Sauvignon Blanc.

Nelson Sauvin shoots emerge quite late, then begin growing with considerable vigor, forming into a clavate-framed vine. This club-like shape makes it quite difficult to pick.

See also NEW ZEALAND.

Beatson, R.A., K. A. Ansell, and L. T. Graham. Breeding, development and characteristics of the hop (Humulus lupulus) cultivar 'Nelson Sauvin.' *New Zealand Journal of Crop and Horticultural Science* 31 (2003): 303–09.

Takoi, K., M. Degueil, S. Shinkaruk, C. Thibon, T. Kurihara, K. Toyoshima, K. Ito, B. Bennetau, D. Dubourdieu, and T. Tominaga. Specific flavor compounds derived from Nelson Sauvin hop and synergy of these compounds. *Brewing Science* 62 (2009): July/August.

Bill Taylor

Netherlands, the is located in northwestern Europe and is bordered by the North Sea to the north and west, Belgium to the south, and Germany to the east. It has a maritime climate favorable for growing brewing barley, which takes place mainly in the southwest and northeast of the country. There are four maltings within Netherlands' borders, and the Netherlands produces approximately 4% of Europe's (and just over 1% of the world's) malt. Of this production about one third is exported to other European countries such as Germany, Belgium, Greece, and France, and the rest is used nationally. Hop farming started in Northern-Drenthe, Brabant, Limburg, and Zeeland around 1450, but over the centuries foreign competition and low prices forced

Calendar motif of a tin-glazed, 18th-century Dutch Delftware plate. The brew year has always started on the first day of October, after the hop and barley harvests are safely stored away. This is when brewers purchase raw materials and roll out barrels for the coming brew season. PRIVATE COLLECTION/© CHARLES PLANTE FINE ARTS/THE BRIDGEMAN ART LIBRARY INTERNATIONAL

most farmers to switch over to more profitable crops and it totally disappeared by 1905. Recent interest in regional produce has resurrected hobby-scale hop fields in Schijndel (2005) and introduced commercial farming in Reijmerstok (1997) in the most southern tip of south-Limburg.

Records of taxes levied on beer appear as early as 1112, although brewing was already taking place in the 11th century. Records from 1350 indicate that brewers typically used a ratio of 75% oats to 25% wheat malt to brew their beer. Barley malt appeared from 1400 onward but it took until 1550 before it made up an average of more than 25% of the typical three-grain grist. Gruit, or gruut, a mixture of bog myrtle and local herbs, was the only preservative used to flavor beer and there are records of taxation on this mixture dating from 1274. See GRUIT. This is the earliest known form of taxation in the Low Countries. See TAXES. Many cities had to apply to regional lords or clergy to get exclusive permission to collect it within their jurisdiction. From the time when the first hopped beers from the

Hanseatic League made their appearance in 1320 the use of hop steadily increased until it became common by 1450. This new style simply became known as "Hoppenbier" and the older un-hopped version as "Ael" (ale). Beer generally fell into three strength categories (in descending order): tappers beer, burgers beer, and ships beer. Ships beer and "scharbier" or "kleinbier," at 1%–2% ABV, were extremely weak untaxed beers that offered an affordable staple for everyday use. Having been boiled they were safer to drink than contaminated water. "Kuyt" or "Koyt" beer was a widely popular name that first appeared in 1358 and was used for hopped and un-hopped beers of many styles, strengths, and qualities, which varied depending on where it was brewed. Hamburg, Joopen (originally from Gdansk), and English beers were so much better in quality and so popular that import taxes of up to 75% had to be levied to protect the local brewers.

Many of the original beer styles brewed in the Netherlands disappeared with industrialization and the entrance of lager brewing in 1864. Ten years later there were 489 breweries in the Netherlands and in 1914 there were 359. The major change came in 1926 when a new law making it illegal to brew low alcohol "small" beers was passed. The result was a decimation of the remaining ale brewers who, for whatever reason, were unable to switch over to lager production. In 1930 only 148 brewers remained and the total continued to spiral down until an all-time low of 16 was reached in 1980. Together these brewers made fewer than 10 beer styles of which more than 99% sold was pilsner. See PILSNER. Heineken pilsner exported worldwide in green bottles had already become an international icon and synonymous with Dutch brewing.

The turnaround came in 1980 with the founding of beer consumer organization PINT, immediately followed by an employee buy-out of the SKOL brewery in Arcen. So many small independent brewers joined the revival that in less than 20 years the pilsner monoculture turned into a specialty beer oasis. There are now 80 breweries and contract brewers in the Netherlands that brew no fewer than 60 styles of beer. Pilsner, brewed by four multinationals, still accounts for 90% of the beer sold, but its market share continues to dwindle in favor of specialty beers.

Out of all the styles available, two remain that can be considered to be Dutch: Oud Bruin and Dort. See OUD BRUIN. Oud Bruin ("Old Brown") was a beer style that existed before the emergence of lager brewing. It was a dark low-alcoholic blend of young and aged ale that had a refreshing sweet and sour character. Only the Gulpener brewery in South-Limburg still makes an authentic version of this style, called Mestreechs Aajt. Currently made by three breweries, Dort was developed in the 1950s as a strong lager specialty. It is much stronger and sweeter than its German ("dortmunder") namesake and is more closely related to Blond Bock.

See also HOLLAND.

Derek Walsh

New Albion Brewing Company. In 1976 Jack McAuliffe, a former sailor seeking to emulate the flavorful beers encountered on his travels beyond American shores, started the New Albion Brewing Company in Sonoma, California, with partners Suzy Stern and Jane Zimmerman. Beginning in a decade which would see the number of US brewers shrink to a mere 44, New Albion, named for Sir Francis Drake's appellation for California, is considered the first American "micro" brewery.

New Albion produced ale, porter, and stout on a concatenation of 55-gallon Coca-Cola syrup drums which served as brewhouse vessels, fermenters, conditioning tanks, and bottling tanks. The malt used was procured from another pioneering craft brewer, Anchor in nearby San Francisco; the hops were Cluster and Cascade; the yeast—wherever it first came from—continues to be used at Mendocino Brewing in Hopland, and now Ukiah, just down the road. The beer was bottled by hand, the bottles labeled by a foot-operated machine, and individual 22-ounce bottles were packaged in wooden boxes, which required a $4 deposit.

It is said that the quality of New Albion's beer was somewhat inconsistent, wonderful at its best but not always at its best. The brewery closed in 1983 due to undercapitalization, as even the beer's high shelf price for the time provided insufficient cash flow back to the company.

In early 2009, in anticipation of San Francisco Beer Week, former New Albion brewer Don Barkley recreated the New Albion ale at his Napa-Smith brewery in Napa, California. It was served at events throughout the week in commemoration of the first steps made by New Albion in the history of California and US craft brewing.

Charriere-Botts, Emily. New Albion Beer revived. *Sonoma News,* Feb. 9, 2009.
Curtin, Jack. Different strokes, different coasts: How craft beer grew on either side of the country. *American Brewer,* Summer 2006.
Holl, John. "New Albion Brewing." http://www.craftbeer.com.

Dick Cantwell

New Belgium Brewing Company, an American craft brewery located in Fort Collins, Colorado, is recognized as a brewing industry leader in the promotion of environmental consciousness and sustainability.

New Belgium was opened in 1991 by Jeff Lebesch, an electrical engineer and homebrewer, and Kim Jordan, a social worker. A European bike tour which included stops at Belgian bars and breweries inspired the couple to take their homebrew operation commercial. Upon returning to Colorado, the pair began their business, with Lebesch designing and building equipment to brew beers patterned after those he experienced in Belgium. Jordan took on the business end of the brewery, handling the marketing, selling, package design, and accounting functions. In 1996 New Belgium recruited Rodenbach brewmaster Peter Bouckaert. From those humble beginnings, New Belgium has grown into the third largest American craft brewery in a matter of 18 years, with a current volume of more than 500,000 US barrels.

The New Belgium line of beers is anchored by the flagship pale ale Fat Tire but also features several beers of Belgian derivation as well as a number of innovative style varieties. These include beers such as Sunshine Wheat, Abbey Ale, Trippel, Frambozen, and the wood-conditioned Flemish-style sour red ale La Folie.

New Belgium has also gained well-deserved recognition for its sensitivity to the environmental impact of its brewing operation. New Belgium is a recognized leader in brewing industry sustainability efforts, including attaining 100% of its electricity from wind power, using evaporative coolers rather than compressors for maintaining building temperatures, recycling Colorado beetle-kill pine trees into interior woodwork, using on-site wastewater treatment, and several other sustainability initiatives.

See also ENVIRONMENTAL ISSUES.

New Belgium Brewing Company. "Follow Your Folly!" http://www.newbelgium.com/ (accessed May 19, 2010).

Jeff Mendel

Newcastle Brown Ale is a distinctive variation of a traditional English beer style that has earned worldwide popularity. The beer was released in 1927 following 3 years of development at the northern England-based Newcastle Breweries Ltd by assistant brewer Lieutenant Colonel James Herbert Porter, DSO, and chemist Archie Jones. Porter had commanded the 6th Battalion of the North Staffordshire Regiment in World War I and had studied brewing after leaving the army. He went to work in Newcastle where, in 1924, his brief was to create a popular new bottled ale using advanced production techniques. The new beer, advertised for the first time in the *Newcastle Daily Journal* on April 25, 1927, proved to be a buoyant prospect from the start, selling at a premium price of nine shillings for a dozen pint bottles. Development had been top secret and on its unveiling, Colonel Porter admitted that they had varied the recipe so much over the 3 years of trials that rivals had been thrown off the scent.

Newcastle Brown Ale was also advertised in that day's local newspaper as: "Entirely New. You have tasted nothing quite the same as this before . . . a good Brown Ale with a rich mellow flavor recalling the famous 'Audit' Ales of bygone days. It's just the right strength . . . not too heavy for summer drinking, yet with sufficient 'body' to satisfy the man who likes good Ale and knows when he gets it." (Audit Ale was a special strong beer served at university colleges on Audit Day, which marked the official inspection of the accounts drawn up at the end of a financial year.)

Newcastle Brown Ale (4.7% ABV) is full-bodied and smooth, showing restrained caramel and notes of bananas and dried fruit. Curiously, it is rarely seen on draught in the UK, where tradition demands it is served in a half-pint schooner to be regularly topped up from the bottle.

Originally it was a blend of two definite styles, a strong dark beer and a lower-alcohol amber ale, on Colonel Porter's understanding that its distinct fruitiness could not exist as a single brew, but this practice was discontinued after ongoing specialist research into raw materials and their influence showed that a stand-alone beer with indistinguishable characteristics could be produced. Newcastle Brown Ale's famous five-pointed blue star logo with its overlaid Newcastle city silhouette represents the five breweries—John Barras & Co, Carr Bros & Carr, JJ & WH Allison (two companies), and Swinburne & Co—that combined to form Newcastle Breweries Ltd in 1890. The gold medals on the label originate from the 1928 International Brewers' Exhibition in London where the beer won the Brewing Trade Review cup for best bottled beer, plus first prize for the best brown ale in a bottle.

James Porter was promoted to head brewer the following year and more than three decades later in 1962 became company chairman. Virtually every English brewery produced a version of the style, but Newcastle Brown Ale's translucent, red-to-brown hue was aimed firmly at the mainstream market, intended to rival the pale ales of Burton upon Trent that were becoming increasingly popular. See BURTON-ON-TRENT. Soon popularly dubbed "Newkie Brown," it quickly became a symbol of working class culture and was particularly associated with the shipbuilding, coal mining, armaments, and steel-forging industries that dominated the North of England at that time. Those industries are now largely gone from the area, but the beer's working class image remains, despite a brief stint as cult beer among British university students in the 1960s and 1970s. Marketers have created a much different image for Newcastle Brown Ale in most of the 40 countries to which it is exported. North America is among the beer's largest markets, and its advertising aims to cultivate an urban chic far removed from Newcastle's old shipyards. In 1996 the beer was awarded Protected Geographic Indication (PGI) by the European Union, meaning it could only be produced in Newcastle upon Tyne, its place of origin. Newcastle Brown Ale thus gained the sort of status afforded to Parma ham in Italy and Champagne in France. But in 2005, parent company Scottish & Newcastle closed its Newcastle brewery and production moved, controversially, across the River Tyne to Gateshead. See SCOTTISH & NEWCASTLE BREWERY. This was barely a two-mile shift, but it upset traditionalists and PGI status was removed.

In 2010, 2 years after Scottish & Newcastle's joint-operation take-over by Heineken and Carlsberg, the 900,000 hectoliter (766,951 US bbl) per year brewing and packaging operation was transferred to Tadcaster in North Yorkshire.

See also BROWN ALE.

Newcastle Daily Journal, April 25, 1927.

Ritchie, Berry. *Good company: The story of Scottish & Newcastle.* London: James & James, 1999.

Alastair Gilmour

New Glarus Brewing Company, an American craft brewery located in the small Swiss-flavored town of New Glarus, Wisconsin, is well known for its world-class interpretations of a wide variety of beer styles, especially its artisanal fruit beers.

New Glarus Brewing Company was founded by Dan and Deb Carey in 1993. Dan, the brewmaster, graduated from University of California–Davis with a degree in Food Science, passed the Institute of Brewing and Distilling Diploma and Master Brewer exams, worked at a small brewery in Germany, and was a production supervisor at Anheuser-Busch before starting New Glarus. Deb Carey uses her entrepreneurial experience to handle the business affairs of the brewery, including sales and marketing. She also obtained the start-up capital for the business.

New Glarus' product line is anchored by six year-round beers, the most notable of which are Wisconsin Belgian red and raspberry tart. These are both Belgian-inspired fruit beers made by traditional brewing methods using fresh fruit—Door County cherries for the Belgian Red and Oregon berries for the Raspberry Tart. The other New Glarus year-round selections are a Belgian-inspired abbey ale, a bottle conditioned farmhouse ale, a nut brown ale, and a pale ale. Several seasonal and one-off beers round out the brewery's offerings.

New Glarus' reputation as one of the finest American craft breweries is bolstered by a litany of awards at national and international competitions. The brewery has grown rapidly over the years, despite a tight geographical distribution limited largely to the surrounding few hundred miles.

New Glarus Brewing Company. "New Glarus Brewing Company." http://www.newglarusbrewing.com/ (accessed May 12, 2010).

Jeff Mendel

New York

See BROOKLYN, NEW YORK, and MANHATTAN, NEW YORK.

New Zealand, a nation of 4.3 million, shares the heritage of New Zealanders of European descent who arrived after Captain Cook in the 18th century and the indigenous minority Maori, whose Polynesian ancestors arrived around 1,000 years ago.

The first beer that we know to be brewed in New Zealand was in 1773. Captain Cook landed in Dusky Sound in the south island during his second voyage to the Pacific region. Probably because of his belief that beer was useful in fighting scurvy, he used some local botanicals, including manuka (a tree with tea-like leaves), together with molasses to make the first New Zealand brew for his thirsty crew.

There are two large brewers in the market today, Lion Nathan (owned by Kirin) and DB (owned by Asia Pacific Breweries). The main brands for Lion Nathan are Steinlager, Lion, Speight's, Canterbury, and Mac's. DB (formerly Dominion Breweries) has Heineken, Tui, DB, and Monteith's. These two historic brewers supply approximately 90% of the New Zealand market with a range of mainstream lagers, international premium beers, and local "craft-style" beers. New Zealand is notable in brewing history for the development of a continuous fermentation (CF) process pioneered by Morton Coutts of Dominion Breweries. Although both breweries used CF for a time, only DB still uses it to produce some local brands.

New Zealand has a vibrant craft beer industry with approx 50 breweries covering almost all geographies. The annual beer competition Brew NZ is growing in significance, as is the associated public event Beervana. New Zealand also has a small but active hop industry that focuses efforts on aroma varieties that find favor with craft and premium beer brewers around the world. The Nelson Sauvin hop is a recently developed New Zealand-specific variety with a vibrant fruity aroma.

See also NELSON SAUVIN (HOP).

Bill Taylor

New Zealand hops were grown at the northern end of the southern island of New Zealand shortly after the arrival of English settlers there in the mid-1800s. The country is particularly well suited for growing organic hops because many of the pests and diseases that are a problem for hops in the Northern hemisphere are not present in remote New Zealand. This greatly reduces or even eliminates the need for plant protection spraying. Most of the cultivars grown in New Zealand are a mix of European and North American genetic material. They are unique to the island country and are bred there. See GREEN BULLET (HOP), NELSON SAUVIN (HOP), PACIFIC GEM (HOP), and SOUTHERN CROSS (HOP). New Zealand grows barely 1% of the world's hops. Among craft brewers, especially in the United States and the UK, New Zealand's claim to hop fame rests largely with the distinctive passion fruit-like Nelson Sauvin, with Southern Cross gaining increasing notice as well.

Val Peacock

Ninkasi was the leading goddess of ancient Sumeria, a culture that thrived from roughly the 5th to the 3rd millennium BC in what is now part of Mesopotamia in Southern Iraq. Among the Sumerians, Ninkasi was considered the mother of all creation. Born of sparkling-fresh water—a likely reference to the rivers Tigris and Euphrates—her name meant "the lady who fills the mouth." In the world beyond, she was in charge of brewing all the beer (and possibly of making all the wine as well) for the great god En-lil and his divine entourage. On Earth, she was revered as the goddess of fertility, which, strangely, put her in charge not only of the harvest, and beer and brewing, but also of drunkenness and seduction, the passionate art of carnal love, and the cruel art of war. She was the mother of nine children, all named after intoxicating drinks or their effects. One was named "the boaster" and another "the brawler." Ninkasi lived on the fictional Mount

Sâbu, which translates into "the mount of the taverner" or "the mount of retailing." It was Ninkasi's responsibility—or, more specifically, that of her priestesses—to provide fermented beverages, especially beer, in all the temples of Sumeria, including the major religious center of Nippur, whose ruins lie some 180 km (111 mi) southwest of present-day Baghdad. Her emblem was an ear of emmer or barley, and in the spring she caused the grain to grow. Grain was at the center of Sumerian culture, and Ninkasi, its goddess, was at the center of Sumerian ritual. A *Hymn to Ninkasi* has come to us through the millenia. It consists of two Sumerian drinking songs dating from the 18th century BC. The hymn is considered one of the world's oldest pieces of literature. The first song outlines in great detail how Mesopotamian beer might have been brewed, whereas the second praises Ninkasi for providing beer drinkers with the opportunity to attain a "blissful mood," with inward joy and a "happy liver." The Sumerians are considered the first civilization to have given up their hunting and gathering ways and become sedentary. Their emphasis was more on the brewing than the martial arts. They treasured their beer and their bread, and beer was their sacred drink, a gift from the gods, to be savored for joy, worship, and peace.

See also BEER GODS.

Bienkowski, P., and A. Millard, eds. *Dictionary of the Ancient Near East.* London: British Museum Press, 2000.

Civil, M. A hymn to the beer goddess and a drinking song. In *Studies presented to A. Leo Oppenheim, June 7th 1964.* Chicago: The Oriental Institute of the University of Chicago, 1964.

Hornsey, I. S. *A history of beer and brewing.* Cambridge, UK: Royal Society of Chemistry, 2003.

Milano, L., ed. *Drinking in ancient societies: History and culture of drinking in the Ancient Near East.* Padua: Sargon srl, 1994.

Ian Hornsey

nitrogen is an element most often found in beer in its gaseous form (N_2) or as a constituent of larger molecules, such as proteins, amino acids, and nucleotides.

In its gaseous state, nitrogen is important to brewers as a plentiful and inert gas (N_2 makes up 78% of the atmosphere). N_2 is often used to purge vessels or packages of unwanted oxygen in applications varying from purging a brew kettle to avoid hot-side aeration to purging packages of hops for storage. Also, N_2 is used as an ingredient in nitrogenated beers, where it adds no flavor but produces very fine, stable bubbles (in comparison to N_2, carbon dioxide produces relatively large bubbles with a tart, acidic flavor). See NITROGENATED BEER. N_2 is usually separated from other atmospheric gasses using a nitrogen generator; the nitrogen can then be used immediately in its gaseous state or liquified for later use.

N_2 in its liquid state (LN_2), which at atmospheric pressure is between −195.8°C and −210°C (−320.8°F and −410°F), can be useful to brewers as a refrigerant for the cryogenic storage of yeast cells. Also, LN_2 can be dripped into bottles or cans before they are filled with beer. In this application, the LN_2 rapidly evaporates upon hitting the bottom of the package and subsequently purges the package of unwanted air.

In bars and restaurants, nitrogen is often part of a gas blend (with CO_2) used to drive draught systems. At normal draught system operating pressures, nitrogen is far less soluble in beer than CO_2 and therefore can be used to help push beer to the tap without concern about dissolution of nitrogen into the beer. The proper ratio of nitrogen to CO_2 will depend on temperature, pressure, and the desired carbonation level of the beer. It is worth noting that nitrogen pressure will not hold CO_2 in beer. Many draught systems that run on a gas blend containing 75% nitrogen, a blend meant for the dispense of Irish stout, will end up serving flat beer as a result.

See also FREE AMINO NITROGEN (FAN).

Kunze, Wolfgang. *Technology brewing and malting,* 3rd international ed. Berlin: VLB Berlin, 2004.

Nick R. Jones

nitrogenated beer occurs when nitrogen gas (N_2) is dissolved in the beer, usually in addition to carbon dioxide gas (CO_2). The ratio of the two gasses is typically around 70% N_2 to 30% CO_2. Although many beers are now served in nitrogenated form, nitrogenation is most closely associated with Irish stouts.

One way that nitrogenated beer can be distinguished from its normally carbonated counterpart is its creamy, persistent head of foam. Also, nitrogenated beer is notably less carbonated than most other beers and as a result has a less acidic flavor.

When a nitrogenated beer is first poured into a glass, it has a distinctive, homogenous, foamy texture. This texture is a result of the relative insolubility of nitrogen in beer (N_2 is approximately 100 times less soluble in beer than CO_2) combined with special dispensing technology. In the case of nitrogenated beer served on draught, the special dispensing technology is a restrictor plate immediately prior to the faucet. This restrictor plate is perforated by a number of small holes, which in conjunction with the sudden pressure drop from one side of the plate to the other encourage extremely small nitrogen bubbles to form. These small bubbles rise to the top of the glass much more slowly than CO_2 bubbles and sometimes even flow downward (the downward-flowing bubbles are the ones closest to the side of the glass. They eventually work their way to the middle of the glass and rise to the top). In the case of canned or bottled nitrogenated beer, the role of the restrictor plate is served by a device called a widget, which like the restrictor plate jets nitrogenated beer through several small holes. See WIDGET.

After its initial foamy stage, a nitrogenated pour will gradually stratify into an attractive glass of beer topped with a dense, creamy head (a process that can take several minutes). Customers often find the pulsating waves that form in the glass during the "settling" of the beer somewhat mesmerizing, and the image of the settling pint has been used very effectively in advertising. The almost imperceptibly small bubbles of N_2 are much more persistent than larger CO_2 bubbles, and the head that they form often lasts longer than the pint of beer itself. Nitrogen bubbles are more stable than CO_2 bubbles, partially resulting from the fact that the surrounding air is mostly nitrogen as well. Because of the creamy head and the lower CO_2 content, nitrogenated beers tend to have a creamy, smooth mouthfeel, even when the beer below is technically light or even thin.

Nitrogenated beer was first mass marketed by Guinness during its 200th anniversary celebration in 1959. Guinness originally called its invention "easy serve" and despite 3 years of research and development at first only released it in England because of concerns that the technology was not yet perfected. It was another 5 years until Guinness finally considered its new nitrogenated beer ready for release in Ireland in 1964.

For Guinness, the advent of nitrogenated beer coincided with the popularization of the use of metal kegs instead of wooden casks in the 1950s. Traditionally, draught beer was delivered to pubs in wooden casks still containing live yeast and unfermented beer. After a conditioning period, the publican would serve the beer by means of gravity or a hand pump, with air displacing the beer as it was served. See CASK CONDITIONING. When Guinness decided to switch to kegged beer, which was far easier to handle and more stable in the marketplace, they looked to duplicate the soft texture of the original. Nitrogenation approximates the product of this traditional serving technique much more closely than dispensing beer under pure CO_2 pressure, while not requiring the publican to devote as much attention to his inventory. Although beer served traditionally through casks is still quite popular in England and beer served under CO_2 pressure has become the worldwide standard, nitrogenated beer remains an important factor thanks to brands such as Guinness and Boddington's, who have developed, refined, and marketed nitrogenation. Today, even craft brewers have begun to experiment with nitrogenation, although the technique requires very high nitrogen pressures in cellar tanks. Many brewers feel that nitrogenated dispense shreds notable character from beer, particularly degrading the crisp qualities of hop bitterness. Others argue that when brewers make beers intended from the outset to be served in nitrogenated form, it is possible to offset any negative effects while taking advantage of the formation of the creamy, long-lasting foam.

Yenne, Bill. *Guinness: The 250-year quest for the perfect pint.* Hoboken, NJ: John Wiley & Sons, 2007.

Nick R. Jones

Noble hops, a term that has an undeniable ring of antiquity and distinction to it, yet is merely a marketing tag and of recent vintage at that. The term was created in the United States only sometime in the 1980s and has no technical meaning. It was meant to set apart from the world's hundreds of hop varieties a select few, venerable Continental

European ones with fairly low alpha acid and fairly high essential oil contents. These were initially the German Hallertauer Mittelfrueh, Spalter, and Tettnanger, and the Czech Saaz from the Žatec region of Bohemia. See HALLERTAUER MITTELFRUEH (HOP), SAAZ (HOP), and TETTNANGER (HOP). The term "Noble hops" has since migrated into other languages, including French (*houblons nobles*), Spanish (*lúpulos nobles*), and even German (*edelhopfen*). What ties these four varieties together, beyond their delicate, elegant, herbal, and floral aromas, is their powerful *terroir*, which is their centuries-old history of having been grown in and having adapted to their home territories. Before the emergence of their "noble" designation, these hops were often referred to just as "fine hops." Today, there is no longer any agreement as to which hops do and which do not belong into the lofty ranks of Humulus lupulus nobility. However, because there is no scientific or legal basis for adjudicating such assignations, that battle is best left for dueling marketers to settle.

Adrian Tierney-Jones

non-alcoholic "beer," also called NA, low-alcohol, near beer, small beer, or small ale, is a malt beverage with very low alcoholic content. Although the name might lead one to believe that a non-alcoholic beverage contains no measurable alcohol, this is not true. Technically speaking, there is no such thing as non-alcoholic beer because beer contains alcohol by definition. In the United States, although these products are colloquially called non-alcoholic beer, the actual labels read "non-alcoholic malt beverage" or "non-alcoholic brew." These NA products may contain up to 0.5% alcohol by volume (ABV), although there are global differences that can lead to confusion. In the United States, the term "non-intoxicating" was applied to all beverages with less than 0.5% ABV during Prohibition and has since morphed into "non-alcoholic." The U.S. Food and Drug Administration does not consider the terms "non-alcoholic" and "alcohol-free" synonymous. The term "alcohol-free" may be used in the United States only when the product contains no detectable alcohol. In the United Kingdom, alcohol-free or zero-alcohol beverages may contain measurable alcohol up to 0.05% ABV. Beverages labeled as dealcoholized, alcohol-removed, or non-alcoholic may not contain more than 0.5% ABV and those labeled low alcohol may not exceed 1.2% ABV. The European Union standard is wider than that of the United States or UK because alcohol-free applies to all beverages containing less than 0.5% ABV. Although there is no global agreement for reduced alcohol beer or wine, the worldwide codex standards for ethanol in some fruit juices, soft drinks, and baked goods are 0.3% to 1.0% ABV maximum; hence, interestingly, these products may contain equal or higher levels of alcohol derived from the use of flavoring extracts or natural fermentation than some categories of beer and wine.

There are hundreds of non-alcoholic and alcohol-free beers in the global marketplace today, currently representing less than 1% of total worldwide beer sales. Many brewers think of NA beer production and sales as part of their overall corporate citizenship effort because profitability can be lower for these products as a result of higher equipment and energy costs. In the United States, NA beers are produced exclusively by large mass-market brewers. Recently, stricter drunk-driving law enforcement and increasing awareness of the reduced calorie content of NA beers (generally half of regular alcohol beers) have resulted in higher volume sales in some markets. Spain has recently reported alcohol-free beer sales as 8% of total beer sales. Several NA beers in the global marketplace are even specifically marketed for dogs.

Alcohol can be reduced and NA beer produced by modifying many different parts of the brewing process singly or in combination, as follows: (1) limiting the malt/water ratio in mashing to yield a calculated lower original gravity and subsequent alcohol level; (2) using lower fermentable brewing materials to retain original gravity, yet yield higher finished beer dextrins with lower ethanol; (3) controlling the dextrin content by warmer infusion mashing in the 70°C–80°C (158°F–176°F) range, which inactivates heat-sensitive enzymes like beta-amylase and slows the conversion of starch dextrins to maltose, thereby lowering the fermentability of wort; (4) fermenting the "second runnings" from a stronger beer mash (e.g., Imperial or Scotch Ale); and (5) using the "cold contact" method of fermentation by pitching brewer's yeast into wort at or near freezing temperatures, effectively limiting fermentation but allowing some beer flavor development.

Beers produced in this manner are often reported as having a "worty" flavor character thought to be caused by aldehydes, such as 3-methylthiopropionaldehyde. Another modification includes (6) interrupting fermentation when the desired gravity and alcohol content are reached via pasteurization or crash cooling or removal of yeast from beer or beer from yeast as in immobilized yeast fermentations. (7) Following a normal fermentation, ethanol can be boiled from the finished beer at temperatures above ethanol's boiling point of 173.5°F (78.6°C) and below the boiling point of water for a minimum of 30 min. Some hop volatiles will be lost by boiling along with higher alcohols and aldehydes. Malt flavors and hop bitterness will remain generally unchanged as long as the beer is not allowed to "cook-on," leading to off-flavors from furfural products. (8) A more elegant but complex method involves passing the finished beer over a semipermeable membrane either under its own pressure (a form of dialysis) or pressure-boosted (reverse osmosis), where small molecules like water and ethanol are pulled away from the larger sugars, proteins, flavor, and color compounds in beer. Ethanol is then evaporated or distilled through application of low heat under a vacuum. Finally, the residual water is recombined with the beer flavor, carbohydrate, and color "soup" to make a dissected-then-reassembled NA beer. (9) Diluting finished beer with deoxygenated brewing water to the desired alcohol level as an extrapolation of the method used by high-gravity brewers is the simplest method of producing non- or lower-alcohol beer, but this method dilutes all beer color and flavor compounds concomitantly. (10) Recognizing that ethanol itself is a significant contributor to beer flavor and mouthfeel and that removal of all or some of it by any method can result in dramatic flavor changes, some flavor houses offer concoctions that claim to make NA beer taste more like real beer. Each method has its advantages and disadvantages of complexity, capital, and operational and energy costs.

See also NEAR BEER.

Kunze, W. *Technology brewing and malting*, 4th ed., pp. 437–46, 577. Berlin: VLB Berlin, 2010.

Rehberger, A. J. *The practical brewer*, pp. 596–608. Madison, WI: Master Brewers Association of the Americas, 1999.

David A. Thomas

The French Department of **Nord-Pas de Calais** is located at the "point" of France, the northernmost region that abuts the English Channel and not inconsequentially shares a border with Belgium. Nord-Pas de Calais is considered the unofficial center of specialty brewing activity in modern-day France. The region can also claim the highest per capita rate of beer consumption in France.

The area has a long history of brewing beer. The territory has been inhabited by Celts, Germanic tribes, and Saxons, all beer-drinking peoples. Geographically, the cooler northern location is well suited to growing cereal grains. As a result, beer-like beverages became, and still remain, a part of the regional identity.

Nord-Pas de Calais was once littered with small, independent farm breweries that served their own needs and those of a limited local population. Today this brewing heritage is evident in the density of breweries in the department. Most are small, consistent with history. The best known is Brasserie Duyck, producers of Jenlain Bière de Garde, with an annual production of 100,000 hl (80,000 US barrels).

Nord-Pas de Calais became the seat of a renaissance of specialty brewing activity in France in the late 1970s and 1980s. Spurred by the success of Jenlain Bière de Garde (and the growing popularity of Belgian specialty ales), other small regional breweries redefined themselves from producers of typical lager beers to guardians of French brewing tradition with noble intent and perhaps to ensure their own survival.

See also BIÈRE DE GARDE, DUYCK, BRASSERIE, FRANCE, and JENLAIN ORIGINAL FRENCH ALE.

Phil Markowski

Northdown (hop), also known as Wye Northdown, was bred at Wye College in Kent, UK, as a first-generation selection of Northern Brewer and a downy mildew-resistant German male parent. See WYE COLLEGE. It was released for commercial cultivation in 1971. Wye Northdown is a dual-purpose hop with excellent aroma and good bittering qualities, imparting a mild, clean, neutral English flavor to beer. At the time of its release, its alpha acid level at up to 10% was considered astounding for a British hop, but it has since been surpassed by the

12.5% of Wye Target. Wye Northdown is most commonly used in English ales, including porters, and can be substituted with Wye Challenger and Northern Brewer. Wye Northdown matures in early-mid season and produces moderate yields of roughly 1,500 to 1,900 kg/ha (1,338 to 1,695 lb/acre). It is fairly stable in storage. Like its male parent, it is very resistant to downy mildew, but it is susceptible to powdery mildew and verticillium wilt. Its alpha acid level is in the range of 7.5% to 10%, of which 30% to 32% are cohumulone. It beta acid level is in the range of 4.4% to 6.2%. It is rich in essential oils, of which myrcene contributes 23% to 29%, humulene 40% to 45%, caryophyllene 13% to 17%, and floral farnesene less than 1%. Northdown is not much used outside the UK, where it remains well respected.

Victoria Carollo Blake

Northern Brewer (hop) was bred by Professor E. S. Salmon at Wye College, England, in 1934. It came from the old Canterbury Golding variety crossed with a male genotype, which in turn had Brewer's Gold and an unnamed American male hop in its background. See BREWER'S GOLD (HOP) and GOLDING (HOP). Professor Salmon experimented extensively with native American hops in the early to mid 1900s and probably obtained high alpha traits from these crosses. Northern Brewer inherited pleasant aroma characteristics from its female and high alpha traits from its male parent. It was grown extensively in England and, in the 1940s, was taken to Belgium and later to Germany because of its high alpha potential and resistance to verticillium wilt. Germans referred to it as "Belgian hop" when it was planted in the Hallertau region, after the famous Hallertauer mittelfrueh had been devastated by verticillium wilt in the 1960s and early 1970s. See HALLERTAU HOP REGION and HALLERTAUER MITTELFRUEH (HOP). Northern Brewer matures early to medium early in the season, is moderately resistant to downy mildew, and is resistant to verticillium wilt. However, it is susceptible to powdery mildew. It has moderately high yields in Europe but produces poor yields in the United States. Its alpha acid level ranges from 9% to 12% and its beta acid level from 4% to 5%, and its cohumulone content averages about 25%. The essential oil levels are 50% to 60% myrcene, 25% humulene, and 8% caryophyllene. It does not contain farnesene. Its storage stability is above average. It is a dual-purpose hop, although most brewers use it as a bittering hop. Today, Northern Brewer has been largely replaced by higher-yielding cultivars with higher alpha acid values.

Burgess, A. H. *Hops*, 46. New York: Interscience Publishers, 1964.
Neve, R. A. *Hops*, 203. London: Chapman & Hall, 1991.
Salmon, E. S. *Four seedlings of the Canterbury Golding*. Kent, England: Wye College, 1944.

Alfred Haunold

Norway (officially the Kingdom of Norway), home to 4.8 million people, is a Nordic country in Northern Europe occupying the western portion of the Scandinavian Peninsula, which it shares with Sweden and part of northern Finland. Brewing has strong traditions in Norway, and since about 1200 BCE it has been very much a part of the national culture. Beer was not only a natural part of all celebrations, funerals and feasts, but it was also a part of everyday life. It is speculated by anthropologists that beer was consumed regularly in part because people ate so much salted fish and meat. Beer acted as a diuretic, aiding the body in getting rid of all excess salt.

In the 17th and 18th centuries, brewing was actually mandatory for all land owners. Failure to brew before Christmas would result in heavy fines and failure to brew for several seasons would result in loss of land and livestock. Brewing in these times was a farm house activity. Most brewing relied on malted barley, with some adding honey or berries for additional fermentables. Very often the malts had a smoky profile, and in some regions the malt was kilned with alder wood to deliberately give a distinctly smoky character. As hops did not grow well in the short, cool summers of Norway, other additives were used for flavoring. Juniper twigs were the main additive, and they were used as a false bottom in the lauter tun, but spruce shoots and a wide variety of herbs were also used in the brew kettle with great local variation.

It was only after about 1820 that commercial brewing became common in Norway. The brewing industry experienced rapid growth, partly because the authorities considered it better for people to drink beer than distilled liquor. In 1857 there were 353 breweries in Norway (and a population of 1.5 million). Fifty years later, the number was about 40, and by 1996, it was at an all-time low of seven. In the years after World War II, the decline in the number of breweries was caused mainly by larger breweries buying smaller ones and then closing them down, concentrating a growing monopoly.

The commercial brewing industry was mainly influenced by German, and later on Danish, brewing culture. Hence, the rich and diverse brewing traditions from farmhouse brewing were never brought into the commercial world. From about 1840, dark lager—including Bavarian-style dunkel and bock—dominated the Norwegian brew scene, and kept its dominance for more than a century. See DUNKEL and BOCK BEER. After World War II the breweries, which were operating in close cooperation to avoid tough competition, agreed that it would be beneficial to increase sales in the postwar tough economic situation by brewing beer with lower alcohol (cheaper) and lighter color (easier to drink as a thirst quencher). This move was highly successful. Lawmakers in 1993 made it illegal to sell beer above 4.75% alcohol in retail shops (stronger beer could only be sold through the government outlet system for alcoholic beverages, known as Vinmonopolet). This move decimated what little diversity was left in the Norwegian beer scene, and by the turn of the century, most breweries had stopped brewing anything but continental light lager, often referred to as "pils." The exception to this is the strong culture for dark Christmas beers. This tradition is still very much alive, but since sales of strong beers were moved to Vinmonopolet in 1993, the Christmas beers are now mainly at 4.5%–4.75% alcohol, instead of the traditional 6.5%.

The temperance movement has had a strong position in Norway for many years. In the 19th century there were various Protestant temperance organizations, while in the early 20th century socialist political parties and trade unions advocated temperance. This resulted in a ban on distilled spirits and fortified wines between 1915 and 1920, the formation of a government-run sales outlet system for strong alcoholic beverages in 1922 (Vinmonopolet), and significant taxes on alcohol. Taxes on beer are the absolute highest in the world. See TAXES. These factors are likely to have had an impact on beer consumption, which is almost half of what it is in Denmark, a country with a very similar culture and population. In 2008 the average Norwegian consumed 54 liters (14 US gal) of beer, while in Denmark the number was 86 liters (22 US gal).

In recent years there has been a change in the Norwegian brew scene. A small number of tiny craft breweries have started operations, and unlike their forerunners, they are focusing on beer styles and brewing techniques that have not previously been available in the country. One has to bear in mind that Norway is more Scandinavian than European, and trends and changes come later and more slowly to this corner of civilization. Still, there is a slow revolution going on. People are becoming more conscious about beer, and beer is now mentioned frequently in the media, often with a strong connection to food. There are many beer importers, with the number of imported beers growing from three to 300 in 5 years. In 2010 Norway had eight brewpubs, nine craft breweries, three contract breweries, seven regional breweries, and two large breweries.

Danish Brewers Association. http://www.bryggeriforeningen.dk/ (accessed May 2, 2011).

Statistics Norway. http://www.ssb.no/ (accessed May 2, 2011).

Kjetil Jikiun

nucleic acids are molecules that reside in cells and carry genetic information. There are two types of nucleic acids, deoxyribonucleic acid (DNA) and ribonucleic acid (RNA), both of which are polymers of small nucleotide molecules, which are called bases and are arranged in variable sequences. Adenosine, cytosine, guanine, and thymine are the bases in DNA, whereas uracil replaces thymine in RNA. The sequence of these bases is unique for each gene in DNA. Codes for the arrangement of amino acids in the protein are specified by the gene.

In yeast, DNA is a fundamental part of the chromosomes in the nucleus, whereas in bacteria, it is a simple, twisted circle in the cytoplasm. This has consequences in the growth and organization of these two microorganisms and generally results in bacteria being faster growing than yeast.

The genetics of a cell depend on the genes specified in its DNA. The genes determine which proteins may be synthesized and thus dictate the structure and activities of the cell. Mutations in DNA change the cell and thus lead to the evolution of new strains and new species. In brewing yeast, mutations occur readily and can lead to changes in flavor, fermentability, and clarity. Such mutations tend to be undesirable, but they occasionally form the basis for new and novel beers. This said, relative genetic stability is one of the most desired qualities in brewer's yeast, especially yeast that may be subject to repeated repitchings. Genetic stability holds the promise of repeatable results in healthy brewery fermentations.

Keith Thomas

Nugget (hop) is one of the earliest "superalpha" hops. It was released by Al Haunold in 1981 from the U.S. Department of Agriculture (USDA) hop breeding program in Corvallis, Oregon. Nugget originated from a 1970 cross between two USDA varieties, each with high-alpha traits. Among Nugget's prominent genetic ancestors are Brewer's Gold, Early Green, and East Kent Golding. See BREWER'S GOLD (HOP) and EAST KENT GOLDING (HOP). When grown in the Pacific Northwest of the United States, Nugget averages between 12% and 15% alpha acids, approximately 5% beta acids, and approximately 27% cohumulone. Nugget keeps well, retaining nearly 70% of its alpha acids after 6 months in storage at room temperature. The total oil content in Nugget ranges from 1.7 to 2.3 ml/100 g of dried cone weight, with myrcene averaging 54%, humulene 19.4%, and caryophyllene 8.9%. Nugget has an herbal, somewhat spicy aroma, but this is eclipsed by its bittering potential, and brewers rarely use it for aroma. The yield potential of Nugget is excellent, typically between 2,000 and 2,700 kg/ha (1,800 to 2,400 lb/acre). Nugget was actually ready for release into commercial cultivation in the late 1970s, but market forces at that time were aligned against superalpha hops. In 1981, however, a worldwide shortage of alpha acids finally provided the needed momentum for superalpha cultivars to successfully enter the market. It was then that another superalpha hop, Galena, was released as well, taking hold in Idaho.

See also GALENA (HOP) and IDAHO (SOUTHERN HOP REGION).

Haunold, A. A., S. T. Likens, G. B. Nickerson, and R. O. Hampton. Registration of Nugget hop. *Crop Science* 24 (1984): 618.

Shaun Townsend

nutmeg is a spice derived from the seed of the fruit of the evergreen tree Myristica fragrans. Long used in European cooking, nutmeg originally comes from the Moluccan "spice island" of Banda, part of Indonesia. International trade brought nutmeg to Europe as early as the 1st century AD, but the spice was rare and exceedingly expensive in Europe until the end of the 18th century. The Dutch waged a bloody campaign on Banda in 1621, seizing the island for the primary purpose of controlling nutmeg production. About 1770, French botanist Pierre Poivre established nutmeg plantings on Mauritius and the Dutch monopoly ended. The British East India Company soon spread plantations throughout the tropical areas where they traded. Today, most nutmeg is grown in Indonesia on the island of Granada in the Caribbean.

The seed of the nutmeg fruit is a marble-size ovoid actually comprising two spices—the seed itself, which is the nutmeg spice, and the seed's lacy bright-red outer covering, which is removed and becomes the sweet spice called mace. The essential oils of nutmeg are pungent and complex, containing camphenes, terpenols, the root beer–like safrole, gerianol (also a hop essential oil constituent), and other aromatic compounds. Although nutmeg is often sold as a ground powder, the essential oils are quickly oxidized after grinding, and therefore nutmeg is best when freshly grated. It can be added to wort in the kettle, usually at the very end of the boil, and is a popular spice in pumpkin ales and holiday beers. Nutmeg is best used sparingly; it is powerfully aromatic, with freshly grated nutmeg showing the greatest potency and complexity of flavor.

When used in great enough quantities, nutmeg becomes hallucinogenic and poisonous, although such quantities are never approached in normal food or beer uses.

Filippone, Peggy Trowbridge. "Nutmeg and mace history." http://homecooking.about.com/od/foodhistory/a/nutmeghistory.htm (accessed December 9, 2010).

Vaughan, John G. *The new Oxford book of food plants.* Oxford, UK: Oxford University Press, 2009.

Garrett Oliver

nutrition

See HEALTH.

oak is a hard, strong, durable, watertight wood that comes from a tree and is from the genus Quercus. There are hundreds of species of oak, which can be classified into two broad categories: red oak and white oak. Red oak is quite porous, however, and is rarely used to make oak barrels. Nearly all barrels used for wine, beer, and spirits are made from white oak.

Before there was stainless steel, oak barrels were the typical vessel in which to store and transport beer. Oak has long been favored above other woods because its structure makes it watertight and also bendable, the latter quality being crucial for the production of barrel staves. While all oak species can impart their own flavors to beer, until recently this aspect of oak was rarely desired. At some European and English breweries, English, German, and Polish oak barrels were often used but did not impart much oak character. In some cases, the barrels were lined with pitch (a dark resin extracted from the conifer tree) which protected the beer from contamination. In Belgium, the lambic breweries have always procured used oak wine barrels from France in which to age their beer. Large oak vats were once the norm for fermentation and storage of beer in England, a fact made notorious when one of these burst in London in 1814, killing eight people. See MEUX REID & CO. In the United States, the historic Ballantine Brewery also aged their beer in oak barrels for up to 1 year. See BALLANTINE IPA. Aging beer in oak barrels eventually took a back seat to stainless steel tanks until a recently renewed interest in barrel-aged beers.

As craft breweries became more popular, especially in the United States, many brewers have looked for new and unique ways to enhance the flavor of their beers. They quickly discovered that the use of used oak barrels that once housed bourbon, whiskey, wine, or, to a lesser extent, brandy, sherry, or port, could produce the bold flavors they sought. Bourbon and whiskey barrels are more often used for bigger styles of beer such as stout and barley wine. French oak is known for its fine mild character and is preferred by many wine producers. As a result, it tends to be much more expensive than American oak. Charred American white oak is used for the production of bourbon barrels, and by law a bourbon barrel can only be used once to produce bourbon whiskey. As a result, the American bourbon distillers produce thousands of once-used oak barrels every year as a by-product. While most of these barrels go on to second uses aging everything from Scotch whisky to high-end tequila to Tabasco sauce, an increasing number end up in the hands of American craft brewers. Bourbon barrels are by far the most common oak barrels used by brewers in the United States. The cost of these barrels has risen dramatically over the past few years due to increased interest from brewers but also from whiskey producers in countries with quickly developing economies, particularly China and India.

The oak itself contains a number of flavors, and those flavors differ widely depending on the oak species, the growing area, and how the wood has been treated. A range of compounds known as lactones are responsible for many of the aromas and flavors we associate with oak. These are derived from lipids within the wood and tend to impart a coconut-like flavor, especially in American oak. Bourbon barrels, therefore, tend to have plenty of

Before stainless steel, oak barrels were typically used to store and transport beer. PHOTOGRAPH BY DENTON TILLMAN

lactone character, and each bourbon producer will choose wood depending largely on its flavor profile. A prevalent secondary characteristic is the vanilla-like aromatics of the compound vanillin, an aldehyde that can be pleasant at low levels but can easily overpower other flavors. Beyond this are the aromatics of volatile phenols such as eugenol (clove-like) and 4-vinyl guiacol (cinnamon-like), and floral, fruity terpenes. Oak also contains astringent tannins, which can leach into beer over time and possibly clash with hop bitterness.

When using newly acquired used bourbon or whiskey barrels, brewers can choose to rinse them or rack the beer directly on top of any leftover liquid. Rinsing or cleaning the barrel first will lead to softer, more subtle flavors. However, it is more common for brewers to rack beer right into the barrel, and if there is a liter or two of the previous tenant still in the barrel, all the better for sanitation if that tenant was a whiskey. If the latter technique is chosen, the brewer may opt to blend some non-barrel aged beer back into the finished beer to cut the strength of the barrel aged beer and soften the overall character.

Brewers using wine barrels often use them in conjunction with the "wild" yeast Brettanomyces and bacteria such as Lactobacillus and Pediococcus. See BACTERIA and BRETTANOMYCES. In some cases, brewers may desire to extract a small amount of remaining oak flavor and tannins from the wood. He or she may also try to extract any residual varietal wine characteristics that might be left in the wood. Lastly, brewers use oak barrels as a place to harbor micro flora including Brettanomyces, Lactobacillus, and Pediococcus. While these microflora are considered the bane of most brewers and winemakers, they are essential in the creation of the many sour beer styles inspired by Belgium's sour ale tradition. See SOUR BEER.

Brettanomyces has several unique characteristics, such as the creation of a floating mat, called a pellicle, on the surface of the beer. Another is its ability to eventually consume almost any type of sugar, including the cellobiose which is created during the toasting of the oak. And a near continuous fermentation by Brettanomyces can create a constant exhaustion of carbon dioxide, thus helping to protect the beer from oxidation.

Micro-oxygenation, the slow and steady ingress of oxygen through the porous wood and into the barrel-aged beer, has many implications for beer. Brewers, as well as winemakers, may choose to use French or American oak barrels. French oak is more porous than American oak, thus allowing more oxygen diffusion through the oak itself. The micro-oxygenation of the beer has a direct effect on the acetic bacterial (acetobacter) development in sour beers. Acetobacter requires oxygen to flourish, and more oxygen means more acetic (vinegar-like) character in the beer, which may or may not be desired. Barrels that are not topped up or completely filled, leaving head space in the barrel, may also develop an acetic character.

Like winemakers, brewers must also take into consideration barrel size. Most brewers would consider a barrel that is 219 to 227 liters (57 to 59 US gal) a standard size barrel. Barrels that are smaller than 219 to 227 liters (57 to 59 US gal) can provide more oak surface area contact for the beer; however, this gives more flavor but can also lead to too much oxygen diffusion. Large oak tanks, called fouders, provide less oak surface area and can potentially protect the beer from too much oxidation. However, most brewers choose to use the more standard size barrel to provide more of an opportunity for blending. These standard size barrels are also easier to obtain.

Brewers who choose to age their beer in barrels without the use of Brettanomyces may pick up some residual oak character and wine flavor. However, the beer is at a greater risk of oxidation since there is no secondary fermentation to provide a protective barrier of carbon dioxide in the barrel and the possibility of no pellicle.

Careful consideration must be given to cleaning a barrel as this will directly affect the outcome of the beer. The most common cleaning methods are water, steam, pressure washing, scraping, chains, or less frequently, chemicals. Regardless of the brewer's choice, how a barrel is cleaned will directly affect the beer being aged in the barrel.

New oak barrels may also be used for aging beer, but they are not common due to high costs. Oak products such as oak chips, cubes, powder, shavings, or immersible staves are useful if ersatz alternatives to new oak flavor is desired. These products have become popular in the wine industry due to their ability to be used in not only stainless steel tanks but also in barrels that have little or no oak character left after repeated uses. Some flavors that new oak will contribute are wood, vanilla, dill, spice, and toastiness. Alternative oak products can be cost effective and are easily accessible to most brewers.

See also BARREL and BARREL-AGING.

Robinson, Jancis, ed. "Oak." In *The Oxford Companion to Wine,* p. 684. Oxford: Oxford University Press, 1994.

Vincent Cilurzo

oast house is a building designed for drying hops before they are compressed, baled or pelletized, packaged, and sold to brewers. Despite a recent fashion for "fresh hop" or "harvest" beers, almost all hops are dried before use. The hop flower contains plenty of moisture, and like most flowers it will turn brown and rot if not properly dried. Oast houses, or "hop kilns" as they are also known, can come in many forms; today, hop drying tends to be industrial and mechanized. But to most people—especially in southern England—the name conjures a specific image of a tall, round building with a distinctive white cone on top, and a cowl and weather vane at its peak.

Oasts traditionally used a wooden fire to dry hops, followed by charcoal, and most recently, oil. The tall cones of the buildings were designed to create a good draught for the fire, and the cowl and vane enabled the roof to turn into the wind to get the best airflow.

Hops would be spread in a layer on a latticed floor of wood and wire, allowing the hot air for the fire below to pass through them. After drying, the hops were then compressed into bales and loaded into hessian sacks known as "pockets."

Hops became popular in England in the 15th century and the earliest description of an oast house dates back to 1574. The oldest surviving example is at Cranbrook near Tunbridge Wells, Kent, and was built around 1750. Perhaps not surprisingly, over the centuries a great many oast houses were consumed by fires. Dried hops are easily flammable and once they caught fire, the design of the building could quickly turn it into a furnace.

With mechanization the traditional oast house became obsolete, but the structures are still a common site around Kent, the "hop garden of England." Many of them have been converted for residential use and are quirky, highly sought-after homes.

See also KENT, ENGLAND.

Pete Brown

oatmeal stout is a sub-style of stout, the distinction being the inclusion of up to 20% oats by weight in the grist. The addition of oats, a cereal grain with high concentrations—relative to barley—of body-enhancing beta-glucans, water-soluble lipids, and proteins, adds a distinctly silky and rich mouth feel to the beer.

Stouts brewed with oatmeal became popular in late 19th-century England, with the stout style in general, and oatmeal stouts in particular, being associated with nourishment and viewed as healthful, restorative drinks. By the middle of the 20th century, however, the style had largely disappeared. A mention of oatmeal stout in Michael Jackson's 1977 tome *The World Guide to Beer* led an American beer importer to commission such a beer from Samuel Smith, a brewery in Yorkshire, England.

Workers unloading fresh hops into traditional oast houses for drying in Kent, England, c. 1900. PIKE MICROBREWERY MUSEUM, SEATTLE, WA

Since the creation of that first modern oatmeal stout, the style has grown in popularity with more than 100 commercially brewed examples available today.

Oats are most often used as rolled oats, added directly to the mash, usually at around 10%–15% of total grist weight. Alcohol content by volume varies from as little as 4% to as high as 7.5%, with most examples below 6%. Oatmeal stouts are often somewhat sweeter than dry stouts, but less sweet than sweet stouts or milk stouts. Hop bitterness varies with each brewer's interpretation of the style but is generally moderate, with an emphasis on bittering, rather than aroma hops.

See also STOUTS.

Jackson, Michael. *Ultimate beer*. New York: DK Publishing, 1998.

Brian Thompson

oats (Avena sativa L.) is a cereal crop. Oats is widespread in the temperate zones of the world, where it is typically grown in the more humid areas and more acidic soils. It has long been a major crop in Scotland and the Scandinavian countries. Oats has traditionally been used for feeding horses and other livestock and for human consumption in porridges, flat breads, or cookies. After de-husking the oat goes through a steaming process that gelatinizes the starch. It can then be either milled to make oatmeal or flaked to make traditional oat flakes. In beer brewing, especially for stouts, oats has been used as flakes and in malted form. See OATMEAL STOUT. Toasted "golden" oat flakes are also now available to brewers. Oats add their own distinct flavor and a notably oily, round mouthfeel. While oat hulls may be used like rice husks to ease lautering in certain beers, oats themselves contain beta-glucans and other gummy substances that tend to clog the mash and impede run-off. Oats may also give cloudy worts and cause strong foaming during fermentation. Hence, most brewers prefer to keep the oat fraction of the grist under 10%, though the adventurous few will push the fraction higher in order to attain qualities they consider desirable.

Briggs, D. E., et al. *Brewing: Science and practice*. Cambridge: Woodhead Publishing, 2004.

Per Kølster

Obesumbacterium proteus is the name given to certain Gram-negative bacteria that occur as contaminants of pitching yeasts. The Irish brewing microbiologist J. L. Shimwell first isolated these bacteria in 1936 and, unsure how to classify them, assigned them to the genus Flavobacterium as F. proteus. In 1963 he realized that this was incorrect and created the monotypic genus Obesumbacterium. These bacteria were very common in beers until the 1980s and could be isolated from virtually every ale yeast in the UK, and less frequently from bottom-fermenting lager yeasts. During fermentation they become associated with the yeast head and are passed to the next fermentation when the yeast is re-pitched. They have relatively little impact on beer flavor when present in low numbers (less than 1% of the yeasts by number) but at higher populations can increase the dimethyl sulfide concentration to produce a fruity, parsnip-like odor. See DIMETHYL SULFIDE (DMS).

During wort fermentation O. proteus reduces nitrate to nitrite, which can react with amines to form N-nitrosodimethylamine (nitrosamine). While the concentrations of nitrosamines so produced are minute and harmless, this led to brewers eliminating the contaminants using acid-washing procedures between fermentations. Together with improved yeast handling and better brewery hygiene this has made O. proteus very rare in breweries. In 2009 several strains from the 1970s were reexamined and shown to represent two very different genera of bacteria, both of which are members of the family Enterobacteriaceae. One retains the name Obesumbacterium proteus but the second has been placed in a new genus, Shimwellia (named after Shimwell) as Shimwellia pseudoproteus.

Priest, Fergus G., and Margaret Barker. Gram-negative bacteria associated with brewery yeasts: Reclassification of *Obesumbacterium proteus* biogroup 2 as *Shimwellia pseudoproteus* gen. nov., sp. nov. and transfer of *Escherichia blattae* to *Shimwellia blattae* comb. nov. *International Journal of Systematic and Evolutionary Microbiology* 60 (2010): 828–33.

Fergus G. Priest

off-flavors in beer are the result of undesirable concentrations of flavor-active compounds. The expected flavor of an alcoholic beverage is a complex but fine balance of hundreds of different organic compounds created by raw materials, the action of yeast, and myriad other factors. More than 1,400 volatile compounds alone have been identified in beer. Many of these compounds may be normally present in beer in concentrations below or just above "taste threshold," the point where they can be tasted or smelled by the human tongue or olfactory sense. When the concentration of one or more of these compounds increases significantly, nuances in taste and aroma differing from the norm may occur, causing flavor faults, or off-flavors, in the beer.

Beers, like other foods and beverages, are consumed with a certain expectation, based on a brand's known flavor and reputation. Up until the point of consumption they should have a consistent flavor, remain stable, and be microbiologically sound. If this expectation is not met, the commercial implications can be significant. Off-flavors in beer made at home will be disappointing to the homebrewer, but off-flavors in commercial beer can spell disaster for a commercial brewery.

Whether a flavor is regarded as undesirable or an off-flavor will depend on several factors: (i) the beverage type or style, (ii) the sensitivity of the taster, and (iii) the consumer expectation. Social and ethnic practices will also influence whether a flavor is regarded as acceptable. Some flavor compounds are regarded as positive under certain circumstances but negative under others, whereas others such as "metallic" or chlorophenol are always considered unacceptable. The "clovelike" spiciness that is characteristic of a Bavarian weissbier would be considered a wild yeast contamination if found in another beer style such as a North American mass market pilsner.

The varying flavor components in beer differ in their importance as well in their concentration. Concentration alone, however, will not be the deciding factor as to the importance of the compounds because the individual thresholds of each compound vary so much. One compound, for example, may greatly influence beer flavor in concentrations below 1 part per billion (ppb), whereas others may be present in several hundreds of parts per million without being of any special importance. The concentration at which an individual compound becomes unacceptable depends very much on the background flavor of the product. An off-flavor will become apparent at lower concentrations in more lightly flavored beers. Diacetyl, a buttery-tasting compound, is a good example of a flavor that is acceptable at different levels in products. In lager beer it is generally regarded as an off-flavor when present at levels greater than 45 ppb, but when present at low levels in an English-style bitter it is considered acceptable. See DIACETYL.

The human palate and nose are extremely sensitive, capable of detecting some undesirable notes such as the compound associated with "skunky" flavor in beer at the parts per trillion level. This aroma is referred to as "lightstruck" character because it is the result of photochemical reactions during improper storage, especially in green glass bottles, which offer little protection. However, the flavor the consumer associates with a particular beer may not be that which the brewer had originally intended. If the sales volume of beers sold in green glass bottles is any indication, some consumers would appear not to find the lightstruck flavor objectionable, although most brewery quality control departments would reject a beer showing such a flavor. See LIGHTSTRUCK.

Although much is known and well documented about the off-flavors associated with beer, research is ongoing and will continue to discover new off-flavors and their origins, together with new pathways and causes of previously identified off-flavors.

Morton Meilgaard, the famous brewing sensory scientist, attempted to classify beer flavors into five categories: desirable, desirable in small amounts, desirable in specialty beers, indifferent unless in excess, and undesirable. Those flavors in the fifth category contain defects that are undesirable at any concentration and beer containing these compounds above the taste threshold would certainly be considered off-flavored. They include moldy, metallic, worty, grainy, strawlike, woody, bready, papery, chlorophenol, rancid, oily, skunky, catty, and stale. In reviewing this list, one can identify many of the above-mentioned compounds as those that are associated with oxidation or staling. See OXIDATION.

The flavor scientist S. J. E. Bennett divided possible sources of off-flavors into six groups: (i) raw materials, (ii) a shortfall in process control, (iii) microbiological spoilage, (iv) packaging, (v) storage, and (vi) accidental contamination. The task of categorizing off-flavors themselves is not as simple as it might seem. An undesirable note may have several potential causes. Diacetyl, for example, may be the result of the individual yeast strain utilized by a brewery, insufficient beer maturation time, or, worse, microbial contamination. The good brewer, therefore, is constantly vigilant and should have a well-formed idea of exactly how the brewery's beer should taste and smell.

See also FAULTS IN BEER.

Bennett, S. J. E. Off-flavours in alcoholic beverages. In *Food taints and off-flavours*, 2nd edition., M. J. Saxby ed. Glasgow, Scotland: Blackie Academic & Professional, 1996.

Christopher Bird

Oktoberfest, locally just called "Wiesn" (meaning "the meadow"), is Germany's largest folk festival, staged for 16 to 18 days on the 31-ha (77-acre) Theresienwiese in Munich from the last 2 weeks of September into the first weekend of October. Since the first Oktoberfest in 1810, it has grown into the most famous beer festival in the world, hosting about 6 million visitors every year (with a record of 7.1 million in 1985). The Munich Oktoberfest has spawned similar festivals from Cincinnati, Ohio, to Blumenau, Brazil. The original festival's popularity is inextricably tied to its large beer tents, many with up to 10,000 seats. Each tent has its own unique décor and character. Schottenhamel (serving Spaten beer) seats 6,000 people inside and 4,000 in the adjoining outdoor beer garden, Hacker-Festhalle seats 6,950 in the beer hall but only 2,400 in the garden, and Hofbräu seats 6,898 inside and 3,022 in the garden. The smaller tents are the relatively cozy Hippodrom (3,200 inside, 1,000 outside) and the posh Käferzelt that seats 1,000 people, usually Munich's high society. Beer is served in the iconic 1-l glasses (the so-called masskrug) only—in an average 16-day season beer sales amount to 6.5 million servings. The image of a woman wearing the traditional Bavarian dirndl and cheerfully carrying several giant "Mass" glasses in each hand is an image recognized almost anywhere.

There are strict regulations regarding the beer served at the Oktoberfest. Only the large breweries that brew inside Munich's city limits are allowed to deliver beer to the Oktoberfest—these are Augustinerbräu München, Hacker–Pschorr, Hofbräu, Löwenbräu, Paulaner, and Spaten-Franziskaner-Bräu. See HACKER–PSCHORR BREWERY.

The smaller breweries (including Forschungsbrauerei and brewpubs like Union Bräu) as well as those from outside town are banned. The ban on out-of-town beer once raised royal ire; Prince Luitpold of Bavaria, until recently the owner of the "Kaltenberg-brewery" south of Munich, made several attempts to bring his own beer to Oktoberfest. Although he was Prince of Bavaria, the rules held fast and his complaints were in vain, but they did make for some excellent public relations for Kaltenberg's König Ludwig beer brand.

There is a popular myth that there is one distinctive style of beer brewed for Oktoberfest—but historical evidence shows that there have been many changes in the beers served at the festival in the past. In the first 60 or so years the then popular Bavarian dunkel seems to have dominated the festival. As is often the case, the historical record makes note of the common beer only when something notably different is introduced. This was obviously the case in the year 1872, but the following story was only reported in a pamphlet 35 years later (and quoted in many Oktoberfest publications ever since). In that particularly hot late summer Michael Schottenhamel, owner of Spaten's tent on the Wiesn, had run out of the traditional dark lager beer—and considered dispensing beer from a different brewery. Joseph Sedlmayr, owner of Spaten-Leistbräu, desperately fearing to lose the contract, suggested he sell a strong version of a Vienna-style lager brewed by his son Gabriel. This beer was in fact an 18°P bock beer and at a probable 8% alcohol by volume (ABV) it was sold at a premium price. It may not have been "traditional" but it proved to be popular and for several years—up until World War I—bock-strength beers dominated the Wiesn. The strength of the beer has changed several times since (being at its lowest point in 1946 and 1947 at two "unofficial" and reputedly illegal Oktoberfest beer bars after World War II) and is now in a range between 5.8% and 6.3% ABV. For decades the reddish–brown marzenbier ruled the tents, but in recent years the style has changed yet again. Since 1990 all Oktoberfest beers brewed in Munich have been of a golden color and a slightly sweetish malty nose, with medium body and a low to moderate bitterness. According to European Union regulations, no beers except those brewed by the authorized large breweries of Munich are allowed to be labeled "Oktoberfest," yet many American breweries brew their own versions of Oktoberfest beers. Boston Beer Company (Samuel Adams) claims to be the largest brewer of Oktoberfest beer because no single brewery in Munich brews more of the festival beer than their American competitor.

The Oktoberfest is not just a beer festival and showcase for Munich's breweries; it is also a sort of pop-up amusement park. The popular funfair features some spectacular fairground attractions, from roller coasters to a real flea circus with live fleas performing amazing tricks that can only be seen only through a magnifying glass. The Oktoberfest is also a part of living Bavarian history. It originated in the year 1810 when Bavaria's king Maximilian I. Joseph organized a 2-day festival (on October 13 and 14) to celebrate the wedding of his son, Crown Prince Ludwig (later Ludwig I) and Princess Therese of Sachsen-Hildburghausen. On this occasion free beer and free food were offered at four different locations in Munich and a horse race was organized in what was to become Theresienwiese (named after the princess). At the raceground innkeepers from downtown Munich had set up tents where food and beer were sold. The entire spectacle was popular enough to make a tradition out of the festival, a tradition kept alive for 200 years and only discontinued in times of war and cholera. It is often forgotten that the first Oktoberfest was a political manifestation to demonstrate national unity during and after the Napoleonic wars (when Bavaria was fighting on the side of the French). This politicized character has been revived several times—during German unification in the 1870s, under the Nazi regime in the 1930s, and after German reunification in the 1990s. And for practical (i.e., weather) reasons, the festival was moved forward in the calendar from early to mid-October in the first decades to the last 2 weeks of September in the 1870s, with only a couple of days reaching into the actual month of October. On noon of the first day of Oktoberfest, the mayor of Munich taps the first keg and proclaims "O'zapft is!" ("It is tapped!") and the world's largest beer party comes to life.

Bauer, Richard, and Fritz Fenzl. *175 Jahre Oktoberfest*. Munich, Germany: Bruckmann, 1985.

Conrad Seidl

old ales, a British ale style that has evolved greatly over the past 2 centuries. Traditionally, these beers were also known as stock ales or strong ales as they emerged to some prominence in the late 18th and early 19th centuries. At first, little separated them from barley wines, and they were big beers. Old ales were normally fermented only from the first, high-gravity runnings of the mash, often in a parti-gyle brewing process See PARTI-GYLE. The second runnings were then fermented as brown ales or other medium-strength beers; sometimes a third running was even performed, yielding small beers of little strength and body. See SMALL BEER. Old ales were invariably higher-alcohol beers of perhaps 6% to 7% alcohol by volume (ABV). But the alcohol level was initially kept in check by mashing techniques that favored unfermentable sugars in the high-gravity wort. The beer was left with notable residual sweetness rather than higher levels of alcohol. The original old ales were literally old by beer standards of the day, matured for months and often years in wooden casks. Long aging in wood allowed the ale to mellow in bitterness but also to acquire some flavor from the raw wood, a slightly stale taste from oxidation, and a dash of sourness from wild yeasts, particularly Brettanomyces, and lactic bacteria with which the brew would invariably come into contact. Old ales received very little to no aroma hops; hop flavor and aroma, even if they survived the long aging, would not have been compatible with the beer's other flavors. The finished beer would have had a low, natural effervescence, a deep tawny color, and a substantial mouthfeel. A long, slow, secondary fermentation would sometimes eventually reduce the "unfermentable" sugars, leaving the beer with a dry finish. Old ales were often blended with young "running ales," thereby conferring to the young beer some of the richer properties of the older fraction. The British brewery Greene King still produces its excellent Strong Suffolk (also known as Olde Suffolk) by this method.

Over time, like most British beer styles, the beers referred to as "old ales" changed substantially. They have kept the original dark color range, and most show a tendency toward a rich fruitiness, but in all but a few examples, the touch of wild or lactic character is gone. Some old ales are simply slightly beefed-up mild ales, barely touching 5% ABV. Wood aging is rare, and aging itself seems optional, although some strong versions do age very well indeed. In the past decade or so, however, craft brewers have sought to bring back types of old ale somewhat closer to those of the mid-1800s, and many of these are very characterful and show good aging potential.

See also BARLEY WINE and STOCK ALE.

Brewing Techniques. *Old, strong and stock ales*. http://www.brewingtechniques.com/library/styles/2_5style.html (accessed April 4, 2011).

Campaign for Real Ale. http://www.camra.org.uk/ (accessed April 4, 2011).

Michael Jackson's Beer Hunter. *Apples and black treacle in a real winter warmer*. http://www.beerhunter.com/documents/19133-000071.html (accessed April 4, 2011).

Horst Dornbusch

Opal (hop) is a hop that was bred by the Hüll Institute in Germany and registered in 2001. It has a complex background with some aroma hop. With 5% to 8% alpha acids, 3.5% to 5.5% beta acids, and 13% to 17% cohumulone, it is largely a dual-purpose hop rather than a true aroma or bittering hop. Nonetheless, this hop has one odd aspect to its aroma profile. When freshly dried, Opal often has a garlic-like note, which fades away after a few months in storage in bales. Then its pleasant hop aroma comes to the fore, becoming more appealing than that of most dual-purpose hops, blending slightly peppery notes with light citrus. Opal has a good tolerance to verticillium wilt, as well as downy and powdery mildew, and it yields a respectable 1,850 kg/ha (1650 lb per acre). The oil profile is Hallertau-like. Storage stability is average. Beer made with Opal tends to have a smooth, pleasant bitterness.

Val Peacock

open fermentation is the name given to fermentations that take place in vessels that are "open" to the environment in which they are situated. Open fermentations were the traditional method of fermentation before closed or lidded fermentation vessels were introduced. Open fermentation vessels were once used in all breweries for all types of beer including lagers as well as ales. Today, open fermentations usually take place in specially constructed rooms with smooth, easily cleaned surfaces (often tiled) to minimize the risk of microbiological contamination, and they must

Wort fermenting in an open fermentation vessel at the J.W. Lees Brewery in Manchester, England. PHOTOGRAPH BY DENTON TILLMAN

have a good air flow to remove carbon dioxide gas that is given off during the fermentation process. Early fermentation rooms were designed with good natural air extraction, which was later replaced by more sophisticated extraction and air conditioning systems, often including cooling systems for lower temperature lager fermentations, or heating systems in breweries in colder climates.

Nearly all modern breweries now use closed fermentation vessels, which have many advantages. Closed vessels are easier to clean using modern automated cleaning equipment, and no carbon dioxide from the fermentation need enter the immediate environment. Carbon dioxide can also be collected and used later in beer processing. Closed vessels can be positioned outside the main brewery buildings and closed vessels can also be built stronger to become pressure vessels which can be used to retain natural carbon dioxide from the fermentation process. While the flow of carbon dioxide (CO_2) off the surface of the liquid protects the beer while fermentation is very active, as soon as this activity ceases the beer must be quickly moved into closed vessels to avoid oxidation and bacterial contamination. Then the vessels often must be cleaned by hand, though some larger breweries have devised ingenious systems to clean open vessels automatically.

All this being said, many brewers feel that open fermentation has advantages as well, and this may be why it remains relatively common in the UK, Germany, and Belgium. One obvious advantage is the brewer's ability to actually see the fermentation and gauge its progress. The vessels used for open fermentation tend to be broad and shallow, and this shape encourages the formation of esters that are often found desirable, especially in beer styles featuring yeast fermentation character, such as weissbier. Top-fermenting ale yeasts often form a thick floating mat on top of the liquid toward the end of fermentation. Open fermentation allows the easy collection of that yeast, which tends to be healthy and unencumbered by dead cells and protein sediment. The vitality of open-fermenting yeast has long been noted, and it forms the basis for the famed Burton Union fermentation system. See BURTON UNION SYSTEM. Finally, let it be noted that open fermentation is not without charm. Many brewers have found themselves enjoying the Zen-like collection of floating islands of yeast off the surface of a vat of beer, deftly using a specially made slotted paddle to lift the thick foam. For brewers, such ancient practices tend to make for pleasantly quiet moments in often hectic days.

See also FERMENTATION VESSELS.

Paul KA Buttrick and Garrett Oliver

Optic (barley), a spring barley bred and grown in the UK for the production of pale ale malt. Derived from the cross Chad × (Corniche × Force), it has grown to be the most widely planted barley in England and Scotland. Optic produces high yields and has moderate resistance to mildew and rust. It matures late and is capable of producing full-flavored, biscuity tasting malts, especially when floor malted, although flavors are considered lighter than those of the variety Pearl, which is also popular. Optic-based malts are widely used in the UK and by American craft brewers, especially for the production of pale ales and India pale ales.

Martha Holley-Paquette

Oregon Brewers Festival. It was with visions of Munich's Oktoberfest that Art Larrance, cofounder of Portland Brewing Company of Portland, Oregon approached other local craft brewers in 1988 with the idea of starting a festival at which craft-brewed Northwest beers would be showcased alongside those from farther afield. Other original organizers were Dick and Nancy Ponzi of BridgePort Brewing and Rob and Kurt Widmer of Widmer Brothers Brewing. The Oregon Brew Crew, a local homebrew club, volunteered its collective services as pourers for the 16 beers offered by a total of 13 breweries. The festival was held in a city park alongside the Willamette River. Five thousand people were expected; 15,000 attended.

The Oregon Brewers Festival continues to be held the last full weekend in July. Many of the same organizers are still involved, and the Brew Crew still arranges the volunteers. Eighty beers are now offered, one from each brewery represented, and in contrast with other festivals given to aggressive promotion and competition, the Oregon festival is unequivocally democratic: the smallest brewpub is presented exactly the same as the largest, most moneyed national producer. The many brewers on hand are expected only to enjoy themselves and their colleagues' beers. The only competition associated with the festival, in fact, is in being invited to participate.

Like Munich's older festival, the mayor participates annually in the tapping of the Oregon festival's first kegs. A parade to the festival grounds is held, and these days some 70,000 people can be counted on to attend.

Oregon Brewers Festival. http://www.oregonbrewfest.com/ (accessed April 23, 2011).

Dick Cantwell

organic acids contain the active carboxyl grouping -COOH. They are produced by living organisms, hence the name "organic." Mineral-based acids are called inorganic. Organic acids in food and beverages tend to be highly flavorful, in addition to being predominantly sour. See SOURNESS. In beer, small amounts of certain acids promote a sense of freshness, whereas an excessive amount—unless a characteristic of a particular beer style—tends to be an indicator that the beer is spoiled, often from an infection by spoilage microbes that produce acetic acid. See ACETIC ACID BACTERIA (ACETOBACTER). Lactic acid bacteria, on the other hand, which are naturally present on malt, acidify the mash and thus the resulting beer, which may contain as much as 1.2% lactic acid in solution. Some Belgian-style beers are intentionally brewed to be sour. These are surprisingly pleasant tasting precisely because of their acidity. Lambics, for instance, are particularly prized for their tartness. They are fermented with both yeast and acid-producing bacteria. Some lambics, such as kriek, acquire some of their acidity from the addition of sour fruit, which contain such organic acids as tartaric, malic, and citric acid. See KRIEK. One malt-derived organic acid, oxalic acid, is of particular concern not because of its flavor, but because of its precipitate, oxalate, which can serve as a collection point for carbon dioxide bubbles in the finished beer and cause gushing when the beer is opened. See GUSHING.

See also ACIDIFICATION, CITRIC ACID, LACTIC ACID, OXALATES, and SOUR BEER.

Kunze, Wolfgang. *Technology brewing and malting*, 2nd ed. Berlin: VLB Berlin, 2003.

Rick Vega

organic ingredients have experienced a great rise in popularity in recent years, mostly as a reaction to the way food is grown throughout the world. The extensive use of chemical fertilizers and pesticides and the advent of genetically modified foods have led to a renewed interest in traditional farming methods. Beer is a "natural" product and even in the largest breweries in the world is still generally made using traditional ingredients and processes that date back centuries. Beer is made from malted barley, malted wheat, and various cereal grains, as well as water, hops, and yeast, along with a number of simple process aids. Most of these can be produced in ways that allows them to be labeled "organic." Brewers of organic beers tend to focus on the organic certifications of the agricultural ingredients they use in their beers, namely barley, wheat, cereal grain, and hops. In order for these to be labeled as organic, they need to be grown without the use of chemical fertilizers and pesticides unless they appear on a list of exempt and thus allowed substances. Soil preparation, planting, growing, harvesting, and processing need to be overseen by a certifying agency to ensure compliance. Great efforts are taken to ensure the organic integrity of the ingredients, including measures to guarantee that there is no possibility of mingling with non-organic ingredients. This strict control extends to the manufacturing process in the brewery as well and involves the creation of a paper trail for the seamless tracing of every ingredient in a beer all the way back to the farmer who grew it. Hops and cereal plants are susceptible to many diseases, and development of organic markets in beer ingredients has been slow. The quality of organic malts and hops, once widely considered marginal, has improved considerably, and interest in these ingredients has continued to increase.

Different countries have different certification systems with varying degrees of stringency and scope. In the United States the certification of maltsters, hop growers, and brewers was originally handled at a local level by private certifying agencies. Each had their own set of rules. Since 2002, however, the US Department of Agriculture (USDA) has offered a USDA certification for organic products that uses the local certifying agencies plus a standardized set of rules that ensure the integrity of products labeled organic. This led to the creation of the National Organic Program (NOP) and a list of ingredients that are non-organic yet still may be included in certified organic products. On this list are the following items of interest to brewers: several acids (as long as they are naturally produced), agar-agar, bentonite, calcium carbonate, calcium chloride, calcium sulfate, carbon dioxide, carrageenan, diatomaceous earth (as a food filtering aid only), enzymes, hydrogen peroxide, magnesium sulfate, malic acid, microorganisms (any food grade bacteria, fungi, and other microorganism), nitrogen, oxygen, peracetic acid, perlite, potassium chloride, potassium iodide, sodium bicarbonate, sodium carbonate, sodium hydroxide, and yeast. Beer that includes these ingredients at levels below 5% of the total dry weight of its ingredients or uses them as process aids are permitted to be labeled as *certified organic*. The items on the NOP list are frequently reviewed and may be removed should a reliable organically produced source become available. Hops were once on the NOP list, but on October 28, 2010 the National Organics Standards Board unanimously voted in favor of the removal of hops from the list, effective January of 2013. After this date, any beer certified organic in the United States will contain organically certified hops only. Certifying agencies—many with differing rules as to what is allowed as a nonorganic beer ingredient—exist in several countries including Australia, Canada, Germany, Great Britain, Sweden, Norway, India, Ireland, Greece, Belgium, China, Japan, and the central offices of the European Union in Belgium.

See also ENVIRONMENTAL ISSUES.

American Organic Hop Grower Association. http://www.usorganichops.com (accessed December 4, 2010).

Steve Parkes

original gravity (OG), sometimes called original extract, is a measure of the solids content originally in the wort, before alcoholic fermentation has commenced to produce the beer. OG is one of the major measurements used by brewers to determine the future alcohol content of a beer fermented from a particular wort. It is measured by a saccharometer, hydrometer, or refractometer as the density of the wort at standard temperature and pressure (STP; usually 20°C and 760 mm) at the final collection point before the yeast is added. Original gravity is expressed as the density above that of distilled water and in the UK is called the excess gravity. Water is deemed to have a density at STP of 1.000. If the wort density is 1.048, it will have 48° of excess gravity and an OG of 48.

Internationally, different units are used to express OG that are unique to the brewing industry and include degrees Plato, degrees Balling, or percent dry matter of the wort, Brix % (for sucrose only). These units take into account the solution factors of carbohydrates and mixtures of carbohydrates typically found in wort made from different cereal/malt recipes (e.g., barley malt, maize, rice, sugar). The numerical figure for these units approximates one-quarter of the excess gravity. In the example above 48/4 = 12% dry matter by weight or 12° Balling or 12° Plato.

Laboratory procedures can be used to establish the original gravity of a beer by measuring both the present or apparent specific gravity of the beer and the alcohol content of the beer, the latter by distillation. Original gravity tables convert the alcohol content back to the amount of carbohydrate fermented to produce it. Then, by the addition of these two values, the wort's original gravity can be established from the tables. Tables for converting alcohol content to a value for carbohydrate fermented were first produced in 1850 by Graham, Hofman, and Redwood and were incorporated into the UK 1880 Inland Revenue Act for excise duty collection calculations as Statutory Tables. They were found to give inaccurate results under certain circumstances (Section 15 of the Act Export drawback, etc.) so in 1910 after a Joint Inquiry led by Sir T. E. Thorpe and Dr H. T. Brown of the Institute of Brewing, they were refined to accord with "brewing operations as carried out in present day brewery practice." The use of high-gravity brewing technology and postfermentation dilution is ignored by this analysis because it measures the OG as if no dilution had occurred.

Brewers seek to achieve consistent original gravities for their worts as part of overall quality assurance for their beers.

See also BALLING SCALE, PLATO GRAVITY SCALE, and SPECIFIC GRAVITY.

Broderick, H. M., ed. *The practical brewer*. St Paul, MN: Master Brewers Association of the Americas, 1993.

Graham, T., A. W. Hofman, and T. Redwood. Report on original gravities. *Quarterly Journal of the Chemical Society* 5 (1852): 229.

Hopkins, R. H., and B. Krause. *Biochemistry applied to malting & brewing*, 2nd imp. London: Allen & Unwin, 1947.

Hough, J. S., D. E. Briggs, R. Stevens, and T. W. Young, eds. *Malting & brewing science*, 2nd ed. London: Chapman & Hall, 1982.

Chris J. Marchbanks

Orval Brewery. Abbaye Notre Dame D'Orval, one of Belgium's six Trappist beer producers, is located in southern Belgium in the province of Luxembourg. The abbey gets its name from a legend in which the widowed countess Mathilda of Tuscany accidentally dropped her wedding ring into a spring on the site of the future abbey and assumed it was lost. She prayed to God for the return of her ring, promising to build a great abbey if she should see the ring again. Within moments a trout swam to the surface with the ring in its mouth. She is said to have exclaimed "This place truly is a 'val d'or,'" meaning "golden valley," and established a church on the site known as Orval. The trout with the ring in its mouth remains the symbol of the abbey. Orval has a long and storied past, with the first evidence of monks arriving in 1070 to begin construction of a church. The church was completed in 1124, and in 1132 joined the Cistercian order. Two events almost destroyed the community. First, a major fire in 1252 caused enough damage to consider closure. After much rebuilding over time, the abbey was burned and looted during the French revolution in 1793 and lay in ruins. In 1887 the Harenne family acquired the ruins of the abbey and its estate, and rebuilding work began in the 1920s. A brewhouse was installed in 1931, Orval regained its rank of "abbey" in 1935, and in 1948 its magnificent new church was finally consecrated and headed by a Trappist abbot. The Harenne family remains involved in the day-to-day affairs of the brewery, which remains inside the walls of the striking Art Deco abbey buildings.

True to the Trappist ideals, the Orval abbey produces both beer and cheese. Although a brewery was probably always present in the abbey, it wasn't until the 1930s that Orval distinguished itself as a brewery.

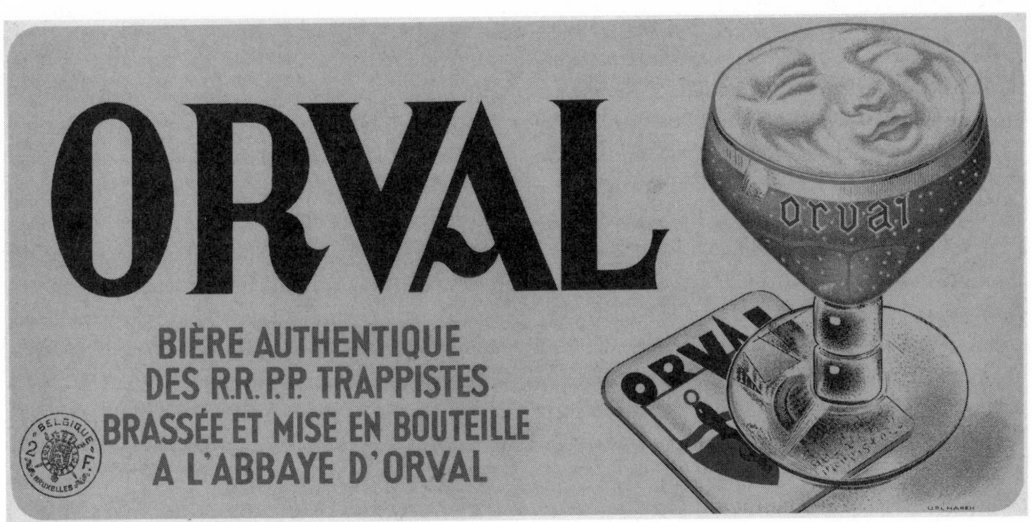

Decal, c. 1930. The Belgian Trappist brewery at Orval produces two beers, only one of which, simply called Orval, is available for public consumption. PIKE MICROBREWERY MUSEUM, SEATTLE, WA

Orval makes only two beers, and only one of these makes it into the outside world. This beer, simply named "Orval," is an outlier among Trappist beers, a honey-colored pale ale of distinctive character. The beer is a relatively light 6.9% ABV, but with a unique taste profile due mainly to the yeast strains used, the dry-hopping with fresh Hallertau, Styrian Goldings, and French Strisselspalt hops. Most unusually, the beer is partially carbonated, then bottled with a small dose of priming sugar and a blend of yeast including the "wild" yeast strain Brettanomyces. See BRETTANOMYCES. The phenolic, estery character of the Brettanomyces, often described in literature as "horse blankets," tends to become apparent after 6 months. Therefore, Orval's beer, which is hoppy and fresh when young, attains a fascinating and complex old age in the bottle. The character of Orval has been hugely influential among craft brewers, particularly in the United States, where many have been moved to experiment with Brettanomyces.

See also CISTERCIAN ORDER and TRAPPIST BREWERIES.

Keith Villa

oud bruin, or (east) Flanders Brown, refers to a blended sour dark ale style that was common in the province of Limburg in the Netherlands and is still popular in the East Flanders city of Oudenaarde in Belgium. The name "oud" (old) refers to the lagering or aging process that can take over a year to complete. If performed in traditional oak vessels, bacteria and wild yeasts residing within the wood will change the beer until it develops a variety of cherry, plum, and raisin-like aromas and fruity flavors, with a slightly acidic and astringent finish. Many of these characteristics are more readily associated with wine than beer. Traditionally it is then blended with younger and sweeter beer to reduce the acidity and introduce the sweetish caramel malt notes that make it more complex and palatable. There are also versions that are neither fermented in wood nor blended and that are drier, hoppier, and more metallic in character. A distant relative of the Flanders red ale, the two styles are often confused and some consider them to be one and the same. Stylistically speaking, however, Flemish brown does not show the "barnyard" Brettanomyces character often present in Flemish red, whereas Flemish red misses the deeper color and caramel nuttiness common in "Vlaams Bruin."

Oudenaarde is considered to be the capital of the style, but to make matters confusing, the geographical location of the brewery used to define which variation of the style was brewed. The city, which is split by the Schelde River, was also split by the Treaty of Verdun from 843 CE. The kingdom of France and its brewers were located on the northwest bank and brewed sweet–sour versions, using gruit as their flavoring preservative, while their German counterparts on the southeast brewed a hopped version with a light roast character.

Oud was a refreshing blended beer popular in the Netherlands until World War I, before the introduction of refrigeration and lager beer. It was born out of necessity, similar to other blended beers of the same era such as porter. See PORTER. If a beer became too old, sour, and astringent, instead of being discarded it was blended with fresh, young beer that could "rejuvenate" it and make it an acceptable pint. Shortly thereafter the Dutch embraced lager beer with such a vengeance that of the original thirty-five breweries in Maastricht in 1870 only eight remained in 1940. "Aajt" (Maastricht's dialect for old) was the name used for their version of Flemish brown. The Marres brewery, the last aajt brewer, tried to beat the lager wave by introducing a stronger and perfected "Dobbel Aajt" (Double Old) but it never caught on and production at the brewery was taken over by local competitor Brand in 1946 until its liquidation in 1959 and demolition in 1979.

The Dutch still produce an artificially sweetened and colored lager version of this style popular with the elderly, nursing mothers and athletes looking for a sweet pick-me-up without the caffeine in cola. Confusingly called "Oud Bruin," it varies from 2%–3.5% ABV and typically has a low bitterness of about 12 IBU.

The Gulpener brewery in the Dutch Limburg village of Gulpen, nestled between Belgium and Germany, reintroduced Mestreechs Aajt in 1984. The base beer for this blend is spontaneously fermented for 11 to 13 months in wooden barrels at De Zwarte Ruiter pub close to the brewery. About 25% of this beer is blended with two other commercial beers, an Oud Bruin at 3.5% ABV and their Dort at 6.5% ABV. The "wild" spontaneously fermented beer, referred to as "oerbier" in the brewery, is quite sour and the Oud Bruin tastes artificially sweet (from saccharine) and is mouth-coating. The final product, Mestreechs Aajt, has a sweet-and-sour character that is totally unique and unlike other Flemish brown ales. Former brewery director Paul Rutten once said, "The taste is so strange that there is very little market for it in Holland" and that it is only brewed to maintain and promote the blended beer tradition. Gulpener stopped producing Meestrechs Aajt in 2005 due to hygiene law issues with the local food and health authorities and has only recently announced plans to reintroduce it. In March of 2009 De Molen brewery from Bodegraven in the province of South-Holland, in collaboration with the Amager Brewery from Denmark, released a 5.7% ABV version of the Flemish brown style called "Vlaams & Hollands" (Flemish & Dutch). It is fermented using a lactic culture and lagered for 4 months in Bordeaux wine and Dutch whiskey barrels. Traditional Belgian examples of sour Flemish brown ales are Cnudde Oudenaards Bruin (4.7% ABV; only available on draught in the direct vicinity of the brewery), Verhaeghe Vichtenaar (5.1% ABV), and, for stronger versions, Liefmans Goudenband (8% ABV) and De Dolle Brouwers Oerbier Special Reserva (12%–13% ABV). Fine non-soured examples are Roman Adriaen Brouwer (5% ABV) and a stronger version called Adriaen Brouwer Finest Dark (8.5% ABV).

See also FLANDERS and NETHERLANDS, THE.

Derek Walsh

oxalates. Oxalic acid is a dicarboxylic acid found in many locations in nature. Of particular significance for brewing, it is found in malt. It has a high affinity for calcium, which has implications for the body, as the resultant precipitates can lead to problems such as kidney stones in individuals who are otherwise at risk for the condition. In the context of beer, precipitated oxalate in the beer leads to particulate and haze formation, gushing, and the white mineral deposit called "beer stone," the latter being responsible for the blocking of beer piping. For this reason, oxalate removal is encouraged in the brewhouse by the addition of sufficient calcium to precipitate out the material in mashing and/or wort boiling. The rule of thumb is that there needs to be 4.5 times more calcium present than oxalic acid, but the factors impacting the level of oxalic acid in malt are not well understood.

Charles W. Bamforth

oxidation, a process that is generally considered ruinous to beer. Exposure to oxygen can happen virtually anywhere in the brewing process, from the brewhouse, to the fermentation cellar, to the packaging line, and even within the bottle in storage after packaging. We perceive the evidence of oxidation as off-putting stale notes that are variously describes as leathery, papery, wet cardboard-like, catty, and *ribes* or black currant. See FAULTS IN BEER. On rare occasions, however, oxidation can improve certain beers, when it is deliberately employed under controlled conditions—such as during the long vat storage and barrel aging of lambics prior to bottling or during gentle bottle aging of barley wines. Such slow and graceful oxidation, which can have similar effects to the oxidation of Madeira wines in an estufa, adds complex flavors, makes the brew robust, and allows it to be kept for years. See AGING OF BEER.

The first chance for oxygen pickup in the brewing process occurs in the mash, where it is referred to as hot-side aeration. See HOT-SIDE AERATION. It can be the result of excessive stirring of the mash or too much splashing of wort during recirculation. Although oxidation accelerates with a rise in temperature, the solubility of oxygen decreases simultaneously. Therefore, boiling wort, which would oxidize if cooler, is too hot to pick up oxygen. Conversely, cold wort, which needs to be saturated with oxygen at the beginning of fermentation to stimulate yeast action, is cold enough that damaging oxidative reactions are slowed; the yeast then strips the oxygen out of solution before any damage can be done. In the mash, however, there is just enough oxygen present at a high enough temperature to make damaging oxidation reactions possible.

A second major oxygen pickup location for beer is the filling line. The amount of oxygen pickup depends largely on the sophistication of the bottling and kegging equipment and the care of the operators, but zero oxygen pickup is virtually impossible to achieve. The more oxygen is in the packaged beer, the faster it will become stale. Importantly, the rate of oxidation accelerates significantly with an increase in the beer's storage temperature. For instance, a particular beer that may have a shelf life of 4 months if kept at a temperature of 6°C (42°F) may have a shelf life of less than 3 months if kept at temperature of 30°C (86°F).

Oxygen picked up throughout the brewing and packaging process can react with many compounds in beer, and the effects are usually negative. Perhaps the most notable flavor-active compounds are trace elements of fatty acids (lipids), which, when combined with oxygen, make beer taste stale and give it a pronounced flavor of wet cardboard. See LIPIDS. Oxygen can also react with melanoidins that are created during the malting process and the kettle boil. See BOILING and MALT. Oxidized melanoidins can give the beer a slight taste of sherry. In the cold brew, oxygen can turn alcohol into almond-tasting aldehydes, which is one reason why wort should never be aerated to alleviate a stuck fermentation.

Chemically speaking, oxidation is the uptake of oxygen on the molecular level by a compound in conjunction with a release of energy. The best proof of that point is perhaps the importance of oxygen for fire. Without oxygen, fire simply does not burn. A good example of the importance of oxygen in brewing is perhaps the oxidation of the carbohydrate glucose in the process of yeast respiration. This is represented by the following equation:

$$C_6H_{12}O_6 + 6O_2 \rightarrow 6CO_2 + 6H_2O + \text{energy}$$

The reaction generates energy and is the primary means by which organisms derive energy from food. In this reaction, oxygen being incorporated into the sugar to generate carbon dioxide and hydrogen is removed to yield water. Another view of oxidation, therefore, is the removal of hydrogen from a molecule.

Hydrogen may be extracted from a substance by materials other than oxygen, and the molecule from which hydrogen is removed is still said to be oxidized, whereas the molecule that has accepted the hydrogen is said to be reduced. When yeast "burns" sugar during fermentation, for instance, there is a stage in which hydrogen is removed from an intermediate in the pathway. The hydrogen does not attach to oxygen, but rather to an enzyme called nicotinamide adenine dinucleotide (NAD) to produce NADH. Later the yeast replenishes the NAD using the NADH to reduce acetaldehyde, thereby making ethanol.

As well as being defined as the addition of oxygen or the removal of hydrogen, oxidation can also be understood as the loss of electrons from a substance, in which case reduction is defined as the opposite of these. Oxidation and reduction work in tandem: when one participant in a reaction is oxidized, another becomes reduced. The overall circumstance is called redox. Substances that oxidize other substances are known as oxidizing agents or electron acceptors. Conversely, substances that reduce other substances are called reducing agents or electron donors. There are numerous redox reactions in malting and brewing. Some examples are as follows:

- The reduction of acetaldehyde to ethanol takes place by way of alcohol dehydrogenase, a yeast enzyme that functions as a catalyst. The enzyme's name, incidentally, highlights the reversible nature of the reaction.
- The reduction of diacetyl to acetoin by yeast. Various enzymes may catalyze this reaction.
- The oxidation of unsaturated fatty acids during malting and brewing—a key source of stale flavors in beer, notably cardboard. It may be catalyzed by the enzyme lipoxygenase but can also be caused by activated forms of oxygen, such as superoxide, perhydroxyl, and hydroxyl. In turn, these activated forms of oxygen are produced by the reduction of oxygen (addition of electrons), whereby the electrons may come from ions such as iron and copper.

Another substance that develops through this reaction of oxygen and metal ions is hydrogen peroxide, which can oxidize polyphenols. This converts them into deeper colored forms, which therefore darken wort and beer. These, in turn, can polymerize and adhere to proteins, which causes hazes. See COLLOIDAL HAZE and HAZE. When speaking of finished beer, outside of the pleasant effects of slow oxidation on a small class of age-worthy beer styles, the word "oxidation" is always pejorative. Unlike the world of wine, which has a number of deliberately oxidized types such as oloroso sherry, tawny port, and vin jaune, there are no beer styles that are deliberately oxidized before reaching the consumer.

Bamforth, C. W., and A. Lentini. "The flavor instability of beer." In C. W. Bamforth, ed., *Beer: a quality perspective*, 85–109. Burlington, VT: Academic Press, 2009.

Garrett Oliver and Horst Dornbusch

oxygen (O_2) is a gas that composes about 20% of air. It is needed by respiring barley during germination and is also required to support the synthesis of unsaturated fatty acids and sterols in yeast. See AERATION. Oxygen can have a number of adverse impacts in wort, notably the production of color, lowering of rates of wort separation, and development of undesirable flavors; however, it also promotes the removal of complexes of oxidized polyphenols and polypeptides, thereby enhancing the colloidal stability of beer. Oxygen in the finished beer is highly undesirable because it promotes beer staling and haze formation.

In all cases it is oxygen in solution that is important rather than that which is present in the headspace above the liquid, whether it is wort, beer, or water.

The concentration of oxygen is dependent on the following:

- the partial pressure of oxygen above the liquid: higher pressures (and proportion of oxygen in the gas phase) give higher oxygen concentration in solution;
- the temperature: higher temperatures mean less oxygen in solution; and
- the concentration of other substances dissolved in the water: high levels of competing solutes make for less oxygen in solution.

The oxygen concentration in deionized water under a headspace of air is 0.34 mM (10.9 ppm) at 10°C (50°F) and 0.28 mM (8.9 ppm) at 20°C (68°F). In 15°Plato wort the equivalent values are 8.0 and 6.6 ppm, respectively. For worts at lower atmospheric pressures (higher altitudes) the concentration of oxygen in wort will be proportionately less. At a given atmospheric pressure the solubility of oxygen in beer is less than in pure water, but greater than in wort.

Ground-state oxygen can be dissociated into its constituent atoms by light energy, and in turn these can react with other oxygen molecules to form ozone, which is also more reactive than ground-state oxygen. Therefore, ozone is a good sterilant.

While oxygen is essential for aerobic life, it is toxic in excess. Some organisms are anaerobic: they have systems readily poisoned by even low levels of oxygen. The electrons used to "activate" oxygen come from metals such iron, copper, and manganese. Therefore, the aim is to minimize both oxygen levels and the amount of these metals if damage to the beer is not to occur.

See also OXIDATION.

Halliwell, B., and J. M. C. Gutteridge. *Free radicals in biology and medicine*. New York: Oxford University Press, 2007.

Charles W. Bamforth

Pabst Brewing Company was founded in 1844 as the Best Brewing Co of Milwaukee, Wisconsin. Frederick Pabst, son-in-law of the brewery owner, would later join the brewery staff and eventually take control. After stewarding it into becoming the largest brewery in the country, Best was renamed Pabst in 1889.

It was around that time when Pabst engaged in one of the country's fiercest competitions for brewery dominance against rival Anheuser-Busch. During the Chicago World's Fair in 1893 the two vied for the ultimate public support—and that of judges—for their brews. Final scores (that still lay in dispute by some) put Pabst 0.3 points ahead. The brewery responded by placing a blue ribbon on its packaging, something that remains to this day.

In the 1930s the brewery merged with Premier Malt Products and expanded its distribution around the United States but was hobbled by Prohibition and some poor business decisions. By the 1950s Pabst, although selling nearly 11 million barrels of beer per year, had been well outpaced by Schlitz and Anheuser-Busch. Twenty years later, after further management missteps, Pabst Blue Ribbon was remarketed as a bargain beer, after years as a premium quality lager. In 1985 Paul Kalmanovitz purchased the company and his Kalmanovitz Charitable Foundation helped Pabst Blue Ribbon, commonly known as PBR (and now being contract brewed by MillerCoors in the United States), become popular with both the college crowd and city dwellers.

In 2010 the company was sold to Connecticut-based Metropoulos & Co, which also took control of the brewery's other brands, Old Milwaukee, Stroh's, and Old Style. It produces about 6 million barrels of beer annually with sales revenue topping more than $500 million.

Daykin, Tom. "New Pabst owner promises to build sales." *Milwaukee Journal Sentinel*, June 28, 2010.

Ogle, Maureen. *Ambitious brew: The story of American beer*. New York: Harcourt Press, 2006.

John Holl

Pacific Gem (hop) is a New Zealand high-alpha variety released in 1987 by the New Zealand Horticulture Research Centre (now HortResearch). It has a few indigenous New Zealand hops as well as Cluster and Fuggle in its genetic background. See CLUSTER (HOP) and FUGGLE (HOP). Pacific Gem matures early to mid-season and averages a very respectable yield of some 2,700 kg/ha (2,380 lb/acre). Because common hop diseases are not present in remote New Zealand, there is no need to spray against them, which makes New Zealand-grown hops sought after by organic brewers. Pacific Gem stores well, too. Pacific Gem averages about 13% to 15% alpha acids, 7% to 9% beta acids, and 40% cohumulone. It has an aroma that is reminiscent of blackberry and dark fruit, and when added during the wort boil, it permeates the brewhouse with whiffs of oak and other woods. This hop has a smooth bittering profile that makes it particularly suited for European-style lagers. Because of its high acid content, it has also become a favorite for the production of hop extract via the supercritical CO_2 method. Although its high alpha pegs it as a bittering hop, some New Zealand craft brewers also use it for its aromatic character.

See also CARBON DIOXIDE HOP EXTRACTS.

Hopsteiner. http://www.hopsteiner.com/pdf/nz/NZPacific Gem.pdf/ (accessed November 8, 2010).

New Zealand Hops Limited. *High alpha hop data sheet.* http://www.nzhops.co.nz/varieties/pacific_gem.html. (accessed November 8, 2010).

Jon Griffin

packaging

See BOTTLING and CANNING.

Pajottenland District (Belgium), a part of the Flemish Brabant province situated west of Brussels, between the Zenne and Dender river valleys. This quiet, rural area is known for the unique microflora of bacteria and wild yeasts responsible for the spontaneous fermentation of lambic beers. See LAMBIC. True lambic beer is only produced here and in the Senne Valley in which Brussels lies. The area has been known for its gastronomical specialties for centuries, and the area was made famous the world over by the paintings of Pieter Brueghel the Elder, who often portrayed the day-to-day life of Pajottenlanders. On Sunday mornings locals can still enjoy the authentic lambic café atmosphere in In de Verzekering tegen de Grote Dorst ("The insurance against the great thirst"), which organizes events such as "The Night of Great Thirst" festival, during which lambic brewers welcome beer lovers from all around the world.

See also BELGIUM and FLANDERS.

In De Verzekering de Grote Dorst. http://www.dorst.be/ (accessed April 4, 2011).

Webb, Tim, Chris Pollard, and Joris Pattyn. *Lambicland,* 2nd ed. Cambridge, UK: Cogan & Mater, 2009.

Lorenzo Dabove

pale ale can denote a specific style of beer in one context, but in its predominant form it is a generic name for a group of copper-colored, hop-forward, bitter beers. These include English and American pale ales, India pale ales, "double" India pale ales, English bitter (ordinary, special, and extra special), and Belgian pale ales. "Pale ale" originated as a catch-all term for any top-fermented beer that was not dark. Up to the 18th century at least, the bulk of beers produced in England were of a dark brown color, brewed largely from amber and brown malts. Those few beers brewed from paler malts were called pale simply to distinguish them from their darker brethren. Malt drying technology was somewhat crude in those days and the so-called pale malts would have been quite dark compared with modern standards. As a result, pale ales of that time would probably have been of a reddish–amber color. Even today, pale ale malts are malted and kilned so that they are slightly darker than pale lager malts, and pale ales made from them are honey to copper in color, rather than straw yellow.

Pale ale certainly existed before 1700, but even in the 18th century it was not a defined style, as its competitor, porter, had become. It began to become a less vague term as malting methods improved and maltsters were better able to control its color. An important milestone came in 1790 when George Hodgson began to ship pale ale to India. See HODGSON, GEORGE. By the first quarter of the 19th century, the Burton-on-Trent brewers had lost their export trade to the Baltic countries as a result of embargoes put in place during the Napoleonic Wars. By this time Hodgson had taken firm control of India exports but had been at odds with the East India Company. So a director of the Company approached Samuel Allsopp in Burton and asked him whether he could brew pale ale for the Indian market. In 1822 the first brew was made, and it was shipped to India in 1823. Burton maltsters supposedly developed a special pale malt for this brew, and certainly the highly mineralized Burton water, whose hardness accentuated hop bitterness in the beer, was admirably suited to the production of what became India pale ale (IPA). While Hodgson did not invent the IPA beer style, he had an impact on its development and made a good trade in IPA until his market position was eventually usurped.

Soon, Burton IPA became popular in England, and brewers from other areas of the country rushed to copy it. IPA was a strong beer, at around 7% alcohol by volume (ABV), but lower-strength versions began to be produced, and these were often referred to simply as "pale ale," whereas some brewers started to use the term "bitter ale." In fact, although pale ales took a good share of the beer market in England it was still the darker, more lightly hopped mild ales that dominated. But the grip of mild ales was to continually loosen through the 20th century as pale beers became the norm.

Yet, in large part as a result of raw materials restrictions during the two World Wars, beer strengths declined in England. Accordingly, "bitter," the weaker version of pale ale, became the most popular beer in the country, until it was overtaken by lager in the last quarter of the 20th century. Bitter itself fragmented into several substyles, with "ordinary" being the weakest, at 3%–4% ABV, "special" and "extra special" covering the range 4.5%–5% ABV, and the oddity of Fuller's "extra special bitter" weighing in at 5.5% ABV. See EXTRA SPECIAL BITTER (ESB).

But pale ale production was not limited to Britain alone. Belgian brewers developed several examples of varying alcoholic strengths. These are more characterized by fruity notes from the distinctive Belgian yeasts used in their production than the malt and hop flavors of British beers. Oddly enough, apart from Cooper's Sparkling Ale from Adelaide, South Australia, pale ale is rare in the countries of the British Commonwealth.

In the United States, because of the surge of German immigrants bringing lager brewing with them, pale ale did not really become a big factor in the 19th century. It was produced on a modest scale, notably in New England; for example, Ballantine IPA survived into the 1980s. See BALLANTINE IPA. But around that time the US craft brewing revolution began. These new brewers, with little brewing heritage to draw on, looked to Europe and Britain in particular for inspiration.

Pale ale was simpler to produce and required less capital investment than lager, and most craft brewers opted for it. These were entrepreneurs and inventive people, and simply copying British beers was not enough. They wanted to go back to the roots of pale ale and to explore the possibilities of the wide variety of American hops available to them. The result was that American IPA became a new style; a stronger version was dubbed by some "double IPA," and the pale ale family of beer styles was lifted and carried forward into the future.

See also AMERICAN PALE ALE, ENGLISH PALE ALE, and INDIA PALE ALE.

Foster, Terry. *Pale ale*, 2nd ed. Boulder, CO: Brewers Publications, 1999.

Jackson, Michael. *Michael Jackson's beer companion*. Philadelphia: Running Press, 1993.

Terry Foster

Palisade (hop) is a proprietary hop owned by Yakima Chief. It was bred by Chuck Zimmerman, who recorded it as an open-pollination product of Tettnanger. Whether this was genuine Tettnanger (U.S. Department of Agriculture 21496, 21497, or 61021) or American Tettnanger (21197) is unclear. The latter is not a true Tettnanger and many believe it to be a Fuggle. See AMERICAN TETTNANGER (HOP), FUGGLE (HOP), and TETTNANGER (HOP). Hence, Palisade may or may not have German heritage. It is an extremely vigorous hop, unlike either Tettnanger or Fuggle, with rather high yields that may reach 2,200 to 3,000 lb/acre. It flourishes in the hot, dry climate of Yakima, but can only survive in Oregon with great difficulty, because it is extremely sensitive to downy mildew, a major problem in Oregon. With 5.5% to 9.5% alpha acids and 6% to 8% beta acids, the alpha-to-beta ratio resembles more that of Tettnanger than Fuggle, but the alpha levels are considerably higher than that of either. Cohumulone content is 24% to 29%, which is similar to that of both Fuggle and Tettnanger. The oil profile, however, is very dissimilar to either. Palisade has average storage characteristics. When harvested early in the season, Palisade has a gentle, pleasant aroma that blends well with beers having a delicate flavor profile, but when harvested later Palisade becomes rather aggressive and pungent. The aroma can vary widely as a result. On average, however, Palisade shows a range of tropical fruit aromatics and is sometimes reminiscent of mango, with notes of apricot and freshly cut grass. Many American craft brewers treat Palisade as a good "blending hop," a character actor that supports other hops in leading roles. It blends particularly well with Amarillo and Cascade and has found its way into many American West Coast pale ales and India pale ales.

See also AMARILLO (HOP), CASCADE (HOP), and INDIA PALE ALE.

Val Peacock

Palm Breweries occupies half of the village of Steenhuffel, Belgium, northwest of Brussels. It began as the Van Roy family's De Hoorn brewery enterprise. Brewing started there in the mid-18th century, although the expansion of the brewery from a small, local operation did not begin until the 1880s.

The product responsible for the company's success has been Palm Speciale, an amber-color, biscuity pale ale with 5.4% alcohol by volume, created in 1904. The brewery almost came to an early end in 1914, when a German bomb destroyed most of it. However, the Van Roys refused to quit, and the brewhouse was quickly rebuilt to an even higher standard.

This refusal to bend before the forces of history became apparent once again in the late 20th century, when the international brew scene became preoccupied with mergers and acquisitions. Although many drinkers considered the 1970s a time that solidified the global triumph of standardized pilsner beers, Palm had a different vision of the brewing future, one in which the beer-drinking public would turn away from conformity. Palm decided to remain an ale producer when others were turning to lagers.

In 1981, Palm acquired a 50% share in Frank Boon's lambic brewery, which strengthened this brewery's distribution and helped it survive. See BOON BREWERY. Then, in 1998, Palm took over the iconic Rodenbach brewery with its hundreds of huge oak tuns, for which Palm built a new brewhouse. See RODENBACH.

Palm had many critics at the time, who predicted that no good would come of these moves. They were proven wrong, however, because the traditional brews made by these companies began to enjoy not only greater market acceptance but also a significant expansion of their market shares.

More recently Palm has started to undertake a revamp of its own beers by returning to traditional bottle conditioning and slowly introducing a greater variety of styles. This was a move, in part, to combat the newly voiced paradoxical charge that perhaps Palm had become "too mainstream for beer aficionados and too distinctive for the mass market." Today, the Palm Breweries Group is a central fixture of the Belgian brewing landscape.

Tim Webb

papain is a protease enzyme that can be added to beer before filtration and packaging. It was the first haze preventative used in the brewing industry. The enzyme is capable of digesting dissolved proteins—with amino acids as a by-product—and thus increasing the clarity of beer. One of the main natural sources of papain is unripe papaya fruit, which contains high levels of the compound. The enzyme can be purified by modern processing techniques and combined with other enzymes to produce specific mixtures suitable for chillproofing in brewing and other applications in the food industry. Among the many traditional uses of papain are as a meat tenderizer, as a medical aid on wounds and stings, and as a digestive aid. Meat wrapped overnight in crushed papaya leaves, for instance, becomes tender and requires less cooking time because of the release of papain in the milk-like papaya juice.

In brewing, papain is used to digest excess proteins after fermentation, because high protein levels can cause hazes, high viscosity, and excess foaming in the finished beer. See CHILL HAZE and FOAM. Using papain, however, is not without risks. The amino acids produced by papain digestion may also serve as nutrients for spoilage microorganisms. Papain is also very resilient and acts under a wide range of conditions including high and low temperatures. This makes it suitable for many applications, particularly in foods with low pH and during beer processing at low temperatures. On the flip side, however, its high temperature resistance may allow it to survive pasteurization and thus continue to be active in packaged beer. If improperly used or allowed to survive into packaged beer, papain can eventually digest foam-positive proteins as well as haze-forming proteins, thereby damaging a beer's foam stability. Largely for this reason, use of papain has declined in recent decades, and it has been replaced by modern adsorbents that are reliably filtered out of finished beer.

Keith Thomas

Papazian, Charles, "Charlie" (1949–), is the president of the Brewers Association in Boulder, Colorado. Papazian is one of the most influential American beer personalities, often referred to as the "father of homebrewing." He has inspired homebrewers through his published works and craft brewers through the trade organization he started in 1978. First, Papazian founded the American

Homebrewers Association for homebrewers and shortly thereafter the Association of Brewers for the burgeoning microbrewery industry of small commercial breweries.

Papazian received a Bachelor of Science in Nuclear Engineering in 1972 from the University of Virginia. While in college, a friend's neighbor showed off his basement homebrewing system, and the budding engineer was intrigued, not only by the taste of the beer but also by the brewing process. After college, Papazian moved to Colorado, where he began brewing at home and later taught others to homebrew.

His notes eventually became the first *Complete Joy of Homebrewing*, initially published as a pamphlet in 1976. Two years later, Papazian self-published a completely revised 80-page version. This eventually became the seminal guide for homebrewers. Later published in an expanded form by HarperCollins, it has since gone through 25 printings and 3 editions, selling more than 1 million copies.

Papazian is also the author of several other books, including *The Homebrewers Companion* and *Microbrewed Adventures*. He now travels the world as a lecturer and presenter at numerous prestigious events, such as the National Press Club, the National Restaurant Association, and Slow Food's Salone del Gusto in Italy.

Jay R. Brooks

parti-gyle is the name given to a number of beers that may be brewed from a single batch of grist ingredients in the brewhouse. The process of brewing a parti-gyle is standard in traditional brewhouses in the UK, where wort from one mash tun may be run off into two or more kettles. See COPPER. Each part of the run-off will have different strengths or gravities; the wort run-off into the first kettle will be stronger, while that run into the second will be weaker. See RUN-OFF. The first high-gravity kettle will also have more yeast nutrients than the weaker second kettle. The wort in each of the kettles may be mixed in different quantities to produce different beers, while different sugars and hops may be added to the kettles to make alternative beers. For example, the strong first worts may be used on their own to brew a strong ale or barley wine; a mixture of two kettles with mostly strong wort in the first copper may be used to brew a "special bitter ale" with an original gravity of 1.050 (14.5°Plato), whereas the worts containing beer from the weaker second kettle may be used to brew a "light ale" of 1.035 (9°P). Parti-gyling is not carried out in modern breweries using "high gravity brewing." That technique involves brewing and fermenting a strong beer that is then diluted to the intended final strength with deoxygenated (deaerated) brewing water before it is packaged.

See also HIGH GRAVITY BREWING.

Paul KA Buttrick

pasteurization is the process of heat treating beer to inhibit the growth of potential beer spoilage microorganisms and prolong the shelf life of the beer. Named after the great French scientist Louis Pasteur, who was able to prolong the drinking quality of beer by holding the beer at 55°C–60°C (131°F–140°F) for a short time, pasteurization is used in the production of most of the draught and bottled/canned beers throughout the world. Pasteurization is often confused with sterilization. In the former, the beer is subject to sufficient heat processing to render the beer free from microbial spoilage during the course of its shelf-life. However, low levels of some microorganisms might still survive the heating, albeit without causing spoilage of beer. In sterilization, the heat treatment applied is of such intensity that it kills all microorganisms present.

Initially, based on a largely empirical observation, holding beer at a temperature of 60°C (140°F) for a few minutes was deemed sufficient to maintain microbiological integrity over its shelf-life of several months. The brewing industry uses this temperature of 60°C as a basis for quantifying the extent of the pasteurization process. For every minute the beer is held at 60°C it is said to be subject to one pasteurization unit (PU). Holding for 15 min at 60°C, therefore, is 15 PUs of treatment.

There are two major methods of beer pasteurization. Bottled and canned beers are pasteurized by passing the filled containers through a long, relatively narrow chamber in which hot water is sprayed over the containers for a fixed time before cooling.

The spraying chamber is called a "tunnel" and the process is therefore called "tunnel pasteurization." For large containers of beer such as kegs, heating the contents of the keg in a tunnel is impractical. Instead, beer is heat treated by being passed through a heat exchanger (hot water gives up its heat by exchanging with cold beer over a large surface area) where the beer will be heated to 70°C–72°C (158°F–162°F) for as little as 30 sec. See HEAT EXCHANGER. This is known as "high-temperature/ short-time" processing or, more commonly, "flash pasteurization." It is calculated that 72°C (162°F) for 30 sec is equivalent to 15 min at 60°C, or 15 PUs. Beer that has been flash pasteurized is then cooled rapidly before being filled into sterile containers. Depending on the perceived risk of microbiological spoilage of the beer, the number of PUs applied will vary but for most beers the range is 5–25 PUs, with 15 PUs the approximate industry standard. Beers with very low alcohol contents will tend to receive more PUs.

Although pasteurization is effective in preventing microbial spoilage in beer, it can adversely impact flavor by accelerating the "staling" or "aging" of beer. Staling is a natural phenomenon, the result of relatively slow chemical changes to the beer components with time, particularly if any quantity of oxygen is present in the beer at the time of filling the beer container. The application of heat during pasteurization increases the rate of the chemical changes. Brewers endeavor to minimize oxygen pickup during packaging and reduce PU application to a minimum to maintain the freshness of the beer for as long as possible. In recent years, instead of pasteurizing the beer, some brewers attempt to exclude beer spoilage microorganisms by a process of microfiltration known as "sterile filtration." See STERILE FILTRATION. This method can be highly effective, but it also tends to strip away flavor, aroma, body, and even color.

See also PASTEUR, LOUIS.

George Philliskirk

Pasteur, Louis (1822–1895), was a famous French scientist credited (among many other achievements) as the first person to understand the process of fermentation and the importance of microorganisms in the production and spoilage of beer. His observations on the heat treatment of beer to prevent microbial spoilage became known as "pasteurization." Before Pasteur's definitive statements on the nature of fermentation, it had been thought that the products of fermentation arose from "spontaneous generation," which, in essence, propounded that "life" was continually being created out of inanimate matter. In 1860 Pasteur wrote, "Alcoholic fermentation is an act correlated with the life and organization of yeast cells, not with the death and putrefaction of the cells, any more than it is a phenomenon of contact, in which case the transformation of sugar would be accomplished in the presence of the ferment without yielding up to it or taking from anything." By 1875 Pasteur had concluded that fermentation was the result of life without oxygen, whereby, in the absence of free oxygen in the atmosphere, cells were able to obtain energy which was liberated by the decomposition of substances containing combined oxygen.

In 1876 Pasteur published his groundbreaking book *Etudes sur la Biere* in which he dealt with the diseases of beer and described how the fermenting yeast was often contaminated by bacteria, filamentous fungi, and other yeasts. For example, long rod-shaped and spherical-shaped organisms (probably lactic acid bacteria) seen under the microscope were responsible for a sour defect. See LACTIC ACID. In Pasteur's own words, "Every unhealthy change in the quality of beer coincides with the development of microscopic germs which are alien to the pure ferment of the beer" (1877). These unwelcome organisms had come into contact with the beer as a result of contamination in the production environment or through contaminated yeast. Pasteur observed that by holding beer at between 131°F and 149°F (55°C–60°C) for a short time the growth of beer spoilage organisms was inhibited and the beer could be rendered palatable for up to 9 months. This is the basis of the process of pasteurization.

Pasteur, it is said, was not a great lover of beer, but as a result of the Franco-Prussian War of 1870, the outcome of which resulted in France ceding the hop-growing region of Alsace-Lorraine, Pasteur had an animosity for all things German. This resulted in his determination to improve the quality of French-made beers, or as Pasteur himself stated, to make the "Beer of National Revenge"!

See also PASTEURIZATION.

Hornsey, Ian S. *A history of beer and brewing*. Cambridge: Royal Society of Chemistry, 2003.

Hutkins, Robert W. *Microbiology and technology of fermented foods*. Ames, IA: IFT Press and Blackwell Publishing, 2006.

George Philliskirk

Paulaner Brauerei GmbH & Co. KG, the largest brewery in Munich and the eighth largest in Germany. The brewery is almost 4 centuries old and was founded as a monastery brewery in 1634. It has been making beer with only brief interruptions ever since. During its sometimes turbulent history, the brewery has changed hands several times, made its own innovative contributions to the world of beer, and generally reflected the development of Bavarian beer at large. See BAVARIA. Today, Paulaner, together with Hacker–Pschorr, the Anheuser-Busch InBev–owned Löwenbräu and Spaten, the State of Bavaria-owned Hofbräuhaus, and the independent Augustiner, is one of Munich's traditional "big six" breweries. The brewery's legal name is now Paulaner Brauerei GmbH & Co. KG. Together with the adjacent Hacker–Pschorr Bräu GmbH, it is part of the Munich-based Brau Holding International AG, which, in turn, is owned 49.9% by the Dutch Heineken N.V. and 50.1% by the Schörghuber Corporate Group, a diversified enterprise with businesses in hotels, aircraft leasing, beverages, real estate, and construction. Paulaner takes its name from the Paulaner monks, a branch of the Benedictines, so named after the Italian Saint Francis of Paola. The monks had come to Munich from Italy in 1627 at the invitation of the pious and austere Duke Maximilian I of Bavaria to do good works. Initially they only brewed for themselves, but they soon obtained a dispensing license for the Munich citizenry. In Benedictine fashion, their beers were strong and malty, a true "liquid bread." The friars called their beer sankt-vater-bier ("Holy Father Beer"), a name that evolved into Salvator, the Latin word for "Savior." During Lent, when, according to ecclesiastic doctrine, the monks were restricted to a liquid diet, these friars eventually used a recipe created in 1774 by one of their brewmasters, Valentin Stephan Still, who stirred the mash as Brother Barnabas. Barnabas' recipe yielded a version of Salvator that was "double" strong ("doppel" in German) and thus invented the first doppelbock. See DOPPELBOCK. However, the Paulaner monks' joy in their Salvator was short lived. Calamity soon came in the person of Napoleon Bonaparte, under whose policy of secularization of church property the Paulaner monastery and its brewery were forced to be shut down and become the property of the State of Bavaria in 1799. The brewery lay in disuse for 7 years until it was rented, in 1806, to Franz Xaver Zacherl, the owner of the Münchener Hellerbräu. Zacherl was able to purchase the old Paulaner Brewery outright in 1813, thus saving Salvator beer from extinction. The revived Paulaner Brewery prospered and in 1928 merged with the Gebrüder Thomas Bierbrauerei of Munich to form the company Paulaner Salvator Thomas Bräu. In 1998, the Hacker–Pschorr Brewery was closed and Paulaner took over the brewing of the Hacker–Pschorr brands. Paulaner is now by far the biggest brewery in Munich.

The Paulaner Group, which currently includes Hacker–Pschorr Brau GmbH Munchen and Auerbrau AG Rosenheim, introduced a light beer with 40% less alcohol in 1989, 3 years after releasing the first non-alcoholic wheat beer. Paulaner roggen, a dark wheat beer brewed with rye, debuted in 1998 but has since been discontinued.

Paulaner bottles five varieties of weissbier, six hellbiers or light lagers, an Oktoberfest (available July–October), and a pilsner brewed exclusively with Hallertau hops. Paulaner produces a portfolio of more than 25 beers, but the Paulaner Salvator doppelbock still takes a special place of honor in that portfolio, especially during an annual 2-week-long Lenten celebration in the hallowed halls of the Paulaner brewery beer hall—built in 1861 and completely renovated after a 1999 fire—at Hochstrasse in the Nockherberg district of Munich. There, the first cask of the new season's Salvator doppelbock is the official opening act of Bavaria's "strong beer season"—with blaring oompah bands, comedians, sausages and pretzels, a star-studded audience, and TV cameras in attendance.

In 2008 Paulaner sold more than 1.8 million barrels of beer, a growth of 1.8% over the previous year. Along with brewhouses in China, Hungary, Indonesia, Russia, South Africa, Singapore, and Thailand, Paulaner currently operates 14 beer gardens in and around Munich. Guided tours of the Munich brewery are offered year round.

Bayerischen Brauerbund. http://www.bayerisch-bier.de/index.php?StoryID=1/ (accessed April 4, 2011).

Bild. "Germany's Largest Beermakers: Oettinger, Krombacher and Bitburger." http://www.bild.de/BILD/ratgeber/geld-karriere/2009/01/26/bier/die-groessten-meistgetrunkenen-biermarken-deutschlands-oettinger-krombacher-bitburger.html/ (accessed December 1, 2010).

Oktoberfest München. *Müncher Brauereien auf dem Oktoberfest.* http://www.oktoberfest-zeitung.de/index.php/brauereien/muenchner-brauereien-auf-dem-oktoberfest/136/ (accessed April 4, 2011).

Paulaner Service Portal. *Paulaner Brauerei in München.* http://www.paulaner-serviceportal.de/ (accessed April 4, 2011).

Typisch München. http://xn--typisch-mnchen-osb.de/muenchen/index.php/essen-trinken/paulaner/46/ (accessed April 4, 2011).

Horst Dornbusch and Ben Keene

pectinatus is a genus of strictly anaerobic, Gram-negative, spherical bacteria of which some species are common contaminants of non-pasteurized, packaged beers. During the 1970s the processing and packaging of beers became more controlled and oxygen concentrations could be kept to an absolute minimum. This improved beer quality but unexpectedly opened the beer to a new bacterial threat: strictly anaerobic organisms that are killed by oxygen. First reported by S. Y. Lee and coworkers at Coors Brewery in 1978, these isolates from packaged beer were assigned to the genus pectinatus as Pectinatus cerevisiiphilus. They have since been encountered widely in Germany, Japan, and Scandinavia. Other species, Pectinatus frisingensis and Pectinatus haikarae, have since been described. Spoilage of packaged beer is evident from turbidity and off-flavors reminiscent of rotten eggs from the production of hydrogen sulfide. See HYDROGEN SULFIDE. Similar anaerobic bacteria isolated from finished beer in Germany in 1979 were classified in the genus megasphaera as Megasphaera cerevisiae. These bacteria are sensitive to ethanol and are therefore more common in low-alcohol products. A strain of a second species isolated from spoiled finished beer, Megasphaera sueciensis, was described in 2006. However, it seems that megasphaera strains are less common than pectinatus as beer contaminants. It should be emphasized that laboratory culture of these organisms requires attention to strict anaerobic techniques; they cannot grow in the presence of oxygen.

See also BACTERIA.

Juvonen, Riikka, Maija-Liisa Suihko. *Megasphaera paucivororans* sp. nov., *Megasphaera sueciensis*, sp. nov. and *Pectinatus haikarae* sp. nov., isolated from brewery samples and emended description of the genus *Pectinatus. International Journal of Systematic and Evolutionary Microbiology* 56 (2006): 695–702.

Fergus G. Priest

pediococcus is a genus of coccoid-shaped (spherical) lactic acid bacteria. Pediococci typically occur in pairs and tetrads and were originally confused with the genus Sarcina, hence the term "sarcina sickness" for beer contaminated with these bacteria. Like other lactic acid bacteria, these Gram-positive organisms have a fermentative physiology (producing lactic acid from sugars) and grow best at low pH (around pH 4–5) and in the absence of air. It is for these reasons that specialized culture media set at a low pH and supplemented with glucose or sucrose are required for their growth in the laboratory.

Pediococci are associated with various food fermentations including vegetable pickles, sausages, and milk products. Of the 16 recognized species, Pediococcus damnosus is by far the most commonly encountered beer contaminant, probably because it has evolved tolerance of hop iso-alpha acids using a variety of molecular mechanisms. See ISO-ALPHA ACIDS. These include several different resistance genes similar to those that confer antibiotic resistance on bacteria and code for proteins referred to as multidrug exporters. P damnosus may be detected in the late fermentation and conditioning or packaged beer but rarely in pitching yeast. Contaminated beer is characterized by the buttery aroma of diacetyl, as well as turbidity and acid formation. Pediococci may produce copious amounts of extracellular polysaccharide, which forms viscous precipitate or "rope" in beers when some fermentable sugar is present.

See also LACTIC ACID.

Suzuki, Koji, Kazumaru Iijima, Kanta Sakamoto, Manabu Sami, and Hiroshi Yamashita. A review of hop resistance in beer spoilage lactic acid bacteria. *Journal of the Institute of Brewing* 112 (2006): 173–91.

Fergus G. Priest

pentanedione, properly called 2,3-pentanedione, is a vicinal diketone (VDK) normally produced by yeast during fermentation. It gives a honey-like flavor in beer and is considered an off-flavor for most beer styles. Pentanedione has a flavor threshold some 10-fold higher than the related buttery-tasting VDK diacetyl, but brewers usually seek to eliminate both from finished beer. Pentanedione is formed in fermenting beer by a spontaneous oxidative decarboxylation of alpha acetohydroxybutyrate, a precursor of the amino acid isoleucine. The pentanedione is reassimilated and removed by active yeast given prolonged contact.

To reduce the effect of 2,3-pentanedione on the overall flavor profile of the finished beer, many brewers employ either a "VDK rest" or kräusening when primary fermentation is complete, especially when fermenting lagers. The former method involves allowing the temperature in the fermenter to slightly rise over a specified period of time, usually from 1 to 3 days. The warmer temperatures raise the metabolic activity of the yeast, speeding the reabsorption of the offending compounds. The latter involves adding a small amount of freshly fermenting wort to beer that has finished its primary fermentation. The active yeast then performs the necessary VDK removal. Lagering, the storage of beer at cold temperatures for long periods, can eventually remove VDKs, but this can take months, and most brewers will use the methods above. 2,3-Pentanedione can be a useful marker for infections within a brewery. Brewery labs can perform gas chromatography tests to determine the ratio of diacetyl to pentanedione in beer. As many spoilage bacteria tend to produce diacetyl but not pentanedione, the presence of a vastly greater proportion of diacetyl than pentanedione is usually symptomatic of a contamination problem.

Bamforth, Charles, and M. Kanauchi. Enzymology of vicinal diketone reduction in brewers yeast. *Journal of the Institute of Brewing* 110 (2004): 83–93.

Goldammer, Ted. *The brewer's handbook: The complete book to brewing beer*, 2nd ed. Clacton on Sea, UK: Apex Publishers, 2008.

Zviely, Michael. Molecule of the month: 2,3-pentanedione. *Perfume & Flavorist* July (2009): 20–22.

Damien Malfara

pentose is a monosaccharide sugar composed of five carbohydrate atoms. In barley and other grains, pentose occurs naturally as the monomer of polymers called pentosans, non-starchy polysaccharides found in the cell walls of the grain endosperm. The principal pentoses are xylose and arabinose; hence, the pentosans are called arabinoxylans. Pentosans are also the main building blocks of barley husks. Pentosan amounts to merely 3% to 4% of all of the carbohydrates in barley, and about 20% of pentosans are hydrolyzed and degraded into pentose during malting. As sugars, therefore, pentosans play only a minor role in beer making, although their survival into beer is said by some to benefit foam stability. They also may be claimed to represent soluble fiber, with possible health benefits.

Oliver Jakob

peracetic acid (PAA), the antimicrobial properties of peroxyacetic acid, was first described in 1902. However, it was more than 50 years before PAA was "rediscovered" and commercially introduced. The long lag time was likely caused by a lack of understanding of how to stabilize PAA solutions and by reports of spontaneous decomposition of highly concentrated solutions. Today, PAA has become a common choice of sanitizer/disinfectant for breweries because of its broad antimicrobial activity and its "compatibility" with beer.

PAA is a clear liquid shipped in specially vented containers similar to those used for bleach and hydrogen peroxide. In concentrate and strong-use solutions, it exhibits a strong, characteristic odor reminiscent of acetic acid or vinegar, especially when handled or agitated. PAA solutions are produced by mixing acetic acid and hydrogen peroxide in an aqueous solution, often assisted through a sulfuric acid catalyst. PAA has a very high oxidation potential and is therefore an ideal antimicrobial agent. PAA has an extremely broad killing spectrum and is effective against bacteriophages and spores. PAA is a very effective cold sanitizer and can be used over a wide range of temperatures (0°C–40°C) as well as a wide range of pH (1–7.5). It is non-foaming and therefore an excellent choice for use in cleaning in place applications.

PAA is relatively unstable and breaks down readily into acetic acid (acetate), water, and atomic oxygen. This form of oxygen poses no risk of oxidation to beers that come into contact with it. These breakdown products are environmentally friendly and PAA is certified for use in the production of organic beers. Brewers appreciate the effectiveness of PAA; however, it must be handled carefully because it is highly concentrated and can cause burns.

Dirk Loeffler

pericarp constitutes remains of the ovary wall that surrounds the embryo and endosperm in cereals. In cereals, such as barley, the pericarp is fused with the testa (seed coat) to form a thin layer that sits immediately below the husk encompassing the embryo, aleurone layer, and endosperm. The pericarp/testa may be revealed in barley by gently stripping the husk from the grain to show the slightly shiny skin of the grain. With cereals such as hull-less barley and wheat, the husk is removed during the threshing phase of harvesting to leave the grain covered by the pericarp/testa.

The role of the pericarp, particularly with hull-less cereals, is to protect the nutrient-rich endosperm, aleurone layer, and embryo from soil microbes. See ALEURONE LAYER. The pericarp also acts somewhat as a barrier to the movement of water into the grain; this may be of interest when conditioning wheat malts before brewing. Some investigations have indicated that the pericarp/testa is relatively rich in polyphenols and tannins, but this is probably of little consequence because the pericarp/testa is a minor component of the grain.

See also BARLEY and ENDOSPERM.

Evan Evans

Perle (hop) is a hop variety that was released in 1978 by the German Hüll Hop Research Institute in the heart of the Hallertau. It was bred from the English hop Northern Brewer and an undisclosed male parent. Perle is a well-balanced and highly versatile hop with both medium bittering and medium aroma characteristics, which make Perle a favored multipurpose hop for bittering, flavor, and aroma. Perle averages 5% to 9.5% alpha acids for a moderate, slightly minty, fruity–spicy up-front bitterness. Perle's mild, fresh-green, almost earthy aroma results in clean and refreshing reverberations in the finished beer. Because of this balance, Perle performs particularly well in pale to medium dark session ales and lagers where aggressive bitterness is not desired. It is also excellently suited to wheat beers. Agronomically, Perle is relatively easy to grow. It is fairly hardy, high yielding, and resistant to many common hop diseases, including wilt (Verticillium albo-atrum, Verticillium dahliae) and downy mildew (Pseudoperonospora humuli). See DOWNY MILDEW and VERTICILLIUM WILT. In its land of origin, Germany, it has become the most planted aroma hop variety. It is also grown in Belgium and, since the late 1980s, in the Pacific Northwest of the United States, where alpha values have been higher than in the German-grown hops.

CMA Hop Variety Portfolio. *The spirit of beer—Hops from Germany*. West Newbury, MA: Association of German Hop Growers, 2005.

Lydia Winkelmann and Horst Dornbusch

Perlick is a Wisconsin-based manufacturing corporation that produces a wide spectrum of equipment for breweries and bars. It has three divisions: bar and beverage equipment, tapping, and brewery fittings. Its fabricated items range from refrigerated cabinets and glass-washing equipment to liquor display cabinets and specialty stainless-steel sinks. The Perlick catalog features a lengthy list of beer faucets, keg couplers, party pumps, and dispensing heads. It offers fittings that are compatible with other manufacturer's products and for virtually every part of the brewing process. The comprehensive nature of the Perlick product line has made it a household name in the North American brewing industry. The company was founded under the name R. Perlick Brass Works by Robert Perlick and his son, Walter, on the second floor of a building in downtown Milwaukee in 1917, with an initial focus on brass items for the automotive industry.

After the repeal of Prohibition, however, the elder Perlick saw opportunities in the brewing industry, and soon Perlick was selected as the exclusive supplier for A. O. Smith glass-lined beer tanks. See PROHIBITION. Perlick also started to manufacture fittings for refrigeration equipment and later launched its own refrigeration division. Perlick now operates an almost 28,000 square meter (roughly 300,000 square foot) production facility as well as representatives in all American states and Canadian provinces.

John Holl

perlite is a siliceous volcanic glass with many uses in construction, horticulture, and the beverage industry. It is mined in North America, South America, Asia, Australia, and Europe and used in its puffed form as a filter aid. Perlite aids filtration by increasing the length of time before a filter becomes clogged with solids. It can also be used as a precoat on which other grades of filtering agents can be applied. For example, a pressure leaf filter can be precoated with perlite, upon which subsequent layers of diatomaceous earth can be applied to form a layered cake. Perlite used in conjunction with other filter media helps brighten beer by trapping suspended solids, like yeast and hop particles, that otherwise might end up in a bright beer tank and subsequently in the packaged product. Use of perlite is popular because it can reduce the amount of diatomaceous earth needed for filtration. Diatomaceous earth, when dispersed into the air, is associated with respiratory problems. See DIATOMACEOUS EARTH. Numerous studies have been conducted to assess the toxicity of perlite and no adverse health effects have been recorded. Perlite dust, however, can be a nuisance, causing eye, nose, and/or lung irritation. The use of a dust mask and goggles while handling perlite is, therefore, advisable.

See also BRIGHT TANK and FILTRATION.

Perlite Institute. http://www.perlite.org/ (accessed May 11, 2011).

Schundler Company. Perlite health issues: Studies and effects. http://www.schundler.com/perlitehealth.htm/ (accessed May 11, 2011).

Rick Vega

Peroni Brewery, founded as the Birra Peroni Brewery in 1846 by the Peroni family in Vigevano, Italy. In 1864 Giovanni Peroni moved the brewery to Rome, where it soon began to prosper. The first advertising for Peroni beer appeared in 1910 and helped popularize the brand. By the 1960s, Peroni beer was widely available throughout Italy and began wider distribution to become a truly international brand by the 1990s. Peroni was purchased by South African Breweries in 2005 and began an international relaunch focused on their premium brand, Nastro Azzuro, a lager beer with a fuller flavor than the beer simply named Peroni. Peroni have built their brand around the Italian sense of style, and this approach has brought the beer to more than 50 countries around the world in five continents. The Daily Telegraph (UK) included Peroni, along with Gucci and Ferrari, among the top Italian icons. The original and most widely known brand in Italy is Peroni Beer, at 4.7% alcohol by volume (ABV). From its early days, Peroni was considered refreshing and well made compared with other Italian-brewed beers. The beer is made in the modern "international lager" style and contains corn grits as well as malt. The second largest brand is Nastro Azzurro, meaning "Blue Ribbon" in Italian. Nastro Azzuro is a premium lager at 5.1% ABV launched in 1963. It also contains corn grits but shows more malt character. The strongest beer made by the brewery is Peroni Gran Riserva, at 6.6% ABV.

See also ITALY and SOUTH AFRICAN BREWERIES LTD.

Keith Villa

pH stands for "power of hydrogen" or "potential of hydrogen." It is the chemical variable that denotes a solution's acidity or alkalinity. The pH value of a solution indicates its concentration of hydrogen ions. As the concentration of hydrogen ions in a solution decreases, it becomes more alkaline (caustic), that is, its pH value increases. Conversely, as the level of hydrogen ions increases, the solution becomes more acid (corrosive), that is, its pH value decreases.

Numerically, pH is measured on a logarithmic scale from 0 (the most acidic) to 14 (the most alkaline), with 7 being neutral. Distilled water (pure H_2O) is the standard for pH neutrality. All acids, therefore, have a pH value of 0 to 7; all bases have a pH value of 7 to 14. An extremely acidic solution with a pH value of 1, for instance, has a 10 times greater concentration of hydrogen ions than a solution with a pH value of 2; it is 100 times more acidic than a solution with a pH value of 3, and so on. On the alkaline side, a base with a pH value of 10 is 10 times more caustic than a solution with a pH value of 9 and 100 times more caustic than one with a pH value of 8. The most common ways of measuring pH values are disposable indicator strips made of litmus or phenolphthalein paper, or pH meters, most of which rely on hydrogen-sensitive electrodes to give LED read-outs. The pH scale was first developed in 1909, by Søren Peder Lauritz Sørensen, the head chemist of the Carlsberg Brewery in Copenhagen, Denmark.

Among the key sources of hydrogen ions in brewing water are mineral salts and the compounds formed by them. More specifically, calcium and to a lesser extent magnesium react with phosphate and other materials to release hydrogen ions and thereby lower the pH. Conversely, waters rich in bicarbonate are alkaline. Next to brewing water, a beer's malt bill is also a significant pH factor, because very dark, heavily kilned, or roasted malts decrease the pH values of the mash, wort, and beer, while pale, gently kilned malts raise them.

Brewers manage pH values mostly to enhance enzyme performance in the mash and yeast performance in the fermenter, as well as the quality of the finished beer. Enzymes perform at their peak only within narrow pH ranges (optima): Gum-converting endo-beta-glucanases have a pH optimum of 4.7 to 5; protein-converting endopeptidase and carboxypeptidase are at 5 to 5.2; and starch-converting beta- and alpha-amylase are at 5.4 to 5.6 and 5.6 to 5.8, respectively. In mashes that are too acidic or too alkaline, enzyme activity is impaired and can even stop. Most mashes, therefore, are kept at a compromise pH range close to 5.4 to 5.6, which is also where proper amounts of zinc, an important yeast nutrient, are leached from the malt into the wort. Some brewers acidify their mashes, for example, to a pH of 5.2, which among other things promotes limited dextrinase activity.

At the start of the boil, the wort pH drops by about 0.2 or 0.3, mostly because of the precipitation of calcium compounds into the trub. This brings the wort pH close to 5, which is ideal for most yeast strains at the start of vigorous fermentation. The yeast's metabolism, in turn, causes another pH drop in the fermenter, usually by about 0.5 to 0.7. At the end of fermentation, the typical pH value of a barley-based beer is usually a pleasant (to humans) 4.1 to 4.5 and that of a wheat-based beer is slightly lower. Some beers, such as the lambics and other sour beer types, have much lower pHs because of acids produced by bacterial strains.

See also ACID, LAMBIC, and MASHING.

Bamforth, C. W. pH in brewing: An overview. *Technical Quarterly of the Master Brewers Association of the Americas* 38 (2001): 1–9.

Coastwide Laboratories. *pH—The power of hydrogen.* http://www.coastwidelabs.com/Technical%20 Articles/ph__the_power_of_hydrogen.htm/ (accessed May 11, 2011).

Horst Dornbusch

phenolic flavors and aromas are often described as clove-like, medicinal, smoky, or "band-aid" and are considered off-flavors in most beer styles.

Beer always contains some form of phenol; polyphenols, such as tannins, are derived directly from hops and malt. Low levels of polyphenol can contribute to mouthfeel, whereas high levels can cause a drying, mouth-puckering astringency.

When a beer is described as phenolic, it is usually with reference to volatile phenols. Volatile phenols have low flavor and aroma thresholds and most people taste and smell them at very low concentrations, sometimes under 10 parts per billion. Although volatile phenols are generally not desirable, certain of these are sought after in particular beer types.

There are three main sources of volatile phenols: ingredients, chemical taints, and yeasts and bacteria.

Ingredients

The two brewing ingredients most likely to contribute volatile phenols are water and smoked malts. Although it should not, mains water may already contain phenols when entering the brewery. (Most countries specify a very low maximum level of phenols, including chlorophenols from added chlorine for mains water.) Breweries relying on their own water supply are typically more at risk of introducing phenols into the brewing process from this source.

Once added, phenols will not be removed by the normal brewing process.

Rauchmalt is a type of malt dried over an open fire made with beechwood logs. It is a specialty of the Bavarian region of Franconia in Germany. Rauchmalt adds the phenols guaiacol and syringol. These give a beer a smoky aroma and taste, sometimes described as "campfire" or "barbecue potato chips." These phenols are a distinguishing characteristic of rauchbier, a Bamberg speciality with powerfully smoky flavors. Craft brewers in the United States and other countries are experimenting with rauchmalt and creating interesting smoky beers that often pair well with food.

Peated malt is produced by smoking malt over burning peat. Although mainly used in the production of whiskey, some brewers are experimenting with peated malt for the resultant smoky, earthy phenols.

Chemical Taints

The main chemicals giving rise to volatile phenols are chlorine and bromine. These two chemicals combine with phenols (including polyphenols) already in the beer to create chlorophenols and bromophenols, respectively.

Chlorine is typically added to main water supplies and must be removed before the water can be used for brewing. Chlorine-based cleaners and sanitizers are very popular in breweries. Poor rinsing can result in chlorine contaminating the beer. Bromine can be introduced by packaging materials.

Chlorophenols and bromophenols are detectable at much lower concentrations than other phenols. Chlorophenols remind people of antiseptics or mouthwash, bromophenols of old television sets, hot Bakelite, or the smell of an electrical short. None of these characteristics is welcome in beer.

Yeasts and Bacteria

Most frequently, beers derive volatile phenols from yeasts or bacteria. 4-Vinyl guaiacol, known as 4VG, is a signature characteristic of Bavarian wheat beer (weizens) and many Belgian beers. Brewers manage their brewing processes and select yeasts known to produce this phenol. 4VG gives beers aromas and flavors described as being clove-like, spicy, or herbal and is considered desirable in these beers at certain levels.

Yeasts produce 4VG through the decarboxylation of ferulic acid. Brewers can increase the concentration of ferulic acid in wort by having a mash rest at 45°C (113°F) and by raising sparge liquor temperatures. Wheat malt and some barley varieties produce elevated ferulic acid levels. Higher fermentation temperatures also promote the production of 4VG. However, as these beers age, 4VG starts breaking down, giving a vanilla-like character and losing the 4VG signature.

A smaller subset of Belgian beers, including lambics, contains the phenol 4-ethylphenol (4-EP). This phenol is produced by the wild yeast type brettanomyces and it reminds people of farmyards, medicines, and mice. *p*-Coumaric acid, from malt, is the precursor to 4-vinylphenol, which in turn is the precursor to 4-EP. See BRETTANOMYCES.

Although 4VG, and to a lesser extent 4-EP, is expected in certain beer styles, in most it is not welcome and is seen as a fault. Brettanomyces also produces 4-ethylguaiacol, which gives beer smoked meat or clovey, spicy character. This phenol is largely unwelcome in beer; however, many craft brewers are experimenting with brettanomyces, especially in the production of sour and "wild" beer styles. Just as brettanomyces character in wine is usually considered a fault, but sometimes considered a desired "complexing agent," so it is in beer. See SOUR BEERS.

Wort spoilage bacteria are those which change the flavor and aroma of beer at the start of fermentation, before the yeast establishes itself. Certain Gram-negative, indole-negative, short-rod, wort spoilage bacteria have been reported to produce a medicinal phenolic taste in the resultant beer. This is always unpleasant and can be a difficult problem for a brewery to eradicate once established.

West, Dwight B., Albert F. Lautenbach, and Donald D. Brumsted. *Phenolic characteristics in brewing. I.* Chicago: J. E. Siebel Sons' Company, Inc., 1965.

West, Dwight B., Albert F. Lautenbach, and Donald D. Brumsted. *Phenolic characteristics in brewing. II—The role of water*. Chicago: J. E. Siebel Sons' Company, Inc., 1965.

Antony Hayes

Philadelphia, located near the east coast of the United States, approximately 90 miles southwest of New York City, is the country's fifth largest city and one steeped in history. Philadelphia played a pivotal role in the American Revolution; the Declaration of Independence was signed there in 1776. Many of the young country's early leaders called the city home for at least a time, including George Washington and Benjamin Franklin, two men who regularly brewed their own ales. George Washington evinced a particular regard for porter beer brewed in the city by Robert Hare. In 1790 Washington's secretary wrote, "Will you be so good as to desire Mr. Hare to have if he continues to make the best Porter in Philadelphia 3 gross of his best put up for Mount Vernon? As the President means to visit that place in the recess of Congress and it is probable there will be a large demand for Porter at that time." However, Philadelphia's beer roots can be traced back to 1680 when the city's founder, William Penn, began construction on a brewery.

Home to nearly 100 commercial breweries by the 1880s, Philadelphia was reputed to be the greatest brewing city in the Western Hemisphere, with a section of the city actually referred to as Brewerytown. But Prohibition effectively shut the industry down entirely, and subsequent economic woes worsened the damage. Philadelphia was not able to regain its footing in the brewing business, and by 1987 the last of the city's breweries, Schmidt's, closed its doors.

The microbrewery movement of the 1990s came to Philadelphia with notable vigor and by 2010 there were roughly 20 small breweries operating in the greater city area. The city is also noted for its array of good beer bars, and it remains the number one market in the United States for specialty beers imported from Belgium.

In 2008 Philadelphia launched its annual Philly Beer Week, quickly establishing it as one of the most celebrated, well-attended, and respected beer events in the United States. Spanning 10 days and host to several hundred events, Philly Beer Week is held every June.

Baron, Stanley. *Brewed in America: A history of beer and ale in the United States*. Boston: Little Brown & Co., 1962.

Bryson, Lew. *Pennsylvania breweries*, 4th ed. Mechanicsburg, PA: Stackpole Books, 2010.

New York Times Philadelphia Travel Guide, Philadelphia. http://travel.nytimes.com/travel/guides/north-america/united-states/pennsylvania/philadelphia/overview.html/ (accessed December 6, 2010).

April Darcy

Philippines

See SOUTHEAST ASIA.

Pilgrim (hop) is a modern British hop that was released for commercial cultivation in 2000. It was bred at the Hop Research Institute Wye as part of its dwarf breeding program. See HEDGE HOPS and WYE COLLEGE. Although both its parents, First Gold and Herald, are dwarf varieties, Pilgrim is not. Young's Brewery was an early commercial consumer of Pilgrim, whereas as of 2010, the largest Pilgrim customer was Molson Coors, who use it in Carling lager. Pilgrim is a dual-purpose bittering and aroma hop, but with relatively high alpha acid levels between 9% and 13%. Its bitterness, however, is often considered slightly harsh, which may be because of its high level of cohumulone (about 36% to 38%). Many consumers who enjoy beers with aggressive hop bitterness, on the other hand, consider the Pilgrim bitterness quality fairly pleasant and slightly citrus-like, especially when compared with that of other high-alpha hops. See BITTERNESS. The Pilgrim aroma is largely dominated by high levels of humulene (roughly 17%) and its flavor is earthy and spicy. Agronomically, Pilgrim matures mid- to late season, is a vigorous grower, and is the most wilt resistant of any variety planted today. It is also highly resistant to both powdery and downy mildew. Its average yield is a solid 1,250 to 1,500 kg (2,756 to 3,307 lb) per acre. It also keeps well in storage.

Charles Faram & Co Ltd. http://www.charlesfaram.co.uk/varietydetail.asp?VarietyID=UK-PL/ (accessed October, 3, 2010).

Jon Griffin

pils

See PILSNER.

Pilsen (Plzeň) is a city in Western Bohemia in the Czech Republic and the birthplace of the pilsner beer style. The term "pilsner" originally meant "from Pilsen," and the most popular beers in the world are based upon the original pilsner. Beer has been brewed in Pilsen since its founding in the

Trade card, c. 1880. The town of Pilsen in the Czech Republic gained worldwide fame as the birthplace of the pilsner beer style. PIKE MICROBREWERY MUSEUM, SEATTLE, WA

Middle Ages, but it was the development of a clear, golden-colored beer that has taken the city's name around the world.

Founded in 1295 by King Wenceslaus II of Bohemia, the city's square is dominated by the gothic cathedral St Bartholomew. From here can be seen the renaissance city hall built in 1554, regarded as one of the most beautiful buildings in Bohemia.

Underneath the city lies a labyrinth of cellars, tunnels, and springs. This underground world provided ideal conditions for the citizens to store food, shelter in times of siege, and make and store beer. On October 5, 1842, Bavarian brewer Josef Groll, working for Pilsen's Bürger Brauerei (later Plzeňský prazdroj, or "Pilsner Urquell"), brewed the first batch of the golden lager that came to be known as pilsner beer.

Pilsen is an historic city with many museums, art galleries, and theatres, but beer unsurprisingly provides many places of interest for today's visitors. The Brewery Museum tells the story of beer from ancient to modern times. It includes a reconstruction of a gothic malt house and Josef Groll's office. Within the complex is a bar serving unfiltered Pilsner Urquell. Visitors can be taken on a walking tour of the city's underground medieval cellars.

The Pilsner Urquell brewery is home to the Pilsner Urquell Brewery Visitor Centre with its tour of the brewery and also the Patton Memorial Pilsen, the only museum in Czech Republic dedicated to the events of 1945, when the American Army fought to liberate the area. The brewery is the site each September for a beer and music festival.

See also CZECH REPUBLIC.

City of Pilsen. http://www.pilsen.eu/ (accessed March 3, 2011).

Tim Hampson

pilsner (or pilsener or pils) is a pale, golden lager, originally from the Czech Republic. It revolutionized the brewing world when it first appeared, thanks to its seductive golden glow and crisp, refreshing taste. And thanks to an oversight that meant neither the name nor the recipe was patented, it was quickly imitated around the world. Today, for most beer drinkers, pilsner is simply synonymous with lager. Imitation pilsners today account for 95% of global beer volume—although most of these beers share little of the character of the original.

The "Original Pilsner"

Like Burton-on-Trent and Munich, the town of Plzeň (or Pilsen) in Bohemia, Czech Republic, is one of those rare towns where nature just happened to leave the perfect combination of ingredients lying around, and phenomenally gifted brewers happened to come along and find them.

The Czechs refer to beer as "Czech Bread"—they have always taken it incredibly seriously and drunk a great deal of it. But for most of beer's history, the ability to brew beers to a high and consistent standard lagged behind the demands for quality. In the mid-19th century, the citizens of Pilsen were becoming increasingly concerned with the quality of their beer, culminating in 1838, when an entire season's brew was solemnly poured away in front of the town hall.

Something had to be done, and the citizens came together to build a new state-of-the-art brewery, the

Bürger Brauerei (Citizens' Brewery), uniting their skill and resources—and stealing as many ideas and resources as they could from the neighboring Bavarians. Martin Stelzer was commissioned to design and build the new brewery. He traveled extensively around Bavaria and met the man he knew he wanted as brewmaster, Josef Groll. See GROLL, JOSEF.

At the time, brown Bavarian lager was the most celebrated beer style across Europe, and Groll was briefed to recreate a Bavarian-style lager at the new Bürger Brauerei. He recruited Bavarian brewing assistants and barrel makers and brought Bavarian lager yeast with him.

But what came out of the tanks in October 1842 was not Bavarian beer. The citizens of Pilsen were handed a "golden beverage with thick snow-white foam . . . [and] the drinkers having tried its sharp delicious taste, welcomed it with such cheers that had never been experienced in Pilsen before."

Bavarian skill had met Czech ingredients. Moravian barley is sweet, Bohemian Saaz hops have little bitterness but a lot of aroma, and the very soft, sandstone-filtered Plzen water allows these flavors to come through. Soon pilsner beer was being discussed excitedly throughout the Austro-Hungarian Empire and beyond.

Perhaps as a result of their intoxicated delight, the burghers of Pilsen didn't get around to trademarking "pilsner bier" until 1859, by which time there were many other beers on the market referring to themselves as pilsner-style beers. Belatedly, in 1898, the Bürger Brauerei registered "the original pilsner" (Pilsner Urquell) as a trademark. See PILSNER URQUELL. The brewery became known as the Pilsner Urquell brewery (Plzeňský Prazdroj). It still brews the beer today.

It would be incorrect to refer to Pilsner Urquell as the world's first golden beer (as the brewery often does) because color is a function of malt. English pale ale brewers had pioneered the use of pale malt decades previously, and Bavarian lager brewers freely admitted to stealing the knowledge to create it. But pilsner was certainly a new style of beer that had not been seen before, and its popularity spread rapidly.

Global Domination

The birth of pilsner lager coincided with the greatest period of scientific innovation in the history of brewing. Railways meant beer could be transported across greater distances, and information traveled faster. Refrigeration meant lager no longer had to be conditioned in cool caves or deep cellars. And the work of Louis Pasteur, and those influenced by him, led to the isolation of single strain yeasts that could guarantee product consistency. See PASTEUR, LOUIS. This consistency became pilsner's byword, and brands emerged in the late 19th century that still dominate the global beer market today.

Styles of "Pilsner"

Pilsners are generally distinguished from other lager styles by their more assertive hop character. Within the style, there are two main geographic variants: Czech pilsners (such as Pilsner Urquell or Žatec) tend to be darker in color but delicate in flavor, with floral, grassy aromas, while German pilsners (such as Bitburger, Warsteiner, and Veltins) can be more bitter and earthy and use a variety of European Noble hops as well as the beloved Czech Saaz. See SAAZ (HOP). The Netherlands and Belgium are also home to world-famous "international pilsner" brands such as Heineken or Jupiler, and these tend to be sweeter with considerably less hop character.

Pilsner created the template for the industrial golden lager that dominates the global beer market and as such it is often misunderstood. Many so-called pilsners have none of the character that truly defines the style, having had their maturation time cut and flavor-giving ingredients reduced sometimes to the point of extinction. Consequently, the first encounter with a true pilsner can be a life-changing revelation to the drinker who has only previously experienced mass-produced pale imitations.

See also CZECH PILSNER, CZECH REPUBLIC, GERMAN PILSNER, and PILSEN (PLZEŇ).

Pete Brown

pilsner malt is a type of pale lager malt made from two-row spring barley that is always highly modified (i.e., good protein degradation) during malting and is kilned to an exceptionally blonde color value of no more than 2.5 to 4 European Brewery Convention (EBC; approx. 1.5° to 2.1° Lovibond). Pale ale malts, by comparison, tend to have a color rating of about 5 to 7 EBC (approximately 2° to 3° Lovibond). Pilsner malt is named after the world's first blonde lager, the pilsner, developed in the Bohemian city of Pilsen in 1842. See PILSEN (PLZEŇ). The base malt of that original Pilsner was made from Haná (also spelled Hanna or Hannah), a common barley variety then grown in Bohemia and Moravia (now part of the Czech Republic). Many of the best modern brewing barley varieties cultivated around the world, including those for pilsner malt, are genetic descendants of the old Haná strain. See HANÁ (BARLEY). In the brewhouse, good pilsner malt should have excellent processing characteristics, including favorable total protein and glucan levels, outstanding enzymatic strength for the conversion of unfermentable grain starches into fermentable malt sugars, excellent lautering properties, and high extract yields. See LAUTERING. Because pilsner malt provides the finished beer with a delicate maltiness, a substantial body and mouthfeel, as well as good foam development and head retention, it is a versatile base malt that is popular not only in traditional pilsner beers and their modern variations but also in low-alcohol beers, light beers, and many blonde Belgian beers, both ales and lagers. See BASE MALT and MOUTHFEEL. In finished beer, the flavor of pilsner malt tends to be soft, round, direct, and sweetly malty, where pale ale malts will give more color along with toasty, biscuity notes.

Thomas Kraus-Weyermann

Pilsner Urquell originated after disgruntled tavern owners in the Bohemian city of Pilsen (Plzeň in Czech, and now within the Czech Republic) poured 36 barrels of the local beer down the drains in 1838 and sparked a revolution in brewing. The beer, probably wheat beer but certainly made by the method of warm fermentation, was sour and undrinkable. Beer drinkers demanded better beer and they had heard of the new method of brewing in neighboring Munich, where so-called Bohemian beer made with the aid of newly invented ice-making machines was meeting with approval. Local businessmen and tavern owners in Pilsen committed to raise funds and build a new brewery, to be called Burghers' (Citizens') Brewery. A leading architect, Martin Stelzer, was hired to design the brewery and he toured Europe and Britain to study modern breweries that used the new technologies of the Industrial Revolution—pure yeast strains, steam power, and artificial refrigeration—to make beer.

He returned to Pilsen to design a brewery on a site in the Bubenc district with a plentiful supply of soft water and sandstone foundations where deep cellars could be dug to store or "lager" beer. He also brought with him from Bavaria a brewer called Josef Groll who had the skills to make the new cold-fermented style of beer. See GROLL, JOSEF. The brewery was built rapidly and its first batch of beer was unveiled at the Martinmas Fair on November 11, 1842. The beer astonished and delighted the people of Pilsen. It was a golden beer, the first truly pale beer ever seen in central Europe, for the lager beers brewed in Bavaria were a deep russet/brown in color as a result of barley malt being kilned or gently roasted over wood fires. A legend in Pilsen says the wrong type of malt was delivered to the brewery by mistake but this seems fanciful. It's more likely that Martin Stelzer brought back from England a malt kiln indirectly fired by coke rather than directly fired by wood. This type of kiln that was used to make pale malt, the basis of the new style of beer brewed in England called pale ale. A model of a kiln in the Pilsen museum of brewing supports this theory.

Groll would also have been aided in his endeavor by the high quality of Moravian barley, which is low in nitrates, which can cause hazes. The clarity of the beer, the extremely soft water of the Pilsen region, and the floral, spicy Saaz hops from the Žatec region all combined to make this beer something special. See SAAZ (HOP). The beer from the Burghers' Brewery was an instant sensation. It coincided with the development of glass on a commercial scale; before then, glassware was all handmade and therefore the province of the wealthy. Now, staring at the beer in clear glasses, consumers could finally see what they were drinking. They reveled in the sparkling, golden nature of the new beer from Pilsen, so different from the cloudy beers they had been drinking from their earthenware tankards. The clarity of the new beer was aided by a slow decoction mashing regime that extracted the maximum sugars from the malt and settled out proteins. The lager yeast strain, which Groll had brought from Bavaria, worked at a low temperature to mature the beer in the cold sandstone cellars beneath the new brewery.

The new beer—golden, clear, malty, hoppy, and bittersweet—appealed to a wider audience than those reached by darker beers.

The reputation of the beer from Pilsen spread like a brush fire. Supplies left via canals and the new railroad network to all parts of the Austro-Hungarian Empire, of which the Czech lands were a part. A "pilsner beer train" left every day for Vienna and the beer became a cult drink in Berlin and Paris. It reached Hamburg and other cities of northern Germany via the River Elbe. By 1874 pilsner beer had arrived in the United States and, with the second wave of immigrants from central Europe, lager brewing began to challenge the hegemony of the English-style ales introduced by the first colonists.

It was the Austrian connection and the role of German as the official language in Bohemia that gave the beer its name. Pilsner means "from Pilsen" but, as the fame of the beer spread, brewers in other countries started to produce their interpretations of the style and were not shy about calling them pilsners or pilseners. In 1898 the Burghers' Brewery labeled its beer Pilsner Urquell, which means "original source of pilsner" (the Czech rendition is Plzensky Prazdroj). The Pilsen company, when it introduced the new label, referred to the "absurdity and illogicality of using the word Pilsner for beers brewed in towns outside Pilsen." Just before World War I, the Czech company took the German brewery Bitburger to court for infringement of copyright when the Germans labeled a new golden lager Bitburger pilsner. The result was not an outright victory for the Czechs, but Bitburg and other German brewers did agree to either shorten the name to "pils" or to place the town of origin on the label to avoid giving the impression their beers came from Pilsen. That convention is still widely followed in Germany today. During the communist period that followed World War II, the name of the brewery was officially changed to Pilsner Urquell. But the original brewing methods were left intact and it was possible to see, even in the late 1980s, the remarkable system used to produce the beer since the 19th century. The entrance to the brewery is through a Napoleonic arch built during the period of empire. Inside, an exhaustive mashing regime was, and is still, used. The system is triple decoction, in two rows of polished copper vessels. One third of the mash is pumped from one vessel to a second one, the temperature is raised, and the mash is then returned to the first vessel. The process is then repeated. See DECOCTION. The sweet wort is then boiled for around two and a half hours with Žatec hops (Saaz in German). Most breweries consider 90 min sufficient, but at Pilsner Urquell brewers believe the long copper boil aids the clarity of the finished beer and develops deeper flavors. Some slight caramelization of the sugars during the boil accounts for the fact that the original pilsner is a shade darker than many modern versions of the style.

Until the 1990s, the hopped wort was cooled and then pumped to small open fermenting vessels made of Bavarian oak. Following primary fermentation, the unfinished beer was pumped down to the sandstone lager cellars and matured there for 70 days in large wooden vessels lined with pitch. The pitch sealed the wood and made sure that wild yeast and bacteria did not infect the maturing beer. The finished beer had mellowness and also a noticeable touch of butterscotch (diacetyl) from the yeast strain. See DIACETYL.

Once the free market replaced communism, the method of fermentation was changed with great rapidity. Since 1993, 3.6 billion Czech crowns ($200 million) have been pumped into the brewery. The aim has been to speed up fermentation and produce more beer. Fermentation and lagering now take place in cylindroconical stainless steel vessels and last for 35 days. Some drinkers—mainly outside the Czech Republic—complained that the beer lacked its old complexity and had a more austere bitterness, reminiscent of a north German pils, than did the original. Since 2005, the brewery has been owned by the SABMiller international group and by 2010 it seemed that the beer had returned to something like its original aroma and flavor.

Archives at Pilsner Urquell. Protz, Roger. *The taste of beer*. London: Weidenfeld & Nicolson, 1988.

Roger Protz

pin is a cask or keg with the capacity of an eighth of a UK barrel, holding 4.5 UK gal (20.46 l) or 5.6 US gal. Pins are often used to hold barley wines and other very strong beers, assuring that the contents of the cask can be served over a reasonably short period of time.

Chris J. Marchbanks

pine, fir, and spruce tips, the green shoots at the tips of the branches of evergreens, can be harvested in spring and used as a flavoring in beer. To the taste they are far less resinous than the more mature needles and twigs (although these can be used as well, to harsher effect) and even somewhat citrusy. When boiled in water they can provide either simple flavoring to the brewing liquor or, if further concentrated, an essence to be added to the ferment, as appears in recipes for spruce and pine ales dating as far back as the 17th century. It is reported that in 1769 when Captain James Cook landed in New Zealand, it was with beer on board made with a mash of spruce tips, a beverage with an added antiscorbutic element.

Like many beers brewed with ingredients alternative to imported British malt and hops, evergreen-flavored beers were common in colonial American brewing, often combining with molasses as the primary fermentable. See BREWING IN COLONIAL AMERICA. Benjamin Franklin brought a recipe for a spruce beer back home after his stint at the French court following the War of Independence, and another was recorded in the journal of General Jeffrey Amherst. Mentions are many throughout history, and across a broad geography, of beers made with the tips of pine, fir, and spruce.

Spruce beers in particular appear from time to time in the repertoires of American craft brewers. Anchor Brewing Company's "Our Special Ale," for example, brewed for the Christmas season each year to slightly different specifications, sometimes contains spruce.

Buhner, Stephen Harrod. *Sacred and herbal healing beers: The secrets of ancient fermentations.* Boulder, CO: Siris Books/Brewers Publications, 1998.

Mosher, Randy. *Radical brewing: Recipes, tales & world-altering meditations in a glass.* Boulder, CO: Brewers Publications, 2004.

Dick Cantwell

Pinkus Müller is a small brewery in the city of Münster, Westphalia, in northwest Germany. The brewery is famous for both its tart altbier and its brewery tap, which is considered one of the main tourist attractions in Münster. The brewery claims to be the oldest producer of organic beer in Germany. It joined Bioland, a farmers organization for organic and health food, in the 1970s and turned all-organic in the late 1980s. The brewery itself is much older. It was founded by Johannes Müller along with a bakery on the same premises in 1816. The name Pinkus is first mentioned in connection with Johannes' great-grandson Carl Müller (1899–1979), who reputedly earned that nickname as a student, when he and a few friends extinguished a gaslight by urinating on it. "Pinculus" is vulgar Latin for "little pisser." Later, the enterprising Carl Germanized and shortened "Pinculus" to Pinkus and turned that little gaslight tale into a branding legend. Over the years, Pinkus beers tended to be top fermented and somewhat sour—an old beer style that until World War II was known as "Münstersch Alt." This beer differed from the better known Düsseldorf altbier, made by such breweries as Uerige, which are darker in color and have a bit more bitterness. See ALTBIER and UERIGE BREWERY. Pinkus Müller's beer is notably retrograde, a blend of fresh pale amber altbier of medium bitterness and a small portion of aged beer, which is deliberately infected with lactic bacteria, to give the finished product its distinctive tartness. Although Pinkus Müller's altbier has lost some of these characteristics in recent years, its eccentricities have been well preserved in the unfiltered version called "Spezial."

Conrad Seidl

The **pint** has been the usual serving quantity for draught beer in the British public house at least since the beginning of the 20th century. In earlier centuries, before the pint became ubiquitous, the "pot," or quart—equal to 2 pints—was the norm. In Britain today, "going for a pint" has become equivalent to "going for a beer."

The pint is one eighth of a gallon, and a gallon was originally the volume of 8 lb of wheat. By the 18th century a number of different "gallons" were recognized in Britain, including the "wine gallon," defined by Parliament in 1707 as equal to 231 in^3, and the beer or ale gallon as equal to 282 in^3.

The United States adopted the wine gallon of 231 in^3 as its standard gallon measure, which made a US pint 28.875 in^3 or 473.176 ml. In the United Kingdom the Imperial Weights and Measures Act of 1824 abolished all other gallon measures and brought in the Imperial gallon, equal to the volume of 10 pounds of distilled water at a precise temperature, or 277.419 in^3. The Imperial pint, one eighth of this, is thus equal to 34.677 in^3 or 568.261 ml.

Both the US and the UK pints are divided into "fluid ounces" each meant to be equal, or approximately equal, to the volume of 1 oz of water at a specific temperature and pressure. The Imperial pint contains 20 British fluid oz equal to 28.413 ml each. The American pint, by contrast, contains 16 US fluid oz equal to 29.574 ml each. This makes the US fluid ounce 4% larger than the Imperial one. The Imperial pint is approximately 20% larger than the US pint.

Martyn Cornell

Pioneer (hop) is a modern English variety developed by Dr Peter Darby at Wye College in Kent in 1984 and released for commercial cultivation in 1996. Pioneer's progenitors are an in-bred female member of Wye's Target hop family—a high alpha line—and a dwarf hop line related to Wye's First Gold hop. See FIRST GOLD (HOP), TARGET (HOP), and WYE COLLEGE. Pioneer has an alpha acid range of 8% to 10%, a mildly citrus-like flavor, and a typically English aroma. It is a dual-purpose variety suitable for both bittering and aroma. It is also excellent for dry hopping. Initially bred primarily for its high agronomic yield, Pioneer won the 2007 (British) Institute for Brewing and Distilling Hop Competition—surprisingly on the merits of its aroma. Alas, it is a stubborn hop to cultivate and sometimes simply dies after planting, either from disease or because of the wrong soil pH. This is a likely reason why Pioneer now enjoys only limited popularity and availability.

Brian Yaeger

Pipkin (barley) is a two-row winter barley with excellent malting quality properties. It resulted from a Sergeant × Maris Otter cross and the breeding program at the Welsh Plant Breeding Station in Aberystwyth, UK (Habgood et al., 1982; BBSRC Small Grains Cereal Collection Database). Pipkin might actually be genetically closer to its grandparent Pioneer—the winter parent of Maris Otter (Rostoks et al., 2006). It is also one of the first UK cultivars developed through doubled haploid technology. In 1986 Pipkin was added to the UK National Institute of Agricultural Botany (NIAB) Recommended List (Jones et al., 1986) and in 1988 garnered the WPBS the Thompson Perpetual Challenge Trophy from the Institute of Brewing for breeding "the most successful and established new variety." Pipkin yields 25% more than Maris Otter and has lower grain nitrogen content. It was also superior in its resistance to powdery mildew (Blumeria graminis), net blotch (Pyrenophora teres), and leaf blotch (Rhynchosporium secalis)—all still serious disease impediments to barley cultivation. Pipkin grain size is smaller than that of its contemporary Halcyon (another Maris Otter offspring) and maltsters, including Ian Hall at Thomas Fawcett & Sons Ltd, found that it yielded 2% to 3% lower extracts. In 1999 Pipkin became outclassed by newer cultivars and was no longer recommended by the NIAB. Today, the only place you might locate a fresh pint brewed with Pipkin malt is at the Penlon Cottage Brewery in Wales, where owners Penny and Stefan Samociuk advocate local production to the extreme by using malt both bred and grown near the brewery.

BBSRC Small Grains Cereal Collection Database at the John Innes Centre. http://data.jic.bbsrc.ac.uk/cgi-bin/germplasm/cereals.asp/ (accessed August 15, 2010).

Habgood, R. M., D. L. Jones, D. M. Jones, R. A. Pickering, P. W. Morgan, B. C. Clifford, R. B. Clothier, R. Cook, T. E. R. Griffiths, E. W. C. Jones, and I. T. Jones. Cereal breeding. In *Report of the Welsh Plant Breeding Station for 1981* (1982): 76.

Jones, J. E., E. Chorlton, R. B. Clothier, R. Cook, T. E. R. Griffiths, D. M. Jones, I. T. Jones, and P. A.York. Cereal breeding. In *Report of the Welsh Plant Breeding Station for 1985* (1986): 74.

Rostoks, N., L. Ramsay, K. MacKenzie, L. Cardle, P. R. Bhat, M. L. Roose, J. T. Svensson, N. Stein, R. K. Varshney, D. F. Marshall, A. Graner, T. J. Close, and R. Waugh. Recent history of artificial outcrossing facilitates whole-genome association mapping in elite inbred crop varieties. *Proceedings of the National Academy of Sciences of the United States of America* 103 (2006): 18656–61.

Eric J. Stockinger

pitching is the process of adding yeast to wort to start fermentation and produce beer. Whereas traditional winemaking still uses "wild" yeast on grape skins and in the winery environment to start fermentation, almost all types of beers are fermented by pitched yeasts.

The term "pitching" may seem to have connotations of a baseball throw, but it should actually be done gently so as to minimize stress on the yeast and ensure rapid growth.

Stored yeast is typically held chilled to minimize deterioration. Removing yeast from such cold hibernation and heating it rapidly may shock the cells and reduce the speed of fermentation, with undesirable results. Gentle treatment will allow yeast to initiate fermentation at the correct time and speed.

The number of yeast cells added per volume of wort is referred to as the "pitching rate." Pitching rates may be expressed in terms of volume of yeast slurry per barrel of wort or as numbers of cells per milliliter. A typical pitching rate for warm-fermented ales would be 1 million cells/ml/degree Plato original gravity. Therefore, a 12°P wort might be pitched at 12 million cells/ml. This is only a guide and pitching rates will increase for strong beers to overcome the inhibition of high alcohol concentrations. Lager yeasts typically require higher pitching rates than do ale yeasts. Lower pitching rates are associated with slower starts to fermentations, higher rates of yeast reproduction, and greater ester production; the converse is true of higher pitching rates. Brewers determine, based on a number of factors, what pitching rate is best for each beer.

Some traditional yeasts have been repitched from previous batches, in succession, for decades and consistently produce the same character in the resulting beer. These yeasts have evolved a stable genetic composition and are a treasure to a brewer. More commonly yeast "drifts" with continual repitching and new cultures are required from the laboratory on a regular basis, typically every 12 or so generations, although some will refresh the yeast more frequently.

Pitching requires careful handling to avoid contaminating the wort. After yeast is cropped from a previous batch, it may be pitched into new wort in any variety of ways. It may be as simple as physically tossing buckets of yeast slurry into the fermenter or as complex as in-line dosing of yeast from brinks on weight load cells tied back to a computer—in this case the program delivers the exact weight of yeast desired. Oxygen may be added to pitching yeast to provide a building block for sterols to enhance growth, but oxygen is more often added to the wort.

Brewing Techniques. http://www.brewingtechniques.com/library/backissues/issue2.3/kingtable.html/ (accessed May 11, 2011).

Edgerton, J. A primer on yeast propagation technique and procedures. *MBAA Technical Quarterly* 38 (2001):167–75.

Keith Thomas

Plato gravity scale is a measurement of the concentration of dissolved solids in a brewery wort. Degrees Plato (°P) is used to quantify the concentration of extract (mainly sugars derived from malt but also including other soluble material in wort) as a percentage by weight. A 10°P wort will contain 10 g of extract per 100 g of wort. The measurement of wort gravity is important to brewers in that it is an indicator of the potential alcoholic strength of the beer. As a very rough guide, every 1°P generates approximately 0.4% alcohol by volume—a 12°P wort will produce an average of approximately 5% alcohol by volume, depending on the extent to which sugars are fermented out.

The Plato scale differs slightly from the Balling scale in that the measurement of the specific gravity used to determine the dissolved solids content is carried out at 20°C for the Plato scale and 17.5°C for the Balling scale. Brewers measure the degrees Plato using either a calibrated refractometer or a hydrometer. See HYDROMETER. The Plato scale is used by most brewers worldwide, although brewers in the UK and those using British brewing traditions prefer to use the specific gravity scale instead. This is derived by measuring the specific gravity of the wort (where water is 1.000), multiplying by 1,000, and then subtracting 1,000 from that figure to give the degrees of gravity. Thus, a wort with a specific gravity of 1.048 is said to have 48 degrees of gravity. The Plato and gravity scales can be approximated by multiplying the °P by 4 to give the degrees of gravity. A 12°P wort is therefore approximately 48 degrees of gravity.

See also BALLING SCALE and SPECIFIC GRAVITY.

George Philliskirk

Poland is a nation of almost 39 million people with a very rich but conservative brewing tradition. In 1321 Konrad, the Duke of Olesnica, granted the city of Namyslow in southwest Poland the privilege to brew beer, and the ducal malt and brewhouse were founded. Seven hundred years later, Browar Namyslow, Poland's oldest brewery, continues to brew its brand Zamkowe on the site of a Gothic castle.

The third republic of Poland has existed for less than a century, and it has undergone a revolution in its brewing industry while surviving Nazi occupation and Communist rule. Nazis confiscated Polish breweries and produced a low-gravity lager for the soldiers on the Russian front. Under Communist rule, brewers were forbidden to sell their beer outside of their region (with the exception of the Żywiec and Okocim breweries in southern Poland, which were allowed to export beer). Poland now boasts some of the most modern and state-of-the-art breweries in the world.

The 1990s were a decade of great change on the Polish brewing landscape. Global brewers entered the market with the first national television and billboard advertising campaigns that the country had ever seen. An Australian conglomerate called Brewpole brought the concept of "Miller Time" to Poland, relabeling it as "EB Time." By the start of the 21st century the major brewers had basically swallowed up Poland's most prominent regional players and successfully consolidated the market. What was once a full-bodied, well-hopped pale lager has become a homogenous, adjunct-infused, characterless pale lager in line with the common international pilsner. See ADJUNCTS. Today, the market is 95% controlled by four large brewers: SAB Miller, Heineken, Carlsberg, and Royal Unibrew. Beer drinkers have shunned their local brewers for the brands of global players who introduced marketing tactics from the Western world.

For those seeking Polish beers with more flavor, there are some beacons of hope. Notable styles that have survived the market upheaval are the Baltic Porter and Kozlak beers. A few independent local brewers have begun producing a non-pasteurized version of their pale lagers, with the first to gain national prominence coming from the Amber Brewery near Gdansk.

The Baltic porter is the most interesting beer style brewed in Poland today. Original gravities for Baltic porter range from 18 to 22°P, alcohol content from 7.5%–9%, and bitterness from 25 to 40 IBUs. The aroma evokes toffee, caramel, sherry, and licorice. The color is copper to dark red, and the flavor is of caramel, dark chocolate, and sour cherries. Baltic porter can be a very complex beer. As with most Polish beers, malty sweetness dominates, and hops are toned down. Baltic porter is fermented with a lager yeast, whereas traditonal porters are fermented with ale yeast. See BALTIC PORTER.

Small craft brewers have realized the opportunity to create a niche by producing the above-mentioned styles, avoiding useless battles over the question of who can produce the cheapest golden lager.

Homebrewing has become increasingly popular in Poland. The community of homebrewers now has access to ingredients from all over the world, and homebrewers are beginning to replicate styles from many different countries. The modern Polish beer consumer is open to trying beers from the UK, Belgium, the United States, and beyond, so one imagines it is only a matter of time until more Polish brewers begin producing beers inspired by craft brewing movements worldwide.

After 2004 robust growth has been seen in the brewpub segment of the market. Today there are almost 20 brewpubs in Poland, and that number continues to increase. The very first brewpub in Poland, Spiz, was opened in Wroclaw in 1992. Since then, Spiz has opened two other locations, in Milkow and Katowice. Another brewpub chain is Bierhalle, with locations in Warsaw, Lodz, Katowice, and a restaurant in Wroclaw. Bierhalle offers Reinheitsgebot-inspired beers brewed in glass coppers from the company Joh. Albrecht. See REINHEITSGEBOT.

The Polish brewpubs tend to brew five styles: pale lager, dark lager, honey lager, wheat beer, and Kozlak, a Polish-style bock. Some of the brewpubs produce strictly German-inspired beers such as pils, märzen, dunkles, weizen, alt, and bock.

A style often written about is a smoked wheat ale from the former Grodzisk brewery. This style has died out, although a Polish businessman has purchased the land where the former brewery was located and plans to resurrect the brewery and Grodzisk beer. The worldwide brewing community eagerly awaits this revival. Grodzisk beer was characterized by effervescence, smokiness, and a dry finish, and could be dubbed Poland's "Champagne of Beers." The beer was relatively light, ranging from 2%–5% ABV. Although this beer is no longer brewed commercially, Polish homebrewers organize a yearly competition to brew this style in its hometown of Grodzisk. The beer writer Michael Jackson once listed the Grodiszk ale as a "world-class beer."

Ryan Gostomski

Polish hops cultivation in Silesia, in the western part of present-day Poland, an area that has been Austrian and German at times, goes back to the 9th century. Today, Silesia is only a minor hop-growing area; most of the Polish production has moved to the southeastern part of Poland, near the city of Lublin. There are other small pockets of hop cultivation in western Poland as well, some of which have been growing hops since before the 15th century. Poland grows several hop cultivars, but the variety Lublin is the most traditional. See LUBLIN (HOP). Poland grows about 3% of the world's hops.

Val Peacock

polymerase chain reaction (PCR) is a testing method that can be used to assess the health and purity of yeast cultures. PCR is a method of studying the genetic material, specifically the deoxyribonucleic acid (DNA), of living organisms. DNA in live cells is composed of two chains of nucleotides (building blocks) linked together to form a double helix. PCR targets specific or random regions of the DNA for analysis by amplifying the number of copies of those regions. The region of the DNA to be amplified is determined by DNA primers that bind to each side of the target sequence and trigger the amplification. The amplicon(s) can be separated according to their size in an agarose gel to generate a single band (specific PCR) or a fingerprint (random PCR). In a brewing context, fingerprints are useful to differentiate and identify yeast strains as well as to detect yeast mutations that may occur during extensive repitching of a particular culture. Specific PCR is useful to detect contaminations in wort, beer, and yeast slurries. Wild yeast or bacteria can also be targeted using species-specific primers. The appearance of a band on the agarose gel indicates the presence of the targeted contaminant, whereas the absence of a band signals that the sample is clean. Most recent technologies eliminate the need for agarose gel, thereby allowing for real-time PCR, which makes it possible to detect and quantify contaminants in as little as 3 h. This can provide brewers with critical information about the quality of potential pitching yeast, information that might previously have taken days to obtain.

Juvonen, R., R. Satokari, K. Mallison, and A. Haikara. Detection of spoilage bacteria in beer by polymerase chain reaction. *Journal of the American Society of Brewing Chemists* 57 (1999): 99–103.

Van Zandycke, S. PCR applications to brewing: Differentiation of brewing yeast strains by PCR fingerprinting. *Journal of the American Society of Brewing Chemists* 66 (2008): 266–70.

Sylvie Van Zandycke

polyphenols are molecules containing one or more aromatic rings and two or more hydroxyl (OH) groups attached to aromatic rings. The polyphenols found in beer include simple polyphenols (two or more hydroxy groups on a single aromatic ring) or multiple ring structures such as the proanthocyanidins, which, in turn, may include catechin, epicatechin, and gallocatechin, as well as various polymers constructed from them. Polyphenols are derived directly from malt and hops and are often involved in haze formation in finished beer. See CHILL HAZE, COLLOIDAL HAZE, and HAZE. They have no aroma, and their major gustatory impact is a perception of astringency. Astringency is not technically a taste sensation, that is, it is not perceived by the taste buds. Rather, it is a so-called chemesthetic sensation, which is essentially tactile, because it is perceived by the trigeminal nerve. Chemically, this astringency is the result of polyphenols combining with proline-rich proteins in our saliva to form insoluble complexes. Usually, proteins in the mouth perform a lubricating function on the mouth's surfaces. When polyphenols rob the palate of lubrication, the mouth feels rough and a mouth-puckering sensation is perceived. Whereas astringency from tannin can be considered a positive aspect of some wines, polyphenol astringency in beer tends to clash with hop bitterness and is rarely appreciated.

Asano, K., K. Shinagawa, and N. Hashimoto. Characterization of haze-forming proteins of beer and their roles in chill haze formation. *Journal of the American Society of Brewing Chemists* 40 (1982):147–54.

McManus, J. P., K. G. Davis, J. E. Beart, S. H. Gaffney, T. E. Lilley, and E. Haslam. Polyphenol interactions. Part 1. Introduction; Some observations on the reversible complexation of polyphenols with proteins and polysaccharides. *Journal of the Chemical Society Perkin Transactions II* (1985): 1429–38.

McMurrough, I., R. Kelly, and J. Byrne. Effect of the removal of sensitive proteins and proanthocyanidins on the colloidal stability of lager beer. *Journal of the American Society of Brewing Chemists* 50 (1992): 67–76.

Siebert, K. J. "Haze in beverages." In *Advances in food and nutrition research*, Vol. 57, ed. S. L. Taylor, 53–86. London: Elsevier Inc, 2009.

Siebert, K. J., and P. Y. Lynn. On the mechanisms of adsorbent interactions with haze-active protein and polyphenol. *Journal of the American Society of Brewing Chemists* 66 (2008):46–54.

Karl Siebert

polyvinylpolypyrrolidone

See PVPP.

Poor Richard's Ale

See FRANKLIN, BENJAMIN.

porridge beers are a type of artisanal, "indigenous" beers that are not subjected to a filtration process during production of the wort and thus have a thick consistency. Many of these are African in origin, and probably the best known is the Sudanese/ Nubian drink *bouza*, which has been known since Pharaonic times. In a bygone age, the drink would have been made from barley or emmer, but nowadays other grains, such as maize, are often used. According to Edward Lane in the 19th century,

> *boozeh* or *boozah*, which is an intoxicating liquor made from barley-bread, crumbled, mixed with water, strained and left to ferment, is commonly drunk by the boatmen of the Nile, and by other persons of the lower orders.

Alfred Lucas examined 16 samples of *bouza* from various Cairo retailers in the 1920s and reported that they were all similar in appearance and all had the texture of thin gruel. Samples contained much yeast and were in a state of active fermentation; they had all been made from coarsely ground wheat. Alcoholic content varied from 6.2% to 8.1% alcohol by volume (average 7.1%). Starting with a late Roman account by Zozimos of Panapolis, the bread-based brewing process for *bouza* is well documented.

Because of the lack of filtration after fermentation, such beers are usually highly nutritious, because nearly all of the nutrients from the raw materials end up in the final product. In this context, there is speculation that *wusa*, an ancient beer of the Israelites, may have been the original "manna from heaven."

Based on their consistency, many African sorghum and millet beers would qualify for inclusion in this beer category; merissa, pito, and pombe are examples. Some types are actually porridge-like and others are merely very turbid. They are often subject to some degree to spontaneous fermentation, and some are sour in flavor. To this day, production of such beers remains a cottage industry throughout parts of Africa and is an important part of traditional village life, as it has been for centuries. In Central and South America, traditional corn-based chicha broadly fits into the porridge beer category as well.

See also CHICHA.

Lane, E. W. *An account of the manners and customs of modern Egyptians*, 5th ed. London: J. Murray, 1860.

Lucas, A. *Ancient Egyptian materials and industries,* 4th ed. Revision by J. R. Harris. London: Edward Arnold, 1962.

Steinkraus, K. H., ed. *Handbook of indigenous fermented foods,* 2nd ed. New York: Marcel Dekker, Inc., 1995.

Tamang, J. P., and K. Kailasapathy, K., eds. *Fermented foods and beverages of the world* Boca Raton, FL: CRC Press, 2010.

Ian Hornsey

porter, a type of dark beer that first saw life in the 1700s, built London's greatest breweries, slaked the thirsts of America's revolution-minded colonists, and then traveled the world, morphing as it went to meet the changing needs of time and place. Porter remains a beer style that is nowadays firmly established in the consciousness of the beer-drinking public all over the world, even if it is difficult to know what it actually tasted like in its heyday. Today, the best renditions of porter are well balanced and aromatic, with predominant notes of rich chocolate as well as hints of coffee, caramel, nuts, and sometimes a faint smokiness, combined with an often dry, even slightly acidic, finish. The origins of this beer style, however, are about as opaque as the beer itself. The most persistent and fanciful tale, for which most objectivists agree there is very little hard evidence, speaks of the "invention" of the porter style by Ralph Harwood, the owner of the Bell Brewhouse in Shoreditch, East London, England, in 1722. See HARWOOD, RALPH. Allegedly, Mr Harwood's beer was created for the convenience of a publican who ran the Blue Last, a working class watering hole on Shoreditch's Great Eastern Street. The Blue Last was then frequented mostly by "porters"—strongmen for hire, who would carry loads of produce, fish, and dry goods on their backs from merchant storehouses to the city's many public markets. In those days, beer in pubs was invariably served cask conditioned, and it was often served as a mix from several casks, or "butts." When the barman poured beer from a butt, the stream of beer was referred to as a "thread"; a blended mug of beer might contain several threads. One of the oft-mentioned popular blends of the day was called "three-threads." See CASK CONDITIONING and THREE-THREADS. There were several reasons for the practice of mixing different beers right into a patron's mug or tankard on the premises. Given the uneven quality of brewing grains and malts—a problem that was only remedied starting in the early 19th century—beer flavors were not always predictable. Thus, blending a single beer from several casks on the spot allowed the publican great flexibility in catering to his clientele's tastes. Mixing threads was also a way for sneaky publicans to sell rather than dump slightly "off" or acetic barrels by diluting them with one or more drinkable threads.

Mr Harwood allegedly decided to do the blending for the publican right at the brewery; this would obviate the need to take the time to blend several types of beer into each glass. He concocted a mash—probably mostly of brown malt—that represented a mixture of the publican's threads and called it "entire butt." It bundled the flavors of several butts into a single, labor-saving, pre-fab "entire" ale that could be poured as a single thread. Because this new beer quickly became the favorite of the hard-working and hard-drinking porters, it eventually became known by the occupation of its best customers—and the name "porter" stuck for the beer.

Thus goes the happy tale of the birth of porter, and it seems vaguely unfortunate that it is probably not true. Three-threads was a reality, but it seems that porter was in fact something else. It is also true that porter was often a blend, and this is where the various stories may have crossed paths and melded. Porter almost certainly emerged as a variant of a beer widely referred to simply as "brown beer," for which a number of early 18th-century recipes exist. Porter seems to have begun its reign as an aged, or "stale" version of brown beer, and this aged character became prized during the 1700s. In 1773, in *The Complete English Brewer*, George Watkins writes of larger, well-experienced porter breweries: "Thus, in brewing porter, they make three and sometimes four mashes; strengthening them with a little fresh malt, or running them as they call it a greater length, that is, making more beer from the same malt, according to their pleasure. These several worts they mix and make the whole of such a strength as experience shews them porter ought to have; and this they work up and barrel accordingly. In the same manner, if a butt of porter be too mild, they will throw into it a small quantity of some that is very strong and too stale; first dissolving in it a little isinglass. This produces a new tho' slight fermentation; and the liquor, in eighteen or twenty days, fines down, and has the expected flavor."

Thus, we do see early mention of porter as a blend within the brewery; this was a practice that was not at all unusual in other brewing cultures of the time. See BLENDING HOUSES.

The American colonies imported porter from London, but as matters became heated between England and the colonies in the late 1760s, American porter breweries took up the slack. George Washington's favorite porter was brewed by one Robert Hare of Philadelphia; we still have Washington's letters extolling its virtues and ordering extra stocks after a fire at the brewery in 1790. Porter was a favorite style in the early United States and was still widely brewed before lager beer pushed it aside in the mid 1800s.

Back in London, by the end of the 18th century porter had become truly big business. Porter brewing reached its peak in London in the 1820s, by which time it had become arguably the first mass-produced commercial beer. In Ireland, too, the original brown porter of London became a popular beer. There it was known as "plain porter," a beer that continued to be made under that name by Guinness until 1974. To this day in Ireland, you still hear the occasional older gentleman ask for "a pint of plain." See ARTHUR GUINNESS & SONS. As the demand for porter grew, not only among the laboring classes but also among the better off, so did the size of the breweries that made it. Some breweries began to specialize in this single beer style and became very prosperous enterprises. In the first half of the 19th century the Truman, Hanbury & Buxton Brewery, for instance, had managed to become Britain's second largest brewery purely on the strength of its porter, of which a record shows it produced about 305,000 hl (260,000 US bbl) in 1845 alone. See TRUMAN, HANBURY, BUXTON & CO. As the Industrial Revolution produced one new mechanical marvel after another, London's porter breweries put them to use with startling speed and ingenuity. Steam engines were in use in London's porter breweries within months of being patented.

Because the best-tasting porters were often matured in holding tanks for months or even up to a year, some of the aging vats became truly gigantic. Some vats were so large that breweries could serve occasional promotional dinners for their patrons inside them when they were empty. The world record in wooden fermenters at the time was set by the Meux Brewery of London, whose largest wooden porter vat could hold about 32,500 hl (roughly 27,750 US bbl). See MEUX REID & CO. On a day in October 1814, however, one of the giant Meux vats suddenly burst, causing rivers of porter to rush through the adjacent streets, crushing houses and drowning several people in beer. The final tally of the destruction included eight people dead from drowning, injuries, or alcohol poisoning of those who took more than their fill from the unexpected free beer running in the gutters. Today, in London's Chiswell Street, there remains an events venue called "The Brewery," and it is still possible to hold large gatherings in a space that was once held the Whitbread Brewery's huge porter tuns. The Whitbread Porter Tun Room is one of the largest unobstructed indoor spaces in London.

Despite the huge popularity of porter in its heyday, we have only a vague understanding of how it must have tasted. The best we can do is to draw some reasonable inferences. The original porter, no doubt, was a deep shade of brown to mahogany, made from a foundation grist of the standard floor-malted brown malt of the day with some smoky notes from the kilning of the grain over open wood, straw, coal, or coke fires. Straw-dried brown malt was considered the best because it had relatively little smoke flavor. Either deliberately or inadvertently, some portion of the grain bill may also have been popcornlike, so-called blown or snap malt. See SNAP MALT. Brown malts were sometimes merely toasted, sometimes quite dark, and often somewhat burned. They were usually left with only a portion of their original starch remaining for subsequent conversion to sugar. Aside from this, depending upon changing laws at any given time, colorings were widely used in porter, a favorite being a type of burnt sugar syrup. Licorice was also a popular additive and colorant. Porters appear to have been highly hopped, although the bitterness would have mellowed over months of aging.

However, there must have been a microbial story to tell as well. Considering the long aging of porter in vast wooden vats, it is impossible not to postulate that these vats were also breeding grounds for wild yeasts and bacteria, including probably lactobacillus and what we now call Brettanomyces, both of which have notable effects on the flavor of finished beer. See BRETTANOMYCES, LACTOBACILLUS, and WILD YEAST. Whereas lactobacillus produces tart lactic acid, the "wild" yeast strain Brettanomyces is responsible for the barnyard and sweaty horse blanket notes we have come to associate with many Belgian spontaneously fermented lambics. See LAMBIC. This interpretation is supported by that fact that Brettanomyces was first identified not in Belgium, but in Britain, in the secondary fermentation of a British stock ale, by N. Hjelte Claussen, the then director of the Laboratory of the New Carlsberg Brewery in Copenhagen, Denmark. Claussen introduced the term "Brettanomyces," meaning "the British yeast," for this microbe at a special meeting of the Institute of Brewing in April 1904 and referred to its flavor as giving beer an "English character." Since then, the British Brettanomyces strain has been known as Brettanomyces clausenii, the stronger Belgian strain as Brettanomyces bruxellensis, and the strain found in many lambics as Brettanomyces lambicus. Admiring mentions of "stale" porter seem to indicate that Brettanomyces, lactic bacteria, or both were partially responsible for the flavors of the best regarded porters of the 1800s.

As brewing techniques improved dramatically during the Industrial Revolution in England in the

19th century, so did the porter. When Daniel Wheeler introduced black "patent" malt in 1817, the makeup of most commercial porters changed quickly and dramatically. Now porter could be brewed largely from pale malt, with the new black malt as the flavoring and coloring. Pale malt could easily give more than 30% more extract than did scorched brown malts. During various periods British breweries paid taxes on the amount of malt used, and therefore the new efficiencies translated very directly to profits for brewers. Porter was often parti-gyled with stronger beers, increasing efficiencies even further. See PARTI-GYLE. Technological advances gave brewers many more choices. Some porters were brewed stronger, either for home or for export. These particularly rich beers were referred to as "stout porters," and it is generally accepted that the most full-bodied and stout porters served as the genesis of stout as a somewhat separate beer style. By the early 20th century, stouts were seen as a different article, as evidenced by Samuel Sadtler, writing in *A Hand-book of Industrial Organic Chemistry*: "'Porter' has now come to mean a dark malt liquor, made partly from brown or black malt, the caramel in which gives it the sweetness and syrupy appearance, and containing four or five per cent of alcohol. Stout is a stronger porter, with larger amount of dissolved solids, and containing six or seven per cent of alcohol." See STOUTS.

For the Baltic trade, a stronger version of porter, the Baltic porter, emerged. These porters are still made in many countries around the Baltic Sea, including in Finland, Sweden, and Estonia. In flavor, they may resemble less roasty imperial stouts and in strength they resemble barley wines, at 7% alcohol by volume (ABV) and above. They are clearly more sipping than quaffing beers and are usually cold fermented with lager yeasts. See BALTIC PORTER. Versions of porter were also popular in "East India" (India itself) and in "West India" (the Caribbean), and variants of these are today referred to as "foreign stouts." These tend to be strong and to have at least a slight tang, an echo of the acidity that would have once been popular. In the days before refrigeration, the acidity would have prevented the beer from seeming overly sweet or malty. No doubt this quality still gives the beer better drinkability in very warm climates.

In Victorian England the porter also underwent a class differentiation, and some porter versions even climbed the social ladder to become favorites of the upper classes. One such was the "robust porter," considered a beer for connoisseurs, not guzzlers. Strangely, this ale was favored more by well-heeled gentlemen than by genuine toiling porters; but considering porter's rough working-class lineage, the term may, therefore, strike the careful linguist as a tautology and the sociologist as a peculiarity. Perhaps the key characteristic of a robust porter is its greater residual sweetness compared with the drier brown and Irish porters. It is also slightly higher in alcohol.

By the 1870s, however, porter's reign was coming to an end. The practice of aging the beer had largely died away, the flavors had changed, and the breweries started to neglect porter. At one end of the flavor spectrum, pale ales were now the fashion in Britain; at the other end, stouts were taking over from porters. By the 1920s, most porters were shadows of their former selves—weak, thin, and not particularly palatable; porter was now considered a beer for old men. Whitbread's great Chiswell Street Brewery brewed its last batch of porter on September 9, 1940, as air raid sirens pealed through the streets of London during the Battle of Britain. London brewers continued to produce porters into the 1950s, but by this time the style had largely faded into oblivion.

Only during the past few decades has the porter made a comeback of sorts, especially in North America, where the beer that once had a roughneck image is now a respectable, almost gentrified, craft beer style. Small British breweries have taken up the style somewhat more gingerly, but porter seems to be regaining steam there as well. Most contemporary craft brewers take porter to have more chocolate and coffeelike roasted flavor than do brown ales, but less of this character than stouts generally have. Most keep to a sessionable strength, or at least below 6% ABV, with many British versions coming in quite a bit lighter than that. Baltic porters, brewed stronger and cold fermented with lager yeasts, have also gained favor among American craft brewers. Some modern porters are even dry hopped, often with very un-English Pacific Northwest hop varieties, and such beers may be labeled as American porters; surely they are at least "Americanized." See AMERICAN HOPS, HISTORY and DRY HOPPING.

Given that porter beer has seen so many changes over its nearly 3 centuries of existence, it is perhaps not surprising to see that it has arrived into the

21st century newly refreshed and ready for another star turn, this time as a foundation beer of the craft brewing movement.

Dornbusch, Horst. "Robust porter: Style profile." *Brew Your Own Magazine*, September (2006).
Foster, Terry. *Porter*. Boulder, CO: Brewers Publications, 1992.
Licker, J. L., T. E. Acree, and T. Henick-Kling. What is "Brett" (Brettanomyces) flavor? A preliminary investigation. *American Chemical Society Symposium Series* 714 (1999): 96–115.
Pattinson, Ronald. *Porter*. Amsterdam: Kilderkin, 2010.
Sadtler, Samuel Philip. *Industrial organic chemistry*, 4th ed. Philadelphia: J. B. Lippincott Company, 1912.

Horst Dornbusch and Garrett Oliver

Porterhouse Brewing Company is a company founded in Dublin, Ireland, in 1989 by cousins Liam La Hart and Oliver Hughes. La Hart, a publican, and Hughes, a barrister, had established Harty's microbrewery in 1982, where they pursued their stated beer-making mission: 100% Irish, 0% chemicals. They were joined at Porterhouse in 1994 by architect Frank Ennis. The initial plan was simply to develop a brewpub and Dublin's first microbrewery, but the business gradually expanded to include a boutique hotel and several pubs in Ireland that have been successfully replicated in London, England and Shanghai, China. Their brewpub location in Dublin's trendy Temple Bar district remains a center of local nightlife. The Porterhouse brewing and business model flourished between 1996 and 2008, when Ireland was experiencing rapid economic growth through state initiatives such as tax incentives and increased foreign investment, transforming it from one of Europe's poorer countries into one of its wealthiest. Over the same period the nation also experienced a significant and enduring craft brewing boom. For now, the boom economy has receded in Ireland, but Porterhouse beers have continued to gain wide acclaim.

All Porterhouse beers are brewed in Dublin using hops from the United States, New Zealand, Germany, England, and the Czech Republic. Locally sourced, Irish barley and a Yorkshire-origin yeast strain contribute to concentrated flavors, aromas, and textures, particularly in their notably characterful Irish stout, Wrasslers.

The Porterhouse Brewery uses direct-fired kettles, which Hughes maintains are "expensive but essential if you want the best results," and produces classically Irish styles such as plain, porter, and red ale from traditional recipes. See DIRECT FIRING. For instance, fresh Carlingford oysters are added to Porterhouse Oyster Stout for an indefinable but complementary briny balance to the coffee notes arising from its use of roasted barley. Porterhouse has also invested in an Irish whiskey distillery in Dingle, County Derry.

See also IRELAND.

Alastair Gilmour

potassium metabisulfite ($K_2S_2O_5$), commonly abbreviated KMS, is a powdery, white, strongly sulfurous-smelling (burned match) chemical used in many food and beverage industries, as well as in breweries as an antioxidant. When dissolved in water or beer, KMS releases free sulfite ions, and these are responsible for the antioxidative properties of the compound. KMS is by far the most popular antioxidant used in the brewing industry. Its popularity within some large breweries is because it is highly effective at preventing oxidation and because the added sulfites improve the naturally occurring sulfites produced by the yeast during fermentation. KMS is also active in limiting growth of wild yeasts and bacteria in beer.

Free sulfite reacts very readily with and thus eliminates free oxygen in foods (including beer), but also with many intermediary chemicals compounds (most important, aldehydes and ketones) that can combine with free oxygen into the stale and papery-tasting compounds so undesirable in beer.

KMS is allowed by Food Health and Safety authorities in most countries (it has the E-number 224 on the EU positive list of food additives) around the world, but it is not permitted by Germany's Reinheitsgebot (the German Purity Law, which is not, however, despite its name, an official law). KMS is rarely used by craft brewers anywhere, but it is common in mass-market beers in many countries. In most countries the use of KMS is regulated by specific limits either to the total concentration of sulfites in beer or by maximum allowed dosing rates.

The reason for these limitations is that sulfites are known to provoke and worsen certain allergies in humans. For example, in the United States, levels above 10 ppm will require the words "contains sulfites" to be printed on the label.

KMS is very widely, almost universally, used in the wine industry for the same purposes as in brewing, but in wine KMS is used at concentrations 10–20 times higher than in beer.

Ilett, D. R. Aspects of the analysis, role, and fate of sulphur dioxide in beer—a review. *Master Brewers Association of the Americas Technical Quarterly* 32(1995): 213–21.

Anders Brinch Kissmeyer

Premiant (hop) is a modern hop variety released in the Czech Republic in 1996. It is named for what the breeder considered its "premium" quality. Until Premiant was released, Saaz was perhaps the only internationally known cultivar of the Czech Republic. See SAAZ (HOP) and ŽATEC HOP REGION. Aiming at producing a dual-purpose hop, the Czech Hop Research Institute in the town of Žatec crossed a bitter American male cultivar with a Czech aroma variety. The aroma of the resulting plant, with Sládek and Northern Brewer in its genealogical makeup, is spicy but with a weaker aromatic profile than that of other Czech varieties. See NORTHERN BREWER (HOP) and SLÁDEK (HOP). But this makes Premiant a popular hop in the production of beer without a strong hoppy character. Premiant is a mid- to late-season hop with green bines and long, egg-shaped cones. It yields well, producing an average of 2,000 to 2,300 kg/ha (roughly 1,800 to 2,050 lb/acre). It has good resistance to red spider mites and hop aphids and, reportedly, to mildew. Alpha acids range from 8% to 12.5%, of which cohumulone is only 23%. This gives Premiant a neutral bitterness with no harsh, bitter aftertaste. Beta acids range from 4.5% to 8%. The fractions of essential oils are myrcene, which imparts a floral aroma, 38%; humulene, which imparts a balsamic, resinous aroma, 25% to 35%; caryophyllene, which imparts a spicy aroma, 5% to 10%; and farnesene, which imparts floral notes, 1% to 1.5%. Although Premiant's aromatics are muted, a few craft breweries have sought to concentrate its aromatics in strong India pale ales, where it is reported to show a grassy, woody character. This hop is fairly stable in storage.

Jelínek, L., M. Šneberger, M. Karabín, and P. Dostálek. Comparison of Czech hop cultivars based on their contents of secondary metabolites. *Czech Journal of Food Science* 28 (2010): 309–16.

Patzak, J. Characterization of Czech hop (*Humulus lupulus* L.) genotypes by molecular methods. *Rostlinná Výroba* 48 (2002): 343–50.

Victoria Carollo Blake

Pride of Ringwood (hop) is a medium to high alpha acid hop named after Ringwood, a suburb of Melbourne, in Victoria, Australia. The hop was bred there by A. S. (Bill) Nash, a hop breeder employed by Carlton United Breweries, in the late 1940s to mid 1950s. This work was later continued by the Australian Hop Marketers Ltd, a company that has since merged with the Barth-Haas Group, the world's largest hop-processing and trading company. The genetic lineage of Pride of Ringwood includes Pride of Kent, an old English aroma hop, as well as an unknown male parent, which probably contributed the hop's high alpha acid content. Pride of Ringwood was added to the U.S. Department of Agriculture Hop World Cultivar collection in 1966. It matures in early to mid-October, which is too late for it to be suitable for growing conditions in the United States. Its alpha acid content ranges from 9% to 10.5% and its beta acid content from 5.5% to 6%; its cohumulone content averages about 32%. Among its essential oils, 53% is myrcene, 9% to 13% is the spicy caryophyllene, and only 2% to 3% is humulene. This hop has no farnesene. Its aroma is described as earthy, herbal, grassy, and strong; some Australian craft brewers find it objectionable, whereas others seem to enjoy its distinctiveness. Pride of Ringwood was one of the first high alpha acid hops in Australia, where it has now largely been replaced by the newer superalpha varieties Millennium and the Australian-bred Super Pride. Its yield in Australia is a substantial: 2,500 to 3,000 kg/ha (2,230 to 2,676 lb/acre).

Hop Products of Australia. *Pride of Ringwood.* http://www.hops.com.au/products/australian_varieties/pride_of_ringwood.html/ (accessed March 8, 2011).

Nash, A. S. (Bill). *Hop Research Annual Report*, 1–2. Melbourne, Australia: Department of Science, Industrial Research, 1949.

Alfred Haunold

priming sugar is any sugar added to a fermented beer with the purpose of starting a secondary re-fermentation in a tank, a cask, a bottle, or more rarely, a keg. The end result is natural carbonation and additional flavor development. The sugar may be added as a solid, but it is most often added in liquid form just prior to racking the beer into a conditioning tank or its final container.

Yeast, which may be added at the same time as the priming sugar, consumes the priming sugars, giving off carbon dioxide and carbonating the beer inside the tank or package. Priming sugars are usually highly fermentable, with the most common being neutrally flavored sucrose, glucose, and dextrose. Under the correct conditions, these sugars will ferment out completely and leave no extra residual sweetness in the finished beer. Other sugars, such as invert sugar and molasses, although rarely used, can contribute their own colors and flavors to a finished beer.

In British cask-conditioned beers, which have a low, but brisk natural carbonation, the addition of priming sugar is usually 1.5 g to 3.0 g/l. The more priming sugar added, the more carbonation is likely to be produced, with some vigorously carbonated Belgian specialty beers using up to 14 g of priming sugar per liter.

Briggs, D. E., et al., eds. *Brewing: Science and practice*. Cambridge: Woodhead Publishing, 2004.
Hind, H. L. *Brewing science and practice*, vol. 2. London: Chapman & Hall, 1943.

Chris J. Marchbanks

Progress (hop) is a modern, English dual-purpose hop used for both aroma and bittering. Grown in Kent, its key flavor characteristics are notes of fruit and juniper berry. It originated at Wye College in Kent in the late 1950s. See WYE COLLEGE. It was brought into the United States by the Department of Agriculture Hop Research Farm in Corvallis, Oregon, in 1966. The hop's pedigree is a Whitbred Golding variety crossed with a wild American hop. Its alpha acid content is generally in the range of 5% to 7%. Although initially considered a replacement for Fuggle, the latter has generally been replaced not by Progress, but by hops with ever higher alpha ratings. This has limited Progress' acceptance. Agronomically, Progress is tolerant to verticillium wilt but not to downy mildew. It matures mid-season and keeps well in storage. Its main use is for classic English-style ales.

Lemmens, Gerard. The breeding of hop varieties. *Brewer's Digest* March (1997).
Neve, R. A. *Hops*. London: Chapman & Hall, 1991.
Wagner, T. *Gene pools of hop countries*. Zalec, Yugoslavia: Institute for Hop Research, 1978.

Brian Yaeger

Prohibition, or "the Noble Experiment," refers to the period between 1919 and 1933 when the sale, manufacture, and distribution of alcohol were illegal in the United States. Although it may have lasted only 14 years, Prohibition was the culmination of decades of protest and lobbying and has ramifications that are still felt today. It remains the focal point of the ongoing debate surrounding the potential dangers and benefits of alcohol and people's right to drink as they please.

Motivations

It is easy for those who enjoy alcohol to dismiss prohibitionists as radical fundamentalists or miserable killjoys, so it is important if we want to understand Prohibition properly to appreciate the conditions by which it came about. Throughout the history of alcohol, epidemics of destructive drinking have always occurred at times of massive social upheaval, when populations face the stressful shattering of their lifestyles and the uncertainty of new economic and societal realities.

One such era was the rapid industrialization of the United States in the latter half of the 19th century. Just as Britain had experienced its own gin epidemic in the world's first Industrial Revolution a century before, so the United States was transformed by forces that ran almost out of control. The big businesses that built railroads, manufacturing industries, and financial centers marched on for a time with unfettered power, with little regard for the social consequences of their actions. Poverty, crime, slavery,

Postcard, c. 1910, illustrating the common prohibitionist charge that the brewing industry harmed the American home. PIKE MICROBREWERY MUSEUM, SEATTLE, WA

prostitution, and alcoholism were seen as blights on the face of a young nation, and the middle classes were keen to define a morality and sense of society that they felt could be described as American.

Alcohol was one of several targets—with some justification. Although many saloons were well run, there were also those that encouraged children to drink to get them into the habit or enticed men with free food or free beer to persuade them to carry on drinking. Alcohol-fueled violence and disorder, although perhaps not epidemic, were certainly significant problems in urban areas.

The Maine Law

In Maine in 1851, a law was passed to prohibit the sale of all alcoholic beverages except for "medicinal, mechanical or manufacturing purposes." It was an attempt to "validate American family values," like the laws against adultery, dueling, and lotteries that were being passed by state legislatures at the time. The Maine example quickly spread elsewhere, and by 1855 a total of 12 states had joined Maine in total prohibition.

The law was highly unpopular, and opposition soon turned violent. Disturbances such as the Lager Beer Riots in Chicago in 1855 ultimately led to repeal in 1856. But these laws were not really working anyway—dry states could do nothing to prevent the transport of liquor across state lines, and some states simply chose not to enforce them. Whereas alcohol consumption was actually declining before the Maine Law was passed, consumption of beer, wine, and whiskey in the United States all increased between 1850 and 1860.

The year 1861 saw the outbreak of the American Civil War. Within the new society's emerging moral compass, the campaign against slavery temporarily pushed the Temperance issue into the background. The anti-drink lobby retreated to reconsider and began to reorganize much more effectively.

The Women's Christian Temperance Movement and the Anti-Saloon League

In 1873, the Women's Christian Temperance Movement came together not, in fact, to advocate temperance—or moderation—but the outright universal Prohibition of alcohol. They did so because they believed the saloon was the center of society's ills and campaigned to have them closed down using a mixture of prayer and direct, confrontational action.

The 1919 Volstead Act prohibited the sale of alcoholic beverages exceeding 0.5% ABV. This postcard is likely from the early 1930s, before the act was repealed in 1933. PIKE MICROBREWERY MUSEUM, SEATTLE, WA

The Movement's most infamous member, Carrie Nation, was an imposing lady, 6 feet tall, dressed in black, and accessorized with an axe. In 1890 Kansas was a dry state, but the law was not being enforced. With a group of her sisters, Nation prayed and read the Bible outside a saloon in the town of Medicine Lodge, hoping God would force it to close. Eventually she grew tired of waiting, strode into the saloon with her axe, and smashed the place to matchwood, while patrons fled and staff stood agape. Between 1900 and 1910 she was arrested 30 times for violent conduct and criminal damage. She paid her fines with fees from lecture tours and sales of souvenir axes. In her own words, she was "a bulldog running along at the feet of Jesus, barking at what He doesn't like."

The Anti-Saloon League (ASL) favored careful politicking over sensational stunts and was ultimately more effective. This, the first real single-issue pressure group, was founded in 1893 in Oberlin, Ohio, by Howard Hyde Russell, who circumvented the politics and infighting that dogged other groups by organizing it more like a bureaucratic corporation than a democratic, committee-led special interest group. The ASL had a clear focus on how politicians voted rather than whether they personally drank. It supported dry political candidates, put pressure on waverers, and succeeded in making Prohibition a vote-winning issue.

Apart from direct pressure on politicians, the ASL carried out a very effective public relations campaign demonizing drink. Using baseless "scientific" studies and scare stories, their simple, effective propaganda portrayed drinkers as victims, lured in and broken down by the saloon. They claimed that alcohol killed 50,000 people a year and that after one taste of alcohol people were hooked and would develop a ruinous habit. Powerful cartoons appeared, such as one showing a man handcuffed to a giant beer bottle labeled "drinking habit" on a saloon bar, while at home his daughter asks, "Mummy, why doesn't Daddy come home?" Another, "Christmas morning in the Drunkard's Home," simply shows children in ragged nightclothes weeping at the sight of their empty stockings.

Over a few decades, popular opinion turned against alcohol. By 1920, some Americans regarded drinkers with such disgust that, at the Fifteenth International Congress Against Alcoholism in Washington, two doctors were able to seriously consider their outright extermination, before pulling back and proposing what they called the more "humane method" of simply rounding them up into concentration camps and sterilizing them.

Against all this, the brewing industry did little to help itself. Unsavory sales promotion practices in saloons continued, and when spirits manufacturers suggested a joint lobbying campaign against Prohibition, the brewers refused to acknowledge the common cause. As late as 1916, a brewing trade publication declared that "All people hate drunkards and whisky makes them. Men drinking beer exclusively may become 'funny' but never drunk."

That same year, Congress passed the Sixteenth Amendment, which gave federal government the right to raise a nationwide income tax. A powerful argument against Prohibition had always been that taxes on alcohol sales provided the government with 40% of its revenue. Now, the Prohibitionists argued, those vital funds could be raised by other means.

The Volstead Act

In January 1917 the 65th Congress convened, in which "dries" outnumbered "wets" by 140 to 64 in the Democratic Party and 138 to 62 among Republicans. With America's declaration of war against Germany in April, the powerful, pro-beer German American lobby was silenced, whereas simultaneously the debate about the best use of raw materials during the war effort added yet another argument to the Prohibitionist's armory.

On December 18, 1917, the Senate proposed the Eighteenth Amendment, establishing a legal definition for intoxicating liquor, outlawing the manufacture, sale, and transportation of any drink stronger than 0.5% alcohol, and setting out penalties for doing so. (Interestingly, the consumption of alcohol was never itself prohibited.) Thirty-three of the then 48 states were already dry by this time: the Act was simply ratifying what many already believed. President Woodrow Wilson exercised his veto, raging,

> These miserable hypocrites in the House and Senate . . . many with their cellars stocked with liquors and not believing in prohibition at all—jumping at the whip of the lobbyists . . . The country would be better off with light wines and beers.

The veto was immediately overturned, and the Eighteenth Amendment was ratified on January 16, 1919, and put into effect a year later.

The Prohibition Era

It quickly became clear that Prohibition was impractical. The first problem was smuggling. It was illegal to transport alcoholic beverages across state lines; it was also illegal to transport them across national borders. But there was a large difference between stating this and enforcing it. There simply were not enough agents to prevent alcohol entering the United States from Canada. As one commentator observed, "You can't stop liquor from dripping through a dotted red line." There are no figures for how much booze was smuggled over the Canadian border, but revenues from liquor taxes to the Canadian government increased fourfold during Prohibition, at the same time as consumption statistics suggest the quantity of spirits drunk by the Canadian population virtually halved.

Spirits also entered the United States from the West Indies. The Rum Runner Bill McCoy became so famous for the quality of his liquor that "The Real McCoy" entered the language to describe the genuine article.

Those who could not get the Real McCoy simply made their own. It is hard to make illegal a process that occurs in nature, and homemade alcohol was easy to manufacture. An estimated 70 million gallons of moonshine were made from corn sugar every year. This was mixed with glycerine and juniper oil to create "bathtub gin" (so called not because it was mixed in bathtubs, but because it was diluted with water from bath taps.)

Most of this imported and home-distilled alcohol was sold in covert drinking clubs or speakeasies. One Prohibition agent reckoned that in 1926 there were 100,000 in New York alone, and although they were sometimes raided, it was futile to make any serious attempt to eradicate them when many numbered city officials and dignitaries among their regular customers.

It is often suggested that Prohibition was such a failure that alcohol consumption actually increased during the years it was enforced. Although there can be no accurate measure of clandestine consumption of illegally brewed booze, this is probably not true. But what is undeniably true is that

Prohibition ultimately had the opposite effect of what the original temperance campaigners intended. Before Prohibition, there had been a steady shift from consumption of spirits toward beer. Once alcohol consumption was illegal, speakeasy customers tended to be dedicated drinkers, favoring the more direct alcohol hit from spirits. Beer was also much harder to produce illegally compared with bathtub gin. Those who defied Prohibition therefore tended to become harder drinkers than they had been before. From a position where beer was by far the dominant drink, during Prohibition spirits rose to account for 75% of all alcohol drunk in the United States.

If hypocrisy allowed Americans to keep drinking while supporting Prohibition (one wag said people would "vote dry as long as they were able to stagger to the polls"), the economics of illegal alcohol sales eventually turned public opinion toward thoughts of repeal. Bootleg booze fueled the growth of organized crime across the United States. Most famously, Chicago became a haven for smugglers, profiteers, and drinkers. Gangsters such as Al Capone and his rival Bugs Moran made millions of dollars from illegal alcohol sales. By the end of the 1920s Capone controlled all of Chicago's 10,000 speakeasies and ruled the bootlegging business from Canada to Florida. But when people started dying in intergang rivalry—most notably in the St Valentine's Day Massacre of 1929—the public began to feel that the power of the gangsters was out of control.

Other events that same year also put an end to one of Prohibition's most persuasive arguments. With income tax in place, Prohibitionists had been able to argue that on the one hand, central government no longer needed liquor tax to keep the treasury running. On the other, they argued that the money being poured into saloons would be freed up and spent on other goods and services, fueling the manufacturing industry rather than lining brewers' pockets. This never happened—those who still chose to drink ended up spending more as prices increased, and the huge cost of attempting to enforce Prohibition further emptied state coffers. And following 1929's Wall Street Crash, the Great Depression left the country broke. The economic arguments for Prohibition—which everyone knew was not working anyway—simply fell apart, and the lost revenue from liquor taxes started to look too good to go without.

In 1932, industrialist John D Rockefeller Junior wrote,

> When Prohibition was introduced, I hoped that it would be widely supported by public opinion and the day would soon come when the evil effects of alcohol would be recognized. I have slowly and reluctantly come to believe that this has not been the result. Instead, drinking has generally increased; the speakeasy has replaced the saloon; a vast army of lawbreakers has appeared; many of our best citizens have openly ignored Prohibition; respect for the law has been greatly lessened; and crime has increased to a level never seen before.

That year, Franklin Roosevelt stood for the Presidency on a repeal platform. He won one of the biggest landslides in electoral history.

Repeal

On March 22, 1933, Roosevelt signed into law an amendment to the Volstead Act known as the Cullen–Harrison Act, allowing the manufacture, transportation, and sale of some alcoholic beverages. Prohibition was repealed at midnight on April 7, 1933. At 12.01 AM, the brewers of Milwaukee and St Louis opened their gates and shipped 15 million bottles of beer. The first consignment from Anheuser-Busch went to the airport, from whence it was delivered to the White House and to pro-repeal lobbyists in New York by the company's new Clydesdale horses. The manufacture of spirits still required various licensing agreements, and by a simple administrative oversight, homebrewing would remain illegal until 1979. By the time Jimmy Carter legalized homebrewing, American beer enthusiasts felt they sorely needed it. See CARTER, JAMES EARL, JR.

The Prohibition Aftermath

By any true measure, Prohibition can only be regarded as a failure. But it has had lasting repercussions for the United States. Anti-alcohol sentiment ebbs and flows, but still runs very high in American society: 35% of the population do not drink, half of them for religious reasons. Neo-Prohibitionists on the religious right still run campaigns attempting to equate beer with heroin or crack cocaine.

America has Prohibition to thank for the growth of organized crime. Mafia groups had largely confined their activities to gambling and theft before 1920. By 1933, with powerful infrastructures in place and corrupted law enforcement officials under their control, gangs and families simply moved into different product lines once alcohol was no longer quite so profitable to them.

And Prohibition had a permanent effect on America's beer palate. Of the 1,392 brewers in operation before Prohibition, only 164 remained afterward. America's fledgling wine industry was destroyed entirely and would take decades to re-emerge. A generation that had known nothing but soft drinks rejected the bitterness of the Bavarian-style beers that had been popular in America before Prohibition and demanded something sweeter. Modern American beer, less characterful than traditional beer styles, became ubiquitous, and it would only be after the 1979 legalization of homebrewing and the growth of craft brewing that America would once again know an interesting variety of beer styles and tastes.

It was not all bad: the popularity of speakeasies did lead directly to the spread of jazz music across America. But although this is obviously a good thing, it is unlikely that those who suffered the lasting effects of organized crime or bad liquor would consider it a worthwhile legacy.

Barr, Andrew. *Drink: A social history.* New York: Carroll & Graf Publishers, 1999.

Ogle, Maureen. *Ambitious brew: The story of American beer.* Orlando, FL: Harcourt Books, 2006.

Peck, Garrett. *The prohibition hangover: Alcohol in America from demon rum to cult Cabernet.* New Brunswick, NJ: Rutgers University Press, 2009.

Pete Brown

A **protein rest** is a period of enzyme activity during mashing when excess protein is removed and digested. It is typically part of a series of temperature holds arranged in a sequence to ensure progressive digestion of beta-glucans, proteins, and starches.

Not all mashes require a protein rest, but if poorly modified malt or high protein adjuncts are used, excess protein is likely to be released into the wort, leading to possible hazes in finished beer.

Removing protein from wort involves both precipitation and enzyme digestion. A temperature of 119°F (43°C) is optimal for these and results in the removal of intact proteins in a precipitate and their breakdown into polypeptides and amino acids.

This digestion is most effectively achieved using natural protease enzymes derived from the barley malt. Whereas the endo-proteinases act best at relatively low temperatures of around 119°F (43°C), the exo-peptidases (notably carboxypeptidase) are much more heat tolerant and are able to act at the higher temperatures used for saccharification.

It is the endo-peptidases whose survival would be facilitated at the lower temperatures, but there is a school of thought that says these enzymes cannot act because they are blocked by endogenous inhibitors from the grist. Accordingly it has been suggested that the term "protein rest" is a misnomer and that it should be called a "beta-glucan rest" because it is the breakdown of beta-glucans by heat-sensitive beta-glucanases that is much more relevant at these lower temperatures. Many brewers seek a middle ground between the optimum temperatures for peptidase and proteinase activity, settling on a rest temperature of 122°F (50°C), with the typical stand lasting from 10 to 20 minutes. Yet other brewers feel that given today's well-modified malts, the protein rest is an unnecessary anachronism. As in many other areas of brewing, actual practice is often assembled from a blend of theory, observation, and tradition, with each brewer deciding individually upon what he thinks works best for his beer and his brewing system.

Keith Thomas

proteins are organic molecules that are essential to life. In the cells of organisms, they perform several roles. Importantly, they function as structural components of cells, and when water soluble, they function as enzymes that catalyze reactions. Organic catalysts initiate chemical reactions without being part of them. Chemically, proteins are composed of linear polymers of 20 different amino acids. These amino acids, in turn, are arranged in various sequences called "primary structures," which determine the way amino acid chains are folded—three-dimensionally—to produce proteins with specific functions. Polypeptides are small proteins of fewer than 100 amino acids; highly complex, large-molecular proteins may have many thousands of polypeptides. Based on these structural distinctions, some proteins—such as collagen—form the fiber of animal tissues, whereas other proteins—those with very complex shapes—may become enzymes.

The brewer has a complex relationship with proteins, which are looked upon as both a curse and a blessing. The nitrogenous compounds that concern the brewer start with nitrogen uptake from soil in the grain fields and then follow through the entire brewing process into the beer drinker's glass. Protein management throughout the malting and brewing process, therefore, is an essential part of making good beer, or, in fact, any beer at all.

Proteins, in the form of enzymes, are the key organic catalysts that break down components in raw barley and make them process compliant for such operations as lautering and filtration and finally suitable for yeast to metabolize during fermentation. Without enzymes doing their catalytic work, we could not break down grain starches into sugars and yeast would, quite literally, have nothing to ferment. Enzymes convert large-molecular starches into yeast-fermentable sugars; they reduce large-molecular proteins into smaller ones, including amino acids, which are essential for healthy yeast growth and development. See ALPHA AMYLASE, FREE AMINO NITROGEN (FAN), MODIFICATION, PROTEOLYSIS, and YEAST NUTRIENTS. Enzymes perform these functions at various stages in the malting plant and in the mashing vessel. The brewer will use the mashing profile to break down certain proteins and leave others intact. The breakup of large-molecular proteins reduces mash viscosity and thus enhances the ability of the brewer to extract sugars through the grain bed during lautering. See FERMENTATION, LAUTERING, MALT, MASHING, and PROTEIN REST.

As malt and other grains become wort, proteins take on other roles, and the brewer begins to attempt to manipulate the protein profile of both the wort and the finished beer. The boiling of the wort coagulates and precipitates proteins that, left intact, would make the resulting beer opaque, viscous, and unstable. In the kettle and whirlpool, proteins leave the wort as a granular sediment called trub. Kettle finings, such as carageenan derivatives, may be added to assist the coagulation and help settle out the trub. Later, after the wort is cooled, more protein will sediment out during the "cold break." The brewer may hope to avoid protein-derived hazes and sediments in beer that is destined to be filtered bright, but he must not go too far. Beer without proteins would have little body or mouthfeel; it would taste thin and empty. The sturdy crown of foam that is prized on most types of beer is largely created by proteins; remove these "foam-positive" proteins, and the beer may end up without proper tactile and visual texture—foamless, wan, and unattractive. Brewing may seem, at its core, to be a simple art, but a look at the conflicting roles of proteins is a window into the true complexity of modern brewing.

See also CHILL HAZE, COLD BREAK, FOAM, and KETTLE FININGS.

Briggs, D. E., J. S. Hough, R. Stevens, and T. W. Young. *Malting and brewing science*, 2nd ed. New York: Chapman & Hall, 1985.

Keith Thomas, Horst Dornbusch, and Garrett Oliver

proteolysis is a general biochemical term covering the breakdown of proteins into peptides and eventually amino acids. In relation to brewing the term refers to one or more steps in step infusion or decoction mashing processes. These steps are in the temperature range between 113°F (45°C) and 131°F (55°C) where the malt's naturally occurring proteolytic enzymes are active. The practical effects of this proteolytic rest are highly questionable, as the theory behind these, as many other older, traditional mashing dogma, stems from a time when the quality of malts was far inferior to those of today. Furthermore, some have suggested that proteolysis does not occur in mashes, even at low temperatures, because of the inhibition of the necessary enzymes.

The older brewing literature and the legends within certain schools of thought in brewing theory say that proteolysis produces more free amino acids needed as nutrients by the yeast, that it helps to form more amylolytic enzymes, thus aiding starch conversion, and that by removing part of the soluble protein improves the chemical stability of the beer. Newer literature and more modern schools of thought claim that the positive effects of proteolysis are negligible, and that the only significant effect is negative as the content of foam active proteins in the finished beer is reduced. As the temperature range for proteolysis coincides very closely with the optimum range for the natural malt beta-glucanases, it is likely that some of the positive effects, previously assigned to proteolysis, were in fact a result of beta-glucan breakdown.

See also MASHING and PROTEIN REST.

Kunze, Wolfgang. *Technology brewing and malting*, 3rd international edition. Berlin: VLB Berlin, 2004.

Anders Brinch Kissmeyer

pub games are an integral part of traditional British pub life, especially in the English countryside. Darts is far and away the most popular pub game throughout the English-speaking world. Most pubs in Britain have a dart board and an area set aside for players. In the past 20 years, the game has moved out of the pub and world championship matches are contested in large arenas packed with supporters.

The game is believed to have started when English archers, who were the backbone of the army before the invention of guns and artillery, practiced their art in inns when they were on leave from military duties. They would mark out a playing surface in chalk on the end of a wooden cask behind the bar and fire whittled-down versions of their arrows to see who could hit the target, including the bull's eye in the center, with the greatest accuracy. In some parts of England, the East End of London in particular, modern darts with their feathered flights are known as arrows, pronounced "arrers."

The game of darts has a standard board with doubles and trebles marked in 20 segments, but it is by no means universal. In some parts of England, boards have only doubles and no trebles, whereas a "fives" board has 12 segments. Darts has long been a popular game in France and Belgium where it is known as fléchettes in French or vogelpik in Flemish. In these countries, players use four darts per round as opposed to three. A vogelpik board is on display in the Bruges Folk Museum as part of a reconstruction of a 19th-century Flemish inn called De Zwarte Kat or the Black Cat.

Skittles is another British pub game with many different versions. Alley skittles is widely played in the southwest counties of England, with hundreds of thriving leagues taking part. The rules of the game vary but there are always nine skittles or pins in a set. Players either bowl a wooden ball at the skittles or aim a large disc known as a cheese. Variations on alley skittles are also played in northwest England and the Midlands. Where pubs do not have space for skittle alleys, the game is played in the main body of the pub on a table. The two main versions are Devil among the Tailors, an 18th-century game in which a ball on a cord is swung to hit the skittles, and Hood Skittles, in which a flat cheese is bounced off the cushioned walls of the table. A version of table skittles played in parts of Kent, southeast England, has the charming name of Daddlums, whereas in Oxfordshire Aunt Sally is played with a single pin and six throwing batons.

Bar billiards was brought to Britain from France and Belgium in the 1930s, although the origins of the game may lie in Russia. A table covered in green baize has nine holes or pockets with each hole guarded by a pin, a wooden sentinel often shaped like a mushroom. Players armed with cues have to sink seven white balls with a red cue ball. If they knock over a pin, then points are deducted from their scores. A similar game is bagatelle, played in France as well as Britain. As one version of bagatelle is known as Mississippi; it may also have been played at one time in the United States. In common with bar billiards, the aim is to sink balls into holes. There are no pins guarding the holes in this game. Both bar billiards and bagatelle have declined markedly in the past 2 decades because of the popularity of an American import into British pubs, namely pool.

Quoits is an outdoor pub game that involves throwing horseshoes or a fully round iron ring over a post or pegs in the earth. Its origins are unclear. Some believe it was a Roman game; others think it came from Ancient Greece—a descendant of discus throwing—whereas still others argue it came from northern Germany and the Low Countries. Certainly the Dutch introduced a version of quoits to North America. It is indisputably an ancient game, with two English kings, Edward III and Henry V, banning a game they called coits or coytes. In 19th- and 20th-century England and Scotland the game became popular, with pub teams vying for supremacy and waging large bets on the outcome. Indoor versions of quoits known as Caves or Flat Board survive in a few pubs, with rubber rings pitched onto a numbered board. Ringing the Bull is distantly related to Quoits: a copper ring suspended on a string has to be lobbed over a horn or hook mounted on the wall.

Other outdoor pub games involve hitting a ball with a stick. They have a spring that throws a ball in to the air and the player has to hit the ball with a stick toward a target or a net. Versions of the game include Bat and Trap and Knur and Spell and are believed to be the forerunners of baseball, cricket, and golf.

Shove Halfpenny (pronounced Shove Ha'penny) is a popular pub game in which pennies or similar coins are shoved or pushed with the player's hand along a board with numbered partitions or beds. In a version of the game that originated in the Netherlands, the pennies have to be pushed through narrow openings into partitions.

Card games are widely played in pubs but the most popular indoor pub game after darts is dominoes, or "doms" for short. It was introduced in the 19th century and is thought to have originated in China. It was played widely in France as well as Britain. The game has many versions but is based on players holding dominoes or tiles with a varied number of pips on each tile. The aim when a player puts down a tile is to ensure that the outer pips, when added up, are either five or three or multiples of five and three. For example, if the pips add up to fifteen, the player scores three points for three fives, plus a further five points for five threes, a total score of eight. The game of dominoes arouses great passion among the participants, no doubt as a result of the copious amounts of beer consumed as the game progresses.

Taylor, Arthur. *Played at the pub.* Swindon, England: English Heritage, 2009.

Roger Protz

The Dove, on the River Thames in London, dates back to the 17th century. CATH HARRIES

public houses (pubs), like fish and chips and village cricket, are a bastion of the English. It is an institution that did not really have a foreign equivalent until the "English/Irish theme pub" became popular a few decades ago. Being such a fundamental part of the UK's heritage, it is unsurprising that such establishments have inspired many great writers, including Shakespeare, Samuel Johnson, G. K. Chesterton, and George Orwell. Johnson in particular, together with the diarist Samuel Pepys, was a devotee of the London drinking house. A quote by the 19th-century lawyer and politician Sir William Harcourt (1827–1904), who served as Home Secretary and Chancellor of the Exchequer under William Gladstone, perhaps summed things up: "As much of the history of England has been brought about in public houses as in the House of Commons."

Although in modern-day parlance there is a blurring of the terms "public house," "inn," "tavern," etc, there was, as we shall see, a definitive difference between these types of "on the premises" drinking establishments. These are not to be confused with "off-licences," where liquor is retailed for consumption off the premises. Thus, we can speak of on-trade and off-trade. The exact derivation of the term "public house" is obscure, although it probably arose as a contracted form of public alehouse (in contrast to small, illicit, private alehouses) and first seems to have been used in the late 17th century. The term became more frequently applied to alehouses in early Hanoverian England. However they are named, the history of these places of refreshment can ultimately be traced back to the Roman occupation of Britain, when roadside watering holes sprang up alongside roads. These establishments, variously known as *diversoria, cauponae,* or *tabernae diversoriae,* were meant to provide respite for the weary traveler (and his horse). The Romano-British equivalents of publicans, therefore, were *diversores* or *caupones.*

Pub heritage may go back even further because, during the Celtic period, there was an order of people called *beatachs* or *brughnibhs,* who were keepers of open houses established for the expressed purpose of hospitality. Like their Roman counterparts, these premises were not merely drinking houses; food and entertainment were also available. Similar premises existed in Italy as well, and we know that in Herculaneum there were no fewer than 900 public houses. It was not until Anglo-Saxon times that something like the alehouse, where consuming strong drink was the main aim, developed—but then the Anglo-Saxons did not consider drunkenness dishonorable.

Further afield, we know that inns existed in classical Greece and Rome and that ancient China harbored similar establishments. *Korschmas,* tavern-like premises, were available to 12th-century peasants in parts of what is now Poland and Russia, and contemporary writings from colonial Mexico indicate the presence of innumerable *pulquerias,* where the indigenous beverage could be purchased. Likewise, visitors to Japan during the 17th century pontificate about numerous small shops/inns selling sake. As the rise of industrialization and urbanization spread throughout Western Europe and North America, so did the influence of the public drinking place. It seems as though Europeans exported their drinking and social habits to the colonies of the New World.

Legend has it that the Roman drinking houses that had been established in Britain were destroyed by the Anglo-Saxon invaders and that for a couple of centuries, at least, there were no public places of rest and refreshment. New establishments evolved, however, and it was in Anglo-Saxon times that Britain saw the first real distinctions between drinking houses open to the public because those ancients recognized the alehouse (*eala-hus*), the winehouse (*win-hus*), and the inn (*cumen-hus*). The latter is certainly of Anglo-Saxon origin, and, like the hostel, was meant to signify a lodging house, not a place for drinking.

Manorial records indicate that local controls over drinking were in force throughout medieval times, but these did little to prevent drunkenness and social disorder. Distinctions between drinking places became more precise when licensing them became a requisite. This aspect of the industry dates from the reign of Edward VI, with acts being passed in 1552 and 1553. The Alehouse Act of 1552 (5 and 6 Edw. VI c.25) was the first attempt to nationally coordinate existing controls, and from this point, an alehouse was a place where only ale (or beer) was sold. An inn provided bed and board, as well as beer, and the tavern provided liquor other than ale and/or beer and might also provide accommodation. The Act of 1552 gave justices of the peace power to license or to suppress houses, and licensees had to supply surety for good behavior and the prevention of drunkenness on their premises.

In 1577, there was a census of alehouses, inns, and taverns in England, and the results showed that there were around 14,000 alehouses, 1,631 inns, and 329 taverns, plus about 3,500 other unclassified licences. The census was to form a basis for making a levy on drinking places to raise money for the repair of Dover Harbor (at the rate of 2 *s* 6 *d* [12½ *p*] per license). The figures obtained from the census indicated there was one license for every 187 people, 9 alehouses to every inn, and around 40 alehouses to every tavern.

The importance of drinking houses to the general populace and the predilection for overindulging in them at this period fostered a vociferous anti-drink faction See PROHIBITION and TEMPERANCE. There was perceived to be a danger that these places were fostering a huge underclass, and the following lines penned by the Elizabethan pamphleteer and moralist, Philip Stubbes, are representative of the anti-drink sentiments of the time. In the 1583 edition of his *The Anatomie of Abuses,* he writes about drunkenness thus:

> I say that it is a horrible vice, and too much used in England. Every county, city, town, village, and other places hath abundance of alehouses, taverns, and inns, which are so fraught with malt-worms, night and day, that you would wonder to see them. You shall have them there sitting at the wine and good-ale all the day long, yea, all the night too, peradventure a whole week together, so long as any money is left; swilling, gulling and carousing from one to another, till never a one can speak a ready word . . . And a man once drunk with wine or strong drink

rather resembling a brute than a Christian man, for do not his eyes begin to stare and be red, fiery and bleared, blubbering forth seas of tears? Doth he not froth and foam at the mouth like a bear? Doth not his tongue falter and stammer in his mouth?

After the Restoration in Great Britain there was a trend toward more extensive, better controlled drinking premises, and magistrates, who supervised licensing matters, started to insist that licensed premises should be equipped with stabling (previously confined to inns) and lodgings. By restricting licenses to specific houses within the community, magistrates gave an incentive to publicans to enlarge and improve their properties. In 1739, a public house for sale in Leeds was described as "a new brick-built house, garret height, well guested, with a good stable . . . good vaulted cellars, brew-house, and a well." All this, of course, meant that property and rental values increased. In the 1690s it was claimed that two-thirds of all pubs in the country paid over £5 (c. $8.15) per annum in rent. Rents were especially high in London and other cities, and in 1725, The *Public-Housekeeper's Monitor* complained of "high rents to which public houses are generally advanced so as very often to exceed double the rents of private ones of the same real goodness." In addition, incoming landlords in London were expected to pay a premium for "goodwill," a practice that continues to this day.

It should be stressed that even up until the early 18th century, the name alehouse was still being widely applied, even for houses with improved facilities. Many of the basic functions of the alehouse persisted, but the ever-increasing demands of a more sophisticated clientele resulted in many more facilities being required (and provided). There was also more respectability, and premises located in cellars, down narrow back-alleys, or on the remote outskirts of town were no longer acceptable. The provision of food might no longer be the major source of income for a publican anymore. As the century progressed, many landlords moved away from brewing to concentrate on retailing beer and other commodities. In any case, the publican who made both beer and food was finding it harder to compete, quality-wise, with ever more competent common brewers. Having said this, the brewpub was to have a resurgence during the late 20th century and would form an important segment of the "microbrewery revolution." See BREWPUB and MICROBREWERY.

By the start of the 19th century, the term "alehouse" had largely been replaced by public house, and within a few decades the "pub" had arrived. Premises increased in size, and a class of professional, prosperous, and well-established landlords was developing. From the 1810s and 1820s, purpose-built pubs began to appear in London and other major centers of population. The old alehouse had essentially been an ordinary dwelling place that had been adapted (to varying degrees) to retail beer. Henceforth, brewers, landowners, and builders started to construct public houses with identifiable facades and fittings that were solely for the purpose of retailing liquor. These new buildings could be expensive; the estimated cost of a new house in London in 1814 was reckoned to be £1,000–£2,000 (1,643–3,286 US dollars), with those in the countryside being around half that.

Many of these new pubs were built on new sites, in expanding urban areas, but many replaced older, smaller premises. Occasionally, established inns were converted into new-style pubs, and it was not uncommon for the more pretentious landlord to present his house as a tavern or an inn, when all he really sold was beer; this further blurred the distinction between the outlets. By the 1830s, an informal hierarchy of public houses was evolving, and this would largely supplant the traditional taxonomy of inns, taverns, and alehouses. The largest and most commercially oriented pubs were mostly in towns, usually along major thoroughfares or on street corners. This maximized their visibility and was aimed at attracting a better-off clientele, especially through passing trade. Smaller, less elaborate houses would be found off of the main roads and served local, generally less affluent, customers. This period also saw the evolution of "ethnic" houses in larger towns and cities.

Illicit, unlicensed drinking houses (hush shops) also abounded during the early 19th century, and pubs had to compete with them. Some were merely small, run-down alehouses, whereas others catered to specific sectors of society, such as "flash houses" (criminals and prostitutes) and "dram shops" (spirit drinkers). The notorious metropolitan gin shops, whose numbers soared at this time, were often little more than a single room in someone's house—then there were the gin palaces, which were starting to emerge. Very often, when a backstreet alehouse lost its license, it would re-emerge as an illicit gin shop.

The high density of drinking houses in prime areas was a cause of concern for magistrates and for publicans, as well as the emerging police force. In 1823, the *Liverpool Mercury* complained that within 300 yards of a new marketplace there were over 100 licensed premises. Magistrates were clearly having a hard time regulating the sale of liquor, and in 1818 some 14,000 Londoners petitioned Parliament against the high price and poor quality of alcoholic drink sold in the capital. By this point, there was a widespread populist belief that public houses were controlled by a corrupt political establishment, and there was a growing movement for the liberalization of the liquor trade.

In 1830, in response to the growing unpopularity of brewers and publicans and concern at the volume of gin being drunk, the burdensome tax on beer was abolished and some licensing laws were changed. This Beer Act (1Wm.IV c.64) reversed the licensing policy of the previous couple of centuries and allowed any rate-paying householder to sell beer, ale, and cider without consent from local justices, but by taking out an excise license from the Excise authorities. It also allowed pubs to open for 18 hours a day, except Sunday (they were already open from 6:00 AM until 9:00 PM), but they could not sell spirits or fortified wines. This was a genuine (if misguided) attempt to "improve the plight of the working classes," but the immediate impact was the mushrooming of "beer-only" premises all over England and Wales, and these were known as "beer shops" or "beer houses." Some 25,000 licenses were taken out in the first 6 months, and this number rose to around 46,000 after 6 years (there were only around 56,000 fully licensed pubs). The Act became known as the Duke of Wellington's Beer House Act, after the then prime minister. The fee for such an establishment was 2 guineas per annum, and the license included permission to brew.

The immediate result was an increase in bad behavior. Sydney Smith, a contemporary Whig reformer, penned the following classic lines: "The new beer bill has begun its operations. Everybody is drunk. Those who are not singing are sprawling. The sovereign people are in a beastly state."

Peter Clark correctly observed that the 1830 Act marked the end of the English alehouse (and, by connotation, its evolution into the pub) and as a kind of obituary penned the following: "The enduring reason for the success of the alehouse in the centuries before 1830 is that it was quintessentially a neighbourhood theatre in the widest sense, in which ordinary people could be actors and observers. Against the backdrop of its flickering fire men could gossip and rant, joke, laugh and posture, sublimate their miseries in drunkenness, applaud their own success in generosity and games."

In cities like London, it seemed as though the construction of public houses was central to the strategies of the developers in many areas between the 1830s and 1860s. At first, most of these new pubs were almost indistinguishable from the rows of terraced houses around them, but by the time of the beer boom of the 1860s and 1870s, their design became increasingly more distinct. Public house building probably reached its acme during the late Victorian/Edwardian period when we witnessed palatial buildings containing numerous rooms, each with its own appeal (public bar, saloon bar, etc), and, very often, rooms designated for meetings, snooker, and the like. Some specimens still exist, and the wondrous Barton Arms, Aston, Birmingham, is one of the finest examples of Victorian pub architecture.

The Beer Act held sway for just under 40 years, for, in the 1869 Wine and Beerhouse Act, the stricter controls of yesteryear were reintroduced. It was now once again necessary for publicans to obtain their licenses from justices. The 1872 Intoxicating Liquor (licensing) Act reinforced this legislation and obliged clerks of licensing divisions to keep a register of all licenses granted. Licenses were only granted, transferred, or renewed at special Licensing Sessions and would only be granted to respectable individuals. The 1869 Act was to form the basis of pub licensing matters for many years.

During the period 1891–1903, Charles Booth penned his mammoth *Life and Labour of the People of London*, which detailed the activities of the poor of that time. From the work it is evident how important the pub was to that unfortunate section of society. He declared, "public houses play a larger part in the lives of the people than clubs or friendly societies, churches or missions, or perhaps than all put together."

World War I had a major effect on both public houses and breweries. Within 4 days of the declaration of war, on August 4, 1914, the first of a series of regulations under the broad title of Defence of the

Realm Acts was introduced. These gave the authorities the power to pass laws necessary for securing public safety and the defense of the realm. Regulation 7 gave naval and military authorities the power to determine licensing hours in or near any defended harbor. Regulation 17 made it an offense to encourage members of His Majesty's armed forces to drink "with the intention of becoming drunk." This Act also gave local magistrates the power to control opening hours of licensed premises in areas that were considered "sensitive," such as railway marshalling yards. Then, on August 31, the Intoxicating Liquor (Temporary Restriction) Act was enacted, which gave magistrates even more power to curtail drinking in sensitive areas, a description that applied to almost 25% of all licensing districts in the UK. Pubs affected by these regulations had their opening hours "temporarily" restricted to 11 AM to 2.30 PM and 6.30 PM to 9.30 PM. By the end of the War, some 94% of all British citizens had been subjected to limited drinking opportunities. The evening limit was increased to 11 PM, and these hours persisted until the 2003 Licensing Act, which, in theory allowed "all-day drinking."

Even with these measures, a shortage of munitions that jeopardized the war effort in early 1915 was attributed to drink. The then chancellor Lloyd George urged moderation, saying: "Drink is doing us more damage in the war than all the German submarines put together . . . We are fighting Germany, Austria, and Drink, and as far as I can see, the greatest of these three deadly foes is Drink."

This speech was monumentally significant because it meant that concern over the drink problem was no longer confined to an enthusiastic temperance lobby, it was now a matter of national importance, and greater powers were considered necessary. Such powers arrived with the Defense of the Realm Amendment, which created a new body, the Central Control Board (Liquor Traffic), which possessed huge powers over licensing hours and other licensing matters and the power to "acquire" pubs and breweries in "sensitive" areas. Within weeks, the sale of alcohol was banned in Newhaven (Sussex) from which munitions were shipped to France. The same happened in other ports, such as Southampton and Bristol. Because of production problems in nearby munitions factories, in January 1916 the Control Board embarked on measures that would see Carlisle's 4 breweries and some 235 pubs in and around the town being taken under government control. These were then run (mostly inefficiently) by managers—an innovation in the industry—and a number of pubs were closed (especially the men-only drinking houses). This Carlisle and District State Management Scheme had a policy of running fewer, but "better" pubs, and by 1920 their estate had been reduced by 40%. The Scheme lasted until 1974, when the property was denationalized and purchased by T. & R. Theakston Ltd, of Masham, Yorkshire. See THEAKSTONS.

Despite a difficult financial climate between the two World Wars, around one-quarter of the UK's pubs were improved in some way. No longer would the majority of the population tolerate the basic "boozer" as a place of recreation. Over the next few decades, the public house milieu would change drastically, and from consisting of a humble cheese roll, food provision has improved beyond recognition. Today's pub is as much about food as drink, and more than 80% serve a variety of food.

Identification of the presence of drinking places has always been critical and originally involved the hanging-up of a recognizable object outside the premises concerned. Objects gradually became painted signs and eventually lettering was added. Names such as Sun and Star became common. The most common pub name in Britain is the Red Lion, followed by Royal Oak, White Hart, Rose and Crown, Kings Head, and Kings Arms. All of these have special significance as far as British history is concerned.

As we enter the second decade of the 21st century, the British pub is at a crossroads. Most are now owned by mammoth pub companies, the "pubcos," many of which are more interested in real estate than selling beer. The number of outlets is in decline, with around 50 closing per week in 2010. The reasons put forward are simple: spiralling costs, declining sales, and the 2007 smoking ban. Beer sales are at their lowest since the Depression of the 1930s. Those pubs not focusing on food have been the hardest hit. Many pubs are now restaurants in all but name and represent 40% of all catering outlets in Britain. Catering now accounts for around one-quarter of pub turnover.

In the past, the public house has been the subject of much literary attention and, keeping in mind the vast amount of pleasure that the pub has brought to its patrons over the years, it is pertinent to take note of the following evocative, oft-quoted words by essayist, poet, and travel writer Hilaire Belloc (1870–1953), which illustrate how much of a British institution the public house was at the beginning of the 20th century.

> When you have lost your inns drown your empty selves, for you will have lost the last of England.

Belloc also wrote *The Four Men*, which describes a journey made on foot with three companions from one end of Sussex to the other. The story commences with the author sitting in the George Inn at Robertsbridge and, in the course of his travels, he winds his way through country lanes, where small rural pubs seemingly jump out at every crossroad. In what is much more than a rustic pub crawl, there is mention of a number of establishments, and we are left in no doubt as to Belloc's love of the English pub: "Is there not the Bridge Inn of Amberley and the White Hart of Storrington, the Spread Eagle of Midhurst, that oldest and most revered of all the prime inns of the world . . . "

At its best, the English pub, through all of its changes, remains a touchstone. The pub is still the home of Britain's national drink, cask-conditioned bitter, although it is not nearly so common as it once was, and cellarmanship seems a waning art. But a pub is not a bar, and there is still something left to the idea that it is a "public house." In most pubs, it remains possible to get a pint of beer at the bar, sit down in a chair, and read a book for the next hour, undisturbed by the patron of the house. In winter, the fireplace may glow with wood or coal. Properly run and well kept by hospitable people, the pub seems a remnant of a more civilized age, even if we know that this age may never have really quite existed.

See also ALE HOUSES, COACHING INNS, and TAVERNS.

Belloc, H. *The four men: A farrago*. Oxford, UK: Oxford University Press, 1984.

Chapman, R. W., ed. *Life of Johnson/James Boswell.* Oxford, UK: Oxford University Press, 2008.

Clark, P. *The English alehouse: A social history, 1200–1830*. London: Longman, 1983.

Fried, A., and R. M. Elman. *Charles Booth's London: A portrait of the poor at the turn of the century*. London: Hutchinson, 1969.

Girouard, M. *Victorian pubs*. New Haven, CT: Yale University Press, 1984.

Hackwood, F. W. *Inns, ales and drinking customs of old England*. London: T. Fisher Unwin, 1910 (reprinted London: Bracken Books, 1987).

Jackson, M. *The English pub*. London: Harper & Row, 1976.

Matthias, P. *The brewing industry in England, 1700–1830*. Cambridge, UK: Cambridge University Press, 1959.

Stubbes, P. *Anatomie of abuses*. London: R. Jones, 1583 (reprinted NewYork: Garland, 1973).

Ian Hornsey

pulque is a fermented alcoholic beverage from Mexico with pre-Hispanic origins, made from the maguey (Agave Americana or century) plant and known by its Nahuatl name as *octli*. Before the Spanish Conquest in the 16th century, it was a sacred drink used for various religious festivals as well as public fiestas.

After the arrival of the Spanish, the drink assumed a wider audience with both Spaniards and the indigenous consuming it, as distilled drinks had yet not developed a production base and importing alcohol from Europe was still difficult. With increasing consumption throughout the 16th and 17th centuries, Spanish authorities decided to impose tighter restrictions on its sale and consumption because of problems with public drunkenness, despite the fact that it accounted for a large percentage of government tax revenue. During this period, pulque came to be associated with the poorer classes, with it being frowned upon by the nobility and wealthy because of its association with alcoholism. Following the Mexican War of Independence (1810–1821), the drink achieved a short-lived renaissance in which rich and poor were imbibing large amounts in celebration of their shared indigenous past; this ended when burgeoning commercial beer interests in the 20th century sought to monopolize the Mexican liquor market. More recently, producers have begun to add fruits to improve the flavor; these are known as *curados*.

Pulque's long and complicated production process has hindered its popularity, since the maguey plant has to initiate the fermentation process, which, once begun, does not stop, eventually making the drink unpalatable. As a result, its distribution has always proven difficult, forcing production and consumption to remain local despite recent attempts to bottle and can it for long-distance sale.

While pulque is not technically related to beer, it tends to occupy a similar socio-cultural space and is therefore worth noting in that context.

See also MEXICO.

De Barrios, Virginia B. *A guide to tequila, mezcal and pulque.* Mexico City: Editorial Minutiae Mexicana, 1991.

Guerrero y Guerrero, Raul. *El pulque.* Mexico City: Editorial Joaquin Mortiz, 1985.

Jai Kharbanda

pumping over has two meanings in the brewery. One meaning refers to the practice of pumping beer from one tank to another via a hose, as, for instance, from a secondary fermentation tank to a lagering tank to leave sedimented yeast and particulate behind. See LAGERING and SECONDARY FERMENTATION. The second, more specific meaning refers to the rousing of the wort by recirculating it externally from the bottom to the top of the tank. See ROUSING. Although the objective implied in the first meaning is obvious and requires no further explanation, the objective of the second meaning is to keep the yeast evenly suspended in the wort during fermentation to ensure complete and prolonged contact of the yeast with all sugars and other nutrients in the wort. Such pumping over must be done carefully, without oxygen pickup. This is why the inlet for the recirculating wort at the top of the tank must be below the beer level. Pumping over should never be done through the spray ball at the top of the tank. Oxygenating fermenting beer would lead to a quick conversion of the precursors acetohydroxy acids into vicinal diketones, including diacetyl. See DIACETYL and VICINAL DIKETONES. Pumping over is usually a last-ditch effort used when the fermentation has slowed significantly or has become stuck altogether because the yeast has prematurely settled at the bottom of the fermenter. Whereas the term "pumping over" is rarely used for other circumstances, some breweries use a similar technique to blend beer or disperse hop material during dry hopping operations.

See also DRY HOPPING, FERMENTATION, and FLOCCULATION.

Kunze, Wolfgang, *Technology brewing and malting,* 2nd ed. Berlin: Verlag der VLB Berlin, 1999.

Narziss, Ludwig. *Abriss der Bierbrauerei,* 5th ed. Stuttgart, Germany: Ferdinand Enke Verlag, 1986 (transation of title: *Outline of beer brewing*).

Oliver Jakob

pumpkin ale is an American original, invented in the 18th century by English colonists in the New World. Pumpkin is a New World plant that is rich in starches and sugars. Pumpkin ale was brewed in England only after the introduction of pumpkins there from North America. The brewing methods for pumpkin ale are about as varied as there are breweries making it. As a general rule, pumpkin ale has an orange to amber color, a biscuit-like malt aroma, and a warming pumpkin aroma. Modern pumpkin ales are almost always made with "pumpkin pie spices," which usually include cinnamon, nutmeg, allspice, and sometimes vanilla and ginger. The finish tends to be dry because of many fermentable sugars derived from the pumpkin. Pumpkins belong to the family of squashes and zucchini, the family of Cucurbitaceae. The English word "pumpkin" is derived from the Greek word *pepon,* meaning large melon. In old English, this fruit was often spelled *pumpion* or *pompion*. Apparently, the term was coined around 1550, and the oldest written reference to *pompion* appears only 100 years later. The oldest known recipe for "pompion ale" is made only from pumpkin juice and, unlike modern pumpkin ale recipes, does not call for any addition of cereal malts. It is thus more a recipe for a pumpkin wine than for a pumpkin beer. The recipe dating precisely from February 1771 was published anonymously by the *American Philosophical Society*:

> RECEIPT FOR POMPION ALE
>
> Let the Pompion be beaten in a Trough and pressed as Apples. The expressed Juice is to be boiled in a Copper a considerable Time and carefully skimmed that there may be no Remains of the fibrous Part of the Pulp. After that Intention is answered let the Liquor be hopped cooled fermented &c. as Malt Beer.

Later recipes started to include malt as well, leading to the modern version of pumpkin ale. There can be little doubt that the American association of the pumpkin with the holiday pie recipe has influenced today's interpretations. Hops are not really the point of most pumpkin ales, so either English or American varieties can be used. The malts are often a combination of grain pale malt, pilsner malt, Munich malt, and caramel malts. The pumpkins, too, can be used in many ways. Some brewers add the pumpkins raw, cut up in small cubes and macerated; others bake the pumpkins first, for about 90 min at about 190°C (375°F), and then remove the seeds, stem, and skin, before macerating the meat to a pulp. Yet others press the pumpkins like apples and add just the juice to the kettle or the fermenter. In terms of process, there are also great variations. Some brewers add the pumpkin to the mash, which has the advantage of allowing the mash enzymes to convert the pumpkin starches. In this case, the pumpkin must be cooked first to gelatinize the starches, allowing the conversion. Others add the pumpkins to the kettle, which may increase the finished beer's turbidity. Larger commercial brewers often use pumpkin puree. Some brewers add the spices to the kettle, often wrapped in cheesecloth and boiled for only 15 min; others add the spices to the fermenter, which can give the beer a harsher, more astringent flavor. There is also a technique of soaking the spices in vodka for several days and then just adding the strained extract to the fermenter. Pumpkin ale can be made by single- or multistep infusion, even by decoction. Given the greater turbidity of pumpkin ale wort, many brewers use plenty of Irish moss as a kettle fining. See CARRAGEENANS. After the kettle, it is pitched with a warm-fermenting yeast and treated like any other ale. Variations in flavor are wide; many pumpkin ales are sweet and heavily spiced, straining for the pie associations. Others taste more like ordinary ales with a nutty background flavor of squash and a light dash of spice. Most appear in American bars, restaurants, brewpubs, and shops in late summer, acting as an annual harbinger of the coming autumn.

Filippone, Peggy Trowbridge. "Pumpkin History—The History of Pumpkins as Food." http://homecooking.about.com/od/foodhistory/a/pumpkinhistory.htm/ (accessed April 4, 2011).

Home Brew Forums. *History of Pumpkin Ale.* http://www.homebrewtalk.com/f12/history-pumpkin-ale-81325/ (accessed April 4, 2011).

Horst Dornbusch

PVPP is short for polyvinylpolypyrrolidone which is a polymerized and water/beer insoluble version of the soluble compound PVP (polyvinylpyrrolidone), a nylon-type polymer that has an even higher affinity for chemical bonding with polyphenols than the proteins present in beer have. This gives PVPP excellent properties as a chemical stabilizer for beer. If finely granulated, high surface area PVPP is dispersed in beer, a very high proportion of the dissolved polyphenols in the beer will bind to the PVPP particles, subsequently to be filtered out. Brewers wish to remove these polyphenols because they will otherwise with time react with beer proteins, forming insoluble complexes that will make the beer hazy. This type of stabilizer is referred to as an adsorbent.

Practical beer stabilization with PVPP can be done two different ways. The simple way is single use PVPP stabilization, where a PVPP product with very low particle size is added to unfiltered beer, which, after a few hours of reaction time, is then kieselguhr (diatomaceous earth) filtered. The PVPP used and the polyphenols removed by it will, being insoluble, form part of the filter cake which is treated as waste. The more advanced method is using "regenerable PVPP." This involves an extra, specific PVPP filter placed after the kieselguhr (or other filter type), where filtered beer is dosed with a high concentration of slightly coarser PVPP particles. These react—en route to the PVPP filter or via a holding pipe/vessel—with the polyphenols in the beer, and finally the combined PVPP-polyphenol particles are filtered out in the extra filter. The advantage of this technique is that the filter cake from the PVPP filter can be washed with hot caustic, dissolving out most of the polyphenols, leaving PVPP particles behind that can then be recycled in the stabilization process. PVPP is expensive, so this re-use can be desirable, especially in large breweries, Some brewers use PVPP in the form of specially impregnated filter sheets that are used after the main beer clarification stage. Regardless, PVPP is not considered an additive, as it is always filtered out and therefore is not contained in the finished beer.

See also ADSORBENTS and POLYPHENOLS.

Kunze, Wolfgang. *Technology brewing and malting,* 3rd international edition. Berlin: VLB Berlin, 2004.

Anders Brinch Kissmeyer

Pyramid Breweries, Inc., a pioneer of Northwest American craft brewing, was established by Beth Hartwell in 1984 as Hart Brewing, Inc., in Kalama, Washington. Pyramid Breweries eventually grew to become one of the five largest craft breweries in the United States and now maintains locations in three states. Pyramid pale ale, the brewery's first release, was followed by wheaten ale a year later and then in 1994 by the debut of apricot ale, a beer that has come to be synonymous with the brewery. Upon changing its name to Pyramid Breweries, Inc., the company increased production and introduced other styles, winning many awards at national and international competitions.

Pyramid no longer brews in Kalama and, after having purchased Portland Brewing Company in 2004, was itself acquired in 2008 by Independent Brewers United, the parent company of Magic Hat Brewing in Burlington, Vermont. In addition to two alehouse restaurants adjacent to its breweries in Berkeley, California, and Portland, Oregon, Pyramid also runs brewpubs in Walnut Creek and Sacramento, California, as well as one in Seattle, Washington. Pyramid sells three year-round beers (Audacious apricot ale, Haywire Hefeweizen, and Thunderhead IPA), four seasonals, and two "unconventional brews" dubbed the "Ignition Series." In August 2010, Pyramid Brewing Company was acquired by North American Breweries, a conglomerate based out of Rochester, New York.

Hamson, Tim. *The beer book*. New York: Dorling Kindersley, 2008.

Jackson, Michael. *Great beer guide*. London: Dorling Kindersley, 2000.

Pryamid Breweries, Inc. *Pyramidbrew.com*. http://www.pyramidbrew.com/company/ (accessed June 7, 2010).

Torres, Bianca. "Seattle's Pyramid Breweries crafts quality strategy." http://seattletimes.nwsource.com/html/businesstechnology/2002155251_pyramid20.html/ (accessed June 6, 2010).

Ben Keene

pyruvate is the molecule produced as the end point of the glycolytic breakdown of glucose. It is a three-carbon compound formed by yeast cells during fermentation. When the yeast cell grows under anaerobic conditions, the pyruvate is converted into carbon dioxide and acetaldehyde. From there, during normal brewery fermentations, acetaldehyde will be converted to ethanol.

Lewis, M. J., and T. W. Young. *Brewing*, 2nd ed. New York: Kluwer Academic/Plenum Publishers, 2001.

Russell, I., and G. G. Stewart. *An introduction to brewing science & technology, series III, Brewer's yeast*. London: The Institute of Brewing, 1998.

Steven J. Pittman

quality control and assurance. Quality control (QC) is a reactive approach, with response to measurements so as to prevent the product from being out of specification. Thus, the emphasis is on prevention rather than detection; the ethos might be called "right the first time." For example, rather than making a QC measurement on beer, such as gushing, the focus would be upstream in ensuring that gushing is not going to be a problem (e.g., the use of noninfected malt). Quality assurance (QA) is an attitude in which one strives to ensure that the product at every stage in its production is within specification. QA naturally embraces QC insofar as it is dependent upon analysis of raw materials, process, and product, but the emphasis is proactive rather than reactive.

Measurements are either made in-line, on-line, or at least at-line, so as to provide real-time information that assures that material is within specification or allows immediate feedback response to correct goods that are off-target. The benefit is reduced waste in terms of product and time.

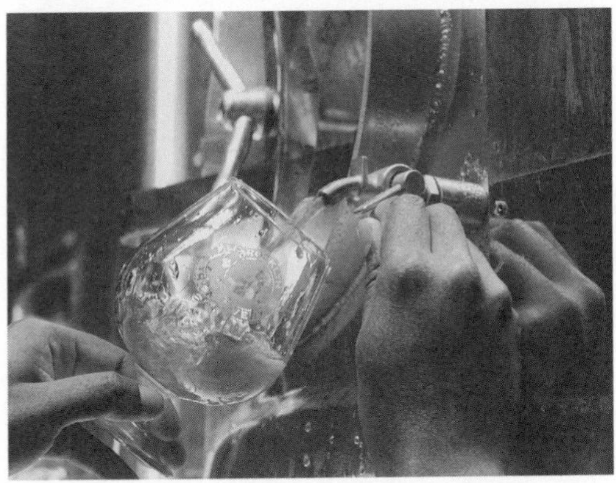

A brewer at the Brooklyn Brewery tastes his latest creation. PHOTOGRAPH BY DENTON TILLMAN

Total quality management (TQM) is a culture whereby everyone in a company is committed to excellence and highest quality delivery in all aspects of the organization, including fabrication. The whole organization is subsumed in and motivated by a determination to be part of quality best practice. The motivation is driven from the highest level of management.

TQM depends on the adoption of a quality system, which may be formalized through standards such as those within the ISO 9000 series. (ISO 9000 was spawned out of Mil-Q-9858a, a standard for military procurement established in the United States in 1959.) The purpose is to focus on and achieve compliance with documented systems. Fundamentally, this means that there is steadfast adherence to a quality manual that delineates everything from raw materials in to product out in terms of specifications, standard operating procedures, and so on.

Specifications should be realistic and meaningful. They must relate to what is expected in a raw material, process stage, or product, but not set to such a rigor that they are unachievable.

Hazard analysis and critical control points (HACCP) is also fundamental to QA. It is a management system designed to assure the safety of food products; however, the principles are broadly applicable to all aspects of delivering a quality product.

Bamforth, C. W. *Standards of brewing.* Boulder, CO: Brewers Publications, 2002.

Charles W. Bamforth

A **quarter** is an ancient and potentially confusing measure applied to English malting barley.

Not to be confused with a "quart" (a measure of liquid), a quarter is the standard measure for barley as bought by a maltster, and it equates to 448 lb, which should yield approximately 80 lb to 100 lb of extract for the brewer.

However, during the malting process, during which malt is dried, the weight of a given quantity of malt decreases. A quarter of malted barley (still in line to give the same yield of extract) weighs approximately 336 lb. Although the actual weight has fallen by around 25%, the projected yield is still the same. A quarter is therefore a measure of weight, but the weight it describes is different depending on whether it is applied to barley or barley malt. Many old British beer recipes are based upon quarters of malt, a measurement that can leave the modern interpreter nonplussed.

Perhaps because of its confusing nature, today a quarter is a measurement rarely quoted outside the malting industry, and it is rarely listed even in glossaries of brewing terms. But it is still in contemporary use.

The capacity of a malting is traditionally measured according to the number of quarters which can be processed through it over a 4-day period. So a "50 quarter malting" does not refer to a plant that has the capacity to hold 50 quarters of malt, but to the quantity of barley that goes through it every 4 days. The floor space of a traditional floor malting is measured in square feet per quarter.

Pete Brown

racking is a term that refers to the transfer of beer from one vessel to another. Although it is used most often to describe the kegging and casking of beer, brewers often refer to "racking" oak-aged beers from barrels into other vessels. In homebrewing, racking may refer to the transferring of beer to a secondary vessel or to bottles. In essence, racking is a simple process but one that can easily ruin a good beer and all the hard work that went into its production. Successful racking involves transferring the beer efficiently, in the shortest time, without causing it damage. Although it is a simple process of fluid flow, racking is more than just pouring or pumping liquid. Ideally it should be pumped quietly and carefully, using sterile hoses or pipes and with no exposure to air or contaminated surfaces. Three major problems may arise during racking: contamination by microorganisms, oxidation, and loss of foam potential. The beer can become contaminated if it comes into contact with microorganisms that may have infested pipework or hoses. Oxidation from contact with air is also a constant danger during transfers. Oxygen pick-up by beer during transfer is one of the major causes of premature staling in finished beer and a contributor to unwanted haze formation. Turbulence is also bad for beer—if the racking of a beer is too vigorous or conducted at too high a speed, the transferred beer may lose its ability to develop a good head of foam. Loss of carbonation is an attendant danger. Racking is a gentle art that, done correctly, can help ensure that the quality put into the beer in the brewery stays intact until the beer reaches its destination in the glass.

Keith Thomas

The **Radeberger Group** is the largest single beer company in the diverse and decentralized German market, with a 15% share by volume. The namesake Radeberger Brewery is one of 14 breweries owned by the company. They brew dozens of classic German beers, some of them national brands and many of them regional specialties. Among them are Jever Pilsner, DAB (Dortmunder Actien Brewery), Dortmunder Union, Henninger, Schultheiss, Berliner Kindl Weisse, Binding, Sion Kolsch, Altenmeunster, and the non-alcoholic brew Clausthaler. On its own, the Radeberger Brewery ranks ninth among all German breweries. The Radeberger Group also imports Corona Beer, Guinness, and Kilkenny. The Radeberger Brewery was founded as Zum Bergkeller in Radeberg, a suburb of Dresden, in 1872. The area has a history of hop growing and is not far from the Czech region of Bohemia. Radeberger pilsner was favored by the King of Saxony, and the first German chancellor, Otto von Bismarck, declared Radeberger the "Kanzler-Brau" (the Chancellor's Brew) in 1887. In 1946, the Communist East German government took control of the brewery. When the Berlin Wall fell in 1989, the brewery underwent extensive renovation. It was purchased by the Oetker Gruppe of Bielefeld, Germany, in 2004. The Oetker Gruppe is an $8 billion Euro private company that has interests in food, beer, wine, spirits, non-alcoholic beverages, shipping, banking, publishing, chemicals, hotels, and retail and wholesale outlets. The beers of the Radeberger Group are brewed according to the specifications of the German Beer Purity Law.

See also REINHEITSGEBOT.

Jackson, Michael. *Ultimate beer*. New York: DK Publishing, Inc, 1998.
Oetker Group. http://www.oetker-gruppe.de/.
Radeberger Gruppe. http://www.radeberger-gruppe.de/

Stephen Hindy

Radlermass (translated: "cyclist's liter"; "mass" is an old Bavarian word for "liter") is a mixed beer-based drink with a long history in German-speaking regions. Its northern German name is "Alsterwasser." Usually consisting of a 50/50 mixture of various types of beer and German-style clear lemon-lemonade, the invention of the Radler has been widely attributed to the Munich gastronomer Franz Xaver Kugler in 1922. Radlermass is the Bavarian equivalent of the British shandy (which is also a mixture of beer and lemonade, or, less often, ginger beer). Kugler's "cyclist's liter" became very popular in Munich, and other beer gardens offered the same mixture.

Today radler is not only drunk in Bavaria but all across Germany and Austria. In Austria it is usually a mixed beer with cloudy orange-lemonade. During the summer months, radler is very popular because of its reputation for being a perfect thirst-quencher—a result of its harmony in sweet-bitter and sour taste—and is bottled premixed and available all over Germany. Until the 1990s in Germany it was forbidden by law to produce radler in bottles (it had to be mixed in the beer garden by adding half a liter of lemonade to half a liter of beer), but nowadays the market share of ready-mixed radler and other beer-based drinks is increasing.

The "Russenmass" is a mixture of hefeweizen and lemonade. The "Diesel" is a mixture of lager and a cola-based beverage. The mixing of these two drinks produces a diesel-fuel-like coloration, which explains the name of the drink. There exist several regional differences in names and variants. Hefeweizen mixed with cola is called a "Colaweizen." Weißbier mixed with cola is called a "Flieger" ("Aviator"), or "Turbo." Pilsner or altbier and cola are known as a "Krefelder."

Wolfgang Stempfl

Rahr Malting Company is a malt producer based in Shakopee, Minnesota. The firm began as the Eagle Brewery, which was founded in 1847 in Manitowoc, Wisconsin, by German immigrant William Rahr. Like many breweries of the era, Eagle produced its own malt. By the 1860s, the company was also supplying malt to other breweries, mainly in the local area. The brewery was closed during Prohibition and never reopened, but the malt production continued.

Today, the company is still controlled by Rahr's descendants and has become the ninth-largest commercial maltster in the world and the fourth largest in North America. Rahr has two malting facilities—one in Shakopee, Minnesota, and one in Alix, Alberta, Canada. The company also has a grain storage elevator in Taft, North Dakota.

Rahr produces roughly 510,000 metric tons (33 million bushels) of malt per year. Although the company does produce some specialty malts, the bulk of its production is pilsner-type base malt, wheat malt, and malt used in the distilling and food industries.

In addition to its own malt, Rahr also distributes imported and domestic specialty malts, hops, and other brewing products (such as adjuncts, head retention agents, and fining agents) to mainly-North American customers through its Brewers Supply Group subsidiary. Among the companies whose malt they distribute are Weyermann (Germany), Briess (United States), and Castle (Belgium).

Rahr is also a part owner of Koda Energy, a power company that burns malting and agricultural byproducts to generate heat and electricity, some of which is then used by Rahr. Koda is a joint venture between Rahr and the Shakopee Mdewakanton Sioux Community.

Rahr Malting Co. http://www.rahr.com

Josh Rubin

Rameses II Usermaatra Setepenra was the third ruler of the 19th Dynasty in ancient Egypt. He became Pharaoh in 1279 BC and during his long reign, until his death in 1213 BC, he excelled as a warrior, a builder, and, somewhat tangentially, a brewer. Some of the greatest Egyptian temples and monuments are to his credit, including the Nubian rock-cut temple at Abu Simbel, numerous temples at Memphis, the court and pylon of Luxor temple, a temple at Abydos, and the Ramesseum, his own mortuary temple at west Thebes, opposite modern Luxor. On the field of combat, he won the crucial Battle of Qadesh (Kadesh), in present-day Syria against the Hittite king Mutwatallis, which preserved Egypt as the mightiest power of his age. The Ramesseum is of particular interest to modern scholars trying to determine the place of beer in ancient Pharaonic society. It was this structure that, incidentally, was incorrectly described by the 1st century BC Greek historian Diodorus Siculus as the "Tomb of Ozymandias," which, in turn inspired the early 19th-century poet Percy Bysshe Shelley to write his well-known sonnet by the same name. The complex contains several mud-brick granaries that are testimony to the importance of grain to the economy of ancient Egypt. To build his massive structures, Rameses II needed vast armies of laborers, who, in turn, required feeding and hydration. In ancient times people knew that although water might not be safe to drink, beer was trustworthy, and therefore it was the latter that constituted the daily beverage of the common man. Near the tomb's construction site, on the west bank of the Nile, was the settlement of Deir el Medina, where Rameses II housed his workers. Extensive excavations there have yielded fascinating insight into the daily lives of the people who lived under the 18th to the 20th dynasties. The many ostraca (shards of pottery) recovered point to brewing on a tremendous scale and establish barley as the most common grain used, next to emmer. The relicts have allowed us to reconstruct the entire sequence of Egyptian brewing and baking techniques, from primitive malting to mashing and spontaneous fermentation in earthenware crocks.

See also EGYPT.

Kitchen, K. A. *Pharaoh triumphant: The life and times of Rameses II, King of Egypt.* Warminster, England: Aris & Phillips, 1982.

Lesko, L. H., ed. *Pharaoh's workers: The villagers of Deir el Medina.* Ithaca, NY: Cornell University Press, 1994.

Samuel, D. "Brewing and baking." In P. T. Nicholson and I. Shaw ed., *Ancient Egyptian materials and technology,* Cambridge, UK: Cambridge University Press, 2000.

Ian Hornsey

rauchbier is a German-style beer brewed with smoked malt. It can be any style, but most commonly

Rauchbier, beer brewed with smoked malt, is a favorite beer style in Bamberg, Germany. CATH HARRIES

it is a medium-strength lager. Rauchbier (German for "smoke beer") is quite popular in Franconia, especially in Bamberg and its surroundings, where it is usually brewed to märzen strength. *Aecht Schlenkerla Rauchbier* from Brauerei Heller-Trum is probably the best known brand. Schlenkerla's historic brewery tap is only 100 m from the Romanesque cathedral of Bamberg, so many tourists make their way over for a beer and some food. The tourists are told quite a tale—that rauchbier originated in a cloister that had been caught on fire, as happened often in medieval cities. As the legend goes, much of the cloister was destroyed, but part of the brewhouse, including a good amount of malt, had been spared. The malt, however, had been exposed to the smoke from the nearby fire and picked up this special flavor, which made the beer famous.

This tale may be full of action and dramatic flames, but it is most unlikely that it has any historic validity. Some smokiness must have been typical for most kilned malts before new malting and kilning technologies were invented in the early

19th century: Combustion gases from the heat chamber would pass through to the kiln's perforated floor and add flavor to the malt. Today this effect is desired only in specific smoked lagers, weizenbiers, bockbiers, and porters—and the malt used for this purpose is produced separately in a kiln where smoke from cured beechwood (for some rare malts it may also be oak) is used to dry the malt.

During the brewing process, the amount of smoked malt in the mash is crucial for the desired smokiness—as is the yeast. Some modern brewers have noticed that their first rauchbier does not taste as smoky as they would like—even when it is brewed from 100% smoked malt. This is because the yeast absorbs a significant portion of the smoky flavor during fermentation. If this "smoked" yeast is subsequently used to ferment a nonsmoked beer, it too may show a hint of smokiness. Schlenkerla uses this fact for good effect in its Helles lager, a brew made without smoked malt, but with repitched rauchbier yeast. More typically, rauchbier yeast is repitched into consecutive rauchbier batches for a consistent smokiness. This yeast trick even works with brews that are not made from 100% smoked malt, that is, when part of the mash is made up of caramel and dark malts for extra body and mouthfeel.

A strong smokiness is especially desirable when rauchbier is paired with food. Typical Franconian pairings often involved smoked meats, which are a local specialty. In general, most any hearty food, German or otherwise, tends to work well with the smoky rauchbier flavors—rauchbier itself is often described as smelling like campfires, bacon, or sausages. Not surprisingly, many cigar aficionados, perhaps enjoying the greatest concentration of smoke flavors they can get, have enjoyed rauchbiers with their favorite cigars.

In recent years brewers have brewed a broader spectrum of smoked beers: a seasonal rauchbock has been brewed for some time in Franconia and American brewers have turned smoked porter into a respected and well-loved beer style. Smoked wheat beers have appeared during the past decade as well. Smoked wheat ales (aka rauchweizen) are brewed from approximately 60% conventional wheat malt and 40% smoked barley malt. They are fermented with a traditional strain of Bavarian Hefeweizen yeast. Because of the smaller amount of smoked malt in the grist and the use of a yeast that produces its own balancing aromas, rauchweizen has become the beer of choice for those who can enjoy some smoked flavor but don't want the intensity of classical rauchbier. Smoked beers generally age well, with the smoky characteristics melding with sherryish notes as the beer slowly oxidizes.

Conrad Seidl

real ale, as frequently quoted from the *Oxford English Dictionary*, is "a name for draught (or bottled) beer brewed from traditional ingredients, matured by secondary fermentation in the container from which it is dispensed, and served without the use of extraneous carbon dioxide."

"Real ale" as an expression was adopted by the Campaign for Real Ale (CAMRA) in 1973. First known as the Campaign for the Revitalization of Ale, its name change was an attempt to simplify and shorten what was an uncomfortable mouthful of letters at the most sober of times. The appellation is a convenient campaigning device that has attracted a number of crass comments about the "realness" of filtered beers. Certainly an excellent India pale ale, even if filtered, is considered by most beer enthusiasts very real indeed.

The simple, accurate, and nondidactic expressions "cask conditioned" or "bottle conditioned" might better describe beer with live yeast. The qualitative difference, of course, between cask-conditioned beers and filtered beers lies in the presence of live yeast, which is able to feed on any fermentable sugars remaining in the beer from the time it is racked into cask at the brewery and to impart its own individual imprint of aromas and flavors as well as life-enhancing carbonation.

However, what might be termed CAMRA's "cause celebre" has inspired the fundamentalists of the campaign to insist that even a noninvasive blanket of carbon dioxide at atmospheric pressure to protect slow-selling beers from the ravages of oxidation must be construed as an unnatural interference with the aroma, flavor, and mouthfeel of cask ale, thereby rendering it "nonreal." However, studies clearly demonstrate that the cask breather system protects the beer without actually adding carbon dioxide to the liquid. Why, then, the controversy?

The strongest claim is that the air drawn into a cask on dispense somehow softens the palate of the beer, resulting in beneficial flavor changes analogous to the effect of oxygen on a young red wine. In fact, research has found this "benefit" to be generally undetectable and a CO_2 blanket produced by a cask breather to provide better overall flavor to the consumer. The fact that not a smidgen of evidence can be produced to support CAMRA's thesis has not deterred the dogmatism at work within the organization. CAMRA's influential "Good Beer Guide" persists in "excommunicating" pubs that protect their beers with cask breather systems. Their beer rendered unreal by this judgment, a country pub can easily fade from public view and finally fail, diminishing the overall beer culture. These are, of course, matters of opinion—some Bavarian brewers might claim that the Reinheitsgebot declares many wonderful British and Belgian beers to be unreal. Perhaps, then, it may be up to brewers and consumers to decide which ales are real and which are somehow false. One hopes that there is an eventual determination that British real ale is a beer that is traditionally brewed and fermented, properly conditioned on live yeast, honestly served with the yeast intact, and without the addition of artificial carbonation. If such a beer emerges beautifully into the glass in front of a happy beer drinker, no doubt it shall be found properly derived and quite real enough to provide genuine pleasure, which is of course the point of beer in the first place.

See also CAMPAIGN FOR REAL ALE (CAMRA), CASK BREATHER, CASK CONDITIONING, and CELLARMANSHIP, ART OF.

Mark Dorber

real degree of fermentation (RDF) measures the degree to which sugar in wort has been fermented into alcohol in beer, defined as "attenuation." A sweet beer has more residual sugar and lower attenuation. The RDF expresses the percentage of extract that was fermented. RDFs in the 50s represent full-bodied beers with over 40% of their original extract left unfermented, whereas RDFs in the 80s represent highly attenuated beers with less than 20% of their original extract unfermented. Mouthfeel is largely determined by RDF percentage; the higher the RDF percentage, the lighter and drier the beer. Conversely, a beer with a lower RDF percentage may have a round and even syrupy mouthfeel. The term "real" in this instance separates this measurement from those that are "apparent." Because alcohol is lighter than water, a sample of beer may "appear," when a hydrometer is used, to have lower residual sugar than it actually does.

See also APPARENT EXTRACT, HYDROMETER, MOUTHFEEL, and REAL EXTRACT.

Paul H. Chlup

real extract (RE) is a precise calculation concerning the gravity of beer. It is related to a boiled wort's gravity, a fermented wort's attenuation, and a finished beer's alcohol level. The specific gravity of wort—its density—is greater than that of water, which sets the mark at 1.000 because of the presence of sugars in solution. Gravity is commonly measured in terms of original gravity or degrees Plato (°P). See ORIGINAL GRAVITY and PLATO GRAVITY SCALE. A standard beer may have an original gravity of 1.048 or 12°P. As beer is being fermented—or attenuated—its gravity decreases because sugars are converted into carbon dioxide gas, which largely escapes, and alcohol, mostly ethanol, which mostly stays in the beer.

Attenuation is thus the extent to which wort sugar has been converted to alcohol. If a beer has plenty of residual sugar after fermentation, it has a lower attenuation value than a beer from the same-gravity wort with next to no residual sugars. If the difference in gravity between the starting wort and the finished beer is measured using a hydrometer, this attenuation value is misleading, because the wort gravity is measured based on sugar dissolved in a reference liquid of water only. The beer gravity is measured based on residual sugars dissolved in a reference liquid that is both water and alcohol. This is significant, because alcohol has a lower density (or gravity) than water. Thus, the difference between the hydrometer readings of wort gravity and of finished beer gravity lead to a value called apparent attenuation—"apparent" rather than actual, because it contains a small error. See ATTENUATION and HYDROMETER.

That error is based on ethanol having only 79% of the gravity of pure water. RE, therefore, is the corrected value for the amount of attenuation. It is derived mathematically from the initial wort gravity and the final beer gravity, both measured in °P, with two correction factors. RE, therefore, takes into account the effect of the presence of alcohol in the finished beer (and the absence of alcohol in the starting wort). The formula for determining RE is (with 0.1808 and 0.8192, respectively, as correction constants)

$$RE = 0.1808 \times °P \text{ (of initial wort)} + 0.8192 \times °P \text{ (of final beer)}.$$

If the original gravity of a wort is 1.048 (or 12°P), for example, and the finishing gravity of the beer is 1.012 (or 3°P)—these are two are very common values in average session beers—using a rounded value of 4 gravity points equal 1°P, RE is

$$RE = [(0.1808 \times 12) + (0.8192 \times 3)]°P$$
$$RE = (2.1696 + 2.4576)°P$$
$$RE = 4.6272°P$$

See also APPARENT EXTRACT, MOUTHFEEL, and REAL DEGREE OF FERMENTATION (RDF).

Paul H. Chlup

Redhook Ale Brewery was founded, like Microsoft, in 1981 in a garage in Washington State. Starbucks Coffee Company cofounder Gordon Bowker recruited marketing analyst Paul Shipman, who was then working for Chateau Ste. Michelle, a Woodinville, Washington, winery. The two started Redhook Ale Brewery inside a transmission shop in Seattle. At the time, almost nobody in America was starting breweries. In 1980 eight craft brewers were registered in the United States, and they were largely ignored by industry experts. With few successful examples to emulate, it took the pair some time to find the right market. Their initial offering of a spicy Belgian ale left Seattle patrons confused. To them, the beer apparently tasted like bananas. Redhook sold fewer than 1,000 barrels in its first year. By 1984, however, after having had some success with their Blackhook porter the previous year, the pair crafted a beer called Ballard bitter (now Ballard bitter IPA). As people sought out this IPA in bars around Seattle, it became clear that the Redhook Ale Brewery had more than just a cult following; the microbrew revolution was gaining traction.

With the success of the Ballard bitter, the brewery soon moved out of the garage and into a 26,000 ft^2 historic Seattle Electric Railway building located in the local neighborhood of Fremont. It was in 1987, in this new facility, that they created their flagship beer, Redhook ESB, in the tradition of an English-style extra special bitter. See EXTRA SPECIAL BITTER (ESB). This beer is crisp and biscuity, showing caramel and fruit flavors, which become more pronounced as the beer warms in the glass.

In 1988, with the ESB gaining popularity, a more sophisticated brewery became a necessity and Redhook expanded and updated the Fremont facility. In 1994, it opened a second brewery in Woodinville, Washington, and in 1996 a third brewery in Portsmouth, New Hampshire. Through a venture called Craft Brewers Alliance, Redhook Ale Brewery is now licensed to brew and sell the successful Widmer Hefeweizen, owns a stake in both the Goose Island Beer Company and the Kona Brewing Company, and has had an advantageous distribution alliance with Anheuser-Busch since 1994. In turn, Anheuser-Busch InBev owns more than 35% of Craft Brewers Alliance, who are estimated to produce more than 400,000 hl (340,867 US bbl) of beer per year.

ESB Review from Beer Advocate. http://beeradvocate.com/articles/719

Funding Universe, company histories. http://www.fundinguniverse.com/company-histories/Redhook-Ale-Brewery-Inc-Company-History.html

Gordon Bowker Bio. http://seattletimes.nwsource.com/html/businesstechnology/2004269843_bowkertimeline09.html

History of microbreweries. http://www.brewersassociation.org/pages/about-us/history-of-craft-brewing

Miscellaneous information. http://www.examiner.com/x-6861-Bartender-Examiner~y2009m7d24-Redhook-Brewery

Redhook Ale Brewery website. http://www.redhook.com/Default.aspx?p=15

Seattle PI Interview with Paul Shipman. http://www.seattlepi.com/business/137100_amomentwith29.html

Jonathan Horowitz

reduction is the gain of electrons or a decrease in oxidation state by an atom in a substance. The greater the degree of reduction, the lower the oxidation state of a given atom. A reduction always occurs in tandem with an oxidation. One reactant is *reduced* (gains electrons or decreases in oxidation state) as another is *oxidized* (loses electrons or increases in oxidation state). If a transfer of electrons occurs, the electron-donating substance is called a *reducing agent* or *reductant*. By donating electrons, it is itself oxidized.

Glucose and other sugars capable of effecting reduction are called *reducing sugars*. In monosaccharides, the carbonyl carbon (number one) in the linear form is oxidized to a carboxyl group. In polysaccharides, the end of a chain with a free anomeric carbon (that is, not linked to another sugar) is commonly called the *reducing end*. So, for example, lactose is a reducing sugar (because it has an anomeric carbon available for oxidation), whereas sucrose is not.

Reductants in beer protect it to a certain extent from the ravages of oxidation. Reductants are initially present in beer; chief among them are products of the Maillard reaction. Increasing boil length will increase formation of melanoidins and thereby reduction potential to an extent. Prolonged boils, however, can lead to faster staling through other mechanisms. It is therefore advised to boil within appropriate limits, neither minimizing nor overextending the boil. Caramel and other highly kilned malts will increase the reduction potential of the beer. Even in very pale beers, it was once common practice to add a small amount of highly kilned malt as an antioxidant. Polyphenols, sulfhydryls, nitrogen compounds, and hops also contribute to reduction potential.

Narziß, Ludwig. *Abriss der Bierbrauerei (Summary of the beer brewery)*, 7th ed. Weinheim, Germany: Wiley-VCH Verlag GmbH & Co KGaA, 2005.

Nelson, David L., and Michael M. Cox. *Lehninger principles of biochemistry*, 4th ed. New York: W. H. Freeman and Company, 2005.

Wolfgang David Lindell

refrigeration is the method of cooling something to a temperature lower than that of the

Beer label, c. 1933, advertising a traditional cave lagering. Before the advent of refrigeration in the late 19th century, caves were ready-made cellars, as they were cool enough to store lagers for aging. PIKE MICROBREWERY MUSEUM, SEATTLE, WA

surrounding environment or, more accurately, the transfer of heat away from one mass and into another. Historically, palatable beer could only be brewed in climates and seasons that allowed sufficient natural cooling of the fermenting beer. Fermentation is an exothermic process—it generates heat. Uncontrolled, fermentation temperatures can quickly rise high enough to cause off-flavors or even kill the yeast itself. Each yeast strain has its unique temperatures it tolerates and a narrower range for the beer it produces to taste ideal. In northern latitudes, this once generally limited brewing to the months of October through April; the brewing season was somewhat longer in steadily cool parts of northern Europe and Britain. Most beer was consumed shortly after fermentation because bacterial spoilage usually set in within weeks. For centuries, ice was harvested in large blocks in winter and stored with the beer in deep underground cellars. This could keep the beer cool for months. Later, cool water was run through piping submerged in the fermenters, but this method was dependent on ambient water temperatures that often fluctuated seasonally.

The genuine breakthrough was "artificial" or mechanical refrigeration, which was invented specifically for brewing. In 1873 Carl von Linde, working for the Spaten Brewery in Munich, invented mechanical refrigeration. See LINDE, CARL VON. Using ether as the refrigerant gas, he was able to make block ice to cool Spaten's cellars. Although expensive, by the 1880s most breweries made their own ice mechanically. In addition to year-round brewing, this allowed for the expanded availability of the colder-processed lager beers versus warm-fermented ales. Breweries could be larger and further from natural ice sources. The invention of mechanical refrigeration was a critical factor in the spread and later dominance of lager brewing throughout the world. As refrigerants, ammonia replaced ether in the 1880s, and the safer freon was developed in the 1920s. Beginning in the 1970s freon was replaced with newer synthetics because of atmospheric ozone depletion.

In most modern breweries, fermentation vessels are fitted with hollow jackets that chill parts of the interior surface of the vessel on demand. This allows brewers to set a maximum temperature during active fermentation and then easily chill the beer for further processing. Refrigeration is also widely applied to heat exchangers, where the bulk of the cooling may be achieved with ambient-temperature water but supplemented by a further refrigerated cooling stage. This allows wort and beer to be quickly chilled to cold temperatures during periods when the ambient water temperature is relatively warm.

See HEAT EXCHANGER.

Brian Hunt

Reinheitsgebot, known in English as the (Beer) Purity Law, refers to a decree issued originally by the Bavarian Duke Wilhelm IV on April 23, 1516, on the occasion of a meeting of the Assembly of Estates, at Ingolstadt, north of Munich. The original text says that "We wish . . . forthwith that . . . in all our towns and markets and in the countryside no other items be used for beer than barley, hops, and water." Since then, this decree has gone through many iterations, revisions, and amendments, and is now part of the modern German tax law, where it resides under the frightfully convoluted title of "Section 9 of the Public Notice concerning the Amendment of the Provisional Beer Law dated July 29, 1993." The Purity Law may be almost 5 centuries old, but its current name of Reinheitsgebot is of much more recent vintage. That term was coined on March 4, 1918, by an obscure member of the Bavarian State Parliament, Hans Rauch, during an impassioned debate about beer taxation. Before then, the law had simply been known by the prosaic name of "Surrogatverbot" (surrogate, or adjunct, prohibition). See ADJUNCTS. Because of its longevity, the Reinheitsgebot is now considered the world's oldest, still valid food safety and consumer protection legislation.

It is perhaps a much underappreciated fact that there are really two Purity Laws today, the Bavarian and the German. While the Bavarian version still restricts the use of anything but barley malt, hops, water, and yeast—an ingredient that was added after its discovery in the late 17th century—for all bottom-fermented beers, it allows for the additional use of malted wheat and malted rye, for instance, in top-fermented beers only. The German version, on the other hand, is slightly more lenient when it comes to bottom-fermented beers. These may also be made with the addition of "technically pure cane sugar, beet sugar, invert sugar, and modified starch sugar, as well as coloring agents made from these sugars." Historically, therefore, it is an anachronism to refer to the German Purity Law of 1516. A "German" version simply did not exist back then, even though this identifier can be found on many German ale and lager labels today. In fact, in northern Germany, the use of malt substitutes such as rice, green starch, and potato starch was legally not only permitted, but protected by the German Imperial Law of 1873, which made sure that brewers operating within the "Northern German Beer Taxation Community" paid brew raw materials taxes on these ingredients, too. Only on June 3, 1906, did the Second German Empire adopt the current understanding of the Purity Law for all of Germany. When Bavaria became a member state of the German Weimar Republic, in 1918, it made it one of the conditions of its joining that the new republic continue to adopt the Purity Law, as had the German Empire before. Bavaria insisted on the same in 1949, when it joined the current German Federal Republic.

German brewers—including in Bavaria—that fail to adhere to the Purity Law may sell their beverages, but may not call them "beer." In 1987, however, the European Court dealt a serious blow to that reading of the Reinheitsgebot, when it ruled that the law amounted to an inadmissible restriction of free trade against beers brewed in the rest of Europe. Non-German brewers, therefore, were allowed, henceforth, to sell even non-Reinheitsgebot brews into Germany and call them "beer," while German brewers, under their domestic law, were still compelled to follow the Reinheitsgebot when brewing beers destined for their own market. But German brewers were now allowed—according to a new Section 9 (7) Amendment of the Provisional Beer Law—to depart from the restrictions of the German Purity Law when making beers for export . . . except in Bavaria, where brewers still had to adhere to the Bavarian version of the law, no matter what.

See also BAVARIA.

Bavarian Brewers Federation, Munich. http://www.bavarianbeer.com.

Horst Dornbusch and Karl-Ullrich Heyse

residual sugars are sugars that are still present in beer after the fermentation process is complete. A beer with a lot of residual sugar will have a fuller body and often taste sweeter, whereas one with less residual sugar will be drier and have a lighter mouthfeel. The sugars present in beer are generally derived from malted barley. Sometimes brewers will use adjuncts, different malted grains, corn, rice, syrup, honey, molasses, or other forms of sugar, in varying quantities, to complement the sugars extracted from the barley. The majority of these sugars are then consumed by yeast during the fermentation process.

Unlike winemakers, brewers rarely stop fermentations to produce a beer with higher residual sugar. Brewers, however, have far more control over the actual sugar profile and can control the amount of residual sugar in a number of ways. They can, for example, use sugars that they know the yeast will not be able to consume. Lactose, for example, is a nonfermentable sugar that is used in brewing milk stouts, also known as sweet stouts. Brewers can also manage the amount of sugar that will be left behind in a beer at various stages of the brewing process. During the mash, as the starches from the barley are being converted into sugar, the brewer can adjust the conditions to influence how many of the resulting sugars will be fermentable. Higher saccharification temperatures, for example, will result in the production of larger dextrins, which yeasts will not ferment. These dextrins will be left in the finished beer to contribute body and possibly sweetness. Brewers can also influence the amount of sugar that is consumed during fermentation by selecting yeast strains that will consume more or less of certain sugars. Yeasts that consume a lot of sugar are referred to as highly attenuative yeasts. The range of residual sugar in various beer styles is quite wide, with the driest well under 1% residual sugar by weight (lambics, some saisons, and other Belgian specialty styles) and some hefty barley wines nearing a syrupy 10% residual sugar. It is important to note, however, that not all sugars actually taste sweet and that the perception of sweetness is based upon a number of factors including temperature, carbonation, and bitterness. Beers with high residual sugars rarely taste as sweet as the sweetest wines. That said, at the dinner table, many beers possess enough residual sugar to make equally good (or excellent) accompaniments to a wide range of desserts and to be very pleasant digestifs.

Fix, George. *Principles of brewing science*, 2nd ed. Boulder, CO: Brewer's Publications, 1999.
Palmer, John. *How to brew*. Boulder, CO: Brewer's Publications, 2006.

Mirella G. Amato

resins in hops are chemical constituents produced by the hop plant, Humulus lupulus, as secondary metabolites. The term "secondary metabolite" refers to substances produced by a plant that do not participate in the primary metabolic process but are nonetheless necessary for the development and life of the plant. Resins are found in the lupulin glands of mature hop cones along with hop oils and some polyphenols. The resins are characterized by their extractability in different solvents, whereby soft resins are soluble in cold methanol and hard resins are soluble in diethyl ether. From a brewing perspective, only the soft resins are considered important because they contain the precursors to bitter flavor in beer. The hop acids, which are part of the soft resins, are composed of two chemically similar groups of compounds, alpha acids, or humulones, and beta acids, or lupulones. Neither of these compounds is bitter per se, but isomerized alpha acids as well as oxidized beta acids are. Isomerized alpha acids are the principal source of bitterness in beer. Therefore, hops are characterized to a large extent by their alpha acid content. Hop resins are not very soluble in water and even less so in beer because of beer's acidic nature. Virtually no amounts of beta acids and only small amounts of alpha acids (less than 14 parts per million) can be found in beer. Hop resins are extracted during wort boiling, during which alpha acids are isomerized to iso-alpha acids. Hop resins can also be extracted from hops using supercritical CO_2 or ethanol. These can then be used during brewing in their pre-extracted form.

See also HULUPONES, ISO-ALPHA ACIDS, HOP ISOMERIZATION, and LUPULIN.

Thomas Shellhammer

respiration of barley is essentially the "breathing" of the live barley kernel. Like our own breathing, it involves the uptake of ambient oxygen and the release of carbon dioxide. During dormancy, the seed's husks and protective coat—called the testa layer and the pericarp layer—serve as barriers to gas exchanges between the internal living cells and the exterior, thus limiting the rate of respiration. But once the grain is awoken during steeping and germination, the grain's respiration rate depends on several factors, most important on the grain's protein and moisture content, the amount of oxygen in the environment, and the ambient temperature. As these values rise, so does the grain's respiratory metabolism. The faster the grain's breathing, the faster will be its acrospire and rootlet growth. Respiration only slows down again or even ceases when the grain is being dried in a kiln or roaster. Sugars are the principal carbon sources for grain respiration during malting, which is why respiration is also considered a "malting loss." This is because sugars used up by barley for its respiration will not be available later for fermentation. Controlling respiration during silo storage, steeping, and germinating, however, is a delicate balancing act between, on the one hand, depriving the grain of oxygen—which impedes the malting process and may even kill the kernel—and excessive oxygenation, on the other hand, which may result in reduced brewhouse yields. Phased adjustments in ventilation, temperature, and moisture, therefore, are the maltster's main tools for maintaining a proper equilibrium between kernel vitality and nutrient preservation for subsequent beer making.

Briggs, Dennis Edward. *Malts and malting*. London: Chapman & Hall, 1997.

Thomas Kraus-Weyermann

respiratory-deficient mutants, also referred to as RD mutants, are defective yeast cells. All yeasts used in brewing have the ability to ferment or respire specific carbon sources. Alcohol is only produced when sugars are fermented; however, respiratory ability, too, appears to be important for yeast's ability to produce acceptable beers.

RD yeast mutants are also called petite (French for small) mutants because of their small colony size when they are propagated on agar medium. These mutants show sublethal damage to their mitochondrial DNA. They occur more frequently than nuclear mutants because of their proximity to the highly oxidative electron chain. Importantly, they lose their ability to respire and use carbon sources such as ethanol or glycerol. But they can still ferment, albeit slowly.

There are two forms of RD mutants, each differing in the nature of their DNA damage: rho⁻ mutants contain incomplete mitochondrial DNA, whereas rho⁰ mutants do not contain mitochondrial DNA at all. Only rho⁻ mutants are observed in brewing and they occur spontaneously in concentrations of up to 4% depending on the yeast strain. Increased mutation rates can develop if brewers yeast is stressed or not handled properly during harvest and storage. Mutations also accumulate during serial repitching. A culture containing high levels of RD mutants—of perhaps 10%—can affect fermentation performance as well as produce noticeable off-flavors, particularly the clove-like 4-vinyl guaiacol. RD mutants are easily detected in brewery lab tests, and high concentrations will spur a brewery to reculture the yeast strain to arrest the development of further yeast health issues.

Jenkins, C., S. Lawrence, A. Kennedy, P. Thurston, J. Hodgson, and K. Smart. Incidence and formation of petite mutants in lager brewing yeast *Saccharomyces cerevisiae* (syn *S. pastorianus*) populations. *Journal of the American Society of Brewing Chemists* 67 (2009): 72–80.

Sylvie Van Zandycke

A **rhizome** is a stem of a plant that grows horizontally underground and is capable of producing new shoots or roots for the plant. The rhizome serves as one means by which this type of plant may spread and propagate itself. A number of plants produce rhizomes, such as hops, ginger, bamboo, and Bermuda grass. The hop plant is a perennial; thus, the material above ground dies back each winter, but the root structure survives and will continue producing new plant material for many years. New shoots will grow from the rhizomes that have overwintered. Rhizomes grow each spring from the main root mass of the hop plant and will travel up to several feet, in some instances underground, before shoots emerge. Hop growers will often use rhizome cuttings in the springtime once new buds appear as a means of propagating a particular hop plant for use in a hop yard. In this fashion the plant material obtained will be genetically identical to its source. Those wishing to plant hops in home gardens can usually find rhizomes for sale in springtime by hop merchants and homebrew supply shops, usually by mid-March.

Thomas Shellhammer

rice, Oryza sativa, is, like all cereals, a grass. In the case of rice there seems to be archaeological evidence for the origins of domestication in the Yangtze Valley in present-day China. There are also strains of rice native to Africa. For successful planting, rice prefers hot, wet conditions and can grow in standing water. Today, rice is second only to maize in terms of agricultural production. However, it is the largest in terms of consumption as food, with around 3 billion people, mostly in the Middle and Far East, relying on it as their dietary staple. Rice has become more popular as a food in the west with consumption in the United States rising sharply, possibly because so much is used to make beer. The vast majority of the rice consumed is white rice, in which the bran coat has been ground away. Anheuser-Busch is the largest single buyer of rice in the United States. Budweiser beer is brewed with rice making up a large portion of the grist.

Traditionally, growing rice involves a low capital outlay but an intensive expenditure of labor. In Asia, the construction of paddy fields has used immense amounts of labor, but flooding the fields brought in nutrients, prevented weeds growing and competing with the crop, and kept down pests. Paddy fields also generate large volumes of methane from decomposing organic matter, thus increasing global warming.

Rice prices have risen rapidly since 2008, partly because of poor harvests in some areas but also because of speculative market activity and government price supports for other cereals, particularly for their use in biofuels. Productivity has fallen by as much as 20% in some areas, and many analysts expect prices to continue to rise.

Rice in Brewing

In the Far East, a lack of barley and plenty of rice, combined with the universal human desire to produce alcohol, led to the invention of sake or so-called rice wine. Although it often has wine-like alcoholic potency, sake is not a wine at all, but a form of beer. Rather than malt the rice, the knowledge of fungal fermentation techniques led to the use of Aspergillus oryzae to hydrolyze the starch in polished rice. The technique involves the removal of as much as 50% of the rice grain by milling, to leave pure endosperm (the starchy storage material). The polished rice is washed and steamed before a culture of A. oryzae is added to the mass of cooked rice. The fungus produces the enzymes to hydrolyze the starch, producing fermentable sugars, which can then be fermented by yeast.

Rice in Beer

It is commonly held, at least among craft brewers, that the use of rice in beer is to be abhorred. To quote Maureen Ogle, from an article in the *LA Times*, "Rice is considered by many brewers to be what the nasty, industrialized brewers use to water down their beer" and "craft brewers treat rice almost as if it were rat poison." The article goes on to state that rice lowers the body, flavor, and color of beers made with elevated rice adjunct levels, which seems rather to reinforce the notion.

In fact, German brewers arrived in America to find that it was difficult to make good beer using the high-protein, six-row barleys available in the United States at the time. Looking for ways to dilute the malt, they began to use rice and corn. The end result bears little resemblance to good German or Czech lagers but their customers enjoyed this form of beer and millions of people still do. Although rice may once have been a cheap alternative to barley malt, it no longer is. Sharply rising prices have resulted in much higher material costs for brewers employing rice in their mashes.

Interestingly, despite the assertions by many American craft brewers and beer enthusiasts that rice is anathema, some craft brewers are experimenting with production of "pre-Prohibition" lagers that mimic the beers made in the United States in the late 1800s. These are relatively highly hopped but are very light bodied, the result of the use of up to 20% rice in the mash. Other craft brewers are experimenting with the use of specialized rice types that actually add interesting flavors to the beers.

As with all starchy adjuncts, the rice must be cooked to gelatinize the starch before it is added to the mash. This is usually done before the grain is mashed, possibly along with the addition of enzymes to prehydrolyze the starch. The addition of more than 30% rice to a mash can lead to problematically low enzymatic activity and high density in the mash bed. High adjunct mashes can also be somewhat sludgy, leading to difficulties in run-off. High levels of starchy adjuncts can also lead to problems with yeast nutrition because the adjuncts lack proteins and vitamins necessary for sustained yeast growth.

Ogle, Maureen. *Ambitious brew.* Orlando, FL: Houghton Mifflin Harcourt, 2006.

The sake brewing process. www.sake-world.com/html/brewing-process.html/

Chris Holliland

rice hulls are the hard outer layers of grains of rice. During normal harvesting of rice, the shard-like hulls are a by-product that later find other uses. After extensive boiling and drying to remove flavors and color, rice hulls are often used in the fruit juice industry as an aid to filtration and pressing operations. In brewing, many craft brewers blend them into mash to ensure good wort flow through the mash (or lauter) bed.

Rice hulls are most often used during the production of beers with high percentages of nonbarley cereal-grain adjuncts such as wheat or rye. These grains have higher levels of protein and beta-glucan compared with barley and lack the husks that create needed porosity in a mash bed. Higher protein and beta-glucan levels increase wort viscosity, sometimes forcing the brewer to increase mash bed porosity artificially. Rice hulls are favored by brewers because they do not contribute flavor or color and do not break down in the mash; they remain stiff and act to "open up" the mash bed. Oat hulls are another option for increasing bed porosity or reducing wort viscosity. As craft brewers produce increasingly stronger beers, they use more malt in their mashes, and the depth of the mash beds increases accordingly. Greater bed depth also decreases wort flow, and once again rice hulls often come to the rescue. Some brewers, looking to push the limits of style and their brewing systems, have sought to use rice hulls to produce beers from grists of 100% hull-less wheat.

Rates of usage can vary with the percentage of adjunct grains, but in general, adding between

1% and 5% of total grist weight in rice hulls directly to the mash helps ensure better wort runoff rates and greater wort clarity.

Lewis, Michael. *Brewing,* 2nd ed. New York: Kluwer Academic/Plenum Publishers, 2002.

Brian Thompson

Ringwood Brewery is named after the historic English town of Ringwood on the River Avon just to the west of the New Forest. It had been an important watering hole for several centuries until it lost its last commercial brewery after World War II. Brewing returned to the town in 1978, however, when Peter Austin, head brewer at Hull Brewery, retired to Hampshire to indulge his passion for sailing.

Apparently unable to keep away from the mash tun, Peter cobbled together various pieces of defunct brewery and dairy equipment and a 10-barrel plant evolved. He put his idiosyncratic Yorkshire yeast to work and went on to help spark the birth of the modern British microbrewery movement. Ringwood's Old Thumper, a robust pale ale, became the brewery's flagship beer. The success of the brewery, along with the rebound of cask-conditioned beer in Britain, persuaded Austin to engage in brewing equipment supply and brewery education. During the next decade or so, he set up breweries all over the world (including in North America), with his Ringwood plant being used for training purposes. To the new breweries he brought his rough-hewn, wooden-clad vessel design and the Ringwood yeast. The yeast's signature fruity/spicy quality became ubiquitous in English and American start-up breweries.

As Ringwood prospered, Peter took on two business partners, David and Nigel Welch, who brought greater financial stability to the concern. Further successes and the acquisition of a few pubs were such that larger premises had to be purchased for the brewery, which they found in Christchurch Road. The new site proved to be large enough to accommodate a couple of capacity increases over the years.

In 2007, with Austin long retired and with the brewery capable of producing 40,000 UK barrels per annum, David Welch sold the concern (and a vineyard) to Marstons plc for £19.2 million (31.4 million US dollars).

Bruning, T. *The microbrewers' handbook,* 2nd ed. Norwich, UK: Paragraph Publishing, 2009.
Protz, R., and A. Millns., eds. *Called to the bar.* St. Albans, UK: Camra Books, 1992.

Ian Hornsey

Ringwood yeast

See BREWPUB.

roasted malts, a general category of specialty malts that have been roasted at high temperatures in a malt roaster and traditionally includes biscuit, caramel (or crystal), brown, chocolate, and black (also called black patent) malts. Malt roasters are also used to produce roasted barley, an unmalted product. Roasted malts contribute a wide range of flavors and aromas including caramel, toffee, burned sugar, nutty, biscuit, chocolate, and coffee and hues ranging from golden to red to black, depending

Roasted barley gives beer a bitter, coffee-like flavor, often associated with stouts. PIKE MICROBREWERY MUSEUM, SEATTLE, WA

upon the roasting process and degree of roast as determined by the maltster and the style. They can add considerable bitterness when used at relatively high proportions, particularly in various types of stout. Roasted caramel malts can also provide enhanced foam creation and stability and increased viscosity (to add body or mouthfeel). Dark roasted malts can be used for flavor, but they can also be used to provide color adjustment without adding significant flavor.

The main purpose of roasting is to create unique colors, flavors, and aromas through intense Maillard reactions, the chemical reaction of amino acids and reducing sugars, and/or caramelization of sugars at high temperatures, followed by polymerization of these newly formed molecular structures to form brown pigments. The high temperatures applied during roasting completely deactivate all enzymes developed during malting. These intense color- and flavor-producing reactions are best initiated using malt roasters, which are specifically designed to produce extremely high yet consistent temperatures, apply heat uniformly to all malt kernels, and allow for precise airflow control.

There are two distinctive categories of roasted malts—roasted "green" malts (caramel malts) and dry roasted malts (brown, chocolate, and black malts).

Caramel malts are characterized by a glassy endosperm with varying degrees of sweet flavor ranging from light caramel to toffee to burned sugar. The typical color range of caramel malts is 10° to 120° Lovibond (13 to 160 standard reference method [SRM]; 25 to 320 European Brewery Convention [EBC]). See COLOR.

Caramel malt is produced by bypassing the kiln and introducing germinated barley (green malt) directly into a roaster at relatively high moisture content. The green malt is quickly heated up and held at the optimum temperature of 60°C–75°C (140°F–167°F) of the starch-degrading enzymes that had developed during germination. Moisture is held inside the roaster during this stage. This process is commonly referred to as "conversion" or "stewing." During conversion, the starchy endosperm of the malt is rapidly broken down by the enzymes into liquefied sugars; essentially, the grain husk now contains heavy wort. Following conversion, moisture is allowed to escape from the roaster and is driven from the kernels at high applied temperatures. The temperature of the kernels increases to over 200°C (400°F), whereby the liquefied sugars are caramelized or crystallized, developing the sweet caramel flavor and glassy endosperm characteristic of this style of malt. Skilled maltsters control the amount of caramelization or degree of roast using hands-on visual, aroma, and flavor sensory and "dye match" control samples.

Caramel malts are produced by malting companies throughout the world and are used in many styles of beer. In the United States, caramel malt is a signature ingredient in amber and red ales and is widely used in brown ales, Scotch ales, stouts, and porters. Used in smaller percentages, they contribute sweetness and develop rich flavors in pale ales, India pale ales, and mild ales. A distinguishing characteristic of caramel malts is their ability to improve foam development and stability and to enhance viscosity resulting from nonfermentable structures they contribute to beer.

Dry roasted malts include biscuit, brown, chocolate, and black malt and are produced by roasting kiln-dried malt at low moisture and very high temperatures to varying degrees of color and flavor. Dry roasted malts do not undergo the conversion or stewing step that caramel malts do, so the colors and flavors produced during this roasting process are the product of intense Maillard reactions and end products and therefore contribute little or no residual sweetness to a beer. There are various gradations of roast, which can be compared with gradations of roast for coffee, which can be roasted lightly, fully, or virtually burned, as is the case with espresso roasts. Brown malt, an archaic type now making a minor comeback, can be used in British mild and brown ales, Scotch ales, stouts, and porters and has a color range of 55°–170° Lovibond (75–230 SRM; 150–450 EBC). Brown malt was used to create the original porter beers that became popular in London in the 1700s. Originally it was often the base malt in porter, but it was largely replaced by a blend of pale malts and other roasted malts when roasting technology improved during the 1800s. For many years, historically minded amateur brewers had to roast approximations of brown malt themselves if they wanted to accurately reproduce early porters, but some maltsters now produce small quantities. Chocolate malt is more deeply roasted than brown malt and is named more for the color than flavor. Chocolate malts generally contribute rich, roasted coffee flavor to porters, stouts, brown ales, Scotch ales, dunkels, and other dark beers. Depending upon the maltster, typical color ratings are 200° to 500° Lovibond (270–680 SRM; 550–1,350 EBC) for pale to dark chocolate malts.

Black malt, also known as "black patent" or just "patent malt," is so highly roasted that many flavor and aroma compounds are volatilized off, leaving only dark roasted, coffee-like, slightly astringent flavors. With a color range of 500° to 650° Lovibond (680–880 SRM; 1,350–1750 EBC), it is often used in small quantities with minimal flavor contribution to the finished beer. However, when used in higher quantities, it can add form of bitterness, an espresso-like roast bite, particularly to stouts.

David Kuske

Robust (barley) is a North American six-row spring barley variety with smooth awns and plump kernels. In the brewhouse, Robust has low beta-glucan levels, which leads to low wort viscosity and a well-draining mash bed. Developed in 1983 by the Minnesota Agricultural Experimental Station, Robust is a cross between the Morex and Manker barley varieties. It has short stalks and good lodging resistance, unlike many long-stalk varieties which often break easily and are difficult to harvest. See LODGING RESISTANCE. Robust barley is resistant to stem blotch and stem rust, but it is susceptible to loose smut. It grows best in well-drained, fertile soils and can thrive on alkaline and heavy substrates. In 2009, it was second in acreage in Minnesota only to Lacey barley plantings, but it does less well in hotter and drier conditions. Robust is used both as a malting and a feed barley. In the United States it is used almost exclusively by large brewers as a base malt; however, craft brewers use Robust widely in the form of roasted and caramel malts.

Star Seed. www.gostarseed.com/products/barley-spring-robust-48-bag Minnesota agricultural news. Barley varieties (accessed September 7, 2009).

Yoon, S. H., P. T. Berglund, and C. E. Fastnaught. Evaluation of selected barley cultivars and their fractions for beta-glucan enrichment and viscosity. *Cereal Chemistry* 72(2, 1995): 187–90.

Chris Holliland

Rochefort Brewery, or Brasserie de Rochefort (Abbaye de Notre-Dame de Saint-Rémy), is a monastery brewery in the province of Namur, Belgium, and a member of the International Trappist Association.

The Abbey of Notre-Dame de Saint-Rémy was founded around the year 1230, initially as a convent for Cistercian nuns. After 2 centuries, the nuns traded location with monks from the abbey of Givet, 18 miles (30 km) away. The site was attacked by French troops in 1653 and destroyed. The monks then defiantly reconstructed the monastery, which survived until the French Revolution, when they were forced to flee once more as their wealth was confiscated and the buildings torn down. Cistercian brothers returned to the site in 1887 and determined to rebuild it.

Today, the abbey stands in a valley, separated from the town of Rochefort by a wooded hill. The monks observe the rule of St. Benedict, which divides the day into equal parts devoted to prayer, work, and rest. Part of the work takes place at the monastery brewery, which is mostly staffed by lay employees but supervised by one of the brothers.

The brewery was given greater importance through modernization in 1952 and again, when it was rebuilt, in the 1960s. Capacity today stands at around 34,000 US barrels (40,000 hl) per year, but to prevent commercialism from destroying the balance of prayer, work, and rest, output is capped at 21,300 US barrels (25,000 hl). The copper brewhouse itself is notable for being among the most beautiful in Belgium.

The brewery's three top-fermented beers are simply numbered 6, 8, and 10. All are bottle-conditioned and, in addition to barley malt and hops, ingredients include wheat starch, brown and white sugars, and a small amount of coriander. Colors deepen in shades of brown and complexity increases as alcoholic strength increases in each of the offerings. The Rochefort beers are bottle-conditioned and, when kept well, tend to age beautifully.

See also ABBEY BEERS, BELGIUM, and TRAPPIST BREWERIES.

Abbaye Notre-Dame de Saint-Remy Rochefort (brochure). Trappistes Rochefort, undated.

Jeff Evans

Rodenbach is a Belgian brewery located in the town of Roeselare, West Flanders, famed for its sour

The Rodenbach cellar in the Belgian town of Roeselar contains nearly 300 giant oak vats known as "foeders."
PHOTOGRAPH BY DENTON TILLMAN

red ales. In the mid-18th century, Ferdinand Rodenbach migrated to Flanders from the German Rhineland. His descendants immersed themselves in local commerce, politics, and culture, and their brewing interests began when Pedro Rodenbach secured a partnership in a Roeselare brewery in 1821, becoming owner in 1836. However, it was Pedro's grandson, Eugene Rodenbach, who set the tone for the business's development when he traveled to England and studied porter-making, learning more about acidification, wood aging, and blending.

Today Rodenbach is part of the Palm Breweries group, whose main production center is at Steenhuffel, Belgium. See PALM BREWERIES. Palm (which is also part-owner of the Boon brewery, in Lembeek) has invested in the premises, commissioning a new brewhouse and showcasing the remarkable cellar filled with nearly 300 giant oak vats. Known in Dutch as "foeders," these range in capacity from 140 hl (120 barrels) to 650 hl (555 barrels).

Rodenbach beers are brewed from a blend of pale ale and colored malts, with pelletized hops, a year or two old, from Poperinge used in the copper. Top fermentation in cylindro-conical vessels with the Rodenbach mixed yeast culture leads to 4 weeks' lagering in horizontal tanks. The beer is then transferred to the oak vats, some of which date back more than 150 years, where it is aged for up to 2 years at 59°F (15°C). Microorganisms in the wood sour the beer and create a complex array of fruity esters.

There are two main products from Rodenbach: Rodenbach Classic is a 5% ABV blend of young (un-soured) beer with aged beer, at a ratio of 1:3 [ratio should be 3:1 in favor of young beer]. The 6% Grand Cru is mostly aged beer, with a little young beer added, then slightly sweetened with sugar.

See also FLANDERS.

Toye, Jan. *The world of Palm & Rodenbach*. Steenhuffel, Belgium: Palm and Rodenbach Breweries, 2002.

Jeff Evans

roggenbier, once a common beer style in medieval Bavaria, is made with at least 30% rye malt, although typically the proportion of rye was often higher. *Roggen* is the German word for rye. The introduction of the Reinheitsgebot (the so-called Bavarian beer purity law) in 1516 and the resulting move to exclude grains besides barley malt from Bavaria's mash tuns all but put an end to the production of roggenbier. For centuries to follow, rye would only be used for baking bread in Bavaria.

The roggen style was resurrected in Germany in the 1980s by the Spezial Brewery in Schielring in eastern Bavaria. The brewery was bought by Thurn und Taxis of Regensburg, which, in turn, became part of Paulaner in 1997. Paulaner still produces a roggenbier and today Spezial, now owned by Kuchlbauer of Adensberg, continues to make a roggen. A small number of German brewers also make roggen.

Typically a roggenbier will be about 5% alcohol by volume and dark in color. A proportion of wheat will be used in the malt as well as rye. When the beer is served unfiltered, it will have a hazy appearance similar to a hefeweizen and a soft earthy/spicy aroma. Roggens are top-fermented beers and often employ weissbier yeast strains for fermentation.

Rye is difficult to brew with because it has no husk, and the grain quickly absorbs water in the mash tun, forming a sticky, gummy mash, which is difficult to lauter. However, this has not stopped many American craft brewers making their own ryes. Because of the difficulties of working with rye, the mashes of the American versions are dominated by barley malt, although better beers show considerable rye character. The annual competition at the Great American Beer Festival judges a "Rye Beer" category, with German-style roggen listed as a substyle. In 2010 there were 32 entries in the category.

See also RYE.

The German Beer Institute. *Brewers Association 2010 Beer Style Guidelines*. http://www.germanbeer institute.com/ (accessed January 18, 2011).

Thomas, Steve. *Good beer guide Germany*. Hertsfordshire, UK: CAMRA, 2006.

Tim Hampson

Rogue Ales started their "small revolution," as the company likes to describe it, in Ashland, Oregon, in 1988. Between June and October of that year, Jack Joyce, Bob Woodell, and Rob Strasser worked with Jeff Schultz, an avid homebrewer (and Bob's accountant), to install a 10-barrel brewing system and a 60-seat pub in a commercial space on Lithia Creek. Roughly 18 months later, in May 1989, Rogue opened the much larger Bay Front Brew Pub in Newport, Oregon's old Front and Case Building on Southwest Bay Boulevard. By this point, John Maier, formerly of Alaska Brewing, had joined the company as brewmaster.

Rogue now owns and operates 10 multitap meeting halls or bars in Oregon, Washington, and California and brews approximately 86,000 barrels of beer annually. It produces Issaquah Frog beers at the namesake brewhouse in Issaquah, Washington, and has sold beers created at the Eugene City Brewery under the Track Town Ales name since October 2004. They also raise seven varieties of hops on a 42-acre property in Independence, Oregon, and harvest barley at their 256-acre farm in the Tygh Valley. The 34 aggressively hopped beers sold under the Rogue Ales brand are fermented with PacMan, their proprietary yeast, and are never pasteurized. Many have won national awards. Since the early days of brewing their American amber (originally Ashland amber) in a basement facility for a local market, Rogue has grown into an international business that distributes its beers to 19 different countries along with all 50 states. In 2003 Rogue also began distilling its own rum, whiskey, and gin.

Hamson, Tim. *The beer book*. New York: Dorling Kindersley, 2008.

Kitsock, Greg. "American originals: Brewers who march to a different beat." http://allaboutbeer.com/live-beer/people/people-features/2001/09/american-originals/1/ (accessed July 5, 2010).

Rogue Ales. *Rogue.com*. http://www.rogue.com (accessed July 5, 2010).

Ben Keene

roller mill is the most common device for crushing malt and grain into grist in preparation for the mash. Roller mills differ by the number of tandem operating rollers and by the treatment of the malt or grain prior to and during the milling operation. There is dry milling, conditioned dry milling, and wet milling. The actual milling takes place between a pair of cylindrical rollers that spin downward in opposite directions. The rollers are flat or, in newer mills, serrated, and they rotate at differing or identical velocities. They are specially cast to have the hard surface necessary for milling. Rollers turning at different velocities cause the grain to press together and shear into smaller pieces, whereas serrated edges also cut the grain. Care must be taken to prevent the serrated edges from dulling on hard objects, such as stone or metal. To prevent this, a stone separator and a magnet are often installed in the malt or grain path right before the mill. The magnet is also an essential precaution against dust explosions that may be sparked by metal objects being scraped by the rollers.

Varying the distance between the rollers determines the fineness of the grind as well as the speed with which the milling can be accomplished. This, in turn, has an effect on overall brewhouse efficiency and yield. Milling malt for a normal brew should not take more than 1 h to 2 h. The time depends on the length of the rollers, the moisture content of the malt, the roller speed, and the type of roller surface. In some roller mills, the grist may be separated by size and some grist fractions may be sent through the mill a second or even third time.

The simplest, most common, but least efficient mill is a two-roller mill, which is usually found in small breweries or brewpubs. Both rollers spin at the same speed. The malt passes through the rollers only once. The use of such mills, therefore, requires well-modified and homogenous malts.

Four-roller mills are more common in mid-size breweries. They consist of two pairs of rollers stacked one on top of the other. Malt passes through the first set of rollers and is directed to a sieve that lets finer grist fall through directly. The remaining, coarser grist is directed to the second pair of rollers.

Six-roller mills are the most flexible. They can be adapted to different dry malts to produce grist for any mash. After the first pair of rollers, the grist is separated into three fractions by a set of two sieves, whereby the finest fraction, which is basically flour, is directed away for collection. A coarser fraction bypasses a second pair of rollers and is sent directly to a third pair to be milled again, whereas the coarsest fraction, which consists of husks with endosperm remnants, is directed to the second pair, also to be milled again. This fraction is then sifted to separate it into husks, coarse grist, and flour. The coarse fraction from this milling step is then directed to the third pair of rollers to be milled a third time.

The fractioning that is possible with four- and six-roller mills allows for the optional separation of husks from the grist. The husks can then be added to the mash later, reducing the leaching of astringent polyphenols. When adding husks to the mash, however, it is essential that the husks be free of endosperm remnants, because these contain unconverted starches that could end up in the wort and beer as hazes.

Some modern roller mills condition the malt with water before the milling process. This process, called "conditioned dry milling," involves moistening the grist to increase the level of water in the husks but not significantly in the endosperm. The moistened grist is than milled normally. The moisture makes the husks less brittle, which results in larger husk fractions. This results in numerous advantages, including more efficient and faster lautering, higher brewhouse yields, and milder beers. One disadvantage is an increased risk of microbiological contamination from moist deposits inside the mill itself. These mills, therefore, must be cleaned thoroughly after use.

In the process called wet milling, the grist is effectively steeped in water until it contains as much as 30% moisture. Done properly, the husks become elastic and the endosperm is squeezed out during milling using a simple two-roller mill.

See also GRIST, MILLING, and WET MILLING.

GEA Brewery Systems GmbH, *Millstar brochure*, Huppmann Tuchenhagen, 2009.

Kunze, Wolfgang. *Technologie Brauer & Mälzer* (Technology for brewers and maltsters), 9th ed. Berlin: VLB Berlin, 2007.

Narziss, Ludwig. *Abriss der Bierbrauerei* (Summary of the beer brewery), 7th ed. Weinheim, Germany: Wiley-VCH Verlag GmbH & Co. KGaA, 2005.

Wolfgang David Lindell

rounds

See DRINKING CUSTOMS.

rousing is an expression used for processes bringing yeast into homogenous suspension in either wort or beer to render the yeast more active with respect to its fermentation performance. Traditionally, the term refers to procedures that are used to prepare the pitching yeast for actual pitching. In the absence of modern techniques for effective, in-line pitching of the yeast homogenously into large volumes of wort, such preparation of the yeast may be necessary to ensure short, complete, and consistent fermentations. In practice, rousing may be performed by pumping or pouring the yeast from one vessel to another, by mechanically agitating the yeast, or by blowing sterile air, oxygen, or CO_2 into the bottom of the yeast-holding vessel.

Rousing may also refer to the process of "revitalizing" yeast that has flocculated and settled to the bottom of the fermentation vessel before the fermentation is complete or before sufficient diacetyl reduction has been achieved. Such yeast may be brought back into suspension in the beer, normally by injecting CO_2—or in rare cases compressed air—into the bottom of the vessel. If this is not sufficiently effective, some breweries will recirculate the entire contents of the fermenting vessel to resuspend all of the yeast in an attempt to "rouse" it from an inactive state.

Kunze, Wolfgang. *Technology brewing and malting,* 3rd international ed. Berlin: VLB Berlin, 2004.

Anders Brinch Kissmeyer

running beers are beers that are imbibed fresh and can be brewed all the year around.

This British term is somewhat archaic but harks back to an earlier age of brewing. In the British Isles, before the role of yeast in fermentation was understood and before brewers knew how to take precautions against contamination, brewing was normally an activity undertaken largely in the cooler months. Everyone knew that beer brewed in summer was prone to quick souring. Grists were often mashed more than once; the first mashes produced a strong wort, resulting in stock ale that could be stored for the summer months in large wooden vats. The secondary mashes were analogous to the re-steeping of a once-used teabag; they produced a lighter "small" beer or "running beer" for immediate consumption. The beer was too light in alcohol to keep fresh for long, but then it didn't need to.

In England there developed the practice of mixing together a stored stock ale, which would often have sour and fruity flavors from the presence of wild Brettanomyces yeast and other microflora, with a fresh "running bitter," often only several days old. Greene King's Strong Suffolk is a surviving example of this practice.

Building on Louis Pasteur's pioneering work in the mid 1800s, scientists such as Horace Tabberer Brown, who started work at Worthington's Brewery in Burton in 1866, began to focus on beer spoilage. Brown believed that spoilage was caused by an organism called Saccharobacillus pastorianus. Brown's scientific work and that of others revolutionized brewery sanitation, enabling beer to be produced all year around. Summer-brewed beers no longer suffered from severe infection, and the terms "running beers" or "running bitters" came to represent lighter beers that were fresh and brewed all year round. Such beers required very short maturation and could be served little more than a week after they'd been brewed.

Gourvish, T.R., and R. G. Wilson. *The brewing industry 1830–1980.* Cambridge: Cambridge University Press, 1994.

Hornsey, Ian S. *Brewing.* London: Royal Society of Chemistry, 1999.

Tim Hampson

run-off is a term used by brewers to describe the extraction or washing through of wort from a mash separation vessel such as a lauter tun, mash tun, or mash filter. In a lauter tun or mash tun, the mash in a vessel is sprayed with hot water, which rinses the soluble material from the mash and is "run-off" from the slatted bottom of the vessel. The rinsing process is called "sparging" and involves brewing water at approximately 168°F (75°C). See SPARGING. This temperature is important because it is a temperature above which malt enzymes are deactivated, removal of sugar is efficient, and the viscosity of the wort is lowered, allowing it to filter down more easily through the grain bed. Optimizing the run-off rate is very important in ensuring an efficient brewhouse operation. The brewer's objective is to run-off wort as fast as possible to achieve the best possible extract and quality from the malt. The run-off rate is determined by the type of vessel used, the depth of mash, and the composition of the grist. In a mash tun (approximate mash depth 1.5–2 m) the run-off will be slower than in a lauter tun (approximate mash depth 0.5 m) with the run-off from a mash filter (approximate mash depth 5 cm) being the fastest. Another very important feature of run-off is wort clarity. Most brewers want clear worts which they believe give beer of the best quality. Generally, the deeper the mash depth, the brighter (clearer) the wort, so mash tuns generally give clearer worts than mash filters. However, modern engineering and process control has enabled clear worts to be produced from lauter tuns and mash filters without slowing the process.

See also LAUTERING and MASH FILTER.

Paul KA Buttrick

Ruppert, Jacob (1867–1939), known as "the colonel" for his service in the New York National Guard, was one of the Empire State's most prominent brewers. The son of German immigrants Jacob Ruppert and Anna Gillig, Ruppert was born August 5, 1867, attended Columbia Grammar School in New York, and went to work in the small Jacob Ruppert's family brewery in 1887. He became president of the brewery upon the death of his father just before Prohibition. The brewery's main beers were Knickerbocker lager and Ruppert's Pale Ale. He was elected to the U.S. Congress for four straight terms starting in 1898. He and Tillinghast L'Hommedieu Huston purchased the New York Highlanders baseball team in 1915, later changing their name to the New York Yankees. They brought the Boston Red Sox pitcher George Herman "Babe" Ruth to New York in 1919. Ruppert also brought Lou Gehrig and Joe DiMaggio to the Yankees. Ruppert bought out Huston in 1922, and opened Yankee Stadium in 1923. Ruppert opened a two million barrel brewery in upper Manhattan in 1913. The $30 million brewery employed 1,000 workers. In 1932 a *Time* magazine reporter asked Ruppert if the biggest thrill of his life was winning baseball championships. He replied, "Looking back now, I doubt if I ever felt more elated than when I was a youngster and on occasion would go galloping out driving the ambulance to bring in one of our ailing brewery wagon horses . . . Those brewery teams were as pretty to see operate as a nicely stepping ball team." Ruppert died January 13, 1939. The brewery, between Second and Third avenues and East 90th and 92nd streets, closed in 1965.

Stephen Hindy

Russia is a relative late-comer as a beer nation, but as of 2010 it had come to rank as the world's fourth-largest beer market, after China, the United States, and Brazil. Beer, *pivo* in Russian, is the second most popular alcoholic beverage, after vodka, and it is generally preferred to wine. Russian beers are mainly lagers, and pale lagers are the most common. In Russia, beer is categorized by color, not by style, or the yeast that ferments it. Beer is therefore looked upon as simply light, red, semi-dark, or dark. Russians purchase beer mostly in cans and PET bottles, and less frequently in glass bottles.

Pivo is often the alcoholic beverage ordinary Russians drink in parks, at sporting events, with *shashlik* (barbecue), and during the warmer summer months. Kiosks in parks, train and metro stations, and on the street sell several varieties of lager. It is legal to carry open containers in public in Russia; it is not uncommon for someone on his or her way home from work to carry an open beer or to head off to the park, beer in hand.

Modern beer in Russia does not have as long a history as a traditional fermented beverage called kvass. This old beer style has been produced for well over 1,000 years, and it became particularly popular during the reign of Peter the Great, who ruled the Russian Empire from 1682 to 1725. Kvass is fermented from rye bread, often dark, and flavored with seasonal herbs and fruit such as apples or berries, and even with birch sap. It is a sweet drink with aromas and flavors of pumpernickel, brown sugar, and prunes. Today, kvass is usually quite low in alcohol, and it is considered more of an alternative to soda, suitable even for children.

Kvass is sold in bottles or cans today, and, in the summer months, is available from street vendors. It is usually served unfiltered, with yeast still in the bottle or can, for its putative nutritional value. Ochakovo Company is the leading producer of kvass in Russia. Nikola Kvass is another popular brand produced by the Deka beverage company.

Russia's brewing industry is dominated by Baltika Brewery, which is now part of the Carlsberg Group. Construction on the first Baltika factory began in 1978, but the first beers were not sold until 1990. The company was privatized in 1992. The brewery now operates out of St. Petersburg. Baltika has expanded to 10 factories throughout Russia, and several of these are located in and around

St. Petersburg and Moscow. Baltika also exports to almost 40 countries.

Baltika produces 14 different beers, all lagers, from a non-alcoholic pale lager to several dark lagers. The most widely distributed of its brews are Baltika No. 3, a pale lager; Baltika No. 7, a pale export lager; and Baltika No. 9, a stronger lager with 9% alcohol by volume. Baltika also offers beer-mix coolers such as Baltika Kuler and Baltika Kuler Lime.

In addition to making Baltika-brand beers, the company produces beers under the labels of Arsenalnoe, Zhigulevskoye, and Leningradskoe. All these are lagers that are generally brewed in the German tradition. Arsenalnoe Zakalennoye, for example, is a strong version of pilsner with 7% alcohol by volume. Before Zhigulevskoye Pivo became part of Baltika, it was the oldest Russian brewery, built by Austrian Alfred Vakano in the late 19th century.

Moscow's Ochakovo Company is another Russian brewery of note. It was built in 1978 as a brewery, but then also expanded into the soft drinks market. Today it produces lagers, kvass, and soft drinks. It even operates a winery, as well as other agricultural enterprises that are related to grain production and malting. Ochakovo is the largest Russian-owned brewery today.

Russia has also experienced a rise in the craft beer market, with microbreweries and brewpubs sprouting up in St. Petersburg and Moscow. Especially in St. Petersburg, which has historically been more Western leaning, the number of microbreweries and brewpubs is rising steadily. Several brewpubs in Moscow, however, have closed in recent years.

Tinkoff Brewery started out as a brewpub in St. Petersburg, in 1998, and has since become a chain of 10 brewpubs, located in various cities. In addition, it now owns a large brewery in Pushkin, outside of St. Petersburg, making it Russia's fourth largest brewery. In 2005, however, Tinkoff was purchased by InBev. Tinkoff now produces German-style lagers at its brewpubs, but bottled Tinkoff is no longer available.

While Russia's brewing until recently has been dominated mostly by kvass, modern lagers have taken over Russian market share and are even gaining market share abroad, while smaller breweries are producing craft lagers, and some specialty beer bars and restaurants that serve English style ales next to German and Czech style lagers are also catching on in the major cities.

Beer business analysis. http://eng.pivnoe-delo.info/russia-results-of-2008-trends-of-2009/ (accessed January 12, 2011).

Russian tourism. http://www.waytorussia.net/ (accessed January 12, 2011).

White, Stephen. *Russia goes dry: Alcohol, state, and society*. Cambridge: Cambridge Universty Press, 1996.

Anda Lincoln

Russian River Brewing Company is situated in Santa Rosa, deep in the heart of Californian wine country. It was established in 1997 by Korbel Champagne Cellars. Vinnie Cilurzo, a young brewer hailed as the creator of the "double IPA" beer style while at the Blind Pig Brewing Company, was hired as the first brewmaster. After being awarded "Small Brewing Company of the Year" and "Small Brewing Company Brewmaster of the Year" at the Great American Beer Festival in 1999, the Russian River business was sold to Vinnie and his wife, Natalie, in 2002. See GREAT AMERICAN BEER FESTIVAL.

As of 2010, Russian River produced approximately 3,000 barrels a year of which more than half was served in the adjacent pub and restaurant in Santa Rosa. It is renowned for its extremely esoteric and innovative approaches to brewing. Cilurzo explores beer's relationship with wood, embraces the art of beer blending, adopts a very liberal attitude to hopping, and even plays music to his yeast in an attempt to further enhance the fermentation process.

Strongly inspired by the Belgian brewing tradition, yet rooted firmly in the American craft brewing movement (for which Cilurzo is a prominent figure and spokesperson) Russian River's range of ales include several Brettanomyces-tinged barrel-aged beers, Belgian-style ales, and highly-hopped American IPAs and "double IPAs." Russian River has been a strong advocate for sour beer styles and their own sour beers have proved highly influential upon an up-and-coming generation of craft brewers.

Russian River's most revered ales include "Pliny the Elder," an American "Imperial IPA" with an IBU of 100 and "Supplication," a brown ale aged with sour cherries in Pinot Noir barrels inoculated with Brettanomyces yeast and Lactobacillus and Pediococcus bacteria. Hop lovers also head to Santa Rosa to sample the original "Blind Pig IPA" now brewed by Russian River.

See also DOUBLE IPA and SOUR BEER.

McFarland, Ben, & Tom Sandham. *Good beer guide: West Coast USA*. St. Albans, UK: Campaign for Real Ale, 2008.

Ben McFarland

rye (Secale cereale L.) is a grain type that is strongly linked to the Northern hemisphere, where it historically has been cropped in Germany, Southern Scandinavia, Poland, the Baltic States, and Russia. It is tolerant to poor soils and drought. Rye has a naked grain that takes up water quickly during malting; it requires less water and steeping time than barley. Because rye has no husk, the acrospire of the kernel is vulnerable to damage during the malting process. See ACROSPIRE. The crop has mostly been used for food consumption in black bread types. Malted and unmalted rye are also used to produce whiskey (United States), gin (Holland), and beer (Russia, Finland, Germany, Poland). Rye increases the complexity of beer flavor, giving a spicy quality and can lend a rounded, smooth mouthfeel. Rye sometimes adds a reddish tinge to beers in which it is used. Normally, only small quantities of malted rye are used in modern brewing of specialty beers. The usual proportion is about 10%–20% of the malt bill, as in German rye beers (roggenbier). See ROGGENBIER. Higher proportions may be used, but rye contains high levels of protein and beta-glucans, which can cause the mash to become gummy and difficult to run-off. Still, many American craft brewers use rye in relatively high proportions, often seeking to concentrate its unique flavors to the extent practicable. In brewing, rye may be used as whole grains (which must be cooked first), rye malt, or pre-gelatinized flakes.

Briggs, D. E., et al. *Brewing: Science and practice*. Cambridge: Woodhead Publishing, 2004.

Purseglove, J. W. *Tropical crops: Monocotyledons*. New York: Longman Group, 1976.

Per Kølster

Saaz (hop), widely considered among the world's great hop varieties, is a "Noble" aroma hop from the Czech Republic. See NOBLE HOPS. It was selected from a landrace that has grown in Central Europe since the Middle Ages. It was named after the town of Žatec (Saaz in German), some 60 km (40 mi) northwest of Prague. Internationally, the hop acquired its German name in the 19th century, when what is now the Czech Republic was part of the German-speaking Austro-Hungarian Empire. Sometimes referred to as Saazer or Bohemian Red Hop, Saaz matures early and has a low yield potential, but it possesses a uniquely pleasant aroma, which is why it is the major hop produced in the Czech Republic and much of it is exported to breweries around the world. Virus-free clones, called Osvald clones, of the original Saaz have been released in the Czech Republic in an effort to boost yield.

Saaz's alpha acid content ranges from 3% to 5%, the beta acid content from 3% to 4%, and the cohumulone content is about 23%. The essential oils are divided between roughly 30% to 40% myrcene, 25% to 30% humulene, 8% caryophyllene, and about 14% farnesene. In terms of growth characteristics, soft resin content, oil composition, and aroma properties, Saaz is very similar to the German Tettnanger and Spalter, which are also often labeled "Noble" and which the hop trade often characterizes by the German terms "Saazer Formenkreis" (literally meaning circle of Saaz-type forms). Saaz is also very similar—some researchers even believe identical—to the Polish cultivar Lublin. See LUBLIN (HOP). Despite its low bittering power, brewers and beer drinkers the world over treasure the Saaz hop for its pleasant aroma and consider the unique marriage of Saaz, pale Bohemian or Moravian malt, and soft brewing water one of the classic beer taste sensations in the form of Bohemian pilsner. Anheuser-Busch, the largest American brewer, has grown significant acreage of Saaz at Bonners Ferry in northern Idaho at a latitude similar to that of Žatec. See IDAHO (NORTHERN HOP REGION). The future of this operation, however, is in doubt after the merger of Anheuser-Busch with InBev to form ABInBev.

Neve, R. A. *Hops,* 201. London: Chapman & Hall, 1991.

Rybacek, Vaclav, ed. *Hop production,* 77. Amsterdam: Elsevier, 1991.

Alfred Haunold

SABMiller plc is a company formed by the 2002 merger between South African Breweries Ltd and the Miller Brewing Company of the United States. South African Breweries Ltd was founded as Castle Brewing in Johannesburg in 1865. The name was changed to South African Breweries Ltd (SAB) 2 years later, when the company was floated on the local stock exchange.

The introduction of apartheid in South Africa in 1948 included a prohibition on alcoholic beverages for the indigenous black population (lifted in 1962). This collapsed the domestic market, and in 1949 SAB initiated a massive expansion program outside South Africa, starting breweries in Bulawayo, Zimbabwe's second largest city, and in Zambia. By 1955, SAB had built a new brewery in Johannesburg, but this coincided with the government's introduction of a heavy beer tax. This led to a drastic fall in consumption and to pressure for the South African brewing industry to consolidate. The result was the acquisition by SAB, in 1956, of its brewing rivals Ohlsson's and Chandlers, which gave SAB a virtual regional beer monopoly. Between 1964 and 1966 SAB was granted licenses to brew Guinness, Amstel, and Carling Black Label, and in 1973, it built additional breweries in Botswana and Angola.

In 1990, when the ban on political parties was lifted in South Africa and when markets behind the Iron Curtain opened up after the 1989 fall of the Berlin Wall, SAB's annual production exceeded a substantial 32 million hl (27,269,373 US bbl). This put SAB in a position to consider acquisitions outside Africa. The first European acquisition was the old Dreher Brewery in Budapest, Hungary, which it took over in 1993. This was followed by a shareholding in the Czech Plzeňský Prazdroj (Pilsner Urquell) in 1994 and that brewery's outright purchase in 1999. In 1995, SAB purchased a majority stake in Lech (Poland), which has been wholly owned by SABMiller since 2009. By 2001, SAB's global production reached 77 million hl (65,616, 928 US bbl), with 42% of this volume produced outside of South Africa.

As of 2010 other European SABMiller holdings included Birra Peroni in Italy, SABMiller RUS LLC in Russia, Pivovary Topvar in Slovakia, Grolsch in The Netherlands, Sarmat in Ukraine, and Ursus in Romania. The company's structurally most significant acquisition, however, came in 2002 with the purchased of the US-based Miller Brewing Company from Philip Morris Corporation for USD$3.6 billion, to become the world's second largest brewer. This was the precursor to further joint ventures and acquisitions, particularly in emerging markets.

One of the main SABMiller targets was the burgeoning Asian markets. SAB had been in China since 1994 through a joint venture called China Resources Snow Breweries (CR Snow). In 2004, CR Snow acquired the Chinese brewing interests of Lion Nathan. In 2006, it added breweries in Dongguan, Lanzhou, Harbin, Yanjiao, and Nanjing, followed by the 2007 purchase of Blue Sword, SABMiller's largest China acquisition. In 2009, CR Snow continues to expand with the acquisition of breweries in Anhui, Liaoning, Zhejiang, and Shandong provinces. SAB made its first foray into the fast-growing Indian market in 2000 with the purchase of the Narang Brewery. The resulting SAB subsidiary Mysore consolidated its position in 2003 by taking over Shaw Wallace to become India's second largest brewer. Another joint venture came in 2006 with Vinamilk in Vietnam, where SABMiller invested in a greenfield brewery with an annual capacity of 5 million hl (4,260,839 US bbl).

Elsewhere, SABMiller was not idle either. In 2005 it acquired a majority interest in South America's second largest brewery, Cerveceria Bavaria, of Colombia. This built on SAB's 2001 entry into Latin America with the purchase of Cerveceria Honduras. And in late 2010 SABMiller purchased Argentina's Isenbeck brewery from Germany's Warsteiner.

In North America, in 2007, SABMiller announced a distribution joint venture with the Canadian-American brewing group Molson Coors Brewing Company to form MillerCoors, which now manages the portfolios of both groups in North America from its new headquarters in Chicago.

In 2009, SABMiller's global production was 210 million hl (178,955,260 US bbl) with revenues of USD$24.53 billion, making SABMiller the world's second largest brewer after Anheuser-Busch InBev.

See also ANHEUSER-BUSCH INBEV, COORS BREWING COMPANY, MILLER BREWING COMPANY, and SOUTH AFRICAN BREWERIES LTD.

International directory of company history, January 1, 2004.
SABMiller report, 2010.
SABMiller.com. Reuters, May 2010.
The Star (SouthAfrica). November 14, 2008.

Glenn A. Payne

saccharification, literally "to make into sugar," the conversion, by enzymes, of starches into sugars and dextrins during the mashing process. Saccharification of cereal starches into fermentable sugars and unfermentable dextrins creates the basis of the wort, a sugary solution that is later fermented into beer. See WORT. Saccharification during the mash is achieved by the activation of malt enzymes at the correct temperatures and moisture levels. To be susceptible to digestion by enzymes, the starches in barley malt must first be gelatinized. Barley malt starches gelatinize at temperatures between 61°C and 65°C (142°F and 149°F). Most adjunct starches, such as corn grits or rice, require higher temperatures for gelatinization and are therefore cooked separately before being added to the mash for saccharification. See CEREAL COOKER. Once the starches are gelatinized, they are broken down by beta amylase and alpha amylase into sugars, principally maltose. Alpha amylase is primarily responsible for the hydrolysis of starches into dextrins, and beta amylase digests dextrins into fermentable sugars. The enzymes themselves are rapidly denatured by higher temperatures. At 65°C (149°F), beta amylase is almost completely deactivated with 30 minutes, whereas alpha amylase survives somewhat longer. The time period and temperature(s) at which the mash is held to effect saccharification is called a "saccharification rest." This temperature is a compromise between the higher temperatures required for starch gelatinization and the lower temperatures that will preserve the activity of the malt enzymes. This rest usually lasts from 30 to 60 min, depending on the enzymatic power of the malt used. Lower saccharification temperatures will favor the production of fermentable sugars by beta amylase, whereas higher temperatures will favor the production of unfermentable sugars and dextrins by alpha amylase. It is therefore possible to manipulate the sugar profile and fermentabilty of the wort through the temperature of the saccharification rest. This will, in turn, help determine the residual sweetness and body of the resulting beer.

During temperature programmed mashing, two or more rests in the range of 61°C–74°C (142°F–165°F) are often employed to achieve efficient conversion of all starches. This will be followed by a rise to approximately 76.6°C (170°F) to arrest enzymatic activity and reduce the viscosity of the first runnings. In single temperature infusion mashing, the mash temperature is usually within a few degrees of 65°C (149°F), a temperature sometimes referred to as *optima*, referring to the optimization of both malt primary enzymes for the purposes of starch digestion.

See also AMYLASES, ALPHA AMYLASE, and MASHING.

Whitehouse, R., and M. van Oort. *Enzymes in food technology,* 2nd ed. New York: Wiley-Blackwell, 2010.

Garrett Oliver

saccharometer

See HYDROMETER.

saccharomyces

See YEAST.

sage. The Latin name for sage, *Salvia officinalis,* indicates the wide use of this perennial herb as a medical plant—the word *salvia* means to heal or save. Sage originated in the Mediterranean area, and today is widespread globally. It is antiseptic, antibacterial, antimicrobial, and anti-inflammatory. Sage is mentioned as a flavoring additive, along with hops, in old brewing literature, and was sometimes part of the brewing herb blend known as gruit. See GRUIT. Together with other herbs of the same botanical family, the Labiatae, sage was used in medicinal beers, which were common in Europe during the Middle Ages. Sage is powerfully flavored and may be used to spice beers, preferably as a late addition in the kettle or as a "dry" flavoring herb in order to add the aroma of the alcohol soluble oils. While most modern beer drinkers find sage unpalatable as a beer flavoring, commercial examples of sage beers have appeared on the market in recent years.

See also HERBS.

Behre, Karl-Ernst. "The history of beer additives in europe—a review." *Veget Hist Archaeobot* 8 (1999): 35–48.
von Hofsten, Nils. "Pors och andra humleersättninger och Ölkryddor i äldre tider." *Akademiska Förlaget,* 1960 (Title translated: Gale and other substitutes and beer-spices in past times).

Per Kølster

sahti, a farmhouse beer style indigenous to Finland, is one of the oldest beer types still brewed today. Sahti is top fermented, unfiltered, unpasteurized, and turbid with an original gravity of at least 19°P and at least 6% alcohol by volume, with the most common alcohol content being between 7% and 8% by volume. See PLATO GRAVITY SCALE. The color may vary from pale yellow to dark brown. Sahti should have a pronounced banana-like aroma and taste slightly sweet, with little hop character. Some examples have a clear indication of rye and juniper in the taste.

Sahti is a relic of an ancient Finnish rustic brewing tradition. It is still brewed much the same way as it was some 500 years ago, to be consumed at weddings and other festive occasions. The sahti heritage is strongest along the "sahti belt," which runs through the old provinces of Satakunta and Häme, a few hundred kilometers north of Helsinki. "Suomen sahtiseura" (the Sahti society of Finland) keeps the tradition alive and arranges a yearly sahti competition for home and farmhouse brewers.

Close relatives to sahti exist on some Baltic islands. Gotland, Sweden, has a farmhouse brew called "dricku" and Saaremaa and Hiiumaa (Estonia) have "koduõlu."

The first modern commercial sahti brewer, Lammin Sahti, in Lammi, Finland, started brewing in 1987. In 2010 half a dozen commercial sahti brewers held a license to sell their beers and a handful of microbreweries occasionally brew commercial sahti as well. After sahti received worldwide attention through the writings of beer author Michael Jackson, the interest in brewing sahti has spread to other parts of the world, notably the United States. See JACKSON, MICHAEL.

In Finland, farmhouses and homebrewers brew sahti in small volumes, often with traditional equipment. Commercial brewers use modern stainless steel brewing vessels, but their brewing procedure still follows the traditional principles.

It takes the small-scale brewer about 20 kg (44 lb) of grain and 50 g (1.6 oz) of compressed baker's yeast to produce around 50 l (13.2 gal) of basic sahti. The grain bill contains malted barley and other malted and/or unmalted grains: rye, wheat, oat, and barley, according to the specific recipe. A commonly used grain bill contains about 90% malted barley and 10% malted rye, but old hands have been known to use an even higher proportion of rye, up to 40%. A small amount of hops and juniper (Juniperus communis) may be added, usually by boiling them and spicing the brewing liquor with the resulting solution. See JUNIPER.

The mashing procedure is a form of temperature-programmed infusion mashing. Hot water is added to the mixture of malt and cereals either in batches of rising temperature or all at once and heated in the mash tun. The traditional vessel used is the "muuripata," a wood-heated built-in cauldron, which is standard equipment for heating water in a Finnish sauna. At the start of mashing, the temperature is around 40°C (104°F), and it is increased gradually to 70°C (158°F). Mashing schedules usually have rests at about 50°C (122°F) and just below 65°C (140°F). There may be one more rest at about 75°C (167°F) as well. Some brewers use single-temperature mashing at a temperature of 65°C (140°F). (Old sahti masters do not use thermometers; they measure the temperature by their fingers and the tip of the elbow.) In some recipes the mashing ends with boiling, which is achieved by different methods and can be short or long in duration. One way to bring the mash to boiling point is to immerse heated stones in the mash. The end product might then be called "kivisahti" (stone sahti). This method is ancient, reaching back to a time when people did not have metal vessels. See STEINBIER.

After approximately 4 h of mashing, the mash is strained. Traditionally this happens in the "kuurna," a trough-like vessel with a false bottom of rye straws and juniper twigs, with or without the berries, boiled to make them sterile. Although now usually made of stainless steel, the trough shape of the kuurna recalls the vessel's origins as a hollowed-out aspen log. The mash, which may be quite porridge-like, is transferred to the kuurna and sparged with hot water. After collecting the high-gravity part of the wort the brewer may ferment that separately, but continue sparging and use the secondary low-gravity batch to make a "naisten sahti" ("ladies' sahti," the name being as ancient as the style). After the run-off is over, the spent grains from the mash make a flavorful ingredient for bread. Some brewers do not boil the wort but others do, especially if the brewer wants to concentrate the wort to reach a higher gravity.

At one time, sahti, like all ancient beer styles, was spontaneously fermented, but this sort of fermentation is no longer performed. Today, the correct fermenting agent for sahti is either commercial baker's yeast or simply harvested yeast from a previous batch (of course, commercial baker's yeast may differ from country to country, but it is quite consistent within Finland). The main fermentation is very vigorous and usually lasts roughly 3 days. The secondary fermentation takes at least 1 week, preferably more.

Sahti should be stored in cool surroundings and consumed within a few weeks. If properly stored, commercial versions have a shelf-life of 2 months. The traditional drinking vessel for sahti is a wooden cup called a "haarikka," which is often passed around, particularly in the sauna.

Because sahti is a farmhouse beer, most variables in sahti brewing are adjustable according to the brewer's fancy, as long as the minimums of the original gravity and the alcohol content are kept; only baker's yeast or harvested yeast is used and the alcohol comes exclusively from the sugars in the grain bill.

Sahti has a certificate of specific character for agricultural products and foodstuffs (TSG) in European Union.

See also FINLAND.

Asplund, Ulla, ed. *Sahtikirja.* Lammi, Finland: Suomen sahtiseura, 1990.

Jackson, Michael. "Sahti." http://www.beerhunter.com/styles/sahti.html/ (accessed February 8, 2010).

Sahti Society of Finland. *Sahtiverkko.* http://www.sahti.org/ (accessed February 8, 2010).

Jussi Rokka

Saison means "season" in French. The origins of Saison ales can be traced to farmhouse breweries located primarily in the French-speaking area of Belgium known as Wallonia, specifically the province of Hainaut. See WALLONIA. According to legend these brews were the drink of the "saisonniers," migrant workers who came to help with the harvest. As was common practice in the days before artificial refrigeration, brewers would make beer seasonally. From late fall to the beginning of spring, the weather was cooler and more favorable for controlled fermentation. In farmhouse breweries this was also the time of year when there was less work to do outdoors. Farm brewers would spend the cooler months building a stock of "provision beer" to drink during the entire year, particularly the summer season.

The practical goals in brewing Saisons were threefold: to refresh the seasonal workers in summer, to make work for the full-time farm workers during the winter (a period of "unemployment" on a farm), and to produce spent grain, which served as quality feed for the livestock in the winter. Beer was therefore brewed in one season, winter, to be drunk in another, summer.

No one alive can be certain of what a typical Saison tasted like several centuries ago, but we can assume that they were different from modern versions. How different is anyone's guess. Given that these ales were produced by farmers (not full-time brewers) and the fact that they were not sold commercially is reason to believe that these Saisons were probably made with little mind to repeatability. With the unpredictability of the growing season and the practice of crop rotation it is probable that these brews were made with varying amounts of different grains such as barley, wheat, rye, and spelt. In years when hops were scarce, herbs and spices were likely substituted. In other words, these farmer-brewers made their Saisons with whatever was at hand. This legacy lives on in the variations—on a rather loose theme—that define modern Saison.

Today, Belgian Saison, along with its French cousin, Bière de Garde, make up the two major subcategories of the family of styles known as Farmhouse ales. See BIÈRE DE GARDE. The two styles may share a common heritage but have clearly evolved to become distinctly different from each other. Saisons tend to be dryer and exhibit more hop character while Bière de Garde are generally malt-accented and full-bodied.

Modern Saisons defy easy categorization. They can be as contradictory as they are uniform. Most are light in color, a few are dark, and some are in between. A few are full-bodied and sweet; many are extraordinarily dry and fruity. Those who like their beer styles neatly arranged in narrow categories will find attempting to pigeonhole Saisons an exercise in frustration. To others, this elusive quality is precisely their allure, as they represent many possibilities within a loose structure. For many modern brewers "Saison" is a nearly blank canvas; its definition, a moveable feast.

Present-day brewers and beer aficionados can agree that, generally speaking, modern Saisons are exceptionally dry, highly carbonated, and fruity ales of average to moderate alcohol strength (5%–8% by volume). Hop bitterness tends to range from 20–40 IBUs. Nearly all of them are re-fermented in the bottle, with many displaying copious sediment.

Despite the varied interpretations of Saison, perhaps the best known and considered by many the standard-bearer of the style is Saison Vieille Provision from Brasserie Dupont. See DUPONT, BRASSERIE. Several Belgian Saisons are made with spices, a throwback to earlier times. Best known are Saison Pipaix from Brasserie Vapeur, Saison 1900 from Brasserie Lefebvre, and the lineup of "seasonal" Saisons from Brasserie Fantome. Recently developed versions are Saison 2000 from Brasserie Ellezelloise, Saison Voisin, a remake of an old regional Saison from Brasserie de Geants, and Saison de Epeautre from Brasserie Blaugies, which uses an old form of wild wheat (considered a close relative of spelt) called Epeautre in the grist. There are a few Flemish versions as well, such as Bink Blonde from Brouwerij Kerkom (perhaps the oldest continuously operated farm brewery in Belgium) and Martens Seizoens, whose fruity, dry, hoppy accents places them closer to Saison than to any other recognized Belgian style.

Although Saison is native to Belgium, perhaps the country that may ultimately expand or redefine the Saison style is the United States. Many American craft brewers embody the creative "no rules" approach that has long defined Saison. There are more numerous and more varied versions of Saison being made in the United States at present. Over time, perception of Saison as a Belgian style may well shift to it being primarily associated with American craft brewers, just as the British-derived India pale ale style has essentially become American.

Jackson, Michael. *Beer companion.* Philadelphia: Running Press, 1993.
Jackson, Michael. *The great beers of Belgium,* 3rd ed. Philadelphia: Running Press, 1998.
Markowski, Phil. *Farmhouse ales.* Boulder, CO: Brewers Publications, 2004.
Woods, John, and Keith Rigley. The beers of Wallonia. Wiscombe, Bristol, England: The Artisan Press, 1996.

Phil Markowski

Saladin box, a pneumatic germination vessel for malting. In the late 1800s French engineer Charles Saladin overcame the main shortcoming of the first designs of a pneumatic germination vessel designed by his compatriot Galland. (The vessel was pneumatic because air was blown through the grain bed to cool and humidify it, in contrast to floor malting, in which cooling occurs by convection and conduction.) See FLOOR MALTING. Galland's design took the leap from shallow (10 cm to 20 cm; 4 in to 8 in) germinating beds to deeper beds of 60 cm to 80 cm (24 in to 32 in) in rectangular boxes, thus reducing dramatically the ground area required for malting. However, his design did not address the turning of the germinating grain, which still called for substantial manual effort and time. Without constant turning, the rootlets of the sprouting barley will quickly tangle together to form an inseparable and useless mat of damp grain. Saladin designed a system of screw turners that were driven by belts and pulleys and that raised the grain from the bottom of the bed in the box to the top. This separated the growing barleycorns and prevented them from matting together and made the germination phase more even throughout the bed by moving corns from the cooler layers to the warmer and vice versa. The Saladin Box design is rectangular and often up to 50 m long, so the sets of screws are mounted on a moving crossbar that slowly traverses the box from one end to the other, usually two or three times each day.

Saladin's design is still recognizable in modern malting plants, with the principal differences being the move to stainless steel construction, the scale of individual vessels, the use of direct drive motors rather than pulleys and belts, and, since the 1980s, the uniform acceptance of circular vessels. A more subtle difference has been the development of open ribbon screws, which turn the grain more effectively and with less damage than the original "Archimedes" style of screw.

See also GERMINATION and MALTING.

Colin J. West

Salt and Co.

See THOMAS SALT AND CO.

Salts

See CALCIUM CHLORIDE and SODIUM CHLORIDE.

Sam Adams

See BOSTON BEER COMPANY.

Samuel Allsopp & Sons brewery in Burton-on-Trent in the English Midlands played a leading role in the development of pale ale in the 19th century. The company dates from the 1740s, when an innkeeper named Benjamin Wilson started to brew beer on the premises. The brewing side prospered and Wilson's son, also named Benjamin, took over the business and was joined by his nephew Samuel Allsopp. In 1807 Allsopp bought out the Wilsons and turned Samuel Allsopp & Sons into a public company.

Burton was a major producer of strong brown ale that was exported to Russia and the Baltic States. The brewing town faced a major crisis in the late 18th and early 19th centuries when England was almost continuously at war with France. When Napoleon blockaded the Baltic ports against the English, the Burton brewers lost their export trade. Between 1780 and the mid-1820s, the number of brewers in Burton fell from thirteen to five. The remaining brewers, who included William Bass and William Worthington as well as Allsopp's, desperately looked for new markets. Their salvation was the British colonies, India in particular. Beer had been supplied to "the Raj," the British rulers of India and their large retinue of servants and soldiers, since early in the 18th century, but dark beers did not satisfy drinkers in the torrid climate of the subcontinent.

Help came to Burton when a small London brewer, George Hodgson, used the East India and West India docks in the capital to export a new, paler beer to India. See HODGSON, GEORGE. Hodgson's "India beer" proved popular but the brewer fell out with his agents in India by not paying his bills. The powerful East India Company, which monopolized trade between the two countries, was determined to break Hodgson's domination of beer supply. See EAST INDIA COMPANY. A director of the company, Campbell Majoribanks, had dinner with Samuel Allsopp in London and urged him to brew a beer suitable for the India market. Allsopp took a bottle of Hodgson's India beer back to Burton and handed it to his head brewer, Job Goodhead. Goodhead spat the beer out, offended by its bitterness, but said he could replicate it. According to a local legend, Goodhead made a small sample of beer using a tea pot as his mashing vessel, with only pale malt. The experiment was triumphant and Allsopp started to export pale ale with such success that in 1859 he built a new brewery in Burton opposite the railway station.

The other Burton brewers rushed to follow in Allsopp's footsteps. They found that the spring waters of the Trent Valley, rich in sulfates, were ideally suited to brewing pale ale; the natural salts in the water enhanced the flavors of malt and hops. Allsopp's was second only in size in Burton to Bass and in the 1830s the two breweries were exporting 6,000 barrels a year to India. Beer was sent by canal to the docks in London and Liverpool. But as the railway system developed in Britain, it carried Burton pale ale to towns and cities for domestic consumption. India pale ales were strong, between 7% and 8% alcohol, and heavily hopped to withstand the long sea journey to Bombay and Calcutta. Beer for the British market, simply called "pale ale," was lower in alcohol and less heavily hopped.

By 1890 Allsopp's was producing 460,000 barrels of beer a year with a workforce of 1,750. Samuel had been succeeded by his sons Charles and Henry but their stewardship of the company was disastrous. In the 1890s, £80,000 was invested in a new 60,000-barrel brewery designed to make lager beer, at a time when there was little demand for lagers in England. The venture failed. As did numerous other brewers, Allsopp's rushed to build large estates of pubs but became so financially stretched that it went into receivership in 1913 and was rescued only by a merger with Ind Coope, which came from Romford in Essex, close to London. In common with several brewers from London, Liverpool, and Manchester, Ind Coope had opened a brewery in Burton to use the local waters to brew pale ale.

Ind Coope & Allsopp, on firmer financial footing, remained a major presence in British brewing. It was best known for its Burton pale ale called Double Diamond; the name came from a branding mark on casks in the 19th century. By this time, the company was known only as Ind Coope, the Allsopp name having been dropped in 1959. In 1971 Ind Coope became part of Allied Breweries, a company that included Ansells of Birmingham and Tetley of Leeds.

The former Ind Coope & Allsopp and Bass breweries in Burton are now owned by the American brewer Coors. A pilot brewery within the Burton complex, called the Samuel Allsopp Brewery, survives but is currently not in use. It was used in the 1990s to produce an India pale ale for a seminar on IPA organized by the British Guild of Beer Writers. The beer was based on an Ind Coope & Allsopps' recipe from the 1920s.

See also BURTON-ON-TRENT and IND COOPE & SONS.

Gourvish, T. R., and R.G. Wilson. *The British brewing industry, 1830–1980.* Cambridge, England: Cambridge University Press, 1994.

Roger Protz

Samuel Smith's Old Brewery is one of the oldest family-owned breweries in Britain. It was founded in 1758 in the Yorkshire town of Tadcaster, where beer has been produced since the 14th century with the aid of water pumped up 85 feet from an underground lake of limestone water. The importance of the water supply gave Tadcaster the nickname of "the Burton of the North" because Burton-on-Trent in the Midlands is also famous for excellent brewing water.

Tadcaster today has three breweries: a former Bass brewery owned by Molson Coors and two breweries named Smith, John and Samuel. The Smiths come from the same family but a major disagreement early in the 20th century led to John Smith opening a rival plant in the town.

Samuel Smith Old Brewery playing card, c. 1920. PIKE MICROBREWERY MUSEUM, SEATTLE, WA

Sam Smith's, as the company is popularly called, is fiercely traditional. It owns more than 200 pubs and delivers to those close to Tadcaster with horse-drawn drays. It is one of the few remaining brewers to use "Yorkshire Squares," a method of fermentation developed in the 19th century to cleanse beer of yeast. See YORKSHIRE SQUARE. Most modern squares are made from stainless steel but Smith's prefers Welsh slate, which they feel helps keep natural carbonation entrained in the beer, imparting a creamier texture.

Sam Smith's Old Brewery bitter—labeled Old Brewery pale ale in the bottle—is a classic Yorkshire pale ale, brewed with pale and crystal malts and hopped with English Fuggles and Goldings. The brewery is also acclaimed for its bottled Oatmeal stout, Imperial stout, and Taddy porter (Taddy is a diminutive of Tadcaster). The brewery also brews a bottled brown ale, organic lager, and alpine lager. For many American craft brewers in the 1980s and early 1990s, Samuel Smith's beers were a singular touchstone and helped popularize classic British beer styles. The brewery is also famous for eccentric behavior. In the early 2000s, they removed all branding and music from their pubs and their delivery trucks became free of logos. Even in the main street of Tadcaster, a casual observer might not notice the brewery at all, hidden as it is behind an unmarked door.

Roger Protz

Sankey kegs, Sankey, or Sanke, are a style of kegs developed in Europe in the 1960s having immediate superiority over existing styles. The greatest advancement was the ability to clean and fill kegs aseptically and with automation. Sankey fittings permit cleaning, filling, and the application of dispense gas all through the same small fitting. Previously, Hoff-Stevens and Golden Gate kegs used bung holes for cleaning and filling, requiring the manual labor of bunging, debunging, and aligning the filling and cleaning equipment. The new Sankey technology allowed for the combined automatic cleaning and filling of kegs in about 2 min, without exposing the keg interior to atmospheric contaminants or human contact.

Cleaning and filling are accomplished through the single-connection dispense port, eliminating the unsanitary traditional bung hole. Cleaning is accomplished upside down, and filling can be accomplished with the keg upright or inverted. Integral to the keg design are domed heads and straight-side walls. During the cleaning cycles, cleaning solutions are pumped through the keg valve and up the internal tube or "spear" and spread evenly by the dome, down the side walls, and across the bottom dome. Previous keg designs had convoluted shapes and made cleaning and dispensing less efficient. Further benefits of this design include the ability to pack kegs more space efficiently, superior stacking stability, and the addition of ergonomic handles at the top of the kegs.

Sankey kegs were first used in the United States by Hamm's in 1973 and by Anheuser-Busch in 1978.

From the dispense perspective, the prime benefits were less skill required to attach and detach the dispense head coupler and therefore less spillage. Just as in the brewery, space efficiency and safety were improved. The Sankey keg and coupler is now the American standard, but there are two varieties, and they are not interchangeable. The smaller American Sankey fitting is twisted and locked into place; the slightly larger European Sankey coupler has a shorter stem and will not fit American Sankey kegs. Many American bars will be equipped with both types of coupler, allowing them to serve beer from either keg type.

See also KEG.

Broderick, Harold. *Beer packaging.* Madison, WI: MBAA Publications, 1982.

Brian Hunt

Santiam (hop) is a European-type aroma hop similar to German Tettnanger. See TETTNANGER (HOP). It was bred in Corvallis, Oregon, in 1988. Its genetics include Tettnanger as well as Hallertauer and Cascade. Santiam is a triploid, which means it produces nearly seedless cones even in the presence of male pollinators. It is adapted to the growing conditions in all major hop-growing areas in Oregon and Washington. In the brewhouse, it can be used as a replacement for German aroma hops. Its yield may be as high as 2,400 kg/ha (2,000 lb/acre), which is significantly higher than that of Tettnanger. Its alpha acid content ranges from 5% to 8% and its beta acid content from 5% to 7%; its cohumulone content is about 22%. It keeps well in storage. Santiam's essential oil composition is similar to that of Tettnanger, averaging about 30% to 50% myrcene, 18% to 28% humulene, 5% to 8% caryophyllene, and 8% to 14% farnesene. The characteristic humulene-to-caryophyllene ratio ranges from 3.2 to 3.6, which is similar to Tettnanger. Santiam seems perhaps to have suffered from poor marketing—it is a hop little spoken of, despite having very good brewing characteristics.

Haunold, Alfred. Flavor characteristics of new hop varieties. *The New Brewer* 15 (1998): 59–64.

Henning, John A., and Alfred Haunold. *Release notice of Santiam, a new aroma hop cultivar.* Washington, DC: U.S. Department of Agriculture, OR Agric. Expt. Station, WA Agric Expt. Station, and ID Agric. Expt. Station, March 9, 1998.

Alfred Haunold

Saphir (hop) is an aroma hop bred by the Hop Research Center in Hüll in the Hallertau and approved for commercial cultivation the Bundessortenamt (the German crop registration agency) in 2002. It is largely grown in the Hallertau. Agronomically, the variety is highly resistant to verticillium wilt and fairly resistant to both downy and powdery mildew. It has medium storage stability. Saphir is low in alpha acids (usually between 2% and 4.5%). Its beta acid content is 4% to 7%, and its cohumulone content is roughly 12% to 17%. In terms of essential oils, Saphir has 25% to 40% myrcene, 20% to 30% humulene, 9% to 14% caryophyllene, and less than 1% farnesene. The result of this combination of acids and oils is a floral, spicy, citrus aroma, which makes Saphir excellently suited primarily as an aroma hop for blonde lagers. It is considered a good substitute for Hallertauer Mittelfrueh, which is among its parents.

Sepp Wejwar

Sapporo Beer is a descendant of a brewery founded in 1876 on Hokkaido, Japan's northernmost major island, and began selling Sapporo brand lager in 1877. The brewery was part of a general movement on the part of the Japanese government to promote economic development on Hokkaido. Beer was considered appropriate for the region because of the cool climate and the availability of barley and hops.

The original company was reorganized in 1887 and re-established as Nippon Bakushu Shuzo Kaisha (Japan Beer Brewery Company). With the addition of capital from several large trading companies, they opened a brewery in the Meguro area of Tokyo and also began producing Yebisu Beer in 1890. In 1906, the company aligned with Asahi Beer to form Dai Nippon Breweries, which commands approximately 70% of the Japanese market. From the start of this alliance, beer consumption in Japan increased dramatically until the start of World War II, when rationing put a brake on beer production. The Yebisu brand of beer was discontinued in 1943.

In 1949, the Dai Nippon alliance was broken up by the Japanese government's Economic Decentralization Act, resulting in two separate entities, Asahi Breweries Ltd and Nippon Breweries Ltd. In 1964, in response to consumer demands, the name of Nippon Breweries was changed to Sapporo Beer. Then, in 1971, Yebisu Beer was reintroduced to the market after a 28-year absence. This 100% malt beer was considered Japan's first authentically German-style beer in the postwar period, and its popularity continues today. In recent years, several versions have been released, including a dark beer and an extra hoppy lager.

The most popular Sapporo product, however, has been Sapporo Black Label beer, which was introduced in 1977 to join the long-selling Sapporo Lager, which remains Japan's only pasteurized beer. Sapporo entered the low-malt "happo-shu" beer market in 2001, and it currently produces a number of products in this lower tax category. In 2006, Sapporo bought Sleeman Breweries of Ontario, Canada's third-largest brewer, which now produces most of the Sapporo beer sold in North America.

See also JAPAN.

Bryan Harrell

sarcina sickness

See PEDIOCOCCUS.

schankbier, a now antiquated German federal beer tax category that was abolished effective January 1, 1993. Literally, the term meant "tap beer" and referred to a brew with an original gravity—measured in degrees Plato—of 7°P to 8°P.

See also ORIGINAL GRAVITY and PLATO GRAVITY SCALE. For an explanation of the old and the new German beer tax law, see VOLLBIER.

Horst Dornbusch

Schlenkerla is without a doubt the most famous brand name of all the rauchbiers in the world. See RAUCHBIER. It is made in Bamberg, Bavaria, by a brewery whose legal name is Heller-Bräu Trum KG, but which is known to the locals simply as the Schlenkerla Brewery. The young owner, Matthias Trum, is the sixth generation of his family to run the brewery, and beers show a strictly conservative bent. The heart of the enterprise is an ancient half-timbered public beer hall at number 6, Dominikanerstrasse, in the old town of Bamberg. Schlenkerla is a hallowed medieval drinking establishment that was first mentioned in a document in 1405, when it was known as Zum Blauen Löwen (At the Blue Lion). Almost hidden behind an unassuming entrance, this venerable beer hall with its dark and cozy recesses framed by heavy, blackened, hand-hewn timbers started out as a full-fledged brewpub, but today the brewery and fermentation cellars, which are not open to the public, are a short walk distant, up on one of the seven hills of Bamberg. The name Schlenkerla is Bamberg slang for "Schlenkerer," a German word denoting a person who is in the habit of swinging his arms while shuffling along. The patrons of the Blue Lion affixed this nickname to a fellow named Andreas Graser, who had acquired the pub in 1877. Soon thereafter, the people began using the publican's epithet as a synonym for his tap room and eventually for his brew, too. Rauchbier of various strengths has always been the singular focus at Schlenkerla. The full name of the brewery's flagship lager is Aecht Schlenkerla Rauchbier, with "aecht" being Franconian dialect for the German "echt," which means "true" or "original." Like all rauchbiers, Aecht Schlenkerla is made from barley malt that has been kiln dried over an open fire of aged beechwood, which imparts a smoky, bacony flavor to the beer. It is not certain when the current version of the rauchbier emerged in and around Bamberg, but Schlenkerla still has its own malting operation, where it employs the traditional open-fire malting methods to this day. It is reasonable to assume that some form of smoked beer has been brewed by this enterprise for at least 5 centuries. Schlenkerla makes several smoky brews. The traditional Aecht Schlenkerla, considered the archetype of all rauchbiers, is brewed and aged much like a märzen, with an alcohol by volume level of 5.1%. See MÄRZENBIER. Schlenkerla lager is a slightly smoky helles-type blond brewed to an alcohol level of 4.8%. The brewery says that smoked malt is not used here, but that a slight smokiness pervades the beer through the repitched yeast and the general brewing facility. See HELLES. Schlenkerla also brews two seasonal smoky offerings, an Urbock sold in October in bottles only, with a bockbier alcohol level of 6.5%; and a fastenbier, a doppelbock-like Lenten strong beer, available only in the spring in cask-conditioned form. See BOCK BEER and DOPPELBOCK. Finally, the brewery makes a smoky weissbier, a wheat ale called Schlenkerla Rauchweizen, with 5.2% alcohol by volume. This beer uses smoked barley malt and unsmoked wheat malt.

See also WEISSBIER.

Schlenkerla. http://www.schlenkerla.de/ (accessed February 18, 2011).

Horst Dornbusch

The **Schneider Weisse Brewery** is a family-owned enterprise that specializes exclusively in the production of weissbier (wheat beer). The brewery is headquartered in Kelheim, Bavaria, on the banks of the Danube, some 110 kilometers (68 miles) northeast of Munich. With an annual output of almost 270,000 hl (230,085 US bbl) per year, Schneider Weisse is the seventh-most popular German wheat beer. It was in Kelheim, where Bavarian Duke Maximilian I (1573 to 1651), owner of the Hofbräuhaus in Munich, built a brand new weissbier brewery in 1607. This was only a few years after the ruling Bavarian dynasty, the Wittelsbach family, had instituted a weissbier monopoly for themselves in 1602—a monopoly that was to last until 1798. After 1602, only the dukes of Bavaria—and no commoner—could brew weissbier, because

Brewhouse entrance at the Schneider Weisse Brewery in Bavaria. Schneider Weisse, in operation since 1872, produces some of the world's most renowned traditional wheat beers. PHOTOGRAPH BY DENTON TILLMAN

the beer was in technical violation of the Bavarian 1516 Beer Purity Law, which permitted only barley, hops, and water to be used in beer. See REINHEITSGEBOT. In 1607, Maximilian built a *Weisses Bräuhaus* (white brewery) specifically for his wheat beer, right next to his "brown beer" Hofbräuhaus brewery. By the middle of the 19th century, however, top-fermented weissbier had fallen out of favor with Bavarians, who preferred the modern, somewhat cleaner tasting bottom-fermented lagers. But Georg Schneider I (1817 to 1890), a brewmaster, continued to believe in weissbier. So he leased the once-profitable *Weisses Bräuhaus* from the Wittelsbach family, in 1855. At that time, weissbier might have completely disappeared from the Bavarian beer map had it not been for Georg Schneider's decision to keep the tradition alive in downtown Munich. Schneider used an old recipe that is still the brewery's flagship beer today. It is called *Schneider Weisse—Unser Original* (our original) or, more recently, just "Tap 7." In 1872, the Bavarian rulers gave up on weissbier brewing altogether, and Schneider obtained permission to transfer his weissbier brew rights to an adjacent brewery, Maderbräu, which he had acquired, and to change his business name to "G. Schneider & Sohn." In 1927, another Schneider, Georg IV, acquired the Kelheim premises—today Schneider's production site, pub, and headquarters—which by then had fallen into the hands of the secular State of Bavaria. In 1907, the Schneider brewery introduced a doppelbock-strength wheat beer, Aventinus. The brew was named after an obscure Bavarian author and philosopher, Johann Georg Turmair (1477 to 1534), who called himself Aventinus. Schneider recently decided to give the draught version of Aventinus the more prosaic name of Tap 6. When the Munich brew site was destroyed during World War II, in 1944, Schneider moved all production to Kelheim, but rebuilt the former Maderbräu as a beer hall, which it still is today. Schneider has broadened its wheat beers portfolio considerably since the turn of the millennium. It now offers a number of wheat beer styles, from a non-alcoholic wheat beer to an extra-strength eisbock-version of Aventinus, and more recently a well-hopped strong weissbier called Hopfen-Weisse, originally a collaboration with The Brooklyn Brewery of New York. The brewery's top-selling beer, usually simply called Schneider Weisse, is 100% bottle-conditioned and well regarded as one of the world's finest traditional wheat beers.

Conrad Seidl

Schulz Brew Systems, based in the Franconian town of Bamberg in northern Bavaria, is the world's oldest brewing equipment manufacturer. Founded in 1677 in Bamberg by Christian Schulz, a coppersmith who had just married the widow of his deceased master, Schulz has been specializing in the fabrication of brewhouses and fermenters ever since. The company is still owned and operated by a 10th-generation descendant of Christian Schulz and is known in Germany as Kaspar Schulz Brauereimaschinenfabrik & Apparatebauanstalt KG. Schulz has the distinction of being the oldest continuously operating industrial enterprise in Bamberg, the city otherwise also known as the home of the Rauchbier style and the Weyermann Malting Company. See RAUCHBIER and WEYERMANN® MALTING.

During the 18th century, aside from brewing equipment, the company also made ornamental copper artifacts for churches and official buildings as well as copper household utensils at a time when copper pots and pans were the standard cooking gear in upscale kitchens. In 1887, then under a 7th-generation Schulz, Kaspar, the company's legal name was changed to what it is today. Kaspar added distillation equipment for schnapps makers, malting equipment, and sterilization equipment to the company's portfolio. Of these, Schulz micromalteries are still available today. Whereas many brewing equipment manufacturers started to make ever larger brew equipment after World War II, when consolidation in the brewing industry created a demand for breweries of giant dimensions, Schulz began to focus on smaller, well-crafted systems that fit the more segmented German market. Since 1947 the company has shifted from strict traditionalist to innovator, leading revolutions in automation, brewpub systems, modular brewhouses, and cutting-edge energy saving technologies. Nearly 3 and a half centuries after its founding, Schulz retains about 100 employees and the firm's work can be seen in more than 400 brewhouses and 50 countries around the world.

Oliver Jakob

schwarzbier, literally "black beer," is a black lager with a light to medium body and a moderate to high bitterness. The alcohol content typically is around 5% alcohol by volume (ABV)—which makes it a "vollbier" in terms of German tax law. But schwarzbier constitutes a style of its own, differing from dunkel both in color and in body. By definition—although this definition does not seem to bother many brewers—schwarzbier should be brewed from Munich and dark (roasted) malts. A toasty to slightly burned malt note in the aftertaste is acceptable if it is balanced with hop bitterness and a hint of hop aroma. Schwarzbier is darker than most dunkels but also drier and lighter bodied. Many are now made with dehusked roasted malts, allowing the beers to attain a very dark brown color and chocolaty flavor while avoiding the acidic bite usually associated with heavily roasted malts. Schwarzbier has been virtually unknown for decades in Western Germany but has made a large impact on the market after Germany's reunification in 1990. The output of schwarzbier has been 1.1 million hl (937,384 US bbl) in Germany in 2009, with the eastern German Köstritzer Schwarzbier being the strongest selling brand at 390,000 hl (332,345 US bbl). See KÖSTRITZER SCHWARZBIERBRAUEREI.

German beer statistics include the relatively small production of "German porter," another beer style that is not clearly defined. Some German porters are similar to Baltic porters, whereas others are simply schwarzbier running under a different name. The German porter style was developed in the 19th century from a bottom-fermented and relatively strong dark lager (typically 13 to 16°Plato) that undergoes a secondary fermentation with a top-fermenting ale yeast and in some cases with Brettanomyces. See BRETTANOMYCES. During World War I, when it seemed "unpatriotic" to drink a British-style beer in Germany, German porter went out of fashion. Relatively pure forms of the style have survived in Karlsruhe's Hoepfner brewery and in Meissner Schwerter brewery in Meissen, Saxonia.

The new popularity of schwarzbier since Germany's reunification has led to a decline in the sales of top-fermented dark altbier, the once-popular style from Northrhine Westphalia that has seen large production losses in the decades after 1990. Whereas altbier tends to be bold and hoppy, most schwarzbier is fairly mild in flavor with bitterness rarely rising above 20 international bitterness units. This has made it a relatively popular beer style among American craft brewers, who enjoy its combination of bold appearance and easygoing character. Interestingly, schwarzbier seems to have become a specialty in Utah, where strict laws limit the sale of beers above 4% ABV. These restrictions appear to have made Utah's brewers proficient in the production of mild but flavorful beer styles, and the popularity of schwarzbier is on the rise.

Leichter Anstieg bei Schwarzbier im Jahr 2009. *Brauwelt* 25/26 (2010): 752.

Conrad Seidl

scooping is a UK outgrowth of the blogosphere, said to be a variant of beer ticking. See TICKING. Beer scoopers not only seek out beers that are new to them but also attempt to record impressions and opinions of the beers, rather than simply "ticking them off" (checking them off) a list. No doubt this is a hobby that will be given new life by the rise of social media such as Twitter.

See also SOCIAL MEDIA.

Beer scooping. http://www.scoopergen.co.uk (accessed January 25, 2011).

Zak Avery

Scotch ale is a traditional, top-fermented beer that is brewed to greatly varying strengths. Sometimes the term "Scotch ale" is reserved just for the heavier versions, while the milder versions are labeled "Scottish ales." Traditionally, the different versions of Scotch ale were classified by a nomenclature that is derived from their per-barrel price in the 19th century, in increments of 10 shillings from 60 to 160 shillings. See SHILLING SYSTEM. A typical 60-shilling "light" ale might have a gravity of 7.5–8.75° Plato (1.03–1.035); a 70-shilling "heavy" ale, of 8.75–10°P (1.035–1.040); an 80-shilling "export" ale, of 10–12.5°P (1.040–1.050); and a 90-shilling "export" ale, of 12.5–16.25°P (1.050–1.065). See PLATO GRAVITY SCALE. Beers rated at 100 shillings and above were usually referred to as "wee heavy." A 120-shilling wee heavy, for instance, might have a gravity of 19.25–23.75°P (1.075–1.095); and a 140-shilling wee heavy, of 23.75–32.5°P (1.095–1.130).

The base malt for Scotch ale is pale ale malt with varying amounts of pale caramel malt and unmalted roasted barley added to the mash. Many homebrewers and craft brewers, particularly in the United States, have taken to adding peat-smoked malts to their Scotch ales, perhaps influenced by the peaty character of Scotch whiskies. Although Scottish malts were traditionally floor-malted and then dried or roasted in peat-fired kilns, giving the malts smoky flavors, malts were once dried over fires almost everywhere; Scottish beers were no smokier than others. Scottish brewers got rid of smoked malts as soon as brewers in other countries; modern Scottish brewers and historians insist that there's nothing "Scottish" about beers with peat flavors. Despite these protests, the romance is hard to cast aside, and modern brewers sometimes imitate this fanciful flavor by adding to the mash a small portion of peat-flavored whiskey malt or even a small percentage of Rauchbier-type smoked malt.

The color of Scotch ale ranges from amber, to light brown, to deep mahogany. Scotch ale is often mashed-in thick for a saccharification rest of 60 to

Two men enjoying strong Scotch Ale, also known as "Wee Heavy," c. 1890. PIKE MICROBREWERY MUSEUM, SEATTLE, WA

90 minutes at a single, relatively high temperature of 158°F (70°C) or above, which favors alpha-amylase instead of beta-amylase activity. This generates a good amount of higher-molecular, unfermentable sugars, which provide body and mouthfeel to the finished beer as well as a rich maltiness.

Traditionally, Scotch ales of differing strengths were brewed by the parti-gyle method, whereby the strong ales were collected just from the first runnings of the mash and boiled and fermented separately. See PARTI-GYLE. These "heavies" may have had an alcohol by volume content of 9%–10%, sometimes more. To achieve proper fermentation volumes for these heavier beers, two or more consecutive batches would be mashed. The second runnings would become one of the weaker ales, yielding perhaps an alcohol by volume brew of 3.5%. Depending on the parsimony of the brewer, even a third running was sometimes performed. Such exceedingly small, low-alcohol brews were then referred to as "two-penny ales." Higher or lower Scotch ale gravities can be achieved by simply increasing or decreasing the size of the grain bill in the mash tun as well as shortening or lengthening the run-off time for each individual gyle.

Scotch ales are top-fermented, but in the cool climates of Scotland, fermentations carried out at ambient temperatures have rarely been very warm, and as a result, levels of fruity esters tend to be low. For the same reason, stronger Scotch ales have traditionally had more residual sugar than their counterparts to the south. Bitterness levels of Scotch ales range widely, usually between 15–25 IBU, but hops have never been a focal point of beers brewed in a land where hops will not grow. Scotch ale aromatics tend toward rich maltiness, with hop character kept very much in the background.

While Scottish brewers may never have had a predilection for peat flavors, they did often use flowers and herbs in their beer before the introduction of hops (imported from warmer, sunnier England), in the 19th century. Use of heather in particular was once quite common. Without the protective qualities of the hop, however, these beers often spoiled quickly, and one wonders whether this pushed the Scots in the direction of their more famous whiskies. That said, the stronger Scotch ales, especially the rich "wee heavies," have long enjoyed an excellent reputation, not only at home but also in the export trade. See WEE HEAVY.

See also SCOTLAND.

Noonan, Greg J. *Scotch ale, classic beer style series #8.* Boulder, CO: Brewers Publications, 1993.

Horst Dornbusch

Scotland, comprising the northernmost region of the United Kingdom, is a country better known for whisky as its preferred restorative, but it has nevertheless given the world some of its most enduring beer styles. The nation has never been short of entrepreneurs, innovators, and free thinkers, and the Scottish family names of McEwan, Younger, Drybrough, and Tennent are forever associated with resourcefulness, ingenuity, and beer. The Edinburgh-based McEwan and Younger businesses came together in 1931 as Scottish Brewers Ltd, and then joined forces with Newcastle Breweries Ltd in 1960 to form Scottish & Newcastle, a powerful force that developed into one of Europe's most progressive companies. The Tennent brewing business that originated in farming has produced lager for the domestic market since 1885 and continues to thrive in Glasgow. See SCOTTISH & NEWCASTLE BREWERY.

Farmers growing barley were closely linked to maltsters and whisky distillers and were instrumental in commercializing beer-making, which had, in pre-industrial times, been a cottage industry. See ALE-WIVES. Historical documents indicate that the commercial brewing trade was developed by Benedictine monks in 12th-century Edinburgh and in neighboring Dunbar, where they took full advantage of fresh spring water sources and locally grown barley. Over the centuries, Scotland gained a reputation for ales of high quality. Belhaven, Scotland's longest-established brewery, gained such a reputation that in 1827 Austrian Emperor Francis I chose its beers for his cellar, describing them as "the burgundy of Scotland."

The ready market for beer consumption and the difficulties of bulk transport meant that brewing was concentrated in the larger towns and cities—Aberdeen, for example, could count 144 brewers in 1693. Glasgow and Edinburgh (with its "charmed circle" of pristine wells lapping below the city) developed the greatest concentration of breweries, yet little, rural Alloa in the Central Lowlands was regarded as second only to Burton-on-Trent as a British brewing center, due to its bountiful local supply of grain and coal and its harbor on the River Forth. For a time, Scotland vied with England for the trade in India pale ale, before Burton finally eclipsed all other sources.

Beer and whiskey share both raw materials and process procedures before they go their separate ways, only to return side by side on more social and convivial occasions. Just as brandy is distilled wine, whisky is essentially distilled beer. Traditional scotch ales are generally characterized by their dark color, their substantial malt flavors, and having little hop content, but a rich—and perceived to be nutritious—sweetness and smooth, rhythmic texture. See SCOTCH ALE. Some beer terminology is exclusively Scottish, such as the "shilling" system derived from the 19th-century cost of a hogshead of beer. "Light," "heavy," and "export" ales were variously known as 60/- (that is, 60 shillings), 70/-, and 80/-. Of course, it is the barley wine-like "wee heavy" beer style that lights the path from Scotland and many US brewers have taken it to heart, often developing it a stage further by using peated malt, despite the protests of actual Scots.

There is some written evidence—and a lot of folklore—to support the notion that bittering ingredients such as heather, myrtle, and broom were used in Scottish beer instead of hops, which are unsuitable for cultivation in harsher climates and were therefore expensive to transport from the south of England and continental Europe. Some contemporary Scottish brewers, such as the Heather Ale Company, have revisited these age-old ingredients to produce beer flavored with pine cones, gooseberries, and even seaweed with notable success.

In the 1950s an "amalgamation rush" had brought about the virtual disappearance of the Scottish independent brewers. Bass Charrington, Allied, Scottish & Newcastle, and Whitbread had taken a large stake in the Scottish trade, following smaller companies such as Vaux of Sunderland in the North of England and Allsopp of Burton-on-Trent which had already acquired a significant brewery-owning foothold in Scotland. Scotland was not exempt from the lager phenomenon that spiralled out of the 1960s with the demand for "younger" and "easier-to-drink beers" typified by dubiously Irish Harp Lager and Skol, a decidedly confused Scottish-Scandinavian synthesis.

The independent spirit has never been conquered, however, and Scottish brewers have always been at the forefront of innovation, being early adopters of bottling, canning, and exporting. Enterprising breweries such as Harviestoun, Fyne Ales, Orkney, Highland, and Black Isle have developed distinct styles and beer ranges. Harviestoun's Ola Dubh, for instance, is produced in various "expressions" having been matured for different periods in former whisky casks. Among recent entries, Aberdeenshire-based BrewDog plays an age-old "bad boy" role, clambering for record amounts of alcohol in their beers and eliciting both delight and disgust by their general antics. These are all beers that exemplify Scotland: spirited and heavily influenced by time and place.

See also BRITAIN.

Donnachie, Ian. *A history of the brewing industry in Scotland*. Edinburgh: John Donald Publishers, 1979.

Murray, Jim. *The complete guide to whisky*. London: Carlton Books, 1997.

Smith, Gavin D. *The Scottish beer bible*. Edinburgh: Mercat Press, 2001.

Alastair Gilmour

Scottish & Newcastle Brewery is an international brewer operating in more than 50 countries. The company's origins in modest but ambitious family businesses in 18th-century Edinburgh, Scotland, and Newcastle in the north of England evolved into one of the UK's most successful corporations, eventually owning three of the best-selling beers in Europe—Baltika, Kronenbourg 1664, and Fosters—plus the smaller but well-known Newcastle brown Ale. See NEWCASTLE BROWN ALE.

In 1931 Edinburgh, the William Younger brewing business, formed in 1749, amalgamated with that of William McEwan (established 1856) to form Scottish Brewers Ltd. A union of five family brewing companies operating around Newcastle had given birth to Newcastle Breweries Ltd in 1890 and the merger of both concerns in 1960 not only created Scottish & Newcastle Breweries but also launched a formidable force in British business.

By 1995 Scottish & Newcastle was the country's number one brewer (and in Europe's top six) through takeovers of Courage and Theakstons and was listed on the London Stock Exchange as "Scottish Courage." Relentless expansion produced a major leisure industry player, developing separate beer and pub divisions while expanding significantly as an international organization through acquisitions of French conglomerate Danone (makers of Dannon yogurt and other food products) and Fosters of Australia and brewing interests in Russia, Finland, the Baltic states, China, and throughout Asia.

In April 2008, Scottish & Newcastle UK Ltd was jointly taken over by Heineken NV and Carlsberg A/S and now operates as a subsidiary of both, with the assets split between the two parent companies. As of 2010, the UK brewing division traded under the name Heineken UK, with the leased pub division operating as the Scottish & Newcastle Pub Company.

See also COURAGE BREWERY, SCOTLAND, and THEAKSTONS.

Ritchie, Berry. *Good company, the story of Scottish & Newcastle*. London: James & James, 1999.

Alastair Gilmour

scuffing is the scratching of bottles caused by bottle-to-bottle and bottle-to-guides rubbing on the bottling line. Particularly returnable, reusable bottles may pass through a bottling line some 20 to 50 times before they break. Every time they return to the brewery, their labels are scraped off. Then they are washed, refilled, capped, and crated. Eventually, they develop very noticeable scuff rings at the bottle height where they are in contact with the guide rails of the filling and packaging system. Aesthetics is subjective, but Europeans seem to be willing to accept the unsightly, "used" look of a scuffed beer bottle, whereas North Americans might not. Bottle manufacturers use various protective coatings, some made of organic compounds, to enhance their bottles' smoothness and abrasion resistance, and thus minimize scratch marks. But scuffing cannot be avoided entirely, especially if the bottles are subjected to a cleaning cycle with caustic solutions. This is because the alkaline cleaning agent eventually damages their organic protective coatings. Some manufacturers, therefore, coat their bottles with tin oxide, which is more resistant than organic coatings to removal by alkaline solutions. Scuff marks are also ideal places for bottle bloom.

See also BLOOM.

Abrasion-resistant coatings for use on returnable glass containers. http://www.sciencedirect.com/science?_ob=ArticleURL&_udi=B6TW0-46SWNFV-2M&_user=10&_coverDate=03%2F06%2F1981&_alid=1748752515&_rdoc=1&_fmt=high&_orig=search&_origin=search&_zone=rslt_list_item&_cdi=5548&_sort=r&_st=13&_docanchor=&view=c&_ct=13&_acct=C000050221&_version=1&_urlVersion=0&_userid=10&md5=1f38e03a36af7a63d21e3917960cf4d7&searchtype=a (accessed October 15, 2010).

On-Line Coating of Glass with Tin Oxide by Atmospheric Pressure Chemical Vapor Deposition. http://www.osti.gov/glass/Best%20Practices%20Documents/Other%20Case%20Studies/On-line%20coating%20of%20glass.pdf (accessed October 15, 2010).

Process for forming tin oxide glass coating. http://www.freepatentsonline.com/4329379.html (accessed October 15, 2010).

Horst Dornbusch

secondary fermentation is a somewhat catch-all term referring to any phase of fermentation following the very active "primary" fermentation, but before complete removal of the yeast. In lager beers, secondary fermentation can refer to the period of maturation and lagering, during which important flavor changes occur, particularly reabsorption of diacetyl by yeast. In traditional German lager brewing, the term can also refer to the krausening process, where actively fermenting wort is added to beer that has finished its primary fermentation. This addition restarts fermentation in the combined batch, reducing diacetyl and, if the reactivated fermentation is in a closed tank, building natural carbonation.

In Britain, secondary fermentation refers to an important part of the traditional ale-brewing process whereby condition (dissolved carbon dioxide) is built up as residual sugar and is slowly taken up by the yeast. This gives sparkle and mouthfeel to the finished beer. Secondary fermentation may also remove unwanted flavor compounds, such as sulfurous character in the beer, giving it a "cleaner," more pleasant palate. Secondary fermentation can take place in the brewery in conditioning tanks or, in the case of traditional beer in the UK, in casks. Secondary fermentation in conditioning tanks can be prompted by the addition of wort or sugar solution to the tank.

When a secondary fermentation takes place in a bottle, giving the beer a natural and often lively carbonation, this is referred to as "bottle conditioning." See BOTTLE CONDITIONING. In the case of bottle-conditioned beer, the wort or sugar solution is added to the beer, which either still has yeast in it or has yeast added before bottling, and the secondary fermentation takes place in the bottle over a period of time. In the case of traditional cask beer in the UK, the beer either has a small amount of fermentable sugar left after primary fermentation or a sugar solution (called priming sugar) is added to the cask, which contains unfiltered beer and clarifying agents (finings). The sugar is fermented by the yeast in the cask, which builds up condition over several days. The cask is ready to serve after the secondary fermentation is finished and the beer has been clarified by the finings.

Amateur brewers often use the term "secondary fermentation" to refer to an aging period after the primary fermentation; this usually involves transferring the young beer to another fermentation vessel to remove it from dormant yeast.

See also CASK CONDITIONING, CONDITIONING, and PRIMING SUGAR.

Paul KA Buttrick

Sedlmayr, Gabriel the Elder purchased a rather unremarkable brewery in Munich, in 1807. Nobody could have imagined then that this commonplace transaction, conducted by an erstwhile brewmaster to the Bavarian Royal Court, would herald the birth of one of the greatest brewing dynasties on earth, and help change the world of brewing forever. The brewery in question was Spaten, which had started life as a Munich brewpub in 1397. Between 1622 and 1704 it was owned by the Späth family, from which the brewery took its name of Spaten (the German word for "spade"). Subsequently, the brewery changed hands a few times, until it was acquired by the Siesmayr family, who sold it to Sedlmayr. The new owner's brewing acumen was to serve the company well, and, coupled with his energy and enterprise, was to transform Spaten from virtual obscurity—ranking last in terms of malt consumption among Munich's 52 brewers at the time—to a position of prominence, having become the third-largest brewery in Munich, after Hacker and Pschorr, by 1820. A decade later, Spaten beer was even respectable enough to be served in Munich's world-renowned Hofbräuhaus, the 1589 former private, now public, watering hole of the Dukes of Wittelsbach, the ruling Bavarian Dynasty between 1180 and 1818. See WITTELSBACHER FAMILY. Much of Sedlmayr's success stemmed from his readiness to embrace the new brewing technologies that were being developed in Europe in the course of the Industrial Revolution. It was under his stewardship, with direction from his son Gabriel the Younger, for instance, that Spaten experimented with new malting techniques in the 1830s. See SEDLMAYR, GABRIEL THE YOUNGER. In the process, Spaten developed a highly aromatic, deep amber malt now known as Munich malt. The brewery used this malt as the foundation grist of a new lager style, the märzen, which it introduced in 1841. See MÄRZENBIER and MUNICH MALT. Gabriel Sedlmayr was fortunate in that he had two sons, Gabriel and Josef, who followed in his footsteps as gifted brewers. They assumed the Spaten reins upon Gabriel the Elder's death in 1839, and immediately began to write their own part of brewing history by turning Spaten into Munich's leading brewery by the end of the 19th century.

Behringer, Wolfgang. *The Spaten brewery from 1397–1997: The story of a Munich-based company from the Middle Ages to the present.* Munich, Germany: Piper, 1997.

Hornsey, I. S. Who was Gabriel Sedlmayr II? *Biologist* 55(4) (August 2008): 160–63.

Ian Hornsey

Sedlmayr, Gabriel the Younger was a brewer who took over the reins of the Spaten Brewery of Munich, with his brother Josef, upon the death of his father, Gabriel Sedlmayr the Elder, in 1839. See SEDLMAYR, GABRIEL THE ELDER. The two brothers inherited their father's innovative zeal and, over the next few years, modernized the brewery at the same pace as their father had done before them. In 1844, Spaten became the first brewery outside England to adopt steam power. A year later, Gabriel bought out his brother and became the sole proprietor of Spaten, which would continue to be a center of brewing innovation. Already during his student days, Gabriel had been an innovator. As part of the requirement for his Master Diploma, young Gabriel embarked upon an extensive grand tour of noted European brewing centers in the early 1830s. On one of his trips, he met fellow brewer Anton Dreher, whose mother owned a small brewery in Klein-Schwechat, just outside Vienna. The meeting, in 1832, marked the beginning of a lifelong friendship and business association. See DREHER, ANTON and VIENNA LAGER. The two travelers visited Great Britain in 1833 to learn more about fermentation—and engaged in what can only be described as a classic case of industrial espionage. By using a specially modified hollow walking cane, they furtively gathered wort and beer samples during their brewery visits und subsequently analyzed them in their hotel. They put the data thus collected to good use after they had returned home by developing two new malts and two new beer styles: Dreher came up with Vienna malt and Vienna lager; Sedlmayr invented Munich malt and märzen beer. See MÄRZENBIER and MUNICH MALT.

In those days it was difficult to brew lagers in the summer; the hot central European climate was inhospitable to brewing in general and lager brewing in particular. Brewers used ice blocks cut from frozen lakes and ponds in the winter and stored them underground for use as coolant in the summer. This was costly and inefficient. So Sedlmayr looked around for a technological solution, which he found in the work of a young Munich engineering professor, Carl Linde. See LINDE, CARL VON. Linde had been tinkering with refrigeration machines, and in 1873, Sedlmayr persuaded Linde to install one of his experimental devices in the Spaten fermentation and lagering cellars. This was, as best as anybody knows, the first time that mechanical refrigeration had been used in a brewery, and Spaten was from then on uniquely equipped to brew bottom-fermented beer reliably year-round. With this new technology in place, Spaten had become the largest of the Munich breweries. Spaten's superb lager-making ability allowed it to experiment with ever more delicate brews, especially one that could compete with the rising popularity of the Bohemian pilsner from just east of the Bavarian border. The result was the introduction, in 1894, of a straw blond beer, the delicate lager that was to become the signature brew for Bavarian beer garden and beer hall lagers for the next century, the Helles.

See also HELLES.

Behringer, Wolfgang. *The Spaten brewery from 1397 to 1997: The story of a Munich-based company from the Middle Ages to the present.* Munich: Piper, 1997.

Hornsey, I. S. Who was Gabriel Sedlmayr II? *Biologist* 55(4) (August 2008): 160–63.

Ian Hornsey

sensory evaluation is a common method of evaluating beer. Unlike other testing methods, which make use of various instruments and equipment, sensory evaluation is conducted by individuals and relies on their sensory perception. This evaluation can be used to assess such subtle aspects of beer as freshness, quality, craftsmanship, balance, conformity to style or brand, and drinkability.

During sensory evaluation, there are four different aspects of beer that come under scrutiny: appearance, aroma, flavor, and mouthfeel. The assessment of a beer's appearance includes notes on its color, which can range from a light straw to black; its clarity, which can be transparent, veiled, cloudy, or opaque; and its foam. Various aspects of the foam are observed, including thickness, color, texture, and retention (how quickly it collapses), as well as the lacing that forms on the inside walls of the glass as the beer is consumed.

When evaluating aroma, there is a wide range of features presented for evaluation. Because beer is made from a minimum of four ingredients, and each of these ingredients can contribute a range of aromas, this often results in a very complex nose. Common descriptors used to characterize a beer's aroma include grain, bread crust, caramel, toffee, molasses, chocolate, coffee, clove, coriander, pepper, grassy, banana, raisin, plum, grapefruit, pine, herbal, earthy, resinous, even "sweaty horse blanket" for some specialty beers such as gueuze. There are also brewing faults that can be detected in the aroma. Some examples include notes of corn, butterscotch, skunk, sulfur, vinegar, chemicals, or plastic.

The flavor of beer combines its taste and its aromas and is equally complex. It is also during this stage of evaluation that bitterness is first perceived. Because bitterness is most readily perceived at the back of the tongue and finish is an important aspect of beer, it is common practice to swallow beer during sensory evaluation in order to better assess these elements. Other taste sensations are often described as malty, sweet, sour, citrus, or acidic. Defects often reveal themselves as imparting flavors of wet cardboard, cat urine, mold, leather, vegetable, rancidity, metal, or astringency.

The final aspect of sensory evaluation, mouthfeel, relates to the texture of the beer. Notes are taken on its weight and body as well as other possible sensations such as warmth, astringency, or slickness. Carbonation levels and carbonation texture also play an important role in the mouthfeel of a beer.

Although sensory evaluation is not as objective or precise as some laboratory tests, which can yield numerical results, it is still often used in breweries, either on its own or as a complement to these other methods because it better reflects the consumer's experience of the beer. Most brewers will taste their beers regularly, at various stages of the brewing process. In addition to this, many breweries have a quality control department, which will conduct sensory evaluation sessions in order to get a wider range of feedback. See QUALITY CONTROL AND ASSURANCE. These sessions can be used to test new products, to assess the impact of a new brewing ingredient or method in an existing product, to learn more about a beer's shelf life and how its flavor evolves over time, and to get an idea of how the brewery's beers compare to other similar products on the market.

There are a number of tools that can be used to assist in the sensory evaluation of beer. The most common of these tools is a beer evaluation sheet. There are many different styles of beer evaluation sheets, but most of them will provide guidelines for features a taster should look for and comment on while assessing beer. Another common tool is the Beer Flavor Wheel. Developed by Morton Meilgaard in the 1970s, the Beer Flavor Wheel provides a wide range of beer descriptors. These are divided first into those perceived by sense of taste and those perceived in the aroma. The descriptors are then organized into 14 categories, each of which contains between one and six descriptors. Meilgaard's aim in creating this wheel was to establish a standard vocabulary for beer evaluation and to this day many organizations use his Beer Flavor Wheel as a reference tool. See FLAVOR WHEEL.

No matter how many tools and guidelines are used, sensory evaluation can never be fully objective. Factors such as the taster's diet, mood, experience, and personal preference, the tasting environment, and the time of day, as well as the sequence in which beers are served can all affect how a beer is perceived.

Brewers Publications, ed. *Evaluating beer.* Boulder, CO: Brewers Publications, 1993.

Ivory, Karen. *Making sense of smells.* Philadelphia: The Monell Connection, 2001.

Meilgaard, Morten, Gail Vance Civille, and B. Thomas Carr. *Sensory evaluation techniques,* 2nd ed. Boca Raton, FL: CRC Press, 1991.

Mosher, Randy. *Tasting beer.* North Adams, MA: Storey Publishing, 2009.

Stone, Herbert, and Joel L Sidel. *Sensory evaluation practices,* 2nd ed. San Diego, CA: Academic Press Inc, 1993.

Mirella G. Amato

Serebrianka (hop) is an old, relatively low-alpha Russian aroma hop of unknown origin and pedigree. It arrived in the U.S. Department of Agriculture Hop Research Center at Corvallis, Oregon, in 1971 as rhizome cuttings from the Institute for Plant Research, Leningrad, USSR (now St. Petersburg, Russia), but it was discarded in 1991 because of poor growth and a lack of disease resistance. Serebrianka is also known by the name Silver hop. Perhaps its most important contribution to beer is that it served as one of the ancestors of the American-developed hop variety Cascade, which has become one of the signature hops of many American craft beers.

See also CASCADE (HOP).

Horner, C. E., S. T. Likens, C. E. Zimmermann, and Alfred Haunold. Cascade, a new continental-type hop variety for the U.S. *Brewer's Digest* 47 (1972): 56–62.

Alfred Haunold

serving beer is a task that in many ways is far trickier than serving most wines. Almost all beer contains some carbonation, and unlike sparkling wine it generally forms a crown of foam. Getting beer into its glass with its carbonation intact and the correct volume of foam while achieving a nice visual presentation is an art form that takes some practice. Once we also take into account draught versus bottled beers, differing beer styles, differing carbonation levels, and widely varying glassware, we arrive at a realization that proper beer service requires attention to a number of details. At home, of course, we can do as we please, paying attention only to our guests and to our mutual enjoyment of the beer and the moment. In restaurant and bar settings, service of both beer and food should be more formalized and designed to maximize the customer's experience.

Restaurant and Bar Service

The service of any beer, whether draught or bottled, starts with the beer glass. First, it must be aroma free and absolutely clean—no oils, dust, detergent residue, or other foreign matter. Within the beer industry, this status is referred to as "beer clean." Beer foam is made up of a liquid/protein matrix that will break down quickly in the presence of even trace amounts of fats, oils, or detergents. Rapidly collapsing foam can be a fault within the beer itself, but it is more often related to glassware contaminants. Dust, foreign particles, and scratches will cause breakout of carbon dioxide from the liquid. A large area of bubbles observed clinging to the sides of a glass is a clear sign that the glass is either dirty or otherwise compromised. In a restaurant setting, dirty glasses should never reach the customer, but if they do, the customer ought to reject them and request replacements.

Most draught beer systems are designed to serve a glass of beer within several seconds. Normally, the glass is placed at a 45 degree angle below the spout and the tap opened quickly, allowing the beer to pour down the side of the glass. The glass is brought to an upright position when the glass is approximately three-quarters full, allowing the foam to rise to the appropriate level. Allowing the foam to settle for several seconds afterward will increase its density and allow the server to add a little more foam for a perfect pour. The appropriate amount of foam varies widely between beer types, but "1.5 fingers" might be said to be average. Many American bars serve beer with very little foam, leaving the beer looking soapy and unappealing. Foam is considered particularly important in Germany, where servers may spend a few minutes building a large head with a consistency approaching that of whipped cream. Weissbier is famous for its high carbonation and voluminous head formation, and traditional weissbier glassware is tall and vase-shaped to accommodate perhaps "3 fingers" of foam.

The service of bottled beer is, of course, different, especially in restaurant settings. The bottle should be presented to the customer before it is opened; this will help avoid any confusion as to what has been ordered. The server can use this as an opportunity to check that the beer is at the appropriate temperature and to see whether it is unfiltered and therefore contains a sediment. The beer should then be opened at the service station and brought back to the table for pouring. If the bottle was sealed with a cork, it is appropriate to present it to the customer, especially if the beer has been aged.

In the majority of cases, especially in more formal restaurants, the glassware should remain in place on the table while the beer is served. This requires skill, a steady hand, and some patience. Many beers, especially wheat beers and beers brewed in Belgian styles, may have very high levels of carbonation; not surprisingly these tend to be very foamy. However, even for most foamy beers, pouring a slow, thin stream down the center of the glass will achieve a fine-looking pour with a good ratio of liquid to foam. In the rare instance that this cannot be achieved with the glass on the table, the server can ask the customer whether the glass can be lifted. Having gained the customer's assent, the server may then lift the glass by its stem and pour the beer gently with the glass at an angle.

Beers that have been intentionally aged will often throw a sediment, even if they were originally filtered. Such beers should be poured very carefully and steadily to assure that no sediment ends up in the customer's glass. Sediments are harmless, but rarely taste particularly good in aged beers and often have unpleasantly gritty textures. The bottle may be left on the table for the customer to decide upon the final pour.

When pouring beers that contain sediment, it is best to pour carefully until the last 1 cm or half inch of beer and then stop, leaving the sediment behind in the bottle. The customer should be asked whether he or she would like the sediment added and, if not, whether the bottle should be removed from the table. Notable exceptions to this rule are Belgian witbiers and German weissbiers, which are always served intentionally hazy. In this case the last 2 cm or inch of beer can be retained in the bottle, the bottle can be swirled gently, and the sediment can be added through the center of the foam to fall through the liquid in a plume.

Serving Temperature

The serving temperature of beer has dramatic effects upon its flavor, aroma, and appearance. Beer has a very wide range of flavors and textures, and it is therefore not surprising that optimal serving temperatures vary as well. Especially in the United States, many beers are served too cold, a legacy of the country's long monoculture of mass market lagers. These beers were said to taste best "ice cold," but better beers rarely taste of anything much at all when served below 3.3°C (38°F). On most draught systems, it can be difficult to serve beer much warmer without experiencing excessive foaming, but warmer serving temperatures are possible when a system is well designed and properly balanced.

For bottled beers, of course, the situation is considerably easier; it is essentially possible to served bottled beer at any temperature. In the home setting, the achievement of the correct temperature can be as simple as taking a bottle out of the refrigerator and waiting. In the restaurant setting, some attention must be paid in advance. Cold temperatures will enhance sensations of bitterness, dryness, carbonation, and tannin and will often give beer a more refreshing quality. Colder temperatures also assist foam retention. However, at colder temperatures, volatilization of aromatic compounds slows dramatically, and beer loses much of its flavor and aroma; it will also tend to taste thinner. Conversely, warmer temperatures bring volatile elements to the fore and allow the beer to display its full range of flavor and aroma while accentuating body, maltiness, sweetness, and acidity. Proper beer serving temperature involves finding a happy balance that accentuates a beer's best qualities and, if necessary, suppresses any negative ones.

The vast majority of beers will show their best somewhere between 5.5°C and 12.7°C (42°F and 55°F). Lager beer flavors are ingredient driven, and cold fermentations do not develop many fruity flavors or aromatics. Colder temperatures tend to suit them because there is less to be lost by chilling. Darker lagers, especially heavier ones such as doppelbock, will enjoy a slightly warmer temperature to let their rich malt flavors evolve. Most wheat beers and popular American craft beer styles, such as India pale ale, do best at the lower end of this range. Many Belgian beers are warm fermented, delicate, and highly aromatic; most will taste their best in the center of this temperature range. The highest temperatures are reserved for British cask-conditioned beers. Contrary to foreign opinion, British ales are not served at "room temperature" (few drinks, including red wine, taste good at temperatures approaching 21°C [70°F]), but at a "cellar temperature" of about 11°C (52°F). Aged or vintage beers should also be served at these temperatures. Below are some general guidelines for best service temperatures.

- Serve pale lagers, wheat beers, pale ales, and India pale ales relatively cold, 5°C–8°C (42°F–46°F).
- Serve darker lagers, brown ales, farmhouse ales, sour beers, and pale abbey styles at cool temperatures, 7°C–9°C (45°F–48°F).
- Serve Irish stouts, darker and stronger abbey ales, and British summer ales at moderate temperatures, 9°C–11°C (48°F–52°F).
- Serve cask-conditioned ales, barley wines, imperial stouts, and aged "vintage beers" at lightly chilled cellar temperatures, 11°C–13°C (52°F–55°F).

Keep in mind that once the beer is in the glass it will tend to warm up, so there is little harm in serving a beer slightly below the ideal temperature and allowing it to warm into its optimal range.

Garrett Oliver

A **sheet filter** is a device for removing suspended particulate from beer. The filter construction consists of 4–5 mm (0.16–0.2 in) sheets pressed between plates with inlet and outlet channels. Modern filter sheets come in various nominally rated porosities, ranging from coarse to fine to sterile. The sheets themselves may be made from any number of materials, but they have traditionally been made from cellulose impregnated with diatomaceous earth. The sheets may be quickly blinded, depending on the turbidity of the beer to be filtered. Although it is easy to use otherwise, sheet filtration of turbid beer can be slow and cumbersome, requiring frequent back-flushing. This is why sheet filters tend to be more popular nowadays with small-batch breweries than with larger ones. Larger breweries tend to prefer membrane candle filters instead. See CANDLE FILTER. Considering that beer making has been around for at least 8,000 years and probably longer, beer filtration has a surprisingly brief history. The first beer filter was registered with the German Imperial Patent Office only on June 4, 1878, by Lorenz Adelbert Enzinger, a Bavarian from Wasserburg who had moved to Worms in the Rhineland. Enzinger's device consisted of several iron plates with paper leaves as a filter medium. These paper sheets had to be replaced after each filtration. That same year, Enzinger formed a company to manufacture and market his filter, and within just 8 years, he had sold his 1,000th filter. The first filter sheet capable of sterile filtration, that is, of trapping even tiny microbes, was developed in 1913 by the German chemist Friedrich Schmitthenner, who worked for the Seitz works, a company founded in 1887 in Bad Kreuznach. The Enzinger and Seitz works merged in 1982 and, after several additional mergers and acquisitions, have evolved into the modern German beverage bottling and packaging technology company KHS.

See also FILTRATION.

Horst Dornbusch

shelf life refers to the length of time during which a beer will stay in a desirable state in the trade. Frequently it is used synonymously with the term *stability*.

Most beers start to deteriorate from the time that they are bottled. While it is true that some beers, especially stronger varieties, can change over time in ways that lead to interesting and desirable flavors (via reactions similar to those occurring in some wines) most do not. See AGING OF BEER.

The shelf life of a beer may be declared on the label, in terms of a "Best Before" date or a filling date. The former refers to the date before which a product is ideally consumed. The latter gives the date on which the package was filled, usually with an injunction regarding how many days the beer will be in its best condition.

As beer is inherently resistant to contamination by pathogenic bacteria, there is no health risk associated with consuming it after the shelf life has expired. Indeed, in many markets some beer has certainly seen its best days well before the end of the allocated shelf life. "Best Before" dates are probably more frequently set on the basis of the time within which the brewer is confident that the beer will not develop undesirable turbidity. The time may even be nothing more than an "artificial" declaration driven by logistical considerations, with not even lip service paid to the flavor quality of the liquid in the container.

The shelf life of beer will depend on the packaging type, ranging from a matter of days for cask-conditioned ale once it has been broached, to several weeks for a kegged beer, to months for beer in bottles and cans, with the latter enjoying the advantage of the most airtight seal.

The instability of beer takes various forms, including susceptibility to certain spoilage organisms, sensitivity to light, and proneness to gushing. However, the most extensively studied forms of instability are colloidal (haze, non-biological) instability and flavor instability (staling). Of these, the biggest challenge by a wide margin is flavor instability. See COLLOIDAL HAZE and FLAVOR.

Even though many modern consumers equate crystalline clarity with quality in beer, the achievement of haze stability still seems to elude some brewers. See HAZE. While both beer drinkers and laboratory methods can agree upon the question of whether a beer is clear or not, there is more debate about the desirability of clarity. Interestingly, there are regional differences apparently developing in the mind of the consumer. In the eastern United States, for example, most beer drinkers expect sparkling clarity in most styles of beer, whereas many in the west of the country regard clarity with suspicion, suspecting that the beer is over-processed.

Among brewers there remain deliberations centering on the merits and demerits of downstream stabilization methods.

Flavor instability is altogether a more complex issue, stemming at least from the fact that a perceptible change in the level of any single flavor component may be construed as instability. Considering there may be some 2,000 flavor active species in beer, many of which display extremely low flavor thresholds, the problem is manifest. Even if brewers take a more conservative approach and suggest that far fewer compounds than this are significant through their changing levels during beer storage, the range of substances is still substantial. Confounding the situation further is the reality that, whereas most brewers deplore classic aged character (cardboard/wet paper flavors and aromas), there appear to be a very many customers who either don't recognize it, don't care about it, or even might desire it (this mirrors winemakers' experiences with cork taint, a problem that affects a fairly high percentage of wine bottles, but goes unnoticed by many wine drinkers). They are used to this aroma in their beers, often because the beer has travelled a long way for a long time to reach them. It has even been suggested that beers should be stressed to their ultimate, achieving aged character before leaving the brewery, with the intent of training the customer to accept aged character as the norm. That would certainly overcome the fundamental problem for brewers: if customers are accustomed to fresh beer, then it is desirable that they should always receive it in that condition, despite the enormous challenges involved. However, if customers are used to drinking a stale product (for example one that has been imported and which has traveled vast distances with agitation), then they will expect that flavor (rightly or wrongly depending on the brewer's philosophy). It is amusing to note that the term "stale," as applied to beer, was once a term describing a desirable aged quality, not the epithet it has become today.

Lewis, M.J., and C. W. Bamforth. *Essays in brewing science.* New York: Springer, 2006.

Charles W. Bamforth

Shepherd Neame Brewery is said to be Britain's oldest brewery, with a heritage that can be traced back to at least 1698. The port of Faversham in southeast England had already enjoyed a tradition of brewing when its mayor, Captain Richard Marsh, founded a brewery conveniently situated over an artesian well. Monks at a neighboring Benedictine abbey had long known that its pure spring water and locally grown malting barley produced a heady concoction.

Around 1741, ownership of Marsh's brewery passed to Samuel Shepherd, who was joined by his sons Julius and John. Obvious visionaries, they installed a revolutionary steam engine to grind malt and to pump water and started buying pubs, some of which are still owned by the brewery. A steam engine survives, as do unlined Russian teak mash tuns installed in 1914, plus the brewery's wood-panelled interior with its decorative hop moldings reflecting its position amid the hop yards of East Kent. An innovative visitor center set in a medieval hall creates a fine harmony.

Shepherd Neame's state-of-the-art brewhouse and its 370 pubs have earned accolades for social responsibility, environmental concerns, and community focus, culminating in a 2006 Queen's Award for sustainable development.

It remains that rarity in modern British brewing—an independent family company—now in its fifth generation from when Percy Beale Neame assumed control from the Shepherds in 1877. Its core ales are Spitfire (4.5% ABV), a malt and citrus-tinged delight, and the generously fruity Bishop's Finger (5.0% ABV).

See also BRITAIN.

Alastair Gilmour

shilling system is not only a traditional, predecimal, British currency denomination but also an old-style, uniquely Scottish measure for a beer's strength. In the 19th century, it referred to the pretax price of a British barrel (36 UK gal, about 43.2 US gal or 164 l) or a hogshead (54 UK gal, about 64.8 US gal) of ale. In those days, Scottish ales were brewed to a wide range of differing strengths, from a very weak gravity of perhaps 7.5 P (OG 1.030) to a whopping gravity of perhaps 32.5 P (OG 1.130). The stronger the brew, the more it cost, from roughly 60 to 160 shillings. The classic way of making Scottish ales is by the parti-gyle method, which involves boiling and fermenting the early, heavier runnings and the later, weaker runnings of the same mash separately. See PARTI-GYLE. Parti-gyle beers are often blended from two consecutive batches and sometimes from different-strength runnings. The strongest finished ales were often called Scotch ales or Wee Heavy ales; the mid-range brews were called Export ales and the weaker ones Scottish ales or Two-Penny ales. This nomenclature, however, was never applied consistently, and the technical dividing lines that separate the various shillings ratings have always been somewhat fluid. A typical 60-shilling Two-Penny may have a gravity of 7.5°Plato–8.75°Plato (1.030–1.035); a 70-shilling Export 8.75°P–10°P (1.035–1.040); an 80-shilling Export 10°P–13.75°P (1.040–1.055); a 90-shilling Wee Heavy 13.75°P–19.25°P (1.055–1.075); and a 140-shilling outlier 23.75°P–32.5°P (1.095–1.130). Shilling ratings are sometimes denoted by the old currency symbol "/-," with "80-shilling" becoming "80/-." The modern drinker, when these antiquated terms are used, simply knows to expect a beer of "normal" strength (4.5% to 5.5% alcohol by volume) to be designated "80 shillings" and something lighter below this number and something heavier above it.

Noonan, Greg J. *Scotch ale, classic beer style,* Series 8. Boulder, CO: Brewers Publications, 1993.

Spake, Neil. *The shilling system.* http://www.scottishbrewing.com/history/shilling.php/ (accessed January 24, 2011).

Horst Dornbusch

Shimwellia

See OBESUMBACTERIUM PROTEUS.

shipping

See BULK TRANSPORT and DISTRIBUTION.

shive is the plug used to close the bunghole in a cask after filling. It resides on the top of the belly of traditional beer casks. Shives are made of wood (usually sycamore or oak) or plastic and driven into the bunghole by a mallet. Nylon is also used but is less flexible than wood as the latter can expand when in contact with the beer, ensuring a tight fit. Nylon shives, however, can be easier to remove for cask cleaning.

Size standardization has been slow and small diameter/thickness variations exist in the UK market. Example dimensions are 50–60 mm in diameter with a tapered thickness of 15–18 mm.

The shive has a thin central section which can be punched through to give a hole of 8 mm diameter for the addition of finings after filling. See FININGS. This is sealed with a tutmade from cork or nylon. The tut is removed and replaced with a spile for traditional cask beer venting. See SPILE. This hole is also the entry point for so-called blanket gas (carbon dioxide) that extends cask beer shelf life; it also provides the access point for a dipstick used to measure liquid/ullage content. Shives are used only once, then removed and discarded when the cask is emptied and washed.

Hornsey, I.S. *Brewing*. Cambridge: Royal Society of Chemistry, 1999.

Chris J. Marchbanks

Siebel Institute of Technology, North America's oldest brewing school, was founded in Chicago as John E. Siebel's Chemical Laboratory by John Ewald Siebel in 1868.

J. E. Siebel was born near Düsseldorf, Germany, in 1845 and earned a PhD from the University of Berlin before moving to Chicago in 1866. Siebel was a very important contributor to brewing technology in the United States, publishing many papers in the journal he edited, *The Western Brewer*, as well as other brewing journals.

In association with a partner, Siebel began conducting brewing classes as early as 1882, but when his sons joined the business in the 1890s, a regular program of classes covering all aspects of brewing and packaging was established, conducted in both German and English. The name was changed from The Zymotechnic Institute to Siebel Institute of Technology in 1910.

After Prohibition a second company called J. E. Siebel and Sons was created to sell specialty items such as yeast and kettle finings to brewers. The Siebel companies remained family businesses for much of their history, managed by brothers Ron and Bill Siebel from the 1960s onward. In 1992 J. E. Siebel and Sons was sold to Quest and in 2000 Siebel Institute of Technology was sold to Montréal-based yeast manufacturer Lallemand.

A full range of brewing classes continues to be taught in Chicago, with fermentation classes in Montreal and other programs offered in cooperation with Doemens, a brewing school in Munich.

See also DOEMENS ACADEMY.

Seibel Institute of Technology. http://www.siebelinstitute.com/ (accessed January 18, 2011).

Randy Mosher

Sierra Nevada Brewing Company is the seventh largest brewing company in the United States. It produces a diversity of year-round and seasonal beers. The flagship brand is Sierra Nevada Pale Ale, with its characteristic grapefruit-like aroma owing to Cascade hops. This beer is widely credited as the progenitor of the American pale ale style. See AMERICAN PALE ALE.

The company was founded in Chico in 1979 by Ken Grossman and Paul Camusi with $100,000 borrowed from family. See GROSSMAN, KEN. Both Grossman and Camusi had been home-brewers; Grossman had previously opened a homebrew store in Chico. Their first brewery was on a dirt road outside the city and used equipment obtained from failed breweries and the soft-drink and dairy industries. The brewery's name came from Ken Grossman's favorite climbing venue.

The first batch of Sierra Nevada Pale Ale was brewed in November 1980 but it and the ensuing eight batches were discarded because they were not of the standard expected by the partners. It was in 1981 that the first satisfactory brew emerged, alongside a porter and a stout. In that year the production output was 500 barrels. All of the beer was bottle-conditioned as funds were insufficient to buy a carbonating device. Slowly, local sales picked up—especially to the students at Chico State University—and soon the product was being shipped to San Francisco, where an early devotee was Jerry Garcia of the Grateful Dead, whose fans in turn started to enjoy the brew. When an article on the exciting new brewing company appeared in the *San Francisco Examiner* Sunday magazine, Sierra Nevada got onto the beer map. Another article in *The Village Voice* in New York alerted the East Coast to the product. In due course the chief beverage buyer for Safeway supermarkets, a man with a daughter at Chico State, brought the Pale Ale onto that store's supermarket shelves.

By 1987 Sierra Nevada was producing some 12,000 US barrels and was in the market in seven states. As the company grew exponentially (despite a reluctance to advertise, a policy that continues today), they relocated to a new site in 1988 and embarked on major expansions, upgrades, and installations. By 1989 output was a little over 30,000 barrels and broke through 100,000 barrels in 1993. Three years later output was 265,000 barrels from 80 employees.

In 1997 Sierra Nevada began construction on a second brewhouse allowing for the production of 600,000 barrels of beer per year, with the possibility of expansion. A wastewater treatment plant was introduced, the first stage in an ongoing drive toward environmental excellence—continued through the installation of fuel cells in 2005. By 1999 production was 420,000 barrels and Grossman had bought out Camusi. A year later the company's conference room/auditorium (The Big Room) was opened, to complement the taproom and restaurant. The beer was now sold in all states of the country. Production was 541,000 barrels in 2001. Two years later, Crossman tested the international market for the first time with shipments to the UK. Volumes as of 2010 are well over 700,000 barrels.

Over the years, Sierra Nevada Brewing has gained a reputation for excellence and technical stringency. Aside from their popular Pale Ale, Sierra Nevada also produces a porter, a stout, a well-loved barley wine called Bigfoot, and several seasonal offerings.

Sierra Nevada Brewing Co. http://www.sierranevada.com/ (accessed September 10, 2010).

Charles W. Bamforth

silica gel is a beer stabilizer that reduces the level of haze that can form in finished beer. It works by removing the small proteins or polypeptides that react with polyphenols, which are the basis for the most common type of beer haze. The use of silica gel as an adsorptive beer stabilizer was first introduced in the 1960s. The two types commonly used in brewing are hydrogel and xerogel.

A difference in production makes for different handling characteristics of these materials but leaves the function of silica gel unchanged. Silica gel adsorbs those hydrophilic, haze-active proteins with a molecular weight of approximately 40,000 kDa and larger, while not interacting with those hydrophobic proteins that promote positive foam development with an approximate molecular weight of 10,000 to 20,000 kDa.

Silica gel is mixed in water prior to use and normally is dosed into unfiltered beer just prior to filtration. Because it is not soluble in beer, the silica gel itself is also removed by the filter, along with the proteins. Its mode of action is very fast, requiring just a few minutes to adsorb proteins.

The main difference between hydrogel and xerogel is that hydrogel has a higher moisture content, usually 60% to 70%, needs greater mixing time to adequately disperse, and is less expensive. Xerogel disperses readily in water, but it is very dusty when handled because of its low moisture content of about 5% and has been known to negatively affect filter flow. Another feature of xerogel is that it does not readily dissolve in a caustic solution, which can have an impact on regenerable filter systems.

See also ADSORBENTS, HAZE, and POLYPHENOLS.

Hough, J. S. "Post-fermentation treatments." In *The biotechnology of malting and brewing*, 139–43. Cambridge, UK: Cambridge University Press, 1994.

O'Rourke, T. Colloidal stabilization of beer. *The Brewer International* 2 (2002): 23–25.

Andrew Fratianni

Simcoe (hop) is a dual-purpose hop that can be used for both bittering and aroma. It was bred by Yakima Chief Ranches and released in 2000. Charles Zimmermann is the published patent inventor. Because this is a proprietary hop, its genealogy has not been disclosed. Simcoe matures early to mid-season and typically yields about 1,040 to 1,130 kg (2,300 to 2,500 lb) per acre. The variety is moderately resistant to powdery mildew and it keeps well in storage. Although not used much as a bittering hop, many craft brewers and homebrewers favor Simcoe for its unique aroma profile composed of piney, woody, and grapefruit citrus notes mixed with slightly dank and spicy notes of onion and garlic. These aromas make the hop resemble Cascade and Chinook, with some elements resembling the key aromas of Amarillo, CTZ, and Summit. See AMARILLO (HOP), CASCADE (HOP), CHINOOK (HOP), and CTZ (HOP). Simcoe has an alpha acid range of 12% to 14%, a beta acid range of 4% to 5%, and a cohumulone content of 15% to 20%. The essential oil spectrum is divided among 60% to 65% myrcene, 10% to 15% humulene, 5% to 8% caryophyllene, and less than 1% farnesene. Simcoe is particular popular in American India pale ales (IPAs) and "double IPAs," especially as a dry hop. Used judiciously in a blend, it can provide a pleasant "orange crush" element to beer aromatics.

See also DOUBLE IPA, DRY HOPPING, and INDIA PALE ALE.

Matthew Brynildson

Sinebrychoff Brewery is a brewery and soft drinks maker that was founded in Helsinki, Finland in 1819 by Russian emigrant Nikolai Sinebrychoff. Today, Sinebrychoff is one of the oldest and largest breweries in Northern Europe and the oldest consumer goods producer in Finland. Sinebrychoff has about 1,000 employees as well as a modern production facility in Kerava, some 30 km (18 mi) north of Helsinki, with an annual output of approximately four million hectoliters. Since 2000, it has been part of the international Carlsberg Group. See CARLSBERG GROUP. Sinebrychoff's best known beers are its lines of Koff and Karhu pale lagers, both brewed in the Bavarian tradition, as well as its well-loved Sinebrychoff Porter, a classic 7.2 ABV Baltic porter. The company claims that the yeast used for the ale originates from the now-defunct Park Royal Brewery in London, once one of the Guinness brewing locations. This porter has a rich mahogany color and a strongly malty aroma of caramel, coffee, and chocolate, with a hint of licorice in the finish. Despite its relatively light ABV, this beer can age quite well for several years. Next to beer, Sinebrychoff produces ciders and various brands of non-alcoholic beverages. It is also Finland's only Coca-Cola bottler.

See also FINLAND.

Gerrit Blüemelhuber

singel, or *single,* is the name given to the relatively light types of beer that Trappist monks brew for their own tables. Although Belgium's Trappist breweries produce some of the world's most beguiling beers, the monks themselves rarely drink the beers they send out into the secular world. Most Trappist beers are quite strong, and it is possible that the monks have thought that drinking strong beers would interfere with prayer and work. Traditionally, however, beer was a major sustenance within monasteries, so the monks developed lighter beers that they largely kept to themselves. The Trappist versions are rarely seen commercially, but a number of secular breweries make beers in the same vein. They sometimes refer to them as singel, taking after the naming tradition set by the stronger "dubbel" and "tripel"; occasionally they are referred to as "patersbier," or "father's beer."

Although these beers cannot necessarily be said to constitute a style per se, they do have a number of things in common. Most are golden, although light amber is sometimes seen as well, and all are top fermenting and dry. They generally have about 5% alcohol by volume, although some are much lighter. They tend to be relatively hoppy versus their light gravities, and this gives the beers a refreshing quality. All are fermented at warm temperatures by Belgian yeasts, giving the beers their trademark fruity and spicy qualities.

Singels probably originally developed as "small beers," brewed from further steepings of the mash after the heavier wort has already been collected for stronger beers. The Trappist versions include the golden Chimay Dorée, Westmalle Extra, and Petite Orval, also known as Orval Verte (Green), and Achel "5," of which there is a blond version and a darker version. Some bottles inevitably escape the walls, but these beers are generally found only at the monasteries and the establishments connected to them. Beer enthusiasts collect, share, and trade them; they are not generally deep or particularly exciting, but they are racy and refreshing, and their rareness gives them a certain caché. The monks, in the meantime, will enjoy these beers daily, saving the stronger beers for holidays. The best known secular commercial example is Witkap Pater Singel, brewed by Brouwerij Slaghmuylder, but a number of American craft breweries have produced their own versions as well.

See also ABBEY BEERS, ACHEL BREWERY, CHIMAY, ORVAL BREWERY, and WESTMALLE BREWERY.

Garrett Oliver

Singha

See BOON RAWD BREWERY.

Sissi (barley) is a Germany spring brewing barley variety that was very popular in the 1990s, especially in southern and eastern Germany. It was bred by Saatzucht Josef Breun GmbH & Co KG of Herzogenaurach near Nuremberg in Bavaria and was registered with the Bundessortenamt (the German government's crop-licensing agency) in 1991. In its heyday, many brewers favored malted Sissi as a pilsner-type base malt because of its good disastatic power and its ability to produce full-bodied, malt-accented beers with good head retention. Sissi had several agronomic drawbacks, however. Its yield per hectare was only average and it was fairly susceptible to mildew (Erysiphe graminis). In the brewhouse, too, its extract yield was only average and it is now easily surpassed in extract values by more recently bred brewing barley varieties. Today, therefore, Sissi has disappeared entirely both from the official list of recommended barley varieties maintained by the Bundessortenamt and from the catalogs of commercial barley breeders and traders. However, Sissi is still planted in very limited quantities, perhaps only a few thousand tons per year, almost exclusively in Bavaria, and usually on a special-order basis just for small brewers who have formulated their recipes specifically for this variety.

Thomas Kraus-Weyermann

A **six-row malt** is derived from the kernels of six-row, instead of two-row, barley varieties. The term "six-row" refers to the morphology of the barley spike or head. Spikelets are arranged in an alternate pattern at each node along the rachis (stem) of the spike. In six-row varieties, the two lateral spikelets along with the central spikelet are fertile and produce a total of three kernels. The kernel count at each node on the rachis, therefore, is six. This arrangement of kernels gives the head a round appearance compared with the flat appearance of the two-row spike. It is only a single gene that distinguishes two-row from six-row barley varieties, but the two types each have their own separate breeding programs and thus constitute entirely different market classes of grain. In general, six-row barley is less plump and has a thicker husk and, after malting, will have lower extract yields, a higher protein content, and greater enzyme activity compared with two-row varieties. Because these characteristics are genetically determined, breeders can manipulate them. In theory, therefore, the differences between two-row and six-row barley traits can even be diminished. For example, breeders are now working on increasing the malt extract potential of six-row barley. The variety Morex is an example of this breeding direction. See MOREX (BARLEY). The only characteristic that cannot be merged in any future barley variety is the kernel shape, because it is strongly influenced by the arrangement of kernels on the spike. In a six-row spike the lateral kernels will tend to be thinner, whereas in a two-row spike all the kernels will generally be more uniformly plump. Related to plumpness is husk content, which will generally be greater in thinner kernels than in plump ones. The result of this difference is a proportionally larger amount of flavor influencing husk-derived phenolic compounds in the finished beer. See PHENOLIC.

Six-row malt is used primarily in North America breweries, whereas two-row malt is used most everywhere else in the world. The key regions for six-row barley cultivation are Mexico, the midwestern United States, and, to a lesser extent, the Prairie Provinces of Canada. In the United States, several large brewers use a blend of two- and six-row malts in their mashes. A number of factors may have contributed to the preference of six-row malt in North America. Historically, six-row barley varieties became more prominent because they are better adapted to growing conditions in the Midwest, where two-row varieties tend to be more susceptible to leaf diseases. Recently bred two-row varieties, however, have exhibited much greater resistance to leaf diseases as well. Many brewers in the United States, especially the large ones, also use enzyme-free adjuncts, such as rice or corn, in their mashes and, therefore, need the enzyme strength of six-row barley to obtain sufficient diastatic power for proper saccharification. See ADJUNCTS and DIASTATIC POWER. In craft breweries, where all-malt mashes are more frequently employed, two-row malts are often used as base malts, whereas caramel malts and roasted malts are frequently six-row varieties. The future of six-row barley supplies, however, is not certain because many farmers in the American Midwest are shifting toward other crops, often induced by the growing demand for biofuels.

See also TWO-ROW MALT.

Kevin Smith

skimming a term referring to the removal of a substance from the surface of a fermentation, usually one taking place in an open vessel. The precise meaning depends on the type of beer being brewed. For lager fermentations, skimming usually refers to the removal of proteinaceous cold break material that floats to the top of the wort soon after it is cooled into the fermenter. This material, which is brown and granular in appearance, is felt by some brewers to be detrimental to beer flavor. Others prefer to leave it intact, citing evidence that it contains nutrients that promote healthy fermentation. Once high krausen is underway, another residue may eventually form on top of the foam. Called brandhefe by German brewers, this may also be skimmed because it contains hop resins that may coarsen the beer's bitterness.

In traditional British ale brewing, skimming refers to the recovery of brewing yeast toward the end of fermentation in a fermenting vessel where a "top cropping yeast" is used. Yeast is normally skimmed from relatively shallow square or round fermenters with wort depths of 2 to 4 m (6.5 to 13.0 ft); the vessel may be open or closed (with a top cover). Yeast is not skimmed from tall cylindro-conical fermenters; yeasts in such tanks will usually sediment to the bottom of the vessels. When a beer is fermented using a top cropping yeast strain, the yeast will separate out from the body of the fermentation and rise to the beer surface. This will happen when most of the nutrients have been used up, so the yeast has no reason to stay in the wort; it will therefore flocculate (combine together in clumps) and form a thick, creamy yeast head on the beer. At a predetermined time, usually when a fermentation has reached a particular gravity, the yeast will be taken from the surface in a number of ways, depending on the brewery. The most common method is to suck the yeast off the vessel using a vacuum pipe attached to a tray that is floating on the surface of the beer; a special skimmer or paddle is used to pull the yeast into the tray and vacuum pipe. The yeast skimmed from a vessel may be collected and stored for use in following fermentations, with the excess often sold another brewery, a distillery, or as a by-product for animal feed.

See also BRANDHEFE, FERMENTATION, FLOCCULATION, and HIGH KRÄUSEN.

Paul KA Buttrick

slack malt is finished malt that has been allowed to pick up moisture during storage.

At the end of the malting process, the finished malt is dried in a kiln, achieving average moisture content, by weight, of approximately 3%–5%. Malt quality stability during storage is critically dependent on its moisture content. Over time, moisture levels above normal specifications can cause two principal problems: a decline of enzymatic power and the toughening of the grain husk. The enzyme degradation erodes the malt's ability to effect conversion of starch into sugars during the mash. The grain hull, having gone from brittle to leathery, doesn't break properly when milled, and this leads to various problems during lautering. For both of these reasons, brewhouse extract will be compromised and subsequent processing may be problematic. See LAUTERING. Normal malt moistures are not conducive to insect proliferation, but damp malt provides a breeding ground for pests, and mold may grow as well. Malt moisture levels above 6% are generally considered unacceptable.

Malt is hygroscopic, meaning that it tends to soak up moisture from its surroundings. It must be protected from any opportunity to pick up moisture after it leaves the kiln—which it will do from air under normal ambient conditions. Before the industrialization of the brewing industry in the 18th century, both malting and brewing were largely cottage industries. In those days, brewers and maltsters could protect a heap of malt by storing it under a layer of dry hay that would absorb moisture from ambient damp air. Modern methods involve tight seals—sacks for malt should be lined with plastic, international shipping containers similarly should have the malt contained in a plastic liner, and silos and conveyors need to be weather-tight. Trucks for road transport will often have roll tops, which need to be inspected before each filling to ensure their integrity. See BULK TRANSPORT.

In storage, malt should be kept separately from any raw barley being stored, as raw barley, having a moisture content of 13%–15%, will exude its moisture into the surrounding air, and the malt will absorb it, resulting in slack malt.

Colin J. West

Sládek (hop) is named after the Czech word for "brewer." It was released by the Hop Research

Institute in Žatec (Saaz) in 1994, after 25 years of breeding efforts. Sládek was bred from a Saaz "Osvald clone" crossed with Northern Brewer. See NORTHERN BREWER (HOP) and SAAZ (HOP). Alpha acids in Sládek range from 4.5% to 8.5%, of which 24% are cohumulone. Beta acids range from 5% to 9%. The alpha acids are slightly unstable in storage. In terms of essential oils, this hop has an unusually low myrcene content of less than 1%. Notably floral hops, by comparison, generally have about 35% myrcene. The balsamic, resinous humulene amounts to about 34% of essential oils, whereas the spicy carophyllene amounts to 12%. The floral farnesene amounts to only 0.5% of the total oils. Sládek matures semilate in the season and has a fairly high average yield, 2,200 to 2,400 kg/ha (roughly 1,950 to 2,150 lb/acre). The variety is resistant to downy mildew but slightly susceptible to powdery mildew. In the brewhouse, Sládek is best used as complement to, rather than a replacement of, Saaz in top-quality lagers.

Jelínek, L., M. Šneberger, M. Karabín, and P. Dostálek. Comparison of Czech hop cultivars based on their contents of secondary metabolites. *Czech Journal of Food Science* 28 (2010): 309–16.

Victoria Carollo Blake

Slovenian hops. Attempts to grow hops in Slovenia date back to 1844. Saaz hops and Bavarian hops were brought to the region but did not grow well. A British hop, mislabeled "Golding," was imported instead, and it flourished. The resulting hops, now known as Styrian Golding, are probably a derivation of Fuggle, not English Golding. Still, they have become the cultivar that is most closely associated with Slovenia. Some Styrian Golding is also cultivated across the border from Slovenia in neighboring Austria. Another uniquely Slovenian cultivar is Bačka. It has a murky background, but is probably of central European origin. Bačka was one of the primary hops of the region through much of the 20th century. Today, Slovenia has a large variety of bitter and aroma hops to offer, most of which are produced from local breeding programs. See BAČKA (HOP), FUGGLE (HOP), and STYRIAN GOLDING (HOP). Once a region of the former Yugoslavia, Slovenia accounts for about 2% of the global hop production.

Val Peacock

small beer, a type of weak beer that from medieval times until the 19th century was the staple drink of most of the population of England in preference to water. Small beer was usually produced by fermentation of wort from the second or third wetting and extraction of a mash after the brewer had drawn off stronger wort for ale production. This procedure had the advantage of economy in giving good yield from the materials, but it generally resulted in a product with suspect keeping qualities and poor flavor. An alternative method, particularly favored when it was necessary to brew small beer in the summer months when demand was greatest, was to make a separate single extraction of a suitably small quantity of a fresh batch of malt. This latter method was generally recognized to yield a superior if more expensive product. Small beer, which was brewed both domestically and by commercial brewers, was drunk throughout the day at meals by all classes and ages of the population. Until modern supplies became common, water quality was often dubious and it was considered potentially dangerous to drink. The alcoholic strength of small beer must necessarily have been variable, with recipes suggesting a likely alcohol content of 1%–3% alcohol by volume (ABV). In colonial America, some versions contained non-malt sugars, often molasses. Modern versions of small beer are rare, but the Anchor Brewery Company of San Francisco produces a small beer with an alcohol content of 3.3% ABV from the second extraction of the grist from production of a barley wine. See ANCHOR BREWING COMPANY. Shakespeare seems to have despised small beer because he mentions it more than once in his plays. In *Othello*, the villainous Iago taunts Desdemona with the phrase, "To suckle fools and chronicle small beer." Over the centuries "small beer" has passed into the English language as a description of something trifling and of little value.

Sambrook, Pamela. *Country house brewing in England 1500–1900*. London: Hambledon Press, 1996.

Ray Anderson

Smaragd (hop) is an aroma hop developed largely as a Hallertauer Mittelfrueh derivative at the Hüll Hop Research Center in the Hallertau region of Bavaria, Germany. See HALLERTAUER MITTELFRUEH (HOP). *Smaragd* is the German word for emerald.

Commercially, this hop is also known as Hallertau Smaragd. Its primary use is in Bavarian lagers and Belgian-style ales. Smaragd is grown almost exclusively in Germany, where it matures mid-late in the season. It has an average yield of roughly of 1,850 kg/ha (1,650 lb/acre), and it has good resistance to downy mildew, but only average to low resistance to powdery mildew. The hop keeps well in storage. The alpha acid rating of this hop is a moderate 4% to 6%, the beta acid rating 3.5% to 5.5%, and the cohumulone a very low 13% to 18% of the alpha acids. Regarding essential oils, this variety has about 20% to 40% myrcene, 30% to 50% humulene, 9% to 14% carophyllene, and less than 1% floral farnesene. The variety also has a relatively high level of linalool, 0.9% to 1.4%. Linalool is an essential oil that imparts a citrus or bergamot aroma to the beer. The bouquet and flavor of Smaragd is somewhat like that of Hallertauer Mittelfrueh, showing predominately fruity, hoppy, and flowery notes.

Steinhaus, M., W. Wilhelm, and P. Schieberle. Comparison of the most odour-active volatiles in different hop varieties by application of a comparative aroma extract dilution analysis. *European Food Research Technology* 226 (2007): 45–55.

Verband Deutscher Hopfenpflanzer (Association of German Hopgrowers). "The spirit of beer. Hops from Germany." http://www.cob.sfasu.edu/csc/gharber/public_html/bb/hopfenm_engl.pdf/ (accessed October 27, 2010).

Victoria Carollo Blake

smoked beers, as the name implies, is a beer that has derived a smoky flavor and aroma from the addition to the grist of a certain portion of smoked malt. Such malt usually picks up its smokiness in the malt house, where it is dried—after steeping and germinating—in a direct-fired kiln that is heated by a smoky fuel such as juniper, beech wood, or peat. See MALT. Before the innovations of the Industrial Revolution and the introduction of the indirect-fired kiln in the early 1800s, all kilns were direct-fired. This meant that virtually all malt had flavors influenced by smoke; less so, if the fuel was fairly clean-burning coke; more so if it was slow-smoldering, high-resin, unseasoned softwood. See KILNING and WHEELER, DANIEL. The most favored wood varieties for smoke-kilning malt are ash, beech, and oak. Peat, too, has been used as a traditional fuel for smoke-kilning malt, especially in the Scottish Highland and Islands. Peat formed from partially decayed vegetation in bogs, marshes, and wetlands after the retreat last ice age some 7,000 to 8,000 years ago. Scottish peat-smoked malts impart aromas and flavors to fermented extracts used to distill many Scotch and Irish whiskeys. Historically, peat malts have not played a significant role in the brewing of Scottish ales, but many modern home-brewers and non-Scottish craftbrewers have started to add such malts to their ale grist for their interpretations of these beer styles.

Because a brewer can add smoked malt to any beer, there is some debate as to whether or not smoked beer can constitute a style proper, or if "smoked" is just one of many possible descriptors in the vocabulary of brewers and beer tasters. There are legitimate arguments on both sides, but, regardless of where one comes down on this issue, there appears to be universal agreement that one type of smoked beer is, indeed, a style of its own, largely for historical reasons. This is the Bamberger rauchbier, an almost bacon-scented lager made with malt that has been smoked-kilned over well-seasoned beech wood logs. The brewing of rauchbier is documented as the early Middle Ages and is considered a regional specialty of Franconia, a region in central Bavaria. Rauchbier is still produced by many small and mid-size Franconian breweries. The most famous of the Franconian rauchbier brewers is Brauerei Heller-Trum, better known as Schlenkerla, a brewery and pub in the old town of Bamberg. See SCHLENKERLA. This brewery still makes its own malt, smoked over a firebox within a barely mechanized malting facility. See BAVARIA and RAUCHBIER.

Most smoked beers nowadays, however, rauchbier and otherwise, are made with commercially available smoked malt, with the most prominent made in Bamberg by the family-owned Weyermann maltings. This malt is made by the traditional method of kiln-drying the germinated grain with seasoned beech wood. It is kilned to a relatively pale color of only 3 to 6 EBC (1.7 to 2.8°L) to preserve the malt's enzymatic power. Rauchmalz can be used for varying degrees of smokiness, in any amount up to 100 percent, in any grist bill. American craft breweries in particular have used these malts to create a dizzying array of flavors in their beers. Other than Schlenkerla, perhaps the best-known beer made with smoked malt is the Alaskan Brewing Company's

Alaskan Smoked Porter, which was first introduced in 1988 and has since won numerous awards at prestigious national and international competitions. This brewery smokes its own malt in small batches using local alder wood in a commercial food smoker. See ALASKAN BREWING COMPANY.

Outside of Franconia, the phenolic character of smoked beer is unfamiliar and somewhat shocking to the average beer drinker, even within Germany. While poorly brewed smoked beers can emerge with unfortunate flavors reminiscent of ashtrays, the best of them can pleasantly evoke campfires. This can give these beers an unparalleled affinity with food, especially smoked meats and fish. Even if the accompanying food isn't smoked, many foods that meld well with smoked flavors will pair nicely with a range of smoked beers.

Horst Dornbush and Sepp Wejwar

smoked malt is the base malt for smoked lagers or ales. The most common use of smoked malt, however, is not for beer, but for whisky, especially Scotch. Many traditional Scottish distilleries—several of whom still have their own maltings—rely on peat-smoked malt for their mashes. Whisky malt is usually dried and cured in peat-fueled, direct-fired kilns. Because peated malt tends to be somewhat acrid, it is rarely used in brewing. When it is used, it is never a base malt, but is only added to the grist in fairly small quantities, just to add flavor complexity.

Smoked malt for brewing—often referred to by its German name of Rauchmalz—is usually based on two-row spring barley and is invariably smoked over hardwood. Softer woods, such as pine, are too resinous to produce a pleasant-tasting smoke. The favored fuel for beer-malt smoking is beechwood, which imparts a slightly bacony flavor to the malt and thus to the finished beer. Other hardwood varieties are also suitable. One North American brewery, the Alaskan Brewing Company in Juneau, Alaska, makes an award-winning smoked porter based on finished pale malt that is smoked over alderwood. The classic beer style using smoked malt, however, is rauchbier, a medieval lager that may be brewed to varying strengths. Rauchbier is still made by several breweries in and around the city of Bamberg in the Franconia region of Bavaria. See RAUCHBIER and SMOKED BEERS. Several traditional Rauchbier breweries, including Schlenkerla and Spezial in Bamberg, continue to make their own beechwood-smoked malt from scratch, exclusively for their own beers. Bamberg is the center of the universe for smoked beers, and the local Weyermann maltings sends beech-smoked malt to craft breweries around the world.

During the steeping and germination phases, smoked malt is treated like any other malt. See MALT. The kiln, however, is a dedicated piece of equipment used only for smoked malt. It may be direct fired with the beechwood logs as the only heating element as well as the smoke source. Alternatively, the kiln may be indirect fired, with an auxiliary beechwood fire used primarily as the smoke source. In either case, the smoke must be allowed to pass through the grain bed. Before beechwood logs can be used for smoke kilning, they must be seasoned in the open air for several years. This reduces, but does not eliminate, their moisture. If the wood is too wet, it will not burn; if it is too dry, it will not smoke. Only if it is correctly aged will it produce a mellow and pleasant smoke. To ensure homogeneous smoking of the drying grain in the kiln, the grain bed must not be deeper than 60 cm (about 2 ft). The kilning process takes about 36 to 48 h. During the first 30 to 40 h, the grain is gently dried to allow the smoke to penetrate past the husks well into the endosperms. During the final 6 to 8 h, the malt is smoke cured at a temperature not exceeding roughly 85°C (185°F). Temperature control is essential to ensure that the grain's enzymes do not become denatured. As a consequence, smoked malt is as capable of conversion in the mash as pale malt. It can be used in any proportion desired, from just a few percent to 100% of the grain bill, and it can be added to any beer style. See BASE MALT. A beer brewed from 100% smoked malt will have the color of a pilsner or a pale ale, whereas darker beers usually acquire their color from varying additions of caramel and roasted malts.

Thomas Kraus-Weyermann

smut is among the most prevalent barley diseases and can be found anywhere the grain is grown. The flowering heads of affected plants are covered by sporing structures of the fungi Ustilago nuda (loose smut) or Ustilago hordei (covered smut). These appear as either olive or dark brown spore masses, respectively, and are easily dispersed to spread the disease through the crop. Some smut

Smut is a fungal disease that can have a catastrophic effect on barley yields. DAMIAN HERDE/SHUTTERSTOCK

spores are covered, that is, contained within a membrane. These are less likely to be dispersed until harvest time when mechanical agitation from the harvesting machinery may release them into the air. Dispersed spores can infect the developing seeds of adjacent plants by penetrating the seed embryos during their development. Smut is a very pernicious disease, and early infections tend to spread systemically through the entire plant, penetrating most of its parts during the growth cycle. Infected plants may appear normal until the seed head emerges. In the seed head smut destroys the embryo and leaves only a small amount of plant tissue intact. The result is a catastrophic effect on yield. A variety of fungicides are effective against the disease, but proper crop rotation and the sowing of uninfected seeds can break the cycle from one harvest to the next.

See also BARLEY DISEASES.

Keith Thomas

snakebite is a mixture of lager and alcoholic cider that is sometimes euphemistically referred to as a "beer cocktail." Technically, as a mix of drinks, it is a cocktail, but beyond that technicality it has little in common with what we generally think of as cocktails.

Snakebite is popular in Britain and had its heyday in the 1980s, when it was a popular drink among students and youth subcultures such as "Goths" and "punks." Often a shot of blackcurrant cordial would be added, to create "snakebite and black," "Diesel," or "Purple Nasty."

These names give some clue as to snakebite's appeal among young, budget-conscious drinkers who are often more interested in the intoxicating qualities of alcohol than its flavor: Snakebite is cloudy, looks and tastes unappetizing, and is commonly believed to get you drunk more quickly than lager or cider separately.

For this reason, there is an urban myth that snakebite is illegal in Britain; this is not true. Pubs are not allowed to serve half pints of snakebite, because this would mean serving incomplete measures of both cider and lager (draught products may only legally be sold in third, half, or full pint measures) but they are perfectly at liberty to serve a half of cider and a half of lager in a pint glass. However, some pubs reserve the right to refuse to do so thanks to the drink's reputation and its tendency to attract undesirable drinkers, particularly in a climate of concern over binge drinking.

Pete Brown

snap malt is a traditional English malt from the days of floor malting and direct-fired kilns. See FLOOR MALTING. It is made much like regular pale malt, except for a final high-heat drying stage in the kiln. One of the best historic descriptions of snap malt making is in an 1885 book about English malting by Henry Stopes, who explains that "barleys selected for snap malt were small, and in other respects of an inferior quality... Color and, to a certain extent, size was immaterial, because the action of the fire when the corn was drying upon the kiln entirely hid both." However, Stopes continued, the barley must be capable of germination, because ungerminated grains do not snap. On the germination floor, "the making of snap malt principally consist in half drying it and sprinkling a little water over what is intended for snapping the following morning, which is done to toughen the skin of the grain." In the kiln, most of the grain's moisture is first dissipated over moderate heat. But then the fire under the kiln wire is quickly stoked to an intense blaze, which causes the grain to swell—to "snap"—by about 25% of its size and to release a popcorn-like empyreumatic scent. Snap malt, therefore, adds flavor complexity to finished beer. In the 19th century, kilning snap malt must have been a hot and dangerous job, because, according to Stopes, the grain had to be spread a mere inch and a half thick on the kiln's wire floor—instead of the usual 4 inches—and needed to be turned at least once every 4 min. The entire kilning process for snap malt lasted only 75 min to 2 h—much shorter than the normal 32 h to 48 h for regular floor malt.

Stopes, Henry. *Malt and malting: An historical, scientific, and practical treatise, showing, as clearly as existing knowledge permits, what malt is, and how to make it.* London: Lyon, 1885.

Thomas Kraus-Weyermann

social media, Internet-based communication platforms that make use of networks modeled on social interactions. Social media utilize Web-based publishing platforms to disseminate text, video, images, and other digital media between users. Social media are user-generated, decentralized, and almost always free. Popular examples of social media in 2010 included blogs, Facebook, Twitter, Myspace, 4Square, Flickr, YouTube, Second Life, and Digg, with others certain to follow.

Craft breweries in the United States have been the most enthusiastic adopters of social media in the brewing world. As of 2010, over half of the 1,500 breweries in the United States had Facebook pages, with slightly less than half using Twitter. Social media have thrived with craft breweries primarily because of the low cost and direct connection to supporters, crucial attributes in an industry focused on affordable marketing, and the authenticity of its personalities.

Twitter has played an increasingly prominent role in American craft brewing, with many small breweries using it to spread information about special releases and to promote event ticket sales to fans.

Twitter and Facebook have also played important roles in grassroots public relations campaigns, such as Vermont-based Rock Art Brewery's successful response to a cease-and-desist letter from soft drink maker Hansen's.

Social media are also used by the world's largest breweries. Facebook pages for brands such as Heineken, Bud Light, Guinness, Coors Light, and Miller Lite have hundreds of thousands of connections to users. That said, large breweries have not embraced Twitter as enthusiastically as their craft counterparts.

Large breweries often use social media to promote contests, giveaways, sponsored events, and other forms of paid marketing. The use of social media as an avenue to amplify paid marketing differs from the strategy of craft brewers, who often have little or no paid marketing to amplify. Craft breweries most commonly use social media to converse directly with supporters and provide images, information, and video from within their respective breweries, with the content usually generated by the brewers themselves. Large brewers rarely provide such personal low-key content, preferring instead to redirect supporters to specially designed Websites, professionally produced videos, and similar content often generated by public relations firms.

Message boards and blogs maintained by craft beer aficionados have played an influential role in the development of craft beer culture. Although typically frequented by a specialized audience, message boards and blogs have built international awareness of small craft breweries and their offerings. Sites like BeerAdvocate.com and Ratebeer.com receive millions of visits per month and host databases containing tens of thousands of beers, which users rate and review. Beer blogs have likewise proliferated, usually offering short-form commentary from beer journalists (both self-styled and professional) and aficionados. Brewers have also made widespread use of blogs to communicate with supporters and build awareness of their breweries and personalities.

Jacob McKean

sodium chloride, commonly known as table salt or sea salt, has the chemical formula NaCl. In water it is completely dissociated into the sodium and chloride ions, each with their own separate characteristics. Well waters nearest oceans are more likely to have higher salt contents than others. Waters high in salt are unsuitable for brewing because of their effect on yeast cell chemistry, as well as their unpleasant effects on beer flavor. Unlike many other ions found in brewing water, neither the sodium nor the chloride ions contribute significantly to the activity of mash enzymes, kettle boil coagulation, or yeast metabolism. Both these ions do, however, contribute immensely to flavor and taste perception in final beer. Sodium ions are generally considered the less desirable of the two. Sodium ions give the familiar "salty" notes and a coarseness and harshness that most brewers try to avoid. Sodium ions are considered usually best restrained to a maximum of 25 mg/l, although some stouts will taste pleasant with levels up to 150 mg/l.

Chloride, however, can give a softness and smoothness, almost sweetness, to beer flavor, in direct counterpoint to the commonly found sulfate ion that contributes a dry sharpness and accentuates bitterness. Brewers add calcium chloride more commonly as a source of chloride rather than sodium chloride. Chloride concentration in certain beers is considered palatable roughly between 50 and 250 mg/l.

In the United States it was once relatively common for some people to add salt to their beer to cause to beer to foam. This practice that has almost completely died out. However, some craft breweries have recently recreated the previously extinct Leipsiger Gose beer style, which contained noteable salt.

See also WATER.

Pollock, J. R. A. *Brewing science*. New York: Academic Press, 1979.

Brian Hunt

solera, a system comprising a number of vessels containing the same beverage, but of consecutive ages, the purpose of which is to create a consistent drink that can be drawn off at regular intervals. This dynamic system of maturation takes place typically in cascading stages of wooden casks. See BARREL-AGING and OAK. Each stage is called a *scale* and includes the *solera*, the oldest barrel or set of barrels, and the *criadera*, a series of barrels of successively younger product. The Spanish terms reflect the fact that the solera is primarily employed in the production of sherry, although it is also used with other wines such as marsala and port, as well as rum, brandy, whiskey, balsamic, and sherry vinegars. Not surprisingly, it is also used for beer.

Author Julian Jeffs believes the terms "solera" and "criadera" first appeared in print around 1849, although they were probably in use much earlier. Gale's in the UK, Ballantine's in the United States, and Bayerska in Sweden were among the early production breweries to employ this technique. Belgian brewers also utilized soleras in the production of some Flemish red ales and oud bruin-style beers. Contemporary brewers utilizing the solera system include the Cambridge Brewing Company, Dogfish Head Craft Brewery, Freetail Brewing Company, and New Belgium Brewing Company in the United States, Birreria Baladin in Italy, and Norrebro Bryghus in Denmark.

Applicable to a wide range of beers including sour ales, barley wines, and strong lagers, a solera enables the consistent creation of complex beers with significant aged characteristics otherwise unattainable in most small production breweries. The process involves drawing off a quantity of the beer from the solera at set intervals and refreshing the casks with slightly younger beer of the same style from the criadera. The final product should come specifically from the oldest casks, with each level then replenished by the next oldest, regardless of the number of scales in the system. In working the scales of a solera, the brewer seeks to maintain an even distribution when topping up each older level.

Therefore, if 50% of one barrel is removed, an equal amount from each barrel in the next scale is drawn out to total the volume extracted from that individual older barrel. This process is then repeated for each barrel of every level in the solera. If this is not done, significant variations can occur in the development of the individual casks.

One challenge for the brewer employing a solera is the intensive labor required to maintain proper blending techniques, particularly when topping up barrels because of evaporation. Additionally, depending upon the style of base beer being aged, the beer can often experience a considerable rise in acidity as a result of invasive or resident microflora because most beer has neither the level of alcohol found in spirits nor the acidity of wine to protect it from infection. See ACETIC ACID BACTERIA, BRETTANOMYCES, LACTOBACILLUS, and SOUR BEER. Therefore, the solera system is well suited to beer styles in which some acidity or wild yeast character, whether originally anticipated or not, may bring about a pleasing complexity. Proportional blending from each barrel in the solera is sometimes required because certain barrels can express a propensity for producing higher degrees of attenuation or acid concentrations than others. A balanced and consistent beer is the goal every year.

Jeffs, Julian. *Sherry*. London: Mitchell Beazley, 2004.
Meyers, Will. La método solera—traditional methods for the production of unique beers. *The New Brewer* 27 (2010): 44–7.

Will Meyers

solventy off-flavors in beer can be described as having pungent, acrid aromas followed by a harsh, burning, or warming sensation on the back of the tongue that persists in extreme cases. Reminiscent of acetone or nail polish remover, it can also be described as paint thinner (e.g., toluene, turpentine), mineral spirits, polyurethane varnishes, lacquer, sanitary cleaners (citrus terpenes), dry cleaning chemicals (e.g., tetrachloroethylene), glue solvents (acetone, methyl acetate, ethyl acetate), spot removers (e.g., hexane, petrol ether), polyester resins, vinyl and adhesives, two-part epoxies, and superglue.

The source of solvent off-flavors in beer can most commonly be traced to two sources, those arising from tainted or contaminated equipment (inferior can liner curing, plasticizer leaching from tank linings, or gaskets), and flavor-active substances produced by yeast cells during fermentation—namely, higher alcohols and their acetate esters.

Some 45 higher alcohols have been identified in beer. Those of importance for aroma, because they occur at concentrations near or above their flavor thresholds are n-propanol, isobutanol, 2-methylbutanol (amyl alcohol), and 3-methylbutanol (isoamyl alcohol). Referred to as aliphatic alcohols, they contribute to beer flavor by general intensification of alcoholic/solvent-like aroma and taste with a corresponding warming effect on the palate. Aromatic alcohols of concern are tryptophol and tyrosol (when present in too high a concentration) are described as chemical or solvent and can cause lingering harshness and after bitter and are generally regarded as negative to beer flavor.

Control of higher alcohol formation during fermentation can be accomplished in three ways: by choice of an appropriate yeast strain, by modification of the wort, and by manipulation of fermentation conditions.

Volatile esters, although present in only trace amounts in beer, comprise the most important set of aroma-active compounds. See ESTERS. While esters are usually associated with fruity or candy-like notes, the most prominent ester, ethyl acetate, has a solvent-like "nail polish remover" aroma when concentrated. Therefore, ethyl acetate can be a pleasant aroma component, but like many aromatics it can present problems if levels dominate beer flavor rather than serve to compliment other, more desirable flavor compounds present.

See also OFF-FLAVORS.

Van Laere, Stijn D. M., Kevin J. Verstrepen, Johan M. Thevelein, Patrick Vandijck, and Freddy R. Delvaux. Formation of higher alcohols and their acetate esters. *Cerevisia* 33(2) (2008).

Christopher Bird

sommelier

See CICERONE.

Sorachi Ace (hop) is a hop developed by Dr Yoshitada Mori of Sapporo Breweries in Japan in the late 1970s. Brewer's Gold was crossed with Saaz, and the progeny was crossed with a Beikei No. 2 male. It was formally released from the Sapporo program in 1984 and was briefly grown in Japan and at Sapporo's hop farms in China. Research plantings were done at the U.S. Department of Agriculture/Oregon State University research farm in 1994, but the hop was not made available commercially in the United States until released in 2006 by Virgil Gamache Farms of Toppenish, Washington.

Sorachi Ace was named after the Sorachi subprefecture of Hokkaido. The breeding goal was a higher-alpha Saaz-type hop, but the result was rather different. Sorachi Ace averages 12%–13% alpha acids, although it has reportedly achieved up to 16% in non-commercial plantings in Japan. Cohumulone is low at 23%, and the hop gives a clean, snappy bitterness. Sorachi Ace matures mid season and is a vigorous grower that resists downy mildew. Yields are considered average at 1,569 to 1,681 per hectacre (1,400 to 1,500 lb per acre). This hop is particularly notable for its flavor and aroma, which is reminiscent of lemongrass, lemon peel, and lemon verbena. Some tasters find an oak-like background note, along with accents of cilantro (coriander leaf), dill, and diesel fuel. Still grown on fewer than 12 acres in the United States in 2010, Sorachi Ace has captured the attention of craft brewers seeking out new flavor characteristics, particularly for India pale ales, saisons, and wheat beers.

Gamache, Darren. *An incomplete history of the Sorachi Ace.*

Gamache, Darren. Virgil Gamache Farms, personal conversation, January 17, 2011.

Garrett Oliver

sorghum is a grass that provides a gluten-free grain that is grown widely as a food crop in Africa and Asia, as well as in parts of the Americas, and in Oceania. Sorghum is related to millet, and although there are numerous species under the sorghum genus, the main crop variety is *sorghum bicolor*. In the United States, it is chiefly cultivated as a substitute for corn for livestock feed and/or bio-ethanol production. It is also turned into sorghum syrup. Sorghum is well adapted to growing in hot, arid climates and requires sustained high temperatures for a high yield. Sorghum subspecies are grouped into grain, grass, sweet, and broom corn varieties. Grain and sweet sorghums can be used in brewing.

The use of sorghum as a brewing grain is traditional in Africa, where sorghum-based alcoholic and non-alcoholic beverages have been made on a small homebrew scale for centuries. Sorghum is also widely used in the modern African industrial brewing, because domestically produced sorghum is less costly than imported barley. Guinness stout, for instance, is made in Nigeria from a sorghum mash and malt extract. Sorghum can be malted in a fashion similar to barley but requires higher temperatures for germination. See MALT. In brewing, too, malted sorghum behaves very similarly to malted barley. In the mash, it is hydrated, its enzymes break down starches to sugars, and the sugar-containing wort is boiled, cooled, and fermented with brewers yeast. Unmalted sorghum can also be used as a starch adjunct in brewing. Notably, some traditional African sorghum-based beverages are fermented with lactobacillus or may be produced by way of a sour mash, to generate a sour-tasting beverage. See AFRICA, TRADITIONAL BREWING IN. Sorghum malt is not widely available in the United States, but sorghum syrups can be used as a substitute.

In North America, the increasing incidence of celiac disease has led to the production of several gluten-free commercial beers, made from sorghum in conjunction with other gluten-free grains, including rice. Lakefront Brewery of Milwaukee, Wisconsin, launched its New Grist in 2006; Anheuser-Busch produced the first nationally distributed gluten-free beer, also in 2006, under the brand name of Redbridge. More recently, the first commercial American beer brewed from 100% malted sorghum was introduced by Bard's Tale Brewing Company, Buffalo, New York.

Dewara, J., et al. Determination of improved steeping conditions for sorghum malting. *Journal of Cereal Science* 26 (1997): 129–36.

Owuama, C. I. Sorghum: A cereal with lager beer brewing potential. *World Journal of Microbiology & Biotechnology* 13 (1997): 253–60.

Martha Holley-Paquette

sour beer. While a certain level and quality of acidity is widely considered desirable in wine, often forming the backbone of its flavor structure, acidity is usually considered a flavor fault in modern beers. When speaking of beer, the word "sour" is usually pejorative. That said, there is a range of older beer styles that are traditionally acidic, and together with modern variants inspired by them, they have been termed, perhaps a bit rakishly, "sour beer." When well made, they can be among the most complex and refreshing of beers, terrific with food and easily pushing the boundaries of what the modern drinker thinks of as "beer."

In the days before modern sanitation, sour flavors in beer were common, if not always welcome. Most people avoided brewing during warm weather, when acidifying bacteria and wild yeast were more prevalent and likely to produce mouth-puckering acidity, sometimes with a vinegary tang, within days or weeks. When souring is intentional, the older "sour" beer styles are usually produced by the aging of beer in wooden barrels and involve the attempt to control acidity levels and produce an agreeable flavor. The classic sour beer styles include the German Berliner Weisse, and the Belgian Oud Bruin, Flanders Red, and lambic beers. All of these styles display a bracing lactic acidity, with the Belgian styles also showing some acetic character and a range of aromatics developed by bacteria and wild yeast during aging in oak barrels.

The rise of craft brewing in the United States and the emergence of upstart small breweries in other parts of the world has produced a new generation of brewers who aspire to create increasingly unique and flavorful beers. Many of these brewers have taken inspiration from classically sour Belgian beer styles. Not content with mimicking Belgian sour beers, they have started to develop what might be termed "new world" sour beers. Many of these new sour beers have no agreed-upon style guidelines and are yet to be classified in any particular category. This, of course, is part of the fun for the brewers who are making them. Some are aged in wine barrels, while others are aged in bourbon or whiskey barrels, successfully blending flavors that typically might not work well together. A handful of these "new world" brewers have even successfully created spontaneously fermented beers, something generally found only in Brussels or the Lambic region of Belgium. Some of these brewers have also installed "cool ships" in which to start the spontaneous fermentation before racking into oak barrels. Brewers who do not have the luxury of a cool ship have even used their mashing vessels as a temporary but suitable substitute in which to start their spontaneous fermentations. See COOLSHIP.

The wild yeast strain Brettanomyces is considered a scourge in most of the world's vineyards, while being cautiously welcomed in others, especially among "natural" winemakers who employ no laboratory yeasts. Cultured Brettanomyces is often used in the making of new world sour beers. See BRETTANOMYCES. Desirable flavors often associated with sour beer using Brettanomyces are earthy, barnyard, mushroom, musty, and a general "funkiness." Brettanomyces can be used with or without the introduction of bacteria, such as Lactobacillus and Pediococcus, during the barrel aging process. Because Pediococcus tends to produce the buttery-tasting compound diacetyl, Brettanomyces is often used in tandem to help minimize the undesirable characteristics that Pediococcus produces. In time, the Brettanomyces yeast will absorb the diacetyl, eventually eliminating unwanted buttery flavors.

Lactobacillus and Pediococcus are the two main bacteria that contribute to the actual acidity, or sourness, in the beer. Lactobacillus can ferment with or without oxygen and produces lactic acid and carbon dioxide, and yields a soft and mild tangy acidity. Fermenations using lactobacillus finish thinner and more cleanly on the palate than those using pediococcus. Conversely, pediococcus adds more rich and complex characteristics to the beer. Pediococcus ferments glucose into lactic acid, but it does not produce carbon dioxide. Skilled brewers of sour beer will blend these bacterial strains carefully, massaging fermentations to create the acid profile they desire in the beer. As individual barrels may progress differently, blending tends to be an essential part of the art of sour beer-making.

Enamored by the pungent flavors wild yeasts can create, some brewers have begun using Brettanomyces yeast for the entire primary fermentation, thus creating a 100% Brettanomyces fermented beer. These beers are generally produced in stainless steel tanks though some aging in oak barrels can make them even more interesting. In some cases, bacteria will be added, developing more mouthfeel and texture, thus adding to the overall complexity and structure of the beer. In this case, it is the addition of Lactobacillus and/or Pediococcus that will give the beer its acidity.

Belgium's lambic brewers are content to have ambient microflora everywhere throughout the brewery, but that is not always the case among new world brewers of sour beer. Wild yeast strains and bacteria that are normally considered "spoilers" of wort and beer can be risky to use in a brewery producing "normal" beers with standard brewer's yeasts; cross-contamination could be disastrous. As a result, most sour beer producers keep their "sour operations" as separate as possible from regular beer production, using different hoses, different bottle fillers, different tanks, and even separate buildings to keep the wild things at bay.

The development, largely by American craft brewers, of entire new categories of beer during the past decade, has resulted in the need for a new nomenclature to describe them. This nomenclature is surely unsettled, but the two terms in general use are "sour beer" and "wild beer." "Wild beer" is generally used to describe any beer that displays the earthy characteristics of Brettanomyces yeast strains, regardless of whether the beer is a light golden ale or a strong dark stout. If the brewer adds acidifying bacteria to the beer, it is termed a "sour beer." If both Brettanomyces character and bacterial acidity are in evidence, then the beer is generally deemed to fit both categories. Debates sometimes stretch into the wee hours, but with considerable humor, with brewers often lovingly referring to their wild yeasts and bacteria as "critters." Regardless of how many angels eventually dance upon the head of this developing nomenclature, what is certain, if improbable, is that sour beers are taking hold, especially in the United States. Just as "natural winemaking" is slowly emerging from cult status, so is the production and enjoyment of sour beer, with some newly minted brewers focusing much of their energy into the development of a brave new world of beer flavor.

See also BERLINER WEISSE, FLANDERS, LAMBIC, OUD BRUIN, and SOURNESS.

Vincent Cilurzo

sourness describes the taste that perceives acidity. See ACIDITY. The mechanism for detecting sour taste is similar to that which detects salt taste. Hydrogen ion channels detect the concentration of hydronium ions that are formed from acids and water. Sour taste is mainly recognized on the left and right sides of the tongue.

By a combination of direct intake of hydrogen ions (which itself depolarizes the cell) and the inhibition of the hyperpolarizing channel, sourness causes the taste cell to fire in this specific manner. It has also been suggested that weak acids—such as carbon dioxide, which is converted into the bicarbonate ion by the enzyme carbonic anhydrase—mediate weak acid transport. The food group that most commonly contains naturally sour foods is fruit, with examples such as lemon or grape.

Sourness normally is not one of the main taste impressions in beer and is usually considered an off-flavor. Sourness in beers usually is indicative of an infection, and acidity tends to clash with hop bitterness. However, Belgian lambic beers (gueuze, kriek), which undergo spontaneous fermentation, traditionally have a significant sour tang. See LAMBIC. The same is true of Flanders brown and red ales. Wild yeasts and bacteria varieties such as *Brettanomyces bruxellensis*, *Brettanomyces lambicus*, and Pediococcus are responsible for the occurring sourness. Other organisms, including Lactobacillus bacteria, produce acids which may cause a sour taste in beer. Sour ales such as Berliner weisse and Leipziger gose are inoculated with lactobacillus bacteria. See LACTOBACILLUS.

The Belgian and old German sour beer styles have inspired considerable interest in the brewing of sour ales among craft brewers, particularly in the United States.

See also SOUR BEER.

Wolfgang Stempfl

South African Breweries Ltd. was founded in 1865 as Castle Brewing in Johannesburg, from which it served the influx of miners and prospectors into the Witwatersrand Goldfield. The company brewed 75,000 hectoliters (63,912 US bbl) in its first year. It changed its name to South African Breweries (SAB) two years later, floating on the local stock exchange, and setting up head offices in London in 1868. In 1910 the founding of the Rhodesian Brewery was its first foreign foray. To develop indigenous raw materials, SAB imported barley seeds in 1911. Then, in 1935, it cooperated with rival Ohlsson's to develop local hop production. Apartheid, introduced by the South African government in 1948, made the sale of alcoholic beverages to and its consumption by the black population illegal. That ban was not lifted until 1962.

In 1949, SAB embarked on a massive expansion program, and brewing operations began in Bulawayo (Rhodesia) and in Zambia. In 1955, SAB built a new brewery in Johannesburg, just about the time when the government introduced a heavy beer tax. This led to a drop in consumption, which SAB weathered better than its rivals, Ohlsson's and Chandlers. SAB acquired them both in 1956, giving them a virtual monopoly of their domestic market. Between 1964 and1966 SAB was granted licenses to brew Guinness, Amstel, and Carling Black Label. It built additional breweries in Botswana and Angola in 1973. By 1990, when the Iron Curtain was coming down, SAB's total production had surpassed 32 million hectoliters (27,269,373 US bbl), and the company embarked on its first acquisitions outside southern Africa. It bought a brewery in Hungary in 1993, followed by the acquisition of the prestigious Pilsner Urquell brewery in Pilsen, Czechoslovakia. Then it purchased Lech in Poland and Ursus in Romania. Then came the grand coup: In 2002, it was able to purchase Miller Brewing in the United States from Phillip Morris for USD 5.55 billion, which made the new company, SABMiller, the world's second largest brewer.

See also SABMILLER.

Glenn A. Payne

Southeast Asia is a region of 10 countries bounded by India, China, and the Pacific and Indian Oceans. There is little indigenous beer tradition in Southeast Asia because all but one of its constituent nations have lived through periods of colonialism. Although these are now independent nations, they retain continuing business links to Europe. Only Thailand avoided colonization, although brewing there has a strong German element. Throughout the area lager styles predominate, although occasionally ales and stouts can be found.

Brunei is a Sultanate in the British commonwealth on the island of Borneo. The sale and public consumption of alcohol is banned with some concessions for foreigners and non-Muslims. Not surprisingly, there are no breweries in Brunei.

Burma (Myanmar) is an independent republic that cut its ties with colonial British rule in 1948. The Mandalay Brewery produces the fruity Mandalay beer and the odd spirulina beer, which has algae added; the brewery claims it has health-giving properties. The Myanmar Brewery in Rangoon brews Myanmar beer and Tiger beer among others, exporting to several surrounding countries. Per capita beer consumption in Myanmar is 1 l (33 oz) per year.

In Cambodia (Kampuchea) local brewing shows little influence of the country's French colonial past. There are two major breweries in the capital city of Phnom Penh, with the Cambodia Brewery producing Gold Crown, a European-style pilsner, and Anchor, a lager found throughout the region. The recently built Kingdom Brewery brews Clouded Yellow pilsner and Kingdom's draught. In the port city of Kompong Som a subsidiary of Cambodia Brewery also brews Anchor and contract brews the Laotian beer Lao. The Heineken-built Cambrew brewery produces Anghor, Bayou beer, and a strong 8.3% alcohol by volume Black Panther stout.

Indonesia is a republic consisting of more than 16,000 islands. It is the world's fourth most populous nation. Independence came in 1949 after 350 years of Dutch rule; some Dutch brewing influence remains. The most popular beer is Bintang Star beer, following the taste and packaging styles of Heineken, the major Dutch brewer. It is brewed throughout the country. The Bintang plant in the capital city of Jakarta also brews Guinness Foreign Export stout. In nearby Bekasi the Delta brewery produces Anker beer and Anker stout and San Miguel, a lager from the Philippines. Storm Brewing of Bali has a large portfolio, including a bronze ale called Red Dawn; a pale ale called Sand Storm; and Black Moon, a dry Irish stout. It also produces occasional specialty ales using interesting ingredients including bananas, chilies, and chocolate.

Laos, a republic that shook off French dominance in 1954, is the only land-locked country in the region. Brewing is by the state-run Laos Brewing Company, supported by foreign investment including Danish brewer Carlsberg. There are two breweries, one in the capital city of Vientiane and the other in the southern province of Champasack. The main products are Beerlao lager, the slightly more flavorful Beerlao dark, and Beerlao gold; all three are lagers. Also brewed is Carlsberg beer.

Malaysia is a monarchy consisting of two areas separated by the South China Sea: half of the Malay peninsula and one-third of the island of Borneo. British influence dates back more than 2 centuries but the Danish company Carlsberg has been in business in the area since 1903. The Carlsberg Brewery (Malaysia) in Selangor has an extensive portfolio of beers including Carlsberg special brew, Connor's original stout, Corona light lager, and Tetley's English ale. The recently formed and smaller Jaz Brewery brews a fresh-tasting lager on a German brewing system.

The Philippines is a republic of many islands in the western Pacific first controlled by Spain and then by the United States, gaining independence in 1946. Several breweries produce the best-selling pale lager San Miguel, including one in the capital, Manila, where a dark lager, Cevera Negra, is also brewed. Red Horse ale and Gold Eagle lager are also in the portfolio. In the ancient capital Cebu, the Asia Brewery produces Colt 45, Beer Na Beer, and beers from Coors' range.

Singapore is an independent city-state on an island off the tip of the Malay Peninsula. One large brewery, Asia Pacific, brews the big Tiger brand, which is exported to 60 countries, and a variety of other styles. Among the several craft brewers and brewpubs, Brewerkz is renowned for its cask-conditioned ales, particularly India pale ale and stout. Archipeligo Brewing, owned by Asia Pacific, is more adventurous and boasts an interesting list of wheat beers, saisons, and various beers based on local cuisine.

Thailand is a constitutional monarchy and has never been colonially controlled. Three groups own all of the major breweries: Thai Bev plc, often called Cosmos, has five breweries with Chang as its major seller; the Boon Rawd Brewery Company owns three breweries, with Singha and Leo the predominate brews; and Thai Asia Pacific is a major brewery and a smaller plant just outside the capital of Bangkok that brews Anchor and San Miguel. See BOON RAWD BREWERY. Among the imported beers is Guinness directly from Dublin. There are several brew pubs now operating.

In Vietnam, after a long French colonial period and decades of war, comparative stability arrived in the 1990s. Beer 333 (known as BabaBa) is brewed in the capital Hanoi and Ho Chi Minh City in the south. The Saigon Beer Company is the largest brewery, producing 5 million hl (4,260,839 US bbl) annually (and targeting 7 million hl [5,965,175 US bbl] by the end of 2010), with Saigon beer its main product. Unique to Vietnam is Bia Hoi (gas beer), which is made fresh every day and sold at stalls and by cycle vendors. Often dispensed out of plastic jugs, it is a very cheap golden "running beer" that rarely lasts more than 24 h before becoming sour and unpalatable.

Barrie Pepper

Southern Cross (hop) is a New Zealand variety that was released in 1994 by the country's HortResearch hop breeding program. Southern Cross is a triploid, which means it is an infertile, seedless plant. Its genetic background includes a New Zealand research variety from the 1950s, a California hop, and the English Fuggle. See FUGGLE (HOP). Southern Cross matures in early-mid season, has good yields of about 2,400 kg/ha (2,141 lbs/acre), and is fairly stable in postharvest storage. Southern Cross is a dual-purpose hop with alpha acids in the 12% to 14.5% range and beta acids in the 6% to 6.4% range. It has a fairly high content of floral myrcene of 59% essential oils. The balsamic, resinous humulene amounts to about 13%; the spicy caryophyllene to about 4%; and the floral farnesene to a relatively high 5%. The resulting aroma of this hop is lemony with slight piney and woody notes. The perceived bitterness is soft. Although New Zealand craft brewers have long been familiar with Southern Cross, it is only in recent years that brewers in the northern hemisphere have taken note of it. Craft brewers from California to Norway are now starting to use this hop, largely for aroma, in a wide variety of beers ranging from wheat beers to saisons and pale ales. See BITTERNESS.

New Zealand Hops Limited. "NZ Hops—Data Sheet. Southern Cross." http://www.nzhops.co.nz/varieties/pdf/southern_cross.pdf/ (accessed October 28, 2010).

Victoria Carollo Blake

South Korea, located in East Asia, occupies the southern half of the Korean Peninsula and many outlying islands to the south and west. One of the most densely populated countries in Asia, South Korea is home to 49 million mostly Christian or Buddhist inhabitants. A country that has consistently been subjected to brutal invasions by its neighbors Japan, China, and Russia, South Korea has experienced a steadily growing economy in recent years and is now home to a multiparty democratic government. The capital of Seoul has a population of 9.5 million people and apparently opened its first brewery in 1908.

Beer is the drink of choice, making up about 60% of the South Korean drinks market. Citizens favor Western-style lager beers, called maekju. South Korea's version of a pub is the hof (hopeu), which serves pints of inexpensive local beer, as well as more expensive and heavily taxed imported beer. The latter are now frequently the drink of choice among young, urban professionals. South Koreans generally favor beers brewed from large proportions of rice, which gives them clean, but bland flavors.

Two major domestic South Korean breweries, Oriental Brewery Co. Ltd. (OB) and Hite Brewery Co., maintain a duopoly on the South Korean beer market. The leader in the market is Hite, founded in 1933 as Chosun Beer Co. Ltd. Hite manufactures beer under the names Hite, Hite Pitcher, Max, Stout, S, and STOUT. It also makes traditional Korean spirits and imports Foster's and Kirin beers. OB, the country's second largest brewery, was started in 1952 and purchased by InBev in 1998. In November 2009, Anheuser-Busch InBev sold the company to Kohlberg Kravis Roberts & Co. for USD $1.8 million. The new owner maintains a strong relationship with OB, using it to distribute such brands as Budweiser and Hoegaarden throughout the country. OB will have the right to buy the company back in 2014 under certain financial conditions. Popular brews produced by OB are OB, Cass, and Cafri. The company is focused especially on developing the Cass brand, which is currently number one in the South Korean market.

De La Merced, Michael J: K.K.R. to Buy Anheuser's South Korean Brewer. http://dealbook.nytimes.com/2009/05/07/kkr-to-buy-anheusers-south-korean-brewer/ (accessed November 10–29, 2010).

Drinking in South Korea: Beer. http://iguide.travel/South_Korea/Drinking/Beer (accessed November 10–29, 2010).

Guide to South Korea. http://www.lonelyplanet.com/south-korea (accessed November 10–29, 2010).

Hite Brewery Companted Limited Company Snapshot. http://www.corporateinformation.com/Company-Snapshot.aspx?cusip=C41000010 (accessed November 10–29, 2010).

Idzelis, Christine. KKR toasts Oriental Brewery. http://www.thedeal.com/newsweekly/deals-of-the-year-2009/kkr-toasts-oriental-brewery.php (accessed November 10–29, 2010).

National Geographic. http://travel.nationalgeographic.com/travel/countries/south-korea-guide/ (accessed November 10–29, 2010).

April Darcy

Spain. The evidence of brewing taking place in what we know as the Iberian Peninsula predates the creation of the country called Spain by several thousand years. Beer was present at the dawn of civilization and has gone hand in hand with the development of social organization in Europe from the outset. It is impossible to say exactly how much of the Neolithic "package," in which the art of brewing beer was well bundled up, was put together by the indigenous people and how much introduced from elsewhere, directly or indirectly from the Middle East. It has, however, been clearly demonstrated that this package (containing, among other things, sedentary communities, the transition from foraging to an agro-pastoral economy, and ceramics) included the brewing of beer in what is now Spain.

The earliest archaeological remains of beer to be discovered in Europe have been uncovered in recent years by a team of archaeologists from the University of Barcelona. Traces of malt and beer were found adhering to grinding stone artifacts and pottery bowls from the Post-Impressed Ware phase in a burial context in a cave, Cova de Can Sadurní (Begues, Barcelona), which had been occupied by post-glacial hunter-gatherers and their successors until Roman times, and have been dated to mid-fifth millennium cal BCE (beginning of the middle Neolithic period). Remains of beer dating from the Bronze Age (second millennium BCE) have also been found at the same site.

Later remains have been discovered on pottery from the late Neolithic period (mid-third millennium cal BCE), called the "Bell Beaker phase" after the type of drinking vessels used at various sites throughout present-day Spain. Further evidence has been found at Bronze Age (second millennium cal BCE) sites, and, in the Iron Age (first millennium cal BCE) beer residues become even more widespread.

The cereals used for malting were barley and wheat, and in some cases the presence of honey and aromatic herbs (Filipendula, Arbutus, Epilobium angustifolium, among others), was detected.

A golden thread of beer running from the distant past to early Roman times thus emerges, but it was destined to lose its luster. The Greeks and Romans looked down on beer as a drink fit only for the hoi polloi or plebeians (respectively) and barbarians. Though brewing evidently went on in Roman provinces—as is clearly demonstrated by an Imperial Decree by Diocletian in 301 BCE that fixed prices throughout the Empire for three types of beer—it tended to be eclipsed by viniculture for a very long time, especially in Southern Europe.

From the fall of Rome to the Industrial Revolution there is little documentation of brewing in Spain, but what can be surmised from indirect sources is that it was a small-scale, local activity and that the resulting beer was not of very high quality and often needed the addition of lemon juice to make it more palatable. There was, however, to be a fleeting glimpse of gold again in Spain. The Holy Roman Emperor Charles V (Charles I of Spain) retired to the monastery of Yuste in Cáceres, and in 1557, missing his favorite drink, had "Mechelschen Bruynen" or "Mechelen Brown" imported from his native Flanders. He immediately followed this up by summoning the Flemish brewer Enrique van der Trehen to commission a brewery in the monastery and practice his arts there. Charles's empire has been described as one on which the sun never sets; it could also be said to be one in which beer started flowing in Spain once again.

The next beer-related event of any significance was the arrival in Barcelona in 1851 of Louis Moritz Trautmann from Pfaffenhoffen, Alsace. Moritz's brother had been a brewer there, and this helped him get a job in a small brewery run by a Frenchman, Ernest Ganivet, in the center of old Barcelona 2 years later. By 1856 he had not only learned his trade but also bought the company, and he went on to take over another rather larger brewery in 1859 from a man of German origin, Juan Maurer. Municipal by-laws prohibited the opening of new breweries in the old city, so Louis Moritz y Compañia moved the short distance out to the Eixample, which would eventually become a district of Barcelona. The new brewery took 2 years to construct but once up and running proved to be a great success.

While Moritz was building up his business another immigrant from Alsace arrived in Barcelona in 1871. August Kuentzmann Damm, a brewer fleeing the Franco-Prussian War, immediately set about finding a Catalan financial partner, and by the following year the new firm of Camps y Kuentzmann was up and brewing. The first partnership was short-lived and by 1876 August was in business with his cousin Joseph, also a refugee, and a third partner, Adolf Leinbacher. On Leinbacher's death the company was renamed Damm y Compañia and by 1897 Joseph Damm was the sole owner, in due course bequeathing the company to his children: Joseph, Maria, and Carles.

At this time there were two other breweries of significance operating in Barcelona: Cammany, established by Catalans in 1899, and La Bohemia, set up by a Czech brewer and a Catalan wine dealer in 1902. Initially known by the founders' surnames, Miklas & Musolas, the firm changed its name to La Bohemia upon the incorporation of an additional nine associates. The new company started building a large brewery in Carrer Rosselló that same year. However, Miklas left before the brewery started operating, in 1905, and the company name was changed again to Joan Musolas (though the brewery kept its original name).

In 1910 Barcelona's four main brewers very nearly merged, but Moritz, the largest at the time, was temporarily under the management of Ernesto Petri, a Swiss who changed the name of the company to Expert. He refused to cooperate, keeping the company independent until 1920 when the Moritz family regained control. The other three brewers duly merged under the name Damm S.A. and decided to operate from La Bohemia—though it was the furthest from the center it was also the largest and had the most modern plant. The new brewery was very successful and in its first 10 years doubled production from 30,000 hl (25,565 US bbl) (a little less than Moritz at the time) to more than 65,000 hl (55,390 US bbl). With increased profits came the temptation to invest outside Catalonia in order to open new markets. In 1929 Damm took over La Alicantina and started planning the construction of a new brewery in Valencia in 1935. There was by now a plethora of small and mid-sized breweries dotted all over Spain, each with its own local market; they would later tempt the bigger brewers, but the predatory phase was delayed by the outbreak of the Civil War in 1936.

Most of the initial growth of industrial brewing had taken place in Catalonia, but the fact that beer could be a good business opportunity did not go unnoticed in the rest of Spain. The turn of the century turned into a liquid gold rush. Most of the breweries that were to be long-term key players were already operating, brewing German-style lagers (the exception being a pale ale, Ambar 1900, from La Zaragozana in Saragossa) and most of the names of the beers still survive today in one form or another.

If the Agrarian Revolution in the Iberian Peninsula probably began in Catalonia, the Civil War sparked another revolution there. Workers collectivized many factories, and the breweries were no exception. Damm and Moritz were run by the anarcho-syndicalist Confederación Nacional del Trabajo (CNT) from June 1936 until the end of the war in 1939. Wages were equalized (this meant better pay for most workers), health insurance was extended to all, and the retirement age was lowered to 60. Raw materials were supplied by agricultural collectives. Profits were plowed back into the factory and provided the workers with a library, a canteen, and sports facilities, as well as financing the CNT militia. Two of the firm's best lorries were sent to the front.

Just 5 months separated the end of the war in Spain and the start of World War II. Raw materials became increasingly scarce. The national association to which most brewers had belonged since 1922 was taken over by the new regime in order to promote and regulate the growing of barley and hops and the production of malt. Today, after various transformations, the industry is served by three organizations: Cerveceros de España, which represents the remaining six big brewers; Malteros de España, which defends the interests of farmers and the seven maltings; and S.A. Española de Fomento del Lúpulo, which aids hop growers and processes the hops. Thanks to the efforts of the latter (set up in 1945 by the then 33 main breweries), Spain is self-sufficient in hops. The majority of these are high alpha varieties, mainly Nugget (since 1993 largely replacing the traditional H-3 and H-8), Magnum, and the more recent Columbus. Perle is also being grown commercially and trials are underway with other aroma hops. Most hops are processed into Type 90 pellets and the rest into extracts. Similarly, efforts are being made to phase out the myriad traditional strains of barley and introduce varieties better suited to brewing. Malteros is promoting the cultivation of Pewter, Scarlett, and Quench for base malts, and Prestige, Henley, and Shakira for special malts. Clarion and Braemar are currently undergoing field trials.

Recent developments among mass-market breweries include the reintroduction of Moritz beers. Although the beers are actually brewed by La Zaragozana, a microbrewery is planned for the Ronda Sant Antoni in Barcelona, where the company formerly had its head office. Moritz recently launched an unpasteurized lager, Alfa. La Zaragozana now brew a bottle-conditioned wheat beer, Ambar Caesaraugusta, and Damm another, called Inedit.

Craft beers have been available for some time now in Spain, if not always easy to find. The birth of craft beer, however, was not an easy one. The main problems were caused by an insensitive, inflexible bureaucracy—or *burrocracia* ("rule by donkeys") as Spanish wit would have it. The first to suffer, in 1989, was Naturbier, a pub-brewery in Madrid, brewing German-style lagers. It operated illegally for 4 years until its owner, a parliamentarian, eventually succeeded in obtaining a license. The second was the Barcelona Brewing Company or BBC, another pub-brewery, which opened in April 1993. The BBC produced Three Graces English-style real ales: a bitter, a special bitter, and a stout. Despite great public acceptance it was not so well-received by the public authorities. Closed by Customs and Excise in 1995, the heroic efforts of brewers and customers to extricate it from the administrative labyrinth ultimately came to naught. At the turn of the decade ridiculous situations arose. What should have been two national chains of brewpubs, one based in Seville and the other in A Coruña, were forced to produce hopped, concentrated wort in sympathetic municipalities and ship it to the others where it would be fermented and conditioned. The only survivor is Magister, in the center of Madrid, though Boris de Messones, the former head brewer, has since fled to Korea, where, among other things, he is running one brewpub and constructing a second. Others from this period closed for technical or financial reasons.

Where craft beer has really taken off in the last few years is in Catalonia in northeast Spain. The seeds were sown in the last days of the Barcelona Brewing Company during a brewing education course, with Alex Padró and Paco Sánchez attending, and in the Wolf Brewery in England, where Pablo Vijande worked during his university summer break. Two beer associations were set up: Humulus Lupulus in the Cerveceria Jazz with Padró as one of the founder members and Catalunya Home Brewers set up by Sánchez and Vijande. These two associations have educated and inspired, directly or indirectly, most of the people now involved in craft beer in Catalonia. If we discount the reopening of the BBC under the name La Cervesera Artesana and the fleeting existence of the Sant Jordi brewery on the Costa Brava, the first microbrewery to open in the region was in 2005, Padró's Glops, brewing Bavarian-style beers, followed by Companyia Cervesera del Montseny, or CCM.

A critical mass is now being reached. Carlos Rodríguez from Agullons, a farmhouse-brewery near Sant Joan de Mediona producing three critically acclaimed ales, finally obtained official permission to operate in 2008. Others, too, are up and brewing: Guzmán Fernández at Ca l'Arenys (who also fabricate microbrewing equipment and supply raw materials) is making Guineu, a wide range of ales and lager including the audacious Riner, a highly hopped 2.5% ABV pale ale. Josep Borrell at Moska, near Girona, is also brewing lagers and ales together with special beers containing indigenous cereals such as buckwheat, under the brand name Kecks. These are meant to be paired with local food.

Some microbreweries in the region are also using exotic additions: La Gardenia (La Rosita) is using rose petals in one beer and hazelnuts in another, Les Clandestines add thyme to one of theirs, and Bleder is using dates. The most recent arrival is another farmhouse brewery, Art Cervesers, set up by Paco Sánchez, brewing Art beers: an IPA, a märzen, and a stout. See INDIA PALE ALE, MÄRZENBIER, and STOUTS. There are also various nanobreweries, such as Almogàvers and Zulogaarden. The Catalan food culture is responding, and various serious restaurateurs are incorporating craft beer lists and beer-pairing menus.

The seeds from Catalonia are spreading to Valencia and further south and look likely to be disseminated all over the country. Spain has become a fount of creativity and innovation for chefs worldwide, and we cannot be surprised if we soon see the emergence of an equally interesting Spanish beer culture.

See also HISTORY OF BEER.

Blasco, A., Edo, M., and Villalba, M. J. *Evidencias de procesado y consumo de cerveza en la cueva de Can Sadurní (Begues, Barcelona) durante la prehistoria* (Evidence of brewing and consumption of beer in the Can Sadurní cave in prehistory). Actas del IV Congreso del Neolítico Peninsular. Museo Arqueológico de Alicante, Diputación de Alicante. Tomo I, pp. 428–31, 2008.

Guerra Doce, E., and Delibes de Castro, G. *The Toast to the Prince: Beer Residues at the Beaker Burial Pit of Fuente Olmedo (Valladolid, Spain) and the Role of Alcohol in the Mortuary Rites of Prehistoric Europe.* Proceedings of the Annual Meeting of the Association Archeologie et Gobelets (Torres Vedras, Portugal), May 2008.

Huxley, S. *La cerveza . . . poesía líquida, un manual para cervesiáfilos* (Beer . . . liquid poetry, a manual for beer lovers). Gijón: Ediciones Trea, 2006.

Sanchez, F., Tintó, A., Vidal, J.M., and Vijande, P. *La cerveza artesanal, cómo hacer cerveza en casa* (Craft beer, how to brew at home). Barcelona: Cerveart, 2006.

Steve Huxley

Spalter Select (hop) is a German aroma hop variety that was bred at the Hop Research Institute in Hüll in the Hallertau in Bavaria. See HALLERTAU HOP REGION. It was released in 1991 and registered for commercial cultivation in 1993. In the hop trade, it is often referred to as simply "Select." This variety has a rather complicated genetic makeup, but it is largely derived from Hallertauer Mittelfrueh and Spalt. See HALLERTAUER MITTELFRUEH (HOP) and SPALT (HOP). The Spalt region of Germany grows a bit more Select than it does the eponymous Spalter-Spalt, but far more Select is grown in the Hallertauer region than in Spalt. Select tends to grow to the top of the trellis without much undergrowth, and it forms a thick clump at the top. This makes it hard to pick with the smaller German picking machines. Some growers have tried the Alsatian practice of stringing the plants at a 30° angle from vertical to lengthen the climb to the top, thus producing less top growth and more undergrowth. See FRENCH HOPS. This reduces picking difficulties and may increase yields. The plant itself tends to turn its lower leaves yellow late in the summer as if it were suffering from a disease or a nutrient shortage, but this is normal and does not seem to impact yields. The dried cones have a duller appearance than most hops and they also have a characteristic yellowish hue. The cone size is often smaller than that of other varieties, and the dried cones tend to shatter more readily.

The aroma of Spalter Select is easy to distinguish from either Hallertauer Mittelfrueh or Spalter-Spalt. It has some background spicy and herbal notes that are similar to these hops, but it also has a characteristic heavy, sweet, almost candy-like aroma that makes it instantly recognizable. Select typically yields 1,900 kg/ha (1,695 lb/ac) and has 3% to 6.5% alpha acids, 2.5% to 5% beta acids, 21% to 27% cohumulone, and 0.6% to 0.9% essential oils. Select has very good resistance to wilt and good resistance to downy mildew, but only fair resistance to powdery mildew. It stores relatively well and is harvested mid- to late season.

Val Peacock

Spalt (hop) is a German landrace hop, sometimes known as "Spalter," from the Spalt region southwest of Nuremburg in Bavaria, which has been a hop growing and trading area since the middle of the 14th century. See SPALT HOP REGION. In 1538, Spalt received the world's first seal of quality for hops, conferred by the Prince-Bishop of Eichstätt. See HOP SEAL. The hop seal was meant to guarantee high quality standards. Spalt is still grown in this region, mostly on small and medium-size farms with deep, loose soil that allows good root development. The area receives 650 mm (25.6 inches) of rain per year as well as ample sunshine, both of which are necessary for the development of the characteristic Spalt hop aroma. Spalt, like its counterparts Hallertauer, Tettnanger, and Saaz, is considered one of the "Noble" hop varieties because of its relatively high aroma content compared with bitterness. Its delicate, spicy aroma works particularly well in such continental European beer styles as pilsner, bock, kölsch, and helles. Spalt is considered the classic hop for altbier, where it supports the beer's gentle fruitiness. Spalt matures early and grows vigorously with red bines and long lateral branches, but it produces only a modest amount of small cones for a relatively low average yield of only about 1,200 to 1,600 kg/ha (roughly 1,070 to 1,430 lb/acre). Alpha and beta acids both range from 4% to 5%, which is consistent with the other Noble hop varieties. The cohumulone content is moderate at 23% to 28% of alpha acids. Among the variety's essential oils, myrcene is a low 15%, humulene 25%, caryophyllene 15%, and the floral farnesene a very high 15%.

Spalter Hopfen. *The history of spalt hop growing*. http://www.spalterhopfen.com/geschichte_eng.html/ (accessed October 28, 2010).

Verband Deutscher Hopfenpflanzer (Association of German Hopgrowers). *The spirit of beer: Hops from Germany*. http://www.cob.sfasu.edu/csc/gharber/public_html/bb/hopfenm_engl.pdf (accessed October 27, 2010).

Victoria Carollo Blake

Spalt hop region is a German hop-growing area centered around the small Franconian town of Spalt, roughly 30 km (18 mi) south of Nuremburg, in Bavaria. It is the home of the classic aroma hop Spalter. The cultivation of hops is documented in the area as early as 1341, and for the next 100 years—considered by many the golden age of hop-growing in the Nuremburg area—the Spalt region, as well as much of the countryside around Nuremburg, was a thriving hop-producing area. In 1538, Spalter hops were so prized that the district became the first to be awarded by the feudal powers of the time the privilege to a use a so-called hop seal. See HOP SEAL. This seal was placed on packaged hops to authenticate that they were in fact genuine Spalter hops, and this allowed them to command a higher price. In later centuries the cultivation of hops in the greater Nuremburg area declined drastically, but the Spalt district always remained viable.

Although the classic Spalter variety is still a major hop grown in the region, Spalt Select has surpassed it in total acreage, and there is just about as much Hallertauer Mittelfrueh in the ground as Spalter. See HALLERTAUER MITTELFRUEH (HOP) and SPALTER SELECT (HOP). In the hop trade, Hallertauer Mittelfrueh grown in Spalt is referred to as Spalter Hallertau to differentiate it from Hallertauer Hallertau. Small amounts of Hallertauer Tradition and Perle are also grown. See HALLERTAUER TRADITION (HOP) and PERLE (HOP). In most years, Spalt produces less than 2% of all German hops.

Val Peacock

sparging is the spraying of fresh hot liquor (brewing water) onto a mash to rinse out residual sugars. It is essential to achieving desirable efficiency of sugar extraction.

Once the malt enzymes have digested starch into sugars, the mash must be drained and separated from the residual solids, particularly the malt husks. The sugary wort produced by mashing will be filtered by these solids which are held on the mash or lauter plates; much will remain on the surface and crevices of the husks. See LAUTERING. Removing this residue requires rinsing with fresh brewing liquor.

Before sparging became mechanized, grains were rinsed by refilling the mash tun with fresh liquor, stirring, and then re-draining. This may have been repeated a number of times until no further sugars could be removed. Historically a number of beers of different strengths could be produced from a single mash by this means, which is called the "parti-gyle system." See PARTI-GYLE.

Mechanical sparging developed as a more efficient system whereby liquor was sprayed onto the top of the mash continuously and drained off from the bottom. Wort was collected continuously in the kettle and a single brew of a target strength was produced.

Successful sparging requires a careful matching of inflow and outflow as too fast or too slow a sparge will result in an overflow or a dry mash. In either of these circumstances, lautering can be inefficient or cease entirely. It is also important to ensure that the sparging liquor is suitably treated, if necessary, to maintain a low pH in the mash. Too high a pH can result in excessive extraction of tannins and silicates from the grain husk, which can give the finished beer an undesirable astringency.

Keith Thomas

sparkler, a small plastic fitting that can be affixed to the spout of a beer engine when dispensing cask-conditioned ales. The most common type of sparkler is essentially a cap perforated with several small holes. When the beer is poured, it sprays forcefully through the holes in the cap. Thus, aerated and agitated, the beer forms a thick cap of foam. In Britain, the home of cask-conditioned draught beer, opinions are sharply divided as to whether the sparkler enhances or diminishes the character of the ales poured through them. That dividing line, although fuzzy, seems to run across the country somewhere north of the Midlands and perhaps just south of Yorkshire. In the north, most cask beer drinkers feel that the sparkler softens, rounds, and opens the beer's flavors while giving it an attractive head of foam. In the south, the sparkler is often seen as an abomination that shreds the light, natural carbonation out of the beer and reduces the appealing bitter characteristics of its hops. A properly conditioned cask ale, they argue, should not require the use of a sparkler to look and taste its best. So heated is the debate over the sparkler that even the usually bombastic Campaign for Real Ale (CAMRA) sidesteps the issue, saying that sparklers should only be used when the brewery has stated a preference for them. See CAMPAIGN FOR REAL ALE (CAMRA). Sparklers are only used in association with beer engines, usually fitted with swan-neck spouts, and never affixed to taps used for gravity dispense.

Garrett Oliver

Spaten Brewery is regarded as the most significant German brewery in the development of lager brewing. Records suggest that there was a Spaten Brewery, a brewpub in fact, in Munich as far back as 1397 but it was not until the early 19th century, under ownership of the Sedlmayrs—arguably Munich's most prestigious brewery family—that Spaten, meaning spade, came into its own. Gabriel Sedlmayr (the Elder) purchased the Spaten Brewery in 1807 and quickly turned it into Munich's leading brewery. See SEDLMAYR, GABRIEL THE ELDER.

Much of the credit for Spaten's place in brewing history must go to Gabriel Sedlmayr (the Younger) who embraced the invention of steam power in more ways than one. He traveled Europe on rail to study brewing techniques in Austria, Switzerland, Prussia, Belgium, and Britain, where brewers were vigorously exploring temperature control.

In 1821, Spaten helped fund the first steam engine in Bavaria. Later, in 1844, Gabriel bolstered brewing production with the introduction of steam power at Spaten and, with this, Spaten cemented its reputation for darker (dunkel) Munich-style lagers. A year later, one of Gabriel's protégés, Jacob Christian Jacobsen, founded the Carlsberg Brewery in Copenhagen using Spaten yeast and specializing in dark lagers as well.

Peerless in its pursuit of brewing excellence, in 1841, just 1 year before the introduction of the pilsner in Pilsen, Bohemia, Spaten introduced the first amber-colored lager in Continental Europe, the Märzen. It reached the Bavarian market roughly at the same time as another amber lager, the Vienna lager of the Dreher Brewery, first graced the taps of the Austrian capital. In 1872, the Franziskaner-Leist Brewery, although not (yet) part of Spaten, but owned by Joseph Sedlmayr, brother of Gabriel the Younger, came out with a special Oktoberfest beer oddly named a "Märzen-Bier" brewed "the Vienna way." The current Spaten Oktoberfest beer is still brewed largely according to that 1872 Franziskaner-Leist recipe. A year later, in 1873, Spaten commissioned the first ever continually operational refrigeration system, designed by Carl von Linde. About 2 decades later, in 1894, it became the first Bavarian brewery to brew a light-hued lager, Spaten Münchner Hell, using a variation of the 1842 Pilsner brewing method. See PILSNER and LINDE, CARL VON.

Spaten adopted the spade logo in 1884 as a ground-breaking marketing move. In 1922, the Spaten and the Franziskaner-Leist breweries formally merged. Then, in 1997, the joined company merged with the Löwenbräu Brewery. In 2003, this new enterprise was subsequently purchased by the company later known as Anheuser-Busch InBev.

Spaten beers include Münchner Hell (5.2% alcohol by volume [ABV]), Doppelbock Optimator (7.2% ABV), Oktoberfestbier (5.9% ABV), and a pils (5% ABV).

Dornbusch, Horst. *Bavarian helles*. Boulder, CO: Brewers Publications, 2000.
McFarland, Ben. *World's best beers*. London: Aurum Press, 2009.

Ben McFarland

spear, a long and narrow metal draw tube that can be found in every modern beer keg. It reaches from the neck valve to within a half inch (1.25 cm) of the bottom of the keg. It allows gas under pressure to enter the keg and drive the beer to the tap. The beer flows up the spear and out of the coupler to the tap by way of a ball valve inside the neck body on the keg head (the top of the upright keg). When the tap is opened to pour the beer, the pressure inside the keg propels the beer. External gas, usually carbon dioxide, is regulated for a particular pressure level and replaces the depleted beer, maintaining a constant keg pressure until the keg is emptied. The spear is usually held in place by a clip or retaining ring. Both can be removed from the keg for cleaning. However, the spear should never be removed while the keg is under pressure because this can turn the spear into a dangerous projectile capable of causing serious injury.

Tim Hampson

specific gravity, sometimes called present gravity, is the density of beer or wort at standard temperature and pressure (20°C, 760 mm Hg) measured by saccharometer, hydrometer, or refractometer. A more accurate laboratory method is by weight using a specific gravity bottle. The units of specific gravity follow the practice of the country for original gravity, namely excess gravity, degrees Plato, degrees Balling, etc. In the case of unfermented wort, the specific gravity is the same as the original gravity. For fermenting wort or beer it is more correctly the apparent specific gravity that is measured by a saccharometer because the alcohol being lighter than water reduces the actual reading given by the floating bulb.

See also BALLING SCALE, ORIGINAL GRAVITY, PLATO GRAVITY SCALE, and REAL DEGREE OF FERMENTATION (RDF).

Briggs, Dennis E., Chris A. Boulton, Peter A. Brookes, and Roger Stevens. *Brewing: science and practice*. Cambridge, UK: Woodhead Publishing, 2004.
Hind, Lloyd. *Brewing science and practice*. New York: Wiley, 1943.

Chris J. Marchbanks

spelt is a hard-grained heirloom wheat, with genes going back to cultivars planted in Neolithic times in the Fertile Crescent of the Middle East. Its scientific name is Triticum spelta, and its often-used German name is Dinkel. Mankind's first known brewers, the Sumerians, almost certainly made beer from spelt. Spelt is the result of a cross between Emmer (Triticum dicoccum) and wild grasses in Mesopotamia some 10,000 years ago. See EMMER. Emmer, in turn, is a cross between Einkorn (Triticum monococcum), which is an even older wheat variety, and wild grasses. See EINKORN WHEAT. In Europe, spelt is known to have been cultivated at least since the late Bronze Age, some 3,000 years ago, mostly in the regions inhabited by the Alemans, a Germanic tribe in what is now the German State of Baden-Württemberg and the German-speaking part of Switzerland. In the Middle Ages, spelt was also known as Schwabenkorn (Swabia grain), because the southwestern German region of Swabia (part of Baden-Württemberg) was then the center of spelt cultivation. Spelt places few demands on soil quality and climate, which means that it can grow where modern wheat (Triticum aestivum) cannot. Today, interest in ancient grains is rising, and craft brewers in Europe and the United States are starting to rediscover spelt. Used at proportions approaching 50% of the grist, spelt malt gives mild, nutty flavors backed by tangy acidic notes.

Horst Dornbusch

spent grain is the compact waste of malt and/or grains left after mashing and lautering in the brew house. It weighs approximately 100–130 kg wet for every 100 kg of dry grist that went into the original mash. Spent grain consists primarily of barley husks (the aleurone and pericarp layers), embryonic remnants, protein, and minerals. When dried, it typically contains approximately 28% protein, 8.2% fat, 41% carbohydrates, 17.5% cellulose, and 5.3% minerals. When wet, water by mass comprises 75%–80%. What is waste to the brewer is valuable to the farmer; because of its many nutrients, spent grain is an excellent animal feed, and most livestock find it highly palatable when it is fresh. Once the spent grain cools, however, it must be processed quickly or it will spoil. Breweries traditionally dispose of it while it is still damp, collecting it in a silo or other container for local farmers or distributors. It is of special value for ruminants (mammals such as cows that partially digest food by chewing a cud) because it better withstands protein degradation in the rumen (a chamber for microbial fermentation of ingested feed) when compared to other feeds. Spent grain is also well suited for silaging (a method of fermenting and storing cattle fodder). No additives are necessary and it yields a high-quality silage with an optimal pH value and minimal protein breakdown. Spent grain can also be dried and then stored or burned as an alternate energy source, or it can be fermented to produce biogas (the generic term for gas produced by the biological breakdown of organic matter in the absence of oxygen). It also is a good additive to compost, and it is widely used as a medium on which to grow mushrooms. Samples of spent grain are often analyzed in the lab to provide quantitative feedback on brewhouse performance. In many small breweries and brewpubs, "digging out the mash tun" is a vigorous daily ritual carried out with a shovel, a welcome portent to the end of the workday.

Kunze, Wolfgang. *Technologie brauer & mälzer (Technology brewers and maltsters)*, 9th ed. Berlin: VLB Berlin, 2007.

MEBAK. *Brautechnische analysenmethoden, Band II*, 4th ed. Freising-Weihenstephan, Germany: MEBAK, 2002.

Süd-Treber GmbH. http://www.suedtreber.de/ (accessed May 26, 2010).

Wolfgang David Lindell

spices have a long history of use in beer. In fact, since the beginning of beer making some 8,000 years ago until the introduction of hops roughly in the High Middle Ages in Europe, spices both local and exotic, along with herbs, had been the dominant beer flavoring. In many Belgian beer styles, they are still popular to this day, and they are once again being used by many modern craft brewers, often for seasonal specialty beers, including Christmas and other holiday beers. During the Age of Discovery, spices became increasingly available to Europeans, who used them in both their food and their beer. Brewers in medieval times often used spices not just for their own flavor but also to cover up acidic, rancid, or medicinal off-flavors in their beer. Medieval physicians often attributed healthful qualities to spices—many of which, of course, have not stood up in the light of modern science—leading to such fanciful prescription as drinking a mug of hot spiced beer, similar to a toddy, mulled wine, or glögg, as an antidote to the plague.

Spices mainly used for bittering in beer and for balancing its malt aroma were bay leaf, juniper, and such seeds of the umbel family (Apiaceae) as anise, caraway, coriander, dill, and fennel. Carrot and parsley belong to this group as well. These seeds not only taste bitter but also impart significant aromas and anise/coriander/licorice flavors. Other spices add a chili-like sharpness to the brew. These include chili peppers, black and green peppers, ginger, quassia, and grains of paradise. Next is the group of "true" spices, each with its own unique flavor. There is allspice, cardamom, cinnamon, clove, licorice, mace/nutmeg, and star anise, as well as the zest of different citrus fruits. Many of these spices have been and still are particular favorites for Christmas cooking, baking, and beer making. Finally, a few nontraditional beer flavorings have been used by many brewers. Vanilla, for example, has become common, whereas saffron is perhaps considered more experimental.

There is some controversy among brewers about the proper techniques for using spices in beer. Some hold that spices should be added only sparingly and must not overpower the flavors put into the beer by malt, hops, and yeast. Others, however, prefer a less nuanced approach and prefer to challenge traditional notions of beer flavor. This often means that a spice that is traditional for a particular kind of beer, such as Curaçao orange peel in Belgian wit, may migrate to a beer style where it has never been used before. In the United States, the most prevalent spiced beers are seasonal pumpkin ales, which are popular in the autumn and winter months. Although most of these beers do contain pumpkin, the flavors are often driven by combinations of cinnamon, allspice, nutmeg, ginger, vanilla, and other spices. The goal is to mimic the aroma and flavor of the traditional American pumpkin pie, which is consumed almost exclusively during the winter holiday season. Aside from Belgium, where spices are used less than is often supposed, brewing with spices is currently seen most frequently among craft brewers in the United States, Denmark, and the UK, with Italian craft brewers swiftly following.

Spices and Their Uses in Beer

Common name	*Scientific name*	*Part used*	*Comment*	*Use (examples)*
Allspice	Pimenta dioica	Seed	Bitterness, significant aroma, healthy, beer preservative	Christmas beers, medieval medicinal beers
Anise	Pimpinella anisum	Seed	Adds a spicy and anise-like bitterness during the boil	Historical beer bittering
Bay leaf	Laurus nobilis	Leaf	Bitterness, significant aroma, healthy, beer preservative	Recent experimental brewing
Caraway	Carum carvi	Seed	Adds a spicy and anise-like bitterness during the boil	Historical beer bittering
Cardamom	Elettaria cardamomum	Seed	Powerfully aromatic, ginger family	Christmas beers, medieval medicinal beers
Chili pepper	Capsicum spp.	Fruit	Both vegetal flavor and capsaicin heat	Original porter, experimental brewing
Cinnamon	Cinnamomum verum	Bark	Popular, but often is actually cassia bark	Pumpkin ales and Christmas beers, medieval medicinal beers
Citrus	Citrus spp.	Peel	Lemon peel; sweet, canned orange peel; Curaçao	Belgian-style ales, particularly witbier
Clove	Syzygium aromaticum	Flower bud	Very powerful, best used sparingly	Pumpkin ales and Christmas beers Medieval medicinal beers
Coriander	Coriandrum sativum	Seed	Widely used	Belgium wit
Dill	Anethum graveolens	Seed	Adds a spicy and anise-like bitterness during the boil	Historical beer bittering

Fennel	Foeniculum vulgare	Seed	Adds a spicy and anise-like bitterness during the boil	Historical beer bittering
Ginger	Zingiber officinale	Root	Highly aromatic	Original porter, medieval medicinal beers
Grains of paradise	Aframomum melegueta	Seed	Pepper-like spice with notes of citrus and pine; once believed to be an aphrodisiac	Old English ales, abandoned in the 17th century by law, experimental brewing
Juniper	Juniperus communis	Berry	Used in the mash or boil	Historical Scandinavian brewing, such as Finnish Sahti, for which boughs, too, are used in the mash
Licorice	Glycyrrhiza glabra	Root	Bitter, medicinal	Original porter and stout
Mace	Myristica fragrans	Fruit/ aril	A sophisticated and delicious alternative to nutmeg	Holiday beers
Nutmeg	Myristica fragrans	Fruit/ nut		Christmas beers, medieval medicinal beers, experimental brewing
Parsley	Petroselinum crispum	Seed	Adds a spicy and anise-like bitterness during the boil	Historical beer bittering
Pepper	Piper nigrum	Seed	Highly fragrant, adds heat if concentrated	Experimental brewing, medieval medicinal beers
Quassia	Quassia amara	Wood	Quinine-like	Historical beer bittering
Saffron	Crocus sativus	Style/ stigma	Very expensive, strong savory flavor	Experimental brewing
Star anise	Illicium verum	Seed	Adds a spicy and anise-like bitterness during the boil	Experimental brewing, Christmas beers
Vanilla	Vanilla planifolia	Fruit	Widely used	Holiday beers, porters

See also CORIANDER, CURAÇAO ORANGES, JUNIPER, and NUTMEG.

Behre, Karl-Ernst. The history of beer additives in Europe—A review. *Vegetation History and Archaeobotany* 8 (1999): 35–48.

Both, Frank, ed. *Gerstensaft und Hirsebier: 5000 Jahre Biergenuss*. Oldenburg, Germany: Verlag Isensee, 1998.

Buhner, H. B. *Sacred and herbal healing beers: The secrets of ancient fermentation*. Boulder, CO: Siris Books, 1998.

Hofsten, Nils von. *Pors och andra humleersättninger och Ölkryddor i äldre tider. Akademiska Förlaget (Gale and other substitutes and beer-spices in past times)*. Uppsala, Sweden: AB Lundequistska Bokhandeln, 1960. Includes an English summary.

Per Kølster

spile, sometimes called a cask peg, is a wooden or plastic peg intended to manually control the venting in and out of carbon dioxide (CO_2) and air from the shive hole during the conditioning and dispense of traditional cask beer. See SHIVE. Spiles have a tapered conical shape approximately 20–30 mm long to fit in the shive hole and are manipulated by hand and mallet.

There are two types of spile. "Soft pegs" are made from a very porous wood such as cane, bamboo, or sapwood, which allows casks to vent off CO_2 slowly during the conditioning period. "Hard pegs," made from hard wood (oak, sycamore) or nylon, retain condition (CO_2 gas) in the beer and exclude air when the beer is not being drawn out. Wooden spiles are discarded after a single use, but plastic spiles can be reused after appropriate cleaning.

Miles, J.G. *Innkeeping*, 9th ed. Boulder, CO: Brewing Publications, 1985.
O'Neill, P. *Cellarmanship*, 4th ed. St. Albans, UK: CAMRA, 2005.

Chris J. Marchbanks

spoilage

See BEER SPOILERS.

spray malt

See DRIED MALT EXTRACT.

spruce

See PINE, FIR, AND SPRUCE TIPS.

Sri Lanka is an island republic off the southeastern coast of India. It was formerly called Ceylon. Brewing began there in 1860 mostly to meet the needs of western tea planters. Sri Lanka's preferred beer styles have changed little since then, and despite the tropical weather, Sri Lankans are fond of strong stouts.

Sri Lanka is home to more than 21 million people, and although many of them do not drink, the nation's beer business is competitive. The largest of Sri Lanka's brewers is the Lion Brewing Company, which produces 83% of the country's beers. The Danish Carlsberg concern owns 25% of Lion Brewing's equity. The company exports to the UK, Japan, Australia, and the Maldives. In 1998, it built a new brewery built in Biyagama some 25 km east of Colombo, the country's largest city, which replaced a century-old, outmoded plant at Nuwara Eliya. Lion Brewing also has a second, smaller facility in Colombo. Three beers constitute the brewery's portfolio: lager, strong, and stout. Lion Stout, a robust foreign-style stout recalling beers of the mid 1800s, is an impressive beer full of chocolate, rum, and dark fruit flavors at 8% ABV. In addition, the company brews Carlsberg beers.

Sri Lanka's second brewer is Asia Pacific Breweries, which moved into the country in 2005. It has a brewery at Mawathagama, where it makes a range of Kings beers, including a lager and a stout. The country's smallest brewer is the Three Coins Brewery in Colombo, which is owned by McCallum. Following the national style preference, it brews Sando Stout.

Jackson, Michael. http://www.beerhunter.com/documents/19133-001402.html/ (accessed January 11, 2011).

Barrie Pepper

staling, a complex set of organic chemical changes that occur in beer over time, transforming its flavor and causing it to diverge from the desired and expected flavor and appearance. Staling, it should be noted, is a different (if related) phenomenon than "aging," which describes intentional and desirable flavor changes over time. See AGING OF BEER. Although the word "stale" is nowadays always pejorative, this was not always so. In 19th-century England, the word "stale" was often synonymous with "old," and the flavor of older beer, sometimes including acidity, was widely considered superior. For most of history, brewers have largely been concerned with the prevention of beer spoilage by microorganisms. Now that microbiological concerns have largely been conquered by modern technology and sanitation, brewers focus on shelf life, which can be defined as stability of flavor, aroma, and appearance.

Many consumers may not recognize the flavor of stale beer. However, most do recognize the normal flavor of their favorite beers and those flavors are usually the flavors of fresh beer. As beer ages, it develops new flavors and the fresh flavors diminish. Most of the changes that occur as fresh beer becomes stale involve oxygen, which is one reason why brewers attempt to avoid oxidation throughout the brewing process. Among the first and most prominent attributes of beer staling is the development of cardboardlike, sherrylike, and/or black currantlike flavors. Caramel flavors may develop in pale beers, even those that did not include any caramelized malts in the brewing process. As beer stales, it becomes darker in color, a change that will be particularly notable in pale beers such as pilsner. Hazes or precipitates will also eventually tend to develop in filtered beers. See HAZE.

Much attention has been concentrated on the development of the oxidative compound (E)-2-nonenal, which has a strong damp cardboard aroma.

However, many other compounds contribute to the flavor of stale beer, particularly a large range of aldehydes. See ALDEHYDES and (E)-2-NONENAL. Maillard reaction products result in sweet, bready, toffeeish, and winelike flavors in stale beers. Controversially, it has been suggested that slight staleness may be partly responsible for the desirable depth of malt character seen in certain beer styles, particularly German doppelbock. Many consumers associate skunklike flavors with beer staling, but this is technically a form of damage by light and will not occur in beer kept under dark conditions. See LIGHTSTRUCK. This is an understandable misconception, especially because beer that has become stale may also have been exposed to light for long periods of time. In beers with strong hop aromatics, for example, India pale ales, the hop aromatics eventually degrade from bright, fresh floral and citrus aromas to duller tealike aromas.

Beer staling is slowed by colder temperatures and accelerated by warmer temperatures. The nature of the staling is itself temperature dependent; beer that is quickly staled at warm temperatures tastes different than beer that slowly stales at cold temperatures. This means that laboratory "forcing" tests, in which beer is stored at elevated temperatures to mimic the effects of age, can give an indication of a beer's shelf life, but not necessarily how the beer will taste when it becomes stale.

The consumer's best protection against buying or serving stale beer is the information hopefully provided by the brewer in the form of a bottling date or, better yet, a "best-before" date. The former will give the consumer an idea of whether the beer can be expected to be fresh, and the latter will involve the brewer's best determination as to how long the beer will look and taste as it should.

See also FAULTS IN BEER, OFF-FLAVORS, and OXIDATION.

Vanderhaegen, B., H. Neven, H. Verachtert, and G. Derdelinckx. The chemistry of beer aging—a critical review. *Food Chemistry* 95 (2006): 357–81.

Garrett Oliver

standard reference method (SRM) is the method for color assessment of wort or beer as published in the recommended methods of the American Society of Brewing Chemists. See AMERICAN SOCIETY OF BREWING CHEMISTS (ASBC). It is measured in a cell of path length 0.5 inches (1.27 cm) with light of wavelength 430 nm. The resultant absorbance value is multiplied by 10 to yield the color value and by any dilution factor if the sample needs to be diluted to bring the color within the reliable measurement range of the spectrophotometer. If a 1 cm path length is used (most spectrophotometer cuvettes are such), then the multiplier is 12.7 rather than 10.

In the color method of the European Brewery Convention (EBC), a 1 cm path length is used but the multiplier is 25. Accordingly, EBC color values are approximately twice those on the ASBC scale. A reading is also taken at 700 nm to assess the level of turbidity in the sample, which may be a particular problem for worts. If A_{700} is less than 0.039 x A_{430}, then the sample is sufficiently bright. If this criterion is not met, then the sample needs to be filtered or centrifuged before repeat analysis.

Shellhammer, T. H. "Beer color." In C. W. Bamforth ed,. *Beer: A quality perspective*, 213–27. Burlington, MA: Academic Press, 2009.

Charles W. Bamforth

Stander (barley) is a six-row malting variety developed by Dr Donald Rasmusson at the University of Minnesota and released in 1993. The variety was named for its enhanced lodging resistance, that is, its ability to "stand up" to strong winds and heavy rains. See LODGING RESISTANCE. Stander was higher-yielding, a little shorter, and matured slightly later than other varieties grown at the time. The parents of Stander were the varieties Excel and the University of Minnesota breeding line M80-224. Stander has resistance to the leaf disease spot blotch, and it carries the *Rpg1* gene, which gives it resistance to strains of stem rust that are currently prevalent in the United States. Stander was grown primarily in the northern Plains (Minnesota, South Dakota, and North Dakota) where, by 1996, it made up almost 40% of the acreage. Though Stander was initially approved as a malting barley variety by the American Malting Barley Association, it quickly fell out of favor with American brewers because its high percentage of soluble protein made it difficult to use in the brewhouse. Farmers also had problems with it, as it had a tendency to sprout before harvesting. As a result, Stander acreage dropped to below 5% by 2000.

Rasmusson, D. C., R. D. Wilcoxson, and J. V. Wiersma, Registration of "Stander" barley. *Crop Science* 33 (1993): 1403.

Kevin Smith

starch, a large-molecule carbohydrate used in making beer. To make any alcoholic beverage, there must be sugar present for yeast to ferment. Plants make glucose, a sugar, during photosynthesis but need to store it until it is needed. Because glucose is a highly soluble and fairly small molecule, it attracts a lot of water into the plant cells. By joining several glucose molecules into fewer larger molecules, the amount of water drawn into the cell is much reduced, which makes storing it much less demanding. The larger molecule in question is called starch. Grain starch will be broken down into sugars to create wort, which will then be fermented into beer.

Starch is a carbohydrate, meaning that it is built up from carbon, oxygen, and hydrogen, literally, carbon and water. Because starch contains many molecules of sugar, it is called a polysaccharide. Starch exists in two slightly differing forms, one a linear molecule and the other branched. The straight chain form is called amylose and is usually about 10% to 30% of the starch present. The branched chain, called amylopectin, makes up 70% to 90%. Corn starch, for example, is 25% amylose and 75% amylopectin.

The starch is packaged as starch grains inside special storage cells until such time as it is required. The starch grains must be gelatinized before the starch can be enzymically attacked and converted into sugars in the brewhouse. Gelatinization occurs at around 65°C for barley starch, which dictates the typical conversion temperatures used by brewers. However, gelatinization occurs at higher temperatures for rice and corn, demanding that they be cooked separately and added later to the main barley malt mash.

The Iodine/Starch Test

To check for conversion of starches into sugars, brewers will often perform a simple starch test in which iodine (as potassium iodide) is added to starch, producing a characteristic blue–black color. The different structure of amylopectin produces a red–violet color with iodine. As starches are hydrolyzed into smaller molecules, this reaction no longer occurs.

Starch is the primary material from which fermentable sugars used in brewing are derived. Yeast is unable to use large and complicated starch molecules, so the starch must first be hydrolyzed into smaller carbohydrates. During the malting, roasting, and then mashing of barley, many of the enzymes normally present in the grain are destroyed. However, two enzymes persist, at least well into the mash. These are alpha- and beta-amylase, which, between them, are capable of hydrolyzing much of the starch present into sugars no larger than three glucose units long. Hydrolysis means literally "to add water," resulting in the starch being broken up and turned back into sugars.

Alpha-amylase attacks the bonds between glucose subunits in starch at any point in the chain, producing random-length carbohydrates. Left long enough, alpha-amylase will reduce amylose into a soup of glucose, maltose (a disaccharide with two glucose rings), and maltotriose (a trisaccharide with three glucose rings).

Beta-amylase starts at one end of the starch molecule and chops it up into pairs of glucose molecules, called maltose. Beta-amylase can only start its work from one end of the starch molecule, which slows things down.

The two enzymes work in concert in the mash tun, the alpha-amylase producing more ends for the beta-amylase and between them producing approximately 80% fermentable sugars in the form of 10% to 15% glucose, 50% to 60% maltose, and 10% to 15% maltotriose from the original starch. The remaining 20% consists of the nonfermentable fragments of amylopectin containing the branch points because neither enzyme is capable of breaking them down. These fragments of the amylopectin molecules are called limit dextrins. Endogenous industrial enzymes such as glucoamylase are able to hydrolyze even branch points and so can produce 100% fermentable sugars from amylopectin.

See also AMYLOPECTIN, AMYLOSE, ENDOSPERM, and MASHING.

Garret, Reginald H., and Charles M. Grisham. *Biochemistry*, international ed. Fort Worth, TX: Saunders College Publishing, 1995.

Scientific Psychic. www.scientificpsychic.com/fitness/carbohydrates1.html/ (accessed January 4, 2011).

Chris Holliland

starkbier, a now antiquated German federal beer tax category that was abolished effective January 1, 1993. Literally, the term meant "strong beer" and referred to a beer with an original gravity—measured in degrees Plato—of more than 16°P. In particular, this designation would have covered doppelbock. See DOPPELBOCK, ORIGINAL GRAVITY, and PLATO GRAVITY SCALE. For an explanation of the old and the new German beer tax law, see VOLLBIER.

Horst Dornbusch

Staropramen Brewery, founded in 1869 and located in the Smíchov district of Prague, was once the largest brewery in the Czech Republic. Currently in the number two spot, its flagship brand, a full-bodied golden lager simply known as Staropramen, is sold in over 30 countries around the world. Following construction of the brewery, the first ceremonial batch was brewed on May 1, 1871, and was available for sale on July 15, 1871.

By 1891 the Staropramen Brewery was producing 140,200 hl (3.7 million gallons) of beer annually. The brewery continued to grow but was hobbled by World War I and its after effects; raw materials for brewing were limited. However, by the 1930s the brewery was once again producing beers at a record pace. In 1939 it brewed 859,561 hl.

Following World War II Staropramen was nationalized but continued to produce beer and by the 1960s was brewing 1 million hl per year. In 1992, the company Pražské pivovary, a. s., was created and assumed ownership of Staropramen and fellow Czech Republic brewery Braník. A third brewery, Ostravar, was added to the company in 1997.

The company was purchased by Belgium-based InterBrew in 2000. In an effort to return to its roots and to make the brewery more identifiable to the public, Pražské pivovary, a. s. was renamed Pivovary Staropramen a.s. in 2003. In 2009 Pivovary Staropramen a.s. was purchased by an investment group that later renamed itself StarBev.

Staropramen continues to produce several brands of lager including the eponymous lager, Světlý (pale), Černý (dark), and the reddish Granát (garnet), brewed from a recipe that the brewery says dates back to 1884.

See also CZECH REPUBLIC.

Official Information from Pivovary Staropramen a.s., InBev and StarBev.

Pivovary Staropramen. http://www.pivovary-staropramen.cz/web/en/o_nas/historie/ (accessed January 10, 2011).

Correspondence with Pavel Barvík, Corporate Affairs Manager, Pivovary Staropramen a.s., in January 2011.

John Holl

steam beer. While in America today the name "steam beer" is claimed by a single San Francisco brewer, it was once a widespread beer style in California. In the mid-to-late 1800s, people streamed into the West, drawn by promises of the Gold Rush and wide open spaces. Beer, of course, went with them. By the late 1800s, an indigenous style called "steam beer" was brewed by perhaps as many as 25 breweries in San Francisco alone. In 1902, Wahl and Heinus's *American Handy Book of Brewing and Malting* tells us, "This beer is largely consumed throughout the state of California. It is called steam beer on account of its highly effervescing properties and the amount of pressure ("steam") it has in the trade packages. The pressure ranges from 40 to 70 pounds in each trade package, according to the amount of kräusen added, temperatures, and time it takes before being consumed and the distance it travels from saloon rack to faucet, etc."

Other explanations abound for the original naming of steam beer, but it is agreed that the style adheres to general production methods: lager ("bottom-fermenting") yeast is allowed to ferment the beer at warmer temperatures, resulting in a crisply nuanced yet hearty hybrid of both styles. The combined factors of the demand for the lager beers then capturing the world's fancy and the lack of refrigeration available to brewers on America's expanding western frontier led to the production of beers which satisfied both taxonomy and capability. Eventually this beer became a style unto itself. Steam beer's rough-and-tumble production origins fit with its favor among the working class of the day, not unlike the role of porter in Industrial Revolution-era London. Literary mention of steam beer also indicates a less-than-sophisticated reputation. As refrigeration and more consistently modern brewing techniques came to the West, brewers moved to more strictly defined lager styles, resulting in the near-extinction of steam beer.

In 1965 Fritz Maytag, an heir to the resources of the Maytag washing machine family, became involved with the Anchor Brewing Company, which had brewed under that name in San Francisco since 1896 but which at the time was on the verge of bankruptcy. He not only rescued the brewery by eventually purchasing it outright but gave new life to its steam beer, which today remains the brewery's flagship product. For years "Anchor Steam" was a strictly San Francisco staple, but in the 1980s it became more widely available throughout the United States and beyond.

Various breweries in America and elsewhere have historically appended the word "steam" to their beer in reference to the power plants firing their kettles and running their machinery. It is thought, however, that true steam beer owed its name to one or another procedural association in its production and serving. One had to do with the "steam," or excess carbonation needing to be let off kegs of fresh beer preparatory to serving; another concerned the method of cooling the wort post-boil by running it into broad and shallow cooling vessels which allowed a proportionately large surface area to come into contact with cold outside air, resulting in distinctive and enveloping clouds of steam. This cooling procedure also adheres to the inherent low-tech aspects of frontier brewing.

Another interesting aspect of the steam beer mythos is the jealous manner in which Anchor Brewing protects the style-designated name of its principal beer. Time and again it has asserted its legally sanctioned (trademarked since 1981, and generally respected) ownership of the word "steam" in connection with beer and brewing. Letters have appeared on the doorsteps of more than a few brewers, requesting them to cease and desist the use of even oblique and playful reference to "steam beer" and threatening legal proceedings to enforce the same. Occasional recalcitrant American brewers have generally been brought to heel, but Anchor has found difficulty enforcing steamy sovereignty beyond American borders. Sleeman's of Canada, for example, has proven able to defy Anchor's attempted prohibition of its marketing of a steam beer under that name by proving the use of the name within Canada prior to Anchor's introduction there. The Maisel Brewery in Bayreuth, Bavaria, produces a "steam beer" (dampfbier) as well, avowedly in reference to the old steam engines these days displayed alongside more modern equipment. An outgrowth of this assertion of right by Anchor has been the designation of the once-ubiquitous American steam beer style by various US judging entities as "California Common Beer," including the Beer Judge Certification Program and the Brewers Association, which oversees both the World Beer Cup competition and the Great American Beer Festival. Smacking of political correctness and lacking all but a vestige of Old West color, the new designation would seem to discourage emulation of a beer with an interesting—as well as democratic—historical pedigree.

Since the Anchor beer stands alone in the legal marketing of American steam beers, some notes on its appearance and effect are perhaps appropriate. Dark amber in color, Anchor Steam displays strong carbonation, a touch beyond the usual. Its crispness of flavor is due both to its lager yeast and the Continental hops used, but there is also malt flavor and the fruitiness of warmer fermentation in evidence. It is noteworthy that such a hybrid would have served, in the infancy of the craft brewing movement, as a "gateway" beer to the uninitiated. Some years later Boston Beer Company (brewers of Samuel Adams Boston Lager) and many other American brewers would take similar approaches with their own beers. Perhaps a steam beer by any other name may yet taste as sweet.

See also ANCHOR BREWING COMPANY.

Anchor Brewing. anchorbrewing.com (accessed October 20, 2010).

Jackson, Michael. *The new world guide to beer.* Philadelphia: Running Press, 1988.

Mosher, Randy. *Radical brewing: Recipes, tales and world-altering meditations in a glass.* Boulder, CO: Brewers Publications, 2004.

Smith, Gregg. "Steam beer." http://www.realbeer.com (accessed August 14, 2010).

Dick Cantwell

Steel's Masher. Developed and patented in England in 1853, Steel's Masher is a device to hydrate the grist, eliminate manual mixing of the mash with paddles or oars, and optimize temperature control during mash-ins. Designed specifically for use in infusion mashing schemes with single temperature rest, a Steel's Masher is a critical piece of equipment that allows the brewer to control both the malt flow (via a slide valve) and the mash water flow into the grain to maintain consistent temperature throughout the mash and obtain excellent wetting and mixing.

During the mash-in process, grist (milled malt) is fed into the top of the Steel's Masher, and makes a right angle turn into a horizontal feed auger. Mash water is supplied either before or at the feed auger, then the mixture transfers through a series of mixing paddles or mixing rods where the malt is thoroughly mixed with the water. By the time the grain exits the masher, it is completely wetted. The mash then is then fed to the mash tun. This is called "doughing in." Modern Steel's Mashers are equipped with sophisticated temperature sensors and water mixing valves that allow precise temperature control of the mash as it enters the mash tun.

Versions of the Steel's Masher remain in use in many English ale breweries and in some American craft breweries.

Mitch Steele

steeping, the first of the three stages of the malting process. See MALTING. The aim of steeping is to take barley that has recovered from dormancy and has been stored at about 11% to 14% moisture and to raise the moisture content of the grain to around 43% to 47% by successive immersions in water over a period of approximately 2 days. See DORMANCY (OF BARLEY).

Modern malting procedure uses interrupted steeping—alternating periods of water immersion and dry periods known as air rests. During each of two or three (occasionally four) wet periods, the grain/water mixture is aerated to maintain aerobic conditions for the grain. In the intervening dry periods, air is drawn through the damp grain to remove the carbon dioxide produced by respiration of the barley seeds. This helps approximate the conditions in which the seeds would normally grow and therefore stimulates them to germinate.

Steeping normally proceeds in the temperature range of 15°C to 20°C (about 60°F to 70°F). It takes place in a purpose-designed vessel of either cylindroconical or flat-bottom design. The latter has a plenum area situated below slotted floor plates to permit even ventilation and aeration.

Water enters the grain primarily through the micropyle at the embryo end of the grain. Accordingly, hydration of the grain occurs from the proximal toward the distal end, and the moisture content of the embryo will be higher than that of the endosperm during wet phases until the grain equilibrates during subsequent dry phases. Increasing the grain moisture performs two main functions: it stimulates the embryo to start to grow and water penetrates the endosperm matrix, allowing enzymic activity to take place during the germination stage.

Rapid, even, and complete hydration allows successful germination to follow—steeping is the key stage in malting to allow satisfactory modification of the grain during the remainder of the process.

See also GERMINATION and MODIFICATION.

Colin J. West

Steffi (barley) has been one of the world's most successful modern two-row spring brewing barleys. Bred by Ackermann Saatzucht GmbH & Co. in Irlbach in eastern Bavaria, it has been popular with farmers, maltsters, and brewers alike ever since its registration for commercial use in 1989. As a brewing base malt, Steffi produces mashes of low viscosity and high extract values that result in worts of good fermentability. According to the official listing by the Bundessortenamt (the German government's seed certification agency), Steffi's favorable all-round qualities include kernel homogeneity, a high percentage of kernels with a diameter greater than 2.5 mm, low protein values, and fairly high agronomic yields, as well as unusually high disease resistance in the field. Steffi seems to be almost uniquely immune to loose smut of barley (Ustilago nuda), a destructive fungal pathogen that easily propagates via sporulation, especially in moist conditions during the plant's maturation period. See SMUT. While most barley varieties have a commercial life cycle—from introduction to phase-out—of about a decade, Steffi has remained in cultivation more than twice that long in both Europe and North America. Though waning, Steffi was still the cultivar of choice in 0.7% of all barley plantings in Germany in 2009. Steffi is still especially sought after by organic farmers, who value its unusual natural hardiness—a key advantage in organic crop production, where chemical herbicides and pesticides are not allowed.

See also TWO-ROW MALT.

Bundessortenamt Blatt für Sortenwesen (German certification agency annual report). http://www.bundessortenamt.de/internet30/index.php?id=23/ (inactive).

Thomas Kraus-Weyermann

stein is the German word for "stone." To non-speakers of German it usually denotes a particular beer-drinking vessel that became ubiquitous in Bavaria in the 19th century. For centuries, Germans would drink beer in pubs from large communal earthenware pitchers, which they often passed around from one eager lip to the next. The Vienna Congress, which ended the Napoleonic Wars in 1815, brought about decades of peace and prosperity, during which more and more pub patrons could afford their own, private beer mugs. These were usually made of superior, high-temperature kilned "stoneware" instead of earthenware, and glazed with salt for a smooth finish. Finer examples were intricately decorated.

Beer gardens shaded by chestnut or linden trees became fashionable in the mid-19th century, which led to the development of the tin-lidded stein for keeping insects and leaves out of beer. See BEER GARDENS. Early steins came in all shapes and sizes, but a set of Bavarian laws, passed between 1809 and 1811, mandated that all steins henceforth had to hold the same amount of beer, namely one Munich "mass," which is exactly 1.069 liters (36.15 fl. oz.). Once Bavaria joined Bismarck's newly forged Second German Empire in 1870, the old Bavarian stein was resized to exactly 1 liter. At the same time, low-cost steins started to be mass-produced with brewery logos, which led to the gradual disappearance of the tin lid.

The final blow to the stein, however, came in 1878, when Lorenz Enzinger, a Bavarian engineer, invented the beer filter. As soon as brewers could make brilliantly clear beer, they switched to serving it in transparent, cheaper glassware, which was now being mass-produced. However, the stein has not gone out of fashion entirely. In many traditional beer halls and beer gardens in Bavaria and, indeed, around the world, publicans sometimes serve their lagers (never ales) in steins—but invariably in unlidded ones for easier and more hygienic cleaning in modern dishwashers. Garishly kitschy "steins" are widely sold to tourists in Bavaria, but antique steins are among the most collectible beer-related objects, and fine examples have sold at auction for many thousands of dollars.

See also BAVARIA.

"Der bayerische Masskrug und das bayerische Bier." www.zur-wurst.at/ (accessed September 10, 2010).

Horst Dornbusch

steinbier, "stone beer," an ale brewed with the use of hot stones, originally without the use of any brewing equipment made from metal. Steinbier breweries were typical for southern Austria and for some parts of Bavaria up to the beginning of the 20th century. The brewing method was supposedly developed by farmers who did not own proper brewing vessels. Heating of the mash and boiling of the wort were induced not by heating a brew kettle but rather by dropping very hot stones into wooden vessels containing the mash or the wort. Most stones are unsuitable for that procedure because sudden temperature changes result in cracking of most types of rock. A certain variety of rock, however, seems to resist extreme temperature changes; it is called "gray wacke." This kind of stone is very common in Carinthia, the southernmost state of Austria, and it was here that steinbier was developed.

Steinbier was produced in wooden brewing vessels. Stones heated over fire were dropped into the mash tun to heat the mash; later, after the run-off, the same or a similar vessel would be used to boil the wort. The effect of adding hot rock to the mash, and even more effectively to the wort, would result in spontaneous boiling of the liquid that came in contact with the surface of the stone. Sugars from the wort would also instantly caramelize, whereas the stone itself released some of the smokiness of the fire in which it had been heated. Not surprisingly, this procedure was highly dangerous and could easily end up with the brewer burned by wort or the brewery consumed by fire.

This rather primitive production method seems to date back millennia and was widespread throughout the world, but gray wacke is particular to this part of Europe. Superheated stones have been used in farmhouse brewing for centuries, but rarely in professional brewing in towns or villages. Professional brewers refused to accept the brewers of steinbier in their guilds because the use of metal vessels was considered crucial for the craft. When state-of-the-art brewing equipment became more widely available in the second half of the 19th century, most steinbier breweries could not survive the stiff competition. Holzleger was the last steinbier brewery in Austria (and presumably in the world); it was opened in the small village of Waidmannsdorf near Klagenfurt in 1645 and was in operation until 1917, probably because of a lack of brewing material in World War I. The production was 690 hl that year.

Long after steinbier had disappeared from the map, the production technique was rediscovered by the Sailer Bräu Franz Sailer in Marktoberdorf, Bavaria. Here gray wacke rocks were put into large metal cages, heated over beechwood, and hauled into a (conventional) brew kettle. The rocks, coated with caramelized sugars, were then later added to the fermenting beer, giving it a unique blend smoke and caramel flavors. The production was given up when Allgäuer Brauhaus (a subsidiary of Radeberger) took over the brewery in Marktoberdorf in 2003. Some other breweries have taken up the production of steinbier, including Leikeim in the Franconian town of Altenkunstadt. Their steinbier is a lager with faint hints of caramel and smoke.

Conrad Seidl

Steinecker

See KRONES.

Stella Artois is an "international pilsner" beer brand currently owned by Anheuser-Busch InBev and distributed all over the world with an alcohol by volume of either 5% or 5.2% depending on the location.

Stella Artois is brewed under contract in Australia and the UK but originates from the Belgian town of Leuven where, according to tax records, the Den Horen (the horn) Brewery resided as far back as 1366. Although the Stella Artois logo of a horn and much of the brand marketing pays homage to the Den Horen name and the date of 1366, the name Artois was not associated with the brewery until the 18th century when Sebastian Artois, the brewmaster, lent it his name in 1717.

More than 200 years later, in 1926, Stella Artois was released as a limited edition Christmas beer meaning "star." Having found favor in its native Belgium, it was launched as a permanent beer and, by 1930, was being exported to other European countries.

Belgium is famous for its distinctive and flavorful ales, so many beer enthusiasts are surprised to find that fairly bland international pilsners account for more than 70% of the Belgian beer market. In Belgium, Stella Artois is considered a very ordinary beer at best—the top selling beer in Belgium is its stablemate, Jupiler.

One of the most successful markets for Stella Artois was in the UK during the 1980s and 1990s when its "Reassuringly Expensive" advertising campaign and strong links with cinema established it as the leading premium lager brand, selling 3 million barrels a year in 2001. However, the Stella star has since waned amid associations with binge drinking, so-called lager louts, and the beer's unfortunate UK nickname, "wife-beater."

Despite this, Stella Artois remains one of the world's most popular lager brands and a leading import brand in the United States. It is brewed using hops, barley, maize, water, and yeast.

Ben McFarland

sterile filtration, a form of filtration fine enough to remove spoilage organisms. For beer, "sterile filtration" is understood to reduce yeast and beer spoilage organisms to extremely low levels, such that the packaged product will last for its intended shelf life, which may vary by brand, region, or market. Sterile filtration does not promise the complete absence of microorganisms and generally describes the reduction of organisms without the heat treatment of beer as used in tunnel or flash pasteurization. It can also be referred to as "cold sterilization" or "draught filtered." A typical laboratory quality assurance value for sterile beer would be less than 1 cell per 100 ml of beer.

Sterile filtration can be accomplished in different ways. It can take place in successive depth filtrations using kieselguhr filters, with depth filtration via a single pass on a sheet filter, or with absolute filtration on a cartridge filter. Normally, any pore rating on a filter with 0.45 μm or less will yield sterile beer.

Proponents of sterile filtration claim that it avoids any negative flavor changes that may come from pasteurization, but the process will have higher costs because of the increased equipment and operating costs. Other brewers, including those brewing more flavorful beers, believe that sterile filtration can remove body, aroma, and color from beer and therefore approach such technologies cautiously. Regardless, sterile filtration cannot be seen as a replacement to poor brewing practices upstream and it only works as the very last step in a well-run brewing process with care toward proper cleanliness and proper maintenance.

European Brewery Convention. "Cold sterilisation." In *Manual of good practice, beer filtration, stabilisation, and sterilisation,* 117–44. Nürnberg, Germany: Fabi and Reichardt Druck, 1999.

Andrew Fratianni

sterilization

See PASTEURIZATION.

Sterling (hop) is a Saaz-type hop developed by the U.S. Department of Agriculture (USDA) hop breeding program in Corvallis, Oregon. Sterling originated in 1990 from a cross by Al Haunold between a virus-free female Saaz clone and a male USDA variety with Cascade and a complex European ancestry in its background. Sterling was released by John Henning and Al Haunold in 1999. For a Saaz-type hop, Sterling typically produces a high alpha acid content (8.1%), whereas its beta acid content averages 4.7%. The cohumulone fraction of the alpha acids averages approximately 24%. The essential oil profile, however, is typically Saaz-like, in part because of its relatively high levels of farnesene. Sterling is somewhat susceptible to downy mildew but tolerant of powdery mildew, spider mites, and hop aphids. Sterling plants often exhibit a distinct yellowing of foliage (chlorosis) during intense summer heat.

Henning, J. A., and A. Haunold. *Notice of release of "Sterling," a high-yielding Saazer-type hop cultivar.* Washington, DC: USDA-ARS Government Press, 1999.

Shaun Townsend

sterols are essential grain-derived yeast nutrients. They are types of cholesterol that form part of the yeast's cell wall membrane. They have two principal functions. They make the cell wall permeable for the metabolic transfer of sugars into and alcohol out of the cell and they make the yeast more tolerant to increasing levels of alcohol. After completing fermentation, yeast sterol levels are low, and repitched yeast needs sterol levels to be restored to carry out the next healthy fermentation. The level of sterols within yeast cells after pitching is an indicator of the yeast's viability during fermentation and its ability to continue to actively ferment wort through the primary fermentation and into any intended conditioning, maturation, or lagering phase. Fermentation scientists, therefore, often refer to the sterol level in yeast by the French descriptor of *facteur de survie,* meaning survival factor.

Yeast uses oxygen to synthesize sterols and unsaturated fatty acids (UFA), largely during the aerobic phase of the fermentation cycle; this is why ample wort aeration at pitching time is essential for successful fermentations. Incomplete or stuck fermentations, by contrast, are often the result of the yeast not having synthesized sufficient sterols because of a lack of dissolved oxygen in the wort at the start of its development. Interesting recent research has suggested the possibility that oxygen addition at the time of yeast storage, used in conjunction with an addition of olive oil to provide the UFA, may be used to replace wort aeration, allowing repitched yeast to begin fermentation with ample levels of both sterols and UFA.

See also AERATION, FERMENTATION, and YEAST.

Hull, Grady. "Olive oil addition to yeast as an alternative to wort aeration." Presented at the Craft Brewers Conference, Philadelphia, PA, 2005.

Reed, Gerald, and Tilak W. Nagodawithana. *Yeast technology*, 2nd ed. New York: Van Nostrand Reinhold, 1991.

Horst Dornbusch

Stewart, Graham, Dr, (b. 1942), born in Cardiff, Wales, has been among the most influential brewing scientists of the past few decades. While heading up the research group at the Labatt Brewing Company in Canada, the team developed and implemented the use of high gravity brewing and ice beer. His research group at Heriot-Watt University in Scotland further increased the brewing industry's understanding of yeast biochemistry as it pertains to the brewing process.

Stewart's research group at Labatt did pioneering work that explained the mechanics of yeast flocculation and was also one of the first brewing groups to carry out advanced genetic research on constructing yeast strains with high temperature tolerance. These were later used in the fuel ethanol industry. Stewart held a number of technical positions with Labatt Brewing and from 1986 to 1994 was the Labatt Brewing Technical Director.

In 1994, Dr Stewart returned to the UK and to the university environment, where he held the position of Director and Professor, International Centre for Brewing and Distilling, at Heriot-Watt University (1994–2007). Many students in the brewing and distilling industry have been trained and mentored by him in this role.

Stewart has made a large contribution to the brewing literature with over 300 publications including books, patents, review papers, articles, and peer-reviewed papers.

He continues to work actively with students and researchers in the brewing industry as an Emeritus Professor in Brewing and Distilling, Heriot-Watt University.

See also FLOCCULATION and HERIOT-WATT UNIVERSITY.

Inge Russell

St. Gallen was a monastery in Switzerland founded as a small hermitage and cloister by an Irish missionary named Gallus around 590 AD. Over centuries, this monastery became an important fount of European brewing culture and knowledge. By the 720s, the cloister had achieved monastery status and around 800, during the reign of Charlemagne, it became an imperial abbey. Little more than 20 years later, its installations included a church, a cloister, a library, a school, a hospital, a pilgrims' hostel, dining halls, the monks' sleeping quarters, dormitories for workers and tradesmen, guest houses for visitors of lofty rank, elaborate gardens and lawns, workshops, bath houses, latrines, a water-powered mill, and three breweries. Eventually, St. Gallen would evolve into the world's largest and most sophisticated brewery operation of its time, and its light of spiritual and material culture would shine into all of Central Europe. We have excellent contemporary accounts of this, preserved in the architectural plan of the monastery of St. Gallen, drawn up in 829 AD, and a 1060 AD chronicle penned by St. Gallen's Abbot Ekkehard IV, entitled *Casus St. Galli* (*The Case of St. Gallen*). Both documents are now in the St. Gallen Library, the Stiftsbibliothek, a UNESCO World Heritage Site.

Each of the monastery's three breweries was dedicated to making a different type of beer. One brew was a strong beer called celia, made from barley, sometimes from wheat, or frequently from both. It was reserved only for the abbot and his inner circle and his high-ranking visitors. The second brew, called cervisa, was a beer of milky-sour taste, usually made from oats, and flavored with herbs and sometimes with honey; the latter version was called cervisa mellita. This was the monks' and pilgrims' everyday beer and was consumed like water throughout the day. The third brew, called conventus, was a thin "small beer" made from the final runnings of the stronger beers and mixed with fresh extract from malted oats. See SMALL BEER. It was brewed specifically for the abbey's lay workers and for beggars.

St. Gallen's three breweries represented the first truly large-scale brewing operation in Europe. They were spread out over 40 buildings and yielded perhaps 10 to 12 hectoliters of beer a day. It took more than a hundred monks, twice as many serfs, and an even larger number of pupils from the monastery school to tend the oat, wheat, and barley fields and to run the breweries. In the granary, the monks threshed the reaped grain and moistened it until it sprouted. They dried it in a separate room, in a kiln that shared its heat source with a brew kettle. Once fully malted, they coarsely crushed the grain in two huge, water-powered mortars. Each brew kettle served as both mash tun and cooker. While most brew kettles at the time were heated by hot stones dropped into the mash or just by an infusion of hot water, the kettles at St. Gallen were direct-fired. They were mounted over round furnaces, whose walls were made from a mesh of willow reed filled with clay. Each furnace was large enough for a monk to stand up in and patch the clay walls. A flue at the top of the furnace led away the smoke, either into the open air or into the kiln. The monks ladled the wort with wooden buckets from the kettles through filters of pressed straw into flat, wooden tubs, made of hollowed tree trunks. These stood in cooling rooms adjacent to the brewhouses. Fermentation occurred in separate wooden tanks placed between the cooling vats. Although yeast and its role in fermentation was unknown at the time, the St. Gallen monks had already learned that adding a bit of already-fermenting beer from a neighboring tank (rich with active yeast) to a fresh batch or pouring fresh wort over the sediments left behind by a previous batch would jump-start fermentation. The monks also learned that mixing the residue from the fermented beer with bread dough would make the bread rise faster. The St. Gallen beer was, by all accounts, of good and consistent quality, a great achievement in the Middle Ages, when mankind's knowledge of microbes was still centuries into the future.

See also SWITZERLAND.

Horst Dornbusch

Sticke bier is a name broadly given to a special version of top-fermented Dusseldorf-style altbier, generally described as being higher in alcohol and more assertive in character than the traditional version.

The term derives from "stickum," old Dusseldorf dialect for "gossiping." In the context of beer, it suggests that the brewer was a bit heavy handed in apportioning the ingredients for a given batch, resulting in a more intense flavor. Legend has it that those in the know would let a select few in on the "secret" that a particular batch was stronger because of the brewer's "generosity." In modern times, the assertive character of Sticke is intentional, the result of exacting recipe design.

Although brewers around the world have used the term "Sticke" to describe a more assertive version of altbier, in Germany the name originated with the Zum Uerige pub brewery, located in the Altstadt or "Old City" section of Dusseldorf. A few of the other Dusseldorf breweries make a seasonal strong altbier, each with a unique name. Zum Schlüssel ("The Key") calls theirs "Stike" (merely dropping the "c" to make the name their own), and another pub brewer, Ferdnand Schumacher, calls their special altbier "Latzenbier," an apparent reference to the high wooden slats where the rare casks traditionally rested out of view of the less privileged customers.

These special altbiers are notably more assertive in hop character when compared with the traditional altbier and other German styles. Hop bitterness in a typical Sticke can be as high as 60 International Bitterness Units (IBUs) compared with a range of 30–40 IBUs in more conventional altbiers. As in other forms of altbier, the color tends toward dark copper to light brown, and the palate will show fruity notes from a warm fermentation. Alcohol by volume may range from 5.5% to 6.0% compared with a more standard 5.0% in the "everyday" altbiers.

The availability of "Sticke bier" or special altbier is considered a special event. At Zum Uerige, Sticke is available just two times per year, the third Tuesdays in January and October. Zum Schlüssel serves "Stike" on the last Wednesdays of March and October. Schumacher releases latzenbier in mid-September and late November.

See also ALTBIER.

German Beer Institute. http://www.germanbeer institute.com/altbier.html/ (accessed May 18, 2011).
Jackson, Michael. *Beer companion.* Philadelphia: Running Press, 1993.
Neidhart, Matthias B. Personal communication. United, International.
Uerige Sticke. http://www.uerige.de/de/produkte/bier/uerige_sticke/ (accessed May 18, 2011).

Phil Markowski

stock ale is one of three related traditional British strong, fruity ale styles, the others being old ale and barley wine. Mention of stock ale begins to appear in brewing books of the late 1700s. The definitions of these categories, however, have never been very precise, either technically or historically. More likely than not stock ales were generally strong, because they were made only from the first, high-gravity runnings of a parti-gyle brew. They also usually needed several months to even a year to mature in casks. This mellowed their heavy, sometimes cloying flavors and made them palatable. Over time, stock ales would oxidize in storage, taking on lactic and musty notes from lactobacillus and brettanomyces organisms in the casks. At one time this acidity, so long as the flavor had not become vinegarlike, was considered desirable. See BRETTANOMYCES, LACTOBACILLUS, OLD ALES, ORIGINAL GRAVITY, OXIDATION, and PARTI-GYLE.

Beers called stock ales, although malt accented, were generally more strongly hopped than old ales and had at least 7.5% alcohol by volume (ABV) but often closer to 9% ABV. Much of the strength came from wort, but some recipes called for up to 25% added sugar in the kettle. The preservative effects of plenty of alcohol and hop bitterness are probably responsible for the brew's name of "stock" ale; it was certainly beer for keeping as opposed to a "running beer" meant to be served soon after fermentation. Publicans who were willing to blend individual pints for customers, including the fabled "three-threads," may well have added stock ale for extra complexity. See THREE-THREADS. A less kind contemporary interpretation of the three-thread pour, however, was that it was a way for publicans to get rid of unpalatable, oxidized cask residues. Barley wine, the third classic British strong ale, was a much later development than stock and old ale. Developed as a house beer for the British aristocracy, barley wine only reached the commercial marketplace at the end of the 19th century. In fact, the first beer marketed as barley wine was released as late as 1903, by Bass, under the brand name of "Bass #1." It, too, was a first-runnings beer. Modern American craft brewed examples of stock ales seem to be less massive than their traditional British forbears, and they generally have no lactic character. These beers, although perhaps slightly stronger than regular pale ales, tend not to reach the alcoholic heights of the British classics, but they may exceed them in hopping rates, both for bittering and for aroma. Most are fairly pale, and this may be traditional, because recipes from around 1900 call for only pale malt.

Lodahl, Martin. "Old, Strong and Stock Ales."http://www.brewingtechniques.com/library/styles/2_5style.html/ (accessed January 27, 2011).

Horst Dornbusch

Stokes' law is named after George Gabriel Stokes, an Irish-born mathematician who studied the behavior of fluids. He developed an equation that describes the force required to move a sphere through a fluid at a particular velocity. His formula can be rearranged to calculate the terminal velocity of a sphere falling through a fluid, which makes it useful for determining the time it takes for solids to settle out of suspension in a brewery tank. Brewers can also use it to understand how to manipulate the variables involved to increase the rate of settling. The law in the form used by brewers is

$$V_S = \frac{2}{9}\frac{(\rho_p - \rho_f)}{\mu} gR^2$$

where V is the particle's velocity in m/s, ρ_p is the mass density of the particle in kg/m^3, ρ_f is the mass density of the fluid in kg/m^3, g is the acceleration as a result of gravity m/s^2, R is the radius of the particle in m, and μ is the viscosity of the fluid in kg/m/s.

A careful look at the equation shows that the greatest impact a brewer can have on the settling velocity of a particle—without affecting beer quality—is an increase in the particle's radius. Doubling the particle's radius, for instance, would cause a fourfold decrease in the settling time. Brewers use this principle to speed up clarification through sedimentation by adding inert agents to the brew that cause yeast and other particulates to bind together, which creates larger-size particulates and speeds up sedimentation. See FININGS. The equation is sometimes written with the 2/9 term replaced with 1/18. The equation can also be adapted to apply to centrifugation, where beer is spun at high velocity, which, in effect, increases particulate acceleration through gravity. Centrifugation is used mainly in the preliminary reduction of suspended particles, especially yeast, after fermentation and before cold storage and maturation.

Lewis, Michael J., and Tom W. Young. *Brewing*, 2nd ed. New York: Kluwer Academic/Plenum Publishers, 2002.

Steve Parkes

storage of beer, a subject not to be confused with *aging of beer*, addressed here separately. See AGING OF BEER. Whereas aging is a practice designed to confer specific benefits upon beer by applying conditions that will produce positive changes over time, storage is largely concerned with preventing negative change over shorter periods. Proper storage will preserve a beer's shelf life and help it reach the customer in peak condition. See STALING.

Once beer has been produced and is technically ready for sale, it needs to be stored. The first storage, generally very short, will be at the brewery. Brewpubs will normally store beer in its original fermentation vessel until it is ready to transfer to a serving vessel. In packaging breweries, storage may involve a matter of hours between a beer's filtration and its kegging or bottling. Normal bottling and kegging operations are performed at cold temperatures, and the brewery will keep kegs in cold storage, at approximately 3°C (38°F), until they are ready for distribution. At this stage, bottles are best kept under cool conditions, approximately 11°C (52°F), minimizing the effects of heat while also avoiding excessive condensation that can ruin bottle labels.

Once the beer has reached a distribution center, proper storage conditions are once again critical. Bottles and kegs should be maintained at the temperature ranges noted above. Flash-pasteurized kegs, which are rare in the United States but common in Europe, may be stored somewhat warmer (below 15°C [60°F]) without fear of ill effects. Beer storage areas should be kept free of strong aromas because it is possible for some aroma compounds to transit the bottle closure and cause off-flavors.

In the retail outlet, where possible, similar conditions should be maintained. However, most bottled beer will be destined for shelves at ambient temperature, and short periods here will do no harm. It is at this point that the beer becomes vulnerable to light, having often been removed from its case box. Light and heat are beer's most potent enemies, the former causing skunky flavors and the latter speeding staling reactions. See LIGHTSTRUCK. Strong light, especially direct sunlight, should be avoided, and any exposure time should be kept short; direct sunlight can damage beer within seconds. Draught beer kept in bars or restaurants, unless it has been flash pasteurized, is vulnerable to microbiological spoilage and resulting off-flavors unless it is kept cold. It is therefore very important for bars and restaurants to manage their stocks in a fashion that prevents warm storage of kegged beer, even for relatively short periods of time. Improper storage at the retail outlet is among the principal reasons for off-flavors in draught beer, especially during warm weather conditions.

In the home, the best storage conditions are found easily—in the refrigerator. The purpose of a refrigerator is to slow microbiological and physical changes in food, and it performs this function admirably for beer as well. When it is not possible to store beer in the refrigerator, it should be stored in the coolest, darkest area available in the house, preferably away from high moisture. Much has been made of the idea that rapid temperature changes will ruin beer, but this is not generally a real concern. Beer should be stored upright when possible, although short periods in other positions will do no harm. Regardless of the storage conditions, most beer is meant to be consumed within a short matter of months after it leaves the brewery. Unless intentionally aged character is desired, it is usually best for the consumer to buy beer more frequently and keep it as fresh as possible, as opposed to purchasing larger amounts and storing it in the home.

See also FAULTS IN BEER, OFF-FLAVORS, and OXIDATION.

Garrett Oliver

stouts are a category of warm-fermented ale styles that are distinguished by their dark color, generally an opaque deep brown or black, as well as a distinct roasted character that is often perceived as dark chocolate or coffee. Both of these qualities derive from the use of roasted grains used to brew these beers. Traditional English stout recipes rely on bitterness from the roasted grain to provide a dry finish and consequently tend to show very little hop character. American craft-brewed versions, however, tend to have a bolder hop presence.

Stouts, as we know them, evolved from the stout porter, which was a very popular style in London in the 1800s. Although the term "stout" first emerged in England in the 1700s to describe the high-alcohol, bolder-flavored version of any beer style, over time it became closely associated with the porter style.

Postcard, c. 1910, showing an early example of the famed "Guinness is Good for You" marketing campaign. E. & J. Burke, a New York-based liquor importing company, bottled and distributed Guinness under a "Guinness Foreign Stout" label, and came to dominate Guinness exports to the United States. PIKE MICROBREWERY MUSEUM, SEATTLE, WA

In the late 1800s, regular porters fell out of favor and the designation stout porter was eventually simplified to stout.

There are many different kinds of stout. The most widely known is the Irish dry stout, popularized by Guinness. Despite the dark color, draught Irish stout is generally a very light style, rarely exceeding the 4% alcohol by volume typified by Guinness. Another common style is oatmeal stout, in which oatmeal is added, resulting in a richer, silkier mouthfeel and full head. The sweet stout, or milk stout, brewed with the addition of lactose, has become less common since its heyday over a century ago. Other stout styles are growing in popularity today. Imperial stout, first brewed in England for Emperor Peter the Great of Russia, has become popular among craft brewers, particularly in the United States. These are usually above 8% in alcohol and the best examples are full bodied, rich, and complex and will often have flavors and aromas of dried fruit, coffee, and dark chocolate.

See also FARSONS LACTO MILK STOUT, IMPERIAL STOUT, MILK STOUT, and OATMEAL STOUT.

Cornell, Martyn. *Beer: The history of the pint.* London: Headline Book Publishing, 2003.

Jackson, Michael, ed. *Beer.* New York: DK Publishing, 2007.

Papazian, Charlie. *Brewers Association 2010 beer style guidelines.* Boulder, CO: Brewers Association, 2010.

Mirella G. Amato

Strainmaster is a device developed and patented by Anheuser-Busch in the late 1950s to separate the solids in the mash—the spent grain—from the liquids—the wort that becomes beer. It essentially functions as an alternative to traditional lauter tuns and mash filters. The Strainmaster is a large rectangular vessel with inward-sloping walls that form a hopper-like enclosure at the bottom. The lower portion of the vessel contains several wort lines, each equipped with a series of draw-off tubes (so-called fins) that are perforated to allow wort to enter the tube while keeping grain particles out. For straining, mash is pumped into the Strainmaster from the top, and once the wort lines and draw-off tubes are covered, wort is drawn off and recirculated back over the top of the grain bed, similar to "vorlaufing" in a lauter tun. See VORLAUF. Once the wort runs clear, it is diverted to the kettle, while wort clarity and gravity are monitored at a grant. The draw-off rate for each wort line is adjusted for maximum straining efficiency. As with conventional mashing and lautering techniques, the grain bed in the Strainmaster is sparged with hot liquor to completely flush out all usable extract. See SPARGING. When the kettle is full, straining is stopped and the hopper bottom opens up, emptying the spent grain into a receiving tank below. The Strainmaster is then hosed down before it is filled with the next mash. The key advantage of the Strainmaster compared with conventional lautering techniques is its drainage speed. Whereas lautering my take 90 to 120 minutes, the Strainmaster usually accomplishes the same task in about an hour. Because the Strainmaster can operate with fairly deep grain beds, it takes up only about half the floor space of a conventional lauter tun. The Strainmaster has a few drawbacks, however. Because it has no rakes or knives to loosen up highly compressed grain beds, it lacks the tools to alleviate a stuck mash. It also produces 5% to 8% less extract than a lauter tun would from the same grain bill, which is one reason why even the Strainmaster's inventor, Anheuser-Busch, abandoned the concept during the 1980s.

See also LAUTERING and STUCK MASH.

Mitch Steele

strike temperature refers to the temperature of the hot liquor (hot brewing water) used to create the mash. Although the term is sometimes used to refer to the initial mash temperature (which may be tepid) of temperature-programmed mashes, it is more often used in reference to the British-style single-temperature infusion mash. In traditional British brewing, both mashing and lautering happen in the same vessel. Mashing grains to extract sugars requires careful management of the mash temperature because this controls the enzymatic activity that breaks down starch, proteins, and cell wall materials to create the wort.

The most suitable range of temperatures for this breakdown in traditional British infusion mashing is 60°C–70°C (140°F–158°F) because this range covers the optimal activity of the amylase starch-digesting enzymes. At the lower end of the range, a highly fermentable wort will be produced, whereas at the upper end a thicker, less fermentable wort will result. Brewers choose their mash temperature according to the character of wort required for the specific brew.

Hitting the target mash temperature is critical and is achieved by adding hot brewing liquor (water) to the grist as it enters the mash/lauter tun. The temperature of this "strike" liquor must be hotter than the target mash temperature because the malt will inevitably be at a lower temperature. Generally this strike temperature is around 75°C–80°C (167°F–176°F). Calculations are typically employed to achieve this and require a measurement of the grist temperature and an estimate of the heat losses of the process. Taking into account the strike temperature of the water, the temperature of the grist, the temperature of the room, and the temperature of the mash vessel, as well as the texture of the mash, the achievement of the desired mash temperature was once as much an art form as a science. It remains so at many small craft breweries.

Having a hotter strike temperature than the final mash temperature also assists in starch digestion because starch grains swell and gelatinize at high temperatures, thus exposing the starch to liquor for dissolving and for enzymatic breakdown.

In decoction and temperature-programmed mashes a lower strike temperature may be required because cell wall material and protein require different temperature steps for their digestion, generally 35°C–50°C (95°F–122°F) for cell walls and 45°C–50°C (113°F–122°F) for protein.

See also INFUSION MASH, MASHING, and TEMPERATURE-PROGRAMMED MASH.

Keith Thomas

Strisselspalt (hop) is the major aroma hop variety grown in the Alsace region of France near Strasbourg. It is a landrace variety, that is, an open-pollinated, domesticated plant adapted to a region. Its profile resembles that of Hersbrucker Spät, also a landrace, from which Strisselspalt is thought to be derived. See HERSBRUCKER SPÄT (HOP). Genetically, it is also similar to Lublin, Northdown, and Progress. See LUBLIN (HOP), NORTHDOWN (HOP), and PROGRESS (HOP). Its aroma is pleasant and hoppy with moderate intensity, and it is used mainly in international-style lagers and wheat beers. A classic Strisselspalt-based beer is the Alsace bière de mars or bière de printemps, the local, slightly strong, well-matured spring beer—the Alsatian concept of a märzenbier. See MÄRZENBIER. In decades past, the American brew giant Anheuser-Busch was by far the largest customer of Strisselspalt, but since the merger of Anheuser-Busch with Brazilian-Belgian InBev in 2008, Strisselspalt has all but vanished from the new entity's hop requirements. Strisselspalt may also be marketed under the names Alsace, Elsasser (or Elsässer in German), Precoce de Bourgogne, and Tardif de Bourgogne. In the brewhouse, it can be substituted with Mount Hood and Crystal. See CRYSTAL (HOP) and MOUNT HOOD (HOP).

Strisselspalt is late maturing and yields about 1,500 to 2,000 kg/ha (some 1,350 to 1,800 lb/acre). It has red–green bines and produces plump, medium-size cones with average postharvest stability, retaining 60% to 70% of the alpha acids after 6 months of room temperature storage. Disease resistance is rather poor because it is susceptible to English and French strains of verticillium wilt and shows no resistance to downy and powdery mildew. In Strisselspalt cones, the alpha:beta acid ratio is approximately 1:1, with alpha acids ranging from 3% to 5%, of which 20% to 25% is cohumulone. Myrcene accounts for about 25% of essential oils in Strisselspalt; humulene accounts for about 20%, carophyllene almost 10%, and farnesene less than 1%.

Murakami, A. Hop variety classification using the genetic distance based on RAPD. *Journal of the Institute of Brewing* 106 (2000): 157–61.

Victoria Carollo Blake

Stroh Brewery Company brands were sold to Pabst and Miller in 2000. Stroh was America's fourth largest brewer at the time of its demise, but it was no longer profitable. The end of Stroh in many ways symbolized the last gasp of the great regional brands that never quite managed to meet the challenge of the US national breweries. Bernhard Stroh, a 28-year-old German immigrant, founded the Lion's Head Brewery in Detroit, Michigan, in 1850, producing "Bohemian-style" light lager beer. Upon his death in 1882, his son, Bernhard Stroh Jr, took over and changed the company name to the B. Stroh Brewing Company. The name was changed again in 1902, this time to The Stroh Brewery Company, the name under which it was incorporated in 1909. In the 20th century, the brewery became famous for its "fire-brewed" beer. The Stroh brewing kettles were heated directly by gas flames instead of by the more modern method of steam. The high heat underneath the kettle slightly caramelized the malt sugars in the wort, which was said to give the Stroh beers a finer and deeper malt flavor. See DIRECT FIRING. The family business struggled through Prohibition making near beer, soft drinks, and ice cream and became one of America's top breweries again after Prohibition ended in 1933. But a workers strike in 1958 shut down the brewery, and this allowed several national brands to gain a foothold in Stroh's main markets, including Detroit. Fourth-generation CEO Peter Stroh took over the company in 1968 and launched a string of acquisitions as a strategy for remaining competitive against the emerging brew giants Anheuser-Busch and Miller. Peter Stroh was replaced in 1995 by CEO William Henry, the first non-family member to run the company. He continued on the acquisition trail, buying the Heileman Brewing Co. in 1996. With these acquisitions and its own long-term brands, Stroh had compiled a long list of weak regional brands in its portfolio: Pabst, Schaefer, Schlitz, Rainier, Olympia, Old Milwaukee, Lone Star, and Colt 45. In addition, the company brewed Sam Adams Boston Lager and Pete's Wicked Ale under contract. These two brands were leaders in the craft brewing world, but their growth was not great enough to fund the $700 million in debt the company had taken on to buy the other regionals. After one and a half centuries in the beer business, the company had ceased to be viable, and it collapsed in 2000. As of 2010, ownership of the entire Stroh portfolio is divided between Pabst and MillerCoors, but all brands are physically brewed by MillerCoors.

"The Stroh Brewery Company." http://www.fundinguniverse.com/company-histories/The-Stroh-Brewery-Company-Company-History.html/ (accessed May 18, 2011).

Stephen Hindy

stuck mash, a dreaded occurrence in breweries large and small, sh occurs when wort will not filter correctly in a mash or lauter tun and leads to a slow or negligible run-off.

Ideally, the wort produced by the mashing process drains through a filter bed of husk particles, leaving solids behind and becoming clarified. In some cases this range of digestion is incomplete and the mash fails to drain easily from the mash or lautering vessel (in British brewing systems, both the mash and the run-off are typically done in a single vessel), leaving a stuck mash. Typically the filter bed becomes clogged with a matrix of semi-digested protein and cell wall gums and cannot filter the wort. Stuck mashes can be a major problem in a brewery and lead to rejected brews and considerable brewer irritation.

A stuck mash is typically caused by poorly modified malt, malt with too high a protein level, high beta-glucans, or the addition of too much adjunct material. Adjuncts typically lack enzymes and their overuse can result in a mash enzyme level too low to achieve proper conversion. See ADJUNCTS. Occasionally a mistake in temperature control may lead to too hot a mash, denaturing the enzymes and rendering them inactive. Overfilling a mash vessel may also cause a stuck mash by pressing down and compressing the mash bed. If malt is milled too finely, the fractured husk material may be too small to filter the wort properly, again leading to the stuck mash. A stuck mash can also occur if the brewer has attempted to run off the mash too quickly, drawing smaller particles down to the bottom of the mash and even forcing the mash down upon the plates of the vessel.

A simple solution is to stir the mash carefully in the hope that a resettlement of the filter bed will be more open and restore filtration. Underletting by pushing fresh hot water through the plates may achieve this with less disturbance. See UNDERLETTING. If this does not work, brewers with mechanical rakes in their lautering vessels may stir the mash in with hot water, once again hoping for a successful resettling of the mash. As a last resort, the addition of enzymes or possibly fresh malt with high enzyme activity may be necessary.

For many brewers, the phrase "stuck mash" conjures up images of late nights in the brewhouse, dinners gone cold, and attempts at Zen-like calm in the face of great frustration.

See also MASH and MASHING.

Keith Thomas

stuykmanden is a Flemish word for a rather large, bucket-shaped, perforated, hand-operated brewing vessel. Early versions were made from wicker; later they were made of copper. The stuykmanden is closely associated with the Flemish wheat beer brewing tradition, specifically the brewing of witbier (bière blanche) in the traditional manner.

When witbier was brewed in preindustrial times, several brewhouse vessels had to be in simultaneous use. In one of these vessels the major part of the mash, called the *goed sakken,* containing coarsely milled barley malt and both raw wheat and raw oats, was mashed in cold water and mixed by hand. After a rest, the resulting wort had to be drawn from this vessel and transferred to one of the wort kettles. But the combined factors of the gummy grist composition and the low temperature made the mash very viscous and starchy. This mash was impossible to run off through the false bottom of the mash tun, and this is where the stuykmanden came into use. It was immersed in the mash from the top, forcing the liquid to run through the perforations into the interior of the stuykmanden, from where it could be siphoned off into buckets that were then emptied into the wort kettle.

Later in the brewing process, the stuykmanden was also in use for drawing of worts of increasing temperature and decreasing strength in the extremely elaborate and complicated process of heating water and wort in some vessels, holding others, transferring water and weak worts onto the two different mashes, and transferring worts to the kettles. Not surprisingly, the use of this brewing practice and the stuykmanden have not survived into the modern era.

See also GOED SAKKEN.

Rajotte, Pierre. *Belgian ale.* Boulder, CO: Brewers Publications, 1992.

Anders Brinch Kissmeyer

Styrian Golding (hop) is an aroma hop grown primarily in Slovenia and the neighboring southern Austrian province of Styria. Other names for the hop are Savinja Golding after a river in Slovenia and Sannthaler after a range in the Alps at the Austro-Slovenian border. The name "Styrian

Golding" is, however, a partial misnomer, because this hop has no relationship to the English hop variety Golding or East Kent Golding. In fact, Styrian Golding is a genetic derivative of the English variety Fuggle. In the 1930s the Savinja growing area was devastated by diseases affecting the German-derived hops grown there. The growers went to England looking for new stock and were under the impression that they had selected a Golding variety, hence the name. Styrian Golding matures relatively early in the season and is fairly resistant to downy mildew, but it is susceptible to hop aphids and mites. The alpha acid content of Styrian Golding is typically between 3.5% and 6%, and beta acids are 2% to 3%, with cohumulone at 25% to 30%. The essential oils have roughly 30% myrcene, 37% humulene, up to 11% caryophyllene, and up to 5% farnesene. The Styrian Golding aroma is delicate and slightly spicy. It is a very versatile hop and can be used in both ales and lagers, with some British breweries using it for dry hopping. It is fairly widely used in Belgium and also used by many craft brewers brewing beers in Belgian styles. Styrian Golding has a number of derivatives, included several higher-alpha "Super Styrians," the most prevalent of which is Aurora, which achieves roughly 8% alpha in most seasons.

Sepp Wejwar

sucrose, a secondary product of photosynthesis and the primary transport sugar in many plants, is a disaccharide composed of glucose and fructose. These are both fully fermentable hexoses and are isomers (they have the same molecular formula but differing structures) of each other. The molecular formula of each is $C_6H_{12}O_6$. Hence, the formula of sucrose is $C_{12}H_{24}O_{12}$. Sucrose has an extract value of 381 degree l per kilo. Because a 40% solution of sucrose is often used for priming, adding 7 ml of the solution to 1 l of beer will add 1 degree l of fermentable extract.

Brewing yeast hydrolyses sucrose using the enzyme invertase prior to transportation of the products glucose and fructose across the cell membrane. The glucose is preferentially taken into the cell before fructose, leading to a cumulative imbalance in the amount of glucose and fructose in partially fermented worts where both are present. Once inside the cell, both sugars enter glycolysis, the first part of fermentation.

Most sucrose is derived from either the sugar cane plant or sugar beets. It is widely used by homebrewers as a priming sugar for bottle conditioning or to make up some of the extract in wort. It is often said that sucrose imparts a "cidery" or "vinous" flavor to beer and that excessive amounts should not be added to wort or beer to make up a shortfall in fermentable extract.

See also SUGAR.

Garret, R. H., and C. M. Grisham. *Biochemistry,* international ed. Fort Worth, TX: Saunders College Publishing, 1995.

Pelczar, M. J., E. C. S. Chan, and N. R. Krieg. *Microbiology—Concepts and applications.* New York: McGraw–Hill, 1993.

Chris Holliland

sugar is a member of the carbohydrate family (literally hydrated carbon molecules). In general, a sugar is any sweet, soluble monosaccharide or disaccharide. The most common example is sucrose (table sugar). Monosaccharides of immediate interest to the brewer include glucose and fructose. Glucose (also known as dextrose) is primarily used by yeast for metabolism followed by maltose, the main sugar in brewers' wort. Fructose (also known as fruit sugar) is the sweetest of all sugars and may enter the brewing process through the use of high-fructose corn syrup adjuncts or in beers flavored with honey. Disaccharides belong to a group of sugars that are formed from the condensation of two monosaccharide sugars. Maltose (malt sugar), ironically, is the least common disaccharide present in nature but is the most important brewing sugar. Maltose is a disaccharide composed of two glucose units linked between the number 1 and number 4 carbon atoms of glucose in its alpha conformation. Maltose is derived during malting and mashing from the breakdown of starch.

See also BROWN SUGAR, CANDI SUGAR, CORN SUGAR, FERMENTATION, INVERT SUGAR, MASHING, PRIMING SUGAR, RESIDUAL SUGARS, and SUCROSE.

Collins, P., and R. Ferrier. *Monosaccharides: Their chemistry and their roles in natural products.* New York: Wiley, 1995.

Gary Spedding

sulfuring (of hops) refers to a traditional method of defending harvested hop cones against the effect of fungal foliar diseases, most commonly downy and powdery mildew, and of improving the appearance of hop flowers after harvest. To sulfur hops, sulfur was burned in the oast house to produce sulfur dioxide, a compound that has a long history of controlling microbial growth in food, wine, and beer and of stabilizing product appearance. Dried fruits, especially apricots, still benefit from sulfuring during the drying process. In modern hop production, however, sulfuring hops has been replaced by the use of foliar fungicides. Also, many hop cultivars have been bred to resist plant diseases that were once difficult to control.

Hop sulfuring typically took place during the early hours of drying at a rate of 1 to 4 kg of sulfur burned per 200 to 400 kg of fresh hops. The sulfur was added to the kiln's fire, with the sulfur dioxide being carried through the hops with the combustion gases during the first 1 to 2 h of drying at a greatly reduced airflow. After sulfuring, the airflow was increased to speed up drying. Sulfured hops could keep for about 1 year. Today, of course, refrigeration allows hops—in hermetically sealed, oxygen-free packaging—to be stored much longer. In the old days, it was essential to sulfur hops as quickly as possible after they were harvested, because moist hop flowers deteriorate extremely quickly, sometimes within just a few hours. The wetter the hop cone, the faster it deteriorates. Yet, sulfuring was often able to restore the appearance, although not the bittering power, of slightly damaged hops. Hop sulfuring is no longer common because sulfur dioxide can react with several flavor-intensive hop resin compounds and thus produce undesirable off-flavors and aromas.

Meeker, E. *Hop culture in the United States.* Puyallup, WA: E. Meeker & Co, 1883.

Thomas Blake

Sumer is often called the "cradle of civilization" because it was said to be the birthplace of writing, the wheel, agriculture, the arch, the plow, irrigation, and possibly beer. Sumer occupied the southern section of the rich plain between the Tigris and Euphrates Rivers and the areas west of the Shatt al-Arab Waterway in what today is known as Iraq. This was the region where hunter-gatherers first decided to settle down and cultivate crops. Dr Solomon Katz of the University of Pennsylvania has theorized that the primary motivation for settlement was a need to grow grain to make beer. "My argument is that the initial discovery of a stable way to produce alcohol provided enormous motivation for continuing to go out and collect these seeds and try to get them to do better, " Katz has said. By about 5000 BC, the Sumerians were practicing year-round agriculture with irrigation and a specialized labor force. The Sumerians produced far more food than they needed, allowing them to reap profit from agriculture and eventually to develop writing to keep track of their production. Some of the earliest evidence of beer brewing was uncovered in Sumer. Archaeologists discovered a cuneiform text in the ancient Sumerian city of Ur that included a recipe for beer. It was contained in the "Hymn to Ninkasi," the goddess of brewing. The recipe employed a twice-baked bread called *bappir* that was fermented and flavored with honey and dates. The beer was served in a large urn. Sumerian beer lovers sat around the urn in communal fashion and drew the beguiling liquid through straws. Ur is believed to be the birthplace of the Hebrew prophet Abraham, although the palace at Ur was at one time adjudged to be an unfit place to live—because of the absence of both beer and bread.

See also HISTORY OF BEER, NINKASI, and PORRIDGE BEERS.

Hornsey, Ian S. *A history of beer and brewing.* Cambridge, UK: RSC Paperbacks, 2003.
Katz, Solomon. Comments in *The New York Times,* March 24, 1987.

Stephen Hindy

Suntory Group is a major Japan-based multinational manufacturer of whiskey, beer, and soft drinks. In addition, it owns food market and restaurant chains in several countries. The company traces its origins back to a small store in Osaka, Japan, that opened in 1899 and initially produced and sold grape wine. In 1907, the store released Akadama port wine, which became one of Suntory's most famous early products. By 1921, the store had grown into a company named Kotobukiya Limited, and by 1924 it had constructed Yamazaki Distillery.

The company's Suntory White Label, introduced in 1929, became Japan's first genuine whiskey, and whiskey production remained the company's mainstay for the next decades. By 1963 the company had named itself after its main whiskey brand, Suntory, and then built the Musashino Brewery, where Suntory beers are still made today. The brewery broadened its portfolio in 1967 with Jun Nama, an unpasteurized beer, and in 1968 with the release of its beers in cans. The first all-malt Suntory beer came in 1986, followed by Suntory The Premium Malt's [sic] in 1989. By 1993, Suntory began brewing Carlsberg draught under license. Today, Suntory is Japan's third largest brewery after Kirin Holdings and Asahi Breweries Ltd. Although most of Suntory's beers are golden, lightly flavored, international-style pilsners, they also produce versions of the beer-like low-malt drink happoshu and a few all-malt specialty beers such as The Premium Malt's Black, a take on the schwarzbier style.

See also JAPAN.

Suntory. http://www.suntory.com/ (accessed May 18, 2011).

Bryan Harrell

A **swan neck** is a long-neck spout fitted to a cask beer engine (hand-pump) featuring a tall arch resembling the long, curved neck of the eponymous bird. Such a spout is primarily designed for use with a tightly fitted Angram sparkler, a restrictor device that causes the beer to be sprayed into the glass. However, as with regular spouts, sparkler use is optional.

The depth of the spout between the curve and the base generally matches the height of a standard Nonic or Tulip 568-ml (20-oz) pint glass, allowing the beer to be served with the tip of the swan neck spout near or at the bottom of the glass. Such a practice, almost always performed with a tight sparkler attached, is standard in Northern England, Wales, and Scotland, areas where sparkler use is normal. The use of a sparkler will remove carbonation while forming thick, creamy foam on a pint of cask beer, and this form of cask beer service is appreciated by many beer drinkers in the aforementioned regions. If a sparkler is used without a swan neck spout, some beer is often lost because of overfoaming. A fresh glass must be used each time if the outside of the swan neck makes contact with the beer being poured, as dictated by British Health and Safety rules. Contrary to popular belief, beer poured through a swan neck without a sparkler attached will bear little or no difference in carbonation and texture to that served unimpeded through a regular spout. The enmity sometimes directed at the swan neck spout is often misguided because any differences in texture are actually caused by the sparkler rather than the spout itself.

Alex Hall

Sweden is a kingdom on the Scandinavian peninsula, in Northern Europe, where brewing and beer drinking have been common household activities for millennia. In excavations, drinking vessels have been found containing residues of beer dating to the Nordic Bronze Age (1700–500 BC), whereas Sweden emerged as a nation only in the Middle Ages. Much is unknown about the pre-Christian era in Scandinavia because there are few written records dating that far back in time. Runic inscriptions from the Viking Age survive, however, and we know that *öl* (ale) and especially *mjöd* (mead) were treasured beverages.

Before the introduction of hops in brewing, and also for a long time afterward, bitter herbs and plant parts were used to season and preserve beer. Some of the more widely used agents for this purpose were rowan berries, sweet gale, and yarrow. See GRUIT.

It has been known for some time that the Order of Cistercians brought hops to Sweden around 1100 AD; however, recent genetic research indicates that hops were present earlier; Vikings had brought hops home from some of their numerous trade expeditions. The first records of the use of hops in brewing in Sweden are from the 13th century. In *Upplandslagen* (the Law of Uppland) from 1296, hops were mentioned among the crops subject to tithe—the peasants were obliged to pay a tenth of their harvest in kind to the church.

As it was in many parts of Europe, beer was the everyday drink of the people, enjoyed even by monks, nuns, and children. Healthy drinking water was not always readily available, and therefore, well into the 18th century it was normal for an adult to drink several liters of beer a day. Nuns in the Vadstena Abbey, for instance, were each entitled to a ration of 3 l (6 pints) of beer a day and those in Solberga Abbey of 5 l (10 pints). These beers would have contained less alcohol than most contemporary beers, but the volumes do give us a clear picture of beer as an important part of the daily diet.

Considering the total beer consumption in Swedish society, it is no wonder that the cultivation of hops played a significant role in the national economy. In order to reduce the dependence on hop imports, peasants were required to grow hops. As specified in *Kristofers landslag*, the civil law in force between 1442 and 1734, each peasant was obligated to cultivate 40 poles of hops. This number was eventually increased to 200 poles, which was the amount still stipulated by law in 1734, as part of a legal system that is still in place in Sweden today. Fortunately for the Swedes, that part of the law has since been eliminated. Hop farming is no longer commercially viable in Sweden, but there is a small, non-profit hop farm, *Humlebygget*, in Näsum in southern Sweden, which grows some 200 hop plants, mostly for homebrewers and small commercial breweries.

Like other parts of Europe, Sweden was once home to many varieties of beer, most of them now lost to history. Two old Swedish beer styles that have survived into our age are *svagdricka* and *Gotlandsdricka*. Svagdricka is dark, sweet, and very low in alcohol content. In fact, current legislation does not consider most svagdricka real beer but *lättdryck* (light drink) because it contains less than 2.25% alcohol by volume. Svagdricka is top fermented, unpasteurized, and these days sweetened with saccharine. Bottom-fermented, pasteurized versions also exist, and the drink bears a resemblance to Russian kvass. See KVASS. Several breweries still produce svagdricka, but the style seems to have an uncertain future because it has not found favor among younger drinkers.

Gotlandsdricka is the only traditional homebrewed beer to survive the emergence of industrial brewing in Sweden. It is still made largely the same way as it was in centuries past. Its origins are on the island of Gotland, in the Baltic Sea east of the Swedish mainland, where it is also known just as *dricke* (drink). Gotlandsdricka is smoky, spicy, and turbid. Traditionally, the barley (and sometimes wheat or rye) was home-malted, too, and some farms still produce their own malt for dricke. Kilning is usually carried out over open hardwood fires, typically of beechwood, giving the malt a strongly smoked, almost tar-like note. The brewing liquor is usually boiled water flavored with generous amounts of juniper berries and twigs. Although stainless-steel and plastic vessels are the mash tuns of choice of modern Gotlandsdricka brewers, traditionally the mash tuns were made of wood. Either way, they are always lined with juniper twigs, preferably with ripe blue juniper berries attached, and these form a false lauter bottom. This contributes to the dricke's distinct spiciness. Lännu (Gotlandsdricka wort) may be boiled briefly or for up to 2 h or could be fermented unboiled. Hops are added to the kettle or to the mash. Some brewers boil just a portion of the lännu with hops. Fermentation is typically by baker's yeast, although brewer's yeast is becoming more common even among traditional Gotlandic homebrewers. Dricke is drunk extremely young, while still fermenting, and sugar can be added to keep the fermentation going and the brew from souring while it is being depleted. Much of the technique here will be familiar to enthusiasts of the Finnish traditional sahti, although modern sahti usually eschews the smoked malt. See SAHTI. Dricke is particularly popular as a holiday brew for Easter, Midsummer, and Christmas; and there is an annual competition that typically gathers some 30 to 60 entries.

Swedish beer styles were all top fermented until things changed radically in the mid 19th century, when Fredrik Rosenquist af Åkershult started *Tyska Bryggeriet* (the German Brewery), the first brewery specializing in the production of bottom-fermented lager beers. The cleaner palate of these beers was well received and lager quickly became the norm, as the Germanic brewing tradition swept aside the old Swedish beer styles.

The next big changes came in the form of legislation. An anti-alcohol movement, which grew strong in the 19th century, remains influential in Sweden. During much of the 20th century, beer was classified exclusively according to its alcohol content, and retail sales were heavily regulated. *Starköl* (strong beer) was even outlawed entirely for more than 3 decades, when only low-alcohol beer was readily available. The upper alcohol limit varied over those years, but it was never higher than 4% alcohol by volume (ABV). Stronger beer, typically porter, was only available in pharmacies—and then only to those lucky enough to get a doctor's prescription for it. A generation grew up without access to good beer, and this sad state of affairs lasted until 1955, when the current government-controlled alcohol retail monopoly *Systembolaget* was established. Starköl was made legal, but only up to an alcohol content of 5.6%, which, of course, left many interesting beer styles still out of reach for Swedes. Even a doctor's prescription could not get you anything else.

Beers over 3.5% ABV were available only in Systembolaget shops, and sales were rather low. This changed dramatically when in 1965 a new tax category, IIb, known as *mellanöl* (medium beer) was introduced for beers of 3.5% to 4.5% ABV, which could, henceforth, be sold in general food stores. Although advertising for these brews was still illegal, they were heavily promoted indirectly. Beer consumption boomed, especially with the younger adults, and breweries were starting to prosper again, after many decades of rather poor business. In fact, mellanöl was too successful, and renewed pressure from the anti-alcohol lobby led to the abolition of the mellanöl tax category in 1977. Today any beer containing more than 3.5% ABV must once again be purchased at Systembolaget.

Nevertheless, around the turn of the millennium, the Swedish beer scene underwent a tremendous evolution driven mostly by three developments, two of them legislative as a result of Sweden's joining the European Union in 1995. First, Sweden had to abolish the upper alcohol limit for starköl; second, it had to abolish the government wholesale monopoly. This meant that virtually all the world's beers could be made available at Systembolaget. Swedes even in the most sparsely populated regions could now drink barley wines, imperial stouts, doppelbocks, and abbey beers at home, not just while traveling abroad. As of 2011, there were 1,070 different beers from 54 countries available at retail through Systembolaget shops all over Sweden. Ironically, this gives Swedes better access to a greater variety of beer than can be found in many countries without such a government monopoly. There are also many private beer wholesalers, and even more beers than those carried by Systembolaget can be found in specialized beer bars.

The third factor of change, which predates the two legislative ones, was the craft brewing revolution. As in many other countries, the 20th century saw a decline in the number of breweries in Sweden. From several hundred in the 19th century, only a handful of starköl breweries were left in the 1980s. Sven-Olle Svensson was the owner of *Sofiero Bryggeri* in Laholm in southern Sweden, an old brewery that had only produced svagdricka and soft drinks for almost a century. In 1989 Svensson bought new equipment and acquired the necessary permit from the authorities to start making starköl. Other brewers soon followed, and today there are more than 40 breweries in Sweden, a number that grows every year. Unlike most German, Czech, or British brewers, who tend to stick to their traditional beer styles, the new Swedish breweries have taken a page from the American craft brewing movement and brew a wide variety of styles. Homebrewing, too, has experienced a similar revival, and most craft breweries are, in turn, established by former homebrewers. There are now reasons for Swedish beer enthusiasts to be optimistic about the future of their favorite beverage. Beer bars are becoming common and the culinary establishment is starting to pay attention to craft-brewed beer as a versatile beverage that suits Swedish food quite well. The annual Stockholm Beer and Whisky Festival, first held in 1992, is now one of Europe's largest beer events, and smaller beer festivals are popping up all over Sweden.

Systembolaget. http://www.systembolaget.se/ (accessed February 6, 2011).Thunaeus, Harald *Ölets historia i Sverige del I—Från äldsta tider till 1600-talets slut* (The history of beer in Sweden part I—from ancient times to the end of the 17th century).

Thunaeus, Harald *Ölets historia i Sverige del II—1700- och 1800-talen* (The history of beer in Sweden part II—the 18th and 19th centuries).

Svante Ekelin

swing-top

See FLIP-TOP.

Switzerland is a small country that has had an outsized role in brewing history. Few modern beer enthusiasts may realize that the Swiss brewing tradition dates back to at least 754 AD, the earliest documentary mention of brewing at the monastery of St. Gallen in what is now northern Switzerland.

See ST. GALLEN. Documents show that the monastery had three breweries, each making different beers. The first and biggest brewery served the cloister community, the monks, farm hands, employees, and students. The second focused on sustenance beers provided to poor pilgrims, and the third brewery made stronger, finer specialty beers for enjoyment by distinguished guests. Brewing and baking used similar ingredients, and next to each brewery there was a bakery. St. Gallen represented the first truly large-scale brewing production anywhere in Europe. More than 100 monks and an even larger number of their pupils worked in the monastery's breweries.

St. Gallen disseminated early brewing knowledge and brought Swiss brewing into the European mainstream. From then on Swiss brewing largely followed the same path as Central European brewing until the second half of the 18th century, when brewing in Switzerland experienced a type of Renaissance; by 1890, there were about 500 domestic breweries slaking the thirst of tiny Switzerland. To protect themselves from competition of imports from neighboring Germany, Swiss brewers founded the Swiss Brewery Club, forerunner of today's Swiss Brewery Association, in 1877. In 1935, Swiss brewers went one step further by establishing a Swiss beer cartel to control distribution channels and set beer prices for restaurants and retail outlets. Publically, the Swiss beer barons called this cartel a "customer protection plan." Each restaurant, henceforth, could deal with only one distributor, who supplied the premises with beer on a long-term contract basis. Selling beers from distributors outside the region was strictly forbidden and led to draconic repercussions by the cartel, including delivery boycotts. Within this system, foreign beer had no chance whatsoever. Even at the end of the 1980s, the market share of foreign beers in Switzerland, therefore, was no more than 1%.

Behind the comfortable protection of the cartel, Swiss breweries failed to innovate or put any effort into exports, and beer drinking declined among the population. Eventually, the cartels collapsed and foreign beers quickly made inroads. In subsequent years the big, but weakened, Swiss brewers became easy prey, one by one, for the takeover strategies of the large international concerns such as Heineken and Carlsberg, which together now hold about two-thirds of the Swiss beer market. Although there were still 45 Swiss breweries in 1990, there were only 24 by 1998. Most hops used in Swiss beers come from Germany; most malt came from Germany and France. More than three-quarters of all Swiss beers nowadays are international blonde lagers; about 15% are specialty beers, including rice, corn, spelt, and wheat beers; and dark beers amount to less than 1%.

However, there is a new beer movement afoot in Switzerland these days, with dozens (more than 100) of new craft breweries opening up. There are the Wädi-Bräu and Turbinen-Bräu in Zurich; brewery Unser Bier (Our Beer) in Basel; Öufi Bier in Solothurn; Luzerner Bier in Lucerne; the idiosyncratic and creative Brasserie Franches-Montagnes in the Jura, and Brasserie Trois Dames in French Switzerland. Many of these new players are financed by their own beer-drinking patrons who purchase shares in these start-up companies. In fact, collecting stock certificates of microbreweries has become a veritable and organized Swiss pastime. By 2010, there were 7.6 million people in Switzerland and a staggering 254 breweries registered with the Swiss beer tax authorities. A new Swiss beer culture is evolving, largely as a reaction against decades of abuse by the "big bad guys," and the Swiss media are taking an ever greater interest in stories of the small breweries and their brewers—stories that seem to resonate more in the Swiss public than the slick advertisements of the big players. As craft brewing rises, it has touched people's hearts, reconnected them with homegrown breweries, and injected new life into the once moribund Swiss beer scene.

Amstutz, Thomas. "*Schweizer Bierbaron* (Swiss Beer Baron)." *Die Weltwoche*. http://www.weltwoche.ch/ausgaben/2008-36/artikel-2008-36-schweizer-bierbaron.html/ (in German) (accessed May 18, 2011).

Dornbusch, Horst. *Prost! The story of German beer.* Boulder, CO: Brewers Publications, 1998.

Lohberg, Rolf. *Das Grosse Lexikon vom Bier* (The great lexicon of beer). Ostfildern, Germany: Scripta Verlags-Gesellschaft mbH, 1982.

Jan Czerny

syrups are adjuncts used in brewing. They are usually added directly to boiling wort in the kettle but can be used during the final stages of brewing, for example, during racking or in the bright beer tank prior to canning and/or bottling. The major syrups used in brewing are either sucrose or starch based. See SUCROSE. Starch-based syrups are produced from cereals (for example, corn and wheat) by hydrolysis of the starch using acid, exogenous enzymes, or a combination of the two to produce a range of syrups with different fermentabilities. Currently, maltodextrin is the most popular and complex of the products of starch conversion. See MALTODEXTRINS. Enzymatic starch conversion is used extensively with syrups produced with sugar composition similar to wort—10%–15% glucose, 2% fructose, 2% sucrose, 50%–60% maltose, 10%–15% maltotriose, and 20%–30% unfermentable dextrins, giving approximately 70%–80% fermentability. Specialist syrups with high levels of dextrins are now available for the production of beer with enhanced body (mouthfeel) and high levels of maltose (>70%) and maltotriose (>15%) for increased fermentability. These latter syrups are used during high-gravity brewing. Belgian brewers and those looking to emulate the flavors of certain Belgian beer styles use a sucrose syrup referred to as "candi sugar." This syrup is very fermentable and often highly caramelized; it is used to give both color and flavor to the beer without adding body.

Graham G. Stewart

table beer is the English translation of the Belgian concept of *tafelbier* (French: *bière de table*). Although this seems to imply that they are equivalent to "table wine," this is not the particularly the case. Table beers are invariably low in alcohol—typically between 1% and 2.5% by volume—although a few nudge up to 3.5%. Their color ranges from light blonde to jet black and all shades of amber and brown in between. Most but not all are sweet, some intensely so. Hopping is low to middling. Whereas the Belgians have their *tafelbier*, the Dutch have their dark sweet lagers, which they refer to, confusingly, as *oud bruin*, which is an entirely different style in Belgium. See OUD BRUIN. But these Dutch beers are clearly related to German *malzbier* and similar brews found occasionally in Scandinavia. Most of these beers are promoted for the health-enhancing qualities of the malt they contain. Many older Belgians remember with affection how they were introduced to beer by their parents over Sunday lunch, with a glass of *tafelbier*, poured from a genuine beer bottle. In the late 19th century, Belgian brewers faced stiff competition from companies that espoused an anti-alcohol philosophy while plying the public with all sorts of herbal "tonics." In Belgium, as in many other countries at the time, sweet low-alcohol beers gave brewers their own tonics to sell. In Belgium, the last brewery to produce only table beers, De Es of Schalkhoven in Limburg, closed in 1992, although Gigi of Gérouville in Luxembourg continued until 2007, while supplementing its production with regular beers. There are roughly 30 *tafelbieren* still in regular production by mainstream Belgian brewers.

Tim Webb

Take-All is the common name of a root-rotting disease that strikes many cereal plants, including barley, wheat, and rye. It tends to strike under cool, moist soil conditions, especially in waterlogged and poorly drained fields. Only oats appear to have some resistance to the disease, and the name "Take-All" is essentially a rueful description of its effects. Take-All is caused by a fungus, Gaeumannomyces graminis, and its most obvious symptom is a browning or blackening of the roots. This discoloration may extend up to the culms (stems) of the plant. It causes root necrosis and eventually the plant becomes stunted and ears look bleached. Some ears may ripen prematurely and produce only small kernels, whereas others may have no kernels at all. The fungus propagates by spore germination and mycelial growth, which occurs typically in late spring, when temperatures start to rise, but it can also affect winter barley during mild autumn weather. Infections may jump from one set of roots to an adjacent one, and because the fungus can survive in crop stubbles and other plant residue after the harvest season, it can infect crops season after season. Rhizomes of grass weeds can also harbor the fungus. Fungicides can combat the disease and these are usually applied to seed. But proper field management by way of crop rotation and biological controls with antagonistic microorganisms such as Pseudomonas bacteria are more effective.

Keith Thomas

tannins occur naturally in the bark of trees and bushes, in the husk of grains, in hops, and in many fruits, such as grapes. They are secondary phenolic metabolites and come in two basic groups: hydrolyzable and condensed. Hydrolysis can turn the former into glucose and phenolic acids. The latter, by contrast, are stable compounds made up of several flavonoid phenols that are polymerized with each other. Tannins are capable of binding and precipitating proteins, and as a result they have been used for thousands of years as organic preservatives, most notably for the tanning of leather. One of the key natural functions of tannins is to protect the fruits and seeds of plants through the fall and winter so that they remain healthy and capable of sprouting new shoots in the spring. In the interim, the bitter, astringent sensation caused by tannins can ward off plant-eating creatures and protect against microbial pests like molds and mildew.

Chemically, tannins are complex polyhydroxy phenols that are soluble in both water and ethanol. They contain phenolic orthodihydroxy groups, which have the capacity to form cross-linkages with proteins and peptides, which are high-molecular-weight nitrogen-based compounds. This linkage capacity is the chemical basis for the ability of tannins—and similar polyphenols present in the brewing process—to promote the precipitation of trub during the kettle boil of the wort.

The amount of tannin in the average finished beer is usually no more than 150 to 330 mg/l. About two-thirds of this is derived from the husk material of barley and about one-third from hops. The exact proportions vary, of course, with the beer's original gravity and the quantity of hops used in the beer. Beers made with a substantial portion of wheat malt, however, tend to be much less astringent than comparable beers made entirely from a barley mash because wheat kernels are essentially free of husks. If the tannin concentration is excessive, it can cause a mouth-puckering astringency, which, depending on a person's subjective sensitivity, could be considered an off-character. Astringency in the mouth is the not an actual flavor, but a tactile sensation. Tannins, when consumed, react with proteins in human saliva, just as they do in wort. When the saliva proteins coagulate, the saliva ceases to be a lubricant in the mouth. As a result, the inside of the mouth feels as if it is contracting and becoming leathery—a condition that we perceive as extreme dryness. This quality, although prized in moderation in red wines, tends to clash with hop bitterness in beer and is therefore generally avoided.

Just as tannins react with proteins and peptides in wort, they also do so in finished beer, where high levels can cause colloidal hazes. Hazes are more likely if the proteins in the grain, from which the beer was made, were not properly modified in the malt house or were not properly degraded in the mash tun. See CHILL HAZE, HAZE, and MODIFICATION. In short, hazes are composed of a combination of condensed polyphenols and proteins. Such tannin–nitrogen complexes are more stable at low temperatures, which is why some turbidity is termed "chill haze." Dry hopping, the addition of hops to beer postfermentation, also tends to cause haze, and although this phenomenon has not been well studied, it is thought to be caused by tannin extraction from the leafy hop material. Many herbs and spices are tannic in nature, so surprises abound for the brewer who uses them indiscriminantly.

Brewers will sometimes make use of the ability of tannins to link up with proteins to help stabilize finished beer against haze formation. The addition of as much as 3 g tannin/hl to the boiling wort can help precipitate unwanted proteins and thereby have a positive effect on both the clarity and the chemical–physical stability of the finished beer. The added tannin joins the precipitate. Such tannin additions are generally considered the simplest and most cost-effective method of beer stabilization. In Germany, however, such additions are a violation of the country's Beer Purity Law (Reinheitsgebot) because some of these "kettle tannins" might reach the finished beer. A more expensive method of finished-beer stabilization is the addition of insoluble polyvinylpolypyrrolidone (PVPP) in conjunction with beer filtration. PVPP adsorbs and thus removes tannin, but because PVPP is filtered out before the beer is packaged, it conforms to the German Beer Purity Law.

See also REINHEITSGEBOT.

MEBAK, Brautechnische Analysenmethoden Bd. IV, 2. Auflage, para. 1.4.
Narziss, Abriss der Bierbrauerei, 6. Auflage, para. 2.5.3 + 7.6.4.

Oliver Jakob

tap is the general term for devices used to dispense beer from a bulk container such as a keg, cask, barrel, or tank. It is also a verb for the act of broaching a keg or barrel of beer so that it can be served.

The classic functions of a tap—broaching and pouring—are separated into two independent pieces of equipment in modern draught systems. At most bars today, consumers see bartenders pull on a tap handle, which connects to a lever-operated valve and allows beer to flow from a spigot into the glass. Although properly called a "faucet," many refer to this most visible chrome- or brass-colored element of the draught system as the tap.

Hidden away in a cooler, whether just below the bar or hundreds of feet and several floors away, another device, properly called a coupler, attaches to the keg to open its sanitary seal and allow beer to flow from the keg to the bar. Some refer to the coupler as a tap. Indeed, the act of placing the coupler upon the keg and engaging it to allow the flow of beer is commonly referred to as "tapping a keg." Thus, the modern act of tapping a keg generally involves a coupler rather than a tap. Couplers used to tap kegs are made of stainless steel and the faucets they pair with may also be made of stainless steel or, more commonly, chrome-plated brass.

But modern draught systems, which drive beer from stainless kegs remote from the drinker's glass, were only invented about 100 years ago. Well into the 20th century, brewers used wooden barrels to transport and serve draught beer both in Europe and in North America. Some breweries continue to use such wooden barrels of various sizes to serve beer, although generally in special or limited situations. Also, stainless-steel casks with a design similar to that of a wood barrel are currently used for cask-conditioned ale served using a traditional tap.

Both wooden barrels and stainless-steel casks for gravity dispensing are made with a small circular opening near the edge of the head, or flat top, and another in the middle of the bowed side of the barrel. During the filling process these openings are plugged with a wooden bung or with specially shaped pieces with the names of shive and keystone. See CASK and GRAVITY DISPENSE.

This style of barrel or cask requires a classic tap. In its simplest form, the tap consists of a straight tube with a valve and spigot at the front. The rear end of the tube is generally tapered slightly and the tube itself is drilled with scores of small perforations. When in use, the rear portion is inside the barrel submerged in beer, whereas the front remains outside to allow for beer service. This classic design allows the tap to be used both for broaching and for pouring.

To initiate service, publicans set a barrel on its curved side, rotated so that the plug or bung in the flat top is at the bottom, closest to the floor or serving shelf on which the barrel rests. Once the barrel is secured, they swiftly hammer the tapered rear section of the tap through the wooden bung or keystone and into the barrel so that it snugly fills the open hole. Once inserted, the tap allows beer into its tubular center via the perforations. When the front spigot is opened, beer flows out of the spigot and into a waiting glass.

Early taps were made of wood and today some are made of highly durable plastic, but for much of their history, taps were made from brass for both strength and durability. Although all have a tubular element, many variations on the basic shape and appearance have been adopted for either functional or decorative reasons.

The classic tap design is still used daily in certain limited applications. The pubs operated by German breweries may tap wooden kegs set upon the bar this way. Those who serve traditional cask-conditioned ale in England and the United States commonly use classic taps as well. Ceremonial tappings at festivals and special events often employ traditional barrels and taps. Hammering the tap through the bung or shive with a wooden mallet makes for a dramatic event—especially when accompanied by a frothy spray of beer at the moment of broaching. In Bavaria, it is usually a prominent political figure who is called upon to tap the first cask at a festival—before the assembled press, of course. A poor performer at this weighty public function may have a hard time getting reelected. Call it politics not by the ballot but by the mallet.

Ray Daniels

Target (hop), also known as Wye Target, is an English bittering hop that was released for commercial cultivation in 1972. It was developed by Dr Ray Neve of Wye College in 1965 from Northern Brewer and Eastwell Golding. See EASTWELL GOLDING (HOP), NORTHERN BREWER (HOP), and WYE COLLEGE. Because of the catastrophic effect of verticillium wilt on Fuggle plantings in Kent in the early 1970s, there was a great demand for wilt-resistant, high-alpha-acid varieties at the time. Developing such a hop was the "target" of the breeding program, and Wye Target was the result. Target has an alpha acid content of 11%, which makes it very suitable as a bittering hop, although some brewers also like the hop's floral notes, especially during dry hopping. See DRY HOPPING. This hop also has an unusually high geraniol oil content, which results in a floral flavor. Target can be used for almost all beer styles, although it is considered too harsh for light lagers. It is particularly popular as a bittering hop for stouts and porters. After its release in 1972, it soon made up about half of all hop plantings in the UK. It has since declined somewhat in popularity but is still today the third most widely grown hop in the UK. One of the hop's drawbacks is its relatively low stability in storage, which also makes it difficult to schedule for pelleting.

Neve, R. A. *Hops.* London: Chapman & Hall, 1991.

Adrian Tierney-Jones

taste

See AFTERTASTE and FLAVOR.

taverns, a word derived from the Latin "taburna," historically has generally denoted a place in which people can gather for food and drink, sometimes lodging, and occasionally various forms of entertainment. In 1700s America, taverns played a large role in colonial public life. One step above an ale house, a tavern was often a place where people might meet to discuss politics and issues of the day. Interestingly, even in the 1700s, the management or ownership of a tavern was considered a respectable profession for a woman and was one of the few acceptable ways that a woman might support herself and her household, especially if she had become widowed.

In England taverns were originally retail establishments of vintners, and, as Bishop Earle wrote in 1628, are "a degree above an ale house, where men are drunk with more credit or apology." For a largely abstemious man, lexicographer Dr Samuel Johnson spent a fair amount of time in the taverns in, and around, London's Fleet Street. Taverns, premises that purveyed a variety of drinks, not solely beer, could attract a different clientele than other drinking places, and they certainly seemed to satisfy the expectations of the good doctor. Johnson's elegant oracular deliverance of March 1776 tells us much of what we need to know about the heyday of the tavern:

> There is nothing which has yet been contrived by man, by which so much happiness is produced as by a good tavern or inn. There is no private house in which people can enjoy themselves so well as in a capital tavern. Let there be ever so great plenty of good things, ever so much grandeur, ever so much elegance, and ever so much desire that everybody should be easy, in the nature of things it cannot be; there must always be some degree of care and anxiety. The master of the house is anxious to entertain his guests, the guests are anxious to be agreeable to him, and no man but a very impudent dog indeed can as freely command what is in another man's house as if it were his own; whereas, at a tavern there is a general freedom from anxiety. You are sure to be welcome, and the more noise you make, the more trouble you give, the more good things you call for, the welcomer you are. No servant will attend you with the alacrity which waiters do who are incited by the prospect of an immediate reward in proportion as they please.

Over the top? Well, some might think so, but perhaps we should remember that, in Johnson's day, the London tavern attained its zenith in terms of social importance. It should also be remembered that Johnson sometimes attempted to justify the fact that London's myriad of taverns were, for an Englishman, a kind of substitute for home life.

See also COACHING INNS and PUBLIC HOUSES (PUBS).

Bickerdyke, John (pseudonym of Charles Henry Cook). *The curiosities of ale and beer.* London: Leadenhall Press, 1886 (reprint, Beer Books, Cleveland, 2008).
Chapman, R. W, ed. *Life of Johnson/James Boswell.* Oxford: Oxford University Press, 2008.
Clark, P. *The English alehouse: A social history, 1200–1830.* London: Longman, 1983.
Hackwood, F. W. *Inns, ales and drinking customs of old England.* London: T. Fisher Unwin, 1910 (reprint, Bracken Books, London. 1987).
Matthias, P. *The brewing industry in England, 1700–1830.* Cambridge: Cambridge University Press, 1959.

Ian Hornsey

taxes are often imposed by governments, which keep a sharp eye on things that the governed seem to greatly enjoy; those that are not banned outright are usually destined to be taxed instead. The recurring question about beer taxes appears to be whether the government in question considers beer a food, a luxury, or a vice that is detrimental to society. Traditionally, beer has been considered primarily a food staple and a necessary part of a healthy diet. It was, therefore, taxed only moderately, if at all. It was even used alongside other foods as a form of payment for work ranging from the building of Egypt's pyramids to service at England's royal court. But just as governments inevitably run into hard times and are forced to find new and novel ways to fill their coffers, beer inevitably went from being recognized as healthy and nutritious to being considered an unnecessary luxury. The taxman soon set upon brewers.

In the United States, the federal taxation of beer began as a temporary war measure in 1863, during the Civil War (1861–1865). Until that time, beer had been treated as "liquid bread," that is, a food not to be taxed. Because of the war, however, many patriotic brewers siding with the North were more than happy to provide the federal government with one dollar for every barrel of beer sold. Many of these brewers had formed the United States Brewers Association in 1862, which was instrumental in creating the first American beer taxation system.

Throughout the war, the members of the Association were very dutiful in their tax obligations. They even assisted the government in collecting these taxes. At war's end, however, it quickly became clear that the emergency excise tax on beer was there to stay, and the Association dispatched a delegation to Europe to investigate how beer taxes were collected there. In Europe the Americans found a veritable jumble of tax collection methods. One exasperated visitor said, "Austro-Hungary taxes according to extract; Bavaria, Great Britain, and Norway tax malt by measure; Württemberg and the German Brewing-Tax Confederation levy on malt by weight; Russia, Belgium and the Netherlands base the tax on capacity of fermenting tuns, while France and Baden tax according to capacity of kettle." In the end, the Association recommended to the U.S. Government a system of taxation based on the amount of finished product, in terms of barrels, which the breweries released into the consumer market. This excluded the beer consumed by brewery employees, of course. This system survives to this day in the United States. Some countries, including the United States, maintain a lower tax burden upon small brewing concerns, and this has proved to be a key factor in the development of the craft brewing segment.

In England, beer taxation was much older. There it started in 1266, when Henry III signed the "Assize of Bread & Ale" into law. This statute contained provisions for a form of beer taxation that we would recognize today as a combination of licensing fees, fines, and direct taxes. Brewers were compelled to make regular payments to the government on the production and sale of beer, and those who transgressed the laws would simply be forced to pay more. Later, during the reign of William III, Parliament enacted the first taxes on malt and hops, thus ushering in Britain's long and complicated string of beer taxation, with taxes levied on malt, hops, and the finished beer. Because beer is made almost entirely from malt, not hops, by weight and ignoring water, and because the amount of malt in the mash is a rough measure of the amount of alcohol in the beer, the malt tax in effect amounted to a tax on alcohol, whereas the hop tax was comparatively negligible. Many British brewers, therefore, tried to reduce their malt tax payment by resorting to alternative fermentables. See ADJUNCTS. But the government was not to be fooled so easily. It responded by slapping a tax, also called a duty, on the strength of the wort, measured in degrees of original gravity. See ORIGINAL GRAVITY. This method of duty collection was changed only in 1993 when so-called duty-at-the-gate replaced it. This was a tax on finished beer calculated on both its volume and the relative volume of alcohol it contains.

On the Continent, too, beer taxation flourished. It is not entirely certain who came up with the idea, but documents reveal that during the time of Charlemagne the most common beer tax was a gruit tax placed on herbs brewers used to flavor their brews before hops became common. See GRUIT and HOPS. By 1220, the city of Ulm in southern Germany had imposed a tax on beer; by 1388, Margrave Friedrich VI of Kulmbach in northeastern Bavaria imposed a "tap penny" of one guilder per barrel on his brewers output and a "drink tax" on the beers dispensed by his innkeepers. Duke Wilhelm IV of Bavaria, best known as the principal author of the Bavaria Beer Purity Law of 1516, has another, less noble deed to his credit. See REINHEITSGEBOT. In 1543, he wanted to purchase three towns in neighboring Swabia—Gundelfingen, Lauingen, and Höchstädt—a transaction for which he needed cash. So, in short order, he placed a general tax, a so-called beer penny, on all beer produced in Bavaria. In the end, he did not buy the town, but the tax stayed, because, thus ran his argument, he had to raise an army because the Ottoman Turks were a constant threat from the south. The beer penny even survived the Thirty Years War (1618–1648), only to rise continuously over the years.

Today, beer is taxed all over the world, often in multiple ways, in the form of license fees on producers, importers, distributors, and retailers; by way of taxes on its original gravity, alcoholic strength, and volume; and by way of consumption taxes such as sales taxes, value-added taxes, and goods and services taxes. In short, the methods of taxing beer are as varied as there are governments searching for ways to tax it.

Dornbusch, Horst. *Prost! The story of German beer.* Boulder, CO: Brewers Publication, 1997.
Durst wird durch Bier erst schön. http://www.bier-lexikon.lauftext.de/biersteuer.htm/ (accessed May 18, 2011).
Hornsey, Ian. *A history of beer and brewing.* Cornwall, England: The Royal Society of Chemistry, 2003.
Martin, Montgomery R. *Taxation of the British Empire.* London: Effingham Wilson, Royal Exchange, 1833.
Rich, H. S. Co. *The Western brewer, one hundred years of brewing, a complete history of the progress made in the art, science and industry of brewing in the world, particularly during the nineteenth century,* 2nd ed. New York: Arno Press, 1974.

Nick R. Jones

Carrie Nation (1846–1911). A heroine to the temperance movement, Kentucky-born Nation vandalized bars and saloons, often using a hatchet for maximum effect. AMERICAN PHOTOGRAPHER, 20TH CENTURY/PRIVATE COLLECTION/THE STAPLETON COLLECTION/THE BRIDGEMAN ART LIBRARY INTERNATIONAL

temperance, the act and philosophy, as self-described by its followers, of moderation or abstinence from alcohol. Temperance left the private realm and became a powerful political movement in several countries in the 19th and early 20th centuries.

The movement began in the United States, where an abstinence pledge had been introduced by churches as early as 1800. However, the earliest temperance organizations seem to have been founded at Saratoga, New York, in 1808 and in Massachusetts in 1813. Its roots are founded deep in the American psyche of the time and historical puritanism. They believed God's challenge should be a spur to undertake social and political reform. With missionary fervor they set about their task—to save America from the slavery of the "demon rum."

Thanks essentially to campaigning sermons by many preachers, some 6,000 local temperance groups in many states were up and running by the 1830s. By 1836, the American Temperance Society had become an abstinence society, and ideas about problems associated with drinking had begun to change—in the minds of temperance campaigners, alcohol was becoming the root of all evil. Temperance had become the stalking horse for Prohibition, which eventually took hold in the United States in 1920 and lasted until 1933.

In the mid-1800s, burgeoned by the ease by which people and messages could now travel large distances relatively quickly, temperance movements also became popular in the UK, Ireland, Scandinavia, Canada, Australia, and New Zealand and spread as far as Africa and South America.

In 1835, the British Association for the Promotion of Temperance was formed. In its early days the movement, as in the United States, was not anti-beer; in fact there was a belief that the consumption of beer, as opposed to spirits, was not harmful. But during the 1840s the issue became highly politicized. The National Temperance Federation was formed in 1884 and became closely associated with the Liberal Party, whereas the Conservative Party tended to support the interests of brewers, publicans, and other drinks producers. Temperance supporters started to campaign for teetotalism and greater control over where and when alcohol could be sold. Beer consumption was on the rise and the temperance movement blamed this on the availability of drink in over 100,000 public houses in Britain. In 1869 the government was persuaded to put the issuing of licences into the hands of local magistrates. This was a move with unintended consequences because it led to brewers beginning to buy pubs so they could maintain guaranteed outlets for their beers. This resulted in the tied house system still practiced in the UK today. See TIED HOUSE SYSTEM.

With the advent of World War I, temperance campaigners called for severe restrictions on the hours on which public houses could be open, in an effort to support the war effort by trying to stop munitions workers drinking. This led to the Defence of the Realm Act, which in October 1915 stopped pubs opening in the afternoon or late at night. It took more than 70 years of campaigning before pubs could open again at these times.

In the United States, the temperance movement is now widely referred to as "neo-prohibitionism" and remains a powerful force. Hundreds of "dry" counties from Kentucky to Alaska still completely prohibit the sale of alcoholic beverages, and as of 2010, 14 states continued to enforce antiquated "blue" laws that prohibit sales of alcoholic beverages on Sundays.

Blocker, Jack S. *American temperance movements: Cycles of reform*. Boston: Twayne Publishers, 1989.
Brogan, Hugh. *History of the United States*. London: Longman Group, 1985.
Gourvish, Terry R. Richard G. Wilson. *The brewing industry 1830–1980*. Cambridge, UK: Cambridge University Press, 1994.

Tim Hampson

temperature-programmed mash is commonly used in modern brewhouses as an efficient means of converting the starch, polysaccharides, and protein material in malt and in other cereal adjuncts into soluble form that can be rinsed by sparging to the wort kettle ready for boiling. See SPARGING. Unlike the older "single temperature infusion mash" which combines the mashing, conversion, and run-off of the wort into one non-heated vessel, called a "mash tun," a temperature-programmed mash takes place in a vessel called a mash mixer, often called a conversion vessel. This vessel has heating panels that are used to heat the mash as it goes through the enzymatic conversion process; it also has a specially designed mixer to ensure thorough mixing and temperature distribution through the mash. The temperature program will vary according to the brewing recipe and the type of malt specified. If the malt used is "under-modified" (e.g., traditional lager malt), a program might include mashing in warm at 40°C–45°C and holding for 45 min, followed by heating to 62°C–65°C for 45 min for saccharification, before a final heat rise to 75°C. At this point the mash is transferred to a lauter tun or mash filter for sparging (rinsing the dissolved malt contents) to the kettle. "Well-modified" malts, such as American lager malts and British ale malts, will tend to have shorter holding times and fewer temperature set points. The different temperatures coincide with the enzyme activity for working on different constituents in the malt (e.g., proteases break down protein and are most active at about 45°C), whereas amylases that convert starch to small glucose units are most active at 61°C–67°C. Some beers have three holding temperatures and are mashed in at 35°C. The mash is heated to 75°C because at this temperature enzymes become deactivated and the wort viscosity decreases, which speeds up wort run-off. Temperature-programmed mashes can also be used to finely tune wort composition. For example, when brewing weissbier some Bavarian brewers will use mash rests that favor the development of organic compounds that yeast will later transform into aromatics typical of that beer style.

Paul KA Buttrick

terpenes are naturally occurring hydrocarbon chains found in all organisms. These hydrocarbons are made up of building blocks of five carbon chains known as isoprenes (isoterpenes, C_5H_8). Terpenes are important in brewing for their role in hops, specifically, but not isolated to, their presence in hop essential oils. These comprise between 0.5% and 3% of the total hop weight. Terpenes in essential oils are broken down into three types of compounds—hydrocarbons (50%–80%), oxygenated hydrocarbons (20%–50%), and hydrocarbons that contain chemically bound sulfur (<1%). The relative concentrations of these can be used to identify different hop varieties.

The most common and important terpenes in hop essential oils are the monoterpene (C_{10}) myrcene and the sesquiterpenes (C_{15}) caryophyllene and humulene. These highly aromatic compounds are so water insoluble that they rarely survive into finished beer unless added during dry hopping. Oxygenated hop terpenes are more likely to survive the kettle boil because they are more water soluble than the unoxidized hydrocarbons. However, their impact on the finished beer is hard to quantify because of additional chemical changes during transesterification by yeast cells during fermentation. Important oxygenated terpenes include linalool and geraniol, which contribute floral characteristics to finished beer, as well as limonene and alpha-terpineol, which contribute citrus characteristics. Little is known about the sulfur-containing hydrocarbons and their aromatic contribution.

Lewis, M. J., and T. W. Young. *Brewing*, 2nd ed. New York: Kluwer Academic/Plenum Publishers, 2001.
Stevens, Roger. "The chemistry of hop constituents." In *Brewing science and technology*. London: The Institute & Guild of Brewing, 1987.

Steven J. Pittman

Tettnanger (hop) is a "landrace" hop grown in the Tettnanger region of Southern Germany. See TETTNANG HOP REGION. The variety's origins are not known, but it has been cultivated there since the mid-1800s. Genetically and in terms of its aroma characteristics, this German Tettnanger is very similar to Czech Saaz. See SAAZ (HOP). However, it should not be confused with American Tettnanger, which is a very different variety. See AMERICAN TETTNANGER (HOP). The German Tettnanger is an early-maturing hop with a reasonable tolerance to verticillium wilt and powdery mildew, but it is sensitive to downy mildew. It has an alpha acid content of 2.5% to 5.5%, a beta acid content of 3% to 5%, and a cohumulone content of 22% to 28%. It yields about 1,300 kg/ha, and the cultivar has average storage properties. Tettnanger is a prestigious aroma hop, and it is considered one of the four classic "noble" varieties, next to Hallertauer Mittelfrueh, Spalt, and Saaz. See HALLERTAUER MITTELFRUEH (HOP). Because of its unique aroma and slightly citrus-like, almost grassy flavor, it is sought after as an import all over the world. The traditional marriage between Tettnanger aromatics and the fresh, blonde, prickly effervescence of a malty German pilsner is considered classic. It can make for a magnificent blend of "spritz and zest," the perfect interplay between malt and hops.

Val Peacock

Tettnang hop region is a small German hop-growing area on the north shore of Lake Constance, near the Swiss border, centered around the town of Tettnang in Baden-Wurttemberg. Although there is documentary evidence of some hop growing in the area as early as 1150, hop production there became significant only in the mid-19th century. Because Tettnang is also a traditional wine-growing area, the fungal organism Botrytis cinera, which imparts the famous and highly prized "noble rot" flavor to some late-harvested wines, is widely present in the environment. Botrytis affects hops as well as grapes, but in the case of hops there are no positive effects, and botrytis is a more prevalent "hop pest" in Tettnang than in other German areas. Fortunately, it is only a minor problem in most years.

The classic aroma variety of the region is its namesake Tettnanger. It is similar to Saaz. See SAAZ (HOP) and TETTNANGER (HOP). The other main cultivar grown in Tettnang is Hallertauer Mittelfrueh.

See HALLERTAUER MITTELFRUEH (HOP). In the hop trade, the latter is usually referred to as Tettnanger Hallertau to differentiate it from Hallertauer Hallertau. Smaller amounts of Perle and Hallertauer Tradition are grown there as well. See HALLERTAUER TRADITION (HOP) and PERLE (HOP). The Tettnang region produces about 5% of the total German hop crop.

The Tettnanger Tettnang variety should not be confused with the hop called "Tettnanger" in the United States. See AMERICAN TETTNANGER (HOP). The American hop is said to have come from Switzerland, just on the other side of Lake Constance. Whereas the cultivar in Tettnang has a characteristic red-striped bine, the American version lacks that stripe. The chemistry and flavor of the American version are more earthy and Fuggle-like than floral and Saaz-like. Although the "American Tettnanger" may well have come from Switzerland, many suspect that its original home was the hop fields of Kent, England. Those brewers wishing true Tettnanger hop character will source them from Germany.

See also FUGGLE (HOP).

Val Peacock

Thailand

See SOUTHEAST ASIA.

Theakstons is a small brewing dynasty with its roots in the rural and farming communities of Masham, North Yorkshire, England. Robert Theakston took a lease on the town's Black Bull Inn and brewhouse in 1827 and the family name has been synonymous with classic northern English ale ever since. His son Thomas took the business forward, building a new brewery in 1875 at the nearby—and appropriately named—Paradise Fields, where it remains. Theakstons, one of only a few British breweries to continue to employ coopers (a maker or repairer of casks and barrels), acquired the neighboring Lightfoot Brewery in 1919 and, less advisedly in 1974, the Carlisle State Management Brewery, which had been nationalized by Chancellor of the Exchequer Lloyd George in 1914 to control excessive drinking by munitions workers.

Families being families meant that ownership battles and business turbulence threatened survival on several occasions, most notably in the 1980s following a merger with Matthew Brown of Blackburn, which in turn was swallowed up by Scottish & Newcastle. See SCOTTISH & NEWCASTLE BREWERY. Paul Theakston split off from the family business, establishing the cheekily named Black Sheep Brewery in Masham in 1991. Despite the strife, the T&R Theakston brands did gain national recognition under Scottish & Newcastle's ownership, particularly the nutty malt flavored and vinous fruit-influenced Old Peculier, which developed from cult brand to international favorite under its watch. Its spelling is based on religious custom, referring to a parish outside a bishop's control (which Masham had become in the 12th century).

Fortunately, families are also peculiarly resilient and although Paul Theakston has kept the well-respected Black Sheep Brewery, the Theakstons Brewery was returned to the other four Theakston brothers in 2003, who represent not only the fifth generation of Theakston brewers but also Yorkshire perseverance, clear vision, and tireless enterprise.

Alastair Gilmour

Thomas Hardy's Ale is regarded by many as the epitome of aged English beer and one of the world's finest barley wines.

Often equated to a beer version of an Oloroso sherry, it was first brewed in 1968 by the now defunct Eldridge Pope Brewery, based in Dorchester. Having stumbled across 2,000 empty Victorian bottles some years earlier, Eldridge Pope's brewers decided to commemorate the 40th anniversary of the novelist Thomas Hardy as part of a local festival celebrating his work.

Adorned with a distinctive gold medallion, it was the liquid embodiment of a passage taken from Hardy's book *Trumpet Major*: "It was of the most beautiful colour than the eye of an artist in beer could desire; full in body yet brisk as a volcano; piquant, yet without a twang; luminous as an autumn sunset; free from streakiness of taste but, finally, rather heady."

At the time, Thomas Hardy's Ale was one of only a handful of British bottle-conditioned beers and, at 11.7% alcohol by volume, was very much an ale-making anomaly and its drinkers were urged to lie it down for up to 25 years. The original bottlings from 1968 drink magnificently to this day and are likely to have decades of life left to them.

As well as a quartet of a quintessential hop varieties (Challenger, Golding, Northdown, and Styrian Golding), Thomas Hardy's Ale was brewed using pale malt, a soupçon of crystal malt, and maltose syrup, yet the beer attained much of its honey-amber hue from a boil lasting longer than 3 hours. Fermented for 3 months, it was hopped for a second time and then matured in oak casks for up to 6 months. As such, it was very similar to the original barley wines devised for the cellars of English aristocratic houses in the late 1700s.

Initially brewed as a one-off, Thomas Hardy's Ale was brewed again in 1974 and then brewed every year (until 1976) until 1997 when Eldridge Pope Brewery closed. Life, however, was breathed back into the beer in 2003 when the brewing rights were bought by a US importer called, rather aptly, Phoenix Imports of Maryland.

Phoenix commissioned O'Hanlon's in Devon to brew the beer for an eager American market, yet in 2009 and despite cult status and critical acclaim, brewing capacity issues—and the fact that the beer took so long to brew—brought production to a halt once again. As of early 2011, a search was on to find a brewery that could restore this legendary beer to the shelves of devotees around the world. As of 2011, well-kept bottles from early "vintages" were worth hundreds of dollars to avid collectors.

See also AGING OF BEER and BARLEY WINE.

Jackson, Michael. *The world guide to beer*. London: Quarto Publishing, 1977.
McFarland, Ben. *World's best beers*. London: Aurum Press, 2009.

Ben McFarland

Thomas Salt and Co. was a brewery based in Burton-on-Trent, England, famous for producing India pale ale. The brewery, established in 1774, was originally a malting company adjacent to another Burton brewery, but later made the transition to brewing independently, possibly to capitalize on Burton's success in the Baltic trade. It was one of the few breweries to survive the collapse of that trade in the early 19th century.

Around 1823, Salt followed Allsopp's lead and began brewing pale ale for the Indian market. See SAMUEL ALLSOPP & SONS. Soon, according to Alfred Barnard, "Salt's pale and Burton ale became well known in all parts of the world."

The brewery grew steadily throughout most of the 19th century. In 1874–1875, near the peak of beer production in Burton, Bass and Allsopp together accounted for 62% of the 2.6 million barrels brewed, whereas Salt's was fourth biggest with 180,000 barrels. This was still large by any reasonable contemporary comparison, and Salt's ale stores dominated the huge eastern façade of St. Pancras station in London.

Like all other Burton brewers, Thomas Salt and Co. suffered financially after coming late to the race to acquire tied houses and entered voluntary liquidation in 1906. See TIED HOUSE SYSTEM. It struggled on for another 20 years before being absorbed by Bass in 1927. The old Salt's well—still running under the streets of Burton—is still used today in the production of traditional Burton ales now brewed under the William Worthington brand name.

See also BURTON-ON-TRENT and INDIA PALE ALE.

Pete Brown

three-threads was a beer drunk in early 18th-century London and is commonly considered to have been a mixture of three types of beer drawn from separate casks in the ale house. The name survives as the cornerstone of an enduring tale concerning the origins of porter. According to the tale, porter was invented in "around 1722" when a brewer succeeded in duplicating three-threads in a single cask for the convenience of the publican. This account, which first appeared in 1760, has been repeated many times in the popular literature, frequently without attribution and sometimes with elaboration. It has been refuted, if not laid to rest, by modern scholarship, which asserts that porter was an existing brown beer that came to be produced on a massive scale by the great London brewers from the 1720s. The scale of production, changes in ingredients, and increased storage time led to changes in the beer's flavor, but there was no single "invention" of porter as such. Three-threads did exist; it is referred to in a "good pub guide" for

London published c. 1718, but it apparently had nothing to do with porter. Although most commonly given as a mixture of pale ale, mild (fresh brown beer), and stale (matured brown beer), there is no definitive information on the combination of beers that went into three-threads. It has even been hypothesized from limited and somewhat ambiguous contemporary evidence that three-threads was not drawn from three separate casks by the barman, but rather was supplied ready blended by the brewery. Therefore, sadly, it seems that we cannot truly know anything for certain about the beer called three-threads other than its name.

See also PORTER.

Cornell, Martyn. *Beer: The story of the pint.* London: Headline Book Publishing, 2003.
Sumner, James. Status, scale and secret ingredients: The retrospective invention of London porter. *History and Technology* 24 (2008): 289–306.

Ray Anderson

ticking is a peculiarly English beer-related hobby involving the tasting of as many different beers as possible—similar to bird watchers keeping list of birds species they have seen. It is also widely compared to trainspotting. Every new beer encountered by a ticking aficionado receives a "tick," as in making a tick (check) mark on a list. Because of the sheer endless list of existing beers, augmented daily by experimental brewers all over the world, the lifetime list of a diligent ticker can be equally endless. Although beer ticking tends to strike many non-English people as oddly obsessive, the growth of social media such as Twitter seems destined to increase the ranks of the hobby.

See also SCOOPING.

Zak Avery

The **tied house system** began when British commercial brewers began to dominate the production and sale of beer in the UK and they inevitably started to vie with each other for trade in specific areas. The more successful breweries readily gained more business and were obliged to expand. Expansion required capital expenditure and, unless newly acquired business could be made permanent and guaranteed, this could involve considerable risk.

Accordingly, long ago these brewers decided that the best way to consolidate the retail outlets for their beer was to purchase them, or control them in some way, and thus create what is called a "tied estate." The "tied house" would sell only the owning brewery's beer, guaranteeing the brewery a loyal retail "customer." An independent pub that was not beholden to any brewery became known as a "free house." The tied house system was always more prevalent among urban brewers, where competition was more intense and, even then, was adopted with varying degrees of enthusiasm.

Tied public houses are a peculiarly British phenomenon; indeed, in many other parts of the world (the United States, for example) the brewery and the bar or restaurant must be independent entities. It was also more a characteristic of England, rather than other parts of the UK. Even as far back as the 17th century, certain English brewers were more interested in controlling business than expanding it. Brewers appreciated the economies of brewing on a large scale but did not want to produce volumes that they could not sell. In those early days, not all beers in any particular pub might be subject to a tie, and a London porter brewer might tie its customers for that product alone, whereas lighter ales could be purchased from anyone.

It quickly became evident that tying oneself to a brewer was not all that it seemed, and many urban publicans became so indebted that they were forced to cede assets and/or to deposit the deeds (or leasehold agreement) with a brewer. Many publicans were forced to sell their pubs to a brewery and then lease the property back. The situation became so dire that, in 1686, the Commissioners of Excise, commenting on the poverty of London publicans, found "most of them in debt to the Brewers and living on their stocks." Many pubs fell into the hands of brewers by accident of bankruptcy and tended to stay in the brewery's estate thereafter.

Rising land and property values (especially in cities), license fees, and the rising cost of equipping a pub made it much more difficult for intending publicans to take up public houses without external financial assistance. Brewers were more than ready to oblige with "loans" in return for guaranteed trade.

Throughout the 19th century, the larger brewers gradually increased their tied estates, mainly by purchasing smaller breweries and their pubs. From 1880 onward, brewery ownership of licensed outlets grew rapidly, and by the mid-1890s, some 90% of the on-trade (the sale of beer to be consumed on the premises) of beer in the larger British cities (Manchester, Liverpool, Birmingham, etc.) was tied.

Throughout the 20th century, British brewers sought to enlarge their tied estates, mainly by buying smaller breweries purely for their outlets. This situation reached a climax during the 1960s, when a "takeover/merger mania" developed (known as "rationalization"), which would ultimately alter the infrastructure of the British brewing industry. From the mayhem, a handful of huge brewing companies, the "Big Six," emerged, and these controlled an unhealthy percentage of the trade in beer. The catalyst for this mania was the merger of Watneys and Mann, Crossman & Paulin to form Watney Mann in 1958. The number of brewery sites in Britain fell from 567 in 1950 to 177 just 20 years later.

Merger mania was followed, in the 1980s, by a "mini merger mania" that involved some larger regional brewers, and this resulted in a far greater reduction of consumer choice. By the late 1980s, the Monopolies and Merger Commission (MMC) was getting involved, and just prior to MMC's March 1989 Report, the *Financial Times* revealed that the Big Six were responsible for 75% of UK beer output and owned 75% of its tied houses. Bass possessed the largest estate with some 7,300 houses, with Whitbread owning 6,500 and Courage 5,100.

The eagerly awaited MMC Report, *The Supply of Beer*, unanimously concluded that a monopoly existed in favor of those brewers who owned tied houses or had tying agreements with free houses in return for loans at favorable interest rates. The Commission remarked upon the differing size of brewery companies, but noted that most of them "brewed beer *and* wholesaled it *and* retailed it."

The MMC concluded that "the complex monopoly has enabled brewers with tied estates to frustrate the growth of brewers without tied estates . . . and that, over time, the monopoly has served to keep the bigger brewers big and the smaller brewers small." The MMC felt that all this was not in the public interest and, among other things, they recommended the following:

> Not the complete abolition of the tie, but a ceiling of 2,000 on the number of on-licensed premises, whether public houses, hotels, or any other type of on-licensed outlet, which any brewing company or group may own.

Brewers affected by the MMC recommendations, which were implemented and widely referred to as the "Beer Orders," immediately sought to find ways of circumventing them. In 1990, Grand Metropolitan and the Fosters Brewing Group of Elders IXL (who owned Courage) with 6,100 and 5,100 pubs, respectively, announced what they described as a "merger" of their breweries and their tied estates. There was one difference, however. Fosters (Courage) would run the breweries, and Grand Met would administer the tied estate, which was run under the name Inntrepreneur Inns. Inntrepreneur was 50% owned by Grand Met and 50% by Elders IXL. Courage was now solely a brewer, because, in effect, this was a pubs-for-breweries swap. Cynics might suggest that this was an ingenious way of circumventing the Beer Orders. The proposal was referred to the Office of Fair Trading, who finally approved it at the end of March 1991. The maneuver meant that Courage then became the UK's second largest brewer, with 20% of the market.

Some (usually poorly performing) pubs were sold off, but after various other maneuvers, the Big Six (or their derivatives) basically divorced themselves from their pub estates. Pub-owning companies were set up (often financed by large brewers), which effectively tied the pubs again. As well as restricting the number of tied houses large breweries could own, their tenants were given the right to buy a beer outside of the tie (a "guest beer"). This provision was partly responsible for the rapid expansion of microbreweries starting in the 1990s. Another effect was that many underperforming pubs were sold off as either characterful family houses or shops, and the number of pubs in the UK fell sharply as a result.

The 1989 Act was revoked in January 2003, by which time the industry had been transformed from one dominated by brewer-owned chains to one dominated by large independent pub-owning groups—the so-called pubcos. For smaller breweries, however, life goes on much as it had in the past, and slowly but surely, enterprising small breweries are enthusiastically building estates of their own pubs.

See also PUBLIC HOUSES (PUBS).

Gourvish, T. R., and R. G. Wilson. *The British brewing industry 1830–1980.* Cambridge: Cambridge University Press, 1994.
Hawkins, K. H., and C. L. Pass. *The brewing industry.* London: Heinemann, 1979.
Hornsey, I. S. *A history of beer and brewing.* Cambridge: Royal Society of Chemistry, 2003.
Matthias, P. *The brewing industry in England, 1700–1830.* Cambridge: Cambridge University Press, 1959.
Monopolies and Mergers Commission. *The supply of beer: A report on the supply of beer for retail sale in the United Kingdom.* London: HMSO, 1989.
Wilson, R. G., and T. R. Gourvish, eds. *The dynamics of the international brewing industry since 1800.* London: Routledge, 1998.

Ian Hornsey

Timothy Taylor Brewery is an independent British brewery in Keighley, Yorkshire, founded by brewer Timothy Taylor in 1858. Today, the business is the last independent brewery of its kind in West Yorkshire and has an international reputation.

It brews a range of cask-conditioned, classic Yorkshire beer styles including a dark mild, a best bitter, Golden Best—a rare example of a pale mild—and Ram Tam, a traditional winter warmer. Each is notable in its own right. But the brewery's reputation revolves around the legendary Timothy Taylor Landlord.

Landlord, at 4.3% alcohol by volume, is a strong (by British ale standards) and hoppy pale ale that has won over 70 prizes at international competitions and British real ale festivals—more than any other beer. It inspires reverence among British beer aficionados, many of whom claim it to be simply the best British cask ale of all time. During a television interview in 2005, pop star Madonna declared that Landlord was the "champagne of ales," an endorsement that helped push Landlord to greater heights, and has even been credited with helping revitalize the British cask ale industry. The beer also had an influence that reached all the way to San Francisco, with Anchor Brewing Company's Fritz Maytag citing Landlord as an inspiration for his own groundbreaking Anchor Liberty Ale.

Cask-conditioned Landlord is a tricky beer to keep well, but in the hands of a cellarman who truly understands its temperament and treats it properly, it becomes a truly memorable taste experience.

Pete Brown

Tomahawk (hop)

See CTZ (HOP).

top fermentation, generally associated with ales, is a mode of fermentation in which the flocculating yeast rises to the surface of the fermenting wort, rendering it possible to "skim" the crop of yeast from the surface of the vessel ready for transfer to the next batch of wort. The yeast concerned, "ale yeast" or Saccharomyces cerevisiae, is relatively hydrophobic, such that upon flocculating it tends to seek the surface of the liquid to escape the aqueous milieu of the fermenter contents. (In "bottom fermentation" on the other hand, the yeast, often described as a "lager yeast" or Saccharomyces pastorianus, drops to the bottom of the fermentation vessel.) See BOTTOM FERMENTATION. Top fermentation is carried out traditionally in open fermenters, which in the modern era are likely to be fabricated from stainless steel. They are usually either square or round in cross-section and typically 2–4 m (6–13 ft) deep. A classic example is the "Yorkshire square" fermentation vessel. See YORKSHIRE SQUARE. An alternative approach is the Burton Union system, where the rising yeast passes from a series of oak barrels in which fermentation is effected into a "top trough." See BURTON UNION SYSTEM. Top fermentations tend to be carried out at higher temperatures (16°C and higher) than bottom fermentations, although some styles of beer using top fermentations also ferment at lower temperatures than this (kölsch beers, for example).

See also ALE YEAST, FERMENTATION, KÖLSCH, and OPEN FERMENTATION.

Briggs, D. E. C. A. Boulton, P. A. Brookes, and R. Stevens. *Brewing: Science and practice.* Cambridge, UK: Woodhead, 2004.

Charles W. Bamforth

total quality management

See QUALITY CONTROL AND ASSURANCE.

Tradition (barley) is a six-row spring barley variety developed by Busch Agricultural Resources, Inc. (BARI), and released in 2003. It was bred in

1992 from 6B89-2126 and ND10981 parents in Fort Collins, Colorado. It is well adapted to the upper Midwest and intermountain regions of the United States and Canada. The parent 6B89-22126 is an experimental accession developed by BARI but never released, whereas ND10981 was developed by North Dakota State University but not released. Tradition contains high levels of malting enzymes and is listed as a malting variety by the American Malting Barley Association, Inc. Tradition exhibits moderate resistance to most foliar pathogens and has resistance to fusarium head blight similar to that of Legacy and Lacey. This variety produces higher yields, matures earlier, and exhibits greater disease resistance than the comparable six-row varieties Robust and Morex and a slightly lower yield than Legacy. Also, Tradition has a "nodding" seed head with semi-smooth awns, white aleurone, and medium-short (81 inch), strong straw that resists lodging.

American Malting Barley Association, Inc. *Barley Variety Dictionary—Tradition.* http://www.ambainc.org/media/AMBA_PDFs/Pubs/Barley_Dictionary/Tradition.pdf/ (accessed April 11, 2011).

North Dakota State University. *Brochures—Tradition.* http://www.ag.ndsu.nodak.edu/aginfo/seedstock/Brochures/Tradition UC.htm/ (accessed April 11, 2011).

Martha Holley-Paquette

trans-2-nonenal

See (E)-2-NONENAL.

Trappist breweries are breweries located within the walls of a Trappist abbey, where brewing is performed by, or under the supervision of, Trappist monks. The name "Trappist" originates from the La Trappe abbey located close to the village of Soligny in Normandy, France, where this reform movement of the Cistercian Order of the Strict Observance was founded in 1664.

Over the past several decades the Trappist beers have become some of the most influential inspirations for commercial brewers large and small. There are seven Trappist breweries—six in Belgium and one in the Netherlands—that brew beer for commercial sale. They are Westmalle, Westvleteren, Chimay, Koningshoeven, Rochefort, Orval, and Achel. Most of the breweries are operated by secular employees who do not live onsite but work under the supervision of a monk from the abbey. Trappist beer is not a categorical style, but there are some common characteristics that almost all Trappist beers share. Each is top fermented, unpasteurized, contains no chemical additives, adds sugar to the wort in the kettle, and is bottle conditioned. Since 1997 authentic Trappist beers can be recognized by a hexagonal logo on their label that guarantees the following:

They are produced within the walls of the monastery.
The monastic community determines the policies and provides the means of production.
The profits are primarily intended to provide for the needs of the community or for social services.

(Beers produced in similar styles and connected, even if only in name, to a religious order are termed "Abbey beers" rather than "Trappist." See ABBEY BEERS.)

Despite beliefs to the contrary, Trappist beers as they are now produced have only existed since the early 1930s, when Orval and Westmalle developed their first commercially available beers. Similarities in flavor among Westmalle, Westvleteren, and Achel are a result of the fact that all three use the same yeast culture. The Westmalle abbey and brewery are located northeast of Antwerp and produces three beers: Extra (5% alcohol by volume [ABV]), Dubbel (6.5% ABV), and Tripel (9.5% ABV). Westvleteren is located northwest of Ypres, 10 km from the French border, and produces three beers: Blond (5.8% ABV), 8 (8% ABV), and 12 (10.2% ABV). They are only available in bottles sold in wooden crates at the abbey gate. Chimay, arguably the most famous of the seven Trappist breweries, is located south of Charleroi, 1 km from the French border, and produces four beers: Dorée (4.8% ABV; not for commercial sale), Rouge (7% ABV), Tripel (8% ABV), and Bleue (9% ABV). Their beers are transferred by tank truck to Baileux, 8 km away, for bottling. The Koningshoeven abbey and brewery, located close to Tilburg, 12 km from the Belgian border in the Netherlands, produces at least eight beers: Tilburg Dutch Brown Ale (5% ABV, for export), Witte Trappist (5.5% ABV), Blond

(6.5% ABV; filtered), Dubbel (7% ABV), Bock (7% ABV; a seasonal beer), Isidór (7.5% ABV), Tripel (8% ABV), and Quadrupel (10% ABV). They are all available in bottles and in kegs. Rochefort is located south of Liege, 30 km from the French border, and produces three beers: 6 is 7.5% ABV, 8 is 9.2% ABV, and 10 is 11.3% ABV, in bottles only. Orval is located less than 1 km from the French border, south of Florenville, and produces two beers: Orval (6.2% ABV) and Petit Orval (3.5% ABV; not for commercial sale). It is the only Trappist that uses a brettanomyces yeast culture for refermentation. See BRETTANOMYCES. Achel is located less than 50 m from the Dutch border northwest of Hamont and produces five beers: Blond and Bruin, both 5% ABV and only on draught at the brewery, Blond and Bruin (8% ABV in bottles), and Extra (9.5% ABV in 75-cl bottles).

Most of the abbeys brew a lower-alcohol beer for consumption of the monks called "refters" beer, enkel (single), and for light-colored versions, blonde. These seldom leave the abbey. Westmalle's version is called Extra (5% ABV), Chimay's Dorée (4.8% ABV), Orval's Petite (3.5% ABV), and at Achel they produce Achel Blond & Brune (5% ABV).

Dubbel (double), tripel (triple), and quadrupel (quadruple) beers are the styles for which the Trappists are most famous. The terms "enkel" (single), "dubbel," "tripel," and "quadrupel" loosely refer to the amount of malt with fermentable sugars and the original gravity of the wort prior to fermentation. Rochefort and Achel are the only Trappists still using the gravity scale of Belgian degrees instead of dubbel, tripel, etc. to refer to their beers. See BELGIAN BREWING DEGREES. Rochefort 6 corresponds to an original gravity of 1.060 (15°Plato) 7.5% ABV, 8 corresponds to 1.080 (20°P) 9.2% ABV, and 10 corresponds to 1.100 (25°P) 11.3% ABV. When these beers were first brewed in the 1950s these figures were close to the actual alcohol content. Today, improved ingredients, temperature control, and yeast management have resulted in much stronger beers using the same amount of raw ingredients.

See also CHIMAY, KONINGSHOEVEN BREWERY, ORVAL BREWERY, ROCHEFORT BREWERY, WESTMALLE BREWERY, and WESTVLETEREN.

Derek Walsh

Traquair House Brewery is situated beneath the chapel of the oldest inhabited house in Scotland. It is beyond doubt that a substantial dwelling had occupied the site for some time before King Alexander I granted Traquair House a royal charter in 1107, since its walls have formed a retreat for 23 monarchs, a refuge for persecuted Catholics, and a bastion of support for the Jacobites' long conflict to regain the Scottish throne lost in 1688.

The brewery was in full operation when Mary Queen of Scots visited Traquair in 1566 and records show that Charles Edward Stuart—Bonnie Prince Charlie—and his entourage sampled its already renowned produce in 1745. It can be little wonder that Traquair's strong, malt-influenced ales come ready laced with nostalgia and wrapped in tradition. One of its current beers, Bear Ale, commemorates the house's grand "Bear Gates" that were closed behind Bonnie Prince Charlie and will never open until the British crown once more sits on a Stuart head.

The brewery had fallen into disuse in the early 1880s but was revived in 1965 by Peter Maxwell Stuart, whose ancestry traces the family line. The brewing equipment was intact, including a Russian memel oak mash tun and open unlined oak fermenters. His first beer, Traquair House Ale (7.2% alcohol by volume), evolved from an 18th-century recipe that determined the brewery's heady, dark, and traditionally Scottish style.

Now run by his daughter Lady Catherine Maxwell Stuart—Traquair's 21st laird—an estimated 70% of the brewery's production is exported to the United States, Canada, Scandinavia, and Japan.

See also SCOTLAND.

Alastair Gilmour

triangular taste test is one of the methods used in the sensory evaluation of beer. As its name implies, the triangular taste test involves the comparison of three separate samples. As a general rule, two of these samples are identical, whereas the third one is slightly different; the samples are assessed through a blind tasting. The test is designed to measure how easily subjects can perceive the difference in the disparate sample.

There are two common scenarios in which this style of testing is used. The most popular of these is when a brewery has tweaked the process or ingredients used to make one of their beers. The goal, in these cases, is to determine whether there is a detectable difference in the finished product. The other common use for the triangular taste test is to screen potential judges for tasting panels and, more specifically, to determine whether their palate is sensitive enough to detect the various compounds they will later be required to identify.

Some attribute the development of the triangular taste test to the research laboratory team at Carlsberg breweries. Records show that the test was first used there in 1923. It then came into common use at Carlsberg in the mid 1930s, when the research laboratory reworked its sensory evaluation program to yield better results. To this day, the triangular taste test is considered one of the more efficient sensory evaluation testing methods and is commonly used at breweries worldwide.

Lawless, Harry T., and Hildegarde Heymann. *Sensory evaluation of food principles and practices.* New York: Aspen Publishers, 1999.

Meilgaard, Morten, Gail Vance Civille, and B. Thomas Carr. *Sensory evaluation techniques,* 2nd ed. Boca Raton, FL: CRC Press, 1991.

Mirella G. Amato

tripel is a strong, golden-colored ale that was first commercialized by Hendrik Verlinden at the secular De Drie Linden brewery in Braaschat, Belgium, as Witkap Pater in 1932. He actually had his beer trademarked as "Witkap Pater = Trappistenbier" (Witkap Pater = Trappist Beer), which was the first legal use of the name "Trappist" as a trademark. The Westmalle Trappist Abbey followed in 1934 with their Superbier that was modified by Brother Thomas and renamed "Tripel" in 1956. It is one of the most popular beer styles in Belgium and there are hundreds of versions brewed worldwide.

The term "tripel" refers to the amount of malt with fermentable sugars and the original gravity of the wort prior to fermentation. One theory of the origin is that it follows a medieval tradition where crosses were used to mark casks: a single X for the weakest beer, XX for a medium-strength beer, and XXX for the strongest beer. Three X's would then be synonymous with the name "tripel." In the days when most people were illiterate, this assured drinkers that they were getting the beer they asked for.

Tripel beers are traditionally brewed using soft water and approximately 80% pilsner malt for sweetness supplemented with fermentable sugar to lighten the perception of body (chaptalization). Hopping is done in multiple additions using classical aroma varieties such as Saaz, Tettnang, Spalt, and Styrian Golding, with flowers being preferred to pellets or extracts. Primary fermentation is done at relatively warm temperatures using Belgian ale yeast and is usually followed by a cool maturation of 2 to 4 weeks. The best versions are then bottle conditioned. The best tripels have 8%–10% alcohol by volume (ABV) and a gold to light amber color (10–20 European Brewery Convention) and are dry on the palate and well-attenuated, generously hopped using aroma varieties (30–40 International Bitterness Units) and highly carbonated using bottle conditioning (6–8 g per 1/3–4 vol). Tripels should show dense and mousse-like foam, bright burnished golden color, and complex spicy, floral, orange, banana, and citrus notes. Flavors are fruity with alcohol and slight maltiness and are supplemented by hop flavor bitterness and spicy yeastiness. The body is medium because of high carbonation, attenuation, and hop bitterness. Despite the high alcohol content, a good tripel remains almost dangerously drinkable. The driest and lighter versions are not cloyingly sweet and are refreshing enough to enjoy as an aperitif, whereas the fuller and more alcoholic versions make an excellent nightcap.

Of all the Trappists, only Chimay sells its tripel in keg form. See CHIMAY. Kegged tripels miss the refreshing carbonation of bottle-conditioned versions because the maximum pressure at which they can be tapped is much lower than the level in the bottle; this is the main reason that Westmalle does not keg its tripel. Recommended Belgian examples of tripels are Westmalle tripel since 1934 (benchmark for the style and called, with unmonastic bombast, the "mother of all tripels" by the brewery; 9.5% ABV and 39 EBU with ripe banana notes and a spicy hop bitterness), Chimay White (also known as "Cinq Cents" in the large bottling) since 1966 (8% ABV and 35 EBU with hints of Muscat grapes and very dry), and De Halve Maan Straffe Hendrik since 2008 (9% ABV; has a malty and fruity character with a spicy and bitter hop finish). Excellent foreign (non-Belgian) examples are Allagash Triple (9% ABV from Portland, Oregon) and Brooklyn Local 1 (9% ABV and 28 EBU; has a complex orange spiciness and hails from Brooklyn, New York).

See also BELGIUM and TRAPPIST BREWERIES.

Derek Walsh

Triumph (barley) is the anglicized name of a spring brewing barley variety that was bred in the former East Germany and released there in 1973 under the name "Trumpf." Triumph has an impressive pedigree that reaches directly back to the hallowed Czech "Old-Haná agroecotype" of the mid-1800s. See HANÁ (BARLEY). It has great malting qualities and generates excellent yields per hectare in most regions. In addition, it has outstanding lodging resistance because of its short, stiff straw, which is the result of gamma ray mutation of one of its ancestors, the Czech cultivar Valtice (or Valtický), developed between the two world wars. A selection among these mutants led to the sturdy Czech Diamant, a variety released in 1965, which was reported to be 15 cm (6 inches) shorter and 12% higher in agricultural yield than Valtice because it carried the *sdw1* dwarfing gene. See LODGING RESISTANCE. Diamant featured in the pedigrees of more than 150 barley varieties, of which Triumph became one of the most successful, both as a cultivar in its own right and as a foundation stock for further spring barley breeding. During malting, Triumph showed rapid modification of the protein matrix, thus releasing starch and giving favorable extract values in the brewhouse. In the field, however, it lacked resistance to scald (Rhynchosporium), whereas extensive cultivation led to breakdown of its mildew and leaf rust resistance. By the mid-1990s, Triumph began to be succeeded by newer cultivars, many of which were bred from Triumph as one of their progenitor varieties.

Ahloowalia, B. S. M. Maluszynski, and K. Nichterlein. Global impact of mutation-derived varieties. *Euphytica* 135 (2004): 187–204.

Bill Thomas

Trommer's Evergreen Brewery in Brooklyn distinguished itself among dozens of breweries in that borough of New York, and indeed among all American breweries, for steadfastly, for more than 50 years, brewing a beer with 100% malted barley and hops, with no adjuncts such as rice or corn. Trommer's White Label beer was known for its high quality, even in the war years when malted barley was costly and in short supply. The brewery was founded by John F. Trommer, who was born in Hersfeld, Germany, immigrated to the United States, and worked in breweries in Maine, Massachusetts, Manhattan, and Brooklyn before purchasing a small brewery in 1897. He died shortly thereafter. His oldest son, George F. Trommer, ran the company until it was sold to the Piels Brewing Co. in 1951. (A younger son, John F. Trommer Jr, died in a sensational suicide in 1907 after a failed love affair with a teacher.) Trommer's was producing 46,000 barrels annually at the dawn of Prohibition in the 1920s. Trommer financed a chain of 950 hot dog restaurants and supplied them with his White Label near beer. In 1929, at the height of Prohibition, Trommer opened a new brewery with a capacity of 300,000 barrels. Serving Trommer's White Label near beer, which remained legal during Prohibition, the restaurant chain and the famous Maple Garden beer garden at the brewery enabled Trommer to grow his business despite the ban on beer. He later purchased a brewery in Orange, New Jersey. The demise of Trommer's began during the 1949 brewery workers strike in New York. Pickets refused to allow management personnel into the brewery during the strike, and Trommer's treasured yeast strain went bad. It was never the same, and neither was Trommer's beer. The brewery closed in 1951.

See also BROOKLYN, NEW YORK.

Anderson, Will. *The breweries of Brooklyn*. Croton Falls, NY: Will Anderson, 1976.

Stephen Hindy

trub, from the German word meaning "sediment," is a collective term covering sediments formed in the brewing process during wort boiling—called hot break—and upon cooling the wort before primary fermentation boiling—called cold break—as well as during cold storage of fermented beer, which is called cold trub. These three types of sediments are collectively called "trub" because they mainly consist of the same type of chemical complexes formed by the reaction between the naturally occurring polyphenols in the wort and parts of the soluble protein.

Trub, regardless of whether it is warm or cold, is a waste product that is discarded with the brewery by-products. The hot break settles along with hop residues and smaller malt particles as so-called hot trub after the wort separation process (normally a whirlpooling process; alternatively centrifugation). The cold break formed at wort cooling will, if not intentionally removed in a separate process step before fermentation, settle in the fermenting vessel along with the yeast after fermentation, and the cold trub formed during cold storage will, along with dead and settled yeast, be removed as well. The desirability of having cold break carried over into fermentation has been debated by brewers for many decades. Traditional German pilsner brewers often remove it for flavor and taste reasons, whereas other brewers claim that the cold trub is flavor neutral, but that its presence speeds up fermentation.

Formation of trub is in any case highly desirable, and thus the brewer seeks to optimize the processes with respect to maximum trub formation. It is important to remove as much as possible of the two main trub components—the polyphenols and the soluble proteins—during the brewing process because over time they will inevitably react to form insoluble complexes, giving rise to the formation of visible haze and/or precipitates in the beer. This may not present a problem in bottle-conditioned beers, but it is usually considered a flaw in pale, filtered beers, which both the brewer and the consumer may expect to be bright and clear.

See also COLD BREAK and HOT BREAK.

Hough, J. S. D.E. Briggs, R. Stevens, and T. W. Young. *Malting and brewing science*, 2nd ed. Cambridge, UK: Cambridge University Press, 1982.

Kunze, Wolfgang. *Technology brewing and malting*, 3rd international ed. Berlin: VLB Berlin, 2004.

Anders Brinch Kissmeyer

Truman, Hanbury, Buxton & Co. was a venerable British brewery that operated for more than 3 centuries before it closed its doors in 1988. The original brewery was built on Lolsworth Field, Spitalhope, London, by Thomas Bucknall in 1669. He was soon joined by Joseph Truman, who became brewery manager in 1694. Joseph Truman brought Joseph Truman Jr into the company in 1716 and his executor, Sir Benjamin Truman, who took ownership of the business in 1722. Two years later a new brewery, The Black Eagle, was built on nearby Brick Lane, which grew to become Britain's second largest brewery, employing some 1,000 people. Sir Benjamin died in 1780 without a direct male heir and left the brewery to his grandsons. In the same year, Sampson Hanbury became a partner and took over control in 1789. His nephew, Thomas Fowler Buxton, joined in 1808. He improved the brewing process by adopting innovations in brewing technology brought about by the Industrial Revolution. Outside his activities in the brewery, Buxton was a renowned philanthropist, and he was elected a member of Parliament in 1818. He was associated with William Wilberforce, a leader in the fight to end the British slave trade. By the time of his death in 1845, the brewery produced about 305,000 hl of porter annually. The brewery is even mentioned in Charles Dickens' *David Copperfield* (1850). Seizing upon the growing influence of Burton as a brewing center in the 19th century, the company acquired the Phillips brewery there in 1887 and 2 years later became a public company. But its fortunes declined with the shift in popular taste away from porter toward pale ale near the end of the 19th century. In 1971, the brewery was acquired by the Grand Metropolitan Group, which, in turn, was merged into Watney Mann 1 year later. Thomas, Hanbury, and Buxton ceased production in 1988 but its brewery still stands on its site in Brick Lane, London, where it has been redeveloped into a complex of residential housing, offices, restaurants, galleries, and shops.

Glenn A. Payne

Tuborg Brewery, Tuborgs Fabrikker A/S, opened in 1875, founded by two of Denmark's leading industrialists at the time, Philip W. Heiman and C. F. Tietgen, as a truly innovative and ambitious enterprise. Situated on the coast in Hellerup just north of Copenhagen, it was established as an impressive "vertically integrated" production conglomerate, including a coal-fired power plant, a malting plant, a glass works (for the bottles used for export), a soft drink factory, the brewery itself, and a complete harbor installation, providing easy access to the export markets.

Tuborg's first beer was "Rød Tuborg" (Tuborg Red), the brewery's interpretation of the dark, Bavarian-style bottom-fermented lager that was the dominant beer style in Denmark at the time. But Tuborg's real claim to fame was the introduction of the pilsner in Denmark with "Grøn Tuborg" (Tuborg Green) in 1880—today the most popular beer in the country. See PILSNER. Internationally, Tuborg is probably best known for its stronger, pale pilsner called Tuborg Gold.

Tuborg formally merged with "big brother" Carlsberg in 1970, but the two had had very close links since 1903, when the two companies entered into a (initially secret) profit-sharing agreement. Production at the original location in Hellerup continued until it was closed in the 1990s. Since then Tuborg has been brewed at the Carlsberg Brewery in Copenhagen and at Carlsberg's Fredericia Brewery in Jutland, which today is the only brewery in Denmark brewing Tuborg.

In the 1970s, television commercials introduced Tuborg Gold to Americans, who were assured that it was "the golden beer of Danish Kings," although the beer was actually being brewed in the United States. In the Danish market Tuborg overtook Carlsberg in sales in the 1980s, driven by a fresh, young, modern marketing campaign. Tuborg is not only bigger than Carlsberg in Denmark but is also sold in more than 70 countries worldwide, often brewed locally in many of these countries and used as "the fighting brand," meaning a brand strategically priced so as to best compete against local competition.

See also CARLSBERG GROUP and DENMARK.

Anders Brinch Kissmeyer

tunnel pasteurization

See PASTEURIZATION.

turbidity

See HAZE.

two-row malt is made from two-row barley, which is distinguished by having two rows of seeds along the flowering head. Two-row barley clearly differs from six-row barley, which has six rows of seeds. A number of generalizations apply to six-row and two-row malts: the latter generally have larger kernel sizes, lower protein levels, lower enzyme activity, and lower huskiness (tannic astringency). Two-row malts also have a higher starch-to-protein ratio because of their smaller aleurone layer compared with the endosperm. Only 2 of the approximately 30,000 genes of barley determine whether a plant became a two-row versus a six-row individual. Therefore, it is possible to breed for a specific malt profile regardless of the row type.

The difference between these two malts arises from different growth patterns of the seeds. Two-row barley varieties produce only a single fertilized seed at each seed point, or node, on their flowering head. The position of the corns alternates at each node, resulting in two-row barley having two rows of seeds along its length. Six-row barley varieties, by contrast, have three fertilized corns develop at each node and thus produce six rows along the length.

Typical differences in protein levels between two-row and six-row malts result in different applications. This relates to the protein in malt containing hydrolytic enzymes used for the modification of starches and proteins. See MODIFICATION.

The usually higher protein level in six-row malt makes them more suitable for beers that are made with greater proportions of adjunct levels or with poorly modified malts. This is because their relatively high enzymatic power assists in the conversion of the added material. Alternatively, well-modified two-row malt tends to be more suitable for all-malt beers. As a general rule, six-row malts are preferred by large mass-market breweries in the United States and Mexico, whereas two-row malts are preferred almost everywhere else.

See also SIX-ROW MALT.

Keith Thomas

Uerige Brewery is one of the four brewpubs in and around the old town of Düsseldorf, Germany, that has defined our modern understanding of the altbier style. The others are Brauerei Ferdinand Schumacher, Im Füchschen, and Zum Schlüssel. See ALTBIER. The site of the Uerige was first mentioned in a 1632 land tax registry of Düsseldorf. It was then shared by a baker named Martin Pütz and an innkeeper named Dietrich Pfeilsticker. It became a brewery in 1862, when Hubert Wilhelm Cürten, a baker and brewmaster, bought the premises. He converted and expanded the building—seemingly without a plan. The result was a completely confusing jumble of Spartan halls, narrow passageways, dark and smoky recesses, and cozy, intimate niches, each with its own decor—as is still the case today. The place got its name from the nickname Cürten's patrons bestowed upon him. He was apparently a man of dour disposition, so they called him the "uerige," which means "grouch" in the local vernacular.

The establishment suffered serious damage during the bombing raids of World War II, but it was restored to its original condition. Today, the Uerige is one of the few breweries left in Germany where draught beer is still served in old-fashioned wooden casks and poured by gravity. See GRAVITY DISPENSE. In the summer, the Uerige puts out high tables in front of the building, turning the street into a veritable beer garden. Next to its traditional altbier, Uerige also produces a weissbier, a top-fermented wheat beer style that has experienced a dramatic revival in Germany in recent decades. See WEISSBIER. Perhaps the most interesting beer at the Uerige is sticke, a bock-like version of the altbier that is brewed to a strength of 6% alcohol by volume, with more malt and more hops than the regular Uerige brew. Sticke is made only twice a year, ready for tapping on the third Tuesday in January and the third Tuesday in October, respectively. According to local lore, the first sticke was simply a brewmaster's mistake, fairly common at a time when beer ingredients were still measured rather haphazardly by the "bucketfull." But the people liked the resulting beer, so the "mistake" was turned into a habit, and the recipe varied from one batch to the next, depending on the brewmaster's whim and inclination. Because the patrons never knew what was going to be in the next sticke, it acquired its peculiar name: "sticke" is a mangled version of the low-German word "stickum," which means "secret." In a certain way, sticke became something similar to the changing "reserve" beers that craft brewers enjoy producing.

In the winter of 2007–2008, Uerige added a distillery and a separate pub in an adjacent building, where it produces two whiskey-like varieties of beer schnapps made from sticke wort that is brewed without hops. They have an alcohol by volume level of 42% and are appropriately named Stickum and Stickum plus.

Dornbusch, Horst. *Altbier.* Boulder, CO: Brewers Publications, 1998.

Uerige. http://www.uerige.de/ (accessed April 11, 2011).

Horst Dornbusch

U Fleku, in Prague, Czech Republic, may not be Europe's oldest brewpub, as it sometimes claims, but is certainly among the most spectacular, with its grand Gothic halls and central courtyard. Its distinctive dark lager adds to the overall impression of stepping back into a distant age.

U Fleku was founded in 1499 by Vit Skremenec, a malt house owner who began to brew his own beer in former monastic buildings. The rambling tavern on Kremencova Street was bought in the 18th century by Jakub and Dorota Flekovskymi and is still named after their shortened surname today. When the communists came to power, U Fleku was nationalized, but after the restoration of democracy it was returned to the previous owners in 1991, the Brtnik family.

The small brewhouse, renewed in the 1980s with copper kettles, has a yearly capacity of 6,000 hl to brew the house beer. Four malts are used and three lots of Žatec (Saaz) hops are added during the copper boil before it is cooled in a large open pan and then fermented in traditional oak vats with yeast from Budweiser Budvar. The 13 degree black lager Flekovsky Tmavy Lezak has a fruity–malty, spicy character, beneath a dense tawny head. It is the only beer U Fleku serves.

Today tourists flock through the entrance beneath the striking clock to see the elaborate wood paneling, stained glass, and murals—and to try the unique beer and traditional Czech food. U Fleku also has a brewery museum in the former malt house, displaying old brewing instruments and drinking vessels.

See also CZECH REPUBLIC.

Brian Glover

Ukraine, a country with a population approaching 46 million, is located on the Black Sea in Eastern Europe. Once considered the breadbasket of the Soviet Union, this vast territory has a relatively short beer history when compared with its western neighbors. The Lviv Brewery, founded in 1715, is the oldest. Of several dozen domestic brands available today, three big companies share the market with Lvivska: Chernigivske, Pshenychne Etalon (gold medal winners at the 2004 World Beer Cup), and Obolon, the first Ukrainian brewer to export to the United States. Started in 1980, Obolon continues to lead its competitors in volume.

Recently, the world's largest brewing companies have taken an interest in Ukraine. The Lvivska Pyvovarnia brewery is now part of the Carlsberg Group (previously Baltic Beverages Holding), which also includes the Slavutych brewery in Kyiv (Kiev). SUN In-Bev, the Russian unit of Anheuser-Busch InBev, operates three breweries in Ukraine, and in 2008 SABMiller acquired Donetsk-based CJSC Sarmat in an effort to gain a foothold in this fast-growing beer market. At present, the majority of imported beer comes from Russia, whereas Ukraine exports its own products to surrounding countries—nearly 10 times what it imports.

Lager, typically low-alcohol brands and inexpensive varieties commonly sold in plastic bottles, remains popular, although a law passed by Ukraine's parliament in 2010 restricts low-alcohol consumption and sales, going so far as to ban the sale of beverages such as fruity "beer mixes" aimed at younger drinkers. In the past decade brewpubs, especially in the capital of Kyiv, have begun to offer a wider variety of styles including amber ales, darker porters, and the occasional stout.

Bharat Book Bureau. *Bharatbook.com*. http://www.bharatbook.com/detail.asp?id=64602&rt=Beer-in-Ukraine.html/ (accessed July 5, 2010).

Matosko, Alexandra. "Beer drinking, Ukrainian-style." http://www.kyivpost.com/news/guide/general/detail/46185/ (accessed July 5, 2010).

Obolon CJSC. Obolon.ua. http://obolon.ua/eng/about/history/ (accessed July 5, 2010).

Sibun, Jonathan. "SABMiller buys one of Ukraine's biggest brewers." http://www.telegraph.co.uk/finance/newsbysector/retailandconsumer/2789703/SABMiller-buys-one-of-Ukraines-biggest-brewers.html/ (accessed July 5, 2010).

Ben Keene

Ukrainian hops accounted for most of the hop production in the former Soviet Union, in the region of Ukraine, now an independent country. The traditional hop there is stern-sounding Clone-18, believed to originate in central Europe. It appears similar to Saaz and Lublin. See LUBLIN (HOP) and SAAZ (HOP). Much of the current Ukrainian hop acreage is in an area that was part of Poland before World War II, which partly explains the similarity between Clone-18 and Lublin. About 75% of Ukrainian hop production is of aroma varieties; the rest is in bittering varieties. Zagrava is a recently developed Ukrainian aroma hop, whereas Promin and Magnat are new bittering varieties. Ukrainian hop production comprises just a bit over 1% of the world total.

Val Peacock

ullage has its roots in Anglo-Norman and Latin and in the 15th century when the word meant the volume by which a container is under-filled—that is, the space above the beer. This remains the common usage in the United States, where the headspace in a keg, a cask, or a bottle (for the latter, when beer or wine has leaked or been evaporated out) is referred to as the ullage. It can also describe the lost liquid itself, especially in cases of leakage or evaporation through corks. The definition is somewhat different in the UK, where "ullage" is used to describe several related features associated with the contents of a cask or keg of beer. It can refer to the process of emptying or drawing beer from a cask or keg of beer—that is, a cask that has been opened and is part full. It is also the amount of beer in a cask when it is not full or the volume of liquid and sediment in a cask after all the saleable beer has been removed. The sediment contains beer, finings, dry hop, and yeast residues. Dipsticks (graduated rods used to measure liquids) calibrated for different cask sizes are used to measure the volume of ullage/beer remaining in the cask by inserting them through the hole in the shive. See SHIVE. In the UK, ullage can also describe the beer lost or spilled at the point of dispense.

Jeffery, E. J. Brewing. *Theory and practice*, 3rd ed. London: Nicholas Kay, 1956.
O'Neill, Patrick. *Cellarmanship*, 4th ed. St. Albans, England: CAMRA: 2005.
Wahl, Robert, and Max Henius. *American handy-book of the brewing, malting, and auxiliary trades*, 3rd ed. Chicago: Wahl & Henius, 1908.

Chris J. Marchbanks

Ultra (hop) is a triploid aroma hop cultivar having 30 chromosomes, a type that produces very few seeds even when grown in the presence of fertile male hops.

Ultra originated from a 1983 cross made at Corvallis, Oregon, between tetraploid (2n = 40) Hallertauer Mittelfrüh and the diploid (2n = 20) male germplasm line 21373M. It was commercially released in 1995.

Ultra matures medium early and is moderately resistant to downy mildew and verticillium wilt. Its average yield is about 2,017 to 2,465 kg/ha (1,800 to 2,200 lb/acre). In many respects, Ultra resembles its female parent, Hallertauer Mittelfrueh. Its alpha acids content ranges from 4% to 6%, its beta acids ranges from 4% to 5%, and it has a cohumulone fraction of 21% to 25%. Its essential oils are divided among 35% myrcene, 38% humulene, and 11% caryophyllene. It has no farnesene. The humulene/caryophyllene ratio is 3.4, which some hop chemists consider to be indicative of continental-type aroma properties.

Although the development of Ultra was initially sponsored by major American breweries under the auspices of the Hop Research Council, this hop is today used mainly used by craft brewers who like it for its aroma quality.

Haunold, A., G. B. Nickerson, U. Gampert, and D. S. Kling. Registration of Ultra hop. *Crop Science* 37 (1997): 291–92.

Alfred Haunold

umami is sometimes called the fifth taste. It was first identified in 1908 by Professor Ikeda Kikunae of Tokyo Imperial University. Popularly referred to as "savoriness," umami has been proposed as one of the basic tastes (in addition to sweet, sour, salty, and bitter) sensed by specialized receptor cells present on the human and animal tongue. *Umami* is a Japanese word meaning "flavor" or "taste." In English, however, "brothy," "meaty," "savory," or even "deliciousness" have been proposed as alternative translations. It describes the flavor common to savory foods such as meat, Parmesan cheese, soy sauce, seaweed, and mushrooms.

The umami taste is caused by the detection of the carboxylate anion of glutamic acid, a naturally occurring amino acid common in meats, cheese, broth, stock, and other protein-heavy foods. Salts of glutamic acid, known as glutamates, easily ionize to give the same carboxylate form and therefore the same taste. For this reason, they are used as flavor enhancers. While the umami taste is caused by glutamates, 5′-ribonucleotides such as guanosine and inosine monophosphate greatly enhance its perceived intensity. Since these ribonucleotides are also acids, their salts are added together with glutamates to obtain a synergistic flavor enhancement effect.

Umami tastes are initiated by specialized receptors, with subsequent steps involving secretion of neurotransmitters, including adenosine triphosphate and serotonin. Other evidence indicates that guanosine derivatives may interact with and boost the initial umami signal. Beers brewed to show notable umami character are rare, but not unknown. For example, the addition of kelp (large seaweeds belonging to the brown algae class of plants) may give an umami taste, especially in stout beer styles, where the roastiness of the malt and the bitterness is enhanced by the umami taste of the kelp. Beers properly aged on yeast sediment can develop umami-like character. See STOUTS. Given that hydrolyzed (heat-treated) yeast is often used as a meat-like flavoring in foods, this cannot be considered surprising. Oenologists are currently studying the possible contribution of lees (yeast sediment) contact to the development of positive umami characteristics in wine.

Wolfgang Stempfl

underback is traditionally a vessel between a mash separation device (e.g., a mash tun, lauter tun, or mash filter) and the kettle. The vessel is essential to maintain wort flow and save time in the brewhouse when more than one full kettle is required from a single mash. When the required volume of wort is reached in the kettle, it is brought to a boil; the wort that continues to run from the separation device is then run into the underback. This wort is held at 70°C–80°C and is run to the kettle once the previous contents have been boiled and sent to the whirlpool or fermenter. In the British parti-gyle system of brewing (where the wort from a single mash is run off to separate vessels in stages), the first wort run into the underback is often called the "first worts" and the next are called "second worts." See PARTI-GYLE. The size of the underback can vary; if the size of a kettle is half the volume that can be extracted from a full parti-gyled brew, the underback will be large enough to take the rest of the wort from that brew. In modern breweries, underbacks are often referred to as "wort holding tanks" and can be anything up to the full brew volume. In most breweries outside the UK, the underback receives the wort from a second mash, while the wort from a previous mash is occupying the kettle. This saves considerable time because the brewery can be collecting one wort while boiling another. Care needs to be taken to ensure that the wort holding vessels are regularly cleaned because holding hot wort can encourage themophilic bacteria to produce undesirable nitroso-compounds called ATNCs (Apparent Total Nitroso Compounds) that can be carried through to finished beer.

Paul KA Buttrick

underletting is a technique used by brewers during run-off or lautering as a method of freeing up a mash bed that has collapsed, "set," or "stuck." Recovery of wort from a mash involves straining the wort through a complex filter bed created by the grain itself. Collecting the wort too quickly can result in the grain bed compressing, preventing liquid from flowing through it. In this case it may be possible to free the blockage by pumping hot brewing water through the mash from below. This can free up the mash bed, but it also has the disadvantage of replacing the wort underneath the vessel false bottom with water rather than wort and possibly diluting the wort before it is collected. Underletting will cause the wort to become turbid, and the brewer usually must then recirculate the wort until it runs clear. See VORLAUF. In general this may be a tactic used by brewers as a "last resort," when wort has stopped flowing through the mash bed altogether. Often brewers will simply wait for slow-flowing wort to collect without risking diluting it with the underletting technique. In rare cases, underletting may be part of the actual intended brewing technique, especially with very heavy or thick mashes.

See also LAUTERING and STUCK MASH.

Steve Parkes

unitanks

See FERMENTATION VESSELS.

United Kingdom

See BRITAIN.

The **United States** has a history of brewing that began with efforts by the earliest English colonists to make beer from the only grain available to them, corn. Thomas Hariot, one of the unsuccessful settlers at Roanoke Island, published his "Narrative of the First English Plantation of Virginia" upon his return to London in 1588. Hariot wrote of the diversely colored corn that made very good bread and "We made of the same in the country some mault, whereof was brued as good ale as was to be desired. So, likewise, by the help of hops, thereof may bee made as good beere." Later, when a colony was established in Virginia, Capt George Thorpe wrote on December 29, 1620, of the difficulty of growing barley in the hot climate of the South. "And the greatest want they complayne of us a good drinke—wine being too dear, and barley chargeable, which though it should be there sowen, it were hard in that country, being so hot, to make malt of it, or, if they had malt, to make good beer . . . they had found a way to make good drink from Indian corn, which (they) preferred to good English beer."

Even the puritanical Pilgrims' landing at Plymouth Rock was influenced by their thirst for beer. Alexander Young's "Chronicles of the Pilgrim Fathers" records the diary of one of the passengers on board the Mayflower in 1620: "So in the morning, after we had called on God for direction, we came to this resolution—to go presently ashore again and to take a better view of two places which we thought most fitting for us; for we could not now take time for further search or consideration, our victuals being much spent, especially our beer, and it now being the 19th of December."

The first brewery on Manhattan Island was established by Dutchmen Adrian Block and Hans Christiansen in 1612. The Dutch administration levied the first excise taxes on beer in the New World. Dutch-run breweries proliferated in New Amsterdam despite the taxes. Philadelphia also prospered as a brewing center. Founder William Penn's early letters indicate the first brewery in Philadelphia was built around 1685. Penn described its proprietor, William Frampton, as "an able man who had set up a large brew-house, in order to furnish the people with good drink." Several breweries also opened in Baltimore during the colonial period.

The brewing industry languished during the Revolutionary War when American ports were blockaded and consumption of beer declined. However, the founding fathers also were partisans of American beer. George Washington had a fondness for taverns; his farewell address in 1783, after the revolutionary war, was held at Fraunces Tavern in lower Manhattan. James Madison and Thomas Jefferson both promoted the benefits of beer and ale over distilled spirits, as did Samuel Adams, a signer of the Declaration of Independence, member of the first national congress and maltster.

After the war, ale and porter breweries flourished in the big cities of the East, Philadelphia, Baltimore, and New York. Among prominent Philadelphia breweries was the Robert Smith India Pale Ale Brewing Co and the Gaul Brewery. The brewing business also caught on in the Lehigh Valley. D. G. Yuengling started a brewery in Pottsville in 1829. In Baltimore there was the Globe Brewery and the James Sterret Brewery. In New York City, the Old Brewery, or Coulter's Brewery, was erected at the junction known as Five Points. The brewing business also took hold in Upstate New York. Matthew Vassar, founder of the eponymous college, ran a brewery in Poughkeepsie, New York. The Evans Brewery started up in Hudson, New York, and the Albany Brewing Co in the state capitol. In the 18th century, Boston developed as a distribution point for the ales and porters brewed in New York, Pennsylvania, and Maryland. The Bunker Hill Brewery was established in Boston in 1821.

Lager beer brewing came to America in 1840 and virtually transformed the American brewing landscape overnight. The advent of lager beer heralded a golden age for brewing in America. Before then, all beers brewed in America were warm-fermented ales. John Wagner brought a bottom-fermenting lager yeast from Bavaria and set up a small, eight-barrel brewery in the rear of his house in Philadelphia. The beer was lagered, or stored, in the cellar. The relatively light-bodied lager beer was immediately popular, and a wave of German immigration insured its success in cities across the United States. In the 1830s, 600,000 immigrants poured into the United States, in the 1840s, 1.7 million, and in the 1850s, 2.6 million. Seventy-five percent

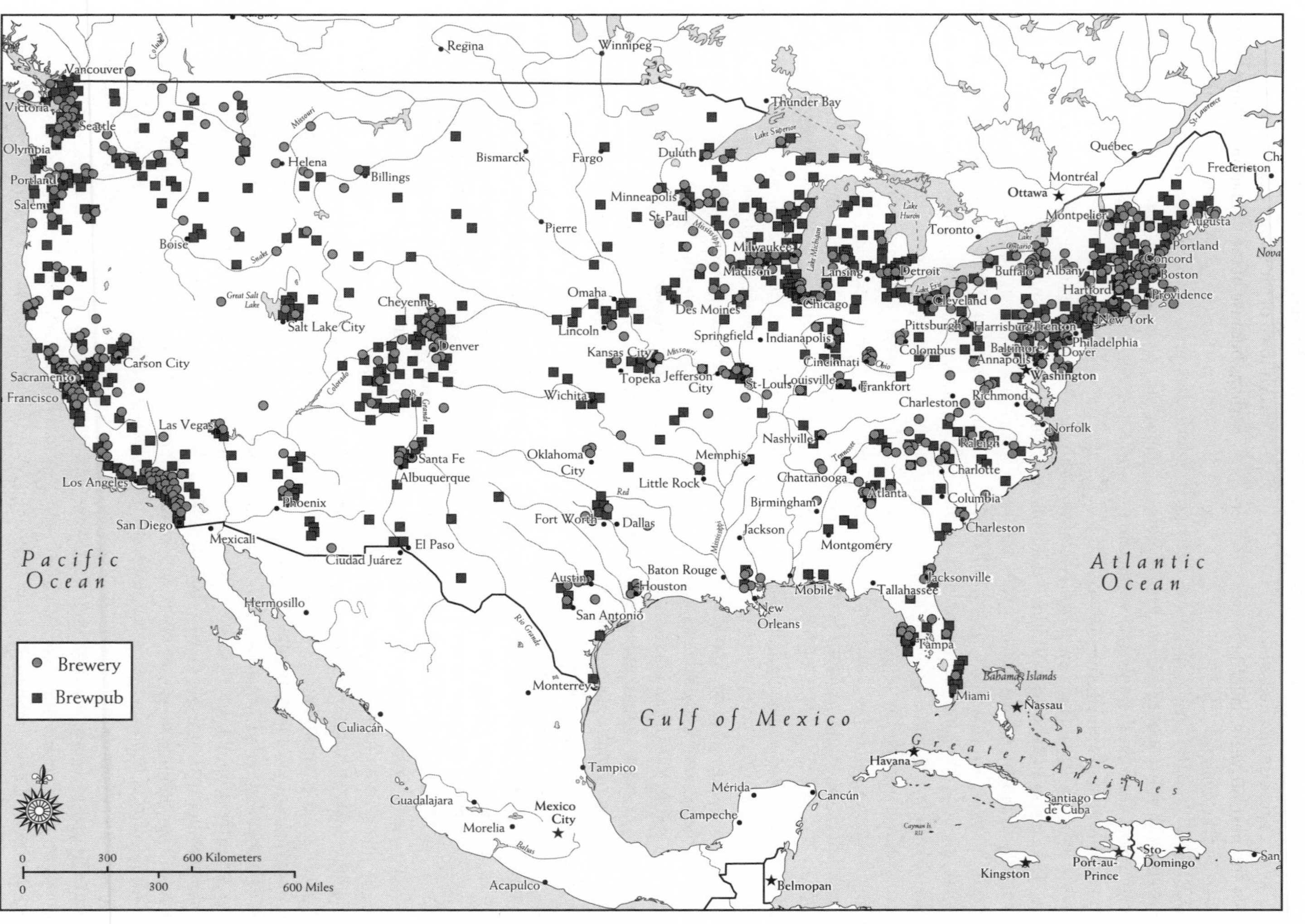

US breweries and brewpubs. GEORGE CHAKVETADZE, ALLIANCE PUBLISHING were beer-loving Irish and Germans. The Irish were fleeing famine and the Germans were fleeing a suffocating culture dominated by feudal lords.

For the next 80 years, lager breweries proliferated across the country. They brewed light lager beer and experimented with corn and rice adjuncts to lighten their beers and hedge against shortages of barley. Virtually every city in the country had a brewery, and the big cities had dozens. New York City, the largest urban center in the nation, was by far the biggest brewing center, with lager breweries established by Frederick and Maximilian Schaefer, Col Jacob Ruppert, and George Ehret. In Brooklyn, then an independent city, the Liebmann family established Rheingold. There were more than 40 other breweries in Brooklyn when it became part of New York City in 1898. There were more than 100 breweries in metropolitan New York. Philadelphia also was a major brewing center, with Schmidt's, Jacob Conrad's Keystone State Brewery, and Ortleib's.

What was not clear at the time was that the future of brewing in the United States would not be written by the big urban brewers of the East, but rather by the German-Americans who had settled in the Midwest. Phillip Best started "Best and Company, Beer Brewery, Whiskey Distillery & Vinegar Refinery," which eventually passed into the hands of Frederick Pabst, who had married Best's daughter Maria. August Krug started a brewery next to his restaurant and saloon in Milwaukee and hired a bookkeeper named Joseph Schlitz. Krug died in a freak accident and Schlitz married his widow and changed the company name to Joseph Schlitz Brewing Company. Phillip Best's brother Carl had opted for the family vinegar business, but he eventually started the Plank Road Brewery with a partner. The partner ran the brewery into the ground and fled, and Carl filed for bankruptcy. Frederick Miller, a 31-year-old German immigrant, purchased the defunct brewery and launched the Miller Brewing Co. These are the men whose beers made Milwaukee famous.

In St Louis, 18-year-old Adolphus Busch went into the brewing supply business and eventually met Eberhard Anheuser, who had acquired a failing brewery in a settlement of debts owed him by the previous owners. Busch married Anheuser's daughter Lilly and went into business with Anheuser. He brewed a beer called Budweiser for a friend, Carl Conrad, an importer of wines and liquors. Conrad had tasted the light, pilsner-like Budweis beer from the Czech town of the same name.

Perhaps because of the limitations of their home markets, perhaps because of the pioneering spirit that drove them West, these Midwestern brewers eventually eclipsed their brethren in the big cities of the East. The Midwestern brewers invested in many new technologies to help them reach new markets far from home: artificial refrigeration, pasteurization, automated bottling lines, and refrigerated rail cars. They built state-of-the-art laboratories and staffed them with well-trained European scientists. In short, they were more entrepreneurial than their Eastern counterparts who could hardly meet the demand for beer in the burgeoning cities around them.

By 1910, there were 1,498 breweries in the United States. In the 1880s and 1990s, price wars broke out among breweries. The advantage, of course, lay with the large breweries that could afford to buy raw materials at lower prices and sell at lower prices. But the seeds of a catastrophe for all American brewers had been planted decades before.

The temperance movement in America, led by religious opposition to alcoholic beverages, had claimed its first victory when Maine passed a prohibition law in 1850. In the next 5 years, two territories and 11 of the 31 states followed Maine's lead. Maine and the other prohibitionist states were small and rural and were not big consumers of beer, so there was little organized opposition from the beer industry.

The greater threat came in 1893 when Howard Hyde Russell founded the National Temperance Society, with support from capitalists J. P. Morgan, John D. Rockefeller, and Andrew Carnegie, who lamented the effects of alcohol abuse on their workers. An even more powerful group, the Women's Christian Temperance Union, had formed in 1873, campaigning against alcoholic beverages and persuading people to sign pledges of abstinence. Opponents of alcoholic beverages eventually coalesced into the Anti-Saloon League (ASL), led by the very effective advocate Wayne Wheeler. By 1902, the ASL had 200 employees and offices in 39 states and territories.

The brewing industry seemed oblivious to the threat to their livelihoods. Many breweries owned the saloons and beer gardens that the ASL was targeting. There were sporadic efforts to oppose local option laws in Texas and other states, but by 1909, 46 million Americans lived in dry territories. Nearly 500 breweries went out of business in the next decade. Brewers seemed unable to put aside their competitive instincts and cooperate against a common enemy. The ASL began attacking the lavish lifestyles of successful brewers like the Uihleins, Ruppert, Ehret, and Adolphus Busch.

The U.S. Brewers Association finally got its act together in 1913, funding the National Association of Commerce and Labor, made up of brewers and the trades that supplied the industry: grain and hop farmers, glass and bottle-cap manufacturers, wholesalers, retailers, saloonkeepers, and hotel workers. The new organization turned to the National German-American Alliance, a group dedicated to preserving German heritage, culture, and language in America, for help combating the "drys."

This alliance backfired when, in 1917, the United States entered the war against Germany. Eventually, the Senate opened hearings into the activities of the National German-American Alliance. In the course of the hearings, the U.S. Brewers Association admitted that it was funding the antitemperance efforts of the Alliance. Wayne Wheeler linked the U.S. brewing industry to the perfidy of the German enemy, completely undercutting the efforts of the U.S. Brewers Association.

Efforts by the brewers and distillers to head off Prohibition were too little and too late. Through decades of patient advocacy and by speciously linking the German-American brewers to the German war effort, Wayne Wheeler and the ASL had engineered a fundamental change in the political landscape. The Eighteenth Amendment to the Constitution was ratified by the necessary 36 states on January 16, 1919, and Prohibition was to come 1 year from that date. In May 1919, the Volstead Act put in place the apparatus for enforcing Prohibition.

Some brewers made "near beer" to get through the dry spell. Some made ice cream. Some were fortified by side businesses: Jacob Ruppert in New York owned the New York Yankees baseball team. Organized crime took over the production and distribution of alcoholic beverages during Prohibition, and violence flared between mobsters and authorities across the country. There were 1,179 brewers in the United States when Prohibition was imposed. Many companies launched when Prohibition was repealed in 1932, but by 1935, there were only 703 breweries in America.

The next 45 years saw consumption of beer rise in America, but paradoxically, the number of breweries in the United States declined. The reasons included consolidation and brewery closings. By 1978, there were 89 breweries in the country, and they were owned by fewer than 50 brewing companies. Advances in refrigeration and the construction of the interstate highway system enabled the big Midwestern breweries to ship beer to all parts of the country economically. Economies of scale enabled them to buy raw materials much more cheaply than their urban counterparts. Mass advertising, particularly through national television, enabled them to persuade consumers that their beer was so special they could ship it to your market and price it competitively against your local beer. Why drink the local stuff when you could drink a beer that was being sold across the country and advertised on national television? The Midwest giants eventually triumphed over the big regional breweries of the East Coast, which had been content to brew and market their beer in their rich urban markets.

But not everyone in America was satisfied with the bland light lager beers that the national giants were peddling. Fritz Maytag, a scion of the Iowa-based washing machine company, purchased the failing Anchor Brewing Co in San Francisco in 1964, after graduating from Stanford University. Maytag revived Anchor Steam Beer, the rich, malty lager beer that was fermented in open vats at higher temperatures, like ale. A few years later, Jack McAuliffe, a submarine technician who served the U.S. Navy in Aberdeen, Scotland, became enamored of English cask-conditioned "real ale," a type of beer that was being rescued by Britain's Campaign for Real Ale, a consumer advocacy group. He came home to Sonoma, California, in 1976 and started the New Albion Brewery, America's first "microbrewery." A microbrewery was simply a small brewery making flavorful beer in small batches and selling to a local market. New Albion lasted only 4 years, but former employees went on to start the Mendocino Brewing Co in Hopland, California, in 1982. Ken Grossman, a former bicycle repair shop owner, cobbled together old dairy equipment to start the Sierra Nevada Brewing Co in Chico,

California, in 1980 with friend Paul Camusi. In the East, William Newman, a former state budget clerk, started Newman Brewing Co in Albany, New York, in 1979, brewing a beer called Newman's Albany Amber. By 1990, there were 284 breweries in America. The new breed of "microbrewer" was making flavorful and strong ales and lagers—big beers that looked, smelled, and tasted very different than the light lager beers made by the national breweries.

In 2010, there were more than 1,700 breweries in the United States, more than existed before Prohibition and more than in Germany. About 500 were production breweries and the rest were brewpubs, small breweries that make beer for a single restaurant. The Brewers Association, the trade association of small brewers, claims that virtually all Americans now live within 10 miles of a brewery. The Brewers Association defined a microbrewery as a brewer making fewer than 16,500 hectoliters (15,000 barrels) of beer a year. Breweries producing more than 15,000 barrels were called "regional breweries." As breweries that had been called microbreweries outgrew their "micro" size, a new term sprang up—"craft" breweries—a term that broadly covered independently owned breweries making flavorful beer by traditional methods. Craft breweries were producing about 5% of the beer sold in America in 2010, but they represented the fastest growing segment of the alcoholic beverage industry, with many producers growing at a pace of more than 10% per year. The passion for craft brewing now has spread to Asia, Europe, South America, and Australia.

The Midwest brewing giants still produce most of the beer consumed in the United States, but they are no longer run by the families that gave them their names and they are now controlled by international brewing conglomerates. Anheuser-Busch brews half of the beer sold in America, but the company was bought by the Belgian-based brewing company InBev in 2008. Anheuser-Busch InBev is run by Brazilians. Miller Brewing Co was purchased by South African Breweries Ltd in 2002. Coors Brewing Co merged with Molson Breweries of Canada in 2005, and then Miller–Coors formed a joint venture in 2007. Miller–Coors sells 30% of the beer in America. Just as craft beer has become a force in the US beer industry, so has imported beer. Imports now account for about 13% of the beer drunk in America. The leading importing countries are Mexico, Holland, and Canada.

By 2010 the United States, a country where a mere 30 years previously there had been little beer to be found beside light mass market lagers, was home to the world's most diverse and dynamic beer culture. Having originally taken their own inspirations from England, Germany, Belgium, and other great brewing nations, American craft brewers are currently at the leading edge of creativity and culinary exploration in the world of brewing. Flavorful, interesting beers from the United States, Europe, and beyond are slowly moving out of the realm of specialty bars and into the mainstream of the American food culture.

Baron, Stanley. *Brewed in America*. New York: Little, Brown & Co, 1962.
Ogle, Maureen. *Ambitious brew, the story of American beer*. New York: Harcourt Books, 2006.
One hundred years of brewing, a supplement to the Western brewer, 1903. New York: Arno Press, 1974.

Steve Hindy

University of California, Davis. Often simply called "Davis" within the wine world, UC Davis is among the world's most influential teaching institutions in matters regarding fermentation. In April 1880 the Regents of the University of California were mandated by the California State Legislature to establish a program of instruction and research in viticulture and enology, reflecting the clear potential for California to develop an international wine business. Upon the repeal of Prohibition in 1933, the department became established on the campus at Davis, near Napa Valley. In 1956 Ruben Schneider, Technical Director of San Francisco's Lucky Lager Brewing Company, wrote to Emil Mrak, then Chair of the Department of Food Technology at UC Davis (later Chancellor), urging the establishment of a brewing program to complement the wine focus. The brewing program was established in 1958 with a grant from the Master Brewers Association of the Americas. See MASTER BREWERS ASSOCIATION OF THE AMERICAS.

The brewing technology course was the first of its kind to be offered in a major American educational institution. The first pilot-scale brewery was dedicated on December 8, 1958. The brewing program started with eminent fungal taxonomist

Herman Phaff, who gave lectures within an Industrial Applications of Yeast course. The first appointed teacher for brewing was T.O.M. ("Tommy") Nakayama, who later moved on to the Miller Brewing Company. From 1964 Michael Lewis took over the teaching of the brewing program. See LEWIS, MICHAEL J. Charles Bamforth was appointed to the Anheuser-Busch Professorship of Malting and Brewing Sciences in 1999. See BAMFORTH, CHARLES W. A new 1.5-barrel brewery was formally opened in 2006 and transferred to new accommodation within the August A. Busch III Brewing and Food Science Laboratory in 2010. There are extensive brewing programs both on campus and through University Extension, through which off-campus students can pursue top-level brewing qualifications. UC Davis also retains a long-standing barley breeding program.

Charles W. Bamforth

vacuum evaporation is a modern, "no-boil" method of wort preparation. See BOILING and WORT. It is based on the physical relationship between a liquid's boiling temperature and the ambient pressure surrounding it. The object of vacuum evaporation is ecological sustainability achieved by reducing the use of primary energy in the brewhouse. A secondary goal is wort quality improvements effected through the reduction of the shear factors that operate on the wort during a long, conventional, rolling boil. In vacuum evaporation, wort preparation is divided into two distinct steps, the simmering phase and the evaporating phase. During simmering, the wort is kept at just below the boiling point, at roughly 98°C (approximately 208°F), for about 50 to 60 min. This guarantees that all of the biochemical processes of a conventional boil take place, including wort sterilization, isomerization of hop alpha acids, the formation of flavor and aroma components, and the coagulation of excess proteins. See MAILLARD REACTION, MELANOIDINS, and PROTEINS. At the end of the no-boil heating phase the wort is pumped into the whirlpool for a conventional trub sedimentation phase. However, at this point, instead of being sent through a heat exchanger, the wort is pumped through an in-line vacuum evaporator with a constant vacuum atmosphere. There, the evaporation of the wort's undesirable volatiles, especially dimethyl sulfide and its precursors, which are usually driven off into the kettle stack during a vigorous and highly energy-intensive boil, are being essentially sucked out of the wort. See DIMETHYL SULFIDE (DMS). There is no need for the large amount of additional thermal evaporation energy that normally initiates the phase change from liquid to vapor. Aside from the substantial energy savings compared with conventional wort kettle treatments, a simmer-type vacuum evaporation technology has the additional advantage of reducing the thermal impact on the wort by reducing its oxidation potential. This, in turn, enhances the beer's overall stability, especially its foam stability. Vacuum evaporation technology can be retrofitted to most conventional brewhouses and can thus serve as one way for environmentally conscious breweries to modernize and upgrade their older, energy-inefficient brewhouses without replacing the entire installation. Currently, there are two major manufacturers of vacuum evaporation brewhouse technologies, Ziemann of Ludwigsburg and Schulz of Bamberg, both from Germany. Schulz's "GentleBoil" technology is designed to function entirely without a kettle boil. Under optimal conditions, it can reduce the primary energy consumption for brewhouse wort processing down to 1 l of fuel oil (or equivalent) per hl of wort, which equals energy savings of roughly 70% compared with conventional wort preparation techniques. In the environmental impact equation, this brings the carbon footprint of a hectoliter of wort down from about 9,000 to 3,000 g of CO_2 emissions for conventionally produced wort.

Dornbusch, Horst. Sustainability in the brewhouse. *The New Brewer* July/August (2009): 40–5.

Oliver Jakob

Vanguard (hop) was selected at Washington State University from a cross between an open-pollinated Hallertauer Mittelfrueh female seedling and a male seedling with generic European ancestry. See HALLERTAUER MITTELFRUEH (HOP). It was first planted in commercial trials in 1989. Vanguard is an early-maturing hop and produces about 1,400 kg/ha (1,250 lb/acre) in the Yakima Valley. See YAKIMA VALLEY HOP REGION. Vanguard contains roughly 5.8% alpha acids, with 18% of the alpha acid as cohumulone. The hop has a very mild bitterness. The essential oils are made up of less than 25% myrcene and more than 40% humulene. Its aroma is one of subtle spiciness with herbal and citrus notes. Its main use in the brewery is as a substitute for Hallertauer hop varieties. Vanguard is well suited to German beer styles, including kölsch, hefeweizen, and lagers.

See also HELLES, KÖLSCH, and PILSNER.

Stephen Kenny

vanilla is a flavoring agent derived from the fruit of the orchid Vanilla planifolia, which is native to Mexico, but is now cultivated in tropical regions around the world. It is the second most expensive spice in the world, after saffron. The vanilla fruit are commonly called beans, because they resemble bean pods, each about 15 to 30 cm (6 to 12 inches) in length. Each fruit is harvested when ripe and then goes through a lengthy curing process, which can take up to 2 years, although 6 months is more common.

Vanilla is most widely available as an alcohol-based liquid extract; vanilla flavor and aroma are extracted from ground pods through maceration in ethanol. Natural vanilla extract is a combination of hundreds of chemical compounds making for a very complex aroma and flavor, but the dominant chemical component is vanillin. Because natural vanilla is so expensive, the vast majority of vanilla flavor used today is actually artificial vanillin, which is derived very inexpensively from lignin, a wood by-product of the paper industry.

When used as a flavoring agent in beer, vanilla is most often found in winter seasonal beers, where the sweet aroma pairs nicely with other festive spices like cinnamon, allspice, and clove. Vanilla can be added at any of several stages in the brewing process. Most commonly, vanilla beans or liquid vanilla extract is added either at the end of the boil during the whirlpool stage before wort is transferred for fermentation or postfermentation before packaging. Whole beans can be used to "dry spice" the beer in the fermenter in a technique similar to dry hopping. Whole vanilla beans can also be added to a firkin or a pin to flavor a beer during cask conditioning.

Rain, Patricia. *Vanilla: The cultural history of the world's favorite flavor and fragrance.* Los Angeles, CA: Tarcher, 2004.

Brian Thompson

Vapeur Brewery (Brasserie à Vapeur) is a small, artisanal brewery situated in the town of Pipaix, Belgium, 74 kilometers southwest of Brussels. The name translates in French to "steam brewery," a name well justified because it is actually powered by an old steam engine. The brewery was originally opened in 1780 on a farm in Pipaix by Cosne-Damien Cuvelier and his wife, Marie Alexandrine Moulin. Descendants of their family ran the brewery, with the last family member, Gaston Biset, operating it from 1930 to 1983. By this time the brewery closed and was in disrepair, facing demolition. In 1984 the brewery was purchased by a young couple, Jean-Louis Dits and his wife Anne-Marie Lemaire (Sittelle), who had always dreamed of owning a brewery. They rebuilt much of the brewery and opened up for business. Tragically, Sittelle was killed in an accident at the brewery in 1990. Jean-Louis pressed on and continued operating the brewery, which brews only on the last Saturday of each month. Brasserie à Vapeur brews several artisanal beers, and despite the brewery's tiny production it has gained an international reputation. The oldest and best known of their beers is an idiosyncratic Saison-style of beer called Saison de Pipaix, whose heritage and recipe date to 1785. See SAISON. It is a very dry ale spiced with black pepper, ginger, sweet orange peel, curacao orange peel, and star anise. It ages quite well, and it is still possible to find bottlings from the late 1980s. Three other beers are also brewed: Vapeur Cochonne, Vapeur Legere, and Vapeur en Folie. All are spiced in the old farmhouse ale tradition. Except for Saison de Pipaix, the labels of the beers feature colorful, cartoon characters designed by Belgian artist Louis-Michel Carpentier.

Keith Villa

Verticillium wilt is a plant disease that can result in severe damage and high yield losses in hop fields. It is caused by two fungi, Verticillium albo-atrum and V. dahliae. An infection initially produces yellow patches on the hop leaves, which become black as the tissues die. Eventually, the leaves turn yellow and black and curl upward at the edges, before they become withered. Once a field is infected, the disease generally spreads rapidly and can affect entire growing areas.

The fungi are wide-ranging and can be transmitted to hop plants from weeds, from other crops such as lucerne, and from the soil where spores often survive for years. Insects, too, can spread the disease over long distances, as can seeds moved from one area to another. Infections typically start at the roots and pass through the plants to the leaves and flowers. Dry conditions encourage the growth of the parasite, as the plants become drought stressed.

Virulent varieties of Verticillium wilt were recorded in the 1930s in the UK and continental Europe, where they caused severe damage. In North America, however, outbreaks of V. albo-atrum have been more limited, and V. dahliae is the more common threat because of its preference for warmer temperatures.

Resistant hop varieties have been developed in recent years, but good farming practices have reduced the impact of the disease, too. These include removing plant residues from fields after the harvest, keeping hop plants separated by patches of grass, and the use of fungicides. Restrictions on plant movement and sourcing of new plants have also been effective.

EPPO data sheets on quarantine pests. "*Verticillium* spp. on hops." ww.eppo.org/QUARANTINE/fungi/Vertilillium/ (accessed August 30, 2010).

Keith Thomas

viability is a percentage measure of the ability of a batch of grain to germinate. (Germination, in nature, is the first step in the development of a new plant from seed. In the malt house, it is the step between steeping the cleaned grain for proper hydration and drying it in a kiln or drum. See GERMINATION.) A grain's viability rate is essential in assessing malt quality, because it is during germination that enzymes in the kernel's skin, the aleuron layer, become active and start breaking down large-molecular nutrients into smaller molecules and thus make them accessible either to the new plant as food or to the brewer as starches that will become wort compounds. Because kernels that fail to germinate do not become malt, depending on their number, they can drastically reduce the quality of a malt shipment. Excessive wetness or drought in the fields, infestations of plant diseases and pests, poor malting procedures, and, most important, improper storage conditions can severely reduce viability. However, a perfect batch of grain, in which all kernels manage to germinate, is a rare occurrence. The brew industry, therefore, uses specific viability values below 100% as reasonable benchmarks for quality. The minimum acceptable viability for brewing barley and wheat varies from one maltster to the next, ranging from 92% to 98% for top-quality specialty malt. For rye, it is usually 85% to 90%. Grains with viability ratings below these thresholds are usually not suitable for brewing and tend to end up as animal feed.

Thomas Kraus-Weyermann

vicinal diketones (VDKs) are a group of flavor components in beer, most notably 2,3-butanedione (generally referred to as diacetyl) and 2,3-pentanedione. Sweet butter, caramel, or butterscotch flavors and aromas are characteristics of diacetyl, while pentanedione contributes more honey-like notes to beer. See DIACETYL. Both compounds are derived from two ketone groups on adjacent (vicinal) carbon atoms. See KETONES. They are formed during beer fermentation in consistent proportions, and derivation in this ratio can indicate possible bacterial contamination. Excessive or unexpected VDK character can be a sign of improper fermentation or infection by bacteria or wild yeasts. In normal healthy fermentations, VDK production levels are strain dependent. Monitoring and controlling VDK levels plays an important role in flavor formation during beer maturation because VDKs are detectable by humans at fairly low levels. In light lagers, diacetyl is perceptible in the range of 20 to 60 parts per billion (ppb). Detection becomes more difficult in darker, more robust beers, in which diacetyl may be noticed at around 60 to 80 ppb. Research indicates that roughly 25% of all humans, however, are genetically blind to diacetyl detection, whereas many other beer drinkers taste it strongly and find the flavor and aroma repellent. Opinions about VDKs are divided among brewers as well. Although many brewers consider any notable trace of VDK character in beer a clear defect, others regard small amounts as desirable for rounding out a beer's flavor and adding complexity.

Although VDKs are formed during fermentation, they are not produced directly by yeast. Instead, they are the result of a long-chain reaction. During synthesis of the amino acids valine and isoleucine, yeast cells excrete alpha-acetolactate and alpha-ketobutyrate, respectively. These are precursors to VDKs, and their levels peak roughly halfway through fermentation. Subsequently, they break down spontaneously into VDKs, whose levels peak near the end of fermentation. During beer maturation, however, VDK levels decrease again because yeast metabolizes them as an energy source. The result of this final process is the conversion of VDKs into less flavor-active molecules. If beer is removed from its yeast before this reabsorption is complete, VDKs may later appear in the finished beer.

As the fermentation progresses, brewers monitor VDK levels as an indication of beer maturity. Reduction of VDKs is one of the main goals of traditional lagering; resting the beer for many weeks after fermentation gives the yeast an opportunity to "mop up" VDKs.

On a practical level, brewers have several tools at their disposal for keeping diacetyl levels in check during fermentation. The most important of these is yeast strain selection. Some yeast strains produce only minimal amounts of VDKs and are capable of quickly metabolizing whatever levels they do generate, whereas others are not. A so-called diacetyl rest is another common way of managing VDK levels. It involves a temperature increase roughly halfway through the fermentation, usually by about 1°C to 2°C (2°F to 5°F). This change in temperature accelerates both the rate at which precursors are converted to VDKs and the rate at which yeast metabolizes and thus removes VDKs.

Kräusening is another time-honored method of diacetyl reduction. See KRÄUSENING. This involves adding actively fermenting beer to maturing beer. The fresh yeast that is introduced through kräusening consumes VDKs fairly quickly, in addition to contributing natural carbonation. Many industrial breweries have found other ways of reducing VDKs without adding maturation time. A Food and Drug Administration–approved enzyme isolated from bacteria (Acetobacter spp.) can be added to wort. It is capable of circumventing diacetyl formation entirely by converting alpha-acetolactate directly into flavorless acetoin. Another strategy is to use genetically modified yeast strains that produce this enzyme. A third method of VDK reduction is to pass warmed beer through an immobilized yeast bioreactor, a system that can drop VDKs to acceptable levels in only a few hours.

See also IMMOBILIZED YEAST REACTOR.

Boulton, Chris, and Quain, David. *Brewing yeast and fermentation.* Oxford, UK: Blackwell Science Ltd, 2001.

Hough, J. S. *The biotechnology of malting and brewing.* Cambridge, UK: Cambridge University Press, 1991.

Kallmeyer, Moritz. *The role of diacetyl in beer.* Pretoria: Silverton, 2004. http://www.draymans.com/articles/arts/03.html/.

Jeff S. Nickel

Vienna lager is an amber-reddish Austrian beer style that closely resembles the golden-amber Märzen style of Munich, Bavaria. Both the Vienna lager and the Märzen were first brought to market in 1841. To put that date in perspective, the world's first golden blond lager, the pilsner, was developed in Plzen, in the Czech Republic, a year later, in 1842. The concurrence of the introduction of the Vienna and Märzen lagers was no accident, because the two brewers who created these styles, Anton Dreher and Gabriel Sedlmayr, were close friends and had cooperated in their development. Dreher was the owner of the Schwechat Brewery near Vienna, which was part of his family's vast brewing holdings, the largest in the Austro-Hungarian Empire, with sites from Trieste on the Adriatic to Budapest, Hungary. See DREHER, ANTON. Sedlmayr was the owner of the Spaten Brewery in Munich. See SEDLMAYR, GABRIEL THE YOUNGER. Both breweries were making mostly dark lagers, or dunkels, at the time.

While the Märzen beer is still fairly popular in much of the modern world, the Vienna lager is now rarely brewed, even in the city for which it is named. Strangely, this beer style is perhaps most popular nowadays in Mexico, where somewhat bowdlerized versions are made on an industrial scale. This may well be a result of the odd period from 1864 to 1867 when Archduke Ferdinand Maximilian Joseph of Austria ruled as Maximilian I, Emperor of Mexico. In the United States, too, Vienna lager has found a solid following among craft beer aficionados.

In central Europe, virtually all beers prior to the appearance of the Vienna, Märzen, and pilsner lagers in the 1840s were some shade of dark brown. This is because the malt kilns in use in those days were direct-fired, with the combustion gases from the kiln's fuel drying the malt. The resulting malt tended to be rather uneven, with some kernels barely dried, and others soundly roasted, and even scorched. In Britain, on the other hand, in the early 1800s, a new, indirect-fired kiln had come into use. It dried the malt using heated air, not fire. This allowed for the reliable production of pale malt, which, in turn, gave rise to a new beer style, the pale ale. Dreher and Sedlmayr became interested in this new British brew and in 1833 they set off on a fact-finding mission to the United Kingdom to learn all they could about making this pale beer. In fact, some beer historians accuse the two friends of outright industrial espionage. Upon their return, they each adapted the progressive British ale-making techniques to their own lager-making, which resulted in the revolutionary Vienna and Märzen lagers.

Both brews were of medium body and, in typical Central European fashion, had plenty of malty notes. However, they also differed from each other. The brew from Munich had a slightly, but not cloyingly, sweet finish, while the one from Vienna finished much drier. The Munich brew—like the prevailing dunkel of the age—placed less emphasis on up-front hop bitterness than did the Vienna brew. Still today, the IBU-values of an authentic Märzen generally range in the low 20s, while those of a Vienna lager range in the high 20s. The lingering hop-aromatic finish, on the other hand, tends to be more pronounced in the Munich than in the Vienna lager style. Technically speaking, the color of a classic golden-amber Märzen tends to be around 18–25 EBC (9–13 SRM), while that of the reddish Vienna lager might be around 22–28 EBC (11–14 SRM). The dominant dunkel lagers of the early 19th century, by comparison, had a typical color rating closer to 40 EBC (20 SRM). In alcohol by volume, the brew from Munich was also a bit stronger than that from Vienna. While the strength of the Märzen was close to 6 ABV, that of the Vienna lager was around 5 ABV, similar to that of a Munich export lager.

The revolutionary aspect of the two new lagers was based on their malts, which were kilned the British way, over hot air instead of direct heat. These malts have survived to our day and are now universally known as Vienna malt and Munich malt. Vienna malt makes up the majority of the grist for a true Vienna lager, which should display some toffeeish, bready flavors.

Both the Schwechat and the Spaten breweries are still in existence today. The Schwechat Brewery, which was founded in 1632 and purchased by the Dreher family in 1796, is now part of the Brau Union Österreich AG conglomerate, while the Spaten Brewery, which can trace its origins all the way back to 1397 and was purchased by the Sedlmayr family in 1807, is now part of the Belgian–Brazilian–American Anheuser-Busch InBev concern.

See also MUNICH MALT.

Dornbusch, Horst. *Bavarian helles*. Boulder, CO: Brewers Publications, 2000.

Dornbusch, Horst. *Prost—The story of German beer*. Boulder, CO: Brewers Publications, 1997.

Dornbusch, Horst. Vienna lager. *Brew Your Own*, 15(3) (2009).

Fix, George, and Fix, Laurie. *Märzen, Oktoberfest, Vienna*. Boulder, CO: Brewers Publications, 1991.

Horst Dornbusch

Vietnam

See SOUTHEAST ASIA.

vinegar

See ACETIC ACID.

VLB Berlin, VLB, is the abbreviation for a world-renowned Berliner educational institution in the brew industry now known under the legal name of *Versuchs- und Lehranstalt für Brauerei in Berlin e. V.* The name means "research and teaching institute for breweries." It was founded in 1883, not as a "mere" academic institution, but—as the name implies—as a cooperative repository of brewing knowledge in which the resources of the brew industry, the scientific community, and the state would be combined to further research, teaching, and practical brewery training. This was a revolutionary concept in Germany at a time when, sociologically, academia, and industry were still considered two very separate spheres of society.

The concept of combining scientific and polytechnic training has proven enormously successful over the years. Today, the VLB offers a complete spectrum of brewery-related training and education programs—some in conjunction with the Technical University of Berlin—from continuing education courses and conferences for brewery professionals employed in breweries, malteries, distilleries, and other beverage industries to academic tracks leading to degrees as diploma brewmaster, as bachelor and master in brewing and beverage technology, and as PhD in engineering. Starting in 1999, the VLB even offered courses toward a certified brewmaster in English. Since then, a craft brewing course and a brewing technology course have been added in English, as well as a brew training program in Russian. The modern VLB is a mature and established institution with a complex set of test facilities, research institutes, and departments specializing in such areas as malting, microbiology, biotechnology, management and logistics, brewing and packaging technologies, raw materials, chemical analytics, water and waste water technologies, and commercial consulting to industry.

Hendel, Olaf. Dienstleister der Brauindustrie seit 125 Jahre, VLB Berlin. *BRAUWELT* 148 (2008), pp. 718–19.

Versuchs- und Lehranstalt für Brauerei in Berlin (VLB). http://www.vlb-berlin.org/ (accessed August 16, 2010).

Winkelmann, Lydia. Ein Prost auf die Gründerväter. *BRAUWELT* 148 (2008), p. 793.

Lydia Winkelmann and Horst Dornbusch

vollbier, a now antiquated German federal beer tax category, which was originally invented by revenue bureaucrats. The first Germany-wide beer tax law dates from 1906, and soon the Kaiser's imperial tax authorities made a distinction between vollbier and other classes of beer for tax purposes. These found their modern codifications, forming the basis of the law that lasted until the 1990s, in the beer tax laws promulgated by Nazi Germany in 1939. The category was abolished by legislation effective January 1, 1993. Literally, the term "vollbier" meant "full beer" or "entire beer" and it referred to all beers with an original wort gravity, in the brewhouse, at the end of the kettle boil—measured in degrees Plato—of 11°P to 14°P. See ORIGINAL GRAVITY and PLATO GRAVITY SCALE. Strangely, this overarching category covered about 99% of all beers made in Germany at the time, whereas the remaining 1% of brews were covered by three additional categories: einfachbier (literally "simple beer") of an original gravity of 2°P to 5.5°P and 0.1% market share, in the early 1990s; schankbier (literally "tap beer") of an original gravity of 7°P to 8°P and 0.2% market share; and starkbier (literally "strong beer") of an original gravity of more than 16°P and 0.7% market share. Note that there are gaps in this tax classification, which meant that, prior to 1993, German brewers could not legally make beers based on wort gravities of 5.6°P to 6.9°P, 8.1°P to 10.9°P, or 14.1°P to 15.9°P! As part of the progressive harmonization of all laws within the European Union, this odd German beer tax scheme was replaced in 1993 by a new, continuous system in which every degree Plato of original gravity constitutes a separate tax category. As of early 2011, therefore, brewers pay slightly less than 0.8 Euro per degree Plato per hectoliter. This rate applies to breweries with an annual volume of 200,000 hl or more. This tax rate is graduated downward for smaller breweries. The lowest tax rate of a little more than one-half of the regular tax applies to breweries with 5,000 hl or less annual volume. The term "vollbier" is now simply used to mean "regular beer," distinguishing it from beers that are particularly light or strong in alcohol.

Harms, Diedrich. Durchschnittswerte bei Bieranalysen. *Brauerei-Forum* 7 (2009): 15.

Conrad Seidl

vorlauf is German for "recirculation." When a mash is transferred to a lauter tun or when the mash rest has finished in an infusion mash tun, some particles of grain remain in suspension under the vessel's false bottom. These materials come mostly from the grain's embryo, which is rich in lipids, and its husk, which contains phenolic compounds.

See LIPIDS and POLYPHENOLS. If they were boiled in the kettle, they would contribute unpleasant flavors to the finished beer. These particles are therefore sent back into the grain bed so that they never enter the wort stream. During the vorlauf sequence, wort is drained by simple gravity from underneath the false bottom into a collection vessel called a grant, from which it is pumped over the top (or just below the surface) of the grain bed. See GRANT. In the process, the grain bed serves as a filter that traps all floating particulate matter. Brewers continue the vorlauf until the recirculating wort runs clear. Only then is the wort lautered, that is, drained into the kettle. Although the technique is standard in the United States and Germany—from whence Americans derived the word "vorlauf"—not all brewers feel that the wort needs to be fully clarified. Some worry that reintroduction of the fine particulate matter into the mash bed will impede the runoff, thus causing more problems than are solved.

See also KETTLE and LAUTERING.

Steve Parkes

Wadworth Brewery is a family-run company in Devizes, Wiltshire, in the south of England. Henry Alfred Wadworth founded this brewery in 1875 after having trained as a brewer in London. He went into business with his brother-in-law, John Smith Bartholomew, whose descendants still run the business today.

Wadworth's brews a range of fine, well-respected session ales. The flagship brand, 6X, is a full-bodied, finely balanced mid-brown beer at 4.3% ABV and has a national following. The brewery's other beers are harder to find outside Wadworth's heartland but include seasonal and limited-edition ales. The brewery has broadened its portfolio in recent years, most notably with Swordfish, introduced in 2009 to commemorate a century of British naval aviation. Swordfish is blended with Pusser's Rum, the traditional booze ration of British sailors.

While its beers are good, Wadworth is more notable for the brewery itself. The Victorian red-brick Northgate brewery in the heart of the town of Devizes is still the center of Wadworth's operations. It is one of the finest surviving examples of a traditional Victorian tower brewery and retains many original features. A new copper house was installed in 2009, but the original open copper is still occasionally used, and a traditional steam engine is still in running order. Wadworth employs the UK's last remaining master brewery cooper, meaning that its beers are still available to be served from wooden barrels, and beer is delivered to local pubs every day by a team of four shire horses.

Wadworth remains an important regional family brewery, which offers a now rare opportunity to see some great, painstakingly preserved British brewing traditions.

See also BRITAIN.

Pete Brown

Wahl-Henius Institute of Fermentology is a brewing research laboratory and school in Chicago that operated between 1886 and 1921.

Founded in 1886 by Dr Robert Wahl and Dr Max Henius as the Wahl & Henius, the name was changed to the Scientific Station for Brewing of Chicago and then to the Institute of Fermentology before becoming the Wahl-Henius Institute. Its educational division, the American Brewing Academy, was created in 1891.

The school and laboratory operated successfully until Prohibition, when the near dissolution of the brewing trade forced its closure and sale to the American Institute of Baking, which retains the nucleus of the Wahl-Henius library.

Wahl-Henius would perhaps be mostly forgotten today if it were not for its role as publisher of two important beer texts. *The Wahl-Henius Handy Book of Brewing, Malting and the Auxillary Trades*, coauthored by Wahl and Henius, is a comprehensive and wide-ranging view into American brewing in 1901. It also contains basic chemical analyses of many contemporary American and European beers, providing an unusually valuable window into the brewing past. J. P. Arnold's 1911 *Origin and History of Beer and Brewing* is an exhaustive romp through thousands of years of beer history.

Randy Mosher

Wales is a mountainous country of three million people located to the west of England and comprising part of the United Kingdom. It is to Wales that the ancient Britons were driven by a succession of invaders, from the Romans to the Anglo-Saxons. The fleeing Celtic tribes were known for their brewing skills. Saxon records from the 7th century onward mention "Welsh ale" (or bragawd/bragot), a heavy brew laced with spices. It was as highly prized as another Celtic drink, mead, made from fermented honey.

Today beer is still the national drink, but the industry has had to make its way in a society far more hostile to alcoholic drinks than neighboring England. In the late 19th century the dominant non-conformist chapels were appalled by public displays of drunkenness. The powerful anti-alcohol movement succeeded in establishing the Welsh Sunday Closing Act in 1881, shutting pubs on Sundays; members of the movement also pressed for prohibition. The country's leading brewing center, Wrexham, in northeast Wales—once known for its strong ales—was largely shut down, though its pioneering lager brewery, Wrexham Lager, continued producing until 2000. When founded in 1883, it had promoted its lager as a temperance drink.

Those that survived concentrated on brewing relatively low-alcohol beers. Wales' leading brewer today, Brains of Cardiff, chiefly brewed a mild, dark ale. "Dark" accounted for the bulk of its production until the 1980s. Stronger pale ales mainly came from England, notably from Bass and Whitbread, which later took over many Welsh breweries. The only other survivor is Felinfoel of Llanelli, which pioneered beer canning in Britain in 1935. But from the 1980s a fresh wave of craft brewers sprang up to meet the demand for local cask beer, with 40 brewing across Wales by 2009.

See also BRITAIN and TEMPERANCE.

Ebenezer, Lyn. *The thirsty dragon*. Llanrwst, UK: Gwasg Carreg Gwalch, 2006.

Glover, Brian. *Prince of ales, the history of brewing in Wales*. Stroud, UK: Alan Sutton Publishing, 1993.

Brian Glover

Wallonia is the southern portion of Belgium, which includes the five French-speaking provinces of Hainaut, Namur, Wallonian Brabant, Liège, and Luxembourg. The Belgian province of Luxembourg is a separate entity from the neighboring Grand Duchy of the same name, which ceded from Belgium in 1839, only 8 years after the official founding of Belgium as an independent country, as part of the reorganization of Europe in the wake of the Napoleonic wars.

Historically, the concept of a Walloon region was based mostly on language. The Walloons speak a variant of French with strong Celtic influences, which are still noticeable in the rural parts of the region.

Historically, Wallonia is perhaps less prominent in the world of brewing than Flanders to the north or the lambic-brewing area around Brussels, yet there are distinct Wallonian beer styles that owe much of their character to the two main forces that shaped the region—agriculture and heavy industry.

Whereas the northern portion of Wallonia consists largely of undulating farmland, the southern portion is made up of the wooded hillsides and swooping valleys of the Ardennes. Between the two is a narrow strip of land, which was responsible, in the 19th century, for turning Belgium into the world's second most powerful industrial economy after Great Britain. In its heyday the region's power derived from the coalfields around Mons and Charleroi and the smelting plants and blast furnaces in and around Liège, with the Sambre and Meuse Rivers as transportation links.

In the Wallonian countryside, especially in northern Hainaut, between Enghien near Brussels and the ancient cathedral city of Tournai, the indigenous beer is the French-style *bière de garde* (stored beer), or the type known locally as *saison* (season). This is a shorthand reference to the brewing and fermenting of this farmhouse style during the cooler months of spring for drinking on hot summer days. Brewing the beer in springtime rather than summer reduced the chance of beer spoilage. Although the Wallonian *saison* bears some relationship to Flemish brewing, the link is only indirect; both brewing traditions resort to high hopping rates as a way to preserve beer. See BIÈRE DE GARDE and SAISON.

An entirely different brewing tradition evolved in the industrial centers of Wallonia, where men who engaged in heavy manual labor sought quaffing beers that helped them slake their thirst after a hard day of toil. These beers were meant to provide plenty of nourishment, but relatively little alcohol.

They were soft, light, and sweet, yet confusingly, they too came to be known as *saison*. Simpler, lighter beers are also tailor-made for brewing on an industrial scale and this spawned the success of such large brewing companies as Piedboeuf at Jupille-sur-Meuse, the eventual creator of Jupiler lager, and one of the founding firms of what eventually became Anheuser-Busch InBev, the world's largest brewer.

Farmhouse brewing, by contrast, has largely avoided the trend toward industrial brewing. Among the more successful small breweries of the region nowadays is the idyllically situated Dupont Brewery in the village of Tourpes, east of Tournai. Its Moinette brands of stronger ales and the iconic Saison Dupont have arguably foreseen and shaped the emerging tastes of a new generation of craft beer lovers worldwide. Using prodigiously high hopping rates, by Belgian standards, these beers have created a Belgian style of delicately spicy (although unspiced), bitter pale ales that are now influencing more recent craft brewers, who regard them as belonging to a distinctly southern Belgian style, in vivid contrast to the styles of the Flemish north.

The overt rivalry between southern and northern Belgian brewers has even drawn in the regional governments, which are keen to support entrepreneurial brewers interested in starting microbreweries in the region. During the first decade of the new millennium, therefore, some 40 new breweries appeared on the scene in the Hainaut and Luxembourg provinces. Several of these, such as Rulles, De Ranke, and Jandrain-Jandrenouille, are starting to gain international reputations.

Ironically, many of the brands that are most associated with the region, such as Leffe and Maredsous, are now physically brewed outside the region. The overall improved fortunes of Belgian brewers, however, have persuaded some established breweries to come out with bold new products. The commercially astute Lefèbvre Brewery, for instance, broke with tradition and now makes a sweet, spicy, heavy, and very hoppy beer called Hopus. Likewise, Dubuisson, whose Bush Beer barley wine is sold as Scaldis in many countries for local reasons, has branched out by producing smaller beers, some with alcohol by volume as low as 7%. The region is also home to the three Trappist breweries of Chimay, Rochefort, and Orval. Orval helps brewers throughout the province of Luxembourg by sharing its yeast with them.

To the world, "Belgian beer" often implies a single beer culture. But to the Belgians themselves, there are subtle differences between the Flemish and the Wallonian ways of brewing. Whereas the beers of Flanders seem more freewheeling and fearless, the beers of Wallonia, although not shy of experimentation, seem perhaps earthier and more grounded in tradition.

See also BELGIUM, FLANDERS, and PAJOTTENLAND DISTRICT.

Tim Webb

Warrior (hop) was developed as a super alpha hop variety by Yakima Chief Ranches in the Yakima Valley. See YAKIMA VALLEY HOP REGION. Because this hop is proprietary, its genetic origins are not disclosed. This variety is characterized by high levels of alpha acids (15% to 17%), low levels of beta acids (4% to 5%), a moderate essential oil content (1–2 ml/100 g), and a low cohumulone content. Warrior has excellent yield potential, is moderately resistant to powdery mildew, and has good storage stability. Warrior has become a favorite bittering hop for brewers wishing to create "double IPAs" or beers with extreme levels of hop bitterness. The hop's aromatics are piney, with notes of citrus and pineapple, and it can deliver a big punch of bitterness without rough edges.

Thomas Shellhammer and Val Peacock

Washington, George. On the day New York was finally evacuated by the British army in November of 1783, George Washington stopped for a beer at the Bull's Head Tavern on what is now the Bowery—one of many mentions of the first American president's devotion to beer and its concerns.

Modern hobbyists and beer enthusiasts are fond of citing Washington as an early practitioner of homebrewing, largely on the strength of a 1737 diary entry from when he served as a colonel in the Virginia militia. In the entry Washington outlines the brewing of a small beer. See SMALL BEER. Whether he turned his own hand to the craft or put it down for the use of those on his estate, it shows a sensibility familiar with the practices of brewing.

Washington was a great aficionado of porter, a beer style that captured such enthusiasm in Britain that it is sometimes credited with having spurred the Industrial Revolution there. America showed a lesser, but still evident fascination with porter. Washington credited the Philadelphia brewer Robert Hare with making the best porter in the city, even to shrewdly attempting to corner remaining supplies of Hare's beer when the brewery was destroyed by fire. Washington's interests ran as well to more general advocacy of American brewers by urging his countrymen to "buy American," boasting in a letter to the Marquis de Lafayette in 1789 that he used no "porter or cheese" in his family that was not produced in America, touting the superior quality of the American articles.

Baron, Stanley Wade. *Brewed in America: The history of beer and ale in the United States.* Boston, MA: Little, Brown & Co., 1962.
Smith, Gregg. Beer in America: The early years 1587–1840. Boulder, CO: Brewers Publications, 1998.

Dick Cantwell

wassail was a very specific Christmas custom in medieval England, which involved the consumption of copious amounts of hot ale. It was a way of passing on good wishes and has only really ceased to have significance over the last century and a quarter or so. The word is derived from the Old Norse *ves heill* and Old English *wes hal*, meaning "be of good health" or "be of good fortune." The use of the wassail as a drinking toast seems to have arisen among the Danish-speaking inhabitants of England, and then spread throughout the whole land. When the Normans conquered England, they erroneously assumed that the wassail was a native English phenomenon.

A little after the Conquest, Geoffrey of Monmouth gave an early account of the practice in his story of Rowena, the daughter of Hengist, which he wrote around 1140 AD. He relates that it had been the custom in early Britain for one who drinks to another to say, "wacht heil!" and for he who pledges in return to answer, "drink heil!" Indeed, legend has it that the night before the Battle of Hastings, the English army had spent their hours revelling amid cries of *wessel* and *drinche-heil*! Originally a general toast, the wassail became to be known as principally a Twelfth Night ceremony in which a bowl of hot, spiced ale was offered to participants. Henry VII's Household Ordinances of December 31, 1494 record procedure and protocol for the wassail. The most complete 17th-century accounts of the custom are to be found in the verses of Robert Herrick (1591–1674), who "quaffed the mighty bowl" with Ben Jonson.

As with most ceremonies, a specialized paraphernalia evolved, and the large (originally wooden) wassail-bowl was a central feature. Elaborate cups were also employed, and most large monasteries and grand houses possessed such items. For many years, the main ingredients of the wassail-bowl were hot strong ale, sugar, spices, and roasted apples; a drink called "lambswool" (similar to a posset, consisting of sugared hot milk curdled by spiced ale). A verse from Herrick's poem *Twelfth Night* is most evocative:

> Next crown the bowle full
> With gentle lamb's-wooll;
> Add sugar, nutmeg and ginger,
> With store of ale, too;
> And thus ye must doe
> To make the wassaile a swinger.

"Drinking the wassail," also sometimes termed "wassailing," has long had an association with song, particularly Christmas carols. An interesting variant was called the "Orchard-visiting wassail," a ceremony which involved drinking to the health of trees in cider-apple orchards.

Bickerdyke, John (pseudonym of Charles Henry Cook). *The curiosities of ale and beer.* London: Leadenhall Press, 1886 (2008 reprint, Beer Books, Cleveland, OH).
Hackwood, F. W. *Inns, ales, and drinking customs of old England.* London: T. Fisher Unwin, 1910 (1987 reprint, Bracken Books, London).
Wilson, C. A. ed. *Liquid nourishment.* Edinburgh: Edinburgh University Press, 1993.

Ian Hornsey

water can easily be argued to be the most important raw material in brewing, representing as it does 85%–95% of most beers. Breweries are heavy users of water throughout the brewing process, where it is used for mashing, sparging, cleaning, sanitizing, wort chilling, steam generation, and more. Even the more efficient breweries will use 4 to 5 liters (or 1.06 to 1.32 gal) of water to every liter of beer produced with the "world record" in 2011 standing at a bit more than 2 to 1. Although all uses of water are important to the brewery, the water that ends up as part of the beer naturally takes precedence.

Water Sources

Historically, significant breweries have always been built close to suitable supplies of good water. The composition of the local water impacted the beer styles and traditions that arose in many of the classical European beer countries or regions such as Plzn (Pilsen) in the Czech Republic, Burton-on-Trent and London in England, Bavaria in Germany, Dublin in Ireland, Munich in Germany, and Vienna in Austria, etc. Fundamentally, the most significant differences in the composition of water are determined by whether it is from a *surface water* source (reservoirs, rivers, streams, or lakes) or a *ground water* source, such as aquifers, wells, or a municipal water supply based on ground water. The basic difference is that surface water is virtually mineral free because it is made up of recent precipitation, whereas ground water can be anything from very soft (low in minerals), as found in Czech Bohemia (Pilsen), to the very mineral-rich water in Burton-on-Trent. See BURTON-ON-TRENT.

These differences depend on local geology, which determines both the time it takes for precipitation on the surface to drain down to the *aquifers* (water-bearing geological layers) from where it is drawn and the chemical composition of the geolayers between the surface and the aquifer. These two factors combined determine which minerals the water takes up and in which concentrations during this process.

Water Treatment

Today, most difficulties with local water supplies can be overcome by technological means. With the introduction early in the 20th century of industrial water treatment, the traditional ties between local water composition and beer quality were eliminated to the extent that today any brewery anywhere in the world can, given a suitable water treatment system, create any desired composition of the water used for brewing, sometimes called "brewing liquor."

Diverse techniques are available for treating brewing water. These vary not only with the desired end quality of the treated water but also with the composition of the untreated water, as well as with the age and technological sophistication of the water treatment systems. Such systems range from simple depth filtration, which uses *sand* to remove just particulate matter, to *reverse osmosis* that removes virtually all "foreign" molecules and ions from the water, leaving it almost as pure as distilled water. Which system—or combination of systems—is used at individual breweries will depend on a multitude of factors, of which by far the most important is, of course, the requirements for producing a brewing liquor that is ideal for the quality of the beer styles the brewery chooses to make. This is clearly the case for larger and more modern breweries, whereas smaller and older breweries often have to live with either an archaic or an overly simplistic system or even no water treatment at all.

Water Hardness

The chemistry of the water has a significant impact on the flavor of the beer brewed with it, and one of the most important elements in water chemistry in this respect is its *hardness*. This is an ancient descriptor of the combined contents of the anions sulfate and bicarbonate and the cations calcium and magnesium. Water containing high concentrations of these minerals is said to be hard water, and conversely water with low mineral content is said to be soft water. Hardness can be divided into *permanent hardness* (calcium and magnesium sulfate) and *temporary hardness* (calcium and magnesium bicarbonate). As the name hints, temporary hardness can be removed by boiling the water, causing precipitation of calcium carbonate and leaving the water softer once it cools. This water can then be removed or decanted off the precipitate. Boiling will not remove permanent hardness, however, a term that generally denotes sulfates and chlorides of calcium and magnesium. Despite the name, water containing high permanent hardness can be softened by the use of chemical additives that react with and precipitate the hardening minerals. Softening can also be achieved by the use of devices that replace calcium and magnesium ions with sodium or potassium ions; these devices are common in many people's home water systems.

Calcium, and to a lesser extent magnesium, lowers the water's pH by reacting with phosphate and other ions. Bicarbonate raises its pH. The net pH that results from the level of calcium, magnesium, and bicarbonate impacts (among other things) the extractability of various malt and hop components into wort and the quality of perceived bitterness.

The calcium and magnesium that make up the permanent hardness are, however, highly desirable in moderate concentrations.

Water Chemistry and Beer Quality

The ions present in water (and other brewing raw materials) have various impacts:

Calcium (Ca^{2+}): Decreases pH (acidifies) and stabilizes alpha-amylase during mashing. Calcium improves the sedimentation of both trub and yeast after fermentation and precipitates calcium oxalate that might otherwise cause gushing in beer.

Magnesium (Mg^{2+}): Enzyme cofactor. However, too much magnesium can result in an astringent bitterness.

Sodium (Na^{+}): Affords saltiness. Gives a fuller, rounder, sweeter taste in moderate concentrations.

Potassium (K^{+}): Can give similar flavor effects to sodium. Although small amounts are necessary for healthy yeast, higher concentrations can interfere with enzymatic activity in the mash. Laxative.

Iron (Fe^{2+}): An oxidizing agent; can cause haze in worts and gives a metallic off-flavor to beer.

Zinc (Zn^{2+}): Stimulates yeast by activating alcohol dehydrogenase. Foam enhancer.

Bicarbonate (HCO_3^{-}): Increases pH. Gives a less fermentable sugar profile from mashes and can produce difficulties in separation of proteins and polyphenol complexes during the cold and hot breaks. This can later cause difficulties in filtration. Causes scaling in brewery vessels and piping.

Sulfate (SO_4^{2+}): Gives a drier and more pleasantly bitter taste and flavor in moderate to high concentrations. Gives rise to a sulfidic aroma and flavor when reduced by yeast.

Chloride (Cl^{-}): Mellows out and increases the fullness of the palate of the beer.

The positive effects, especially in the brewing of many traditional English style ales, of the calcium, sulfate, and chloride ions has given the name to a very specific adjustment of water used for brewing such beers. It is called *Burtonization*—named after the well water in Burton-on-Trent—and involves an addition of calcium sulfate (gypsum) and calcium chloride to the water. See BURTONIZATION.

In many areas of the world, the public water supply is chlorinated and it is essential that such chlorine be removed from the water before it is used for brewing. If it is not, the chlorine will react chemically with diverse organic compounds in the malt, resulting in the formation of organochlorines that have strong, penetrating, unpleasant bandaid like phenolic off-flavors. Dechlorination is most commonly carried out with activated carbon filters that also remove any organohalogens created by the chlorination.

Hough, J. S., D. E. Briggs, R. Stevens, and T. W. Young. *Malting and brewing science*, 2nd ed. Cambridge, UK: University Press, 1982.

Kunze, Wolfgang. *Technology brewing and malting*, 3rd international ed. Berlin: VLB Berlin, 2004.

Anders Brinch Kissmeyer

wee heavy is a complex, strong beer originating in Scotland and characterized by substantial malt-influenced flavors. Wee heavy remains one of Scotland's definitive beers and the style has gained a worldwide following. This strong ale is traditionally served in small ("wee") measures, although this owes more to an alcohol strength that can range from 5.5% to 9.0% ABV rather than any alleged Scottish canniness with money and portions. And, confusingly, "heavy" in Scottish ale terms can refer to any beer between 3.5% and 4.0% ABV, which equates roughly with the relatively light "ordinary bitter," that of most English ales.

As a general rule, a wee heavy is strong, dark, and malty with little hop character and moderate carbonation. Malt is the major aroma—which follows through on the palate as toffee and caramel—but earthy and smoky secondary aromas may also be present, accentuating the style's renowned complexity.

The wee heavy mouthfeel is medium-full to full-bodied with some versions offering a thick, chewy viscosity. The style has traveled well and has found niche audiences in North America and parts of Europe where indigenous beer styles are readily endorsed but others of interest are taken seriously.

Wee heavy was originally a product of its time and place: 18th-century Scotland. Hops aren't native to the country and were therefore an expensive commodity to ship from the traditional English growing centers of Kent, Hereford, and

Worcestershire, let alone from abroad. But what Scotland does produce in quantity is high-quality malting barley which, from the earliest days of managed agriculture, was concentrated in key areas: Berwickshire, the Lothians, Fife, Angus, and the Buchan region of the northwest, to be malted for beer and whiskey production. So when it came to making beer at a reasonable cost, the hop content was invariably kept to a minimum.

Soft water has also been a key component in Scottish brewing, and in the wee heavy style flavors come from high mash temperatures and kettle caramelization rather than from crystal malts. Scotch ale—an alternative name for wee heavy—traditionally goes through a long boil in the kettle that caramelizes the wort. This was particularly the case in days when kettles were direct-fired by flames, and some of the better examples are still brewed this way. This also produces a deep copper-colored sweet beer with roasted malt caramel flavors (even some liquorice and coffee flavors) and wee heavies should be full-bodied and strong.

Belgians are particularly fond of Scottish-derivative ales and they have become something of a tradition in the Walloon region; their malty sweet, dark body and hint of fruit appear in several guises from Scotch Silly (8.0% ABV) to Abbaye Des Rocs Brune (9.0% ABV).

The Baltic countries were traditional Scottish beer trading grounds, with Norway, Denmark, and Holland also of great importance. But it is in North America that the wee heavy style has flourished and developed through the curiosity, knowledge, and enthusiasm of craft brewers. Its evolution in America is well documented and started early. There is evidence from around the 1750s of beer exported from Scotland to the new colonies in North America which tended to follow in the wake of Scottish emigration. Initial demand for strong Scottish beers came from the merchants and planters in those colonies and in the West Indies where their influence was also strong. By 1785 North America and the West Indies soaked up 80% of Scottish strong ale export, reflecting the concentration of Scottish emigrants to Maryland, Virginia, and the Carolinas with Jamaica and Grenada being important settlements in the West Indies. Today, wee heavy is brewed by dozens of craft brewers across the United States, often as a seasonal beer for the cold weather months.

See also SCOTCH ALE and SCOTLAND.

Donnachie, Ian. *A history of the brewing industry in Scotland*. Edinburgh: John Donald Publishers, 1979.

Alastair Gilmour

weevils, small beetles distinguished by their long snouts and their voracious appetite for grain and malt.

The grain weevil (Sitophylus granarius) infests stores of barley, wheat, oats, rye, rice, and corn. In 16th-century England they were known as "maltworms" and the playwright William Shakespeare made several references to them and the damage they could do to grain.

Wingless, the weevil is about 2–4 mm long (3/16 inch) and has been the bane of maltsters' lives for generations. In the 19th century the "ravages" to barley that had been stored for only 6 to 8 months could be enormous. Females can lay several hundred eggs at a time, one inside each grain kernel. As the larva develops, it can eat the whole of the inside of a kernel, leaving the husk to appear intact. Researchers estimate that one pair of weevils may produce up to 6,000 offspring a year. The larvae live for 5 weeks during the summer months but they can live up to 5 months in cooler temperatures. The adults, which can live for up to 8 months, feed on the outside of grain kernels.

Once established in a grain store, weevils are notoriously difficult to eradicate. Henry Stopes, the author of *Malt & Malting* in 1895 and a designer of malting facilities, despaired at the limited effectiveness of eradication methods, advising, "short of demolition of the building, few (methods) are really successful."

Today good hygiene and the judicious use of approved pesticides can prevent weevil infestation of grain stores.

Patton, Jeffrey. *Additives, adulterants and contaminants in beer*. Oldham, UK: Patton Publications, 1989.
Stopes, Henry. *Malt & malting*. London: F. W. Lyon, 1895.
Wahl, Robert, and Max Henius. *American handy book brewing and malting, volume II*. Chicago: Wahl-Henius, 1908.

Tim Hampson

Weihenstephan The faculty for Brewing Science and Beverage Technology at the Technical University of Munich in Weihenstephan, a small town north of Munich in the Freising District of Germany, has historically been considered the epicenter for education in the world of brewing. In 1021 Weihenstephan was established by Benedictine monks as an abbey and beer brewery. Commercial beer brewing commenced in 1040, making Weihenstephan reputedly the oldest continuously operating brewery in the world. When the Benedictine Abbey ceased in 1803 and the property was taken over by the Bavarian State Government, it became the founding location for the Agricultural and Brewing College. Later, in 1907, the Weihenstephan research brewery was established. The college achieved full university status in 1920 and was allowed to issue doctorate degrees. In 1930 it was merged into the Technical University of Munich, Germany. Current fields of study at Weihenstephan have since been broadened to include forestry, horticulture, nutrition, biotechnology, food technology, and appliance engineering. The campus is now a large modern university referred to as the Center of Life Science with 80 professors and over 3,000 students. The campus has two breweries: the original Research Brewery and the Bavarian State Brewery, with an annual output of over 200,000 barrels, and a distillery. There are five high-tech, small-scale research breweries on campus for student projects as well as commercial consulting projects for Brewing Science majors to use. As an interdisciplinary major, there are two different educational paths for students. The 4 and a half year Masters in Engineering program is highly academic and requires the students to publish a thesis of significant scientific relevance in the brewing disciplines of process engineering, malting, mechanical engineering, microbiology, business administration, packaging, or energy technology. Course work in microbiology, biochemistry, mechanical engineering, brewing and malting technology, fermentation science, analytical chemistry, accounting, business administration, food chemistry, process engineering and microbiological quality control are among the 45 required classes necessary to graduate. The graduates are considered among the elite in the brewing world, as the program is highly competitive with less than 20% of the accepted students meeting the graduation requirements.

Also offered at the University of Munich is the 2-year Diploma Braumeister (Graduated Brew master) program. Students can qualify for this program if they have completed a journeyman-training program at a brewery administered by a certified brewing engineer and a total of 3 years working in the industry. The classes that correspond to the Braumeister program are at the lower division level and the degree does not require a thesis. All classes in both programs are taught entirely in German.

Among the industry services provided by Weihenstephan are the yeast bank, technical consulting, and financial consulting. The Weihenstephan yeast bank, established in 1940, supplies yeast to breweries around the world. It has the largest collection of bottom and top fermenting strains in the world. The various strains were differentiated using modern research methods conducted by the graduate students at Weihenstephan. Yeast is shipped to breweries in various forms: yeast in agar, yeast on cotton, one-liter flask, or pressed cakes. Throughout the world, many yeast strains are known largely by their Weihenstephan catalog numbers. This is especially the case with Bavarian weissbier yeast, which some brewers and enthusiasts persist in simply calling "Weihenstephan yeast," even though Weihenstephan makes hundreds of other yeast strains available.

As far as technical consulting goes, the majority of brewing machinery technology developments is initiated by the major German brewing machinery manufacturing firms. Most of these companies send their new developments to be tested and have their results certified by the Brewery Testing and Research Institute (Staatliche Brautechnische Prüf und Versuchsanstalt) at Weihenstephan. The institute is staffed with 51 technical staff members that focus primarily on analytical chemistry.

Financial Consulting to the brewing industry is offered by the Financial Advisory Group Weihenstephan (Unternehmungsberatung Weihenstephan). Founded in 1976, this company was purchased by Delloite Touche Tohmatsu and continues to offer financial consulting to the brewing and beverage industry worldwide. The company specializes in brewery valuations, supply chain management, structural reorganizations, and controlling.

The Abbey Brewery of Weihenstephan became the Bavarian State Brewery at Weihenstephan in 1921. The brewery is particularly well-known for its hefeweizen, which is exported worldwide. See HEFEWEIZEN. It is a modern state-of-the-art brewery and bottling facility that incorporates much of the technology that is developed through cooperative efforts with current and former students at the Technical University of Munich at Weihenstephan.

See also GERMANY and MUNICH.

Geschichte Weihenstephans (History of Weihenstephan). http://www.weihenstephan.de/weihenstephan/wegweiser/campgeschi.html/ (accessed November 2, 2009).

Staatsbrauerei Weihenstephan (Weihenstephan brewery). http://www.brauerei-weihenstephan.de/ (accessed November 4, 2009).

Uhl, Bodo. Die hofmarks—und braurechte des klosters weihenstephan. (The royal brand and brewing rights of weihenstephan and the history of Freising.) *Sammelblatt des Historischen Vereins Freising* 29 (1979): S.9–53.

Wissenschaftszentrum Weihenstephan (Research Center Weihenstephan). http://www.wzw.tum.de/ (accessed November 4, 2009).

Dan Gordon

weissbier is the classical wheat beer of Bavaria and one of Germany's greatest and most distinctive beer styles. Weissbier means "white beer" in German. This name derives from the yellowish-white tinge that is imparted by the pale wheat and barley malts from which the beer is made. Outside Bavaria, most weissbier is better known as *hefeweizen*, literally "yeast wheat" in German. This name is derived from the fact that it is a wheat-based beer that is usually packaged unfiltered, with plenty of yeast turbidity in the finished beer. According to German law, a beer that is labeled hefeweizen, weizenbier, or weissbier (these three terms are largely interchangeable, but there is also a filtered version of weissbier called "kristallweizen") must be made with at least 50% malted wheat. Most weissbiers, however, use more wheat than the law requires and are made with 60%–70% malted wheat. The rest of the grist is malted barley. In other countries, where German laws do not apply, of course, wheat beers may be brewed with any percentage of wheat, although it would be difficult to get true weissbier character from a mash containing much less than 50% wheat. Making beer with 100% wheat, however, would be exceedingly difficult, because wheat has no husks and an all-wheat mash would be nearly impossible to lauter. Therefore, beers made with 100% wheat are largely confined to laboratories and pilot plants, although craft brewers will occasionally produce such a beer, usually using rice hulls to help loosen up the gummy mash. See LAUTERING and MASH.

The origins of wheat beer reach back into antiquity, some 6,000 years ago, and probably even earlier. The first wheat beer brewers were the Sumerians of Mesopotamia, between the rivers Tigris and Euphrates, in what is now southern Iraq. We know so from archaeological finds from the region. The grains they brewed with next to barley were einkorn, emmer, and spelt, which are genetic predecessors of our modern wheat. See WHEAT. Therefore, the oldest known depiction of beer drinking, which dates to about 3400 BC, is one of wheat beer drinking. It is an ornamentation on an earthenware crock showing a scene of two ladies drinking beer through straws. The Egyptians, too, followed the Sumerians' pioneering example and made their brews mostly from wheat. Further proof of the ancient roots of wheat beer is the Code of Hammurabi, the world's oldest body of laws. It dates to the 1700s BC and contains elaborate rules for making and dispensing wheat beer.

Today, we associate weissbier mostly with Bavaria, where it is always made with top-fermenting yeast. This makes weissbier one of the very few warm-fermented ales made in this beer culture, which is considered the cradle of lager brewing. See BAVARIA. The geographical origins of the modern weissbier probably go back to the 12th or 13th century in Bohemia in today's Czech Republic, from where weissbier brewing spilled over into the neighboring Bavarian Forest. There, in 1520, the Degenberg family, a noble dynasty from the village of Schwarzach, was able to obtain from the ruling Wittelsbach dynasty of Bavaria the exclusive and perpetual (and, in those days, probably deemed inconsequential) privilege to make wheat beer. See WITTELSBACHER FAMILY. To the chagrin of the Bavarian dukes, however, this brewing privilege, granted in recognition of the Degenberg vassal services, turned out to generate more profits than anticipated. It also diverted plenty of wheat from the people's baking ovens to the Degenberg brew kettles. In 1567, therefore, an unhappy Wittelsbach Duke Albrecht V declared wheat beer to be "a useless drink that neither nourishes nor gives strength, but only encourages drunkenness," and he categorically outlawed wheat beer making in his entire realm. Unfortunately for him, by the rules of feudal etiquette, he still had to grant the Degenberg clan an exemption from his draconian prohibition. In 1602, however, the Bavarian dukes got lucky. That year, Hans Sigmund of Degenberg died without leaving an heir. This meant that the Wittelsbach duke Maximilian I could finally reclaim the right to brew wheat beer; he promptly turned wheat beer brewing into a monopoly for himself and his heirs. Soon every innkeeper in his realm had to pour weissbier purchased exclusively from the network of breweries owned by the Dukes of Bavaria. That wheat beer monopoly lasted roughly 200 years, until 1798, when several monasteries and burgher breweries were given permission to brew weissbier too. This was only allowed because, by that time, weissbier had fallen out of fashion and the Wittelsbach breweries were running losses. Subsequently, the Bavarian dukes offered the weissbier rights for sale or lease to various breweries, both civil and monastic, on a nonexclusive basis. As it turned out, none of them could make a go of it, simply because demand for weissbier kept declining. In the 19th century, in part because of improvements in brewing techniques, Bavarian lagers were gaining in quality and had become much more competitive with weissbier. By 1872, the dukes finally gave up for good on the erstwhile weissbier cash cow and sold the rights to one intrepid brewmaster named Georg Schneider I. See SCHNEIDER WEISSE BREWERY.

Weissbier sales decline steadily until, in the 1950s and early 1960s, they had fallen to below 3% of the overall Bavarian beer production. Many breweries stopped making weissbier altogether and the style seemed headed for extinction. Despite this, George Schneider and his heirs, perhaps strangely, kept the weissbier faith, albeit on a fairly modest sales volume. They set themselves apart as weissbier specialists, which eventually proved to be a successful long-term strategy, because in the 1960s, more than a century after its seeming demise, weissbier sales bounced back with a vengeance. A sudden—and largely inexplicable—shift in consumer taste reversed weissbier's downward spiral from about 1965 onward, not only in Bavaria but also throughout the world. Today, weissbier is the most popular beer style in Bavaria, holding greater than one-third of the market share. In Germany overall, weissbier holds almost one-tenth of the market. Although helles may rule the summer beer gardens, a glass of weissbier remains an integral part of brotzeit, the "second breakfast" enjoyed in the mid-morning. Completing the beer style's reversal of fortune is its popularity among craft brewers, who now make weissbier all over the world, from Japan to Brazil.

Because wheat has a high protein content, modern weissbier brewing often employs long rests to break down proteins and reduce wort viscosity. Decoction mashing is still widely employed in Germany for similar purposes. A rest at about 44°C–45°C (111°F–113°F) is often used to develop ferulic acid in the mash. Ferulic acid is a precursor compound—weissbier yeasts convert it to 4-vinyl guaiacol, a phenol with a distinctly clovelike aroma that is part of the typical character of weissbier. See 4-VINYL GUAIACOL. Original gravities are usually between 11.5° and 13.2° Plato and fermentations finish with some notable residual sugar at around 3° Plato. Weissbier is fermented by a family of closely related yeast strains that produce many of the classical flavors of the style. Whereas wheat itself gives the beers a certain lightness of the palate and a zing of acidity, the aromas of cloves (4-vinyl guaiacol), bubblegum, bananas (isoamyl acetate), and smoke (4-vinyl syringol) that characterize weissbier are all products of fermentation of these specialized yeasts. For many years, craft brewers outside Bavaria referred to this yeast as the "Weihenstephan strain" because that brewing school's famous yeast bank was once the only source for genuine weissbier yeast. Some breweries outside Germany, particularly in the United States, use the word "hefeweizen" to describe and market beers fermented with standard lager or ale yeasts; these beers are misnamed; they have no classical hefeweizen character. See AMERICAN WHEAT BEER. Although it is often now used in cylindroconical fermenters, weissbier yeast naturally flocculates to the top of the fermenting vessel, making it a good candidate for open fermentation. Many weissbier producers note that open fermentation deepens the beer's ester profile. Primary fermentation usually proceeds at 20°C–22°C (68°F–72°F) and is completed within 2 to 4 days. After a short aging period in closed tanks, typically only 10–14 days, the beer is ready for bottling or kegging. Traditionally weissbier is refermented in the bottle, using speise (literally "food" in German, speise is wort, sometimes with fresh yeast blended in) as the priming sugar to meet the strictures of the Reinheitsgebot. Refermentation may be performed by the original weisse yeast, but lager yeasts are occasionally preferred for their powdery texture in the bottle. Unfortunately, true bottle conditioning has become increasingly rare, especially among the large brands, and most weissbier seen outside of Bavaria is pasteurized. Bottle conditioning gives a fresher flavor and achieves high levels of carbonation, often at about 4 volumes (8 g/l), about 30% higher than the average pilsner.

Weissbier now comes in several variations. There is the classic weissbier or hefeweizen, a pale beer with plenty of yeast in suspension and capped with a tall, robust crown of white foam. Then there is the terminological contradiction of dunkelweissbier or dunkelweizen ("dark white beer" or "dark wheat"), which is weissbier made with the addition of dark malts, such as caramel, crystal, or roasted malts. Weissbier with an amber color is sometimes called "bernsteinfarbenes weisse," literally "amber white"—many of these are considered especially traditional because the color predates the wide availability of pale malts. There is a low-alcohol version on the market called leichtes weissbier. See LEICHTES WEISSBIER. Then there is the filtered kristallweizen ("crystal wheat"), as well as weizenbock (a wheat-based bock beer). On rare occasions brewers also make weizendoppelbock or weizeneisbock, both wheat equivalents of their all-barley-based cousins.

All are served in tall vaselike glassware, chunky at the base, cinching in to an elegant waist, and then flaring dramatically at the lip. High carbonation and high protein in the beer combine to produce voluminous foam, and this is very much part of the beer's presentation and the reason for the shape of the glass. Bottles of hefeweizen are poured carefully to achieve the beautiful mousse-like foam, and then the bottle is swirled with the last of the beer to collect the yeast, which is added to the glass as the finishing touch. There has been some conjecture that it is weissbier's yeastiness that may have precipitated its revival. The mid-1960s saw a renewed interest in natural foods, and brewer's yeast is an excellent source of vitamins.

In Germany, hefeweizen is never served with the slices of lemon that became strangely ubiquitous in the United States in the 1980s and 1990s. The aroma of the lemon overwhelms the beer's delicate aroma, and the oil of the lemon peel quickly destroys the beer's trademark foam. American tourists who ask for lemon with their weissbier in Bavarian beer gardens are generally greeted with faint smiles of pity.

See also BOCK BEER, DOPPELBOCK, and EISBOCK.

Bavarian Beer. *The history of Bavarian hefeweizen.* http://www.bavarianbeer.com/index.php?StoryID=101/ (accessed January 29, 2011).

Bavarian Beer. *Weissbier/weizenbier/hefeweizen.* http://www.bavarianbeer.com/index.php?StoryID=135/ (accessed January 29, 2011).

Horst Dornbusch and Garrett Oliver

Weltenburger, an abbey brewery in Bavaria, Germany. Although the Belgian Trappist breweries have become justly famous worldwide, they are not the only monastic breweries in Europe. Among the others are the followers of St Colombanus, who established a religious settlement on a bend in the River Danube in northern Bavaria in the 7th century.

The abbey has been abandoned on a number of occasions because of flooding and was also relinquished by the monks during Napoleon's period of monastery secularization. After some time in private hands, and later in the care of the Bavarian state, it was returned to the brotherhood in 1843.

The Weltenburger Abbey today is a major tourist attraction, drawing 750,000 visitors a year, many of whom arrive by leisure boat from Kelheim. Its highly ornate Baroque church is open to outsiders, as is the beer garden in the courtyard, where beer brewed in the small brewhouse opposite is served.

According to abbey literature, brewing has taken place here since at least 1050 AD, but it is no longer in the hands of monks. In 1973, with investment needed in the brewhouse, the brothers assigned brewing rights to the Bischofshof Brewery in nearby Regensburg. This means that Bischofshof employees man the abbey's brewhouse and produce dark lagers and a dark wheat beer for sale under the Weltenburger Kloster name. The best known is Asam bock, a dark lager matured for 12 weeks and named after two brothers who built the abbey church.

Bischofshof also brews beers for Weltenburger at its Regensburg brewery. These include Barock Hell

Weltenburg Abbey, Bavaria, Germany. This Benedictine monastery has operated a brewery since at least 1050 BCE, and it is the oldest continuously operating monastery brewery in the world. CATH HARRIES

and are sold under the differentiating "Marke Weltenburger" label.

See also ABBEY BEERS and TRAPPIST BREWERIES.

Evans, Jeff. On the beautiful Blue Danube. *Beers of the World* 15 (2007): 46–9.

Weltenburger. *Weltenburger.de.* http://www.weltenburger.de/die_klosterbrauerei.htm/ (accessed 23 November 2009).

Jeff Evans

Westmalle Brewery resides in a Trappist abbey (officially known as Our Lady of the Sacred Heart) located in the town of Westmalle, Belgium, in the province of Antwerp. It was founded as a religious house, or priory, in 1794 by several Cistercian monks. It became a Trappist abbey in 1836, and for the sustenance of the monks a small brewery was built within the walls. In 1856 the abbey began selling beer to the public in very small quantities directly from their abbey. The demand for their beer gradually increased, leading to construction of additional brewing capacity in 1865 and again in 1897. By 1921 the beer from Westmalle abbey was offered for the first time in the general marketplace. The popularity of the beer necessitated another brewery expansion in the 1930s, and since then the brewery has generally been a leader in environmental and safety standards. It has also been a leader in brewing, as the Westmalle beers have proven to be highly influential. The ingredients used for brewing Westmalle beers include water, yeast, barley malt, hops, and sugar. The water comes from a deep well on the brewery property and is considered hard water, with many dissolved minerals. It is treated before being used in the brewery. Even though the law did not require it at the time, a waste treatment plant was installed in the 1960s to ensure that water was returned to the environment in a clean state. The brewery's use of hops is a bit unusual in that only whole cone hops are used, while many modern breweries, including some Trappists, now use either liquid hop extract or pelletized hops. The yeast at Westmalle is a proprietary strain that is cultured by the brewery. It imparts some of the distinctive spicy and floral aromas found in the beers. Finally, the sugar used for brewing is Belgian candi sugar, which is fully fermentable and gives the beer a lighter body than expected, thus providing a smooth balance to the beer. See CANDI SUGAR. The candi sugar is liquid in form and comes in a light color with a light flavor, or a dark color with a complex toffee-like flavor.

The Westmalle abbey produces three types of beer: Westmalle Extra, Westmalle Dubbel, and Westmalle Tripel. The extra is a low alcohol (4.8% ABV) beer brewed twice a year for the monks to consume at the abbey during lunch. It is a golden-colored "table beer" with a smooth light flavor and is not available to the general public. The dubbel is a 7% ABV beer with a chestnut brown color and high amount of carbonation resulting in a very rich head of foam. The dubbel and extra are the two oldest styles of beer made by the brewery and date to the start of the brewery in 1836. The dubbel is a very flavorful, complex beer and the modern version can be traced to a reformulation of the beer that took place in the 1920s. The tripel is a 9.5% ABV beer with a pale, golden color. It has a very complex flavor as a result of the balance between the light malt, yeast, and hops. Westmalle Tripel was first brewed in 1934 and is widely considered to be the original of the tripel style. In 1956 it was reformulated and has remained the same since then. All of the Westmalle beers are partially bottle-conditioned and so develop a mature flavor in the bottle, as well as a very full level of carbonation. Both beers are available in both 33 cl (11.2 ounces) bottles and a 75 cl (25.4 ounces) bottle sealed with a cork and wirecage.

In 1998, Brother Thomas, the recently retired head brewer of Westmalle, acted as the technical advisor for the revival of brewing at the Trappist monastery Achel. He brought the distinctive Westmalle yeast with him, and thus the influence of the Westmalle brewers reached one step further down through time.

See also ACHEL BREWERY, BELGIUM, and TRAPPIST BREWERIES.

Keith Villa

Westvleteren Brewery is the smallest of the six Belgian Trappist breweries, with yearly production around 5,000 hl (4,200 US barrels). In 1831, the prior of the recently founded Catsburg monastery took a few of his monks into the woods of Westvleteren, near the hop fields of Poperinge. There they founded the Trappist Abbey of St Sixtus in Westvleteren. Brewing commenced in 1839, with a strict focus on the support of the monastic life of the community. The monks brew only about once per week, and they remain resolutely noncommercial, showing no interest in increasing their output. By the time they replaced their brewing equipment in 1990, the former brewhouse was nearly a century old.

Westvleteren allows little contact with the outside world and is the only Trappist brewery where all the work is done by the monks themselves. The monastery itself rarely allows guests, and the Westvleteren beers are difficult to obtain, even in Belgium. It is available only from a drive-up outlet at the monastery, through a telephone-based lottery system that is cross-checked against the license plates of drivers who arrive hoping to pick up beer they've reserved. The beers themselves are rather inexpensive, topping out at 38 euros per case of 24 bottles, but each customer may only buy one case. The rules for the phone lottery and the beer pickup are so strict as to be nearly comical. The monks are entirely aware of the popularity of their beer, telling prospective buyers on their Website:

> Please take into account that you may often get a busy signal when you call to make a reservation, due to the fact that our beer lines are overburdened! You're not the only one who is calling at that moment. Due to our small-scale production, the number of telephone calls is much greater than the number of available reservations. That means it's a matter of having a lot of patience as well as a lot of luck.

If anyone tries to reserve beer more than once in a month from the same phone number, the call is automatically cut off. Beer can sometimes be bought at their visitor's center and café called In De Vrede, but amounts are strictly limited, and often they do not have any beer at all. Westvleteren's marketing is nonexistent. The bottles have no labels, only wooden crates, and the three beers are to be recognized by only their crown caps. All of the beers are made from pale malt, along with a range of sugars added in the kettle, and they are all fully bottle conditioned. The dark Westvleteren "8," 8% alcohol by volume (ABV) and sporting a blue cap, and "12,"

10.5% ABV and sporting a yellow cap, are both russet brown in color, with complex earthy rum and fruit flavors backed by aggressive hop bitterness. In 1999 the blond "6" was added to the range, replacing the monks' own table beers. This is a modern "singel" at 5.8% ABV and has a green cap, a powerful earthy, an herbal aroma, a light, firm body, and an intensely appetizing hop bitterness. Westvleteren's beers, both because of their quality and also inevitably because of their scarcity, are among the most highly sought in the world. The monks forbid the resale of the beer, but this, of course, is widely ignored.

Ben Vinken

wet hopping is the process of using un-kilned, hence "wet," hops in brewing. In the Northern Hemisphere, aroma hops are typically harvested in late August and early September and high alpha-acid hops used for mostly bittering are typically harvested in mid to late September. Wet hops are approximately 80% moisture and this is reduced in a hop kiln right after the harvest to about 9%. Getting the hops dried correctly is critical. If left too dry, hops may oxidize, and there is the heightened risk of warehouse fires. If left too wet, baled hops may "sweat," become moldy, and develop off aromas. When brewers use hops wet, therefore, they must be loosely packed in cardboard boxes right after picking and shipped via the fastest method straight to the brewery, where they are used immediately. If they aren't used right away, the hops will deteriorate quickly, becoming unusable for use in wort or beer.

Beers produced with un-kilned hops are referred to as "wet hop" beers, "fresh hop" beers, "green hop" beers, or "harvest" beers. These beers have emerged largely in the past 10 years and are almost exclusively produced by American craft brewers located in hop-growing areas. Because of the high moisture content of wet hops, brewers typically use at least four to five times the weight of wet hops as they would of the same variety in its kiln-dried state. Wet hops, just like kilned hops, can be added at any point in the boil, or into a hop-back. Adding wet hops to cool, finished beer is also gaining in popularity. The reason behind such "wet dry hopping" is the desire to capture the hops' most delicate and volatile aroma oils in the finished beer. Like traditional dry hopping, "wet dry hopping" captures volatiles driven off during a kettle boil but also those that may be driven off by the hop kilning process. Some beer enthusiasts enjoy the uniquely "green" delicate character of these beers, while others are put off by the distinctly grassy chlorophyll-like aromatics. Regardless, these beers are very unique creations driven by a particular time and place, and therefore represent a fascinating evolution of the brewer's art.

Jeremy Marshall

wet milling is a modern technique used to grind malt in preparation for mashing, and it is said to bring significant benefits compared to traditional dry milling. It is a practice recommended by the major German brewing plant manufacturers and used in conjunction with a lauter tun. See LAUTER TUN. It is often called "continuous steep milling" and requires that milling take place in the time taken to mash a grist, normally about 20 minutes. Traditional dry milling takes place independently of the mashing process and usually takes longer as a result. In wet milling, malt is steeped in a continuous stream of warm water to bring the husk moisture content up to 15%, before the malt is ground on a pair of specially designed rollers. In wet milling, the grain husk remains mainly complete, whereas in a dry mill it can fragment. This fragmentation can slow run-offs and cause quality problems. Because of the higher moisture content during wet milling, there is no dust produced, so explosion risks are eliminated and dust removal equipment unnecessary. Because the husk remains complete, wet milling also allows a faster run-off time and a greater loading on a lauter tun (deeper grain depth), as well as reduced oxidation of the grain and the resulting wort. Wet milling systems are expensive and rarely seen in small breweries. See OXIDATION.

Paul KA Buttrick

Weyermann® Malting of Bamberg is today one of the leading producers of German specialty malts. They also produce pilsner and other base malts, but are perhaps best known for a series of specialties designated by the prefix "Cara." Carapils, a Weyermann trademark since 1908, is a pale dextrin malt and Carafa, a chocolaty roasted malt used in the production of dark beers. See CARAPILS. In addition, they offer a line of organic malts, rye and wheat malts, as well as roasted unmalted grains, which because of the strictures of the German Purity Law (Reinheitsgebot) are intended for use in making beer beyond German borders. See REINHEITSGEBOT. A Reinheitsgebot-approved liquid coloring agent called Sinamar is also manufactured.

In 1879 Johann Baptist Weyermann expanded his father's grain store to include a malt-roasting facility that in its earliest days produced malt coffee. Soon a germination room was added for the production of brewing malt. Several expansions were undertaken over succeeding decades, and in 1902 a second facility, largely for the production of the malt-based Sinamar, was opened in Potsdam on the outskirts of Berlin. This plant was damaged in the closing days of World War II, subsequently placed under Russian control, and never reopened.

Perhaps more than any other German maltster, Weyermann has striven to make itself integral to the growth of the craft brewing movement, especially in America. Its specialty malts in particular are part of recipes devised by hundreds of breweries from Colorado to Japan. The company remains family-run. While the German brewing community can be insular, Sabine Weyermann and Thomas Kraus-Weyermann, invariably garbed in the distinctive red and yellow of their brand, are often seen at beer festivals and conferences, and have been tireless over the years in their attention to small brewers worldwide.

Weyermann. http://www.weyermann.de/eng/ (accessed October 20, 2010).

Brewing Techniques. http://www.brewingtechniques.com/bmg/weyermann.html/ (accessed October 20, 2010).

Dick Cantwell

WGV

See WHITBREAD GOLDING VARIETY (HOP).

wheat cultivation for both bread and beer making is as old as civilization itself. Human nutrition—in fact all creature nutrition on earth—is based essentially on only three major groups of compounds: carbohydrates in the form of starches and sugars, nitrogen-based proteins, and water. Less bulky, but also critical for human health, are a large number of trace elements such as minerals and vitamins. The seeds of grasses, which we call cereals, especially wheat, happen to contain an almost perfect natural combination of all these essential ingredients of human sustenance. They are rich in starches and proteins and they contain small amounts of lipids (fats) in the form of germ oils (concentrated carbohydrates) as well as a varied assortment of trace elements. They even have some fiber in the form of cellulose to make the entire package excellently suited for the human system. Our predilection for grass seeds is fortunate, because grasses are both ubiquitous and infinitely versatile; and humans have learned to turn them into many basic food preparations, including breads, porridges, and beers.

Of all the grass seeds, wheat is probably the best suited for bread making, because four-fifths of its proteins are made up of gummy glutens. These are the characteristic wheat proteins that make dough sticky, cohesive, and elastic. For brewing, however, these proteins must be degraded, because a viscous, gummy drink is a rather poor thirst quencher and a difficult dinner companion. Wheat, unlike other cereals, also lacks enzymes that can convert unfermentable starches into fermentable sugars. See AMYLASES and ENZYMES. Finally, wheat lacks husks. If a mash were made up entirely of wheat, it could combine into a pasty mass, which would prevent proper wort extraction during the lautering process. See HUSK, LAUTERING, MASH, and WORT. Barley, by contrast, is virtually perfect for beer making. It is relatively low in gluten and it has great diastatic power for starch conversion. See BARLEY and DIASTATIC POWER. It also has plenty of husk material, which gives it double the cellulose content of wheat—0.5% of dry weight versus 0.25% of dry weight. This is why barley, unlike wheat, makes for a natural filter bed for great extraction values during wort run-off. When using wheat in beer making, it is essential that it is paired with a good portion of barley malt or other husk- and enzyme-rich malt. Only a mixed mash ensures that there are enough enzymes to effect conversion of all starches, including those contained in the wheat. In practice, wheat beer brewers tend to use at least 30% non-wheat grist in the mash. The table contains a comparison of barley, wheat, corn, rye, and oats in terms of compounds relevant to beer making.

Given the composition of wheat, it is somewhat surprising that even mankind's earliest brewers, who obviously had no understanding of enzymatic mash activities, used not only barley but also several

Approximate Average (%) of Kernel Weight

Compound	*Barley*	*Wheat*	*Oats*	*Rye*	*Corn*
Starch	53	58	40	55	61
Proteins	9.5–13.5 (rarely more)	12–14.5 (often more, rarely less)	11	10–11	0.93
Water	13	13	13	13	13
Lipids*	2.5–4.4	1.5	3	1.5	7–10

*Roughly half of the lipid content is degraded during malting.

varieties of wheat—usually in combination—in their mashes. According to the best archaeological evidence, the first brewing of both barley- and wheat-based beers was concurrent with mankind's first settlements and earliest agriculture—both considered breakthroughs in human social evolution. This was about 8,000 to 10,000 years ago in what is now Iraq, in the fertile plains between the rivers Tigris and Euphrates, where a people called the Sumerians abandoned their hunter-and-gatherer ways and became farmers, bakers, and brewers. See SUMER. We consider that change in lifestyle the beginning of history and civilization as we know it, and beer making was part of that transformation. The grains available to these Neolithic brewers were the heirloom ancestors of today's barley and wheat varieties.

When brewing started, the Sumerians probably used a wheat variety called Triticum monococcum. It has very hard kernels as well as firm husks and is still occasionally grown today, mostly as an heirloom cereal for specialty foods. It is now commonly referred to by its German name of Einkorn, and we consider it the primordial progenitor of all modern wheat (Triticum aestivum). See EINKORN WHEAT. In Sumerian times, Einkorn got crossed somehow, probably by open pollination, with wild grasses, which resulted in an advanced, relatively softer, husked wheat, Triticum dicoccum, which is now known also by a common German name, emmer. This wheat, in turn, spawned another cross, again with wild grasses, called spelt (Triticum spelta), which represented the next advancement in wheat cultivars. Spelt, also known by its German name of dinkel, is still planted today, and it is used for both specialty bread and beer, often organic. See EMMER and SPELT. Spelt cultivation moved from the fertile crescent of the Middle East to other parts of the ancient world, perhaps in part because it places few demands on soil quality and climate. It can grow where modern wheat cannot. In central Europe, for instance, spelt is known to have been cultivated at least since the late Bronze Age, some 3,000 years ago, mostly in the regions inhabited by the Alemans, a Germanic tribe that roamed what is now the German State of Baden-Wurttemberg and the German-speaking part of Switzerland. Spelt is fairly high in protein content, up to about 17% compared with modern wheat, which has about 12% to 14.5%. This is why spelt-beer mashes rarely contain more than 50% spelt. Although spelt husks would be useful as a filtration substrate in the mash, they are usually removed in the malt house nowadays because of their high astringency, which would make the beer taste too rough for a modern palate. Centuries of breeding improvements eventually turned the ancient spelt into our modern, now huskless, wheat.

The world grows about 650 to 700 million metric tons (MT) of wheat per year. The exact quantity varies from year to year, with the variation mostly dependent on weather conditions. Given an overall world cereal production of roughly 2.25 billion MT—which includes corn, barley, sorghum, and millet—almost one-third of all cereal cultivation is wheat. Roughly 20% of that wheat is grown in the European Union and slightly less than that in China. India accounts for slightly more than 10% of world wheat production, whereas Russia and the United States each account for slightly less than 10%. Other significant producers of wheat are Australia, Kazakhstan, Pakistan, and Ukraine, each with roughly 3% to 4% of world production.

Only a tiny fraction of the world's wheat goes into brewing. In fact, given the small worldwide demand for wheat by the brewing industry compared with the food-processing and feed-lot industries, virtually all wheat is bred and cultivated exclusively for non-beer purposes. Even in Germany, with its strong weissbier market, where almost 1 of every 10 beers consumed is a wheat beer, only 0.5% of the roughly 25 million metric tons of wheat produced there make it to a malt house and from there to a brewhouse. See WEISSBIER. Unlike barley, of which many strains are bred in many countries by public institutions and commercial crop breeders specifically for brewing, no similar breeding programs exist for brewing wheat strains, which means that maltsters often cannot get the wheat selection they like at harvest time. Brewers, unless they have made their own arrangements with farmers, are invariably stuck with whatever the maltster can procure in markets that are not geared toward brewing.

To be sure, there are some wheat varieties with characteristics that make them much better suited for malting and brewing than others. However, these are often only marginal varieties as far as breeders and farmers are concerned. Although maltsters and brewers prefer grains with a protein content below 12%, the core of wheat-strain breeding focuses on varieties with the highest amount of protein, called E-wheat in Europe, which stands for "elite wheat." E-wheat has at least 13.3% protein and generates the best economic return for farmers and breeders. In terms of quality rankings, E-wheat is followed by A-wheat ("quality wheat" with at least 12.5% protein), B-wheat ("bread wheat" with at least 12.2% protein), K-wheat ("cookie wheat" with at least 12.5% protein), and C-wheat (all others). In either of these categories, the wheat may be planted as winter or spring wheat, although the majority of the world's wheat is winter wheat. Breeders have very little incentive to focus on varieties other than E because the return on investment from licenses and the sale of seeds for cultivation is insufficient to amortize the high cost of research and development, which some breeders in Europe report as being in the neighborhood of 17% of sales revenues, not counting the cost of regulatory compliance and marketing. This up-front investment is fairly high by overall industrial standards. Even the American pharmaceutical industry, which has unusually high research and development costs, tends to invest only about 18% of its annual domestic sales in research and development activities.

The challenge for maltsters is to select brewing wheat from what is essentially a stream of baking wheat while using trade-atypical criteria. The only alternative for maltsters is to enter into special forward contracts with farmers, who will then grow malting- and brewing-friendly wheat varieties because they have a guaranteed market and a guaranteed price. Only contracts can also guarantee that a batch of raw wheat is of only a single variety instead of a mix of several varieties, which would not have uniform malting characteristics. Current wheat varieties that are considered of high malting and brewing quality include Anthus, Tabasco, Skalmeje, Hermann, and Mythos. In recent years, when wheat supplies have been low and prices high, some wheat beer brewers have found that even their signed contracts did not always protect them, with the farmer having found a suitcase full of cash a more compelling offer.

Interestingly, although the introduction of brewing barley varieties into commercial cultivation is strictly regulated by certification processes in most countries, there are no equivalent certification standards for brewing wheat, which means there are no variety registries for the maltster and brewer to consult when choosing wheat for brewing. The selection criteria for good brewing wheat, therefore, are more a matter of practical experience. In this process, it helps if the maltster knows for which type of beer the wheat is intended. The key difference is whether the beer will be yeast-turbid like a German weissbier or filtered like a German kristallweizen. See KRISTALLWEIZEN. Whereas the protein- and gluten-related viscosity of the wort and beer is less important for unfiltered beers, it is crucially important for filtered beers. See FILTRATION. Quality barley base malts, for instance, tend to have a viscosity rating of 1.4 to 1.58 mPa second, whereas wheat malts are more likely to have a rating of 1.60 to 2.10 mPa second. A value greater than 1.75 mPa second is considered high, regardless of mash composition, and is likely to cause lautering and sometimes even filtration problems. The higher the viscosity value of the wheat malt, therefore, the less of it can be used in the mash. This makes the mash composition a delicate balancing act for the brewer trying to make a yeast-turbid beer, because too much viscosity causes process problems, whereas too little viscosity may allow the yeast to settle out quickly, giving the beer an unwanted clarified appearance. In yeast-turbid wheat beers, a good amount of suspended proteins is a plus, helping to stabilize the beer's turbid appearance, because, perhaps unknown to the consumer, much of the opacity of many wheat beers is derived not only from yeast in suspension but also indirectly from hazes. Haze-forming complexes can envelop yeast cells and thus prevent them from becoming part of the sediment. See CHILL HAZE, COLLOIDAL HAZE, and HAZE.

In general, large proportions of wheat also tend to give beer a certain lightness of mouthfeel along with a dash of refreshingly crisp acidity. Wheat varietal differences can have significant implications for the flavors and aromas of the finished beer. For instance, differences in the composition of a wheat variety's amino acids influence the ester content of the beer after fermentation. See ESTERS. This, in turn, influences the beer's flavor and aroma. Many wheat beer styles have estery notes as part of their normal style profile. The amount of variety-specific ferulic acid is crucial too, because this acid is largely responsible for the synthesis of 4-vinyl guaiacol, which is the very compound that generates the signature fruity–clovey flavors generally associated with German wheat beers. See 4-VINYL GUAIACOL and FERULIC ACID. For weissbier wheat malts, therefore, the ferulic acid character is even more important than the malt's modification, whereas for quality barley malt, by contrast, modification is one of the key selection criteria. See MODIFICATION. For these reasons, brewers look for wheat malt specifications and descriptions that include such phrases as a "phenolic aromas," "ester aromas," "yeasty aromas," and "malty aromas," depending on the type of wheat beer they wish to produce. Also crucial in the selection of wheat for malting and brewing is the variety's known resistance to fusarium, a common mold whose toxins can leach into the beer. There the toxins can serve as nuclei for the aggregation of large carbon dioxide bubbles, which, when the bottle is opened, can cause the sudden and vigorous eruption of the beer—a defect known as gushing. See FUSARIUM and GUSHING.

The production of malt from wheat is not different in principle from the production of barley malt. See MALT and MALTING. However, because wheat has no husks, "naked" wheat kernels absorb water much faster during the steeping phase than do husk-wrapped barley kernels, which is why steeping times for wheat tend to be much shorter than for barley. Once transferred to the germination chamber, the lack of husks also causes wheat kernels to be much more closely packed than barley kernels. This, in turn, results in more germination heat to be generated and retained, thus potentially accelerating germination out of control. To slow the process down and to ensure germination homogeneity, the maltster must reduce the temperature in the germination chamber and keep the wheat layer at a lower depth than a comparable barley layer. However, because the lower temperature slows down germination, it also favors higher protein modification, even to a point of causing portions of the degraded proteins to ooze out of the aleurone layer and to glue the wheat kernels together. See ALEURONE LAYER. Reducing the water content during germination is one way to keep excessive modification in check. Increased turning of the germinating wheat malt, on the other hand, which could alleviate clumping, would run the risk of damaging the delicate kernels, especially the acrospires. This would cause a slowdown of the kernel's internal chemical changes and reduce the malt's quality for brewing. See ACROSPIRE.

Clumping can also pose problems in the kiln, because aeration of the malt would not be even, and the sticky kernels would not dry homogeneously. Because of the lack of husks, the initial kilning temperature of green wheat malt is generally kept lower than for green barley malt—by roughly 5°C (10°F). This prevents an excessive coloring of the malt from the relatively large amount of amino acids (a degradation product of proteins) in wheat malt. See AMINO ACIDS. After kilning, wheat malt, just like barley malt, is polished to remove the rootlets and the now dead, protein-rich acrospires. In barley, the acrospire grows inside the husk and only the protruding portion is removed in the polishing process, whereas in wheat, without the husk, the entire acrospire is removed. As a result, wheat malt loses about 0.5% to 0.7% of its protein content during the polishing process. Analytically, the finished wheat malt differs from barley malt mostly in terms of the chemical structure of the proteins. In wheat malt, the proteins are mostly large-molecular compounds, whereas in barley malt they are largely modified into small-molecular structures. This leaves plenty of wheat proteins for the brewer to degrade in the mash tun, which means a multistep mashing process is definitely advisable in wheat beer making. Once properly degraded in the brewhouse, these proteins are then responsible for the firm and long-lasting creamy head, which is one of the characteristics of a well-brewed wheat beer.

A brewer can add any proportion of wheat to the grist, except in Germany, where a brew may be called a weissbier only if the mash contains at least 50% wheat malt and if the brew is fermented with top-fermenting yeast only; that is, in Germany, all wheat beers are warm-fermented ales. Highly malt-accented wheat beers usually have a good portion of caramel malts in the grain bill as well. See CARAMEL MALTS. Pale, spritzy weissbiers, on the other hand, are generally less malty, whereas their fruity, banana, bubblegum, clove-type notes—produced by specialty weissbier yeast strains—dominate the taste and aroma. Next to the German weissbier, perhaps the most common wheat beer style is the Belgian wit beer or *bière blanche,* which is usually made with about 20% unmalted wheat. Then there is the sour Berliner weisse, a sparkling ale made from a mash with a wheat malt portion rarely exceeding 30%. Belgian lambics, too, contain unmalted wheat, sometimes up to 40%. Finally, American craft brewers now make a large variety of wheat ales, which usually contain anywhere from 10% to 35% malted wheat and are often fermented with regular ale or lager yeasts as opposed to weissbier strains. See AMERICAN WHEAT BEER. These are sometimes mislabeled as "hefeweizen," although they have no classic hefeweizen (weissbier) yeast character. There is an increasing interest in wheat varieties among craft brewers worldwide, with many brewers exploring spelt, emmer, and other ancient wheat varieties alongside the modern ones.

Deutsche Tiernahrung Rohstofflexikon "Weizen" (German animal feed raw materials dictionary "Wheat"). http://www.deutsche-tiernahrung.de/open/brand_id/3/action/glossary%3Blist/menu/19/letter/W/M/kGnbIg#Weizen/ (accessed January 15, 2011).

Rentel, Dirk, and Meyer, Dieter. Fünf Jahre neues Klassifizierungssystem bei Weizen—Rückblickende Bewertung (Five years of a new classification system for wheat—a retrospective evaluation). http://www.agfdt.de/loads/GT01/RENTEL.PDF/ (accessed January 15, 2011).

Ziesemer, Andrea. E-Weizen rechnet sich (E-wheat is worth it). Gülzow: Landesforschungsanstalt für Landwirtschaft und Fischerei, Innovation 3/2009. http://www.dsv-saaten.de/export/sites/dsv-saaten.de/extras/dokumente/innovation/e-weizen-rechnet-sich-3-09.pdf/ (accessed January 15, 2011).

Walter König

wheat malt is the second most common malted grain used in brewing, after barley malt. Typical wheat-accented brews are German weissbier (also known as hefeweizen or weizenbier), which must contain at least 50% wheat malt by law; German Berliner weisse, a sour, sparkling ale, whose wheat malt portion rarely exceeds 30%; and the more modern "American wheat beer," which usually contains 10% to 35% malted wheat. Some American craft brewers have recently become enamored of a barley wine variant dubbed "wheat wine," replacing a large proportion of barley malt in the grist with wheat malt. Because modern wheat (Triticum aestivum) has a relatively high glucan and protein content compared to barley and has no husks—properties that can create lauter problems in the brewhouse—mashes rarely contain more than 70% wheat malt. Some adventurous brewers have made beers from 100% wheat malt, but this feat invariable requires a number of tricks in the brewhouse, as the husk-less grain cannot create its own filter bed through which to run off the wort.

When used in beer, wheat malt imparts a lighter body than does barley malt, often coupled with a gently refreshing touch of acidity. These qualities tend to make many wheat-based beer styles suitable for pairing with light dishes and seafood, and consumption of wheat beer tends to soar in hot weather. Contrary to popular misconception, the banana and clove-like flavors of German wheat beers are due to the special yeast used rather than the use of wheat malts. Wheat malts do, however, give these beers their delicacy of texture. Most wheat malts will tend to create a wort with a honey-orange color, but different malting houses will have their own specifications, and dark wheat malts are now available as well. In modern Bavaria, wheat-based weissbier was once a particular province of the Bavarian royal family, who held to themselves the right to brew wheat beers until finally giving way in 1872. Until then, wheat, valuable for making bread and other foods, was considered too lofty an ingredient to be used to make beer for commoners.

See also WEISSBIER, WHEAT, and WHEAT WINE.

Dornbusch, Horst. *The ultimate almanac of world beer recipes.* West Newbury, MA: Cerevisia Communications, 2010.

Horst Dornbusch

wheat wine is essentially a wheat-based version of a traditional barley wine. See BARLEY WINE. Brewers have surely made strong beers from wheat for millennia, from ancient Egypt to the American colonial period. However, the modern wheat wine style seems to have emerged out of the American craft brewing scene in the 1980s. There is no set convention regarding the proportion of wheat a wheat wine must contain, but it is generally accepted that the wheat portion should be at least half of the beer's grain bill. Most brewers will ferment at moderate temperatures with British ale yeasts or more neutral American or Canadian strains. Because of the protein content of wheat and the resulting viscosity of the mash and wort, rice hulls are often employed in the mash. Compared with barley wines, most wheat wines are less aggressively hopped, but will still often have bitterness levels ranging from 50 to 70 International Bitterness Units. Most are deep gold to amber in color, have alcohol contents between 8.5% and 12%, and are full-bodied beers showing notable residual sugar. Wheat wines can be very fruity, but because wheat malt is lighter on the palate than barley malt, a certain bright elegance on the palate is generally preferred.

See also INTERNATIONAL BITTERNESS UNITS (IBUS) and RICE HULLS.

Hieronymus, Stan. *Brewing with wheat: The "wit" and "weizen" of world wheat beer styles*. Boulder, CO: Brewers Publications, 2010.

Brian Yaeger

Wheeler, Daniel, a 19th-century British engineer and inventor, was the creator of a revolutionary device for kilning and roasting malt, which he patented in 1818 as an "Improved Method of Drying and Preparing Malt." See FLOOR MALTING, KILNING, and MALT. In traditional kilns, the germinated grain was dried by placing it in a layer on a perforated, usually metal, floor. Then the maltster would light a wood, coal, or coke fire underneath, and the hot, often smoky, combustion gasses passing through the grain would carry the moisture away through a flue. In the process, of course, some of the malt would invariably get slightly to severely scorched, while some of it might remain fairly green. The average malt color, therefore, would always be some shade of brown, and the malt would always pick up smoky flavors from the fuel—more so from dirty-burning coal or certain types of wood, less so from clean-burning coke. In Wheeler's invention, by contrast, the perforated-floor kiln was replaced by a revolving metal drum. Thus, the malt was never exposed directly to the kiln's fire. Wheeler had picked up the idea for his "improved method" from watching coffee being roasted. In Wheeler's adaptation of the coffee roaster for malt-making, malt could now remain smoke-free. It could also be dried more homogeneously. Importantly, maltsters could now for the first time adjust the temperature and length of the drying processes with ease and thereby control the color and flavor of the finished malt—from gently kilned pale malt all the way to severely roasted black malt. This new flexibility in malt drying led not only to a vast array of new malts; it also spawned a revolution in beer-making. Simply put, new malts begat new beer styles, including various types of porter, stout, and pale ale on the British Isles, and märzen, Vienna, pilsner, Oktoberfest, and helles lagers on the Continent.

It was around that time, too, that the hydrometer—especially a practical model developed in 1790 by the English chemist William Nicholson—came into wide use in the brewing industry. See HYDROMETER. This new gadget told brewers for the first time, in no uncertain terms, that pale malts generally produce more sugar extract per pound than do dark malts. With the hydrometer in the brewhouse and the new plethora of pale and color malts in the loft, brewers no longer needed to rely on traditional brown malt and variations in the grist-to-water ratio to make different beers. Instead, they could now make any shade and flavor of beer by simply mixing extract-rich pale malts with various amounts and types of dark malt, and do so much more economically and efficiently than ever before. Among the early adopters of the new brewing techniques made possible by the Wheeler malts were such London brewers as Whitbread and Barclay Perkins, as well as the St. James's Gate Brewery in Dublin, makers of Guinness.

Cornell, Martyn. "Raise a glass (darkly) to Daniel Wheeler." http://www.beerconnoisseur.com/Raise-a-Glass-to-Daniel-Wheeler/ (accessed November 16, 2010).

Mosher, Randy. *Tasting beer*. North Adams, MA: Storey Publishing, 2009.

Winship, Kihm. "Black patent malt and the evolution of porter." http://home.earthlink.net/~ggsurplus/blackpatentmalt.html/ (accessed November 16, 2010).

Nick Kaye

whirlpool. First developed at the Moosehead Brewery in New Brunswick, Canada in 1960, the whirlpool vessel is now a common method of separating hop fragments and other solid particles from hot wort. This vessel is also sometimes referred to as "hot wort settling tank." The principle of the whirlpool tank is that centripetal forces will cause solid particles suspended in a rotating mass of liquid to migrate to the center of the bottom of the vessel in a cone-shaped mass. Trub, a sediment containing hop fragments and solid protein-based particles, must be removed before the wort can be chilled and sent to a fermenting vessel. In order to work properly, a whirlpool tank must be a vertical cylinder with a flat bottom and the tank diameter must be at least equal to the depth of the wort when the tank is full. Deep tanks with a small diameter will not work well. The whirlpool effect is achieved by pumping the wort through an inlet line located above a height over 1/3 of the tank's depth; the inlet pipe must be turned tangentially and can even be sized less than the diameter of the main wort line so as to increase the wort rotation inside of the tank. It is important to note that any obstruction inside the tank will create eddy-currents that will upset the smooth rotation of the wort, delay settling, and decrease the compactness of the trub pile. The bottom of the tank should have a 1% gradient incline toward the tank outlet, which should be located near the tank wall and not in the middle of the tank. As the hot wort is swirled in the whirpool tank, the sediment gathers into the center, forming a "trub cone" and leaving the rest of the wort clear. Once the wort comes to a rest, it will be pumped to the chilling apparatus from a port near the wall of the vessel, leaving the trub cone in the center. Once the wort is cast out to the fermentation vessel, the trub cone can be discarded though a port located in the center of the vessel.

The invention of the whirlpool vessel made the use of pelletized hops common in brewing; without it, the small fragments of hops contained in the pellets are very difficult to remove from the wort. While the whirlpool is usually a separate vessel in larger breweries, many smaller breweries will use a combined kettle/whirlpool vessel. This vessel can accomplish both the boiling function and the subsequent whirlpool function, but is considered a compromise, as it rarely can do either of these tasks quite as well as separate vessels specifically designed to do each.

De Clerck, Jean. *A textbook of brewing.* London: Chapman & Hall, 1957. Trans. by Kathleen Barton-Wright.

Ray Klimovitz

Whitbread Brewery was one of the great brewing houses of the London porter boom, and later one of the "Big Six" brewers that dominated British brewing in the late 20th century. Samuel Whitbread began brewing in London in 1742, and in 1750 moved to the famous Chiswell Street brewery, which no longer brews but still stands in London. Whitbread seized the opportunities presented by the Industrial Revolution and invested in steam power to create the first purpose-built mass-production brewery in Britain. Porter—the beer that was sweeping London at the time—thrived on large-scale brewing, and the economies of scale made Whitbread the largest brewer in London by the end of the 18th century, when the city was arguably the most influential in the beer world.

Whitbread Brewery went on to produce a range of beer styles and brands, and acquired a large estate of tied pubs. See TIED HOUSE SYSTEM. In the late 20th century the company entered licensing agreements with lager brewers such as Stella Artois and Heineken to sell their brands throughout its estate.

When entrepreneur Eddie Taylor precipitated a rapid consolidation in British brewing in the 1960s, Whitbread's "umbrella scheme"—taking shares in smaller breweries to protect them from being swallowed by Taylor's empire—eventually saw it become one of the Big Six breweries that between them accounted for 75% of Britain's beer output.

The power of the Big Six eventually led to legislation restricting the number of pubs (2,000) that a brewery could own. The numbers of pubs they held before that was so vast (around 15,000–18,000) that the British beer and pub industry tends to refer to the legislation as the end of the tied house system. The new limit meant that a national brewer could no longer achieve their accustomed presence. Not a ban, yet because of the legislation, no national brewers own pubs any more.

In 2001 Whitbread sold its brewing operations to Interbrew (now Anheuser-Busch InBev). Today it refers to itself as "the UK's largest hotel and restaurant group."

Pete Brown

Whitbread Golding Variety (hop) is an English hop with a traditional lineage. It dates from 1911, when it was derived from a seedling of an old hop variety called Bate's Brewers. It takes its name from its place of origin, which was then a farm owned by the Whitbread Brewery, in Kent, UK. It is also known as Whitbread's Golding or WGV. Despite its name, neither Whitbread Golding Variety nor its parent Bate's Brewer is a true Golding hop. See GOLDING (HOP). In the brewhouse, WGV can be used as an all-purpose aroma variety. It has a mild, clean bitterness as well as a sweet, fruity flavor that is more intense than that of true Golding varieties. Its primary use nowadays is in English-style ales, and it may be substituted with Fuggle, Stryian Golding, or East Kent Golding. See EAST KENT GOLDING (HOP), FUGGLE (HOP), and STYRIAN GOLDING (HOP). WGV matures in mid-season and yields a modest 1,350 to 1,450 kg/ha (1,204 to 1,294 lb/acre). Its main advantage over true Golding is its resistance to verticillium wilt. It is, however, susceptible to downy and powdery mildew. WGV has a moderate alpha acid rating of 5% to 7.5%, with a rather high cohumulone fraction of 33% to 35%. Its beta acid rating is a low 2% to 2.7%. As for essential oils, myrcene accounts for 27%, humulene 42%, caryophyllene 13%, and farnesene 2.1%.

De Keukeleire, J., G. Ooms, A. Heyerick, I. Roldan-Ruiz, E. Van Bockstaele, and D. De Keukeleire. Formation and accumulation of α-acids, β-acids, desmethylxanthohumol, and xanthohumol during flowering of hops (*Humulus lupulus L.*). *Journal of Agricultural and Food Chemistry* 51 (2003): 4436–41.

Victoria Carollo Blake

white beer is an unfiltered, top-fermented style of wheat beer also known as wit bier (Flemish) and bière blanche (French). "White" refers to the unfiltered, cloudy whiteness of the beer as it appears in a glass. This style originated in the Middle Ages in Belgium and is uniquely different from other traditional wheat beers, such as those of Germany. Whereas the German white or wheat beers are made with only malted wheat, malted barley, and hops, the white beers of Belgium usually include unmalted wheat as an adjunct, spices, and sometimes oats. The percentage of unmalted grains in the grist can approach 50%, though 30% to 40% is more common. Specifically, Belgian style white beers were traditionally produced in the Flemish region of Belgium where brewers had access to cereal grains from the region's farms, and access to spices from the neighboring country of Netherlands.

White beer, though popular since the Middle Ages, decreased in popularity in the early 1900s, mainly due to the advent of golden lager. The low point in white beer history came in the 1950s when the last white beer brewery, in Hoegaarden, Belgium closed its doors. The revival of this style of beer can be attributed to one man, Pierre Celis. See CELIS, PIERRE. Celis was a milkman who in the mid-1960s started a new brewery called De Kluis. See DE KLUIS (BREWERY). De Kluis was dedicated to brewing a white beer called Hoegaarden, named after the town in which it was brewed. See HOEGAARDEN. Celis had worked as a young man in the Tomsin brewery in Hoegaarden before it ceased production. He remembered a lot about white beer brewing from his early days in the brewery and from talking to townspeople who remembered the taste of white beers when they were commercially available. Hoegaarden white beer soon became quite popular and has been emulated by many brewers in Belgium and around the world.

From the 1990s onward white beer production increased in volume significantly, due mainly to two commercially available examples, Hoegaarden, a traditional Belgian-style white beer, and MillerCoors' Blue Moon Belgian White, a "Belgo-American-style" white beer.

Traditional Belgian-style white beer is made with malted barley and unmalted wheat. Some variations include other grains, such as oats or spelt. It is spiced with a small quantity of hops to keep the bitterness low. Other spices traditionally include coriander and Curacao orange peel. Further, some variations add more unique spices to achieve an even more complex flavor. The yeast should typically be a Belgian ale yeast that produces unique fruity and spicy flavor notes. During the mashing process, many traditional white beer brewers employ a long, tepid mash rest, which promotes lactic acid production. This gives the beer a slight, refreshing tartness that is no doubt a throwback to the days when many beers, especially in warmer weather, had an unintentional tang of acidity from bacterial activity. The appearance of a traditional white beer is very pale yellow in color with a slight haziness and a rich, foamy head. The haze is mainly protein with a small amount of yeast. The aroma is citrusy, spicy, and fruity and the body is light. The taste is slightly tart, but balanced with light malt and wheat flavors, as well as complex citrus and spice notes for a refreshing taste. Americans have been given to putting slices of lemon or orange into white beers, perhaps wishing to accentuate the beer's bright citrus character. While white beer isn't treated this way in Belgium, some bars in the Netherlands have adopted the practice, occasionally going so far as to provide plastic muddlers for those wishing even more lemon character in the beer. The alcohol content of traditional white beer is between 4.5% and 5.0% ABV.

Unmalted wheat is difficult to work with, and some brewers have produced their own variants on Belgian white beer, particularly in the United States where the popular Blue Moon brand has brought greater attention to the style. This beer is spiced with a small quantity of hops to keep the bitterness low, approximately two-thirds the bitterness of traditional white beer. In addition to hops, it is spiced with coriander and Valencia orange peel. No lactic acid production is promoted during the mashing step, the yeast flavors are clean and mild, and the beer is a very cloudy gold color in appearance. At 5.4% ABV, this medium-bodied beer is slightly stronger than the traditional version and has an overall orange-citrusy flavor and aroma. The brewery has promoted the use of an orange slice to garnish the glass since 1997.

In addition to white beer, some brewers have produced stronger "grand cru" versions of white beer for holidays or special occasions. Grand cru white beers have similar tastes and aromas as regular white beers, but are more full-bodied and intense. These usually have between 8% and 10% ABV, but if well brewed can be pleasantly balanced and expressive beers.

See also BELGIUM.

Keith Villa

White Horse, The

See DORBER, MARK.

White Labs is a commercial yeast bank based in San Diego, California. It was founded in 1995 by Chris White after he had completed his PhD work at a yeast laboratory in San Diego. Today, White Labs services clients—mostly commercial brewers, but also homebrewers—in North America and some 80 countries around the world. White Labs maintains approximately 500 yeast strains, of which some 60 are grown to commercial quantities in any given week. Several of these are custom strains, which White Labs maintains under private agreement for individual breweries. Most of White Lab's sales come from 11 strains. White Labs offers yeast only in liquid form.

The White Labs yeast strains range from standard English ale yeast to wheat beer yeasts, special strains for high-gravity brewing, to various kinds of semiwild Brettanomyces for Belgian-style sour ales. In addition to yeast, White Labs sells several strains of bacteria, such as Lactobacillus and Pediococcus, for the production of sour beer styles, including Berliner weisse and lambic-influenced beers.

The company's most popular strains are being constantly propagated and are therefore usually in stock for immediate delivery, often within a day.

White Labs. http://www.whitelabs.com/ (accessed January 25, 2011).

Josh Rubin

White Shield

See WORTHINGTON BREWERY.

A **widget** is a small, hollow device designed to release gas into beer upon the opening of a can or bottle. The widget, usually a plastic disk, has a tiny circular aperture of 0.02 to 0.25 cm in its center. Because it is constructed to be heavier than beer, it does not float and sits at the bottom of the container. The operating principle is very simple: beer is usually kept under pressure and saturated with gas in solution—carbon dioxide, nitrogen, or a mixture of the two—before it reaches the filling line. Once the beer is bottled or canned, the gas builds up pressure inside the container, and, if a widget is present, beer also enters the hollow of the widget until the gaseous pressures in the container and inside the widget are at equilibrium. As soon as the container is opened, the pressure in the container drops, but the pressure inside the widget cannot escape so quickly. The widget shoots a jet of beer and gas into the surrounding beer, causing more gas to break out of solution and a sturdy, thick head to form. The effect of the widget, therefore, is to help canned or bottled beer to imitate the appearance and mouthfeel of a draught beer dispensed from a tap under normal or nitrogen dispense.

The widget was invented after years of development by two brewers, Tony Carey and Sammy Hildebrand, of Guinness in Dublin, in 1968. It was granted a patent in the UK in 1972 and in the United States 1989. It was introduced commercially by Guinness in cans in 1988 and in bottles in 1999. The widget won the UK's Queen's Award for Technological Achievement in 1991.

Tim Hampson

wild yeast is any species of yeast in fermentation other than the pitching yeast, often derived from the environment in or surrounding the brewery. The introduction of wild yeast into wort or beer can be intentional, as in the production of spontaneously fermented lambic, or unintentional, through contamination in the brewery. With the exception of lambic and other spontaneously fermented beers, wild yeasts are considered spoilage organisms in brewing and are avoided at all costs. See LAMBIC.

Although the microbiology of beer is complex, the wild yeasts most often associated with brewing are natural strains of Saccharomyces and Brettanomyces (Dekkera) and, to a much lesser extent, the yeasts Candida and Pichia, as well as other oxidative yeasts. Wild Saccharomyces may include both natural strains of the ale, wine, and bread yeast Saccharomyces cerevisiae or the lager yeast Saccharomyces pastorianus. Although S. cerevisiae is known to exist independently of human activity and can be found on a variety of substrates including the surfaces of fruits and plants, as well as in soil and tree sap, there is a tendency for it to thrive in environments rich in simple sugars, such as ripe fruit. Wild Saccharomyces yeast contamination is only encouraged in spontaneously fermented beers. Brettanomyces, which is the bane of winemakers, is also found on the surfaces of fruits and is generally avoided, except in spontaneous fermentation or when intentionally pitched as a pure culture. Candida, Pichia, and other oxidative yeasts in beer are always unintentional because these yeasts can contribute high levels of acetic acid when exposed to oxygen.

During the crafting of lambic beers, which are spontaneously fermented in the Senne Valley region of Belgium, wild strains of both Saccharomyces and Brettanomyces are major determinants of the sensory profile and attenuation level of the beer. For production of lambic, the hot wort is cooled while being exposed to the ambient brewery environment, which invites inoculation of wild yeast from the air. The local flora of wild yeast and bacteria is thought to give the beers of each brewery their unique taste, and it is often said that the microbes for fermenting lambics take up residence in the "cobwebs" of breweries. The more likely scenario is that the microbes for lambic fermentation live in the porous wooden beams and fermentation vessels inside the brewery. These microbes are often local to the brewery producing the lambic, so certain lambics cannot be reproduced in another brewery because the brewery does not have the same natural flora. Such differences may be said to represent part of the terroir of these unique beers.

Although not technically "wild" yeast, many brewers are now experimenting with the controlled pitching of pure cultures of Brettanomyces, often in conjunction with acid-producing bacteria such as Lactobacillus and Pediococcus. A classic example of a beer that uses Brettanomyces in a controlled setting is Orval. Several North American craft breweries also use this method, some producing highly regarded, Brettanomyces-influenced sour beers. See SOUR BEER.

In this new generation of sour beers, the introduction of wild yeast into cooled wort or beer is not always encouraged as it is with lambic brewing.

Wild yeast can also be introduced unintentionally during fermentation or conditioning; this is termed wild yeast contamination. This contamination is undesirable because most brewers control the fermentation and/or conditioning process using the yeast(s) of their choice, which allows them to have control over the quality of the final product. Wild yeasts are frequently more robust fermenters than brewing strains and can survive and thrive under more adverse conditions, so these wild yeasts can outcompete the pitching yeast during fermentation. This presents a problem if the brewer repitches the yeast at the end of fermentation because the contaminating wild yeast will then be the majority yeast during the start of the next fermentation. Because of this phenomenon, brewers often employ rigorous tests to determine the presence of wild yeast before repitching yeast.

Wild yeast contamination can lead to unpredictable fermentation results because the characteristics of the wild yeast are unknown. They may differ from the pitching yeast in the level of sugar attenuation, production of esters, fusel alcohols, sulfur compounds, or other secondary metabolites that are important in beer flavor and aroma. The characteristic sign of wild Saccharomyces contamination is the presence of medicinal/phenolic or clove-like notes, which is not a characteristic of brewing yeasts, with the exception of German wheat beer yeasts. Flocculation is also generally lower in contaminating Saccharomyces, so contaminated beer that is unfiltered will tend to be turbid. Brettanomyces yeasts are able to metabolize higher sugars such as dextrins, so contamination with Brettanomyces can result in a highly attenuated, thin beer; if bottle conditioned and aged, these beers can become highly carbonated from the slow fermentation of dextrins that the Saccharomyces was unable to ferment. Brettanomyces is also responsible for the tastes and smells often colorfully described as "mousy," "barnyard," or "wet horse blanket." As with some wines, these characteristics are considered "complexing agents" when found desirable, but ruinous when they are not. Wild yeast can be picked up during the brewing process any time that cooled wort or beer comes in contact with a nonsanitized surface or the air, such as during postboil wort transfer to the fermenter or during postfermentation conditioning or packaging. Along with spoilage bacteria, wild yeasts pose a biological threat to the intended quality of conventionally brewed beers.

See also BRETTANOMYCES.

Campbell, Iain. "Wild yeasts in brewing and distilling." In *Brewing microbiology*, 3rd ed, 247–66. New York: Kluwer Academic/Plenum Publishers, 2003.

Lewis, Michael J., and Charles W. Bamforth. "Microbiology." In *Essays in brewing science*, 58–68. New York: Springer, 2006.

Sparrow, Jeff. *Wild brews: Culture and craftsmanship in the Belgian tradition*. Boulder, CO: Brewers Publications, 2005.

Daniel J. Kvitek

Willamette (hop) is an American aroma hop bred by Al Haunold and released in 1976. It has been used expansively by Anheuser-Busch, primarily as a replacement of the English Fuggle and other aroma hops that became increasingly sparse on world markets. See FUGGLE (HOP). Willamette was developed by the U.S. Department of Agriculture hop breeding program in Corvallis, Oregon. It originated from a controlled 1967 cross between two Fuggle derivatives. Its breeding objective was an aroma hop with European characteristics and a yield that is 40% greater than that of Fuggle. Willamette is a triploid, which means it matures as a virtually seedless plant. It has a moderately low alpha acid content of 4% to 8% and a low beta acid count of 3% to 4.5%. Its aroma is mild, pleasant, earthy, and slightly spicy. Currently, it is planted on roughly 40% of all hop acreage in the Willamette Valley acreage of Oregon and is America's most important aroma variety. For large breweries and small, Willamette remains an important workhorse hop that can deliver fine-tuned bitterness in the kettle and a pleasant aroma as well. See WILLAMETTE VALLEY HOP REGION.

Thomas Shellhammer and Val Peacock

The **Willamette Valley hop region** is the second largest hop-growing area in the United States. The valley lies between the Coast Range and the Cascade Mountains, some 70 km (40 miles) south of Portland, Oregon. It is one of the most verdant agricultural areas in the world, producing not only hops but also more than 250 different agricultural commodities. Among wine lovers, the Willamette Valley is well known for growing excellent pinot noir. Situated at a latitude of approximately

45° north, this region's climate is similar to that of the Hallertau hop-growing region in southern Germany, although the Willamette Valley has warmer winters. It offers many conditions that are ideal for hop cultivation. These include long days with 15.5 h of sunlight during the summer months, moderate summer temperatures with an average high of 28°C (82°F), temperate winters with an average low of 1°C (34°F), and consistent rainfall throughout the fall, winter, and spring, but very light rainfall during the summer, when precipitations averages about 1 cm (0.5 in) per month. Total rainfall for the year averages about 100 cm (40 in).

Although the climate in the Willamette Valley is ideally suited for hops cultivation, especially of delicate aroma varieties, many hop growers have implement some form of irrigation as a safety backup. The region produces almost 20% of all US hops, compared with about 75% from the Yakima Valley in the state of Washington and almost 10% from Idaho. Among the roughly 20 hop varieties that grow in the region, Cascade, Glacier, Golding, Millennium, Mount Hood, Nugget, Sterling, Super Galena, and Willamette are perhaps the best known. The most prevalent varieties are Nugget and Willamette, which are planted on about 70% of the total acreage.

Thomas Shellhammer and Val Peacock

wine yeast, any of a number of yeasts, mainly from the species Saccharomyces cerevisiae, that are used to ferment fruit juice (usually grape) to produce wine. Approximately 150 different wine yeasts are available from commercial producers; most have been isolated from spontaneous (uninoculated) wine fermentations from around the world. These strains are chosen for their beneficial fermentation and/or flavor profiles, for their ability to ferment specific grape types, or for specific technical reasons, for example, the ability to restart "stuck" fermentations. See FERMENTATION. Although most commercial wine yeasts are S. cerevisiae, some are hybrids between S. cerevisiae and other closely related Saccharomyces species and are similar to the hybrid lager yeast, Saccharomyces pastorianus. Although wine and ale yeasts are both members of the S. cerevisiae species, DNA analyses have shown that wine and ale strains form separate groups that are genetically distinct. Because wines generally contain more alcohol than beers, most wine yeasts tolerate higher alcohol levels than beer yeasts. Wine yeasts, however, are generally not considered good fermentation agents for quality beers because they produce flavors and aromas that are not compatible with typical beer sensory profiles. In addition, the spectrum of sugars that they best ferment (mostly glucose and fructose) is not generally the one that most worts represent. However, high-alcohol tolerant "champagne yeasts" are occasionally used in brewing, mostly by craft brewers and amateur brewers, either when a fermentation is stuck or to fully attenuate a high-gravity fermentation. This is often a method of last resort and an indication that the original yeast was either ill-chosen or not healthy at the time of pitching. The yeast strains referred to as champagne yeasts include the popular Prise de Mousse, used by many craft brewers for bottle conditioning. This yeast is highly active and will tolerate alcohol levels as high as 18%, although like many wine yeasts it is a producer of diacetyl (widely tolerated or even desired in wine), which it will usually reabsorb given proper time and conditions.

See also YEAST.

Barbara Dunn

winter ale, although not technically a beer style per se, can certainly be considered a widespread brewing tradition. The custom of brewing a stronger-than-normal dark ale for drinking against the chills of the coldest months of the year is doubtless as old as brewing in Northern Europe itself. As an anonymously written verse from 1656 put it, "When the chill Sirocco blows/And winter tells a heavy tale/O, give me stout brown ale."

Earlier unhopped or lightly hopped ales were particularly suitable for being heated and spiced, giving rise to such winter's drinks as ale posset, a drink mixing piping hot ale mixed with bread, milk, sugar, ginger, and nutmeg. Other beer-based winter drinks included lamb's wool, a combination of spiced hot ale and roasted apples, and egg flip, hot, mild ale mixed with eggs, brandy, and nutmeg.

British winter ales were also flavored by the traditional method of floating spiced toast on the surface, a habit that survived until at least the start of the 19th century, judging by the description in a memoir in *Chambers's Edinburgh Journal* from March 15, 1845, of "the tankard of winter ale, its creamy top half hidden by the crisp brown toast."

The rise of hopped beer, which reacts badly to being heated, seems to have meant the decline of hot ale drinks. However, drinkers continued to express a desire for stronger, sweeter, and often darker beers in the winter months. In London, in particular, this was met by the original Burton ale, a type made by the brewers of Burton-on-Trent before they began producing highly hopped pale ales for the Indian market. See BURTON-ON-TRENT.

Burton ale became a widely available style of beer in the UK, particularly during the colder months. Bass No. 1, the strongest Burton ale in that company's range, was called in advertisements around 1909 "THE winter drink." It was a very robust beer, and bottles from the first decade of the 1900s are still enjoyed in fine condition today. In 1949, the journalist Maurice Gorham wrote that Burton, "darker and sweeter than bitter . . . is also known as 'old' . . . many pubs do not keep Burton during the hot weather, counting it a winter drink." The beer writer Andrew Campbell wrote in 1956 that Burton or Old, "a still stronger type of dark beer" than Best Mild, was on sale "in winter months," with gravities from 1,040 to 1,050. Barclay Perkins in Southwark, London, renamed its 4K Burton Ale Winter Brew. At least eight London brewers were still making a Burton in the mid-1950s, and Courage at the Horsleydown brewery would send out show-cards to its pubs saying, "Courage Burton is now on sale for the winter season."

However, the fall in popularity of darker ales in the 1960s meant that Burton ale rapidly almost disappeared, about the last one left being made by Young's brewery in Wandsworth. In 1971 Young's changed the name of its Burton ale to Winter Warmer, reflecting its seasonal nature and its particular appeal.

Another London brewer, Fuller, Smith & Turner, replaced its Burton ale with a strong bitter, Winter Beer, in 1969. See FULLER, SMITH & TURNER. Two years later, Winter Beer was renamed Extra Special Bitter, also known as ESB. As the strongest bitter brewed in the UK at that time, it quickly became popular and moved from a seasonal to a year-round brew, inspiring a host of imitators.

The tradition of winter warmer beers or seasonal old ales was revived, like so many other beer styles, from the mid-1970s onward by the growing craft beer sector in the United States, the UK, and elsewhere. These seasonal beers, generally at 5% to 8% alcohol by volume, have an emphasis on darker malts and sometimes use spices alongside hops, recalling the old heated spiced ales. At least one brewer, Hepworth, in Sussex England, encourages consumers to "gently mull" its dark Classic Old Ale, which it describes as "a traditional style of winter beer." Many winter ales in Europe are dubbed "Christmas ales," and this is an old tradition, although in the United States this is translated to "holiday ale" out of cultural sensitivity. Spices are common in the American craft brewed beers as well. First brewed in 1975, Anchor Brewing Company's Christmas Ale has been influential for decades, its name predating worries about religious overtones.

Martyn Cornell

witbier

See WHITE BEER.

The **Wittelsbacher family** is a dynasty that ruled Bavaria for 738 years, from 1180 until 1918, first as dukes and then, from 1806, as kings. The Wittelsbachs were, next to the Habsburgs of Austria, one of the most important dynasties in European history because their marriage policy throughout the centuries ensured that members of their family became part of the bloodlines of just about every ruling house of note in Europe. One Wittelsbach or another held, at various times, such titles as Duke of Luxembourg, Duke of Palatine, King of Bohemia, King of Greece, King of Hungary, King of Sweden, and Emperor of Germany. Perhaps uniquely, however, the House of Wittelsbach played almost as great a role in the history of beer as it did in the history of Europe. The following are some of the milestones in the annals of the House of Wittelsbach and of beer: in 1269, the chronologically fourth Wittelsbach Duke of Bavaria, Ludwig "the Severe," started Munich's first brewery. In 1516, the Wittelsbach Duke Wilhelm IV proclaimed the "Bavarian Beer Purity Law" (Reinheitsgebot), which later evolved into a federal German law restricting beer ingredients to just water, yeast, malt, and hops.

See REINHEITSGEBOT. In 1553, Duke Albrecht V issued the Bavarian summer brewing prohibition for the period between April 23 and September 29—a regulation that remained in force until 1850 and laid the foundation for the Bavarian lager as well as the emergence of the märzen beer style. See BAVARIA and MÄRZENBIER. In 1602, Duke Maximilian I instituted a highly profitable weissbier (wheat beer) brewing monopoly for the Wittelsbach family and forced every innkeeper in his realm to pour the crown-brewed wheat ale. See WEISSBIER. The monopoly lasted until 1798, by which time weissbier had fallen out of favor. Meanwhile, however, it had garnered substantial revenues for the ducal coffers. In 1810, the wedding celebrations of Crown Prince Ludwig I and Princess Therese of Saxe-Hildburghausen became the first Munich Oktoberfest, the forerunner of what is today by far the world's biggest beer fest, with 6 to 7 million visitors annually. See OKTOBERFEST. And in 1868, King Ludwig II of Bavaria established a "Polytechnic School of Munich" at the old Benedictine Abbey of Weihenstephan outside Munich, which had received its brew right in 1040. This school was renamed the "Royal Bavarian Academy for Agriculture and Breweries" in 1895. Since then, it has evolved into one of the world's foremost brew research and teaching institutions and is now part of the Technical University of Munich. Even today, a Wittelsbach, His Royal Highness Prince Luitpold of Bavaria, is in the brewing industry. He is the chief executive officer of his family's Kaltenberg Brewery, now part of the Warsteiner group of breweries and one of Germany's largest makers of dunkel. See DUNKEL, KALTENBERG BREWERY, and LUITPOLD, PRINCE OF BAVARIA.

Sepp Wejwar

women in brewing have a long history. For most of recorded human history, women have been responsible for supplying the world's beer. From the brewing goddesses of the ancient near east and the disenfranchised brewsters of medieval England to the ladies fighting on both sides of the US Temperance movement and the women asserting themselves in every aspect of the modern brewing industry, the story of women's role in brewing is as long and complex as human history itself.

In many ancient societies, beer was seen as a gift of joy, love, happiness, and spirituality sent from the heavens. In both ancient Sumerian and Egyptian societies the giving of the gift of fermentation to humanity was attributed to a goddess, and in both societies its earthly production was also entrusted to females. In Sumeria, the society with the earliest records of beer production, the goddess Ninkasi watched over all brewing activities. She was the only female deity associated with an actual profession. The tablet describing one of the first recipes of beer, dated back to 1800 BC, has been dubbed the "Hymn to Ninkasi." The Hymn is less a practical text than it is a celebration of Ninkasi's gift of the brewing process itself. In ancient Egypt, the goddess Hathor was called "the inventress of brewing" and "the mistress of intoxication." Both Hathor the goddess and beer itself were associated with fertility, pleasure, joy, and music. See BEER GODS and NINKASI.

In both ancient Sumeria and ancient Egypt, the brewing process was similar to the process of making bread and even shared the same facilities. Baking and brewing, often done with the same dough, were considered daily chores that naturally fell to the women of the household. Most depictions of the brewing process from this time show women straining mash or grinding grain for baking and brewing. Some women also used their brewing skills to turn a small profit by operating taverns or drinking houses where beer was both brewed and sold by the glass. These taverns, much like later European ones, often doubled as brothels, with the brewster and the madame being one and the same. These woman-run taverns were so common that the Code of Hammurabi (c. 1700 BC) has four laws (clauses 108–11) pertaining to them, in which the language is exclusively directed toward female operators.

Similarly to brewing in ancient Sumeria and ancient Egypt, in Europe brewing was a task that fell primarily to the women of the household until the turn of the first millenium AD. However, around the year 1000 AD, various monasteries around mainland Europe took up the practice of brewing and distributing beer. This practice began to establish beer production as a more profitable and esteemed profession, soon to be practiced on a scale that would no longer be feasible for women to conduct casually from their homes.

The most recent and best documented transition of brewing from small-scale "women's work" to a profitable industry run almost exclusively by men occurred in medieval England and was brought on by several factors. Before 1348 AD, beer production was mostly confined to the home, as was once the case throughout Europe, and the brew of choice was traditional, unhopped English ale. Brewing was often a part of a woman's work at home, did not entail a huge up-front investment, and was a decent source of income in times of need for both single and married women. Brewing was therefore small scale and ale supplies were inconsistent.

After the plague ravaged England, consumption of ale greatly increased. This increasing demand favored suppliers who could finance and run larger operations that put out a steady supply of ale and disadvantaged the mostly female-run home businesses requiring little capital and producing inconsistent output. Single women generally did not have access to the kind of wealth or political clout that was required for large-scale commercial brewing operations, so the late 14th century saw a surge in breweries run by married couples, with the wives providing the brewing know-how and the husbands providing the capital and political connections. The establishment of brewers' guilds and increased regulation of the brewing industry further increased the advantages of breweries with well-connected male figureheads. The participation of women in the guilds was limited and was nonexistent in government. Therefore, a brewery had a higher chance of success if led by a man able to effect the political and economic decisions crucial to a business.

The introduction of hopped ale to England further solidified women's role away from the commercial brewery. The already male-dominated and well-established beer industry of mainland Europe had long given up sweet ales, gruits, and other unhopped beers in favor of beer brewed with the bitter and aromatic hop. Dutch and German immigrants imported their hoppy brews into England and eventually built breweries to supply the growing population of beer drinkers. Although hopped beer was slow to supplant unhopped ale as England's beverage of choice, the larger English breweries soon recognized the advantages in terms of quality and shelf life of producing European-style hopped beers and ales. As hopped beer's popularity grew, its production required new brewing technology and education to which the remaining brewsters had little to no access.

Another social force that shifted brewing from brewsters to the more regulated and male-dominated industry was that England began to see negative depictions of brewsters in art. These depictions originated from the age-old fear of being cheated by false measures and deceitful tavern owners, but developed into vicious descriptions of the physical appearance, moral composition, and unsanitary brewing practices of alewives and brewsters generally. See ALE-WIVES. The most famous such depiction is a poem written by John Skelton in 1517 called "The Tunning of Elynour Rummyng." Catchy and humorous to this day, poems like this, describing alewives as horrifically ugly, possibly allied with the Devil, preying on customers, and operating in the most disgusting conditions, acted as an expression of social feelings of the time, as well as a possible deterrent to doing business with alewives and brewsters. Eventually, the majority of women involved with beer were found selling pints in taverns or in the streets rather than making beer in the brewhouse.

And so the world has seen women passing on the skills and knowledge of beer brewing down to their daughters for thousands of years. The brewing traditions of women continued in most beer-drinking societies until such money and prestige accompanied brewing that it became a profession only available to men. The recent growth of craft breweries throughout the United States, however, has marked a clear resurgence of women playing crucial roles in the modern beer industry. In addition to the myriad skills that women bring to breweries, they are recognized as having a superior sense of taste and smell as well as a greater ability to remember and recount sensory experiences. These skills have earned women valued seats on educated beer sensory analysis panels around the world. There are several organizations created to support women in the beer industry, from brewers to brewery owners, managers, salespeople, advocates, and educators. One such organization, the Pink Boots Society, currently registers over 500 members. Along with the resurgence of beer in all its variations, the role of women in brewing today continues to expand and evolve.

Bennett, Judith. *Ale, beer, and brewsters in England: Women's work in a changing world, 1300–1600.* New York: Oxford University Press, 1996.

Bickerdyke, John. *The curiosities of ale & beer*, 2nd ed. London: Spring Books, 1965.

Hornsey, Ian. *A history of beer and brewing*. Cornwall, England: The Royal Society of Chemistry, 2003.

Alana R. Jones

woodruff. Also known in English as "sweet woodruff" and in German as "Waldmeister," woodruff is an herbaceous perennial best known in beermaking as one of the commonly used sweetened flavorings for Berliner weiss (the other being raspberry). Though the brilliant green imparted by the "schuss" in the glass is mainly owing to the enhancement of dye, woodruff syrup adds both a mitigating sweetness and an herbal note to the sour wheat beer. It is important to note that the flavoring is added at serving; to do so earlier would be in violation of Germany's Beer Purity Law, Reinheitsgebot. See REINHEITSGEBOT.

American craft breweries have sometimes produced beer with woodruff; in these, dried leaves are added either to the boil or to cold, conditioning beer. San Andreas Brewing of Hollister, California, has brewed its Woodruff Ale since the early 1990s and Elysian Brewing of Seattle, Washington, produces a woodruff-accented version of its Ambrosia Spring Bock. Woodruff has also traditionally been used in Germany and Austria as a flavoring and garnish for the young May wine.

Woodruff is low-growing, its leaves in lanceolate whorls of from six to nine, with small white flowers. It is often planted as a decorative ground cover. The green leaves are fragrant, imparting notes akin to nutmeg or cinnamon. Its aroma and flavor contribution intensify upon drying of the leaves.

Cram, Alice B. "The abc of herbs: The scent of sweet woodruff." homepages.sover.net/~garden/Woodruff.html/ (accessed October 20, 2010).

Graeve, Maud. *A modern herbal*. New York: Harcourt, Brace, 1931.

Dick Cantwell

The **World Beer Cup,** sometimes referred to as the "Olympics of Beer," is the world's biggest international beer competition, typically featuring well over 3,300 beers entered by some 650 breweries from almost 50 countries. The competition was founded in 1996 by the Brewers Association and takes place every other year in parallel with the Association's Craft Brew Conference and BrewExpo America, which moves from city to city on an annual basis.

Brewers enter their beers in one of over 90 beer style categories to be judged by an international panel of experts in blind tastings. The judges award gold, silver, and bronze medals in each category, whereby the principal criterion for evaluation is the beer's adherence to its style definition. The judging is highly technical and discussions among judges are often spirited.

World Beer Cup judges are selected based on their demonstrated knowledge of beer styles, the brewing process, and sensory aspects of beer, as well as on their experience in judging. Peer recommendations are also given consideration. Considering the large number of beers that need to be evaluated, as of 2010 World Beer Cup competitions required close to 200 judges working over more than 2 days. In recent World Beer Cup competitions, the judges hailed from almost 30 countries. Roughly half came from countries other than the United States.

In addition to selecting individual beers for medals, the judges also honor breweries with Champion Brewers Awards in the five categories of small and large brewpub as well as small, mid-size, and large brewery. These awards go to the companies that garnered the most overall medal points with their beer entries. Because of the high quality of the judging, World Beer Cup awards are widely respected and coveted by brewers.

Brewers Association. *World Beer Cup 2010*. http://www.worldbeercup.org/ (accessed April 21, 2010).

Jeff Mendel

World Brewing Congress

See AMERICAN SOCIETY OF BREWING CHEMISTS (ASBC).

wort is an aqueous solution of extract made from grain, intended for fermentation by yeast into beer. For most beer styles, the finished wort that reaches the fermentation vessel is between 80% and 90% water by weight. Wort is created by the process of mashing and then separated from grain husk material in the lautering process. See LAUTERING and MASHING. Wort is then collected in the brew kettle, where it is boiled with hops. See KETTLE. When yeast is added to cooled wort, fermentation transforms the hopped wort into beer.

The composition of the wort depends on the composition of the grain bill, the mashing process, the brewing water, and the hops. A standard all-malt wort will contain approximately 12% monosaccharides, 5% sucrose, 47% maltose, 15% maltotriose, and 25% higher saccharides, such as dextrins. Most of these wort sugars are produced in the mash tun, where enzymes in the grain convert starches to sugars. See ENZYMES, SACCHARIFICATION, and SUGAR. Mash temperature and thickness will have large effects on the sugar profile of the wort, and this will affect the wort's fermentability. Some beer styles call for the addition of non-grain-derived sugars—both fermentable and unfermentable—to the wort to give the finished beer extra flavor and/or to develop a higher alcohol content without heaviness of texture. Besides carbohydrates, wort components include nitrogen compounds (mostly proteins), salts and minerals, acids, phenols, hop bitter substances, hop essential oils, and lipids.

Other grains aside from barley, including wheat, rye, or oats, may be part of the mash and thus become part of the wort. Many beer styles are brewed with the addition of adjuncts such as corn grits or rice, which require specialized brewhouse equipment, including dedicated mills and cereal cookers to generate a fermentable wort. See ADJUNCTS. Several mash raw materials such as sorghum or buckwheat can produce gluten-free wort for gluten-free beer. See BUCKWHEAT, GLUTEN-FREE BEER, and SORGHUM.

Wort is physically and microbiologically unstable. Boiling renders wort sterile, preparing it for the introduction of brewer's yeast. The wort boil also extracts bitterness, flavors, and aromas from hops, concentrates the wort through evaporation, drives off unwanted volatiles and off-flavor precursors, denatures malt enzymes, and causes the coagulation of proteins and phenolic substances that can later be removed.

The kettle boil also has the effect of darkening the wort's color and deepening its malt flavors as a result of the Maillard reaction. See MAILLARD REACTION. The pH of the wort drops as well largely because of the precipitation of calcium phosphate. In most worts, the drop is from roughly 5.6 to 5.8 to roughly 5.2 to 5.4, a pH range that is acceptable to most yeast strains for the start of fermentation. See FERMENTATION and YEAST.

Hops are added to the brew kettle as cone hops, pelletized hops, or liquid extracts, usually in several doses at different stages of the boil. Hops contain dozens of bittering, flavor, and aroma compounds that are extracted from the plant material during the boil. See ALPHA ACIDS, AROMA UNIT (AU), and HOP OILS. If brewers use herbs and/or spices in their beers, they too are usually added to the boil. See GRUIT, HERBS, and SPICES.

The next important function of the boil is to coagulate malt proteins, which gather into visible flocs called hot break or trub. See HOT BREAK and TRUB. Trub also contains phenols and tannins as well as spent hop material. Much of the trub settles out at the bottom of the brew kettle. Traditionally, this would have been removed by recirculating the wort through a bed of whole flower hops, allowing the hops to act as a form of filter. This is still practiced at many small breweries. These days, however, trub is usually removed from the wort in a special vessel called a whirlpool into which the hot wort is pumped tangentially at high speed after the kettle boil. See WHIRLPOOL. Trub particles and hop fragments are forced to the sidewalls and finally to the center of the whirlpool floor. Clear wort is then siphoned off through an outlet near the edge of the whirlpool floor and sent through a heat exchanger for cooling. See HEAT EXCHANGER. Once it is cooled to fermentation temperature, the wort is aerated or oxygenated and then usually pumped into a fermentation vessel, where the yeast transforms wort into beer. See FERMENTATION. Some wort may also be moved directly into a packaging area to become an unfermented non-alcoholic malt beverage, such as Malta. It can also be moved into a vacuum evaporator to be concentrated into a syrupy malt extract, widely used in the food industry and by homebrewers.

For most beer styles, the finished wort that reaches the fermenter has a gravity between 9°P and 16°P, but some strong beer styles call for much more concentrated worts, with some barley wines produced from worts of more than 30°P.

David Kapral

Worthington Brewery was established by William Worthington in the English town of Burton-on-Trent in 1744. It became one of a handful of companies to trade lucratively with the Baltic states along with the better-known Burton entrepreneurial brewers run by the Wilson, Sketchley, Bass, and Evans families. By the 1820s a worsening relationship with Napoleon Bonaparte soured much of this trade, and an alternative market had to be found.

Since at least the 1780s the East India Company had exported beers to the Indian sub-continent, following in the wake of the administrators and troops who left the United Kingdom to work in settlements there. Records show that some of the first shipments took place in 1697.

The trade was dominated by London brewer Abbot & Hodgsons, but the Burton brewers recognized a business opportunity when they saw one. When the London brewer faltered, the trade quickly became dominated by Burton brewers Bass and Allsop, and, to a lesser extent, Worthington. They first began to imitate the London brewers' beer but discovered that a Burton IPA had the attribute of arriving in Calcutta pale, clear, and sparkling. See BURTON-ON-TRENT and INDIA PALE ALE. Sometime around the start of the 20th century the term "India pale ale" disappeared from White Shield's label and became known by its heart shield and dagger label design, which was first registered as a trademark in 1863.

Worthington was never one of the big Burton brewers and was subsumed within the growing Bass empire in 1927. Somehow, nonetheless, the beer survived as a bottled beer. It was a curiosity as it still contained yeast in the bottle, long after the practice of bottle-conditioning had largely disappeared from British brewing. Drinkers' conversations often focused on whether the beer should be poured clear or have the yeast tipped into the glass too. Many beer enthusiasts have commented upon the beer's ability to age well, gaining character in the bottle over a year or two.

Over time several attempts were made to revive the brand. By the 1990s its production was so small that it was farmed out to contract brewers around the country. But in 2000, Steve Wellington, brewer at Burton's Museum brewery, persuaded the then-brand owner Bass to bring production of White Shield back to Burton. The Museum brewery, built in the classic English tower style, continues its work to restore the beer to its former glory and repute. At 5.6%, it is lighter than IPA was in its heyday, but is bottle-conditioned and retains a fine hop bitterness and aroma. Today the brand is owned by MolsonCoors Brewing Company.

See also BURTON ALE, BURTON-ON-TRENT, and INDIA PALE ALE.

Gourvish, T. R., and R. G. Wilson. *The brewing industry 1830–1980*. Cambridge: Cambridge University Press, 1994.

Matthias, Peter. *The brewing industry in England 1700–1830*. Cambridge: Cambridge University Press, 1959.

Tim Hampson

Wyeast Laboratories is a yeast bank and supplier located in the hamlet of Odell, Oregon. Wyeast Laboratories, Inc, was founded by David and Jeanette Logsdon in 1985. The company takes its name from its location on Oregon's Mount Hood, which the native inhabitants used to call Wy'East. David Logsdon was a homebrewer who once maintained the yeast and bacteria library at Mount Hood Community College. He helped two pioneering Portland microbreweries, Bridgeport and Widmer Brothers, manage their yeasts when they first opened. In 1987 he became the first brewer for the start-up Full Sail Brewery in Hood River. Wyeast was launched to supply yeast to homebrewers and to the emerging craft brewing industry. It initially offered only three strains—one ale yeast, one lager yeast, and one champagne yeast. Since then, the Logsdons collected yeast cultures from all over the world, and Wyeast currently maintains a collection of hundreds of yeast strains, offering about 70 strains to homebrewers and 100 to commercial brewers. Wyeast's unique "smack-pack," developed by Logsdon and introduced in 1986, revolutionized pitching for homebrewers by providing active liquid yeast in a small pouch surrounded by a larger pouch of liquid yeast nutrient. By "smacking" the pack, the inner pouch bursts and the yeast and yeast nutrient can combine. As the yeast begins to ferment, it creates a small starter, causing the package to swell. This indicates that the yeast is viable and ready to be pitched. Wyeast was also the first company to supply pure liquid yeast to craft breweries. It now supplies fermentation cultures not only to breweries in the United States but also around the globe. In 2009 Dave Logsdon sold his shares in the company to Jeanette Logsdon, the current owner.

Abram Goldman-Armstrong

Wye Challenger (hop)

See CHALLENGER (HOP).

Wye College, officially The College of St. Gregory and St. Martin at Wye, was established by John Kempe, Archbishop of York, as a seminary in 1447. Wye College developed an outstanding reputation as a center for rural and agronomy studies over centuries to eventually become an independent School of Agriculture, which affiliated to the University of London in 1898.

The site near Ashford covers 400 ha, including a 320-ha farm with woodland and glasshouses and two sites of special scientific interest. In 2000 the college merged with Imperial College of the University of London, but activities declined because of financial difficulties and the college is now being relaunched as PhoenixWyeCollege in collaboration with the University of Buckingham.

Because of its location in the center of Kent, Wye College specialized in hop research and during the later part of the 20th century developed many novel varieties including Northern Brewer, Challenger, and Brewers Gold. Some varieties such as Target and Yeoman were developed for increased yield of alpha acid, whereas others showed improved disease resistance.

More recently, Dr Ray Neve and Dr Peter Darby of Wye pioneered the major development of dwarf hops based on finding a mutant plant with reduced internode length. Dwarf hops provide a major advance in growth and harvesting efficiencies and have promise to greatly improve the efficiency of hop production. To a large extent, in its heyday Wye College was widely viewed as being virtually synonymous with English hop research, breeding, and development.

Hop research has transferred to other locations such as Wye Hops Ltd in Canterbury, but the advances made at Wye provided the brewing industry with major hop varieties that are still in popular use today by commercial and amateur brewers.

Keith Thomas

Wye Northdown (hop)

See NORTHDOWN (HOP).

Wye Target (hop)

See TARGET (HOP).

xanthohumol, a prenylated flavonoid (a type of polyphenol), found in the hard resin fraction of hops. It is somewhat unique, because nearly all other poly- and monophenols are found in nonlupulin plant material in the hop cone. Hop resins are divided between soft resins—those that are soluble in hexane—and hard resins—those that are soluble in ether. The soft resin fraction contains the hop's alpha and beta acids, whereas the hard resin fraction contains the hop's oxidized alpha and beta acids, as well as xanthohumol and its isomerized counterpart isoxanthohumol. Xanthohumol is the most abundant prenyl flavonoid in hops and may amount to nearly 1% of the hop-cone dry weight, depending on variety. Xanthohumol has no brewing value, because it does not contribute to or modify beer flavor. However, it does offer potentially very significant human health benefits. It has been identified as having strong anti-inflammatory, antioxidative, and broad-spectrum anticarcinogenic properties. It inhibits the metabolic activation of procarcinogens, it induces carcinogen-detoxifying enzymes, and it inhibits tumor growth at an early stage. In particular, it has been shown to be chemopreventive against breast and prostate cancer. Within the class of plant-based polyphenols, both xanthohumol and isoxanthohumol have high antioxidant properties, higher than genistein (which is found in soy) but not as high as quercetin (which is found in onions and fruit). Despite the high levels of xanthohumol in some hops, its presence in beer is very low because it isomerizes rapidly during kettle boil. Traditionally hopped lager beer may have between 0 and 30 parts per billion (ppb) xanthohumol, whereas more heavily hopped ales and porters can have as much as 100 to 700 ppb. The low concentrations in beer combined with its very low bioavailability means that the amount of xanthohumol obtained by drinking beer is negligible. Isoxanthohumol, on the other hand, is found at up to 100 times higher levels in beer. Heavily hopped beers may have between 800 and 3,500 ppb (or 0.8 and 3.5 ppm) isoxanthohumol. There is some evidence that intestinal microbiota can isomerize isoxanthohumol back to xanthohumol during the digestion process. If true, this may bring new attention to the possible health benefits of xanthohumol. See LUPULIN.

Thomas Shellhammer

xerogel

See SILICA GEL.

xylose is a five-carbon sugar (or pentose) that is the principal monosaccharide of hemicellulose and one of the most abundant sugars in nature. Most of the xylose in wheat or barley is joined into larger molecules with arabinose, another pentose; together they are referred to as arabinoxylan. This polymer usually consists of roughly equal parts xylose and arabinose and can constitute up to 10% of brewing grains. Most of this arabinoxylan is nonsoluble and will remain in the spent grain following lautering. However, 1–2 g/l arabinoxylan is found in a typical hopped wort and has been shown to affect the wort's viscosity. Some of the simpler arabinoxylo-oligosaccharides created by breakdown of the arabinoxylans are found in beer, anywhere from 0.8 to 2 g/l. These polysaccharides can affect the mouthfeel of a beer, giving roundness, and are generally considered taste-neutral. Yeast strains used in brewing do not ferment xylose, so if any were present in the wort, it would not be fermented.

See also SUGAR.

Jared W. Wenger

Yakima Valley hop region is the largest hop-growing area in the United States. It is located approximately 230 km southeast of Seattle, Washington, at roughly 46 north latitude. This region experiences long days of up to 16 h of sunlight during the summer months, moderate summer temperatures with an average high of 31°C (87°F), and cold winters with an average low of –7°C (20°F). Because the region is also in the rain shadow of the Cascade Range, rainfall is very light, averaging 21 cm (8 inches) per year, which translates into less than 2 cm per month. Rain in the summer months is rare. Although the name "Yakima" is now iconic among American brewers and beer enthusiasts, it is not a natural hop-growing region. Once just a stretch of sagebrush country, Yakima Valley actually has a desert climate, and most agriculture in the valley depends upon irrigation. Fortunately, water is available from the Yakima River Watershed. The arrival of settlers from the East began in the 1860s

Photograph of oast houses in Yakima Valley, Washington State, c. 1910. Yakima Valley is the largest hop-growing region in the United States. PIKE MICROBREWERY MUSEUM, SEATTLE, WA

and they quickly turned the valley into a verdant fruit-growing region, which it still is today. The first hop rhizomes in the Yakima Valley were planted in 1872, and just 4 years later Yakima hop growers shipped 80 bales of hops to breweries westward. Hop growing as well as other agricultural activities accelerated rapidly after the completion of the Northern Pacific Railroad from the Great Lakes to the Pacific in 1883. Once irrigation is established, the region's climate is well suited for growing hops, and new plants can produce a harvest in their first year. Yakima varieties range across the full spectrum from superhigh alpha hops to bittering hops and aroma hops. Generally, more than 25 different varieties are cultivated in the region on a commercial scale. These include the higher-alpha varieties Columbus/Tomahawk/Zeus (CTZ), Nugget, and Galena, as well as the important American aroma varieties Willamette, Cascade, and Mount Hood. The higher-alpha varieties account for more than half of the total hop acreage in Washington State. In contrast to the small farm sizes of just a few acres in European hop growing regions, the average farm size in the Yakima Valley is about 450 acres (180 ha). In most years, roughly 75% of the entire American hop harvest comes from the Yakima Valley, whereas not quite 20% comes from the Willamette Valley in Oregon and not quite 10% from two hop-growing regions in Idaho.

The Free Encyclopedia of Washington State History. "Yakima County—Thumbnail History." http://www.historylink.org/index.cfm?DisplayPage=output.cfm&file_id=7651 (accessed March 8, 2011).

Thomas Shellhammer and Val Peacock

yeast transforms wort made by the brewer into beer.

Introduction

Although it is the brewer who makes wort, it is yeast that transforms it into beer. Yeast are unicellular fungi that include several genera including Saccharomyces, the name of which is Latin for "sugar fungus." And indeed the name is apt—during fermentation Saccharomyces yeasts consume wort sugars and give off alcohol, carbon dioxide, and a range of flavors that we associate with beer. The genus Saccharomyces itself comprises several species, some of them more relevant than others for the beverage industry. The most common species used in the alcohol industry is Saccharomyces cerevisiae, cerevisiae meaning "of beer." In winemaking, different selected strains can produce many different wines with varied flavor characteristics. The production of distilled spirits and industrial production of ethanol also use specific strains of S. cerevisiae; this species is an ideal candidate because it is able to produce and then tolerate high concentrations of alcohol. It is also utilized in the baking industry for its leavening ability and, of course, for beer brewing purposes. Saccharomyces yeasts are round or oval in shape and reproduce by multilateral budding. Traditional identification of genera revolves around reproduction and morphology. Physiological tests are the norm to differentiate yeast species and include fermentation and assimilation of various carbon sources and growth under different environmental conditions. However, recent technologies involving DNA are widely used these days for genus/species determination. They are based on the detection of DNA sequences that are specific to a particular genus/species of yeast. These methods are mostly used to identify wild yeast contaminants in brewing; large breweries may employ this particular technology as part of their quality assurance program.

Yeast Composition

Saccharomyces yeasts are mainly composed of carbohydrates, proteins, lipids, minerals, and DNA/RNA; the various proportions of these components will vary depending on growing conditions. Yeast also contains vitamins and spent yeast is commonly used for nutritional supplement. Each cell contains various organelles indispensable to yeast functions.

The nucleus contains the genetic information in the form of chromosomes. A haploid cell contains 16 chromosomes (one single copy of the genome) and in contrast brewer's yeasts are either polyploid (multiple copies of each chromosome) or aneuploid (different multiples of the various chromosomes). Because genes of importance are present in multiple copies in true brewing yeast strains, they are less susceptible to mutations when compared with a haploid yeast (also called "lab" yeast because of its use in research). This is relevant because brewer's yeast cultures are typically reused many times and therefore require extra protection against mutations and physiological changes. The yeast genome of a haploid strain of S. cerevisiae was published in 1996 and was the first eukaryote to be sequenced. This major step opened news avenues toward understanding yeast behavior and stress resistance, which is key to improving yeast efficiency in brewing.

Mitochondria are the sites of respiration, where most of the energy is produced when sugar levels are low and oxygen is present. Under anaerobiosis, promitochondria are present (a not fully developed form of the organelle) and they play an important role in fermentation and flavor outcome of the beer. Respiratory-deficient or "petite" mutants have been shown to produce elevated amounts of 4-vinyl guaiacol (clovelike flavors) and to exhibit aberrant flocculation and fermentation profiles. See FLOCCULATION and 4-VINYL GUAIACOL. Mitochondria and the nucleus both contain DNA, the composition of which is unique to each yeast strain. This represents a useful tool when looking at differentiating strains within a culture collection or for taxonomic purposes. Large breweries may use many different yeast strains in production; being able to identify and differentiate them all is an essential step to process control. Many smaller craft breweries also use many different yeast strains, but usually they do not have access to DNA profiling technology and therefore must rely on good practice to avoid cross-contaminations.

Also contained within the cytoplasm, vacuoles are present in various numbers depending on the growth phase and physiological condition of the yeast. They serve to store nutrients and also provide a site for the breakdown of macromolecules including proteins.

The plasma membrane of the yeast cell represents a barrier between the cytoplasm and the environment and regulates the exchange necessary for the cell to survive. It is composed of lipids and proteins; the lipid component of the membrane will be of importance for cell proliferation. Indeed, the concentration of sterols and unsaturated fatty acids will eventually dictate how many times yeast cells can divide. When depleted, oxygen will be needed to replenish the membranes to ensure further division. See AERATION. This is the reason chilled wort is oxygenated, so that the yeast can reproduce three or four times during the first hours of fermentation. Changes in lipid composition also regulate membrane fluidity and are triggered in response to changes in environment such as temperature or alcohol concentration. A yeast that has the ability to trigger membrane fluidity changes is more likely to be resistant to alcohol. It is therefore important to select the right strain depending on the type of beer to be produced.

In contrast to the plasma membrane, the cell wall is a rigid structure composed mainly of carbohydrates (glucans and mannans) and proteins (10%–20%), but it is not indispensible to the survival of the cell. Its primary role in brewing is flocculation, which is the result of interactions between cell wall proteins on one cell and carbohydrate residues on the other cell. Calcium is a necessary element for these connections. The process of flocculation is reversible and is an invaluable step for beer clarification and yeast repitching; however, some less flocculent strains can be desired for producing wheat beers, many of which are traditionally served with a yeast haze. Flocculation can also be assisted with the addition of specific process aids to encourage sedimentation and achieve beer clarification. See FININGS and FLOCCULATION.

Finally, the periplasm is the space between the plasma membrane and the cell wall. It is the location of specific enzymes including invertase, which breaks down sucrose to glucose and fructose units, which are then readily assimilated by the yeast. This enzyme is of little use in most brewing fermentations because brewer's wort is mainly composed of maltose, which is broken down inside the cells.

Ale and Lager Yeasts

From a brewing point of view, S. cerevisiae is more familiarly known as ale yeast or top-fermenting yeast. These yeast types have been known for thousands of years, although the nature of microorganisms was a mystery to ancient brewers 3,000 years ago. In contrast, the more recently domesticated lager yeast is a different species known as Saccharomyces pastorianus. It was recently found to be a natural hybrid of S. cerevisiae and Saccharomyces bayanus (a species sometimes used in winemaking). Taxonomists had previously identified the organism as being Saccharomyces carsbengensis, Saccharomyces uvarum, and even S. cerevisiae. Lager yeasts were first used by Bavarian brewers 200 years ago and rapidly made their way into breweries around the world to become by far the most used yeast in the brewing industry. See LAGER YEAST. Because of their relatively recent usage, lager yeasts are not as genetically diverse as ale yeasts and, as a consequence, lager beers tend to have a rather similar flavor profile when compared with the variety of ale yeasts found in breweries across the world. Yeast species other than S. cerevisiae and S. pastorianus have also been identified in most alcohol-producing processes. They are sometimes desired because they contribute to the quality and particularly to the taste and aroma of the final product. Brettanomyces species in particular have been used to produce beers such as sour ales and Belgian lambics. See BRETTANOMYCES, LAMBICS, and SOUR BEER. However, in most instances such yeasts are considered "contaminants" because they can affect fermentation performance and generate off-flavors. Contaminating yeast or "wild" yeast can be of either the Saccharomyces or the non-Sacharomyces genera. Among the Saccharomyces wild yeasts, Saccharomyces diastaticus is particularly undesirable because it has the ability to use some of the sugars that brewers yeast leave behind (dextrins), which contribute to the body of the beer. Among non-Saccharomyces wild yeast, those such as Pichia, Rhodotorula, Kluyveromyces, and Candida can negatively affect the quality of beer by causing haze or a film on the surface. Additionally, they may produce off-flavors such as diacetyl or phenolic compounds. See DIACETYL, PHENOLIC, and WILD YEAST. Microscopic examination can sometimes provide clues to the presence of contaminated yeast because they are smaller and/or different shapes than typical brewer's yeast. Otherwise, they can be detected using specific growth medium or genetic techniques.

Ale and lager yeast are easily differentiated from each other physiologically by their ability to use the disaccharide melibiose (lager yeast does use this sugar, but ale yeast does not), growth at temperature above 37°C (98.6°F; lager does not and ale does), and the ability of the yeast culture to rise (ale) or drop (lager) in the fermenter. The latter quality, however, is these days no longer strictly true because the use of cyclindroconical vessels has encouraged selection of ale yeasts that flocculate to the bottom of the tank, easing their reuse. Beyond the differentiation of ale and lager yeast it is possible to distinguish individual strains based on their unique DNA sequence. Genetic techniques have been developed to obtain DNA profiles for each strain; these are unique and easily differentiated.

Propagation and Fermentation

Ale and lager yeast can grow aerobically and anaerobically. In the presence of oxygen, cells are encouraged to divide and produce biomass instead of alcohol. However, this is only strictly true if the sugar concentration is kept below a level of 0.2 g/L. Once the level of sugar is higher than 0.2 g/L, yeast will produce alcohol regardless of the presence of oxygen—this has been defined as the Crabtree effect. In breweries propagation (biomass production) is usually conducted in low-gravity worts in the presence of oxygen. In sophisticated yeast propagation systems, oxygen will be introduced and sugars will be continuously fed at very low concentrations. Cell division will occur with low alcohol production and prepare the cells for fermentation conditions. During the first few hours of fermentation, when the yeast cells are under aerobic conditions, they divide and produce ethanol simultaneously. Once the oxygen is exhausted, the yeast enters an anaerobic environment and will keep producing ethanol at a slower rate. Beside ethanol, yeast will produce other by-products that will impact on beer flavor and aroma. Higher alcohols, esters, sulfur compounds, or vicinal diketones are all produced as a result of yeast metabolism and their concentration can be modulated by influencing parameters such as temperature, pitching rate, aeration, or pressure. See ESTERS, FUSEL ALCOHOLS, and VICINAL DIKETONES.

Yeast Growth

When cells grow, they undergo an asymmetric form of cell division called "budding" and go through a cell cycle to generate a new cell. When the conditions are adequate, a mother cell gives rise to a daughter cell (called a "virgin" cell) and becomes itself a generation older. This implies that a yeast culture always contain 50% virgin cells, 25% generation 1 cells, 12.5% generation 2 cells, etc. The average age of a yeast culture is therefore very young. This means that theoretically a yeast culture could be used indefinitely. The reality is quite different;

despite maintaining a young age status, yeast cells accumulate stress and are exposed to mutations. To avoid genetic and behavioral changes new yeast is usually reintroduced regularly. The form of aging focusing on cell division is referred to as *replicative* and is not to be confused with *chronological* aging, which represents the time-related age of a culture (days, weeks, etc). The age of a culture also refers to the number of times the yeast has been used (repitched) for fermentation.

Yeast Division and Storage

The division of a yeast cell or cell cycle is genetically programmed and influenced by environmental factors. A culture contains cells of different stages of the cell cycle. The first phase of the cycle is a rest phase called G_1 where no budding occurs. Toward the end of G_1 the keypoint "START" senses that the environment and the cell itself are adequate for division and allow entrance into the reproductive cycle and DNA synthesis. The bud starts to emerge before reaching another rest phase, G_2. Past G_2, mitosis will then take place and nuclear division will occur. The last step is the cytokinesis where the daughter and mother cells physically separate. The separation process leaves a bud scar on the mother cell and a birth scar on the daughter cell. Both types of scars are composed of chitin and can be easily visualized using the fluorescent dyes calcofluor or wheat-germ agglutinin in combination with a fluorescent microscope. A single cell is able to accumulate many bud scars on its surface, each the result of the birth of a daughter. Realistically, under brewing conditions a cell is likely to die of stress before it reaches its genetically determined division potential. When cells are dormant (reversible nondividing state or stationary phase), they enter a G_0 phase until the conditions are again suitable to pass START. Cells can survive for long periods of time in the G_0 state but will deteriorate with time. A yeast culture in storage between brews will contain cells in G_0 phase. When pitched into a new wort for fermentation, the cells will re-enter the cell cycle until a growth-limiting factor will again arrest cell division. When repitching yeast, cells consistently enter and exit the cell cycle; when damages occur as a result of accumulated stress, they may become permanently deactivated and eventually die, hence the need to constantly grow new yeast cultures.

Yeast Maintenance

After a determined number of repitchings, new yeast should be used, either obtained in a dry form or propagated by a third party or in-house. See YEAST BANK. Propagations are typically started from a stock culture. Yeast stocks should be kept at cold temperatures to maintain the integrity of the DNA through time; spontaneous mutations do occur and can affect the characteristics and performance of yeast. To protect yeast strains against mutation for a long period of time, cryopreservation is recommended, with the safest method being storage in the gas phase of liquid nitrogen in a specific container. Working stocks can be maintained frozen at –80°C for long-term storage. Agar slants may be kept at 4°C (39°F); however, this is only for short-term storage because there is a higher risk of mutation and contamination. The number of times a yeast culture can be reused depends on numerous factors; however, it is well documented that cultures should be replaced regularly to ensure fermentation performance and consistency. Although this is the norm, there are exceptions, and some breweries have been reported to have used a single yeast culture for years or even decades without notable mutation of loss of vitality. The genetic stability of the strain used, hygiene process, brewing frequency and schedule, the yeast maintenance program, and type of beer produced will eventually determine how many times a particular yeast culture can be repitched.

Boulton, Chris, and David Quain. *Brewing yeast and fermentation*. Oxford, UK: Blackwell Science Publications, 2001.

Gibson, B. R., S. J. Lawrence, J. P. Leclaire, C. D. Powell, and K. A. Smart. Yeast responses to stresses associated with industrial brewery handling. *FEMS Microbiology Reviews* 31 (2007): 535–69.

Powell, Chris D., and Andrew N. Diacetis. Long term serial repitching and the genetic and phenotypic stability of brewer's yeast. *Journal of the Institute of Brewing* 113 (2007): 67–74.

Rose, Anthony H., and J. Stewart Harrison. *The yeasts*, 2nd ed. London: Academic Press, 1993.

Verstrepen, K. J., G. Derdelinckx, H. Verachtert, and F. R. Delvaux. Yeast flocculation: What brewers should know. *Applied Microbiology and Biotechnology* 61 (2003): 197–205.

White, Chris, and Jamil Zainasheff. *Yeast: The practical guide to yeast fermentation*. Boulder, CO: Brewers Publications, 2010.

Sylvie Van Zandycke

yeast bank, a term referring either to a collection of yeast cultures (culture collection) or to an entity that holds a culture collection. A yeast bank can be held at a university, at a private company, or by individuals. Yeast banks exist throughout the world. The yeast may be stored for scientific purposes, commercial applications, or food and agricultural applications.

The yeast cultures stored in a yeast bank are usually purified yeast cultures. Yeast was first purified by Emil Christian Hansen in 1883. See HANSEN, EMIL CHRISTIAN. Once yeast was in pure form, laboratories started keeping a bank of strains and supplying them to breweries. In 1885, the Scientific Station for Brewing in Munich reported distributing 107 cultures to breweries. Today, it is possible for brewers, both amateur and professionals, to order yeast from yeast banks and have it shipped worldwide in various forms.

Yeast can be stored in a yeast bank in a number of ways. One of the earliest methods, still in use today, is to store yeast on agar plates or slants (slopes); these are then subcultured every 3–6 months to maintain viability. This method is not the best for long-term storage of the overall yeast bank, because yeast will mutate over time. Some yeast banks store their yeast in freeze-dried format, but this is less common because of reports of low viability, flocculation changes, and mutation. The most common way yeast is stored in a yeast bank is to deep freeze the cultures at either –80°C (ultrafreezers) or –196°C (liquid nitrogen).

Boulton, C., and D. Quain. *Brewing yeast and fermentation.* Oxford, England: Blackwell Science Ltd, 2001.

Laufer, S., and R. Schwarz. *Yeast fermentation and pure culture systems.* New York: Schwarz Laboratories, 1936.

Chris White

yeast, dry

See DRY YEAST.

yeast nutrients are compounds and elements that are essential to vigorous yeast health and viability. Brewers must ensure optimum yeast health to avoid slow or stuck fermentations, off-flavors, and other problems with beer. The key yeast nutrients are carbohydrates, amino acids, vitamins, and minerals. Malted barley naturally contains a balanced set of these, but high-gravity worts, especially those containing high levels of adjuncts in the form of refined sugars, may not be properly balanced, and yeast performance in these environments may be sluggish. Yeast cultures that have been repitched many times may be particularly prone to inefficient uptakes of nutrients, especially in demanding environments. Many fermentations can be aided by the addition of yeast nutrient preparations, even in all-malt worts. Simple carbohydrates such as glucose, fructose, sucrose, and maltose and often maltotriose are easily metabolized by brewer's yeast. Yeast cannot, however, assimilate higher polysaccharides (namely dextrins). Therefore, these stay in the finished beer. Amino acids, also referred as free amino nitrogen (FAN), are the yeast's main nitrogen source, whereas yeast cannot metabolize peptides and proteins. FAN is incorporated into new yeast proteins but the FAN levels influence the yeast's fermentation performance. Especially for beers with high levels of alcohol, judicious additions of a nitrogen source may be indicated. Vitamins such as biotin, panthotenic acid, thiamine, and inositol are essential for enzyme function and yeast growth. Minerals including phosphate, potassium, calcium, magnesium, and especially zinc are crucial to yeast health and thus successful fermentations. Zinc can be deficient even in all-malt worts, because most of it tends to be lost during lautering. Extra zinc can be added in mineral form ($ZnSO_4$ or $ZnCl_2$), or it can be incorporated in inactive yeast for a more complete nutritional product. German brewers technically adhering to the Reinheitsgebot, which does not allow the addition of mineral salts, have found many ingenious ways to ensure that their yeast gets the zinc it needs. These range from zinc fittings inside the kettle or lauter tun, zinc chains attached to the paddles in the mash mixer, or the old brewer's trick of adding some live yeast to the kettle. Sometimes a block of zinc is simply hidden at the brewery; shavings will occasionally be taken from it. Weissbier fermentations are particularly susceptible to zinc deficiencies because wheat is rich in manganese, which can block zinc uptake by yeast cells. Finally, yeast needs oxygen to synthesize sterols and unsaturated fatty acids in the yeast cell membrane. This, in turn, allows for ample cell divisions during the yeast's aerobic phase. Yeast nutrients, judiciously applied, can speed fermentations and promote better attenuation, better flocculation, better yeast storage capability, and better overall beer flavor. As such they have become a standard part of the brewer's husbandry of yeast.

See also AMINO ACIDS, CARBOHYDRATES, NITROGEN, and OXYGEN.

Fischborn, T., J. McLaren, E. Geiger, F. Briem, K. Glas, and J. Englmann. Servomyces—A biological nutrient. *Technical Quarterly of the Master Brewers Association of the Americas* 41 (2004): 366–70.

Van Zandycke, S., and T. Fischborn. The impact of yeast nutrients on fermentation performance and beer quality. *Technical Quarterly of the Master Brewers Association of the Americas* 45 (2008): 290–93.

Sylvie Van Zandycke

yield is a measure of the amount of a raw material that survives a process as a percentage of the amount of that same raw material used as input into that process. Two important yields that brewers are concerned with are brewing material efficiency (BME) and hop utilization. See HOP UTILIZATION. BME is a measure of the amount of extract that is actually delivered to the fermenter compared to the amount of extract that is theoretically extractable from the grist. Most breweries aim for a BME in the mid- to upper-ninety percent range. Hop utilization is a measure of the amount of bitterness, as measured in International Bitterness Units (ppm of iso-alpha acid), contained in the beer versus the amount of alpha acids of the raw hops that was added to the kettle. See INTERNATIONAL BITTERNESS UNITS (IBUS). Hop utilization rates vary widely as a result of many factors, including variations in kettle boils, hop products, yeasts, and fermentation performance. Process consistency is the key for any given brewery to maximize its yields.

Downstream from the brewhouse, yield is often measured in terms of beer loss, which is often expressed in terms of extract rather than raw volume losses, because this removes the variable of concentration and/or dilution from the equation. In most breweries, beer losses are measured and tracked for each step of the beer-making process, rather than simply as the amount brewed versus the amount packaged. At the packaging line, too, yield is measured as beer loss.

Gebauer, E. A European approach to brewhouse yield. *MBAA Technical Quarterly* 5(1) (1968): 94–9.

Lieberman, C. E. Control of brewing processing losses. *MBAA Technical Quarterly* 13(1) (1976): 44–50.

Jim Kuhr

Yorkshire square is a unique fermenting vessel that originated in the north of England. The vessels were originally made of stone, followed by slate, and modern vessels are made of stainless steel. They are cubic in shape and were originally quite small (50 hl) but modern squares can be 250–300 hl in size. The vessel is specially designed to assist in yeast collection. The vessels have a lower compartment that is separated from an upper deck with a 1-meter wide hole in the center. A highly flocculant, top-fermenting yeast is used to ferment the ale style and the fermenting wort is occasionally roused (circulated by pump) from the lower to upper deck to keep the fermentation going and yeast in suspension. See FLOCCULATION. During fermentation, yeast foam wells up through the hole onto the upper deck where it remains; beer retained in the yeast separates from the foam and runs back into a pipe that runs from the upper deck through to the bottom of the vessel below. Because of its appearance, this pipe is referred to as the "organ pipe." At the end of fermentation the rousing is stopped and fresh yeast is skimmed from the upper deck. The Samuel Smith's Brewery of Tadcaster still uses the Yorkshire square system and the Black Sheep Brewery in Masham adopted this classic fermentation system when they started up in 1991. Tetley's Cask Bitter was a well-known ale fermented in these vessels. The system is now rare, but beers fermented in Yorkshire squares are said to be full bodied and often fruity in character.

Paul KA Buttrick

Young's Brewery. Young's is an iconic, much-loved London beer brand.

Charles Allen Young and his business partner took over the Ram Brewery in the London district of Wandsworth in 1831. The Ram was reputedly Britain's oldest brewing site in continuous operation, with a history dating back to the 1550s.

The brewery stayed within the Young family for its entire existence. In the 1970s chairman John Young,

Charles' great-great-grandson, stuck resolutely to his traditional beliefs and insisted that the brewery should continue to brew cask-conditioned ales even as many of his peers were moving to pasteurized and filtered keg products. He was widely derided for his decision at the time, but was proven right by the real ale revolution he helped create. See REAL ALE.

Over the decades, Wandsworth grew around the Young's Brewery until the brewery was essentially right in the middle of the town. Although the brewery was successful, the land on which it sat became very valuable, and eventually shareholders could no longer resist the allure of offers. In 2006 Young's closed the Ram Brewery and moved its brewing operations to a joint venture with Charles Wells of Bedford. Young's continued to run an estate of around 200 pubs as a separate company. In September 2006, as the Ram Brewery's final brew before closure was running, its flamboyant chairman died at age 85.

Diehard Young's devotees had decided the beers were not as good as they used to be before brewing had even commenced at their new home. But Young's remains a source of classic and widely respected traditional beers.

Young's Bitter, affectionately known as "Ordinary," is a light, hoppy session pint at 3.8% ABV. Young's Special London Ale is particularly notable as traditional, full-bodied IPA with a cult following.

Pete Brown

yucca

See MANIOC.

Yuengling, David G., (1808–77) founded the Eagle Brewery in 1829, which was later renamed D. G. Yuengling & Son, currently the oldest brewery in the United States.

David Gottlob Yuengling's birth name was Jüngling, but he anglicized it to Yuengling after emigrating to the United Stated in 1823 from his home in Aldingen, Germany. Aldingen is a small town located in Baden-Württemberg, in the southwest corner of Germany. He is believed to have been trained as a brewer before embarking for America when he was 25 years old.

After spending at least his first year in America in Reading and Lancaster, Pennsylvania, he eventually settled farther north in the coal regions of Schuylkill County in the town of Pottsville. There, he founded the Eagle Brewery on Centre Street in 1829, only to see it burn to the ground 2 years later. A second brewery was then built at the present site on Mahantongo Street.

Yuengling's son Frederick joined his father at the brewery in 1873 and the name was changed to D. G. Yuengling & Son. Frederick was succeeded by his son, Frank, and in 1963, Frank's sons Richard L. Yuengling and F. Dohrman Yuengling assumed the helm. In 1985, fifth-generation Richard L. Yuengling Jr bought the brewery from his father. Richard "Dick" Yuengling is the current (2010) president and owner. Dick Yuengling has four daughters, Jennifer, Sheryl, Wendy, and Deborah—and they all work at the Yuengling Brewery.

Jay R. Brooks

Zastrow, Klaus, Dr, a native of Berlin, Germany, is a retired brewmaster who spent most of his career with Anheuser-Busch. Zastrow began his brewing career in 1949 as an apprentice at the Englehardt Brauerei in Berlin. He then worked at several other breweries and malt houses in Germany and Switzerland, including Spaten Brauerei and Kronenburg Brauerei. He graduated as a certified brewery engineer from the Technical University in Berlin and earned his PhD in agricultural science from the university in 1963.

He then joined the staff of Anheuser-Busch as a brewing technologist and scientific advisor to the senior vice president of brewing. Later, he spent 15 years as vice president for brewing technical services, where he was responsible for applied brewing research, product development, serving as a liaison for international, government, and legal affairs, and plant protection for raw materials.

Upon his retirement from the company in 1993 he became an instructor for the Budweiser Mobile Beer Schools and worked as a primary instructor for the Budweiser Beer School (a promotional program featuring a short class designed to teach members of the general public the basics of beer production and tasting), where he was responsible for both conducting and coordinating activities related to the program. Greatly admired and respected in the brewing world, he is the author of several scientific papers and was a sought-after lecturer because of his extensive brewing knowledge and innovation in the field.

Zastrow is also a member of the extended faculty for the Siebel Institute of Technology and serves as an independent consultant in the brewing industry. See also SIEBEL INSTITUTE OF TECHNOLOGY.

Official Archives and Biographies from Anheuser-Busch. 1985, 2004.

John Holl and Wolfgang David Lindell

Žatec hop

See SAAZ (HOP).

Žatec hop region is the main hop-growing region of the Czech Republic. It is centered on the town of Žatec near the western border of the country. This is also the origin of what may be the world's most prestigious hop, Saaz. See CZECH REPUBLIC and SAAZ HOP. There are two other hop-producing regions in the Czech Republic, Trschitz and Auscha, both of which also grow Saaz (also known as Saazer); however, combined they are less than half the size of Žatec. Hop cultivation in Žatec probably goes back 1,000 years, but it did not become a center of world production until the 15th and 16th centuries, when many of the area's small hop centers were granted the right to use a "hop seal" to guard against fraud and forgeries in the trade. See HOP SEAL. These seals evolved into the Žatec seal that is still in use today. Before World War II, hop farming was a business consisting of many small, family-owned farms, similar to those in Germany. See HALLERTAU HOP REGION. After the war, however, the communist Czechoslovak regime confiscated all private farms and merged them into very large collective farms the size of present-day American hop farms (about 200 ha/500 acres).

With the return of private enterprise, however, these farms were broken up again, but not into the mosaic of small plots that existed in days past. Hop research activity in the region dates as far back as 1925, and a state-sponsored Hop Research Institute was founded in 1950. After the fall of communism, this became the Hop Research Institute Co Ltd. The institute researches and promotes agricultural practices, breeds new hop varieties, and has become one of the world's leading hop research centers. See PREMIANT (HOP) and SLÁDEK (HOP).

Val Peacock

Zentner is a German unit of mass related to the Latin *centum* (hundred) and *centeni* (per hundred). Although the measure has generally fallen into disuse, it is still sometimes used to express large weights relating to hop crops. The abbreviation for Zentner is "Ztr." Over time, Zentner has denoted various quantities, mostly defined as 100 German pounds ("Pfund" in German), which, in turn was not itself a uniform quantity. In 1833, however, members of the *Zollverein* (German Customs Union) agreed to standardize all units of measurements, and they set 1 German pound to be equal to 500 grams, and 1 Zentner to be 50 kilograms. But these designations applied to Germany only. Pounds in other systems remained different. One "avoirdupois pound," for instance, which is a measure invented by London merchants in 1303 and is still the pound in use today in the United States, is 453.5924 grams; while 1 troy pound, a French measure from medieval times and now used mainly to weight precious metals, is 373.2417 grams. The Zentner, too, had a different meaning outside Germany. In Austria and Switzerland, for instance, 1 Zentner is still considered the equivalent of 100 kilograms, that is, the Austrian/Swiss Zentner is twice as heavy as a German Zentner. In Germany, there is also a Doppelzentner (double Zentner). Its abbreviation is "dz," and it means 100 kilograms. Confusingly, therefore, one German Doppelzentner is one Swiss or Austrian Zentner.

Wolfgang David Lindell

Zeus (hop)

See CTZ (HOP).

zinc is a key component at the active site of several yeast enzymes, most notably alcohol dehydrogenase. In most worts the zinc content is relatively low and therefore many brewers add it (typically at 0.2 ppm) to stimulate fermentation. Some options for the brewer to enhance the zinc content in wort are as follows:

Adding zinc salts to the boiling wort
Using zinc-enriched yeast
Incorporating zinc plates into the wort kettle

Zinc at higher levels (e.g., 2 ppm) is very beneficial to beer foam stability and cling, probably through an involvement in the bridging of hydrophobic polypeptides with iso-alpha acids. See CLING. Many so-called yeast nutrients are zinc-based preparations. Amusingly, many German breweries, forbidden by the Reinheitsgebot to add zinc to their worts, nonetheless have strategies for introducing it. These range from attaching zinc chains to the blades of the mash mixer to hiding a pure block of zinc somewhere within the brewery and shaving bits off of it when needed to aid fermentations.

Zinc is also beneficial for the human body and is used in many medications. One of the richest stores of zinc in the body is the prostate gland.

Charles W. Bamforth

Zymomonas is a Gram-negative beer-spoilage bacterium. It has a notorious legacy as a historic contaminant of breweries. Zymomonas bacteria are similar to Gluconobacter and are distinguished by their short rods and very active polar flagellae. These give the cells a strong motility indicated by their rapid movement under a microscope. This bacterium is distinctive in that it can ferment glucose, fructose, and sucrose—as can brewers yeasts—but it cannot ferment maltose. Also like yeast, it produces ethanol and carbon dioxide, but at a more efficient rate. However, its fermentation by-products include acetaldehyde as well as hydrogen sulphide, which is rapidly converted into objectionable vegetal flavors. Zymomonas is also resistant to acidic conditions and may thrive together with acetic acid bacteria. A Zymomonas infection can therefore result in a very sour beer. Because Zymomonas does not flourish in a habitat with high levels of maltose, it does not grow well in wort.

As soon as yeast has converted maltose into alcohol, however, Zymomonas can become a problem and spread quickly. This is why in the 1950s and 1960s, when the priming of cask-conditioned ales with glucose or sucrose was fairly common in the UK, outbreaks of Zymomonas in a brewery were common, too—a problem that may have hastened the decline of cask beer and the general shift to filtered kegged beer. Once Zymomonas has colonized brewery equipment, it is difficult to eradicate. Sometimes contaminated equipment even needs to be replaced. Today, Zymomonas has become relatively rare in breweries, mostly because of much improved hygiene management and because priming with sugars is rarely employed nowadays. Zymomonas has one promising modern application, though: Its efficient production of ethanol makes it highly valuable in the manufacture of bioethanol and other chemical products.

"Zymomonas." In *Brewing microbiology*, 3rd ed., eds. F. G. Priest and I. Campbell, 233–35. New York: Kluwer Academic/Plenum, 2003.

Keith Thomas

zymurgical heraldry, or the heraldry of beer and brewing, is a common yet underappreciated facet of beer-related art and labeling. Many beers and breweries incorporate heraldic badges and coats of arms as a part of their identities. Logos and trademarks are essentially the modern counterparts of coats of arms, although the former are used to identify beers on store shelves as opposed to warriors on the field of battle.

Often these coats of arms reveal the location where the beer is produced. The use of civic or civic-derived arms is one of the most prevalent forms of zymurgical heraldry. Just as European wines such as Bordeaux and Champagne are associated with specific regions, beers are also associated with places. For example, the pilsner style of beer was originally developed in Pilsen (Plzeň), Bohemia (modern-day Czech Republic). The label on bottles of Pilsner Urquell (the original pilsner beer brewed by Plzeňský Prazdroj, now part of the SABMiller group of companies), displays the coat of arms of the city of Pilsen.

Another Czech city with beers named after it is Budweis (České Budějovice). The Budweiser Budvar (Budějovický Budvar) Brewery produces a brand of beer known as Budweiser Budvar in the European Union; for legal reasons this beer is called Czechvar in the United States and Canada. The label on bottles of this beer shows the coat of arms of the city of Budweis, the city gates behind a shield with the double-tailed lion of the Kingdom of Bohemia.

Another example of civic arms (albeit with slight modification) is found on the label of Beck's beer. Beck's beer (produced by Brauerei Beck & Co., part of Anheuser-Busch InBev) is brewed in Bremen, Germany, and features a coat of arms with a silver key (the so-called Bremen key) on a red background in mirror image to the coat of arms of the city of Bremen. The Beck's coat of arms also functions as a registered trademark.

In recognition of the beer's origins, companies also take local historical arms, modify those arms, and add elements relevant to the business. The arms associated with the Christoffel brand of beer (brewed by the Bierbrouwerij St Christoffel of the Netherlands) are one example of the use of civic-derived heraldry. The arms are based on those of the Dutch town of Roermond where the brewery is located. The brewery's version has different tinctures (colors) on each of the shield's divisions, with hops and grains adding a distinctive beer-themed background. Barley and hops, of course, are ubiquitous symbols in the industry. It is not necessary that the proper heraldic tinctures be followed, only that the modified arms are distinct and recognizable.

In addition to civic and civic-derived arms, personal arms can also be found on beer labels. One example is Morocco ale brewed by Daleside Brewery in England. Daleside brews the beer on behalf of Levens Hall in Westmoreland. The goat's-head crest that dominates the label is that of the current owners of Levens Hall, the Bagot family.

Royal arms are also found on beer labels. Blanche de Chambly is produced by the Unibroue Brewery in Quebec, Canada. In this example, the arms on the label, three gold fleurs-de-lis on a blue background, are those of the Kingdom of France, a nod to the historical origins of the province.

Another example is found on the bottle of Organic English ale brewed for Duchy Originals Limited, established in 1990 to promote organic food and farming by HRH The Prince of Wales,

Left: The coat of arms of the Dutch municipality of Roermond. *Right*: The Christoffel Bier logo, based on the coat of arms of the Dutch town of Roermond, where the brewery is located. COURTESY OF CHRISTOFFEL BIER

who is also the present Duke of Cornwall. The label of Organic English ale bears the Arms of the Duke of Cornwall. A small shield bearing these arms appears on the Prince of Wales' heraldic achievement below the main shield. Also found on the label is the Prince's badge, which has been used in royal heraldry since the 14th century.

Whether establishing associations with a person or place, emphasizing a historical connection, or simply being used as a modern marketing tool, the heraldry of beer and brewing continues to be a relevant means of identity for today's brewers. A look through late beer writer Michael Jackson's *Great Beer Guide* (2000) illustrates this clearly; of the 500 beers featured in the book, approximately 20% of the labels display coats of arms.

Jackson, Michael. *Michael Jackson's great beer guide*. UK: Dorling Kindersley, 2000.

David L. Smisek

zymurgy is the chemistry and science of fermentation by yeast. Coined in the mid-19th century, the word fuses the Greek "zymo" (leaven) with the suffix "urgy," meaning "work." The word, which is alternatively rendered as "zymology," follows the pattern of the word "metallurgy." It is the last word in many English language dictionaries and is used more often to describe brewing than to describe winemaking or distilling. In recent years the word has been popularized by *Zymurgy*, a magazine for amateur brewers first published by the American Homebrewers Association in 1978.

See also AMERICAN HOMEBREWERS ASSOCIATION (AHA).

Amercian Homebrewers Association. *Zymurgy*. Journal of the American Homebrewers Association. http://www.homebrewersassociation.org/pages/zymurgy (accessed February 16, 2011).

Garrett Oliver

ABBREVIATIONS

ABV	Alcohol by Volume
ASBC	American Society of Brewing Chemists
AE	Apparent Extract
BA	Brewers Association
°P	Degrees Plato
DP	Diastatic Power
DE	Diatomaceous Earth
EBC	European Brewer's Convention
FMB	Flavored Malt Beverage
GABF	Great American Beer Festival
GBBF	Great British Beer Festival
IPA	India Pale Ale
IBD	The Institute of Brewing and Distilling
IBU	International Bitterness Unit
LME	Liquid Malt Extract
MBAA	Master Brewers Association of the Americas
MT	Metric Tons
OG	Original Gravity
PPM	Parts per Million
SRM	Standard Reference Method

Please note that wort and beer gravities are rendered in degrees Plato (°P), which is the standard scale used in most of the world. Brewers in the UK and many amateur brewers use the specific gravity scale. For an approximate conversion from °Plato to specific gravity, multiply °P × 4 and add 1,000. For example: 15 °P × 4 = 60 + 1,000 = specific gravity of 1,060 (sometimes rendered as 1.060).

CONVERSION FACTOR

To Convert	*Multiply by*
Acres to hectares	0.405
Atmospheres to pounds per square inch	14.7
Beer barrels to cubic feet	4.144
Beer barrels to gallons (US)	31.0
Beer barrels to hectoliters	1.1734
Beer barrels (US) to barrels (Imp)	0.728
Beer barrels (Imp) to barrels (US)	1.373
Beer barrels (Imp) to gallons (Imp)	36.0
Beer barrels (US) to gallons (Imp)	26.23
Beer barrels (Imp) to gallons (US)	43.23
Fluid ounces (Imp) to liters	0.0208
Fluid ounces (US) to liters	0.0296
Gallons (US) to beer barrels	0.0323
Gallons (Imp) to liters	4.546
Gallons (US) to liters	3.7853
Gallons (Imp) to gallons (US)	1.2009
Gallons (US) to gallons (Imp)	0.8327
Gallons (Imp) to ounces (Imp)	160.00
Gallons (Imp) to ounces (US)	153.72
Gallons (US) to ounces (US)	128.0
Grams to ounces	0.0353
Grams to pounds	0.0022
Hectares to acres	2.471
Hectoliters to beer barrels (US)	0.8522
Hectoliters to liters	100.00

To Convert	*Multiply by*
Kilograms per square centimeters to atmospheres	0.96
Kilograms per square centimeters to pounds per square inch	14.22
Kilograms to ounces	35.27
Kilograms to pounds	2.204
Liters to fluid ounces (Imp)	35.196
Liters to fluid ounces (US)	33.814
Liters to gallons (Imp)	0.2199
Liters to gallons (US)	0.2642
Liters to hectoliters	0.01
Liters to pints (Imp)	1.7598
Liters to pints (US)	2.1134
Liters to quarts (Imp)	0.8779
Liters to quarts (US)	1.0567
Milliliters to ounces (Imp)	0.0352
Milliliters to ounces (US)	0.0338
Ounces (Imp) to gallons (Imp)	0.0063
Ounces (US) to gallons (US)	0.0078
Ounces (US) to liters	0.0295
Ounces (Imp) to milliliters	28.41
Ounces (US) to milliliters	29.57
Ounces (Imp) to ounces (US)	0.960
Ounces (US) to ounces (Imp)	1.041
Ounces (US) to kilograms	0.0284

To Convert	Multiply by
Parts per million oxygen to milliliters air per ounce (Imp)	0.0993
Parts per million oxygen to milliliters air per ounce (US)	0.1034
Parts per million oxygen to milliliters oxygen per ounce (Imp)	0.0199
Parts per million oxygen to milliliters oxygen per ounce (US)	0.0207
Pints (Imp) to liters	0.568
Pints (US) to liters	0.4732
Pints (US) to pints (Imp)	1.20009
Pints (Imp) to pints (US)	0.8327
Pounds to grams	453.6
Pounds to kilograms	0.45
Pounds to ounces	16.0
Pounds per square inch to atmospheres	0.068
Pounds per square inch to kilograms per square centimeter	0.0703
Quarts (Imp) to liters	1.1365
Quarts (US) to liters	0.946
Tons, metric to kilograms	1000
Tons, metric to pounds	22204.62
Liters of carbon dioxide to grams of carbon dioxide	1.976
Percentage of carbon dioxide by volume to percentage of carbon dioxide by weight	0.1943
Percentage of carbon dioxide by weight to percentage of carbon dioxide by volume	5.1470

Excerpted with the permission of the Master Brewers Association of the Americas from *The Practical Brewer*, 3rd ed., 1999. Originally compiled by the late Dr William C. Cooper and first appeared in *Brewers Digest*, October 1976.

APPENDIXES

BEER ORGANIZATIONS AND ENTHUSIAST CLUBS

Wherever in the world beer is produced there are organized alliances actively advocating for its promotion and appreciation, and the protection of its consumers and producers. Professional brewers from nations across the globe, as well as individual states in the United States, have formed associations to reinforce the political and economic integrity of their trade, as well as to promote social and environmental responsibility; consumer organizations have been formed to ensure product integrity, preserve brewing history and traditions, and promote new products; various enthusiast clubs demonstrate appreciation and preservation by producing events including festivals and competitions, sharing and studying homebrewed beer, and collecting various breweriana. Below is a sampling of associations, societies, and guilds fortified by beer.

American Breweriana Association
Collectors club and "historical corporation" founded in 1982 with almost 3,000 members worldwide.

http://www.americanbreweriana.org/

American Homebrewers Association
Amateur brewing organization with 19,000 members, publisher of the bimonthly magazine *Zymurgy* and producer of the National Homebrewers Conference (San Diego, CA).

http://www.homebrewersassociation.org/

American Malting Barley Association
Organization aiming to support barley production and research, and advocate for the malting industry.

http://www.ambainc.org/

American Society of Brewing Chemists
Association aiming to "improve and bring uniformity to the brewing industry on a technical level" since 1932.

http://www.asbcnet.org/

Beer Institute
Organization representing the US beer industry at federal, state, and community sectors since 1986.

http://www.beerinstitute.org/

Belgian Brewers Association
Described as "one of the oldest professional associations in the world," protects the legal, economic, and social interests of Belgian brewers.

http://www.beerparadise.be/

Brewers Association
Founded in 1942, with a present membership of more than 1,000 US breweries dedicated to "promote and protect small and independent American brewers, their craft beers and the community of brewing enthusiasts." Producer of The Great American Beer Festival (Denver, CO), World Beer Cup international beer competition, Craft Brewers Conference, and the "Support Your Local Brewery" campaign (http://www.sylb.org/).

http://www.brewersassociation.org/

Brewers Association of Canada
Organization of Canadian breweries founded in 1934 aimed to "progressively improve the marketplace for beer while encouraging the responsible use of beer and the protection of the environment."

http://www.brewers.ca/

Brewers Association of Japan
Founded in 1953, organization monitoring fair competition, advocating for reduced taxes, promoting responsible drinking, and facilitating research.

http://www.brewers.or.jp/english/index.html/

Brewers Guild of New Zealand
Association that "represents the interests of the brewing industry" in New Zealand through political and social activities.
http://brewersguild.org.nz/

Brewers of Europe
"To equip Europe's brewers with the tools to freely, cost-effectively and responsibly brew and market beer" since 1958, members comprise brewers associations from over 20 countries in Europe, including Portugal, Hungary, Italy, Turkey, Belgium, France, Romania, England, Denmark, Spain, Cyprus, Czech Republic, Germany, Luxembourg, Greece, Lithuania, the Netherlands, Norway, Finland, Slovakia, Sweden, Switzerland, Ireland, Malta, Poland, Bulgaria, and Austria. Coordinator of the European Brewery Convention.
http://www.brewersofeurope.org/

Brewery Collectibles Club of America
Members club since 1970 dedicated to the collection of beer cans and various breweriana. Publisher of the bimonthly *Beer Cans & Brewery Collectibles* magazine.
http://www.bcca.com/

The Brewery History Society
Founded in 1972, acting as "the society for all who are interested in the history of British breweries" and brewing history.
http://breweryhistory.com/

British Beer and Pub Association
Organization advocating for UK beer and pubs with an extensive membership consisting of brewery and pub owners.
http://www.beerandpub.com/

British Beermat Collectors Society
Since 1960, club dedicated to collecting coasters, consisting of self-described "tegestologists," from the Latin "teg" meaning small rug or mat.
http://www.britishbeermats.org.uk/

Campaign for Real Ale
With over 100,000 members, "CAMRA promotes good-quality real ale and pubs, as well as acting as the consumer's champion in relation to the UK and European beer and drinks industry." Publisher of the annual *Good Beer Guide*, quarterly *BEER Magazine*, and monthly *What's Brewing* newspaper.
http://www.camra.org.uk/

Chicago Beer Society
A "nonprofit educational association dedicated to the appreciation of beer" run by volunteers since 1977.
http://chibeer.org/

Craft Brewing Association
Considered by CAMRA to be "the UK's national homebrewing organization," promoting homebrewing with events and publishing the *Brewer's Contact* amateur brewing magazine.
http://www.craftbrewing.org.uk/

Danish Beer Enthusiasts
National association supporting Danish breweries and beer, advocating homebrewing, and promoting the history of beer in Denmark.
http://www.ale.dk/

Durden Park Beer Circle
Club founded in 1971 that researches and reproduces historical British beers, as well as "quality beers of any type."
http://www.durdenparkbeer.org.uk/

European Beer Consumers Union
Organization with members including associations from a dozen nations that protects the beer culture of Europe, promotes traditional European beers and breweries, and represents consumer demands. Represented countries include Switzerland, Austria, Poland, the United Kingdom, Denmark, Norway, Finland, Czech Republic, Sweden, Italy, the Netherlands, and Belgium.
http://www.ebcu.org/

German Hop Growers Association
Organization advocating for the interests of German hop producers for more than 125 years. Publishes the monthly *Hopfen-Rundschau* magazine.
http://www.deutscher-hopfen.de/

Hop Growers of America
Association of hop producers that "represents and promotes the interests of US growers both domestically and internationally."
http://www.usahops.org/

Institute of Brewing & Distilling
Founded in 1886, a non-profit organization dedicated to "the advancement of education and professional development in the science and technologies of brewing, distilling and related industries."
http://www.ibd.org.uk/

Japan Craft Beer Association

Organization promoting the appreciation of international craft beers, beer culture, and history. Producer of both Japan's largest beer festival and competition.

http://www.beertaster.org/

Master Brewers Association of the Americas

Since 1887, organization with 24 international districts "promoting, advancing, and improving the professional interest of brew and malt house production and technical personnel."

http://www.mbaa.com/

Movimento Birrario Italiano (MoBI)

Organization promoting craft beer and beer culture in Italy, conducting conferences, competitions and seminars, and advocating for consumer rights. Publisher of *Movimentobirra* magazine.

http://www.movimentobirra.it/

National Beer Wholesalers Association

US organization founded in 1938 that strives to strengthen the regulations that maintain a "balanced and orderly marketplace," practices political and social advocacy, and promotes responsible drinking.

http://nbwa.org/

North American Brewers Association

Non-profit organization working to "secure beer's role in our culture and society through the advancement of brewing quality and consumer education."

http://www.northamericanbrewers.org/

Oregon Brewers Guild

Founded in 1992, one of the oldest brewers associations in the United States "with the primary goal of promoting the common interests of the members and the brewing industry in Oregon."

http://oregonbeer.org/

PINT

Enthusiast group founded in 1980 championing Dutch beer culture, presently with almost 3,000 members and described as "the largest association of beer in the Netherlands." Producer of beer festivals including the Bokbier Festival (Amsterdam, the Netherlands) and publisher of *PINT* magazine.

http://www.pint.nl/

Society of Beer Advocates (SOBA)

New Zealand enthusiast organization promoting craft beer appreciation and knowledge, and informing and protecting consumers.

http://www.soba.org.nz/

Society of Independent Brewers (SIBA)

Since 1980, UK organization with the mission to "campaign on behalf of independent brewers to ensure that they have the best possible opportunity to bring their goods to market."

http://siba.co.uk/

Stein Collectors International

Collectors club founded in 1965 "dedicated to advancing the state of knowledge and the appreciation of beer steins and other drinking vessels." Publishes a quarterly journal, *Prosit*, featuring information on stein collection.

http://www.steincollectors.org/

Unionbirrai

Association that "promotes the dissemination of the culture of craft beer in Italy" through events, conferences, and courses, and provides professional support to brewers. Publisher of the quarterly *Unionbirrai News* magazine.

http://www.unionbirrai.it/

Zythos vzw

Organization in Belgium with a mission to "preserve and promote the Belgian beer culture." Produces the Zythos Bier Festival (Sint-Niklaas, Belgium) and hosts a number of regional beer appreciation clubs.

http://www.zythos.be/

References

http://www.brewersassociation.org/pages/directories/

BEER FESTIVALS

In 2010, there were over 1,200 festivals across the globe varying in size and focus, taking place at venues including bars, stadiums, zoos, parks, beaches, mountains, resorts, city streets, and bridges. Some festivals have been in existence for only a few years, and others for decades, having become a part of the local culture; some run for only 1 day, and others flow on over a span of weeks, hosting thousands of participants from around the world. Some feature hundreds of international beers, while others focus on regional or specialty beers such as winter beers, strong beers, and barleywines. Most festivals incorporate food and live music, and many also feature wine, spirits, ciders, and perries, in addition to providing festival goers with souvenir commemorative glassware. Festivals are a prime venue for judging competitions, and many are staffed by volunteers and donate proceeds to non-profit charitable organizations. In the United States, beer festivals are often produced by brewers associations and beer-related publications; in the United Kingdom, the majority is put together by local chapters of CAMRA, the Campaign for Real Ale.

This collection is by no means a complete listing, but rather an overview of some of the most notable beer festivals from over 15 countries. Before attending any festival, it is important to confirm the event details with the organizing body.

American Craft Beer Fest, Boston, MA. A Friday and Saturday in June. Produced by BeerAdvocate.com. "The East coast's largest celebration of American craft beer," featuring more than 400 craft beers from 85 American breweries.

http://beeradvocate.com/acbf/

American Craft Beer Week, United States. Seven days in May. Produced by the Brewers Association. More than 200 breweries will partake in over 500 events across the country celebrating the work of craft and independent brewers. A "Declaration of Beer Independence" pledging allegiance to the support of craft beer was signed by mayors, governors, and brewers.

http://www.americancraftbeerweek.org/

Autumn Brew Review, Minneapolis, MN. A Saturday in October; 10th annual in 2010. More than 200 beers from 60 breweries, as well as seminars, panels, and tours.

http://www.mncraftbrew.org/festivals/autumn-brew-review

Bedford Beer and Cider Festival, Bedford, England. A Wednesday through Saturday in October; 33rd annual in 2010. Around 110 real ales, 30 ciders and perries, a selection of international beers, hot and cold food, soft drinks, and live performances.

http://www.northbedscamra.org.uk/beerfestival.html

Beerfest Asia, Singapore. A Thursday through Saturday in June. More than 250 international beers from 30 countries, food, games, live entertainment, and World Cup screenings.

http://www.beerfestasia.com/

Beer Summit Winter Jubilee, Boston, MA. A Friday and Saturday in January. More than 200 selections from 60 breweries with a focus on big beers.

http://beersummit.com/

Belgrade Beer Festival, Belgrade, Serbia. A Wednesday through Sunday in August. Past festivals have featured 45 beers from 20 breweries and 40 musical acts.

http://www.belgradebeerfest.com/active/en/home.html

Big Red Pour International Craft Beer and Music Festival, Glendale, AZ. A Saturday and Sunday in December. Sponsored by Draft Magazine. Hundreds of US and international craft beers, seminars and lessons on pairing beer with food, and live music.

http://www.draftmag.com/bigpour/

Boston Beer Week, Boston, MA. Ten days from May to June. Citywide events including tastings, meet-the-brewer events, beer dinners, special beer offers, homebrew meetings, and the American Craft Beer Fest.

http://beeradvocate.com/bbw/

Brass City Brew Fest, Waterbury, CT. A Saturday in September. More than 300 beers from over 125 US and international breweries, seminars, food from local producers, live music, and a "classic" car show.

http://www.brasscitybrewfest.com/

Brewmasters International Beer Festival, Galveston, TX. Four days in September. Hundreds of beers from across the globe, seminars, culinary delights, food and beer pairings, and live music.

http://www.brewmastersinternationalbeerfestival.com/

BrewNZ Beervana, Wellington, New Zealand. A Friday and Saturday in August. Almost 175 beers from New Zealand and Australia, a beer and food matching competition, and "beer enlightenment" seminars.

http://brewersguild.org.nz/beervana

Bruges Beer Festival, Bruges, Belgium. A Saturday and Sunday in September. More than 275 beers from nearly 60 breweries, food, beer cooking demonstrations, seminars, and live music.

http://www.brugsbierfestival.be/en/beer_festival_bruges-1.html

Buffalo Brewfest, Buffalo, NY. A Friday in August. More than 100 beers with an emphasis on sampling different varieties, live music, raffles, and giveaways.

http://www.askbhsc.org/content/pages/buffalo-brewfest

Burton Beer Festival, Burton-on-Trent, England. A Thursday through Saturday in March; 31st annual in 2010. More than 100 beers from across the UK, as well as a large selection of real ciders, perries, and country wine, live entertainment, and food vendors.

http://www.burtoncamra.org.uk/festival_1.html

California Brewers Festival, Sacramento, CA. A Saturday in September; 16th annual in 2010. Past festivals have featured more than 150 craft beers from over 60 breweries from across the United States, including a variety of international beers, food, and live music.

http://www.calbrewfest.com/

Cambridge Beer Festival, Cambridge, England. A Monday through Saturday in May; 37th annual in 2010, the longest running beer festival in the United Kingdom. More than 200 ales and 80 ciders and perries, as well as a selection of international beers, wine, and mead, a renowned offering of British cheeses, and local savory foods.

http://www.cambridgebeerfestival.com/

Cannstatter Volksfest, Stuttgart, Germany. Two weeks from September to October; second largest festival in Germany after Oktoberfest. Multiple beer tents, live music, carnival rides, and fireworks.

http://www.stgt.com/stuttgart/volkfste.htm

Carribean Rum and Beer Festival, St. James, Barbados. A Friday and Saturday in November. More than 100 beers and rums from the Caribbean, the "Caribbean Alcohol Beverage Awards" judging competition, seminars and demonstrations, food, and live performances.

http://www.rumandbeerfestival.com/

Chappel Beer Festival, Chappel, England. A Tuesday through Saturday in September; 24th annual in 2010. More than 400 beers, featuring a selection of new, rare, and local offerings, as well as ciders, perries, and food.

http://www.essex-camra.org.uk/chappel/

Charlotte Oktoberfest Beer Festival, Charlotte, NC. A Saturday in September. More than 350 beers from over 100 Southeast US and international breweries.

http://www.charlotteoktoberfest.com/

Chelmsford Summer Beer Festival, Chelmsford, England. A Tuesday through Saturday in July. More than 300 real ales, 120 real ciders and perries, as well as a selection of Belgian beer and wine from regional vintners, live music, and food.

http://www.chelmsfordbeerfestival.org.uk/

Cincinnati Beer Fest, Cincinnati, OH. A Friday through Sunday in September. Over 200 beers and almost 30 musical performers.

http://myfountainsquare.com/beerfest

Classic City Brew Fest, Athens, GA. A Sunday in April; 15th annual in 2010. Almost 250 international beers, live music, and food.

http://www.classiccitybrew.com/brewfest.html

Cleveland Beer Week, Cleveland, OH. Nine days in October. More than 700 citywide events including craft beer tastings, dinners, demonstrations, seminars, and beer specials at more than 100 locations.

http://www.clevelandbeerweek.org/

Copenhagen Beer Festival, Copenhagen, Denmark. A Thursday through Saturday in May; 10th annual in 2010. Features hundreds of beers from Danish microbreweries, the majority of Europe, and a selection of international offerings.

http://www.ale.dk/

Cotswold Beer Festival, Winchcombe, England. A Friday through Sunday in July; 34th annual in 2010. More than 80 beers, as well as ciders and perries, food, and live entertainment.

http://www.gloucestershirecamra.org.uk/cbf/

Czech Beer Festival, Prague, Czech Republic. Seventeen days in May. More than 70 Czech beers, featuring a wide array of artisanal food from regional chefs and restaurants.

http://www.ceskypivnifestival.cz/en/index.shtml

Decatur Craft Beer Tasting Festival, Decatur, GA. A Saturday in October. More than 100 regional, US and international beers, food from local restaurants, and live music.

http://decaturbeerfestival.org/

Diksmuide Beer Festival, Diksmuide, Belgium. First four Saturdays in October; taken place for more than 50 years. New beers are offered in addition to well-known Belgian selections, wine, food, and a live Oompah band.

http://www.beerfestivaldiksmuide.be/

Durham Beer Festival, Durham City, England. A Thursday through Saturday in September; 30th annual in 2010. More than 80 real ales, many from local breweries, as well as a selection of over 20 ciders and perries and 20 bottled beers.

http://www.camradurham.org.uk/beerFestivals.php

Festival of Beer and Flowers, Lasko, Slovenia. A Thursday through Sunday in July; 46th annual in 2010; the most populated tourist event in Slovenia. Multiple beer tents across the town, live music from many bands, games, a parade, and fireworks.

http://www.pivocvetje.com/?language=ENG

Fete de la Biere, Switzerland. A Friday through Saturday in May; 17th annual in 2010. More than 170 beers, live music nightly.

http://www.fetedelabiere.ch/

Great Alaska Beer and Barleywine Festival, Anchorage Alaska. A Friday and Saturday in January. More than 200 beers and barleywine-style ales from over 50 regional breweries.

http://auroraproductions.net/beer-barley.html

Great American Beer Festival, Denver, CO. A Thursday through Saturday in September; 29th annual in 2010. Presented by the Brewers Association, more than 2,000 beers from over 450 American breweries, geographically arranged, including the most renowned judging competition in the United States, food and beer pairings, beer dinners, brewing seminars, and live music.

http://www.greatamericanbeerfestival.com/

Great Arizona Beer Festival, Tempe, AZ. A Saturday in March. More than 200 craft beers, live music, food, and a beer judging event.

http://www.azbeer.com/tempe.htm

Great British Beer Festival, London, Earls Court. A Tuesday through Saturday in August. More than 700 real ales, in addition to ciders and perries, international beers, food, live music, games, and beer tasting seminars.

http://gbbf.camra.org.uk/home

Great Canadian Beer Festival, Victoria, BC, Canada. First weekend after Labor Day; 18th annual in 2010. More than 45 craft breweries from Canada, northwest United States, and Belgium, food from local producers, and live music.

http://www.gcbf.com/

Great European Beerfest, Pittsburgh, PA. A Saturday and Sunday in June; 14th annual in 2010. Past festivals have featured 135 European beers, including 40 Belgian varieties, a raffle, live music, and local food.

http://www.sharpedgebeer.com/beerfest.htm

Great International Beer Festival, Providence, RI. A Saturday in November; 18th annual in 2010. "America's Largest International Beer Festival," past festivals had more than 230 beers entered into its Great International Beer Competition. Live music and food.

http://www.beerfestamerica.com/

Great Japan Beer Festival, Tokyo, Japan. A Saturday and Sunday in June; 13th annual in 2010. More than 120 craft beers.

http://www.beertaster.org/index-e.html

Great Lakes Brew Fest, Racine, WI. A Friday and Saturday in September. More than 250 craft beers from almost 100 breweries, food from local establishments, and live music.

http://www.greatlakesbrewfest.com/main.html

Great Taste of the Midwest, Madison, WI. A Saturday in August; 24th annual in 2010. More than 500 beers from over 100 Midwest brewers, beer and food pairings, a real ale tent, live music, a homebrew supply shop, and an exhibit from the Museum of Beer and Brewing.

http://www.mhtg.org/great-taste-of-the-midwest

Great World Beer Fest, New York, NY. A Friday and Saturday in October. Hundreds of craft beers from around the world, live music, and food.

http://www.brewtopiafest.com/

Helsinki Beer Festival, Helsinki, Finland. A Friday and Saturday in April; 13th annual in 2010. Past festivals have included hundreds of international beers, as well as ciders and whiskies, a judging competition, food, and live music from popular Finnish bands.

http://www.helsinkibeerfestival.com/

High Country Beer Festival, Boone, NC. A Saturday in September. Over 200 beers from almost 60 breweries.

http://www.hcbeerfest.com/

International Berlin Beer Festival, Berlin, Germany. A Friday through Sunday in August; 14th annual in 2010. More 2,000 beers from over 300 breweries representing almost 90 countries, food, and live entertainment on multiple stages.

http://www.bierfestival-berlin.de/

Kitchener Waterloo Oktoberfest, Kitchener and Waterloo, ON, Canada. A full week in October; 42nd annual in 2010. The "largest Bavarian festival in North America," over 40 family and cultural events including a renowned Thanksgiving parade; funds raised for more than 70 non-profit organizations and charities.

http://www.oktoberfest.ca/

Kona Brewers Festival, Kollua-Kona, HI. A Saturday in March; 15th Annual in 2010. Features 30 craft breweries, 25 chefs, a fashion show, and live music.

http://www.konabrewersfestival.com/

Liverpool Beer Festival, Liverpool England. A Thursday through Saturday in February. 200 real ales, ciders and perries, artisanal food, and live entertainment.

http://www.merseycamra.org.uk/page9/page9.html

Loughborough Beer Festival, Loughborough, England. A Thursday through Saturday in March; 34th annual in 2010. More than 70 real ales, international bottled beers, fruit beers, ciders and perries, locally produced wine and mead, and live music.

http://www.loughboroughcamra.org.uk/loug_beer_festival.htm

Luton Beer Festival, Luton, England. A Thursday through Saturday in February; 27th annual in 2010. 100 real ales from across England with an emphasis on local breweries, food, and live music.

http://www.sbedscamra.org.uk/luton-beer-festival.asp

Maine Brewers Festival, Portland, ME. A Friday and Saturday in November; 17th annual in 2010. Beer from 20 Maine breweries, food, live music, and a meet-the-brewer dinner.

http://learnyourbeer.com/maine_festival/default.asp

Midwest Beerfest, Wichita, KS. A Thursday, Friday, and Saturday in October. Past festivals have featured more than 500 international and regional beers, food from local producers, and a silent auction.

http://www.midwestbeerfest.com/

Mondial de la Biere, Montreal, QC, Canada. A Wednesday to Sunday in June; 17th annual in 2010. The "largest international beer event in North America," more than 300 beers from breweries representing five continents.

http://festivalmondialbiere.qc.ca/

National Capital Craft Beer Festival, Canberra, Australia. A Saturday and Sunday in April. Almost 80 beers, food from local producers, live entertainment and giveaways.

http://www.canberrabeerfest.com/

National Cask Ale Week, United Kingdom. Eight days from March to April. Over 6,000 pubs across the UK promote and celebrate cask-conditioned "real" ale.

http://www.caskaleweek.co.uk/

National Winter Ales Festival, Manchester, England. A Wednesday to Saturday in January. More than 200 British and international beers, bottled real ale, ciders and perries, food, live music, a raffle, and the "Champion Beer of Britain" judging competition.

http://www.alefestival.org.uk/winterales/

New England Real Ale Exhibition, Somerville, MA. A Wednesday through Saturday in March; 14th annual in 2010. More than 80 cask-conditioned real ales from the UK and New England.

http://www.nerax.org/nerax/

New York Craft Beer Week, New York, NY. Ten days from September to October. Citywide celebration of craft beer, featuring bar specials, festivals, food pairings, beer dinners, and pub crawls.

http://www.nycbeerweek.com/

North American Organic Brewers Festival, Portland, OR. A Friday through Sunday in June. The "most earth-friendly beer festival in North America," 50 organic beers, organic food, and compostable glassware.

http://www.naobf.org/

Norwich Beer Festival, Norwich, England. A Monday to Saturday in October; 33rd annual in 2010. More than 200 real ales, in addition to a selection of draft and bottled European beers, as well as over 25 different ciders and perries.

http://www.norwichcamra.org.uk/festival/fest2010.htm

Nottingham Robin Hood Beer Festival, Nottingham, England. A Thursday to Sunday in October; 34th annual in 2010. Past festivals have featured almost 700 real ales, in addition to an array of various beer styles, ciders and perries, country wine, food, and live entertainers.

http://www.nottinghamcamra.org/NottFest/web%20site/festivalindex.html

Oktoberfest Blumenau, Blumenau, Brazil. Eighteen days in October; 27th annual in 2010. "The largest German party in the Americas," national and regional Brazilian beer, German food, live music, games, performances, and parades.

http://www.oktoberfestblumenau.com.br/

Oktoberfest, Munich, Germany. Mid September to the first week of October; 200th anniversary in 2010. The largest festival in the world, featuring numerous themed beer tents, carnival rides, games, a costume parade, food and live performances of modern and traditional Bavarian music.

http://www.oktoberfest.de/en/

Oktoberfest Zinzinnati, Cincinnati, OH. A Saturday and Sunday in October; 35th annual in 2010. "America's largest and most authentic Oktoberfest," more than 800 barrels of beer, over 40 beer varieties from a dozen breweries, German music, and food.

http://www.oktoberfest-zinzinnati.com/

Olletoober, Oitme, Estonia. A Friday and Saturday in July. More than 100 beers and ciders, games, competitions, and live performances from local bands.

http://www.olletoober.ee/

Oregon Brewers Festival, Portland, OR. Last full weekend in July; 23rd annual in 2010. More than 80 craft beers from across the United States, homebrew demonstrations, memorabilia exhibits, food, a program of live music, and a famous kick-off parade.

http://www.oregonbrewfest.com/

Oregon Craft Beer Month, OR. July. Statewide celebration of craft beer featuring special bar deals, beer dinners, festivals, new beer releases, brewery tours, and meet-the-brewer events.

http://www.oregoncraftbeermonth.com/

Paisley Beer Festival, Paisley, Scotland. A Wednesday to Saturday in April. Past festivals have featured 170 real ales, international beers, ciders and perries, mead, food, live entertainment, and participant voting for the festival's best beer.

http://www.paisleybeerfestival.org.uk/

Peoria Jaycees International Beer Festival, Peoria, IL. A Friday and Saturday in April; 18th annual in 2010. More than 325 beers, local food, and live performers.

http://www.peoriajaycees.org/

Peterborough Beer Festival, Peterborough, England. A Tuesday to Saturday in August. More than 350 real ales, bottled beers, ciders and perries, a variety of food, games, and a raffle.

http://www.peterborough-camra.org.uk/

Philly Beer Week, Philadelphia, PA. Ten days in June. Citywide celebration featuring hundreds of events including festivals, tastings, pub crawls, tours, seminars, beer dinners, and new beer releases.

http://www.phillybeerweek.org/

Philly Craft Beer Festival, Philadelphia, PA. A Saturday in March. More than 100 beers from over 50 breweries, seminars, demonstrations, and food.

http://www.phillycraftbeerfest.com/

Pig's Ear Beer and Cider Festival, London, England. Produced by the CAMRA East London and City branch. A Tuesday through Friday in late November; 27th annual in 2010. More than 100 real ales, as well as bottled and international beers and cider.

http://www.pigsear.org.uk/

Reading CAMRA Beer and Cider Festival, Reading, England. A Thursday through Sunday in April; 16th annual in 2010. More than 500 real ales, 100 international beers, 45 English wines, over 150 ciders and perries, food, and the "CAMRA National Cider and Perry Awards."

http://www.readingbeerfestival.org.uk/2010/general/main

Riverside Festival, Stamford, England. A Saturday in July; 30th annual in 2010. Past festivals have offered 40 real ales from predominately local breweries, 20 real ciders, 30 bands performing on three stages, food, a craft market, and a fireworks display.

http://www.creationbooth.co.uk/riversidefestival/

Rotherham Real Ale and Music Festival (previously the Great British Northern Beer Festival), Rotherham, England. A Wednesday through Saturday in February. More than 200 real ales, over 30 wines and ciders, international bottled beers, food, and an array of live performances including music, dance, and comedy.

http://www.magnarealale.co.uk/

Rujanfest, Zagreb, Croatia. Eleven days in September. Oktoberfest-style celebration featuring 25 types of beer, themed food tents, and live entertainment on three stages.

http://rujanfest.com/

San Francisco Beer Week, San Francisco, CA. Ten days in February. Citywide celebration with 100 events promoting the region's craft beer featuring festivals, beer dinners, food and beer pairings events, special beer releases, meet-the-brewer events, and demonstrations, in addition to live music and film showings.

http://www.sfbeerweek.org/

San Francisco International Beer Festival, San Francisco, CA. A Saturday in April. More than 300 international craft beers and food from local restaurants.

http://www.sfbeerfest.com/index.html

Savor Craft Beer, Washington, DC. A Friday and Saturday in June. More than 160 craft beers from 80 breweries will be served alongside sweet and savory appetizers.

http://www.savorcraftbeer.com/

South African International Beer Festival, Cape Town in February; Durban in July; Gauteng in November. Beer from international and regional brewers as well as homebrewers, beer and food matching, beer culture and history seminars, artifacts, food, and live entertainment.

http://www.saibf.co.za/

South Devon CAMRA Beer Festival, Newton Abbot, England. A Friday and Saturday in September; 28th annual in 2010. More than 50 real ales, a dozen ciders and perries, food, and live music.

http://www.southdevoncamra.com/southdevonbeerfest.html

Springfest and Chili Cook-Off, New London, CT. A Friday in May. More than 100 beers from the US abroad, featuring two dozen microbreweries, live music, and a "chili crown" competition featuring local restaurants.

http://www.newlondonrotary.org/

Steel City Beer & Cider Festival, Sheffield, England. A Thursday to Saturday in October; 36th annual in 2010. More than 100 real ales, bottled beers, ciders and perries, a selection of country wines, food, and music.

http://www.sheffieldcamra.org.uk/beerfestival.htm

Stockholm Beer and Whisky Festival, Stockholm, Sweden. Last weekend in September and first weekend in October; 19th annual in 2010. Past festivals have featured hundreds of international beers, ciders and whiskies, a wide range of food, seminars, and live bands.

http://www.stockholmbeer.se/en

Stoke Beer Festival, Stoke, England. A Thursday through Saturday in October; 30th annual in 2010. More than 200 real ales, 40 ciders and perries, a selection of international bottled beers, and English country wines.

http://www.camrapotteries.co.uk/StokeBeerFestival.html

Tasmanian Beer Fest, Hobart, Tasmania, Australia. A Friday and Saturday in November. "Australia's largest beer festival," hundreds of beers from regional and international breweries, food from local producers, live music, seminars, beer and food matching, and a homebrew competition.

http://www.tasmanianbeerfest.com.au/

Telford Beer Festival, Telford, England. A Thursday to Monday in September; 29th annual in 2010. "Britain's biggest cooled-hand-pulled, pub-based beer festival," past years have featured nearly 35 hand-pulled beers, over 50 new beers in addition to real ciders and perries.

http://www.crown.oakengates.net/2010/09/29th-telford-beer-festival/

Toronto's Festival of Beer, Toronto, ON, Canada. A Thursday through Sunday in August; 16th annual in 2010. More than 120 beers from over 60 international breweries, live music, and cooking demonstrations.

http://www.beerfestival.ca/

Vermont Brewers Festival, Burlington, VT. A Friday and Saturday in July; 18th annual in 2010. Features hundreds of beers from 35 breweries, food, and music.

http://www.vtbrewfest.com/

Village of the Beers, Bibbiano, Italy. A Saturday and Sunday in September. A "festival of small breweries," featuring a selection of Italian craft beers, traditional Belgian beers and homebrews, food made with beer, workshops, live music, and an art exhibition.

http://www.villaggiodellabirra.com/english.htm

Washington Brewers Festival, Kenmore, WA. A Friday through Sunday in June. Selections from over 35 Washington breweries on Friday, and almost 200 beers on Saturday and Sunday, cider and wine, music, food, games, and a craft fair.

http://www.washingtonbeer.com/wabf.htm

Wazoo, Tampa, FL. A Saturday in August; 15th annual in 2010. More than 200 international beers, food from local restaurants, and live music.

http://www.lowryparkzoo.com/wazoo/index.html

World Beer Festival, Columbia, SC in January; Raleigh, NC in April; Durham, NC in October; Richmond, VA in June. Presented by All About Beer. Past festivals have featured 300 beers from 150 breweries.

http://allaboutbeer.com/wbfcolumbia/index.html

World of Beer Festival, Menononee Falls, WI. A Saturday in June. More than 150 beers from over 50 breweries, including a homebrew section and live music.

http://www.worldofbeerfestival.com/index.html

WYES International Beer Tasting, New Orleans, LA. A Saturday in June; 27th annual in 2010. More than 200 US and international beers, including a selection of homebrews.

http://wyes.org/events/beer.shtml

York Beer and Cider Festival, York Knavesmire, England. A Thursday through Saturday in September. Nearly 250 beers, in addition to an international selection, as well as 50 ciders and perries, wine, live music, and food.

http://www.yorkbeerfestival.org.uk/

Zythos Bier Festival, Sint-Niklaas, Belgium. A Saturday and Sunday in March. More than 200 beers from 60 breweries, as well as food, a beer market, and a raffle.

http://www.zbf.be/nl/index.htm

References

http://www.beerfestivals.org/
http://beeradvocate.com/
http://www.camra.org.uk/

WEBSITES, MAGAZINES, AND NEWSPAPERS

The majority of information published on beer falls into three categories: culture, industry, and homebrewing. Culture publications promote and support craft beer with features including beer news, reviews, events, and interviews and articles on brewers and breweries; guides to finding good beers, bars, and breweries when traveling to different cities and countries are common; as well as food recipes involving beer and suggested pairings. Amateur brewers will find technical advice, recipes, style guides, equipment reviews, as well as news and events. Industry professionals will be informed and assisted by resources providing intelligence and reporting on business trends and analysis.

There are numerous print publications and countless websites and blogs devoted to beer; of the latter, it is not unlikely that with each day comes a new arrival. Advantages of storing information online include providing updates with greater ease, hosting richer and more dynamic databases, and the ability to post blogs, videos, photographs, forums, and user reviews and comments. Publications are often accompanied by a corresponding website mirroring much of the printed content and introducing multimedia.

Below are but some examples of the many sources of cultural, political, social, and economic beer information.

Ale Street News

Bimonthly newspaper with the mission to "promote the appreciation of the finest beers available in the US and throughout the world," featuring events, new beer and bar announcements, reviews and articles on travel, beer-and-food, cooking, homebrewing techniques, and recipes.

http://www.alestreetnews.com/

All About Beer

Bimonthly magazine featuring news, reviews, columns, features and events, history and tradition, brewing methods, politics of beer, and amateur brewing information. Website features news and new releases, reviews, events, beer history and knowledge, food and travel information, and a beer and bar finder.

http://www.allaboutbeer.com/

Alltop

Website featuring a comprehensive collection of news feeds aggregated from top beer websites and blogs.

http://beer.alltop.com/

American Brewer

Quarterly trade magazine with a focus on "the business of beer" reporting on trends and offering industry analysis.

http://www.ambrew.com/

BeerAdvocate

Website with more than 1.2 million user-based beer reviews of over 55,000 beers, news, events and festivals, beer education, forum, and travel guide. Accompanied by a print publication including staff reviews, columns, news, and articles on beer culture. Producer of the American Craft Beer Fest (Boston, MA).

http://beeradvocate.com/

Beer and Brewer

Magazine with a focus on beer in Australia and New Zealand featuring news, events, trends, travel and beer-and-food guides, reviews on beer, cider, and whiskey, including a separate "Homebrewer" section providing information for amateur brewers. Website features articles, news, events, and beer finder.

http://www.beerandbrewer.com/

Beer Business Daily
Daily newsletter providing news and analysis with a focus on the US brewing industry.
http://www.beernet.com/

Beer Connoisseur
Quarterly magazine with style information, articles on beers, brewers and industry leaders, beer-and-food, reviews, style guide, beer culture, travel guide, brewery information, events, and general beer education. Website includes articles, blogs, forum, news, and events.
http://www.beerconnoisseur.com/

Beer Info
Online database of beer information including listings of breweries, homebrew resources and brewing equipment, beer festivals, beer associations, style guides, publications, and beer-of-the-month clubs.
http://www.beerinfo.com/

Beer Insights
Subscription based e-newsletters providing news and insights on the US beer industry.
http://www.beerinsights.com/

Beer Magazine
Bimonthly magazine featuring beer culture, reviews, events and beer-and-food offering both a print and digital subscription. Website includes articles, forum, videos, and style guide.
http://www.thebeermag.com/

Beer News
Website providing information on new beer releases, brewery news and press releases, and where to purchase beer online.
http://beernews.org/

Beer West
Quarterly magazine covering beer culture, events, bars, food-and-beer, including seasonal feature articles. Website includes news, events, beer finder, forum, and blog.
http://www.beerwestmag.com/

Beverage World
Monthly magazine providing "business intelligence" on alcoholic and non-alcoholic drinks, including news, research on trends, and feature articles on companies and industry professionals. A digital copy is available via e-mail as well as a daily e-newsletter covering the latest news.
http://www.beverageworld.com/

Bierpassie Magazine
Quarterly Belgian "Beer Passion" magazine with interviews and articles on breweries, food, and beer, and recommended beers and bars. Producer of the Beer Passion Weekend beer festival (Antwerp, Belgium).
http://www.beerpassion.com/

BRAUWELT
German trade magazine issued three times each month in conjunction with a free newsletter covering a wide range of economical issues and technical advancements in the beer industry, as well as news and events.
http://www.brauwelt.de/

Brewbound
Beer themed website produced by BevNET.com featuring consumer-focused reviews, news, events, videos, brewery directory, and forum.
http://www.brewbound.com/

Brewers' Guardian
Bimonthly UK trade magazine first published in 1871 and distributed to 120 countries including reports on industry developments, politics and trends, technology and marketing updates, and interviews with industry leaders. Website includes news articles, columns, events, and resources for aspiring brewers.
http://www.brewersguardian.com/

Brewing News
Bimonthly, regionally distributed newspaper publishing news and articles on craft beer, including travel guides and homebrewing information, available at bars, breweries, and stores. Comprises *Great Lakes Brewing News*, *Mid-Atlantic Brewing News*, *Northwest Brewing News*, *Rocky Mountain Brewing News*, *Southern Brew News*, *Southwest Brewing News*, and *Yankee Brew News*.
http://www.brewingnews.com/

Brew Your Own
Amateur brewing magazine published eight times a year offering technical advice, recipes, and style guides. Website contains news, blogs, reference charts, recipes, and videos.
http://www.byo.com/

CAMRA BEER Magazine

Quarterly UK publication exclusive to members of the Campaign for Real Ale (CAMRA), including articles on beers, breweries, and pubs. CAMRA also publishes its annual *Good Beer Guide*, a directory of breweries and pubs, as well as the monthly newspaper *What's Brewing*, covering brewing industry politics, events, pubs, brewers, homebrewing, and beer-and-food.

http://www.camra.org.uk

Celebrator Beer News

Bimonthly magazine featuring reviews, feature articles, events, and columns. Website includes videos and featured blogs.

http://www.celebrator.com/

Craft Beer

Website maintained by the Brewers Association featuring news, events, feature articles, style guide, beer and brewery finder, beer-and-food, beer history, and general beer knowledge.

http://www.craftbeer.com/

DRAFT Magazine

Bimonthly magazine including reviews, videos, events, beer finder, general beer knowledge, newsletter, food, and travel. Website includes videos, featured blogs, and giveaways. Producer of the Big Red Pour beer festival (Phoenix, AZ).

http://draftmag.com/

The Full Pint

Website featuring craft beer news, reviews, and events.

http://thefullpint.com/

Imbibe Magazine

Bimonthly "magazine of liquid culture" covering the components, production, and history of alcoholic and non-alcoholic beverages, including reviews and articles on industry figures. Website contains articles, a blog, and drink and food recipes.

http://www.imbibemagazine.com/

Japan Beer Times

Free, quarterly, bilingual Japanese magazine with beer reviews, news, interviews, education, travel guides, and brewery features.

http://japanbeertimes.com/

Modern Brewery Age

The "oldest continuously published US beer industry trade magazine and newsletter," offering news, interviews, and statistics in the form of a weekly e-newsletter and quarterly electronic magazine. Publisher of the "Blue Book" professional directory.

http://www.breweryage.com/

Mutineer Magazine

Magazine focused on covering the culture of beer, wine, and spirits. Website contains a blog, videos, and interviews.

http://www.mutineermagazine.com/

New Brewer

The "Journal of the Brewers Association," providing support for breweries of all sizes with industry news and articles on business and technology, as well as reporting on annual US brewery production.

http://www.brewersassociation.org/pages/publications/the-new-brewer/current-issue

Ølentusiasten

Bimonthly Danish "Beerenthusiasts" magazine covering news, events, and feature articles. Website contains a forum and links to beer knowledge, history, and references. Producers of the Copenhagen Beer Festival.

http://www.ale.dk/

The Oxford Bottled Beer Database

Website containing beer reviews and information on almost 4,000 beers listed from nearly 80 countries, news, and a discussion board.

http://www.bottledbeer.co.uk/

Pro Brewer

Website providing industry and technical information for beer professionals with news, events, classifieds, forum, and supplier directory.

http://www.probrewer.com/

Rate Beer

Website with more than 2.4 million user-based beer reviews of 110,000 beers, events, beer and brewer information, beer locator, beer-and-food, style guide, travel tips, and articles via The Hop Press (http://hoppress.com/).

http://www.ratebeer.com/

Real Beer

Website featuring beer education, news, events, forum, brewery and bar finder, and travel guides.

http://www.realbeer.com/

Taps

Quarterly Canadian beer culture magazine containing news, reviews, interviews, feature articles, beer-and-food, and homebrewing information. Website has a blog, videos, and free newsletter.

http://www.tapsmedia.ca/

Zymurgy

Bimonthly North American amateur brewer magazine published for more than 25 years, featuring recipes, equipment analysis, technical demonstrations, and beer culture and science. Subscriptions are accompanied by a year-long membership to the American Homebrewers Association. Website includes homebrewing history and techniques, recommended reading and resources, recipes, forum, videos, blog, club directory, and competition guide.

http://www.homebrewersassociation.org/pages/zymurgy/current-issue

BEER MUSEUMS

The majority of beer museums are located in Europe, where the cultural value and historical significance of beer is more prominent than anywhere else in the world. A number of museums are housed on the sites of historic breweries that are no longer in operation, or at the location of active, long-standing, and successful breweries. At these exhibitions, it is likely that visitors will learn the process by which beer is made and find a history of brewing techniques and related artifacts, in addition to "breweriana," a general term referring to beer memorabilia such as coasters, labels, trays, glassware, openers, and signs. In addition, one can almost always expect to enjoy a sample of beer, generally at the conclusion of the tour, particularly if the museum operates out of a working brewery.

This list is a sampling of what one might expect to encounter when visiting a beer museum. It is strongly recommended to contact any museum directly to confirm hours, location, programming, and costs.

American Hop Museum, Toppenish, Washington

Located in Washington's Yakima Valley, the largest producer of hops in the United States, exhibits feature displays of machinery, photographs, and other artifacts involved in the process of growing and harvesting hops, covering the complete history of the hop industry in America.

http://www.americanhopmuseum.org/

August Schell Museum of Brewing, New Ulm, Minnesota

The August Schell Brewing Company houses an exhibit of old brewing equipment as well as artifacts related to the history of the brewery and the Schell family.

http://www.schellsbrewery.com/

Bavarian Brewery Museum, Kulmbach, Germany

Exhibits touch on the cultural, historical, and economical importance of beer and brewing in Bavaria and Franconia, and include a world history of beer, beer advertisements, artifacts, and brewing demonstrations.

http://www.bayerisches-brauereimuseum.de/

Beck's Beer Museum, Bremen, Germany

The museum focuses on the history of Beck's beer and its current production methods, including films and presentations.

http://www.becks.de/index.php

Beer Advertising Museum, Breda, the Netherlands

An array of beer signs and posters, advertisements, equipment, glassware, labels, coasters, and other paraphernalia are on display. Most artifacts originate from Holland, Belgium, France, Germany, and England.

http://www.bierreclamemuseum.nl/english%20page.htm

Beer and Oktoberfest Museum, Munich, Germany

Situated in a centuries-old historical building, the museum promotes the heritage of Oktoberfest with displays of memorabilia, highlights the history of the festival and Munich's brewing history, and offers food and beer tastings as well as brewing demonstrations.

http://www.bier-und-oktoberfestmuseum.de/

http://www.bier-und-oktoberfestmuseum.de/dahoam.html

Beer Can Museum, East Taunton, Massachusetts

More than 4,500 beer cans are on display in addition to a wide selection of breweriana including coasters, openers, trays, towels, hats, and various items crafted from beer cans.

http://www.beercanmuseum.org/

Belgian Brewers Museum, Brussels, Belgium

The Confederation of Belgian Breweries curates a variety of traditional brewing equipment from the 18th century, including decorated tubs, porcelain tanks, pitchers, and pint pots. An exhibit of modern brewing techniques is also on display.

http://www.beerparadise.be/emc.asp

Bocholter Brewery Museum, Bocholt, Belgium

The history and technology of beer from the mid-18th century until modern times is portrayed through artifacts of "industrial archaeological" including barrels, bottles, and carts.

http://www.bocholterbrouwerijmuseum.be/

Brussels Museum of Gueuze, Brussels, Belgium

In this "living museum" visitors can learn about the history of the Cantillon brewery and the science behind the spontaneous fermentation of lambic-style beer. On display are antique brewing equipment, a cellar, and bottling line.

http://www.cantillon.be/

Carlsberg Visitors Centre, Copenhagen, Denmark

Interactive exhibits display the history of the Carlsberg brewery, featuring the "world's largest collection of beer bottles," brewing equipment, a horse stable, and a sculpture garden.

http://www.visitcarlsberg.dk/

Dortmund Brewery Museum, Dortmund, Germany

Exhibits focus on the brewing tradition of Dortmund's many breweries and provide information on historical and modern beer production and consumption.

http://brauereimuseum.dortmund.de/

European Beer Museum, Stenay, France

Featuring themed exhibits on various floors, the museum displays the history of the ingredients, production, consumption, and advertising of beer.

http://www.musee-de-la-biere.com/

Felsenkeller Brewery Museum, Monschau, Germany

The exhibits include brewing equipment and documents from the last 150 years, as well as bottles and cans, barrels, a collection of photographs, and a cellar constructed in 1830.

http://www.brauerei-museum.de/

Franconian Brewery Museum, Bamberg, Germany

Located in the vaults of the Benedictine Abbey, where beer was produced in the 12th century, over 1,300 exhibits display the production of beer with extensive displays of malting and brewing.

http://www.brauereimuseum.de/

German Hops Museum, Wolnzach, Germany

Covering the science, cultivation, and industry of hops in Germany over the last thousand years, including machinery displays.

http://www.hopfenmuseum.de/

Guinness Storehouse, Dublin, Ireland

Located at the St. James's Gate Brewery, exhibits on multiple floors cover the history of Guinness and its beer with displays including the brewing process, barrel making, and the company's popular advertisements. At the top sits a bar with a panoramic view of Dublin.

http://www.guinness-storehouse.com/en/Index.aspx

Heineken Experience, Amsterdam, the Netherlands

Visitors can take a tour of the old factory, learn about the history of Heineken, witness the brewing process, and partake in interactive exhibits.

http://www.heinekenexperience.com/

Lüneburg Beer Museum, Lüneburg, Germany

Visitors witness the entire brewing process, including bottling, and explore beer production exhibits on four floors featuring an antique kettle and malt mill.

http://www.brauereimuseum-lueneburg.de/

Maisel's Brewery and Cooperage Museum, Bayreuth, Germany

In this operating brewery, a variety of exhibits in 20 rooms demonstrate each element of the brewing process, including barrel-making, in addition to showcasing more than 3,000 glasses and jugs, 400 signs, and a range of coasters.

http://www.maisel.com/museum

Museum of Belgian Beers, Lustin, Belgium
On display are more than 15,000 Belgian beer bottles and glasses, as well as an array of breweriana and advertisements.
http://www.museebieresbelges.centerall.com/

National Beer Museum, Alkmaar, the Netherlands
Through displays of various antique equipment and machinery, visitors learn how beer was made over the last two centuries, and they can view exhibits of bottles, glassware, and advertisements.
http://www.biermuseum.nl/

National Brewery Centre, Burton upon Trent, England
Visitors learn about brewing techniques throughout history with displays of hundreds of artifacts, including vehicles and train cars. Character actors brew and serve beer.
http://www.nationalbrewerycentre.co.uk/

National Brewery Museum and Research Library, Potosi, Wisconsin
Courtesy of the American Breweriana Association, themed exhibits of various artifacts and equipment are on display. The museum also features a library for the purposes of beer research.
http://nationalbrewerymuseum.org/

Pivovarske Museum, Plzen, Czech Republic
An original brewery from the 15th-century houses an exhibit on the history of brewing and malting featuring equipment from the early 20th century, laboratory instruments, antique beer bottles, photographs, glassware, and vehicles.
http://www.prazdrojvisit.cz/cz/pivovarske-muzeum/

Poperinge Hop Museum, Poperinge, Belgium
Guided tours of four floors survey the history and harvesting of hops with displays of documents, photographs, and tools.
http://www.hopmuseum.be/home.php?lang=EN

Sapporo Beer Museum, Sapporo, Japan
Exhibits illustrate the history of beer in Japan, and that of the Sapporo Brewery, through displays including beer bottles, signs, and brewing equipment.
http://www.sapporobeer.jp/

Saxon Brewery Museum, Rechenberg, Germany
Visitors learn the history of this nearly 450-year-old brewery, in addition to the process of brewing beer, and visit the late 18th-century brewhouse, cellars, and working brewing equipment.
http://www.museumsbrauerei.de/

Schaerbeek Museum of Beer, Schaerbeek, Belgium
Ancient and modern brewing history and techniques are on display in conjunction with nearly a thousand Belgian beer bottles and hundreds of coasters, as well as advertisements.
http://users.skynet.be/museedelabiere/

Seattle Micro Brewery Museum, Seattle, Washington
The Pike Brewing Company houses a display educating visitors on the history of beer from ancient to modern times, featuring a wide assortment of vintage regional breweriana.
http://www.pikebrewing.com/history.shtml

Stepan Razin Beer Museum, Saint Petersburg, Russia
At the oldest brewery in Russia, exhibits show Russia's brewing history with some artifacts over 300 years old, as well as industrial and home brewing methods.
http://www.saint-petersburg.com/museums/beer-museum.asp

Stiegl Brauwelt Brewery Museum, Salzburg, Austria
The "largest private brewery in Austria since 1492" showcases a large exhibit on the history of beer and various brewing techniques.
http://www.stiegl.at/de/brauwelt/

Yuengling Museum and Gift Shop, Pottsville, Pennsylvania
America's Oldest Brewery teaches visitors the process of brewing and displays antique labels and packaging, as well as pre-refrigeration storage cellars that were excavated by hand.
http://www.yuengling.com/

Zywiec Brewery Museum, Zywiec, Poland
Exhibits in nearly 20 rooms cover the history of beer in Poland and the Zywiec Brewery itself featuring interactive brewing demonstrations.
http://www.muzeumbrowaru.pl/

DIRECTORY OF CONTRIBUTORS

Mirella G. Amato
Founder, Beerology, Toronto, Ontario, Canada

Ray Anderson
President, Brewery History Society, Swadlincote, UK

Zak Avery
Founder, The Beer Boy, UK

Charles W. Bamforth
Anheuser-Busch Endowed Professor of Malting and Brewing Sciences, University of California, Davis, California

Christopher Bird
CMB Brewing Services, Lexington, Kentucky

Thomas Blake
Professor, Department of Plant Sciences & Plant Pathology, Montana State University, Bozeman, Montana

Victoria Carollo Blake
Assistant Research Professor, Department of Plant Sciences & Plant Pathology, Montana State University, Bozeman, Montana

Gerrit Blüemelhuber
Managing Director Consulting, Doemens Academy, Gräfelfing, Germany

Peter Bouckaert
Brewmaster, New Belgium Brewing Company, Fort Collins, Colorado

Fritz Briem
Managing Director, Lupex Hops, Au/Hallertau, Germany

Jay R. Brooks
Beer Journalist, Novato, California

Pete Brown
Author of *Hops and Glory* and *Man Walks into a Pub: A Sociable History of Beer,* London, UK

Matthew Brynildson
Brewmaster, Firestone Walker Brewing Company, San Simeon, California

Paul KA Buttrick
Founder, Beer Dimensions, Knutsford, Cheshire, UK

Dick Cantwell
Founder and Head Brewer, Elysian Brewing Company, Seattle, Washington

Marcelo Carneiro
Founder and Brewmaster, Cervejaria Colorado, Ribeirão Preto, Brazil

Paul H. Chlup
Quality Manager, SweetWater Brewing Company, Atlanta, Georgia

Vincent Cilurzo
Owner and Brewer, Russian River Brewing Company, Santa Rosa, California

Martyn Cornell

Author of *Beer: The Story of the Pint* and *Amber, Gold & Black: The History of Britain's Great Beers*, Teddington, Middlesex, UK

Jan Czerny

Brewmaster, Unser Bier, Basel, Switzerland

Lorenzo Dabove

Beer Television Host and Judge, Milan, Italy

Curtis Dale

Founder and Brewer, Dale Bros. Brewery, Upland, California

Ray Daniels

Founder, Cicerone Certification Program and Real Ale Festival, Author of *Designing Great Beers*, Chicago, Illinois

Peter Darby

Wye Hops Ltd, Canterbury, UK

April Darcy

Travel Writer, Jersey City, New Jersey

Geoff Deman

Head Brewer of Brewpub Operations, Free State Brewing Company, Lawrence, Kansas

Dan D'Ippolito

Communications Coordinator, Brooklyn Brewery, Brooklyn, New York

Mark Dorber

Co-Director, The Beer Academy and Owner, The Anchor, Walberswick, Suffolk, UK

Horst Dornbusch

Founder, Cerevisia Communications, Brew Industry Consultant, Beer Columnist, and Author, West Newbury, Massachusetts

Jonathan Downing

President, Downing International Brewery Consulting, Oakville, Ontario, Canada

Hans-Peter Drexler

Brewmaster, Weisses Bräuhaus G. Schneider & Sohn, Kelheim, Germany

Stanley H. Duke

Professor, Department of Agronomy, University of Wisconsin, Madison, Wisconsin

Barbara Dunn

Senior Research Scientist, Department of Genetics, Stanford University, Stanford, California

Michael J. Edney

Program Manager, Applied Barley Research Unit, Grain Research Laboratory, Winnipeg, Manitoba, Canada

Jason Eglinton

Associate Professor, Barley Program Leader, University of Adelaide, Adelaide, South Australia

Jens Eiken

Director of Technical and Supply Chain Strategy, Molson Coors UK, Lichfield, Stafford, UK

Svante Ekelin

Co-Founder, Swedish Homebrewers Association, Sweden

Evan Evans

Research Fellow, School of Agricultural Science, University of Tasmania, Australia

Jeff Evans

Author of *A Beer a Day* and *The Book of Beer Knowledge*, Newbury, Berkshire, UK

Roland Folz

Head of Brewing & Beverage Science and Application, Research and Teaching Institute for Brewing in Berlin (VLB), Berlin, Germany

Erik Fortmeyer

Historian and Bottle Collector, Brooklyn, New York

Terry Foster

Author of *Pale Ale* and *Porter*, Stratford, Connecticut

Andrew Fratianni

Institute of Brewing and Distilling Diploma Brewer, Ossining, New York

Alastair Gilmour

Beer Journalist, Newcastle upon Tyne, UK

Gary Glass

Director, American Homebrewers Association, Boulder, Colorado

Brian Glover

Author of *The World Encyclopedia of Beer* and Former Editor of Publications for the Campaign for Real Ale (CAMRA), Cardiff, UK

Abram Goldman-Armstrong

Beer Writer, Portland, Oregon

Dan Gordon

Co-Founder and Director of Brewing Operations, Gordon Biersch Brewing Company, San Jose, California

Ryan Gostomski

President and Brewmaster, Namysłów Brewery, Namysłów, Poland

Jon Griffin

Instructor, University of Nevada, Las Vegas, Nevada

Ken Grossman

Founder, Sierra Nevada Brewing Company, Chico, California

John Haggerty

Brewmaster, New Holland Brewing Company, Holland, Michigan

Alex Hall

Beer Columnist and Editor, New York, New York

Tim Hampson

Author, *Greet Beers: The Best Beers from Around the World* and Co-Author, *The Beer Book*, Oxford, UK

Bryan Harrell

Beer Commentator and Journalist, Tokyo, Japan

Bryan Harvey

Professor, Department of Plant Sciences, University of Saskatchewan, Saskatoon, Saskatchewan, Canada

Alfred Haunold

Professor, Crop and Soil Science Department, Oregon State University, Corvallis, Oregon

Antony Hayes

Beer Writer and Judge, Tonbridge, Kent, UK

Patrick Hayes

Professor, Department of Crop and Soil Science, Oregon State University, Corvallis, Oregon

Scott E. Heisel

Vice President and Technical Director, American Malting Barley Association, Inc., Milwaukee, Wisconsin

Cynthia A. Henson

Associate Professor, Department of Agronomy, University of Wisconsin, Madison, Wisconsin

Karl-Ullrich Heyse

Editor of Brauwelt, Nuremberg, Germany

Stephen Hindy

Co-Founder and President, The Brooklyn Brewery, Brooklyn, New York

John Holl

Beer Journalist and Author of *Indiana Breweries*, Jersey City, New Jersey

Martha Holley-Paquette

Co-Founder, Pretty Things Beer and Ale Project, Cambridge, Massachusetts

Chris Holliland

Independent Consultant, Sunderland, UK

Ian Hornsey

Founder Brewer, Nethergate Brewery, Clare, Suffolk, UK, and Author of *Brewing* and *A History of Beer and Brewing*, Clare, Suffolk, UK

Jonathan Horowitz

Brooklyn, New York

Oliver Hughes

Co-Founder, Porterhouse Brewing Company, Dublin, Ireland

Brian Hunt

Founder, Moonlight Brewery, Fulton, California

Steve Huxley

Partner, Steve's Beer, and Author of *Cerveza, La Poesía Líquida*, Barcelona, Spain

Oliver Jakob

Brewmaster, Project Manager, and Product Manager, GEA Brewery Systems, Kitzingen, Germany

Kjetil Jikiun
Head Brewer, Nøgne-ø Brewery, Grimstad, Norway

Alana R. Jones
General Manager, Santa Fe Brewing Company, Santa Fe, New Mexico

Nick R. Jones
Brewer, Santa Fe Brewing Company, Santa Fe, New Mexico

Kim Jordan
Co-Founder, New Belgium Brewing Company, Fort Collins, Colorado

Colin Kaminski
Brewmaster, Downtown Joe's Brewery and Restaurant, Napa, California

David Kapral
Owner, Brewing Consulting Services, Boise, Idaho

Csilla Kato
Enologist, Beringer Vineyards, Napa, California

Nick Kaye
Managing Editor, *The Beer Connoisseur Magazine*, Atlanta, Georgia

Ben Keene
Beer Journalist and Travel Writer, Brooklyn, New York

Stephen Kenny
Assistant Scientist, Department of Crop and Soil Sciences, Washington State University

Jai Kharbanda
Food Scholar, Mexico City, Mexico

Ritchie S. King
Science Journalist, New York, New York

Anders Brinch Kissmeyer
Founder, Nørrebro Bryghus and Kissmeyer Beer & Brewing, Charlottenlund, Denmark

Ray Klimovitz
Technical Director, Master Brewers Association of the Americas, Chippewa Falls, Wisconsin

Jennifer Kling
Professor, Department of Crop and Soil Science, Oregon State University, Corvallis, Oregon

Per Kølster
Manager and Director, Fuglebjerggaard (farm and brewery), Helsinge, Denmark

Walter König
General Manager, Bavarian Brewers Federation, Munich, Germany

Thomas Kraus-Weyermann
Co-President, Weyermann® Malting Company, Bamberg, Germany

Jim Kuhr
Brewmaster, The Matt Brewing Company, Utica, New York

David Kuske
Director of Malting Operations, Briess Malt & Ingredients Company, Chilton, Wisconsin

Daniel J. Kvitek
Department of Genetics, Stanford University Medical Center, Stanford, California

Mike Laur
Founder, The Beer Drinker's Guide to Colorado, Colorado Springs, Colorado

Anda Lincoln
Writer and Attorney, Fort Collins, Colorado

Wolfgang David Lindell
Brewmaster, Old Harbor Brewery, Old San Juan, Puerto Rico

Dirk Loeffler
President and CEO, Loeffler Chemical Corporation, Atlanta, Georgia

Damien Malfara
Founder and Brewer, Old Forge Brewing Company, Danville, Pennsylvania

Chris J. Marchbanks
Master Brewer and Brewing technologist, Burton upon Trent, Staffordshire, UK

Phil Markowski
Brewmaster, Southampton Brewery, Southampton, New York

Jeremy Marshall
Head Brewer, The Lagunitas Brewing Company, Petaluma, California

Ben McFarland
Author of *World's Best Beers,* London, UK

Jacob McKean
Social Media Coordinator, Stone Brewing Company, Escondido, California

Jeff Mendel
Partner and Director, Left Hand Brewing Company, Longmont, Colorado

Juliano Borges Mendes
Co-Founder, Cervejaria Eisenbahn, Blumenau, Brazil

Will Meyers
Brewmaster, Cambridge Brewing Company, Cambridge, Massachusetts

Randy Mosher
Author of *Brewer's Companion* and *Radical Brewing,* Chicago, Illinois

Larry Nelson
Publisher and Editor, *Brewers' Guardian* and *The Brewery Manual,* Surrey, UK

Jeff S. Nickel
AC Golden Brewing Company, Golden, CO

Garrett Oliver
Brewmaster, The Brooklyn Brewery, and Author of *The Brewmaster's Table,* Brooklyn, New York

Geoff H. Palmer, OBE
Professor Emeritus of Brewing, Heriot-Watt University and Author of *The Enlightenment Abolished,* Penicuik, Scotland

John Palmer
Author of *How to Brew* and Co-Host of *Brew Strong,* Los Angeles, California

Daniel Paquette
Co-Founder, Pretty Things Beer and Ale Project, Cambridge, Massachusetts

Steve Parkes
Owner and Lead Instructor, American Brewers Guild, Salisbury, Vermont

Ron Pattinson
Beer Historian, Amsterdam, Holland

Joris Pattyn
Co-author of *100 Belgian Beers to Try Before You Die* and *The Beer Book,* Ursel, Belgium

Glenn A. Payne
Non-Executive Director, Meantime Brewing Company Ltd., London, UK

Val Peacock
President, Hop Solutions, Inc., Edwardsville, Illinois

Barrie Pepper
British Guild of Beer Writers and Author of *The International Book of Beer* and *Beer Glorious Beer,* Leeds, UK

George Philliskirk
Co-Director, The Beer Academy, London, UK

Steven J. Pittman
Brewer, Lagunitas Brewing Company, Petaluma, California

Fergus G. Priest
Professor Emeritus of Microbiology, Heriot-Watt University, Edinburgh, Scotland

Roger Protz
Author of *300 Beers to Try Before You Die, The Taste of Beer,* and the *World Guide to Beer,* St Albans, Hertfordshire, UK

Dan Rabin
Beer Journalist and Co-Author of the *Dictionary of Beer & Brewing,* Boulder, Colorado

Bev Robertson
Professor Emeritus, Department of Physics, University of Regina, Regina, Saskatchewan, Canada

Jussi Rokka

Beer Journalist, *Helsingin Sanomat*, Helsinki, Finland

Josh Rubin

Beer Columnist, *The Toronto Star*, Toronto, Ontario, Canada

Jose R. Ruiz

Founder and President, Maltas e Insumos Cerveceros SA de CV, Chihuahua, Mexico

Inge Russell

Editor, *The Journal of the Institute of Brewing*, Ontario, Canada

Conrad Seidl

Beer Journalist and Author of *Conrad Seidl's Bier Guide*, Austria, Vienna

Thomas Shellhammer

Professor, Department of Food Science and Technology, Oregon State University, Corvallis, Oregon

Gavin Sherlock

Associate Professor, Department of Genetics, Stanford University, Stanford, California

Karl Siebert

Professor, Department of Food Science and Technology, Cornell University, Geneva, New York

Tony Simmons

President and Head Brewer, Pagosa Brewing Company, Pagosa Springs, Colorado

David L. Smisek

Chemical Engineer and Heraldist, Ringoes, New Jersey

Kevin Smith

Associate Professor, Department of Agronomy and Plant Genetics, University of Minnesota, St. Paul, Minnesota

Gary Spedding

Founder, Brewing and Distilling Analytical Services, Lexington, Kentucky

Mitch Steele

Brewmaster, Stone Brewing Company, Escondido, California

Benjamin Steinman

Editor, *Beer Marketer's Insights*, Suffern, New York

Wolfgang Stempfl

CEO, Doemens Academy, Gräfelfing, Germany

Graham G. Stewart

Professor Emeritus in Brewing and Distilling, Heriot-Watt University, Edinburgh, Scotland

Eric J. Stockinger

Associate Professor, Department of Horticulture and Crop Science, Ohio State University, Columbus, Ohio

Stuart Swanston

Genetics Programme, SCRI Technology, Dundee, Scotland

Bill Taylor

Chief Brewer, Lion Nathan Breweries, Sydney, Australia

David A. Thomas

Principal, Beer Sleuth Ltd., Golden, Colorado

Bill Thomas

Genetics Programme, SCRI Technology, Dundee, Scotland

Keith Thomas

Founder, Brewlab Ltd. and Senior Lecturer, Faculty of Applied Science, University of Sunderland, Sunderland, UK

Brian Thompson

Founder, Telegraph Brewing Company, Santa Barbara, California

Adrian Tierney-Jones

Beer Journalist, Somerset, UK

Shaun Townsend

Assistant Professor, Senior Research, Crop and Soil Sciences Department, Oregon State University, Corvallis, Oregon

Rick Vega

Night Brewer, Lagunitas Brewing Company, Petaluma, California

Keith Villa

Master Brewer, MillerCoors, Arvada, Colorado

Ben Vinken

Beer Journalist, *Bierpassie Magazine/El Gusto,* and Host of *The Beer Sommelier*, Antwerp, Belgium

Derek Walsh

Consultant, (Inter)national Judge, Writer, Brewer, BrewingInformationEducationResearch+ (B.I.E.R.+), Zaandam, the Netherlands

Ian L. Ward

President, Brewers Supply Group, Napa, California

Tim Webb

Beer Columnist and Author of the *Good Beer Guide Belgium*, Cambridge, UK

Sepp Wejwar

Beer Writer and Sommelier, Vienna, Austria

Jared W. Wenger

Department of Genetics, Stanford University, Stanford, California

Colin J. West

Executive Director, Maltsters' Association of Great Britain, Dedham, Essex, UK

Chris White

President, White Labs, Inc., San Diego, California

Lydia Winkelmann

Editor, *BRAUWELT, BRAUWELT International* and *BrewingScience*, Nuremberg, Germany

David Wondrich

Cocktail Historian and Author of *Imbibe!* and *Killer Cocktails: An Intoxicating Guide to Sophisticated Drinking*, Brooklyn, New York

Brian Yaeger

Author of *Red, White and Brew: An American Beer Odyssey*, San Francisco, California

Chad Michael Yakobson

Owner and Brewer, Crooked Stave Artisan Beer Project, Denver, Colorado

Sylvie Van Zandycke

Technical Sales Manager, Lallemand, Inc., Lawrenceville, New Jersey

Michael Zepf

Managing Director Seminars, Doemens Academy, Gräfelfing, Germany

INDEX

Page numbers in *italics* refer to illustrations, figures, and tables.